THE BORDERLINES OF TORT LAW

THE BORDERLINES OF TORT LAW

Interactions with Contract Law

Edited by
Miquel MARTIN-CASALS

INTERSENTIA

Intersentia Ltd
8 Wellington Street | Cambridge
CB1 1HW | United Kingdom
Tel.: +44 1223 736 170
Email: mail@intersentia.co.uk
www.intersentia.com | www.intersentia.co.uk

Distribution for the UK and Ireland:
NBN International
Airport Business Centre, 10 Thornbury Road
Plymouth, PL6 7PP
United Kingdom
Tel.: +44 1752 202 301 | Fax: +44 1752 202 331
Email: orders@nbninternational.com

Distribution for Europe and all other countries:
Intersentia Publishing nv
Groenstraat 31
2640 Mortsel
Belgium
Tel.: +32 3 680 15 50 | Fax: +32 3 658 71 21
Email: mail@intersentia.be

Distribution for the USA and Canada:
Independent Publishers Group
Order Department
814 North Franklin Street
Chicago, IL 60610
USA
Tel.: +1 800 888 4741 (toll free) | Fax: +1 312 337 5985
Email: orders@ipgbook.com

The Borderlines of Tort Law. Interactions with Contract Law

ISBN 978-1-78068-248-8
D/2019/7849/89
NUR 822

British Library Cataloguing in Publication Data. A catalogue record for this book is available from the British Library.

À notre collègue Suzanne Carval, *in memoriam*

PREFACE

This book by the European Group on Tort Law (EGTL) deals with the borderlines between tort and contract and, more specifically, with the distinctions between liability in contract and liability in tort established in the legal systems under analysis. By exploring the main differences between the tortious and contractual legal regimes when damage occurs, it aims to shed some light on where the respective borderlines are currently traced in the corresponding legal systems, and what trends there are to suggest the course of the future development of the distinction.

The book includes 15 national reports, a report giving the perspective of an economic analysis of law and, finally, a comparative report. The reports analyse the differences across legal systems as regards the rules that may be relevant to the issues at the borderline between contract and tort and the extent to which actions in tort and actions in contract are mutually exclusive and, when this is not the case, how their concurrence is regulated. The reports also devote some attention to specific situations, such as pre-contractual liability and professional liability, where the contractual or tortious nature of the claim is hotly debated in some legal systems, and end with an analysis of the borderlines problems between tort and contract posed by 16 hypothetical case scenarios. Finally, the comparative report, based on the national reports and on other materials, provides a number of comparative conclusions.

The book has been made possible thanks to the ongoing financial and organisational support of the European Centre of Tort and Insurance Law (ECTIL) and the Institute for European Tort Law (ETL) in Vienna, as well as that of the Institute of European and Comparative Private Law (IECPL) at the University of Girona. The generosity of the National Research Program of the Spanish Ministry of Sciences, Innovation and Universities, through research grants (DER2013-40613-R and DER2016-77229-R) awarded to the IECPL in Girona over the last few years, has also been crucial in allowing the organisation of several meetings of the EGTL.

On behalf of the Group, I would like to thank the current director of the ECTIL and the ETL, Ernst Karner, and the former director of both institutions and one of the founding fathers of the EGTL, Helmut Koziol, from whom many of us have learned so much, for their ongoing support and encouragement. I would also like to thank the staff of the Institutions that have made this project possible, especially Lisa Zeiler, Donna Stockenhuber, Kathrin Karner and Andrew Bell at the ECTIL and the ETL, in Vienna, and Maria Olivas and Maria Subirós at the IECPL in Girona. Our thanks are also owed to Ann-Christin Maak-Scherpe and Ahmed Hegazi at Intersentia.

As editor of this book, I would also like to thank personally my colleagues who have written the national and the economic perspective reports for their infinite patience with a project that has been ongoing for many years.

Finally, I would like to emphasise that at a meeting of the Group held in Girona in 2018, the European Group on Tort Law decided to dedicate this book to our late colleague, Suzanne Carval, whom we all miss very much and will never forget.

Miquel Martín-Casals
Girona, June 2019

CONTENTS

Preface vii
List of Authors xi

Introduction 1

Questionnaire and Hypothetical Cases 7

Austria
Ernst KARNER and Bernhard A KOCH 13

Czech Republic
Luboš TICHÝ 45

England and Wales
Ken OLIPHANT and Vanessa WILCOX 69

France
Jean-Sébastien BORGHETTI 131

Germany
Ulrich MAGNUS 171

Greece
Eugenia DACORONIA 213

Israel
Israel GILEAD 253

Italy
Cristina AMATO and Giovanni COMANDÉ 281

The Netherlands
Anne LM KEIRSE 331

Norway
Bjarte ASKELAND 383

Poland
Ewa BAGIŃSKA 419

South Africa
Johann NEETHLING 467

Spain
Miquel MARTÍN-CASALS and Albert RUDA-GONZÁLEZ 507

Switzerland
Pierre WIDMER, Bénédict WINIGER and Caroline DURET 569

United States
W Jonathan CARDI and Michael D GREEN 617

Economic Perspectives
Michael FAURE and Wenqing LIAO 669

Comparative Report
Miquel MARTÍN-CASALS 711

LIST OF AUTHORS

Cristina Amato
Professor of Comparative Law, University of Brescia, Italy

Bjarte Askeland
Appeal court judge, Gulating Lagmannsrett, Bergen; former, until 2019, Professor of Private Law, University of Bergen, Norway

Ewa Bagińska
Professor of Civil Law, University of Gdańsk, Poland

Jean-Sébastien Borghetti
Professor of Private Law, University Panthéon-Assas (Paris II), France

Jonathan Cardi
Professor of Law, Wake Forest School of Law, United States

Giovanni Comandé
Professor of Comparative Law, Sant'Anna School of Advanced Studies, Pisa, Italy

Eugenia Dacoronia
Associate Professor of Civil Law, University of Athens, Greece

Caroline Duret
Doctoral Candidate, Faculty of Law, University of Geneva, Switzerland

Michael Faure
Professor of Comparative and Environmental Law, Maastricht University; Professor of Comparative Private Law and Economics, Erasmus School of Law, Rotterdam, The Netherlands

Israel Gilead
Emeritus Professor of Law, Hebrew University of Jerusalem; Professor, Sha'arey Mada Umishpat Academic Center, Israel

Michael D Green
Williams Professor of Law, Wake Forest School of Law, United States

Ernst Karner
Professor of Civil Law, University of Vienna; Director of the Institute for European Tort Law and the European Centre of Tort and Insurance Law, Austria

Anne LM Keirse
Professor of Private Law, Utrecht University; Judge at the Court of Appeal, Amsterdam, The Netherlands

Bernhard A Koch
Professor of Civil and Comparative Law, University of Innsbruck, Austria

Wenqing Liao
Legal Counsel Alter Domus; Doctorate in Law and Economics, Maastricht University, The Netherlands

Ulrich Magnus
Emeritus Professor of Law, University of Hamburg; Affiliate Researcher, Max Planck Institute for Comparative and International Private Law, Hamburg; Judge (retired) at the Court of Appeal, Hamburg, Germany

Miquel Martín-Casals
Professor of Civil Law, University of Girona, Spain

Johann Neethling
Research Fellow of Private Law, University of the Free State, Bloemfontein; Emeritus Professor, University of South Africa, Pretoria, South Africa

Ken Oliphant
Professor of Tort Law, University of Bristol, United Kingdom

Albert Ruda-González
Associate Professor in Civil Law, University of Girona, Spain

Luboš Tichý
Professor of European, International Private Law and Civil Law, Charles University, Prague, Czech Republic

Pierre Widmer
Emeritus Professor, Swiss Institute of Comparative Law, Lausanne/Berne, Switzerland

Vanessa Wilcox
Secretary General of the European Law Institute, Former Assistant to the European Group on Tort Law, Austria

Bénédict Winiger
Professor of Law, University of Geneva, Switzerland

INTRODUCTION

I. Tort Law: An Area with Many Borderlines 1
II. The Borderliness between Tort and Contract 2
III. Investigative and Jurisdictional Scope 4

I. TORT LAW: AN AREA WITH MANY BORDERLINES

This book is the third in a new series inaugurated in 2016 entitled 'Principles of European Tort Law'. As in the two previous books,[1] it aims to reflect on certain aspects that were not subject to specific and detailed treatment throughout the 10 volumes[2] that served as the basis for the elaboration of the 'Principles of European Tort Law (PETL)' in 2005.[3] Together with the already existing volumes, as well as the volumes to come, it should contribute to a revised edition of the PETL which, if time and energy permit, should see the light of day within the next decade. 1

By contrast to other soft law projects,[4] the PETL strive to delimit the area of extracontractual liability, but make no specific effort to trace its borderlines with other branches of the law of obligations – such as contractual liability, unjust enrichment or *negotiorum gestio* – or with other branches of the law, either public (for instance, in some countries, the liability of public authorities) 2

1 The 'Principles of European Tort Law' series (Intersentia), with the following volumes: Piotr Machnikowski (ed.), *European Product Liability. An Analysis of the State of Art in the Era of New Technologies* (2016); and Ken Oliphant (ed.), *Liability of Public Authorities in Comparative Perspective* (2016).

2 See the series 'Principles of European Tort Law' (Kluwer International, The Hague) with the following volumes: Jaap Spier (ed.), *The Limits of Liability: Keeping the Floodgates Shut* (1996); Jaap Spier (ed.), *The Limits of Expanding Liability* (1998); Helmut Koziol (ed.), *Unification of Tort Law: Wrongfulness* (1998); Jaap Spier (ed.), *Unification of Tort Law: Causation* (2000); Ulrich Magnus (ed.), *Unification of Tort Law: Damages* (2001); Bernhard A Koch and Helmut Koziol (eds.), *Unification of Tort Law: Strict Liability* (2002); Jaap Spier (ed.), *Unification of Tort Law: Liability for the Acts of the Others* (2003); Ulrich Magnus and Miquel Martín-Casals (eds.), *Unification of Tort Law: Contributory Negligence* (2004); WVH Rogers (ed.), *Unification of Tort Law: Multiple Tortfeasors* (2004); and Pierre Widmer (ed.) *Unification of Tort Law: Fault* (2005).

3 European Group on Tort Law, *Principles of European Tort Law. Text and Commentary* (2005).

4 See, for instance art. VI.-1:103 *Scope of Application* DCFR.

or private (notably, also in some countries, liability for damage arising in the context of family relationships).

3 A first caveat to this book is that it does not deal with all the possible borderlines of tort law, but only with its interaction with contract law. When the Group first met in Graz in April 2013 to discuss the borderlines issue, the original proposal embraced most of the abovementioned borderlines in a single Project. However, the vast majority of the members of the Group rightly pointed out that, although the project was very attractive, it was hardly feasible as a single Project, and that it was better to concentrate first on an area where border frictions were: more common, i.e. happened in most of the countries under survey; important, i.e. had a greater complexity and practical importance; and that were also more frequent. The obvious candidate was then the borderlines between contract and tort and a new draft questionnaire was presented in October 2013 in Girona and submitted to discussion by the Group.

4 I must confess that at first I was quite reluctant to confine the object of analysis to the border area between tort and contract, since I thought it was not as unexplored as some other areas. Not only because in the different jurisdictions most tort law books, even the most elementary ones, already pay some specific attention to the tort-contract divide, but also because there were already some studies that included a thorough treatment of this borderline which had been published in the not too distant past.[5]

5 However, now I do not regret that choice. When one delves into the analysis of this border area, one perceives that although the core of the distinction between tort and contract and, more specifically, between liability in tort and liability in contract, is quite clear and uniform, it is rather elusive in its details and varies considerably across legal systems.

II. THE BORDERLINESS BETWEEN TORT AND CONTRACT

6 In some legal systems, it is contended that, for practical purposes, it is still fundamental to establish whether a certain relationship is to be governed by tort law rules or by contractual ones. In others, in contrast, the ascription to one of the two domains is considered much less important, since there are areas where case law, legislation or both have gradually unified the applicable legal rules. This has been the case, for instance, with the prescription rules,

---

[5] Most notably, Christian von Bar and Ulrich Drobnig, *The Interaction of Contract Law and Tort and Property Law in Europe: A Comparative Study* (2004).

including general prescription periods, which have undergone a strong unification process in most legal systems over the last twenty years. Currently, only a few of the countries under analysis still maintain different general prescription periods for contract and tort, and the trend clearly points towards unification. This is also the case with non-pecuniary losses, which in many legal systems were not recoverable in the case of contractual liability, despite being recoverable under non-contractual liability. Here the current trend also favours unification.

The fact that the boundary, depending on the legal system under analysis, is drawn in one place or another may give rise to the paradox that what is considered a matter of contractual law in one legal system is exclusively governed by tort law in another. Allowing a particular circumstance to be governed by the law of contract might be an indirect response to the lack of satisfactory solutions provided by tort law or by the established interaction between the two domains. An example of a response to the first problem is the growth and expansion of the German doctrine of the so-called 'contract with protective effects to third parties' (*Vertrag mit Schutzwirkung zungunsten Dritter*), which aims at regaining for the area of contract law those cases that are not perceived as properly solved according to tort law rules. An example of a response to problems posed by the established interaction between both domains is the proliferation of the so-called '*obligations de sécurité*' in French law, which in many cases aim to protect within the contract those interests that are regularly protected by tort law rules, but which cannot be protected in the case in question because of the application of the *non-cumul* rule. 7

To put an end to the problems raised by the distinction, some legal systems have even established a 'third track' or a 'third lane' between contract and tort in order to absorb some of the disputed borderline grey areas. This is the case of pre-contractual liability in Germany and in some other countries, where it is not considered either contractual or tortious, but a *sui generis* liability by virtue of law. 8

In many cases, even within the same legal system, the respective domains of tort and contract are subject to passionate doctrinal disputes, often with practical significance, which may lead the borderlines to shift over time. The various different reform projects recently completed in France provide us with a paradigm demonstration as regards this shift between contract and tort. Being the only jurisdiction in this survey that sticks to a sharp division providing that cases must fall either on the contractual or on the tortious side (the *non-cumul* or non-option rule), the 2016 *Avant-projet* and the 2017 *Project* redistribute the borderlines areas and make important inroads into an optional system. Thus, for instance, when personal injury occurs in the context of the contractual relationship between injurer and victim, the 2016 *Avant-project*, with the aim to 9 protect victims, removes liability from the domain of contract law and confines it to tort law (cf. art. 1233). In all likelihood, further reflection pointed out that, occasionally, liability in contract may be more favourable to the victim than liability in tort. Accordingly, the 2017 *Project*, despite maintaining the traditional *non-cumul* rule (cf. art. 1233), provides now that '... the victim may invoke express stipulations of a contract which are more favourable to him than the application of the rules of extra-contractual liability' (cf. art. 1233-1).[6] If this distinction finally becomes law, one may rightly ask whether this differentiation according to the protected interest marks the beginning of the end of the *non-cumul* rule.

III. INVESTIGATIVE AND JURISDICTIONAL SCOPE

10 A quick glance at the questionnaire shows that the project aims to analyse all legal areas of friction between both domains, i.e. all those areas of law that may be relevant in the application of tort or contract law rules. A first objective is to determine whether the problems that are addressed are resolved with the same rules, regardless of the contractual or tortious qualification of the case, or are subject to different ones. If the rules are different, a second objective is to analyse what the differences are and to what reasons they can be attributed.

11 Thus, the reports analyse the differences across legal systems as regards the issues that may be relevant to the borderline between contract and tort. Some of these issues are the foundations of liability, the nature and amount of the compensation to be paid, the extent of the liability of the persons involved and whether defences and limitation periods corresponding to the distinct causes of action give rise to substantially different outcomes.

12 The 16 cases at the end of the reports put to the test the application of the rules and doctrines specified in the national reports so that, in some cases, they just offer the practical application aspects already treated in the report. However, some of these cases develop specific aspects that, due to the necessary concision of the answers, national reports have not been able to tackle in all their required extension. This is the case, for instance, of cases 6 and 7, which deal with the so-called 'spreading damage' (*weiterfressenden Mangel* or *Weiterfresserschaden*), well known in some jurisdictions, but almost unknown

6 The quotation refers to the English translation of the Reform Bill (March 2017), made by Professor Simon Whittaker, for the French Ministry of Justice, available at: http://www.textes.justice.gouv.fr/art_pix/reform_bill_on_civil_liability_march_2017.pdf (accessed 11.07.2019).

in others. Most of the cases are inspired in actual cases of the jurisdictions represented in this Project.

As regards the jurisdictions included in this book, they represent a broad cross-section of national systems in Europe, two mixed legal systems and the United States.[7] Needless to mention is the richness with which mixed legal systems contribute to the analysis of the tort-contract divide, in particular when in these legal systems tort and contractual law are sometimes inspired by different legal traditions. Or the great contribution of the US law, with the great variety of solutions provided by the different state jurisdictions, that turn this report into a difficult comparatist exercise. 13

Finally, the report regarding the Economic Perspectives does not intend to work as a sort of 'litmus test', which says what solutions adopted by national systems are correct and which are not, but aims at incorporating a different approach which can contribute to a deeper reflection of the topics dealt with in the book. 14

The book closes with a Comparative law report where, in this case perhaps more than in others, the comparative reporter cannot confine himself to collecting and ordering the important contributions of the national reports. As a sort of cement that allows him to build a clear and systematic discourse, he must seek assistance in the study of complementary national and comparative materials. 15

[7] In alphabetical order, the national reports included in this volume cover: Austria, the Czech Republic, England and Wales, France, Germany, Greece, Israel, Italy, the Netherlands, Norway, Poland, South Africa, Spain, Switzerland and the United States of America.

QUESTIONNAIRE AND HYPOTHETICAL CASES

QUESTIONS

I. TRACING THE BORDERLINES

A. How and why does your legal system distinguish between tort and contract?

B. Does your system recognise a 'grey zone' between the two (as, for instance, in the case of *culpa in contrahendo*)?

C. Are there common or different rules regulating tort and contract?

D. Do courts apply rules which are common to tort and contract in different ways?

II. MAIN DIFFERENCES BETWEEN TORTIOUS AND CONTRACTUAL LIABILITY

A. What are the differences in the regulation of liability based on tort and liability based on contract as regards the foundations of liability?

1) The role of intention
2) The roles of wrongfulness and fault and their variations
3) The role of strict liability

B. What are the differences as regards *causation* (both causation in fact and scope of liability)?

C. What are the differences as regards *remedies*? Namely:

1) The degree of certainty of the damage
2) Compensation for non-pecuniary loss
3) Compensation for loss of earnings and for loss of chance
4) Restitutionary damages
5) Aggravated and exemplary (or punitive) damages
6) Others (such as specific performance, injunctions, etc)

D. What are the differences as regards the recoverability of 'pure economic losses' between contracting and non-contracting parties?

E. What are the differences as regards liability for others? Namely:

1) Liability for auxiliaries and for independent contractors
2) Liability for the legal representatives or organs of a company
3) Liability of representatives of natural persons
4) Liability of the auxiliary/organ itself

F. What are the differences as regards liability in the case of multiple tortfeasors/breaching parties?

G. What are the differences as regards the persons who may be protected under tort/contract?

H. What are the differences as regards defences (in particular, in the case of contributory negligence)?

I. What are the differences as regards limitation periods (in particular as regards length of periods, '*dies a quo*', liability arising from a crime, specific rules, etc)?

J. What are the differences as regards proof?

K. Are there any other differences?

L. What are the reasons for all these differences?

III. LIMITATION OR EXCLUSION OF LIABILITY ARISING FROM TORT AND FROM CONTRACT

A. Are there any statutory provisions in tort and/or contract authorising a limitation or exclusion of liability under certain conditions or giving the courts the power to do so?

B. Is limitation or exclusion of contractual and tortious liability by contract *ex ante/ex post* possible? Namely:

1) If so, to what extent (if accepted, what are the limits and conditions)? Are there any differences?
2) To what extent can a contractual exclusion provide a defence to a third party to the contract? Does it make a difference whether the claim against the third party is contractual or tortious?

IV. NON-CONCURRENCE OR CONCURRENCE OF ACTIONS

A. Provide an overview of the areas of overlap and the different approaches (in particular as regards the approach to the non-concurrence and concurrence of actions).

B. Non-concurrence and concurrence for the protection against personal injury and damage to property: what is your country's approach?

C. Non-concurrence and concurrence in the case of interference with contractual rights: what is your country's approach? In particular as regards:

1) Interference with a contractual relationship
2) Loss of business due to personal injury to someone else's employees or clients or due to property damage incurred by the entrepreneur

V. SPECIFIC SITUATIONS

A. Pre-contractual liability

B. Liability of professionals (physicians and health care personnel, lawyers, architects, etc (professional = regulated profession))

CASES

Case 1. The unattractive shopping mall

D owns a shopping mall and lets a store therein to Z, who is to sell shoes. The contract allows Z to sublet the store and he does so to C, without informing D. In breach of his obligations to Z and other tenants, D fails to keep the shopping mall clean and attractive. Because of this, C's business is on the decline and the number of shoes he sells keeps declining. Can C bring a claim for lost earnings against D (in contract/tort/both)?

Case 2. The idle lawyer

After having a terrible fight with his two daughters, W had asked his solicitor D to cut his daughters out of his will, which request was duly implemented shortly thereafter. Before W died, however, he reconciled with his daughters. W subsequently asked D to change the will back, so that £9,000 would be bequeathed to each of his daughters, but due to D's unreasonable delay, the will was not prepared for execution before W's death. His heirs were unwilling to share the estate with the two daughters and pointed to the language of the will at the time of death. Can the daughters bring a claim against D in contract/tort/both to recover the amount promised to them by their late father? (Please disregard potential claims against the estate or heirs arising out of the laws of inheritance such as the daughter's legal share).

Case 3. The defective house

Contractor D builds a house for Z. The contract contains an exclusion clause whereby D shall not be liable to Z if the house's negligent construction causes property damage to the latter. Two years after the house has been built, Z sells it to C. Three years later, part of the house falls down due to a defect caused by D's negligence, and C also suffers personal injury. Can he sue D for compensation of his bodily injury and/or the damage caused to the house (in contract/tort/both)?

Case 4. Apartment in flames

C is a tenant living in a rented apartment. Her landlord, D, has negligently failed to monitor the circuit breaker, which causes fire in the apartment while C is inside. She is able to escape the burning apartment, but suffers severe physical injury. Does C have a valid claim against D (in contract/tort/both)?

Case 5. Injured skier

C had bought a ski pass which entitled him to use the ski lift in a ski resort during his holidays. For reasons that were not fully clarified, there was a derailment of the ski lift while C was using it, and the cable fell, causing significant personal injury to C. C brings a claim against D1, the owner of the ski resort and issuer of the ski pass, as well as against D2, the insurance company with whom D1 had liability insurance. This policy states that the insurance company 'would cover up to the amount of €900,000, any compensation which the contracting party would have to pay arising from liability in tort pursuant to the general clause of liability for fault by reason of the operation of the resort'. D2, however, refuses to cover the insured accident and to pay any compensation, alleging that this was a case of contractual liability which was not covered under D1's policy.

Case 6. Exploding car

C buys a brand new car from D1, produced by D2, which has a two-year full warranty against all defects. Three years later, while on a trip to the mountains, C parks the car, and when he is 300 metres away enjoying sightseeing the car suddenly explodes and is totally destroyed. Experts say that the car's fuel line was defective. C brings a claim against D1 and D2.

Case 7. Burning racing boat

Y sells a racing boat to D. D adds special electronic equipment to improve navigation on the high seas. After using the boat for two years, D sells it to C with a two-year full warranty against all defects. Three years later, C decides to participate in a race around the world. Once the race has started, and after C has sailed only 400 miles, the equipment added by D, which was defective from the beginning, catches fire, and the fire destroys the boat entirely. C is rescued by X's boat and taken to shore where he catches a flight home. C suffers no personal injury but sues D, claiming the value of the destroyed boat and the cost of his repatriation expenses.

Case 8. Insidious report

D, acting as C's employee, is the contact person for company Z, which manufactures a product exclusively for C. D files a disparaging report on company Z, based on false and insidious statements, which leads C to terminate its contract with company Z. A few weeks later, D, while still working for company C, sets up his own company and signs a distribution contract for the same product with company Z. C files a claim against its former employee D.

Case 9. Circular letter

C is an industrial property agent acting for company D. After many disagreements between agent and company, C leaves D and sets up his own company Z. D then sends a circular to all its customers alleging that C no longer works for the company because he had to be dismissed for misconduct; it claimed further that C's new company Z cannot legally manage industrial property rights; and that C had been reported to the authorities for professional intrusion. Finally, D asks its customers to refrain from dealing with C and to correspond directly with D. C files a claim against D.

Case 10. Shortage of supply

D, X and Z provide C with the same component parts he needs for his product. When D learns that X is bankrupt and that Z had to reduce its production dramatically for other reasons, D tells C that it will discontinue distribution of component parts if C does not accept a 20% increase in prices, furthermore that payments shall be made in less than 30 days instead of 90 as agreed in the original supply contract. Since C has no alternative supply sources, he accepts the new conditions, but brings an action against D.

Case 11. Injured rock star

X, a famous retired rock star, agrees with C, promoter, to perform a comeback concert. On his way to the concert X suffers an accident caused by D, and the concert must be cancelled. C brings a claim against D for the cancellation costs and for loss of profits.

Case 12. Equipment destroyed

X, a famous retired rock star, agrees with C to perform a comeback concert. C concludes a transport contract with D1 to transport the electronic equipment needed for the concert. On its way to the concert the truck suffers an accident caused by D2, the driver of a colliding bus. The equipment was destroyed and as a result the concert had to be cancelled. C brings a claim against D1 and D2. Does it make a difference if C was the owner of the equipment or not?

Case 13. Slipping on a lettuce leaf

C enters D's premises, a grocery shop. Before buying anything, C slips on a lettuce leaf and breaks her leg. C brings a claim against D (in contract/tort/both?).

Case 14. Test drive

D wants to buy a second-hand car from C, a car dealer. Before buying it D drives the car along the main street in front of C's premises and smashes the front part of the car against a tree. C brings a claim against D.

Case 15. Breaking off negotiations

D enters into negotiations to sell an antique to C. C says that he will be on a business trip for a couple of days and that he will continue negotiations on Friday of the same week, to which D agrees. On Thursday D sells the antique to X. C brings a claim against D for the costs incurred.

Case 16. Non-disclosure of relevant facts

C wants to buy a specific machine ('type X') to harvest corn on his land. C does not mention where he intends to use this machine, but D knows through a friend that C owns fields of corn on steep hills in a distant part of the country. Although it works on all terrains, the type X machine has a dramatically reduced performance when used on steep fields. D does not say anything and sells the harvester to C.

THE BORDERLINES OF TORT LAW IN AUSTRIA

Ernst KARNER and Bernhard A KOCH

QUESTIONS

I. Tracing the Borderlines 15
II. Main Differences between Tortious and Contractual Liability 16
 A. Differences as Regards the Foundations of Liability 16
  1) Role of Intention 16
  2) Role of Wrongfulness and Fault and their Variations 17
  3) Role of Strict Liability 18
 B. Differences as Regards Causation 19
 C. Differences as Regards Remedies 20
  1) Degree of Certainty of the Damage 20
  2) Compensation for Non-Pecuniary Loss 20
  3) Compensation for Loss of Earnings and for Loss of Chance 20
  4) Restitutionary Damages 21
  5) Aggravated and Exemplary (or Punitive) Damages 21
  6) Other Remedies 21
 D. Differences as Regards Recoverability of 'Pure Economic Losses' 22
 E. Differences as Regards Liability for Others 22
  1) Liability for Auxiliaries and for Independent Contractors 22
  2) Liability for Legal Representatives or Organs of a Company 22
  3) Liability of Representatives of Natural Persons 23
  4) Liability of the Auxiliary/Organ Itself 23
 F. Differences as Regards Liability in the Case of Multiple Tortfeasors/Breaching Parties 23
 G. Differences as Regards the Persons Who May be Protected 23
 H. Differences as Regards Defences 24
 I. Differences as Regards Limitation Periods 24
 J. Differences as Regards Proof 25
 K. Other Differences 25
 L. Reasons for the Differences 25

III. Limitation or Exclusion of Liability Arising from Tort and from Contract . . . 26
A. Statutory Provisions Authorising a Limitation or Exclusion of Liability . . . 26
B. Limitation or Exclusion of Contractual and Tortious Liability by Contract . . . 26
1) Is it Possible to Limit or Exclude Contractual or Tortious Liability under a Contract? . . . 26
a) Statutory Provisions for Specific Contracts . . . 26
b) Statutory Provisions for Specific Torts . . . 27
c) General Approach Towards Contractual Limitation of Liability in Practice . . . 27
2) To What Extent can a Contractual Exclusion Provide a Defence to a Third Party to the Contract? . . . 29
IV. Non-Concurrence or Concurrence of Actions . . . 30
A. Overview . . . 30
B. Concurrence/Exclusion of Actions for the Protection against Personal Injury . . . 31
C. Concurrence/Exclusion of Actions for the Protection of Property . . . 31
D. Concurrence/Exclusion in the Case of Interference with Contractual Rights . . . 32
1) Interference with a Contractual Relationship . . . 32
2) Loss of Business due to Personal Injury to Someone Else's Employees or Clients or to Property Damage Incurred by the Entrepreneur . . . 32
V. Specific Situations . . . 33
A. Pre-Contractual Liability . . . 33
B. Liability of Professionals . . . 34

CASES

Case 1. The Unattractive Shopping Mall . . . 34
Case 2. The Idle Lawyer . . . 35
Case 3. The Defective House . . . 36
Case 4. Apartment in Flames . . . 37
Case 5. Injured Skier . . . 38
Case 6. Exploding Car . . . 38
Case 7. Racing Boat Burning . . . 40
Case 8. Insidious Report . . . 40
Case 9. Circular Letter . . . 41
Case 10. Shortage of Supply . . . 41
Case 11. Injured Rock Star . . . 41

Case 12. Equipment Destroyed 41
Case 13. Slipping on a Lettuce Leaf 42
Case 14. Test Drive 43
Case 15. Breach of Negotiations 43
Case 16. Non-Disclosure of Relevant Facts 44

QUESTIONS

I. TRACING THE BORDERLINES[1]

Unlike in many other European legal systems, contractual and tortious liability are jointly regulated under the same set of provisions in Austrian law (§1293 ff *Allgemeines bürgerliches Gesetzbuch* [Austrian Civil Code, ABGB]). This is in line with the Austrian point of view that basic problems such as causation concern contractual and tortious liability alike. Accordingly, §1295 para 1 ABGB stipulates that everyone is entitled to seek compensation from the injuring party for culpably inflicted damage and emphasises that 'the damage may have been caused by the breach of a contractual duty or independently of any contract'.[2] 1

Nonetheless, there are significant differences between the two forms of liability.[3] Firstly, pure economic loss is, in principle, not recoverable under tort law, while it is generally compensable under contract law. Secondly, in tort law, the plaintiff has to prove the tortfeasor's fault, whereas §1298 ABGB provides for a reversal of the burden of proof in the case of contractual liability: the defendant must prove that he was not at fault in relation to the breach of the obligation.[4] 2

---

1 See also *H Koziol*, The Borderline Between Tort Liability and Contract, in: H Koziol (ed), Unification of Tort Law: Wrongfulness (1998) 25.

2 All quotations from the ABGB are taken from the translation provided by *BC Steininger* in: E Karner/K Oliphant/BC Steininger (eds), European Tort Law: Basic Texts (2nd edn 2018) 1.

3 *E Karner* in: H Koziol/P Bydlinski/R Bollenberger (eds), Kurzkommentar zum ABGB (5th edn 2017) §1295 no 1.

4 *H Koziol*, Basic Questions of Tort Law from a Germanic Perspective (2012) no 4/4. §1298 ABGB reads: 'Whosoever claims to have been prevented from fulfilling his contractual or statutory duties without fault on his part has the burden of proving such. If, by reason of a contractual agreement, he is liable only for gross negligence, he also has to prove its absence.' The second sentence is interpreted *e contrario* to limit the reversal of the burden of proving fault to slight negligence, whereas it remains for the claimant to prove (also in contractual liability) that the defendant acted with gross negligence or intent unless the contract expressly limits liability to such qualified fault (which is the direct meaning of the second sentence).

Thirdly, in the field of tort, vicarious liability is confined to instances where the principal employs incapable or knowingly dangerous auxiliaries (§1315 ABGB[5]), whereas under contract law, the principal has comprehensive vicarious liability for negligent conduct on the part of auxiliaries he deploys to fulfil his contractual obligations (§1313a ABGB).[6] Other distinctions are considered under II below.

3 Despite these differences, contractual and tortious liability are not considered two strictly separate areas.[7] In Austrian law, an interim area is acknowledged, in which one has to determine whether to apply contractual or tortious provisions in order to reach an appropriate result.[8] Such interim legal areas arise, for example, in the case of *culpa in contrahendo* and with regard to the liability of experts towards third parties based on objective legal duties of care.[9]

II. MAIN DIFFERENCES BETWEEN TORTIOUS AND CONTRACTUAL LIABILITY

A. DIFFERENCES AS REGARDS THE FOUNDATIONS OF LIABILITY

1) *Role of Intention*

4 While the focus of this report is on the main differences between liability in tort and contract, insofar as intention is concerned, the position under Austrian law is very much alike. Both contractual and tortious liability are based on fault. In both areas, the extent of compensation depends on the degree of fault according to the general rule of §§1323 and 1324 ABGB:[10] slight negligence obliges the tortfeasor to compensate actual loss only, whereas full compensation, including loss of profits, is due if the tortfeasor acts with gross negligence or intent.

5 This provision reads: 'Whosoever, for the conduct of his affairs, avails himself either of an unfit person, or knowingly of a dangerous person, is liable for the harm such a person causes to another in that capacity.'

6 *Koziol* (fn 4) no 4/4. §1313a ABGB reads: 'Whosoever is under an obligation of performance to another is liable to that person for the fault of his legal representative, and of persons he engages to perform the obligation, as if it were his own fault.'

7 *Koziol* (fn 4) no 4/2 ff; *id*, Delikt, Verletzung von Schuldverhältnissen und Zwischenbereich, Juristische Blätter (JBl) 1994, 209.

8 'There is no sharp dividing line between the core areas of breach of contract and tort, instead there is a fluid transition with many interim gradations in respect of which it is necessary to re-examine the extent to which the principles of one or both of the core areas apply.' *Koziol* (fn 4) no 6/56.

9 *E Karner*, Haftung für Rat und Auskunft zwischen Vertrag und Delikt, in: FS Koziol (2010) 695 ff.

10 *Karner* (fn 3) §1293 no 3 ff.

A special rule applies to B2B contracts, where loss of profits is compensable even in the case of slight negligence (§349 *Unternehmensgesetzbuch* [Commercial Code, UGB][11]).

5 Intention plays a role in several respects, but still irrespective of whether the claim arises under tort or contract: one who intentionally damages another's property in violation of criminal law or through wantonness and spitefulness not only has to compensate the damage to the property as such, but in addition also has to make good the sentimental value attributed to the property by the victim (*Affektionsinteresse*, §1331 ABGB[12]).

6 While pure economic loss is generally deemed compensable under contract law but not in the law of delict as mentioned before, §1295 para 2 ABGB provides for an exception to that difference by providing for compensation also under tort law if such harm is inflicted intentionally and in violation of public morals.[13] Furthermore, pure economic loss is also compensable under tort law when false advice or misinformation is given knowingly (§1300 ABGB[14]).

7 Finally, in the field of labour law, an employee who intentionally causes damage is not entitled to a reduction of liability under the Employees' Liability Act (*Dienstnehmerhaftpflichtgesetz*, DHG), just as the intentionally acting employer cannot invoke the employer's liability privilege (§333 *Allgemeines Sozialversicherungsgesetz* [Social Security Act, ASVG]). In any case, a contractual disclaimer meant to apply to intentional wrongdoing is void.

2) *Role of Wrongfulness and Fault and their Variations*

8 As with intention, there are also far-reaching similarities under this category. Regarding wrongfulness, the theory of unlawfulness of conduct (*Verhaltensunrechtslehre*) applies both in Austrian tort as well as in contract law.[15]

---

11 §349 UGB determines that '[a]mong entrepreneurs, the damage to be compensated includes lost profit'.

12 This provision reads: 'If a person's patrimony is damaged through the intent or conspicuous negligence of another, he is also entitled to claim lost profits and, if the damage has been caused through an act forbidden by the criminal law, or through wantonness and spitefulness, such value as is attributable to his particular preferences.'

13 §1295 para 2 reads: 'A person who intentionally inflicts damage in a manner contrary to public morals is also liable; however, if the damage was inflicted in the exercise of a right, he is liable only if the exercise of the right clearly had the object of harming the other.'

14 *Koziol* (fn 4) no 6/48; *Karner* (fn 3) §1300 no 4. According to §1300 ABGB, '[a]n expert is also liable if, for payment, he negligently gives detrimental advice in a matter pertaining to his art or science. Apart from this case an advisor is liable only for damage he has knowingly caused to another by giving the advice.'

15 *H Koziol*, Österreichisches Haftpflichtrecht I (3rd edn 1997) no 4/2; *id*, Wrongfulness under Austrian Law, in: H Koziol (ed), Unification of Tort Law: Wrongfulness (1998) 11, 13 f.

According to this doctrine, liability depends on whether the conduct leading to the damage is considered unlawful or not. Contrary to German doctrine, wrongfulness cannot be deduced from the mere result of the conduct (*Erfolgsunrechtslehre*).

9 In tort, wrongfulness may result from either a negligent or intentional infringement of absolute rights (eg life, health, property), a violation of a protective statutory norm (*Schutzgesetz*, §1311 ABGB) or a wilful infliction of damage *contra bonos mores* (§1295 para 2 ABGB).[16]

10 In contract, wrongfulness may arise out of the breach of primary or secondary contractual duties or out of the infringement of duties of care and duties to inform.

11 Unlike in most European legal systems, a subjective standard of fault is to be applied in principle under both tort and contract law (§1297 ABGB). Thus, the liability of the injurer depends on his personal abilities and knowledge.[17] However, as far as the tortious and contractual liability of experts is concerned, an objective yardstick of fault applies (§1299 ABGB).[18]

12 In respect of the burden of proof regarding fault, a significant difference exists between contract and tort law: in tort, the plaintiff has to prove that the injurer is liable (§1296 ABGB), whereas in contract, the burden of proof is reversed at the expense of the injurer (§1298 ABGB[19]).

3) *Role of Strict Liability*

13 Austrian law provides for strict liability in a range of specific provisions, mainly regarding the keeper of a source of special danger: motor vehicles and railways (*Eisenbahn- und Kraftfahrzeughaftpflichtgesetz* [Statute on liability for keeping railways and motor vehicles, EKHG]); airplanes (*Luftfahrtgesetz* [Aviation Act, LFG]); radioactivity (*Atomhaftungsgesetz* [Nuclear Liability Act, AtomHG]); mains for electricity and gas, as well as installations for their distribution (*Reichshaftpflichtgesetz* [Reich Liability Act, RHG]); pipelines (*Rohrleitungsgesetz* [Pipelines Act, RohrlG]); mines (*Mineralrohstoffgesetz* [Mineral Resources Act, MinroG]); and operations with genetically modified organisms (*Gentechnikgesetz* [Gene Technology Act, GTG]). Such a multitude of specific provisions, dating from different times and based on diverse policy reasoning, as well as the lack of a general rule has led to gaps in protection and inconsistences.

[16] *Karner* (fn 3) §1294 no 4. See also supra fn 13.
[17] *H Koziol*, Austria, in: P Widmer (ed), Unification of Tort Law: Fault (2005) 14 f; *Karner* (fn 3) §1294 no 7.
[18] *R Reischauer* in: P Rummel, ABGB (3rd edn 2007) §1299 no 5; *Karner* (fn 3) §1299 no 1.
[19] Cited supra fn 4.

However, these drawbacks are alleviated as Austrian courts accept, at least in principle, that strict liability can be applied analogously to sources of risk comparable to those covered by specific legislation.[20] Furthermore, it should be pointed out that, according to Austrian doctrine, liability based on fault and strict liability based on dangerousness are not completely separate areas as between these two core areas – which represent the ends of an unbroken chain – there is a broad interim area with many gradations: the more dangerous an activity or object, the stricter the liability.[21]

These instances of strict liability introduced by specific legislation do not require 14
the proof of fault within the sphere of the operator at all, whereas liability for breaches of contractual duties merely reverses the burden of proving fault by shifting it onto the debtor.

B. DIFFERENCES AS REGARDS CAUSATION

With regard to causation, there are no differences in principle. In tort as well as 15
in contract law, the *conditio sine qua non* rule applies, according to which, one has to ask whether, but for the defendant's conduct, the harmful result would still have occurred.[22]

A limitation of imputation (*wertende Begrenzung der Zurechnung*) restricts the 16
otherwise overly extensive liability for wrongful and faulty conduct. However, this instrument, which in many countries is called 'legal causality', is not a question of causation in Austrian understanding.[23] Rather, the adequate causation theory and the notion of scope of protection are manifestations of a limitation of imputation.[24]

Such instruments are in principle equally applicable in tort and contract law 17
except for certain natural modifications. If a protective statutory norm is violated, the protective purpose of the norm is to be examined: in other words, one has to examine whether the violated norm was intended to avoid (inter alia) precisely the harm which in fact was inflicted. In contract law, liability attaches to a breach of a contractual duty that aimed at preventing the damage in question.[25]

---

20 *Karner* (fn 3) §1306 no 2 with further references (refs).

21 *BC Steininger*, Verschärfung der Verschuldenshaftung (1997) 143 ff; *Koziol* (fn 4) no 6/188 ff.

22 *R Zimmermann* in: B Winiger/H Koziol/BA Koch/R Zimmermann (eds), Digest of European Tort Law, vol 1: Essential Cases on Natural Causation (2007) no 1/29; *Koziol*, Haftpflichtrecht I (fn 15) no 3/5 ff; *Koziol* (fn 4) no 5/57 ff.

23 *H Koziol* in: J Spier (ed), Unification of Tort Law: Causation (2000) 11 ff.

24 *Karner* (fn 3) §1295 no 6 ff; *Koziol*, Haftpflichtrecht I (fn 15) no 8/1 ff.

25 *Koziol*, Haftpflichtrecht I (fn 15) no 8/49 ff.

C. DIFFERENCES AS REGARDS REMEDIES

18 In general, contract law offers a much wider range of remedies than tort law, which is basically limited to damages, even though the default rule provides for restitution in kind (§1323 ABGB).[26] As mentioned above, the provisions of the ABGB concerning liability (§§1293 ff) principally apply to both contract and tort law, except for rules on the burden of proof, vicarious liability and compensation for pure economic loss. However, the parties to a contract have certain autonomy to agree on modifications of legal regulations, for example by stipulating lump sum damages in advance (§1336 ABGB).

1) Degree of Certainty of the Damage

19 As far as the standard of certainty of damage is concerned, there are no differences between tort and contract law. In both fields, the law requires the judge to be convinced beyond reasonable doubt ('probability bordering on certainty') or at least to a very high probability that the damage was the consequence of the conduct in question.[27] Preponderant probability does not suffice.

2) Compensation for Non-Pecuniary Loss

20 According to the general rule of §§1323 and 1324 ABGB, which is applicable both to tortious and contractual liability, monetary compensation for immaterial harm is due if the tortfeasor acted with at least gross negligence.[28] Specific provisions extend,[29] restrict[30] or exclude compensation.[31] Furthermore, the Austrian Supreme Court holds the view that non-pecuniary losses are only recoverable (in money) if expressly provided for by law.

3) Compensation for Loss of Earnings and for Loss of Chance

21 As mentioned before, §§1323 and 1324 ABGB apply to tort and contract law alike and stipulate that actual loss is recoverable even if the harmful conduct was

---

26 See infra no 22.

27 *E Karner* in: H Koziol/BC Steininger (eds), European Tort Law 2008 (2009) 71 f with further refs; *T Klicka*, Die Beweislastverteilung im Zivilverfahrensrecht (1995) 33; *W Rechberger/DA Simotta*, Grundriss des österreichischen Zivilprozessrechts (9th edn 2017) no 813.

28 *E Karner/H Koziol*, Non-Pecuniary Loss under Austrian Law, in: WVH Rogers (ed), Damages for Non-Pecuniary Loss in a Comparative Perspective (2001) 1 ff.

29 According to §1325 ABGB, damages for pain and suffering triggered by bodily injury are recoverable in the case of slight negligence as well as where a strict liability provision applies.

30 The sentimental value for damaged property is only recoverable in the case of intent (§1331 ABGB).

31 §1330 ABGB: defamation.

slightly negligent. Loss of profits is only compensable if the tortfeasor acted with gross negligence or intent, whereas slight negligence suffices in B2B contracts (§349 UGB).[32] Loss of a chance is not recoverable under Austrian law; however, under certain circumstances, proportional liability in cases of uncertain causation may serve a similar goal.[33]

4) *Restitutionary Damages*

According to §1323 ABGB, damage has to be compensated – in tort law as well as in contractual law – primarily by restitution in kind, meaning that the injurer must create a situation similar and equal to that which would have existed without the damage. This serves best the function of compensation. If restitution in kind is impossible or impractical, the damage has to be compensated in money, with impracticality already given if the plaintiff prefers pecuniary compensation and this is not in conflict with the higher interests of the defendant.[34] 22

5) *Aggravated and Exemplary (or Punitive) Damages*

Punitive damages are unknown to Austrian law. As damages always aim at compensation, the plaintiff is never entitled to more than what his damage amounts to.[35] This is also true in the field of non-pecuniary losses as compensation in money shall enable the victim to obtain amenities to alleviate their situation.[36] Penalisation is reserved for criminal law. 23

6) *Other Remedies*

As mentioned before, in contract law the plaintiff can benefit from a wider range of remedies than in tort, including termination of contract, claim for specific performance and price reduction. As far as these remedies do not aim at the compensation of losses, fault is not required since those means have different objectives. However, overlaps are possible: as termination also restores the parties' private autonomy it may equally serve the purpose of a claim for restitution in kind, which then requires a faulty breach of contractual duties.[37] 24

---

32 Supra fn 11.

33 See eg *BA Koch*, Proportional liability for causal uncertainty: How it works on the basis of a 200-year-old code, in: M Martín-Casals/D Papayannis (eds), Uncertain Causation in Tort Law (2016) 67, 79 f.

34 *H Koziol*, Austria, in: U Magnus (ed), Unification of Tort Law: Damages (2001) 9.

35 On this *Koziol* (fn 4) no 2/55 ff.

36 *Karner/Koziol* (fn 28) 7 f.

37 Cf §933a ABGB (compensation instead of warranty).

D. DIFFERENCES AS REGARDS RECOVERABILITY OF 'PURE ECONOMIC LOSSES'

25 Whereas pure economic loss is more freely recoverable under contract law, the ABGB provides for compensation of such losses also under tort law, albeit only in exceptional cases,[38] particularly if the damage was inflicted intentionally and in violation of public morals (§1295 para 2 ABGB),[39] or when false advice or misinformation is given knowingly (§1300 ABGB).[40]

E. DIFFERENCES AS REGARDS LIABILITY FOR OTHERS

1) *Liability for Auxiliaries and for Independent Contractors*

26 In respect of liability for auxiliaries, Austrian law makes a sharp distinction between tort and contract law. Whereas in tort the principal is only liable if he employs an incapable auxiliary or one whom he knows to be dangerous (§1315 ABGB), he is responsible for all harmful conduct of a person employed to assist him in fulfilling a contractual obligation (§1313a ABGB).[41] However, the principal is not vicariously liable for independent contractors in tort, while he may be in contract if they assist him in meeting his contractual duties.[42]

2) *Liability for Legal Representatives or Organs of a Company*

27 Legal entities are liable for their organs and representatives (ie power-holders) under tort as well as under contract law. Representatives in the sense of §337 ABGB are persons who exercise a responsible, leading or supervisory function within the organisation.[43] In recent years liability for representatives has been extended to natural persons.[44] Furthermore, legal entities are, like natural persons, responsible for their auxiliaries according to the general rules (§§1313a, 1315 ABGB).

---

38 See *Karner* (fn 3) §1295 no 2; *H Koziol*, Schadenersatz für reine Vermögensschäden, JBl 2004, 273 ff.

39 Supra fn 13.

40 Supra fn 14.

41 *H Koziol/K Vogel*, Austria, in: J Spier (ed), Unification of Tort Law: Liability for Damage Caused by Others (2003) 11 ff. See supra at fn 5 f.

42 *Karner* (fn 3) §1313a no 4, §1315 no 2.

43 *Koziol* (fn 4) no 6/126 f.

44 *Karner* (fn 3) §1315 no 7.

3) *Liability of Representatives of Natural Persons*

28 As laid down in §1309 ABGB, parents (or other people in charge) are liable for a child if they culpably violate a duty of supervising such minor. Regarding vicarious liability and contributory negligence (§1304 ABGB), there is a difference between tort and contract law: if parents act as auxiliaries on behalf of their children under contract law, the former's conduct is imputed to the latter. In tort, children cannot be held liable for their parents because parents are meant to protect them, and children cannot freely select them.[45]

4) *Liability of the Auxiliary/Organ Itself*

29 As auxiliaries are typically not parties to the contract in fulfilment of which they are employed, they are in principle not bound by the contractual duties, but may only be liable in tort instead, where only general duties of care apply and not the specific ones introduced by the contract. As an exception, an auxiliary deployed for contract negotiations may also be liable *ex contractu* if he makes extensive use of the other party's personal trust and has a significant economic interest in the contract.[46]

F. DIFFERENCES AS REGARDS LIABILITY IN THE CASE OF MULTIPLE TORTFEASORS/BREACHING PARTIES

30 With respect to the liability of multiple tortfeasors, the same rules are applicable in tortious and contractual liability, namely §§1301 f ABGB:[47] where several persons have acted in concert (*Mittäter*), they are jointly liable irrespective of whether the damage caused is separable or not. If the tortfeasors acted independently from each other (*Nebentäter*) and the damage is separable, each of them is liable for the part of the damage he has caused; if the damage is inseparable, they are jointly liable.

G. DIFFERENCES AS REGARDS THE PERSONS WHO MAY BE PROTECTED

31 According to the privity of contract rule, in principle the liability of the promisor only protects the promisee: only the parties to the contract are protected and

---

45 *A Kletečka*, Mitverschulden durch Gehilfenverhalten (1991) 67 ff; *Koziol*, Haftpflichtrecht I (fn 15) no 12/73 f; *Karner* (fn 3) §1304 no 2.

46 *Karner* (fn 3) §1313a no 10.

47 *Karner* (fn 3) §1301 no 1 ff and §1302 no 1 ff.

only they can raise contractual claims against each other. However, like in Germany, the concept of the so-called contract with protective effects towards third persons (*Vertrag mit Schutzwirkung zugunsten Dritter*) applies in Austria:[48] third parties are also protected by the contract if they are endangered by an incorrect fulfilment of the duties arising from it, as long as they are foreseeably proximate to one of the contracting parties. According to established case law, no protection exists if third parties have a contractual claim of their own.[49]

H. DIFFERENCES AS REGARDS DEFENCES

32 With regard to defences, there are basically no differences between tort and contract law. Contributory negligence (§1304 ABGB), self-defence (§3 *Strafgesetzbuch* [Penal Code, StGB]) and self-help (§§19, 344 ABGB) can be raised in both fields alike. Even so, contractual agreement may modify or even exclude such defences where legally permissible.

I. DIFFERENCES AS REGARDS LIMITATION PERIODS

33 According to §1489 ABGB, claims for compensation prescribe within three years starting from the time when the plaintiff harmed becomes aware of the damage and the identity of the injurer. If the damage or the identity of the injurer have not become known to the person harmed or if the damage arose from a criminal act which can only be committed intentionally and is punishable with imprisonment of more than one year, the claim only expires after 30 years, however – according to constant jurisdiction – starting from the harmful event and not from the materialisation of the ensuing harm.[50] In practice, the expansion of the prescription period for criminal offences is particularly relevant in cases

48 For a groundbreaking analysis see *F Bydlinski*, Vertragliche Sorgfaltspflichten zugunsten Dritter, JBl 1960, 359 ff; see further *G Schmaranzer*, Der Vertrag mit Schutzwirkung zugunsten Dritter (2006); *Karner* (fn 3) §1295 no 19.

49 OGH 7.12.1978, 2 Ob 133/78 = JBl 1980, 39 with cmt by *H Koziol*; 26.11.1992, 1 Ob 601/92 = JBl 1994, 331 with cmt by *M Karollus*.

50 See OGH 16.1.1979, 4 Ob 57/78 = Das Recht der Arbeit (DRdA) 1980, 27 with critical cmt by *H Koziol*; *W Dehn* in: H Koziol/P Bydlinski/R Bollenberger (eds), Kurzkommentar zum ABGB (5th edn 2017) §1489 no 9; *R Rebhahn*, Zur neuen Regelung der Verjährung im BGB und zur langen Verjährung von Schadenersatzansprüchen, in: FS Welser (2004) 868 ff. Firmly dissenting *Koziol*, Haftpflichtrecht I (fn 15) no 15/19; *id* (fn 17) no 21 ff; *R Madl*, Beginn der langen Verjährung nach §1489 Satz 2 ABGB unabhängig vom Eintritt eines Schadens? in: FS Koziol (2010) 759 ff; *P Vollmaier* in: A Fenyves/F Kerschner/A Vonkilch (eds), Klang-Kommentar zum Allgemeinen Bürgerlichen Gesetzbuch (3rd edn 2012) §1489 no 48.

of sexual abuse.[51] These prescription periods, as well as rules on suspension and interruption, apply to both contract and tort law alike. A contractual extension of prescription terms is not valid (§1502 ABGB).

J. DIFFERENCES AS REGARDS PROOF

As mentioned above, differences concerning proof are significant. In tort, the plaintiff has to prove all preconditions for the injurer's liability, particularly that the injurer acted culpably (§1296 ABGB). In contract, the burden of proof is reversed at the expense of the defendant: he has to prove that the he was not at fault (§1298 ABGB).[52] 34

As far as the standard of proof is concerned, there are no differences between tort and contract law: the evidence must support a probability bordering on certainty or at least very high probability.[53] Preponderant probability does not suffice. 35

K. OTHER DIFFERENCES

According to §176 ABGB, a minor is responsible for torts from the age of 14 onwards. However, some tensions exist in respect of the relationship between the responsibility for torts on the one hand, and the legal capacity for entering into contracts, fully gained at the age of 18 (§21 ABGB), on the other. Consequently, it is disputed whether a minor between the age of 14 and 18 can be held liable on the basis of *culpa in contrahendo*, particularly for obscuring his true age and misleading potential contract partners, or if the rules of legal capacity, which aim at the protection of minors, bar such a liability.[54] 36

L. REASONS FOR THE DIFFERENCES

As has already been pointed out, contractual liability is more favourable for the plaintiff than tortious liability:[55] pure economic losses are recoverable, 37

---

[51] Cf *M Spitzer/F Kernbichler*, Kindesmissbrauch und §1489 ABGB – Brüche zwischen strafrechtlicher und zivilrechtlicher Verjährung, ÖJZ 2010, 330 ff.

[52] Supra fn 4.

[53] *Klicka* (fn 27) 33; *Rechberger/Simotta* (fn 27) no 813.

[54] *C Fischer-Czermak*, Zur Haftung beschränkt Geschäftsfähiger aus culpa in contrahendo, in: FS Reischauer (2010) 117 ff with further refs.

[55] *Karner* (fn 3) §1295 no 1 with further refs.

the burden of proving fault is reversed at the expense of the injuring party (§1298 ABGB) and the tortfeasor is liable for all his auxiliaries according to §1313a ABGB. The reasons for the different levels of protection are manifold:[56] insofar as the protection of pure economic interests is concerned, the main reason is that liability would incalculably increase if pure economic losses were generally compensable under tort law. On the other hand, if someone enters into an obligation and forms a special relationship with another person, it seems reasonable to impose greater duties of care as both parties have an enhanced influence not only on the legal goods but also on the pure economic interest of their counterpart. Hence, it is in the interest of both parties to minimise the possibility of damage to their relationship. This objective is ensured by the stricter rules of contractual liability.

III. LIMITATION OR EXCLUSION OF LIABILITY ARISING FROM TORT AND FROM CONTRACT

A. STATUTORY PROVISIONS AUTHORISING A LIMITATION OR EXCLUSION OF LIABILITY

38 Austrian law in principle does not provide for reduction clauses or similar provisions allowing judges to mitigate the duty imposed upon the liable person, neither in tort nor in contract law. However, according to §§2 ff DHG, the courts can reduce the liability of employees towards their employers if they acted only (slightly or grossly) negligently: in the case of slightest negligence, they may even be relieved from liability altogether.

B. LIMITATION OR EXCLUSION OF CONTRACTUAL AND TORTIOUS LIABILITY BY CONTRACT

1) Is it Possible to Limit or Exclude Contractual or Tortious Liability under a Contract?

a) Statutory Provisions for Specific Contracts

39 The Austrian Consumer Protection Statute (*Konsumentenschutzgesetz*, KSchG) in its art 6 para 1 no 9 prevents entrepreneurs from including in their B2C contracts provisions whereby 'an obligation on the entrepreneur's part to make

56 See *Koziol* (fn 4) no 4/5.

good any damage for personal injuries is excluded or limited or an obligation on the entrepreneur's part to make good any other damage is excluded or limited if he or a person for whom he is responsible causes the damage deliberately or as a result of gross negligence'.[57] Paragraph 2 of said article requires an express stipulation of a clause providing that 'an obligation on the part of the entrepreneur to make good any damage to an article which he has accepted for processing is excluded or limited', thereby at least ruling out such clauses in standard form contracts. §12 para 4 sent 2 of the Package Travel Act (*Pauschalreisegesetz*, PRG) now provides that there can be no contractual limitation in advance of the liability in damages of a travel operator under the statute.

According to §970a ABGB, hotel-keepers cannot exclude their special liability according to §§970 ff ABGB by merely posting a notice. Article 160 LFG prevents air carriers from excluding or limiting liability under the carriage contract. 40

b) Statutory Provisions for Specific Torts

Some strict liability statutes specifically rule out or at least restrict the contractual freedom to limit or exclude liability. 41

Article 9 Product Liability Act (*Produkthaftungsgesetz*, PHG) and art 21 AtomHG[58] stipulate that liability foreseen by these statutes 'may be neither excluded nor limited beforehand'. The same is true for art 5 Reich Liability Act (*Reichshaftpflichtgesetz*, RHPflG).

According to art 10 EKHG, train operators or keepers of motor vehicles must not exclude or limit their liability for fatal or bodily injuries suffered by paying passengers beforehand, which not only allows them to still provide for such limitations regarding property damage, but also if they carry passengers for free under an *ex ante* contractual agreement. A similar policy underlies art 167 MinroG: the holder of a mining operation must not limit or exclude liability for the death or personal injury of workers, paying visitors or other people present in the mine 'for a justified cause'.

c) General Approach Towards Contractual Limitation of Liability in Practice

Even in the absence of express rules on contractual modifications of liability, the general rule of §879 para 1 ABGB may still preclude such alterations if deemed unconscionable.[59] Several express rules already mentioned were subsequently 42

57 Translation according to <https://www.ris.bka.gv.at/Dokument.wxe?Abfrage=Erv&Dokumentnummer=ERV_1979_140> accessed 28.1.2018.

58 'Liability for damages under this Federal Act may be neither excluded nor limited beforehand.'

59 *Koziol*, Haftpflichtrecht I (fn 15) no 18/4.

considered to be just a codification of a specific case otherwise governed by §879 ABGB.[60]

43 This is commonly agreed to be the case with respect to intentional harm. Opinions are split, however, when it comes to excluding or limiting liability for gross negligence. Courts are less favourable towards such provisions if only contained in standard form contracts, whereas individual specific agreements might stand the test. Some decisions do not disapprove of the exclusion of liability for gross negligence in general, only if it is 'particularly gross' (even though such category of fault otherwise does not exist).[61] The type of harm is also decisive: courts are hostile towards provisions limiting or excluding liability for bodily harm and disallow them in standard form contracts even for slight negligence,[62] while liability for grossly negligently inflicted personal injury cannot be excluded at all, not even by individual arrangement. Furthermore, some cases allow *ex ante* restrictions with respect to foreseeable harm but forbid them when it comes to atypical risks.[63]

44 While it is highly unlikely that tortious liability will have been mutually modified by the parties *ex ante*, the question remains whether someone can unilaterally exclude liability up to a certain limit under certain (needless to say: very specific) circumstances. This is the case, for example, if someone gives access to or grants passage through his property for free without entering into an agreement with the beneficiaries (mere toleration of passage). While it is – again – impossible to exclude liability for personal injury caused by gross negligence, it is commonly understood that one can at least rule out liability for lower degrees of negligence in such cases. This is supported by §1319a ABGB, which already by statute only holds persons in charge of some road, way or passage liable for harm to those passing through only in cases of gross negligence or intent.[64]

45 If parties legitimately agree *ex ante* to modify or exclude each other's or one side's liability, this applies to both contractual and delictual liability unless specified expressly in the language of the agreement.

46 After the harmful event, parties can also agree to modify or exclude liability. Since liability in such cases has already arisen, any reduction thereof constitutes a waiver of existing rights and is consequently governed by the general rules on waiving rights.

---

60 See eg OGH 24.3.1998, 1 Ob 400/97y = Entscheidungen des Österreichischen Obersten Gerichtshofes in Zivil- (und Justizverwaltungs-)sachen (SZ) 71/58.

61 Cf OGH 19.12.2013, 3 Ob 196/13i = Zivilrecht aktuell (Zak) 2014/173.

62 See eg OGH 22.2.2001, 6 Ob 160/00y = JBl 2001, 590.

63 See eg OGH 15.7.1997, 1 Ob 2374/96s = SZ 70/142; *Koziol*, Haftpflichtrecht I (fn 15) no 18/5 (see also the criticism to the practice regarding atypical risks, no 18/6 ff).

64 *Koziol*, Haftpflichtrecht I (fn 15) no 18/36, who also emphasises that liability may not arise at all in such cases if the person passing through another's property acts at his own risk.

If more than one individual is liable for the same loss (for example, in the case of joint, concurrent or alternative wrongdoing triggering joint and several liability), and one of them has *ex ante* stipulated with the victim to exclude or reduce liability, the remaining wrongdoer still has to compensate the whole loss under his joint and several liability vis-à-vis the victim. The issue arises, however, to what extent the payor can seek recourse from the other wrongdoer in light of the latter's exclusion or reduction of liability. This has to be seen in light of §896 ABGB, whose last sentence in essence provides that releasing someone from a solidary obligation cannot affect the rights of the remaining persons liable to claim recourse. This is also supported by the fact that a contractual agreement must not impose burdens upon a third party.[65] However, since the contractual modification of liability primarily intended to allocate risks, the beneficiary of an agreement limiting or excluding his liability can pass on any duties arising under the aforementioned recourse claims of a third party to his contractual partner, ie the victim, who effectively had negotiated with the beneficiary upfront that any loss arising in the course of their contractual arrangement would have to be borne by himself rather than by the beneficiary.[66] 47

2) To What Extent can a Contractual Exclusion Provide a Defence to a Third Party to the Contract?

Third parties may benefit from a contractual exclusion if the parties to the contract intended not to pursue any such claims against these third parties. This may be the case, for example, if the contracting parties lawfully limit or exclude liability vis-à-vis each other and want to extend such restrictions to their respective auxiliaries, who might otherwise face a more far-reaching liability than their employers (though only in delict).[67] 48

The reverse is not true – it is impossible to curtail potential claims of third parties by some *ex ante* agreement: a contract at the expense of third parties (*Vertrag zu Lasten Dritter*) is void. The question is particularly relevant for contracts with a protective purpose vis-à-vis third parties (*Vertrag mit Schutzwirkung zugunsten Dritter*), which may provide for limitations *inter partes* to the extent permissible. In such constellations one has to differentiate: if the interests of the third parties coincide with those of the contracting parties, the rights of these third parties cannot exceed those arising under the contract itself, so that contractual modifications of liability would also affect potential claims of such third parties. This is the case, for example, if someone buys services 49

65 *Koziol*, Haftpflichtrecht I (fn 15) no 14/32 ff (no 14/34).
66 *Koziol*, Haftpflichtrecht I (fn 15) no 14/35.
67 *Koziol*, Haftpflichtrecht I (fn 15) no 18/39.

from another in order to fulfil his own obligations vis-à-vis a third party. If the service provider is aware of this and his services are at least also targeted on the interests of the ultimate beneficiary, ie the third party, any exemption of liability stipulated by the service provider must also extend to such third party.[68] However, if the interests of the contracting parties deviate from those of the third parties, the former cannot reduce or even exclude their liabilities vis-à-vis the latter.[69] This is debated with respect to the quasi-contractual liability of producers to ultimate consumers – if a manufacturer limited his liability for product defects in his distribution contracts, this will only concern claims by retailers and other distributors, but must not affect the rights of the ultimate consumers, even if Austrian court practice tends to think otherwise, since the interests of the parties to the distribution contract are not in line with those of the ultimate consumers.[70]

IV. NON-CONCURRENCE OR CONCURRENCE OF ACTIONS

A. OVERVIEW

50 Since the ABGB treats both tortious and contractual liability under the same rules, it does not draw a strict line between the two by ordering a rule of *non cumul* or the like. If the requirements of both paths towards liability are given, the plaintiff can choose between the two or file suit on both counts, even though he will obviously only recover once.[71] For practical reasons, however, a plaintiff will typically prefer a contractual cause of action in light of the advantages this alternative offers (burden of proving fault reversed, easier access to compensation for pure economic loss, and in particular the by far more preferable rules on vicarious liability). Since the law maintains that rather generous approach by allowing concurrent actions throughout, it does not matter what kind of harm the victim has suffered, as treated separately by the next subsections. The fact that pure economic loss is more readily indemnified under a contractual cause

68 Take the example of an attorney who asks an expert to assist him internally in a case with one of his clients. The substance of the expert's advice targets the interests of the attorney's client, and if the expert is only willing to provide his services subject to a limitation of his potential liability, this impacts upon the subsequent personal claims of the client as well. Cf *Karner* (fn 9) 708 ff, 718 f; *E Karner/H Koziol*, Mangelfolgeschäden in Veräußerungsketten (2012) 63 ff, 77 ff.

69 *Koziol*, Haftpflichtrecht I (fn 15) no 18/40 f.

70 Cf *Koziol*, Haftpflichtrecht I (fn 15) no 18/40; OGH 28.11.1978, 5 Ob 707/78 = SZ 51/169.

71 While this can be seen as two separate (though concurrent) causes of action or just one with a dual line of reasoning, the latter interpretation is to be preferred in light of the Austrian legislative peculiarity that contractual and tortious liability are treated as one in the ABGB; cf *Koziol* (fn 4) no 4/18 f.

of action does not as such exclude a claim filed in tort – the plaintiff is just much less likely to succeed.

B. CONCURRENCE/EXCLUSION OF ACTIONS FOR THE PROTECTION AGAINST PERSONAL INJURY

As can be seen particularly in medical malpractice cases, victims who sustained 51
personal injuries or the surviving relatives of a deceased victim can claim compensation both on a tort as well as on a contractual basis, while only recovering once, of course.

The tort cause of action rests upon an interference with a so-called absolute right of the victim, ie an interest that is protected against harmful interference by anybody. However, the interference per se does not suffice to establish wrongfulness, it is merely deemed to serve as an indication of unlawful conduct.[72] The consent of the victim may serve as a defence, which – if valid – justifies medical treatment that otherwise would be regarded as an illegal infliction of bodily harm. As a defence, the (informed) consent of the patient has to be proven by the defendant doctor or hospital, whereas it is up to the patient to prove any deficiencies in the information provided to him if his action rests solely on the reasoning that the doctor failed to properly reveal all risks associated with the treatment (as obliged under the treatment contract).[73]

C. CONCURRENCE/EXCLUSION OF ACTIONS FOR THE PROTECTION OF PROPERTY

Claims for compensation of property damage can be based both on a contract as 52
well as on a tort basis. Damage to property constitutes a violation of an absolute right that indicates (though not per se fully establishes) wrongfulness, whereas it will arise from a breach of some contractual duty in the former case.[74] It is not unlikely that victims will sue on both grounds.[75]

---

72 See supra no 8 on Austria's preference for the so-called '*Verhaltensunrecht*' (unlawfulness of conduct).

73 See *BA Koch*, Medical Liability in Austria, in: BA Koch (ed), Medical Liability in Europe (2011) 1 (no 72).

74 Cf supra no 8.

75 Cf eg OGH 2.7.1998, 2 Ob 153/98f: The claimant's car had been destroyed in an accident while being (negligently) driven by the defendant. Whereas the claimant argued that he had lent the defendant his car and that the latter was therefore liable for breaching his contractual duty to return it, the court questioned whether the two parties had indeed entered into a legally binding agreement. It nevertheless confirmed liability by referring to the defendant's interference with the claimant's absolute property right, ie to a tort cause of action.

D. CONCURRENCE/EXCLUSION IN THE CASE OF INTERFERENCE WITH CONTRACTUAL RIGHTS

1) *Interference with a Contractual Relationship*

53 Generally, tort law only provides remedies for the intentional interference with another's contractual rights. It does not suffice that the tortfeasor knows of the existence of the victim's rights as a creditor and that these may be impaired by the tortfeasor's pursuance of his own interests. Instead, the latter's conduct must be aimed at preventing the creditor from obtaining what he can claim under the contract. The tortfeasor must specifically induce the debtor to breach the contract.[76] Merely negligent interference with another's contractual rights only triggers (tortious) liability if such rights are evident to third parties such as the tortfeasor.[77] The latter would be confirmed, for example, in a case where land had been sold twice and the (chronologically) first buyer had not yet been entered into the land register as the new owner (which is required under Austrian law for the title to pass). If that buyer had already taken possession of the land and made installations thereupon, a subsequent buyer of the same land should have realised that it had already been promised to another, so that he was acting in bad faith at the time he entered into the (second) sales contract with the seller.[78]

2) *Loss of Business due to Personal Injury to Someone Else's Employees or Clients or to Property Damage Incurred by the Entrepreneur*

54 Austrian law is quite reluctant to indemnify secondary or tertiary losses (*mittelbarer Schaden*) that a third party incurs as a domino effect of some primary injury to the immediate victim, particularly if it is a pure economic loss that this third party incurs and not one that is merely consequential to some primary harm (like the recoverable loss of business an entrepreneur suffers due to damage to *his* property). If an employee is injured, his employer will at some point no longer have to pay his salaries (subject to the restrictions of labour law), from which time onwards the loss of income will be incurred by the immediate victim. This loss of income is recoverable (§1325 ABGB). As far as it was shifted from the immediate victim to the employer due to regulations of labour law, the claim of the immediate victim is transferred to the employer by

---

76 OGH 10.4.1968, 6 Ob 97/68 = SZ 41/45.

77 The fact that contractual rights are usually not evident to third parties is the prime reason why their interference with such rights only triggers liability under certain strict conditions; cf *H Koziol*, The Nature of the Interests Protected by Tort Law, in: H Koziol (ed), Unification of Tort Law: Wrongfulness (1998) 29, 30; *id*, Österreichisches Haftpflichtrecht II (3rd edn 2018) no A/2/199 ff.

78 Eg OGH 19.10.1976, 5 Ob 671/76 = JBl 1977, 257.

law (so-called *Drittschadensliquidation*).[79] The fact that the employer has to seek a replacement or cannot fulfil his own obligations vis-à-vis his clients because he is missing a crucial employee is by contrast a separate loss that will not have to be indemnified by the employee's injurer, since the link between the latter's conduct and the damage incurred by the employer is not strong enough to justify liability, particularly in light of the floodgates argument, and thereby falls outside the scope of tortious liability: the purpose of the duty not to injure the employee is solely to protect the employee and not the employer.[80]

V. SPECIFIC SITUATIONS

A. PRE-CONTRACTUAL LIABILITY

As has long been established in practice, the (more favourable) rules of contractual liability (§§1298, 1313a ABGB)[81] extend to harmful conduct by parties who have not yet entered into a contract (and perhaps never will), but who have at least already approached each other with an eye towards possibly concluding a contract (so-called *culpa in contrahendo*). The approximation of either side's sphere singles them out vis-à-vis each other and gradually creates specific duties of care the closer they get.[82] This is obviously not necessarily physical proximity, even though the latter is particularly relevant if one of them is bodily injured during such a pre-contractual phase. Knowledge of each other's actual identity is not required either, even though it may further increase or at least specify the duties of care owed. A shop-owner, for example, has to create and maintain an environment for his prospective customers that prevents them from suffering harm. 55

The interests potentially harmed play a significant role in defining these duties of care – the higher the interest, the further such duties extend. The latter rule is equally valid in the law of delict, of course, but the proximity between potential contracting parties specifies and at least thereby extends the range of duties owed, as the contact between them allows them to identify specific needs, for example. In the shop example, its owner knows or at least should know the expectations and experiences possible customers have with respect to the environment in which they enter into contractual negotiations, and which

79 *Karner* (fn 3) §1295 no 17 with further refs.

80 *Koziol*, Haftpflichtrecht I (fn 15) no 13/13.

81 See supra no 2.

82 This is not exclusive to pre-contractual relations – such special proximity triggering special duties may also exist in a relationship based on mere courtesy rather than actual willingness to enter into a legally binding agreement; cf *Koziol*, Haftpflichtrecht I (fn 15) no 4/46; *id* (fn 4) no 4/11.

the owner specifically establishes for such purpose. The mirror image of this is equally true, though – whoever is about to shop for groceries should be aware of the possibility that lettuce leaves may be on the floor in the immediate vicinity of the vegetables section, which has an impact on the appropriate frequency of cleaning that area.[83]

B. LIABILITY OF PROFESSIONALS

56 Irrespective of the basis of the claim – whether tort or contract – professionals have to abide by a higher standard of care set by §1299 ABGB. Contrary to the general rule of §1297 ABGB, which stipulates a subjective standard of fault taking into account the abilities of the individual tortfeasor,[84] an objective standard of care is applied as far as experts are concerned: they are responsible for skills typical of their profession and may not argue that their personal abilities are below average. This can be justified given the fact that, firstly, a person who carries out an activity requiring special skills despite not possessing them creates a particular danger to his contractual partners as well as to third parties. Secondly, the expert in question can be expected to omit the dangerous activity without greater difficulty, and thirdly, the expert earns a special profit through his activity. In this respect, the strict standard of liability serves deterrent and preventive purposes.[85] Yet even experts may prove that they were subjectively incapable of complying with the objective standard of care, for example due to unconsciousness.[86]

57 As with other defendants, plaintiffs can choose between tort and contract actions (and even pursue their claims on both grounds), though contractual liability provides for certain advantages which are also present in cases filed against professionals, in particular if these employ auxiliaries, in which case the more beneficial rule of vicarious liability (§1313a ABGB) applies.

CASES

CASE 1. THE UNATTRACTIVE SHOPPING MALL

58 C cannot bring a tort-based claim against D, since the loss he incurs constitutes a pure economic loss, which is in principle not recoverable under tort law.[87]

---

83 See infra no 77.

84 *Karner* (fn 3) §1294 no 7; *Koziol*, Haftpflichtrecht I (fn 15) no 5/1; *id*, Fault under Austrian Law, in: P Widmer (ed), Unification of Tort Law: Fault (2005) 15 f.

85 *Koziol*, Fault (fn 84) 16 ff; *id* (fn 4) no 6/89.

86 *R Reischauer* (fn 18) §1299 no 5; *Karner* (fn 3) §1299 no 1.

87 *Karner* (fn 3) §1295 no 2 with further refs.

Furthermore, no direct contractual claim is available to C because C and D did not conclude a contract. However, C is foreseeably affected by the fulfilment of the contract between D and Z, since this contract allows Z to sublet the store. Therefore, it was foreseeable at the time the contract was concluded that the tenant himself or any of his subtenants, to whom Z is entitled to sublet the store according to the tenancy agreement, would be affected by its fulfilment. It is therefore not necessary that the specific person actually affected was already known to the parties at the time of conclusion of the contract, which is why it does not matter that D was not informed of the fact of subletting or the identity of subtenant C.[88] Consequently, the contract between D and Z becomes a contract with protective effect vis-à-vis a third party C (*Vertrag mit Schutzwirkung zugunsten Dritter*). Compensation claims for pure economic losses generally cannot be based on such contracts with positive protective effects, in order to avoid excessively extending the debtor's liability. This principle does not apply, however, in cases where the third party should be the beneficiary of the main contractual duty.[89] This is exactly the case here, since C should benefit from the duties arising out of the contract between D and Z. In addition, only C incurs a loss and therefore there is no risk of extending D's liability. If C could not claim damages from D, D could not be held liable by anyone, neither by C nor by Z, who does not incur a loss. Insofar as the decline in sales constitutes a loss of profits, §349 UGB can be applied to the B2B contract, which means that even in cases of slight negligence, contrary to the general rule of §§1323 and 1324 ABGB, a loss of profits is compensable.[90]

CASE 2. THE IDLE LAWYER

The loss incurred by the daughters constitutes a pure economic loss and 59
consequently they cannot bring a tort-based claim. Although they are not party to a contract with D, the contract between W and D can be regarded as a contract with protective effect vis-à-vis the daughters (*Vertrag mit Schutzwirkung zugunsten Dritter*), since the daughters should have benefitted from the main contractual duty, namely the change of W's last will.[91] As already noted,[92] pure economic losses are usually not compensable in such cases, since the debtor's

[88] *Koziol*, Haftpflichtrecht II (fn 77) no A/2/361 ff; for a detailed analysis of contracts with protective effects vis-à-vis third parties, see also *F Bydlinski*, Vertragliche Sorgfaltspflichten zugunsten Dritter, JBl 1960, 359 ff.

[89] *Koziol* (fn 4) no 4/13; *id*, Haftpflichtrecht II (fn 77) A/2/372 ff.

[90] §349 UGB determines that '[a]mong entrepreneurs, the damage to be compensated includes lost profit'; see supra no 4.

[91] See also Case 1 and infra no 61.

[92] Cf supra no 58.

liability should not be extended unreasonably. In this case, however, there is no risk of extending D's liability: if the daughters were not able to file a claim against D, D could not be held liable by anyone even though he acted negligently.[93] Consequently, the daughters may claim compensation for their pure economic loss based on the protective effect of the contract between D and W.

CASE 3. THE DEFECTIVE HOUSE

60 In a first step, the question is whether C can file a tort-based claim against D. As regards the collapse of the house, C's damage constitutes a pure economic loss: the loss incurred by C results from the fact that C paid the price for a flawless house but received a defective one. Therefore, the amount by which the buying price for the house was excessive must be regarded as the loss suffered by C. Since the loss incurred by C results from a disturbance of the balance between performance and counter-performance, none of C's absolute rights have been infringed and C suffers only pure economic loss. Consequently, C cannot claim tort-based compensation for the damage caused to the house. However, a different view must be taken with regard to the physical injury. By building a defective house, D created a source of danger. Therefore, legal duties to maintain safety (*Verkehrssicherungspflichten*) ought to have been observed vis-à-vis third parties in general and not only vis-à-vis contracting parties.[94] C can therefore claim compensation for his bodily injury based on tortious liability. The exclusion of liability agreed between D and Z does not have any effect on C with regard to tort-based claims, since it is not possible for D and Z to make an agreement that impairs the legal position of third parties.

61 In addition, it must be determined whether C has contractual liability claims against D. Again, claims for compensation of the damage caused to the house must be strictly distinguished from those regarding bodily injury. Since there is no direct contractual relationship between C and D, the question arises whether the contract between D and Z includes protective duties vis-à-vis third parties (*Vertrag mit Schutzwirkung zugunsten Dritter*). For a contract to have such protective duties, it is a prerequisite that the third party is foreseeably endangered at the time the contract was concluded by an incorrect fulfilment of

---

93 Regarding the problem of a debtor not being liable vis-à-vis anyone, neither his contractual partner nor the beneficiary of the main contractual duty, see *Koziol*, Haftpflichtrecht II (fn 77) no A/2/373.

94 *Koziol*, Haftpflichtrecht II (fn 77) no B/1/1 ff. The basic idea behind these legal duties to maintain safety is that a person who created a source of danger should also be responsible for removing it; otherwise he or she can be held liable for damage caused by this special source of danger.

duties arising from that contract.[95] In our case, however, it is rather questionable whether a third party (in this case C) was foreseeably affected – at least in the abstract – by the contract between D and Z. Even if we assume that C was foreseeably endangered and therefore the contract between D and Z had a protective effect towards him, further problems arise: the damage caused to the house represents a pure economic loss for C and is therefore generally not compensable.[96] In addition, only duties of protection and care are extended to third parties, whereas the main contractual duties can only be enforced by the contracting parties themselves.[97] Consequently, C cannot claim compensation for the damage caused to the house, since the delivery of a flawless house constitutes the main contractual duty under the contract between D and Z. In contrast to the damage to the house, the physical injury suffered by C would in principle be encompassed by the protective effect of the contract between D and Z.[98] However, the exclusion of liability laid down in this contract must be taken into account. Here, the liability exclusion is restricted to property damage, which is why C's claim for compensation of the physical injury is not at all affected by it. But what would be the solution to the case if the liability exclusion also encompassed bodily injury? According to the prevalent opinion in Austria, a contractual exclusion of liability is also effective in respect of third parties who base their claims on a contract with protective effects. However, we must examine whether such a liability exclusion clause would actually be valid. If D was an entrepreneur and Z a consumer, liability for physical harm could not be excluded at all and liability for other damage could only be reduced to cases of gross negligence or intent according to §6 para 1 no 9 of the Austrian Consumer Protection Statute (*Konsumentenschutzgesetz*, KSchG). Otherwise, the validity of the clause must be examined on the basis of the general rule of §879 ABGB.[99]

CASE 4. APARTMENT IN FLAMES

C can sue D both on a contract and on a tort basis. Her landlord, D, obviously 62
owes her certain duties of care under the rental agreement, which necessarily provides inter alia for reasonable and adequate efforts to maintain safety in the

95 Although it is not necessary for the contracting parties to know exactly who this third party will be, there must be at least some reasonable possibility that a third party will be affected by the contract; see *Koziol*, Haftpflichtrecht II (fn 77) no A/2/363 ff; see also Case 1.

96 See already Case 1.

97 See also Case 6.

98 This of course requires that the contract between D and Z actually includes protective duties vis-à-vis C.

99 See *Koziol*, Haftpflichtrecht I (fn 15) no 18/11 ff; *G Kodek* in: A Kletečka/M Schauer (eds), ABGB-ON – Kommentar zum Allgemeinen bürgerlichen Gesetzbuch (1.10.2013) §1295 no 93 ff.

building. Such (contractual!) duties are typically even held to extend to third parties such as cohabitants, who can then also sue D on a contractual basis instead of relying on a pure delictual cause of action. The rental agreement thereby becomes a contract with protective effect vis-à-vis third parties (*Vertrag mit Schutzwirkung zugunsten Dritter*) since cohabiting family members have to be expected to be present on the rented premises at least temporarily, which means that the duties owed by the landlord to the immediate tenant regarding building safety are stretched to also protect such non-parties to the rental agreement.

63 While D would probably also be considered to owe certain duties of care to the public at large and therefore might also be sued in tort, it will be more difficult to establish liability for practical reasons: if D had employed auxiliaries to monitor the circuit breaker, for example, he would only have to account for their failure to do so had they met the highly restrictive standard of §1315 ABGB, so if they were objectively unfit or otherwise dangerous to do the job. This is probably one of the prime reasons why the theory of a contract with protective effect vis-à-vis third parties is applied so readily in such cases, since the plaintiff can instead rely upon the more generous vicarious liability provision of §1313a ABGB.

CASE 5. INJURED SKIER

64 D2 may succeed on the latter count since the insurance contract language clearly reduced cover to cases of tortious liability. If it just said 'liability' instead, courts would hold that this includes both tortious and contractual liability, which also brings the latter under the insurance cover.

65 However, even if the policy had excluded contractual liability as suggested by D2, D1 may be liable in tort as well, such that D2 would still have to provide cover. Ski lifts fall under a statutory regime of strict liability, so that the more restrictive approach towards vicarious liability in tort does not play any significant role here. If the conditions of the EKHG that applies here are fulfilled, which very well may be the case if the lift derailed, D1's concurrent liability in contract (and the issue raised by D2) would only play a role if C's claim exceeded the monetary caps of the EKHG.

CASE 6. EXPLODING CAR

66 Considering that a defect in the fuel line is a flaw within the sphere of D2 only, D1 will not be liable unless he was aware of the defect at the time of sale and failed to warn C of such risks. D2 is not an auxiliary of D1, so the defect can also not be attributed to the latter via vicarious liability.

D2 will not be liable under strict product liability in light of art 1 para 1 PHG, which implemented art 9 lit b of the EC Product Liability Directive, limiting its scope for property losses to 'damage to, or destruction of, any item of property other than the defective product itself'.[100] 67

While a claim under fault-based liability in tort is theoretically possible, it seems unlikely (notwithstanding further facts) that D2 personally (!) is to blame for the defect, and his vicarious liability for his employees is extremely limited by §1315 ABGB. 68

The only remaining potential basis of a claim against D2 is the predecessor of the strict liability statute, a theory commonly referred to as *Produzentenhaftung* (producers' liability) rather than the statutory *Produkthaftung* (product liability). It developed in the absence of a special legislative regime at the time, inter alia to circumvent the narrow boundaries of §1315 ABGB. Under this theory, the original contract of the producer with his distributor(s) includes protective duties vis-à-vis third parties (*Vertrag mit Schutzwirkung zugunsten Dritter*), since the ultimate consumers/product users are foreseeably exposed to any risks associated with the product upon putting it into circulation. C is therefore within the protective scope of D2's distribution contract and may consequently avail himself of a (quasi-)contractual claim including in particular the benefit of a more generous vicarious liability rule (§1313a ABGB) and a reversal of the burden of proving fault to D2 (§1298 ABGB).[101] This theory can still be applied despite the European Court of Justice's (ECJ) rulings regarding the exclusivity of the EC product liability regime since the latter is confined to no-fault tort claims, whereas not only fault-based, but in particular also contractual claims remain possible.[102] Such a claim would also not yet be time-barred since, according to §1489 ABGB, the prescription period begins to run three years from the date when C became aware of both damage and D2 as the person possibly liable for it.[103] 69

However, this theory only applies to losses caused by the defective product to other items or to persons, but not if the product itself is damaged: such a diminution of its value is deemed to be a pure economic loss in the relationship between D2 and C, and the aforementioned theory of producers' liability does not cover such losses according to prevailing theory and court practice.[104] 70

---

[100] Whether or not P has a claim against the producer of the component (the fuel line) under product liability is disputed, but should be answered in the affirmative; see *H Koziol/P Apathy/BA Koch*, Österreichisches Haftpflichtrecht III (3rd edn 2014) no B/97 ff.

[101] See *Koziol/Apathy/Koch* (fn 100) no B/4 f.

[102] See eg ECJ 25.4.2002, C-183/00, *González Sánchez v Medicina Asturiana SA*, ECLI:EU:C:2002:255.

[103] The long-stop period of 30 years running from the day the car was put into circulation has not expired yet either according to the facts.

[104] Austrian Supreme Court (Oberster Gerichtshof, OGH) 28.11.1978, 5 Ob 707/78 = SZ 51/169.

Moreover, one has to bear in mind that only duties of protection and care are extended to third parties, whereas the main contractual duties regarding the product itself can only be enforced by the contracting parties themselves. Even if C had suffered some personal injury or loss to other property in the course of the explosion, his claim under said theory may still fail if D2's distribution contract excluded liability for slight negligence, which will – according to constant jurisdiction – extend to third parties as well and thereby preclude C's claim if D2 can prove that the negligence within his sphere did not exceed that threshold.[105]

CASE 7. RACING BOAT BURNING

71 C might have a contractual liability claim against D based on fault, which is not excluded by the warranty clause unless its interpretation leads to the conclusion that the parties to the sales contract wanted to cut off any claims after the expiration of the two-year period. However, this would require fault within D's sphere, such as knowledge of the defect or mishandling of the device upon installation. While it is, according to §1298 ABGB, D's burden to prove that neither he nor his auxiliaries were at fault, that task is not unmanageable. Tort-based claims are not possible in light of the pure economic loss incurred by C (purchase price for the defective boat, repatriation expenses).

CASE 8. INSIDIOUS REPORT

72 C could sue D for compensation on the basis of a culpable breach of the latter's contractual fiduciary duties. As an employee, D is obligated to maintain loyalty towards C, which he clearly violated. This would not only be a valid reason for firing D under art 27 para 1 Employees Act (*Angestelltengesetz*, AngG), but also provides for compensatory remedies.[106] If D had acted after terminating his employment with C, the latter's claim could also be based upon art 1 Unfair Competition Act (*Bundesgesetz gegen den unlauteren Wettbewerb*, UWG).[107]

---

105 Cf the Austrian Supreme Court case cited in fn 104 and the criticism against such an extended scope of an exoneration clause to third parties cited in *Koziol/Apathy/Koch* (fn 100) no B/4 fn 6.

106 Cf OGH 10.2.1993, 9 ObA 1/93 = Sammlung arbeitsrechtlicher Entscheidungen (Arb) 11.072 (defendant employee solicited colleagues from the plaintiff to a competitor company the defendant had founded while still employed by the plaintiff).

107 This would require that D systematically poached staff from C with the intent to harm the latter or for similarly reprehensible motives; cf OGH 26.9.1990, 9 ObA 231, 232/90 = Österreichisches Recht der Wirtschaft (RdW) 1991, 119. Offering better conditions per se would not suffice, eg as this is part of the ordinary competition on the labour market. However, it were unfair within the meaning of the UWG if someone for example entices

CASE 9. CIRCULAR LETTER

Such conduct by D would fall under art 7 UWG, which, inter alia, provides for compensatory relief against any harm ensuing from such anti-competitive behaviour.[108] 73

CASE 10. SHORTAGE OF SUPPLY

Whether or not C actually has a valid claim against D depends upon the exact circumstances of the case that are missing from the hypothetical (such as whether this was a long-term relationship or just a singular acquisition, to what extent the changes on the supply side were due to altered general market conditions and how foreseeable these were to both parties, etc). More importantly, the modification of essential contract terms evidently accepted by C would have to be scrutinised further, and to what extent it can be avoided. If C intends to seek compensation, one imaginable path may be opened (again) by the rules against unfair competition or the more general rules on unconscionability (§1295 para 2 ABGB). 74

CASE 11. INJURED ROCK STAR

Koziol solved a similar hypothetical by arguing that if C is relieved from his duty to pay X due to the latter's inability to perform, it is X who incurs a loss of income (as a consequence of and in addition to his physical injuries), whereas C's loss is additional and distinct therefrom. In light of its purely economic nature, such loss must remain uncompensated.[109] 75

CASE 12. EQUIPMENT DESTROYED

While claims against D1 will be governed by the general rules of freight contracts and by the specific terms of his arrangements with C (that potentially include specific safeguards for the untimely arrival of the equipment), claims 76

an employee of his competitor to leave the latter's employment inter alia by promising to pay any liquidated damages owed by the employee under a non-competitive clause in his employment contract, which not only evidences that the prospective new employer knew of such obligations, but acted specifically to induce his future employee to breach such duties; cf OGH 18.2.2003, 4 Ob 290/02d = SZ 2003/12.

[108] OGH 20.3.2007, 4 Ob 247/06m = Medien und Recht (MR) 2007, 203.

[109] *Koziol*, Haftpflichtrecht I (fn 15) no 13/13.

against D2 will depend upon whether he was only the driver or also the keeper of the truck, in which case strict liability rules apply. Neither these nor the general rules on fault liability that apply to the driver will provide for compensation of the economic loss incurred by C resulting from the delay of the equipment. However, if C was the owner of the equipment that was damaged or even destroyed, he may not only claim the cost of repair or replacement of the equipment, which is capped at €1.2 million by art 16 para 1 no 1 EKHG if the claim is based upon strict liability, but may – in the case of gross negligence – also claim the consequential loss resulting from the non-usability of his equipment, which consists in his loss of earnings due to the cancellation of the concert and might be recoverable as *lucrum cessans* according to §§1323, 1324 ABGB.[110] If C was already indemnified by D1 under the freight contract, he may obviously not be compensated twice, now based upon tort law, but the claims as such do not exclude each other.

CASE 13. SLIPPING ON A LETTUCE LEAF

77 This is a common classroom hypothetical in Austria, based upon German cases.[111] Just as in Germany, meanwhile,[112] Austrian courts would also apply the theory of *culpa in contrahendo* here and would grant C a (quasi-)contractual claim against D,[113] which may be preferable to an equally possible concurrent tort action,[114] if it was not D personally who is to blame for the inadequate

---

110 Cf *Koziol*, Haftpflichtrecht I (fn 15) no 2/40 f.

111 The immediate equivalent would be the vegetable leaf case Bundesgerichtshof (BGH) 28.1.1976 BGHZ 66, 51 (English translation at <http://www.utexas.edu/law/academics/centers/transnational/work_new/german/case.php?id=796> accessed 28.1.2018), where the German Supreme Court confirmed a *culpa in contrahendo* of a self-service store owner vis-à-vis potential buyers, the latter role being presumed of those entering the store. The court, however, obiter denied such liability if it is clear that the person entering the store had no intention to buy (such as someone merely seeking shelter from the rain). The original precedent was Reichsgericht 7.12.1911 RGZ 78, 239 (English translation at: <http://www.utexas.edu/law/academics/centers/transnational/work_new/german/case.php?id=807> accessed 28.1.2018), where the prospective buyer and her child fell on rolls of linoleum floor-cover dropped by a shop assistant. In this case, the court still distinguished between potential clients who had already entered into actual negotiations with the store (as here) and the situation where someone merely enters the store without yet entering into negotiations (in which case the Reichsgericht obiter denied liability).

112 This was not always the case, see eg OGH 18.5.1955, 2 Ob 260/55 = SZ 28/135: no contractual duty of care to keep the premises safe for potential clients. Similarly also OGH 18.12.1973, 3 Ob 167/73 = Evidenzblatt der Rechtsmittelentscheidungen (EvBl) in Österreichische Juristenzeitung (ÖJZ) 1974/109.

113 *Karner* (fn 3) §1294 no 5 with further refs.

114 Based upon the concept of so-called '*Verkehrssicherungspflichten*' (duties of care securing public passage or – as the literal translation would suggest – 'traffic'). Since extending to the public at large, the latter are typically narrower than duties owed among actual or prospective contractual partners.

cleaning of his store but rather one of his employees for whom he is liable comprehensively according to §1313a ABGB.

However, irrespective of whether based upon contractual or tortious liability, Austrian courts seem to define a storekeeper's duties of care rather narrowly and are anxious not to stretch his obligations vis-à-vis his (potential) clients too far. In a tort case where a client, before making a purchase, had also slipped on a lettuce leaf, the court denied liability by arguing that customers have to watch out themselves where they walk, that lettuce leaves can easily be discerned on a shop floor, and that it is quite common that pieces of fruit and vegetables fall on the ground in the part of the store where they are sold. The court stressed that it would be too burdensome for the storekeeper to have that area monitored constantly. Liability would only arise if the leaf on which the plaintiff had slipped had already been on the floor for so long that it should have been detected during the ordinary maintenance routine.[115] 78

CASE 14. TEST DRIVE

By smashing the front part of the car against a tree, D culpably infringes C's absolute right of property. Consequently, C may file a tort-based claim against D. In addition, C has a quasi-contractual liability claim against D based on *culpa in contrahendo*:[116] although there is no contract between C and D yet, the parties are in the process of concluding a contract. Therefore, they have more extensive duties of protection and care towards each other than towards other third parties and fault is presumed according to §1298 ABGB. By damaging C's car, D violated these duties and can therefore be held liable by C. 79

CASE 15. BREACH OF NEGOTIATIONS

In general, breaking off negotiations does not trigger any liability.[117] As long as there is no agreement, each party may break off negotiations even if the other party suffers damage due to the non-agreement. While negotiating, the parties should be free to refuse further negotiation without having to justify their decision. A claim for damages is therefore only possible in extreme cases, for example if a party abruptly breaks off negotiations without reasonable cause 80

---

115 OGH 26.3.1987, 7 Ob 558/87 = Zeitschrift für Verkehrsrecht (ZVR) 1989/28.

116 Regarding the concept of *culpa in contrahendo* see already Case 13.

117 OGH 10 Ob 10/05a; a detailed analysis regarding the legal consequences of a breach of negotiations can be found in *M Lukas*, Abbruch von Vertragsverhandlungen, JBl 2009, 751 ff and JBl 2010, 23; see also *Koziol*, Haftpflichtrecht II (fn 77) no A/2/311 ff.

even though it has acted as if the contract would certainly be concluded. In our case, the negotiations between C and D are still ongoing. Therefore D is free to break off negotiations without triggering any liability.

CASE 16. NON-DISCLOSURE OF RELEVANT FACTS

81 The question is whether D can be held liable for the non-disclosure of relevant facts to C. Since C only incurs a pure economic loss, a tort-based claim is precluded. However, C might bring a quasi-contractual claim based on *culpa in contrahendo*. Generally speaking, an omission can only be unlawful if there is a duty to act in order to prevent damage. Consequently, in order to be held liable, D must have violated a duty that obliged him to provide information to C: otherwise, ie if no such duty existed, D cannot be held liable. An obligation to disclose might arise out of pre-contractual duties between the contracting parties.[118] Although there is no general duty to inform the contracting partner about all circumstances that could be relevant for his decision, such a duty does exist if the other party can reasonably expect a disclosure of relevant facts.[119] This is especially true in situations where one contracting party addresses a specific topic and the other party fails to disclose relevant information on it. In our case, however, C did not tell D that he intended to use the machine on steep hills: D only knew of C's plans from a friend. Furthermore, according to the case, the machine works on all terrains and is therefore in principle suitable for any kind of corn field. Consequently, it must be established in light of the circumstances of the case whether C could have reasonably expected to be informed by D about the reduced performance of the machine on steep hills. Since D in fact knew about C's plans and disclosing the relevant facts would have been possible for him without further difficulty,[120] it can be argued that D violated his duties vis-à-vis C. Consequently, D can be held liable for the damage caused by a breach of trust (*Vertrauensschaden*). C must be put in the position he would have been in if D had disclosed the relevant facts to him, ie C would either have bought the machine at a lower price or not bought the machine at all.

118 *Koziol*, Haftpflichtrecht II (fn 77) no A/2/276 ff.

119 OGH 21.4.1982, 1 Ob 778/81 = SZ 55/51; OGH 12.12.1991, 7 Ob 625/91 = JBl 1992, 450; OGH 24.10.2000, 1 Ob 183/00v = SZ 73/160.

120 *R Bollenberger* in: H Koziol/P Bydlinski/R Bollenberger (eds), Kurzkommentar zum ABGB (5th edn 2017) §870 no 1.

THE BORDERLINES OF TORT LAW IN THE CZECH REPUBLIC

Luboš TICHÝ*

QUESTIONS

I. Tracing the Borderlines 46
   A. Distinction between Tort and Contract 46
      1) Liability Regime Until 2013 46
      2) Liability Regime Since 2014 47
         a) Liability in Tort 47
         b) Liability in Contract 48
   B. Existence of a 'Grey Zone'? 49
   C. Common or Different Rules Regulating Tort and Contract 50
   D. Application of Common Rules in a Different Way 50
II. Main Differences between Tortious and Contractual Liability 51
   A. Differences as Regards the Foundations of Liability 51
      1) Role of Intention 51
      2) Role of Wrongfulness and Fault and their Variations 52
         a) Wrongfulness 52
         b) Fault 53
   B. Differences as Regards Causation 54
   C. Differences as Regards Remedies 55
      1) Degree of Certainty of the Damage 56
      2) Compensation for Non-Pecuniary Loss 56
      3) Compensation for Loss of Earnings and for Loss of Chance 56
      4) Restitutionary Damages 56
      5) Aggravated and Exemplary Damages 56
   D. Differences as Regards Recoverability of 'Pure Economic Losses' 56
   E. Differences as Regards Liability for Others 57
      1) Liability for Auxiliaries 57
      2) Liability for Legal Representatives or Organs of a Company 58
      3) Liability of Representatives of Natural Persons 58
      4) Liability of the Auxiliary/Organ Itself 58

* The author wishes to express his indebtedness to Dr Jiří Hrádek for his initial cooperation on this chapter.

F. Differences as Regards Liability in the Case of Multiple Tortfeasors/Breaching Parties. . . . 59
G. Differences as Regards the Persons Who May be Protected 59
H. Differences as Regards Defences 60
I. Differences as Regards Limitation Periods. . . . 60
J. Differences as Regards Proof 61
III. Limitation or Exclusion of Liability Arising from Tort and from Contract 62
A. Statutory Provisions Authorising a Limitation or Exclusion of Liability 62
B. Limitation or Exclusion of Contractual and Tortious Liability under Contract 63
IV. Non-Concurrence or Concurrence of Actions 63

CASES

Case 1. The Unattractive Shopping Mall 64
Case 2. The Idle Lawyer 64
Case 3. The Defective House 64
Case 4. Apartment in Flames 65
Case 5. Injured Skier 65
Case 6. Exploding Car. 65
Case 7. Racing Boat Burning 65
Case 8. Insidious Report. 66
Case 9. Circular Letter. 66
Case 10. Shortage of Supply 66
Case 11. Injured Rock Star 66
Case 12. Equipment Destroyed 66
Case 13. Slipping on a Lettuce Leaf. 67
Case 14. Test Drive 67
Case 15. Breach of Negotiations 67
Case 16. Non-Disclosure of Relevant Facts 67

QUESTIONS

I. TRACING THE BORDERLINES

A. DISTINCTION BETWEEN TORT AND CONTRACT

1) Liability Regime Until 2013

1 The regulation of compensation for damage was set forth in Act 40/1964 Coll, the Civil Code, until the end of 2013, based on §420, which stipulated a general

clause defining the conditions for liability of legal and natural persons in delict. §420 of the Civil Code provided that *every person is liable for damage which he causes by breaching a legal obligation.* This means that, under this condition, the distinction between liability based on breach of contract and liability based on delicts could not be determined.

The civil law theory required the following elements for liability to be established: (i) breach of a legal duty or an event qualified by the law; (ii) damage; and (iii) causation between the breach and the harm consequently inflicted. In most cases of liability, fault was required, either in the form of negligence or intention. This was the case for matters which were not deemed cases of strict liability. 2

The provisions relating to strict liability are located in §§420a–437 of the Civil Code (with the exception of §§422–424). These are cases which do not require fault to be established. For the fulfilment of the facts of a particular case, only three conditions must be met: a legally specified event causing damage; damage; and causation between the incident and the harm incurred. A number of such cases related directly to breach of contract as they comprised liability for worn items, protected or handed-over items, as well as liability for damage caused by used items. 3

2) Liability Regime Since 2014

Unlike the former Civil Code, which was based on a general clause on damages, Act no 89/2012 Coll, the new Civil Code (CC 2012), establishes a new basis for liability based on breached norms, ie it differentiates between contractual and non-contractual damages. 4

The basic difference between these two types of liability is that while tortious liability is based on fault, liability for breach of contract is qualified as strict liability, where the potential wrongdoer can exempt himself if he proves that he was temporarily or permanently prevented from the fulfilment of his obligation under the contract by an extraordinary, unpredictable burden that occurred independently of his will. 5

a) Liability in Tort

The basic provisions for non-contractual liability are laid down in §§2904, 2909 and 2910 CC 2012. They establish liability for an accident, liability for breach of good morals and liability for breach of law. 6

- The provisions of §2904 CC 2012, which establish liability for a coincidence, are very specific, as Czech civil law traditionally follows the principle of *casum sentit dominus.* A coincidence which is subject to §2904 (*casus mixtus*) is one of the culpable acts, and it is based on the fact that the wrongdoer breached its legal obligation by a culpable act or omission and in causation herewith damage occurred.

- Pursuant to §2909, a wrongdoer who causes damage to a victim by wilful breach of good morals is obliged to compensate it; but if he was acting in the exercise of a right, he is obliged to compensate the damage only if he intended to damage another.
- The third case of liability for delict is based on §2910 CC 2012, which sets forth liability for a breach of a legal duty. The duty to provide compensation for a breach of legal obligations under the law is associated with the culpable breach of the legal duty.

7 The CC 2012 newly includes a differentiation of cases where a violation of legal obligations affected absolute rights and cases where another law is subject to interference. If absolute rights are breached, the law requires a culpable breach of legal duties by the wrongdoer. If a relative right of the injured party is harmed, the injured party has a claim if this happened due to a culpable breach of a legal duty which is laid down in order to protect such a right.

b) Liability in Contract

8 As regards liability in contract, a distinction must be made between cases specifically regulated under particular types of contracts, such as liability under a mandate, etc, and a general provision stipulated in the Part on Obligations in delict, in particular under §2913 CC 2012.

9 Pursuant to §2913, if a contractually obligated party incurs damage due to a breach of contract, the victim is entitled to compensation regardless of the fault of the wrongdoer. According to this provision, however, the person whose interest the agreed obligations obviously should have served also has a right to compensation. As a result, when concluding a contract, in relation to third parties, the wrongdoer must now at least take into account the possibility that the other party has an interest in the protection of a third party or the fulfilment should have served the interests of the third party.

10 However, in cases where damage is caused to a third party while fulfilling contractual obligations and the above conditions are not met, the question of whether the wrongdoer is obliged to compensate shall be considered pursuant to the provisions on tort liability.

11 The regulation (under §2913, see above no 9) in the Part on Obligations dealing with special cases of liability is basically compatible with the general one. The cases of special liability are as follows: liability of minors and mentally ill people;

liability for persons with dangerous qualities; liability for damage caused by operational activities; damage caused by means of transport; damage caused by an animal; damage caused by a thing and product liability; damage to a received thing, a thing brought in or put aside; and damage caused by information or counsel. The legal reasoning of the CC 2012 defines such cases as examples of strict liability where fault is not decisive for establishing liability and the wrongdoer can exempt himself from liability only based on specific reasons stipulated by law.

B. EXISTENCE OF A 'GREY ZONE'?

Czech law explicitly acknowledges cases of *culpa in contrahendo* in the CC 2012, and since the CC 2012 lacks explicit regulation of the nature of the relationship (compared to the German BGB, which stipulates that cases of *culpa in contrahendo* are contractual in nature), *culpa in contrahendo* may be described as a 'grey zone' case. 12

The regulation of *culpa in contrahendo* is found in §§1728–1730 CC 2012 and it establishes four basic cases under which damages shall be granted in the pre-contractual relationship. 13

- The basic rule, which is based on the principle of free contractual process, is that anybody can lead contract negotiations freely and he is not responsible for the fact that he does not enter into the contract unless contract negotiations begin or continues to do so without the intention of concluding the contract.
- However, during contractual negotiations, certain duties exist which may lead to damages if one party violates those duties. The contracting parties shall notify each other as to all the factual and legal circumstances which they know or must know, so that each party can learn about the possibility to conclude a valid contract and that each party manifests its interest in the contract entered into. This is a case of breach of information duty, which corresponds to information that is known to only one party and may influence the behaviour of the other party with respect to the conclusion of the contract.
- If the negotiations reach a point that the conclusion of a contract seems highly probable, no party shall breach reasonable expectations of the other party in the contract negotiations and terminate the contract negotiations without having a good reason for so doing. A party who acts unfairly in such a sense shall compensate any damage which arises; however, only to the amount that corresponds to the loss resulting from the contract in similar cases.
- The fourth case of *culpa in contrahendo* is breach of confidential information. In accordance with this, if a party to the negotiations provides the other party

with data or communications, the other party shall take care not to allow these to be copied and to prevent their disclosure without lawful reason. The sanctions in such a matter consist in the duty to return any enrichment which was lawfully obtained from the disclosed information.

C. COMMON OR DIFFERENT RULES REGULATING TORT AND CONTRACT

14 The provisions on liability for damage are systematically arranged at the end of the CC 2012, namely in §2894 ff, and the legislation also regulates some cases of liability for damage that are currently regulated in other laws, in particular product liability set forth in Act No 59/1998 Coll.[1]

15 The regulation of liability for damage is based on the principle that anybody who is at fault for breaching his legal duty shall be obliged to compensate for damage. Due to this uniform approach, the CC 2012 uses a system of general provisions regulating basic issues such as prevention and defences, and it also regulates the manner and scope of compensation.

16 In consequence, the major difference is based on the fact that cases of delictual liability are based on fault, whereas cases of contractual liability are strict.

17 In the case of non-contractual liability, the rebuttable presumption of fault in private relationships is formed in such a way that a person is negligent if he acts carelessly and without the kind of knowledge and skills typically expected of a person of average abilities. If a certain person shows special knowledge, skills or accuracy, the person is consequently at fault if he does not make use of such qualities.

18 By contrast to this, in cases of damage caused by a breach of contractual duty, the wrongdoer is required to show that the fulfilment of the duty, which was accepted by contract, was prevented by an extraordinary impediment which could not have been foreseen or prevented by exercising due care and which does not originate in the personal conditions of the wrongdoer.

D. APPLICATION OF COMMON RULES IN A DIFFERENT WAY

19 There are no differences in the approaches of the courts due to the recent development of tort and contract law, which were subject to uniform regulation contained in §420 of the Civil Code.

---

1 Zákon č 59/1998 Sb, o odpovědnosti za škodu způsobenou vadou výrobku, Act no. 59/1998 Coll. (on liability for damage caused by defective products).

Although CC 2012 changed the approach and set forth different rules for the establishment of compensation for damage caused by contract, the general principles remain the same. 20

II. MAIN DIFFERENCES BETWEEN TORTIOUS AND CONTRACTUAL LIABILITY

A. DIFFERENCES AS REGARDS THE FOUNDATIONS OF LIABILITY

1) Role of Intention

Pursuant to §2913, if a contractually obligated party incurs damage due to a breach of contract, the victim is entitled to compensation regardless of the fault of the wrongdoer. Therefore, intention does not play any role when establishing liability. 21

As a result, fault only plays a dominant role in tortious liability if no strict liability is stipulated. 22

The cases of special liability are as follows: liability of minors and mentally ill people; liability for persons with dangerous qualities; liability for damage caused by operational activities; damage caused by means of transport; damage caused by an animal; damage caused by a thing and product liability; damage to a received thing, a thing brought in or put aside; and damage caused by information or counsel. 23

Nevertheless, some of these cases are cases of contractual liability. Moreover, some do not allow for any exemption from liability. 24

Despite qualifying contractual liability as strict, even in these matters, the degree of fault plays an important role. CC 2012 sets forth the following cases: 25

- The degree of fault plays a significant role in the compensation of damage. The role of the individual degrees is important for the application of §2954[2] or §2971,[3] which set out the scope of damages.

---

2 If the wrongdoer caused damage by an intentional criminal offence from which he had a property benefit, the court may decide upon the injured party's motion of satisfaction from the things obtained by the wrongdoer from the property benefit, even if such things are not otherwise subject to the enforcement of a judicial decision. Until satisfaction of the right to compensation for damage, the wrongdoer may not dispose of the things stated in the decision.

3 If so justified by special circumstances under which the wrongdoer caused damage by an illegal act, particularly if the wrongdoer breached, by gross negligence, a major legal duty,

- Intent will be relevant in acting against good morals pursuant to §2909 CC 2012. In accordance with this provision, which applies both to breach of legal act or contract, a wrongdoer who causes damage to the injured party by an intentional breach of good morals is obliged to compensate it; if he is exercising his rights, the wrongdoer is obliged to compensate the damage only if he purposefully intended to cause damage.
- The degree of fault plays an important role in assessing the participation of individual wrongdoers under §2916,[4] even though the CC 2012 speaks about the level of participation and it can therefore consist in other aspects of the liability relationship.
- Degree of fault is also important in assessing the limitation period under §636 para 2, pursuant to which, if damage or injury is caused intentionally, the objective limitation period is extended to 15 years.
- The degree of fault makes it impossible to agree on limitation of exclusion of rights and claims. In particular, the parties cannot agree on limitation of damages pursuant to §2898 if damage was caused intentionally or was the result of gross negligence.
- An insurer may limit insurance payments in cases of intentional misconduct.
- Finally, provided that the damaged party caused a certain part or all of the damage intentionally, to the extent of such conduct of the person damaged, the liable party shall be exempted from liability.

2) *Role of Wrongfulness and Fault and their Variations*

26 Under Czech law, wrongfulness and fault are two independent institutes of law which must be assessed independently.

a) Wrongfulness

27 Application of wrongfulness must be divided into tortious and contractual liability since the background of wrongfulness results from the relationship between the parties.

28 Pursuant to §2910 CC 2012, a wrongdoer who wilfully breaches an obligation set by law and thus interferes with an absolute right of the injured party shall

or if the wrongdoer has intentionally caused the damage because of his desire to destroy, to cause harm or on the basis of another especially despicable motive, the wrongdoer shall also provide compensation for immaterial harm to any person who legitimately feels such loss as a personal misfortune that may not be otherwise redressed.

4 A person who is obliged to compensate damage jointly and severally together with others shall settle with them in accordance with their participation in causing the occurred damage.

compensate what he has caused by so doing. Thus, one of the basic conditions for attributability of a wrongdoer's activity is, pursuant to §2910 CC 2012, unlawfulness, ie such act or omission of a natural or legal person which is contrary to objective law.

The same applies to contractual liability. Pursuant to §2913, if any party breaches an obligation under a contract, it shall compensate the damage caused as a result thereof to the other party or even to a person whose interests the fulfilment of the obligation should have apparently served. Therefore, as regards contractual breach, wrongfulness is traditionally considered to be identical with actions against contractual obligations, which is based on the existence of relations between the contracting parties. What is, therefore, contrary to the contractual arrangements is illegal. 29

Wrongfulness is not presumed and it will be the injured party who has to prove that a breach of such an obligation occurred. Moreover, wrongfulness is always subject to correction by reasons excluding unlawfulness. Unfortunately, with the exceptions of self-defence and nuisance, none of the provisions of the CC 2012 defines the grounds of justification and these are defined by the legal theory (see below no 74 f). 30

b) Fault

As already mentioned, fault is not a prerequisite for contractual liability which is deemed strict. Thus, fault is only relevant to tortious liability. 31

The provisions of §2912[5] set out the basic prerequisite for the existence of fault, which is a violation of the standard of care, which every single legal entity must follow. In the event of a breach, an unlawful act occurs. 32

Under Czech law, the standard of care must always be deemed objective because its objectivity is essential for the protection of every person in everyday life. The applicable standard of conduct is therefore governed by the average requirements of similar members of a group of persons depending on the specific situation. In doing so, no consideration will be given to individual experience, knowledge, ability or physical capabilities, as the main measure shall be the average ability of a person belonging to the group. 33

---

5 (1) If the wrongdoer does not act in a way that could be reasonably expected from a person of average abilities in private relationships, it shall be deemed that he acted carelessly. (2) If the wrongdoer demonstrates specific knowledge, ability or diligence or if he commits to perform an activity for which a specific knowledge, ability or diligence is required, and he does not make use of this specific knowledge, ability or diligence, it shall be deemed that he acted carelessly.

34 §2912 para 2 sets the standard of care in specific cases where the wrongdoer, before his illegal activities, shows some knowledge, skill or diligence, ie in some way increases the expectations of third parties in its standard behaviour.

35 Nevertheless, the CC 2012 establishes certain cases where no fault is relevant:

- Cases of contractual liability. A party may exempt himself if he proves that he was prevented from fulfilling his contractual duty temporarily or permanently by an extraordinary, unforeseeable and unpreventable obstacle that occurred independently of his will. An obstacle that occurred from the wrongdoer's personal circumstances or that occurred when the wrongdoer was in delay with the fulfilment of his contractual obligation, as well as an obstacle that the wrongdoer was obliged to overcome under the agreement, shall not exempt him from liability.
- In three cases absolute strict liability without a possibility of exemption exists: (i) damage caused by a defective item (§2936); (ii) damage caused to taken-over items (§2944); and damage to a thing left aside (§2945).
- In the case of an item brought onto premises intended for accommodation (a hotel, etc) the accommodator is liable for damage to this item (§2946). If the accommodator proves that the damage would also have occurred otherwise or that it was caused by the accommodated party or by the person who accompanies the accommodated party on the basis of his own will, the accommodator shall be relieved of the obligation to provide compensation for damage (§2946 para 2).
- In the case of damage caused by information or advice, a person who presents himself as having a specific profession or occupation required for a professional performance or otherwise claims to be an expert shall provide compensation for damage caused by his incomplete or incorrect information or harmful advice provided for a fee in a matter relating to his knowledge or skills. Otherwise, only damage caused intentionally by information or advice shall be compensated.

B. DIFFERENCES AS REGARDS CAUSATION

36 Causation, as one of the basic conditions of a liability relationship, is not described in the CC 2012, with two exceptions: alternative and partial causation.

37 Therefore, it can be assumed that both the doctrine and case law will continue to apply the current concept of causation, which is based predominantly on the theory of adequacy.

38 The theory of adequacy uses the criterion that damage is considered a result of a wrongful activity if, besides being the condition of the damage, the wrongful act

or wrongful event is, due to its general nature, or, according to the usual course of events and experience, a common result of the damage. For the theory of adequacy, therefore, a cause of a wrongful result is only such a wrongful act or event which would have been objectively foreseeable to an average person: that is, also to the person to whom the relevant cause is attributable.

Nevertheless, there is no difference in causation as regards causation in fact. 39

C. DIFFERENCES AS REGARDS REMEDIES

Compensation for damage is based on the concept that proprietary damage shall be compensated, whereas non-material harm shall be subject to compensation only in special cases determined by law. This dualistic approach is also strongly reflected in the terminology used when §2894 CC 2012 provides for a legal definition of pecuniary damage which is compensable (recoverable) as a rule, while non-pecuniary harm can be compensated (recovered) only if the law specifically provides for it. 40

Under this rule, damage shall mean harm to assets of the injured party and any other harm is thus considered as non-pecuniary damage, which is subject to specific provisions on compensation of damage to health (pain and suffering, worsening of social position and other harm), interference with natural human rights, etc. 41

As regards the scope and manner of compensation, the CC 2012 is based on the approach that restitution in kind must take precedence over compensation in money. If restitution in kind is not possible or if requested by the injured party, the wrongdoer shall be obliged to provide damages in money. Therefore, if restitution in kind is possible, the type of compensation for damage shall depend on the will of the victim, and the court cannot consider whether the chosen method of compensation is 'useful' or 'usual' as it currently can. Pursuant to §2952 CC 2012, the scope of such damages shall be determined by the actual damage and lost profit. 42

Damages for pure economic loss shall also be recoverable, but only in special cases. Compensation for non-material harm must be granted especially in cases of interference with the personality rights of an individual or a legal entity and if it is justified by special circumstances under which the wrongdoer caused damage by acting illegally. The CC 2012 sets a basic provision that pure economic loss shall be compensated. 43

The manner and extent of the reasonable satisfaction must be determined in such a way that circumstances which merit special consideration are compensated. This term encompasses causing harm through the use of deceit, threats, 44 abuse of the victim's dependence on the wrongdoer, public attacks as well as discrimination with regard to sex, health, ethnic origin, belief or other similarly serious reasons. Also relevant to the determination of the satisfaction shall be whether the victim reasonably fears death or serious injury as a result of threats attributable to the wrongdoer.

1) Degree of Certainty of the Damage

45 There is no difference and the fundamental rule consists in the certainty of the damage.

2) Compensation for Non-Pecuniary Loss

46 There is no difference and both legal provisions and contract serve as a basis for consideration as to whether non-pecuniary loss was incurred.

3) Compensation for Loss of Earnings and for Loss of Chance

47 There is no difference. Loss of earnings must always be documented and it must be evidenced for sure that the earnings were not only probable, but certain.

48 As regards the loss of chance doctrine, Czech law does not acknowledge this approach to damages. The corrective is under Czech law theory of causation.

4) Restitutionary Damages

49 Restitutionary damages do not exist in Czech law. There is no difference.

5) Aggravated and Exemplary Damages

50 There is no difference as the Czech law does not acknowledge damage other than that which actually occurred as a direct result of an unlawful act or omission of the wrongdoer.

D. DIFFERENCES AS REGARDS RECOVERABILITY OF 'PURE ECONOMIC LOSSES'

51 The CC 2012 newly establishes recoverability of pure economic loss in tort law cases.

52 Pursuant to §2909, the duty to provide compensation arises in the case of a wrongdoer who interferes with a right of the injured party by breaching a legally stipulated duty set by law for the protection of such right.

Based on the provision §2910 second sentence, pure economic loss represents cases where compensation is conditioned by the existence of violations of absolute rights, acts contrary to good morals or violations of safety standards and, therefore, most cases relate to indirect or consequential damage. 53

In Czech law, the concept of pure economic loss is new. 54

With respect to contractual damages, no similar provision is established. 55

Czech law addresses the issue of successive and indirect damage through the theory of causation, which does not place an emphasis so much on the foreseeability of damage but rather on the existence of a direct causal link, without which damages are rejected. 56

E. DIFFERENCES AS REGARDS LIABILITY FOR OTHERS

Pursuant to §2914, a person who uses a proxy, employee or other helper in the course of performing an activity shall be obliged to compensate damage caused by this proxy, employee or other helper in the same way as if he had caused the damage himself. If anyone took over an obligation during the performance of another to fulfil a certain activity on his own, he shall not be deemed a helper. If the other person did not choose him diligently or did not supervise him sufficiently, the former shall guarantee the fulfilment of his duty to compensate for damage. 57

From a systematic point of view, the provisions of §2914 are rather problematic. Its inclusion gives the impression that the provision contains only an obligation to compensate damage caused by auxiliary persons for breach of contract, which further supports the content of the explanatory memorandum. In such a case, however, the tort area of liability for others remained completely unregulated, which probably was not the purpose of the current legislation, as in such a case neither the scope nor conditions of third party liability are deductible. 58

1) *Liability for Auxiliaries*

The breach of a legal obligation is attributed directly to the principal, and the principal is obliged to pay damages just as if he himself caused the damage. However, the principal can call in his favour those circumstances that would exempt the auxiliary if he were liable directly. 59

Based on the above, the principal is liable for damages only if the auxiliary person causes damage in connection with the performance of duties with which it was conferred. Damage must be caused in the performance of activities and not by accident while performing duties. 60

2) *Liability for Legal Representatives or Organs of a Company*

61 In the case of a legal entity, the conduct of its institutions and other persons referred to in §129 shall not be deemed as acts of third parties, but as the acts of the legal person itself. The concept of such liability is based on the principle that conduct of a body is considered to be an act of the legal entity. For bodies of a legal entity shall be deemed only statutory bodies (determined by law); employees, including senior executives, will constitute auxiliaries within the meaning of §2914.

3) *Liability of Representatives of Natural Persons*

62 The liability of a legal representative of a natural person who is a parent is stipulated in §2921. This provision sets forth that anyone who omitted to provide due supervision of a minor who has not gained full legal capacity or anyone who suffers from a mental disorder shall be jointly and severally liable with the wrongdoer to compensate the damage. If the wrongdoer is not obliged to compensate the damage, compensation shall be paid to the injured party by the person who omitted to provide due supervision of the wrongdoer.

63 Because there are no special conditions regarding the liability of parents, the liability of parents for acts of their children should be governed by the same principles as other cases of liability based on negligence, ie liability shall be subject to §2910. In other words, the parent shall be held liable if he/she has caused damage as a result of breaching his/her legal duty to properly carry out parental responsibility – inter alia the duty to supervise the child.

64 The breach of parental duty may also consist of an omission of proper performance. However, a basic condition is that the parent must be subject to the imposed duty to take action before a causal link between damage and behaviour can be established. Because parental responsibility includes all elements of care of the child – including the upbringing, supervisory or protective duty of the parent – parental care shall be understood as the duty to take action.

4) *Liability of the Auxiliary/Organ Itself*

65 There is a general principle that an auxiliary shall not be directly liable if no excess occurs. An excess is a case when an action does not fit into the general framework of authorised activities, which will be, for example, a criminal offence or conduct in clear breach of the general duty of protection.

66 As regards subcontractors, the conditions of liability are different and the subcontractor shall be liable for wrong caused.

As a result of a violation of the selection or supervision, the principal will not be liable for damage caused by the principal's subcontractor who carries out an activity independently. Guarantees for the obligations of subcontractors will be thus subsidiary and dependent on the existence of a primary obligation whereas the principal will be obliged (liability of *culpa in eligendo*) to pay compensation when the subcontractor causes a damage in excess of his/her competence and does not pay compensation. 67

F. DIFFERENCES AS REGARDS LIABILITY IN THE CASE OF MULTIPLE TORTFEASORS/BREACHING PARTIES

The regulation of contributory fault or the liability of multiple tortfeasors is based on the rule contained in §2915 CC 2012, pursuant to which the liability of multiple tortfeasors is joint and several, unless in justified cases when the liability qualifies as being proportionate (several). 68

However, in the internal relationship, wrongdoers shall always settle according to their respective shares in the fault. This provision covers: (i) situations where damage was caused by joint fault, ie where each wrongdoer has a psychological relationship not only to his own act or omission but also to the activities of other persons; or (ii) cases of concurrent contribution, ie a case when damage occurs based on independent acts of wrongdoers. 69

In cases meriting special consideration (proportional, several liability), the court may decide that the wrongdoer shall compensate damage in accordance with his participation in the harmful consequences. If the participation cannot be determined, the degree of probability shall be taken into consideration. Such an approach is not possible, however, if the wrongdoer knowingly participated in causing harm with another wrongdoer or encouraged the wrongdoer to cause harm, or if the damage can be attributed to each wrongdoer even though they acted independently. 70

However, there is no different approach in tort or contractual law. 71

G. DIFFERENCES AS REGARDS THE PERSONS WHO MAY BE PROTECTED

There are no differences, as the liability or protective purpose will be subject to general rules. However, the CC 2012 establishes specific contractual liability. 72

The second case relates to the protective purpose of a contract. According to the provisions of §2912, the person in whose interests the agreed obligations 73 obviously should have served also has a right to compensation for a breach of contract. As a result, when concluding a contract, in relation to third parties the wrongdoer must now at least take into account the possibility that the other party is interested in the protection of a third party or the fulfilment should have served the interests of the third party.

H. DIFFERENCES AS REGARDS DEFENCES

74 In general, the following defences based on justification are acknowledged both by legal theory and case law:

- fulfilment of legal obligations;
- exercise of a subjective right (*neminem laedit qui iure suo utitur*); the exercise thereof must not interfere with the rights of third parties without a legal reason and must not violate 'proper morals';
- self-help;
- self-defence;
- necessity; and
- approval of the injured party.

75 Beside these defences, contributory conduct creates another case which can lead to a release from liability. Pursuant to §2918 CC 2012, if damage occurred or increased as a result of circumstances that are attributed to the injured party, the wrongdoer's duty to compensate damage shall be diminished accordingly. However if the circumstances which are to the detriment of one or the other party have contributed to the damage only to a negligible extent, the damage is not divided.

76 However, there is no different approach in tort or contract law.

I. DIFFERENCES AS REGARDS LIMITATION PERIODS

77 Save for the exceptions (eg ownership rights), pursuant to §§619, 620 and 629 CC 2012, a claim for compensation for pecuniary damage becomes statute-barred three years from the date when the injured party realised for the first time that he had suffered damage and determined who was liable for the damage. Such a claim generally becomes time-barred 10 years after the wrongful event, regardless of when the knowledge was gained (§636 – objective upper time limit); however, case law also considers the occurrence of the damage for the commencement of such a period as decisive.

Furthermore, should damage have been caused intentionally or as a result of bribery, the right only becomes statute-barred 15 years after the objective occurrence. 78

This differentiation means that two kinds of limitation periods are laid down by law in the Czech Republic; firstly, a subjective three-year limitation period, and secondly, a 10-year or 15-year objective period. The subjective period commences with knowledge of the damage and the objective period with the wrongful event (occurrence of the damage). 79

There is an exception regarding damage to health; only a subjective limitation period is allowed for this damage and all components of the damage to health, for instance, the loss of earnings or payments for compensation of physical injury, are understood as independent claims for compensation. 80

A claim for compensation of damage caused by defective products shall become statute-barred 10 years after the product was put on the market. 81

However, there is no different approach in tort or contract law. 82

J. DIFFERENCES AS REGARDS PROOF

The Czech concept of burden of proof is based on the fact that the plaintiff always has to prove all facts in order to establish his claim. The burden of proof arises from the presented arguments and facts (burden of allegation), which is set forth in §101 para 1 lit a of the Civil Procedure Code (CPC) and the obligation to provide evidence according to §101 para 1 lit b in connection with §120 para 1 sent 1 CPC. As such it is stipulated in §120 para 3 CPC. 83

The extent of the burden of proof, that is, the range of particular facts which the party has to prove, is basically determined by substantive law, that is, a legal provision which is applied to the relationship under dispute. Substantive law stipulates who has to bear the burden of proof and which facts each of the parties are obliged to prove. If one party fails to provide the required evidence, it is possible to decide against the party only if the evaluation of evidence which was conducted during the proceedings (§120 3 sent 2 CPC) does not make it possible for the court to accept either the conclusion or the truth of the assertions made by the party, or that such assertions were in fact false.[6] 84

The concept of the burden of proof correlates closely with the topic of the principle of judicial evaluation of evidence (Czech legal theory uses the term 85

6 Supreme Court, 23 Odo 1722/2006.

'free evaluation of evidence'), as governed by §132 CPC, according to which the court evaluates evidence at its own discretion, considering all evidence on its merits and in context, while carefully taking into consideration everything which occurred during the proceedings, including everything which was alleged and presented by the parties.

86 An important exemption is contained in §133a CPC, which states that alleged facts about direct or indirect discrimination shall be deemed proved if the other party does not prove otherwise in the respective proceedings. A similar provision is contained in §2988 CC, which regulates unfair competition claims.

87 However, there is no different approach in tort or contract law.

III. LIMITATION OR EXCLUSION OF LIABILITY ARISING FROM TORT AND FROM CONTRACT

A. STATUTORY PROVISIONS AUTHORISING A LIMITATION OR EXCLUSION OF LIABILITY

88 Within the legal order of the Czech Republic (CC 2012), there are relevant provisions whose purpose it is to argue against the limitation or exclusion of liability for damage caused by breach of statutory or contractual obligations.

89 Pursuant to §2896 CC 2012, a unilateral act (expression of will) which restricts or excludes an obligation to compensate damage caused by third parties is absolutely void. It is irrelevant whether such a manifestation of will is made before or after the date of the occurrence of harm.

90 According to §2898 CC 2012, juridical acts (manifestations of will) which exclude or limit in advance the obligation to compensate damage caused to a person's natural rights or caused intentionally or by gross negligence or right of a weaker party for compensation are absolutely void.

91 One has to stress that such acts are void if performed before the date of the damage. This is how the words 'in advance' should be interpreted. Juridical acts concern fundamental rights which must be respected, regardless of how such harm has occurred. Those acts are then void, regardless of their subject matter that exclude damages for the harm caused by wilful acts or grossly negligent conduct. Regardless of the subject matter and way of occurrence of damage, any restrictions in the rights of the weaker party are not allowed.

92 In accordance with the last sentence of §2898, a waiver of rights is void, ie a unilateral declaration of will on the part of the (potentially) damaged party.

B. LIMITATION OR EXCLUSION OF CONTRACTUAL AND TORTIOUS LIABILITY UNDER CONTRACT

In this regime (above no 87 f), two exceptions apply. According to §2897 CC 2012, anyone may waive the right to claim compensation for damage caused to the property. In this case, the waiver, which is registered in the public register, also applies to subsequent owners. This provision is an exception in several regards. A waiver of rights can occur in this case also in advance and the waiver is valid and effective regardless of the way of causing harm (this includes intentional or grossly negligent acts). Finally, even a weaker party may waive his/her rights against the stronger in such a case. 93

The second exception to the prohibition on limitations of liability for damage is a set of cases that are not subject to the restrictions under §§2896, 2898 and 2899 CC 2012. This exception therefore concerns all cases of damage, and its compensation, regardless of the way in which it occurred and the object of protection. After the occurrence of harm (damage), the damages can therefore be limited or even excluded without any restrictions. 94

Not a limitation or exclusion of liability itself, but a limitation of damages (which consequently may be the same) can occur pursuant to §2953 CC 2012 if the case merits special consideration. A court may order such a reduction, which shall take into account how the damage occurred, the personal and financial situation of the wrongdoer, respectively the liable party, as well as the circumstances of the victim. The compensation cannot be reduced if the damage was caused intentionally. This right of the court to reduce damages cannot be used in cases when the damage was caused by a person who claimed professional performance as a member of a certain profession and breached the applicable professional standard of care. 95

IV. NON-CONCURRENCE OR CONCURRENCE OF ACTIONS

There are many overlaps between tort and contract. An example is the liability for damage caused by things. A buyer may suffer damage which is caused either by movables or immovables. In the case of building collapses due to defects, owners shall compensate the damage, but jointly and severally with any previous owner if the cause of the collapse has its origin in a deficiency in the structure which occurred during the duration of his ownership rights. 96

Damages may be claimed both based on breach of contract and on liability in tort. In both cases, the previous owner shall be held liable without fault. 97

98 A different situation exists in the case of damage caused to things taken over or handed into the custody of another (§§2944 and 2945 CC 2012). In these cases, compensation may be claimed from the holder based on 'factual' contracts or from a person who damaged or stole the thing, ie on the basis of tort liability.

99 The difference is rather substantial. The first case is a case of strict liability, the second case is undoubtedly a case of liability based on fault.

100 If there is choice between the claims, the victim cannot assert both claims simultaneously.

CASES

CASE 1. THE UNATTRACTIVE SHOPPING MALL

101 C has a claim to compensation from D which arises from the protection of legitimate interests of third parties based on damage resulting from a breach of contractual duties. Under §2913 para 1 of the Civil Code, the breaching party shall also compensate the damage caused to the person who was evidently intended to benefit from the fulfilment of the breached duty.

CASE 2. THE IDLE LAWYER

102 The daughters are entitled to damages from D's advocate as they are the persons evidently intended to benefit from the fulfilment of the breached duty. This is a case that is also governed by §2913 para 1 of the Civil Code which provides for such protection.

CASE 3. THE DEFECTIVE HOUSE

103 D's liability towards C for the damage is established by the operation of law as it results from a delict. Even if the clause stipulating the possibility to be released from liability was valid, it would be effective solely towards Z. The liability would arise under the regime of §2910, as D interfered with C's absolute right.

104 C may raise a damage claim against D from its position as a third party with whose right D interfered when breaching its contractual duty. As a result, C shall proceed in accordance with §2913 para 1 of the Civil Code.

CASE 4. APARTMENT IN FLAMES

D breached both its legal duty and duty arising from the lease contract. The following solution is based on the presumption that the landlord owned the flat. The owner's duties are stipulated in the Constitution of the Czech Republic and in §1012 CC 2012. It is the landlord's duty under the lease contract to maintain the premises (flat, house) in the same condition that the premises were in at the beginning of the lease. 105

It follows from the aforementioned that actions brought by the tenant may be based on both grounds (see §§2910 and 2913 CC 2012). A presumption of negligence under §2910 CC 2012 is met, while grounds for a release from liability under §2913 para 2 are not. Both contractual and tort liability lead to compensation for damage. 106

CASE 5. INJURED SKIER

D1 breached a legal duty as well as duty arising from a contract. The piste's owner is liable under general safety provisions for the proper functioning of the funicular (tortious, no-fault liability). A duty of care was also undoubtedly established under the contract concluded with P. 107

As D1 is liable on both grounds, D2 is liable to payment of the insurance claim. 108

CASE 6. EXPLODING CAR

D1 is not liable for damage even if the gas pipes were defective or they constituted a hidden defect since the damage occurred as a result of another defect for which the seller would be liable only in case the purchaser reported the said defect within a two-year period from the product's delivery (see §2112 CC 2012). D2's liability is not imposed by virtue of contract or by law provided that P is not a consumer and the damage was not caused to any other object apart from the vehicle. In such a case, liability for a defective product arises. 109

CASE 7. RACING BOAT BURNING

D would be liable under the contract since effect occurred after the expiry of reclamation period of two years. (The boat had been used for three years.) D 110 is liable for any defects in the product provided that the boat is not used for business purposes (§2943 CC 2012).

CASE 8. INSIDIOUS REPORT

111 D is liable for breach of his/her duties under the Labour Code, unless his/her labour contract stipulate otherwise in favour of employee.

112 C is not allowed to file a claim based on contract.

CASE 9. CIRCULAR LETTER

113 D fulfils the scope of prohibitive behaviour under the regime of unfair competition (§2984 CC 2012: 'competitor states or spreads a false statement about the situation, performance or product of another competitor, where such a statement is capable of causing harm to that competitor') as it disseminated untrue information about C and Z. Furthermore, D may have violated the right to protection of name of the legal entity or may have committed defamation, etc. Also, such an act can be qualified as an intentional breach of good morals (§2909 CC 2012).

CASE 10. SHORTAGE OF SUPPLY

114 D is liable in tort as it has abused its position and thus violates the provisions of §8 CC 2012. (Evident abuse of a right does not enjoy legal protection.) The court may rule that the price in excess of contract is not enforceable. Furthermore a qualification as intentional breach of good morals (§2909 CC 2012).

CASE 11. INJURED ROCK STAR

115 This is a case of pure economic loss. D is liable in tort because D's liability is not restricted within the meaning of §2910 CC 2012. D violated an absolute right or breached a duty imposed by law.

CASE 12. EQUIPMENT DESTROYED

116 D is released from the duty to provide damages under §2913 para 2 CC 2012 since 'the fulfilment of its duty was precluded due to an unforeseeable and

insurmountable obstacle created independently of its will.' Thus it is not liable under the contract. Tortious liability may arise in a situation similar to D in Case 11.

CASE 13. SLIPPING ON A LETTUCE LEAF

D breached its legal duty. D's duty to maintain the shop premises in a state adequate to a professional level (§2912 para 2 CC 2012) is a duty arising from administrative regulations governing retail. 117

A breach of administrative regulations simultaneously forms a basis for tortious liability under §2910 CC 2012 and leads to an award of damages. A claim based on tort only is permissible. 118

CASE 14. TEST DRIVE

D is liable in tort (and not contractually) as the contractual liability regime of the Civil Code does not apply to this case. General elements of tortious liability are met. 119

CASE 15. BREACH OF NEGOTIATIONS

See Case 11. D is liable under the regime of *culpa in contrahendo* pursuant to §1729 CC 2012, ie for termination of contract negotiations without a just cause. Thus D is liable to the extent stipulated by §1729 para 2 CC 2012, ie for positive damage. 120

CASE 16. NON-DISCLOSURE OF RELEVANT FACTS

D is liable for *culpa in contrahendo* under §1729 para 2 CC 2012 as it did not act in good faith. 121

THE BORDERLINES OF TORT LAW IN ENGLAND AND WALES

Ken OLIPHANT and Vanessa WILCOX

QUESTIONS

I. Tracing the Borderlines 71
A. Distinction between Tort and Contract 71
1) Justification for Distinguishing Tort from Contract 71
a) Historical Distinction 71
b) Theories Justifying Continued Division 72
2) Differences between Torts and Contracts 73
B. Existence of a 'Grey Zone'? 75
1) *Culpa in Contrahendo* 75
2) Misrepresentation 76
3) Bailment 78
C. Common or Different Rules Regulating Tort and Contract 78
D. Application of Common Rules in a Different Way 79
II. Main Differences between Tortious and Contractual Liability 79
A. Differences as Regards the Foundations of Liability 79
1) Role of Intention 79
a) Contract 79
b) Tort 82
2) Role of Wrongfulness and Fault and their Variations 84
3) Role of Strict Liability 85
a) Contract 85
b) Tort 87
B. Differences as Regards Causation 88
1) Factual Causation 88
2) Legal Causation 89
C. Differences as Regards Remedies 91
1) Degree of Certainty of the Damage 91
2) Compensation for Non-Pecuniary Loss 92
3) Compensation for Loss of Earnings and for Loss of Chance 94
4) Restitutionary Damages 96

5) Aggravated and Exemplary (or Punitive) Damages. 98
a) Exemplary Damages. 98
b) Aggravated Damages 100
6) Other Remedies. 100
D. Differences as Regards Recoverability of 'Pure Economic Losses'. . . . 101
E. Differences as Regards Liability for Others. 102
1) Liability for Auxiliaries and for Independent Contractors 102
2) Liability for Legal Representatives or Organs of a Company 103
3) Liability of Representatives of Natural Persons. 104
a) Minors. 104
b) Mental Disability. 105
4) Liability of the Auxiliary/Organ Itself 105
F. Differences as Regards Liability in the Case of Multiple Tortfeasors/ Breaching Parties 106
G. Differences as Regards the Persons Who May be Protected. 106
H. Differences as Regards Defences 108
I. Differences as Regards Limitation Periods 109
1) Applicable Time Limits 109
2) When Time Begins to Run ('Dies a Quo'). 110
3) Particular Rules. 111
a) Longstop. 111
b) Extinction. 112
c) Extension 112
d) Exclusion 112
e) Suspension 113
f) Restarting the Clock from Zero 113
g) Contracting Out 113
J. Differences as Regards Proof 113
K. Reasons for the Differences. 113
III. Limitation or Exclusion of Liability Arising from Tort and from Contract 114
A. Statutory Provisions Authorising a Limitation or Exclusion of Liability 114
B. Limitation or Exclusion of Contractual and Tortious Liability by Contract 114
1) Introduction. 114
2) Exemption Clauses and Third Parties 115
3) Statutory Regulation of Exemption Clauses 116
4) Ex post Exclusion of Liability 117
IV. Non-Concurrence or Concurrence of Actions. 118
A. Overview 118
1) Areas of Overlap between Tort and Contract. 118
2) Approach to Non-Concurrence and Concurrence of Actions . . . 118
B. Concurrence/Exclusion of Actions for the Protection against Personal Injury 120

C. Concurrence/Exclusion of Actions for the Protection of Property... 120
D. Concurrence/Exclusion in the Case of Interference with Contractual Rights ... 120
1) Interference with a Contractual Relationship ... 120
2) Loss of Business due to Personal Injury to Someone Else's Employees or Clients or to Property Damage to the Entrepreneur ... 121
V. Specific Situations ... 121
A. Pre-Contractual Liability ... 121
B. Liability of Professionals ... 122

CASES

Case 1. The Unattractive Shopping Mall ... 122
Case 2. The Idle Lawyer ... 122
Case 3. The Defective House ... 123
Case 4. Apartment in Flames ... 124
Case 5. Injured Skier ... 124
Case 6. Exploding Car ... 125
Case 7. Racing Boat Burning ... 125
Case 8. Insidious Report ... 125
Case 9. Circular Letter ... 126
Case 10. Shortage of Supply ... 127
Case 11. Injured Rock Star ... 128
Case 12. Equipment Destroyed ... 128
Case 13. Slipping on a Lettuce Leaf ... 129
Case 14. Test Drive ... 129
Case 15. Breach of Negotiations ... 129
Case 16. Non-Disclosure of Relevant Facts ... 129

QUESTIONS

I. TRACING THE BORDERLINES

A. DISTINCTION BETWEEN TORT AND CONTRACT

1) *Justification for Distinguishing Tort from Contract*

a) Historical Distinction

The categories contract and tort are not to be found in the early common law. 1
It was not until the end of the 17th century that they began to emerge and that

the distinction between them came to have significance, initially for primarily procedural reasons. With the abolition of the old 'forms of action' in the mid-19th century, the question of classification had to be addressed more systematically and on the level of substance, and various theoretical analyses of the distinction between the two causes of action began to emerge.[1]

b) Theories Justifying Continued Division

2 The classic justification, under the 'will theory', is that contractual duties are based on voluntary obligations: it is for the law to set out the prerequisites for the formation of a contract and to enforce it but it is for the parties to negotiate its substantive terms.[2] Tortious obligations, on the other hand, are coercive: they are imposed by law and not on the basis of agreement between the parties.[3]

3 In practice, however, the *laissez-faire* theory of contract is only true as a starting point. First, because terms may be implied into contracts by the courts[4] or the legislature[5] and some terms that have expressly been negotiated by the parties may be struck down.[6] Indeed, entire agreements may be struck down on the grounds, inter alia, of illegality, incapacity, mistake, duress, misrepresentation, frustration and restraint of trade.[7] Second, much judicial ingenuity is also expended on the interpretation of the parties' agreement so as to avoid unjust consequences. As a result of the *contra proferentem* rule, for example, exemption clauses are construed strictly against the party who seeks to rely on them.[8] Third, the classification of terms also allows courts some latitude for intervention. This is the case, for example, with 'innominate terms', intermediate terms that may transpire to be either conditions or warranties on the *ex post* application of the 'consequences of the breach' test.[9] The notion of freedom and sanctity of

---

1 Chitty on Contracts, vol 1 (31st edn 2013) para 1–138. See also *D Ibbetson*, Historical Introduction to the Law of Obligations (2001); *JH Baker*, An Introduction to English Legal History (4th edn 2005); *AWB Simpson*, A History of the Common Law of Contract (1987); *JW Salmond*, The History of Contract (1887) 3 Law Quarterly Review 166.

2 The will theory's foremost English proponent was Sir Frederick Pollock: see *FW Pollock*, Principles of Contract (1876). The influence of Savigny on Pollock's thought is well known: see eg *N Duxbury*, Frederick Pollock and the English Juristic Tradition (2004) 207.

3 In Winfield's classic definition: 'Tortious liability arises from the breach of a duty primarily fixed by law' (*PH Winfield*, The Province of the Law of Tort (1931) 23).

4 Eg the duty of utmost good faith in insurance contracts.

5 Eg in the sale of goods and the provision of services.

6 Eg under the Unfair Contract Terms Act 1977 and the Unfair Terms in Consumer Contracts Regulations 1999. See further Chitty on Contracts (fn 1) para 1–139; *PS Atiyah*, The Rise and Fall of Freedom of Contract (1979); *A Robertson*, On the Distinction Between Contract and Tort, in: A Robertson (ed), The Law of Obligations: Connections and Boundaries (2004) 87 ff.

7 Halsbury's Laws of England, vol 22: Contract (2012) para 213.

8 *Burton v English* (1883) 12 Law Reports, Queen's Bench Division (QBD) 218, 220 per Brett MR, and 222 per Bowen LJ.

9 *Hong Kong Fir Shipping Co Ltd v Kawasaki Kisen Kaisha Ltd* [1962] 2 Queen's Bench (QB) 26.

contract is further eroded by the fact that it is the law that outlines the remedies that are available following a breach of contract. Some such remedies – notably, specific performance – are equitable and therefore discretionary. Despite these observations, there is still strong support for the principle that '[c]ommercial men must be given the utmost liberty of contracting'.[10]

Conversely, individual choice may also be a relevant factor in relation to tortious 4
duties and liabilities. For example, a duty of care may be voluntarily assumed by one person to another (eg in the provision of information or advice)[11] while an injured person may have voluntarily assumed the risk inherent in the dangerous conduct of another such as to absolve the latter from liability (*volenti non fit iuiuria*).

A second purported justification for distinguishing tort and contract is that it 5
is the expectation interest that is protected under contract law,[12] as mirrored by the aim of contractual damages, in contrast to reliance damages in tort, which thus protects reliance interests. However, this dichotomy is questionable since damages for a change in position following detrimental reliance are available under contract law. Chitty on Contracts equally points out that 'damages in tort can compensate the injured party's disappointed expectations, for example, his expectation to be able to earn a living, although … this expectation is general, unlike contractual expectations which are induced by making the contract.'[13]

Finally, tortious obligations are said to be *in rem* (against the world at large) in 6
contrast to contractual ones which are *in personam* (directed toward a particular person). In practice, however, a duty in tort may be owed to an individual or to a limited group of persons.[14]

2) *Differences between Torts and Contracts*

A crucial difference between contract and tort is that liability in contract 7
is prima facie strict (ie arises in the absence of fault), while liability in tort is predominantly fault-based. Strict liability is exceptional in the modern English law of tort.[15] In a contract, it is of course open to the parties to agree that the

10 Per Lord Bingham in *Homburg Houtimport BV v Agrosin Private Ltd (The Starsin)* [2003] 3 Weekly Law Reports (WLR) 711 at [57]. See also *Attorney General of Belize v Belize Telecom Ltd* [2009] United Kingdom Privy Council (UKPC) 10 at [27], per Lord Hoffmann and *Liverpool City Council v Irwin* [1977] Appeal Cases (AC) 239, 254.

11 *Hedley Byrne & Co Ltd v Heller & Partners* [1964] AC 465.

12 *A Burrows*, Understanding the Law of Obligations (1998) ch 1.

13 Chitty on Contracts (fn 1) para 1–140.

14 *K Oliphant* (ed), The Law of Tort (3rd edn 2015) para 1.2; *MA Jones* (ed), Clerk & Lindsell on Torts (22nd edn 2018) para 1–03.

15 *Oliphant* (fn 14) para 1.26 ff.

obligation on the promisor is one of reasonable care, and not to ensure a specified result, and in such cases the standard of liability is the same as that in tort.

8 Another difference relates to *remoteness* of damage. Though remoteness is a central principle in both contracts and torts, with the concept of reasonable foreseeability being used to limit liability, the tests differ, both in the extent to which remote incidents are considered compensable and in their temporal application. As to the former, whereas extremely unlikely events may trigger liability in tort, a very substantial degree of probability is required in contract.[16] As to the latter, the relevant enquiry for reasonable foreseeability is at the time the tort took place, on the one hand, and at the time of concluding the contract, on the other.[17]

9 One must also mention differences as regards the *nature of the interests* which the two causes of action seek to protect. Whereas contract law primarily protects economic interests, tort law's main concern is to remedy physical damage, whether this be to persons or property.

10 Differences also lie in the area of *defences*. For example, sec 1 of the Law Reform (Contributory Negligence) Act 1945 has been construed, subject to one caveat, as limiting the defence of contributory negligence to tort law (see no 85). The power to apportion arises in the case of breach of contract only where the claim is based on the breach of a contractual duty to take reasonable care, where contractual liability is concurrent with liability in tort.[18]

11 A further distinction worthy of mention is the fact that *different remedies* attach to the two causes of action. This is the case in respect of specific performance (no 68 f), rescission and rectification, for example, which are exclusive to contract,[19] whereas punitive damages (no 64 ff) are only available in tort. Nominal damages are generally restricted to torts actionable per se but are more widely available for breach of contract. A classic difference between contracts and torts is that *damages* in the former case are calculated to put the claimant in a position comparable to that he would have been in had the defendant performed the contract and in the latter to restore the party who has suffered loss to the position he would have been in had the tort not been committed. The extent to which damages are available for non-pecuniary loss may also be noted: 'In tort non-pecuniary losses flourish, since a large part of the protection given by the law of tort is to such interests as personal safety and personal reputation,

[16] *Koufos v C Czarnikow Ltd, The Heron II* [1969] 1 AC 350, 388–9 per Lord Reid. See also *Parsons (Livestock) Ltd v Uttley Ingham & Co Ltd* [1978] QB 791 and *Oliphant* (fn 14) para 1.4.

[17] *Oliphant* (fn 14) para 1.4.

[18] *Forsikringsaktieselskapet Vesta v Butcher* [1988] 2 All England Law Reports (All ER) 43.

[19] Clerk & Lindsell on Torts (fn 14) para 1–04.

which are interests not immediately connected with monetary considerations.'[20] By contrast, while damages for non-pecuniary loss may exceptionally be available for breach of contract, this is limited to specific circumstances (see no 54 f below).

Aside from the nature of damages pursuable, differences arise insofar as the *calculation of interest* on damages is concerned. Section 35A of the Senior Courts Act 1981 empowers the court to award simple interest on 'all or any part of the debt or damages in respect of which judgment is given … for all or any part of the period between the date *when the cause of action arose* and … the date of the judgment'.[21] As will be seen below (no 92 ff), causes of action for breach of contract and in tort arise at different times. 12

Procedural consequences, for example in respect of jurisdiction,[22] choice of law[23] and pleading[24] also attach to the decision to sue in contract or tort. In addition, the two legal fields differ insofar as *limitation periods* (as discussed in no 86 ff below) are concerned. 13

A miscellany of other distinctions exist, including the assignability of contractual rights, contrary to the general position in tort, and as regards rules on *capacity*. 14

B. EXISTENCE OF A 'GREY ZONE'?

1) Culpa in Contrahendo

The phrase *culpa in contrahendo* is not common parlance in English law. Indeed 'despite the huge inroads made by first the common law and then statute', it has been observed, 'the underlying principle of English contract law is still *caveat emptor*, let the buyer beware',[25] in contrast to the notion of *caveat venditor* ('let the seller beware'), a basic facet of civil law. As such, English judges have considered the civilian concept of *culpa in contrahendo*, a duty to carry on 15

20 McGregor on Damages (19th edn 2014) para 5–002.

21 Emphasis added. See *Nykredit Mortgage Bank plc v Edward Erdman Group Ltd (No 2)* [1997] 1 WLR 1627.

22 Cf art 5(1) and (2) Regulation (EC) No 44/2001 of 2001 on jurisdiction and the recognition and enforcement of judgments in civil and commercial matters [2001] Official Journal (OJ) L 12/1.

23 Cf Regulation (EC) No 593/2008 on the law applicable to contractual obligations ('Rome I') [2008] OJ L 177/6; Regulation (EC) No 864/2007 applicable to non-contractual obligations ('Rome II Regulation') [2007] OJ L 199/40.

24 Civil Procedure Rules, Practice Direction 16, para 7.

25 *KG Bominflot Bunkergesellschaft für Mineraloele mbH & Co v Petroplus Marketing AG (The Mercini Lady)* [2010] Court of Appeal (Civil Division) (EWCA Civ) 1145 at [45] per Rix LJ. See also *Smith v Hughes* (1870–71) LR 6 QB 597.

contractual negotiations in good faith, 'inherently repugnant to the adversarial position of the parties when involved in negotiations';[26] 'silence is golden'![27] Despite the absence of an overriding principle of good faith in the formation of contract, as is characteristic of civil law systems, English law has developed 'piecemeal solutions in response to demonstrated problems of unfairness … [E]quity has intervened to strike down unconscionable bargains. Parliament has stepped in to regulate the imposition of exemption clauses … The common law also has made its contribution, by holding that certain classes of contract require the utmost good faith, by treating as irrecoverable what purport to be agreed estimates of damage but are in truth a disguised penalty for breach, and in many other ways.'[28] These examples, however, do not constitute 'grey zone' solutions, but rather contractual ones since the prerequisites of contract formation (offer, acceptance, consideration and intention to create legal relations) must be present before the law will intervene to resolve issues that arose prior to the conclusion of the contract. This contrasts with the *culpa in contrahendo* doctrine which can operate where no contract is concluded.

2) *Misrepresentation*

16 English law's reluctance to extend the boundary of contract law absent a contract has led to the reliance on other areas, for example the law of unjust enrichment and tort law, for intervention. The former is limited to the extent that it requires an identifiable *enrichment*, whereas tort's appeal lies in the compensability of *losses*.[29] Intervention, however, is conditioned on the existence of wrongful behaviour. In the area of misrepresentation, a number of distinct tortious liabilities may arise. The tort of deceit (*fraudulent misrepresentation*) is committed where a false representation has been made knowingly or without belief in its truth, or recklessly, without caring whether it was true or false.[30] Where there is a fraudulent inducement of one person by another to contract, a contractual remedy – rescission – may be available in addition to an entitlement to damages, but the measure of damages is tortious. Misrepresentation is thus an area in which tortious and contractual liabilities overlap. (Indeed, tortious liabilities

---

26 *Walford v Miles* (1992) 64 Planning (Property) and Compensation Reports (P & CR) 166, 173 per Lord Ackner.

27 *ING Bank NV v Ros Roca SA* [2011] All ER 39 at [92] per Rix LJ.

28 *Interfoto Picture Library Ltd v Stiletto Visual Programmes Ltd* [1989] QB 433, 439 per Bingham LJ.

29 *P Giliker*, A Role for Tort in Pre-Contractual Negotiations? An Examination of English, French and Canadian Law (2003) 52 International and Comparative Law Quarterly 969. See also *P Giliker*, Pre-Contractual Good Faith and the Common European Sales Law (2013) 21 European Review of Private Law (ERPL) 79, 83.

30 *Derry v Peek* (1889) LR 14 Law Reports, Appeal Cases (App Cas) 337.

other than for deceit might also arise in this context, for example *procuring a breach of contract* or *causing loss by unlawful means.*[31])

Negligent misrepresentation, by contrast, falls more clearly within the grey area because of the way in which tort principles have been adapted to allow for a *voluntarily assumed* responsibility. The tortious liability for negligent misrepresentation was first authoritatively recognised in principle in the well-known case of *Hedley Byrne v Heller.*[32] There, a firm, Hedley Byrne, detrimentally extended credit to a client, Easipower, having sought advice from Easipower's bank, Heller. In the absence of a contract between Hedley Byrne and Heller, the action for damages for pure economic loss was brought in tort. The court ruled that if someone possessing special skill undertakes, quite irrespective of contract, to apply that skill for the assistance of another person who reasonably relies upon it or upon his ability to make careful inquiry, a duty of care will arise. Although there was no contractual relationship, the idea of 'assumption of responsibility' was introduced to address the problem of indeterminate liability. Had Heller not expressly disclaimed its liability in providing the advice, it would have assumed responsibility towards Hedley Byrne by voluntarily entering into a special relationship equivalent to contract, thereby creating a duty of care. The *Hedley Byrne* principle was applied in *Esso Petroleum Co Ltd v Mardon*[33] to impose liability for a negligent *pre-contractual* statement. Lord Denning there ruled that 'if a man, who has or professes to have special knowledge or skill, makes a representation by virtue thereof to another – be it advice, information or opinion – with the intention of inducing him to enter into a contract with him, he is under a duty to use reasonable care to see that the representation is correct, and that the advice, information or opinion is reliable. If he negligently gives unsound advice or misleading information or expresses an erroneous opinion, and thereby induces the other side to enter into a contract with him, he is liable in damages.' Applying this principle, the court found that the defendant oil company had induced the claimant to enter into a tenancy of one of their petrol-filling stations by negligently overstating its throughput and were liable in damages for his consequent losses. The material facts of that case pre-dated the Misrepresentation Act 1967, sec 2(1) of which now provides an alternative, statutory liability in damages. The statutory action applies where a person has *entered into a contract after a misrepresentation* has been made to him. In such cases, the negligent misstatement need not be a term of the contract such as to give rise to an action for breach of contract. Under the statute, damages are assessed on a tortious basis, but applying the approach employed in the tort 17

31 *Oliphant* (fn 14) ch 29.

32 [1964] AC 465, noted by *K Oliphant/V Wilcox*, England and Wales, in: B Winiger/E Karner/K Oliphant (eds), Digest of European Tort Law, vol 3: Essential Cases on Misconduct (2018).

33 [1976] QB 801, 820 per Lord Denning MR.

of deceit rather than that used for negligent misrepresentation at common law (which is somewhat less generous to the claimant).[34]

18 Additionally, it should be noted that a liability for *innocent misrepresentation* may arise under the Misrepresentation Act 1967. The remedies are rescission (sec 1) or damages in lieu of rescission (sec 2(2)). The aim of such damages is to put the claimant so far as money can into the position he would have been in had rescission been granted.[35] This liability, which by definition arises in the absence of fault, has been characterised as one which is *sui generis*, sounding neither in contract nor in tort.[36]

3) Bailment

19 'Bailment', as Lord Denning MR put it, is 'not … an action in contract, nor in tort, but … an action on its own, sui generis'.[37] It describes a legal relationship recognised at common law whereby a bailor temporarily transfers physical possession of property to a bailee for safekeeping. In so doing, the bailee assumes a responsibility to take reasonable care of his bailor's goods and not to convert them.[38] The parties may or may not be in a contractual relationship. It is not easy to label certain obligations owed by the bailee as either contractual or tortious. This is the case, for example, with respect to the imposition of strict liability on the bailee for loss or damage resulting from his unlawful departure from the terms of the bailment which can be visited not only on a contractual bailee but also on the unrewarded bailee under a gratuitous bailment.[39] Depending on the precise facts, a claim against a bailee can be brought in contract, tort, bailment or restitution.[40]

C. COMMON OR DIFFERENT RULES REGULATING TORT AND CONTRACT

20 Although the questionnaire sought to solicit common or *different* rules regulating tort and contract, this section will concentrate on rules common to both causes of action since much of this report details the distinctions between them. As

34 McGregor on Damages (fn 20) para 47–048 ff.

35 McGregor on Damages (fn 20) para 47–067 ff.

36 *Farley Health Products Ltd v Babylon Trading Co* (1987) Times, 29 July, obiter per Lawson J. See also Halsbury's Laws of England, vol 97: Tort (2010) para 409.

37 *Building and Civil Engineering Holidays Scheme Management Ltd v Post Office* [1966] 1 QB 247, 261; Halsbury's Laws of England (fn 36) para 409.

38 *Morris v CW Martin & Sons Ltd* [1966] 1 QB 716, 726, 732, 738.

39 Halsbury's Laws of England (fn 36) para 407.

40 Ibid.

a starting point, it may be noted that contract and tort are both creatures of the common law and large parts of both emerged from what in the days of the forms of action was known as the action on the case. Given their close historical links, it should not be a surprise that certain legal concepts have a role to play in both areas.

As respects *substantive commonalities*, contract and tort are subject to broadly the same (common law) law of damages, though there are some differences of detail (eg in the law of remoteness of damage: see no 8). Contractual obligations are generally strict but where there is a contractual duty of care its practical content is assessed within the same framework of principle that applies within the tort of negligence (see no 37 ff). 21

A number of *procedural similarities* also apply. Thus, the golden rule is that it is incumbent upon the claimant to prove what he contends[41] in respect of both causes of action and the standard of proof is 'the balance of probabilities' or 'more probable than not'.[42] 22

D. APPLICATION OF COMMON RULES IN A DIFFERENT WAY

To a great extent, this question can be answered with reference to the information produced under no 7 ff above. 23

II. MAIN DIFFERENCES BETWEEN TORTIOUS AND CONTRACTUAL LIABILITY

A. DIFFERENCES AS REGARDS THE FOUNDATIONS OF LIABILITY

1) *Role of Intention*

a) Contract

In contract law, the term 'intention' usually appears in the context of 'intention to create legal relations', one of the basic ingredients required for the creation of a valid contract. There is also an action for intentional interference with contractual relations. However, this is classed as a tort and the action, in any 24

41 *Chapman v Oakleigh Animal Products Ltd* (1970) 8 Knight's Industrial Reports (KIR) 1063, 1072 per Davies LJ.

42 *Miller v Minister of Pensions* [1947] 2 All ER 372, 373 f per Lord Denning.

case, is against a third party who procures the breach of the contract, or uses unlawful means to interfere with its performance, and not the other contracting party. That said, there is a concept of *deliberate breach* under English law, which falls under the broader notion of 'fundamental breach'.[43] Such a breach has a number of implications.

25 The first such implication relates to *future performance*: 'where there is a contract which is to be performed in future, if one of the parties has said to the other in effect, "If you go on and perform your side of the contract I will not perform mine"... that in effect amounts to saying, "I will not perform the contract." In that case the other party may say, "You have given me distinct notice that you will not perform the contract. I will not wait until you have broken it, but I will treat you as having put an end to the contract, and if necessary I will sue you for damages, but at all events I will not go on with the contract."'[44] A deliberate breach thus 'indicates the other party's attitude towards future performance',[45] which in turn may dictate the appropriate *remedy*. However, even a deliberate breach, actual or threatened, will not necessarily entitle the innocent party to treat himself as discharged, since it may be that such a breach can appropriately be remedied by damages.[46] This is especially the case with deliberate breaches of a minor character.[47] The effect of an intimation of non-performance thus depends on the facts: 'You must look at the actual circumstances of the case in order to see whether the one party to the contract is relieved from its future performance by the conduct of the other; you must examine what that conduct is so as to see whether it amounts to a renunciation, to an absolute refusal to perform the contract … and whether the other party may accept it as a reason for not performing his part.'[48]

26 The deliberate character of the breach may also be relevant to other remedies. A 'flagrant contravention' of obligations may influence the court's judgment as to the appropriate amount of damages due.[49] In some circumstances, a deliberate *and cynical* breach may trigger the exceptional remedy of an account of profits. Deliberate breaches of contract are a frequent occurrence in the commercial world so that more is needed to justify ordering such a remedy, particularly when another remedy is available.[50] While the House of Lords in *Attorney*

---

[43] *Suisse Atlantique Société d'Armement Maritime SA v NV Rotterdamsche Kolen Centrale* [1967] 1 AC 261, 435.

[44] *Mersey Steel & Iron Co Ltd v Naylor Benzon & Co* (1884) 9 Law Reports, Appeal Cases (3rd Series) (App Cas) 434, 442 per Lord Blackburn.

[45] *Suisse Atlantique Société d'Armement Maritime SA* [1967] 1 AC 261, 435 per Lord Wilberforce.

[46] *Suisse Atlantique Société d'Armement Maritime SA* [1967] 1 AC 261, 365.

[47] *Suisse Atlantique Société d'Armement Maritime SA* [1967] 1 AC 261, 435 per Lord Wilberforce.

[48] *Mersey Steel and Iron Co v Naylor Benzon & Co* (1884) 9 App Cas 434, 438 per Lord Selborne.

[49] *Experience Hendrix LLC v PPX Enterprises Inc* [2003] EWCA Civ 323 at [54] per Gibson LJ.

[50] *Experience Hendrix LLC* [2003] EWCA Civ 323 at [55] per Gibson LJ.

General v Blake was not prepared to rule that any 'of [the following] facts would be, by itself, a good reason for ordering an account of profits',[51] this suggests that all three may: that is, '*the fact that the breach was cynical and deliberate*; the fact that the breach enabled the defendant to enter into a more profitable contract elsewhere; and the fact that by entering into a new and more profitable contract the defendant put it out of his power to perform his contract with the plaintiff.'[52]

A further implication relates to *exemption clauses*. Deliberate breaches often arise against the backdrop of clauses limiting liability. But, whereas liability for deliberate and negligent acts can generally be excluded, liability for fraud, malice or recklessness cannot. As has been said: 'A deliberate act, in the sense of an intentional act, will in nearly all cases fall well short of the fraudulent, reckless or malicious.'[53] Parliament has also intervened in this area: in respect of one who deals with a consumer on his written standard terms of business, sec 3 of the Unfair Contract Terms Act 1977 provides that a contract term which purports to exclude or restrict any liability of a party must satisfy the requirement of reasonableness (see no 111 ff below). Moreover, such words will be approached with the aid of the *contra proferentem* rule which construes words *contra* the *proferens* (the party who seeks to rely upon them). Thus a court could well construe a purported exclusion of liability as applying only to innocent and not deliberate breaches of contract.[54] However, in the case of 'commercial contracts negotiated between business-men capable of looking after their own interests and of deciding how risks inherent in the performance of various kinds of contract can be most economically borne (generally by insurance)', it has been judicially observed that it is 'wrong to place a strained construction upon words in an exclusion clause which are clear and fairly susceptible of one meaning only'.[55] Thus, if sufficiently clear and unambiguous terms are used (and the more radical the clause, the clearer must be the language), an exclusion of liability even for deliberate breaches of contract would prima facie apply.[56] 27

---

51 *Attorney General v Blake* [2001] 1 AC 268, 286 per Lord Nicholls.

52 Emphasis added. *Attorney General v Blake* [1998] Law Reports, Chancery Division (3rd Series) (Ch) 439, 457, 458 per Lord Woolf MR. Referred to in *Attorney General v Blake* [2001] 1 AC 268, 286 by Lord Nicholls.

53 *Regus (UK) Ltd v Epcot Solutions Ltd* [2008] EWCA Civ 361 at [35].

54 There is conflicting authority as to whether there is a presumption against exemption clauses being construed so as to cover deliberate, repudiatory breach. In *Internet Broadcasting Corporation (trading as NetTV) v MAR LLC (trading as MARHedge)* [2009] England & Wales High Court (EWHC) 844 at [33], Gabriel Moss GC found such a presumption to exist, but in the subsequent case of *Astrazeneca UK Ltd v Albemarle International Corp* [2011] 2 Current Law Consolidation (CLC) 252, 290 Flaux J indicated (obiter) that he would decline to follow *Internet Broadcasting Corporation*, stating that the judge there quoted selectively to support his position and that the cases do not support that proposition.

55 *Photo Production Ltd v Securicor Transport Ltd* [1980] AC 827, 851 per Lord Diplock.

56 *Internet Broadcasting Corporation (trading as NetTV) v MAR LLC (trading as MARHedge)* [2009] EWHC 844 at [32] f per Gabriel Moss GC. See also *Photo Production Ltd v Securicor Transport Ltd* [1980] AC 827.

28 Lastly, it may be noted that in *insurance contracts* cover may expressly exclude claims for deliberate acts.

b) Tort

29 English law may be analysed in terms of a tripartite classification of torts according to standards of liability: intention, negligence and strict liability. As will be seen, the role of intent is more significant in tort than in contract.[57] Whereas with some torts it is the particular *conduct that must be intended* (and not the injury that results from such conduct), *intent to harm* is relevant in others. *Intentional harm* plays various roles in various torts. First, there are some torts that require an intention to harm as a basis of liability, for example misfeasance in public office, malicious prosecution, malicious falsehood and causing harm by unlawful means. Second, while not an absolute prerequisite, a malicious motive or intent may be a relevant factor in determining liability in certain torts. In the case of nuisance, for example, the intention with which the defendant acted is taken into consideration in deciding whether the conduct complained of was unreasonable.[58] Third, an intent to injure may amount to malice depriving a defendant of the right to invoke a defence (eg the defence of qualified privilege in the law of defamation). Lastly, in terms of the overall structure of the law of tort, torts of intention may justifiably protect a wider set of interests than torts of negligence.[59]

30 Though it was once considered that a person intends the natural and probable consequences of his conduct,[60] a subjective approach now prevails: the focus is on the defendant's own thoughts and not those that might be imputed to a reasonable

57 See generally *Oliphant* (fn 14) para 1.22 f; *K Oliphant*, The Structure of the Intentional Torts, in: J Neyers/S Pitel/E Chamberlain (eds), Emerging Issues in Tort Law (2007) 509 ff; *JM Finnis*, Intention in Tort Law, in: DG Owens (ed), Philosophical Foundations of Tort Law (1995) 229 ff.

58 *Christie v Davey* [1893] 1 Ch 316, noted by *Oliphant/Wilcox* (fn 32).

59 'I do not resile from the proposition that the policy considerations which limit the heads of recoverable damage in negligence do not apply equally to torts of intention. If someone actually intends to cause harm by a wrongful act and does so, there is ordinarily no reason why he should not have to pay compensation. But I think that if you adopt such a principle, you have to be very careful about what you mean by intend. … If … one is going to draw a principled distinction which justifies abandoning the rule that damages for mere distress are not recoverable, imputed intention will not do. The defendant must actually have acted in a way which he knew to be unjustifiable and either intended to cause harm or at least acted without caring whether he caused harm or not': *Wainwright v Home Office* [2004] 2 AC 406, 425 per Lord Hoffmann.

60 *South Wales Miners' Federation v Glamorgan Coal Co* [1905] AC 239, 244 per Lord Halsbury LC.

person. A distinction is drawn between consequences that are intended as an end in themselves, or as a means to an end, and consequences that are merely foreseeable.[61] Conduct that the defendant knows will necessarily be injurious to the claimant will also be regarded as intended to harm.[62] Conduct that the defendant knows *might* be injurious to the claimant is reckless and is considered tantamount to intention in some torts[63] but not others.[64] Motive is extraneous to the question of liability but it may serve as a ground for justification.[65] Purpose is largely synonymous with intention but, in the anomalous tort of conspiracy to injure, a predominant purpose to injure, going beyond a mere intention, is required.[66]

Intentional torts seek to protect a variety of interests, namely persons (eg assault, battery, false imprisonment, the intentional infliction of emotional harm, malicious prosecution), property (eg conversion, trespass to land and chattels, malicious falsehood), economic interests (eg deceit, procuring a breach of contract, intimidation, conspiracy and causing loss by unlawful means) and reputation and privacy (defamation, the misuse of private information). Some of these torts are *actionable per se*, that is without proof of damage (cf negligence).[67] Moreover, they *cover a broader range of interests* than torts of negligence (eg pure economic interests). Where liability is established, the rules on the *calculation of damages* are more generous in torts of intentional injury than torts of negligence because even unforeseen and unforeseeable losses may be recoverable.[68] 31

It may also be noted that exemplary and aggravated damages (no 64 ff) are more readily available in the case of intent.[69] As seen above, the presence of intention 32

61 *OBG Ltd v Allan* [2007] United Kingdom House of Lords (UKHL) 21, [2008] 1 AC 1.

62 *OBG Ltd v Allan* [2007] UKHL 21, [2008] 1 AC 1 at [167] per Lord Nicholls.

63 *Three Rivers DC v Bank of England (No 3)* [2003] 2 AC 1, 192 per Lord Stein (misfeasance in public office); *Cooperative Group v Pritchard* [2012] QB 320 (trespass to the person). See further Clerk & Lindsell on Torts (fn 14) para 1–58 ff.

64 Eg causing harm by unlawful means: *OBG Ltd v Allan* [2007] UKHL 21, [2008] 1 AC 1.

65 See Clerk & Lindsell on Torts (fn 14) para 1–61 ff.

66 *Crofter Hand Woven Harris Tweed Co Ltd v Veitch* [1942] AC 435.

67 See eg *Cooperative Group v Pritchard* [2012] QB 320, 331 per Aikens LJ.

68 *Smith New Court Securities Ltd v Citibank NA* [1997] AC 254, 279 per Lord Steyn (deceit). In the case of conversion, a different test applies depending on the defendant's state of mind: see *Kuwait Airways Corp v Iraq Airways Co* [2002] UKHL 19 at [100] ff ('foreseeability, as the more restrictive test, is appropriate for those who act in good faith. … Persons who knowingly convert another's goods stand differently. Such persons are acting dishonestly. I can see no good reason why the remoteness test of "directly and naturally" applied in cases of deceit should not apply in cases of conversion where the defendant acted dishonestly').

69 *V Wilcox*, England, and *AJ Seebok/V Wilcox*, Aggravated Damages, in: H Koziol/V Wilcox (eds), Punitive Damages: Common Law and Civil Law Perspectives (2009) 7 and 257.

may also have an impact on the availability of defences (eg contributory negligence)[70] and the imposition of vicarious liability.[71] Evidence of a defendant's intention to repeat a wrongful act may justify the grant of an injunction.[72]

2) Role of Wrongfulness and Fault and their Variations

33 The word 'tort', meaning 'wrong', is rooted in French. In that sense, wrongfulness is at the foundation of all tort claims. The term is sometimes to be found in the English law reports but it is generally used in a non-technical sense.[73] Conduct such as to give rise to liability in tort, or that amounts to a breach of contract, may thus be described as wrongful, though wrongfulness as such is not a formal element of liability in either contract or tort.[74]

34 What it is that makes conduct wrongful in this admittedly rather loose sense is context specific. It varies from tort to tort and as between tort and contract. It may refer to a breach of the duty of care in the tort of negligence or, in the tort of private nuisance, an unreasonable interference with another's use or enjoyment of land. In torts of intention, it is the defendant's state of mind when acting that makes his conduct wrongful. This last proposition makes it clear that English law does not make a clear distinction between wrongfulness and fault: sometimes it is the fault with which it is done that makes the conduct wrongful. It might be more accurate to say, however, that fault is really an aspect of wrongfulness, though there are aspects of wrongfulness that go beyond whether or not there was fault on the facts,[75] for example whether the defendant owed the claimant a duty of care. Thus, conduct may be 'faulty' but not 'wrongful' (eg in the absence of a duty of care) and vice versa (as in respect of torts of strict liability).[76]

35 Fault entails the violation of a reasonable standard of conduct, assessed objectively; it is often referred to as the standard of the reasonable person. The required standard is varied, however, according to age (in the case of children) and the defendant's mental or physical incapacity, if there should be one. To that (limited) extent, the standard of conduct has a subjective component. There is also another sense in which the reasonable person test involves a subjective assessment: 'It is still left to the judge to decide what, in the circumstances of the

---

70 *Standard Chartered Bank v Pakistan National Shipping Corpn (No 2)* [2002] UKHL 43; *Corporacion Nacional del Cobre de Chile v Sogemin Metals Ltd* [1997] 2 All ER 917.

71 Halsbury's Laws of England (fn 36) para 492.

72 *Oliphant* (fn 14) para 8.2.

73 See *Oliphant/Wilcox* (fn 32).

74 *WV Horton Rogers*, England, in: H Koziol (ed), Unification of Tort Law: Wrongfulness (1998) 39.

75 *K Oliphant*, Basic Questions on Tort Law from the Perspective of England and the Commonwealth, in: H Koziol (ed), Basic Questions on Tort Law from a Comparative Perspective (2015) no 5/118.

76 *WV Horton Rogers*, England, in: P Widmer (ed) Unification of Tort Law: Fault (2005) 68.

particular case, the reasonable man would have had in contemplation, and what, accordingly, the party sought to be made liable ought to have foreseen. Here there is room for diversity of view … What to one judge may seem far-fetched may seem to another both natural and probable.'[77]

In the law of contract, the roles of wrongfulness and fault are somewhat easier to separate because contractual obligations are usually strict and liability for breach of contract is thus generally independent of proof of fault. However, the theory of 'efficient breach', which denies that breach of contract is even wrongful,[78] has attracted few adherents in the UK. In fact, fault may be seen to be a pervasive aspect of contract. As mentioned below (no 37 ff), while contractual obligations are generally obligations of result, some contracts stipulate merely for the exercise of reasonable care. This is especially the case where there is concurrence of contractual and tortious duties (eg in the contexts of occupational safety and medical treatment). The use of terms implied by custom or statute (no 40) may also import fault standards, as does the concept of deliberate breach (no 24 ff) and the interpretive approaches employed by the courts (no 24 ff). Fault is also evident in the duty to mitigate which must be undertaken with reasonable efforts. That the law establishes behavioural guidelines based on the conduct of the parties in negotiating their contract is also evident from the existence of torts in the contractual setting: the intentional procurement of another's breach of contract is itself tortious vis-à-vis the other contracting party, while a breach of contract may be the 'unlawful means' required by the torts of conspiracy, intimidation and intentional interference with economic interests.[79] This is said to relieve the pressure to inject a general fault standard into contract law itself.[80] 36

3) *Role of Strict Liability*

a) Contract

Contract liability is normally strict in the sense that there is usually no prerequisite to prove fault in order to seek a remedy. In practice, however, much depends on the terms of the contract, both express and implied. 37

Strict liability is implied by law in the case of certain types of contracts including contracts of sale: sec 13 of the Sale of Goods Act 1979, for example, provides 38

---

77 *Glasgow Corporation v Muir* [1943] AC 448, 457 per Macmillan LJ.

78 Consider Holmes's famous view, summarised by *R Posner*, Let Us Never Blame a Contract Breaker (2009) 107 Michigan Law Review 1349, 1349: 'A contract is an option to perform or pay, and a "breach" is therefore not a wrongful act but merely triggers the duty to pay liquidated or other damages.'

79 See *Oliphant* (fn 14) ch 29 (passim).

80 *RA Hillman*, The Importance of Fault in Contract Law (2012) Cornell Law Faculty Working Papers 111, 16.

that, where there is a contract for the sale of goods by description, there is an implied term that the goods will correspond with the description, and sec 14 that goods sold in the course of a business are of satisfactory quality and reasonably fit for purpose. 'How or why they fall short of that standard is immaterial so far as the law is concerned. The seller may well offer goods designed, made, packed and distributed by other parties over whom he has no control, but he must still in effect guarantee the reasonable suitability and safety of such goods. He remains liable, in other words, whether the defect is known or unknown, and whether or not he tries or is able to remedy it.'[81] Liability is justified by the need to protect buyers and by the fact that the seller will invariably have a contract with the supplier and he with his supplier until liability is traced back to the manufacturer. Other examples of legislation imposing strict liability include contracts on package travel,[82] contracts between innkeepers and their guests[83] and contracts for the electronic transfer of funds.[84] A regime of strict liability may also be imposed by common law, as is the case with contracts for the carriage of goods by land by common carriers.[85]

39 While one can contract out of such liability in some cases (eg common carriers[86]), the obligation cannot be modified in others (eg innkeepers[87]). Conversely, a common carrier's strict liability under common law is mitigated to some extent by statute.[88]

40 The contract may impose a fault standard instead, again either expressly or impliedly. In that case, a negligence standard applies (so that a contractual duty of care, breach – that is, fault, which is assessed objectively – causation and damage need to exist). Such an obligation is quite commonly inferred in many contexts where liability is concurrent in contract and tort (no 117 ff). A standard of 'reasonable care and skill' may also be implied by statute. This is the case in respect of the supply of services in a commercial setting: see sec 13 of the Supply of Goods and Services Act 1982, for example.[89] Parties can, however, contract in

---

81 *MH Whincup*, Contract Law and Practice: The English System with Scottish, Commonwealth and Continental Comparisons (2006) para 6.47. See also *WV Horton Rogers*, England, in: J Spier (ed), Unification of Tort Law: Strict Liability (1996).

82 Package Travel, Package Holiday and Package Tours Regulations 1992, reg 15, subject to exceptions.

83 Hotel Proprietors Act 1956, sec 1(2), subject to exceptions and limitations.

84 Payment Services Regulations 2009, sec 61, implementing the EC Payment Services Directive 2007/64/EC.

85 Chitty on Contracts (fn 1) para 36–014 ff.

86 Ibid.

87 Ibid, para 33–100.

88 Carriers Act 1830, sec 1.

89 'In a contract for the supply of a service where the supplier is acting in the course of a business, there is an implied term that the supplier will carry out the service with reasonable care and skill.'

favour of a higher standard. Section 16(1) thus provides that the 'standard may (subject to exceptions) be negatived or varied by express agreement, or by the course of dealing between the parties, or by such usage as binds both parties to the contract.' Moreover, the provision does not prejudice any rule of law which imposes a stricter duty on the supplier than that imposed by sec 13.[90] This refers to innkeepers' liability (no 39), for example. Note that strict liability in all the above cases is not necessarily absolute liability. Defences may thus apply.

b) Tort

As is the case with certain contractual duties, certain torts are classed as strict liability torts. It is no answer to such torts that reasonable care was taken. Unlike in contract, parties cannot agree to modify the standard set by tort law as there is no standard of required conduct to modify (although they can agree to waive liability: see no 107 f). Strict liability torts include the rule in *Rylands v Fletcher* (for the non-natural use of land),[91] conversion,[92] and breach of statutory duty (depending on the construction of the statutory obligation). Other torts also contain elements of strict liability, for example false imprisonment, in which an intentional deprivation of liberty is tortious even if there is a reasonable belief in justificatory circumstances.[93] Additionally, certain statutes – for example, the Gas Act 1965,[94] the Nuclear Installations Act 1965,[95] the Animals Act 1971,[96] the Reservoirs Act 1975,[97] the Civil Aviation Act 1982,[98] the Consumer Protection Act 1987,[99] the Copyright Designs and Patents Act 1988,[100] the Environmental Protection Act 1990,[101] the Water Industry Act 1991 (for escapes of water)[102] and the Merchant Shipping Act 1995 (in respect of oil pollution)[103] – give rise to strict liability. The list is by no means exhaustive. Although vicarious liability borrows from the principle of strict liability, as no fault is required on the part of the employer, the employer's vicarious liability is not in itself a 'strict liability' since it requires the commission of a tort by the employee. 41

90 Section 16(3)(a).
91 See *Rylands v Fletcher* (1868) LR 3 HL 330.
92 *OBG Ltd v Allan* [2007] UKHL 21, [2008] 1 AC 1 at [95] per Lord Hoffmann.
93 *R v Governor of Brockhill Prison ex parte Evans (No 2)* [2001] 2 AC 19, 26 per Lord Slynn.
94 Section 14.
95 Section 7.
96 Sections 2 and 3.
97 See schedule 2.
98 Section 76(2).
99 Implementing EC Directive 85/374/EEC on defective products.
100 Section 296ZD.
101 Section 73(6).
102 Section 209.
103 Sections 153 and 154.

B. DIFFERENCES AS REGARDS CAUSATION

42 Whether under tort or contract, a claimant needs to establish that the defendant's tortious act or omission, on the one hand, or breach of contract, on the other, was a causative one. In addition to causation, scope of protection (an issue of policy) – see the discussion of remoteness of damage at no 8 above – is also a relevant consideration. Causation plays a more prominent role in tort than it does in contract, perhaps because the commission of a tort generally requires proof of damage, whereas a breach of contract does not. Nevertheless, in both contract and tort, damages are awarded for losses sustained by the claimant only if such losses are causally attributable to the defendant. A conventional distinction is drawn between factual and legal causation. There is *factual causation* if the claimant establishes, on the balance of probabilities, that a defendant's wrongful conduct caused the claimant's loss. There is *legal causation* if the defendant's wrongful conduct can be regarded as the operative cause of the claimant's loss.

1) Factual Causation

43 The 'but for' test, construed simply as 'if not that, then not this',[104] is the first enquiry. There will be instances, however, where this simplistic test is ill equipped to establish the relevant cause. This is the case, for example, where there are two or more acts or events which would each be sufficient to bring about the claimant's injury but the latter is unable to prove which act or event caused the loss (*alternative causes*). In such instances, a broader view of causation is taken – on grounds of fairness and reasonableness – provided it can be shown that the defendant's conduct 'materially contributed' to the claimant's injury[105] or to the risk of the same.[106] A literal application of the 'but for' test is also inappropriate in the case of *overtaken causes*: that is, where a claimant is injured by a defendant's negligence but prior to trial suffers similar loss as a result of an independent supervening event for the consequences of which he seeks to hold the defendant liable. 'But for' the defendant's conduct, the claimant would still have suffered the loss. The rule is, however, that the initial injury is still considered the cause of the damage.[107] Conversely, this is not the case

---

[104] See *Barnett v Chelsea & Kensington Hospital* [1969] 1 QB 428 where, although said to have acted negligently, a doctor was not held liable for failing to see and examine a deceased, the claimant's husband, since he would have died of poisoning even if he had been admitted and treated with all care.

[105] *Bonnington Castings Ltd v Wardlaw* [1956] AC 613.

[106] *McGhee v National Coal Board* [1973] 1 WLR 1; *Fairchild v Glenhaven Funeral Services Ltd* [2003] 1 AC 32.

[107] *Baker v Willoughby* [1970] AC 467.

where the supervening event was non-tortious.[108] Where the successive event is hypothetical rather than actual, a reduction of damages will ensue.[109]

2) *Legal Causation*

44 Legal causation constitutes 'the law's attempt to place limits on liability for damage for which the defendant's negligence has factually been a cause but for which, as a matter of legal policy, no liability should attach.'[110] In both contract and tort, a defendant is liable for all *reasonably foreseeable damage* that arose as a result of his wrongful conduct. In practice, the requirement of reasonable foreseeability will generally[111] not inhibit the imposition of liability in the case of personal injuries since a wide view is taken of the type of harm that needs to be reasonably foreseeable.[112] Additionally, a wrongdoer takes his victim as he finds him (*talem qualem* or eggshell-skull rule),[113] while, where an 'accident was caused by a known source of danger, but caused in a way which could not have been foreseen ... that affords no defence' to the tortfeasor.[114] However, whereas 'extremely unlikely results'[115] are considered reasonably foreseeable in tort, the test in contract is kinder to the defendant: only events which have 'a very substantial degree of probability' are relevant.[116] Yet there is authority to suggest that, where the claimant suffers physical as opposed to economic damage, the tortious rather than contractual standard of remoteness should be applied.[117] Nevertheless, a difference lies in the *temporal assessment* of reasonable foreseeability. In the case of a tort, the enquiry is whether a thing was reasonably foreseeable at the time the tortious conduct took place,[118] and in contract it is at the time of entering into the contract, not that of the breach.[119]

45 Having considered the issue on 'direct consequences', we now turn to the question of intervening actions. There are by far more authorities on this issue in tort than contract. In the latter field, the real issues tend to be obscured

[108] *Jobling v Associated Dairies* [1982] AC 794.
[109] *Heil v Rankin* [2001] QB 272.
[110] *M Lunney/K Oliphant*, Tort Law: Text and Materials (5th edn 2013) 265.
[111] Cf *Doughty v Turner Manufacturing Company* [1964] 1 QB 518; *Tremain v Pike* [1969] 1 WLR 1556.
[112] *Page v Smith* [1996] AC 155.
[113] *Smith v Leech Brain & Co* [1962] 2 QB 405.
[114] *Hughes v Lord Advocate* [1963] AC 837, 847 per Lord Reid.
[115] *Koufos v C Czarnikow Ltd, The Heron II* [1969] 1 AC 350, 389 per Lord Reid.
[116] *Koufos v C Czarnikow Ltd, The Heron II* [1969] 1 AC 350, 388 f per Lord Reid. See also *Overseas Tankship (UK) Ltd v Miller Steamship Co Pty Ltd (The Wagon Mound)* [1967] 1 AC 617.
[117] *Parsons (Livestock) Ltd v Uttley Ingham & Co Ltd* [1978] QB 791 per Lord Denning.
[118] *Doughty v Turner Manufacturing Co Ltd* [1964] 1 QB 518, 528 per Harman LJ.
[119] *Hydraulic Engineering Co Ltd v McHaffie, Goslett & Co* (1878) 4 QBD 670, 676 per Brett LJ.

by the rather vague proposition that the defendant's act or omission must be a 'dominant' or 'effective' cause of the alleged consequence. In the absence of any formal tests for causation in contract law, this task is ultimately approached as a matter of common sense on the part of the courts.[120] In the absence of precedent, it is thought that the rules applicable in tort apply *mutatis mutandis* in contract. There is thus quite some overlap in the two fields insofar as this aspect of causation is concerned. The starting point, both in terms of contract and tort, is that a *voluntary intervening act of a third party* breaks the chain of causation, thus becoming 'a new and independent cause.'[121] An exception applies where the defendant was under an exceptional duty to protect against third-party interference.[122]

46 With respect to intervening acts by *third parties*, the starting point is to ask whether their intervention was reasonably foreseeable. If it was, and there are no other counter-indications, causation is likely to be established unless the defendant ought reasonably to have anticipated the intervention and foreseen that damage would result.[123] Causation may thus be traced through the intervention of a child[124] or a person 'acting on the impulse of personal peril'[125] (that is, to protect himself), the defendant remaining liable; in the latter situation, the doctrine of 'alternative danger' is applied. Similarly, where a defendant acts negligently and a third party intervenes in an attempt to avoid such negligence (ie in safeguarding his interests), the defendant cannot shelter behind the acts of the latter in respect of damage caused to an innocent casualty (which is akin to the alternative danger doctrine).[126] This is also the case where contractual damage is caused to a third party, in seeking to safeguard himself or his property from the defendant's wrongful act.[127]

47 In the case of an intervention by *the claimant* who is not fully responsible, in particular in the case of children,[128] or a person acting on the impulse of personal peril,[129] the chain of causation remains intact. Where a defendant acts negligently and a claimant, in seeking to avoid such negligence

120 *Galoo Ltd v Bright Grahame Murray* [1994] 1 WLR 1360.
121 *Weld-Blundell v Stephens* [1920] AC 956, 986 per Lord Summer.
122 See *Lamb v Camden LBC* [1981] 2 All ER 408 for tort and *London Joint Stock Bank v Macmillan* [1918] AC 777 for contract.
123 *Latham v R Johnson & Nephew Ltd* [1913] 1 King's Bench (KB) 398, 413 per Hamilton LJ.
124 Ibid. See also *Martin v Stanborough* (1924) 41 Times Law Reports (TLR) 1; *Shiffman v Order of St John* [1936] 1 All ER 557.
125 *Latham v R Johnson & Nephew Ltd* [1913] 1 KB 398, 413 per Hamilton LJ. See also *Scott v Shepherd* (1773) 2 William Blackstone's King's Bench Reports (WmBl) 892.
126 *Clark v Chambers* (1878) 3 QBD 327.
127 Analogous to *Haynes v Harwood* [1935] 1 KB 146.
128 *Lynch v Nurdin* (1841) 1 QB 29; *Yachuk v Oliver Blais Co Ltd* [1949] AC 386.
129 *Jones v Boyce* [1816] 1 Starkie's Nisi Prius Reports (Stark) 493; *Pigney v Pointers Transport Services Ltd* [1957] 1 WLR 1121.

(ie in safeguarding his interests) intervenes and suffers damage, the latter's act does not constitute a *novus actus interveniens*.[130] This is also the case where damage is caused to the intervener, himself, in seeking to safeguard the interests (ie person or property) of another.[131] Where a claimant who was subject to a disability imposed by the defendant's tort suffers further injury as a result of that disability, the chain of causation remains unbroken.[132]

Both in contract and tort, a defendant is likely to be discharged from liability 48
in the case of an intervention by a deliberate act of a claimant,[133] unless in circumstances where this could be considered non-voluntary (eg acts done to avoid personal peril).

C. DIFFERENCES AS REGARDS REMEDIES

1) *Degree of Certainty of the Damage*

There are no differences between tort and contract law in so far as proof of 49
damage is concerned (see no 22): in both cases 'the damage must be proved with reasonable certainty'.[134] A claimant who fails to prove this, whether under contract or tort, will be entitled to nominal damages at most. Nevertheless, it could generally be said that in practice tort claims often involve somewhat uncertain damage but the courts are nonetheless prepared to compensate it. For example, there are torts in respect of which damage is presumed to have arisen; moreover, non-pecuniary losses – which are more prevalent in tort – are not amenable to precise mathematical assessment. The uncertainty of future pecuniary loss is also more pronounced in the case of tort because of the large role played there by personal injury claims. The area of loss of chance (see no 57 f) is also relevant to the question of the degree of certainty of the damage. Whereas the balance of probability test applies in the case of past events, the court can only 'make an estimate as to what are the chances that a particular thing will or would have happened and reflect those chances, whether they are more or less than even, in the amount of damages it awards'.[135] As was said: 'You can prove that a past event happened, but you cannot prove that a future event will happen and I do not think that the law is so foolish as to suppose that you can. All that you can do is to evaluate the chance. Sometimes it is virtually

130 *Dee Conservancy Board v McConnell* [1928] 2 KB 159; *Sayers v Harlow UDC* [1958] 1 WLR 623.

131 *Haynes v Harwood* [1935] 1 KB 146.

132 *Wieland v Cyril Lord Carpets* [1969] 3 All ER 1006.

133 McGregor on Damages (fn 20) paras 6–073 ff and 8–145 ff.

134 McGregor on Damages (fn 20) para 10–002.

135 *Mallett v McMonagle* [1970] AC 166, 176 per Lord Diplock.

100 per cent: sometimes virtually nil. But often it is somewhere in between. *And if it somewhere in between I do not see much difference between a probability of 51 per cent and a probability of 49 per cent.*'[136] This approach applies to both contracts and torts.

2) Compensation for Non-Pecuniary Loss

50 As McGregor, the leading textbook on damages in English law puts it, '[t]he pattern of non-pecuniary losses shows a much greater difference between tort and breach of contract: in tort they are the rule, in contract the exception.'[137] This dichotomy is due to the fact that 'a large part of the protection given by the law of tort is to such interests as personal safety and personal reputation, which are interests not immediately connected with monetary considerations.'[138] McGregor goes on to list the five heads under which non-pecuniary damages are available in English law: (a) pain and suffering and loss of amenity; (b) physical inconvenience and discomfort; (c) mental distress; (d) social discredit; and (e) loss of society. While non-pecuniary losses do indeed 'flourish'[139] in tort law, not all torts allow for such damages. This is the case with the economic torts[140] and private nuisance,[141] for example.

51 Most heads of non-pecuniary damages are objectively assessed. Loss of amenity is one such example. Subjective appreciation is required in the case of pain and suffering, on the other hand, with the effect that a person in a coma would not qualify for an award. Damages for bereavement are statutorily regulated and currently set at a fixed sum of £12,980 which is payable to the spouse or, on the death of a child, parents.[142]

52 Until the recent changes ushered in by the Defamation Act 2013 (sec 1(2) in particular[143]), it was possible for all corporate claimants to claim non-pecuniary

136 Emphasis added. *Davies v Taylor* [1974] AC 207, 213 per Lord Reid.

137 McGregor on Damages (fn 20) para 5–001.

138 Ibid, para 5–002.

139 Ibid.

140 Eg conspiracy: *Lonrho Plc v Fayed (No 5)* [1993] 1 WLR 1489, 1494 ff per Dillon LJ. According to one of the present authors, cases in which non-pecuniary damages have apparently been awarded in such actions can be explained on the basis that the underlying loss was in reality pecuniary or that the cause of action was really for interference with the person: *K Oliphant*, The Economic Torts, in: K Oliphant (ed), The Law of Tort (3rd edn 2015) para 29.88. See eg *Mbasogo v Logo Ltd (No 1)* [2006] EWCA Civ 1370, [2007] QB 846.

141 *Hunter v Canary Wharf* Ltd [1997] AC 655.

142 Fatal Accidents Act 1976 (as amended).

143 Section 1(1) reads: 'A statement is not defamatory unless its publication has caused or is likely to cause serious harm to the reputation of the claimant.' And sec 1(2): 'For the purposes of this section, harm to the reputation of a body that trades for profit is not "serious harm" unless it has caused or is likely to cause the body serious financial loss.'

damages for social discredit. It is not altogether clear, once having satisfied the financial loss test under that section, whether trading companies will still be entitled to non-pecuniary damages for injury to reputation. The anomaly (since pecuniary loss and non-pecuniary loss lead to two separate and distinct recoveries) of the legislation is that non-pecuniary damages now hinge on proof of actual or likely pecuniary damage. While corporations are not entitled to pursue the other heads of non-pecuniary damages under English law, English judges are obliged to look to the jurisprudence of the Human Rights Court in Strasbourg in matters pertaining to violations of the European Convention on Human Rights.[144] One of the present authors has highlighted both the Court's acceptance that corporations themselves can suffer heads of non-pecuniary damage ordinarily restricted to natural persons (eg distress) and the more tenable alternative that natural components within such corporations can suffer such damage and, to the extent that they do, that damage should be 'attributed' to corporations for the purpose of computing the latter's non-pecuniary award.[145]

Aggravated damages are also non-pecuniary in nature (see no 57). Incidentally, the oddity of the law as it stands is that such damages may still be available for torts in respect of which 'basic' non-pecuniary damages are not awardable. As has been judicially observed, 'basic' non-pecuniary damages in this sense are being awarded in a disguised fashion.[146] 53

In contract, non-pecuniary damages are available in respect of the same heads as in tort.[147] While this principle was established early in respect of some heads (eg physical inconvenience and discomfort),[148] the courts have only recently begun to accept it in respect of others. Thus, the position was long understood to be that a claimant could not successfully claim damages for mental distress occasioned by a breach of contract.[149] The basis for that approach was the notion that contracts are primarily commercial in nature; as such 'mental suffering on 54

[144] Human Rights Act 1998, sec 8(4).

[145] *V Wilcox*, A Company's Right to Damages for Non-Pecuniary Loss (2016), discussing at length whether such attribution would be accepted outside the Convention arena and under general English law.

[146] *Joyce v Sengupta* [1993] 1 WLR 337, 348 f per Sir Donald Nicholls VC: 'I do not see how, if only pecuniary loss is recoverable, the amount awarded can be increased to reflect the plaintiff's distress. That would be a contradiction in terms. It would be to award damages for distress in a disguised fashion. If distress can inflame the damages recoverable for pecuniary loss, the difference between awarding aggravated damages for that reason and awarding damages for distress as a separate head of loss is a difference of words only.'

[147] McGregor on Damages (fn 20) para 5-016.

[148] *Burton v Pinkerton* (1867) Law Report (LR) 2 Exchequer Cases (Ex) 340.

[149] *Hamlin v GN Ry* (1856) 1 Hurlstone & Norman's Exchequer Reports (H & N) 408. See *P Giliker*, New Head of Damages: Damages for Mental Distress in the English Law of Torts (2000) 20 Legal Studies 19 for a more detailed exposition.

breach is not in the contemplation of the parties as part of the business risk of the transaction',[150] and indeed, the rule continues to be that:[151]

> 'A contract-breaker is not in general liable for any distress, frustration, anxiety, displeasure, vexation, tension or aggravation which his breach of contract may cause to the innocent party. This rule is not, I think, founded on the assumption that such reactions are not foreseeable, which they surely are or may be, but on considerations of policy. But the rule is not absolute. Where the very object of a contract is to provide pleasure, relaxation, peace of mind or freedom from molestation, damages will be awarded if the fruit of the contract is not provided or if the contrary result is procured instead.'

55 In the subsequent case of *Farley v Skinner* it was said to suffice that pleasure, relaxation, peace of mind or freedom from molestation were the principal though not the sole or entire object of the contract.[152] Although not a view shared in some other common law jurisdictions, English law does not compensate additionally for aggravation of a breach of contract (see no 67).

3) *Compensation for Loss of Earnings and for Loss of Chance*

56 Loss of earnings may be claimed in respect of both contractual and tortious breaches. Unlike the position in tort, a contract may specify a particular sum payable as liquidated damages in the event of a breach. In both cases, it is generally the claimant's *net* earnings (ie less income tax, national insurance contributions and other deductibles[153]) that will be compensated and any tax credits claimable by the claimant will be taken into consideration. The period for which loss of earnings are payable has the potential to be longer in tort cases, and in particular personal injury where post-trial loss of earnings could extend for the rest of the claimant's working life. In fixed-term contracts, the computation prima facie ends at the end of that term and, where the contract is terminable by notice, at the end of the notice period. In both cases, parties are expected to mitigate their losses and a deduction must be made for accelerated receipt in the case of lump-sum damages (which is the usual case).[154] Differences may also exist in respect of the date when interest begins to run. Periodic payments may only be ordered in an action for personal injury,[155] and this will typically, though not invariably, be an action in tort.

---

150 McGregor on Damages (fn 20) para 5–024.

151 Per Bingham LJ in *Watts v Morrow* [1991] 1 WLR 1421, 1445.

152 [2002] 2 AC 732.

153 *British Transport Commission v Gourley* [1956] AC 185.

154 For contract: *Lavarack v Woods of Colchester Ltd* [1967] 1 QB 278; for tort: *Lim Poh Choo v Camden and Islington Area Health Authority* [1980] AC 174.

155 Damages Act 1996, sec 2(1).

As regards loss of a chance (no 57 f),[156] the distinguishing factor is not the basis of the liability but the nature of the chance lost. Indeed, several loss of chance cases arise in contexts in which liability in contract is concurrent with that in tort, for example in claims against solicitors, insurance brokers, accountants, surveyors and professional advisers.[157] The cases that have arisen against such defendants illustrate that damages for loss of a chance to secure economic gains or avoid economic losses are well recognised. In the case of reduced prospects of successful medical treatment, however, the courts have so far declined to apply the doctrine, even though the House of Lords was twice invited to do so (in *Hotson v East Berkshire Area Health Authority*[158] and *Gregg v Scott*[159]). The main reason, as described by McGregor, has been that:[160] 57

> 'The existing loss of a chance cases are dependent upon human activity and human decisions which are in their very nature uncertain, and where such uncertainties come into the assessment of damages, the loss of a chance approach makes sense. By contrast, with physical injury there is no inherent uncertainty as to cause but only a lack of knowledge, and lack of knowledge is dealt with in the law by the burden of proof, so that it is appropriate to apply the balance of probabilities rule to the situation, an approach which will favour sometimes the defendant and, also, sometimes the claimant. It may of course be said that this distinction has only legal principle and legal consistency, and not fairness and justice, on its side, and that whether such a difference should be reflected in the law of damages, so as to cause loss of a chance not to be moved into the personal injury and fatal accident sphere, may be open to question and will be doubted by some.'

The analysis above applies to the establishment of the claimant's cause of action against the defendant. Once the cause of action is established, the inquiry shifts to the quantification of damages and at this stage percentage chance assessments are routinely made by the courts, for example in making allowances in the damages for the possibility that, absent the injury, the claimant might have embarked upon some new, more lucrative career.[161] However, it would be impracticably cumbersome to identify and take specific account of every single uncertainty regarding future losses of this nature, and the courts typically adopt a simpler albeit coarser approach: 'it is a truism that the assessment of future loss in this field is in a broad sense the assessment of a chance or, more accurately, a series of chances as to the likely future progress of the claimant in obtaining, retaining or changing his employment, obtaining promotion, or otherwise increasing his remuneration. Nonetheless, such assessment has not traditionally been regarded 58

156 See generally *K Oliphant*, Loss of Chance in English Law (2008) 16 ERPL 1061.
157 McGregor on Damages (fn 20) para 10–068 ff.
158 [1987] AC 750.
159 [2005] 2 AC 176.
160 McGregor on Damages (fn 20) para 10–058.
161 *Oliphant* (fn 156) 1068.

as necessitating application of the technique of percentage assessment for "loss of a chance" based on the likely actions of third parties.'[162] Rather, a conventional ('Ogden') multiplier, discounted for contingencies, and applied to a multiplicand based on the claimant's putative earnings is preferred. Again, although personal injury claims tend to be pleaded in tort, this is not to say that the difference turns on the cause of action itself. It would be difficult to imagine, for example, that loss of the chance of recovery would be available in a medical case where treatment was private (and under contract) rather than on the National Health Service (NHS) (and therefore not under contract).

4) Restitutionary Damages

59 It was only in the 1990s that the then House of Lords formally recognised restitution as a distinct category of liability based on the unjust enrichment of the defendant.[163] Before then, restitution had traditionally been considered 'an appendix to the law of contract'.[164] Notwithstanding this development, however, the role that restitution continues to play in the law of contract and tort remains to be fully clarified.

60 The analytical structure of restitution continues to be debated by scholars. For present purposes, it will suffice, however, to adopt the approach to the topic advanced by the English Law Commission, making a fundamental distinction between unjust enrichment by subtraction (or autonomous unjust enrichment) and unjust enrichment by wrongdoing (or dependent unjust enrichment).[165] As its name suggests, and unlike unjust enrichment by subtraction, *unjust enrichment by wrongdoing* requires the commission of a wrong by the defendant. Having satisfied the court as to his cause of action in tort, there are some circumstances in which a claimant may waive his right to compensatory damages and opt instead for a restitutionary (or gain-based) remedy. Restitutionary remedies have mostly been granted in respect of proprietary torts (eg conversion, trespass to goods, trespass to land), including intellectual property torts, and less frequently in respect to non-proprietary torts (eg deceit, breach of confidence, intimidation and inducing breach of contract).[166] It has been noted that there is 'no unifying principle which governs the circumstances in which a claimant, relying on a cause of action in tort, may recover damages calculated by reference to the defendant's gain.'[167]

---

162 *Herring v Ministry of Defence* [2004] 1 All ER 44 at [25].

163 *Lipkin Gorman v Karpnale Ltd* [1991] 2 AC 548.

164 *Henderson v Merrett Syndicates Ltd* [1995] 2 AC 145, 184 per Lord Goff.

165 *Law Commission for England and Wales*, Aggravated, Exemplary and Restitutionary Damages, Law Com No 247 (1997) Part III.

166 Ibid, para 1.6 ff.

167 Halsbury's Laws of England, vol 88: Restitution (2012) para 560.

As regards contract, the parties generally regulate the rights and obligations until the contract is terminated, whereupon restitution may play a role insofar as remedies are concerned. In *Attorney General v Blake*,[168] the celebrated 'Spycatcher' case, the House of Lords ruled for the first time that 'restitutionary damages' (or 'an account of profits') could be available for breach of contract where compensatory damages would be an inadequate remedy. The House of Lords emphasised that such awards should be treated as exceptional (see further no 26 above) and, in practice, the courts have shied away from looking to the gain made by a defendant as a measure of contractual damages. These are thus normally limited to such sum of money as is necessary to put the claimant in the same position as if the contract had been performed. The deprivation of the defendant of the fruits of his conduct is thought of as unjustifiably punitive and especially inappropriate where commercial interests are involved:[169] 'if some more extensive principle of awarding non-compensatory damages for breach of contract is to be introduced into our commercial law the consequences will be very far reaching and disruptive.'[170] 61

One general issue that has arisen, straddling both contract and tort, is the nature of the damages that may in certain circumstances[171] be awarded in lieu of an injunction pursuant to sec 50 of the Senior Courts Act 1981 (previously, under Lord Cairns' Act of 1858). Such awards in effect entail the court's allowing the defendant to pay for the right to go on committing a wrong (typically a tort or the breach of a restrictive covenant applying to land) because the court objects to the grant of an injunction for whatever reason.[172] In assessing the appropriate amount of damages due, *a portion of* the defendants anticipated profits may be ordered.[173] These are not regarded as truly restitutionary but merely as constituting a reasonable price for what the defendant has acquired.[174] 62

Restitution in *unjust enrichment by subtraction* tends to be based on 'factors vitiating or qualifying the plaintiff's true consent to a transfer of his or her wealth to the defendant: for example, mistake, duress, undue influence, and failure of consideration.'[175] As such, it does not raise issues related to remedies for tort or *breach* of contract. 63

168 [2001] 1 AC 268.
169 Halsbury's Laws of England (fn 167) para 559.
170 *Attorney General v Blake (Jonathan Cape Ltd, third party)* [2001] 1 AC 268, 299 per Lord Hobhouse.
171 *Oliphant* (fn 140) para 8.51 ff.
172 *Lawrence v Fen Tigers Ltd* [2014] AC 822 at [160] per Lord Sumption JSC.
173 *Wrotham Park Estate Co Ltd v Parkside Homes Ltd* [1974] 1 WLR 798.
174 *Oliphant* (fn 140) para 8.59.
175 *Law Commission for England and Wales* (fn 165) Part III, para 1.1.

5) *Aggravated and Exemplary (or Punitive) Damages*

a) Exemplary Damages

64 While some common law jurisdictions allow the recovery of exemplary damages in contract, this is not the case in England: 'if [one] should choose to seek redress in the form of an action for breach of contract, he lets in all the consequences of that form of action … One of these consequences is, I think, this: that he is to be paid adequate compensation in money for the loss of that which he would have received had his contract been kept, and no more.'[176] Where liability is concurrent in contract and tort, however, exemplary damages may still be available. The case against punitive damages in contractual settings was summarised by the English Law Commission in its 1997 report on Aggravated, Exemplary and Restitutionary Damages:[177]

- The Commission argued first that 'exemplary damages have never been awarded for breach of contract'. This premise is now superfluous, however, following the case of *Kuddus v Chief Constable of Leicestershire*,[178] in which the then House of Lords ruled that punitive damages were no longer limited to cases in which they were awardable prior to 1964 (the date of decision of *Rookes v Barnard*,[179] the seminal case recognising such damages in tort).
- 'Second, contract primarily involves pecuniary, rather than non-pecuniary, losses; in contrast, the torts for which exemplary damages are most commonly awarded, and are likely to continue to be most commonly awarded, usually give rise to claims for non-pecuniary losses'.
- 'Thirdly, the need for certainty is perceived to be greater in relation to contract than tort and, arguably, there is therefore less scope for the sort of discretion which the courts must have in determining the availability and quantum of exemplary damages'.
- 'Fourthly, a contract is a private arrangement in which parties negotiate rights and duties, whereas the duties which obtain under the law of tort are imposed by law; it can accordingly be argued that the notion of state punishment is more readily applicable to the latter than to the former'.

---

176 *Addis v Gramophone Co Ltd* [1909] AC 488, 496 per Lord Atkinson. See *V Wilcox*, Punitive Damages in England, in: H Koziol/V Wilcox (eds), Punitive Damages: Common Law and Civil Law Perspectives (2009) no 36 f. See also *S Rowan*, Reflections on the Introduction of Punitive Damages for Breach of Contract (2010) 30 Oxford Journal of Legal Studies 495. For further references on the topic see fn 4.

177 *Law Commission for England and Wales* (fn 165) Part II para 1.72.

178 [2002] 2 AC 122.

179 [1964] AC 1129.

- 'Fifthly, the doctrine of efficient breach dictates that contracting parties should have available the option of breaking the contract and paying compensatory damages, if they are able to find a more remunerative use for the subject matter of the promise. To award exemplary damages would tend to discourage efficient breach.'

In so far as the action is tortious, such damages are available under the three categories recognised in *Rookes v Barnard*: (a) oppressive, arbitrary or unconstitutional action by servants of the government; (b) conduct calculated by the defendant to make a profit for himself which may well exceed the compensation payable to the claimant; and (c) express statutory authorisation.[180] Until recently, only one statutory provision, sec 13 of the Reserve and Auxiliary Forces (Protection of Civil Interests) Act 1951, expressly made mention of such damages. Section 34 ff of the Crime and Courts Act 2013, however, now expressly provide for such damages against publishers of news-related material who publish statements in deliberate or reckless disregard of an outrageous nature for the claimant's rights. The enactment is part of the government response to the strong criticism of press conduct in an official report of 2012 which recommended such damages in actions for breach of privacy, breach of confidence and similar media torts,[181] as well as for libel and slander.[182] 65

It is also relevant to note here that contractual penalty clauses (as opposed to liquidated damages clauses incorporating a genuine pre-estimate of loss or otherwise imposing a detriment on the contract-breaker proportionate to a legitimate interest of the innocent party in the enforcement of the contractual obligation) are not enforceable in English law even though expressly agreed by the parties. Despite being lamented by some as a 'blatant interference with freedom of contract',[183] the Supreme Court has recently upheld the rule against penalties, having regard to its long-established character, its consistency with judicial control over contractual penalties in other legal systems, and its continued utility in protecting against oppressive bargains even if not subject to statutory regulation.[184] 66

180 *Wilcox* (fn 176) no 4 ff. See also Civil Procedure Rules, Rule 14.4.

181 *Wilcox* (fn 176) no 38.

182 See *Lunney/Oliphant* (fn 110) 848 ff for such damages generally and 851 f for details of the recent enactment. See also *A Morris/K Oliphant*, England and Wales, in: E Karner/BC Steininger (eds), European Tort Law 2013 (2014) 183, no 4 f.

183 *Makdessi v Cavendish Square Holdings BV* [2013] EWCA Civ 1539 at [44] per Christopher Clarke LJ. See also *Ranger v GW Ry Co* (1854) 5 Clark & Finnelly's House of Lords Reports New Series (HLC) 72, 94 f, 118 f; *S Worthington*, Common Law Values: the Role of Party Autonomy in Private Law, in: A Robertson/M Tilbury (eds), The Common Law of Obligations: Divergence and Unity (2016).

184 *Cavendish Square Holding BV v Makdessi* [2015] UKSC 67, [2016] AC 1172.

b) Aggravated Damages

67 Like exemplary damages, aggravated damages[185] are not available for breach of contract.[186] Rather, recoverability has so far been limited to torts where damages are at large – that is to say, where the award is not limited to the pecuniary loss that can be specifically proved.[187] Unlike exemplary damages, which are extra-compensatory, aggravated damages are considered to provide compensation for non-pecuniary harm. Apart from the justifications given in no 64 above, a further reason for the irrecoverability of such damages in contract is said to be that they seek to compensate additional injury caused to the claimant's feelings (or mental distress[188]) both up to and including the trial, whereas contract law, which concerns itself mainly with pecuniary losses, to a large extent in the commercial sphere, has traditionally been slow to allow recovery for mental distress.[189] The rule is one of policy. However, it is not an absolute rule. As is the case with non-pecuniary damages for breach of contract (no 54 f), it has been suggested that a contract-breaker could well be liable for aggravation which his breach of contract may cause an innocent party where the 'very [or predominant] object of a contract is to provide pleasure, relaxation, peace of mind or freedom from molestation.'[190]

6) Other Remedies

68 Specific performance is an equitable remedy that operates to compel a defendant to perform his contractual obligation(s). As with all equitable remedies, it is discretionary and subject to equitable defences. It is regarded as an exceptional remedy and the courts will only grant specific performance where damages are not an adequate remedy. Even in such a case, other factors may militate against specific performance, for example the need for the constant supervision of the court to ensure the fulfilment of the contract. It is accordingly settled practice not to make any order requiring the carrying on of a business.[191] Specific performance as such is not available for an action in tort, but the same effect can be achieved by the award of a mandatory injunction.

69 Injunctions, in contrast with specific performance, can be awarded for both torts and breach of contract. Prohibitory injunctions seek to restrain a defendant

185 See also Civil Procedure Rules, Rule 14.4.

186 *Addis v Gramophone Co Ltd* [1909] AC 488. *Kralj v McGrath* [1986] 1 All ER 54, 60 f. See also *Johnson v Gore Wood & Co* [2002] 2 AC 1.

187 *Rookes v Barnard* [1964] 1 All ER 407. See *Sebok/Wilcox* (fn 69) no 1 ff.

188 *Law Commission for England and Wales* (fn 165) Part II, para 1.4

189 McGregor on Damages (fn 20) para 5–023.

190 *Watts v Morrow* [1991] 1 WLR 1421, 1445 per Bingham LJ.

191 *Co-Operative Insurance Society Ltd Respondents v Argyll Stores (Holdings) Ltd* [1998] AC 1.

from doing a particular thing. Mandatory injunctions direct the positive performance of a specific duty. Either can be interim or perpetual and both can be awarded *quia timet*, that is, where an act is threatened or imminent but has not yet commenced. In both cases, an injunction will only be granted where the remedy at law (ie damages) is inappropriate. An injunction may be awarded in respect of a breach of contract in circumstances where specific performance would be inappropriate, for example because it would involve the enforcement of an obligation of personal service.[192] That said, an injunction should not be granted if its effect would be the enforcement of an obligation which it would be inappropriate to enforce through specific performance.[193] If the contract can be severed, the court may do so with a view to ordering an injunction in respect of part of the obligation owed.[194] Non-compliance with an order for specific performance or an injunction, whether in respect of a tort or a breach of contract, is punishable as a contempt of court.

D. DIFFERENCES AS REGARDS RECOVERABILITY OF 'PURE ECONOMIC LOSSES'

70 Traditionally, the recovery of economic loss absent physical or material damage (ie pure economic losses) lay almost exclusively within the territory of contract law on the one hand and the economic torts (eg procuring a breach of contract, conspiracy and intimidation) and a few other heads of tortious liability (eg public nuisance[195]) on the other. The economic torts are torts of intentional wrongdoing; negligence is not enough to establish liability in them. Indeed, the negligent infliction of pure economic loss generally gives rise to no tortious liability at all, reflecting in part a concern about opening the floodgates of liability to a large and indeterminate number of claims,[196] in part a concern not to intrude into spheres already adequately regulated by contract – as evident in the perceived necessity of avoiding, in the context of defective product economic loss, the imposition via tort law of 'the obligations of an indefinitely transmissible warranty of quality'.[197]

71 Contract, whose historical concern has mainly been with commercial matters, primarily protects against financial or 'pure economic loss'. Moreover, such losses

192 See eg *Lumley v Wagner* (1852) 1 De Gex Macnaghten & Gordon 604.

193 *Page One Records v Britton* [1968] 1 WLR 157.

194 *Warner Bros v Nelson* [1937] 1 KB 209.

195 A few other heads of tortious liability also allowed the recovery of pure economic losses, eg public nuisance: see *Rose v Miles* (1815) 4 Maule & Selwyn's King's Bench Reports (M & S) 101.

196 *Cattle v Stockton Waterworks* (1875) LR 10 QB 453.

197 *Murphy v Brentwood DC* [1991] 1 AC 398, 480 per Lord Bridge.

are usually to be anticipated as the result of a breach of contract. By contrast, it was only with the House of Lords' ruling in the case of *Hedley Byrne & Co Ltd v Heller & Partners* (no 17) that negligently inflicted pure economic losses came to be recoverable in tort, albeit only in exceptional circumstances where the fear of indeterminacy is overcome by the close relationship of proximity between the parties involving the defendant's voluntary assumption of responsibility to the claimant either individually or as the member of an identifiable class. In rare cases, the responsibility may be deemed to extend to a third party to a transaction in which the defendant was involved.[198] But there is a risk – in both two-party and three-party situations – of upsetting contractual allocations of risk so the courts tend to tread cautiously. Consequently, in a typical construction project, the fact that a contractor and a sub-contractor engaged by him *act closely in concert* will not enable the recovery of pure economic loss under the *Hedley Byrne* type of liability in the absence of the assumption of responsibility by the sub-contractor to the property owner.[199] Allowing a claim of that nature would undermine the general requirement of privity in the law of contract (see, however, no 81 f).

E. DIFFERENCES AS REGARDS LIABILITY FOR OTHERS

1) *Liability for Auxiliaries and for Independent Contractors*

72 In the first place, it must be pointed out that not all contracts are such that their performance may be delegated to a third party. Whether a contract can be vicariously performed depends 'on the proper inference to be drawn from the contract itself, the subject matter of it, and other material surrounding circumstances'.[200] In general, contracts involving special personal qualities or qualifications cannot be delegated. Where performance is delegated, the original contractee remains liable on the contract.

73 For vicarious liability to arise in tort, it is necessary that that the tort is 'so closely connected with [the employee's] employment that it would be fair and just to hold the [employer] vicariously liable'.[201] By a wider principle, liability for another person's tort may arise on the basis that the defendant authorised its commission or subsequently ratified it. Vicarious tortious liability as such is

198 See eg *Smith v Eric S Bush* [1990] 1 AC 831 (building valuation prepared for lender; claim by purchaser); *White v Jones* [1995] AC 207 (will; claim by beneficiary).

199 *D&F Estates Ltd v Church Commissioners for England and Wales* [1989] AC 177. For the exceptional recognition of a duty of care, see *Junior Books Co Ltd v Veitchi Co Ltd* [1983] 1 AC 520.

200 *Davies v Collins* [1945] 1 All ER 247, 250.

201 *Lister v Hesley Hall Ltd* [2002] 1 AC 215 at [28] per Lord Millett.

limited to the employer–employee relationship and certain other relationships deeded to be 'akin to employment'.[202]

2) *Liability for Legal Representatives or Organs of a Company*

A company is a legal person and is thus capable of entering into binding contractual relations.[203] Section 40 of the Companies Act 2006 provides that: 'In favour of a person dealing with a company in good faith, the power of the directors to bind the company, or authorise others to do so, is deemed to be free of any limitation under the company's constitution.' Subject to certain exceptions,[204] such a contract is thus enforceable against the company by a third party. However, the section does not affect any right of a member of the company to bring proceedings to *restrain* the doing of an action that is beyond the powers of the directors (ie prior to the event).[205] Moreover, the section does not prejudice any actions against the director personally. 74

A company, which achieves its objects through the instrumentality and agency of individuals, is liable for the tortious activities of those individuals *in the same way a natural person would be for the acts of his agents or employees*.[206] Its liability can either be direct (ie for acts or omissions deemed to be those of the company itself) or vicarious. The latter liability is strict insofar as the company is concerned; the company stands in the employee's shoes and no blame need be established on its part.[207] A claim may lie against a company where the act complained of is one which: (a) constitutes an actionable wrong committed by an individual; (b) is within the scope of the individual's authority or is done in the course of his employment or in circumstances sufficiently connected to his employment; and (c) the company is or might possibly be authorised by its constitution to commit.[208] A company is thus liable for the failures of its legal representatives acting within their powers in the same way as it is for those of its employees and the board. A company can elect to assume personal liability in the case of acts done without authority by subsequently ratifying such acts, provided such acts are indeed ratifiable.[209] 75

---

202 *Various Claimants v Catholic Child Welfare Society* [2012] UKSC 56, [2013] 2 AC 1. See further *WV Horton Rogers*, England, in: J Spier (ed) Unification of Tort Law: Liability for Damage Caused by Others (2003) nos 15 ff and 28 ff in particular in respect of the differences between vicarious liability in torts and in contract. See also Clerk & Lindsell on Torts (fn 14) para 6–01 ff; *Oliphant* (fn 14) para 3.1 ff.

203 *Bateman v Ashton-under-Lyne Corpn* (1858) 3 H & N 323, 335 per Martin B.

204 Section 40(6).

205 Section 40(4).

206 *William Ranger v Great Western Railway* (1854) 5 House of Lords Cases (Clark's) 72, 86.

207 *Lister v Hesley Hall Ltd* [2001] UKHL 22 at [64] per Lord Millet.

208 See Halsbury's Laws of England, vol 24: Corporations (5th edn 2010) para 477 and vol 14: Companies (5th edn 2009) para 296.

209 *Poulton v London and South Western Rly Co* (1867) LR 2 QB 534.

3) *Liability of Representatives of Natural Persons*

a) Minors

76 English law classes a person who has not yet attained the age of 18 as a minor.[210] Contracts by minors are valid, but voidable. The exception is where the minor is not 'old enough to understand the nature of the transaction and, if the transaction involves obligations on the minor of a continuing nature, the nature of those obligations.'[211] Contracts of necessity – defined as contracts for necessary goods and services supplied to the minor on the one hand and contracts of apprenticeship, education and service on the other – are, however, binding on minors.[212] All other contracts are voidable at the minor's instigation in the sense that the other contracting party continues to be bound by them but the minor is not. Where a minor is given permission to contract on his parent's behalf, such authorisation being either express or implied, the parent will be liable. This is also the case where the child is authorised by another person who has authority to pledge the parent's credit.[213] Other than that, a parent 'is no more liable to pay a debt contracted by the child with a third party (even for necessaries) than a mere stranger would be. The same principles apply in the case of a guardian and ward.'[214]

77 In contrast to contract, there is 'no defence of minority as such known to the law of tort … a child may be sued in tort as if he were of full age'.[215] That said, a child's age is taken into consideration in determining the question of breach of duty of care. Thus, while the objective test seeks to 'eliminates the personal equation and is independent of the idiosyncrasies of the particular person whose conduct is in question',[216] the courts have ruled that 'it would be a retrograde step to visit liability on a 13-year-old for simply playing a game in the area where he was allowed to do so.'[217] Thus, the question is whether an ordinarily prudent and reasonable child of that particular age would have appreciated the risks involved in the tortious activity in question. As with contract, one cannot without more fix liability on parents for acts committed by their children.

---

210 Family Law Reform Act 1969, sec 1. See also Children Act 198, sec 105.

211 *R v Oldham Metropolitan BC ex parte Garlick* [1993] 1 Family Law Reports (FLR) 645, 662 per Scott LJ.

212 Chitty on Contracts (fn 1) para 8–002 ff.

213 See eg *Bazeley v Forder* (1868) LR 3 QB 559. See also Chitty on Contracts (fn 1) para 8–062.

214 Chitty on Contracts (fn 1) para 8–062.

215 Clerk & Lindsell on Torts (fn 14) para 5–51; *Oliphant* (fn 14) para 2.39 ff. See further *K Oliphant*, Children as Tortfeasors under the Law of England and Wales, in: M Martín Casals (ed), Children in Tort Law, Part I: Children as Tortfeasors (2006).

216 *Glasgow Corporation v Muir* [1943] AC 448, 458 per Lord Macmillan.

217 *Orchard v Lee* [2009] EWCA Civ 295 at [19] per Waller LJ. See generally *Mullin v Richards* [1998] 1 WLR 1304.

The exceptions are where vicarious liability can be established on the basis of an employer–employee relationship, where the parent authorises or subsequently ratifies the child's act or where the parent was negligent, for example in leaving a dangerous thing which he ought to have anticipated his mischievous child would use to injure another. The parent will then be liable for the reasonable and probable results of the wrongful act by the child.[218] It may be worth adding here that household insurance normally includes third-party cover. Persons charged with supervision duties are subject to the standard of a careful parent, breach of which will result in liability in negligence.[219]

b) Mental Disability

Lack of mental capacity is defined in sec 2 of the Mental Capacity Act 2005 as a situation in which a person is 'unable to make a decision for himself in relation to [a] matter because of an impairment of, or a disturbance in the functioning of, the mind or brain.' The approach taken as regards the liability of minors in contract broadly applies to mentally disabled persons. One who has a mental disability is liable for his torts unless his disability is of such a grave degree that he does not know what he is doing.[220] In that case, his mental disability will negate fault or intention where this is a prerequisite of a particular tort. As with children, persons charged with supervisory duties may be personally liable in negligence for the actions of mentally disturbed persons.[221] 78

4) Liability of the Auxiliary/Organ Itself

An employee is under a contractual obligation of care to his employer in the performance of his duties. Additionally, joint and several liability is imposed on an employee and his employer for torts the former committed in the course of employment. In theory, a company is entitled to recover an indemnity equivalent to any damages it covered on its employee's behalf.[222] In practice, however, where the risk of a servant's *negligence* is covered by insurance, it is considered unjust for the employer to exercise the right to an indemnity,[223] and collective agreements often preclude this in practice.[224] Where an indemnity is in fact sought (eg in respect of intentional wrongdoing), courts have the power to apportion the overall 79

218 Halsbury's Laws of England (fn 36) para 437.
219 *Carmarthenshire CC v Lewis* [1955] AC 549, 561.
220 *Morriss v Marsden* [1952] 1 All ER 925, 927 per Stable J. See *Oliphant/Wilcox* (fn 32).
221 *Partington v Wandsworth LBC*, 8 November 1989. On the liability of and for minors and mentally disturbed persons, see also *Horton Rogers* (fn 202) nos 12 f and 37 ff.
222 *Lister v Romford Ice and Cold Storage Co Ltd* [1957] AC 555.
223 *Morris v Ford Motor Co* [1973] QB 792.
224 See *R Lewis*, Insurers' Agreements Not to Enforce Strict Legal Rights: Bargaining with Government and in the Shadow of the Law (1985) 45 Modern Law Review 275.

award of damages as is just and equitable between the company and the employee, having regard to the extent of the latter's responsibility for the damage.[225] This rule is equally applicable to a member or members of the board and is not only limited to instances where they exceed delegated powers but also in the case of breaches of directors' duties.[226] Section 239 of the Companies Act 2006 provides for the possible ratification by a company of conduct by a director amounting to negligence, default, breach of duty or breach of trust in relation to the company. Moreover, a company is likely to have taken out directors and officers insurance which extends to a 'wrongful act' committed by its directors acting in their capacity as directors. The director may in any case be subjected to personal claims by shareholders, and/or dismissed or disqualified for his conduct.[227]

F. DIFFERENCES AS REGARDS LIABILITY IN THE CASE OF MULTIPLE TORTFEASORS/BREACHING PARTIES

80 A contractual promise made by two or more persons is presumed to impose joint liability on the promisees. However, the parties may agree otherwise. Persons acting in concert in tort are jointly and severally liable for the damage caused. As seen, this rule extends to employers and employees when the former incur vicarious liability for the torts of the latter (see no 73). Several concurrent liability applies where two or more persons independently cause the same or indivisible damage to another.[228] Where two or more persons are liable in respect of the same damage, they may resort to sec 1(1) of the Civil Liability (Contribution) Act 1978, which provides that any person liable in respect of any damage suffered by another person may recover contribution from any other person liable in respect of the same damage (whether jointly with him or otherwise). This is the case whether liability is in contract or tort.[229]

G. DIFFERENCES AS REGARDS THE PERSONS WHO MAY BE PROTECTED

81 The doctrine of privity provides that persons who are not parties to a contract cannot generally sue to enforce rights in that contract. It is closely linked to the common law doctrine of consideration, in particular the rule that consideration

225 Civil Liability (Contribution) Act 1978, sec 2(1).

226 Companies Act 2006, sec 170 ff.

227 *PL Davies/S Worthington*, Gower & Davies: Principles of Modern Company Law (2012) ch 10.

228 *Devonshire (Owners) v Barge Leslie (Owners)* [1912] AC 634, 657 per Lord Atkinson. See generally *K Oliphant* (ed), Aggregation and Divisibility of Damage (2009).

229 *WV Horton Rogers*, England, in: WVH Rogers (ed) Unification of Tort Law: Multiple Tortfeasors (2004). As regards tort, see further *Oliphant* (fn 14) ch 4.

must move from the promisee.[230] A further effect of the rule is that obligations generally cannot be imposed on third parties to a contract. Several exceptions to the rule exist under the common law (eg agency, assignment and torts), equity and statute (eg Companies Act 2006, sec 33(1),[231] and Occupiers' Liability Act 1957, sec 3(1)).[232]

A significant departure from the privity rule was ushered in by the Contracts (Rights of Third Parties) Act 1999. By sec 1(1) and (2), a person who is not a party to a contract (a 'third party') may enforce a term of the contract in his own right provided only that the contract expressly provides this or if a term purports to confer a benefit on him. The third party must be expressly identified in the contract by name, as a member of a class or as answering a particular description but need not be in existence when the contract is entered into.[233] Indeed, once a third party has communicated his assent to the term to the promisor and the latter has relied on the term, it is no longer open to the parties to the contract to rescind or vary that right without his consent.[234] Such a third party is entitled to any remedy that would have been available to him in an action for breach of contract if he had been a party to the contract.[235] The third party can also rely on a term excluding or limiting his liability.[236] Various defences are open to the promisor under sec 3 of the Act. The Act does not generally apply in relation to contracts entered into before 11 May 2000[237] or contracts specified in sec 6 (the most important being contracts of employment). 82

In tort, at least so far as unintentional injury is concerned, the main limiting device is the duty of care, recognised as the chief organisational precept of the tort of negligence in Lord Atkin's celebrated 'neighbour principle' in *Donoghue v Stevenson*:[238] 83

> '[A]cts or omissions which any moral code would censure cannot in a practical world be treated so as to give a right to every person injured by them to demand relief. In

230 *Tweddle v Atkinson* [1861] 1 Best & Smith's Queen's Bench Reports (B & S) 393.

231 Which reads: 'The provisions of a company's constitution bind the company and its members to the same extent as if there were covenants on the part of the company and of each member to observe those provisions.'

232 Which reads: 'Where an occupier of premises is bound by contract to permit persons who are strangers to the contract to enter or use the premises, the duty of care which he owes to them as his visitors cannot be restricted or excluded by that contract, but (subject to any provision of the contract to the contrary) shall include the duty to perform his obligations under the contract, whether undertaken for their protection or not, in so far as those obligations go beyond the obligations otherwise involved in that duty.'

233 Section 1(3).

234 Section 2(1).

235 Section 1(5).

236 Section 1(6).

237 See sec 10(2) and (3) for exceptions.

238 [1932] AC 562, 581.

> this way rules of law arise which limit the range of complainants and the extent of their remedy. The rule that you are to love your neighbour becomes in law, you must not injure your neighbour; and the lawyer's question, Who is my neighbour? receives a restricted reply. You must take reasonable care to avoid acts or omissions which you can reasonably foresee would be likely to injure your neighbour. Who, then, in law is my neighbour? The answer seems to be – persons who are so closely and directly affected by my act that I ought reasonably to have them in contemplation as being so affected when I am directing my mind to the acts or omissions which are called in question.'

84 The question of whether to impose a duty of care is one of foreseeability, proximity and whether it is fair, just and reasonable to recognise such a duty.[239] The duty concept may be seen as a limiting device employed in light of the potential of indeterminate liability to an indeterminate class of potential litigants. The three-stage analysis of duty has been the subject of much discussion,[240] but in practice it generates little dispute in the vast majority of cases. It becomes the object of dispute only in specific contexts such as where the claimant's injury takes the form of psychiatric illness or pure economic loss, or where it was caused by an omission, the act of a third party or the breach of public duties.[241] In the case of intentional torts (see no 29 ff), questions of foreseeability, proximity and fairness, justice and reasonableness do not come into play. Rather, different sets of prerequisites arise in respect of each nominate tort which in effect impose their own controlling device on the potential scope of possible claimants.[242]

H. DIFFERENCES AS REGARDS DEFENCES

85 Contributory negligence is regulated by the Law Reform (Contributory Negligence) Act 1945, which provides for the apportionment of liability with regard to the claimant's share in the responsibility for the damage. Save for one exception – namely, where a claim is based on breach of a contractual duty to take reasonable care – contributory negligence is a defence only to tortious liability. It applies to liability for breach of a contractual duty of care only where this is concurrent with a duty of care in tort, in which case the liability is concurrent in contract and tort.[243]

---

239 *Caparo Industries plc v Dickman* [1990] 2 AC 605.

240 *Lunney/Oliphant* (fn 110) 137. See now *Robinson v Chief Constable of West Yorkshire Police* [2018] AC 736.

241 Ibid, 138.

242 *K Oliphant*, The Structure of the Intentional Torts, in: JW Neyers/E Chamberlain/SGA Pitel, Emerging Issues in Tort Law (2007) 509 ff.

243 *Forsikringsaktieselskapet Vesta v Butcher* [1989] AC 852.

I. DIFFERENCES AS REGARDS LIMITATION PERIODS

1) *Applicable Time Limits*

Limitation periods are regulated by a number of statutes, primarily the Limitation Act 1980. The starting point is that the same limitation period applies in respect of both breaches of contract and torts – namely, six years. Beyond this general statement lie several differences. 86

In particular, the primary limitation period of six years applies in respect of actions founded on 'simple contract', a phrase that is not defined by statute.[244] In essence, it refers to a contract that is not created by deed. Thus, the time limit for the recovery of rent arrears, for example, is six years.[245] In the case of a contract by deed, the limitation period is 12 years.[246] This applies to a claim for the recovery of land and proceeds of sale of land, for example.[247] In the case of restitutionary claims, although the correct approach has yet to be authoritatively decided, it is thought that these would be classified as contractual obligations for the purpose of limitations.[248] 87

A number of exceptions to the six-year rule also apply in the case of tort.[249] First, a one-year limitation period applies in respect of actions in *libel, slander and malicious prosecution*.[250] Second, a three-year limitation period applies where the damages claimed consist of or include damages for *personal injury or death*.[251] It should be noted that the three-year period applies even where personal injury was caused by a contractual breach. The same period applies to dependants seeking to bring an action under the Fatal Accidents Act 1976.[252] 88

Third, a three-year limitation period applies to claims under the Consumer Protection Act 1987 in respect of damage caused by *defective products* whether the damage arsing is personal injury, death or property loss or damage.[253] 89

Lastly, a special provision applies in the case of *latent damage*. The provision does not apply in respect of actions based on contract and is limited to those caused 90

---

244 Limitation Act 1980, sec 5.
245 Limitation Act 1980, sec 19.
246 Limitation Act 1980, sec 8.
247 Limitation Act 1980, secs 15 and 17.
248 *A McGee*, Limitation Periods (7th edn 2014) para 4.008.
249 See Limitation Act 1980, sec 2 for the rule.
250 Limitation Act 1980, sec 4A.
251 Limitation Act 1980, sec 11. 'Personal injuries' includes any disease and any impairment of a person's physical or mental condition, and 'injury' and cognate expressions shall be construed accordingly: Limitation Act 1980, sec 38(1).
252 Limitation Act 1980, sec 12.
253 Consumer Protection Act 1987, sec 11A(4).

by a negligent act (other than personal injuries or death[254]). If facts relevant to a cause of action are not known by the expiry of a period of six years from the date on which the cause of action accrued, a three-year period from the date of discovery applies.[255]

91 Where concurrent duties in contract and tort exist, a claimant can sue in both and in so doing take advantage of whichever limitation period is most advantageous to him.[256]

2) When Time Begins to Run ('Dies a Quo')

92 A further distinction between actions in contract and actions in tort is that time runs from different dates. The rule in both cases is that the period runs from the date on which the cause of action accrued (or the day after the cause of action arose, to be more precise[257]). In the case of contract, the cause of action accrues on the date the contract was breached,[258] whereas different rules apply in the case of tort: the cause of action accrues when the damage occurred in the case of torts not actionable per se (ie torts actionable on proof of damage, such as negligence and nuisance). In the case of torts actionable per se (ie torts actionable without proof of damage, such as libel and trespass to land), the clock begins to tick when the act constituting the tort was committed. In the case of a continuing tort (eg a continuous nuisance or passing off), a fresh cause of action accrues each day. A fresh cause of action also begins from the date of each act where the tort in question is repeated, as in the case of multiple trespasses. A similar rule formerly applied in defamation cases so that every subsequent publication of a statement published previously in substantially the same form gave rise to a fresh cause of action. The Defamation Act 2013 introduces a single publication rule, which treats the cause of action in such cases as having accrued on the date of the first publication.[259]

93 Where *personal injury or death* results, the choice is between the date on which the damage occurred (or the date of the deceased's death) or, if later, the date of knowledge of the person injured[260] (or the personal representative).[261] The facts of which the latter must have knowledge are detailed in the governing legislation.[262]

---

254 In addition to personal injuries and death, the provision does not apply in the case of defective products or in respect of claims under the Fatal Accidents Act 1972.

255 Limitation Act 1980, sec 14A(1) and (4).

256 *Henderson v Merrett Syndicates Ltd* [1995] 2 AC 145.

257 *Marren v Dawson Bentley & Co Ltd* [1961] 2 QB 135.

258 *Gould v Johnson* (1702) 2 Salkeld's King's Bench Reports (Salk) 422.

259 Section 8.

260 Limitation Act 1980, sec 11(4).

261 Limitation Act 1980, sec 11(5).

262 Limitation Act 1980, sec 14(1): 'References to a person's date of knowledge are references to the date on which he first had knowledge of the following facts – (a) that the injury in

Similarly, the commencement of the period in *product liability* cases is either the date on which the cause of action accrues or the date on which the claimant knew or ought to have known of the facts,[263] whichever is later.[264] In the case of death, it is three years from the date of death or the date of the personal representative's knowledge, whichever is later. 94

With *latent damage*, the relevant date in respect of the six-year period is the date the tort was committed or, if later, three years[265] from the date on which the claimant had or ought to have had knowledge of the facts.[266] 95

The start of the six-year limitation period is similarly postponed in the case of *fraud, concealment or mistake*,[267] and does not begin until the plaintiff has discovered the fraud, concealment or mistake or could with reasonable diligence have discovered it. 96

3) *Particular Rules*

a) Longstop

In some cases, an overriding time limit or longstop date is imposed. In the case of *latent damage*, the claim expires 15 years after the date of the negligent act or omission.[268] The longstop also applies in the case of *fraud and mistake* but not in the case of deliberate *concealment*.[269] A longstop period of 10 years (from the date of supply by a producer, own brander or the first EU importer[270]) applies in the case of *defective product* claims under the Consumer Protection Act 1987.[271] 97

---

question was significant; and (b) that the injury was attributable in whole or in part to the act or omission which is alleged to constitute negligence, nuisance or breach of duty; and (c) the identity of the defendant; and (d) if it is alleged that the act or omission was that of a person other than the defendant, the identity of that person and the additional facts supporting the bringing of an action against the defendant.' Under sec 14(3): 'For the purposes of this section a person's knowledge includes knowledge which he might reasonably have been expected to acquire – (a) from facts observable or ascertainable by him; or (b) from facts ascertainable by him with the help of medical or other appropriate expert advice which it is reasonable for him to seek; but a person shall not be fixed under this subsection with knowledge of a fact ascertainable only with the help of expert advice so long as he has taken all reasonable steps to obtain (and, where appropriate, to act on) that advice.' See also sec 12 in respect of claims under the Fatal Accidents Act 1976.

263 As defined in sec 14(1A) and (3).

264 Limitation Act 1980, sec 11A(4).

265 Limitation Act 1980, sec 14A(4) and (5).

266 Limitation Act 1980, sec 14A(6)–(8) and (1A).

267 Limitation Act 1980, sec 32.

268 Limitation Act 1980, sec 14B; Consumer Protection Act 1987, secs 4(2) and 2(2).

269 Limitation Act 1980, sec 32(5).

270 Consumer Protection Act 1987, sec 2(2).

271 Section 11A(3).

b) Extinction

98 Where the period prescribed for bringing an action has expired, a claimant may nonetheless petition the court to exercise its discretion to allow an action to proceed. This is because the expiry of the period generally does not *extinguish* a claimant's right of action but merely *bars* him from bringing an action. In the case of conversion[272] and actions to recover land,[273] however, the effect is extinction. This is also the case with respect to the longstop period in respect of defective products. In such cases, it is for the defendant to plead extinction as a defence.

c) Extension

99 The above limitation periods may be extended in the case of disability.[274] A person is treated as under a disability while he is an infant (ie under 18[275]) or lacks capacity (within the meaning of the Mental Capacity Act 2005) to conduct legal proceedings.[276] The extension in question is for a period of six years from the date when the person ceases to be under a disability or dies, unless some alternative period is specified. It is perhaps worth noting that children and those who lack mental capacity can actually issue proceedings (where necessary, through a 'litigation friend').[277]

d) Exclusion

100 The court may in the exercise of its equitable discretion direct that the time limits specified in no 88 above shall not apply to an action for defamation and malicious falsehood[278] or one in respect of personal injuries or death.[279] This also applies where the personal injury or death was caused by a defective product.[280] However, the court cannot set the overriding limitation period aside in the latter case.[281]

---

272 Limitation Act 1980, sec 3.
273 Limitation Act 1980, sec 13.
274 Limitation Act 1980, secs 28 and 28A.
275 Family Law Reform Act 1969, sec 1.
276 Limitation Act 1980, sec 38(2).
277 Civil Procedure Rules, Rule 21.
278 Limitation Act 1980, sec 32A.
279 Limitation Act 1980, sec 33. For an example, see *A v Hoare* [2008] EWHC 1573 (QB) (lottery win by man convicted and imprisoned for attempt rape of claimant 16 years previously).
280 Limitation Act 1980, sec 33.
281 Limitation Act 1980, sec 33(1A).

e) Suspension

There are number of instances in which the running of time may be suspended. Under sec 12 of the Arbitration Act 1996, for example, the period between the commencement of the arbitration and the date of a court order to set it aside or to declare it to be of no effect may be excluded from the computation. The limitation period is also suspended under sec 1 of the Limitation (Enemies and War Prisoner) Act 1945, where a party was an enemy or detained in enemy territory so that the period is deemed not to have run while the said person was an enemy or was so detained.[282] 101

f) Restarting the Clock from Zero

In respect of certain claims (eg for the recovery of land or in relation to mortgages), acknowledgment or part-payment have the effect of restarting the limitation period. In cases of deliberate concealment occurring *before* a cause of action has arisen, time does not run until the concealment is or could reasonably be discovered.[283] But if it occurs *after*, the effect is to restart the limitation period on the claim.[284] 102

g) Contracting Out

Parties may agree to vary (eg extend, postpone or suspended) or exclude limitation periods,[285] subject to the provisions of the Unfair Contract Terms Act 1977 and the Unfair Terms in Consumer Contracts Regulations 1999 (see no 111 ff). Where there is no consideration, the contract must be executed as a deed. 103

J. DIFFERENCES AS REGARDS PROOF

See nos 22 and 49 above. 104

K. REASONS FOR THE DIFFERENCES

See no 1 ff above. 105

---

282 See *McGee* (fn 248) para 2.012 f.
283 Limitation Act 1980, sec 32(1)(b).
284 *Sheldon v Outhwaite* [1995] 2 All ER 558.
285 *Lade v Trill* (1842) 11 Law Journal Reports, Chancery New Series (LJ Ch) 102.

III. LIMITATION OR EXCLUSION OF LIABILITY ARISING FROM TORT AND FROM CONTRACT

A. STATUTORY PROVISIONS AUTHORISING A LIMITATION OR EXCLUSION OF LIABILITY

106 The limitation or exclusion of liability is normally addressed as a matter of common law and only occasionally addressed specifically in statute. A rare example is sec 2(1) of the Occupiers' Liability Act 1957 ('except in so far as he is free to and does extend, restrict, modify or exclude his duty'). The correct construction here seems to be that the ability to restrict or exclude (etc) the duty arises at common law and is only adverted to in the statute for the avoidance of doubt.

B. LIMITATION OR EXCLUSION OF CONTRACTUAL AND TORTIOUS LIABILITY BY CONTRACT

1) *Introduction*

107 A party to a contract may exclude or restrict his liability as a corollary of the doctrine of freedom of contract. The only question is whether the party who seeks to rely on the term did what was reasonably sufficient to give the other party notice of it.[286] Liabilities in both contract and tort can be subject to such provisions, which are construed strictly with any ambiguities resolved against the party that seeks to rely upon the exclusion (see the discussion of the *contra proferentem* rule of construction in nos 3 and 27 above). In addition to express incorporation, exempting or limiting conditions may also be brought into a contract by a course of dealing between the parties or by custom.

108 An individual may also voluntarily agree to absolve another of liability in tort. Disclaimer of liability is a defence. The disclaimer may be agreed by contract but non-contractual disclaimers (eg by notice) are also recognised. As with the exclusion or limitation of liability under contract, for a person to be bound by a disclaimer reasonable steps must be taken to bring it to his notice.[287] Full knowledge of the nature and extent of the precise risk is not a prerequisite. The defence of disclaimer thus differs from the defence of *volenti non fit iniuria*

[286] See eg *Parker v South Eastern Ry* (1877) 2 Law Reports, Common Pleas Division (CPD) 416.
[287] *Ashdown v Samuel Williams & Sons Ltd* [1957] 1 QB 409.

(voluntary assumption of risk) which requires the victim's express or implied agreement to incur a known risk.[288]

2) Exemption Clauses and Third Parties

The doctrine of privity of contracts obstructs the extension of the protection provided by the exemption clauses to third parties.[289] By virtue of sec 1(6) of the Contracts (Rights of Third Parties) Act 1999, however, '[w]here a term of a contract excludes or limits liability in relation to any matter references in this Act to the third party enforcing the term shall be construed as references to his availing himself of the exclusion or limitation.'[290] The effect is thus to circumvent the common law position by allowing a third party to rely on an exemption clause if the contract expressly provides that he may or if the term purports to confer a benefit on him (sec 1(1)). A third party may enforce a term in his own right only if he is expressly identified in the contract by name, as a member of a class or as answering a particular description, but need not be in existence when the contract is entered into (sec 1(3)). Enforcement must obviously be consistent with the terms of the contract (sec 1(4)). The third party is entitled to the same remedies for breach of contract as if he had been a party to the contract (sec 1(5)). The Act is subject to certain exclusions (in respect of certain types of contracts, for example) as detailed in sec 6. 109

The starting point in tort is also that a contractual limitation or exclusion of liability does not extend to a third party. However, as tortious liabilities can be limited or excluded by (non-contractual) notice, a contractual clause of which the third party was aware, or of which he was given reasonable notice, could prima facie be sufficient to limit or exclude liability in respect of things done after the date of notice. Consequently, courts do generally tend to accept clauses limiting the liability of subcontractors in commercial cases. The inclusion of an exemption clause in a main contract may also negative the existence of a *duty of care* by a person not in a relationship of privity of contract to the other contracting party. Damage purported to be limited or excluded in this way need not be constrained to pure economic loss but could extend to physical damage to property or persons.[291] A person may also impose contractual limitations on 110

288 See *A Mullis/K Oliphant*, Torts (4th edn 2011) para 11.2.

289 See eg *Haseldine v CA Daw & Son Ltd* [1941] 2 KB 343.

290 Note that the common law doctrine of privity of contract remains unaltered: sec 7(1) provides that sec 1 of the Act 'does not affect any right or remedy of a third party that exists or is available apart from this Act.'

291 *Norwich City Council v Harvey* [1989] 1 WLR 828.

the tortious liability of third parties in line with the Contracts (Rights of Third Parties) Act 1999.

3) *Statutory Regulation of Exemption Clauses*

111 Several statutory provisions serve to regulate certain exempting terms. An important early landmark was the Unfair Contract Terms Act 1977 which despite its name applies not just to exclusion clauses, etc, in contracts but also to clauses which seek to affect liability in tort. Its ambit also encompasses non-contractual exclusions or limitations of liability which may be effective in tort. The effect of the 1977 Act is either to invalidate a clause or subject it to the requirement of reasonableness (see sec 11). For the most part, the Act applies to business liability, which is defined as liability for breach of duties arising from things done or to be done by a person in the course of a business or from the occupation of premises used for business purposes of the occupier.[292]

112 Section 2(1) of the 1977 Act prevents a party from seeking to rely on a term which purports to exclude or restrict his liability for death or personal injury resulting from negligence. It is immaterial whether the liability arises in contract or tort.[293] In the case of other loss or damage, the exclusion or restriction is valid in so far as the term or notice satisfies the requirement of reasonableness. The Act also applies to terms purporting to exclude the existence of a duty of care.[294]

113 As regards contract in particular, sec 3 of the Act prevents a party in breach of contract from excluding or restricting his liability in respect of the breach, from rendering a contractual performance substantially different from that which was reasonably expected of him or from rendering no performance at all. This applies as between contracting parties where one of them deals as consumer or on the other's written standard terms of business. The Act also invalidates terms which exclude or restrict liability in contracts for the sale of goods, hire purchase and in other contracts for the supply of goods.[295]

114 In practical terms, the 1977 Act has now been overtaken in importance by the Consumer Rights Act 2015. The Act aims to consolidate the consumer protection provisions of the Unfair Contract Terms Act 1977 and Unfair

---

292 See sec 1(3). Certain exceptions apply.

293 Negligence is defined broadly under sec 1. It means the breach: (a) of any obligation, arising from the express or implied terms of a contract, to take reasonable care or exercise reasonable skill in the performance of the contract; (b) of any common law duty to take reasonable care or exercise reasonable skill (but not any stricter duty); (c) of the common duty of care imposed by the Occupiers' Liability Act 1957.

294 *Smith v Eric S Bush* [1990] 1 AC 831.

295 See sec 5 ff.

Terms in Consumer Contracts Regulations 1999,[296] which ran parallel to the 1977 Act, into a single Act. The exclusion or limitation of liability in so far as non-consumers are concerned will continue to be regulated by the 1977 Act. Part 2 of the 2015 Act regulates unfair terms in contracts between traders and consumers. By sec 62, neither an unfair term nor an unfair notice is binding on a consumer. A term is unfair if, contrary to the requirement of good faith, it causes a significant imbalance in the parties' rights and obligations under the contract to the detriment of the consumer. By sec 65, a trader cannot by a term of a consumer contract or by a consumer notice exclude or restrict liability for death or personal injury resulting from negligence. Where a term of a consumer contract is not binding on the consumer as a result of Part 2 of the Act, sec 67 provides that the contract continues, so far as practicable, to have effect in every other respect. The Act is subject to certain qualifications (eg it does not apply to contracts of insurance).[297] There are clearly differences in the precise wording of the Act but, as regards the exclusion of liability, its effect is analogous to that of its predecessors.

Other statutory limitations upon the exclusion or limitation of liability include 115
sec 149 of the Road Traffic Act 1988,[298] sec 7 of the Consumer Protection Act 1987[299] and sec 6(3) of the Defective Premises Act 1972.[300]

4) *Ex post Exclusion of Liability*

English lawyers would not speak of an 'ex post exclusion of liability' but it is of 116
course possible to compromise an existing claim on a no-liability basis.

---

296 Implementing Directive 93/13/EEC of 5 April 1993 on unfair terms in consumer contracts [1993] OJ L 95/29.

297 See sec 66.

298 The section applies where a person uses a motor vehicle that is subject to compulsory insurance against third-party risks. Sec 149(2) reads: 'If any other person is carried in or upon the vehicle while the user is so using it, any antecedent agreement or understanding between them (whether intended to be legally binding or not) shall be of no effect so far as it purports or might be held: (a) to negative or restrict any such liability of the user in respect of persons carried in or upon the vehicle as is required by section 145 of this Act to be covered by a policy of insurance, or (b) to impose any conditions with respect to the enforcement of any such liability of the user.' Sec 149(3) adds: 'The fact that a person so carried has willingly accepted as his the risk of negligence on the part of the user shall not be treated as negativing any such liability of the user.' See also sec 148.

299 'The liability of a person by virtue of this Part to a person who has suffered damage caused wholly or partly by a defect in a product, or to a dependant or relative of such a person, shall not be limited or excluded by any contract term, by any notice or by any other provision.'

300 'Any term of an agreement which purports to exclude or restrict, or has the effect of excluding or restricting, the operation of any of the provisions of this Act, or any liability arising by virtue of any such provision, shall be void.' For further statutes regulating exemption clauses see Chitty on Contracts (fn 1) para 14–115.

IV. NON-CONCURRENCE OR CONCURRENCE OF ACTIONS

A. OVERVIEW

1) *Areas of Overlap between Tort and Contract*

117 English law generally has no problem with the concurrence of actions in contract and tort, and indeed negligently causing loss in the performance of a contract has traditionally been addressed as a matter of tort law in such spheres as medical negligence, professional negligence generally, employers' liability and the liability of common carriers.[301] Admittedly, the 'privity of contract fallacy'[302] was long considered to exclude a manufacturer's liability to the ultimate consumer of his product, on the basis that the manufacturer's duty was (subject to exceptions) only to the other party to the initial contract of supply, but the fallacy was exploded by *Donoghue v Stevenson*[303] in 1932, recognising the manufacturer's tortious duty of care to the ultimate consumer.

2) *Approach to Non-Concurrence and Concurrence of Actions*

118 English law's basic position as regards concurrence of actions was authoritatively stated by Lord Goff in *Henderson v Merrett Syndicates Ltd:*[304]

> 'My own belief is that, in the present context, the common law is not antipathetic to concurrent liability, and that there is no sound basis for a rule which automatically restricts the claimant to either a tortious or a contractual remedy. The result may be untidy; but, given that the tortious duty is imposed by the general law, and the contractual duty is attributable to the will of the parties, I do not find it objectionable that the claimant may be entitled to take advantage of the remedy which is most advantageous to him, subject only to ascertaining whether the tortious duty is so inconsistent with the applicable contract that, in accordance with ordinary principle, the parties must be taken to have agreed that the tortious remedy is to be limited or excluded.'

---

301 See eg *Brown v Boorman* (1842) 3 QB 511, 525 f per Tindal CJ, (1844) 11 Clark & Finnely's House of Lords Cases (Cl & F) 1, 44 per Lord Campbell ('wherever there is a contract, and something to be done in the course of the employment which is the subject of that contract, if there is a breach of a duty in the course of that employment, the plaintiff may either recover in tort or in contract').

302 Normally attributed to *Winterbottom v Wright* (1842) 10 Meeson & Welsby's Exchequer Reports (M & W) 109.

303 [1932] AC 562.

304 [1995] 2 AC 145, 194.

Thus parties are free to pursue their remedy either in contract or in tort, provided that they are not prevented from framing their liability in tort by virtue of, inter alia, the relevant contractual terms.[305] Such an exclusion would, in any case, be subject to the *contra proferentem* rule (nos 3 and 27) and the provisions of the Unfair Contract Terms Act 1977 and Consumer Rights Act 2015 (see no 111 ff). 119

Henderson v Merrett may be taken as a decisive rejection of the approach adopted by the Privy Council in *Tai Hing Cotton Mill Ltd v Liu Chong Hing Bank Ltd (No 1)* where their Lordships stated that they 'do not believe that there is anything to the advantage of the law's development in searching for a liability in tort where the parties are in a contractual relationship'.[306] That said, it must be noted that Lord Goff conceded that there would be situations in which 'the tortious duty is so inconsistent with the applicable contract that, in accordance with ordinary principle, the parties must be taken to have agreed that the tortious remedy is to be limited or excluded.'[307] The difficulty is in identifying when such circumstances arise, though they are quite likely to be inferred to be present in large-scale construction projects and other commercial settings. 120

In addition, there are other specific types of case where the courts will not permit a party to exploit the concurrency of regimes. This is the case, for example, with respect to the liability of children. As seen above (no 76 f), a child's liability is generally broader in tort than it is in contract. Thus, where a tort is tightly connected to a contract, an action in tort may be barred to the extent that it seeks to avoid the law's protection over child contractors. Where, however, the conduct is 'wholly independent of any contract'[308] an action in tort may proceed. A similar approach applies with respect to damages with a view to ensuring that the claimant does not get a windfall merely as a result of framing his action in one form or the other: where the contract imposes a duty of care, the damages awarded will have more in common with tortious damages and where the duty is strict, contractual damages serve as a reference point.[309] The courts are also sensitive of the different ways the regimes regulate remoteness, limitation of actions, contributory negligence and conflict of laws and will in all cases seek to ensure that the claimant's election does not unfairly disadvantage the defendant.[310] 121

---

305 For more extensive coverage see *Mullis/Oliphant* (fn 288) para 5.7.

306 [1986] AC 80, 107 per Lord Scarman.

307 [1995] 2 AC 145, 194.

308 *Burnard v Haggis* (1863) 32 Law Journal Reports, New Series (LJNS) 189, 191 per Keating J. See also Chitty on Contracts (fn 1) para 1–183.

309 Chitty on Contracts (fn 1) para 1–184.

310 Ibid, para 1–186 ff.

B. CONCURRENCE/EXCLUSION OF ACTIONS FOR THE PROTECTION AGAINST PERSONAL INJURY

122 Concurrent liabilities run in the case of personal injury even where a contract actually existed prior to the injury in question. This will usually be the case in an employment or private medical setting. Liability for personal injury in both contexts is typically treated as a matter of tort law, though it is acknowledged that there may be a concurrent liability in contract and that the claimant is free to choose between them depending on which is the more advantageous to him on the facts.[311] Parties can of course agree to a contractual obligation that is more extensive than the obligation arising in tort. There are dicta to the effect that no duty can arise in tort that is not inherent in the contract,[312] but it seems nevertheless that a tort obligation may arise even though there is no subsisting contract – for example, a duty to inform a prospective employee of risks inherent in the employment.[313]

C. CONCURRENCE/EXCLUSION OF ACTIONS FOR THE PROTECTION OF PROPERTY

123 Again, it is well established that liability for property damage can be concurrent in contract and tort.

D. CONCURRENCE/EXCLUSION IN THE CASE OF INTERFERENCE WITH CONTRACTUAL RIGHTS

1) Interference with a Contractual Relationship

124 Several of the economic torts in English law seek to tackle interferences with prospective economic advantages arising from pre-existing contractual relationships.[314] This is the case, for example, with the tort of inducing breach of contract. The tort arises where A intentionally induces or procures B to breach his contract with C resulting in damage to the latter. A's conduct is actionable by C. Liability is subject to the defence of justification. Intention is manifest

311 Eg in terms of private international law. In the context of employers' liability, see *Matthews v Kuwait Bechtel Corpn* [1959] 2 QB 57 (claim in contract); *Coupland v Arabian Gulf Oil Co* [1983] 1 WLR 1136; *Base Metal Trading Ltd v Shamurin* [2004] EWCA Civ 1316, [2005] 1 WLR 1157 (claims in tort). As regards concurrency in the context of employer's liability generally, see *Oliphant* (fn 14) para 20.5.

312 *Scally v Southern Health and Social Services Board* [1992] 1 AC 294, 302 f per Lord Bridge.

313 *White v Holbrook Precision Castings Ltd* [1985] Industrial Relations Law Reports (IRLR) 215.

314 *Oliphant* (fn 14) ch 29. See also Halsbury's Laws of England (fn 36) para 612 ff.

where A knew of the existence of the contract between B and C and intended to procure its breach. Where A merely prevents B from performing B's obligations under the contract, C can bring an action in the tort of causing loss by unlawful means – provided A employs unlawful means.[315] As its title suggests, there must be some independent illegality for the tort to arise. Where A *threatens* to use unlawful means to prevent the performance of the contract, this gives rise to liability in the tort of intimidation[316] (which may also be considered a specific instantiation of the general tort of causing loss by unlawful means).

2) Loss of Business due to Personal Injury to Someone Else's Employees or Clients or to Property Damage to the Entrepreneur

Consequential economic loss is loss that arises as a result of injury to one's 125
person or property.[317] Such losses are recoverable without any special restriction. Absent damage of the above kind, the claim is one for pure economic loss and the rules accompanying such losses apply. *West Bromwich Albion Football Club Ltd v Mohammed El Safty* was an action in which an injured football player had to retire from the sport following negligent advice from a surgeon after a sporting injury. In an action in which the club, which had signed the player on a long-term contract, sued the surgeon, the Court of Appeal ruled, dismissing the case, that there was no contract between the club and the surgeon and there was no necessity for one to be implied. As far as the claim in tort was concerned, even if it was assumed that there was foreseeability by the surgeon and reliance by the club, there was no assumption of responsibility by the surgeon to advise the club, and the question of conflict of interest arose, because the surgeon's primary concern was the player's well-being, not the financial circumstances of the football club.[318]

V. SPECIFIC SITUATIONS

A. PRE-CONTRACTUAL LIABILITY

Pre-contractual liability can arise in tort, but is not a distinct species of liability 126
in its own right. See no 15 ff above.

---

315 *Oliphant* (fn 14), paras 29.66 f and 29.84 ff. See also Halsbury's Laws of England (fn 36) para 621.

316 *Tarleton v M'Gawley* (1793) Peake's Nisi Prius Reports (Peake) 270. See further *Oliphant* (fn 14) para 29.57 ff.

317 *Spartan Steel & Alloys Ltd v Martin & Co* [1973] 1 QB 27; *Leigh & Sillavan Ltd v Aliakmon Shipping Co Ltd* [1986] AC 785. Cf the position on relational economic loss in Canada: *Canadian National Railway Co v Norsk Pacific Steamship Co* [1992] 1 Supreme Court Reports (SCR) 1021, in *M Lunney/K Oliphant*, Tort Law: Text and Materials (5th edn 2013) 374.

318 [2006] EWCA Civ 1299.

B. LIABILITY OF PROFESSIONALS

127 In English law, professional liability is generally concurrent in contract and tort (see no 117 ff above), though habitually treated in works on tort rather than contract.[319]

CASES

CASE 1. THE UNATTRACTIVE SHOPPING MALL

128 The tenancy agreement is between D and Z. Z can thus maintain an action for breach of covenant by D. As Z is under a duty to inform his landlord of the intention to sublet,[320] D can countersue for breach of contract not to assign without licence.

129 As against Z, C has an interest which is valid and so the sub-lease is binding. The question then is whether C has a sufficient interest in the premises to have rights conferred by the Landlord and Tenant Act 1954. Despite Z's breach of covenant not to sublet, C in fact acquires statutory protection under Part II of that Act (on the Security of Tenure for Business, Professional and other Tenants) against D, the superior landlord, until such time as D forfeits the agreement or when C or Z's tenancy expires.[321] Since C is considered 'a tenant … by an agreement … for an underlease' within the definition in sec 69(1) of the Act, he is entitled to pursue D for breach of covenant.

130 Z may have an action in private nuisance against D. As C has sufficient interest in the premises to have the rights conferred on a sub-tenant by the Landlord and Tenant Act 1954, he may also pursue an action. Compensation is available, inter alia, for loss of profits which are the result of inability to use the land for its intended purposes. But, in accordance with the general requirements of private nuisance, it must be shown that D unreasonably interfered with Z and/or C's use or enjoyment of the land affected.

CASE 2. THE IDLE LAWYER

131 The facts are on all fours with those in *White v Jones*,[322] a leading case on professional negligence. Although there was no contract between the daughters

---

319 See eg *Oliphant* (fn 14) ch 16. The main specialist work is Jackson & Powell on Professional Liability (8th edn 2017).

320 Landlord and Tenant Act 1954, sec 40.

321 *D'Silva v Lister House Development Ltd* [1971] ch 17. See Woodfall: Landlord and Tenant (2014) paras 22.008 and 22.022.

322 [1995] 2 AC 207.

and the solicitor and no fiduciary relationship, the House of Lords ruled that it was fair, just and reasonable that the law should impose a duty on the solicitor. The general rule is that, subject to his duties to the court and the professional duties imposed upon his profession, a solicitor when acting for his client owes no duty to third parties. However, the solicitor in this case was said to have assumed responsibility to give effect to his client's testamentary wishes, and this responsibility extended to the beneficiaries under the will whose interests crystallised on the death of the testator, their father. Moreover, the solicitor could reasonably foresee that his negligence might result in the loss of the intended legacy without either the testator or his estate having a remedy against him. Further, there was no risk of an open-ended liability that it might be impractical to insure against; in fact, solicitors have no difficulty in practice in obtaining cover in respect of such risks under their ordinary professional indemnity policies.[323]

The House of Lords had regard to the fact that the claim was based on a loss of expectation which is traditionally the exclusive domain of the law of contract (see no 3). The decision was said to be justified nonetheless as it enabled the solicitor's contractual duty of care to be effectively enforced. As has already been adverted to, the daughters had no action under contract law and the Contracts (Rights of Third Parties) Act 1999 was no aid in this case as it was decided long before its enactment. 132

CASE 3. THE DEFECTIVE HOUSE

By sec 1 of the Defective Premises Act 1972 a person taking on work for or in connection with the provision of a dwelling owes a duty to the commissioner of the building and to every person who acquires an interest (whether legal or equitable) in the dwelling to see that the work which he takes on is done in a workmanlike or professional manner, with proper materials and so that the dwelling will be fit for habitation when completed. D thus owes the above duty to Z and C since sec 3 provides that that duty 'shall not be abated by the subsequent disposal of the premises by the person who owed the duty.' Any term of an agreement which purports to exclude or restrict, or has the effect of excluding or restricting, the operation of any of the provisions of this Act, or any liability arising by virtue of any such provision, is void: sec 6(3). D is thus liable in respect of actual damage to property belonging to C and personal injury. 133

C has no contract with D and so cannot maintain an action for breach of contract. 134

323 [1995] 2 AC 207, 239.

CASE 4. APARTMENT IN FLAMES

135 Landlords have a common law immunity from liability in negligence insofar as the injury arises from their nonfeasance relating to the premises (eg a failure to monitor and maintain),[324] but sec 4 of the Defective Premises Act 1972 imposes a statutory duty on landlords to take such care as is reasonable in all the circumstances to maintain or repair leased premises where such a duty is agreed under the lease,[325] or where the tenancy gives him the right to enter to carry out such work.[326] The landlord need not be possessed of actual notice of the defect.[327] In addition, an action for breach of the repair covenant could be maintained if one exists.[328]

CASE 5. INJURED SKIER

136 C has a valid claim in both contract and tort against D1. He has no right to pursue an action directly against D2 either in contract or tort. While the Third Parties (Rights against Insurers) Act 2010 applies to transfer to and vest rights to a third party like C, this is only the case where D1 is insolvent. The Act seeks to avoid insurance monies being paid to insolvent insureds and divided between the latter's creditors in insolvency proceedings. The Act only applies where a body either incurs a liability or becomes insolvent after the commencement of the Act.

---

324 *Cavalier v Pope* [1906] AC 428; *Rimmer v Liverpool City Council* [1985] QB 1.

325 Section 4(1) reads: 'Where premises are let under a tenancy which puts on the landlord an obligation to the tenant for the maintenance or repair of the premises, the landlord owes to all persons who might reasonably be expected to be affected by defects in the state of the premises a duty to take such care as is reasonable in all the circumstances to see that they are reasonably safe from personal injury or from damage to their property caused by a relevant defect.'

326 The rather wordy sec 4(4) reads: 'Where premises are let under a tenancy which expressly or impliedly gives the landlord the right to enter the premises to carry out any description of maintenance or repair of the premises, then, as from the time when he first is, or by notice or otherwise can put himself, in a position to exercise the right and so long as he is or can put himself in that position, he shall be treated for the purposes of subsections (1) to (3) above (but for no other purpose) as if he were under an obligation to the tenant for that description of maintenance or repair of the premises; but the landlord shall not owe the tenant any duty by virtue of this subsection in respect of any defect in the state of the premises arising from, or continuing because of, a failure to carry out an obligation expressly imposed on the tenant by the tenancy.'

327 *Sykes v Harry* [2001] QB 1014.

328 See eg the implied obligation in Landlord and Tenant Act 1985, sec 11.

CASE 6. EXPLODING CAR

C can maintain an action under the Consumer Protection Act 1987 against D1, if the latter is a supplier, and he fails to identify D2 as the car's manufacturer, and D2 as the producer.[329] He can also bring an action in negligence against both D1 and D2. 137

It is not stated in the facts whether the warranty is offered by the seller (D1) or the manufacturer (D2). If the latter, it could act as a collateral warranty which has legal effect independently of C's contract to purchase the car from D1. But the accident occurs outside the warranty period anyway, so the issue is to that extent redundant. C does, of course, have a contract and therefore a valid claim against D1 for breach of the implied term about quality and fitness under sec 14 of the Sale of Goods Act 1979. The extent to which he can rely upon it, however, depends on the agreed terms. 138

CASE 7. RACING BOAT BURNING

Assuming D is not the producer of the equipment that he installs (which would provide a separate basis of liability), he could be liable as a supplier under the Consumer Protection Act 1987 but can escape that liability by identifying the person who supplied the equipment to him or its producer. An action in negligence and one for breach of contract could also be pursued; the precise terms of the contract would govern the extent of liability, if any. As it does not appear that D sells the goods in the course of a business, the implied warranty of quality under the Sale of Goods Act 1979 does not come into play, and the express warranty would presumably define the limits of D's contractual obligation. 139

CASE 8. INSIDIOUS REPORT

C can pursue an action against D for inducing or procuring breach of contract on the basis that: (a) there was a contract between C and Z; (b) that contract was breached; (c) D's conduct procured or induced the breach; (d) D knew about the contract; and (e) he realised that his conduct would produce the results that it did. Conceivably, there might also be tortious causes of action in malicious falsehood and defamation (see Case 9 below). 140

329 See Consumer Protection Act 1987, sec 2.

141 D also owes a contractual duty of care to C, breach of which founds an action for damages for breach of contract. In addition, there is an implied undertaking by D to exercise reasonable skill or competence throughout his period of employment where he held himself out as holding a particular set of skills. At the very minimum, he is under a duty to exercise reasonable care in discharging his duties. A further implied term in a contract of employment is the duty to serve one's employer with fidelity and good faith. This applies in particular to the solicitation of customers which is prohibited where a non-compete clause was negotiated into his employment contract.[330] The duty of fidelity also extends to prohibit wilful disruption.[331] A host of other implied obligations and duties, including the obligation not to work for another employer while still employed and where such work would be inconsistent with that under the first employment, a duty not to disclose confidential information learnt by virtue of employment, a duty to account for a secret profit or commission earned, could have been breached as a result of D's actions.[332] An action for breach of the implied obligation of mutual trust and confidence could also arise and C may well be within his rights to dismiss D.

CASE 9. CIRCULAR LETTER

142 C may file an action against D in defamation. To establish this liability, he must show that the statements were indeed defamatory and that their publication has caused or is likely to cause serious harm to his reputation. If the action is brought by Z, which presumably trades for profit, Z will have to show that the publication is likely to cause it serious financial loss.[333] C may also pursue an action in malicious falsehood (which is more difficult to establish than defamation) on the basis that D maliciously published false oral or written statements to third parties which referred to him, his property or business and special damage arose thereof. Finally, there is the option of an action under the Protection from Harassment Act 1997 for the repeated false and malicious assertions against him, if this was indeed the case.[334]

143 The facts do not say anything about post-termination obligations in the contract, but naturally these could provide a basis of claim if they exist.

---

330 See Chitty on Contracts (fn 1) para 39–058 for a comprehensive list of cases.

331 See Chitty on Contracts (fn 1) para 39–061.

332 Ibid, para 39–055 ff.

333 Defamation Act 2013, sec 1.

334 *Plavelil v Director of Public Prosecutions* [2014] EWHC 736.

CASE 10. SHORTAGE OF SUPPLY

The first question to ask is whether the variation in the price constitutes a valid contract. For a valid contract to arise, the promisee must normally provide consideration for the promisor's performance, and performance of an existing contractual obligation is prima facie not consideration at all.[335] However, the courts will in some circumstances find that a 'practical benefit' derived by the promisee from continuing the relationship on a new basis may constitute good consideration,[336] which could be the case here. One must then ask whether C enters the contract of variation under economic duress. If so, the contract is voidable and C can recover the overpayment. However, several of the cases on the topic have fallen on the basis of affirmation. The following section in Chitty was quoted with approval by Mocatta J in *North Ocean Shipping Co Ltd v Hyundai Construction Co Ltd*: 'a person who has entered into a contract under duress, may either affirm or avoid such contract after the duress has ceased; and if he has so voluntarily acted under it with a full knowledge of all the circumstances he may be held bound on the ground of ratification, or if, after escaping from the duress, he takes no steps to set aside the transaction, he may be found to have affirmed it.' On the facts, although Mocatta J accepted that a 10% increase (without legal justification) or threatened termination amounted to economic duress, the claimant affirmed it by making the final payments without protest and also by their delay of several months before making a claim for the return of the extra payments. C must, therefore, be careful not to conduct himself as to affirm the variation in price. In particular, he may accept delivery and commence litigation or he may pay for the goods and seek a return of the extra payments immediately after. The courts will inspect the facts surrounding the case carefully. Lord Scarman, sitting in Privy Council, gave further useful guidance on this point in *Pao On v Lau Yiu Long*: 'In determining whether there was a coercion of will such that there was no true consent, it is material to inquire whether the person alleged to have been coerced did or did not protest; whether, at the time he was allegedly coerced into making the contract, he did or did not have an alternative course open to him such as an adequate legal remedy; whether he was independently advised; and whether after entering the contract he took steps to avoid it.'[337] As has been said, 'there remains considerable doubt and some disagreement over the circumstances in which relief will be granted, and how the decisions are best explained.'[338] In addition to the nature of the threat, the 144

[335] *Stilk v Myrick* [1809] 2 Campbell's Nisi Prius Cases (Camp) 317.
[336] *Williams v Roffey* [1991] 1 QB 1.
[337] [1980] AC 614, 635.
[338] Chitty on Contracts (fn 1) para 7–022.

courts will take the causative effect of the threat on C into consideration. In the latter instance, C needs to prove that he had no reasonable alternative and that a reasonable person in his position would have reacted the way he did (see no 36). It would seem the legitimacy of the demand is also a relevant consideration.[339]

145 Broadly the same analysis applies if the variation of price has no contractual effect: C would seem to be able to recover the overpayment on the basis that it was made under economic duress.[340]

146 Theoretically, an action may also lie in the tort of causing loss by unlawful means (formally the tort of intimidation, in particular two-party intimidation). As mentioned in no 124, the tort extends to threatened breach of contract. As stated in *News Group Newspapers v SOGAT*, however, it is essential to show that D intended his threat to injure C.[341] A simple disappointment of C's expectations by D does not suffice.[342] On the facts, D's conduct appears to be motivated by matters in X and Z's spheres and nothing more.

CASE 11. INJURED ROCK STAR

147 No contract exists between C and D. An action against D in tort would fail unless X died as a result of the accident and C is a dependant entitled to bring an action under the Fatal Accidents Act 1976 (which is not applicable to expected benefits under a business relationship with the deceased).[343] C's claim is relational or purely economic, recovery of which is subject to strict restrictions in tort. See nos 70 f and 125.

CASE 12. EQUIPMENT DESTROYED

148 C has a valid claim against D1 for breach of contract but not against D2. C's case against D2 in tort is bound to fail. The loss is purely economic and there is no basis on which D2 could be said to have assumed responsibility for C's purely economic interests. Negligently preventing performance of a contract is not a tort in English law.

---

339 Ibid, para 7–023 f.

340 *Adam Opel GmbH v Mitras Automotive (UK) Ltd* [2008] EWHC 3205 (QB), [2008] Business Law Reports (Bus LR) D55.

341 [1987] Industrial Court Reports (ICR) 181, 204 per Stuart-Smith J.

342 *J Murphy/C Witting*, Street on Torts (13th edn 2012) 410.

343 *Burgess v Florence Nightingale Hospital for Gentlewomen* [1955] 1 QB 349.

CASE 13. SLIPPING ON A LETTUCE LEAF

An occupier of premises owes a duty to see that a visitor will be reasonably safe in using the premises for the purposes for which he is invited or permitted by the occupier to be there: sec 2(1) and (2) Occupiers' Liability Act 1957. D thus owes a duty to C. In determining whether D has discharged the common duty of care to C, regard will be had, inter alia, to whether C was warned not to step on the leaf. No contract has yet arisen between C and D and there is no category of 'pre-contractual liability' in English law (see no 15). 149

CASE 14. TEST DRIVE

No contract has yet arisen between C and D and so an action for breach of contract is out of the question. C may, however, pursue damages against D under the tort of negligence. 150

CASE 15. BREACH OF NEGOTIATIONS

No action arises in tort: it seems highly unlikely in these circumstances that a seller would be held to owe a duty of care to a prospective purchaser in respect of the latter's purely economic interest in acquiring the property. In addition, it does not appear that the parties have reached an agreement on essential matters of principle relating to the sale, so there is not as yet a valid contract between them. This does not seem to be a case in which an agreement to negotiate could be inferred: there is insufficient evidence of any intention to create legal relations.[344] There is also no evidence that C has suffered any loss by being deprived of the opportunity to buy the antique (or, more precisely, to negotiate further for its purchase). 151

CASE 16. NON-DISCLOSURE OF RELEVANT FACTS

C's failure to mention where he intended to use the machine means that he failed to take advantage of an opportunity to include an express material term in the contract. Section 14(3) of the Sale of Goods Act 1979 provides that where 152

---

344 Cf *Emirates Trading Agency LLC v Prime Mineral Exports Private Ltd* [2014] EWHC 2104 (Comm).

a buyer, expressly or *by implication*, makes known to the seller *any particular purpose for which the goods are being bought*, there is an implied term that the goods supplied under the contract are reasonably fit for that purpose. Although D has implied knowledge, this does not come from C directly, so C seems not to satisfy the 'makes known' requirement. It is therefore doubtful that C's action for breach of contract would succeed. In principle, a defendant may attract liability for pre-contractual non-disclosure of material facts under the tort of negligence. This is the case where the defendant has voluntarily accepted responsibility to the other party. The context in which the authorities on this point have arisen is one which seeks to tackle information asymmetry, however.[345] It is thus doubtful that an action in tort would be successful here. There is no suggestion that D possessed special knowledge or skill relative to C.

345 *Banque Keyser Ullmann SA v Skandia (UK) Insurance Co Ltd* [1990] 1 QB 665, 794 per Slade LJ. See generally nos 17 and 70 f.

THE BORDERLINES OF TORT LAW IN FRANCE

Jean-Sébastien BORGHETTI

QUESTIONS

I. Tracing the Borderlines 133
A. Distinction between Tort and Contract 133
B. Existence of a 'Grey Zone'? 135
C. Common or Different Rules Regulating Tort and Contract 136
D. Application of Common Rules in a Different Way 138
II. Main Differences between Tortious and Contractual Liability 138
A. Differences as Regards the Foundations of Liability 138
B. Differences as Regards Causation 140
C. Differences as Regards Remedies 141
D. Differences as Regards Recoverability of 'Pure Economic Losses' 143
E. Differences as Regards Liability for Others 144
1) Liability for Auxiliaries and for Independent Contractors 144
2) Liability for Legal Representatives or Organs of a Company 144
3) Liability of Representatives of Natural Persons 144
4) Liability of the Auxiliary/Organ Itself 145
F. Differences as Regards Liability in the Case of Multiple Tortfeasors/Breaching Parties 146
G. Differences as Regards the Persons Who May be Protected 146
H. Differences as Regards Defences 147
I. Differences as Regards Limitation Periods 149
J. Differences as Regards Proof 150
K. Other Differences 151
L. Reasons for the Differences 152

III. Limitation or Exclusion of Liability Arising from Tort and from Contract . . . 153
A. Statutory Provisions Authorising a Limitation or Exclusion of Liability . . . 153
B. Limitation or Exclusion of Contractual and Tortious Liability by Contract . . . 154
1) Is it Possible to Limit or Exclude Contractual or Tortious Liability under a Contract? . . . 154
2) To What Extent can a Contractual Exclusion Provide a Defence to a Third Party to the Contract? . . . 155
IV. Non-Concurrence or Concurrence of Actions . . . 156
A. Overview . . . 156
B. Concurrence/Exclusion of Actions for the Protection against Personal Injury and of Property . . . 157
C. Concurrence/Exclusion in the Case of Interference with Contractual Rights . . . 158
1) Interference with a Contractual Relationship . . . 158
2) Loss of Business due to Personal Injury to Someone Else's Employees or Clients or to Property Damage to the Entrepreneur . . . 158
V. Specific Situations . . . 159
A. Pre-Contractual Liability . . . 159
B. Liability of Professionals . . . 160

CASES

Case 1. The Unattractive Shopping Mall . . . 160
Case 2. The Idle Lawyer . . . 161
Case 3. The Defective House . . . 161
Case 4. Apartment in Flames . . . 162
Case 5. Injured Skier . . . 162
Case 6. Exploding Car . . . 163
Case 7. Racing Boat Burning . . . 165
Case 8. Insidious Report . . . 165
Case 9. Circular Letter . . . 165
Case 10. Shortage of Supply . . . 166
Case 11. Injured Rock Star . . . 166
Case 12. Equipment Destroyed . . . 167
Case 13. Slipping on a Lettuce Leaf . . . 167
Case 14. Test Drive . . . 168
Case 15. Breach of Negotiations . . . 168
Case 16. Non-Disclosure of Relevant Facts . . . 169

QUESTIONS

I. TRACING THE BORDERLINES

A. DISTINCTION BETWEEN TORT AND CONTRACT

Contract (*contrat*) and tort (*responsabilité délictuelle*) are primarily regarded as two different sources of obligations, following the traditional presentation of the *jus commune*, which was carried over into the Civil Code. Within the third book of the original Code, which was actually somewhat of a melting pot, the third part dealt with 'contracts and contractual obligations in general' ('*Des contrats et des obligations conventionnelles en général*'), whereas the fourth one dealt with 'undertakings formed without a convention' ('*Des engagements qui se forment sans convention*'). Tort[1] belonged to the latter, along with 'quasi contracts' ('*quasi-contrats*'), which are basically unjust enrichment[2] and *negotiorum gestio*. 1

The recent reform of the French law of obligations,[3] which, however, does not cover civil liability,[4] has clarified the presentation of the various sources of obligations, without putting into question the distinction between tort and contract. The first part of the third book of the Civil Code is now explicitly devoted to the 'sources of obligations' and deals successively with contract, with 'extra-contractual liability', ie liability in tort, and with 'other sources of obligations' (unjust enrichment, 'payment not owed', and *negotiorum gestio*). 2

The French Government is now preparing the reform of civil liability law. A consultation was organised in 2016 on the basis of draft project published in April 2016, and a revised draft reform bill on civil liability, *le projet réforme du* 3

---

1 The Code dealt with tort under the heading of *délits et quasi-délits* (delicts and quasi-delicts), but this denomination, inherited from *jus commune*, is now quite out of date and lawyers usually talk of *responsabilité délictuelle*.

2 French law actually distinguishes two scenarios that would both fall under 'unjust enrichment' in other legal systems: *paiement indu* ('payment not owed') and *enrichissement sans cause* ('enrichment without a cause').

3 A regulation which entered into force on 1 October 2016 (ordonnance no 2016-131 du 10 février 2016 portant réforme du droit des contrats, du régime général et de la preuve des obligations) has recast the parts of the Code devoted to the general law of contract (ie rules applicable to contracts in general, as opposed to rules applicable to specific contracts), to the general law of obligations (ie rules applicable to all obligations, regardless of their source), and to the proof of obligations. The purpose of this reform was first of all to confirm existing law and to integrate solutions developed by case law into the Code, in order to make the French law of obligations more clear and accessible, but some changes have also been made.

4 The Civil Code provisions on tort liability have thus not been modified. They have been renumbered, however, due to the general reorganisation of the parts of the Code devoted to the law of obligations.

droit de la responsabilité civile (*Projet*), was published in March 2017.[5] Since then, nothing much has happened, but there is still hope that Parliament will discuss this project at the end of 2019 or at the beginning of 2020.[6] The draft published in 2017 nevertheless deserves to be mentioned, because it runs counter to traditional solutions of French liability law on a few points.[7] One of them is that the draft deals with liability in tort (*responsabilité délictuelle ou extracontractuelle*) and liability in contract (*responsabilité contractuelle*) as a whole. It does preserve the distinction between those two types of liability, but regards them as forming one sole source of obligations, as opposed to contract. Consequently, it presents a certain number of rules as being common to both types of liability.[8] Should the reform materialise along those lines, the provisions on contractual damages, which are now in the 'contract' part of the Code,[9] would be thus moved to the 'civil liability' part. This choice is extremely questionable from a theoretical point of view. It does not fundamentally call into question the basic distinction between contract and tort, however, which would still be regarded as two distinct sources of obligations.

4 The basic reason why French law distinguishes between tort and contract is, therefore, that contracts are a source of voluntarily assumed obligations, arising out of an agreement between the debtor and the creditor,[10] whereas tort gives rise to obligations which do not originate in an agreement and have not been voluntarily assumed. It is sometimes said that a contract is an '*acte juridique*', ie a manifestation of will intended to produce legal effects (in this case one or several obligations), whereas tort is a '*fait juridique*', ie a fact that has legal consequences, but without these having been sought as such.

5 One could question if this basic reason is still fully valid, especially since the legislator and judges have been pouring into contracts new obligations, which

---

5 For a general view of the reform (in French), see *J-S Borghetti*, Vue d'ensemble de l'avant-projet de réforme de la responsabilité civile, Recueil Dalloz (D) 2016, 1386; Commentaire des principales dispositions de l'avant-projet de réforme de la responsabilité civile, D 2016, 1442; Un pas de plus vers la réforme de la responsabilité civile: présentation du projet de réforme rendu public le 13 mars 2017, D 2017, 770.

6 An English translation of the *Projet* by S Whittaker and J-S Borghetti is available at <http://www.textes.justice.gouv.fr/art_pix/reform_bill_on_civil_liability_march_2017.pdf>.

7 Hereinafter, this report will not go into the details of the *Projet* on those points – a majority – on which the latter purports to confirm existing rules or solutions.

8 The draft reform project draws on two earlier academic reform projects: the Catala Project (2005, named after its initiator, Prof Pierre Catala) and the Terré project (2011, named after its initiator, Prof François Terré). On the issue of contractual liability, the draft reform project draws heavily on the Catala Project, which also purports to regulate civil liability in general and sets out general rules common to tort and contract, which are followed by tort-specific rules and contract-specific rules. The Terré project, on the other hand, sharply distinguishes tort liability and liability in contract.

9 Arts 1231–1231-7 new Civil Code.

10 There are of course some exceptions: cf contracts for the benefit of third parties (*stipulation pour autrui*).

the parties may not have wanted or even considered, but which they are not free to set aside: many contract-born obligations have, therefore, not been voluntarily assumed by the parties. The fact remains, however, that entering into the contract remains an act of free will, even if some individual obligations that result from it have not been desired or even known by the parties. It is, therefore, not altogether false to link contract with the intention to assume obligations, and not tort.

B. EXISTENCE OF A 'GREY ZONE'?

There is officially no grey zone between contract and tort, in the sense that any obligation to compensate arises necessarily either out of a tort or out of the breach of a contract.[11] In contrast to some other legal systems, French law does not recognise a third order of liability, such as liability based on a breach of confidence (*Vertrauenshaftung*). 6

The fact remains, however, that it is difficult to ascribe some cases of liability to either tort or contract. In particular, in the case of *culpa in contrahendo*,[12] liability is sometimes presented by the courts as being in contract, and sometimes as being in tort.[13] But the uncertainty carries hardly any consequences with it, since there is no difference between contract and tort in such circumstances: liability for *culpa in contrahendo* is always fault-based,[14] pure economic loss can be compensated whatever the nature of liability,[15] and a defendant cannot exonerate himself in tort by demonstrating that it was his auxiliary who was at fault and that he himself had not been at fault in choosing or monitoring him. 7

---

11 French law distinguishes 'civil liability' (*responsabilité civile*), which encompasses tort and any liability arising out of contract, and which is borne by private persons, from administrative liability (*responsabilité administrative*), which is the liability of the State and public bodies. The specificity of administrative liability does not lie in the specificity of the facts that give rise to it (and which is usually either a tort or a breach of contract), however, but in the identity of the person liable.

12 The expression *culpa in contrahendo* is actually seldom used in France. Lawyers usually speak of *faute précontractuelle*, the most common occurrence of which is the violation of a duty to inform or to advise the other party.

13 Contrary to the old Civil Code, the new Code explicitly deals with pre-contractual liability (see arts 1212–1212-2), basically confirming the solutions developed by case law, but remains silent on its nature.

14 Even if the appreciation of fault can be very harsh for defendants.

15 This does not mean, however, that the expectation interest will be compensated in the case of *culpa in contrahendo*. In line with pre-existing case law, the reform of French contract law has confirmed that: 'In the case of fault committed during the negotiations, the reparation of the resulting loss is not calculated so as to compensate the loss of benefits which were expected from the contract that was not concluded' (art 1112 al 2).

8 Some scholars have also suggested that the existence of a third type of liability, professional liability, should be recognised alongside liability in tort and liability in contract.[16] They argue that the liability of professionals is sometimes quite independent from any contractual link they may have to the claimant and, therefore, should fall outside the two traditional categories of civil liability. This argument might be difficult to understand if one does not have in mind the French *non-cumul* rule, whereby tort liability cannot apply whenever a contractual relationship exists between the parties and damage bears some relation to this relation; as a result, the nature of the liability of a professional will vary depending on the existence of a contract between the latter and the claimant, even when damage was only caused *on the occasion of* the execution of the contract, and not as the result of the breach of an essential obligation created by the contract.[17] The recognition of a new type of liability – professional liability – alongside liability in tort and liability in contract, would thus be a way of avoiding differences of treatment between claimants, in cases in which they appear not to be justified.

9 So far, however, the idea of such a professional liability has not really developed in legislation or in court practice. Admittedly, some liability regimes have been created, which apply regardless of the existence of a contractual relationship between the parties.[18] But liability under these regimes is regarded as being in tort.[19] They thus do not incarnate a new brand of liability, professional liability, but rather constitute exceptions to the traditional *non-cumul* rule.[20]

C. COMMON OR DIFFERENT RULES REGULATING TORT AND CONTRACT

10 The Civil Code provides for no specific rules regulating both liability in tort and liability in contract. There are of course rules common to all types of obligations,

---

16 *P Serlooten*, Vers une responsabilité professionnelle ?, in: Mélanges offerts à Pierre Hébraud (1981) 805–822; *G Viney*, Introduction à la responsabilité (3rd edn 2008) 661–667.

17 This will be the case, for example, when the professional negligently injures the client in the course of the execution of the contract, even if the purpose of the contract has nothing to do with the preservation of the client's bodily integrity.

18 There are mainly two such regimes: liability for traffic accidents, created by a statute of 5 July 1985, and liability for defective products, deriving from the European Directive of 25 July 1985, which was implemented in the Civil Code (previously art 1386-1 ff, now art 1245 ff) by a statute of 19 May 1998.

19 The issue is actually debated as far as product liability is concerned. Some authors argue that this liability may be based in tort or in contract, depending on the existence or absence of a contract between the parties. Nobody contends, however, that product liability would not fall into one of these two categories.

20 See below sec IV.

like in all continental civil codes,[21] but there is no 'general part' on liability which would encompass liability in tort and in contract. Only one exception can be mentioned, which dates back to the 2008 reform of the law of prescription: under art 2226 of the Civil Code, a 10-year prescription period applies to claims for compensation arising out of personal injuries, regardless of the nature of liability (the normal prescription period being five years: art 2224).

In practice, however, the courts tend to apply the same rules to certain aspects of 11
tort liability and contractual liability.

As far as damage is concerned, art 1231-2 (formerly art 1149) of the Civil 12
Code, which normally applies to contractual damages, provides: 'In general, damages due to the creditor are for the loss that he has incurred or the gain of which he has been deprived'.[22] This principle, according to which the defendant must compensate the loss suffered by the plaintiff as well as the lost profit ('*la perte faite et le gain manqué*'), is also applied in tort.

As far as causation is concerned, when consequential damage questions are 13
raised in the context of breach of contract, courts normally apply the same rules as in tort. These rules are judge-made, however, and are quite fluid.

As far as the damaging act (*fait générateur*) is concerned, there is normally a 14
sharp distinction between contract and tort. There is a tendency, however, both among scholars and in case law, to define breach of contract as *faute contractuelle* ('contractual fault') and to regard this fault as the equivalent of *faute délictuelle*, ie the type of fault that gives rise to liability in tort under art 1240 (formerly art 1382) of the Civil Code.

The draft reform project of civil liability law suggests a substantial change 15
in that respect. As explained earlier, it encompasses both liability in tort and in contract and intends to submit both of them to a certain number of common rules, which would cover the definition of damage,[23] causation,[24] and the 'effects' of liability,[25] ie the rules pertaining to compensation. Only the 'damaging acts' would be regulated separately,[26] as well as some defences,[27] and conventions pertaining to liability.[28]

---

21 Rules on the payment of obligations, for example.

22 Unless otherwise stated, in this report all English translations of the former or unmodified *Code civil* provisions are borrowed from the *Code civil* in English on the web site <legifrance.gouv. fr> (updated in September 2014, ed by Alain Levasseur, David Grunning and Randy Trahan). Translations of the new provisions of the Code are borrowed from the translation of ordonnance no 2016-131 of 10 February 2016 by J Cartwright, B Fauvarque-Cosson and S Whittaker.

23 Arts 1235–1238 *Projet*.

24 Arts 1239–1240 *Projet*.

25 Arts 1258–1280 *Projet*.

26 Arts 1241–1252 *Projet*.

27 Art 1253 *Projet*.

28 Arts 1282–1284 *Projet*.

D. APPLICATION OF COMMON RULES IN A DIFFERENT WAY

16 Since there are no legislative rules that are common to tort and contract, this question is not really applicable in the French context.[29] Besides, judge-made rules are too fluid to allow for the identification of clear differences in the way they are applied in tort or in contract.

II. MAIN DIFFERENCES BETWEEN TORTIOUS AND CONTRACTUAL LIABILITY

A. DIFFERENCES AS REGARDS THE FOUNDATIONS OF LIABILITY

17 Tortious liability in French law can be either based on fault (now art 1240 *Code civil* and formerly art 1382)[30] or strict. Many strict liability regimes have been created by the legislator or developed by the courts since the end of the 19th century. In practice, strict liability plays a great role in modern French tort law.

18 When liability for fault applies, the intensity of fault is normally irrelevant. The slightest fault is enough to give rise to liability if it caused damage. Besides, fault is a purely objective notion and is assessed against the standard of a reasonable adult person. Infants and mentally disabled persons can therefore be held liable in tort on the basis of fault if their behaviour was negligent in comparison to the behaviour of a reasonable adult person in similar circumstances.

19 French law ignores the distinction between wrongfulness and fault; or, rather, fault is regarded as boiling down to wrongfulness, the latter being defined as the violation of a statutory duty or the general duty to act with reasonable care.

20 Liability in contract is based on art 1231 ff (formerly art 1146 ff) *Code civil*. In the system of the Code, this liability is independent from the debtor's fault. Article 1231-1 (formerly art 1147) provides: 'A debtor is condemned, where appropriate, to the payment of damages either on the ground of the non-performance or a delay in performance of an obligation, unless he justifies

---

[29] The only exception is the prescription rule in the case of personal injury, but there are no cases so far that would suggest that this rule is applied differently depending on the tortious or contractual context.

[30] 'Tout fait quelconque de l'homme, qui cause à autrui un dommage, oblige celui par la faute duquel il est arrivé à le réparer.' ('Every act whatever of man that causes damage to another obliges him by whose fault it occurred to repair it.')

this on the ground that performance was prevented by force majeure.'[31] In the 20th century, however, under the influence of authors such as René Demogue († 1938), the courts developed the well-known distinction between *obligations de résultat* and *obligations de moyens*. Under this distinction, art 1231-1 should apply only to *obligations de résultat*, whereas a creditor could claim damages for breach of an *obligation de moyens* only if he demonstrates that the debtor was at fault. This distinction is actually extremely debatable and, in practice, it is mostly used in connection with so-called *obligations de sécurité*, which are secondary contractual obligations, whereby the debtor is bound to protect the creditor's physical security during the execution of the contract. 'Main' contractual obligations are most often regarded as *obligations de résultat*. Liability arising out of their breach can therefore be regarded as strict.[32]

However, when the result to which the creditor is entitled consists in the debtor behaving in a manner that must meet a certain standard, strict liability arising out of the non-fulfilment of the contract comes very close to liability for fault, as this non-fulfilment constitutes sub-standard behaviour. This is typically the case for a contract concluded between a doctor and a patient:[33] the patient is entitled to receive from the doctor 'careful and up-to-date medical care', and medical care not meeting this standard can be regarded both as a non-fulfilment of the doctor's contractual obligation and as a fault. But when the debtor is under an obligation to perform a certain act and to behave in a certain way, the standard which this behaviour must meet is normally an objective one.[34] 21

31 'Le débiteur est condamné, s'il y a lieu, au paiement de dommages et intérêts, soit à raison de l'inexécution de l'obligation, soit à raison du retard dans l'exécution, s'il ne justifie pas que l'inexécution a été empêchée par la force majeure.' The drafting of this provision is slightly different from that of former art 1147, but the substance has remained the same.

32 It should be noted that the distinction between *obligations de résultat* and *obligations de moyens* has not been introduced into the new Civil Code, and is also absent from the draft reform project of civil liability law.

33 Following the famous *Mercier* case (Cour de cassation, chambre civile, 20 May 1936, D 1936, 1, 88 conclusions Matter, report Josserand), medical liability used to be regarded as being in contract. The Cour de cassation apparently changed its position a few years ago and now regards it as being in tort: Cour de cassation, première chambre civile (Cass civ 1), 3 June 2010, no 09-13591, D 2010, 1522, note *P Sargos*.

34 See for instance former art 1137 of the Civil Code: 'L'obligation de veiller à la conservation de la chose, soit que la convention n'ait pour objet que l'utilité de l'une des parties, soit qu'elle ait pour objet leur utilité commune, soumet celui qui en est chargé à y apporter tous les soins d'un bon père de famille' ('The obligation to look after a thing, whether the agreement is for the benefit of one party only or for their common benefit, compels the one in charge to bring to it all the care of a prudent administrator'). This provision has been replaced by the new art 1197: 'L'obligation de délivrer la chose emporte obligation de la conserver jusqu'à la délivrance, en y apportant tous les soins d'une personne raisonnable' ('An obligation to deliver a thing entails an obligation to look after it until delivery, taking all the care of a reasonable person in doing so').

If this standard has not been met, the debtor owes damages to the creditor, regardless of his personal aptitudes or state of mind. Negligence or intention on his part, for example, need not be proven. It is only in exceptional cases that the *Code civil* provides that the debtor should be held not to an objective standard of care, but to the same standard of care as the one he applies to his own business.[35]

22 Quite independently from the distinction between *obligations de résultat* and *obligations de moyens*, French contract law does attach some importance to the debtor's fault under certain circumstances. In some contracts, first of all, the debtor only answers for his fault, and sometimes his *faute qualifiée*, ie a fault of particular intensity.[36] Besides, former art 1150 provided that when breach of contract is the result of the debtor's *dol*, ie intentional fault, unforeseeable damage resulting from the breach of contract becomes recoverable.[37] Case law has extended this rule in two directions. First of all, *faute lourde*, ie gross negligence,[38] is regarded as having the same effects as *dol*. Secondly, both *dol* and *faute lourde* render contract terms aimed at limiting damages ineffective. The recent reform of French contract law has confirmed the assimilation of *faute lourde* to *dol* as far as the compensation of unforeseen damage is concerned (art 1231-3 *Code civil*).

B. DIFFERENCES AS REGARDS CAUSATION

23 In tort law, causation between the damaging act (*fait générateur*) and damage must be direct and certain. Although French law does not recognise the difference between cause in fact and cause in law, the requirement that causation be certain is not unlike the test of cause in fact, whereas the requirement that causation be direct is a way of selecting the legal cause of damage among all its

35 See eg art 1927 of the Civil Code: 'A depositary must bring the same care in the custody of the thing deposited as he does in the custody of the things which belong to him.'

36 See eg art 1992, al 2 of the Civil Code on *mandat*, which provides that a principal's agent should be held to a lower standard of care when he acts for free than when he receives a salary. In an employment contract (*contrat de travail*), the worker can be made liable to his employer for breach of contract only if this breach is the result of gross negligence equating to intentional fault (*faute lourde équipollente au dol*): Cour de cassation, chambre sociale (Cass soc), 27 November 1958, D 1959, 20, note *R Lindon*.

37 See below sec II.B.

38 French courts define *faute lourde* as an extremely serious behaviour, which borders on *dol* and betrays the debtor's inaptitude to fulfil the contractual task he had accepted ('un comportement d'une extrême gravité, confinant au dol et dénotant l'inaptitude du débiteur de l'obligation à l'accomplissement de la mission contractuelle qu'il avait acceptée'): see Cass civ 1, 29 October 2014, no 13-21.980.

antecedents. In practice, however, French courts can be quite plaintiff-friendly when it comes to assessing causation, and the requirement of a *cause direct* is not as selective as the cause in law test in some other legal systems. Besides, French law has no equivalent of those instruments that are used in some countries to limit the scope of liability, such as *Schutzzweck der Norm* or *relativité aquilienne*.

In contract law, art 1231-3 (formerly 1150) *Code civil* provides that only damage foreseeable at the time of the conclusion of the contract must be compensated in the case of breach of contract: 'A debtor is bound only to damages which were either foreseen or which could have been foreseen at the time of conclusion of the contract, except where non-performance was due to a gross or dishonest fault [*dol* or *faute lourde*]'. The requirement that damage be foreseeable is not regarded by French lawyers as pertaining to causation, however, but to the definition of compensable damage. Speaking of it, they would therefore not describe it as a test for causation. 24

Furthermore, when physical injury results from a breach of contract, courts tend to lay the foreseeable damage test aside and differences between liability in tort and liability in contract are then hard to see; this is especially true in the field of medical liability, which is often contractual under French law, but to which art 1150 has never been applied. 25

When the breach of contract is the result of the debtor's *faute lourde*, the limitation of damages to foreseeable damage does not apply and the debtor must then compensate any damage that is a direct consequence of the breach (art 1231-4, formerly art 1151 *Code civil*); it is thus the same rule as in tort that applies. 26

C. DIFFERENCES AS REGARDS REMEDIES

All types of damage are normally compensable, both in tort and in contract. The rule applies to non-pecuniary loss, to loss of earnings and loss of chance, as well as to pure economic loss.[39] 27

Restitutionary damages, as well as aggravated and exemplary damages, are normally prohibited in tort law. This is seen as a consequence of the 'full compensation principle' (*principe de la réparation intégrale*), whereby the plaintiff must be compensated for his full damage, but not in excess of it. There are a 28

39 See above sec I.C on the applicability both in tort and in contract of art 1149, which provides that the defendant must compensate the loss suffered by the plaintiff as well the lost profit (*la perte faite et le gain manqué*).

few legislative exceptions to this principle, but they remain of limited scope and importance.[40] Besides, the parties are not allowed to organise in advance by contract any liability in tort that may arise between them. They cannot therefore contract out of the full compensation principle in the field of tort.[41]

29 In contract law, the full compensation principle applies (subject to the foreseeable damage limit), but the parties are allowed to contract out of it. They can do so by a *clause limitative ou exclusive de responsabilité*, whereby a party restricts or suppresses in advance his liability in the case of a breach of contract. The legislator and the courts monitor these terms quite strictly, however, and they are sometimes illegal, especially when they purport to reduce or exclude compensation in the case of physical injury.

30 *Clauses pénales* are another exception to the full compensation principle in contract law. Such terms, which are usually considered equivalent to penalty clauses under common law, are clauses which set in advance the amount of damages due should a party to a contract breach its terms. They bear some resemblance to punitive damages, since they can result in a debtor paying damages in excess of the harm he caused. Besides, such clauses are very often intended to punish the debtor should he fail to fulfil his duties, just like punitive damages. *Clauses pénales* are valid under French law, but only in contract law. The first paragraph of art 1231-5 (formerly art 1152) of the Civil Code sets this out: 'Where a contract stipulates that the person who fails to perform shall pay a certain sum of money by way of damages, the other party may be awarded neither a higher nor a lower sum'. As some creditors imposed excessive *clauses pénales* on their debtors in the past, in 1975 the legislator decided to provide an exception to the sanctity of contract rule, which is now to be found in the second paragraph of art 1235-2: 'Nevertheless, a court may, even of its own initiative, moderate or increase the penalty so agreed if it is manifestly excessive or derisory'. Courts regularly do resort to this rule, but mostly in order to moderate excessive penalties, in which case they are not allowed to award the creditor less than the amount of the loss which he actually suffered. Moreover, when the courts do increase penalties which are ridiculously low, they cannot set them at a level which would exceed the loss suffered by the plaintiff.

31 In the field of contract law, remedies other than damages are normally applicable, such as specific performance or termination of contract. Contractual

---

40 See especially art L331-1-3 *Code de la propriété intellectuelle*, which provides for the possibility of punitive damages in the case of counterfeiting (see on the issue, in English, *J-S Borghetti*, Punitive Damages in France, in: H Koziol/V Wilcox (eds), Punitive Damages: Common Law and Civil Law Perspectives (2009) 55–73).

41 The *Projet* wants to authorise contracts that limit in advance liability in tort, provided the latter is not based on fault and the contract does not cover liability for personal injuries; see arts 1281 and 1282.

remedies can be cumulated if they are not incompatible.[42] Some of these alternative remedies make no sense in tort law. It is accepted, however, that non-pecuniary compensation can apply outside the field of contract. It can consist in the restitution of a stolen or destroyed object, for example. In practice, non-pecuniary compensation seems to be most frequent in cases of privacy infringements, and can consist, for example, in the publication of an official statement in a newspaper that the defendant breached the law. An injunction is also a remedy that can be available in tort as in contract.

When the debtor's contractual obligation consists in an abstention, the judge can issue an injunction against him that he should stop acting in violation of his obligation. The new art 1222 further provides: 'Having given notice to perform, a creditor may also himself, within a reasonable time and at a reasonable cost, have an obligation performed or, with the prior authorisation of the court, may have something which has been done in breach of an obligation destroyed. He may claim reimbursement of sums of money employed for this purpose from the debtor'.[43] Outside the field of contract, although there is no general legislative provision on this issue, it is now generally accepted that the judge can issue an injunction against a defendant that he should abstain from conduct in which he has engaged, or undo what he has done, if this conduct or action is contrary to law and creates a risk of damage for the plaintiff.[44] 32

D. DIFFERENCES AS REGARDS RECOVERABILITY OF 'PURE ECONOMIC LOSSES'

French law ignores the concept of pure economic loss and this type of damage is normally recoverable both under contract law and under tort law, under the full compensation principle. 33

---

42 See new art 1217 *Code civil*: 'La partie envers laquelle l'engagement n'a pas été exécuté, ou l'a été imparfaitement, peut: – refuser d'exécuter ou suspendre l'exécution de sa propre obligation; – poursuivre l'exécution forcée en nature de l'obligation; – solliciter une réduction du prix; – provoquer la résolution du contrat; – demander réparation des conséquences de l'inexécution. Les sanctions qui ne sont pas incompatibles peuvent être cumulées; des dommages et intérêts peuvent toujours s'y ajouter' ('A party towards whom an undertaking has not been performed or has been performed imperfectly, may: – refuse to perform or suspend performance of his own obligations; – seek enforced performance in kind of the undertaking; – request a reduction in price; – provoke the termination of the contract; – claim reparation of the consequences of non-performance. Sanctions which are not incompatible may be combined; damages may always be added to any of the others').

43 'Après mise en demeure, le créancier peut aussi, dans un délai et à un coût raisonnables, faire exécuter lui-même l'obligation ou, sur autorisation préalable du juge, détruire ce qui a été fait en violation de celle-ci. Il peut demander au débiteur le remboursement des sommes engagées à cette fin'.

44 The *Projet* purports to introduce an injunction as a remedy in tort: see art 1266.

E. DIFFERENCES AS REGARDS LIABILITY FOR OTHERS

34 French tort law recognises several cases of liability for others: liability of parents for their children (art 1242 al 4, formerly art 1384 al 4 of the Civil Code), liability of principals for their agents (art 1242 al 5, formerly 1384 al 5 of the Civil Code), etc. In the field of contract law, on the other hand, the concept of liability for others is usually regarded as useless. The question, as a matter of fact, is not who was in breach of the contract, but only whether the debtor should answer for that breach. And the answer, under art 1231-1 Civil Code, is that the debtor should answer for any breach unless he can prove that it was due to force majeure. The mere fact that the debtor did not fulfil the contract himself and that it was thus not he personally who failed to fulfil it correctly is of course not an excuse, and the implication of a third party in the fulfilment of the contract, at the request of the debtor, cannot qualify as force majeure.

1) *Liability for Auxiliaries and for Independent Contractors*

35 In practice, a substantial difference between contract and tort as far as liability for others is concerned relates to damage caused by a contractor. In tort, he who *employs* someone is liable for any damage caused by this person's fault in the course of the performance of his task, under art 1242 al 4 of the Civil Code; but he who contracts with an independent contractor to have the latter do work for him will normally not answer for this person's fault in tort. The reason for this discrepancy is that the employee is regarded as an agent (*préposé*), because he is subordinated to his employer, whereas the contractor retains his independence and is thus not an agent. In contract, on the other hand, the debtor answers for any breach materially committed by the person to whom he entrusted the fulfilment of the contract, regardless of whether this person is an employee, an independent contractor, etc.

2) *Liability for Legal Representatives or Organs of a Company*

36 Liability for legal representatives or organs of a company is a tort law question and is hardly ever mentioned in a contractual context. Once again, the identity of the person who materially (mis)performs the contract, and who may or may not be a legal representative of the debtor company, is normally irrelevant.

3) *Liability of Representatives of Natural Persons*

37 Liability of representatives of natural persons (eg parents for their children) is also a typical tort law question and is normally not an issue in a contractual

context. It must be noted, however, that, as a result of the *non-cumul* rule,[45] liability in contract under French law normally includes not only liability arising out of the non- or misperformance of the contract, but also liability for damage arising in the course of the contract. In specific cases, the Civil Code provides that a party to an agreement must answer in contract not only for damage he personally caused to the other party in the course of the contract, but also for damage caused by his relatives, including his child. The best example is art 1735, on lease contracts, which provides: 'A lessee is responsible for the deteriorations and losses that occur on account of the act of persons of his household or of his sub-lessees'.[46]

4) *Liability of the Auxiliary/Organ Itself*

Liability of the auxiliary/organ itself to the contractual partner of the person or entity for whom he acted can only be in tort, as the auxiliary or organ normally has no contractual relationship to that contractual partner. The auxiliary or organ will thus normally answer for damage caused to that contractual partner through his fault, under art 1240 of the Civil Code. If the defendant is an agent of the contractual partner, however, he will be immune from any liability for his fault, provided he did not act outside the scope of the task entrusted to him and his fault was neither intentional, ie committed with an intention to cause harm, nor a criminal offence.[47] Another exception to the rule of art 1240 applies when the defendant is a representative or an organ of a company. In that case, he only answers to third parties if he committed a fault that can be 'separated from his functions' (*une faute séparable des fonctions*).[48] In practice, such a fault is difficult to prove. 38

The auxiliary or organ can also be liable to his principal or to the entity he represents if his fault has resulted in the principal or entity being in breach of their contractual obligations. When the defendant is an employee, however, the rules of labour law provide that the he can only be liable to his employer if his fault consisted in 'gross negligence equating to intentional fault' (*faute lourde équipollente au dol*).[49] 39

---

45 See below sec IV.

46 'Le preneur est tenu des dégradations et des pertes qui arrivent par le fait des personnes de sa maison ou de ses sous-locataires.'

47 The solution has been established by Cour de cassation, assemblée plénière (Cass ass plén), 25 February 2000, 97-17378 and 97-20152, JCP G, 2000, II, 10295, concl *R Kessous*, note *M Billiau*, ibid I, 241, no 16, obs *G Viney*, RTD civ 2000, 582, obs *P Jourdain*, D 2000, jur 673, note *P Brun*.

48 Cour de cassation, chambre commerciale (Cass com), 20 May 2003, 99-17.092.

49 Cass soc, 27 November 1958, D 1959, 20, note *R Lindon*.

F. DIFFERENCES AS REGARDS LIABILITY IN THE CASE OF MULTIPLE TORTFEASORS/BREACHING PARTIES

40 In tort law, multiple tortfeasors are jointly and severally liable.[50] In contract law, the default rule is that multiple debtors are severally bound to the creditor.[51] This rule applies first of all to claims for the performance of the contract, but it is suggested that it should also apply to liability claims based on breach of contract, even though the issue does not seem to have come before the courts often. In other words, if each party in breach was only bound to fulfil his own part of the obligation, and not the full obligation, then he should answer only for the violation of his part of the obligation. On the other hand, if the breaching parties were solidarily bound to the creditor, ie if the creditor could require the complete fulfilment of the obligation from any one of them, then the breaching parties (and even non-breaching solidary debtors, as the case may be) should be jointly and severally liable to the creditor.[52]

G. DIFFERENCES AS REGARDS THE PERSONS WHO MAY BE PROTECTED

41 Under tort law, any person who suffered damage as a direct consequence of a damaging act (*fait générateur*) is entitled to claim damages. The requirement that the damage be direct is understood rather laxly by case law and it has been admitted for a very long time that persons suffering damage as a consequence of somebody else's damage may claim compensation from the person who must answer for the damaging act that caused that other person's damage. These indirect or secondary victims are called *victimes par ricochet*. According to the very general statements that are to be found in French case law, a *victime par ricochet* may be anyone suffering damage as a consequence of somebody else's damage, and he need not be a relative, for example; besides, he may claim compensation for any type of damage he personally suffered, as is normally the case in French law. In practice, however, *victimes par ricochet* who claim and obtain compensation are almost always relatives of the direct victim, who suffer financial loss and/or pain and suffering due to the latter's death or injury. Courts tend to reject claims for financial loss brought by the direct victim's economic partner, but they usually do so on the not very convincing basis that damage is not then a direct consequence of the damaging act.

---

50 In the case of multiple tortfeasors, French law actually draws a subtle distinction between *responsabilité solidaire* and *responsabilité in solidum*. They are very close to each other, however, and both substantially amount to joint and several liability.

51 Art 1309 (formerly art 1202) of the Civil Code.

52 This has now been confirmed by art 1319 of the Civil Code.

On the other hand, only parties to the contract can normally claim damages in contract for the breach of the contract. It is the privity of contract rule, which derives from art 1199 (formerly art 1165) of the Civil Code. There are several exceptions to that rule under French law, however. 42

A well-known exception concerns chains of contracts, whereby ownership of a good is transferred through several contracts successively. In such cases, when the good sold proves to be defective, any buyer has an action in contract against any seller higher up the chain of contracts. 43

A more recent and practically important exception to privity of contract results from a 2006 decision of the Cour de cassation, France's highest court in civil matters.[53] On that occasion, the court ruled that 'a third party to a contract may, on the basis of delictual liability, invoke a breach of contract whenever this breach has caused him harm'.[54] In effect, this rule 'kills' privity of contract in many cases. The liability it creates, however, is in tort and not in contract. 44

H. DIFFERENCES AS REGARDS DEFENCES

In French tort law, a distinction is usually made between *faits justificatifs* (grounds of justification) and *causes d'exonération* (exoneration causes). Both can be regarded as defences, however. *Faits justificatifs* are facts which suppress the wrongfulness of acts that would otherwise be tortious, and thus prevent their author from being made liable in the first place. The Penal Code provides a list of *faits justificatifs* at art L122-3 ff, which are also regarded as applicable in tort law.[55] The one which seems to be the most commonly relied on is self-defence (*légitime défense*). *Causes d'exonération*, on the other hand, do not suppress the wrongfulness of the damaging act, but they result in the defendant not being liable, even though the normal conditions of his being liable were met. Each liability regime has its own *causes d'exonération*.[56] *Causes d'exonération* under the liability for things regime (art 1242 al 1, formerly art 1384 al 1 *Code civil*), 45

---

[53] Cass ass plén, 6 October 2006, *Myr'Ho*, Bull ass plén, no 9, D 2006, 2825, note *G Viney*, JCP 2006, II, 10181, avis *Gariazzo* and note *M Billiau*, RTD civ 2007, 123, obs *P Jourdain*: 'le tiers à un contrat peut invoquer, sur le fondement de la responsabilité délictuelle, un manquement contractuel dès lors que ce manquement lui a causé un dommage'.

[54] On this subject, see *J-S Borghetti*, Breach of contract and liability to third parties in French law: how to break deadlock?, ZEuP 2 (2010) 279–303.

[55] The only exception is the so-called 'statutory authorisation' (*autorisation de la loi*; art L122-4 al 1 of the Penal Code), whereby there can be no criminal liability arising out of an act authorised by statute. Statutory authorisation does not necessarily suppress tortious liability.

[56] This, however, is not made clear in the draft reform project, whose presentation suggests that most defences are common to all hypotheses of liability; see arts 1253–1257.

for example, are not the same as those under the traffic accident liability regime or the product liability regime. Force majeure is often presented as a general *cause d'exonération* in French tort law, but it actually only applies in some strict liability regimes, mostly liability for things. Contributory negligence, however, is almost always a *cause d'exonération*, except in some extra strict liability regimes.[57] There is no clear rule on how to measure the reduction of the defendant's liability due to the plaintiff's contributory fault, and this question is basically abandoned to the lower judges' discretion. The only limit to this discretion is that the plaintiff's contributory fault can fully exclude the defendant's liability only when this fault qualifies as force majeure vis-à-vis the defendant.

46 In contract law, under art 1231-1 *Code civil*, the debtor can only escape liability for breach of contract if he proves that the breach was excusable, ie that it was caused by force majeure. Force majeure traditionally received the same definition in tort and in contract law, although it is debatable if it is really the same thing in both contexts. The recent reform of contract law has conveniently given a definition of force majeure, at art 1218 al 1 *Code civil*, which only applies to contract law: 'In contractual matters, there is force majeure where an event beyond the control of the debtor, which could not reasonably have been foreseen at the time of the conclusion of the contract and whose effects could not be avoided by appropriate measures, prevents performance of his obligation by the debtor'.[58] Under certain specific provisions, in the case of a breach of contract, it will be enough for the debtor to demonstrate that he was not at fault in order to escape liability for breach.[59]

47 The Civil Code does not mention contributory negligence in the contractual context, but it has long been accepted that the creditor's contributory fault reduces the debtor's liability. The rules that apply to contributory negligence in contract are not clearly defined by the courts, but they appear to be substantially the same as in tort law: lower judges therefore enjoy considerable discretion in measuring to what extent the creditor's fault reduces his right to be compensated. Grounds of justification, on the other hand, never seem to apply in contract.

---

57 Under the traffic accidents liability regime, the victim's contributory negligence hardly ever exonerates the defendant at all when the victim was not a driver.

58 'Il y a force majeure en matière contractuelle lorsqu'un événement échappant au contrôle du débiteur, qui ne pouvait être raisonnablement prévu lors de la conclusion du contrat et dont les effets ne peuvent être évités par des mesures appropriées, empêche l'exécution de son obligation par le débiteur'. Art 1253 al 2 *Projet* confirms that force majeure should be defined differently in tort law.

59 See eg art 1732 of the Civil Code, pertaining to the lessee's situation in a lease contract: 'He is answerable for the deteriorations or losses occurring during his enjoyment, unless he proves that they did not occur through any fault of his.'

I. DIFFERENCES AS REGARDS LIMITATION PERIODS

Until a 2008 statute reforming limitation periods, these periods used to be different in tort law (10 years) and contract law (30 years). Limitation periods have now been harmonised and depend on the type of harm for which compensation is claimed. The normal period is five years (art 2224 of the Civil Code), but a 10-year period applies in the case of personal injury (art 2226 al 1 of the Civil Code). 48

Besides, special rules apply to some tortious liability regimes (eg product liability) as well as to certain contracts (see eg art L133-6 Commercial Code, the transportation contract). 49

In tort as in contract, the prescription period normally starts to run 'from the day the holder of a right knew or should have known the facts enabling him to exercise his right.'[60] In practice, however, this rule is often paralysed by other rules that either set another starting point or postpone the starting point. In case of personal injuries, the 10-year prescription period starts to run 'from the date of the consolidation of the initial or of the aggravated injury.'[61] Besides, art 2234 of the Civil Code provides that 'prescription does not run or is suspended against one for whom it is impossible to act following an obstacle resulting from the law, from an agreement, or from force majeure.'[62] Article 2233 further provides that, as a rule, prescription 'does not run or is suspended against unemancipated minors or adults in tutorship'.[63] All these rules are also common to contract and tort. 50

The 2008 reform of prescription also generalised the long-stop mechanism, which used to be unknown in French law but was initially introduced by international legal instruments, including the 1985 Directive on Product Liability. Under art 2232 of the Civil Code, 'the deferral of the starting point, the suspension or the interruption of the prescription cannot have the effect of extending the period of the extinctive prescription beyond twenty years 51

60 Art 2224 of the Civil Code: 'Les actions personnelles ou mobilières se prescrivent par cinq ans à compter du jour où le titulaire d'un droit a connu ou aurait dû connaître les faits lui permettant de l'exercer.'

61 Art 2226 al 1 of the Civil Code: 'L'action en responsabilité née à raison d'un événement ayant entraîné un dommage corporel, engagée par la victime directe ou indirecte des préjudices qui en résultent, se prescrit par dix ans à compter de la date de la consolidation du dommage initial ou aggravé.'

62 'La prescription ne court pas ou est suspendue contre celui qui est dans l'impossibilité d'agir par suite d'un empêchement résultant de la loi, de la convention ou de la force majeure.'

63 'Elle ne court pas ou est suspendue contre les mineurs non émancipés et les majeurs en tutelle, sauf pour les actions en paiement ou en répétition des salaires, arrérages de rente, pensions alimentaires, loyers, fermages, charges locatives, intérêts des sommes prêtées et, généralement, les actions en paiement de tout ce qui est payable par années ou à des termes périodiques plus courts.'

from the day of the birth of the right'.[64] This long-stop applies both to claims in contract and to claims in tort. The *Code civil* excludes its application in certain circumstances, however. One of them is when the plaintiff claims damages for personal injury (regardless of whether his claim is in tort or in contract).

J. DIFFERENCES AS REGARDS PROOF

52 The burden of proof normally lies on the party claiming damages, regardless of whether the claim is brought in tort or in contract. This is a consequence of a basic procedural rule: 'Each party must prove, according to the law, the facts necessary for the success of his claim' (art 9 *Code de procédure civile*).

53 In order to be awarded damages under tort law, a plaintiff must prove damage, the existence of a damaging act (*fait générateur*) and causation.

54 In contract law, it is normally for the debtor to prove that he performed his obligation.[65] However, when the creditor contends that the debtor did not perform correctly, as is often the case, he, as plaintiff, must normally prove a breach of contract and his ensuing damage in order to be awarded damages.[66] Besides, there is some controversy on how breach of contract should be proven. The Civil Code suggested that a formal notice to the debtor (*mise en demeure*) was requested before damages could be claimed (former art 1146). Such a formal notice characterises the breach of the contract and the creditor can then claim damages if he demonstrates ensuing damage, without having to bring other elements to prove that breach. It is accepted, however, that no formal notice is required for an action in damages when the creditor can prove the breach of contract through other means. This has been basically confirmed by the recent reform of contract law.[67] In practice, the requirement of a formal notice

---

[64] Art 2232 al 1: 'Le report du point de départ, la suspension ou l'interruption de la prescription ne peut avoir pour effet de porter le délai de la prescription extinctive au-delà de vingt ans à compter du jour de la naissance du droit.'

[65] Art 1353 al 2 (formerly art 1315 al 2) *Code civil*: 'celui qui se prétend libéré doit justifier le paiement ou le fait qui a produit l'extinction de son obligation' ('a person who claims to have been discharged must establish satisfaction or circumstances which have resulted in the extinction of the obligation').

[66] There used to be an exception, however. When the breach consisted in the violation of an obligation not to do something (*obligation de ne pas faire*), damage necessarily ensued, according to former art 1145 *Code civil*. Damage therefore did not have to be proven in such a case: it was enough to demonstrate breach of contract (even though it could be argued that the exact nature of damage still had to be proven, in order to assess the amount of damages). The recent reform of contract law, however, has removed this special rule.

[67] Art 1231: 'A moins que l'inexécution soit définitive, les dommages et intérêts ne sont dus que si le débiteur a préalablement été mis en demeure de s'exécuter dans un délai raisonnable' ('Unless non-performance is permanent, damages are due only if the debtor has previously been put on notice to perform his obligation within a reasonable time').

therefore plays a limited role in contract law, as far as claims for damages are concerned, and the difference from tort law is rather small on that count.

K. OTHER DIFFERENCES

It is necessary to be legally capable in order to enter into a contract under French law. The new art 1145 al 1 of the Civil Code provides that 'every natural person is able to conclude a contract, except in the case of lack of capacity provided for by legislation',[68] and new art 1146 immediately adds that minors, if not emancipated, and 'protected' adults are incapable of contracting.[69] Since 1974, the age of majority has been set at 18 years of age. Contracts concluded by persons who do not have the capacity to do so are not valid. Since liability in contract presupposes the existence of a valid contract, minors and 'protected' adults cannot normally be liable in contract. 55

Liability in tort, on the other hand, requires no specific capacity under French law. There is no such thing as 'delictual capacity' in the Civil Code. Besides, French law has adopted a purely objective conception of fault, whereby any behaviour falling below a reasonable standard of care constitutes fault, regardless of the particular abilities of the person who adopted that behaviour.[70] A three-year-old child can thus commit a fault and be held liable in tort if he acts in an unreasonably dangerous way, as compared to a reasonable adult. 56

There are some further differences between tort and contract law as far as rules of jurisdiction are concerned. The basic rule under French law is that 'the territorially competent court is, unless otherwise provided, that of the place where the defendant lives' (art 42, al 1 *Code de procécure civile*). Different subsidiary rules apply in tort and contract law, however. Article 46 *Code de procédure civile* provides: 'The plaintiff may bring his case, at his choosing, besides the court of the place where the defendant lives, before: in contractual matters, the court of the place of the actual delivery of the chattel or the place of performance of the agreed service; in tort matters, the court of the place of the event causing liability or the one in whose district the damage was suffered.' 57

There are no specific rules on the transfer of liability claims in the *Code civil*. The principle is that such claims are transferable, either voluntarily or at the death of their holder, just like any other asset. Case law apparently sets a limit 58

---

68 'Toute personne physique peut contracter sauf en cas d'incapacité prévue par la loi'.

69 'Sont incapables de contracter, dans la mesure définie par la loi : Les mineurs non émancipés; Les majeurs protégés au sens de l'article 425'.

70 See the leading case: Cass ass plén, 9 May 1984, Lemaire 80-93.031, Bull ass plén no 2, JCP éd G 1984.II.20256, note *P Jourdain*, D 1984, jur 525, concl *J Cabannes*, note *F Chabas*, Defrénois 1984, 557, note *D Legeais*, GAJC, no 193.

on the voluntary transfer of claims, however, and seems to consider that such a transfer is not possible for claims for the compensation of non-pecuniary damage.[71] There is no reason why this restriction should not apply to all liability claims, whether in tort or in contract. Previously, courts also refused to transfer claims aiming at the compensation of pain and suffering if the victim had not brought her claim before a court before her death, but the Cour de cassation lifted this restriction in 1976[72] and all liability claims are now transferred at the death of their holder, just like any other claim or asset.

59 There are also some differences between tortious and contractual liabilities in international private law.

L. REASONS FOR THE DIFFERENCES

60 There is an ongoing debate among French authors on the justification of the differences between liability in tort and liability in contract. Some authors rightly insist on the fact that, according to the *Code civil*, the first function of damages in contract is to provide the creditor with an equivalent of what he would have received if the contract had been fulfilled as promised.[73] Yet it cannot be denied that damages in contract now have other functions: the compensation of damage subsequent to the breach of contract (as distinct from the mere absence of what had been promised), as well as the compensation of damage caused on the occasion of the fulfilment of the contract.[74] These functions tend to blur the distinction between liability in contract and liability in tort, and they question the justification of the differences that exist between the two regimes. Those differences are on the wane, anyhow. One of the most important seems to be the limitation of compensation to foreseeable damage in contractual cases. This limitation is usually seen as a consequence of the nature of contract, which is basically a tool for anticipating. The 2006 rule on liability of debtors vis-à-vis third parties seriously questions the effectiveness of the foreseeability of damage rule, however.[75]

61 It could actually be said that the differences between liability in tort and liability in contract have grown too thin and that the current state of French law does not adequately reflect the fundamental difference between liability in tort and damages for breach of contract: the latter are a consequence of the

71 See eg Cass civ 1, 30 May 2006, Bull civ I, no 273.

72 Cour de cassation, chambre mixte, 30 April 1976, Bull civ no 2.

73 See foremost *P Remy*, La "responsabilité contractuelle", histoire d'un faux concept, RTD civ 1997, 323.

74 On this issue, see *J-S Borghetti*, Strict Liability in Tort and the Boundaries of Tort Law, in: Essays in Honour of Jaap Spier (2016) 19.

75 See above sec II.G.

violation of a pre-existing obligation, and result from a promised performance not having been fulfilled, whereas the former is a consequence of the wrongful disruption of an existing state of things.

Interestingly, the two doctrinal reform projects of the French law of obligations, which preceded the contract law reform and the draft reform bill on liability law, took quite opposing views on the difference between tortious and contractual liability. The *projet Catala* regarded them as having the same nature and deals with them in the same place, separately from the other contractual remedies. On the other hand, the *projet Terré* insisted on their being different and regulates damages in contract with the other remedies for breach of contract, while it deals separately with tort law. The Government's draft project clearly adopts the first approach, as explained above. 62

III. LIMITATION OR EXCLUSION OF LIABILITY ARISING FROM TORT AND FROM CONTRACT

A. STATUTORY PROVISIONS AUTHORISING A LIMITATION OR EXCLUSION OF LIABILITY

Article 1231-5 (formerly art 1152) *Code civil* implicitly authorises limitations of liability in the case of breach of contract, by mentioning clauses whereby the parties set in advance damages owed in the case of breach: 'Where an agreement provides that he who fails to perform it will pay a certain sum as damages, the other party may not be awarded a greater or lesser sum.' As shall be seen, however, the validity and effectiveness of such clauses is subject to a certain number of limitations.[76] 63

Aside from the general and implicit authorisation resulting from art 1231-5, there seems to be only one legislative provision which explicitly allows for limitations or exclusions of liability, in the context of product liability. Article 1245-14 (formerly art 1386-15) *Code civil* provides: 'The clauses which tend to exempt from or to limit the liability for defective products are forbidden and shall be deemed not written. Nevertheless, as to damage caused to property not used by the injured party mainly for his own private use or consumption, the clauses stipulated between professionals are valid.' This authorisation is of limited scope and is an exception to the principle set in the first sentence of the article.[77] 64

---

76 See below sec III.B.

77 It covers a type of damage that cannot be recovered under the 1985 Directive, but which the French legislator has chosen to include within the scope of the special product liability regime derived from the Directive.

65 Statutory caps on compensation are to a large extent alien to the French legal traditions. A few could be cited, which often find their origin in an international convention,[78] but they are not specific to either contract or tort law, and their justification never seems to be linked to the existence or absence of a contract.

B. LIMITATION OR EXCLUSION OF CONTRACTUAL AND TORTIOUS LIABILITY BY CONTRACT

1) *Is it Possible to Limit or Exclude Contractual or Tortious Liability under a Contract?*

66 It has always been accepted that parties to a contract could limit or even suppress liability incurred in the case of breach. This is regarded as an element of freedom of contract. As far as exclusions or limitations of liability are concerned, however, this freedom tends to be increasingly fenced. In consumer contracts, clauses that suppress or limit the right of the consumer or of a non-professional party to be compensated in the case of a breach of contract by the professional party are regarded as necessarily unfair, and therefore void.[79] Outside the field of consumer law, limitation or exclusion clauses, though theoretically valid, cannot apply when a party breaches the contract intentionally or as a result of 'gross fault'.[80] This rule is not stated explicitly in the Civil Code, but is an extension of the rule set in art 1231-3 (formerly art 1150), which provides that the limitation of damages to foreseeable damage does not apply in the case of intentional breach of contract or gross fault.[81]

67 Furthermore, the recent reform of contract law has confirmed a rule initially developed by case law,[82] whereby exclusion or limitation clauses must be regarded as void when they deprive the 'essential' obligation of a contract of its substance, by providing that its breach shall have no consequences, or only ludicrous ones (art 1170).[83] It has also extended the control of unfair contract

---

78 There is, for example, a cap on the compensation of damage caused by nuclear installations. But the French legislator did not make use of the possibility provided by the 1985 Directive on product liability to put a cap on the liability of producers of defective products.

79 Art R 212-1, 6 Code de la consommation.

80 This applies whether the intentional breach is attributable to the contracting party himself, or to his employee.

81 See above sec II.A.

82 Cass com, 22 October, Bull civ IV, no 261; Cass com, 29 June 2010, Bull civ IV, no 115.

83 'Toute clause qui prive de sa substance l'obligation essentielle du débiteur est réputée non écrite' ('Any contract term which deprives a debtor's essential obligation of its substance is deemed not written').

terms to all standard form contracts, even if they are not consumer contracts (art 1171).[84] Even though limitation or exclusion clauses should not be regarded as systematically unfair in contracts that are not consumer contracts, this new rule will most probably be used to neutralise such clauses when they create a significant imbalance in the rights and obligations of the parties.

The scope of valid and effective limitation or exclusion clauses in contract is therefore seriously bounded. Besides, many authors are also of the opinion that such clauses should never be valid, whatever the type of contract or the origin of the breach, when they purport to exclude or limit damages in the case where a breach of contract causes a personal injury.[85] It is suggested that French courts might have some sympathy with this opinion, but have hardly any occasion to express it, since such clauses, if they exist, never seem to come up before the courts. 68

Contractual exclusion or limitation clauses, if valid, may only restrict liability *in contract*. Under French law, it is not possible to exclude or limit in advance liability in tort, except in the case provided for by art 1245-14 *Code civil*.[86] This impossibility is actually not mentioned in the Civil Code, but it is regarded as being a consequence of the fact that liability in tort belongs to *ordre public*. Although this justification is open to criticism,[87] the little case law there is on the subject does confirm that any exclusion or limitation of liability in tort is not possible.[88] 69

2) *To What Extent can a Contractual Exclusion Provide a Defence to a Third Party to the Contract?*

A plaintiff bringing a claim *in contract* against a party to a contract to which he is not himself a party must normally bear any limitation or exclusion of liability contained in that contract.[89] 70

[84] 'Dans un contrat d'adhésion, toute clause qui crée un déséquilibre significatif entre les droits et obligations des parties au contrat est réputée non écrite. L'appréciation du déséquilibre significatif ne porte ni sur l'objet principal du contrat ni sur l'adéquation du prix à la prestation' ('Any term of a standard form contract which creates a significant imbalance in the rights and obligations of the parties to the contract is deemed not written. The assessment of significant imbalance must not concern either the main subject matter of the contract nor the adequacy of the price in relation to the act of performance').

[85] Art 1281 al 2 *Projet* explicitly adopts this position.

[86] See above sec III.A.

[87] See *J-S Borghetti*, La responsabilité du fait des choses, un régime qui a fait son temps, RTD civ 2010, 1, no 60.

[88] The *Projet* purports to modify this rule, however; see above fn 41.

[89] This will be the case, for example, when the buyer of a good brings a claim in contract (*action directe*) against the person who sold the good to his own seller, as is possible under French law.

71 On the other hand, when a plaintiff brings a claim *in tort* against a party to a contract to which he is not himself a party, and seeks compensation for damage caused by the breach of this contract, the defendant cannot raise as a defence any exclusion or limitation contained in the contract. This, at least, is the majority opinion among scholars, even though there is little case law on the subject. The justification for this solution is that the plaintiff did not accept the limitation or exclusion contained in the contract to which he is not a party. While this justification holds when the breach of contract is also a delictual fault under art 1382 *Code civil*, it is hardly convincing when the plaintiff relies on the breach of contract per se, as has been possible since 2006.[90] It is suggested that the plaintiff who relies on a contract to which he is not a party must take this contract as it is, ie with the limitations or exclusions it may contain, unless the breach of this contract constitutes a fault under art 1382, in which case the plaintiff can act on this basis, regardless of the limitations or exclusions set by the contract.

IV. NON-CONCURRENCE OR CONCURRENCE OF ACTIONS

A. OVERVIEW

72 French law sets a non-concurrence of actions principle, combined with a priority rule: according to the so-called *non-cumul* rule, whenever there is a valid contract between the parties and damage is connected to this contract, the plaintiff may only sue in contract. There is, therefore, a precedence of contract over tort. This rule applies to all types of damage (personal injury, damage to property, pure economic loss, etc). As a result, there is normally no overlap between tort and contract. As soon as there is a contract, there can be no tort.

73 The *non-cumul* rule is not in the *Code civil*, but the courts and most French scholars regard it today as self-evident.[91] The justification put forward for it is that tort rules should not enable parties to circumvent contract rules. When one looks at case law, however, one sees that the rule was not always applied and that it really established itself in the 1930s. It is suggested that this is a consequence of the development of wide-ranging strict liability regimes in tort, such as *responsabilité du fait des choses*, whose application in contractual settings threatened to upset the allocation of risks between the parties.[92]

---

90 See above sec II.G.

91 Unsurprisingly, the rule is endorsed by the *Projet* (art 1233).

92 See *J-S Borghetti*, RTD civ 2010, 1, no 60; *idem* (fn 73).

There are some exceptions to the *non-cumul* rule, however. Some strict liability regimes, which are regarded as being in tort, apply regardless of the existence of a contractual relationship between the parties. This is especially the case for the traffic accidents strict liability regime[93] and the product liability regime derived from the 1985 European Directive on Product Liability.[94] Case law also considers that certain obligations which may apply between parties to a contract are of a statutory nature and give rise to a liability in tort if breached, even though a valid contract exists between the parties. The exact list of these obligations is not known, however, and not many have been identified so far.[95] Besides, the Commercial Code prohibits a certain number of actions between partners to an 'established commercial relationship', and the Cour de cassation considers that a violation of these prohibitions renders the defendant liable in tort, even though there is usually a valid contract between the partners. 74

B. CONCURRENCE/EXCLUSION OF ACTIONS FOR THE PROTECTION AGAINST PERSONAL INJURY AND OF PROPERTY

The exclusion of tort when a contract exists between the parties applies to personal injury. In some cases, however, the courts disregard the existence of a contract so as apply tort law. This is not a formal exception to the *non-cumul* rule, however. Rather, courts displace the boundary of the contract in such cases, so that damage, even though it occurred on the occasion of the execution of the contract, will be regarded as having occurred outside the contract. Courts resort to this subterfuge in circumstances where plaintiffs who have entered a contract with the defendant are in a situation very similar to that of plaintiffs with no contractual relationship to the defendant: in the case of an accident in a railway station (where victims may be passengers with a ticket or visitors without a ticket), or in the case of an accident in a self-service store (where the plaintiff may or may not have concluded a contract with the shop at the time when the accident takes place). This allows all plaintiffs to rely on tort rules, which are sometimes more favourable than contractual ones, and avoids plaintiffs in very similar situations being treated differently. 75

In order to avoid this difference of treatment between victims of personal injuries, the *Projet*, following various doctrinal suggestions,[96] provides that 76

[93] Law of 5 July 1985.

[94] Art 1245-1 to 1245-17 *Code civil.*

[95] The most significant one is probably the obligation to clean an industrial site after the industrial activity has stopped. If someone sells such a site without having cleaned it, the buyer's liability will be in tort, even though there is a sales contract between the parties.

[96] See eg art 3 *projet Terré.*

compensation of personal injuries should always be governed by liability in tort, even if there is a contract between the parties (art 1233-1). The *non-cumul* rule would thus be maintained, but its meaning would be reversed when personal injuries are at stake.

77 The exclusion of tort when a contract exists between the parties also applies with respect to damage of property.

C. CONCURRENCE/EXCLUSION IN THE CASE OF INTERFERENCE WITH CONTRACTUAL RIGHTS

1) *Interference with a Contractual Relationship*

78 If a person knowingly induces a party to a contract to breach this contract, he will normally be regarded as being at fault, and will thus be liable in tort to the other party to the contract, on the basis of art 1240 *Code civil*. For example, a company hiring an employee of a competing company whom it knows is bound by a valid non-competition clause commits a fault and will be liable in tort to the latter company.

2) *Loss of Business due to Personal Injury to Someone Else's Employees or Clients or to Property Damage to the Entrepreneur*

79 Loss of business due to personal injury to one's employees or clients constitutes under French law a *préjudice par ricochet*, ie damage suffered by someone as a result of someone else's damage. There is a requirement set by case law under French law that damage be direct in order to be compensated, but *préjudice par ricochet* is not regarded as necessarily indirect. When the plaintiff is a relative of the 'direct' victim, *préjudice par ricochet* is normally compensated, whether it be pecuniary or non-pecuniary. As has already been observed,[97] however, courts are obviously reluctant to compensate pecuniary damage suffered by a plaintiff as a result of damage caused to the direct victim when the relationship between the two is of a professional nature. This has never been expressed explicitly; rather, courts tend to regard damage as not being direct in such cases. This justification is debatable, as one hardly sees why this damage is less direct than damage suffered by a relative of the direct victim due to the loss of maintenance payments. But French courts are probably aware, even if they do not formulate things this way, that compensating the economic losses of business or professional partners of the direct victim would be going too far and could generate massive litigation.

---

97 See above sec II.G.

Yet this cautious approach is now being challenged by the recently developed rule whereby 'a third party to a contract may, on the basis of delictual liability, invoke a breach of contract whenever this breach has caused him harm'.[98] On the basis of this rule, the Cour de cassation has accepted, for example on one occasion at least, that the parent company of a car retailer could bring a claim in tort against a car-maker that had abused its right to terminate a contract with the retailer.[99] More generally, as damage suffered by a third party as a result of the violation of a contract is often a consequence of damage suffered by the contractual partner itself, this rule could lead to an extension of compensation for *préjudice par ricochet* suffered by business or professional partners of the contract's creditor. 80

When an entrepreneur suffers a loss of business as a result of damage caused to its own property, this loss can be compensated, provided it does not appear too remote, in which case it would not be regarded as direct. This solution has never really been disputed. 81

V. SPECIFIC SITUATIONS

A. PRE-CONTRACTUAL LIABILITY

Pre-contractual liability under French law could qualify as rather untidy, at least from a conceptual point of view. The original Civil Code did not deal with it, and, if one looked at cases, it was not clear if this liability was based in contract or in tort. When the Cour de cassation recognised such liability, it sometimes grounded it on art 1147 of the Civil Code, ie liability in contract, and sometimes on art 1382 of the Civil Code, ie liability in tort. In practice, however, this did not make any difference, as the basis of liability (fault) and the scope of compensable damage are the same in both cases. Pre-contractual liability was thus a field where the distinction between liability in tort and liability in contract appeared extremely blurred. 82

The recent reform of contract law has introduced a specific provision on pre-contractual liability (art 1112 al 2), which basically confirms pre-existing solutions, but does make the nature of the liability explicit: 'In case of fault committed during the negotiations, the reparation of the resulting loss is not calculated so as to compensate the loss of benefits which were expected 83

[98] See above sec II.G.

[99] Cass com, 21 October 2008, JCP G 2009, I, 123, obs *P Stoffel-Munck*, RDC 2009, 504, obs *J-S Borghetti*.

from the contract that was not concluded'.[100] As explained, however, this is not very important, since the nature of liability does not entail significant consequences in this context.

B. LIABILITY OF PROFESSIONALS

84 There are normally no special rules applying to professionals under French law. The latter are of course submitted to a certain number of duties in connection with their profession, but the violation of these duties does not give rise to a special type of responsibility. The liability of professionals is thus normally contractual vis-à-vis their clients, and tortious vis-à-vis other plaintiffs. It has been observed, however, that the liability of professionals is often assessed quite independently from the existence of a contract. This is, for example, the case with public notaries (*notaires*), who may or may not have a contract with the persons they serve, depending on the cases, but whose liability always seems to be assessed in the same way. Some authors are therefore of the opinion that the liability of professionals could be regarded as a third type of liability, distinct from both liability in tort and liability in contract, but this has not yet been fully confirmed by case law.

85 It must also be mentioned that, in the field of medicine, special legislative provisions apply, which restate the traditional principle whereby a medical doctor normally only answers for his fault, and which apply regardless of the existence of a contract between the doctor and the patient.

CASES

CASE 1. THE UNATTRACTIVE SHOPPING MALL

86 This is exactly the context in which the Cour de cassation recently established this surprising rule, whereby 'a third party to a contract may, on the basis of delictual liability, invoke a breach of contract whenever this breach has caused him harm'.[101] On the basis of this rule, C therefore has a claim in tort against D and can obtain damages for lost earnings. But C has no claim in contract, as he has no direct contractual relationship to D.[102]

[100] 'En cas de faute commise dans les négociations, la réparation du préjudice qui en résulte ne peut avoir pour objet de compenser la perte des avantages attendus du contrat non conclu'.

[101] See above sec II.G.

[102] There are some cases where contractual liability may apply despite the existence of a direct contractual relationship between the parties (see above sec II.G), but the present case is not one of them.

CASE 2. THE IDLE LAWYER

As there is no contractual relationship between the solicitor and the daughters, any liability arising between them should normally be in tort. Yet one might analyse the contract that existed between the solicitor and W as including a stipulation for the benefit of W's daughters, as is possible under art 1205 of the Civil Code.[103] The daughters would then have a claim in contract against the solicitor. But, although such a stipulation for the benefit of a third party can be implicit, it is doubtful if such a stipulation could be recognised in such a case, if only because it would run counter to the absolute freedom to change one's will under French law. 87

Any action of the daughters against the solicitor should thus normally be in tort. Under traditional conceptions that prevailed until recently, however, the daughters would probably not have had any cause of action against the solicitor, as the latter had not committed a delictual fault in the sense of art 1240 of the Civil Code. But the situation has changed since the Cour de cassation has established that 'a third party to a contract may, on the basis of delictual liability, invoke a breach of contract whenever this breach has caused him harm'.[104] This rule would perfectly fit in the present case and would enable the daughters to be compensated for the full economic loss caused by the solicitor's breach of contract as against W. This rule can lead to rather extreme results, however, and it remains to be seen if French judges are ready to apply it in every case where it is theoretically applicable. The present case, typically, is one where judges may be tempted to shy away from the rule and restrict its field of application. But this is only a supposition, and, to the best of my knowledge, no such case has yet come before French courts. 88

CASE 3. THE DEFECTIVE HOUSE

Under art 1792 al 1 of the Civil Code, 'any builder of a work is liable as a matter of law to the owner or to the buyer of the work for the damage, even that resulting from a defect of the ground that compromises the stability of the 89

---

103 Art 1205 *Code civil*: 'On peut stipuler pour autrui. L'un des contractants, le stipulant, peut faire promettre à l'autre, le promettant, d'accomplir une prestation au profit d'un tiers, le bénéficiaire. Ce dernier peut être une personne future mais doit être précisément désigné ou pouvoir être déterminé lors de l'exécution de la promesse' ('A person may make a stipulation for another person. One of the parties to a contract (the "stipulator") may require a promise from the other party (the "promisor") to accomplish an act of performance for the benefit of a third party (the "beneficiary"). The third party may be a future person but must be exactly identified or must be able to be determined at the time of the performance of the promise').

104 See above sec II.G.

building or that, by affecting it in one of its essential component parts or one of its complementary elements, that renders it unsuitable for its purposes.'[105] This warranty lasts 10 years after the work has been accepted (art 1792-4-1 of the Civil Code), and is transferred along with the building if the latter is sold. It cannot be excluded by contract (art 1792-5 of the Civil Code).

90 In the present case, the falling down of the house establishes a defect in the sense of art 1792 and D is liable for any damage caused by this defect, notwithstanding the exclusion clause that was introduced in the contract between D and Z. C can thus bring a claim against D for the compensation of both his personal injury and damage caused to the house. This claim would be regarded as being in contract, although this is a typical case where the concept of professional liability might apply,[106] since the contractor's liability is to a large extent independent from the existence of a contract between him and the claimant.

CASE 4. APARTMENT IN FLAMES

91 Given the existence of a lease contract between C and D, any claim brought by C against D in relation to the rented apartment should be in contract. Article 1721 of the Civil Code provides: 'A warranty is owed to the tenant against all vices or defects of the thing leased that prevent its use, even if the lessor did not know of them at the time of the lease. Should the lessee suffer any loss because of such vices or defects, the lessor is required to indemnify him.'[107] In the present case, the failure of the circuit breaker would probably qualify as a defect within the meaning of art 1721, and D would thus be liable in contract to C for his personal injuries.

CASE 5. INJURED SKIER

92 It is an established solution in French case law that the operator of a ski lift owes an *obligation de sécurité de résultat* to the people using the lift with a

---

[105] 'Tout constructeur d'un ouvrage est responsable de plein droit, envers le maître ou l'acquéreur de l'ouvrage, des dommages, même résultant d'un vice du sol, qui compromettent la solidité de l'ouvrage ou qui, l'affectant dans l'un de ses éléments constitutifs ou l'un de ses éléments d'équipement, le rendent impropre à sa destination.'

[106] See above secs I.B and V.B.

[107] 'Il est dû garantie au preneur pour tous les vices ou défauts de la chose louée qui en empêchent l'usage, quand même le bailleur ne les aurait pas connus lors du bail. S'il résulte de ces vices ou défauts quelque perte pour le preneur, le bailleur est tenu de l'indemniser.'

ticket when they are on the lift. This means that he is liable in contract for any damage caused to the user of the lift, unless he proves that this damage was actually the result of force majeure. In the present case, unless force majeure were proven by D1, he would be liable in contract to C for the personal injury caused.

Whether D2 should cover D1's liability to C is a matter of insurance law. 93
Normally, the insurance contract should apply and D2 would therefore be entitled to refuse to cover the accident, since D1's liability is in contract and not in tort. Insurance contract clauses which exclude contractual liability from the insurer's guaranty are not per se illegal, although some regard them as outrageous.[108] Courts tend to interpret such clauses as restrictively as possible, and sometimes find other ways to neutralise them. In the French context, where the liability of ski lift operators is almost always in contract, having liability insurance that only covers liability in tort is nearly useless and one could argue that the contract was without cause, and thus void. This would not be of much help to the operator, but there is no obvious way in which the clause could be neutralised and the contract regarded as also covering liability in contract.

CASE 6. EXPLODING CAR

C undoubtedly has a contractual claim against D1. Independently from the 94
contractual two-year full warranty against all defects, art 1641 of the Civil Code provides that 'the seller is bound to a warranty against hidden defects in the thing sold that render it unfit for its intended use, or that so impair its use that the buyer would not have bought it, or would only have paid a lower price for it if he had known of the defects.'[109] Under this 'latent defects warranty', which cannot be excluded or limited by contract when the seller is a professional,[110] the seller, if he is a professional, must compensate any damage caused by the defect in the thing sold.[111] In the present case, D1 would thus have to pay damages to C, in an amount equivalent to the value of the destroyed car.

---

108 See eg *Y Lambert-Faivre/L Leveneur*, Droit des assurances (13th edn 2011) no 635.

109 'Le vendeur est tenu de la garantie à raison des défauts cachés de la chose vendue qui la rendent impropre à l'usage auquel on la destine, ou qui diminuent tellement cet usage que l'acheteur ne l'aurait pas acquise, ou n'en aurait donné qu'un moindre prix, s'il les avait connus.'

110 Unless the buyer is also a professional and of the same specialty as the seller, which does not seem to be the case here.

111 In application of art 1645 of the Civil Code. This text provides that damages are owed by the seller only when he was aware of the defect at the time of the sale, but case law has developed a rule whereby professional sellers are irrebuttably presumed to have had knowledge of the defect.

Prescription would not be an obstacle, as an action based on the warranty for latent defects must be brought by the buyer within two years from the discovery of the vice (art 1648 of the Civil Code).

95 Besides this, when the same thing is the object of a succession of sales contracts,[112] it is an established solution under French case law that warranties arising out of one contract are so to say 'attached' to the thing sold, so that their benefit passes to the successive buyers of the thing, just like ownership of the thing itself. If A sells a thing to B and B resells it to C, C can thus bring a claim in contract against A, on the basis of the contractual guaranty to which the contract between A and B has given birth. This contractual claim between two parties that have no direct contractual relationship is called an *action directe*.

96 In the present case, C thus has a claim in contract against D2, based on the latent defects warranty arising from the sales contract concluded between D2 and D1, and which was transferred by D1 to C when the former sold the car to the latter.[113]

97 C could also consider a claim against D2 based on the product liability provisions, derived from the 1985 Directive. This claim would be in tort but would not be barred by the existence of a contractual *action directe* against D2, despite the *non-cumul* rule, since art 1245-17 of the Civil Code, following art 13 of the Directive, expressly introduced an exception to the latter,[114] and the European Court of Justice (ECJ) confirmed that 'the reference in Art 13 of the Directive to the rights which an injured person may rely on under the rules of the law of contractual or non-contractual liability must be interpreted as meaning that the system of rules put in place by the Directive ... does not preclude the application of other systems of contractual or non-contractual liability based on other grounds, such as fault or a warranty in respect of latent defects.'[115] However, following art 9 of the Directive, art 1245-1 of the Civil Code excludes the compensation of damage caused to the defective product itself. In the present case, C could therefore not claim compensation against D2, on the basis

112 Or of any contracts which transfer ownership of the thing.

113 If D1 and D2 are professionals of the same specialty, however, D2 had the possibility to validly exclude the latent defects warranty from the contract concluded with D1. If that was the case, then no latent defects warranty arising out of the first contract could be transferred from D1 to C, and C thus has no claim in tort against D2.

114 Art 1245-17 *Code civil*: 'Les dispositions du présent chapitre ne portent pas atteinte aux droits dont la victime d'un dommage peut se prévaloir au titre du droit de la responsabilité contractuelle ou extracontractuelle ou au titre d'un régime spécial de responsabilité' ('The provisions [on product liability] cannot affect any right which a victim may claim on the basis of the rules of contractual or extra-contractual liability or on the basis of a special liability regime').

115 ECJ 25 April 2002, *María Victoria González Sánchez and Medicina Asturiana SA*, C-183/00, no 31.

of the special product liability provisions, for the loss of the car, which is the very product that D2 produced and that was defective.

CASE 7. RACING BOAT BURNING

Since the accident took place more than two years after the sale of the boat by D to C, the contractual full warranty no longer applies. Under art 1641 of the Civil Code, however, D is still bound by the latent defects warranty. This warranty can be excluded when the seller is not a professional, as is apparently the case with D, but the mere fact that D offered a two-year full warranty does not amount to such an exclusion. Unless the latent defects warranty was explicitly excluded by the contract, C can thus rescind the contract, because of the boat's defectiveness, and be reimbursed for the price he paid (art 1644 of the Civil Code). But D would not have to compensate C for his repatriation expenses, unless it were proven that he knew of the defect at the time of the sale.[116] Given the *non-cumul* rule, it would not be possible for C to try and claim damages to compensate these expenses on the basis of art 1240 of the Civil Code (liability in tort). 98

CASE 8. INSIDIOUS REPORT

D's undoubtedly faulty behaviour took place whilst he was still an employee of C. His liability to C, if it exists, is therefore in contract. According to a well-established case law rule, an employee can be held liable to his employer for breach of contract only if this breach is the result of gross negligence equating to intentional fault (*faute lourde équipollente au dol*).[117] In the present case, D's fault is grave enough to meet the requirement set by the courts, and D should thus be liable in contract to C for the loss he caused. 99

CASE 9. CIRCULAR LETTER

C's claim against D is necessarily in tort. To wilfully spread false and defamatory information about someone else undoubtedly constitutes a fault under art 1240 of the Civil Code, and C could thus ground his claim on this 100

---

116 Art 1645 of the Civil Code provides that damages are owed by the seller only when he was aware of the defect at the time of the sale. Case law has developed a rule whereby professional sellers are irrebuttably presumed to have had knowledge of the defect, but D is apparently not a professional, and his knowledge of the defect should thus be proven by C.

117 Cass soc, 27 November 1958, D 1959, 20, note *R Lindon*.

provision in order to obtain compensation for the loss he suffered. The fact that this loss is purely economic is not an obstacle to its being compensated under French tort law. It would probably be regarded as falling within the loss of chance category.

CASE 10. SHORTAGE OF SUPPLY

101 In view of the abusive pressure that some companies exert on their commercial partners, the French legislator has developed legislation to fight against abuses. Article L442-6 of the Commercial Code (*Code de commerce*) thus provides that a certain number of abusive commercial practices shall give rise to liability. The courts regard this liability as being necessarily in tort, even though there is very often a valid contract between the parties. According to art L442-6, I, 4°, 'Any producer, trader, manufacturer (…) who commits the following offences shall be held liable and obliged to make good the damage caused: (…) 4° Obtaining, or seeking to obtain clearly abusive terms concerning prices, payment times, terms of sale or services that do not come under the purchase or sale obligations, under the threat of an abrupt total or partial termination of business relations'.[118] The behaviour of D in the present case clearly falls within the ambit of this provision, and D would thus be liable in tort to C for damage caused by his abusive behaviour.

CASE 11. INJURED ROCK STAR

102 Under French law, D would be regarded as a *victime par ricochet* of damage suffered by X.[119] In principle, nothing bars *victimes par ricochet* from seeking compensation of any damage, including pure economic loss, which they have suffered as a result of damage suffered by the direct victim (X, in this case). As has been said, however, French courts are clearly reluctant to allow claims by commercial partners of the direct victim, and they tend to regard the alleged loss as indirect, and thus not compensable. In the present case, although C's loss is theoretically compensable on the basis of D's liability in tort,[120]

118 'I. – Engage la responsabilité de son auteur et l'oblige à réparer le préjudice causé le fait, par tout producteur, commerçant, industriel …: 4° D'obtenir ou de tenter d'obtenir, sous la menace d'une rupture brutale totale ou partielle des relations commerciales, des conditions manifestement abusives concernant les prix, les délais de paiement, les modalités de vente ou les services ne relevant pas des obligations d'achat et de vente'.

119 See above sec II.G.

120 Since there was a traffic accident and D was presumably a driver, his liability necessarily rests on the Law of 5 July 1985 on traffic accidents.

a French court would thus probably regard the loss as too remote and thus deny its compensation on the ground that it was not directly caused by the traffic accident.

CASE 12. EQUIPMENT DESTROYED

C can bring an action in contract against D1, on the basis of the transport contract concluded between them. According to art L133-2 of the Commercial Code, the carrier is liable in the case of late delivery, unless he can prove that the delay was caused by force majeure. In order to qualify as force majeure, however, an event must be unforeseeable, and this is certainly not the case with a traffic accident. D1 is thus liable to C in contract under art L133-2 of the Commercial Code. The extent to which he must compensate C's loss can be disputed, however. Unless the parties have agreed otherwise, a transportation contract includes the clauses contained in the 'standard transportation contract' ('*contrat-type*') negotiated under the Government's authority. According to clause 22.3 of this contract, damages in the case of late delivery cannot exceed the price of the contract. But the client has the possibility to make a 'declaration of interest' when he concludes the contract, in which case the declaration will set the upper limit of damages owed by the carrier. In the present case, how much D owes to C thus depends on whether or not such a declaration of interest was made. If not, C will not get more than the price he paid under the contract, which is presumably much less than the loss he suffered as a result of the concert being cancelled. It must further be noted that, under art L133-6 of the Commercial Code, any claim must be brought within one year of the day on which the goods should have been delivered. 103

If C was the owner of the equipment, he could bring a claim in tort against D2 for the loss of it. This claim would be based on the special strict liability regime applicable to traffic accidents. As far as the economic loss resulting from the concert's cancellation is concerned, the solution would normally be the same as in the previous case. 104

CASE 13. SLIPPING ON A LETTUCE LEAF

Given the absence of a contract at the time of the accident, normal rules would require that, in such a case, liability, if any, be in tort. It may however be difficult, in cases like this one, to decide if the accident happened before or after a contract was concluded (especially as, under French law, the mere fact of displaying a product with a price qualifies as an offer, and a sales contract could thus be regarded as concluded as soon as the client puts the product in 105 his basket). To avoid subtle discussions on that count, the Cour de cassation has decided that liability arising out of an accident in a self-service shop is necessarily in tort. This is probably a good rule, even if it does not fit in easily with the *non-cumul* rule. The practical result of it is that the plaintiff will very often be able to rely on the liability for things regime of art 1242 al 1 of the Civil Code. In the present case, D can be regarded as the 'keeper' of the lettuce leaf, and it is thus liable for any damage caused by the abnormal position of the leaf. C therefore has a claim in tort against D based on art 1242 al 1 of the Civil Code.[121]

CASE 14. TEST DRIVE

106 In the case of a traffic accident, any action brought against the driver of a motor vehicle involved in the accident must necessarily be in tort and based on the Law of 5 July 1985. This text subjects drivers to an extra strict liability, totally independent from fault, but which is backed by compulsory third-party insurance. In the present case, C would thus be liable to D on the basis of this Law. It could be, however, that C was not personally insured to drive this car and that his potential liability was covered by D's insurance contract, in which case it will be this contract that determines whether or not D can be compensated for damage caused to his vehicle by a driver to whom he had willingly entrusted it.

CASE 15. BREACH OF NEGOTIATIONS

107 The new art 1112 al 1 of the Civil Code provides: 'The commencement, continuation and breaking-off of pre-contractual negotiations are free from control. They must mandatorily satisfy the requirements of good faith'. In the present case, it is quite clear that, under French law, D's behaviour is contrary to good faith, and thus constitutes a fault. Article 1112 al 2, further provides: 'In the case of a fault committed during the negotiations, the reparation of the resulting loss is not calculated so as to compensate the loss of benefits which were expected from the contract that was not concluded'. If C has incurred some expenses because he has relied on D's promise that negotiations would continue, these will therefore be compensable.

---

[121] C could also invoke art 1240 of the Civil Code (liability for fault, in tort), but art 1242 al 1 is more favourable, since its application does not require that fault be demonstrated.

CASE 16. NON-DISCLOSURE OF RELEVANT FACTS

Article 1112-1 *Code civil* now explicitly provides for the existence of a pre-contractual information duty, the violation of which gives rise to liability.[122] Although the nature of this liability is not specified in the Code, it is generally accepted that it should be regarded as tortious, as the violation of the duty takes place before the contract is concluded. In the present case, a court would probably consider that D's knowledge of the special use to which C intended to put the machine created a duty to warn on the part of the seller. The violation of this duty is the source of D's liability to C under art 1112-1 al 6. C could also rescind the contract on the basis that its conclusion was the result of *reticence dolosive*. *Reticence dolosive* is behaviour whereby a contracting party remains intentionally silent on a point which he knows is essential for the other party's consent and about which he had a duty to inform the latter (art 1137 al 2). It makes the contract voidable, but the plaintiff can also claim damages in addition to rescission (if *reticence dolosive* caused damage that has not been erased by rescission) or in lieu of it. 108

[122] 'Celle des parties qui connaît une information dont l'importance est déterminante pour le consentement de l'autre doit l'en informer dès lors que, légitimement, cette dernière ignore cette information ou fait confiance à son cocontractant. Néanmoins, ce devoir d'information ne porte pas sur l'estimation de la valeur de la prestation. Ont une importance déterminante les informations qui ont un lien direct et nécessaire avec le contenu du contrat ou la qualité des parties. Il incombe à celui qui prétend qu'une information lui était due de prouver que l'autre partie la lui devait, à charge pour cette autre partie de prouver qu'elle l'a fournie. Les parties ne peuvent ni limiter, ni exclure ce devoir. Outre la responsabilité de celui qui en était tenu, le manquement à ce devoir d'information peut entraîner l'annulation du contrat dans les conditions prévues aux articles 1130 et suivants' ('The party who knows information which is of decisive importance for the consent of the other must inform him of it where the latter legitimately does not know the information or relies on the contracting party. However, this duty to inform does not apply to an assessment of the value of the act of performance. Information is of decisive importance if it has a direct and necessary relationship with the content of the contract or the status of the parties. A person who claims that information was due to him has the burden of proving that the other party had the duty to provide it, and that other party has the burden of proving that he has provided it. The parties may neither limit nor exclude this duty. In addition to imposing liability on the party who had the duty to inform, his failure to fulfil the duty may lead to annulment of the contract under the conditions provided by articles 1130 and following').

THE BORDERLINES OF TORT LAW IN GERMANY

Ulrich Magnus

QUESTIONS

I. Tracing the Borderlines . . . 173
  A. Distinction between Tort and Contract . . . 173
  B. Existence of a 'Grey Zone'? . . . 174
  C. Common or Different Rules Regulating Tort and Contract . . . 175
  D. Application of Common Rules in a Different Way . . . 175
II. Main Differences between Tortious and Contractual Liability . . . 176
  A. Differences as Regards the Foundations of Liability . . . 176
    1) Role of Intention . . . 176
    2) Role of Wrongfulness and Fault . . . 177
    3) Role of Strict Liability . . . 178
  B. Differences as Regards Causation . . . 179
  C. Differences as Regards Remedies . . . 179
    1) Degree of Certainty of the Damage . . . 180
    2) Compensation for Non-Pecuniary Loss . . . 180
    3) Compensation for Loss of Earnings and Loss of Chance . . . 181
    4) Restitutionary Damages . . . 181
    5) Aggravated and Exemplary (or Punitive) Damages . . . 181
    6) Other Remedies . . . 182
  D. Differences as Regards Recoverability of 'Pure Economic Losses' . . . 182
  E. Differences as Regards Liability for Others . . . 183
    1) Liability for Auxiliaries and for Independent Contractors . . . 183
    2) Liability for Legal Representatives or Organs of a Company . . . 184
    3) Liability of Representatives of Natural Persons . . . 184
    4) Liability of the Auxiliary/Organ Itself . . . 184
  F. Differences as Regards Liability in the Case of Multiple Tortfeasors/Breaching Parties . . . 184
  G. Differences as Regards the Persons Who May be Protected . . . 185
  H. Differences as Regards Defences . . . 185
  I. Differences as Regards Limitation Periods . . . 186
  J. Differences as Regards Proof . . . 187

K. Other Differences ... 187
L. Reasons for the Differences ... 188
III. Limitation or Exclusion of Liability Arising from Tort and from Contract ... 189
A. Statutory Provisions Authorising a Limitation or Exclusion of Liability ... 189
B. Limitation or Exclusion of Contractual and Tortious Liability by Contract ... 191
1) Is it Possible to Limit or Exclude Contractual and Tortious Liability under a Contract? ... 191
2) To What Extent can a Contractual Exclusion Provide a Defence to a Third Party to the Contract? ... 191
IV. Non-Concurrence or Concurrence of Actions ... 192
A. Overview ... 192
1) Areas of Overlap between Tort and Contract ... 192
2) Approach to Non-Concurrence and Concurrence of Actions ... 192
B. Concurrence/Exclusion of Actions for the Protection against Personal Injury ... 194
C. Concurrence/Exclusion of Actions for the Protection of Property ... 194
D. Concurrence/Exclusion in the Case of Interference with Contractual Rights ... 195
1) Interference with a Contractual Relationship ... 195
2) Loss of Business due to Personal Injury to Someone Else's Employee or Client or to Property Damage to the Entrepreneur ... 196
V. Specific Situations ... 196
A. Pre-Contractual Liability ... 196
B. Liability of Professionals ... 197

CASES

Case 1. The Unattractive Shopping Mall ... 198
Case 2. The Idle Lawyer ... 200
Case 3. The Defective House ... 200
Case 4. Apartment in Flames ... 201
Case 5. Injured Skier ... 201
Case 6. Exploding Car ... 202
Case 7. Racing Boat Burning ... 204
Case 8. Insidious Report ... 205
Case 9. Circular Letter ... 206
Case 10. Shortage of Supply ... 206
Case 11. Injured Rock Star ... 207

Case 12. Equipment Destroyed 208
Case 13. Slipping on a Lettuce Leaf. 208
Case 14. Test Drive 209
Case 15. Breach of Negotiations 210
Case 16. Non-Disclosure of Relevant Facts 210

QUESTIONS

I. TRACING THE BORDERLINES

A. DISTINCTION BETWEEN TORT AND CONTRACT

1 In theory, German law draws a strict distinction between contract law and tort law. The main reason is the different function of both areas of law: contract law depends on and secures the agreement between two or more parties. It is a private act based on their free will that creates binding obligations between them. Tort law on the contrary formulates rules that every member of the society which these rules enacted must observe. While contract law aims at giving the private agreement effect within reasonable borders, tort law aims in general to prevent activities which are unacceptably detrimental to other members of society and to award compensation where damage has occurred as a result of such activities.[1] It defines, as has rightly been said,[2] the conditions under which a person should generally become liable or remain free from liability.

2 The German Civil Code (*Bürgerliches Gesetzbuch*, BGB) follows a peculiar line: it assembles together contract and tort law – and other obligations – in its second Book: Law of Obligations (*Recht der Schuldverhältnisse*)[3] and regulates as much as possible *in abstracto* what all kinds of obligations including contract and tort have in common (general part of the law of obligations).[4] Some of the provisions of this general part of obligations exclusively address contracts,[5] while many others are formulated in an abstract manner to theoretically apply to the other obligations as well.[6] Further, in the special part of the law of obligations, many

1 See on the different functions, eg, *J Esser*, Schuldrecht (2nd edn 1960) 827 f; *H Kötz/G Wagner*, Deliktsrecht (13th edn 2016) no 56 ff; *D Looschelders*, Schuldrecht Besonderer Teil (13th edn 2018) no 1167.

2 See *Kötz/Wagner* (fn 1) no 57.

3 §§241–853 BGB.

4 §§241–432 BGB.

5 See §§311–362 BGB.

6 An example of that kind is §278 BGB which regulates the liability for employees and auxiliaries. The provision is drafted in terms that fit all kinds of obligations. However, since its application requires an already existing legal relationship between the creditor and the debtor, the provision does not apply to torts where the tort only creates such a relationship

types of contracts and also torts are dealt with in separate chapters.[7] It is thus a rather complex picture that the German regulation of contract and tort law presents.

B. EXISTENCE OF A 'GREY ZONE'?

3 German law acknowledges a 'grey zone' between contract and tort law in the sense that provisions which normally require a contract are applied to certain tort-like situations although no contract exists. Since the modernisation of the German law of obligations in 2002, §311 (2) and (3) BGB provide for a specific regulation for these cases which the Civil Code terms '*rechtsgeschäftsähnliche Schuldverhältnisse*' ('obligations similar to legal transactions').[8] §311 (2) BGB lists three different types of cases which can create duties to take account of the rights and interests of the other party, namely: (1) the commencement of contractual negotiations;[9] (2) the initiation of a contract where one party, with regard to a potential contractual relationship, gives the other party the possibility of affecting his rights, legal interests and other interests, or entrusts these to him;[10] and (3) similar business contacts.[11] §311 (3) BGB extends the scope of the contract to third persons; in particular an intermeddler can become personally liable if he, 'by laying claim to being given a particularly high degree of trust, substantially influences the pre-contract negotiations or the entering into of the contract.'[12] With these provisions the legislator codified the pre-existing case law. The relationship between the parties does not create obligations to perform the envisaged contract but to respect the rights and interests of the other person. As in tort law, the main consequence of any neglect of that duty is the liability to pay damages.

4 A further instrument of German law that may be seen as belonging to the 'grey zone' is the legal institute of the contract with protective effects in favour of third persons (*Vertrag mit Schutzwirkung zugunsten Dritter*). This instrument has

---

between the tortfeasor and the victim. Before the commission of the tort, no such relationship normally exists between the tortfeasor and the victim. Therefore, §831 BGB contains a specific and rather different rule for the imputation of the conduct of employees in tort law.

7 §§433–853 BGB.

8 This is the semi-official translation recommended by the Federal Ministry of Justice.

9 §311 (2) no 1 BGB: 'die Aufnahme von Vertragsverhandlungen'.

10 §311 (2) no 2 BGB: 'die Anbahnung eines Vertrags, bei welcher der eine Teil im Hinblick auf eine etwaige, rechtsgeschäftliche Beziehung dem anderen Teil die Möglichkeit zur Einwirkung auf seine Rechte, Rechtsgüter und Interessen gewährt oder ihm diese anvertraut'.

11 §311 (2) no 3 BGB: 'ähnliche geschäftliche Kontakte'.

12 §311 (3) sent 2 BGB: 'Ein solches Schuldverhältnis entsteht insbesondere, wenn der Dritte in besonderem Maße Vertrauen für sich in Anspruch nimmt und dadurch die Vertragsverhandlungen oder den Vertragsschluss erheblich beeinflusst.'

been developed by the courts; it owes its existence to shortcomings in German tort law and is now commonly recognised. Its main purpose is to provide better protection through contract law where the aggrieved person is in more or less the same position as the principle contractual party but has no own contract with the debtor. In consequence, the institute serves a merely subsidiary function: where the aggrieved person already has a comparable claim on another basis, in particular in contract or tort, the rules on contracts with protective effects in favour of third persons do not apply.[13]

C. COMMON OR DIFFERENT RULES REGULATING TORT AND CONTRACT

Originally, the general part of the BGB on the law of obligations intended to regulate only those aspects that were common to all kinds of obligations, whereas the specific part provided rules for individual contracts and non-contractual obligations. In the meantime, legislative interventions have changed this clear distinction. As already indicated, quite a number of provisions of the general part deal exclusively with contracts. However, there are still parts which function for contracts as well as for torts. This is particularly the case with the general provisions on damages in §§249–254 BGB, which are common for both torts and contracts – and other obligations, even outside the BGB. However, the tort provisions of the BGB contain some additional norms on damages which generally do not apply to contract situations.[14] On one occasion, these provisions refer back to the general damages rule: as regards contributory negligence, §846 BGB refers to the general provision on that issue (§254 BGB) when providing that the contributory negligence of a deceased victim may reduce the claims of any descendants. 5

In sum, the Civil Code couples different possibilities to regulate contract and tort issues: partly it provides for common rules; partly it contains rules applicable to only tort or only contract matters; partly the technique of reference to a specific general rule is used. 6

D. APPLICATION OF COMMON RULES IN A DIFFERENT WAY

In general, the courts apply provisions which are common to tort and contract in the same way. A certain difference exists, however, with respect to damages. The difference is not due to different legal principles but to the different functions 7

13 See BGHZ 70, 330; BGHZ 129, 169; BGH Neue Juristische Wochenschrift (NJW) 2014, 2577.

14 See §§842–853 BGB.

of contract and tort law. The main aim and principle of the law of damages is to restore, as far as possible, the state in which the victim would have been had the damaging event not occurred.[15] In contract law, this requires that the so-called positive interest must be compensated where a party is liable for breach of contract. According to the courts, the aggrieved party must be placed in the situation it would have been in if the contract had been correctly performed.[16] In tort law (including cases of §311 BGB), only the so-called negative interest has to be compensated, ie where the tort led to a disadvantageous contract or to the omission of an advantageous contract. The victim must be put in the position he/she would have been in if he/she had not relied on the tortious act.[17] He/she thus cannot claim damages, for example, on the basis of the consequences of a duly performed contract but only due to the expenditure caused by the tort. Often, though not necessarily, the negative interest is lower than the positive interest. The difference is explained by the different protective functions of contract and tort law: contract law safeguards contractual expectations; tort law secures the existing positions of the victim.

II. MAIN DIFFERENCES BETWEEN TORTIOUS AND CONTRACTUAL LIABILITY

A. DIFFERENCES AS REGARDS THE FOUNDATIONS OF LIABILITY

1) *Role of Intention*

8 In German law, the issue of intent is relevant in tort and contract law but in a different manner. However, it has a similar effect.

9 In tort, §826 BGB provides that a tortfeasor is liable for damage if he/she acted both intentionally and against good morals. If that is the case, the typical restriction of the most general provision of German tort law (§823 (1) BGB) that pure economic loss is not recoverable does not apply. Intention (*Vorsatz*) coupled with the violation of good morals is regarded as so unacceptable that even mere economic loss – without any further violation of one of the rights absolutely protected by §823 (1) BGB (life, body, freedom, property, etc) – must

[15] See already the formulation of §249 (1) BGB: 'A person who is liable in damages must restore the position that would exist if the circumstance obliging him to pay damages had not occurred' ('Wer zum Schadensersatz verpflichtet ist, hat den Zustand herzustellen, der bestehen würde, wenn der zum Ersatz verpflichtende Umstand nicht eingetreten wäre').

[16] BGH NJW 1998, 2902; *Grüneberg* in: Palandt, BGB (77th edn 2018) Vor §249 no 16.

[17] See BGH NJW 1972, 36; BGH NJW 2011, 1962.

be compensated. A further field of tort law where intent is significant is public liability. The acting civil servant is exempted from personal liability except in the case of intent or gross negligence where the public employer has a recourse claim against the civil servant.[18]

In contract, in order to establish liability, it is generally irrelevant whether the party in breach of a contract acted negligently or intentionally unless the parties have agreed otherwise.[19] A certain exception is accepted for labour contracts. If, in the course of employment, an employee caused damage to property (machinery, etc) or to the person of the employer, the employee is fully liable only in the case of intent.[20] Mere negligence leads to a restriction or even exclusion of the employee's liability in damages. If an employee caused damage to third persons, he/she is held fully liable but has a recourse claim against the employer in proportion to the degree of negligence, except in the case of intentional conduct.[21] A further exception where intent is significant is the contractual exclusion of liability. Liability for intent cannot be excluded in advance, neither by standard contract terms nor by individual agreement.[22] 10

There is, thus, both in tort and in contract, a tendency to insist on rather stringent liability requirements for intentionally caused damage. 11

2) *Role of Wrongfulness and Fault*

The basic provision in German tort law, §823 (1) BGB, requires that a tortfeasor acted wrongfully *and* with fault. For a long time this was regarded as the rule in tort law and any other concept as the exception. However, with the growth of strict liabilities in many diverse fields, the picture has changed. Fault liability – requiring also wrongful conduct – and strict liability, where neither wrongfulness nor fault play a role, are today the two pillars of tort law (often called '*Zweispurigkeit des Deliktsrechts*': 'the two lanes of tort law').[23] One could even add a third category in between where fault is presumed.[24] Depending 12

18 See §839 BGB in connection with art 34 GG (Grundgesetz, Constitution): the civil servant is not personally liable to the person who suffered damage but the State (or its agency) has to compensate that damage. However, if the servant acted with intent, the State has a recourse action against the servant.

19 See §280 (1) in connection with §276 (1) BGB.

20 BAG NJW 1995, 210.

21 See thereto *C Bittner*, Neue Zeitschrift für Arbeits- und Sozialrecht (NZA) 2002, 835; *Weidenkaff* in: Palandt, BGB (77th edn 2018) §611 no 159.

22 See §276 (3) BGB.

23 See in particular, *J Esser*, Die Zweispurigkeit unseres Haftungsrechts, Juristenzeitung (JZ) 1953, 129; see also *N Jansen*, Die Struktur des Haftungsrechts (2003) 25, 60.

24 For instance §831 BGB (liability for others), §832 BGB (liability of parents for acts of children), etc.

on the threshold a rebuttal of the presumption must overcome, this presumed liability may be nearer to fault or to strict liability.

13 In German contract law, the general rule also requires that, in order to become liable in damages, a party must have acted in breach of a duty *and* with fault.[25] Yet, it has to be noted that contract law recognises a broader arsenal of remedies than tort law, for instance termination of contract or price reduction. For the latter remedies, fault is not required, although a breach of a – generally contractual – duty still is.

14 Therefore, wrongfulness in the form of a breach of an objective duty is always necessary in contract law for any kind of contractual remedy whereas in tort law legal conduct, for instance driving a car on a road, may lead to the establishment of liability when it causes damage to others. And while in contract law liability for damage always requires fault (although fault is in most cases presumed)[26] today's tort law accepts many liabilities without fault.

3) Role of Strict Liability

15 In the 19th century, in the wake of strict liberalism, tort law in Germany was based almost exclusively on fault. According to a famous quote at that time: 'It is not the damage but fault that establishes the obligation to pay compensation.'[27] This prevented enterprises and entrepreneurs from bearing the burden of unexpected consequences of their activities. But already the Prussian Act on Railways of 1838 introduced a strict liability for damage caused by railways and, gradually over time, about 20 special acts have been introduced which today provide for strict liability in different sectors, mainly where high risks from new technical developments are involved. To date, the courts have refused the possibility to extend the existing strict liabilities to analogous cases.[28] The argument still is that only the legislator is allowed to introduce a strict liability as a further exception from fault liability. However, the courts do their best to extend the limits of fault liability, in particular by continually inventing higher duties of care which a tortfeasor has to observe.

16 Contract law saw no comparable development from fault to strict liability. It is still the general rule that, in contract, damages are not owed unless the debtor acted with fault, at least with negligence,[29] unless the parties have agreed otherwise.

---

25 See §280 (1) BGB.

26 See §280 (1) sent 2 BGB.

27 *R von Jhering*, Das Schuldmoment im römischen Privatrecht, in: id, Vermischte Schriften juristischen Inhalts (1879) 199 ('nicht der Schaden verpflichtet zum Schadensersatz, sondern die Schuld').

28 BGHZ 55, 229 (234); BGHZ 63, 234 (237).

29 See again §280 (1) BGB.

B. DIFFERENCES AS REGARDS CAUSATION

With respect to the general concept of causation, there are no dogmatic differences between contract and tort law. The identical starting point is the *conditio sine qua non* rule, moderated by the so-called adequate causation theory. This theory excludes very unlikely causes.[30] However, in difficult causation cases further policy considerations are necessarily examined, in particular the protective purpose of the violated norm or duty.[31] The protective purpose requires an examination of which damage the violated norm or duty was intended to avoid. In contract, the parties may define this purpose, while in tort law it is exclusively the legislator or the judge who determines this protective scope. 17

German law does not directly distinguish between causation in fact and causation in law. However, the three steps mentioned above (*conditio* rule, adequate causation, policy considerations) come close to such a division. 18

It has further to be mentioned that the German law on causation recognises a distinction between *haftungsbegründende Kausalität* (liability founding causation) and *haftungsausfüllende Kausalität* (liability implementing causation). The distinction is relevant with regard to proof. Full proof is necessary as regards causation that is the basis of a claim (normally the proof that a certain conduct has caused a violation of the victim's rights). As far as liability implementing causation is concerned (that the primary damage had further negative consequences for the victim), no strict proof of causation is required but the judge can estimate the amount of damages if the victim otherwise would be left without compensation.[32] This distinction applies both to contract and tort cases. 19

C. DIFFERENCES AS REGARDS REMEDIES

Generally, contract law provides for many more kinds of remedies than tort law where damages are the normal and almost exclusive remedy. For the law of damages, the German Civil Code contains provisions in its general part of the law of obligations (§§249–255 BGB). These provisions provide rules on the assessment of damages which apply both to contract and tort claims.[33] 20

---

30 See for instance BGH NJW 1998, 138 (140); BGH NJW 2005, 1420.

31 See thereto *D Looschelders*, Schuldrecht Allgmeiner Teil (16th edn 2018) no 894 ff; *Magnus* in: Nomos Kommentar BGB (3rd edn 2016) Vor §§249–255 no 64 ff; Palandt/*Grüneberg* (fn 16) Vorbem §249 no 25 ff.

32 §287 ZPO.

33 Nomos Kommentar/*Magnus* (fn 31) Vor §§249–255 no 3; Palandt/*Grüneberg* (fn 16) Vorbem §249 no 4; *Schiemann* in: Staudinger, Bürgerliches Gesetzbuch mit Einführungsgesetz und Nebengesetzen (2017) Vorbem zu §§249 ff no 5 ff.

Therefore, in theory, no differences exist in this respect between the two fields of law. However, in contract, the parties may agree in advance on the amount of damages (even by way of penalty) or on the mode of assessment, whereas this is normally not possible in tort cases (unless there is an accompanying contract, as often in product liability cases).

1) *Degree of Certainty of the Damage*

21 In both contract and tort, the same standard of certainty of damage is applied. As far as liability founding causation is concerned, the judge must have reached a state of conviction that comes close to certainty that the damage was the consequence of the relevant conduct. Mere probability or prevailing probability does not suffice. As already mentioned, this is different with respect to liability implementing causation and consequential losses. Here the judge can assess the damage and the amount of damages even if strict proof was not possible.

2) *Compensation for Non-Pecuniary Loss*

22 Theoretically, no differences between contract and tort law exist in the field of compensation for non-pecuniary loss. In general, such losses are not recoverable under German law unless provided for by law.[34] Because of the high subjective element of non-pecuniary losses and the difficulty in assessing them in terms of money, there are only a few provisions which provide for their compensation.[35] However, in practical terms, compensation for immaterial loss is the exception in contract,[36] whereas it is very often granted in tort.[37] Until very recently, German law denied compensation for the immaterial harm persons suffer when a close relative or other close person has been killed unless the claimant suffered a medically diagnosable injury much more severe than an average person would suffer. Due to the implementation of a new Act,[38] since 22 July 2017 such bereavement damages can now be claimed without further restrictions if a special personal relationship (*besonderes persönliches Näheverhältnis*) existed between the claimant and the deceased. Such a relationship is presumed between spouses, partners and parents and children.

---

34 §253 (1) BGB.

35 Palandt/*Grüneberg* (fn 16) §253 no 2 provides a survey of these provisions.

36 Provisions which explicitly allow compensation for immaterial loss in contract are §253 (2) and §651 f (2) BGB, §15 (2) and §21 (3) AGG, §40 (3) SeemG.

37 Because tort law often involves bodily harm or violation of personality rights. For the former, §253 (2) BGB provides for compensation for non-pecuniary harm; for the latter, the courts have developed a respective remedy (since BGH NJW 1958, 827).

38 §844 (3) BGB introduced by 'Gesetz zur Einführung eines Anspruchs auf Hinterbliebenengeld' of 17 July 2017 (BGBl I 2421).

3) *Compensation for Loss of Earnings and Loss of Chance*

Also with respect to the compensation for loss of earnings and loss of chance, German law does not make a difference between tort and contract cases. Loss of earnings is generally recoverable if the earnings were likely to occur.[39] On the contrary, loss of chance cannot be recovered under German law because the expected gain is too uncertain. 23

4) *Restitutionary Damages*

The starting point of the German law on damages is that the damage has to be made good *in natura*. The debtor of a damages claim is primarily obliged to restore the state that would have existed without the damaging act.[40] In reality, where damage has occurred, the victim almost always claims compensation in money instead of restitution in kind. §249 (2) sent 1 BGB grants the victim the choice between restitution and compensation in money. Again, there is no relevant difference between contract and tort law in this respect. Insofar as the term restitutionary damages refers to gain-based damages, this is a method of assessing damages that is available only in certain specific situations, namely where immaterial property rights have been infringed. In such a case, the claimant can choose between compensation of the actual loss (including loss of profits), the payment of an adequate licence fee or the stripping of the tortfeasor's gain.[41] Moreover, unlawful gains can be recovered under the law of unjust enrichment if the special requirements for this cause of action are also fulfilled. Unjust enrichment claims can then concur with a tort claim; in the contractual field, they come into play if a contract is invalid. 24

5) *Aggravated and Exemplary (or Punitive) Damages*

Neither in tort nor in contract does German law allow damages that primarily aim at penalising the debtor. The main aim of damages is compensation and, to a lesser extent, prevention;[42] in particular, the function of damages for pain and suffering is also to provide the victim satisfaction (*Genugtuung*).[43] Punitive purposes are left to penal law with its specific rules, which attempt to treat the 25

---

39 See §252 BGB which lowers the standard of proof for future losses from almost certainty to probability.

40 §249 (1) BGB.

41 See, eg, §97 para 2 UrhG (Copyright Act) and BGHZ 57, 116 (117); BGHZ 137, 374 (377); BGHZ 176, 311 (326).

42 See *Looschelders* (fn 31) no 873; Palandt/*Grüneberg* (fn 16) Vorbem v §249 no 1.

43 BGHZ 18, 149 (155).

individual against whom a claim has been brought fairly and, in case of doubt, to favour him/her.[44]

26 However, where mass media infringe personality rights of persons, the courts demand that damages must produce a 'real avoiding effect' (*echter Hemmungseffekt*) on the tortfeasor.[45] The amount of damages for the immaterial loss is, therefore, often considerable. Nonetheless, the primary aim remains the prevention of further infringements and not the imposition of a quasi-penal sanction on the tortfeasor.

6) Other Remedies

27 As already mentioned, German contract law – like most contract laws – provides for more and a wider range of remedies than tort law, in particular for the termination of a contract, a claim for specific performance or price reduction. Partly, these other remedies may serve as an equivalent to a damages claim but in most cases their aim is different from that of a damages claim. For instance, termination normally aims at bringing the contract to an end instead of compensating certain losses. However, since termination also restores the parties' freedom to contract, in certain cases this may also be the aim of a damages claim for compensation *in natura*. Additionally, a contractual claim for specific performance may sometimes coincide with a damages claim for compensation *in natura* but normally their aim is different: performance of the contract on the one hand and compensation of a specific loss on the other.

28 Thus, there remains a different arsenal of remedies in contract and tort law.

D. DIFFERENCES AS REGARDS RECOVERABILITY OF 'PURE ECONOMIC LOSSES'

29 In German law, there is a sharp difference between the recoverability of pure economic loss in contract law and in tort law. In contract law, it is a matter of course that any pure economic loss can be recovered. One of the central aims of contract law is the protection of the – mainly economic – expectations of the parties, the gain that they want to make and expect from their contract.

30 The situation is different in tort law. The aim of tort law is the protection of the existing rights and positions of the victim, not of future expectations. Thus, German tort law generally refuses to award compensation for pure economic

---

[44] BGH NJW 1992, 3096 (3103).

[45] BGHZ 128, 1 (16); BGH NJW 1996, 984 (985).

loss where no presently existing right or position has been infringed. Future income (*das Vermögen*) is not among the rights that the central tort norm of §823 (1) BGB lists and absolutely protects against everybody. Only under further conditions can pure economic loss be recovered, for instance if the tortfeasor acted with intent and in violation of good morals[46] or if specific laws such as the Act against Unfair Trade[47] or the Antitrust Act[48] so provide.

E. DIFFERENCES AS REGARDS LIABILITY FOR OTHERS

There are also considerable differences between German tort and contract law with respect to the liability for others. 31

1) *Liability for Auxiliaries and for Independent Contractors*

In contract law, a party is liable for damage that is the consequence of an at least negligent breach of contract by a person whom the contractual party employs or involves for the performance of the contract.[49] The contractual party is responsible for this auxiliary's fault in the same way as for his/her own fault; the responsible party cannot invoke any excuse of sufficient control or supervision of the auxiliary so employed or involved. Even if the auxiliary is an independent contractor who acted in the performance of the party's contract, the party is liable for any fault on the contractor's part. 32

In tort law, liability for others is much more limited. §831 BGB obliges a person whose employees have caused damage to others to compensate that damage unless the person cannot prove adequate selection, supervision and control of the employee. Thus the employer has to answer for his/her own fault and he/she can be released from liability if it can be proven that they adequately selected and supervised the employee. The act of the employee must have occurred in the course of his/her employment. Further, the conduct must have been wrongful but fault on the part of the employee is not required. The provision does not apply to independent contractors because they are not under the control of the employer.[50] The independent contractors themselves may be liable but not the person who engaged them. 33

46 See §826 BGB.

47 §9 UWG.

48 §33 (3) GWB.

49 See §278 BGB.

50 BGHZ 26, 152 (159); BGHZ 80, 1 (3 f); *Wagner* in: Münchener Kommentar zum Bürgerlichen Gesetzbuch Bd 5 (7th edn 2017) §831 no 16; *Sprau* in: Palandt, BGB (77th edn 2018) §831 no 5.

2) *Liability for Legal Representatives or Organs of a Company*

34 Where, on the other hand, the employee has the rank of an organ in the enterprise of the employer, the latter is liable for any fault such an employee committed in the course of his/her employment.[51] The same is true for organs or legal representatives of a company. The company is identified with their wrongful and faulty conduct which caused damage. No excuse as regards adequate selection and supervision is available.

3) *Liability of Representatives of Natural Persons*

35 With respect to the liability of representatives of natural persons, German law distinguishes in almost the same way as for auxiliaries. In contract law, the representee (child or ward) is liable for the wrongful and faulty acts of his/her legal representative without the possibility of being released from liability due to adequate supervision or similar.[52] Thus, in contractual situations, children can be held liable for faults of their parents in performing the child's contract.

36 In tort law, parents and other legal representatives are held liable for damage which a child or the represented person wrongfully (though not necessarily with fault) causes unless the parents or representatives can prove that they adequately supervised and controlled the child or the represented person.[53]

4) *Liability of the Auxiliary/Organ Itself*

37 Where the auxiliary/organ caused damage to others, the auxiliary/organ is liable in tort if a tort was committed. In contract, no liability is incurred because it is not the auxiliary/organ who is personally obliged towards the third party but the employer or company with which the contract was concluded.

F. DIFFERENCES AS REGARDS LIABILITY IN THE CASE OF MULTIPLE TORTFEASORS/BREACHING PARTIES

38 With respect to joint liability, the general rule is identical for tort and contract cases: where several persons acted in concert and caused damage, either by breaching their contract or by committing a tort, they are held jointly liable.[54]

---

51 See §31 BGB.

52 §278 BGB.

53 See §832 BGB.

54 See §427 in connection with §421 BGB (joint contract) and §840 BGB (tort).

The situation is more difficult where several persons did not act in concert but nonetheless caused one inseparable damage. It is likely the prevailing view that, in such a case again, both in contract and tort, the contributing persons are held jointly liable.[55] 39

G. DIFFERENCES AS REGARDS THE PERSONS WHO MAY BE PROTECTED

In general terms, contract law is regarded as primarily protecting the expectations which the parties can reasonably expect from their contract (expectation interests) while tort law mainly protects the presently existing rights of a person (integrity interests). Due to these different aims, the scope of protection varies between contract and tort, in particular with respect to compensation for pure economic loss. Moreover, in contract law, the freedom of the parties to conclude agreements concerning compensation of future losses is generally available, whereas in tort law for factual reasons parties can rarely make an agreement in advance. 40

The personal scope of protection varies likewise. The contract generally protects only the parties and no one else. A party has contractual claims only against the other party to the contract. By contrast, in tort, the victim has a claim against the tortfeasor but may claim injunctive relief against anybody who threatens to infringe his/her rights. Everybody else has to respect the victim's sphere of rights. 41

However, German contract law has extended the protective scope of contracts to further persons who, although not formal contractual parties, are close to the contracting party. The so-called contract with protective effects in favour of third persons (*Vertrag mit Schutzwirkung zugunsten Dritter*) grants contractual rights to at least damages to persons who are close to the contracting party (for instance, the children of a tenant), who foreseeably come into contact with the contractual performance of the other party (for instance, with the dangers of a flat rented by a father from a landlord) and have no other effective remedy.[56] 42

H. DIFFERENCES AS REGARDS DEFENCES

The most important defence is that of contributory negligence, which applies in tort as well as in contract.[57] However, as for other differences between contract 43

55 See MünchKommBGB/*Wagner* (fn 50) §840 no 10 with many further references.

56 See in particular, BGHZ 49, 353.

57 See *Oetker* in: Münchener Kommentar zum Bürgerlichen Gesetzbuch Bd 5 (7th edn 2016) §254 no 7; Palandt/*Grüneberg* (fn 16) §254 no 2.

and tort, contractual agreements may influence what has to be regarded as contributory negligence.

44 With respect to other defences, such as self-help, etc, there is likewise no difference in their application except where contractual agreements may validly vary or exclude them.

I. DIFFERENCES AS REGARDS LIMITATION PERIODS

45 Since the reform of the German Law of Obligations in 2002, the general period of limitation is three years.[58] The period starts when the claim accrued *and* the creditor knew, or did not know due to gross negligence, of the person of the debtor and of the facts giving rise to the claim.[59] Irrespective of the creditor's knowledge or grossly negligent lack of knowledge, claims lapse after 10 years from the date when they arose[60] or, where they concern damages for bodily harm, after 30 years.[61]

46 In principle these limitation periods apply to tort and contract claims alike. However, special limitation periods exist for certain common and important contractual claims: claims of buyers for damage caused by non-conforming goods generally lapse after two years.[62] The same period applies to damages claims for the non-conforming performance of contracts for work.[63] The limitation period for damages claims of a landlord against a tenant for damage caused to the rented thing (flat, car, etc) and for claims of a tenant against a landlord for compensation of certain expenditure is only six months.[64]

47 A further special limitation rule which is relevant only for tort cases concerns the suspension (*Hemmung*) of limitation. For damages claims based on a violation of the sexual self-determination of a minor, the limitation period is suspended until the minor has become 21 years old.[65] Even if an adult person raises such a

---

58 §195 BGB.

59 §199 (1) BGB.

60 §199 (4) BGB. However, damages claims other than for bodily harm lapse also after 30 years after the debtor acted, irrespective of the creditor's knowledge or grossly negligent unawareness and irrespective of the date when the claim arose which may be later than the date of the debtor's action (§199 (3) BGB). In case of conflict between these periods, the shorter one applies (§199 (3) sent 2 BGB).

61 §199 (2) BGB.

62 §437 (1) no 3 BGB (however a five-year period applies to claims if the non-conformity concerns buildings and 30 years where the claim concerns defects of the property title; §437 (1) nos 1 and 2 BGB).

63 §634a (1) no 1 BGB (again a five-year period applies where work on buildings is involved; §634a (1) no 2 BGB).

64 §548 (1) and (2) BGB.

65 §208 sent 1 BGB.

claim against a debtor, the limitation period is suspended as long as the creditor and the debtor live together in community in the same flat.[66]

J. DIFFERENCES AS REGARDS PROOF

With respect to the burden of proof, there are differences between contract and tort claims. In tort cases the general rule is that the claimant bears the burden of proving all elements which justify his/her claim.[67] In particular, fault must be proved unless one of those rules or provisions applies where fault is presumed or where liability is strict.[68] In contract, on the contrary, fault is generally presumed[69] and the burden is on the defendant to prove that he/she was not at fault. Also here some exceptions exist, for instance specific contracts where fault is not presumed.[70] 48

The general standard of proof applies both to tort and contract cases: the judge must be convinced of the relevant facts. Absolute certainty or probability close to such certainty is not required, but nonetheless a rather high degree of certainty is necessary, namely 'a degree of certainty that is useable for practical life and commands silence to doubts.'[71] Mere probability generally does not suffice. However, there are cases where the required degree of certainty is lowered, for instance in order to establish liability implementing causation[72] or to assess future losses.[73] 49

K. OTHER DIFFERENCES

Differences exist between contract and tort as regards the respective capacity. Under German tort law, a minor under the age of seven is not liable for damage 50

66 §208 sent 2 BGB; *Ellenberger* in: Palandt, BGB (77th edn 2018) §208 no 4; *Peters/Jacoby* in: Staudinger Bürgerliches Gesetzbuch mit Einführungsgesetz und Nebengesetzen (2014) §208 no 5.

67 Nomos Kommentar/*Magnus* (fn 31) Vor 33 §§249–255 no 181; Palandt/*Sprau* (fn 50) §823 no 80 ff.

68 For instance, if a medical doctor causes damage and a grave violation of medical duties is proved, then the burden of proof is reversed and the doctor has the burden of proving that he/she was not at fault, see BGH NJW 2004, 2011; BGH NJW 2007, 2767. This rule applies both in contract and tort.

69 §28 (1) BGB.

70 For instance in employment contracts where the employer, in a damages claim against an employee, must prove the fault of the employee (§619a BGB).

71 BGH NJW 2004, 777 (778).

72 See BGH NJW 2004, 777 (778); BGH NJW 2003, 1116 ff.

73 See §252 BGB.

he/she has caused.[74] Between the ages of seven and 18, the minor is liable if he/she had sufficient insight to recognise their own responsibility.[75] Where the damage resulted from a traffic accident, minors below the age of 10 cannot be held responsible for their actions.[76] In contract law, minors below the age of seven are likewise unable to conclude valid contracts. Only their legal representatives can act for them. Minors between the ages of seven and 18 also lack capacity to conclude valid contracts,[77] unless their legal representative has given his/her consent,[78] or where the contract is exclusively to the advantage of the minor,[79] or where the minor could pay with his/her own means which he/she can freely dispose of.[80]

L. REASONS FOR THE DIFFERENCES

51 The differences between German tort and contract law are, on the whole, not dramatic. They lie rather in the details than in deep structural diversities. Nonetheless, they have considerable practical importance.

- Intent plays a role – albeit a different one – in both fields.
- Strict liability for damage can be found much more frequently in tort than in contract law.
- Compensation for non-pecuniary loss is, in practice, the exception in contract law and the rule in tort law.
- Liability for others is more limited in tort law than in contract law.
- The scope of protection is different: in tort law, everybody's sphere of rights is protected against everybody else; in contract law, claims exist in principle only between the parties.
- Although the general limitation period is identical for tort and contract claims, for certain frequent contract claims, different periods apply.
- In contract law, fault is generally presumed and the debtor has the burden of rebutting this presumption; in tort law, the claimant must generally prove the fault of the tortfeasor – although a number of exceptions exist.

52 The main reason for the differences between tort law and contract law lies in the different functions of these two fields of law. Contract law should protect

---

74 §828 (1) BGB.
75 §828 (3) BGB.
76 §828 (2) BGB.
77 §106 BGB.
78 §107 BGB.
79 §107 BGB.
80 §110 BGB.

the expectations which the parties set out in the contract and for which they have concluded the contract. Generally, a party expects a future gain from the contract and in order to achieve this, a party, in most cases, gives something in exchange. Contract law ensures that promises are fulfilled and, if they are not, that such is sanctioned by a remedy. For this reason, in particular the frustrated economic expectation in the form of pure economic loss must be recoverable in contract law.

On the other hand, the central function of tort law is to protect a person's existing rights and positions to which expectations of future gains normally do not belong. 53

Moreover, the differences concerning liability for others still stem from the beginnings of the German BGB when, in the age of liberalism, efforts were made to secure far-reaching economic and commercial freedom for employers and enterprises. 54

III. LIMITATION OR EXCLUSION OF LIABILITY ARISING FROM TORT AND FROM CONTRACT

A. STATUTORY PROVISIONS AUTHORISING A LIMITATION OR EXCLUSION OF LIABILITY

First, statutory provisions of German law which directly limit the amount of damages that can be claimed and which the courts have to apply *ex officio* should be mentioned.[81] This is normally the case with strict liability statutes. With few exceptions, they provide for maximum amounts (caps) that the liable person has to compensate. For instance, §12 *Straßenverkehrsgesetz* (Road Traffic Act, StVG) limits the maximum amount that can be claimed for death or personal injury to €5 million and to €1 million for property damage.[82] Any damage which exceeds these amounts is recoverable only if the tortfeasor's fault can be proved.[83] The maximum amount cannot be lowered by the parties' agreement. 55

A cap is also provided for auditors who have violated their duties concerning the auditing of a company. They are liable in damages for intentional or negligent violations of their duties. However, if an auditor acted with negligence, the 56

[81] See for example OLG Celle OLGR 2007, 505.

[82] Maximum damages amounts (though different ones) are also prescribed, for instance, by §9 Haftpflichtgesetz (Liability Act), §10 Produkthaftungsgesetz (Product Liability Act) or §15 Umwelthaftungsgesetz (Environmental Liability Act).

[83] See §16 StVG which provides that other provisions – in particular the fault liability under §823 BGB – remain unaffected.

liability is limited to €1 million (€4 million with respect to listed companies).[84] It is irrelevant whether the violation was contractual or tortious in nature.

57 A general statutory rule that can lead to a reduction or – in exceptional cases – even to the full exclusion of damages and which has also to be applied *ex officio* is §254 BGB, which regulates contributory negligence. This provision has a wide range of application and often results in a reduction of the amount that can be recovered. It thus also reduces the liability of the debtor and applies both to contract and tort cases.

58 Less frequent than cap provisions are statutory regulations that explicitly allow for the limitation or exclusion of liability. Possibilities to limit or exclude liability are particularly relevant for contractual relationships. Nonetheless, these possibilities also apply to tortious relationships where either after the damaging event or in combination with a contract the tortious liability may be limited or excluded. The German Civil Code in general provides that a party can limit or exclude its liability except in the case of own intent (§276 (3) BGB). This means that liability for slight and gross negligence – and even for the intent of auxiliaries[85] – can be excluded. Further restrictions exist where the limitation or exclusion is foreseen in standard contract terms. Terms which limit or exclude damages for negligently caused death or injury are invalid, as are terms which restrict liability for property damage that was caused with gross negligence.[86] These restrictions actually apply to consumer contracts only.[87] However, the German courts apply their main essence to businesses as well.[88] The use of an incriminating clause between businesses is an indication that the clause is unfair unless circumstances to the contrary can be advanced. If an admissible limitation or exclusion of liability shall take effect between the two or more involved parties, it hardly needs mentioning that any limitation or exclusion of liability can only be achieved by an agreement between the involved persons. Thus, a valid agreement or valid incorporation of standard terms into the contract is always required.

59 There are further statutory provisions for single contracts which only indirectly allow for the limitation or exclusion of liability. An example is §444 BGB. According to this provision, a seller cannot rely on a contractual exclusion of warranty rights with regard to a defect if 'the seller fraudulently concealed

84 See §323 (2) Handelsgesetzbuch (Commercial Code, HGB).
85 See §278 sent 2 BGB.
86 See §309 no 7 (a) and (b) BGB. The provisions include the party's own conduct as well as that of its auxiliary or representative. The liability for the latter's intentional causing of damage can also not be restricted by standard contract terms (though by individual agreement).
87 See §310 (1) BGB.
88 See BGHZ 90, 278; BGHZ 103, 328; BGH NJW 2007, 3774; further Palandt/*Grüneberg* (fn 16) §307 no 40.

the defect or gave a guarantee of the quality of the thing'.[89] The provision implicitly acknowledges the contractual exclusion of warranty rights (within the boundaries mentioned in the preceding paragraph) but restricts its effect under certain circumstances.

B. LIMITATION OR EXCLUSION OF CONTRACTUAL AND TORTIOUS LIABILITY BY CONTRACT

1) *Is it Possible to Limit or Exclude Contractual and Tortious Liability under a Contract?*

Within the borders described above, the parties can limit or exclude their contractual and tortious liability in a contract. Whether a clause limits or excludes only contract damages or tort damages as well is always a matter of interpretation.[90] 60

The main distinction concerns the degree of fault that can be excluded: the individual intent of the party to the limiting or excluding agreement is never excludable,[91] whereas other forms of fault (slight, ordinary and gross negligence) can be excluded by individually negotiated agreement. 61

Thus, a further relevant differentiation concerns the form in which any limitation or exclusion is agreed upon and the protected interest which is involved. Where the respective clause is contained in standard contract terms, any limitation or reduction of damages for negligently caused personal harm (death or injury) is ineffective.[92] Where property damage is involved, liability for intentional or grossly negligent conduct cannot be excluded or limited.[93] 62

The differences between B2C and B2B cases are irrelevant. The courts apply the statutory standards in an almost similar manner to both. 63

With respect to contract and tort, the courts apply the stated rules without, in principle, making a distinction between both fields of law. 64

2) *To What Extent can a Contractual Exclusion Provide a Defence to a Third Party to the Contract?*

As a matter of principle, a (valid) contractual exclusion clause has effect towards the other contracting party only. A tortfeasor can generally not invoke 65

89 Semi-official translation recommended by the German Federal Ministry of Justice.
90 BGH 1977, 379 (381); BGH NJW 1979, 2148.
91 §276 (3) BGB.
92 §309 no 7 (a) BGB.
93 §309 no 7 (b) BGB.

a contract with another person or between other persons as a defence towards the victim. But again, there are some exceptions. Where the effects of a contract are extended to third parties, in particular under a contract with protective effects (*Vertrag mit Schutzwirkung*), contractual restrictions are also extended to the third party.[94] The victim who relies on the contract then must accept that the liability of the tortfeasor is restricted in accordance with a contract clause that validly limits or excludes liability. A further quasi-exception is to be found in labour law, where an employee who causes damage to third persons in the course of his/her employment is liable in principle in tort but has a redress claim or even a claim to be entirely exempted from liability against the employer if the employee acted with slight negligence; in the case of ordinary and sometimes even gross negligence, the employee must bear part of the damage depending on the circumstances. Only in the case of intent does he/she remain entirely liable.[95] The same allocation of damage applies where the employee has injured or damaged rights or goods of the employer.[96] However, in this case, this allocation may directly limit or exclude the employer's claim in tort and contract.

IV. NON-CONCURRENCE OR CONCURRENCE OF ACTIONS

A. OVERVIEW

1) Areas of Overlap between Tort and Contract

66 Tortious and contractual causes of action can overlap under German law where both areas of law protect the same interests of the aggrieved person. Since contract law regularly knows of an inherent obligation not to infringe the interests and rights of the other party,[97] a claim in contract is also frequently accompanied by a claim in tort. Where a contract exists and the bodily integrity of a contract party or his/her property has been infringed, generally a claim in tort also exists.

2) Approach to Non-Concurrence and Concurrence of Actions

67 In principle, German law follows the doctrine of cumulation of actions or claims (*Anspruchskonkurrenz*).[98] Where different bases for claims exist for identical

---

94 BGHZ 56, 259.

95 See BGH NJW 1996, 1532; BAG NJW 1999, 966; BAG NJW 2011, 1096.

96 See the references in the preceding footnote; further Palandt/*Weidenkaff* (fn 21) §611 no 156 ff.

97 See also §241 (2) BGB.

98 See BGH NJW 1987, 2008; also, eg, *Looschelders* (fn 1) no 23; Palandt/*Sprau* (fn 50) Vor §823 no 8.

damage (for instance, in contract and in tort), the victim can claim damages under both causes of action but can recover only once. If there are different requirements for the different causes of action, the victim can generally choose the most favourable basis for his/her claim.[99] However, there are exceptions where the purpose of the involved norms requires a different solution. For instance, the shorter period of limitation has been applied where the purpose of the period was to ensure that a specific situation between the parties was to be dealt with promptly.[100] Yet, it is necessary that the contractual and tortious protection concerns the same interest: where a party, for example, has damaged a rented car, the other party can claim damages in contract and tort. The integrity interest is identical in tort and contract in such a case. The courts then only apply the short contractual limitation period of six months.[101] The application of the tortious limitation period of three years[102] would run counter to the aim of the short period, namely to clear claims between the parties to the rental contract within a short time after the return of the rented good (car), mainly in order to avoid difficulties of proof. On the other hand, where the interest protected by contract and by tort is different, the limitation period for each claim applies independently.[103] Therefore, in a case where a garage had incorrectly repaired a truck which, due to the repair developed further damage afterwards, the Federal Court held that the contractual period of limitation applied to contractual remedies; to the tort claim (damage to property which did not directly follow from the repair but because the owner trusted the repair and transported heavier goods), the Court applied the tortious limitation period.[104]

Furthermore, where the statutory law provides for a reduced standard of fault for certain types of contracts, this standard must also be respected in regard of torts concerning the same situation. For instance, according to §521 BGB, someone who presents a gift to another is liable only for intent and gross negligence if he/she causes damage by the present. This standard cannot be overturned by general tort law, according to which the tortfeasor is liable for any kind of negligence (and intent).[105] 68

99 See eg BGH NJW 1987, 2008 (2010); BGH NJW-RR 2005, 172; BGHZ 101, 337 (for a tort claim, no notice requirement that is precondition for contract claim for damages because defective goods caused damage); see also *Grothe* in: Münchener Kommentar zum Bürgerlichen Gesetzbuch Bd 5 (7th edn 2015) §195 no 46 ff; Palandt/*Sprau* (fn 50) Vor §823 no 4 ff.

100 See BGHZ 54, 264.

101 See §548 BGB and BGH ibid.

102 §195 BGB.

103 See BGHZ 55, 392.

104 BGH ibid.

105 See Palandt/*Sprau* (fn 50) Vor §823 no 5; however, also BGH NJW 1992, 2474 (there the Court denied the analogous application of a specific contractual fault standard (liability only for intent and gross negligence for gratuitous loan contracts, §599 BGB) where the defendant, just for friendship, had loaned a horse to the claimant who was thrown off and considerably

69 Similar considerations apply where the parties agree on the exclusion or reduction of liability. Here it is always a matter of interpretation of the agreement and its intended purpose whether it shall only cover contractual claims or also extend to tortious or further causes of action.

B. CONCURRENCE/EXCLUSION OF ACTIONS FOR THE PROTECTION AGAINST PERSONAL INJURY

70 Where personal injury is caused in the performance of a contract (for instance, during medical treatment), in principle contractual and tortious liability apply alike. The requirements of both causes of action must be met. As far as they differ for each cause, the respective requirements must be fulfilled. However, contractual agreements which validly limit the liability of the debtor will regularly also limit tortious liability unless their interpretation requires another result.[106] Statutory provisions, which limit contractual liability but which also aim at a regulation of the situation irrespective of whether the cause of action originates in contract or tort, have the same effect. As mentioned above, for instance, §521 BGB excludes – not only in contract but also in tort – the liability for simple negligence of a person who provides another with a gift if the gift causes bodily injury.[107]

71 Generally, a claim based on *culpa in contrahendo* can also concur with contractual and tortious claims unless a situation is exclusively regulated by a specific set of provisions. For instance, the rules of sales law that provide remedies in the case of delivery of defective goods (§§433 ff BGB) in principle exclude the redress to *culpa in contrahendo*.[108]

C. CONCURRENCE/EXCLUSION OF ACTIONS FOR THE PROTECTION OF PROPERTY

72 German law does not provide for different rules of concurrence of actions if the damage concerns property.[109] Claims in contract, tort and *culpa in contrahendo*

injured. Under tort law, the defendant was liable without fault (§833 sent 1 BGB). The Federal Court refused any correction of the tort law standard because there was no loan contract between the parties and no reason for an analogous application of the reduced fault standard).

106 See BGH NJW 1979, 2148.

107 See BGHZ 46, 140; BGHZ 93, 23 (although neither decision concerned a case of bodily injury but both expressed the general principle).

108 BGH NJW 2009, 2120; BGH NJW 2010, 858 (exception when party acts with intent).

109 See BGHZ 46, 140; BGHZ 93, 23.

can concur if the requirements of each cause of action are met. Again, whether contractual limitations also extend to the other causes of action is a matter of interpretation. Similarly, whether limitations of contractual liability shall also apply to tortious liability will be determined by the purpose of statutory provisions. The example of the short limitation period that also applies to the tort claim where a rented car is damaged has already been mentioned. On the contrary, it has been held that a buyer of defective goods who has lost all contractual remedies because of delayed notice of the defects[110] can still pursue a claim in tort for damage that the defective goods caused to the buyer's property.[111] The legislative purpose of the exclusion of contractual claims (prompt processing of possible claims) does not 'infect' the tort claim which serves other purposes (the protection of the integrity of the victim's absolute rights).[112]

D. CONCURRENCE/EXCLUSION IN THE CASE OF INTERFERENCE WITH CONTRACTUAL RIGHTS

1) *Interference with a Contractual Relationship*

Where interference with a contractual relationship means the mere non- 73
performance of a contract, this conduct will generally trigger contractual liability. Non-performance of a contract as such does not generally lead to tortious liability unless the non-performance violates absolute rights of the aggrieved party, which are protected by §823 (1) BGB. If this is not the case, the mere non-performance of a contract can trigger tortious liability only if further circumstances stamp this conduct as a violation of good morals and if the author acts intentionally. Then, the aggrieved party will be entitled to damages under §826 BGB. In the field of unfair trade practices or unfair competition, further claims under the respective special acts can arise.

Where the tortfeasor interferes with contractual relationships of the tort victim 74
with third parties, the tort victim generally cannot raise a contractual claim against the third party. A claim against the tortfeasor in these cases generally requires the latter's intention and a violation of good morals (§826 BGB) because the central tort provision, §823 (1) BGB, is generally not applicable as contractual relations do not belong to the absolute rights protected by this provision.

110 Pursuant to §377 HGB, the buyer must immediately examine the goods and notify the seller of defects. Otherwise all contractual claims are lost.

111 BGHZ 101, 337.

112 See BGHZ 101, 337.

2) *Loss of Business due to Personal Injury to Someone Else's Employee or Client or to Property Damage to the Entrepreneur*

75 Where a person suffers loss because his/her employee has been injured by someone else, the employer generally has no cause of action against the wrongdoer. Contract law provides no remedy for such cases. German tort law follows the principle that only the direct victim is entitled to damages.[113] Moreover, the employer suffers mere economic loss that is generally not protected in tort.[114] An exception is recognised if the enterprise of the employer is directly and intentionally attacked (infringement of the so-called 'right of an established and operating business').[115]

76 The same principles apply if a client of the claimant has been injured.

77 Where property of a person – entrepreneur or consumer – has been damaged, any consequential loss is recoverable including loss of profits (§252 BGB). This rule applies irrespective of whether the cause of action sounds in contract or tort or *culpa in contrahendo*.

V. SPECIFIC SITUATIONS

A. PRE-CONTRACTUAL LIABILITY

78 It is a special feature of German law that it developed and accepted the institute of *culpa in contrahendo* a considerably long time ago – already in the 19th century.[116] The pre-contractual phase of negotiations is regarded as a quasi-contractual relationship which justifies the application of all those rules which apply to contracts and which often provide a better protection than that granted by tort law. Since the modernisation of the German law of obligations in 2002, the institute of *culpa in contrahendo* has been expressly acknowledged in the text of the Civil Code in §311 (2) BGB, although the provision does not define special requirements for a damages claim. In this respect, the general provisions of the law of obligations apply. A damages claim therefore requires that, during the

113 The only exceptions are provided for by §844 BGB (claims of dependents of a person who has been killed) and §845 BGB (claims of persons who have lost the services of the injured person if that person was obliged by statute to render these services (only children in the household of the parents have such an obligation)).

114 Only if the requirements of §826 BGB (intent and violation of good morals) are met or if a statutory provision, the purpose of which is to protect the economic interests of the victim, has been violated (§823 (2) BGB).

115 See for instance BGH NJW 2003, 1041; BGH NJW 2006, 830.

116 See thereto *Medicus/Lorenz*, Schuldrecht I Allgemeiner Teil (21st edn 2015) no 103.

pre-contractual phase, the debtor at least negligently violated a pre-contractual duty (§280 (1) sent 1 BGB). The fault of the debtor is presumed (§280 (1) sent 2 BGB). The extent of damages is regulated by §§249–254 BGB.

B. LIABILITY OF PROFESSIONALS

79 In principle, the general contract and tort rules apply when professionals cause damage. Contractual liability therefore requires the violation of a contractual duty and fault which is, however, rebuttably presumed (§280 (1) BGB). To engage tortious liability, the requirements of §823 (1), §823 (2) or §826 BGB must be fulfilled. In contrast to contract law, under §823 (1) BGB, an absolutely protected right must have been infringed and in principle the victim must prove fault on the part of the professional.

80 In certain professional fields, modified rules have developed. This is particularly true for the field of medical and health treatment. The contractual duties and the contractual liability of doctors and other medical staff have rather recently (2013) been specifically regulated in §§630a–630h BGB. §630h BGB specifies the presumption of fault and also of causation: para 1 of the provision presumes an error by the doctor 'if a general treatment risk has materialised which was fully manageable for the treating party and which led to the injury to the life, limb or health of the patient.' Further, para 5 sent 1 provides: 'If gross malpractice has [sc been] committed, and if this is susceptible as a matter of principle to cause an injury to life, limb or health of the nature which in fact took place, it is to be presumed that the malpractice was the cause of this injury.'[117] Simplified, fault is only presumed if the injury can be traced back to treatment whose risks can be fully mastered (such as placing a patient on the operating table, etc); and if the doctor or other staff committed gross malpractice, its causal link to the injury is presumed. These rules apply not only to contractual claims but also to tort claims where the courts first developed these rules.[118] To a certain extent, they level the traditional differences between contract and tort law for this particular professional field.

81 A similarly regulated field is prospectus liability. Special legislative acts provide for the liability of those (professionals) who have issued prospectus if the latter is incorrect, incomplete or misleading.[119]

---

117 The translation is recommended by the German Ministry of Justice, see <www.gesetze-im-internet.de/englisch_bgb/englisch_bgb.html>.

118 See eg BGH NJW 1995, 1618; BGH MDR 1997, 147.

119 See §§20–22 Vermögensanlagengesetz (Act on Capital Investments, VermAnlG); §306 Kapitalanlagegesetzbuch (Code on Capital Investments, KAGB).

82 In a similar vein, the courts, in particular the Federal Supreme Court, have developed stricter liability rules where professional 'experts' cause damage – primarily pure economic loss – to third persons with whom no contractual relationship exists.[120] The main reason for this development is the lack of protection of purely financial interests in §823 (1) BGB and an increased need for such protection since professional experts often give opinions, advice, certifications etc, upon which third parties rely and shall rely (eg, creditors, investors). The courts use several instruments to avoid the shortcomings of traditional tort law: sometimes they imply a contract, for instance of information,[121] or a contract in favour of the third person.[122] More often the courts assume a contract with protective effects towards the third person.[123] Further, the institute of *culpa in contrahendo* is used to hold personally liable professionals who actually act only as agents, intermeddlers or the like but who have a strong individual interest in the intermeddled transaction and often use their own reputation to influence the decision of the third party.[124]

83 However, developments in the contrary direction can also be observed. Partly, the liability of professional experts towards third parties is limited, for instance the liability of public notaries (only subsidiary liability),[125] or the liability of accountants for certain professional activities (limited amount).[126] Yet these regulations attempt to achieve a fair balance between the principally increased liability of professionals and a reasonable extent of this liability.

CASES

CASE 1. THE UNATTRACTIVE SHOPPING MALL

84 Despite the fact that C has no lease contract with D but only with Z, C may nonetheless have a claim in contract against D. The basis of such a claim is the legal institute of contract with protective effects in favour of third persons. As indicated above, the institute serves a subsidiary function: where the aggrieved person already has a full claim for the same damage on a different basis, the rules

---

120 See thereon in particular *H Zugehör*, Berufliche "Dritthaftung" – insbesondere der Rechtsanwälte, Steuerberater, Wirtschaftsprüfer und Notare – in der deutschen Rechtsprechung, NJW 2000, 1601 (the author was judge at the BGH).

121 See BGH NJW 1972, 678; BGH NJW 1992, 2080.

122 OLG Karlsruhe WM 1997, 1476.

123 See already above no 4.

124 See for instance BGH NJW 1987, 2512; BGH NJW-RR 1990, 459; BGH NJW 2006, 993.

125 See §19 Notarordnung (Ordinance for Notaries, NotO).

126 See §323 (2) HGB; see thereto BGHZ 138, 257 (266).

of this institute do not apply.[127] However, in the present case, C in all likelihood has no contractual claim against Z; most probably the sub-lease contract does not oblige Z to ensure the attractiveness of the shopping mall. The rules on contracts with protective effects therefore apply.

This legal institute primarily requires a contract or comparable relationship between the defendant and another party; this contract must extend its effects to the claimant. This requires that: (1) the claimant must be endangered by the defendant's behaviour in the same way as the defendant's contract partner (*Leistungsnähe*);[128] (2) the contract partner must be interested in the extension of the contractual effects and it must be possible to interpret the contract in this way (*Einbeziehungsinteresse*);[129] and (3) the defendant must have been able to have known of the claimant's endangerment and interest (*Erkennbarkeit*).[130] 85

In the case at hand, the lease between D and Z is a contract that in principle can have protective effects. This has been so held for the employee of a tenant who worked and was injured in the leased rooms due to a defective window.[131] In the case at hand, C is affected by D's omission in the same way as Z and Z as sub-landlord has an interest in the protection of C, who otherwise may terminate the sublease. Furthermore, D could know that a subtenant would be interested in the attractiveness of the shopping mall and the performance of D's respective obligations since D's contract with Z allowed the sublease. It is not required that the defendant knew the claimant in person or knew the details of the concrete sublease. Since the principle lease contract allowed the sublease, C was entitled to use the let rooms. 86

German courts would therefore allow C's claim. C would be entitled to be compensated for the loss caused by D's omission. It is the clearly prevailing view that in such situations damages are to be granted not only for personal injuries but also for property damage and pure economic loss.[132] 87

Under German law, C is, however, not entitled to damages in tort (or on any other basis). German tort law (§823 (1) BGB) does not protect pure economic loss that is caused by mere negligence and which does not violate any statutory law. 88

---

127 See BGHZ 70, 330; BGHZ 129, 169; BGH NJW 2014, 2577.

128 BGHZ 49, 354; BGH NJW 2008, 2245.

129 See BGHZ 51, 96; BGHZ 128, 168 (173); BGH NJW 2012, 3165.

130 BGHZ 49, 354; NJW 1996, 2929.

131 BGHZ 61, 233; BGH NJW 2010, 3152.

132 BGH NJW-RR 1986, 1307; BGHZ 133, 168 (171 f.); *Gottwald* in: Münchener Kommentar zum Bürgerlichen Gesetzbuch Bd 5 (7th edn 2016) §328 no 187; Palandt/*Grüneberg* (fn 16) §328 no 15.

CASE 2. THE IDLE LAWYER

89 The case is very similar to the case in BGH JZ 1966, 141, where a father intended to make his daughter the sole heir and asked a solicitor to assist him. The latter promised his assistance but did not do so before the father died.[133] The Federal Supreme Court held the contract between the deceased and the lawyer to execute a valid last will to be a contract with protective effects in favour of the intended heir who therefore was entitled to the full amount that she would have inherited had the lawyer reacted in time. It was held not to be an argument that the real heirs inherited more than they should according to the (invalid) will of the deceased. These heirs had, so to speak, a windfall profit but were not obliged to contribute to the loss of the intended heir.

90 Thus, in the hypothetical, the daughters could claim £9,000 each from D.

91 The only basis of the claim would be the contract with protective effects. German tort law, again, would not allow for the compensation of the pure economic loss of the daughters.

CASE 3. THE DEFECTIVE HOUSE

92 Under German tort law, C would have a damages claim against D based on §823 (1) BGB. This requires the wrongful and faulty causing of damage to the aggrieved party's absolutely protected rights such as bodily integrity and property. These rights are infringed here and D acted in a wrongful and negligent manner. Problematic are two points: the exclusion clause agreed with Z and the passage of time since the erection of the building.

93 Unless Z passed the exclusion on to C when selling the house, the clause has no effect on the relation between D and C. The reason is that in German law a contract to the disadvantage of third parties is invalid.[134] Such a contract would offend the central principle of party autonomy. When D and Z agree that D shall not be liable for property damage to C (or any eventual future buyer), this would be a contract to the detriment of a person who had not participated in the conclusion of the exclusion clause. This result cannot be circumvented by the assumption that the contract between D and Z could be regarded as a contract with protective effects. Under such contracts, the protected third

133 Cases of this kind were given the name 'the laughing double heirs' ('die lachenden Doppelerben') because the intended heir(s) received full compensation but could inherit in future also the estate or parts of it; *G Kegel* in: FS Flume (1978) 545 ff coined this expression; see also BGH NJW 1979, 2033.

134 See BGHZ 54, 247; BGHZ 61, 361; BGHZ 78, 374 s.

person would be entitled to damages (not to performance claims)[135] in the same way as the principle contractual party. This means that also a contractual exemption or exclusion clause in the principle contract would be valid against the third party.[136] However, as mentioned above, the institute of the contract with protective effects serves only as a supplementary 'gap-filler'. Where a person already has a full claim – as here in tort – the institute is not applicable.

With respect to the time element, the German law of limitation provides for a general limitation period of three years (§195 BGB). However, the period starts to run only after the cause of action has accrued and the creditor gains knowledge of the facts and the person of the debtor or grossly negligently ignored these facts (§199 (1) BGB). These rules apply without restriction to tort claims concerning defects in the construction of buildings although for the limitation of contractual rights in such cases the BGB provides a specific period of five years (§634a (1) no 2 BGB).[137] 94

Under German law, in the hypothetical, C would have no further claims based on other causes of action. 95

CASE 4. APARTMENT IN FLAMES

C would have a claim against D both in contract and in tort. Under the lease contract, D is obliged to ensure the security of the – electrical and other dangerous – installations which are part of the let rooms. Since D was negligent in fulfilling this duty, he is liable for the damage (§536a (1) BGB). 96

Also under German tort law (§823 (1) BGB), C could claim damages because D wrongfully and negligently caused her physical injuries. 97

C could claim damages under, and base her claim on, both causes of action (although would only be awarded compensation once). It is not necessary to choose between the contract and tort basis. However, in this case there would be no difference between the two with respect to the outcome. 98

CASE 5. INJURED SKIER

On the assumption that D1 is also the operator – or at least responsible for the operation – of the ski lift, D1 could be liable in contract. The contract would 99

---

135 BGHZ 49, 353; BGH NJW 2012, 3165.

136 BGHZ 56, 269.

137 This period starts with the taking over of the building (§634a (2) BGB) and operates also against a successor (BGHZ 60, 240).

include the obligation to transport C safely. This obligation has been violated. However, contractual liability for damage requires fault. In contract law, fault is presumed (§280 (1) sent 2 BGB). Since the reasons for the accident are unclear, it is very likely that D1 cannot prove the absence of fault and would therefore be held liable.

100 Under German tort law, D1 would not be held liable. First, there is no strict liability statute for ski lifts. §1 *Haftpflichtgesetz* (Liability Act, HaftpflG) provides strict liability only for railways and cable railways but not for drag lifts as which ski lifts are normally constructed.[138] Under §823 (1) BGB, C has to prove D1's fault, which in the circumstances appears to be impossible. In the absence of further telling circumstances (for instance, repeated prior accidents, etc), it is unlikely that German courts would reverse the burden of proof.

101 Since the insurance contract between D1 and D2 covers only tortious liability and D1 is not liable in tort, C has no claim against D2.[139] Anyway, C would have no direct claim against D2; however, D2 would be obliged towards D1 to cover a tortious claim of C against D1.[140]

CASE 6. EXPLODING CAR

102 Under German sales law, C would not be entitled to claim damages from D1. The defective fuel line is a defect that in principle entitles C to damages (§437 no 3 BGB) although generally only after C has given D1 the opportunity to perform the contract and to deliver a new car (§§440, 281 BGB). Further, damages would only be recoverable if D1 was at fault, which may be doubtful (although fault is presumed, §280 (1) sent 2 BGB). However, §438 (1) no 3 BGB provides for a limitation period of two years for damages claims – as well as for the other remedies in the case of delivery of defective movable goods. At least if D1 invokes this provision (which is most likely), C has no contractual claim against D1.

103 The success of a tort claim against D1 is also rather unlikely. C could base his claim on §823 (1) BGB since his property – an absolutely protected right – was destroyed. However, since C bought the already defective car, it cannot be D1's act that caused the damage to C's property. D1 only sold a car of much lower value at too high a price. The normal contractual remedies of performance,

138 See BGH NJW 1960, 1345; *W Filthaut*, Haftpflichtgesetz (9th edn 2015) §1 no 19.

139 A direct claim exists only in the case of mandatory insurance as for instance in the case of insurance for car accidents; see §115 Versicherungsvertragsgesetz (Insurance Contract Act, VVG) in connection with the Pflichtversicherungsgesetz (Mandatory Insurance Act, PflVersG).

140 See §106 VVG.

termination or price reduction (even to zero) are, however, barred by the lapse of the limitation period. Furthermore, the negligence of D1, which would be required for a claim under §823 (1) BGB and which C must prove, would be more than questionable. D1 as a car dealer must know and recognise those defects of the cars he sells which would be revealed by an ordinarily thorough inspection. Since the fuel line is generally invisible inside the car, it is rather unlikely that D1 could discover the defect in the course of a normal inspection. Only if D1 was already aware of similar accidents with this type of car should he have reacted and should have stopped selling this type of car. But only then could he be held liable for a breach of a pre-contractual information duty or even for a violation of §826 BGB if he acted with intent and against good morals.

C can base his claims against D2 only in tort. Even if C could directly rely on 104
the two-year warranty as a contract of guaranty between him and D2, this contract has already terminated due to the passage of time. In tort, either the *Produkthaftungsgesetz* (Product Liability Act, ProdHaftG) or the general tort law of the BGB can constitute a basis for a claim. It is disputed in Germany whether §1 ProdHaftG covers cases where – as here – damage is caused to the product itself.[141] The probably prevailing view denies such a claim.[142] According to this view, the ProdHaftG would not apply here.

In general tort law, it is recognised that, in principle, defects of a product 105
itself cannot trigger liability.[143] Since the aggrieved party in these cases never owned property that was free from defects, the defect cannot have violated this party's property. Thus, in principle C has no tort claim against D2. However, the courts have developed an important exception from the mentioned principle: the case of the so-called '*Weiterfresserschäden*' (literally, 'damage which continues to eat up the good'), where a separate element, that serves a functionally separate purpose and can be installed into, and removed from, a greater entity (machine, car, etc) without great difficulty, destroys the entity; this is regarded as an infringement of the property (the machine, car, etc).[144] The courts divide the damaged good into two parts: the defective separate element and the rest of the good that is free from defects. Yet, in order not to confuse the purposes of tort and contract law, the damage that the separate element causes to the whole good must not only be equal to the reduced value of the good. If that is the case, only remedies in contract apply.[145]

---

141 For applicability of §1 in such cases: *Oechlser* in: Staudinger, Bürgerliches Gesetzbuch mit Einführungsgesetz und Nebengesetzen (2018) §1 ProdHaftG no 16; against: MünchKommBGB/*Wagner* (fn 50) §1 ProdhaftG no 11 ff.

142 See MünchKommBGB/*Wagner* (fn 50) §1 ProdhaftG no 9 ff with further references.

143 See Palandt/*Sprau* (fn 50) §823 no 178.

144 BGHZ 67, 359; BGHZ 86, 256.

145 BGH NJW 1985, 2420; BGHZ 117, 183; BGH NJW 2011, 594.

106 In the case at hand, it is a matter of fact whether the fuel line of the specific car was a separate element that could rather easily be removed and re-installed in the car. Only if that was the case would C be able to file a damages claim for the full loss against D2. D2's fault would be presumed since the courts reverse the burden of proof in product liability cases.[146] It is unlikely that D2 could rebut this presumption. The claim would also not be time-barred. The limitation period of three years (§195 BGB) would only start when the cause of action accrues (§199 (3) BGB), ie in this case when the car exploded.

CASE 7. RACING BOAT BURNING

107 C would not be entitled to damages from D under contract law. Any contractual remedies for the defect are time-barred (§438 (1) no 3 BGB, which provides for a two-year limitation period for remedies for delivery of defective goods).

108 In tort law, a claim based on §1 ProdHaftG would probably be denied because D is likely not the manufacturer of the boat even though he added electronic equipment. But it is highly unlikely that D produced this equipment. He therefore is not a 'producer' in the sense of §4 ProdHaftG. §4 (1) sent 1 ProdHaftG requires – in line with art 3(1) Product Liability Directive – that the person who adds component parts also has manufactured them in order to qualify as a producer.[147]

109 Under general tort law (§823 (1) BGB), D must have been at least negligent in installing the electronic equipment. Under the circumstances of the case, the reversed burden of proof for fault, which the courts accept under general product liability law,[148] would not apply since D would not be regarded as the producer of the boat. The mere installation of a device that others have manufactured does not make a person a producer of the final product.[149] Therefore, C would have to prove D's fault. Unless D made mistakes in installing the equipment or negligently overlooked the fact that the equipment was defective or unfit for its purpose, he would not be at fault and thus not be liable.

---

146 BGHZ 51, 91; BGHZ 116, 104.

147 See OLG Stuttgart VersR 2001, 465 (466): a construction enterprise which installs material that others have fabricated is not liable as a producer if the building is defective because of the defective material; MünchKommBGB/*Wagner* (fn 50) §4 ProdHaftG no 6 f.

148 BGHZ 51, 91; BGHZ 116, 104.

149 Also there, a producer is only the party who has produced the final product or its parts; see BGH BB 1977, 1117 (1118).

CASE 8. INSIDIOUS REPORT

C can have a contract claim against D for breach of inherent obligations of the employment contract. Evidently, there is no express contractual provision that prohibits D from establishing an enterprise that competes with the business activities of one's own employer C. However, §60 *Handelsgesetzbuch* (Commercial Code, HGB) contains a prohibition of competing business activities of employees during the course of their employment. This provision has been extended to any kind of employment contract not only to those falling within the scope of the HGB.[150] Since D has violated this provision, he is liable in accordance with §61 HGB either in damages or can – instead – claim that D's contract with Z is treated as C's contract or that D transfers or assigns what he received or will receive from Z. 110

Moreover, C may also have a claim in tort based on §826 BGB. The provision requires intent and the violation of good morals (*die guten Sitten*). The intent – *dolus directus* or *dolus eventualis* – must refer to the damage.[151] In the present case, it is very likely that C can prove that D intended the damage. The aim of D's false and defaming report was evidently to influence C to terminate and thus to lose the contract with Z so that D could conclude his own contract with Z. Such conduct would also violate good morals. Communicating intentionally wrong facts in order to influence a commercial contract to be concluded or terminated is generally regarded as a violation of good morals.[152] 111

Most likely C is also entitled to claim damages under §9 *Gesetz gegen den unlauteren Wettbewerb* (Act against Unfair Competition, UWG). Although the UWG is in principle applicable only if entrepreneurs (*Unternehmer*) are involved, D is not only an employee but acts here as an entrepreneur for his own business which he has illegally established.[153] §4 no 11 UWG prohibits the violation of statutory provisions which are designed to regulate the commercial conduct in the interest of market participants. §60 HGB, which D has violated, is a provision that aims at the protection of employers against the competition of their own employees.[154] This constitutes a market regulation in the interest of 112

150 See BAG NJW 2008, 392; *von Hoyningen-Huene* in: Münchener Kommentar zum Handelsgesetzbuch (4th edn 2016) §60 no 8 f with further references.

151 BGH NJW 2004, 406; BGH NJW 2004, 2664; BGH NJW-RR 2013, 550.

152 BGH NJW-RR 2005, 611; Palandt/*Sprau* (fn 50) §826 no 20.

153 It is sufficient that the person acts with a view to becoming an entrepreneur (*Existenzgründer*); OLG Köln GRUR-RR 2011, 370; *H Harte-Bavendamm/F Henning-Bodewig* (eds), Gesetz gegen den unlauteren Wettbewerb (UWG) (4th edn 2016) (-Keller) §2 no 218.

154 See BAG Arbeitsrechtliche Praxis (AP) §60 HGB no 4; MünchKommHGB/*von Hoyningen-Huene* (fn 150) §60 no 2.

market participants. Problematic could be that §4 no 11 UWG merely mentions the market conduct and no longer – as it did prior to the amendment of 2004 – the entry into the market. Whether §60 HGB regulates the market conduct or the market entry is doubtful. Employees who compete with their employer have probably already entered the market although §60 HGB aims at their being kept out. The question may be left open here since C can claim damages under §61 HGB and §826 BGB.

CASE 9. CIRCULAR LETTER

113 On the assumption that the allegations in the circular letter are false, it is most likely that C can claim damages on the basis of §826 BGB and §9 UWG. As already mentioned in Case 8, §826 BGB requires intent and violation of good morals. Whether C can prove intent is always a matter of the available evidence. In the present case, intent is hardly doubtful.[155] Further, the dissemination of false facts concerning commercial conduct in order to damage another market participant is generally regarded as offending good morals.[156]

114 The requirements for a claim under §9 UWG are also met: §4 no 8 UWG mentions as one of the forms of unfair trade practices the dissemination of facts which cannot be proven as true and which are able to damage another's business or creditworthiness (so-called '*Anschwärzen*' ('denigrate')). This is what D did here. §9 UWG further requires only fault so that negligence suffices. There is no question here that D was at fault.

CASE 10. SHORTAGE OF SUPPLY

115 C could have a contractual remedy, namely to insist on the old contract if the new contract would be invalid because of a violation of good morals. The basis for the invalidity of the new contract would be §138 BGB. §138 (2) BGB requires that 'a person, by exploiting the predicament, inexperience, lack of sound judgment or considerable weakness of will of another, causes himself or a third party, in exchange for an act of performance, to be promised or granted pecuniary advantages which are clearly disproportionate to the performance.'[157] In the present case D uses the situation that C depends on D's deliveries. It is doubtful

---

155 The intent in the form of *dolus directus* and *dolus eventualis* can be inferred from certain behaviour or indicia; see BGH NJW-RR 2012, 404.

156 BGH NJW-RR 2005, 611; Palandt/*Sprau* (fn 50) §826 no 20.

157 The translation is recommended by the German Ministry of Justice, see <www.gesetze-im-internet.de/englisch_bgb/englisch_bgb.html>.

whether this could be regarded as an exploitation of a predicament. It is actually a normal commercial situation that can occur and for which a party should have taken precautions. However, where a gross disproportion between performance and counter-performance exists, the courts generally invalidate the contract already for this reason alone. A gross disproportion is regularly a 100% over- or undervalue in favour of the defendant.[158] In cases of such a disproportion, the contract is per se invalid.[159] In the present case, the price increase and the new payment term do not reach the level of a gross disproportion (in any case, what the market price of the agreed goods at the relevant time was would still have to be determined). It should be added that C was not obliged to accept D's new offer. If D had stopped delivering under the old conditions in breach of the old contract, C would have been entitled to damages for the ensuing loss.

C can also not claim damages on the basis of §826 BGB because, also under 116
that provision, the new contract was not concluded in violation of good morals. §823 (1) BGB does not allow for compensation of pure economic loss as was caused here. §823 (2) in connection with §240 *Strafgesetzbuch* (Criminal Code, StGB) also provides no cause of action. §823 (2) BGB provides for a damages claim if certain provisions of statutory law have been at least negligently violated. One of those provisions is §240 (1) StGB, which requires that a person 'unlawfully with force or threat of serious harm causes a person to commit, suffer or omit an act'. In the present case, it could be argued that D threatened to stop further deliveries unless C increased the price. In C's situation this might be seen as serious harm since C had no alternative supply sources. However, the threat must be unlawful, which §240 (2) StGB defines as 'inappropriate for the purpose of achieving the desired outcome.' The threat to breach a contract if the other party does not accept higher prices is generally not unlawful in this sense. The threatened party may use the means of contract law but it is inappropriate to employ the sanctions of criminal law for pure cases of breach of contract.[160]

CASE 11. INJURED ROCK STAR

German law does not grant C a damages claim. If at all, only tort law could 117
deliver a basis for a cause of action. However, §823 BGB only entitles directly injured persons to compensation and furthermore excludes compensation for pure economic loss. C is not directly injured but suffered only an indirect loss which is of a purely economic nature.

158 BGH NJW 2001, 1127; BGH NJW 2002, 429; BGH NJW 2002, 3165; BGH WM 2008, 967; 90% in case of land sale: BGH NJW 2014, 1652.

159 See BGH NJW 2014, 1652.

160 See BGH NJW 1999, 800 (threat to stop business relations can be unlawful in the sense of §240 StGB if it is used to achieve bribes in one's own favour).

CASE 12. EQUIPMENT DESTROYED

118 C can file a contractual damages claim against D1, who was obliged to transport the equipment safely and timely to the place of the concert. The basis for the claim is §425 HGB, which provides for a rather strict liability. However, this liability is limited to the value of the transported goods and to 8.33 Special Drawing Rights per kilo. Moreover, the carrier is exempted from liability if he could not have avoided the damage to the transported goods despite the application of utmost care (§425 HGB). It thus depends on the circumstances of the traffic accident if D1 is exempted from this – limited – liability. Compensation of further consequential losses caused by the damage to the transported goods is excluded by §433 HGB. Therefore, C cannot claim compensation for the cancelled concert.

119 The limits which the Commercial Code provides for contractual carriers also apply to tort claims (§434 HGB).

120 A claim against D2 could only be based on tort law in this case. Under §823 (1) BGB, pure economic loss cannot be recovered, but the so-called '*Recht am eingerichteten und ausgeübten Gewerbebetrieb*' ('right of an established and operating business') is also protected as an absolute right in the sense of this provision. It could have been infringed here since C's business in organising this special concert was impaired. However, the courts require that the infringement must be directly targeted towards the business.[161] The aim of the infringement must have been to impair the business. This is not the case here. The traffic accident was not targeted towards C's business but occurred by chance. Therefore, D2 is not liable.

CASE 13. SLIPPING ON A LETTUCE LEAF

121 The German Supreme Court decided a similar case in 1961[162] following the case law of the former *Reichsgericht* (Imperial Court).[163] Since C has not yet bought anything, a contract has not yet been concluded. Thus, a claim cannot be directly based on a contract. For a tort claim, D must have acted negligently (§823 (1) BGB) or be responsible for an employee under §831 BGB. Pursuant to §823 (1) BGB, C must prove D's negligence, which appears to be difficult if not impossible. Under §831 BGB, D can avoid liability by proving that he selected

161 BGHZ 138, 311; BGH NJW 2012, 2579.
162 BGH NJW 1962, 31.
163 See RGZ 78, 239.

and supervised his employees with ordinary care. It is likely that D can prove careful selection and sufficient supervision.

In order to prevent victims such as C from not being compensated, the courts employ the institute of *culpa in contrahendo*. The pre-contractual phase, where a creditor is already in the sphere of the debtor and exposed to the risks there, is regarded as a quasi-contractual situation where, in particular, the contractual presumption applies that damage was caused by the debtor's – here D's – fault (§280 (1) sent 2 BGB). In a situation such as the present one, the debtor is generally not in a position to rebut this presumption. C would therefore be entitled to damages from D on the basis of *culpa in contrahendo*. 122

CASE 14. TEST DRIVE

C could base a claim on contract (a gratuitous lease, §598 BGB) or on general tort law (§823 (1) BGB). Under both causes of action it suffices that D wrongfully damaged C's property and that the circumstances also suggest that D was negligent. In cases such as the present one, German courts however deny liability where the negligence was only slight (not gross negligence or even intent) and where the special test-drive risks have realised.[164] The Federal Supreme Court upheld a lower decision which had assumed a tacit agreement of the parties to exclude liability of the driver for slight negligence. The Federal Court confirmed this construction of an implied contractual agreement.[165] 123

The main arguments were that the test driver is in a specific and potentially dangerous situation where the risk of an accident is increased: he does not know the peculiarities of the car and is often not used to its order of instruments; on the other hand, he will test the qualities of the car and may drive faster and more demandingly than he ordinarily would. Further, the seller could easily insure the risk that its cars are damaged whereas it would be difficult for the driver to get insurance coverage for such test driving of cars belonging to other persons. At least the seller had the duty to inform the interested driver that he would be liable for any negligently caused damage. If a seller omits to pass on this information, the driver can trust that he would not be held liable for damage through simple negligence.[166] Therefore C would not be entitled to damages if D was simply negligent. Only in case of gross negligence (or intent) would a claim arise. 124

164 See BGH NJW 1972, 1363.
165 BGH NJW 1972, 1363.
166 See BGH NJW 1972, 1363.

CASE 15. BREACH OF NEGOTIATIONS

125 C can have a claim under *culpa in contrahendo* aspects.[167] Other causes of actions in contract or tort are not available. Generally, under German law, parties are free to retreat from contractual negotiations (before the conclusion of the contract) without becoming liable for any damage the other party may thereby have suffered.[168] However, under specific conditions, the retreating party may nonetheless be liable on the basis of *culpa in contrahendo*. In order to establish a claim, it is necessary that the party retreats without justification after having induced the other party's impression and reliance that the contract will be concluded.[169] This is for instance the case if a party has expressly declared that it will conclude the contract,[170] or if a party has induced the other to make investments in regard of the expected contract and then retreats without a justifying reason.[171] The other party can then claim damages, however, only for such expenditure which it incurred in expectation of the contract.[172]

126 In the case at hand, D merely declared that he would continue the negotiations after returning from his business trip. This could not give C the impression that D would conclude the contract. In addition, C appears to have incurred thus far no expenditure in expectation of the contract. German courts would therefore reject the claim.

CASE 16. NON-DISCLOSURE OF RELEVANT FACTS

127 C could be entitled to contractual remedies under sales law or under *culpa in contrahendo*. In principle, as far as sales law provides a remedy, *culpa in contrahendo* is excluded.[173] However, at least where a party acted with intent, both causes of action are applicable.[174]

128 Under sales law, the fact that the harvester is not fit for steep fields can be a defect in accordance with §434 (1) BGB. This would be, first, the case if the parties agreed on the use of the harvester on steep fields. Such an agreement on specific qualities of the sales object can be concluded even impliedly.[175] One-sided

---

167 The institute of *culpa in contrahendo* is recognised as such in §311 BGB. The provision does, however, not regulate the requirements for a damages claim. They follow from case law.

168 General opinion, see Palandt/*Grüneberg* (fn 16) §311 no 30.

169 See BGH NJW 1980, 1683; BGH NJW 1996, 1884; BGH NJW 2013, 928.

170 BGH NJW 1970, 1840.

171 BGH NJW 1961, 169; BGH NJW 1985, 1778 (1781).

172 BGH NJW 1996, 1884.

173 BGH NJW 2009, 2120.

174 BGH NJW 2009, 2120; BGH NJW 2010, 858.

175 BGH NJW 2009, 2807.

expectations of the buyer, even if the seller is aware of them, do not, however, suffice for an agreement. It is necessary that the seller positively reacts to the buyer's expectations.[176] The courts would likely regard it as lack of consent if a seller who knows the expectations of the buyer merely delivers the sales object.

Moreover, the requirements of fitness for the contractual purpose or for the general purpose of goods of the same kind (§434 (1) nos 1 and 2 BGB) would also be met here since the harvester is fit for normal harvesting and nothing else has been agreed upon. 129

Therefore, it is likely that German courts would refuse remedies under sales law. 130

Although sales law as basis for a cause of action is probably excluded, D could still be held liable on the basis of *culpa in contrahendo* for omitting to pass on the information that the harvester was unfit for C's purpose. This requires a duty on D's part to disclose the fact that the harvester does not suit C's needs. If a seller has recognised that the buyer cannot use the intended object of sale, he must disclose this fact.[177] Generally, in contractual negotiations, each party is obliged to inform the other party before the conclusion of a contract of circumstances which can frustrate the purpose of the contract and are decisive for the other party's decision to conclude the contract if the general opinion (*Verkehrsauffassung*) would expect such information.[178] 131

In the present case, German courts would expect D to disclose the fact that the harvester is unusable for C's purposes. In knowingly omitting this information, D would be liable in damages (§280 (1) in connection with §311 (2) and §241 (2) BGB). 132

---

176 BGH NJW 2009, 2807.

177 See BGH NJW 1962, 1196; BGH NJW 1985, 1771; BGH NJW 2009, 2120 (omission to pass on information that house contained asbestos); BGH NJW 2010, 858 (duty to inform a buyer of a car that the car had been bought from a dealer who was not registered in the car certificate).

178 BGH NJW 2001, 2163; BGH NJW 2007, 3057; BGH NJW 2010, 858.

THE BORDERLINES OF TORT LAW IN GREECE

Eugenia Dacoronia

QUESTIONS

I. Tracing the Borderlines . . . 215
A. Distinction between Tort and Contract . . . 215
B. Existence of a 'Grey Zone'? . . . 216
C. Common or Different Rules Regulating Tort and Contract . . . 216
D. Application of Common Rules in a Different Way . . . 217
II. Main Differences between Tortious and Contractual Liability . . . 218
A. Differences as Regards the Foundations of Liability . . . 218
1) Role of Intention . . . 218
2) Role of Wrongfulness and Fault and their Variations . . . 218
3) Role of Strict Liability . . . 218
B. Differences as Regards Causation . . . 219
C. Differences as Regards Remedies . . . 219
1) Degree of Certainty of the Damage . . . 219
2) Compensation for Non-Pecuniary Loss . . . 220
3) Compensation for Loss of Earnings and for Loss of Chance . . . 221
4) Restitutionary Damages . . . 222
5) Aggravated and Exemplary (or Punitive) Damages . . . 222
6) Other Remedies . . . 222
D. Differences as Regards Recoverability of 'Pure Economic Losses' . . . 223
E. Differences as Regards Liability for Others . . . 224
1) Liability for Auxiliaries and for Independent Contractors . . . 224
2) Liability for Legal Representatives or Organs of a Company . . . 225
3) Liability of Representatives of Natural Persons . . . 225
4) Liability of the Auxiliary/Organ Itself . . . 226
F. Differences as Regards Liability in the Case of Multiple Tortfeasors/Breaching Parties . . . 227
G. Differences as Regards the Persons Who May be Protected . . . 230
1) Persons Protected under Tort . . . 230
2) Persons Protected under Contract . . . 230

H. Differences as Regards Defences 231
I. Differences as Regards Limitation Periods 232
J. Differences as Regards Proof 233
K. Other Differences 234
L. Reasons for the Differences 235
III. Limitation or Exclusion of Liability Arising from Tort and from Contract 236
A. Statutory Provisions Authorising a Limitation or Exclusion of Liability 236
B. Limitation or Exclusion of Contractual and Tortious Liability by Contract 237
1) Is it Possible to Limit or Exclude Contractual and Tortious Liability under a Contract? 237
2) To What Extent can a Contractual Exclusion Provide a Defence to a Third Party to the Contract? 237
IV. Non-Concurrence or Concurrence of Actions 237
A. Overview 237
B. Concurrence/Exclusion of Actions for the Protection against Personal Injury 239
C. Concurrence/Exclusion of Actions for the Protection of Property 239
D. Concurrence/Exclusion in the Case of Interference with Contractual Rights 239
1) Interference with a Contractual Relationship 239
2) Loss of Business due to Personal Injury to Someone Else's Employees or Clients or to Property Damage to the Entrepreneur 240
V. Specific Situations 241
A. Pre-Contractual Liability 241
B. Liability of Professionals 241

CASES

Case 1. The Unattractive Shopping Mall 243
Case 2. The Idle Lawyer 243
Case 3. The Defective House 244
Case 4. Apartment in Flames 244
Case 5. Injured Skier 245
Case 6. Exploding Car 245
Case 7. Racing Boat Burning 247
Case 8. Insidious Report 247
Case 9. Circular Letter 247
Case 10. Shortage of Supply 248
Case 11. Injured Rock Star 249

Case 12. Equipment Destroyed 249
Case 13. Slipping on a Lettuce Leaf. 249
Case 14. Test Drive 250
Case 15. Breach of Negotiations 250
Case 16. Non-Disclosure of Relevant Facts 251

QUESTIONS

I. TRACING THE BORDERLINES

A. DISTINCTION BETWEEN TORT AND CONTRACT

1 As the making of a contract creates a duty to perform and the commission of a tort a liability to pay reparation, both torts and contracts are, according to the Greek legal system, sources of liability.[1] However, as explained in Greek doctrine: 'Tortious liability according to Article 914 CC is primary, since the obligation between the person causing the prejudice and the person prejudiced is created for the first time in the form of this liability (for compensation) when the conditions of the provision are met. Liability for compensation from non-performance of a contractual obligation is, on the other hand, secondary, since it presupposes precisely a pre-existent (primary) obligation between the parties, the obligation to perform the contract, that is, to fulfil the promised (original) performance.'[2] This secondary liability for compensation is regulated mainly in arts 330, 335 f, 362 f, and 382 f of the Greek Civil Code (GCC).

2 It has been stated that:

> '[T]he distinction between contractual and tortious liability is not as fundamental as used to be believed, nor does it stem from any logical necessity. Often, also, the inclusion of a consequence in law in contractual or tortious liability, such as of the liability of the producer for defective products in accordance with Community Directive 83/374 and the relevant provisions of adaptation of Greek law (art 6 L 2251/1994), should be a matter of indifference to the extent that a recourse to the general law for the filling of any gaps in the special regulation of this liability is not required. This distinction is based chiefly on the fact that, in the case of liability within a contract, we must accept a closer bond between debtor and creditor by reason of the binding nature of the contractual obligation which pre-existed and which had been created by the parties' own will – a binding element absent in tortious liability.'[3]

---

1 See, among others, *P Christodoulou* in: KD Kerameus/PJ Kozyris (eds), Introduction to Greek Law (in English) (3rd rev edn 2008) ch 6, 103.

2 See *A Georgiades*, Law of Obligations – General Part (2nd edn 2015) §59 nos 6, 7, 643.

3 *M Stathopoulos/A Karampatzos*, Contract Law in Greece (in English) (3rd edn 2014) no 40.

B. EXISTENCE OF A 'GREY ZONE'?

3 According to Greek law, at the stage of negotiations for the conclusion of a contract, the parties must deal with each other according to the dictates of good faith and conventional mores (art 197 GCC) and a person who, in the course of negotiations for the conclusion of a contract, has through his fault caused prejudice to the other party is liable for compensation even if the contract has not been concluded (art 198 GCC). So, pre-contractual liability or otherwise, liability from negotiations originates against the person with whom the responsible person has entered into negotiations.

4 As far as the nature of the pre-contractual liability is concerned, it is accepted that pre-contractual liability is a special case of liability *ex lege*, given that it is provided in art 198 GCC.[4] It has been argued that it resembles tort liability because it does not presuppose the existence of a contract,[5] or that it resembles more contractual liability due to the personal bond and the relation of trust which are created between the parties during the stage of negotiations, which contribute to the forming of a legal obligation in a wide sense.[6]

5 There is no unanimity in Greek theory on the issue of how the gaps in the regulation of pre-contractual liability are to be filled. Some scholars argue that the provisions on tort liability apply by analogy, others that the provisions on contractual liability apply by analogy, others are of the intermediate opinion that from the provisions governing contractual or tortious liability, the provision that fits each particular case is to be chosen.[7] It is to be noted, however, that art 198 §2 GCC explicitly provides that the provision on the prescription of the tortious claim (art 937 GCC) applies by analogy for the prescription of the claim deriving from pre-contractual liability, indicating, in the author's view, the tortious nature of pre-contractual liability.

C. COMMON OR DIFFERENT RULES REGULATING TORT AND CONTRACT

6 The rules regulating the extent of damages to be paid, the way of calculating the claim of damages, the time of payment, contributory negligence and the set-off of profit and damage can be considered as constituting the general part of the

---

4 *A Georgiades*, General Principles of Civil Law (5th edn 2019) §34 no 3; *G Lekkas* in: Georgiades/SEAK (= Short Interpretation of the Civil Code), vol 1 (2010) arts 197–198 no 1 with more references to the related Greek literature; *Stathopoulos/Karampatzos* (fn 3) no 84.

5 See, among others, *Lekkas* (fn 4).

6 *M Stathopoulos*, Law of Obligations, General Part (5th edn 2019) §3 no 51.

7 See for more details *Lekkas* (fn 4) arts 197 f no 2.

law on damages. These rules can be found in arts 297–300 GCC,[8] in the chapter regulating the obligation for performance in general. However, it is a unanimous view both in Greek doctrine and jurisprudence that said rules also apply to tortious liability[9] to the extent that there are no exceptions in the chapter on torts (as eg art 930 §3 GCC, which provides that the claim for damages shall not be precluded on the grounds that another person is liable to indemnify or to maintain the victim).[10] Also regarding the requirement of fault (culpability), it has been held that art 330 GCC regulating the responsibility for one's own conduct,[11] though in the chapter on obligation to perform in general, provides for a general definition of culpability and is applicable not only to contracts but to torts as well.[12]

D. APPLICATION OF COMMON RULES IN A DIFFERENT WAY

To the author's knowledge, courts do not apply rules which are common to tort and contract in a different way. 7

---

8 Art 297 GCC: 'Interest. A person who is obliged to pay damages shall use money. Nevertheless, the court may, taking into consideration (any) special circumstances, order, in lieu of compensation in money, the restoration of the former state of affairs (*status quo ante*), if this is not contrary to the interests of the creditor.'
Art 298 GCC: 'Damages shall include the decrease in the existing property of the creditor (positive damage), as well as lost profits. That which can be expected as a probable profit in the usual course of events or by reference to the special circumstances and particularly to the preparatory measures taken shall be reckoned as loss of profit.'
Art 299 GCC: 'Non-pecuniary damage. For non-pecuniary damage, compensation in money shall be due only in the cases provided for in the law.'
Art 300 GCC: 'Damage due to concurrent fault. If the party who sustained the damage has contributed to it or to its extent by his own fault, the court may either not adjudicate damages or reduce the amount due. This also applies where the party who sustained the damage omitted to avert or mitigate the damage or did not draw the attention of the debtor to the danger of the unusually big damage, which the debtor neither knew nor should have known. This provision also applies to the fault of the persons for whom the party who sustained the damage is liable.'

9 *P Kornilakis*, Law of Obligations – Special Part (2002) §99 II 1, 593; *M Stathopoulos* in: A Georgiades/M Stathopoulos (eds), Civil Code, vol II (1979) art 297 f nos 7, 8; *V Peraki* in: Georgiadis/SEAK, vol 1 (2010) art 297 no 5.

10 *A Georgiades* in: A Georgiades/M Stathopoulos (eds), Civil Code, vol IV (1982) art 914 nos 80, 81.

11 Art 330 GCC provides that a debtor is liable, unless it is otherwise provided, for any shortfall in the performance of his obligation resulting from willful misconduct or negligence imputable to him or to his legal representatives. Even though art 330 GCC provides for two forms of culpability, (*dolus*/intention and negligence), it only defines negligence by stating: 'Negligence exists when the care normally required in conducting business is not exercised'.

12 Greek Court of Cassation (Areios Pagos, AP, sitting in full bench) 8/2005 Nomiko Vima (NoV = Legal Tribune) 53 (2005) 1063 = Elliniki Dikaiossini (EllDni = Greek Justice) 46 (2005) 694; AP 9/2005, published in NOMOS data bank; AP 10/2005 Chronika Idiotikou Dikaiou (ChrID = Chronicles of Private Law) E/2005, 504; AP 11/2005 Archeio Nomologias (ArchN = Archive of Jurisprudence) 56 (2005) 456; AP 12/2005 ChrID ΣΤ/2006, 40; AP 13/2005, published in NOMOS.

II. MAIN DIFFERENCES BETWEEN TORTIOUS AND CONTRACTUAL LIABILITY

A. DIFFERENCES AS REGARDS THE FOUNDATIONS OF LIABILITY

1) *Role of Intention*

8 As a rule, the fault principle applies in both contractual and tortious liability. Exceptions, mainly in the direction of the mitigation of the liability (eg liability only for wilful conduct and gross negligence) are more frequent in the case of contractual liability.[13]

2) *Role of Wrongfulness and Fault and their Variations*

9 According to Greek jurisprudence, behaviour is unlawful according to art 914 GCC not only when it contravenes a provision of the law, but also when it is contrary to the unwritten rules of prudence and diligence to be expected from all members of society when acting. Such unwritten rules of behaviour are dictated either by explicit provisions of the GCC (arts 281 and 288) or by the general spirit of the legislation and the need of each member of society to expect a minimum standard of care from other members of society. This principle of prudence and diligence obliges members of society not to provoke damage to somebody else culpably.[14]

3) *Role of Strict Liability*

10 In the chapter regulating tortious liability of the GCC, strict liability is introduced only as an exception[15] in two cases: in the case of non-domestic animals (art 924 §1 GCC) and in the case of liability for employees (art 922 GCC); it also makes liability for fault approximate strict liability by means of reversing the burden of proof, in the case of harm inflicted by a person under supervision (art 923 GCC) or by a domestic animal (art 924 GCC) or in the case of damage caused by the collapse of buildings or structures (art 925 GCC) from natural causes and without the intervention of human force.[16] The supervisor, or respectively the keeper or the owner, are then presumed to be liable. The duty

---

13 *Stathopoulos/Karampatzos* (fn 3) no 40 (d).

14 For the general obligation of prudence and diligence see, among others, *Georgiades* (fn 10) art 914 no 29; *Kornilakis* (fn 9) §84 3 II, 492–494; *Stathopoulos* (fn 6) §15 no 39.

15 For the notion of strict liability see, among others, *Georgiades* (fn 10) Introductory Remarks to arts 914–938 nos 21–38.

16 Athens Court of First Instance 284/2001 ChrID A/2001, 321, 322.

to make reparation arises only if they do not satisfy the requirements of the exculpatory proof, as provided under arts 923, 924 §2 or 925 GCC respectively.[17] A *general* rule comparable to art 914 GCC and regarding strict liability is not provided in the GCC. No-fault liability is also found in special laws,[18] which impose strict liability in certain cases. The most usual basis of justification for these cases is that the activity of the person causing the prejudice constituted a source of risk and, usually, a source from which benefits could be drawn for himself (in which case, it seems even more justifiable that the beneficiary should also shoulder the losses stemming from the same source).[19]

B. DIFFERENCES AS REGARDS CAUSATION

In Greek law, a causal relation between the legal ground of liability (contract or tort) and the damage caused should exist in order for the liability for damages to arise. This can be clearly deduced from the wording of, for example, art 914 GCC ('whoever causes damage to another unlawfully and culpably …') and art 335 GCC ('if during the performance, the performance is wholly or in part impossible for reasons either of a general nature or relating to the debtor, the latter is obliged to pay damages to the creditor for the damage due to this impossibility'), etc.[20] 11

C. DIFFERENCES AS REGARDS REMEDIES

1) *Degree of Certainty of the Damage*

In the Greek law of damages, the 'all or nothing' principle (no compensation or full compensation) applies. As in German law, so also in Greek law the judge freely assesses the evidence but he must firmly believe that the facts exist in order to base his judgment on these facts. Full forensic evidence is required by the Greek Code of Civil Procedure (GCCP).[21] Both under contract and tort, from the moment the judge is convinced that the damage occurred, the damages to be paid cover the whole damage suffered (positive damage and loss of earnings). 12

---

17 *Christodoulou* (fn 1) 147. For an analysis of said articles see, among others, *Kornilakis* (fn 9) §§117–119, 384–394.

18 For the common features of these laws see *E Dacoronia*, Mass Torts: A Greek Approach, Revue Hellenique de Droit International (RHDI) 47 (1994) 94–96.

19 *Stathopoulos/Karampatzos* (fn 3) no 39. See also *E Dacoronia*, Tort Law in Greece. The State of Art (in English), in: Studia in Honorem Pelayia Yessiou-Faltsi (2007) 58.

20 *Stathopoulos* (fn 6) §8 no 104.

21 For this rule, in particular in relation to the issue of causality, see *P Kargados*, Thoughts on the Criteria of Proof of Causality, NoV 36 (1988) 1549 f.

2) *Compensation for Non-Pecuniary Loss*

13 According to Greek law,[22] in principle, the violation of a contractual obligation as such generates only an obligation to pay damages and not an additional obligation for compensation for moral harm. The mere non-execution of contractual obligations as such cannot provoke moral harm and, accordingly, no relevant compensation can be granted according to the Greek legislator, which has opted for a system where compensation for moral harm is exceptionally recognised and only where it is specifically provided by law (art 299 GCC).[23] Compensation for moral harm is recognised, for example, in the case of an infringement of the personality (arts 57 and 59 GCC)[24] and in the case of tort, especially for a person who suffered an attack of his health, honour or chastity or who was deprived of his liberty and, in the case of causing death, for the distress and anxiety of third parties belonging to the victim's family (art 932 GCC).[25] In principle, moral damages in connection with the breach of a contract will be unavailable, unless the breach is concurrently a delict[26] or, on an alternative ground, if the non-performance of the contract infringes one of the plaintiff's personality rights.[27] In the contract setting, it seems to be more often the latter ground rather than the former which accounts for the recovery of moral damages.[28]

14 In view of the above possibilities, it has been mentioned that: 'the practical importance of art 299 GCC is perceptibly reduced, and it is located chiefly in the legislative confirmation of the fact that breach of contractual obligations of the debtor does not in itself involve a prejudice to the goods other than those

---

22 See, among others, *Stathopoulos* (fn 6) §15 no 8.

23 *Stathopoulos/Karampatzos* (fn 3) no 40 (b).

24 See *S Paterakis*, Monetary Compensation for Moral Harm (2nd edn 2001) 262, 263; *K Fountedaki* in: Georgiades/SEAK, vol 1 (2010) art 57 no 5.

25 See *Stathopoulos* (fn 6) §8 no 65.

26 *Stathopoulos* (fn 6) §8 no 66; *Stathopoulos/Karampatzos* (fn 3) no 40 (b). See, eg, the Athens Court of Appeal (decision no 1531/2011 (Episkopisi Emporikou Dikaiou (= EpiskEmpD, Survey of Commercial Law) 17 (2011) 861 with an introductory note of *K Pampoukis*) = Dikaio Etaireion kai Epicheiriseon (DEE, Business and Company Law) 17 (2011) 936, presented (in English) by *E Dacoronia*, Greece, in: K Oliphant/BC Steininger (eds), European Tort Law 2011 (2012) 279 nos 3, 6), which denied an award of moral damages to air travellers because the airline's breach (delayed take off and lost luggage) was not considered a delict (no concurrence).

27 See also, *V Palmer* (ed), The Recovery of Non-Pecuniary Loss in European Contract Law (2016), where, based on the Greek report by the present author, Palmer mentions that Greece qualifies as a liberal regime because it frequently perceives and redresses violations of personality rights in contractual settings, or when the breach of the contract is concurrently a delict, thus allowing compensation for non-pecuniary loss in such cases.

28 Cf, however, *Fountedaki* (fn 24) art 59 no 12, who notes that it is doubtful whether it is consistent with the system of the GCC to accept that arts 57 and 59 GCC apply whenever there is an offence to emotions and thus an offence of the personality even in cases of violation of a contract.

of property of the creditor. Impossibility of performance, default of the debtor, etc, in themselves do not – the legislator has pronounced – injure the creditor morally'.[29]

3) *Compensation for Loss of Earnings and for Loss of Chance*

In contractual liability, the damage which is to be compensated is that arising from the non-fulfilment of the contract, an issue which does not arise in the case of tortious liability, as there is no pre-existing contract between the tortfeasor and the person who sustained the damage.[30] 15

As in the case of contractual liability, so also in the case of tortious liability is compensation for the loss of earnings included in the damages to be paid (art 914 GCC in combination with art 298 GCC, which provides that damages should cover not only the positive damage but also the loss of earnings).[31] 16

Greek jurisprudence has rarely dealt with issues of loss of a chance, while Greek scholars have not long been looking into the subject matter.[32] Since Greek jurisprudence and doctrine were unfamiliar with the concept of 'loss of a chance', it is not surprising that it has been considered appropriate by the Greek Court of Cassation to examine a case of loss of a chance from the scope of art 298 sent 2 GCC on *lucrum cessans*, that is as a case of pecuniary damage consisting in the loss of profits.[33] One can easily discern from art 298 GCC that – unlike positive damage – the legislator has set certain limits as to the level of the legally relevant loss of profit ('that which can be expected as probable profit in the usual course of events or by reference to the special circumstances and particularly to the preparatory measures taken'). The need for such limits arises from the fact that while positive damage is as a rule a fact that already exists, loss of profit can only be determined hypothetically. The limits on the loss of profit provided for in art 298 sent 2 GCC aim at imposing 'a check on unbridled hypotheses'.[34] Accordingly, the probable result of art 298 sent 2 GCC does not refer to any possible development, but only to that development which is expected to occur in the usual course of events.[35] 17

---

29 *Stathopoulos/Karampatzos* (fn 3) no 40 (b).

30 See *Stathopoulos* (fn 6) §8 nos 18 and 20.

31 *Georgiades* (fn 10) art 914 no 83; *G Georgiades* in: Georgiades/SEAK, vol 1 (2010) art 914 no 45; *Kornilakis* (fn 9) §99 1I 2, at 594.

32 *K Fountedaki*, The problem of causation in medical liability, EllDni 35 (1994) 1234 ff; *M Kanellopoulou-Bottis*, The offence against the chance as damage to patrimony or moral harm, Critical Revue (KritE) 2003/2, 253–307; *Stathopoulos* (fn 6) §8 no 90.

33 AP 447/1957 (Section A') – AP 742/1958 (Section C') NoV 6 (1958) 102, cmt by *D Manousakis* – NoV 7, 380, cmt by *A Lipovats*.

34 *Stathopoulos/Karampatzos* (fn 3) no 305.

35 See also *E Dacoronia*, Greece, in: B Winiger/H Koziol/BA Koch/R Zimmermann (eds), Digest of European Tort Law, vol 2: Essential Cases on Damage (2011) 26/5 no 4, 1081, 1082.

4) *Restitutionary Damages*

18 Restitutionary damages can be sought if the conditions for unjust enrichment, which is a third basic source of obligation after contract and tort, are fulfilled. The institution of unjust enrichment, which is regulated in arts 904–913 GCC,[36] presupposes an increase of the patrimony of a person to the detriment of another, which the legal order considers unjustified; it aims at the restitution of this unjustifiable patrimonial change and the setting aside of this injustice, according to the commands of morality and of restorative justice (*iustitia commutativa*).[37]

5) *Aggravated and Exemplary (or Punitive) Damages*

19 As it is a general principle of Greek law that damages have an exclusively compensatory character, punitive damages are not generally recognised either in contractual or tortious liability. However, the Court of Cassation (in full bench) held,[38] though with two dissenting views,[39] that a judgment of a US court, in which punitive damages were awarded on grounds of contractual liability due to the fact that the debtor fraudulently breached the contract, did not violate the national public order and might be declared enforceable in Greece, provided that the 'penal sanction' in favour of the creditor was not excessive.

6) *Other Remedies*

20 As stated in the doctrine:

> 'The first and fundamental protection of the creditor in the Greek law of contracts is the recognition to him of the claim for performance of the obligation of the debtor in the form (non-monetary or monetary) in which it has been undertaken. The law makes

---

36 Art 924 GCC provides that: 'A person enriched without a lawful cause from the patrimony or to the detriment of another person is obliged to restitute the benefit. This obligation arises in particular if a person has received a payment for a debt which was not owed, or if a transfer or a performance has been made on a ground which did not come about or subsequently ceased to exist or was illegal or immoral.'

37 *Stathopoulos* (fn 6) §16 no 1.

38 AP 17/1999 (in full bench) EllDni 40 (1999) 1288 = DEE 6 (2000) 181.

39 On the above-mentioned decision 17/1999, which generated much discussion in legal literature, and for a critical approach of the views expressed therein, see *K Kerameus/S Vrellis/A Grammatikaki*, Order of Execution of a Foreign Decision Awarding Punitive Damages in Greece, Koinodikion (Common Law) 2000, 31; the notes by *I Karakostas* and *C Michailidou* under the decision, DEE 6 (2000) 183 f; *I Komnios*, Public Order and the Institution of Punitive Damages in the Light of the Decision 17/1999; *G Nikolaidis*, Contradiction to the Greek Public Order or not of Punitive Damages, KritE 2000, 319 f; *G Panopoulos*, Punitive Damages and the Greek Public Order of Art 33 GCC (2003); *K Stamatis*, Recognition of a Foreign Court Decision Awarding Punitive Damages, NoV 51 (2003) 1553 f; *E Vassilakakis*, Possibility to Execute a Foreign Arbitrators' Decision, DEE 12 (2006) 461 f.

> it possible for the creditor to enforce the initial performance itself. On this basic issue, Greek law resembles most continental European systems of law and differs from the Anglo-Saxon systems, in which the sanction for non-performance consists mainly in the payment of compensation or in the discharge from the contract, with provision only by way of exception, as a supplementary remedy (which, moreover, remains at the discretion of the court) for specific performance, that is, the possibility of the court directing the defendant to perform the contract which he has made and in accordance with its terms.'[40]

On the contrary, in the Greek law of torts, damages are paid in principle *in money*. Only as an exception can damages be paid *in natura*, ie the restoration of the former state of affairs (*status quo ante*) can be sought (art 297 sent a' and b' GCC).[41] 21

D. DIFFERENCES AS REGARDS RECOVERABILITY OF 'PURE ECONOMIC LOSSES'

'Pure economic losses' of the person who directly sustained the damage are covered as long as they are causally connected to the legal ground of liability (in particular to the unlawful and culpable character of the act that caused the damage). An exclusion of the indirect damage in advance does not derive from the law.[42] When the economic losses are suffered by other, third persons, apart from the person who directly sustained the damage ('indirectly damaged third persons'), in the case of contractual liability, third persons are not entitled to damages, as the debtor who caused damage because he breached his contractual obligations is not in principle liable vis-à-vis third persons.[43] 22

Also in tortious liability, it is accepted that only the person directly damaged is covered and not persons indirectly damaged, with the exception of arts 928 sent 2 and 929 sent 2 GGC. It has been argued, however, that this generalisation is not justified, that when the same detrimental fact caused (direct or indirect) damage to several persons, the legal ground of liability cannot be excluded in advance; it is the protective ambit of the rule of law that has been violated and the causal relation which will determine whether or not damages have to be paid to third parties.[44] 23

---

40 *Stathopoulos/Karampatzos* (fn 3) no 246.

41 For the subject matter see, among many others, *Kornilakis* (fn 9) §99 1 I 2, at 594; *Stathopoulos* (fn 6) §8 76 ff and the monography of *E Zervogianni*, The Restoration of the *Status Quo Ante* as a Form of Damage Compensation (Athens 2006), very shortly presented (in English) by *E Dacoronia* in: H Koziol/BC Steininger (eds), European Tort Law 2006 (2007) 268 no 84.

42 *Stathopoulos* (fn 6) §8 no 111.

43 Ibid, §8 no 115.

44 Ibid, §8 no 116 and §15 no 61.

E. DIFFERENCES AS REGARDS LIABILITY FOR OTHERS

1) *Liability for Auxiliaries and for Independent Contractors*

24 It is accepted by the prevailing view in Greece and by interpretation of the crucial provisions ('Liability for the fault of vicarious agents', arts 334 and 922 GCC)[45] that in contractual liability, fault of the vicarious agent (employee, agent, servant and other ancillary persons whom the debtor employs in performing his contractual obligations) is more easily transferred to the debtor than to the tortfeasor in *tortious* liability.[46]

25 In particular, the differences between arts 334 and 922 GCC are as follows:[47]

(a) Article 334 presupposes an existing relationship between the debtor and the person who sustained the damage (the creditor), while for the application of art 922 GCC, such a relationship is not necessarily required between the master or the person who appoints another person to perform a function and the third party who sustained the damage.
(b) In art 334 GCC, the auxiliary is used for the performance of the undertaken obligation, while in art 922 GCC the auxiliary is used for the execution of a certain service, not related as a principle to the performance of an undertaken obligation.
(c) Article 334 GCC presupposes fault of the auxiliary in the course of the performance of the undertaken obligation, while art 922 GCC presupposes a tort of the auxiliary when executing his service.
(d) On the basis of art 334 GCC, the person who sustained the damage (the creditor) can seek damages for the contractual breach only from the debtor, while art 922 GCC creates liability of the master or the person who appoints another person to perform a function which is parallel and additional to the liability of the auxiliary according to art 914 f GCC.
(e) Liability pursuant to art 922 GCC presupposes, according to the prevailing view, a relation of dependence between the two persons, so that the auxiliary should follow the commands or instructions or accept the control or

---

45 Art 334 GCC: '1. A debtor is responsible for the fault of the person whom he employs in performing his obligation to the same extent as for his own fault. 2. Such liability may in principle be limited or excluded in advance, unless any of the cases of art 332 GCC exist. (As §2 is replaced by art 2 §2 L 3043/2002).' Art 922 GCC: 'The master or the person who appoints another person to perform a function is liable towards a third party for the damage unlawfully caused to the latter by the servant or this other person in the execution of his task.' For a comparative analysis of arts 334 and 922 GCC see the monograph of *Z Tsolakidis*, Contractual and Delictual Liability for Assistants (2008).

46 *Stathopoulos/Karampatzos* (fn 3) no 40 (c).

47 *Kornilakis* (fn 9) §91 2 IV 5, 548.

supervision during the execution of the duty assigned.[48] On the other hand, the debtor is vicariously liable for the persons he employs in performing his contractual obligations according to art 334 GCC even if the latter do not depend on the debtor (for example, because they are independent contractors).

2) Liability for Legal Representatives or Organs of a Company

According to art 70 GCC, juridical acts entered into within the bounds of his powers by the organ administrating the legal person are binding on the legal person. According to art 71 GCC, the legal person is held liable for the acts or omissions of the organs that represent it, as long as the acts or omissions took place in the course of the performance of their duties. 26

3) Liability of Representatives of Natural Persons

According to art 923 GCC, as amended by art 21 L 2447/1996, whoever has the supervision of a minor or of a person of age placed under judicial assistance is liable for the damage that such person unlawfully causes to a third party unless he proves that he properly exercised the duty of supervision or that the damage could not have been avoided. The person who performs the duty of supervision by virtue of a contract will be held liable on the same grounds. 27

In order to assist the victim in establishing his claim, art 923 GCC introduces the following rebuttable presumptions: (a) that the supervisor, through fault, neglected his obligation to supervise; and (b) that a causal link exists between the neglect and the damage caused. If the supervisor does not rebut the said presumptions, he is held liable towards the victim. The preconditions required for establishing the supervisor's liability are as follows: 28

(a) An obligation to supervise must exist, stemming from either the law or a contract. In case more persons are obliged to supervise, all of them are held jointly and severally liable according to art 926 GCC (eg the minor's parents both exercising parental care).
(b) The supervisor must have culpably neglected the supervision. As already mentioned, according to art 923 GCC, if the minor illegally caused damage, the supervisor is presumed to have been at fault in his supervision.
(c) The person under supervision must have caused damage to a third person, ie all of the preconditions stipulated by art 914 GCC, apart from fault, must

48 See relatively *Stathopoulos* (fn 6) §7 no 46; AP 280/2009 DEE 15 (2009) 1396 f.

be fulfilled. If the person under supervision is capable of imputation and has acted with fault, he is also held liable according to art 914 GCC, while the joint and several liability of the supervisor is also preserved.

(d) The supervisor's neglect and the tortious behaviour of the person under supervision must be causally linked. Such a causal link is presumed according to art 923 GCC.

29 Should the aforementioned preconditions be met, the supervisor must make reparations for the victim's material and non-pecuniary damage (art 932 GCC). In order to rebut the aforementioned presumptions, the supervisor must invoke and prove either that he exercised proper supervision or that the damage could not have been averted or that no fault can be imputed to him for neglecting supervision or that – given the circumstances – supervision could not have been exercised.[49]

30 Article 923 GCC aims at protecting third persons and not at protecting the persons under supervision.[50] If the supervisor has neglected his obligation to supervise and this has caused damage to the person under supervision, the supervisor is liable not according to art 923 GCC but according to the provisions from which the obligation for supervision derives (eg arts 1523, 1531, 1632, 1634 and 1680 GCC, which are found in Family Law and establish an obligation to supervise, and arts 335 ff and 383 ff GCC, when such an obligation derives from a contract) or according to art 914 GCC.[51]

4) *Liability of the Auxiliary/Organ Itself*

31 According to art 71 sent 2 GCC, in case the act or omission of the competent organ is culpable and creates an obligation for remuneration, the organ is also held jointly and severally liable with the legal person. As far as corporations are concerned, the directors cannot be held personally liable for the debts of the company, but the principle of their non-liability does not apply when fault can be attributed to them, in which case they are held personally liable according to the general provisions on torts (art 914 ff GCC).[52]

---

49 Athens Court of Appeal 777/2005 EllDni 46 (2005) 1493. See also AP 422/2008 ChrID H/2008, 785 (for a brief summary of the facts of the decision and the judgment of the Court (in English) see *E Dacoronia*, Greece, in: H Koziol/BC Steininger (eds), European Tort Law 2008 (2009) 324 nos 12, 13, 15.

50 *Georgiades* (fn 10) art 923 no 3; *Kornilakis* (fn 9) §92 3I, 549.

51 For an analysis of art 923 GCC see, among others, *Georgiades* (fn 10) art 923; *Kornilakis* (fn 9) §92 3, 548–555; *Georgiades* in: *Georgiades* /SEAK (fn 31) art 923.

52 See, among others, AP 29/2006 DEE 12 (2006), 930 = EllDni 47 (2006), 1031 = ChrID ΣΤ/2006, 410, followed by a note by *K Christakakou*.

F. DIFFERENCES AS REGARDS LIABILITY IN THE CASE OF MULTIPLE TORTFEASORS/BREACHING PARTIES

Multiple parties under contract. According to art 480 GCC, if more persons owe a divisible performance or if more persons are entitled to a divisible performance, in case of doubt, every debtor has the obligation to pay an equal part and every creditor has the right to receive an equal part. 32

Liability of joint tortfeasors under tort. Article 926 GCC, establishing joint and several liability when the damage is caused by a collective act of multiple tortfeasors, clarifies the way liability is shared among several persons who have acted jointly and each one of them independently fulfils the requirements of tortious liability. 33

In particular, art 926 GCC establishes joint and several liability in the following cases. 34

(a) When the damage is caused by a collective act of multiple tortfeasors: The term 'collective act' is interpreted widely as to include any kind of causal collaboration or participation in the perpetration of the tort and the provocation of the damage, irrespective of whether the acts of the multiple tortfeasors occurred simultaneously, successively or parallel to each other;[53] therefore it includes: 35

(i) complicity by means of co-deciding and co-executing the tort, ie cases where several persons act jointly and each one of them fulfils the requirements of tortious liability, as identified herein above;[54]
(ii) the acts of the instigator of the tortfeasor,[55] the direct accessory[56] and the simple accessory;[57]
(iii) cases of several persons committing the tort by acting independently and individually and without any conscious cooperation (lateral abettors);[58]

---

53 *Georgiades* (fn 10) art 926 no 5; *I Deliyannis/P Kornilakis*, Law of Obligations – Special Part, vol III (1992) 218.

54 Eg A and B attack C and jointly beat him; workmen G and H omit to take preventive measures at the ditch they are digging which results in the fall and injury of V. The last example clarifies that the term 'collective act' in art 926 GCC is not restricted to intentional complicity but it also includes so-called 'negligent complicity' (*Georgiades* (fn 15) art 926 no 6, *Deliyannis/Kornilakis* (fn 53); contra *P Filios*, Law of Obligations – Special Part, vol II/2 (4th edn 1998) 92: the author adheres to the doctrine of the penal law which requires intention).

55 The instigator is the person who has brought about the tortfeasor's decision to commit the tort (see art 46 §1 case a' of the Greek Penal Code (GPC)).

56 The direct accessory is the people who assisted the actor directly in and during the commission of the tort (see art 46 §1 case b' GPC).

57 The simple accessory is the person who aided the tortfeasor in any way before or during the commission of the tort (see art 47 §1 GPC).

58 Eg a pedestrian is injured by the collision of two cars. See respectively *A Georgiades*, in: A Georgiades/M Stathopoulos (eds), Civil Code vol IV (1982) art 926 no 8; *Deliyannis/Kornilakis* (fn 53) 219.

(iv) cases of necessary causality, that is cases where the acts of multiple tortfeasors were a necessary condition for the damage to be caused (in the sense that, if any of such acts had not taken place, the damage would not have been caused) but none of the multiple tortfeasors' acts alone could have caused the damage.[59] When the act is not a necessary condition for the detrimental result (in the sense that, even if the act had not taken place, the damage would still have been caused), then there is no necessary causality and no joint liability arises;

(v) cases where damage is caused by the simultaneous acts of multiple tortfeasors, each of which in itself would have been sufficient to cause the victim's loss (cumulative causation);

(vi) cases of posterior complicity: art 926 GCC applies by analogy when an act – though not causally connected with the provocation of the damage – preserves and augments the damage already caused.[60]

36 *(b) When multiple tortfeasors are held liable in parallel*, eg the driver and the insurance company for damage caused when driving;[61] the employer and the

59 *Georgiades* (fn 10) art 926 no 9. Eg A's factory emits harmless chemical waste and so does B's factory. However, when these harmless chemical wastes are fused, they produce – by a chemical reaction – a poisonous substance which contaminates the river and results in the death of fish. A and B are held jointly and severally liable according to art 926 GCC, because the damage was caused by their 'collective act' (wide interpretation of the term). However, it has been maintained that these cases fall under art 926 sent a subpara b GCC concerning liability in parallel (see respectively *M Karasis*, Joint and several debt (1990) 279, fn 87a, 282; *Filios* (fn 54) 93). It must be noted, however, that the discord between the scholars is strictly theoretical because, regardless of where the cases of '*notwendig koindizierende Kausalität*' are placed – ie either in art 926 sent a subpara a GCC concerning collective act or in art 926 sent a subpara b GCC concerning liability in parallel – the actors are in any case held jointly and severally liable.

60 *Georgiades* (fn 10) art 926 no 12; *Deliyannis/Kornilakis* (fn 53) 220. Eg the person who hides stolen goods is obviously not causally connected with the theft, but he is responsible for the preservation of the harm already caused, thus he is held jointly and severally liable according to art 926 GCC applied by analogy. Seen from the point of view of the victim, it is only fair that not only the thief, but anyone who hides the stolen goods also is to compensate the victim, because the latter's property is damaged by both acts.

61 Compulsory liability insurance is required in Greece by either the automobile owner or the possessor of the car (L 489/1976, art 2 §1). In Greek practice, it is the automobile owner who usually chooses the insurance company, negotiates the terms of the contract with the latter and signs the contract. However, the insurance contract covers not only the owner's liability but the possessor's and the driver's liability as well (L 489/1976, art 6 §1). In the case of a car accident, the automobile owner, the possessor, the driver as well as the insurance company are all held jointly and severally liable in damages (*A Kritikos*, Compensation for car accidents (3rd edn 1998) no 2013; *Filios* (fn 54) 156). Art 6 §3 of L 489/1976 explicitly proclaims the insurance company to be liable towards third persons for the damage they suffered from the use of the car, while art 10 §1 of L 489/1976 provides that third persons are entitled to seek compensation directly from the insurer, against whom they can file an action.

employee for the tort the latter committed in the course of their employment (art 926 GCC sent 1 read with art 922 GCC).[62]

(c) When more than one person acted either simultaneously or successively and it is impossible to determine whose action caused the damage (art 926 sent 2 GCC): Article 926 sent 2 GCC is applicable provided that the following requirements are met:[63] 37

(i) acts of more than one person: it is irrelevant whether the acts occurred simultaneously or successively; whether or not they were similar; whether or not they were based on a prior agreement between the wrongdoers;
(ii) each one of the acts of the several persons is required to be independently adequate to have caused the damage, ie is required to be regarded as a potential cause of the wrong complained of. Should one of the two or more possible tortfeasors prove the lack of adequate causation between his act and the damage, he is excluded from liability;
(iii) each one of the acts of the several persons is required to be tortious.;
(iv) it must be impossible to ascertain whose act in fact led to the damage or the extent to which the damage was caused by each of the tortfeasors;
(v) finally, according to art 926 sent 2 GCC, each of the several potential tortfeasors is held jointly and severally liable for the damage if it cannot be ascertained whose action caused the damage or to which percentage each of them contributed to the damage caused.[64] When the probability of having caused the damage is the same for all the possible tortfeasors, art 926 GCC is applicable. In such a case, as far as the relations between the several possible tortfeasors inter se and their right of recourse against each other (art 927 GCC) are concerned, the damage is equally distributed among them. If the causal relationship of the behaviour of one or more tortfeasors with the damage suffered is fully established, whereas such causal relationship cannot be fully established as far as the remainder of the tortfeasors are concerned, the latter will not be held liable.[65]

The aforementioned provisions of L 489/1976 aim at adding one more person as an additional liable person on top of the already existing ones (car owner, possessor and driver), from whom the person suffered the damage is entitled to seek damages. Therefore, under Greek law, the insurer's role is not only to insure the tortfeasor – it is regarded as being liable itself.

62 *Georgiades* (fn 10) art 926 no 16.

63 *Georgiades* (fn 10) art 926 no 20 f; *Deliyannis/Kornilakis* (fn 53) 223 f.

64 Needless to say, all actions have to be tortious in the sense of arts 914 or 919 GCC according to the principle of personal liability.

65 *Stathopoulos* (fn 6) §15 no 110.

G. DIFFERENCES AS REGARDS THE PERSONS WHO MAY BE PROTECTED

1) *Persons Protected under Tort*

38 The Court of Cassation[66] has considered that those in a general partnership do not have a right to seek damages from the person who caused the death of a partner, from whose commercial activity the partnership also earned gains, because the said partnership was only *indirectly* prejudiced by the unlawful act. It can be deduced from arts 914, 297 and 298 GCC that only the person who has been *directly* prejudiced may seek reparation. On the contrary, the person who has been *indirectly* prejudiced, that is the one who has sustained damage from the injury of a legal good belonging to another person, has a right to damages only if such a right is specifically provided by law.[67] Such a right is provided: (a) in art 928 sent 2 GCC, according to which, in the case of death, the person bound to pay damages is also bound to make reparation for the loss of maintenance or services to the person who is entitled by law to claim maintenance or the performance of services from the victim;[68] and (b) in art 929 sent 2 GCC, according to which, in the case of injury to the body or the health of a person, the person bound to pay damages must also compensate a third party, who, being entitled by law to claim the performance of services from the victim, is now deprived of the services because of the delict committed against the victim.

39 Also under tort and, according to art 932 sent 3 GCC, if the victim dies, his family has a claim for monetary compensation for pain and suffering, as being directly prejudiced.

2) *Persons Protected under Contract*

40 One of the basic characteristics of an obligation is *relativity*, that is to say the fact that its effect develops only between the creditor and the debtor, as it does not create rights or obligations vis-à-vis third parties. For third parties, the contract of others is *res inter alios acta*. In English terminology, the principle of relativity corresponds to the 'doctrine of privity'.[69]

---

66 AP 1504/2000 DEE 7/2001, 497.

67 See relatively *Kornilakis* (fn 9) §124, 407, 408.

68 It has to be noted that, according to AP 857/2001 ChrID A'/2001, 704, 705, this obligation continues to exist even if the person entitled by law to claim maintenance cohabits later permanently with another person in a free union, as the said obligation does not constitute a duty to alimony – which ceases, according to art 1444 §2 GCC, when the person entitled to it remarries or lives with somebody else in free union – but it has a compensatory character.

69 *Stathopoulos/Karampatzos* (fn 3) no 185.

Nevertheless, a strict implementation of the privity of obligations would not correspond to the *spirit* and *needs* of our times and, therefore, legislation today lays down as a basis the principle of the privity of contracts, but accepts exceptions from that principle (particularly from the relative effect of contracts).[70] This is the case, for example, when the *lease of a thing* (art 574 GCC) is combined with sub-leasing by the lessee; or a *contract for work* (art 681 GCC) with the engagement by the contractor of employees for its completion; or a *mandate* (art 713 GCC) with the entrusting of the matter by the mandatory to his substitute; or a *loan for use* (art 810 GCC) with ceding of the use of the thing by the user (borrower) to a third party; or *deposit* (art 822 GCC) with the depositing of the thing by the depositary with a third party. In these trilateral relations, only the intermediary has a contractual bond with the other two. Between the latter there is no contract. In spite of this, the GCC, recognising that the second contract is based on the first and that to detach one from the other and to make them independent of one another is not socially and economically justifiable, puts aside relativity and permits (apart from claims against the counterparty): the lessor to ask for the return of the thing leased directly from the sublessee (art 599 §2 GCC); workmen whom the contractor employs for the construction of a building or other work related to immovables to have, in respect of their wages and salaries, a direct claim against the master of work up to the amount the latter owes the contractor (art 702 GCC); the mandatory to take action directly against the mandatory's substitute (art 716 §3 GCC); the lender or depositor to seek the restitution of the thing by the person to whom the user or depositary has given it (arts 819, 825 §2 GCC). This creates, so to speak, a direct obligation between the two persons who do not have a bond between them by contract (without, of course, abolishing the existing obligation between the contracting parties).[71] 41

A *genuine contract in favour of a third party* ie a contract in which the third party to whom the debtor has undertaken to effect the performance acquires a direct contractual right (claim) against the debtor to seek the performance himself, though he is not a contracting party, is also provided for in arts 411–414 GCC and constitutes an exception from privity of contracts.[72] 42

H. DIFFERENCES AS REGARDS DEFENCES

In Greek law, the recognition of the contributory negligence of the victim has as a consequence the reduction of the liability of the tortfeasor to a certain percentage (art 300 GCC). See also below under sec III.A. 43

70 Ibid, no 186.
71 Ibid, no 187.
72 Ibid, no 193.

I. DIFFERENCES AS REGARDS LIMITATION PERIODS

44 In contractual liability,[73] a claim prescribes after 20 years, according to the general rule on the term of prescription provided in art 249 GCC. Exceptionally (eg, in the case of commercial claims or claims for a salary, fees, interest or rent, etc) the term of prescription is five years (art 250 GCC). There are also provisions providing for different terms of prescription depending on the type of the contract, such as in a contract of sale,[74] a contract of lease,[75] a contract for work,[76] or a contract of a loan for use.[77]

45 In the case of tortious liability, in order to avoid keeping tort claims pending indefinitely and in order to ensure legal certainty, the relevant claim must be submitted within a certain period, explicitly provided in art 937 GCC.[78] More particularly, according to art 937 §1 GCC, the claim arising from a tort is barred by prescription five years after the time the injured party gained knowledge of the damage and of the person liable to pay damages; in any case, a claim in tort prescribes 20 years from the commission of the act. The Court of Cassation has ruled that the term 'knowledge of the damage' is to be understood as the knowledge of the detrimental consequences of the act and not the knowledge of the exact extent of the prejudice or of the extent of the damage; furthermore, in the case of a continuing damage, the claim for damages is not 'reborn' continuously; as for future damage, any relevant claim arises when the act started to cause detrimental consequences, provided that, according to the usual course of events, such future damage could be foreseen.[79] From this moment the

---

73 See *Kornilakis* (fn 9) §78 3 I 5, 459; *Stathopoulos* (fn 6) §15 no 8; *Stathopoulos/Karampatzos* (fn 3) nos 40 (e) and 321.

74 Art 554 GCC, as replaced by art 1 §1 L 3043/2002, stipulates that: 'The rights of the seller because of material defects or lack of an agreed quality are time-barred for immovable things after the elapse of five years and for movable things after the elapse of two years'.

75 Art 602 GCC stipulates that: 'The claims of the lessor for damages due to modification or deterioration of the leased thing are time-barred after six months from when the lessor has taken back the thing. In any case these claims are time-barred with the claim for the recovery of the leased thing'.

76 Art 693 GCC stipulates that: 'The claims of the master of the work, arising out of defective performance, are time-barred, in the case of buildings or other immovable things when ten years have elapsed from taking delivery; in all other cases the claims of the master of the work are time-barred in six months'.

77 Art 820 GCC stipulates that: 'Claims of a lender for use for damages due to alterations or deterioration of the thing are time-barred after the lapse of six months as from the date on which the lender received the thing back; in any case they are time-barred with the lender's right to recover the thing'.

78 *Georgiades* (fn 10) art 937 no 34; *G Georgiades* (fn 31) art 937, 1913; *Deliyannis/Kornilakis* (fn 53) 304.

79 See *Georgiades* (fn 10) art 937 no 19; *Kornilakis* (fn 9) §107 9 I, 657, note 6 and (in English) *E Dacoronia*, Greece, in: H Koziol/BC Steininger (eds), European Tort Law 2001 (2002) 269 nos 57–59.

five-year prescription period provided by art 937 §1 GCC starts running for the whole damage.[80]

Also, according to art 937 §2 GCC: 'If the unlawful act constitutes at the same time a punishable offence, which according to the criminal law is subject to a longer prescription period, such (longer) prescription shall also be applicable in regard to the claim for damages'.[81] 46

Prescription is *suspended* in those cases stipulated by law (art 255 ff GCC), for example, in cases of cessation of administration of justice or force majeure within the last six months of the period of prescription. Special protection is provided at this point for claims brought by minors or against spouses or parents or (minor) children. Furthermore, prescription is *interrupted* if the obligor acknowledges the claim or the holder of the right institutes legal action or other legal proceedings (arts 260 ff GCC).[82] 47

These rules on suspension and interruption of prescription also apply to the prescription of a claim arising from tortious liability.[83] 48

J. DIFFERENCES AS REGARDS PROOF

In contractual liability, the fault of the person who caused the damage is presumed (rebuttable presumption – see arts 336 sent 1, 342, 363 sent 1 GCC).[84] As a consequence, he has to prove that he has no fault in order to be discharged. To the contrary, in the field of tortious liability, the burden of proof of all facts for the claim to be substantiated lies with the person who sustained the damage in accordance with the general procedural rule that the burden of proof lies on the plaintiff; therefore, the person who sustained the damage also has to prove the fault of the tortfeasor.[85] 49

---

80 AP 1239/2000 ChrID A'/2001, 313, 314. See also *Georgiades* (fn 10) art 937; *G Georgiades* (fn 31) art 937, 1910 f; *I Karakostas*, Civil Code, Law of Obligations – Special Part, vol 6 (2009) 1264 f.

81 For an analysis of art 937 GCC see, among others, *Kornilakis* (fn 9) §107 9, 655 f.

82 *Stathopoulos/Karampatzos* (fn 3) no 321.

83 *Georgiades* (fn 10) art 937 nos 1 and 52; *Kornilakis* (fn 9) §107 9 III, 661.

84 Art 336 sent 1 GCC: 'The debtor is released from the obligation to furnish the performance, if he proves that the impossibility was due to an event for which the debtor has no liability.'
Art 342 GCC: 'The debtor is not in default, if the delay in performance is due to an event for which the debtor has no liability.'
Art 363 sent 1 GCC: 'The debtor, unless the law provides otherwise, shall be free from every obligation which stems from the promise of impossible performance, if, during the concluding of the contract, he ignored without his own fault that the fulfillment was impossible.'

85 See, among others, *Kornilakis* (fn 9) §78 3 I 4, 458, 459; *Stathopoulos* (fn 6) §15 no 8; *Stathopoulos/Karampatzos* (fn 3) no 40 (a).

K. OTHER DIFFERENCES

50 In the case of a tort, the court can always: (a) declare its judgment to be provisionally enforceable (art 908 §1 d' GCCP), as well as (b) order the collection of the claim by threatening the tortfeasor with detention (art 1047 §1 sent b' GCCP). In the case of a breach of contract, the court has the above possibilities (not always but) only for cases provided by law (arts 908 f, 1047 GCCP), for example in the case of commercial debts.[86]

51 In Greece, different rules exist regarding contractual and tortious capacity. Though minors under the age of 10 have neither contractual capacity (art 128 GCC) nor tortious capacity (art 916 GCC), minors can be held fully liable in tort at the age of 14, whereas full contractual capacity is only gained at the age of 18. Below this age, minors have a reduced contractual capacity depending on their age and the subject matter of the contract (arts 129, 134–136 GCC); minors who have entered into a marriage contract can also undertake certain juridical acts, amongst others current matters of everyday life (art 137 GCC).[87] In tort, a person who is above the age of 10 but below 14 is liable for the damage he caused unless he acted without discretion, ie without the necessary mental maturity, so as to diagnose the unlawful character of his behaviour.[88] The power of 'discretion' is examined on the basis of the particular facts of a case and depends on the degree of the emotional and mental development of the particular minor as well as on the nature of the act.[89] The standard of conduct expected of a child who possesses discretion is the standard of an average child of his age.[90]

52 Another difference, which refers to the transmissibility of claims, has in fact more to do with the type of loss for which compensation is being claimed than with the contract–tort divide. In Greece, the claim to compensation for pain and suffering is independent from the claim of the injured victim to compensation of his moral harm which, in the case of his death, is inherited by his heirs but only if such claim was acknowledged by contract or the victim had filed and served the relevant action before his death according to art 933 GCC. Accordingly, it has been held[91] that it clearly derives from the combination of arts 932 and

---

86 *Kornilakis* (fn 9) §78 3 I 7, 459. See also *P Yessiou-Faltsi*, Civil Procedure in Hellas (1995) (in English) 398.

87 For an analysis of art 137 GCC see, from the most recent bibliography, *A Koutsouradis* in: A Georgiades/M Stathopoulos (eds), Civil Code I^{B} (2nd edn 2016) art 137.

88 AP 731/2008, published in ISOKRATIS and NOMOS.

89 Larissa Court of Appeal 225/2007, published in NOMOS; *Karakostas* (fn 80) 161. See also AP 1410/2006 NoV 55 (2007) 335.

90 *K Christakakou-Fotiadi*, Liability in Tort of Minors and their Parents or Guardians (2008) 44.

91 AP 416/2012, published in NOMOS (for a brief summary (in English) of the facts and the judgments of said decision as well as a short commentary thereof see *E Dacoronia*, Greece,

933 GCC that if a person has been injured by another's tortious behaviour and, while alive, filed an action seeking monetary compensation for moral harm because of his injury and later dies because of this same injury, then the members of his family are entitled to claim monetary compensation for pain and suffering because of his death and, in parallel, continue the court action filed by the victim while alive, as his heirs. This is due to the fact that the claim of the members of the family of the deceased deriving from art 932 sent 3 GCC is a claim they have in their own right, aiming at their relief from the mental pain caused by the death of their beloved relative, and is born independently of their quality as the heirs of the victim. This claim is different from that of the injured person who files an action for compensation of his moral harm according to art 932 sent 1 and 2 GCC, which is inherited according to art 933 GCC, being an asset of the estate that evolves, after the death of the victim, to his heirs.

As regards the rules of conflicts of laws, obligations arising from tort are 53
governed by the law of the place where the tort was committed (art 26 GCC).[92] By contrast, the contractual claim is governed by the law to which the parties have submitted. Absent such a law, the law which is appropriate in relation to the contract, considering the circumstances as a whole, applies (art 25 GCC).[93]

L. REASONS FOR THE DIFFERENCES

The fact that there is a pre-existing bond between the parties to a contract, whilst 54
such a bond does not exist in the case of a tort, mainly explains the existence of some differences between the two forms of liability which may arise. The possibility to have a judgment against the tortfeasor declared as provisionally enforceable and an order for the collection of the claim by threatening the tortfeasor with detention in the case of a tort whilst in the case of contractual liability this is recognised only in certain cases (eg in commercial matters) is justified by the idea that the person who sustained damage as a consequence of tortious behaviour is considered by the legislator as requiring immediate protection and that the behaviour of the tortfeasor is disapproved of by the legal order more than the behaviour of a person who merely violates a contract, provided that the latter is not a merchant, in which case the same possibilities

---

in: K Oliphant/BC Steininger (eds), European Tort Law 2012 (2013) 301 nos 31–33). See also AP 519/1977 (in full bench) NoV 26 (1978) 182.

92 For the field of application of art 26 GCC after the Regulation 864/2007 (Rome II) see *A Grammatikaki-Alexiou* in: A Georgiades/M Stathopoulos (eds), Civil Code I^{A} (2nd edn 2016) art 26 no 2.

93 For the field of application of art 25 GCC after the Regulation 593/2008 (Rome I), see *Grammatikaki-Alexiou* (fn 92) art 25 no 3.

regarding the enforcement of the judgment and the threat of detaining the debtor exist.

III. LIMITATION OR EXCLUSION OF LIABILITY ARISING FROM TORT AND FROM CONTRACT

A. STATUTORY PROVISIONS AUTHORISING A LIMITATION OR EXCLUSION OF LIABILITY

55 The law may provide for a limitation of liability,[94] for example it may be provided that liability exists: (a) only for *dolus*/intention, as is the case of art 812 GCC, according to which the lender of a thing for use is liable for damages for defects of said thing only if he concealed their existence out of *dolus*/intention; or (b) only for *dolus*/intention and gross negligence (thus excluding slight negligence),[95] as is the case of art 499 §1 GCC, according to which a donor is liable only for wilful conduct and gross negligence. Liability only for slight, concrete negligence is provided by law in cases where the parties involved (creditor and debtor) are connected by a close personal relationship,[96] for example spouses in their relation between themselves (art 1396 GCC provides that: 'Spouses, when fulfilling their mutual obligations which derive from marriage, are liable for the level of care they show in their own cases'), parents towards their children (art 1531 GCC provides that: 'Parents, when exercising parental care, are obliged to display the care they exert also in their own affairs'), etc.

56 On the other hand, as already mentioned, according to art 300 GCC,[97] which also applies to torts,[98] if the party who sustained the damage has contributed to it or to its extent by his own fault, the court may either not award damages or reduce the amount due. This also applies where the party who sustained the damage omitted to avert or mitigate the damage or did not draw the attention of the debtor to the danger of the unusually extensive damage, which the debtor neither knew nor should have known. This provision also applies to the fault of persons for whom the party who sustained the damage is liable. Thus, in Greek law, the recognition of the contributory negligence of the victim has as a consequence the reduction of the liability of the tortfeasor to a certain percentage.

---

94 See, among others, *Stathopoulos* (fn 6) §6 no 121.

95 See, among others, ibid, §6 no 90.

96 See, among others, ibid, §6 no 95.

97 For a detailed analysis of art 300 GCC, see the thesis of *A Kontogianni*, Contributory Negligence in Civil Law (2006).

98 *Georgiades* (fn 2) §60 no 44, 666.

B. LIMITATION OR EXCLUSION OF CONTRACTUAL AND TORTIOUS LIABILITY BY CONTRACT

1) Is it Possible to Limit or Exclude Contractual and Tortious Liability under a Contract?

The GCC regulates the agreement for exclusion of liability for fault in art 332 GCC, which, as replaced by art 2 §1 L 3043/2002, provides the following: 'Any agreement excluding or limiting beforehand liability resulting from wilful conduct or gross negligence is null. 57

Void is also any agreement excluding in advance a debtor's liability even for slight negligence if the creditor is in the service of the debtor, or if the liability arises from conducting an enterprise for which prior concession by the competent authority was granted. The same also applies if the exclusion clause is included in a clause of the contract which did not constitute an object of an individual negotiation or if, with the clause, the debtor is discharged from his liability for the infringement of goods which derive from the personality and especially for the infringement of life, health, liberty or honour'.[99] 58

Article 332 GCC refers to the exclusion of the debtor from his contractual liability. However, it is accepted in both Greek theory and jurisprudence[100] that it may also apply to cases of tortious liability, if this is the wish of the parties. 59

2) To What Extent can a Contractual Exclusion Provide a Defence to a Third Party to the Contract?

The exclusion clause cannot be invoked against third parties who have sustained damage.[101] 60

IV. NON-CONCURRENCE OR CONCURRENCE OF ACTIONS

A. OVERVIEW

Although it may be argued that the specific provisions governing the violation of contractual obligations (arts 330, 335 f, 362 f, 382 f GCC), as special provisions, 61

99 For an analysis of art 332 GCC (in English), see *Stathopoulos/Karampatzos* (fn 3) no 158 ff.

100 *Georgiades* (fn 2) §60 no 43, 665; *S Koumanis* in: Georgiades/SEAK (2010) 332 no 8; *M Stathopoulos* in: A Georgiades/M Stathopoulos (eds), Civil Code, vol II (1979) art 332 no 23; *Stathopoulos* (fn 6) §6 no 143; AP 1139/2006 ChrID 2006, 889; Athens Court of Appeal 10390/1979 NoV 28 (1980) 827.

101 *Stathopoulos* (fn 6) §6 no 143; AP 1139/2006 (fn 100).

prevail over those regarding tortious liability and they do not concur with them (principle of *non cumul*), the Greek jurisprudence adopts the principle of 'free concurrence of claims'.[102] According to this principle, when the act or omission which constitutes the contractual non-performance is simultaneously and in itself unlawful, the two liabilities, delictual and contractual, concur;[103] for example, if the depositary or lessee of a thing through his fault destroys an object in his possession, or if an employee or a contractor, in the course of his work, destroys a thing belonging to the employer or to the master of the work, etc, the party who suffered the damage can ground his claim either on the provisions on contractual or those on tortious liability.[104] The relevant claims are submitted to different prescription periods depending on the different legal basis. It has to be noted here that when the two liabilities, delictual and contractual, concur, the majority of Greek scholars consider that it is more correct dogmatically to accept that not two independent claims are born (*Anspruchskonkurrenz*) but only one, founded on two different legal bases (*Anspruchsnormenkonkurrenz*).[105] There are no important practical reasons, however, that dictate this choice.[106]

62 Regarding the presupposition of unlawful behaviour, it has to be said that behaviour is unlawful not only when it contravenes a provision of the law, but also when it is contrary to the unwritten rules of prudence and diligence to be expected from all members of society when acting. Such unwritten rules of behaviour are dictated either by explicit provisions of the GCC (arts 281 and 288 GCC) or by the general spirit of the legislation and the need of each member of society to expect a minimum standard of care from other members of society. This principle of prudence and diligence obliges members of society not to provoke damage to somebody else culpably.[107] When a contractual non-performance is not in itself unlawful, ie it is not contrary to this general duty of 'not culpably damaging another' in specific situations, which is imposed by law, no concurrence of contractual and delictual liability exists. In such a case, only

---

102 For the disadvantages of the free concurrence of claims see, among others, *Kornilakis* (fn 9) §79 4 IIβ, 463 f.

103 See *Kornilakis* (fn 9) §79 4, 461 ff, where also (at 462, fn 3) reference to the abundant relative jurisprudence is made; *Stathopoulos/Karampatzos* (fn 3) no 41; *Stathopoulos* (fn 6) §15 no 10.

104 *Stathopoulos/Karampatzos* (fn 3).

105 For the advantages of the said view, mainly expressed by *A Georgiades*, Die Anspruchskonkurrenz im Zivilrecht und Zivilprozeßrecht (1968), see, from the most recent bibliography, *Kornilakis* (fn 9) §79 4 II 3, 465, 466; *Stathopoulos* (fn 6) §15 no 12. See also the article of *S Kousoulis*, Concurrence of Contractual and Delictual Liability, Honorary Volume to Ap. Georgiades, vol I (2006) 441 ff.

106 *Stathopoulos* (fn 6) §15 no 13.

107 For the general obligation of prudence and diligence see, among others, *A Georgiades* in: A Georgiades/M Stathopoulos (eds), Civil Code, vol IV (1982) art 914 no 29; *Kornilakis* (fn 9) §84 3 II, 492–494.

the provisions regarding the violation of contractual obligations apply;[108] for example, as a failure to pay a contractual debt only conflicts with the rule of law, insofar as the relevant obligation derived from the contract, only contractual liability is applicable.[109]

B. CONCURRENCE/EXCLUSION OF ACTIONS FOR THE PROTECTION AGAINST PERSONAL INJURY

According to the principle of *cumul* adopted by the Greek jurisprudence, 63
when the act or omission which constitutes the contractual non-performance is simultaneously and in itself unlawful, the two liabilities, delictual and contractual, concur. It has to be noted once again, however, that when a contractual non-performance is not in itself unlawful, ie it is not contrary to this general duty of 'not culpably damaging another' in specific situations, which is imposed by law, no concurrence of contractual and delictual liability arises. In such a case, only the provisions regarding the violation of contractual obligations apply.

C. CONCURRENCE/EXCLUSION OF ACTIONS FOR THE PROTECTION OF PROPERTY

The above-mentioned principle of *cumul* exists for the protection from personal 64
injury as well as for the protection of property.

D. CONCURRENCE/EXCLUSION IN THE CASE OF INTERFERENCE WITH CONTRACTUAL RIGHTS

1) *Interference with a Contractual Relationship*

For a long time, the Greek legislator has regulated issues of unfair competition. 65
In particular, art 1of L 146/1914 stipulates that: 'In commercial, industrial or agricultural transactions, any act which is opposed to morality is prohibited. The transgressor may be sued in order to refrain from such acts and for damages.'[110] Articles 914, 919, 281 and 57–59 GCC are complementary to the

---

108 See *Stathopoulos/Karampatzos* (fn 3) no 41; *Stathopoulos* (fn 6) §15 no 11.

109 *Stathopoulos/Karampatzos* (fn 3).

110 See *N Deloukas* in: KD Kerameus/PJ Kozyris (eds), Introduction to Greek Law (1988) (in English) ch 10, 163 and *N Deloukas* revised by *E Perakis* in: KD Kerameus/PJ Kozyris (eds), Introduction to Greek Law (3rd rev edn 2008) (in English) ch 11, 229, Thessaloniki Court of Appeal 1465/2009 and 3000/2005, both published in ISOKRATIS, the data bank of the Athens Bar.

special provisions of L 146/1914. However, the application of the provisions of the special L 146/1914, and in particular of art 1 thereof, does not exclude the provisions of arts 914 and 919 GCC; as a consequence, said provisions can be used cumulatively when the competitive behaviour at the same time constitutes a tort.[111]

66 According to the Greek jurisprudence, attempts to hire competitor's employees or to take over competitor's clients fall under the interdiction of the above Law only when there is an intent to harm the particular competitor.[112]

2) *Loss of Business due to Personal Injury to Someone Else's Employees or Clients or to Property Damage to the Entrepreneur*

67 According to the Greek jurisprudence, *direct* damage is a presupposition for the liability of art 914 GCC. In particular, it is stated in the decisions of the Greek Court of Cassation[113] that it derives from arts 297, 298, 914 and 930 §3 GCC that only the person who has been directly prejudiced may seek reparation, ie only the subject of the right or of the protected interest who has been offended by the tort. In the case of personal injury, the subject of the offended right is the person against whom the tort is directed and this person is entitled to damages, ie only the direct subject of the offence can claim damages. Third persons, even if they belong to the family of the direct victim, who sustain damage to their pecuniary interests as a result of the tort committed against the direct victim, are indirectly and not directly prejudiced and are not substituted to the damages claim of the victim nor do they acquire a direct claim for damages themselves, because their indirect damage does not fall under the protective field of arts 914 and 929 sent a GCC. Indirectly prejudiced third persons fall under the protective field and can claim damages for their indirect damage only in the exceptional cases provided in arts 928 sent 2 and 929 sent 2 GCC,[114] which cannot be

---

[111] *E Aggelopoulos* in: G Triantafyllakis (ed), Applications of Commercial Law, 3B (2007) 1338; Athens Multi-Member Court of First Instance 1748/2004 Dikaio Meson Enimerosis kai Epikoinonias (DiMEE = Law Media and Communication) 2005, 252; Athens Multi-Member Court of First Instance 1540/2004 DiMEE 2005, 261.

[112] Athens Court of Appeal, 2692/2009, 3594/2008, 4530/2002, Athens Multi-Member Court of First Instance 3416/2010, all of them published in ISOKRATIS. See also *N Rokas*, Industrial Property (2004) 196–198.

[113] See, among others, AP 243/2011 published in NOMOS; AP 153/2005 EllDni 47, 429; AP1504/2000 DEE 7/2001, 497.

[114] Art 928 sent 2 GCC states : 'In case of death, the person bound to pay damages is also bound to make reparations, for the loss of maintenance or services, to the person who is entitled by law to claim maintenance or the performance of services by the victim.' And art 928 sent 2 GCC states : 'In case of injury to the body or the health of a person, the person bound to pay damages, must also compensate the third party, who, being entitled by law to claim the performance of services by the victim, is now deprived of the services because of the delict committed against the victim.'

applied by analogy.[115] Persons whose damage arises as a result of the injury of another person are not included in the above-mentioned persons and do not have a claim for lost profit.

V. SPECIFIC SITUATIONS

A. PRE-CONTRACTUAL LIABILITY

As mentioned above, according to Greek law, at the stage of negotiations for 68
the conclusion of a contract, the parties must deal with each other according to the dictates of good faith and conventional mores (art 197 GCC). A person who, in the course of negotiations for the conclusion of a contract, has, through his fault, caused prejudice to the other party is liable for compensation even if the contract has not been concluded (pre-contractual liability, art 198 GCC).

B. LIABILITY OF PROFESSIONALS

Although the EU has not yet issued a directive regarding the liability of persons 69
rendering services, the Greek legislator has taken a step in this direction with L 2251/1994, which introduces provisions regarding not only the liability of producers, but also the liability of persons rendering services (art 8). Hence, art 8 of L 2251/1994 was drafted in conformity with the draft of the EU Directive on liability of persons rendering services (CONSOM 20/ECO 86/6378/92, 12 May 1992) and provides for the civil liability of persons rendering services.

There is no unanimity in theory on whether the legal ground for the liability 70
of said persons is contract, tort or L 2251/1994. Also, although it functions as a form of liability complementary to the liability of the producer for defective products provided in art 6 of the aforementioned Law, the liability of persons rendering services is not a strict liability but a hybrid strict liability, which means that fault is required but there is a reversal of the burden of proof.[116]

Of special interest is the decision 18/1999 of the Court of Cassation (full 71
bench),[117] as it deals with the liability of lawyers. The Court of Cassation with this decision and with a large minority (nine dissenting members) decided

---

115 AP 1918/2005 EllDni 47 (2006) 429.

116 *A Georgiades* (fn 2) §63 no 3, 723.

117 NoV 48 (2000) 465–469 = EllDni 40 (1999) 1290 = DEE 5 (1999) 1172 = EEN 2000, 230 = Digesta 1999–2000, 109, followed by a note of *K Panagopoulos*. For a brief summary of the facts (in English) see *Dacoronia* (fn 79) 269 no 82.

that, as a result of the special nature of the profession of lawyers, on the one hand, and the scope of L 2251/1994 for the protection of the consumer, which incorporated Directive 85/374/EEC, on the other, lawyers are exempted from the scope of the said Law; hence lawyers do not fall under the category of persons (architects, doctors, etc) who are liable vis-à-vis their clients, according to art 8 of the above Law,[118] but continue to be liable according to art 73 of the Introductory Law of the GCCP, which provides for an action for mis-trial against lawyers, notaries, arbitrators, court secretaries and bailiffs.

72 It has been held[119] that L 2251/1994 did not abolish art 73 of the Introductory Law of the GCCP which provides for an action for mistrial against lawyers, notaries, arbitrators, court secretaries and bailiffs and which stipulates that a relevant action is only permitted if it is based on intent or gross negligence and the plaintiff sustained damage from the acts or omissions of said persons (art 73 §4). According to §5 of said article, the court action is not allowed if six months have elapsed from the act or omission invoked. The Greek Court of Cassation (in full bench) has held that the six-month limitation period begins to run not from the moment of the act or omission but from the moment the person who gave the mandate gained knowledge of the damaging behaviour. In this way, art 73 §5 does not contravene art 20 §1 of the Greek Constitution on the right to legal protection which it would do if the provision stood as it reads (six months from the act or omission).[120] It has also been held that art 73 of the Introductory Law of the GCCP is the only basis for a legal action against said persons; a claim based on contractual liability (art 713 GCC regulating the mandate) or on tortious liability (art 914 GCC) or on the above-mentioned art 8 of L 2251/1994 is not possible.[121]

---

118 The said decision has become the object of a lively criticism for the view of its majority in an article by *G Arnokouros*, DEE 7 (2001) 467–474. The said author adopts the view of the minority of the Court, according to which, lawyers should not be exempted as, while exercising their professional activity, they offer services in an independent way; this view was already expressed by *A Georgiades*, The Liability of the Person Rendering Services, Volume dedicated to A Kiantou-Pambouki (1998) 154, 155.

119 Thessaloniki Multi-Member Court of First Instance 10725/1997 Digesta 2000, 118.

120 AP 20/2000 (full bench), published in NOMOS; AP 829/2008 published in NOMOS; 1744/2008 EllDni 52 (2011) 1371; 1057/2009 NoV 57 (2009) 2392; 2217/2013 published in NOMOS; 1892/2014 published in NOMOS. See also *A Karampatzos*, The Institution of Prescription in the Common Frame of Reference as *Occasio* for a Reform of the Law of Prescription of the Greek Civil Code, ChrID ID' (2014) fn 11, 573, 574.
AP 400/2001 EllDni 42 (2001), 848 = NoV 49 (2001) 1501, has held that the six-month limitation period starting from the act or omission is contrary not only to the Greek Constitution but also to art 6(1) of the European Convention on Human Rights.

121 See AP 1057/2009 (fn 120); AP 1892/2014 (fn 120); Larissa Court of Appeal 62/2005 EllDni 46 (2005), 1536. See also *F Triantafyllou-Albanidou*, Peremption for the Filing of an Action for Mistrial against Lawyers, Notaries, Arbitrators, Court Secretaries and Bailiffs (art 73 of the Introductory Law GCCP), in: P Papanikolaou (ed), Issues of the Law of Prescription (2015) 980.

Article 73 GCCP has been tacitly amended, as regards lawyers, by art 161 §1 of the 'Code for Lawyers',[122] which stipulates that claims against lawyers, who, by their act or omission, unlawfully cause damage out of intent or gross negligence to their clients, are time-barred three years after the act or omission invoked by the plaintiff.[123] The provision of the 'Code for Lawyers', though enacted after the settled position of the jurisprudence, according to which the limitation period should start to run not from the moment of the act or omission but from the moment the person who gave the mandate gained knowledge of the damaging behaviour, extends the prescription period from six months to three years but continues to have as its starting point the moment of the act or omission. It has been said[124] that it is possible that the drafters of the Code were of the opinion that the extension of the limitation period from six months to three years would widen the possibility to gain knowledge and, as such, fulfils the requirements of the principle of proportionality. This supposition, though, as mentioned, is not confirmed by the preamble of the Code. It must be noted, however, that, to date, there has been no decision of the courts holding that the three-year limitation period starts to run not from the moment of the act or omission but from the moment the person who gave the mandate gained knowledge of the damaging behaviour. 73

CASES

CASE 1. THE UNATTRACTIVE SHOPPING MALL

Only Z can bring a claim in contract against D for breach of his contractual obligations. Although the principle of *cumul* exists in Greece, this breach cannot qualify as a tort, so Z has no claim in tort against D. 74

C cannot bring a claim in contract against D, as there is no direct contractual relationship between D and C, although D has allowed Z to sublet the store.[125] Only if Z fails to bring an action against D can C substitute Z in the exercise of his judicial protection, by filing Z's claim against D (art 72 GCCP). 75

CASE 2. THE IDLE LAWYER

As mentioned above, according to Greek jurisprudence, art 73 of the Introductory Law of the GCCP is the only basis for W to file a legal action against D. 76

---

122 L 4194/2013 (Official Gazette, FEK A', 208).

123 See also *Triantafyllou-Albanidou* (fn 121) 982 fn 22.

124 Ibid, 986.

125 See, among others, *E Dacoronia*, Sublease of a Thing (1994) 90.

According to the Greek Court of Cassation, a claim based on contractual liability (art 713 GCC regulating the mandate) or on tortious liability (art 914 GCC) or on the above-mentioned art 8 of L 2251/1994 is not possible. Article 73 GCCP has been tacitly amended, as regards lawyers, by art 161 §1 of the 'Code for Lawyers', which stipulates that claims against lawyers, who, by their act or omission unlawfully caused damage out of intent or gross negligence to their clients are time-barred three years after the act or omission invoked by the plaintiff, thus giving the plaintiff a longer period to act.

77 Thus, if W did not file a claim against D within three years from the moment he asked D to change the will back, we are afraid that, under the existing jurisprudence, W's daughters cannot bring a claim against D in contract/tort/both to recover the amount promised to them by their late father.

CASE 3. THE DEFECTIVE HOUSE

78 The exclusion clause, even if valid according to art 332 GCC, does not bind C, as he has no contractual relationship with D. C can sue D for compensation of his bodily injury and/or the damage caused to the house in tort.

79 Article 937 GCC on the limitation period of torts is not an obstacle for C, as the five-year time limit starts to run from the moment C gains knowledge of the damage and of the tortfeasor.

CASE 4. APARTMENT IN FLAMES

80 C can bring a claim against D both in contract and tort.

81 Article 575 GCC on the obligations of the lessor stipulates that: 'the lessor is bound to hand over the leased thing to the lessee in a condition appropriate for the use stipulated and to keep it in such condition during the term of the lease', and art 576 GCC on deficiencies or material defects stipulates that: 'if, during the time of its delivery to the lessee, the leased thing has a defect which destroys or diminishes its fitness for the stipulated use (material defect), or if during the lease such a defect appeared which prevents it from being suitable to be used for the purpose for which it was leased as well as for similar defects which appear later on, the lessee is entitled to claim reduction or non-payment of the rent'.[126] When interpreting said provisions, it is accepted that

[126] For an analysis of arts 575 and 576 GCC see, among others, *M Rapsomanikis* in: A Georgiades/M Stathopoulos (eds), Civil Code, vol III (1980) arts 575 and 576; *R Pantelidou* in: Georgiades/SEAK (2010) arts 575 and 576.

the poor maintenance of parts of a leased thing, such as the poor maintenance of the central heating, constitutes a material defect.[127] Therefore, D, by negligently failing to monitor the circuit breaker, is liable in contract regarding the material defect. Furthermore, this liability arises irrespectively of any fault regarding the existence of the defect; the existence of fault increases his liability (arts 577 sent b, 578, 580 GCC[128]).[129]

C can also bring a claim for damages and compensation of her moral harm against D in tort. According to the Greek jurisprudence, the omission of taking precautionary measures for the avoidance of the danger of fire constitutes unlawful behaviour according to art 914 GCC).[130] 82

CASE 5. INJURED SKIER

As mentioned above, according to the principle of *cumul* adopted by the Greek jurisprudence, when the act or omission which constitutes the contractual non-performance is simultaneously and in itself unlawful, there is delictual as well as contractual liability. Therefore, if D1 is found liable for the derailment of the ski lift and the fall of the cable, C can file a claim for damages in tort against D1 and a claim against D2 according to the terms of the liability insurance. It is irrelevant that C had a contract with D1 as, if it is proven that the accident was due to D1's negligence in maintenance, his behaviour is unlawful and can generate a claim in tort. 83

CASE 6. EXPLODING CAR

In principle, C could base his claim both in contract and in tort. In particular, according to art 548 GCC, as replaced by art 1 §1 L 3043/2002, on 84

---

127 *A Georgiades*, Law of Obligations – Special Part, vol I (2004) §25 II no 10, 345.

128 Art 577 GCC: 'If at the time of concluding the lease, the agreed quality of the leasehold lacks, the lessee has the right to claim damages for non-performance of the contract, instead of the reduction or non-payment of the rent. The same rule also applies if the lessor knew or was bound to know of the material defect which existed at the time of the conclusion of the lease.'
Art 578 GCC: 'The lessee has also the right of the previous article if, by fault of the lessor, the agreed quality ceased to exist or the material defect of the leasehold appeared after the conclusion of the lease.'
Art 580 GCC: 'The lessor is not liable for material defects that the lessee ignored out of gross negligence at the time of the conclusion of the contract, unless the lessor had promised that there is no such defect or he concealed it with malice.'

129 *Georgiades* (fn 127) §25 II no 14, 346.

130 AP 510/1959 NoV 8 (1960) 251; AP 812/1998 EllDni 39 (1998) 1548. See also *Stathopoulos* (fn 6) §15 no 45.

'Destruction or deterioration of the thing', the purchaser has the right to ask for the replacement or to rescind from the contract or to reduce the price even if the thing was destroyed or deteriorated due to its defect. However, art 554 GCC on prescription stipulates that the rights of the seller on account of material defects or lack of conceded qualities are subject to prescription after the end of five years for immovables and two years for movables. Furthermore, according to art 555 §1, as replaced by art 1 §1 L 3043/2002, 'prescription starts with the delivery of the thing to the purchaser even if the purchaser discovered the defects or the lack of quality later', but according to art 556 GCC, as replaced by art 1 §1 L 3043/2002, 'if a time period for the liability of the seller for a defect or lack of the agreed quality was agreed, this in case of doubt means that the prescription for the defects which took place during this time period starts from the time the defects manifested'.[131]

85 Accordingly, although a time period for the liability of the seller for a defect was agreed, C cannot bring an action against D1, as the defect manifested after the lapse of the two-year full warranty.[132]

86 Article 557 GCC, as replaced by art 1 §1 L 3043/2002, according to which the seller cannot invoke the prescription of the previous articles if he concealed or failed to reveal out of intent the defect or lack of agreed quality, cannot apply here, as it cannot be invoked that D1 maliciously concealed or failed to reveal the defect.

87 L 2251/1994 concerning the protection of consumers, and in particular art 6 thereof, stipulates that a producer is strictly liability for defective products.[133] Hence, P has a claim against D2 according to the special legislation for the protection of the consumer, as the claim against the producer is time-barred, according to art 6 §13 L 2251/1994, three years after the person who sustained the damage gained knowledge of it.

88 C also has a claim against D1 and D2 according to arts 914 ff GCC, as their behaviour is unlawful (omission to check the deficiency of the fuel line, as they were obliged to do in accordance with the principle of good faith). This claim is time-barred, according to art 937 GCC, five years after C gained knowledge of the damage and of the tortfeasor.[134]

---

131 For an analysis of arts 548 and 554–556 GCC, see *A Karampatzos* in: Georgiades/SEAK (2010) arts 548, 554–556.

132 See *Karampatzos* (fn 131) art 556, 1096.

133 For an analysis of arts 1–10 L 2251/1994 in English, see *I Karakostas*, Consumer Protection Law (2012).

134 For a comparison of the tortious liability of the GCC and the special liability of art 6 L 2251/1994 and for the advantages of the choice of each as a legal basis for the liability, see *Karakostas* (fn 133) 212–214.

CASE 7. RACING BOAT BURNING

The answer is the same as for Case 6 above regarding the value of the boat. Regarding the expenses for C's repatriation, said expenses constitute indirect damage.[135] Compensation for indirect damage can be sought only if said damage is causally connected to the damaging act.[136] The expenses incurred for the repatriation are causally connected to the destruction of the boat and, therefore, C can claim compensation for them.[137] 89

CASE 8. INSIDIOUS REPORT

C can file a claim against D in contract based on the violation of the contractual obligation not to undertake any act which is competitive to C during the period of the contract. This obligation (referred to as an 'obligation of faith') derives from the contract of work,[138] as a secondary effect,[139] even if it is not explicitly agreed. 90

Apart from the claim in contract, C has a claim for damages based on art 1 of L 146/1914. He also has a claim in tort according to arts 914 and 919 GCC, which can be used cumulatively. 91

CASE 9. CIRCULAR LETTER

C can file a claim against D in contract based on the violation of the contractual obligation of confidentiality even after the termination of the contract of work. This obligation for both contracting parties derives from permanent contracts, such as the contract for work, as a secondary effect,[140] even if it is not explicitly agreed. 92

---

135 Direct damage is provoked directly by the infringement of rights or interests protected by the law, whereas indirect damage is constituted in regard to further unfavourable consequences to the victim's entire property (*M Stathopoulos* in: A Georgiades/M Stathopoulos (eds), Civil Code, vol II (1979) art 297–298 no 44; *Kornilakis* (fn 9) 519).

136 See Athens Court of Appeal 9835/1984 Armenopoulos (Arm) 39 (1985) 118; Crete Court of Appeal 29/1964 NoV 12 (1964) 483; *A Kritikos*, Damages from Car Accidents (2008) §14 I no 10, 198.

137 See *Kritikos* (fn 136) §22 V no 133, 502, for the costs of repatriation in the case of damage to cars.

138 According to art 652 GCC, the employee is bound to diligently perform the services he undertook.

139 See, among others, *D Travlos-Tzanetatos* in: A Georgiades/M Stathopoulos (eds), Civil Code, vol III (1980) art 652 no 126 ff and in particular no 132.

140 See, among others, *Stathopoulos* (fn 135) art 287 no 37 ff and in particular art 288 no 47; *Travlos-Tzanetatos* (fn 139) art 652 nos 127, 128.

93 C can file a claim in tort, as he can invoke that D committed a tort by sending a circular to all its customers with the said content. In particular, D acted unlawfully as he violated the provisions of art 362 of the Greek Penal Code (GPC) on defamation, which forbids the communication, in any way, to third persons of facts that can harm the honour or reputation of a person.

94 Furthermore, C could bring a claim based on the provisions of arts 57 and 59 GCC (protection of the right to personality). Honour and reputation are among the elements that encompass the right to the personality and their violation constitutes an offence of the entire notion of personality. Therefore, a claim for damages and compensation of the moral harm can be brought pursuant to arts 57 and 59 GCC.

95 Finally, C can also file a claim against D in tort according to art 23 L 2472/1997 on the 'Protection of a person from the processing of personal data', which provides for the civil liability of the physical or legal person who causes damage or moral harm to physical persons in violation of the provisions of said Law.[141] The amount awarded as moral harm, according to art 23 §2 sent a' of the above-mentioned Law, cannot be less than GRD 2,000,000 (the equivalent of €5,869.41), unless a smaller amount has been sought or the violation is due to negligence. The award of an amount of money as compensation of moral harm is possible even if the damage is minimal or does not exist.[142] According to art 2 of said Law, 'personal data' is any information related to the subject of the data and 'processing' includes the communication of such information. The processing of data is not permitted without the consent of the subject of the data according to art 7 of the Law.

CASE 10. SHORTAGE OF SUPPLY

96 According to art 178 GCC, a juridical act which is contrary to good morals shall be null and void. Furthermore, void as contrary to good morals are, in particular, according to art 179 GCC, a juridical act that unduly restricts the liberty of the individual, or a juridical act whereby one party exploits the need, weakness or inexperience and succeeds in concluding or gaining for himself or others benefits that are obviously disproportionate to his own performance. Hence, given that C has no alternative supply sources and D, knowing that X has gone bankrupt and Z had to reduce its production dramatically, exploits C's need in order to gain for himself benefits that are disproportionate to his own

141 For an analysis of the presuppositions required for the said liability, see, among others, *Georgiades* (fn 2) §63 V3 nos 33–35, 664, 665.

142 See also ibid, §63 nos 24–26, 731, 732.

performance (20% increase in prices, payments to be made in less than 30 days instead of 90). Accordingly, the new contract between C and D is null and void.

In addition, according to art 919 GCC, whoever intentionally in a manner which violates the commands of morality causes damage to another is bound to make reparation to the other for any damage thus caused. Thus, C also has a claim in tort against D. A claim for damages based on art 1 of L 146/1914 cannot be excluded either. 97

CASE 11. INJURED ROCK STAR

There is no contractual bond between C and D, so there is no claim in contract. 98
There is no claim in tort either because C is indirectly damaged from the accident and, as mentioned above, according to the Greek jurisprudence, *direct* damage is a presupposition for the liability of art 914 GCC.

CASE 12. EQUIPMENT DESTROYED

According to the contract, D1 is obliged to transport the electronic equipment 99
needed for the concert but he is unable to render his performance (impossibility of performance) due not to his fault but to D2's fault. According to art 380 GCC, C is also released from the obligation to counter-perform ie to pay for the transport. Thus, C does not have a claim in contract against D1.

C can bring a claim in tort against D2 for the destroyed electronic equipment. 100
He can also seek compensation for the loss of profit from the cancellation of the concert, as, according to art 298 GCC, 'damages include the decrease in the existing property of the creditor (positive damage), as well as lost profits. That which can be expected as a probable profit in the usual course of events or by reference to the special circumstances and particularly to the preparatory measures taken is presumed as loss of profit.' The proof of the amount of the profit lost 'expected as a probable profit' might be difficult in our case as X is famous but retired, so it is not certain how many tickets would be sold for the comeback concert, unless the tickets had already been sold.

CASE 13. SLIPPING ON A LETTUCE LEAF

C can bring a claim against D in tort. 101

According to Greek jurisprudence, an omission can also lead to an obligation 102
to pay damages according to art 914 GCC, as long as it is unlawful. Such is

the case when the tortfeasor omitted to act, although he was obliged to do so either by law, by contract, by good faith according to the prevailing social understanding, by his previous behaviour or by the general spirit of the law;[143] the person who provokes perilous situations is obliged, according to good faith, to take all necessary measures required by the rules of science and common experience to avert damage, even if such an obligation is not specifically provided by law; otherwise, the violation of the rule specifically providing for such an obligation would alone constitute the element of unlawfulness required by art 914 GCC.[144]

103 D, being a grocery shop, must be aware that people buying in the premises may slip on lettuce leaves, spinach leaves, etc that have fallen to the ground while other customers are shopping. For this reason, D has to have adequate personnel who will immediately clean the premises in order to prevent the creation of a perilous situation for other customers. If D has not taken the necessary precautionary measures, then he may be held liable in tort for C's broken leg.

104 C could further bring a claim against D on the basis of arts 197, 198 GCC on pre-contractual liability.

CASE 14. TEST DRIVE

105 No contract exists between D and C when D negligently smashes the front part of the car against a tree. D has a claim in tort against C.

CASE 15. BREACH OF NEGOTIATIONS

106 As already mentioned, according to Greek law, at the stage of negotiations for the conclusion of a contract, the parties must deal with each other according to the dictates of good faith and conventional mores (art 197 GCC) and a person who, in the course of negotiations for the conclusion of a contract, has through his fault caused prejudice to the other party is liable for compensation even if the contract has not been concluded (art 198 GCC).[145] Accordingly, although D is free to choose the person with whom he concludes a contract (principle of freedom of contracts), he must deal with the person he had entered into

---

143 See, among others, AP 174/2005 Ephimeris Ellinon Nomikon (EEN) 2005, 496; 381/2005 ChrID E'/2005, 710. For a brief summary of the facts of said decisions (in English), see *E Dacoronia*, Greece, in: H Koziol/BC Steininger (eds), European Tort Law 2005 (2006) nos 2, 3.

144 AP 381/2005 (fn 143).

145 For the nature of the pre-contractual liability, see above sec I.B.

negotiations with in conformity with the dictates of good faith and conventional mores. D did not act accordingly and, therefore, C can bring a claim against D for the costs incurred, as what is compensated on the basis of arts 197, 198 GCC is the 'negative interest',[146] ie what C would have had if the prejudicial event had not taken place. It has to be noted that C could not seek that which he would have had if the contract had been concluded, since D had no obligation to conclude the contract with him.

CASE 16. NON-DISCLOSURE OF RELEVANT FACTS

According to arts 534 and 535 GCC, as replaced by art 1 §1 L 3043/2002, the seller is obliged to deliver the thing in the agreed qualities and without material defects. The seller does not fulfil his obligation according to the previous article if the thing which he delivers to the buyer does not correspond to the contract and especially if: 107

(a) the thing does not correspond to the description which was given by the seller or to the sample or example the seller presented to the buyer;
(b) the thing sold is not good for the purpose of the specific contract and in particular for its special use in accordance with the contract's purpose;
(c) the thing is not good for the use that things of the same kind are usually intended;
(d) the thing does not correspond to the quality or effectiveness the buyer reasonably expects from things of the same kind, in view also of the public statements made by the seller, producer or his representative, especially in the context of the relevant advertising or labelling, unless the seller had no knowledge or was not obliged to know about such statements.

According to the prevailing view in Greece,[147] the provisions of arts 534 ff GCC exclude pre-contractual liability, unless other behaviour of the seller that is not covered by said provisions is at stake.[148] 108

In the particular case, P wanted to buy the machine type X, not mentioning where he intended to use this machine, so it seems that D's behaviour was in conformity with art 534 GCC, as he delivered exactly the machine that P wanted 109

[146] See *Georgiades* (fn 4) §34 no 10; *Lekkas* (fn 4) arts 197–198 no 37 with more references to the related Greek literature and jurisprudence; *Stathopoulos/Karampatzos* (fn 3) no 88.

[147] *K Spiliopoulos*, ErmAK, 1954, Introductory Remarks to arts 534–562 no 72. Contra *P Doris* in: A Georgiades/M Stathopoulos (eds), Civil Code, vol III (1980) Introductory Remarks to arts 534–562 no 32 ff.

[148] See *Kornilakis* (fn 9) §51 14, 319.

to buy which worked on all terrains, even if its performance reduced dramatically when used on steep fields. The latter cannot be considered as a material defect. Accordingly, D seems to have fulfilled his obligation under the contract.

110 P may have a claim in tort against D if his behaviour is considered as contrary to the unwritten rules of prudence and diligence to be expected from all members of society when acting. However, we do not think that, under the particular facts of the case, D had an obligation to inform P about the performance of the machine in steep fields, just because he knew through a friend that P owned fields of corn on steep hills in a distant part of the country.

THE BORDERLINES OF TORT LAW IN ISRAEL

Israel Gilead

QUESTIONS

I. Tracing the Borderlines . . . 255
  A. Distinction between Tort and Contract . . . 255
  B. Existence of a 'Grey Zone'? . . . 255
  C. Common or Different Rules Regulating Tort and Contract . . . 255
  D. Application of Common Rules in a Different Way . . . 256
II. Main Differences between Tortious and Contractual Liability . . . 257
  A. Differences as Regards the Foundations of Liability . . . 257
    1) Role of Intention . . . 258
    2) Role of Wrongfulness and Fault and their Variations . . . 259
    3) Role of Strict Liability . . . 259
  B. Differences as Regards Causation . . . 259
  C. Differences as Regards Remedies . . . 260
    1) Degree of Certainty of the Damage . . . 260
    2) Compensation for Non-Pecuniary Loss . . . 261
    3) Compensation for Loss of Earnings and for Loss of Chance . . . 261
    4) Restitutionary Damages . . . 262
    5) Aggravated and Exemplary (or Punitive) Damages . . . 262
    6) Other Remedies . . . 263
  D. Differences as Regards Recoverability of 'Pure Economic Losses' . . . 263
  E. Differences as Regards Liability for Others . . . 263
    1) Liability for Auxiliaries and for Independent Contractors . . . 264
    2) Liability for Legal Representatives or Organs of a Company . . . 264
    3) Liability of Representatives of Natural Persons . . . 264
    4) Liability of the Auxiliary/Organ Itself . . . 265
  F. Differences as Regards Liability in the Case of Multiple Tortfeasors/Breaching Parties . . . 265
  G. Differences as Regards the Persons Who May be Protected . . . 265
  H. Differences as Regards Defences . . . 266
  I. Differences as Regards Limitation Periods . . . 267

J. Differences as Regards Proof ... 268
K. Other Differences ... 268
L. Reasons for the Differences ... 269
III. Limitation or Exclusion of Liability Arising from Tort and from Contract ... 269
A. Statutory Provisions Authorising a Limitation or Exclusion of Liability ... 269
B. Limitation or Exclusion of Contractual and Tortious Liability by Contract ... 270
1) Is it Possible to Limit or Exclude Contractual and Tortious Liability under a Contract? ... 270
2) To What Extent can a Contractual Exclusion Provide a Defence to a Third Party to the Contract? ... 270
IV. Non-Concurrence or Concurrence of Actions ... 270
A. Overview ... 270
1) Areas of Overlap between Tort and Contract ... 270
2) Approach to Non-Concurrence and Concurrence of Actions ... 271
B. Concurrence/Exclusion of Actions for the Protection against Personal Injury and of Property ... 272
C. Concurrence/Exclusion in the Case of Interference with Contractual Rights ... 272
1) Interference with a Contractual Relationship ... 272
2) Loss of Business due to Personal Injury to Someone Else's Employees or Clients or to Property Damage to the Entrepreneur ... 273
V. Specific Situations ... 273
A. Pre-Contractual Liability ... 273
B. Liability of Professionals ... 274

CASES

Case 1. The Unattractive Shopping Mall ... 274
Case 2. The Idle Lawyer ... 274
Case 3. The Defective House ... 275
Case 4. Apartment in Flames ... 275
Case 5. Injured Skier ... 276
Case 6. Exploding Car ... 276
Case 7. Racing Boat Burning ... 276
Case 8. Insidious Report ... 276
Case 9. Circular Letter ... 277
Case 10. Shortage of Supply ... 277
Case 11. Injured Rock Star ... 277
Case 12. Equipment Destroyed ... 278

Case 13. Slipping on a Lettuce Leaf 278
Case 14. Test Drive 278
Case 15. Breach of Negotiations 278
Case 16. Non-Disclosure of Relevant Facts 279

QUESTIONS

I. TRACING THE BORDERLINES

A. DISTINCTION BETWEEN TORT AND CONTRACT

1 The distinction between tort and contract is in principle based on the facts that have to be established in order to constitute a cause of action. *Contract law* (statutory and case law) requires the claimant (C) to establish that an obligation under a valid contract was breached, that the contract has defects, that a pre-contractual obligation was breached, etc. Tort law (statutory and case law) requires C to establish that a specified tort was committed or that a duty which is classified as part of tort law has been breached.

B. EXISTENCE OF A 'GREY ZONE'?

2 A 'grey zone' between contract and tort exists where the facts of a case constitute both a cause of action in contract and a cause of action in tort. This, for example, may happen in cases of lack of good faith in pre-contractual negotiations. Absence of good faith may constitute a cause of action under contract law for breach of the pre-contractual duty of 'bona fide' negotiations,[1] and also a cause of action in tort law, usually for negligent misrepresentation.[2] Yet, remedies may differ under these different causes of action.[3]

C. COMMON OR DIFFERENT RULES REGULATING TORT AND CONTRACT

3 At present each field of law is governed by the statutory provisions that are classified as being either 'tort' law or 'contract' law. The same applies to case

1 Law of Contracts (General Part) 1973 art 12.
2 Civil Wrong Ordinance (New Version) (CWO) art 35 f.
3 See eg Civil Appeal (CivA) 4948/13 *Harkabi v Avni* (15.3.2015) holding that the remedies for 'bad faith' pre-contractual negotiations may include compensation for lost profits under contract law but not under tort law.

law, which interprets and supplements those provisions. Therefore, in principle, there are no rules common to tort and contract but rather different rules, for example regarding legal causation, remoteness of damage, joint liability and, most importantly, remedies. The remedy of specific performance (enforcement), for instance, is traditionally considered primary in contract[4] law but only secondary in tort law.[5]

4 Notably, there is both a legislative and judicial tendency to unify contractual rules and rules in tort. The proposed Civil Code of 2011,[6] for example, to a considerable extent unifies remedies under tort and under contract. Another step already taken toward unification is the application of the statutory tort defence of 'contributory (comparative) negligence'[7] by the courts to contract law,[8] although absent in statutory law. But even if this trend continues, and the proposed Civil Code of 2011 be enacted, it would not change the basic perception that tort and contract are different fields of law which can be unified only to a limited degree.

5 In this regard it is important to emphasise that, in Israel, tort law and contract law originate in quite different legal environments. Tort law has been always based on the English common law tradition. The major statute which governs tort law, the Civil Wrong Ordinance (CWO), is actually a codified restatement of English tort law, and was originally enacted by the British Mandate government of Palestine in 1947. In contrast, contract law was enacted in the 1960s and 1970s, and was influenced to a large degree by the European continental tradition.

D. APPLICATION OF COMMON RULES IN A DIFFERENT WAY

6 As noted above, tort law and contract law, statutory and judicial, are usually not governed by the same rules. When the same rule applies, its application is adjusted to the different context of tort and contract. An example is the common defence of 'contributory negligence' which has been applied by case law to contract.[9] In principle, the basic goals of the defence are the same in both fields – where the harmed party was at fault, she should bear part of the cost of the harm for reasons of fairness and deterrence. Yet, fairness and deterrence may have different meanings and consequences in the contractual context and in the context of tort.

4 Law of Contracts (Remedies for Breach of Contract) 1970 art 3.
5 CWO arts 73 and 74.
6 Arts 454–492.
7 CWO art 68.
8 CivA 3912/90 *Eximin SA v Textile and Shoes Ferarry*, 47 (IV) Piskey Din (PD) 64.
9 Ibid.

II. MAIN DIFFERENCES BETWEEN TORTIOUS AND CONTRACTUAL LIABILITY

A. DIFFERENCES AS REGARDS THE FOUNDATIONS OF LIABILITY

Generally speaking, the major difference between the foundations of contract law and the foundations of tort law is the following: while liability under contract law is basically founded on breach of a voluntarily taken obligation, liability in tort is founded on the breach of a duty imposed by law. This basic distinction, however, has been eroded to a significant degree by two developments. 7

One development, in contract law, is the emergence of a general duty to act in good faith and in a customary manner in the performance of contractual obligation, in the way contractual rights are used,[10] and in negotiating a contract.[11] The Supreme Court has ruled that this obligation to act in good faith and in a customary manner is objective rather than subjective, namely that even where a party to a contract feels and thinks that she is acting in good faith, the court may still find that she failed to do so. Therefore, one can hardly say that the contractual duty to act in objective good faith is one taken voluntarily by the contractual parties. Actually, this is a duty, imposed by law, to act in a manner which the court, the law, approves of. In fact, these kinds of contractual duties are duties imposed by law, similar to the duties imposed by tort law. 8

Another development in tort law is the emergence of tort liability in negligence for 'pure economic loss', namely loss which is not consequential on physical harm to a plaintiff's body or property. One aspect of this development is that when courts consider whether to impose liability for pure economic loss in cases of misrepresentation, professional malpractice and negligent provision of services, they take into account contractual or semi-contractual considerations. They do so with three requirements by which they monitor the scope of liability for 'pure economic loss'. These requirements are: 'special relations', 'reasonable reliance' and 'assumption of responsibility'. Traditionally, courts have tended to impose tort liability for pure economic loss when all these requirements are met, and to limit or deny liability when one or more are lacking. All these requirements are closely related to contractual relations: a voluntary obligation or promise made by a party to a contract constitutes *special relations* between the promisor and the other party, it creates *reasonable reliance* on the promise and it justifies attributing to the promisor an *assumption of responsibility* if the promise is breached. 9

10 Law of Contracts (General Part) 1973art 39.

11 Ibid, art 12.

10 This 'contractual foundation' of tort liability exists also when the parties are not directly related by the same contract but indirectly through a 'chain of contracts' or relations 'akin to a contract'.

11 To sum up, contract liability has a 'tort law foundation' whenever based on objective duties imposed by law, and tort law has a 'contractual foundation' when imposing liability on the ground that 'promises should be kept'.

1) Role of Intention

12 One can distinguish between two meanings of 'intention'. One meaning is that the actor is aware of the facts concerning her conduct, namely that she *knowingly* breaches a contract or inflicts harm upon another. The other meaning is 'bad intention', namely awareness accompanied by the will to cause harm to another person or at least indifference to causing this harm.

13 *In contract*, liability for breaching a contractual obligation may be strict (obligation to secure a specified outcome) or fault-based (obligation to act reasonably in the performance of the contract). Therefore intention, in both its meanings, is not necessarily a precondition to liability. Contractual strict liability, and even fault-based liability, may be imposed even where the non-performing party was unaware of the breach and acted in subjective good faith.

14 Although intention is not necessarily a precondition for contractual liability, it may well be a relevant consideration affecting contractual liability and its scope. For example, where the non-performing party was aware of the failure to perform, this may induce the court to hold that he breached his objective duty to act in good faith. 'Bad intention', for another example, may induce the court to award compensation for non-pecuniary loss (which is discretionary).

15 *In tort*, 'bad intention' was required by a few torts such as 'fraud' and 'unlawful detention', but this requirement has been circumvented by the law of negligence – it was held that, in cases of negligent misrepresentation and negligent arrest, liability can be imposed under negligence law in the absence of 'bad intention'. As to intention in the sense of awareness of the facts that constitute tortious conduct (acting *knowingly*), this requirement is now limited to the torts of false imprisonment, assault and causing breach of contract.[12]

16 However, 'bad intention' and awareness may make a difference in tort law. If the existence of bad intention, for example, is established, this may lead to an award of punitive damages. Intention in the sense of awareness may render

12 CWO arts 26, 23 and 61.

conduct which is reasonable without awareness unreasonable (reasonable people do not *knowingly* act in this manner).

2) Role of Wrongfulness and Fault and their Variations

17 'Wrongfulness' in the continental European sense is not a concept used in Israel. As mentioned, contractual liability is strict (unless the obligation is to act in a non-negligent manner), while tort liability is basically based on objective fault, with 'islands' of strict liability, discussed below,[13] and islands of torts which require bad intention.[14]

3) Role of Strict Liability

18 *Contractual liability*, as mentioned, may be strict (obligation to secure an outcome) or fault-based (obligation to act reasonably in performance).

19 Liability in tort is usually fault-based, with 'islands' or 'pockets' of strict liability. These 'islands' can be classified into two groups. One group is '*modern* strict liability', based on considerations of loss-spreading, fairness and deterrence (it applies to harm suffered in road accidents, by defective products and in the workplace). Another group is '*traditional* strict liability' for torts protecting the body (assault, false imprisonment) and physical property (conversion, trespass to land).

B. DIFFERENCES AS REGARDS CAUSATION

20 As to *factual* causation, in both contract and tort, the governing test is the 'but for' test (*causa sine qua non*), which requires that the tortious activity or the breach of the contract is a *necessary* link in the causal chain that leads to P's harm. In cases in which two (or more) independent causes caused the same harm independently, so that none is a 'but for' cause, the *sufficiency* test applies – each cause is considered as a factual cause although not a 'necessary' cause. Proportional liability, namely liability adjusted to the probability that D caused C harm, actually exists only in cases of 'lost chances of healing', which are considered tort cases.[15]

21 As to legal causation, in both fields, the leading test is the 'scope of risk test', which often takes the form of a 'foreseeability test'.[16] As indicated above,

13 See below no 19.

14 Such as Fraud (CWO art 56) and Malicious Prosecution (CWO art 60).

15 CivA 10399/08 *Fruts v Tzergiev* (4.4.2008).

16 CivA 4394/09 *Landerman v Sagiv Engineering* (30.12.2010).

however, the content of the 'scope of risk' and foreseeability tests differs in tort and contract given the different foundation of each field.

22 In *tort*, where the obligation is imposed by law, the 'scope of risk' is also determined by law. Legal causation is established where the risk that actually materialised (*ex post*) was a risk which, *according to law*, rendered the conduct tortious when it took place (*ex ante*). For example, as under negligence law only reasonably *foreseeable* risks are considered tortious, legal causation is recognised only where harm is *objectively foreseeable*.

23 In contract law, which is founded on voluntary obligations, the 'scope of risk' within which legal causation is recognised is determined by the party who voluntarily undertook the obligation. The question is: 'What is the scope of liability assumed by the party?' In this regard, the law provides that subjective foreseeability of a harm by a party to a contract is an indication that that party voluntarily assumed liability for this harm.[17]

C. DIFFERENCES AS REGARDS REMEDIES

24 As a general observation, it is the different foundations of contract and tort that result in the differences between the remedies provided by each field of law. In a nutshell, although the aim of remedies in both fields is the same – *restitutio in integrum*, restoration to original position – the 'original position' has different meanings in contract and tort. In tort, it means restoration to the condition in which the plaintiff would have been in the past and in the future were she not harmed by the tortfeasor. In contract, the original condition refers to the condition in which the plaintiff would have been in the past and in the future had the contract not been breached.

1) Degree of Certainty of the Damage

25 As to *past* losses, rules of evidence which apply both to contract and tort require that these losses should be established by the 'preponderance of evidence' test, namely *that it is more probable than not* that the damage was caused by the tort or by the breach of contract. As mentioned, the only exception is proportional liability *in tort* for 'lost chances of healing'. This exceptional tort liability is adjusted to the probability that the loss was caused by the defendant, even if it is more probable than not that the loss was not caused by the unlawful conduct.

---

[17] Law of Contracts (Remedies for Breach of Contract) 1970 art 10.

As to future losses, in both tort and contract, courts are more flexible with the required certainty: they may well award compensation for future loss which is discounted by the probability that this loss will indeed occur, even if the probability is less than 50%. However, no compensation is awarded for future losses which are considered speculative.[18] 26

2) *Compensation for Non-Pecuniary Loss*

Tort law has traditionally awarded compensation for non-pecuniary loss which is consequential on the plaintiff's bodily injury, for example for pain and suffering, loss of life amenities and loss of life expectancy. Tort law has also traditionally awarded compensation for non-pecuniary loss which arises following damage to the plaintiff's property. As to 'pure' non-pecuniary loss (which is not consequential on physical harm to the plaintiff or his property), until the mid-1980s, this loss was not compensable under negligence law, only under torts which protect dignity (defamation) and privacy. In 1985, the Supreme Court allowed liability in negligence for pure non-pecuniary loss[19] and since then the scope of this liability has been expanded dramatically, especially in cases when the autonomy of a person is infringed. 27

In contract, the law provides that courts may award compensation for non-pecuniary loss to the extent that it finds proper in the circumstances of the case.[20] Where a breach of contract causes physical harm accompanied by non-pecuniary loss (consequential loss), it appears that contractual compensation for this loss would be similar to tort compensation for such loss. Where the breach leads to a pure non-pecuniary loss, courts differentiate between commercial contracts (usually no compensation) and contracts which by their nature affect a party's emotional welfare, such as marriage contracts or vacation contracts. Still, even in commercial contracts, compensation may be awarded when the breach was executed in 'bad intention' or where it caused severe emotional harm or inconvenience. 28

3) *Compensation for Loss of Earnings and for Loss of Chance*

Compensation for loss of earnings and for loss of chance, in contract and in tort, is discussed in nos 25 and 26 above. 29

[18] CivA 591/80 *Chayu v Ventura*, 38 (IV) PD 393 (1984).
[19] CivA 243/83 *City of Jerusalem v Gordon*, 39 (I) PD 113 (1985).
[20] Law of Contracts (Remedies for Breach of Contract) 1970 art 13.

4) *Restitutionary Damages*

30 The Law of Unjust Enrichment 1979 has been interpreted by the courts as establishing an independent branch of private law, alongside tort and contract. As such, this field of law has become the general as well as the major source for the remedy of restitution. Claims for restitution, therefore, have to be based on this Law, unless other branches of law provide a specific remedy of restitution. Such specific remedy of restitution is provided by contract law. The law of contractual remedies provides that when a contract is rescinded due to breach, the breaching party owes a duty of restitution – to give back what was given to him under the contract or to pay its value.[21] A corresponding duty of restitution lies upon the other party.[22] Mutual restitution is also provided in cases of contract frustration.[23] Claims for other types of restitution in the contractual context must be submitted under the law of unjust enrichment. For example, when the contract is not rescinded, claims for the restitution of benefits attained by the breaching party from the breach have to be filed under the law of unjust enrichment.

31 Tort law provides for restitution only in the context of contribution among tortfeasors. Otherwise, restitution of benefits gained by the tortfeasor from the commission of a tort can be claimed only under the law of unjust enrichment. However, when the benefits gained by the tortfeasor correspond with the victim's harm, compensation for the harm will actually have the effect of restitution. For example, when a tenant remains on the premises after the rental period expires, the harm to the landlord and the benefit to the tenant may be the same – the unpaid rent.

5) *Aggravated and Exemplary (or Punitive) Damages*

32 Punitive damages are awarded in tort only in rare cases where it has been established that the tortfeasor acted in 'bad intention' or 'maliciously', namely intended to harm the plaintiff by the unlawful conduct. Contract law, in contrast, does not provide the sanction of punitive damages. Moreover, contract law does not allow the parties to a contract to 'punish' each other for breach by agreeing on damages which significantly exceed the actual loss.

33 Aggravated damages are awarded to compensate the harmed person for the additional emotional harm suffered by her due to the knowledge that the defendant harmed her intentionally. Tort law explicitly allows such damages,

---

21 Law of Contracts (Remedies for Breach of Contract) 1970 art 9.

22 Ibid.

23 Ibid, art 18.

while contract law allows them implicitly by authorising courts to award compensation for non-pecuniary loss at their discretion.

6) Other Remedies

As mentioned, given the different foundations of tort and contract, specific performance (and injunctions) are considered, subject to exceptions, as *primary* remedies in contract law, while under tort law this remedy is *secondary* and *discretionary*. The difference, in essence, lies in the different nature of the obligations. Contractual obligations are voluntary and *in personam*, and that makes their enforcement justified (people should keep their promises) and limited in scope. Duties of tort law, in contrast, are imposed by law against the will of the liable party, and are usually *in rem*, which makes their enforcement much more difficult. Moreover, an injunction is irrelevant where tort liability is strict – liability for harm caused by reasonable and even desirable conduct. Although the harm should be compensated, the conduct itself should not be stopped or reduced by court orders. 34

D. DIFFERENCES AS REGARDS RECOVERABILITY OF 'PURE ECONOMIC LOSSES'

Since the mid-1980s, as mentioned,[24] 'pure economic loss' has been recoverable in tort, not only under specific torts such as fraud or passing off, but also under the general tort of negligence. The difference between tort and contract in this regard is that, under negligence law, compensation for pure economic loss is recoverable only where the breaching party acted negligently while, in the case of contract law, strict liability may be imposed for pure economic loss caused by non-negligent conduct. Yet, despite this difference, there is a large area where tort and contract may overlap in imposing liability for pure economic loss. This overlap and its implications are discussed below.[25] 35

E. DIFFERENCES AS REGARDS LIABILITY FOR OTHERS

D's liability for harm caused to C by A's conduct may be either *personal* or by way of *attribution* – A's liability or A's conduct are attributed to D. 36

The liability of D is *personal* where D's conduct, harming P, meets a required condition for making D personally liable to P. Such personal liability for 37

24 Above no 27.

25 Below nos 64 and 69.

harm caused by others is very common both in contract and in tort. *In tort*, for example, where employee A injures employee C because the employer D failed to instruct the employees on how to avoid workplace risks, employer D is *personally* liable to C for the harm to C caused by A's conduct. A's conduct led to a materialisation of the risk that employer D created and the latter is personally liable for the materialisation of that risk. In contract, for example, where D is unable to fulfil his contractual obligation to deliver goods to C because A destroyed the goods, D is personally liable *in contract* to C for personally breaching the delivery contract.

38 D's liability for the conduct of another (A) is *non-personal, attributed liability*, pursuant to two major theories: vicarious liability and the *organ doctrine*. Vicarious liability usually attributes to employer D the liability of employee A for a tort committed by A against C in the course of A's employment for D. Both D and A are held liable to P.[26] The 'organ doctrine' attributes to a corporate legal entity D the conduct and mental state of those who are considered organs of the company while acting as organs.[27] Therefore, a corporate body D may be held liable for the conduct and state of mind of its organs.

39 Notably, both kinds of attributed liability, vicarious and that under organ theory, are imposed in tort, not in contract. Contract law imposes liability on D for the acts of A only where A acted as D's agent.

1) Liability for Auxiliaries and for Independent Contractors

40 Liability for harm caused by auxiliaries, as explained,[28] may be personal or vicarious. Liability for harm caused by independent contractors is not vicarious – only personal.

2) Liability for Legal Representatives or Organs of a Company

41 Pursuant to the organ theory, corporate bodies are held liable to third parties for harm caused by an organ while acting as an organ.[29]

3) Liability of Representatives of Natural Persons

42 The law does not impose vicarious liability on parents for the conduct of their children. Such liability has to be personal – it should be established that the parents (or other representatives) *personally* committed a tort against C.

---

26 CWO art 13.
27 Companies Law 1999 art 47.
28 Above no 38.
29 Above fn 27.

4) *Liability of the Auxiliary/Organ Itself*

Under vicarious liability, the auxiliary has to be liable in order to render D liable as well. D's liability is derived from the auxiliary's liability.[30] Under the organ theory, the organ may *not* be liable although the corporate body is liable for the organ's conduct.[31] 43

F. DIFFERENCES AS REGARDS LIABILITY IN THE CASE OF MULTIPLE TORTFEASORS/BREACHING PARTIES

In both tort and contract, multiple tortfeasors/beaching parties, respectively, are jointly and severally liable vis-à-vis the plaintiff.[32] As to their relative shares inter se, under tort law these shares are basically determined in accordance with the parties' relative degree of fault, also taking into account their relative causal contribution to the harm.[33] Contract law in this regard takes a different starting point. It presumes that the joint and several liability should be apportioned *equally* among the liable parties.[34] The apparent explanation for this difference is that while tort liability is basically fault-based, so that the relative fault of the multiple tortfeasors can be compared, contract liability is often strict, so that the fault is either absent or unknown and therefore cannot be compared for apportionment purposes. 44

When one party pays more than her inter se share, both tort and contract provide her with a claim of contribution (recourse) against the other parties for the share that she paid. 45

There seems to be a difference between contract and tort regarding the effect of waivers and compromises between the creditor and a member of the liable group. 46

G. DIFFERENCES AS REGARDS THE PERSONS WHO MAY BE PROTECTED

The scope of protection provided by *contract law* is determined and limited by the scope of obligations undertaken by the parties. These are usually obligations taken vis-à-vis the other parties to the contract (*in personam*). The scope 47

---

30 Above no 38.

31 Ibid.

32 CWO art 11; Law of Contracts (General Part) 1973 art 54.

33 CWO art 84.

34 Law of Contracts (General Part) 1973 art 56(a).

of protection is widened where one party undertakes an obligation which benefits another person who is not party to the contract, and the contract implies that it confers upon the latter beneficiary a legal claim against the former (contract for the benefit of a third party).[35] The scope of protection may also be shifted from one person to another where the former effectively transfers the contractual right to another person, or where the right is transmitted by law. Otherwise, contract law does not extend the scope of protection of a contract to persons who are not parties to the contract.

48 The scope of protection provided by *tort law* is determined in each case by the conditions that have to be met in order to impose liability. In negligence law, for example, the requirements of *proximity or special relations* between the parties narrow the scope of the protected persons,[36] as does the requirement of *reasonable reliance* – people whose expectations are not reasonable are not protected.[37]

H. DIFFERENCES AS REGARDS DEFENCES

49 There are four defences in both contract and tort. As mentioned, the conditions for their application and the actual manner in which they are applied may well differ from tort to contract given the different foundations and aims of each branch of law.[38]

50 The defence of 'contributory negligence/fault' is a statutory defence in tort law. It does not exist as a statutory defence in contract law but was embraced by the Supreme Court in 1993.[39] In both fields, the *aim* of this defence is to promote fairness and deterrence by shifting part of the cost of loss to a plaintiff C whose faulty conduct contributed to the harm suffered by him. It has also been argued that inclusion of the defence in contract law will increase the trust in contracts and their reliability. In tort and in contract, the defence reduces the amount of compensation. The apportionment of the cost of harm between the parties is also governed by the same principles: the comparative degree of the parties' fault (or of lack of good faith in contract), and the relative causal contribution to harm. Yet, their application in tort and contract may differ as explained.[40]

51 Another defence which exists in contract and in tort is 'mitigation of damage'. The establishment of a *failure* on the part of the plaintiff to mitigate harm – to

[35] Ibid, art 34.
[36] CivA 106/54 *Wienstein v Kadima*, 8 PD 1317 (1954).
[37] Ibid.
[38] See above no 3.
[39] See above fn 8.
[40] See above no 3.

reasonably avoid an increase in the scope of harm – leads to a corresponding reduction of compensation. This defence is statutory in contract law.[41] In tort it is applied by courts as an extension of the *legal causation* rules regarding 'remoteness of damage'. Harm that could reasonably have been avoided is considered as being 'remote' and therefore non-compensable. The basic idea behind the defence in both contract and tort is similar to that of 'contributory negligence' – fairness and deterrence. However, the actual application of the defence in each field may differ given the different foundations of contract and tort.

A third defence is *ex turpi causa non oritor actio* – 'a sinner shall not benefit from his sin'. A cause of action which originates in *morally undesirable* activity of the plaintiff should not be recognised. *In contract* this *traditional* defence was transformed into a statutory provision which annuls a contract (or part of a contract) where its formation, content or aim are illegal, immoral or contradict public policy.[42] The extent of the required ensuing restitution and the scope of annulment are determined by the court.[43] *In tort law* the defence is not statutory – it has been embraced by the Supreme Court as being a general principle that does not need to be enacted. It has been applied where the plaintiff's conduct which exposed him to the risk of harm was significantly immoral, and there was a typical, 'strong' causal link between this reprehensible conduct and the harm caused and sued for. Therefore, there is a major difference between contract and tort with regard to this defence. 52

The fourth defence which applies in contract is limitation of actions – discussed in nos 55–56 below. 53

Defence claims which obviously apply only to contract are the right to annul a contract in cases of mistake, misrepresentation, duress and undue influence/unconsciousness. Exemption from the fulfilment of obligations is provided in cases of unexpected and unavoidable force majeure or inability to perform (frustration).[44] Statutory defences in tort, absent in contract statutory law, are necessity and self-protection, *de minimis*, voluntary assumption of risk and state and the immunity of public officials. 54

I. DIFFERENCES AS REGARDS LIMITATION PERIODS

The general law of limitation of civil actions applies to contract and tort, as to all other civil actions. It sets a general limitation period of seven years, and 55

41 Law of Contracts (Remedies for Breach of Contract) 1970 art 14.
42 Law of Contracts (General Part) 1973, art 30.
43 Ibid, art 31.
44 Law of Contracts (Remedies for Breach of Contract) 1970 art 18.

enumerates causes for suspension, extension and renewal of the limitation period. All the above apply to contract and tort. There are, though, some special provisions regarding limitation of actions in *tort*,[45] but they have been interpreted narrowly and in accordance with the general law of limitation and therefore hardly make any real difference. There are shorter limitation periods, of two years for tort claims regarding breach of privacy[46] and of three years for strict product liability,[47] but such a shorter period also applies to contractual claims against insurers.

56 That contract and tort are basically governed by the same general law of limitation does not mean that the outcome of applying this law would be the same given the differences between the two. For example, if the same occurrence gives rise to claims in contract and in tort, it may be that the contractual claim will be barred before or after the tort claim because the causes of action are composed of different facts and therefore the contractual cause of action may accrue before or after that in tort.

J. DIFFERENCES AS REGARDS PROOF

57 In principle, the burden of proof is the same for all civil actions ('more probable than not'). In practice, however, evidential presumptions concerning fault and causation often shift the burden of proof to the defendant in tort cases. The major presumptions are *res ipsa loquitor*[48] and the judicial 'evidential loss' presumption.[49]

K. OTHER DIFFERENCES

58 Another difference between contract and tort concerns the age of legal capacity. The threshold age for tort liability is 12, while the general legal capacity to undertake contractual obligation is acquired at the age of 18. Yet another difference is that tort rights are inalienable[50] (although inheritable[51]), while contractual rights can, in principle, be transferred.

45 CWO art 89.
46 Privacy Protection Law art 26.
47 Defective Products Liability Law 1980 art 6.
48 CWO art 41.
49 CivA 8151/98 *Shterenberg v Chechik*, 56 (i) PD 539 (2001).
50 CWO art 22.
51 Ibid, art 19.

L. REASONS FOR THE DIFFERENCES

The reasons for the above differences between tort and contract were discussed above.[52] *Contract law* regulates voluntary obligations to specific persons (*in personam*). Its major aim is to incentivise people to keep their promises and to facilitate and protect socially desirable transactions. Therefore, the aim of contractual remedies is to restore the plaintiff to the condition in which he would have been if the obligation had been performed. *Tort law* imposes non-consensual duties that aim to protect the public at large (*in rem*) from risks of harm that are socially undesirable. Accordingly, the aim of tort remedies is to restore the plaintiff to the condition in which he would have been if the tort had not been committed.[53] 59

III. LIMITATION OR EXCLUSION OF LIABILITY ARISING FROM TORT AND FROM CONTRACT

A. STATUTORY PROVISIONS AUTHORISING A LIMITATION OR EXCLUSION OF LIABILITY

In principle, once the conditions for tort or contractual liability are met, and no recognised defence or immunity applies, liability has to be established and imposed as a matter of right. There are, however, two major doctrines that actually empower the courts to exercise judicial discretion to deny and limit liability or remedies. One doctrine, which has been described as 'imperial', is the statutory doctrine of 'good faith', which originates in contract law[54] but governs all branches of private law.[55] According to this doctrine, rights should be exercised in good faith and courts may limit rights or entitlement to remedies not exercised in good faith. The other doctrine by which courts empower themselves to limit rights and remedies is the 'public policy' doctrine – courts may deny or limit rights and remedies if their recognition or provision conflicts with 'public policy'. It was held, for example, that a victim of a road accident who due to disability is unable to establish normal sexual relations is nevertheless not entitled to pecuniary compensation for costs of paid-for sex, although legal, because such an award would conflict with public policy. 60

52 Above nos 3, 5 and 6.

53 The difference between the aims of tort remedies and contractual remedies was recently highlighted by the decision of the Supreme Court in *Harkabi v Avni* (fn 3).

54 Law of Contracts (General Part) 1973 arts 12 and 39.

55 Ibid, art 61(a).

B. LIMITATION OR EXCLUSION OF CONTRACTUAL AND TORTIOUS LIABILITY BY CONTRACT

1) Is it Possible to Limit or Exclude Contractual and Tortious Liability under a Contract?

61 In principle, contractual and tort liability can be excluded by contract but this may be deemed invalid if illegal, immoral or if it contradicts public policy.[56] In this regard it was held that exclusion by contract of tort liability for bodily injury contradicts public policy and therefore is invalid. Exclusion of liability for harm caused by malicious or intentional conduct would probably also be considered invalid. The Standard Contracts Law may also deny the validity of contractual terms that exclude or limit liability if such terms are considered 'depriving'.

2) To What Extent can a Contractual Exclusion Provide a Defence to a Third Party to the Contract?

62 Under contract law, where there are multiple debtors who are jointly and severally liable, and the creditor excludes the liability of one debtor, wholly or partially, the liability of other debtors will also be reduced accordingly, unless the creditor provides otherwise.[57] Whether this rule applies to tort liability is uncertain.

IV. NON-CONCURRENCE OR CONCURRENCE OF ACTIONS

A. OVERVIEW

1) Areas of Overlap between Tort and Contract

63 Tort and contract do actually overlap in the very wide range of cases regarding professional malpractice, negligent provision of services and production of defective products. The reason for this overlap is that the malfunction of the professional (eg physician, lawyer, engineer, appraiser, etc) or of another service provider (bank, insurance company, consulting firms, etc) or of product producers (including houses and buildings) may constitute both negligence (or strict liability in cases of products) and a breach of contract. It is a breach of contract because contracts for professional and other services and products are

56 Law of Contracts (General Part) 1973 art 30.
57 Ibid, art 55.

assumed to contain an implied term – an obligation of the service provider to act reasonably. Therefore, failure to do so amounts to both negligence and a breach of contract. Moreover, theoretically, breach of every contract can also be deemed to be negligence if it is established that the breach was objectively unreasonable.

It is noteworthy that the extent of the overlap of tort and contract has been significantly increased since it was held that, in principle, 'pure economic loss' is recoverable under negligence law. Under the 'exclusionary rule', which denies liability in negligence for pure economic loss, only contract law provided remedies for such loss. With the relaxation of the exclusionary rule and the rapid expansion of negligence liability for pure economic loss caused by misrepresentation, professional negligence and negligent provision of services and production of products, tort law stepped into the domain of contract law. The implications of this 'invasion' are discussed below. 64

An overlap will also take place in cases of misrepresentation in pre-contractual negotiations.[58] 65

2) *Approach to Non-Concurrence and Concurrence of Actions*

The governing principle regarding the relation among different branches of private law is the following: *as a rule*, whenever a given occurrence constitutes different causes of actions in different fields of law, these causes of action may concur. For example, it was held that a tenant who did not evacuate the premises after the rental period expired is liable in contract (breach of rental contract), tort (trespass) and unjust enrichment (not paying rent).[59] 66

As an exception, concurrence would not be recognised where liability for an occurrence is denied or limited under one branch of law, and the court finds that this denial or limitation should also apply to other potential causes of action. Cases of product imitation exemplify this approach. D imitates P's aesthetic design of a product, sells the imitated product and benefits from it, thereby reducing P's revenues. Let us assume that tort law denies D's liability because C has not yet acquired a reputation as the maker of this product (no *passing off*), and that property law also denies D's liability because C failed to register the design. Can C nevertheless succeed in a claim based on the law of unjust enrichment? It was held that, in the absence of bad faith or unfairness on D's part, the denial of liability in tort law and property law should also bar liability in unjust enrichment law – no concurrence.[60] 67

When different causes of action do concur, each one providing its remedies, the plaintiff, as a rule, is entitled to 'add up' these remedies (accumulation), 68

---

58 See above no 2.

59 CivA 7452/96 *State of Israel v Aharon Contracting Co*, 51 (IV) PD 874 (1998).

60 See CivA 5768/94 *A Sh IR Import v Forum Accessories*, 52 (IV) PD 289 (1998).

unless they overlap (to avoid double compensation) or contradict one another. Accordingly, if tort law provides a remedy for harms X and Y, and contract law provides remedies for harm Y and Z, the plaintiff would be entitled to X+Y+Z (unless X and Z contradict each other).

69 Given the principle of concurrence, the ensuing 'invasion' of negligence law into the domain of contract law (after the relaxation of the 'exclusionary rule') raises difficult questions. The problem was rightly described as the bull (tort law) in the china shop (contract law) or the elephant in the rose garden. The danger is that the mutual, consensual, fine-tuning reached by the parties to a contract will be interfered with by the non-consensual liability imposed by tort law. Another danger is that limitations on liability in contract (prescription, for example) may be circumvented by resorting to tort law. This problem can be avoided or mitigated by an exception to the concurrence which will provide that denial or limitations of liability in contract should not be circumvented by negligence law. Such a restriction can be imposed with the help of the 'duty of care' concept. Courts can rule that no duty of care in tort exists between parties to a contract regarding the contract where contract law denies or limits liability. Unfortunately, this 'invasion' problem and its possible solution have hardly been discussed by the courts.

B. CONCURRENCE/EXCLUSION OF ACTIONS FOR THE PROTECTION AGAINST PERSONAL INJURY AND OF PROPERTY

70 The above general rules that allow concurrence of different causes (unless the denial of one cause is interpreted as denying the other cause) and aggregation of remedies (unless they overlap or contradict each other) apply to the protection of bodily integrity and property. Such protection, however, is usually adjudicated in the framework of tort liability.

C. CONCURRENCE/EXCLUSION IN THE CASE OF INTERFERENCE WITH CONTRACTUAL RIGHTS

1) *Interference with a Contractual Relationship*

71 Protection against interference with contractual relations is provided by tort law. The special tort that directly protects contractual relations is 'causing breach of contract'.[61] This tort states that a person who knowingly, and without sufficient

[61] CWO art 62.

justification, causes any other person to break a legally binding contract with a third person is liable in tort, provided that the third party suffered pecuniary loss. It excludes marriage from the definition of 'contract' and strikes and lockouts in respect of trade disputes from the definition of 'causing breach'. Other torts that may provide such protection are defamation,[62] injurious falsehood,[63] false description[64] and negligence.[65] Contract law may protect one contract from another contract by denying the validity of the latter if it interferes with the former in ways which are illegal, immoral or conflict with public policy[66] or if such interference is not done in 'good faith'.[67]

2) Loss of Business due to Personal Injury to Someone Else's Employees or Clients or to Property Damage to the Entrepreneur

As a rule, where physical harm to one person leads to consequential pure economic loss to another person, the latter, who is a secondary, indirect, loss-sufferer, cannot sue in negligence, which is tort law's major vehicle for compensation of pure economic loss. Such a claim is allowed, by special statutory provision,[68] only with regard to the dependents of a person who was killed by D's tortious conduct. P's *dependents* can sue for the loss of economic support by the descendent. 72

V. SPECIFIC SITUATIONS

A. PRE-CONTRACTUAL LIABILITY

Pre-contractual liability for improper negotiations may be imposed in contract and in tort. The contractual liability originates in a special statutory provision, which is part of the general law of contract.[69] It provides that, in negotiating a contract, a party has to conduct the negotiations in good faith and in a customary manner. Failure to do so triggers liability to compensate the other party for losses according to the law of contract remedies. Liability in tort for improper contractual negotiations may be imposed for negligent misrepresentation under the tort of negligence.[70] 73

62 Defamation Prohibition Law 1965.
63 CWO art 58.
64 Commercial Torts Law 1999 art 2.
65 CWO art 35 f.
66 Law of Contracts (General Part) 1973 art 30.
67 Ibid, art 39.
68 CWO arts 78–80.
69 Law of Contracts (General Part) 1973 art 12.
70 CWO art 35 f.

B. LIABILITY OF PROFESSIONALS

74 Liability of professionals vis-à-vis their customers or patients is commonly perceived of as *tort liability* for *negligent malpractice*, although it may also be based on contract law. Negligence law is the major venue for claims against professionals because service and treatment relations are often not regulated by explicit, formal contracts that specify the agreed quality of service. Contractual liability, therefore, has to be based on the assumption that professionals *implicitly* undertake a commitment to provide the service or the treatment in a reasonable, non-negligent manner. In other words, contractual liability actually 'duplicates' tort liability in this regard. Yet, where the contractual liability of the professional is strict, or where the contract otherwise contains obligations other than to act reasonably, a claim may well be brought in contract.

CASES

CASE 1. THE UNATTRACTIVE SHOPPING MALL

75 *In contract.* The question is whether C would be considered a *third-party beneficiary* under the contract between D and Z. Since the contract refers explicitly to the issue of subletting, although not specifically to C, *and* since the contract may be interpreted as implying that D made her commitment not just to Z but also to other tenants, C may be considered a third-party beneficiary who has a contractual claim against D.

76 *In tort.* The traditional conditions for holding D liable to C in negligence for C's pure economic loss are apparently met in these circumstances:[71] there are *special relations* between Z and C – a chain of contracts that links them; C has a legitimate expectation that D would fulfil his contractual obligations and, therefore, C has *reasonable reliance* on D's contractual commitments; it is justified to attribute to D an *assumption of responsibility* toward C for breach of D's commitment.

CASE 2. THE IDLE LAWYER

77 *In contract.* As in Case 1, the question is whether the daughters (C) would be considered a *third-party beneficiary* under the contract between D and W. Unlike Case 1, it is doubtful whether the answer would be in the affirmative.

71 See above nos 9 and 48.

It is questionable whether D's commitment to W can be extended and interpreted as a commitment to C.

78 *In tort.* As in Case 1, the question is whether the three traditional conditions for holding D liable in negligence to C for the pure economic loss of the forgone inheritance are met. Unlike Case 1, it is less probable that the answer would be in the affirmative. Obviously, there was no reasonable reliance on C's part (unless C establish that they knew about the inheritance and suffered a loss because they reasonably relied on it). There are hardly any *special relations* between C and D in the absence of any contractual relations, and it is questionable whether the law should attribute to D an assumption of responsibility to C (as opposed to an *assumption of responsibility* to W). However, courts may nevertheless waive or relax the traditional conditions on grounds of deterrence, because otherwise D, who was negligent and caused foreseeable harm, escapes responsibility after W is dead. The deterrence justification, however, cannot justify tort liability where D can be found liable in contract.[72]

CASE 3. THE DEFECTIVE HOUSE

79 *In contract.* C has a contractual claim only if Z's contractual rights were transferred to him. In that case, however, the exclusion clause will be binding and undermine C's claim regarding the *property injury.*

80 *In tort.* C can certainly sue in tort for the bodily injury. Firstly, the exclusion refers only to *property damage.* Secondly, even if the exclusion was extended to *bodily injury*, it would be considered void as it conflicts with public policy.[73] As to the *property damage*, it is yet an unanswered question whether D owes a duty of care to C if no such duty was owed to Z given the exclusion. The answer may depend on whether C knew about the exclusion clause and whether he paid less to Z because of it. In such a case, the court may deny D's liability. If C did not know about the exclusion, D's liability may nevertheless be denied on the ground that C has a claim against Z.

CASE 4. APARTMENT IN FLAMES

81 P can and probably will bring claims in tort and in contract, as there is an actual contract between the two. Yet, the 'major' claim would be in tort because the contractual claim is for breach of an implied term to act reasonably with regard to safety risks, and that in fact 'duplicates' the tort claim.[74]

---

72 See above no 6.

73 Law of Contracts (General Part) 1973 art 30.

74 In that regard contractual liability is not strict – see above no 13.

CASE 5. INJURED SKIER

82 Given the concurrence of causes of action in tort and contract,[75] C has claims in tort and in contract against D1, and therefore the insurer D2 is liable under the policy.

CASE 6. EXPLODING CAR

83 Assuming that the defect in design was due to D2's negligence, D2 would be liable to C in both contract and tort[76] were there no warranty. The question, accordingly, is whether the limitation of the warranty period to two years *restricts* D2's liability. The answer depends on the wording of the warranty. If the wording is ambiguous, courts would apparently interpret it as limiting liability to two years *only with regard to claims which are not fault-based.* The alternative interpretation, namely that the warranty *restricts* D2's fault-based liability, is clearly undesirable. After all, warranties are intended to extend liability, not to restrict it.

CASE 7. RACING BOAT BURNING

84 As in the former case, the question is whether the warranty provided by D is interpreted as limiting his liability to two years for all claims or only for claims which are *not* fault-based. Assuming that D was negligent in adding and selling the equipment, and that the warranty did not bar C's fault-based claim, the scope of D's liability, namely whether he should be liable for the boat and the cost of repatriation, depends on the foreseeability of these risks given the defect in the equipment.[77]

CASE 8. INSIDIOUS REPORT

85 D knowingly, and without sufficient justification, caused C to terminate its contract with Z. C cannot sue D under the tort of causing breach of contract[78] as this tort protects *the other party* against C's breach. However, C may sue D in contract for breach of its employment contract, and sue D in tort for negligent

---

[75] See above no 66.

[76] Ibid.

[77] Law of Contracts (Remedies for Breach of Contract) 1970 art 10.

[78] CWO art 62.

misrepresentation or even fraud. Z, on the other hand, can sue D in tort for causing breach of contract, injurious falsehood (if Z acted 'maliciously'), false description and defamation.[79]

CASE 9. CIRCULAR LETTER

It is unclear from the case whether D's allegations regarding C and Z are true or false. If they are false, it appears that C can sue D for committing the following torts:[80] causing breach of contract (if other parties breached their contract with C because of these allegations), injurious falsehood, false description, defamation,[81] negligence and possibly infringement of privacy. Assuming that the allegations are not false, C may still succeed in filing a claim based on causing breach of contract, defamation, negligence and infringement of privacy if D fails to establish that the publication of these allegations was legally justified given their detrimental effect on C. P can possibly sue D for breaching his *contractual* obligation to act in good faith.[82] 86

CASE 10. SHORTAGE OF SUPPLY

In contract, C may well succeed against D in a claim asking the court to declare that the new conditions should be set aside, relying on the statutory provision regarding the revocability of contracts or terms when entered into under undue influence/unconsciousness. *In tort*, C may argue that D was negligent in trying to benefit from C's distress and therefore liable in negligence to C for the additional costs of the increased prices but such claim is unprecedented. 87

CASE 11. INJURED ROCK STAR

Being a 'secondary' or 'indirect' or 'par ricochet' sufferer from D's tort, C is not entitled to compensation under negligence law for his 'pure economic loss'. Compensation to 'indirect' or 'secondary' sufferers has been denied on policy grounds (over-deterrence, administrative costs, etc).[83] 88

---

79 Respectively CWO arts 62 and 56; Commercial Torts Law 1999 art 2; Defamation Prohibition Law 1965.

80 Ibid.

81 Privacy Protection Law 1981.

82 Law of Contracts (General Part) 1973 art 39.

83 See *I Gilead*, Tort Law – The Limits of Liability (2012) 904–925.

CASE 12. EQUIPMENT DESTROYED

89 *Claim against D2.* C is a 'secondary' or 'indirect' or 'by ricochet' sufferer of D2's negligence, if there was such negligence, and therefore not entitled to compensation from D2 under negligence law for C's pure economic loss.[84]

90 *Claim against D1.* If D1 was somehow negligent, C may have a claim in tort and in contract. Absent negligence, a contractual claim will succeed only if D1's liability under the contract was strict and not fault-based. Assuming that liability was strict, D1 may establish the defence of *frustration*, namely that the breach was unforeseeable and unavoidable.[85] If D is held strictly liable in contract, C still has to establish that the scope of his loss caused by cancellation was foreseeable when the contract was made.[86]

CASE 13. SLIPPING ON A LETTUCE LEAF

91 The claim will be brought by C *in tort* – for negligent maintenance of the shop which involves risk of physical injury to potential shoppers. The option of a *contractual claim* for breaching an implied term in an implied contract between C and D to keep the place secure for potential shoppers may also exist but is hardly ever used in practice, being unnecessary – it 'duplicates' the tort claim.

CASE 14. TEST DRIVE

92 Such claim will usually be brought by C *in tort* for D's negligent driving. A corresponding claim in contract can be based on an implied term in an implied contract – the implied obligation of D to drive carefully. Such contractual claim, however, actually 'duplicates' the tort claim.

CASE 15. BREACH OF NEGOTIATIONS

93 The claim would usually be brought in contract for breaching the pre-contractual obligation to act in good faith. A corresponding action for negligent misrepresentation may also succeed.[87]

---

84 Ibid.

85 Law of Contracts (Remedies for Breach of Contract) 1970 art 18.

86 Ibid, art 10.

87 See above no 2.

CASE 16. NON-DISCLOSURE OF RELEVANT FACTS

The law of contract explicitly states that failure to disclose relevant facts is 'misrepresentation' that entitles the misrepresented party to cancel the contract if she contracted on the basis of this misrepresentation.[88] An alternative is to sue for compensation for the breach of the contractual obligation to act in good faith in pre-contractual negotiations. In tort, P can sue for negligent misrepresentation.[89] 94

88 Law of Contracts (General Part) 1973 art 15.
89 CWO, art 35 f.

THE BORDERLINES OF TORT LAW IN ITALY

Cristina Amato and Giovanni Comandé

QUESTIONS

I. Tracing the Borderlines . . . 283
- A. Distinction between Tort and Contract . . . 283
  - 1) Contractual Liability . . . 283
  - 2) Non-Contractual/Tort Liability . . . 283
- B. Existence of a 'Grey Zone'? . . . 284
- C. Common or Different Rules Regulating Tort and Contract . . . 286
  - 1) Contract . . . 287
  - 2) Tort . . . 288
- D. Application of Common Rules in a Different Way . . . 288

II. Main Differences between Tortious and Contractual Liability . . . 289
- A. Differences as Regards the Foundations of Liability . . . 289
  - 1) Role of Intention . . . 289
  - 2) Role of Wrongfulness and Fault and their Variations . . . 290
  - 3) Role of Strict Liability . . . 291
- B. Differences as Regards Causation . . . 292
- C. Differences as Regards Remedies . . . 293
  - 1) Degree of Certainty of the Damage . . . 293
  - 2) Compensation for Non-Pecuniary Losses . . . 293
  - 3) Compensation for Loss of Earnings and for Loss of Chance . . . 295
  - 4) Restitutionary Damages . . . 296
  - 5) Aggravated and Exemplary (or Punitive) Damages . . . 297
  - 6) Other Remedies . . . 300
- D. Differences as Regards Recoverability of 'Pure Economic Losses' . . . 301
- E. Differences as Regards Liability . . . 302
  - 1) Liability for Auxiliaries and for Independent Contractors . . . 302
  - 2) Liability for Legal Representatives or Organs of a Company . . . 303
  - 3) Liability of Representatives of Natural Persons . . . 303
  - 4) Liability of the Auxiliary/Organ Itself . . . 303
- F. Differences as Regards Liability in the Case of Multiple Tortfeasors/Breaching Parties . . . 303
- G. Differences as Regards the Persons Who May be Protected . . . 304

H. Differences as Regards Defences. 305
I. Differences as Regards Limitation Periods 306
J. Differences as Regards Proof. 307
K. Other Differences 308
L. Reasons for the Differences 309
III. Limitation or Exclusion of Liability Arising from Tort and from Contract. 310
A. Statutory Provisions Authorising a Limitation or Exclusion of Liability 310
B. Limitation or Exclusion of Contractual and Tortious Liability by Contract 311
IV. Non-Concurrence or Concurrence of Actions 312
A. Overview 312
1) Areas of Overlap between Tort and Contract 312
2) Approach to Non-Concurrence and Concurrence of Actions 314
B. Concurrence/Exclusion of Actions for the Protection against Personal Injury and of Property 315
C. Concurrence/Exclusion in the Case of Interference with Contractual Rights. 315
V. Specific Situations 316
A. Pre-Contractual Liability. 316
B. Liability of Professionals 316

CASES

Case 1. The Unattractive Shopping Mall. 319
Case 2. The Idle Lawyer. 319
Case 3. The Defective House 320
Case 4. Apartment in Flames 321
Case 5. Injured Skier 322
Case 6. Exploding Car. 324
Case 7. Racing Boat Burning 324
Case 8. Insidious Report. 325
Case 9. Circular Letter. 325
Case 10. Shortage of Supply 325
Case 11. Injured Rock Star 326
Case 12. Equipment Destroyed 327
Case 13. Slipping on a Lettuce Leaf. 328
Case 14. Test Drive. 328
Case 15. Breaking Off Negotiations. 329
Case 16. Non-Disclosure of Relevant Facts 330

QUESTIONS

I. TRACING THE BORDERLINES

A. DISTINCTION BETWEEN TORT AND CONTRACT

The distinction between tort and contract in the Italian legal system can be explained as follows. 1

1) Contractual Liability

The *nomen iuris* defines the obligation to pay compensation for damage resulting from the non-fulfilment of a pre-existing agreement (hereinafter: obligation), leaving out of consideration whether or not the origin of the agreement is the contract. Indeed, scholars, instead of referring to contractual liability, frequently refer to the breach of a pre-existent duty.[1] 2

Contractual liability is based on the general provision of art 1218 of the Italian Civil Code (It cc), founding liability of the debtor on his/her objective fault in failing to fulfil a contractual obligation, within the limits of force majeure and act of God. 3

Italian law includes a special set of rules to regulate some contractual types (so-called typified contracts) either under art 1470 ff It cc or under special statutes. Within the limits of the law concerning any contract, one can face specific provisions as regards contractual liability that integrate the general rule provided for by art 1218 It cc. 4

2) Non-Contractual/Tort Liability

Liability arising in the absence of a contractual relationship is liability in tort: it is an unlawful action, a wrong that causes damage that shall be compensated. The unlawful action is the direct source of the duty to compensate damage. 5

Liability in tort is supported by the general clause of liability for fault under art 2043 It cc. 6

Italian law provides for special rules for tort liability caused both by the wrongdoer's own actions and by the action of a third party for whom he/she is liable. These rules are governed either by the Civil Code (art 2049 ff) or by special statutes (ie the Law on Product Liability, Decreto Presidente della Repubblica: d PR no 224/1998, now arts 114 ff Consumer Code; or the Law concerning 7

---

1 *Ex plurimis*: *F Giardina*, Responsabilità contrattuale e responsabilità extracontrattuale (1993) 14 ff, 75 ff.

Liability for Nuclear Damage, 31 December 1962, no 1860, as modified by the d PR 10 May 1975, no 519).

8 To sum up: the original frame of the Italian Civil Code organises non-contractual liability as a special kind of liability, regulated at the end of the fourth book devoted to the law of obligations. Contractual liability (that is, default/breach of an obligation) instead is regulated at the beginning of the fourth book devoted generally to the law of obligations.

9 The structural differences between contract and tort explain why the Italian system draws a clear line between the two sources of obligations. This is why a different set of rules is provided for both sources (see below sec I.C).

B. EXISTENCE OF A 'GREY ZONE'?

10 The Italian Civil Code recognises *culpa in contrahendo* at arts 1337 and 1338, dealing with pre-contractual liability (*responsabilità precontrattuale*).[2] Pre-contractual liability represents an original and innovative peculiarity of the Italian Civil Code. Article 1337 It cc bestows on the prospective parties of a contract (that may never be stipulated) a general duty to bargain in good faith. Article 1338 It cc applies the above-mentioned general duty to cases where a contract has been concluded though it revealed itself ineffective (for any reason): in this case the party who knew or should have known of the reason that rendered the contract ineffective is held liable vis-à-vis the innocent party who reasonably relied on the validity of the contract. The breach of the above-mentioned duty to bargain in good faith gives the innocent party a right to reliance damages (*interesse negativo*), even if a valid contract has been concluded:[3] because a contract has not been concluded, what is restored is *neither* the breach of an obligation *nor* the (positive) interest to the performance of the obligation. Reliance damages, on the contrary, consist in restoring either the detriment suffered or the increase of damage, including loss of earnings and any direct damage, suffered by the innocent party.[4]

---

2 *PG Monateri*, La responsabilità contrattuale e precontrattuale (1998); *G D'Amico*, La responsabilità precontrattuale, in: V Roppo (ed), Trattato del contratto, vol V, t 2 (2006); *P Trimarchi*, La responsabilità civile: atti illeciti, rischio, danno (2017) 85 ff.; *B Marucci*, La responsabilità precontrattuale (2018) 2 Rassegna di diritto civile 528 ff.

3 Cassazione civile (Italian High Court, Cass civ) 8 October 2008, no 24795 (2009) I Nuova giurisprudenza civile commentata 205; Cassazione civile, Sezioni Unite (Cass civ, Sez Un), 19 December 2007, no 26725 (2008) II Rivista di diritto commerciale 17; (2008) Danno e responsabilità 525 note *V Roppo*, La nullità virtuale del contratto dopo la sentenza Rordorf. See recently: *C Miriello*, La responsabilità precontrattuale in ipotesi di contratto valido e efficace, ma pregiudizievole (2006) La responsabilità civile 649.

4 Cass civ, Sez Un, 19 December 2007, no 26725; Cass civ, 29 September 2005, no 19024.

The duty to bargain in good faith is a general clause, whose meaning has been identified by courts as having three main specific features: (1) unfair withdrawal from negotiations;[5] (2) duty to disclose relevant information to the other party;[6] and (3) confidentiality duty.[7] It is important to stress that, in any of the situations listed, what is relevant is not the failure to sign a contract, but the relevance of the reliance of the innocent party on the honest behaviour of the other. 11

As for the nature and discipline of the general duty to bargain in good faith, case law and scholars do not agree. The majority of the opinions of the High Court consider this liability as tortious.[8] This principle is also affirmed in cases where the pre-contractual relationship involves a public entity.[9] Though most 12

5 Cass civ, 10 March 2016, no 4718; Cass civ, 10 January 2013, no 477; Cass civ, 10 June 2005, no 12313 (2006) I Nuova giurisprudenza civile commentata 349; Cass civ, 14 February 2000, no 1632 (2000) Giurisprudenza italiana 2250; Cass civ, 10 June 2005, no 12313 (2006) I Nuova giurisprudenza civile commentata 349.

6 Cass civ, 23 March 2016, no 5762; Cass civ, 20 December 2011, no 27648 (2012) I Contratti 235.

7 Tribunale Amministrativo Regionale (TAR) Catania, 11 July 2013, no 2005.

8 Recently: Cass civ, 16 January 2013, no 1000 (2013) Giustizia civile Massimario; Cass civ, Sez Un, ord 19 October 2012, no 18092 (2012) 22 ottobre Diritto e giustizia online; Cass civ, 20 March 2012, no 4382 (2012) Responsabilità civile e previdenza 1166 note *M Mattioni*, Contratto 'interinale' concluso durante una trattativa e responsabilità precontrattuale; Cass civ, Sez Un, ord 27 February 2012, no 2926 (2012) Giustizia civile Massimario 222; Cass civ, Sez Un, 10 July 2003, no 19896; Cass civ, 11 September 2003, no 13390 (2004) Responsabilità civile e previdenza 400 note *L Vedovato*, Competenza giurisdizionale e natura aquiliana della responsabilità precontrattuale: il responso della Corte di giustizia e gli oblii della Corte di Cassazione. For an opposite affirming the contractual nature of pre-contractual liability see Cass civ, 20 December 2011, no 27648 (2012) Responsabilità civile e previdenza 1949 note *R Scognamiglio*, Tutela dell'affidamento, violazione dell'obbligo della buona fede e natura della responsabilità precontrattuale; *C Castronovo*, La Cassazione supera se stessa e rivede la responsabilità precontrattuale (2012) Europa e diritto privato 4; *F Della Negra*, *Culpa in contrahendo*, contatto sociale e modelli di responsabilità (2012) I Contratti 4; *E Fasoli*, Contatto sociale, dovere di buona fede e fonti delle obbligazioni: una sentenza (quasi) 'tedesca' (2012) Giurisprudenza italiana 12; Corte di Appello (App) Milano, 2 February 1990 (1991) Giurisprudenza di merito 744; Tribunale (Trib) Milano, 11 January 1988 (1988) Responsabilità civile e previdenza 772.

9 Cass civ, Sez Un, 11 January 1977, no 93; Cass civ, 25 May 1985, no 3178 (1985) Giustizia civile Massimario fascicolo 5. Cf recently: Cass civ, 10 June 2005, no 12313 (2005) Diritto e giustizia 15 note *C Garufi*, Nelle trattative l'ente è come il privato; Cass civ, 1 March 2007, no 4856 (2008) Responsabilità civile e previdenza 1608 note *MG Anghelone*, Sospensione delle trattative e responsabilità precontrattuale della P.A.; Cass civ, Sez Un, 12 May 2008, no 11656 (2009) Rivista del notariato 1487 note *M Graziano*, Le Sezioni Unite intervengono nella materia dei rapporti tra vendita di cosa futura e appalto; Cass civ, 10 January 2013, no 477 (2013) I Foro italiano 845. Recently, an important judgment rendered by the Supreme Administrative Court, Consiglio di Stato, has argued in favour of the pre-contractual liability of the public administration before the award of contract: Cons Stato, Adunanza Plenaria, 04 May 2018, no 5 (2018) 12 Corriere giuridico 1547 note *F Trimarchi Banfi*, La responsabilità dell'amministrazione per il danno da affidamento nella sentenza dell'adunanza plenaria n. 5 del 2018.

scholars agree with this solution,[10] there is an important and authoritative thesis according to which pre-contractual liability is contractual in nature. From this perspective, the principle of good faith is the direct source of the duty to compensate reliance damage suffered by one party caused by the other during negotiations. The breach of the general duty triggers a liability different in its nature from liability in tort, as it is rooted in a 'special relationship', or 'social contact' (*contatto sociale*)[11] existing between the prospective parties to a contract. The obligation to pay damages arises whenever there is evidence that breaking off negotiations has caused a detriment to the innocent party who relied on the fair conduct of the counterparty, who should behave in true respect of the interests of the innocent party. In compliance with the latter approach, recent opinions delivered by the High Court (Corte di Cassazione)[12] have referred pre-contractual liability to the law (art 1173 It cc) as a direct source of such a special obligation.

C. COMMON OR DIFFERENT RULES REGULATING TORT AND CONTRACT

13 The Italian Civil Code devotes Title I of Book IV to the law of obligations as a general part, dealing with several events in the life of an obligation, regardless of its source (contract or tort). Therefore, fulfilment of an obligation, liability for breach of the obligation (damages), joint and several liability, assignment of debts, and termination of the obligation are all topics regulated by the Italian Civil Code through common general rules.

---

10 Cf *CM Bianca*, Il contratto, Diritto civile, vol III (2000) 158 ff; *R Sacco/G De Nova*, Il contratto, t 2, in: R Sacco (ed), Trattato di diritto civile (2004) 235 ff.

11 *C Castronovo*, Information Duties and Precontractual Good Faith (2009) European Review of Private Law (ERPL) 559; *A Di Majo*, Delle obbligazioni in generale, in: V Scialoja/G Branca (eds), Commentario al codice civile (1988) 162 ff; *CA Cannata*, Sulle fonti delle obbligazioni, in: G Visintini (ed), Trattato della responsabilità contrattuale, vol I (2009) 29 ff. See recently: G Varanese, "Sonderverbindung" e responsabilità precontrattuale da contatto sociale (2018) 1 Rivista di diritto civile 116–143; *P Gallo*, 1 Quale futuro per il contatto sociale in Italia? (2017) 12 Nuova Giurisprudenza Civile Commentata 1759 ff.; *A Albanese*, La lunga marcia della responsabilità precontrattuale: dalla "culpa in contrahendo" alla violazione di obblighi di protezione (2017) 3 Europa e diritto private 1129 ff.

12 Cass 12 July 2016, no 14188 note *A Di Majo*, La culpa in contrahendo tra contratto e torto (2016) 12 Giurisprudenza italiana 2565; *C Scognamiglio*, Verso il definitivo accreditamento della tesi della natura contrattuale della responsabilità precontrattuale (2016) 11 Nuova giurisprudenza civile commentata 1515; *id*, Responsabilità precontrattuale e 'contatto sociale qualificato' (2016) 6 Responsabilità civile e previdenza 1950; Cass civ, 20 December 2011, no 27648; Cass civ, 10 August 2012, no 14400; Cass civ, 21 November 2011, no 24438. *V Giovanna*, Il dibattito sulla natura della responsabilità precontrattuale rivisitato alla luce della casistica (2017) 3 Contratto e impresa 335–355.

The general theory on damages is set out in arts 1223–1227 It cc, that is in the part of the Civil Code devoted to common general rules to which some rules in tort law refer. In particular, art 2056 It cc on the evaluation of damages in tort merely states that 'damages to the injured person must be calculated according to arts 1223, 1226, 1227', mainly referring to cases of breach of contract. Nevertheless, it must be underlined that this original framework has been questioned by scholars' interpretation, case law and special statutes: Italy has experienced a mutual exchange in the central role of contractual and tortious liability with regard to the law of damages. Tort law constantly seems to appear as the general framework of liability, while contractual liability seems a special framework. A clear example is given by non-economic loss (see below at no 20). Yet in some areas, such as medical liability, it appears that courts are applying contract rules as default rules in order to make the burden of proof easier for plaintiffs. 14

In addition to a general part, there are some special rules devoted to contract or to tort liability. 15

As explained above in sec I.A, the different structure of the two sources of obligations necessarily implies different sets of rules. Below a list of different rules regulating contract and tort are provided. 16

1) Contract

(a) The creditor only has the burden of proving the non-fulfilment of an obligation by the debtor. It is up to the debtor in breach to demonstrate that his default was due to factors beyond his will, and which cannot be imputed to him. The Corte di Cassazione has established[13] that the creditor's burden of proof is limited to alleging the existence of a previous contractual relationship and the breach of the obligation by the debtor: the creditor has no further burden of proof. 17

(b) The statutory limitation period for claiming compensation for damage is 10 years, unless otherwise provided by the law (eg credit deriving from professional unpaid invoices have a short limitation period of three years: art 2956, para 1, no 2 It cc; credit deriving from a contract of education are subject to a limitation period of one year: art 2955 It cc, para 1, no 1). 18

(c) Under contract law, only damage which was foreseeable can be restored. Foreseeability is assessed on the date of the conclusion of the contract. 19

---

13 Cass civ, Sez Un, 30 October 2001, no 13533 (2002) I Foro italiano 770 note *P Laghezza*, Inadempimento ed onere della prova: le sezioni unite e la difficile arte del rammendo.

20 *(d)* Non-economic losses were not recognised in contract law according to a previous interpretation of the Civil Code. As shall be argued below (no 45), a recent decision of the High Court superseded this approach: art 2059 It cc was originally interpreted to apply only to the law of tort but today it can also be applied to obligations deriving from a previous contractual relationship.[14]

2) *Tort*

21 *(a)* Under the law of tort, art 2043 It cc recognises a heavier burden of proof: it is up to the victim to demonstrate intent or fault on the part of the injurer, together with damage and causation between the two.

22 *(b)* There are shorter limitation periods: five years is the general statutory limitation period, but in several cases, both in the Civil Code or in special statutes, the limitation periods can be even shorter (eg three years for product liability: art 125 Italian Consumer Code).

23 *(c)* In tort, any damage deriving from an unlawful act shall be restored, provided that the creditor gives evidence of the direct causal link between the wrongful act and the wrongful damage. Because no relationship existed before the wrongful act, the question of foreseeability cannot even be raised.

24 *(d)* Non-economic losses are recognised in tort law, within the limits of art 2059 It cc as recently interpreted by the Constitutional Court[15] and by the High Court.[16]

D. APPLICATION OF COMMON RULES IN A DIFFERENT WAY

25 Usually courts do not apply the rules common to tort and contract differently. A few exceptions concern damages:

(a) In contract law, where the obligation has a previous monetary value, damages assessed by the court are defined as monetary debts (*debito di valuta*), and

[14] Cass civ, Sez Un, 11 November 2008, nos 26972, 26973, 26974, 26975 (2009) Responsabilità civile e previdenza 63 note *E Navarretta*, Il valore della persona nei diritti inviolabili e la complessità dei danni non patrimoniali; (2009) Rivista italiana di medicina legale 460 note *M Bona*, La riparazione delle lesioni personali dopo le Sezioni Unite di San Martino: nessuna novità per i medici legali, scompiglio nel diritto; (2009) Giustizia civile 930 note *M Rossetti*, *Post nubila phoebus*, ovvero gli effetti concreti della sentenza delle Sezioni Unite no 26972 del 2008 in tema di danno non patrimoniale; (2009) Rivista italiana di diritto del lavoro 486 note *R Scognamiglio*, Il danno non patrimoniale innanzi alle Sezioni Unite.

[15] Corte Costituzionale (Corte Cost), 11 July 2003, no 233 (2003) Responsabilità civile e previdenza 1041 note *P Ziviz*, Il nuovo volto dell'art 2059 c.c.; Corte Cost, 06 October 2014, no 235 (2015) 1 Rivista Italiana di Medicina Legale (e del Diritto in campo sanitario) 295.

[16] See fn 14 above.

they are subject to the principle according to which the damage is liquidated on its face value (art 1277 It cc). In tort law, because there is no previous obligation, damages are always assessed by courts at the very moment when the unlawfulness of the tort is assessed, that is on the date of trial; therefore, damages are assessed on their face value when the decision is rendered (*debito di valore*).

(b) In contract law, non-economic losses have only recently been admitted by courts (see above no 20).

(c) In tort law, pure economic losses have only recently been admitted by courts (see below, sec II.D; see also Case 11: Injured rock star), and are awarded only when the unlawfulness of the damage has been assessed.

(d) Loss of chance is a controversial head of damage, recently considered by the Italian courts as general damage, instead of loss of profits. In contract law, courts would qualify the loss of chance as economic damage;[17] in tort law, courts would qualify it as a non-economic loss.[18] This is true especially in cases of medical malpractice, where the plaintiff claims the loss of opportunity of living longer and/or better.

II. MAIN DIFFERENCES BETWEEN TORTIOUS AND CONTRACTUAL LIABILITY

A. DIFFERENCES AS REGARDS THE FOUNDATIONS OF LIABILITY

1) *Role of Intention*

In contract law, the role of intention in breaching the contract is taken into 26
consideration as a criterion for attributing non-foreseeable damage to the party intentionally in breach (art 1225 It cc).[19] This rule cannot be applied to non-contractual liability because art 1225 is not mentioned by art 2056 and above all because the structure of the two sources of obligations is different. An obligation in contract derives from a previous agreement, from which

17 The most common cases concern the loss of opportunity of a candidate to be successful (Cass civ, 7 October 2010, no 20808 (2010) Giustizia civile Massimario 1300; Trib Roma, 20 October 1999 (2000) Giurisprudenza romana 297); or the loss of opportunity of a worker to be promoted because of the unlawful conduct of his/her employer (Cass civ, Sez Lav, 2 December 1996, no 10748 (1996) Giustizia civile Massimario 1656); or the loss of opportunity of a client to be successful in a suit because of the negligent conduct of his/her lawyer (Cass civ, 27 May 2009, no 12354 (2009) Giustizia civile Massimario 846).

18 Cass civ, 18 September 2008, no 23846 (2010) Rivista italiana di medicina legale 174 note *A Fiori*, Il più probabile che improbabile ed il più improbabile che probabile.

19 See *P Cendon*, Il dolo nella responsabilità civile (1974).

damages are assessed. On the other hand, an obligation in tort has no previous reference to which damages can be related; as a matter of fact, the obligation in tort arises when the unlawful conduct causes damage. Therefore, it is commonly acknowledged that damages awarded as a consequence of a tort always include, by definition, compensation even for unforeseeable injuries, notwithstanding the intention of the tortfeasor.

2) Role of Wrongfulness and Fault and their Variations

27 In tort law, fault is a sufficient ground to establish liability. Nevertheless, there are some 'intentional torts': nuisance (art 833 It cc), unlawful interference with contract, unlawful diversion of employees/auxiliaries,[20] and dismissal of a complaint for a criminal offence.[21] Moreover, intention coupled with gross negligence often justifies aggravated damages with a punitive/retributive function: see below sec II.C.5.

28 Intentional liability can be neither excluded nor limited in contract as in tort under art 1229 It cc: see extensively sec III.B.1 below.

29 In contract law, the role of fault is not limited to a 'subjective' notion (personal difficulty or negligence). The 'objective' definition of fault (*diligenza*: art 1176 It cc) refers to an objective notion of impossibility, the contents of which are represented by the impossibility of satisfying the creditors' interests by applying a regular standard of care. 'The regular standard of care' can be ascertained through a cross-reference to the rule of good faith and fair dealing (art 1175 It cc), according to which it is possible to determine and limit the content of the contractual relationship and consequently the obligations of the debtor.[22]

30 In tort law, the role of fault and fraud represents the very foundations of liability, that is the general rule upon which tort law is founded.

31 Fraud consists in the intention to provoke an injury, or it may consist in accepting the risk that an injury to a third party may result from one's conduct the aim of which is to achieve one's own final purpose.

32 Fault, on the other hand, consists in the infringement of the standard of care imposed by the legal system. As for the definition of the 'standard of care', it is an objective standard, though different in content from contract law. In tort law, since no previous agreement exists, the objective standard guidelines are expressed in 'statutes, regulations, orders and disciplines' (art 43, para 1

---

20 Cass civ, 8 June 2012, no 9386 (2012) Giustizia civile Massimario 767.

21 Cass civ, 12 January 2012, no 300 (2012) Diritto e giustizia online 103 note *G Tarantino*, Querela archiviata: chi non ha denunciato deve risarcire solo se ha agito con dolo.

22 *U Breccia*, Le obbligazioni (1992) 461 ff.

It Criminal Code); negligence, imprudence or malpractice can be affirmed only by taking into account all the relevant circumstances of the case.

3) Role of Strict Liability

In contract law, strict liability has no specific role: as previously affirmed, the contractual standard of care (objective diligence) is necessarily carved out depending on the content and type of the contract. While the burden of proof to provide good reasons for the non-fulfilment of the obligation rests on the debtor, the creditor only needs to show the existence of the contractual relationship and non-fulfilment of the obligation. 33

On the other hand, Italian law provides special rules for tort liability caused both by the wrongdoer's own actions or by the action of a third party for whom he/she is liable (see below sec II.E). The most relevant rules on strict liability within the Civil Code concern: 34

- the employer, for damage caused by employees to third parties (art 2049 It cc);
- the owner, for damage caused by the building in his/her property (art 2053 It cc);
- the owner of an automobile and the driver, in the case of a car accident (art 2054, para 4 It cc).

In all the above cases there are no caps and ceilings, but for the following exceptions: 35

- the manager of a nuclear installation (arts 15–24, L 31.12.1962, no 1860, as modified by d PR no 519/1975): in this case, art 19 provides ceilings to the 'indemnity' (financial guarantee), while damage is covered by the state for the amount exceeding the manager's financial guarantee;
- product liability (art 114 ff It Consumer Code): in this case, art 123 of the Italian Consumer Code (implementing Directive 85/374/CEE of 25 July 1985) provides a threshold of €387,00. Moreover, it is often defined as a 'limited' strict liability, as it is not enough for the plaintiff to prove damage and causation. The plaintiff has to prove the defectiveness of the product according to a regular standard of care in the production as well as in the use of the product.[23]

23 Cf *G Ponzanelli/L Frata*, La responsabilità del produttore dal 1988 al 2012: una lunga evoluzione venticinquennale, in: E Tosi (ed), La tutela dei consumatori in Internet e nel commercio elettronico (2012) 819 ff. Cass. civ., 29 May 2013, no 13458 (2013) I Foro italiano 2118.

36 Finally, there are some special rules which fall under the heading of so-called 'aggravated liability', or quasi-strict liability. According to such rules, the fault of the tortfeasor is presumed; moreover, the defendant cannot rebut the presumption by demonstrating his/her diligence, he/she has to provide evidence of the external fact interfering with the agent's (diligent) conduct (force majeure, act of God: *caso fortuito, forza maggiore*). This is the case for:

- supervisors, as regards damage caused by those without legal capacity (art 2047 It cc);
- parents, tutors and educational supervisors, as regards damage caused by minors (art 2048 It cc);[24]
- agents carrying out a dangerous activity (art 2050 It cc), such as producing electric energy, producing explosive materials, running a building enterprise, or doing sporting activities (skiing, automobile/bike races, etc.);
- damage caused by goods under the keeper's custody (art 2051 It cc);
- damage caused by animals under the owner's custody (art 2052 It cc).

B. DIFFERENCES AS REGARDS CAUSATION

37 Both in contract and in tort, causation is regulated by art 1223 It cc, according to which damage includes general damage and loss of earnings, provided that both can be considered as consequential damage, that is damage directly deriving from the conduct of the party in breach or the party who acted unlawfully, as well as foreseeable damage. This two-tier test can be summarised in causation in fact, and remoteness of damage.

38 The notion of remoteness of damage is subject to the rule of conflicting proceedings applicable to both contract and tort contained in the Criminal Code, art 41, according to which conflicting proceedings do not exclude causation. This rule has been interpreted in different ways in criminal law and private law over the course of time. At present, courts dealing with damages in private law would apply the test of *causalità adeguata*, rather that the test of *conditio sine qua non*. According to the first test, there is remoteness of damage when the conduct is normally (that is, according to rules of experience) adequate to cause a specific harmful event. The scope of this rule is to exclude that damage which cannot be considered as foreseeable to a reasonable person. This is why courts, in the case of liability based on fault, usually apply this test.

---

[24] Cass civ, 20 March 2012, no 4395.

It also gives courts the additional possibility to award compensation for indirect damage, provided that it was foreseeable.

On the other hand, the test of *conditio sine qua non* provides that all behaviour can be considered as materially linked to a specific harmful event if, without their occurrence, the same event would not have occurred. 39

C. DIFFERENCES AS REGARDS REMEDIES

Both in contract and in tort law, the compensation of damage is regulated by arts 1223, 1226 and 1227.[25] Therefore, courts, within the limits already described above in secs I.C and I.D, apply the same rules. As regards the equitable evaluation of loss of earnings, see below at no 46. 40

1) *Degree of Certainty of the Damage*

As regards the degree of certainty, the rule of causation and remoteness of damage expressed by art 1223 It cc is equally applied by courts, regardless of whether the damage derives from a contract or from unlawful conduct. In the case of loss of chance, certainty of damage is ascertained with reference to the principle 'more probable than not'.[26] 41

Damage is compensated with reference to the date of trial, not to the time when the damage occurred. At that moment, both actual and future damage is compensated. Loss of a chance is a future damage for which compensation will be awarded, provided that it is 'more probable than not' that it will arise after the date of trial. On the other hand, loss of earnings is future damage and will be compensated provided that the plaintiff can provide evidence that the likelihood of it occurring is very close to certainty. 42

Damage deriving from tort liability shall be compensated on its face value at the date of trial, being qualified as a monetary debt (*debito di valore*); damage deriving from breach of contract shall take into account the interests accrued on the face value of the original obligation (see above at no 25). 43

2) *Compensation for Non-Pecuniary Losses*

After a very controversial debate that started during the 1970s, the limits of compensation for non-pecuniary losses have recently been clearly stated by the 44

25 *FD Busnelli/S Patti*, Danno e responsabilità civile (2013) 24 ff.
26 Cass civ, 14 December 2001, no 15810 (2001) Giustizia civile Massimario 2155.

High Court[27] and by the Constitutional Court.[28] Both courts have proposed a construction of the statutory discipline (art 2059 It cc) broadening the original meaning of the rule,[29] linking art 2059 It cc to the Italian Charter (1948). In sum,[30] according to the above-mentioned case law, compensation for non-pecuniary losses, whether deriving from breach of contract or from unlawful conduct, is recognised in three situations: (a) when the non-pecuniary loss is a consequence of a tort which is also a criminal offence; (b) when the recoverability of the non-pecuniary loss is clearly provided by a statutory provision;[31] and (c) when the non-pecuniary loss derives from the infringement of a fundamental right related to the person, directly protected by the Constitution.[32] Notwithstanding the three-tier distinction, non-pecuniary losses shall be quantified by courts as a unified notion.

---

27 Cass civ, 31 May 2003, nos 8827, 8828 (2003) Danno e responsabilità 816; Cass civ, Sez Un, 11 November 2008, nos 26972, 26973, 26974, 26975 (fn 14). This construction has been constantly reaffirmed: Cass civ, 15 January 2009, no 794 (2009) Responsabilità civile e previdenza 793. The construction of art 2059 It cc linked to the Charter was originally supported by: *GB Ferri*, Oggetto del diritto della personalità e danno non patrimoniale (1984) I Rivista di diritto commerciale 155; *E Navarretta*, Diritti inviolabili e risarcimento del danno (1996); *id* (ed), Il danno non patrimoniale. Principi, regole e tabella per la liquidazione (2010); *Busnelli/Patti* (fn 25) 68 ff.

28 Corte Cost, 11 July 2003, no 233 (fn 15).

29 The application of art 2059 It cc was limited to cases where non-pecuniary losses were a consequence of criminal offences.

30 See *G Ponzanelli*, Il 'nuovo' danno non patrimoniale (2004) 60 ff.

31 As is certainly the case for the infringement of privacy (art 152, decreto legislativo (d lgs) 30.06.2003, no 196), for the infringement of the copyright (art 159 L 22.04.1941, no 633), for non-pecuniary loss deriving from the unreasonable duration of a trial (L 24.03.2001, no 89), or for non-pecuniary loss arising from a spoilt vacation (art 47 d lgs 22.05.2011, no 79 – Code of Tourism).

32 As is certainly the case for any right and fundamental freedom that cannot be questioned or even limited by the law, nor by any public or private authority: right to psycho-physical health integrity, the right to life, the right to personality, the right to personal freedom, the right to dignity. Coherently, the High Court has recently ruled that damages cannot be awarded in cases of constant train delays and discomfort suffered by subscribers to the railway service, as the nuisance suffered cannot be qualified as a fundamental right: Cass civ, 08 February 2019, no 3720 (2019) Diritto & Giustizia 11 February 2019, note *R Savoia*, Treno sistematicamente in ritardo? Certamente fastidioso, ma non lesivo dei diritti inviolabili della persona. As concerns the right to psycho-physical health integrity in particular, the Italian High Court has recently pointed out that the injuries may in special cases affect the relation life of the injured, which should therefore be restored as such. Moreover, pain and suffering (not necessarily having a medical basis), shall be awarded as non-pecuniary losses related to the person and thus falling within the infringement of a fundamental right, as a separate and autonomous heading of damages: Cass civ 17 January 2018, no 901, (2018) Foro italiano 923; Cass civ, 27 March 2018, no 7513 (2018) 2 Nuova giurisprudenza civile commentata 836; Cass civ, 31 May 2018, no 13770 (2018) Danno e responsabilità 465; Cass civ 31 January 2019, no 278 (2019) 2 Nuova giurisprudenza civile commentata 278 note *G Ponzanelli*, Il nuovo statuto del danno alla persona è stato fissato, ma quali sono le tabelle giuste?

Nevertheless, the modern construction of art 2059 It cc has been questioned by scholars and by some courts under two main arguments: 45

(a) The first does not accept the limitation of recovery of non-pecuniary losses to fundamental constitutional rights. According to this opinion,[33] such a limitation would leave the infringement of a significant number of rights that – though not included in the list of fundamental rights – represent a substantial part of human life and personality without a remedy.[34]
(b) The second argument considers as inappropriate the narrow range of application of non-pecuniary losses when a contractual source of obligation is concerned. According to this view,[35] the different structures of the two sources of obligations (contract and tort) do not allow an overall definition of non-pecuniary loss. In truth, in an obligation to pay damages in tort, the selection of the relevant interests infringed by unlawful conduct can be limited by a statutory provision (art 2059 It cc) as narrowly constructed by courts. On the contrary, in the case of non-pecuniary losses caused by a breach of a previous obligation, the assessment of the relevant interests by the parties, in compliance with the principle of freedom of contract, is relevant. In other words, the parties can include within the contractual liability non-pecuniary interests the infringement of which by the party in breach can provoke a non-pecuniary loss that courts may recognise as recoverable.

3) *Compensation for Loss of Earnings and for Loss of Chance*

Article 2056, para 2 It cc states that a loss of earnings is always assessed through an equitable evaluation of the case at stake in the case of liability in tort.[36] 46

---

33 *P Cendon* (ed), Il *quantum* nel danno esistenziale: giurisprudenza e tabelle (2010); *P Cendon/ P Ziviz*, Il risarcimento del danno esistenziale (2003).

34 As is the case for the right to happiness, the right to moral integrity, or the right to develop one's own personality.

35 *CM Bianca*, Diritto civile, vol 5: La responsabilità (1994) 171 ff; *C Scognamiglio*, Il danno non patrimoniale contrattuale, in: S Mazzamuto (ed), Il contratto e le tutele. Prospettive di diritto europeo (2002) 467 ff; *G Conte*, Considerazioni critiche sull'applicazione del paradigma risarcitorio ricavato dall'art 2059 c.c. anche al danno non patrimoniale contrattuale (2010) I Contratti 709; *C Amato*, Danno non patrimoniale da inadempimento contrattuale (2011) Digesto delle discipline privatistiche, Sezione civile (aggiornamento) 302 ff. Pretura (Pret) Salerno, 17 February 1997 (1998) II Giustizia civile 203; Trib Roma, 21 July 2009 (2009) Giurisprudenza di merito 2764; Trib Genova, 4 May 2009 (2009) Giurisprudenza di merito 2764; Giudice di Pace di Piacenza, 30 December 2008 (2009) Danno e responsabilità 2 note *C Amato*, I primi passi del danno non patrimoniale per inadempimento contrattuale dopo le Sezioni Unite di San Martino.

36 See extensively *P Rescigno*, Valutazione equitativa: profili comuni, in: G Visintini (ed), Risarcimento del danno contrattuale ed extracontrattuale (1984) 84 ff; *G Afferni*, Il quantum del danno nella responsabilità precontrattuale (2008) 82 ff.

47 As concerns pre-contractual liability (see above at no 10), the assessment of loss of earnings is admitted, together with general damages, though what differs is the general principle underpinning such awards. According to the Corte di Cassazione, damages to be awarded to an innocent party in the case of frustration of negotiations (art 1337 It cc) or conclusion of an invalid contract (art 1338 It cc) must be limited to so-called 'reliance damage' (*interesse negativo*) suffered by the innocent party, as opposed to 'expectation damage' (*interesse positivo*) to be awarded in the case of breach of a (valid) contract. Such 'reliance damages' shall be assessed by taking into account either the lower enrichment or the highest costs deriving from the breach of the duty of good faith in the pre-contractual phase.[37] This is because such damages are not connected to the non-conclusion of a contract: they instead represent compensation for the infringement of an interest (in not suffering bad faith conduct) rather than a true contractual interest (the performance of a contractual obligation).

48 Compensation for loss of a chance was questioned by Italian scholarship and case law in the past century until the end of the 1960s.[38] At present, it is admitted especially in the areas of labour law (loss of a chance of promotion of civil servants, loss of a chance of recruitment), professional liability, and public procurement procedures. It is not clear, though, whether this damage can be qualified as general damage or loss of earnings. In the last case, the difference between loss of a chance and loss of earnings lies in the degree of certainty: while the latter are very close to certain, the former are subject to the 'more probable than not' principle.

4) Restitutionary Damages

49 Restitutionary damages are awarded where an obligation was not due or unjustified enrichment occurred.[39] More precisely, they are awarded whenever unjustified displacements of assets took place. They do not aim at recovering a loss deriving from the violation of a previous right; they instead aim at protecting a different interest, which is the lawful movement of assets. Their main characteristic is the enrichment of one party at the other's expense/damage.

---

[37] Cass civ, Sez Un, 19 December 2007, no 26725 (2008) Responsabilità civile e previdenza 556 note *F Greco*, Intermediazione finanziaria: violazione di regole comportamentali e tutela secondo le Sezioni Unite; Cass civ, 29 September 2005, no 19024 (2006) Giurisprudenza commerciale 626 note *CE Salodini*, Obblighi informativi degli intermediari finanziari e risarcimento del danno. La Cassazione e l'interpretazione evolutiva della responsabilità precontrattuale. Cf *B Scumace*, Lucro cessante e interesse negativo (2018) 4 I Contratti 467-473.

[38] See *MF Lo Moro Biglia*, Il risarcimento della chance frustrata. Un itinerario incrementale (2006); *M Feola*, Il danno da perdita di *chance* (2004).

[39] *A Di Majo*, La tutela civile dei diritti (2003) 320 ff.

Recovery of undue payments together with contractual damages are prescribed in two cases. Firstly, when a payment was not due at all (*indebito oggettivo*): art 2033 It cc. This is the case whenever an executed contract is terminated (breach, rescission, impossibility of performance, invalidity: see arts 422, 1463 It cc). The same restitutionary remedy applies when a payment was rendered to the wrong creditor (*indebito soggettivo ex latere accipientis*). Secondly, when a payment was wrongly rendered by a false debtor (*indebito soggettivo ex latere solventis*): art 2036 It cc.[40] Moreover, specific rules are provided by the Civil Code, aiming at avoiding unjust enrichment at the other party's expenses.[41] Finally, a general action against the unjustified enrichment is regulated by the Civil Code: arts 2041 and 2042 affirm that this general remedy can be triggered when no other remedy exists, provided that the victim can prove his/her loss and the causal connection to the other party's enrichment.[42] 50

As concerns the relationship between restitutionary damages and damages in tort, they are concurrent, in the sense that they can both be claimed whenever the conditions of admissibility of either of them are met.[43] In particular, unjustified enrichment and restitutionary damages represent a valid alternative to liability in tort and restoration damages in the area of protection of intellectual property[44] and competition law.[45] 51

5) Aggravated and Exemplary (or Punitive) Damages

As a general rule, exemplary (punitive) damages as such are not recognised, neither in contract nor in tort.[46] 52

---

40 Ibid, 348 ff.

41 A typical case occurs when the owner has initiated a proprietary action against a third party who is in possession of the thing, and the former has obtained the restitution of the good: in this instance, the owner is requested to refund the third party of any expenses actually incurred to maintain the thing: arts 1149, 1150 It cc.

42 Cf *C Amato*, Unjustified Enrichment in Book VII DCFR: Beyond the European Models, in: B Pasa/L Morra (eds), Translating the DCFR and Drafting the CESL. A Pragmatic Perspective (2014).

43 *Di Majo* (fn 39) 356 ff.

44 *A Nicolussi*, Proprietà intellettuale e arricchimento ingiustificato: la restituzione degli utili nell'art 465 TRIPs (2002) Rivista di diritto civile 1030; *C Castronovo*, La violazione della proprietà intellettuale come lesione del potere di disposizione. Dal danno all'arricchimento (2003) Diritto industriale 11; *A Plaia*, Proprietà intellettuale e risarcimento del danno (2003); *P Sirena*, Il risarcimento dei c.d. danni punitivi e la restituzione dell'arricchimento senza causa (2006) I Rivista di diritto civile 531.

45 Cf *A Genovese*, Il risarcimento del danno da illecito concorrenziale (2005).

46 *G Ponzanelli*, I danni punitivi (2008) II Nuova giurisprudenza civile commentata 27. See in particular: Cass civ, 19 January 2007, no 1183 (2007) I Foro italiano 1460, which set aside a North American decision awarding punitive damages as contrary to the Italian public order.

53 Aggravated damages can be awarded in contract law whenever one party is intentionally in breach of contract: in this case compensation for non-foreseeable damage is awarded (see above at no 26).

54 Nevertheless, the punitive and retributive function of civil liability is not completely unknown to the Italian legal system.[47] A recent important decision of the Corte di Cassazione admitted the exequatur of a foreign judgment (in the case at stake, an American judgment) awarding punitive damages as it cannot be considered as contrary to the public order, although the Court warned that the punitive function of liability in tort cannot be admitted in the Italian legal system, unless expressly introduced by law.[48]

55 Setting aside the controversial nature of non-pecuniary losses and the multiple functions of tortious liability, there are several statutory rules reflecting – according to the interpretation of relevant scholarship[49] – a punitive and/or retributive function quite different from the traditional compensatory nature of damages. Here follows a non-exhaustive list:

- art 614-*bis* It Code of Civil Procedure,[50] according to which the judge may order payments due to the party in breach of an affirmative duty;[51]
- art 709-*ter* It Code of Civil Procedure,[52] providing damages to the parent and/or to minor offspring in case the other parent has violated fundamental rights of family members;
- art 96 It Code of Civil Procedure, according to which the right to a trial might turn into unlawful conduct should the plaintiff abuse his/her right with

---

47 *MG Baratella*, Le pene private (2006); *A D'Angelo*, La funzione 'sanzionatoria' della responsabilità civile nella giurisprudenza dei giudici di pace dopo le SS.UU. del novembre 2008, in: G Comandé (ed), Il danno nella giurisprudenza dei giudici di pace. Itinerari tematici e istruzioni per l'uso (2009) 45 ff. Trib Venezia, 14 May 2009 (2009) Responsabilità civile e previdenza 1885.

48 Cass civ, Sez Un, 5 July 2017, no 16601. Cf *G Ponzanelli*, Le Sezioni Unite sui danni punitivi tra diritto internazionale privato e diritto interno (2017) 10 Nuova giurisprudenza civile commentata 1413 ff.

49 *R Pardolesi*, Tutela specifica e tutela per equivalente nella prospettiva dell'analisi economica del diritto, in: S Mazzamuto (ed), Processo e tecniche di attuazione dei diritti, vol I (1989) 522 ff; *U Mattei*, Analisi economica e comparata delle clausole penali nel diritto dei contratti (1996) Rivista critica di diritto privato 603; *FD Busnelli/G Scalfi* (eds), Le pene private (1985).

50 Recently introduced by L 06.08.2015, no 132, art 13.

51 See Cass civ, 15 April 2015, no 7613 (2016) 3 Giurisprudenza italiana 562: this was a case where the Italian High Court recognised the conformity to the Italian public order of a Belgian judgment that had condemned a Belgian corporation to pay a daily penalty clause in favour of the custodian trustee. The payment order referred to the delay in delivering the corporation shares. According to the Italian High Court, such payments should be classified as '*astreintes*', that is as pecuniary sanctions aiming at deterrence, similar to the provision of art 614-*bis* It Code of Civil Procedure.

52 Recently introduced by L 08.02.2006, no 54.

fraud or gross negligence; in this case the judge may award compensation for non-pecuniary losses in favour of the innocent defendant;[53]

- art 129-*bis* It cc, imposing an indemnity to the spouse liable of the invalidity of the marriage, in favour of the spouse in good faith who relied on the validity of the marriage;[54]
- arts 311, para 3, and 313 d lgs 03.04.2006, no 152 (Environmental Code), according to which, where specific performance is not possible, or is impracticable, or has not been complied with by the tortfeasor, the amount of compensation for environmental damage due to the State shall be assessed by the judge taking into account the amount of pecuniary and future losses;[55]
- Art 12 L 08.02.1948, no 47 (regulating the press) introduces a pecuniary award (supplementing non-pecuniary loss) to be paid by a journalist;[56]
- Art 140 para 7, It Consumer Code: this provision gives the judge (who orders an injunction) the power to condemn the party who has not complied with the injunction to the payment of a sum (from €516 to €1,032) per any day of delay;
- Art 1382 It cc (penalty clause) recognises for the creditor – in the case of breach of contract – the right to liquidated damages, without the need to provide any proof either of the existence or of the extension of damage after

---

53 *G Bongiorno*, Responsabilità aggravate, in: Enciclopedia giuridica Treccani, vol XXVI (1991) 1 ff; *R Breda*, Recenti sviluppi interpretativi in materia di responsabilità processuale aggravata (2007) Danno e responsabilità 1045; *id*, Responsabilità aggravata ed effetti regolatori, in: PG Monateri/A Somma (eds), Patrimonio, persona e nuove tecniche di 'governo del diritto'. Incentivi, premi, sanzioni. XIX Colloquio biennale Associazione Italiana di diritto comparato, Ferrara 10–12 maggio 2007 (2009) 991; *id*, Responsabilità processuale aggravata tra risarcimento del danno e sanzione (2010) II Nuova giurisprudenza civile commentata 490. Cass civ, Sez Un, 30 September 1989, no 3948 (1989) I Giustizia civile 2535; Cass civ, 6 June 2003, no 9060 (2003) Giustizia civile Massimario 6.

54 *C Marti*, L'art 129-*bis* c.c. nella prospettiva dei rapporti tra pena privata e diritto di famiglia, in: FD Busnelli/G Scalfi (eds), Le pene private (1985) 209 ff.

55 *B Pozzo*, La responsabilità civile per danno all'ambiente tra vecchia e nuova disciplina (2007) Rivista giuridica dell'ambiente 815; *id*, Nuove tecniche di governo del diritto: incentivi, premi, sanzioni. Il territorio della responsabilità civile in campo ambientale, in: PG Monateri/A Somma (eds), Patrimonio, persona e nuove tecniche di 'governo del diritto'. Incentivi, premi, sanzioni. XIX Colloquio biennale Associazione Italiana di diritto comparato, Ferrara 10–12 maggio 2007 (2009) 880; *D Morgante*, La responsabilità per danno all'ambiente, in: P Fava (ed), La responsabilità civile: trattato teorico-pratico (2009) 1841 ff; *S Patti*, La valutazione del danno ambientale (1992) II Rivista di diritto civile 447; *id*, La quantificazione del danno ambientale (2010) Responsabilità civile 485; *M Franzoni*, Il nuovo danno all'ambiente (2009) Responsabilità civile 785.

56 *V Zeno-Zencovich*, Il risarcimento esemplare per diffamazione nel diritto americano e la riparazione pecuniaria *ex* art 12 della legge sulla stampa (1983) Responsabilità civile e previdenza 40; *id*, Revirement della Cassazione sulle sanzioni civili punitive contro la stampa (1986) Diritto dell'informazione e dell'informatica 473; *MG Baratella*, La riparazione pecuniaria (2001) Responsabilità comunicazione e impresa 295. Cass civ, 7 November 2000, no 14485 (2001) Giurisprudenza italiana 1360: the High Court has expressly recognised the punitive function of this provision.

the breach. In order to avoid abuse, the Code (at art 1384) also gives the judge the power to reduce the original amount of the penalty clause, provided that it be may considered as grossly excessive,[57] or that the obligation has been partly executed by the party in breach, having regard to the interest of the creditor to the performance.[58]

6) Other Remedies

56 Having regard to the statutory texts and to case law, it can be inferred that both specific performance and restoration in kind are secondary remedies, whereas damages remain the primary remedy.

57 Specific performance in contract law always seems possible in principle (art 1453 It cc), but for the irreplaceable nature of the object of the contract or the destruction of the object of the contract.[59]

58 Restoration in kind in tort law is expressly regulated by art 2058 It cc: the statutory text provides for the possibility of restoration in kind, as an alternative to damages, provided that it is requested by the injured party and that it is not unreasonably expensive for the injurer.

59 Examples of specific performance in tort law are:

- the publication of the court's decision in newspapers in cases of infringement of honour or reputation (art 186 Criminal Code; art 120, para 1, Civil Procedure Code);
- the release of a mortgage in the case of professional liability of a notary public who has registered a mortgage but has not mentioned the existence of the mortgage into the deed for the sale of a real estate.[60]

60 As concerns injunctions, they are unanimously considered as remedies that have no *general* application in private law. They aim at restoring the previous situation, notwithstanding the damage suffered by the victims (that may be claimed in a separate action).

---

57 The Supreme Court has interpreted the function of the judiciary power to reduce the penalty clause as corrective of the parties' freedom of contract, in order to bring the agreement to an equitable balance, in the name of a public interest (and not only on behalf of the debtor's inequality of bargaining power): Cass civ, Sez Un, 13 September 2005, no 18128 (2006) I Giurisprudenza italiana 2279.

58 *A Spatuzzi*, L'entità della penale, tra 'lex contractus' ed eterointegrazione giudiziale (2016) I Contratti 15; *FP Patti*, Penalty Clauses in Italian Law (2015) 3 ERPL 297; *FP Patti*, Il controllo giudiziale della caparra confirmatoria (2014) Rivista di diritto civile 685; *G Pardi*, Osservazioni e spunti critici sulla clausola penale (2011) II Giustizia civile 511.

59 *Di Majo* (fn 39) 287 ff.

60 Cass civ, 16 January 2013, no 903.

Special injunctions in tort are recognised by statutory provisions in the areas of: 61

- unlawful competition (art 1599 It cc);
- environmental damage (art 311 ff d lgs 03.04.2006, no 152);
- protection of proprietary rights (art 949, para 2 It cc).

Special injunctions in contractual relationships are recognised by statutory provisions, in the areas of: 62

- unfair terms in B2C contracts (arts 37, 139, 140 d lgs 06.09.2005, no 206: Consumer Code);
- abuse of economic position in subcontracting agreements (art 9, L 18.06.1998, no 192);
- late payments in commercial transactions (art 8 d lgs 09.10.2002, no 231, as modified by d lgs 09.11.2012, no 192, implementing Directive 2011/7/EC).

D. DIFFERENCES AS REGARDS RECOVERABILITY OF 'PURE ECONOMIC LOSSES'

In contract law, the recoverability of pure economic loss is a general rule. 63

In tort law, since 1971[61] courts have recognised the recoverability of pure economic loss, within the limits of unlawful conduct (such as negligent interference of a third party within a contractual obligation; see below, Case 11). At present, the recoverability of pure economic loss is admitted *in principle*, provided that all the elements of the unlawful conduct required by the law and by case law exist. In particular, the recoverability of pure economic loss which 64

61 Cass civ, Sez Un, 26 January 1971, no 174 ('Meroni' case), confirmed by: Cass civ, Sez I, 14 July 1987 no 6132; Cass civ, Sez III, 25 June 1993, no 7063, Cass civ, Sez III, 8 January 1999, no 108. On the unlawful conduct that may include pure economic loss, cf: *FD Busnelli*, La lesione del credito da parte di terzi (1964); *id*, La tutela aquiliana del credito: evoluzione giurisprudenziale e significato attuale del principio (1987) Rivista Critica del Diritto Privato 273 ff; *id*, Itinerari europei nella 'terra di nessuno' tra contratto e fatto illecito: la responsabilità da informazioni inesatte (1991) Contratto e impresa 545; *G Alpa*, La responsabilità civile. Parte generale (2010) 358 ff; *E Navarretta*, L'ingiustizia del danno e i problemi di confine tra responsabilità contrattuale e extracontrattuale, in: N Lipari/P Rescigno/A Zoppini (eds), Diritto civile, vol IV, t III, Attuazione e tutela dei diritti. La responsabilità e il danno (2009) 242 ff. For a different perspective on pure economic loss (considered as recoverable under the application of the general principle of good faith and fair dealing: arts 1337, 1338 It cc) cf: *C Castronovo*, La nuova responsabilità civile (2006) 443, 474; *id*, Ritorno all'obbligazione senza prestazione (2009) Europa e diritto privato 694; *id*, Vaga *culpa in contrahendo*: invalidità, responsabilità e la ricerca della chance perduta (2010) Europa e diritto privato 679 ff.

results from false/misleading information outside a contractual relationship has been recognised as unlawful conduct in several situations:

- prospectus liability,[62] including the liability of the independent authority controlling the financial market (CONSOB);[63] and
- false/misleading information rendered by a professional. This instance covers different situations ruled by the Supreme Court in favour of the recoverability of pure economic loss, where the unlawfulness of the conduct consists – according to the Corte di Cassazione – in the infringement of the right to self-determination also in the area of economic interests. This rationale was used for the first time to establish the recoverability of the pure economic loss suffered by the purchaser of a painting falsely attributed to a famous Italian artist.[64] The same rationale was used in cases where the false/misleading information was rendered by banks' employees to professionals who, though outside a contractual relationship, were provided with false/misleading financial information concerning clients of the bank (*benefondi bancario*).[65]

E. DIFFERENCES AS REGARDS LIABILITY

1) *Liability for Auxiliaries and for Independent Contractors*

65 In the Italian Civil Code, liability for auxiliaries is regulated by two different norms: arts 1228 (liability in contract) and 2049 (liability in tort). Recently, scholars have stressed the different foundations of liabilities.[66] In the case of art 1228 It cc, the foundation of the debtor's liability acting through an agent is fault (as defined above at no 29) and it is a direct form of liability; in the case of art 2049 It cc the foundation for the employer's liability is strict (see above at no 34) and this type of liability is indirect. Moreover, in the case of art 1228, the existence of a master/servant relationship is not necessary, as required in art 2049. Therefore, liability under art 1228 can be attributed to a debtor for the breach of contract caused by an independent contractor, which is not the case under art 2049.

---

[62] See recently: Cass civ, 11 June 2010, no 14056 (2011) Le Società 411.

[63] Cass civ, 3 March 2001, no 3132 (2001) I Foro italiano 1139.

[64] Cass civ, 4 May 1982, no 2765 (1982) II Giustizia civile 1745.

[65] Cass civ, 1 August 2001, no 10492 (2002) Danno e responsabilità 90; Cass civ, 9 June 1998, no 5659 (1998) Danno e responsabilità 1048.

[66] See *G Ceccherini*, Responsabilità per fatto degli ausiliari. Clausole di esonero dalla responsabilità, in: P Schlesinger/FD Busnelli (eds), Commentario al codice civile (2nd edn 2016).

2) *Liability for Legal Representatives or Organs of a Company*

Legal representatives and organs of corporations with share capitals are liable in contract vis-à-vis the company, its partners, the creditors and third parties. For each of these situations there are different actions provided by the Civil Code. The claim brought by the company is contractual in nature (art 2392 It cc); the claim brought by creditors (art 2394) is directly founded on the violations of the representatives' duties imposed by the law; the claim brought by partners and third parties is traditionally considered as grounded on the law of tort.[67] 66

3) *Liability of Representatives of Natural Persons*

Representatives of natural persons with full capacity (parents or tutors) are liable in tort under art 2048 It cc, provided that they live with parents or tutors. This is a case of aggravated and vicarious liability. In the case of persons without full capacity, parents or tutors shall be liable under art 2047 It cc, which provides for direct and strict liability[68] (see above at no 36). 67

4) *Liability of the Auxiliary/Organ Itself*

In all the situations discussed above at no 66, the auxiliary/organ is liable together with the principal, both in contract and in tort. In compliance with the rule of joint and several liability (see below at no 69 f), the principal can file a recourse claim against the auxiliary/organ, and he/she can rebut the presumption of equivalent responsibility by demonstrating the unique fault/negligence of the auxiliary/organ.[69] 68

F. DIFFERENCES AS REGARDS LIABILITY IN THE CASE OF MULTIPLE TORTFEASORS/BREACHING PARTIES

Joint and several liability is the general rule expressed in arts 1292–1313 It cc: because this is regulated in the general and common part of the law of obligations (see above at sec I.C), it applies to contract as well as to tort law (see also art 2055, para 1). Negligence in contract and fault in tort are presumed as equally shared among tortfeasors. 69

This general rule may sometimes be set aside by special statutory provisions, as is the case of environmental liability, where art 311, para 2, d lgs 03.04.2006, 70

[67] See *G Cottino*, Diritto societario (2011) 432 ff.
[68] Cass civ, 2 March 2012, no 3242.
[69] See *A Torrente/P Schlesinger*, Manuale di diritto privato (23rd edn 2017) 889 f.

no 152, has clearly established that if the damage to the environment was produced by multiple tortfeasors, 'each of them shall be liable within the limits of his/her own negligence'.

G. DIFFERENCES AS REGARDS THE PERSONS WHO MAY BE PROTECTED

71 Under contract law, the privity doctrine (art 1372 It cc) would eliminate any protection for third parties. Nevertheless, authoritative scholars have proposed a different interpretation of contractual liability.

72 Some authors[70] – inspired by the German law of obligations – have proposed the theory of protective interests, according to which autonomous duties of good faith can spring from a 'social contact', regardless of the existence of a primary (that is: contractual) obligation. Such supplementary duties maintain the contractual nature of any 'special relationship', different from tort law and very similar to contract law. Their source lies in the law (arts 1175, 1337 It cc). Courts have accepted this view: since 1999, the Corte di Cassazione has afforded protection to third parties under this doctrine.[71]

73 Other authors have proposed an interpretation of contractual duties and liability more respectful of the Italian Civil Code (arts 1176 and 1218). According to this different view, protection of third parties may derive from subsidiary duties of good faith that represent the very essence of a contractual obligation, having regard to the object and type of the contract.[72] In other words, the criterion of diligence mentioned in art 1176 It cc and imposed on the debtor in order to satisfy the creditor's contractual interest is suitable to identify a number of further

[70] *F Benatti*, Osservazioni in tema di 'doveri di protezione' (1960) Rivista trimestrale di diritto e procedura civile 1342; *A Di Majo*, Delle obbligazioni in generale. Artt. 1173–1176, Commentario Scialoja-Branca, Libro IV delle Obbligazioni (1988) 121 ff; *C Castronovo*, Obblighi di protezione e tutela del terzo (1976) Jus 123; *id*, voce 'Obblighi di protezione', in: Enciclopedia giuridica Treccani (1990) 2 ff; *id*, Ritorno all'obbligazione senza prestazione (2009) Europa e diritto privato 679; *L Lambo*, Obblighi di protezione (2007) 110 ff.

[71] Cass civ, 22 December 1999, no 589 (2000) Giurisprudenza italiana 740; Cass civ, 10 May 2002, no 6735 (2001) I Foro italiano 3115, where liability of a doctor for wrongful birth was extended to the father; Cass civ, 15 March 1999, no 2284 (1999) I Foro italiano 1165; Cass civ, 21 June 2004, no 11488 (2005) Rivista critica del diritto privato 361; Cass civ, 19 April 2006, no 9085 (2006) Corriere giuridico 914; Cass civ, 13 April 2007, no 8826 (2007) II Nuova giurisprudenza civile commentata 445; Cass civ, Sez Un, 16 June 2007, no 14712 (2008) Danno e responsabilità 160; Cass civ, Sez Un, 11 November 2008, no 577 (2008) Danno e responsabilità 788; Cass civ, Sez Un, 11 November 2008, nos 26972–26975 (2009) fn 14; Cass civ, 21 July 2011, no 15992 (2012) I Nuova giurisprudenza civile commentata 1172.

[72] See *U Natoli*, L'attuazione del rapporto obbligatorio, in: A Cicu Messineo (ed), Trattato di diritto civile e commerciale, vol XVI, t I (1974) 11–12 ff; *CM Bianca*, Diritto civile. Le obbligazioni (2002) 37 ff.

'instrumental' duties that – though they do not form part of the contractual obligation – can be identified through the good faith principle. According to this view, contractual liability in violation of the primary obligation arises whenever a third party beneficiary suffers damage derived from the breach of contract. This is the case for investors who suffer damage deriving from wrongful information provided by the board of directors or by auditors ('prospectus liability'), and third party victims of professional liability (patients/victims of medical malpractice suffered in a hospital; victims of professional negligence of teachers supervising students in a college).[73]

In sum, compared to the protection of third parties under the law of tort, contract law does not offer the same certainty and privileged regime than liability in tort. 74

Under tort law, statutory provisions directly protect minors, persons lacking capacity, victims of auxiliaries/employees/organs, or of a building in ruin, or of dangerous activities or of a car crash. Not only are they expressly mentioned by the law, but a separate regime is provided, aiming at protecting them through a facilitated burden of proof and through the direct or vicarious liability of persons financially more reliable (see above sec II.E). 75

H. DIFFERENCES AS REGARDS DEFENCES

Contributory negligence is the general rule expressed in art 1227 It cc: because this is settled in the general and common part of the law of obligations (see above sec I.C), it applies to both contract and tort law. The provision distinguishes between a case where the causation of the damage can be attributed to the contributory negligence of the victim (art 1227, para 1 It cc); and a case where the victim was in breach of the duty to mitigate damage (art 1227, para 2 It cc). In the first instance, the rule of apportionment of damage shall apply, and damages shall be awarded to the victim pro quota.[74] In the second instance, instead, the victim shall bear all the costs that he/she could have avoided if he/she had acted with diligence in mitigating damage.[75] 76

As regards defences, if we define 'defence' as the exclusion of the consequences of the breach, once liability has been assessed, then in contract law, there are no defences. Impossibility of performance (arts 1463–1466 It cc) or economic 77

[73] Cf *C Amato*, Affidamento e responsabilità (2012) 205 ff.

[74] Cass civ, Sez Un, 21 November 2011, no 24406: the High Court endorsed the argument according to which the victim's negligence does not concern the attribution of liability: it rather concerns the causation of the damage. Cf *M Franzoni*, Fatti illeciti, in: V Scialoja/G Branca (eds), Commentario al codice civile, sub art 2043 (2004) 40 ff.

[75] Cass civ, 20 December 2011, no 29864.

impracticability in relational contracts (arts 1467–1469 It cc) would not be qualified as 'defences', as they exclude contractual liability and justify the breach.

78 The right to withhold performance (*exceptio inadimpleti contractus*) is classified as a self-defence remedy that is an exception to the general principle that prohibits self-defence in favour of judicial settlement.[76] It may be triggered in bilateral contracts, against the other party's breach, or when both obligations should be performed at the same time, provided that the innocent party acted in good faith, having regard to the particular circumstances of the case (art 1460 It cc).[77]

79 A right of retention is given to one innocent party of a bilateral contract who is expected to perform his/her obligation *before* the counterparty, provided that he/she can give evidence that the counterparty shall not perform because the latter is experiencing difficulties in terms of his/her creditworthiness (art 1461 It cc).[78] The provision of real or personal guarantees by the party in default excludes the possibility of triggering the right of retention. This case especially occurs in the sales of goods, when the seller does not deliver the goods, because he/she has reason to believe that the buyer will not pay for the goods after delivery.

80 The only possible defence in tort law that excludes liability is capacity: that occurs when the tortfeasor was not capable at the time when the injury took place (art 2046 It cc). This is true only if we define 'defence' as the exclusion of the consequences of the injury once liability has been established. The exercise of a right, the fulfilment of preceding obligations, self-defence (art 2044 It cc), act of necessity (art 2045 It cc), consensus or running a dangerous but lawful activity cannot be qualified as 'defences', because they all exclude the unlawfulness of the conduct and consequently they do not give rise to any liability in tort.

I. DIFFERENCES AS REGARDS LIMITATION PERIODS

81 The statutory limitation period for claiming damages is 10 years in contract, unless otherwise provided by law (art 2946 It cc).

---

76 *F Camilletti*, Brevi considerazioni su alcuni strumenti di autotutela contrattuale (2015) 12 I Contratti 1142 ff.

77 Case law affirms that the violation of the duty of good faith by the innocent party can be stated after balancing the breaches of the parties, in respect to their proportion to the economic basis ('*causa*') of the bilateral contract. See recently: Cass civ, 4 May 2016, no 8912.

78 *F Piraino*, Il 'mutamento' delle condizioni patrimoniali e l'eccezione dilatoria ex art. 1461 c.c. 2 (2015) Osservatorio del diritto civile e commerciale 387 ff. Providing real or personal guarantees by the party in default excludes the possibility of triggering the right of retention.

Under tort law, there are shorter limitation periods: five years is the general statutory limitation period (art 2947 It cc), but in several instances, both in the Civil Code and in special statutes, the limitation periods are even shorter (see above at no 22). 82

Rules of suspension and interruption apply to both contract and tort liability. 83

The discipline of *dies a quo* presents many more problems as regards tort law. As a general rule, it runs from the moment when the conduct of the agent and the consequential injury are objectively detectable. Within this general principle, we can distinguish two different situations. The first occurs when the unlawful act and the personal injury are not instantaneous: the *dies a quo* starts from the time when the first appearance of the injury was objectively perceivable. Nevertheless, in the case of 'development' damage, that is damage which appears a very long time after the unlawful conduct (*danni lungolatenti*), the *dies a quo* starts from the time when the victim has perceived that his/her injury was due to previous and specific wrongful conduct.[79] The second situation occurs when the unlawful conduct is permanent (as is often the case with environmental damage): in this case the *dies a quo* starts from any day after the date when the damage occurred.[80] 84

J. DIFFERENCES AS REGARDS PROOF

Both the burden and standard of proof are different in contract and tort, as provided both by statutory law (Civil Code) and by courts. See extensively above at nos 17 and 21. 85

It should be remarked that in contract law the burden of proof has been assessed by case law for any kind of contract. In particular, the only burden of proof upon the creditor is to prove the non-fulfilment of the obligation by the debtor. It is up to the debtor in breach to demonstrate that his default was due to factors beyond his will, not imputable to him (see above at no 17). The situation is different as regards the standard of proof, which varies according to the type and object of the contract to which diligence must be referred. 86

In tort law, the burden of proof as well as the standard of proof vary with reference to the subjects involved in tort and to the nature of the activity carried out by the tortfeasor. 87

---

79 The most relevant cases concern physical damage caused by a compulsory vaccination: Cass civ, Sez Un, 11 January 2008, nos 576, 580, 582, 584 (2009) Giustizia civile 2531–2533 note *C Blaiotta*, Causalità e colpa: diritto civile e diritto penale si confrontano.

80 Cass civ, 28 May 2013, no 13201.

K. OTHER DIFFERENCES

88 Other differences concern: capacity, jurisdiction, conflicts of law, and transmissibility of claims.

89 As regards capacity, contract law applies the general rules on statutory capacity (age of majority, insanity, temporary incapacity). As a consequence, the contract is voidable (art 1425 It cc), unless the minor (but not the insane) has fraudulently concealed his/her age (art 1426 It cc), or – in cases of temporary incapacity – the counterparty knew of the status of temporary insanity (art 428 It cc). In tort law, on the contrary, capacity is determined on a case-by-case basis (art 2047 It cc);[81] damages (or indemnity) are due from the person in charge of the tortfeasor.

90 As regards jurisdiction, conflicts of law in contract law are regulated by art 57 L 31.05.1995, no 218, which refers to the Rome Convention. In B2C sales, the conflicts of law rule in favour of consumers imposes jurisdiction according to the place of residence of the consumer (art 33, para 2, lit u) Italian Consumer Code).

91 Articles 62–63 L 31.05.1995, no 218 regulate tort law and product liability. In the first case, unless the injured party prefers the application of the law of the State where the damaging event occurred, the applicable law is the law of the State where the damage was suffered. In the second instance, the victim can choose between the jurisdiction of the State where the registered office of the producer is located and the jurisdiction of the State where the product was bought.

92 As regards transmissibility of claims, contract law has detailed rules concerning bilateral contracts not executed (arts 1406–1410 It cc). As regards tort law, the most relevant problem in the transmission of claims concerns the claims of secondary victims for non-pecuniary losses deriving from the primary victim's death. Traditionally, and until recently, Italian courts have recognised the claims of secondary victims exclusively in cases when the primary victim survived for a significant[82] period of time before dying. Such non-pecuniary losses were, in fact, considered as damage to the psycho-physical integrity of the primary victim (*iure proprio*), that could be transmitted to the victim's heirs (*iure hereditario*).[83] From this perspective, compensation for pain and suffering was denied in those cases where the victim died instantaneously, or after a period

---

81 Cass civ, 19 November 2010, no 23464.

82 Only 16 hours were needed by Cass civ, 20 February 2015, no 3374: 16 hours of survival were deemed sufficient; Cass civ, 8 April 2010, no 8360: 30 minutes of survival were deemed sufficient.

83 See Corte Cost, 27 October 1994, no 372 (1994) Responsabilità civile e previdenza 996 ff.

of unconsciousness.[84] In contrast, the High Court – in a recent and controversial judgment[85] – questioned the traditional courts' and scholars' opinion,[86] thus awarding non-pecuniary losses to secondary victims also in a case where the primary victim's death was instantaneous. As an obvious consequence, this judgment has created a contrast in case law that brought the matter at stake before the Joint Chambers of the High Court.[87] According to the last ruling, the Corte di Cassazione restated the older course, that is: bereavement damages can be claimed by secondary victims only when the primary victim survived consciously for a significant period of time. The main reason for this decision is rooted in the traditional argument: damages for instant death do not affect health, but life; as such, the right to life can be claimed by the conscious victim only, and subsequently transmitted to the heirs.

L. REASONS FOR THE DIFFERENCES

The main reason for all these differences lies in the divergent structure of the two sources of obligations. Contractual liability aims at restoring damage caused by the breach of a previous (and 'primary') obligation; consequently, all the main features of contractual liability are strictly connected to its secondary nature.[88] On the other hand, damage deriving from a wrong as defined in art 2043 It cc finds its primary source in the law itself, which contains all the fundamental features of the obligation but at the same time is much more flexible. From this perspective, several differences that relate to historical reasons, the different functions of liability in contract and in tort, and the different categories, rules and remedies that they imply still remain. 93

As regards the historical reasons, suffice it to say that art 1173 It cc, dealing with the sources of obligations, distinguishes clearly between obligations deriving 94

84 See *ex plurimis*: Cass civ, 20 February 2015, no 3374.

85 Cass civ, 19 November 2013, no 1361. In support of this original decision: *CM Bianca*, La tutela risarcitoria del diritto alla vita: una parola nuova della Cassazione attesa da tempo (2014) Responsabilità civile e previdenza 492 ff.

86 See *ex plurimis*: *E Navarretta*, Danni da morte e danno alla salute, in: FD Busnelli/M Bargagna (eds), La valutazione del danno alla salute (4th edn 2001) 261 ff.

87 Cass civ, Sez Un, 22 July 2015, no 15530. For a favourable comment, see *E Navarretta*, Con il risarcimento del danno 'E' forse il sonno della morte men duro?' Riflessioni in margine alla Sezioni Unite della Cassazione no 1530 del 2015 (2015) 9 Giustizia Civile com 2 ff; *id*, La 'vera' giustizia ed il 'giusto' responso delle S.U. sul danno tanatologico *iure hereditario* (2015) Responsabilità civile e previdenza 1416; for a more critical position, see *FD Busnelli*, Tanto tuonò, che … non piovve. Le Sezioni Unite sigillano il 'sistema' (2015) 10 Corriere giuridico 1206.

88 In truth, the different limitation periods in contract and in tort cannot be explained having regard to the different structure of the two sources of obligation. Indeed, there is no reasonable justification of the divergence in the application of the remedies: *Giardina* (fn 1) 160 ff.

from a contract and obligations deriving from an unlawful act. The second source was ancillary to the first, although at present this statement is no longer true: case law and statutory interventions have almost reversed the relationship between the two sources.[89]

95 As concerns the different functions, contract law has the main goal of providing enforcement to conventional promises recognised by the law. Another important goal is to assess risks. Liability in tort has several functions: to compensate damage suffered by individuals, to punish unlawful behaviour, and to deter injurious conduct.[90]

96 As regards the different categories, rules and remedies, see in detail above in sec I.C.

III. LIMITATION OR EXCLUSION OF LIABILITY ARISING FROM TORT AND FROM CONTRACT

A. STATUTORY PROVISIONS AUTHORISING A LIMITATION OR EXCLUSION OF LIABILITY

97 As we shall argue below in sec III.B, limitation clauses in contracts as well as in tort are admitted within very restrictive conditions that can be thus summarised: *culpa lieve*, or the existence of express statutory provisions.

98 Nevertheless, there are still some statutory provisions providing a limitation/exclusion of liability, or caps on damages, under special circumstances (see also at no 35):

- Strict liability: at 123 It Consumer Code, in compliance with the European legislation and case law, has implemented a threshold of €387.00, in case of product liability, and in favour of the producer. The strict liability of professionals in cases concerning environmental damage was established by art 311 d lgs 03.04.2006, no 152 (implementing Directive 2004/35/EU, as amended by L 06.08.2013, no 97). Paragraph 2 of this provision provides the exclusion of restoration in kind in favour of specific performance.
- Transport law:[91] caps on damages have been established by European regulations that interact or sometimes even implement international conventions. A limitation of damages occurs both in cases of delay or cancellation of flights, trains, ships and in cases of death or injury of passengers.

---

89 *PG Monateri*, La responsabilità civile (2006) 8, 12.
90 *G Ponzanelli*, La responsabilità civile. Profili di diritto comparato (1996) 9 ff.
91 *V Zeno Zencovich*, Transport Law (2nd edn 2016) 131 ff.

B. LIMITATION OR EXCLUSION OF CONTRACTUAL AND TORTIOUS LIABILITY BY CONTRACT

Limitation/exclusion of liability is regulated by a complex set of rules that can be found in the Italian Civil Code and in the Italian Consumer Code (d lgs 06.09.2005, no 206). 99

Article 1229 It cc states at para 1 the possibility of limiting or excluding liability of the debtor (and his/her auxiliary) only in cases of *culpa lieve* ('soft' negligence). More clearly, the rule prescribes that an agreement which admits a limitation/exclusion of liability in cases of fraud and gross negligence is to be considered void. At para 2, the same article states that when the conduct of the debtor or his auxiliaries represents a breach of the obligations arising from public policy (psycho-physical personal integrity, family relationships, criminal sanctions), terms limiting/excluding liability are void, even in the case of *culpa lieve*.[92] As a general rule, art 1229 is constructed in a very broad manner: therefore, it can also be applied to limitation of liability admitted by special statutory provisions (see transport regulations) with reference to the quantum, insofar as they infringe fundamental constitutional rights.[93] 100

This rule seems to be carved out over an existing legal relationship; therefore, it was exclusively applied to contractual relationships.[94] This thesis seemed to be supported by the logical argument according to which art 2056 It cc did not mention art 1229 among the general rules on obligations applicable to tortious liability. Nevertheless, Italian doctrine has recently admitted the application of the rule to the law of tort by analogy.[95] This opinion is confirmed by Italian courts, which admitted the extension of art 1229 to tortious liability, especially by considering that an agreement excluding/limiting tortious liability is always void under the second paragraph or art 1229 as it is against public policy.[96] 101

Article 1341, para 2 It cc sets out the general regulation of contractual terms and conditions in B2B contracts. According to this rule, exclusion/limitation clauses included in one-sided standard contracts are ineffective if they are not expressly signed in writing by the subscriber. In sum, after the entry into force of the Consumer Code, this article applies: 102

- to B2B contracts only; and
- even in cases of *culpa lieve* vis-à-vis the party who drafted the contract.

---

92 *Ceccherini* (fn 66) 42 ff; *Monateri* (fn 2) 57 ff.

93 Corte Cost, 6 May 1985, no 132 (1985) Vita notarile 709, affirming that some Italian rules applying the Warsaw Convention were against the constitutional protection of personal integrity.

94 *C Castronovo*, Problema e sistema del danno da prodotti (1979) 537 ff.

95 *G Ponzanelli*, Le clausole di esonero dalla responsabilità civile (1984) 222 ff.

96 The leading case is Cass civ, 3 July 1968, no 2240.

103 Articles 33–38 It Consumer Code[97] deal with unfair terms in B2C contracts. In compliance with Directive 93/13/EU, these rules prescribe a control[98] over unfair terms based on the significant imbalance of rights and duties, provided that:

- the terms were not individually negotiated (art 34, para 4 It Consumer Code); and
- they do not reflect mandatory statutory, or regulatory domestic or international, provisions or principles (art 34, para 3 It Consumer Code).

104 Article 124 It Consumer Code[99] considers as void any agreement excluding or limiting liability attributed to producers or retailers under arts 114 ff for damage to person or to property caused to consumers by products delivered on the market.

105 A contractual exclusion/limitation clause admitted within the limits described above (at no 100) cannot provide a defence to a third party to a contract because of the privity rule (see art 1372 It cc). On the other hand, an exclusion/limitation provision triggered in a tortious claim would probably meet the same limits set out by art 1229 It cc and art 124 It Consumer Code; however, no case law can be quoted in support of this statement.

IV. NON-CONCURRENCE OR CONCURRENCE OF ACTIONS

A. OVERVIEW

1) Areas of Overlap between Tort and Contract

106 Under Italian law, there is a large range of issues characterised by the overlap between contractual and extra-contractual liability (*concorso proprio*).

107 Indeed, the entire matter is based on the assumption that, under certain circumstances, the same behaviour causes both the non-fulfilment of a pre-existing agreement and a tort. In these cases, many different regulations

---

97 These rules implement Directive 93/13/EC on Unfair Contract Terms.

98 In the Italian implementation of Directive 93/13/EC, the control over unfair terms is distributed between ordinary courts (in the case of individual claims for damages) and an independent administrative authority, AGCM (in the case of injunction aiming at cancelling the unfair terms from the terms and conditions of a one-sided contract).

99 Arts 114–127 Italian Consumer Code implementing Directive 1985/374/EC on Product Liability.

concur at the same time on the same event: the convergence is between the contractual liability of the debtor (special or general) and the debtor's liability in tort (special or general). From a procedural point of view, the convergence of many different regulations corresponds to the convergence between actions *ex contractu* and actions *ex delicto*. However, the application of one excludes the application of the other. It is obvious that damage compensation assessed according to one rule shall pay off the debt: a creditor cannot receive damages twice.

It is always the judge who determines the legal qualifications applicable to the action according to the facts sustaining it (the so-called *causa petendi*). 108

No specific express statutory rule regulates the phenomenon of overlapping between liability in contract and in tort: the solution is left open to interpretation. 109

After some initial doubts, since the 1970s case law has admitted the possibility of the option between tort and contract liability when the same fact can be considered as not fulfilling some contractual obligation and in the meanwhile as infringing an individual's rights, apart from the contract, then the overlapping between contract and tort liability is permissible. Rare and scarcely significant are the decisions against the effectiveness of the overlapping. From an analysis of the decisions and *rationes decidendi* it quickly becomes apparent that concurrence does not cover all cases. Actually the overlapping of the rules regulating the two different ranges of liability deals exclusively with those circumstances where the fact integrates the non-fulfilment of a pre-existing obligation. The circumstances leading to concurrence are alternatively: 110

- prejudice to an absolute right of the debtor, and, in particular infringement of the right to property, right to life and physical integrity. In these cases, the logical and juridical requirement for the overlapping is that the contract itself generates a duty to avoid causing damage to the tort victim. These instances occur most often in cases of contract of carriage,[100] medical care contracts,[101] and labour contracts;[102]
- the actions of an individual were intended to infringe upon someone else's right;
- the actions of an individual is a crime.

100 Cass civ, 24 May 1993, no 5831; Cass civ, 20 April 1989, no 1855 (1990) I Foro italiano 67 ff; App Napoli, 26 February 1990.

101 As concerns medical malpractice, the High Court has supported the theory of concurrence since 1979. See recently: Cass civ, 23 June 1994, no 6064 (1995) I Foro italiano 202.

102 Cass civ, 19 June 2001, no 8331 (2001) Foro italiano, Repertorio, voce 'Esecuzione in genere' no 58.

111 Several decisions of the High Court state a general rule that includes all possible overlapping of actions provided for in arts 1218 and 2043 It cc.[103]

2) Approach to Non-Concurrence and Concurrence of Actions

112 The main borders of the issue under Italian law having been described, we can turn now to the legal reasons explaining the rule. The possibility to accumulate the advantages connected to both types of liability rules makes it possible to mitigate any unjustified discrimination caused by the different effects of tort and contract liability rules. To deny concurrence would indeed lead to different results for similar cases since the rules in tort and contract liability remain different. The first instance is the case of non-economic loss which, without a rule of concurrence of claims and without a theory of protective interests, would lead to the denial of this form of compensation even though the damage (to the person) would be the same in contract and in tort. A second reason is provided by the different statutory limitation periods. This is the prevailing reason in motivating the creditor to sue in tort. It is the case especially in contracts for the carriage of persons when personal injuries occur. In fact, the action under contract expires after one year, according to art 2951 It cc, while, in tort, an action for personal injury becomes time-barred after five years.

113 Therefore, under Italian law, the rule for concurrence is mainly grounded on equitable reasons because it allows judges to neutralise possible discriminatory consequences which would otherwise arise from the different rules governing liability for tort and for breach of contract in actual cases.

114 However, it is clear that if concurrence is useful to prevent the consequences of an irrational and incoherent system, it does not help in eliminating them.

115 Though scholars seemed to agree on the possible cumulative presence of both contract and tort liability,[104] the theory of concurrence has been severely questioned on legal and systemic grounds. In particular, the concurrence rule can be avoided if a different approach to contractual liability and its effects on third parties is adopted. This is the opinion of an Italian scholar[105] who, in the main stream of the German experience, assumes it is possible

---

103 *Breccia* (fn 22) 671. The leading case is: Cass 13 March 1980, no 1696; more recently: Cass 8 May 2008, no 11410.

104 *PG Monateri*, Cumulo di responsabilità contrattuale ed extracontrattuale (1989) 17 ff; *R Sacco*, Concorso della azione contrattuale ed extracontrattuale, in: G Visintini (ed), Risarcimento del danno contrattuale ed extracontrattuale (1999) 161 ff; *M Rossello*, Responsabilità contrattuale ed aquiliana: il punto sulla giurisprudenza (1996) Contratto e impresa 659–661.

105 *C Castronovo*, Obblighi di protezione e tutela del terzo (1976) Jus 123; *id*, voce 'Obblighi di protezione', in: Enciclopedia giuridica Treccani (1990) 2 ff; *id*, Ritorno all'obbligazione senza prestazione (2009) Europa e diritto privato 679.

to derive several collateral duties from the principal duty upon which the whole contract relies. These are the so-called duties to protect third parties, aiming to protect the physical person of the creditor. The legal source of such collateral duties is usually found in the general principle of objective good faith, which is understood as a general rule suitable for integration of the contract (see above sec II.G). Inserting these duties into the contract would cause a 'contractualisation' of damages to the person expanding the reach of the rule for concurrence. This opinion has recently been supported by a ruling of the High Court,[106] according to which the existence of protective interests, even towards third parties, triggers a contractual liability that can be restored as non-pecuniary loss. At present, this argument prevails over the traditional arguments concerning the overlap between contract and tort. Therefore, the theory of concurrence of the two claims has lost its original goals and roots. Within a legal proceeding, the rule of concurring tort and contract liability allows the highest protection for the plaintiff. The plaintiff can choose between them but he can also accumulate the advantages of both.

B. CONCURRENCE/EXCLUSION OF ACTIONS FOR THE PROTECTION AGAINST PERSONAL INJURY AND OF PROPERTY

As argued at no 110, under Italian case law and according to the majority of scholarly opinions, the circumstances leading to concurrence of actions in tort/contract for protection against personal injury are primarily linked to the infringement of the right to life and physical integrity, as well as to labour law cases. 116

In the case of protection of property, the circumstances leading to concurrence are linked to the infringement of an absolute right, such as the right to property. 117

C. CONCURRENCE/EXCLUSION IN THE CASE OF INTERFERENCE WITH CONTRACTUAL RIGHTS

Interference with contractual rights is, in principle, treated under tort law, unless a specific different action (whether in contract or in tort) is available (eg competition law rules). 118

This is also true where a pure economic loss is derived from a personal injury to someone else's employees or to property damage to an entrepreneur. 119

[106] Cass civ, Sez Un, 11 November 2008, nos 26972, 26973, 26974, 26975 (fn 14) para 4.

Since 1971[107] Italian courts have admitted damages in tort also in cases where a third party caused damage to economic interests deriving from a previous contractual relationship. These are situations where a debtor has been injured by a third party thus becoming unable to satisfy the creditors' interests, who consequently suffer economic loss as a result of the breach of the contract. In such situations the creditor can file a claim in tort against the injurer who provoked the damage to her debtor. The very foundation of a broad construction of art 2043 It cc is that the definition of 'unlawful damage' provided by the above quoted provision cannot be limited to identify property rights, or rights to the integrity of the person, or personality rights ('absolute interests'). On the contrary, the definition of 'unlawful damage' also includes rights *in personam*.

V. SPECIFIC SITUATIONS

A. PRE-CONTRACTUAL LIABILITY

120 As extensively explained in sec I.B, pre-contractual liability in the Italian system is recognised by the Civil Code at arts 1337 and 1338, under the general clause of good faith in negotiations. This form of liability has recently been extended by case law even to situations where a contract has been validly concluded, though without properly informed consent so that one party has accepted conditions that he/she would never have accepted. This liability leads to the recovery of damage limited to reliance damage (*interesse negativo*), though there is a great debate on the opportunity of recognising expectation damage in all those instances where a contract has been validly concluded. According to case law and a majority of scholarly opinions, such liability is non-contractual in nature: therefore, the regulation concerning tort liability would apply, in particular as regards the burden of proof (plaintiff has to demonstrate the defendant's negligence) and the limitation period (five years).

B. LIABILITY OF PROFESSIONALS

121 Professional liability (physicians and health care personnel, lawyers, architects and other professionals belonging to regulated professions) is contractual in nature. Therefore, the general rules on contractual negligence apply, with a relevant adaptation to medical malpractice, with the result that the latter is considered as a sub-system within professional liability.[108] Here follow

---

[107] Cass civ, Sez Un, 26 January 1971, no 174 (fn 61).

[108] *De Matteis*, La responsabilità medica. Un sottosistema della responsabilità civile (1995); *id*, La responsabilità medica tra *scientia iuris* e regole di formazione giurisprudenziale (1999)

the relevant special rules on medical malpractice, aiming at facilitating the attribution of liability to the physician and, above all, to the health care facility as the last instance payer:[109]

(a) The burden of proof on the victim of medical malpractice has been relieved by case law: the patient has to provide evidence of the existence of a contractual relationship with the professional, alleging (without providing material evidence) the breach of the contractual obligations by the professional/defendant. It is up to the professional/defendant to discharge the proof by either providing evidence of the non-existence of any contractual relationship, or by demonstrating (by providing material evidence) that his/her behaviour strictly complied with the required professional diligence, and that the event that led to the injury of the patient was due to supervening and extraordinary circumstances.[110]
(b) The Italian Civil Code provides a special liability rule for professional obligations in general, at art 2236. According to this particular provision, debtors of professional obligations that raise special difficulties can be held liable only if the breach of contract was caused through malice or gross negligence. The above-mentioned (apparent) 'limitation of liability' applies only when the professional has 'to solve technical problems of special difficulty' (art 2236 It cc). This means that if the obligation implies a special technical skill/knowledge, the victim has a right to

---

Danno e responsabilità 781; *M Franzoni*, Dalla colpa grave alla responsabilità professionale (2011).

109 The High Court has clearly affirmed the contractual liability of health care facilities since 2008 (Cass civ, Sez Un, 11 January 2008, no 577). According to case law, the relationship between the hospital and the patient is atypical, as the obligations of the former include not only medical care, but also other obligations, such as, to provide an efficient organisation of the services, to provide a healthy and comfortable recovery (*contratto di spedalità*): Cass civ, 8 January 1999, no 103; Cass civ, Sez Un, 1 July 2002, no 9556. The health care facility may be liable in contract notwithstanding that the physician who has provoked an injury to the patient is not held liable (Cass civ, 8 January 1999, no 103). More complicated has always been the qualification of the liability of a physician operating within a health care facility (either public or private). According to the most recent opinions of the High Court, this is a case of 'social contact' between the physician and the patient (see above sec I.B (no 12)): liability springs from the frustration of the patient's reliance in the professional skills of the physician operating within the health care facility: Cass civ, 22 January 1999, no 589; Cass civ, Sez Un, 11 January 2008, no 577.

110 This rule has been established since 2004 (Cass civ, 21 June 2004, no 11488), and it has been confirmed by Cass civ, Sez Un, 11 January 2008, no 577 (2008) Responsabilità civile e previdenza 856 note *M Gorgoni*, Dalla matrice contrattuale della responsabilità nosocomiale e professionale al superamento della distinzione tra obbligazioni di mezzo/di risultato. Please note that this opinion rendered by the Joint Chambers of the High Court superseded the traditional distinction between obligations aiming at a positive satisfaction for the creditor (*obbligazioni di risultato*), and obligations implying the debtor's compliance to standards of professional diligence (*obbligazioni di mezzi*). See also recently: Cass civ, 18 June 2015, no 18307.

recovery, limited to cases of malice and gross negligence. Nevertheless, if – within the same case – the professional infringes the ordinary rules of professionals through trivial negligence, or he/she acts with imprudence, then the ordinary rule of diligence would apply (art 1176 It cc), and he/she would be liable for damages.[111] In medical malpractice cases, evidence of the special difficulty must be provided by the physician; by the same token, the physician shall provide evidence of supervening events that caused the damage to the patient, notwithstanding the special technical knowledge demonstrated by the physician.[112]

122 From the special process concerning liability for medical malpractice, Italy eventually witnessed a shift from the liability of the physician to the liability of the health care facilities.[113] This shift was confirmed by the recent statutory interventions (see below fn 114 and 115) that highlight the health care facility's liability, and provide special measures on risk management.

123 The most recent statutory reform in force at present, dealing with medical health care practice (L 08.03.2017, no 24, '*legge Gelli Bianchi*')[114] has introduced substantial changes in the medical malpractice regime, with the intent of mitigating the burden of proof on professionals, and reducing litigation. Consequently, case law constructions as illustrated above have been dramatically challenged. In particular:

- criminal liability is excluded in cases of trivial negligence, provided that the physician has respected guidelines and good practices imposed by the scientific community *in similar cases* (art 6 *legge Gelli Bianchi*); and
- in any case, notwithstanding the level of negligence and the criminal liability, physicians are liable in tort vis-à-vis patients, while the hospital is liable in contract (art 7 *legge Gelli Bianchi*).

---

111 The leading case defining the regime (especially in terms of burden of proof) of the 'special difficulties' cases is Cass 21 December 1978, no 6141.

112 See fn 110.

113 *G Comandé*, Dalla responsabilità sanitaria al *no-blame* regionale tra conciliazione e risarcimento (2010) Danno responsabilità 977. Arts 1–3 of the *Gelli Bianchi* law deal with prevention of risks and risk management.

114 *M Lovo/L Nocco*, La nuova responsabilità sanitaria (2017); *G Ponzanelli*, 'Medical malpractice': la legge Bianco-Gelli (2017) Contratto e impresa 356; *L Bettiol*, Riforma Gelli-Bianco: il ruolo delle linee guida nel giudizio di responsabilità penale in campo sanitario (2017) 142(6) Il Foro italiano 236; *C Scognamiglio*, Regole di condotta, modelli di responsabilità e risarcimento del danno nella nuova legge sulla responsabilità sanitaria (2017) 34(6) Corriere giuridico 740; *R Pardolesi*, Chi (vince e chi) perde nella riforma della responsabilità sanitaria (2017) 3 Danno e responsabilità 261 ff. Before this statute, a similar reform had been implemented by the L 08.11.2012, no 189 ('legge Balduzzi'): *R De Matteis*, La responsabilità professionale del medico. L'art. 3 del d.l. 158/2012 tra passato e futuro della responsabilità medica (2014) Contratto e impresa 123.

This provision has mitigated the former statutory approach of the *legge Balduzzi* (L 08.11.2012, no 189), as it provides patients with a double cause of action, in tort and in contract, vis-à-vis two different defendants (*concorso improprio*) thus covering all the possible situations without excessively burdening physicians with a contractual liability imposed through a reversal of the burden of proof. The previous law, on the contrary, had tried to cancel over 80 years of case law concerning the contractual nature of medical malpractice, as well as 40 years of case law concerning the distribution of the burden of proof by recognising tortious liability for physicians only. This explains why the former provision was met with severe criticism from scholars[115] and the courts.[116] 124

CASES

CASE 1. THE UNATTRACTIVE SHOPPING MALL

C can bring a claim in tort against D, as the landlord is liable for damage caused by the immovable which is under his/her custody (art 2051 It cc).[117] Whether C can also sue D in contract is, however, controversial. While it is uncontroversial that Z has a right to sue D in contract (see below Case 4), there is no statutory provision or case law affirming the right of the subtenant to sue D in contract, especially if – as in the case at stake – the landlord was not given notice of the sublet. 125

CASE 2. THE IDLE LAWYER

There is no specific statutory provision or case law concerning the case at stake. Strictly speaking, it would not be possible for the daughters to sue D, 126

---

115 *F Cembrani*, La Legge Balduzzi e le pericolose derive di un drafting normativo che (forse) cambia l'ambito alla responsabilità giuridica del professionista della salute (2013) Rivista italiana di medicina legale 799; *M Bona*, La R. C. medica dopo il decreto-legge no 158/2012: indicazioni per la corretta interpretazione e per la (dis)applicazione delle nuove disposizioni, in: F Martini/U Genovese (eds), La valutazione della colpa medica e la sua tutela assicurativa (2012) 29 ff; *M Bona*, La responsabilità medica civile e penale dopo il Decreto Balduzzi (2013).

116 Cass civ, 19 February 2013, no 4030 (2013) Danno e responsabilità 367; Trib Milano, 21 March 2013 (2013) Rivista italiana di medicina legale 1171. According to some first instance courts, the new statutory liability based on tort law would only apply in cases where the professional is employed by the health care facility: Trib Torino, 26 February 2013 (2013) Danno responsabilità 373; Trib Varese, 26 November 2012 (2013) Danno e responsabilità 375. Trib Enna, 18 May 2013 (2014) Danno responsabilità 74: according to the Court, the reform would imply a two-tier regime: contractual liability as regards the health care facility and liability in tort for the physicians employed by the hospital.

117 Cass civ, 13 December 1988, no 6774 (1989) Giustizia civile 896; Cass civ, 27 July 2011, no 16422 (2011) Diritto & Giustizia 282.

neither under the rules concerning general contract law (as there is no privity of contract between the solicitor and the two daughters) or under the general rules of tort law (as there is no unlawful conduct of the professional vis-à-vis the two daughters, who have not yet acquired a right to the father's estate). Nevertheless, the possible solutions to the case at stake are both rooted in a contractual claim.

127 Application of the recent doctrine of 'social contact' (see above at no 12), according to which a contractual obligation may include – besides the fundamental obligation towards the creditor – protective duties due by the debtor towards third parties who are in a 'special relationship' with the creditor. This doctrine has been acknowledged by the High Court in two sets of cases[118] that share with the case at stake the existence of a contract whose protective effects should be extended to third parties/intended beneficiaries (ie the two daughters).

128 Application of the general contract law rules in compliance with the theory of contractual liability that examines – by means of the principle of good faith – the contents of the contract and consequently the extension of the fundamental obligation.[119] From this perspective, the obligation undertaken by a professional towards his/her client may imply an obligation towards an intended beneficiary, who relies on the correct and diligent fulfilment of the obligation and has therefore a right to sue (in contract) the professional in breach of his/her commitment.

CASE 3. THE DEFECTIVE HOUSE

129 The case at stake is governed by the provisions dealing with procurement contracts (art 1655 ff It cc). In particular, art 1669, para 1 provides the solution: if the contract concerns immovable property, the contractor is liable vis-à-vis the principal, *and his/her assignees/successors in title* for the damage caused by building defects (or even by defects due to the characteristic of the ground), provided that C has given notice of the defect (to the contractor D) within one year from discovery. The action for compensation of the damage caused to the house has a limitation period of 10 years from the termination of the building and the acceptance of the principal, although it expires one year after the notice.

[118] The two sets of cases concern: (1) the liability of a doctor on service in a hospital vis-à-vis the patient admitted to the hospital: Cass civ, 20 January 1999, no 589 (1999) Responsabilità civile e previdenza 652; (2) the liability of a teacher on service in a school vis-à-vis a minor student who injured himself: Cass, Sez Un, 27 June 2002, no 9346 (2002) I Foro italiano 2635; recently confirmed by: Cass civ, 10 May 2013, no 11143 (2014) Danno e responsabilità 605.

[119] See *Breccia* (fn 22) 237; *Amato* (fn 73) 216 f.

Because C also suffered personal injuries, he may also claim compensation for the non-pecuniary losses, as the injury affects a fundamental right protected by the Constitution (see no 44, fn 27). 130

The nature of the action provided by art 1669 is not qualified by the Code as either contractual or tortious. In any case, an action in tort (art 2043) would not have any practical advantage for C; it would instead make the burden of proof more demanding for him (see no 21). 131

As concerns the exclusion of liability clause, it should be considered as void, because the injury has in fact violated the public order (see art 1229, para 2, at no 100) in two aspects. First, it caused damage to the physical integrity of C; second, the provision itself in art 1669 is considered by the High Court[120] as mandatory. 132

The rationale is that immovables have a long-lasting nature; therefore their preservation and functionality must be considered as a matter of public order, and the contractor is strictly liable not only with respect to the contractual partner, but also with respect to his/her assignees/successors in title. 133

CASE 4. APARTMENT IN FLAMES

C can bring a claim in damages against D, who is liable in contract under arts 1575, lit 2), 1576 and 1577 It cc, according to which the landlord has a duty to maintain the immovable in a good state (arts 1575, lit 2), and 1576),[121] and a duty to repair the immovable (art 1577). C can concurrently bring a claim in tort, under art 2051 It cc (affirming the liability of the person who has the custody of a movable item or immovable) and art 2053 It cc (affirming the liability of the landlord in cases where the immovable is destroyed). The latter rule can also be applied to cases where the person injured by the thing in custody or by the immovable is the tenant.[122] What is relevant in order for both actions to succeed is that the tenant has to prove that, notwithstanding the contract of lease, the landlord maintained a power of control over the immovable, and that the tenant gave the landlord prompt notice of the danger.[123] 134

120 Cass civ, 12 December 1987, no 9635.

121 See recently: Cass civ, 22 May 2014, no 11353.

122 Cass civ, 13 December 1988, no 6774 (1989) Giustizia civile 896; Cass civ, 27 July 2011, no 16422 (2011) Diritto & Giustizia 282.

123 See Cass civ, 30 March 2001, no 4737 (2001) I Rivista giuridica dell'edilizia 827: where the action is filed in tort, the landlord held liable has a right of recourse against the tenant who did not promptly inform the landlord of the imminent danger; Cass civ, 11 July 1995, no 7578 (1995) Giustizia civile Massimario 1354 side structures of the immovable are under the tenant's control, and therefore under his/her responsibility. On the definition of control over

135 The statutory references are arts 1576, 1577, 2051 and 2053 It cc.

136 The rationale is that art 1576 (Maintenance of the immovable in a good state) and art 1577 (Occurrence of repairs) refers to the contractual duties of landlords and tenants as regards the rented immovable. The landlord has to diligently maintain the immovable property in a sound condition by repairing it, provided that the tenant has given him/her prompt notice of the dangers deriving from the deterioration. Minor maintenance work, for which only the tenant is liable, is excluded. Statutory law clearly describes the obligations of landlords and their liabilities in contract: the action in tort is therefore subsidiary and concurrent.

137 Notwithstanding that statutory law provides a contractual cause of action to tenants, the majority of claims are filed under tort law, and therefore art 2051 (Damage caused by goods under the keeper's custody) or art 2053 It cc (Deterioration of real property) would more frequently apply. This is probably due to long-standing case law that has held keepers of immovables directly liable under a reversal of the burden of the proof or under a strict liability basis, without any consideration of the respective positions of landlord and tenant, or to their contractual duties. Moreover, a claim in tort also provides the tenant/plaintiff with the possibility to recover compensation for non-economic damage.

CASE 5. INJURED SKIER

138 C can bring a claim in tort (art 2043 It cc) against the owner of the ski resort (D1): the insurance company (D2) will therefore honour its contractual obligations towards D1. Both D1 and D2 can be sued by C. According to a recent decision of the Italian High Court, the personal injury suffered by the skier can be classified as non-economic loss, which can be fully restored where fundamental rights (like health) protected by the Italian Constitution have been infringed. A homogeneous definition of non-economic loss has in fact been adopted by the Italian High Court, regulated by the law of tort (art 2059 It cc) but applicable to any non-economic damage, regardless of the source of the obligation (cf above fn 14).

---

the landlord, and on the apportionment of liability between landlord and tenant according to the distinction between finishing work (under the landlord's control) and side structures (under the tenant's control), see the leading case: Cass civ, Sez Un, 11 November 1991, no 12019 (1993) I Foro italiano 922 (the branch of a tree fell on a member of an association whose registered seat was located on a property owned by the local municipality and rented to the association: according to the Italian High Court, a tree is a 'side structure' whose maintenance is to be executed by tenants).

The statutory reference is art 2059 It cc. 139

As regards the rationale, this is a controversial case, as it involves an unwritten rule. The alternative or cumulative actions rule (*concorso proprio*)[124] adopted by Italian courts and consisting in allowing the plaintiff to choose between a claim in contract or in tort (alternative), or in submitting to courts both claims (cumulative actions), whereas the choice or aggregation would depend on which of the two actions can be considered as more convenient to the plaintiff. Such a choice has traditionally been recognised by Italian courts when one person is under an obligation to protect a counterpart from personal injury.[125] This may happen when – as in the case here – there is both a contractual obligation to protect the party and a legal duty in tort (art 2043 It cc). Because the fact that the injured plaintiff can choose is not supported by convincing legal arguments, and following the enlargement of the notion of non-economic loss, the Italian High Court has coherently declared the opportunity of abandoning this unwritten rule in favour of a general claim in tort.[126] 140

In terms of the case law, notwithstanding the arguments provided recently by the Italian High Court against alternative and cumulative claims, some courts still admit the alternative/cumulative actions' unwritten rule, or they dismiss the rule in favour of a contractual claim. 141

In a case in the area of labour injuries, a teacher was injured to such an extent that she died on the premises of the kindergarten where she was on duty.[127] The Italian High Court recognised the liability of the local authority under both claims in contract (art 2087: liability of employers for breach of contractual obligations to protect physical and mental distress of his/her employees) and in tort (art 7 L no 444/1968, establishing a legal duty to take care of the immovable 142

124 It must be distinguished from *concorso improprio* occurring in cases where damage deriving from the same injury can be claimed against two different defendants. In such cases, damages shall ultimately only be awarded in one case (contract) or the other (tort): it give plaintiffs a double path to damages, it does not duplicate damages.

125 Cass civ, 25 September 2002, no 13942 (2003) Giustizia civile 2034; Cass civ, 20 June 2001, no 8381 (2002) Giustizia civile 2204 note *AV Doronzo*, Sulla responsabilità del datore di lavoro ex art. 2049 c.c.; Cass civ, 2 March 1982, no 1295 (1982) Giustizia civile Massimario fascicolo 3; Cass civ, 2 May 1981, no 2654 (1981) Giustizia civile Massimario fascicolo 5; Cass civ, 5 January 1980, no 28 (1980) I Giurisprudenza italiana 1599. In the area of transportation: Cass civ, 24 May 1993, no 5831; Cass civ, 20 April 1989, no 1855 (1990) I Foro italiano 1970; also in (1990) I Nuova giurisprudenza civile commentata 424; App Napoli, 26 February 1990. In the area of medical malpractice, see recently: Cass civ, 23 June 1994, no 6064 (1995) I Foro italiano 202. In the area of labour law: Cass civ, 14 May 1987, no 4441 (1987) I Giustizia civile 1631.

126 Cf fn 14. Before the famous decision quoted above, when a title does exist, most scholars would insist on abandoning the unwritten rule of alternative/cumulative actions in favour of a claim in contract: *Breccia* (fn 22) 665, 676; *C Castronovo*, Le due specie della responsabilità civile e il problema del concorso (2008) Europa e diritto privato 81.

127 Cass civ 27 June 2011, no 14107.

where the kindergarten is located). In a set of cases the Italian High Court instead chose the contractual action only.[128]

CASE 6. EXPLODING CAR

143 C can sue D2 in tort under art 2043 It cc, affirming a general principle of *neminem laedere* based on fault, and aiming to protect property rights (the destruction of the car in this case). C can also claim damages from D1 in contract under art 1494 It cc, according to which – setting aside the provisions concerning warranties – the seller is liable vis-à-vis the purchaser within the ordinary time limits (10 years), provided that the former has recognised the defect, and/or he/she has not succeeded in excluding his/her fault in ignoring the defect.

144 According to art 123, para 1, lit b) Consumer Code, implementing Directive 1985/374/EC of 25 July 1985 on Product Liability, C has no cause of action against the producer pursuant to this Directive and based on strict liability, as only the product (car) itself was damaged.

145 On the other hand, a warranty claim would fail either under arts 128–135 Consumer Code, implementing Directive 1999/44/EU,[129] or under arts 1490 ff It cc, dealing with the general regime of contractual warranties in the sale of goods. As concerns arts 128–135 Consumer Code, the two-year warranty of conformity with the contract has already expired (art 132, para 1 It Consumer Code), as it starts to run from delivery of the good: therefore, C cannot sue D1 under the special regime. As regards the general regime of sale of goods in the Italian Civil Code, the warranties for defects (art 1490 It cc) or for lack of a fundamental characteristic of the good (art 1497 It cc) are both subject to the draconian limitation period of one year from the time of delivery (provided that the purchaser has informed the seller of the defect or of a lack of the fundamental characteristic after eight days from the time of the discovery): art 1495, para 3 It cc.

CASE 7. RACING BOAT BURNING

146 C can sue D in tort under art 2043 It cc, provided that he can give evidence of D's fault. As in the previous case, C can also claim damages from D in contract

[128] Cass civ 23 April 2009, no 9689; Cass civ 17 February 2009, no 3788; Cass civ 17 February 2009, no 3786; Cass civ 15 December 2008, no 29323; Cass civ 13 August 2008, no 21590; Cass civ 23 April 2008, no 10529.

[129] Directive 1999/44/EU has been modified by Directive 2011/83/EU and implemented into Italian law by d lgs 24.02.2014, no 21 (thus modifying several provisions of the Consumer Code).

under art 1494 It cc, setting aside the provision on warranties: the seller is liable vis-à-vis the purchaser for damage within the ordinary time limits (10 years), provided that the former has recognised the defect and/or he/she has not succeeded in excluding his/her fault in ignoring the defect.

As in the previous case, the action in tort is possible according to Italian law because the plaintiff suffered damage to property. He can claim the value of the destroyed boat at the time of the fire. 147

The very nature of the good (a boat) also admits a claim to recover the costs of repatriation, though it may be arguable that the airplane is the only possible way to be repatriated, pursuant to the doctrine of mitigation of damage. 148

For the same reasons explained under the previous case (time limits), a warranty claim would fail under art 1490 ff It cc, dealing with the general regime of contractual warranties in the sale of goods. 149

CASE 8. INSIDIOUS REPORT

C can sue D in tort for unfair competition. According to art 2598, para 1 (3) It cc D has caused economic damage to Z through conduct contrary to good faith. As D acted fraudulently (art 2600, para 1), C can claim damages at art 2600 It cc, and in compliance with the criteria set out in d lgs 19.03.2017, no 3, implementing Directive 2014/104/EU. C can also claim the publication of the decision (art 2600, para 2 It cc), as well as an injunction before the ordinary trial, together with restitutionary remedies (art 2599 It cc). C can also sue D for breach of contract, as the latter violated a general duty of trust (art 2105 It cc). 150

CASE 9. CIRCULAR LETTER

As in the previous case, C can file a claim against D under arts 2598, para 1 (3), 2599 and 2600 It cc for unfair competition. D may also be held liable of the criminal offences of slander (honour and defamation: arts 594, 595 It Criminal Code). 151

CASE 10. SHORTAGE OF SUPPLY

Special legislation deals with abuse of a dominant position in the supply of goods/service contracts: L 18.06.1998, no 192, art 9, defines the abuse of a dominant position as a 'situation where one business is able to determine – within a contractual relationship with another business – an excessive imbalance 152 in the parties' rights and obligations. The economically dominant position shall be estimated also by taking into account the actual possibilities of the business which claims the abuse of a dominant position to enter the market with alternative goods. The situation described by the law applies to the case at stake: the contractual term determining a 20% increase in prices may therefore be considered as void' (art 9, para 3). Consequently, the previous terms of the original contract shall be restored. As regards payments, the Italian law quoted above assumes that the buyer is in a dominant position vis-à-vis the supplier. Therefore, art 3 imposes maximum payment terms that cannot be applied to this case. In the present case, because the supplier D is in a dominant position vis-à-vis C, the contractual terms concerning early payments can be considered as void (see art 9, para 3) under art 9, para 2 ('The abuse may also consist in the refusal to sell or the refusal to buy, in the imposition of contractual conditions unduly burdensome or discriminatory, or in the arbitrary interruption of an ongoing trade relationship').

153 Moreover, C can sue D alleging the infringement of competition law rules, that is an abuse of a dominant position (see art 102 of TFEU; art 3 L 10.10.1990, no 287; art 2598, para 1 (3) It cc). In particular, C can either trigger public enforcement rules and/or seek compensation under private enforcement rules. Through the first claim, C can ask the Italian Autorità Garante per la Concorrenza e del Mercato (AGCM) to order D to cease the unlawful conduct and/or to impose a fine. Through the second claim, C can obtain an injunction the aim of which is cessation of D's conduct (art 2599 It cc), as well as damages in the case of intentional conduct (see art 2600 It cc, and d lgs 19.03.2017, no 3, implementing Directive 2014/104/EU).

154 The statutory references are art 9 L 18.06.1998, no 192; art 3, para 1 (a) L 10.10.1990, no 287; arts 2598, para 1 (3), 2599 and 2600 It cc; d lgs 19.03.2017, no 3.

CASE 11. INJURED ROCK STAR

155 C has a cause of action against D in tort under art 2043 It cc. This case clearly describes a situation where a debtor has been injured by a third party, thus becoming unable to satisfy the creditor's interests, who consequently suffers economic loss from the breach of the contract. The case that has introduced a broader construction of the notion of *danno ingiusto* in art 2043 It cc was decided in 1971 (the *Meroni* case) and was subsequently confirmed by several decisions (see above at no 64, fn 61). Since this decision, the expression *danno ingiusto* has been extended not only to the violation of rights *in rem* (property rights, personal rights, such as health and personality) but to rights *in personam* as well (*diritti relativi*, or *diritti di credito*), thus including (pure) economic loss

deriving from the breach of a contract due to a tort committed by a third person against the debtor, provided that the creditor can give evidence of causation and of the damage suffered. In particular, in the *Meroni* case, although the principle admitting the recovery of economic loss was stated, a strict test concerning causation is required. In particular: obligations consisting of an interchangeable transfer of goods (*prestazioni di dare*) cannot be considered as a direct and immediate consequence of the tortious event; on the contrary, fundamental and personal obligations (*obbligazioni di fare*) can be considered as a direct and immediate consequence of the tortious event, provided that the debtor's commitment is strictly personal, founded on personal trust and personal sills (reputation, technical skills, professional abilities). The relativity of such a personal obligation lies in the fact that the creditor can possibly obtain the same service/product in the market from another person for the same price: if this is the case, causation cannot be assessed. This important decision overruled a previous and opposite view of the Italian High Court, which, in a very similar case, had rejected the argument of the creditor (a soccer society) who, under art 2043 It cc, sued a third party (an aircraft company) for the economic damage deriving from an airplane accident that led to the death of the entire soccer team (the so-called *Superga* case).[130] At that time, a pure economic loss classified as right *in personam* was not considered as embraced by the definition of 'unlawful damage' of art 2043 It cc. From the information we have in the case at stake, we may infer that the injury provoked by D to the rock star X can be considered as direct and immediate damage to C, provided that the latter can demonstrate that he had to cancel the concert because he could not have replaced X with any other rock star for a similar price.

CASE 12. EQUIPMENT DESTROYED

If the accident is entirely caused by D2, and no contributory negligence can 156
be attributed to D1, the contractual action of C vis-à-vis D1 would be defeated by the doctrine of impossibility of performance (art 1463 It cc). Nevertheless, the concurrence of an action in tort has been established by the High Court in the *Meroni* case (see Case 11). Therefore, C has a cause of action in tort against D2, provided that C is able to pass the strict test on causation and direct damage. While damages concerning the destruction of the equipment can be considered as direct damages (to be paid to the owner), in the case at stake it is doubtful that C may recover damages for the cancelled concert, unless he is able to demonstrate that he cannot replace the equipment for the same price.

[130] Cass civ, Sez III, 4 July 1953, no 2085.

CASE 13. SLIPPING ON A LETTUCE LEAF

157 C can sue D in tort under art 2051 It cc (Damage caused by goods under the keeper's custody). This provision applies to situations where inactive things cause damage within premises. It is a rule of the law of tort that does not adopt the traditional imputation of liability based on fault or fraud (art 2043 It cc). Recently, a stream of case law,[131] supported by the opinion of some scholars,[132] considered the liability imposed on the good's keeper as strict.

158 Therefore, C has to prove that the damage was caused by the lettuce leaf lying on the floor of the grocery shop, subject to D's custody, while evidence of unknown events must be provided by D, which is definitely difficult to prove in the case at stake.

159 No actions as regards contractual or pre-contractual liability can be taken, as respectively:

- no contract has been concluded. In any case, it can hardly be argued that, under a contract for the sale of goods, protective obligations can extend to personal damage suffered after the creditors' interests have already been satisfied; and
- pre-contractual liability is limited to damage affecting the protected interests of (both) perspective parties to a contract, that is relying on the counterparty's fair dealing concerning the sale of goods.

CASE 14. TEST DRIVE

160 C can sue D in tort under art 2054, para 1 It cc, which holds a car driver (and in general the driver of a vehicle) strictly liable in the case of damage to persons and/or things (the tree, if damaged), unless he proves that the car crash occurred notwithstanding his utmost diligence.

161 No action under pre-contractual liability can be taken, as explained in Case 13.

---

[131] Cass civ, 10 December 2012, no 22384 (2013) Responsabilità civile e previdenza 1532; Cass civ, 24 February 2011 no 4476 (2011) Foro italiano, Repertorio 2011, voce Responsabilità civile, no 124; Cass civ, 19 May 2011, no 11016, ibid, no 147; Cass civ, 24 February 2011, no 4484 (2011) Foro italiano I 1082; Cass civ, 6 July 2006, no 15384 (2006) I ibid 2006 3358. The leading cases were: Cass civ, Sez Un, 11 November 1991, no 12019 (1992) I Giurisprudenza italiana 2218 note *E Corradi*, La custodia di cose quale criterio di imputazione della responsabilità ex art 2051 c.c. nel quadro del rapporto di locazione; Cass civ, 20 May 1998, no 5031 (1998) Danno e responsabilità 1101 note *P Laghezza*, Responsabilità oggettiva e danni da cose in custodia.
See among several first instance holdings: Trib Rovereto, 13 January 2010 (2010) Danno e responsabilità 412; Trib Siracusa, 31 October 2010 (2011) Danno e responsabilità 508.

[132] *Monateri* (fn 89) 1033 ff; *Franzoni* (fn 74) 545 ff.

CASE 15. BREAKING OFF NEGOTIATIONS

C can sue D under art 1337 It cc, affirming a legal duty to act in good faith during negotiations and before the formation of a contract. 162

In particular, C can argue that D implicitly accepted to refuse parallel negotiations by accepting C's proposal to continue negotiations the next Friday, after C's return from his business trip. 163

Nevertheless, this is a controversial case: breach of negotiations, in fact, is a situation where Italian courts have the difficult task of balancing two opposing interests, equally protected by the law of obligations, that is: freedom of contract and reliance on fair dealing. Therefore, in a free-market economy, what is relevant is not withdrawal from negotiations, but a withdrawal without cause and with the conscious (though not necessarily malicious) attitude of one party who has already started parallel negotiations.[133] 164

In the case at stake, should the courts recognise D's bad faith in the withdrawal from negotiations, C may obtain reliance damages. According to case law, reliance damages (*interesse negativo*) correspond either to the minor advantage or to the highest detriment (including loss of profits) suffered by the innocent party.[134] 165

---

133 Cass civ, 25 February 1992, no 2335 (1993) I Foro padano 149; Cass civ, 6 March 1992, no 2704 (1993) I Giurisprudenza italiana 1560; Cass civ, 30 August 1995, no 9157 (1995) Giustizia civile Massimario 1568; Cass civ, 13 March 1996, no 2057 (1996) I Foro italiano 2065; Cass civ, 27 October 2006, no 23289 (2006) Giustizia civile Massimario 10; Cass civ, 14 February 2000, no 1632 (2000) Giurisprudenza italiana 2250 note *A Musy*, Comportamenti affidanti e valutazione del danno risarcibile; (2000) Danno e responsabilità 982 note *P Maninetti*, Responsabilità precontrattuale e risarcimento dei danni: verso una concezione sempre più estensiva; Cass civ, 10 June 2005, no 12313 (2006) I Nuova giurisprudenza civile commentata 349 note *R Morese*, La responsabilità precontrattuale della pubblica amministrazione per recesso ingiustificato da trattative con privato e risarcimento del danno; Cass civ, 5 August 2004, no 15040 (2005) Danno e responsabilità 599 ff note *P Pardolesi*, Recesso nelle trattative: un esercizio di *comparative law and economics*. Cf *G Meruzzi*, La trattativa maliziosa (2002) 266 ff; Cass civ, 16 January 2013, no 1000 (2013) Giustizia civile Massimario; Cass civ, Sez Un, ord 19 October 2012, no 18092 (2012) 22 ottobre Diritto e giustizia online; Cass civ, 20 March 2012, no 4382 (2012) Danno e responsabilità 1103 ff note *V Montani*, Responsabilità precontrattuale e abbandono ingiustificato delle trattative: un rapporto da *genus* a *species*; Cass civ, Sez Un, ord 27 February 2012, no 2926 (2012) Guida diritto 45; Cass civ, 10 August 2012, no 14400 (2013) II Giurisprudenza commerciale 202 note *FM Mucciarelli*, Il risarcimento del danno per mancata proposizione dell'Opa obbligatoria: l'epilogo del caso Sai/Fondiaria?

134 Cass civ, Sez Un, 19 December 2007, no 26725 (2008) Giustizia civile 2785 note *T Febbrajo*, Violazione delle regole di comportamento nell'intermediazione finanziaria e nullità del contratto: la decisione delle Sezioni Unite; Cass civ, 29 September 2005, no 19024 (2006) Responsabilità civile e previdenza 1087 note *F Greco*, Difetto di accordo e nullità dell'intermediazione finanziaria; cf *A Luminoso*, La lesione dell'interesse contrattuale negativo (e dell'interesse positivo) nella responsabilità civile (1988) Contratto

CASE 16. NON-DISCLOSURE OF RELEVANT FACTS

166 C can sue D, provided that he can provide evidence of D's knowledge of C's needs:

(a) Under pre-contractual liability (art 1337 It cc): violation of the duty to disclose, as part of the duty to act in good faith during the formation of the contract (see Case 15). The Italian High Court has in fact stated that reliance damages can be awarded under pre-contractual liability even though a contract has been entered into.[135]
(b) Under contract law, as a fraudulent omission to inform of facts relevant to the conclusion of the contract (C would not have bought the type X, but a completely different type of machine, if one existed on the market) (art 1439, para 1 It cc (reticenza dolosa)): according to this provision, C may claim the invalidity of the contract (annullamento) that will eventually be terminated, restitutionary remedies would be triggered, and expectation damages awarded to C.
(c) Under contract law (art 1497 It cc): breach of a warranty of quality implied by the law. In this case, C can ask for the termination of the contract and expectation damages, provided that the lack of quality exceeds the sustainability in compliance with customs, and that C informed the seller of the lack of quality within eight days from the discovery of the defect, and the action is taken within one year from discovery (art 1495 It cc).

e impresa 792; *P Gallo*, Responsabilità precontrattuale: il quantum (2004) I Rivista di diritto civile 487; *C Turco*, L'interesse negativo nella *culpa in contrahendo* (verità e distorsioni della teoria di Jhering nel sistema tedesco e italiano) (2007) II Rivista di diritto civile 165 ff; *D'Amico* (fn 2) 122 ff.

135 Cass civ, 8 October 2008, no 24795; Cass, Sez Un, 19 December 2007, no 26725 (fn 3).

THE BORDERLINES OF TORT LAW IN THE NETHERLANDS

Anne LM Keirse*

QUESTIONS

I. Tracing the Borderlines ... 333
A. Distinction between Tort and Contract ... 333
1) Contractual Norms and Consequent Liability ... 334
2) Tortious Norms and Consequent Liability ... 334
B. Existence of a 'Grey Zone'? ... 335
1) Reasonableness and Fairness ... 335
2) Pre-Contractual Liability ... 336
3) Unfair Business Practices ... 336
4) Fading Borders ... 336
C. Common or Different Rules Regulating Tort and Contract ... 337
1) Damages and Attribution ... 337
2) Obligations as Assets ... 337
D. Application of Common Rules in a Different Way ... 337
II. Main Differences between Tortious and Contractual Liability ... 338
A. Differences as Regards the Foundations of Liability ... 338
1) Role of Intention ... 339
2) Role of Wrongfulness and Fault and their Variations ... 342
3) Role of Strict Liability ... 343
B. Differences as Regards Causation ... 343
C. Differences as Regards Remedies ... 344
1) Degree of Certainty of the Damage ... 345
2) Compensation for Non-Pecuniary Loss ... 345
3) Compensation for Loss of Earnings and for Loss of Chance ... 346
4) Restitutionary Damages ... 346

* The author thanks Thijmen Nuninga, a student research assistant at the time, for his enormous work, without whom this contribution would not have seen the light of day.

5) Aggravated and Exemplary (or Punitive) Damages. 346
6) Other Remedies. 347
D. Differences as Regards 'Pure Economic Losses'. 347
E. Differences as Regards Liability for Others. 348
F. Differences as Regards Liability in the Case of Multiple Tortfeasors/Breaching Parties. 348
G. Differences as Regards the Persons Who May be Protected. 348
H. Differences as Regards Defences 349
I. Differences as Regards Limitation Periods 349
J. Differences as Regards Proof 350
K. Other Differences 350
L. Reasons for the Differences. 351
III. Limitation or Exclusion of Liability Arising from Tort and from Contract 351
A. Statutory Provisions Authorising a Limitation or Exclusion of Liability 351
1) Statutory Limitation 351
2) Judicial Limitation 352
B. Limitation or Exclusion of Contractual and Tortious Liability by Contract 352
1) Exclusion or Limitation of Liability Contained in the Contract 352
2) Exclusion or Limitation of Liability Contained in Standard Terms and Conditions 353
3) Extent of Exclusion 353
4) Third Party. 353
a) Exclusion Clauses Formulated by a Superior 353
b) Exclusion Clauses Formulated for the Benefit of a Third Party 354
c) Exclusion Clauses Invoked against Third Parties 354
IV. Non-Concurrence or Concurrence of Actions. 355
A. Overview 355
1) Areas of Overlap between Tort and Contract. 355
2) Approach to Non-Concurrence and Concurrence of Actions . . . 357
B. Concurrence/Exclusion of Actions for the Protection against Personal Injury 358
C. Concurrence/Exclusion of Actions for the Protection of Property. . . 358
D. Concurrence/Exclusion in the Case of Interference with Contractual Rights. 359
1) Interference with a Contractual Relationship. 359
2) Loss of Business due to Personal Injury to Someone Else's Employees or Clients or to or Property Damage to the Entrepreneur. 360

V. Specific Situations 361
A. Pre-Contractual Liability 361
1) Reasonableness and Fairness 361
2) Pre-Contractual Liability for Failing to Inform Properly 361
3) Pre-Contractual Liability for Breaking off Negotiations 362
B. Liability of Professionals 363
1) Basis of Liability 363
2) Content of Contractual Duty of Care 363
3) Third Parties 365
4) Exclusion Clauses 365

CASES

Case 1. The Unattractive Shopping Mall 366
Case 2. The Idle Lawyer 367
Case 3. The Defective House 368
Case 4. Apartment in Flames 369
Case 5. Injured Skier 370
Case 6. Exploding Car 371
Case 7. Racing Boat Burning 372
Case 8. Insidious Report 372
Case 9. Circular Letter 373
Case 10. Shortage of Supply 374
Case 11. Injured Rock Star 375
Case 12. Equipment Destroyed 376
Case 13. Slipping on a Lettuce Leaf 377
Case 14. Test Drive 378
Case 15. Breach of Negotiations 378
Case 16. Non-Disclosure of Relevant Facts 380

QUESTIONS

I. TRACING THE BORDERLINES

A. DISTINCTION BETWEEN TORT AND CONTRACT

The main reason for distinguishing between contract and tort lies with a person's will or intention to be bound by the norm at issue. In the standard situation, contractual liability only arises if a party breaches a norm that she previously agreed to act in accordance with.[1] Tortious liability, 1

[1] Articles 3:31, 6:213 and 6:74 Dutch CC.

on the other hand, arises if a person breaches a norm that is imposed upon that party by operation of law.

1) *Contractual Norms and Consequent Liability*

2 The importance of the concept 'will' (or 'intention) in contract law can, for instance, be seen in the following basic rules of Dutch contract law. First, a contract is concluded if there is a 'concurrence of wills or intentions.'[2] Normally, this occurs when an offer is met by acceptance,[3] but even if offer and acceptance cannot be unequivocally identified, a court may hold that a contract has been concluded if there is sufficient evidence that the parties' wills or intentions concurred.[4] Secondly, most – although not all[5] – contractual rules allowing for (partial) avoidance of the contract relate to some defect in one party's will or both parties' wills.[6] There are some instances in which contracts create obligations other than those envisaged by the parties – for instance, requirements by mandatory law, customary law and/or reasonableness and fairness[7] – but at its core, the law of contract is based on the idea that parties are only bound by the obligations they have assumed willingly.

2) *Tortious Norms and Consequent Liability*

3 Tortious liability is generally based on art 6:162 of the Dutch Civil Code (Dutch CC) or one of the specific torts.[8] In establishing liability under art 6:162 Dutch CC or one of the specific torts, the tortfeasor's will or intention to be bound by that norm (or: duty of care) is irrelevant.[9] This does not mean that the concepts of good faith, intent or fault have no application in Dutch tort law. Indeed these concepts are often an essential part of establishing liability. However, the will or intention of the tortfeasor to be bound by the norm is

2 Articles 6:217, 6:218 and 3:32 ff Dutch CC.

3 Article 6:217 Dutch CC.

4 Cf Asser/Hartkamp & Sieburgh 6-III 2014/189 f.

5 Some obligations are void or voidable for incompatibility with mandatory law, morality, public order (art 3:40 Dutch CC) or for being detrimental to third parties where this was known or should have been known (art 3:45 Dutch CC).

6 Examples include: mistake (art 6:228 Dutch CC), threat, fraud, or abuse of circumstance (art 3:44 Dutch CC) mental incapacity (art 3:34 Dutch CC), or any other case in which will and declaration do not coincide (art 3:33 Dutch CC).

7 Articles 6:2 and 6:248 Dutch CC.

8 Including: liability for persons and things/property (sec 6.3.2 Dutch CC), product liability (sec 6.3.4 Dutch CC), patent infringement (arts 53 and 70 of the Dutch Patent Act), traffic liability (art 185 Roads and Traffic Act 1994), etc.

9 Cf *J Spier et al*, Verbintenissen uit de wet en schadevergoeding (2015) 3.

irrelevant for the existence of the tortious duty: it arises by operation of law. This is the primary distinction between Dutch tort law and contract law.

B. EXISTENCE OF A 'GREY ZONE'?

1) Reasonableness and Fairness

4 The norms of reasonableness and fairness that govern the contract and the surrounding relationship of the parties are of a dubitable nature. These norms can create obligations for the parties both before and after the contract has been concluded.[10] The central provisions are:

> Article 6:2 Dutch CC:
>
> '1. The creditor and debtor must act towards each other in accordance with the standards of reasonableness and fairness.
> 2. A rule in force between a creditor and his debtor by virtue of law, common practice or a juridical act does not apply as far as this would be unacceptable, in the circumstances, by standards of reasonableness and fairness.'
>
> Article 6:248 Dutch CC:
>
> '1. A contract not only has the legal effects which parties have agreed upon, but also those which, according to the nature of the agreement, arise from law, usage (common practice) or the standards of reasonableness and fairness.
> 2. A rule, to be observed by parties as a result of their agreement, is not applicable insofar as this, given the circumstances, would be unacceptable to standards of reasonableness and fairness.'

5 Both rules allow for the creation of obligations that the parties did not agree upon. This can either be by derogating from the agreement for incompatibility (arts 6:2(2) and 6:248(2) Dutch CC) or by implying terms that are necessary for the contract to operate (arts 6:2(1) and 6:248(1) Dutch CC). Thus, obligations are imposed by external normative rules, which are highly similar to tortious duties. In general, this is not considered to be a 'grey zone' per se, but it must be submitted that this is an important derogation from the central idea that the parties' wills are the sole determinant in contract law.[11]

---

[10] Dutch Supreme Court (DSC) 15 November 1957, Nederlandse Jurisprudentie (NJ) 1958, 67 (*Baris/Riezenkamp*).

[11] Note that this is not a rule on interpretation. Interpretation is generally governed by the idea that a contract must be given the meaning that the parties could, given the circumstance, objectively give to the contract (see DSC 13 March 1981, NJ 1981/635 (*Ermes/Haviltex*)).

2) *Pre-Contractual Liability*

6 The Dutch judiciary has established an extensive practice of pre-contractual liability. It has done so for discontinuance of negotiations,[12] and for a failure to inform or for incorrectly informing the other party about certain essential facts.[13] The precise circumstances under which such liability arises will be discussed in sec V below, but it can be noted here that there is disagreement amongst scholars as to whether this liability is contractual or tortious in nature. In sec V below it will be argued that the safest assumption is that this liability is tortious in nature. Nevertheless, as disagreement amongst scholars remains, these rules inevitably operate in a grey zone.

3) *Unfair Business Practices*

7 In the specific situation where a professional trader supplies misleading information to a consumer (or misleadingly or unfairly fails to do so), liability will be based on sec 6.3.3A Dutch CC on unfair business practices.[14] This liability is without doubt tortious in nature. If, however, for any reason such liability is not within this section,[15] liability is established in the aforementioned grey zone.

4) *Fading Borders*

8 In some specific situations, mandatory contractual and tortious duties of care are identical. For instance, in the seminal wrongful birth case *Baby Kelly*, the liability towards the mother (contractual) and towards the father and the child (tortious) was based on the identical standard of care.[16] Similarly, the standard of care to be observed by schools towards their pupils is identical, regardless of whether it is based on contract or tort.[17] It is submitted that such a convergence could imply the development of a more situation-based approach in which the factual or social situation is more important than the distinction between tort and contract.

---

12 DSC 18 June 1983, NJ 1983/723 (*Plas/Valburg*); DSC 23 October 1987, NJ 1988/1017 (*VSH/Shell*); DSC 14 June 1996, NJ 1997/481 (*MBO/De Ruiterij*); DSC 4 October 1996, NJ 1997/65 (*ABB/Staat*); DSC 12 August 2005, NJ 2005/467 (*CBB/JPO*); DSC 9 December 2011, NJ 2013/273 (*X/Y*); DSC 3 May 2013, NJ 2013/572 (*KLM (private procurement)*).

13 Cf DSC 2 April 1993, NJ 1995/94 (*Cattier/Waanders*); DSC 25 January 2002, NJ 2003/31 (*Paalman/Lampenier*); DSC 5 June 2009, NJ 2012/182 (*Dexio*); DSC 5 June 2009, NJ 2012/184 (*Aegon*); DSC 5 June 2009, NJ 2012/183 (*Levob Bank*).

14 Articles 6:193a–193c Dutch CC.

15 Eg for not being between trader and consumer or for not qualifying as 'unfair'.

16 See the application of art 7:453 in DSC 18 March 2005, NJ 2006/606 (*Baby Kelly*).

17 *BM Paijmans*, De zorgplicht van scholen (diss 2013).

C. COMMON OR DIFFERENT RULES REGULATING TORT AND CONTRACT

1) *Damages and Attribution*

The rules on damages arising from both contractual and tortious liability are governed by sec 6.1.10 Dutch CC. The application of sec 6.1.10 to contractual liability can be excluded by contract. The application of art 6:96(4) Dutch CC (rules on damages for extra-judicial costs in obtaining damages) and art 6:109(1) Dutch CC (moderation of damages by the judge) cannot be excluded by contract. Section 6.1.10 Dutch CC does not apply to penalties, pre-determined liability, and other initial contractual obligations to pay damages (ie obligations that are not the result of a breach of contract). 9

Section 6.1.10 Dutch CC is not the only part of Dutch private law that has an impact on when and how damages can be claimed. For instance, art 7:21 Dutch CC provides, in the context of consumer sales, that in the case of non-delivery or non-compliance, the professional supplying or failing to supply the product must first be given the chance to (i) deliver the missing product, (ii) repair the non-compliant product, or (iii) replace it, before the consumer can claim damages. Once damages are claimed, secs 6.1.9 and 6.1.10 Dutch CC apply.[18] Another example is art 7:658 Dutch CC on an employer's duty to provide a safe working space. This liability cannot be reduced by contributory negligence as provided for in art 6:101 Dutch CC.[19] 10

2) *Obligations as Assets*

The status of contractual claims (arising from the contract or from the breach of the contract) and tortious claims as 'assets' is governed by Book 3 (titles 1–9) of the Dutch CC. Rules relating to specific performance of both contractual and tortious claims are found in arts 3:296–3:300 Dutch CC. Rules on limitation of both contractual and tortious liability are found in art 3:310 Dutch CC (although there are some specific rules). 11

D. APPLICATION OF COMMON RULES IN A DIFFERENT WAY

It has been argued that, although sec 6.1.10 Dutch CC governs both tortious and contractual liability, the application need not be exactly the same.[20] 12

---

[18] Article 7:24 Dutch CC explicitly refers to that section.

[19] Cf DSC 27 March 1992, NJ 1992/496 (*Morsink/Nebem*); DSC 12 September 2003, NJ 2004/177 (*Peters/Hofkens*); DSC 14 October 2005, NJ 2005/539 (*City Tax/Y*).

[20] Cf Asser/Hartkamp & Sieburgh 6-II 2013/6.

It must be submitted, however, that this is only true in the sense that the question as to what damages are recoverable is partly answered by the norm (or obligation or duty of care) the party was supposed to act in accordance with. The application of sec 6.1.10 Dutch CC is not different. An example may clarify this. Article 6:98 Dutch CC governing attribution of damage (or: remoteness of damage) requires the court to assess whether the damage can be reasonably attributed to the person causing the damage.[21] It could be argued that a clear contractual norm has a broader scope than a similar tortious norm because the extent of damage was more easily foreseeable given the precise description of the norm. Thus, it would *appear* attribution is broader in relation to the contractual norm. Note, however, that the application of art 6:98 Dutch CC does *not change*, but that it is the starting point of the analysis, the norm and its scope, that changes.

II. MAIN DIFFERENCES BETWEEN TORTIOUS AND CONTRACTUAL LIABILITY

A. DIFFERENCES AS REGARDS THE FOUNDATIONS OF LIABILITY

13 Non-contractual liability is regulated in art 6:162 and further of the Dutch CC. The general tort clause, art 6:162, reads as follows:

> '1. A person who commits a tortious act which can be attributed to him, against another person, must compensate the damage that the other person has suffered in consequence thereof.
> 2. A violation of a right and an act or omission in violation of a duty imposed by law or of what according to unwritten law has to be regarded as proper social conduct, is to be regarded as a tortious act insofar as there was no justification for it.
> 3. A tortious act can be attributed to the tortfeasor if it results from his fault or from a cause for which he is accountable by virtue of law or generally accepted principles.'

14 Contractual liability is regulated in art 6:74 and further of the Dutch CC. The general clause regarding contractual liability, art 6:74, reads as follows:

> '1. Every imperfection in the compliance with an obligation is a non-performance of the debtor and makes him liable for the damage which the creditor suffers as a result, unless the non-performance is not attributable to the debtor.

[21] Asser/Hartkamp & Sieburgh 6-II 2013/69, citing: DSC 1 July 1977, NJ 1978/84; DSC 13 November 1987, NJ 1988/210.

2. As far as it is not yet permanently impossible to accomplish the indebted performance, para 1 of this article only applies with due observance of what is regulated in subsec 2 for a debtor who is in default.'

The Dutch law of damages is a general law which includes contract law as well as tort law. It is codified in sec 10 of title 1 of Book 6 of the Dutch CC (6.1.10). In specific situations the concrete provisions offer sufficient possibilities to distinguish between tort and contract law situations. 15

1) *Role of Intention*

Both contractual and non-contractual liabilities require that the breach of contract or the fault can be attributed to the person acting. A tortious act can be attributed to the debtor or tortfeasor if it results from his fault or from a cause for which he is accountable by virtue of law, contractual clause or generally accepted principles. This criterion of attribution can be fulfilled by intent of the debtor or tortfeasor, but intent is not required; fault suffices for establishment of liability, be it contractual or non-contractual. 16

The factor of deliberateness is thus not relevant as regards the foundations of liability. Nevertheless this factor does in certain circumstances influence the law or the court in applying certain remedies. Intent or deliberateness can be relevant in the area of assessment of damages, both in tort and contract law. A deliberate breach of contract or an intentional tort may give the creditor or plaintiff a claim for a higher level of damages or could give access to another, extra type of damages. 17

However, here it should be mentioned that while in doctrine regarding contract law it is argued that the bad intention of the debtor as well as the greater probability of foreseeing damage are reasons for increasing the level of damages,[22] this statement is, as far as I can see, not supported by any case law in Dutch contract law. By contrast, reference can be made to tort law cases where it is explicitly mentioned that the more culpable the behaviour or the more serious the wrongfulness of the act, the sooner the damage will be attributed to the wrongdoer as a consequence of the behaviour, and thus the higher the level of damages.[23] 18

A straightforward example of the relevance of intention in the law of damage for the type of damage can be found in art 6:106 Dutch CC regarding an award for 19

22 *HB Krans*, Schadevergoeding bij wanprestatie (diss 1999) 141 f; *M Van Kogelenberg*, Motive matters (diss 2013) 109.

23 Rechtbank (Rb) Haarlem 25 July 2012, 519915/CV EXPL 11-9476; Hof Amsterdam (Eigen arrest).

non-pecuniary loss. According to art 6:95 Dutch CC, the damage that has to be compensated in the case of a tort or a breach of contract consists of material loss and other disadvantages, but the latter only insofar as the law confers a right to compensation thereof. Article 6:106 sec 1a Dutch CC allows for compensation for damage that does not consist of material loss, assessed in conformity with the standards of reasonableness and fairness, if the liable person inflicting the damage specifically aimed at causing such non-pecuniary damage to the aggrieved party.

20 Another example is that the damages may more readily be estimated on the basis of account of profits as a form of compensatory damages on the basis of art 6:104 Dutch CC if the liable person acted with intent. In this provision it is stated that if a person who is liable towards another on the basis of a tortious act or a failure in the performance of an obligation has derived profits from that tortious act or failure, the court may, upon the demand of such other person, assess the damage at the amount of such profit or at a part thereof. Although the relevance of deliberateness is not openly recognised in this provision, the lawmaker has, in its comments on this provision, explicitly mentioned that the degree of culpability can be relevant for the court to use its discretionary powers.[24]

21 Moreover, in assessing contributory negligence, the element of intention is relevant. The gravity of the faults of the tortfeasor or debtor and plaintiff or creditor may influence the apportionment of the damage. Article 6:101 Dutch CC concerning contributory negligence reads as follows:

> 'When the damage is caused as well by circumstances which are attributable to the harmed person himself, then the obligation to compensate damage is reduced by imputing the total damage to the harmed person and to the liable person in proportion to the degree in which the circumstances which have contributed to the damage can be attributed to them individually, on the understanding that another imputation occurs or the obligation to compensate damage extinguishes or stays in force totally, if this is required by fairness in view of the significance of the various faults or of other circumstances in the prevailing situation.'

22 Article 6:101 Dutch CC contains a double apportionment criterion that offers sufficient scope to weigh the circumstances that pertain to a particular situation. The basic rule is the extent to which each of the parties contributed to the damage. However, in the interest of equity, apportionment may also be governed by other factors. The equity correction of art 6:101 allows a different apportionment if

[24] Parlementaire Geschiedenis Nieuw BW, Boek 3,5,6 (Parliamentary History New Civil Code, Book 3,5,6) 1267. See for an example: DSC 28 June 2010, LJN BM0893 (*Doerga/Stichting Ymeren*). See further *Van Kogelenberg* (fn 22) 139–141.

the relative causal contributions appear to offer an unsatisfactory result. The relative gravity of the faults is offered as the first criterion that can be used for that purpose, but the text also indicates other criteria, such as degree of culpability, the nature of the tortfeasor's liability, the type and gravity of the damage incurred. Age and the social, physical and psychological circumstances of both parties can be taken into account, as can economic conditions or the presence of insurance cover. In short, the circumstances of an individual case, considered in relation to each other and in their overall context, determine the equity correction. This can result in any form of apportionment, ranging from a completely upheld to a completely extinguished duty to compensate. In general, if the tortfeasor or debtor acts intentionally, the duty to compensate the damage may be completely upheld, even if there is some contributory negligence. On the other hand, intentional behaviour on the part of the harmed person may completely extinguish the duty to compensate.

It should be noted that the liability of an employer in the case of industrial accidents and employment related illnesses holds a different contributory negligence regime, while this regime does consider the element of intent as decisive.[25] In art 7:658 subsec 2 Dutch CC, this exceptional regime digresses in more than one way from the general regulation concerning contributory negligence in art 6:101 of the Code. First of all, contributory negligence of the employee with regard to the employer's liability only applies if the negligence has evolved intentionally or by reckless behaviour. Unlike art 6:101, art 7:658 Dutch CC sets aside less severe cases of contributory negligence. Secondly, in order to apply the atypical contributory negligence rule as meant in art 7:658 subsec 2, the damage of the employee must be a distinct result of the employee's own actions. The aforementioned criterion is thus interpreted in jurisprudence that if reckless behaviour carried out by the employee is such an overt contribution to the accident, the employer's negligence as a possible cause unswervingly pales into insignificance. In the third place, art 7:658 Dutch CC holds the all-or-nothing principle. Unlike art 6:101 of the Dutch CC, art 7:658 does not work from the premise that the damage is split between the tortfeasor and the plaintiff. If the employer is capable of proving intentional behaviour or lucid recklessness to be the cause of the damage, the obligation to compensate is obliterated in its entirety. However, if it is a question of contributory negligence without premeditation or lucid recklessness, liability for the damage in its entirety pertains.[26] 23

Furthermore, intent plays a similar role of influence in the case of joint and several liability of the employer and employee. If the subordinate and the person in whose service he was are both liable for damage caused to a third person, then 24

25 See *ALM Keirse/MY Schaub*, Employer's liability for an injured employee's suicide in Dutch law (2013) 18(3) European Review of Private Law (ERPL) 631, 642.

26 See further ibid.

in their internal relationship, the subordinate does not need to contribute to the payable damages, unless he caused the damage on purpose or he knowingly behaved recklessly. The circumstances of the case and the nature of their legal relationship may demand a different result than the one mentioned in the previous sentence. This is stated in art 6:170 subsec 3 Dutch CC.

25 More generally, the gravity of fault and intent play a role in assessing the internal contribution of jointly and severally liable persons towards each other. Article 6:102 Dutch CC reads as follows in this regard:

> 'When two or more persons are individually liable for the same damage, then they are jointly and severally liable for it. In order to assess what each of them has to contribute by virtue of Article 6:10 on account of their internal relationship with each other, the damage is imputed to them in accordance with Article 6:101, unless a different imputation results from law or a juridical act.'

The applicability of the double apportionment criterion laid down in art 6:101 Dutch CC entails that the gravity of the fault is relevant.

26 Finally, it is relevant to mention that exclusion clauses cannot be upheld in the case of deliberate behaviour of the party attempting to rely on the exclusion clause. A party who acts deliberately or in gross negligence cannot invoke an exclusion clause. Deliberate actions to frustrate performance prohibit a successful reliance on exclusion clauses.

2) Role of Wrongfulness and Fault and their Variations

27 Both tort and contractual liability require 'attributable' behaviour.

28 With regard to having damages granted in tort law, several conditions have to be met: the conduct should be considered unlawful (and thus a tort), this unlawful conduct needs to be attributable, there needs to be harm, a sufficient causal connection between this conduct and this harm has to be established, and the requirement of relativity should be fulfilled. Conduct is considered unlawful (and a tort) if it infringes someone's right, is in violation of the wrongdoer's statutory duty imposed by law, or if it violates an unwritten rule of duty of care, except when there are grounds for justification. A tortious act can be attributed to the tortfeasor if it results from his fault or from a cause for which he is accountable by virtue of law or generally accepted principles.

29 With regard to having damages granted in contract law, similar conditions have to be met: a non-performance has to be established, this non-performance needs to be attributable, there has to be a loss, and a sufficient causal connection between this non-performance and the loss has to be established. Every imperfection in the compliance with an obligation is in principle regarded as a non-performance of the debtor and is as a rule attributable to the debtor, but

a non-performance cannot be attributed to the debtor if he is not to blame for it nor accountable for it by virtue of law, a juridical act or generally accepted principles (common opinion).

If we look into arts 6:74 and 6:162 Dutch CC, we see a difference in formulation. 30
In the case of contract law, liability is assumed *unless* the non-performance cannot be attributed to the debtor and, in the case of tort law, liability is established *if* the wrongful act can be attributed to the tortfeasor. In contract law, it is up to the debtor to argue and, if contested, prove that the breach of contract cannot be attributed to him. This means that in contract law the attributability of the breach to the debtor is presumed until the defendant proves otherwise, whilst in tort law the attributability is a constitutive requirement for liability and therefore should be proven by the plaintiff. However, this difference is not significant, since it has been accepted in case law that it is actually the defendant who has to prove that a wrongful action cannot be attributed to him, as it is very exceptional that the offender has no fault if the wrongfulness of the act has been established.

Case law regarding the liability of schools towards their pupils shows that it is 31
not necessary to establish whether the liability is based on contract or tort to formulate the required standard of care.[27] In other words, the required standard of care of a certain actor in a certain situation does not vary from the presence of a contract to the absence thereof.

3) *Role of Strict Liability*

Both Dutch tort law and Dutch contract law recognise strict liabilities under 32
certain circumstances. As a general starting point, there is no liability without wrongfulness and fault, but in both tort and contract law there are exceptions to this rule. There is room for the generally accepted practice and laws to lay the risk of damage at a particular side, without requiring fault or wrongfulness. Both for tort and contract law, the Dutch CC outlines several instances of strict liability.

B. DIFFERENCES AS REGARDS CAUSATION

The rules and criteria for the establishment of causation and for the assessment 33
of the scope of liability are the same for tortious and contractual liability. Causation is a requirement to establish both tortious and contractual liability. The requirement of causation consists of two stages: causation in fact and legal causation.

---

[27] See *Paijmans* (fn 17).

34 The first stage, which relates to the factual establishment of a causal link between the tortious act or breach of contract and the damage suffered, is embodied in the wording of arts 6:162 and 6:74 Dutch CC respectively. Factual causation concerns the *conditio sine qua non*, which is established in the situation that the damage would not have arisen if the tortious act or breach had not occurred.

35 The second stage is addressed in art 6:98 Dutch CC. This provision is part of sec 6.1.10 Dutch CC and therefore applicable to both tortious and contractual liability cases. It reads:

> 'Only damage that is related in such a way to the event giving rise to the liability of the debtor that it, in regard to the nature of liability and the damage, it can be attributed to him as a consequence of the event is eligible for compensation.'

36 Tort liability can be restricted via the defence of relativity or the so-called legal causation condition (*relativiteit*). The requirement of relativity (*relativiteitseis*) follows from the wording of art 6:162 – requiring that one has acted tortiously 'against another' – in conjunction with art 6:163 Dutch CC. The breached norm that the injured party invokes needs to serve to protect the injured party from the harm for which he tries to obtain compensation. On a closer look, there are three aspects to this condition: relativity is required with regard to the injured party, the harm suffered and the way the harm was caused. These aspects relate to the questions for which harmful consequences the tortfeasor should be held liable and against whom this liability should be established. It is required that the harm (as it is suffered by the claimant and caused by the tortfeasor) falls within the protective scope of the violated norm. In other words: the claimant should bring forward that a legal norm, the aim of which is to protect his interest and to prevent such harm, was breached. This condition can serve as a tool to restrict liability, because answering the question of whether or not the breached norm serves to protect the injured party is at the same time an answer to whether or not the tortfeasor should be liable for the injured party's harm. The fact that other parties have also caused the harm – ie in a more direct way, being the primary tortfeasor – can be a factor in deciding whether or not the requirement of relativity is met.

C. DIFFERENCES AS REGARDS REMEDIES

37 There are, in principle, no differences between tort and contract as regards remedies. Remedies and damages for tort liability and contractual liability are regulated by the same rules, those contained in sec 6.1.10 of the Dutch Civil Code.

1) *Degree of Certainty of the Damage*

For both tortious and contractual liability, Dutch law prescribes in art 6:97 Dutch CC that the court assesses the extent of the damage in the way which is most consistent with the nature of the damage. Where the extent of the damage cannot be determined exactly, it shall be estimated. 38

Furthermore, under certain circumstances, the court may choose the abstract determination of damage, regardless of whether the liability is tortious or contractual in nature. Damage to property, for example, is generally assessed in an abstract manner. 39

Article 6:105 Dutch CC foresees the possibility of compensation for future damage, again both for tortious and contractual liability. 40

2) *Compensation for Non-Pecuniary Loss*

According to Dutch law, an award of compensation for non-pecuniary losses is only possible when a specific foundation in law can be identified (art 6:95 Dutch CC). 41

The most important foundation is art 6:106 Dutch CC, which is applicable to tort as well as contract situations. It reads as follows:

> '1. The injured person has a right to compensation for damage that does not consist of material loss, assessed in conformity with the standards of reasonableness and fairness:
>   a. if the liable person had the intention to inflict such damage;
>   b. if the injured person has sustained physical injuries, if his honour or reputation is injured or if he is otherwise harmed as a person;
>   c. if the damage consists of harm to the memory of a deceased person and is inflicted on the spouse if not legally separated, the registered partner or a blood relative up until the second degree of the deceased, provided that the memory of the deceased is harmed in such a way that the deceased himself, if he was still alive, could have claimed compensation for injury to his honour or reputation.
>
> 2. A claim for compensation as mentioned in the previous paragraph cannot be conveyed or seized, unless the existence of the claim has been recognised by contract or unless a claim for compensation as mentioned above has been filed. For a conveyance by universal title it is, however, sufficient that the entitled person has notified the liable person that he demands compensation.'

The criteria that have to be met make it clear that this provision is more relevant in tort situations and in breach of contract situations if the breach also constitutes a tort than in 'simple' breach of contract cases.

3) *Compensation for Loss of Earnings and for Loss of Chance*

42 For both tortious and contractual liability, the loss of earnings is explicitly included in the definition of the financial loss that has to be compensated, according to arts 6:95 and 6:96 Dutch CC.

Article 6:95 Dutch CC reads as follows:

> 'The damage that has to be compensated by virtue of a statutory obligation consists of material loss and other disadvantages, the latter insofar as the law confers a right to compensation thereof.'

Article 6:96 Dutch CC states that material loss includes sustained losses as well as lost profits.

43 In case law, the Dutch Hoge Raad has established that a loss of a chance can be compensated for, regardless of whether the liability is tortious or contractual.[28]

4) *Restitutionary Damages*

44 As regards restitutionary damages, there is again no difference between tort and contract. A general provision regarding this type of damages is laid down in art 6:104 Dutch CC of sec 6.1.10 Dutch CC:

> 'If someone who is liable towards another on the basis of a tortious act or a failure in the performance of an obligation has gained a profit because of the tortious act or failure, the court may, upon the request of the injured person, assess the damage in line with the amount of the profit or a part of it.'

This rule gives the judge the power to award damages taking into account the profits gained. This provision is a means of assessing the amount of damages. It is not applicable if no damage has been caused.[29]

5) *Aggravated and Exemplary (or Punitive) Damages*

45 According to Dutch law, punitive damages are not available in tort or in the case of a breach of contract. Penalty clauses are of course a possibility in contract.[30]

---

28 See further *ALM Keirse*, Going Dutch: How to address cases of causal uncertainty, in: I Gilead et al (eds), Proportional Liability: Analytical and Comparative Perspectives (2013) 227 ff.

29 DSC 18 June 2010, ECLI:NL:HR:2010:BL9662, NJ 2015/33; DSC 24 June 2016, ECLI:NL:HR:2016:1309.

30 See *RC Meurkens*, Punitive Damages. The Civil Remedy in American Law, Lessons and Caveats for Continental Europe (diss 2014).

6) *Other Remedies*

Both in tort and contract law actual performance serves as the primary remedy; the remedy of damages is secondary. 46

Following art 3:296 Dutch CC, an injunction or order for performance can be sought both in tort and contract law. According to this provision, the court must honour a claim to perform without any discretion beyond the exceptions mentioned in the same provision. Art 3:296 Dutch CC regarding the legal action to claim specific performance reads as follows:

> '1. Where a person is legally obliged towards another person to give, to do or not to do something, the court shall order him, upon a request or claim of the entitled person, to carry out this specific performance, unless something else results from law, the nature of the obligation or a juridical act.
>
> 2. Where a person is legally obliged to perform something under an effective date or expiration date or under a condition precedent or subsequent, the court may order him to do so with observance of that time stipulation or condition.'

D. DIFFERENCES AS REGARDS 'PURE ECONOMIC LOSSES'

As mentioned before, Dutch law makes no distinction between damages arising from tortious or contractual liability when dealing with compensation of damage. Section 6.1.10 of the Dutch CC states what kinds of damage are eligible for compensation, how the damage should be appraised and how it has to be compensated. This section is applicable to any legal obligation to compensate damage regardless of the foundation of this obligation. 47

Unlike other jurisdictions, Dutch law does not start out by making a distinction between damage to the person, damage to property and pure economic loss.[31] They are treated as instances of material loss and are as such fully recoverable. Pure economic loss is thus included in the patrimonial damage that has to be compensated according this section, both in case of tortious and contractual liability. There is no exclusion of such losses from the scope of liability law, given the fact that there is no separate category of pure economic loss.[32] 48

---

31 *MH Wissink/WH van Boom*, The Netherlands: Damages under Dutch law, in: U Magnus (ed), Unification of Tort Law: Damages (2001) 147.

32 *R de Graaff*, Concurrent Claims in Contract and Tort: A Comparative Perspective (2017) 25(4) ERPL 719.

E. DIFFERENCES AS REGARDS LIABILITY FOR OTHERS

49 Liability for others (such as auxiliaries, independent contractors, legal representatives or organs of a company) depends on different provisions for tort liability and contract liability, but the rationale for this type of liability is similar for tort and contract law. There are no differences worth mentioning. The same is true for the liability of the auxiliary or the organ itself and for the liability of representatives of natural persons.

F. DIFFERENCES AS REGARDS LIABILITY IN THE CASE OF MULTIPLE TORTFEASORS/BREACHING PARTIES

50 There are no differences worth mentioning. The default rule is joint and several liability. This general rule is laid down in art 6:102 Dutch CC, which applies to both tort law and contract law. It reads as follows:

> 'When two or more persons are individually liable for the same damage, then they are jointly and severally liable for it. In order to assess what each of them has to contribute by virtue of Article 6:10 on account of their internal relationship with each other, the damage is imputed to them in accordance with Article 6:101, unless a different imputation results from law or a juridical act.'

Due to the applicability of the double apportionment criterion laid down in art 6:101 Dutch CC, any apportionment from 1% to 99% is possible.

G. DIFFERENCES AS REGARDS THE PERSONS WHO MAY BE PROTECTED

51 The persons protected under Dutch tort law are primarily those against whom the tortious act was committed. Those who are to be protected by the norm breached by the tortfeasor can claim damages. In other words: the claimant should bring forward that a legal norm, the aim of which is to protect his interest, was breached (see also the next section on defences and the doctrine of relativity). Dutch tort law does recognise the entitlement of third parties to damages in cases of personal injury or death of the primary victim (arts 6:107 and 6:108 Dutch CC), albeit under strict conditions and rather limited.

52 The persons protected under Dutch contract law are primarily the parties to the contract. As a principle, third parties cannot be forced to perform an obligation created by a contract to which they are not a party, nor can they oblige others to do so. However, there are both codified exceptions and exceptions in case

law to this contractual doctrine of relativity. An example is the possibility to incorporate a so-called third party clause into the contract.

H. DIFFERENCES AS REGARDS DEFENCES

In principle, there are no differences. The rule of contributory negligence is part of sec 10 of title 1 of Book 6 of the Dutch Civil Code and is therefore applicable to both tort and contract law. However, for some specific tortious liabilities, there are special rules regarding contributory negligence. An example is the rule in art 7:658 Dutch CC (mentioned above) concerning an employer's liability towards his employee. Another example is to be found in the case law regarding traffic accidents between a motorised tortfeasor, on the one hand, and a pedestrian or cyclist, on the other hand.[33] 53

Article 6:162(2) Dutch CC provides that a certain action will not be unlawful if it can be 'justified.' Such justifications are, for instance, force majeure, self-defence, lawful conduct, and consent.[34] These defences are not codified as contractual defences. The former three grounds, however, appear to be implicit in art 6:75 Dutch CC's rule on non-attribution. Consent could, theoretically, either be considered to be implicit in art 6:75 Dutch CC too, or, given that there is no need for consideration, give rise to a new contract. 54

I. DIFFERENCES AS REGARDS LIMITATION PERIODS

The same rules apply in both contract and tort law. Article 3:310 Dutch CC offers the general rules on limitation periods for bringing a compensation claim, irrespective of the cause of action. It reads as follows: 55

> '1. A right of action to claim damages or a contractual penalty becomes prescribed on the expiry of five years from the day following the one on which the injured person has become aware of both the inflicted damage or the fact that the contractual penalty has become due and demandable and the identity of the person who is liable for this damage or contractual penalty, and in any event twenty years from the day on which the event occurred that caused the damage or that made the contractual penalty become due and demandable (exigible).
> 2. When the inflicted damage is caused by air, water or soil pollution, by the realisation of a danger as meant in Article 6:175 of the Civil Code or by ground

---

33 Cf DSC 28 February 1992, NJ 1993/566 (*CJHB*); DSC 2 June 1995, NJ 1997/700–702 (*Marloes de Vos*); DSC 5 December 1997, NJ 1998/400–402 (*Saïd Hyati*); DSC 30 March 2007, NJ 2008/64 (*X/Noord-Hollandsche Verzekeringen*).

34 Asser/Hartkamp & Sieburgh 6-IV 2015/88–93.

movements as meant in Article 6:177, first paragraph, under point (b) of the Civil Code, then – contrary to what is stated at the end of paragraph 1 – the right of action to claim damages becomes prescribed on the expiry of thirty years from the day on which the event that caused the damage occurred.

3. For the purpose of paragraph 2, an "event" is understood as a suddenly occurring fact, a continuously occurring fact or a series of facts arising from the same cause. If the event forms a continuously occurring fact, then the period of thirty years meant in paragraph 2 starts to run after this fact has stopped occurring. If the event forms a series of facts arising from the same cause, then this period starts to run after the last fact in line has occurred.
4. If the event that caused the damage constitutes a criminal offence to which the Dutch Penal Code is applicable, the right of action to claim damages against the person who committed the criminal offence shall not become prescribed as long as the penal action has not ceased to exist due to its prescription or the death of the liable person.
5. Contrary to paragraph 1 and 2, a right of action to claim damages on account of an injury or death becomes prescribed on the expiry of five years from the day following the one on which the injured person becomes aware of both the damage and the identity of the person who is liable for it. Where the injured person was a minor on the day on which he became aware of both the damage and the identity of the person liable for it, the right of action shall only become prescribed after the expiry of five years from the day following the one on which he reached the age of legal majority.'

This general clause concerns claims for damages of all types, such as claims due to breach of contract, tort and unjustified enrichment.

56 Noteworthy is that some particular causes of action have their own limitation periods as there are *leges speciales* derogating from the general clause of art 3:310 Dutch CC. In the case of product liability, for example, European law limits the period for action. The limitation periods are also shorter in the case of a sale contract and in the case of personal transportation.

J. DIFFERENCES AS REGARDS PROOF

57 As regards the law of evidence, in particular relating to the burden of proof and the standard of proof, the same rules apply in both contract and tort law.

K. OTHER DIFFERENCES

58 As regards the liability of minors, there is difference between tort and contract. If a minor acts with the permission of her legal guardians or can be deemed to have acted with such permission, she will be able to enter into a contract and, hence, be liable for non-performance (arts 1:234 and 3:32 Dutch CC). On the

other hand, a minor who has not reached the age of 14 cannot be held liable for tortious acts (art 164 of Book 6 Dutch CC). Instead, her legal guardians will be liable (art 169 of Book 6 Dutch CC).

L. REASONS FOR THE DIFFERENCES

The Dutch law of damages is a general law which regulates contract law as well as tort law. It is codified in sec 10 of title 1 of Book 6 of the Dutch Civil Code (6.1.10). That explains why there are not so many differences. In principle, the same rules apply. In specific situations the concrete provisions offer sufficient possibilities to distinguish between tort and contract law situations. 59

III. LIMITATION OR EXCLUSION OF LIABILITY ARISING FROM TORT AND FROM CONTRACT

A. STATUTORY PROVISIONS AUTHORISING A LIMITATION OR EXCLUSION OF LIABILITY

1) Statutory Limitation

Statutory limitations of liability are rare under Dutch law.[35] Examples can be found in transportation law, where limitation is generally based on the idea that the party suffering the damage is best placed to insure against damages above a certain value,[36] and in rules on nuclear accidents and oil pollution.[37] 60

Article 6:110 Dutch CC does, however, provide that additional rules on maximum damages may be set by Ordinal Decree. The main reason for this rule is the fear that the numerous strict liabilities in the Dutch CC may lead to the award of excessive damages. Nevertheless, art 6:110 Dutch CC is not limited to cases of strict liability.[38] The only example of limitation by decree based on art 6:110 Dutch CC related to liability for terrorist attacks.[39] This decree was temporary and is no longer in force. 61

---

35 Cf *Spier et al* (fn 9) no 264.

36 Cf *Spier et al* (fn 9) no 262, citing arts 8:73, 8:85(2), 8:110, 8:366, 8:388, 8:518, 8:905, 8:983, 8:1105, 8:1157, 8:1182, 8:1218 and 8:1678 Dutch CC.

37 Cf Asser/Hartkamp & Sieburgh 6-II 2013/188, citing art 3 Wet Aansprakelijkheid kernongevallen (Staatsblad (Stb) 1979, 225) and art V International Convention on Civil Liability for Oil Pollution Damage (Tractatenblad (Trb) 1970, 196).

38 Asser/Hartkamp & Sieburgh 6-II 2013/189, citing Parliamentary History Book 6 (1981) 770, 655, 753, 746.

39 Ordinal Decree (*AM v B*) of 9 July 2004, Stb 2004, 358.

2) *Judicial Limitation*

62 Article 6:109 allows courts to mitigate damages. It applies to both contractual and tortious liability. It reads as follows:

> '1. The court may reduce the amount of an obligation to pay for damages if a full award of damages would lead to obviously unacceptable results in view of the circumstances of the given situation, among which the nature of the liability, the legal relationship between parties and their financial resources.
> 2. The amount of the obligation to pay for damages cannot be reduced to a lower amount than that for which the debtor has covered his liability by insurance or was compelled to do so.
> 3. Every contractual provision in derogation from paragraph 1 is null and void.'

The judge must take into account all relevant circumstances and must be cautious in moderating the award.[40] Contractual penalties can, in certain circumstances, be moderated too.[41] As subsec 2 prescribes, the judge cannot moderate the award to an amount for which the injured party has covered his liability by insurance or was compelled to do so.

63 As regards liability for immaterial damage, art 6:106 Dutch CC provides that damages must be assessed in conformity with standards of reasonableness and fairness. A judge may set the award under art 6:106 Dutch CC at nil.[42]

B. LIMITATION OR EXCLUSION OF CONTRACTUAL AND TORTIOUS LIABILITY BY CONTRACT

1) *Exclusion or Limitation of Liability Contained in the Contract*

64 In principle, it is possible to limit or exclude contractual and tortious liability under a contract. Such clauses can be voidable for being contrary to law, common practice or the standards of reasonableness and fairness (art 6:248 Dutch CC), or *ordre public* or morality (art 3:40 Dutch CC). Excluding or limiting liability for intentionally caused damage will generally fall short of this standard.[43] Excluding or limiting liability for damage caused by the injured party's own gross negligence will generally not be allowed either.[44]

---

40 Cf DSC 28 May 1999, NJ 1999/510 (*G/H*).
41 Asser/Hartkamp & Sieburgh 6-I 2016/425.
42 DSC 27 April 2001, NJ 2002/91 (*B/C*).
43 Cf Asser/Hartkamp & Sieburgh 6-I 2016/365, citing DSC 27 March 1987, NJ 1987/658, 659 and DSC 11 September 1998, NJ 1999/664.
44 Cf Asser/Hartkamp & Sieburgh 6-I 2016/365, citing DSC 14 April 1950, NJ 1951/17.

2) *Exclusion or Limitation of Liability Contained in Standard Terms and Conditions*

If limitation or exclusion clauses are contained in standard terms and conditions, they could be voidable if they can be considered unreasonably burdensome (art 6:233(a) Dutch CC). If such clauses are relied upon *against* an individual not acting in course of her profession or business (a consumer),[45] there is a *presumption* that they are unreasonably burdensome for that consumer (art 6:237(f) Dutch CC). If the counterparty is not a consumer but nevertheless contracts for the benefit of a consumer, that consumer can invoke arts 6:237(f) and 6:233(a) Dutch CC on the basis of art 6:213(2).[46] If the counterparty is not a consumer and contracts for herself or another person who is not a consumer, the exclusion clause contained in the standard terms and conditions can still be considered unreasonably burdensome, but to reach that conclusion other circumstances will have to be taken into account.[47] 65

3) *Extent of Exclusion*

The question as to whether the exclusion of 'liability' refers to both contractual and non-contractual liability or only one of the two, and the question as to what damage is excluded is a matter of contractual interpretation.[48] 66

4) *Third Party*

a) Exclusion Clauses Formulated by a Superior

A contractual exclusion can, under certain circumstances, provide a defence to a third party to the contract. 67

The person in whose service a subordinate fulfils his duty can be liable for damage caused to a third person by a fault of this subordinate (see arts 6:76, 6:170(3) and 7:661 Dutch CC). As a result, both the subordinate who commits the tort and the superior in whose service the subordinate was acting are liable for the damage. If the superior has excluded liability or has another defence against her contractual party, thus escaping liability caused by the subordinate,

---

45 Theoretically, it is possible for these rules to apply to contracts *between* consumers. Note, however, that it is difficult to see how a consumer could be using standard terms and conditions (on which she must rely frequently, cf art 6:231(a) Dutch CC) and still qualify as a consumer in that particular transaction. Cf *J Hijma et al*, Rechtshandeling en overeenkomst (2010) 251; Asser/Hartkamp & Sieburgh 6-III 2014/466.

46 Nota II, Parlementaire Geschiedenis Invoerings Wet 6, p 1663.

47 Cf Asser/Hartkamp & Sieburgh 6-III 2014/502.

48 DSC 19 February 1993, NJ 1994/290 (*Groningen/Zuidema*) at 3.5.

the subordinate, too, can rely on the clause or the defence except for cases where the damage was caused intentionally or as a result of own gross negligence (see art 6:257 Dutch CC). It is irrelevant whether the exclusion clause is formulated to exclude tortious or contractual liability. This provision is mandatory law (art 6:250 Dutch CC).

b) Exclusion Clauses Formulated for the Benefit of a Third Party

68 Under Dutch law, it is possible to include a 'third party clause' in the contract on which the third party may rely after she has accepted it (art 6:253 Dutch CC). This can be an exclusion clause.[49] If the circumstances allow it, the third party can rely on the exclusion clause with retroactive effect, which means actions that took place before the third party's acceptance but after the conclusion of the initial contract can be covered by the exclusion clause (art 6:254(2) Dutch CC). Whether and to what extent the third party can rely on the clause will depend on the interpretation of the contract.[50] It should be noted that, upon acceptance, the third party is formally considered to be a party to the agreement.

c) Exclusion Clauses Invoked against Third Parties

69 Under certain circumstances, the parties to a contract may rely on an exclusion clause not only against each other, but also against a third party. The Dutch Supreme Court has held that this exception to contractual relativity is possible if it would be unreasonable not do so. The reasons for extension must be found in the specific circumstances of the case.[51] Circumstances that appear to be of relevance could be: the conduct of the third party (ie whether the third party has given the contractual party reason to believe that the exclusion clause could also be invoked against her); the special nature of the relation between the three parties; and the special nature of the agreement.[52] An example may elucidate this. Party A contracts party B to deliver goods. Party A allows party B to find another carrier if necessary. Party B contracts party C to deliver the goods in her stead. Party C negotiates a normal exclusion clause for risks that are often excluded in the carrier's business with party B. Party A knows party C's business and from time to time supervises party C's work. Due to party C's negligence, the risk materialises and the goods are damaged. Under such circumstances, party A can probably not claim damages as it would be

---

[49] Cf Asser/Hartkamp & Sieburgh 6-III 2014/564.

[50] Cf DSC 1 October 2004, NJ 2004/499 (*TCM/Gesink*).

[51] DSC 20 June 1986, NJ 198/35 (*Citronas*) in which the Dutch Supreme Court cites DSC 7 March 1969, NJ 1969/249 (*Gegaste Uien*) and DSC 12 January 1979, NJ 1979/362 (*Securicor*); see also: DSC 21 January 2000, NJ 2000/553 (*ODS/CPS*).

[52] Cf DSC 21 January 2000, NJ 2000/553 (*ODS/CPS*).

unreasonable for party C not to be able to rely on the exclusion clause because: (i) A allowed B to subcontract, (ii) A knew C's business and was likely to know what normal exclusion clauses in that business were, (iii) A supervised C from time to time, and (iv) on the basis of A's behaviour, C would have suspected B of having been allowed to negotiate the contract as they did.[53]

IV. NON-CONCURRENCE OR CONCURRENCE OF ACTIONS

A. OVERVIEW

1) Areas of Overlap between Tort and Contract

In principle, a breach of contract does not qualify as a tortious act towards the counterparty and/or a third party. In certain exceptional situations, the act qualifying as a breach of contract can simultaneously qualify as a breach of a tortious norm.[54] This concurrence arises only where the conduct of the party breaching the contract would also give rise to tortious liability had the contract not been concluded, ie where the breach of contract constitutes an independent tortious act against the counterparty. In other words, an act or omission may constitute both a failure in the performance of an obligation and a ground for liability in tort provided the tortious liability exists independently of the breach of the contractual obligation. 70

A simple example would be the situation where one party assumes the obligation not to injure the other party whilst they go on a cycling trip together. Injuring the other party is clearly a breach of contract, but it also qualifies as an independent tortious act. The party will be able to choose between the two. Another example would be a contract in which the tortious norm is implicit. If one party lends property to the other, damaging the property clearly is a breach of contract, but it also qualifies as a breach of a tortious norm.[55] Note that in both examples the liable party will have assumed – explicitly or implicitly – to act in accordance with a norm that was already imposed on her by law. 71

Another form of concurrence occurs where the act qualifying as a breach of contract also constitutes an independent tortious act against a third party.[56] 72

---

53 This example is loosely based on the facts of DSC 21 January 2000, NJ 2000/553 (*ODS/CPS*). Note, however, that the case is far more nuanced in reality. See also: Asser/Hartkamp & Sieburgh 6-III 2014/525.

54 Asser/Hartkamp & Sieburgh 6-IV 2015/10.

55 Ibid.

56 Cf *CE du Perron*, Overeenkomst en derden: een analyse van de relativiteit van de contractswerking (1999) 256 ff.

In that case the behaviour of the party must be tortious against the third party regardless of the contract.[57]

73 An example of this would be the situation where one party lends her car to another, stipulating that it be returned without damage in one week. If the party driving the car damages it by negligently hitting another car, this clearly is a breach of the contract. The act of hitting the other car, however, also constitutes a tortious act to the other driver because the party driving the car had a duty of care towards other drivers.

74 The Dutch Supreme Court has decided that when someone enters into a contract and the contractual relationship he entered into thereby becomes – in legal matters – a chain in a network of contracts also concerning third parties and their interests, this party is not under all circumstances free to ignore the interests third parties have in the proper performance of the contract.[58] If the interests of a third party are so closely connected with the proper performance of the contract that the third party can suffer damage or other disadvantages if a party to the contract falls short in the performance of the contract, the norms of what is generally accepted according to unwritten law pertaining to proper social conduct may imply that the party to the contract has to safeguard the interests of that third party by guiding his conduct – partly – in consideration of these interests. In order to determine whether these norms imply this, one has to look at the circumstances of the case, such as the capacity of all parties that are involved, the nature and purport of the agreement involved, the way in which the interests of the third party are involved, the question of whether the contracting party knew about the involvement of the third party, the question of whether the third party could trust that his interests would be taken account of, the question to what extent it would be inconvenient for the contracting parties to take into account the third party's interests, the nature and the extent of the disadvantages the third party could be faced with, the question of whether the third party could reasonably be required to have covered himself against these disadvantages, and the reasonableness of the compensation offered to the third party, where applicable. Noteworthy is that the Dutch Supreme Court has held that a breach of contract is not required in order to invoke this assessment framework.[59] Decisive for tortious liability vis-à-vis the third party is whether or not the debtor should have guided his behaviour in the context of the contract by the third party's interests. Thus, for

---

57 Ibid, 305.

58 DCS 24 September 2004, ECLI:NL:HR:2004:AO9069, NJ 2008/587; DCS 20 January 2012, ECLI:NL:HR:2012:BT7496, NJ 2012/59; DCS 14 July 2017, ECLI:NL:HR:2017:1355, Jurisprudentie Aansprakelijkheid (JA) 2017, 140.

59 DCS 14 July 2017, ECLI:NL:HR:2017:1355, JA 2017, 140.

this tortious liability towards a third person to be established, it is not required that the debtor breached the contract and a debtor can also be held liability towards his contractual party on a contractual basis. For concurrence of these actions this is, of course, required.

2) *Approach to Non-Concurrence and Concurrence of Actions*

The question of which regime (or regimes) applies (or apply) if some event gives rise to two legal claims is unsettled amongst Dutch legal scholars. It would appear that most support exists for the suggestion that both regimes will apply (accumulation). First, leading commentaries suggest that, lacking a rule to the contrary, both regimes apply if two grounds coincide.[60] Second, as art 48 of the Dutch Code of Civil Procedure (Dutch CCP) requires the judge to 'supplement' the legal grounds advanced by the claimant – a provision that allows the judge to decide the case if the claimant's lawyer fails to correctly state the grounds for the claim – it has been suggested that even if the claimant chooses, the judge must rule on both issues.[61] Third, the Dutch Supreme Court has held that the claimant *may* choose,[62] which could be taken to imply that there is no room for accumulation. It should be emphasised, however, that the Dutch Supreme Court has left open the question of whether the claimant *must* choose. It is safer to assume, therefore, that this case law entails no implications for the accumulation debate yet. Recently, the Dutch Supreme Court held that, if a contracting party suffers damage due to the performance of a contract by the debtor, damages can be claimed on the basis of breach of contract – except when otherwise provided by the agreement and provided that the breach of contract is attributable to the debtor – even if the damage is caused by a tortious act of an employee or an auxiliary person of the debtor.[63] Furthermore, the Dutch Supreme Court clarifies that the claimant in such a case can also choose – again, except when otherwise provided by the agreement – to claim damages on the basis of non-contractual tortious liability; provided that the employee involved committed a tortious act vis-à-vis the claimant, the claimant can either claim damages from the employer on the basis of vicarious liability or from the employee himself. 75

Nevertheless, there is an argument to be made for the other side, too. Some authors suggest that it would be contrary to party autonomy for the judge to 76

---

60 Asser/Hartkamp & Sieburgh 6-IV 2015/165.

61 Cf *J Drion*, Handelingen der Nederlandse Juristenvereniging 1960 II (1960) 17.

62 Cf DSC 6 March 1959, NJ 1959/349; DSC 21 December 1973, NJ 1974/308; DSC 18 September 1992, NJ 1992/747; DSC 14 June 2002, NJ 2003/112; DSC 15 November 2002, NJ 2003/48; DSC 14 July 2017, Jurisprudentie in Nederland (JIN) 2017, 162.

63 DSC 14 July 2017, JIN 2017, 162.

decide on both issues if the parties explicitly choose.[64] This argument certainly has some appeal, but it should be emphasised that, regardless of whether it is compatible with art 48 Dutch CCP, it is irrelevant for the situation where the claimant does not choose.

77 Bearing in mind that this is an unsettled debate, it should be emphasised that the practical relevance of this debate is limited. First, art 6:98 Dutch CC on causality does not allow for double compensation. Second, once liability is established – which is premised in this debate, of course – the rules for awarding damages are identical (sec 6.1.10 Dutch CC). Third, once a judge awards a claim on the basis of one basis, she can disregard the other for lack of judicial interest.

B. CONCURRENCE/EXCLUSION OF ACTIONS FOR THE PROTECTION AGAINST PERSONAL INJURY

78 If a contractual obligation includes an obligation, explicitly or implicitly, not to (negligently) injure another person – for instance, a contract between a chauffeur and his passenger – breach of this contractual norm may constitute a tortious act as well.[65]

79 Third parties – ie parties that are not within either contractual relativity or tortious relativity – can claim for the costs incurred for the benefit of the injured party (art 6:107 Dutch CC). The injured party cannot claim these damages, as he did not incur them.[66] If the third party himself suffers personal injury, he can only claim these costs if he has an independent claim in tort or contract.

C. CONCURRENCE/EXCLUSION OF ACTIONS FOR THE PROTECTION OF PROPERTY

80 If a contractual obligation includes an obligation, explicitly or implicitly, not to destroy another person's property – for instance, a contract for the loan of a book with a library – breach of this contractual norm may constitute a tortious act as well. The injured party may opt for both routes, but double compensation is prohibited.

[64] *JJ Vriesendorp*, Ambsthalve aanvullen van rechtsgronden in het burgerlijk geding (1970) 158; *H Nieuwenhuis*, Anders en eender. Beschouwingen over samenloop van wanprestatie en onrechtmatige daad (1982) 23 f.

[65] Cf DSC 9 December 1955, NJ 1956/157.

[66] Cf *R Rijnhout*, Schadevergoeding voor derden in personenschadezaken (2012) 8 ff.

D. CONCURRENCE/EXCLUSION IN THE CASE OF INTERFERENCE WITH CONTRACTUAL RIGHTS

1) *Interference with a Contractual Relationship*

Unlawful interference with a contractual relationship of another person is tortious in nature.[67] A claim based on the contract itself is precluded as the doctrine of contractual relativity prevents a party to the contract from relying on it against a third party.[68] 81

In establishing tortious liability, it is important to assess under what circumstances interference with a contractual relationship of other persons is unlawful. Dutch tort law imposes liability for the infringement of another person's 'personal right', which could imply that any interference with a contract is unlawful. Nevertheless, the DSC has rejected that argument.[69] Instead, the DSC has held that interference can only be unlawful if the tortfeasor's interference is not in accordance with the standards of public prudence (*maatschappelijke zorgvuldigheid*).[70] It should be emphasised that these actions are rarely allowed. Although it is impossible to give a catalogue of circumstances that make such interference unlawful, a brief summary of several cases may illustrate just how seldom this action is applied.[71] 82

Interference with a contract was first held to be unlawful in the Kolynos ruling.[72] In that case, one dealer (A) had the exclusive right to distribute toothpaste from producer X. A retailer (B) obtained the toothpaste unlawfully and sold it at a lower price. A claimed damages from B. The DSC held that, under these circumstances, B's interference was unlawful against A and allowed the claim. 83

---

67 Cf *LM van Bochove*, Betrokkenheid van derden bij contractbreuk (2013) 39 f.

68 Asser/Hartkamp & Sieburgh 6-III 2014/518, citing arts 6:231 and 6:261 Dutch CC; DSC 1 February 1985, NJ 1985/466; DSC 26 May 2000, NJ 2000/640; DSC 30 September 2005, NJ 2008/513. Although the principle was explicitly left out of the 1992 Dutch Civil Code (DCC), it is generally accepted to be part of Dutch law as it can be deduced from art 6:248 DCC, the principle of party autonomy, and the explicit codification of several exceptions. Cf *CE du Perron*, Rechtsbeginselen en de derdenwerking van overeenkomsten (1991/10) Ars Aequi: Juridisch Studentenblad (AA) 133 f; The principle (in Dutch: '*het relativiteitsbeginsel*') used to be codified in art 1376 of the Dutch Civil Code (old), but the legislator opted for removal in order to leave room for the judiciary to further develop exceptions to the rule, of which many already existed also under the old Dutch Civil Code. See also *JBM Vranken*, De derde in het overeenkomstenrecht (I), Weekblad voor Privaatrecht, Notariaat en Registratie (WPNR) 6288 (1997) 715.

69 DSC 17 May 1985, NJ 1986/760 (*Curacao/Boyé*).

70 Cf DSC 11 November 1937, NJ 1937/1096 (*Kolynos*); DSC 13 January 1961, NJ 1962/245 (*KIM/Sieverding*); DSC 12 January 1962, NJ 1962/246 (*Nibeja/Grundig*). See also: *van Bochove* (fn 67) 30–35.

71 See also <http://uitspraken.rechtspraak.nl/inziendocument?id=ECLI:NL:HR:2014:1627>.

72 DSC 11 November 1937, NJ 1937/1096 (*Kolynos*).

84 In the 1960s the German company, Grundig had a network of exclusive dealers in Germany, which it enforced through contracts. This gave rise to two DSC rulings. In the first case, one Dutch retailer (C) obtained products from these licensed dealers. Another Dutch retailer (D) obtained products from an unlicensed German dealer. C claimed damages from D. The DSC refused C's claim, as C was not a party to the original contract with Grundig that some unidentified German dealer violated.[73] In a later case, another Dutch retailer (E) obtained products from an unlicensed German dealer. This time Grundig itself (G) claimed from C. The DSC held, however, that again this was not unlawful against E. The main reason was that the E did not compete with G, but with other retailers.[74]

85 What can be deduced from these cases is that interference can – not 'is', as the judge must still deem the behaviour to fall short of standards of social prudence – only be unlawful if the interfering party interferes with a contract of a direct competitor. Both Grundig cases did not qualify: in the first case, the competitor sued, but it was not her contract that was interfered with, and in the second case, it was not a competitor who sued. Of course, not every interference with contracts of direct competitors is unlawful, but those circumstances cannot be catalogued.

86 A third party who, together with an ex-franchisee competes with the ex-franchisor, could, under certain circumstances, be held liable in tort against the ex-franchisor. In order to qualify as a tort, it should concern a systematic, consistent and substantial detriment to the business of the ex-franchisor.[75]

2) Loss of Business due to Personal Injury to Someone Else's Employees or Clients or to or Property Damage to the Entrepreneur

87 Inflicting personal injury on someone else's employees or clients or causing property damage to an entrepreneur could qualify as a tort against the entrepreneur if he suffers loss of business as a result. Assuming that the tortfeasor and entrepreneur/employer are not in a contractual relationship, only the tortious route is an option.

88 Causing personal injury to another person's employee is a breach of norm against the employee. The personal strand of the tortious doctrine of relativity (art 6:162(1) Dutch CC) prevents the employer from bringing an action against the tortfeasor. If the employer incurs costs for the benefit of the employee – either

---

73 DSC 13 January 1961, NJ 1962/245 (*KIM/Sieverding*).

74 Ibid.

75 Rb Overijssel 12 April 2013, ECLI:NL:RBOVE:2013:201. See also *JH Kolenbrander*, Het postcontractuele non-concurrentiebedig in de franchiseovereenkomst: een update, Contracteren 2015-1 28 ff.

voluntarily or because she is obligated by law to do so[76] – and the employee could have claimed those costs under arts 6:162 and 6:98 Dutch CC had she incurred them herself, then the employer can claim these from the tortfeasor directly (art 6:107 Dutch CC). Article 6:107 Dutch CC has an exclusive or derogating effect, which means that the entrepreneur can *only* claim costs incurred for the benefit of the employee.[77] The same limitation applies to causing damage to clients, as art 6:107 Dutch CC lays down the general regime for third party damages in injury cases.

Causing property damage is unlawful against the entrepreneur directly. The question as to whether compensation for loss of business can be recovered depends on whether the damage falls within the scope of the norm breached (ie satisfies the second strand of the doctrine of relativity (art 6:163 Dutch CC)) and/or can be considered to be 'reasonably caused' by the tortious act (art 6:98 Dutch CC). Depending on what property is damaged, where it is damaged, and how it is damaged, a judge may conclude the loss of business which is (i) protected by the norm, and (ii) caused by the tortious act. Relevant factors include the foreseeability of loss of business, and the nature of liability (intention, culpability, etc).[78] 89

V. SPECIFIC SITUATIONS

A. PRE-CONTRACTUAL LIABILITY

1) Reasonableness and Fairness

Parties must observe the standards of reasonableness and fairness in conducting themselves towards each other in the pre-contractual phase.[79] There are two types of pre-contractual liability that emerge from this under Dutch law: (i) liability for failure to inform (properly), and (ii) liability for breaking off negotiations. 90

2) Pre-Contractual Liability for Failing to Inform Properly

A party can be liable for failing to inform or incorrectly informing the other party about certain essential facts.[80] This liability is partly shaped by the rules on 91

76 This often occurs where an employee is injured and the employer is obligated to pay 70% of the employee's wages for 52 weeks on the basis of art 7:629 Dutch CC.

77 Cf DSC 9 October 2009, NJ 2010/387 (*Vilt*) at 3.5; *Rijnhout* (fn 66) 8 ff.

78 Cf DSC 25 April 2008, NJ 2008/262.

79 DSC 15 November 1957, NJ 1958/67 (*Baris/Riezenkamp*).

80 Cf DSC 2 April 1993, NJ 1995/94 (*Cattier/Waanders*); DSC 25 January 2002, NJ 2003/31 (*Paalman/Lampenier*); DSC 5 June 2009, NJ 2012/182 (*Dexio*); DSC 5 June 2009, NJ 2012/184 (*Aegon*); DSC 5 June 2009, NJ 2012/183 (*Levob Bank*).

mistake (art 6:228 Dutch CC) but is by no means based on those rules. Instead there is an independent duty of care to inform correctly. To what extent such a duty of care exists will depend on the nature of the agreement, the nature of the information, and the parties' knowledge of these matters.[81] There is disagreement amongst academics as to whether this liability should be based on general tort law or on the requirements of reasonableness and fairness independently.[82] It should be submitted that, again, it is more sensible to construe this obligation as a tortious obligation that is shaped by the requirements of reasonableness and fairness, but this is not uncontested.

3) Pre-Contractual Liability for Breaking off Negotiations

92 The Dutch judiciary has established an extensive practice of pre-contractual liability for discontinuance of negotiations.[83] The key norm for establishing pre-contractual liability is whether the injured party could 'legitimately rely' on the other party to continue negotiations.[84] Legal academics tend to disagree as to whether pre-contractual liability for breaking off negotiations is contractual or tortious in nature.[85] It would appear that, given the fact that obligations arise regardless of whether a contract is actually concluded, it is more sensible to construe this general obligation as a tortious obligation on

[81] Cf DSC 5 June 2009, NJ 2012/182 (*Dexio*) at 4.8.4; DSC 5 June 2009, NJ 2012/184 (*Aegon*) at 4.6.2; DSC 5 June 2009, NJ 2012/183 (*Levob Bank*) at 4.5.4.

[82] In favour of qualifying it as tortious: *KJO Jansen*, Informatieplichten: over kennis en verantwoordelijkheid in contractenrecht en buitencontractueel aansprakelijkheidsrecht (diss 2011) 287 f; *C Brunner*, Note DSC 2 April 1993, NJ 1995/94 (*Cattier/Waanders*) NJ 1995/94. In favour of qualifying it as contractual: *B Wessels*, Zelfstandig recht op schadevergoeding bij schending mededelingsplicht, WPNR 6187 (1995) 476.

[83] DSC 18 June 1983, NJ 1983/723 (*Plas/Valburg*); DSC 23 October 1987, NJ 1988/1017 (*VSH/Shell*); DSC 14 June 1996, NJ 1997/481 (*MBO/De Ruiterij*); DSC 4 October 1996, NJ 1997/65 (*ABB/Staat*); DSC 12 August 2005, NJ 2005/467 (*CBB/JPO*); DSC 9 December 2011, NJ 2013/273 (*X/Y*); DSC 3 May 2013, NJ 2013/572 (*KLM (private procurement)*).

[84] Cf DSC 12 August 2005, NJ 2005/467 (*CBB/JPO*) at 3.6.

[85] Asser/Hartkamp & Sieburgh 6-III 2014/202 citing *HFC Schoordijk*, Onderhandelen te goeder trouw (1984) 61 ff; *P van Schilfgaarde*, Note *Plas/Valburg*, AA 1983, 758 ff; *BJ Engelen*, TvPr 1983, 1255; *M Van Delft-Baas*, NJB 1984/131 and Kwartaalbericht Nieuw BW 1984, 74; *P Abas*, WPNR 5691 (1984) 197 ff; *AHM Santen*, Aanbod en aanvaarding bij het kopen van een woning (rede Amsterdam) 4 ff; *JH Nieuwenhuis* in: Bijleveld et al (ed), Bundel Recht vooruit: 150 jaar BW (1988) 114; *J Van Duijvendijk-Brand*, Afrekenen bij echtscheiding (1990) 90 ff; *GJ Rijken*, Redelijkheid en billijkheid (Mon. Nieuw BW no A5) 1994/36; *B Wessels* in: Moltmaker-Bundel (1998) 304, fn 2; *MM van Rossum*, WPNR 6472 (2002) 79; *MJ Van Laarhoven*, WPNR 6484 (2002) 290, all favouring the interpretation that these rules are contractual or *sui generis*, and citing *J Drion*, WPNR (1947) 3992 ff, *Hofmann/Drion/Wiersma*, Nederlands Verbintenissenrecht (1959) 177 *CJH Brunner* and *LH Pels Rijcken* annotating NJ 1983/2305 ff and Bouwrecht 1983, 405 ff; *WSM Schut*, Letters of intent (1986) 82; *HJ De Kluiver*, WPNR (1987) 5816; *MR Ruijgvoorn*, Afbreken van onderhandelingen (2005) 70 ff, favouring the tortious construction.

the basis of art 6:162 Dutch CC merely coloured by the behavioural norm of art 6:2 Dutch CC. Nevertheless, as disagreement amongst scholars remains, these rules inevitably operate in a grey zone.

B. LIABILITY OF PROFESSIONALS

1) *Basis of Liability*

The liability of professionals is generally governed by art 7:401 Dutch CC. This article provides for a general duty of care for 'service providers.' The article reads: 'During his work the service provider must observe the care of a prudent service provider.' 93

Although this article may read as a duty of care, it is generally accepted that claims for breach of this duty must be brought on the basis of breach of contract.[86] In other words art 7:401 Dutch CC implies a duty of care for service providers in all service contracts.[87] The main consequence of this construct is that the contractual defences and rules of attribution are applicable.[88] If the breach of this duty of care also constitutes a breach of the general duty of care of art 6:162 Dutch CC, a claim can be brought either for breach of contract and/or for a tortious act (barring, of course, double compensation). In either case, the burden of proof is on the defendant.[89] 94

2) *Content of Contractual Duty of Care*

Generally, case law requires a service provider to act as a reasonably competent and reasonably acting professional.[90] This standard of care depends on the specific profession at issue. The obligation that art 7:401 Dutch CC imposes can be inspired by specific rules of conduct of the profession at issue.[91] Some specific features of some professional (ie regulated profession) liability are worth mentioning here. 95

A lawyer (*advocaat*) is obligated to: (i) further all legitimate interests of her client in the case with which the client entrusted her, such as inquiring at any moment whether the client has a right to legal aid;[92] (ii) give a client a choice as 96

86 Asser/Tjong Tjin Tai 7-IV 2014/198.
87 Note that this is *not* an obligation to deliver certain results.
88 Cf arts 6:75–6:80 Dutch CC.
89 Asser/Tjong Tjin Tai 7-IV 2014/205.
90 Ibid, 200.
91 Ibid, 202.
92 DSC 1 November 1991, NJ 1992/121 (*De Kort/Blok*) at 3.2.

to whether to proceed with the case, even if the chance of success is slim;[93] and (iii) sufficiently acquaint herself with the relevant branch of law when drafting a contract.[94] A public notary (*notaris*) must perform all necessary checks and acts to ensure that deeds are validly passed,[95] and has an enhanced duty of care to ensure juridical acts have the intended results.[96] A bank employee (*bankmedewerker*) must inform her clients of all exchange clauses (*deviezenbepalingen*), provided she was aware of these.[97] A bailiff must perform her assignments correctly and must, under certain circumstances, put her client's interests before her own.[98] The receiver (*faillissementscurator*) must act in the interest of the creditors and the general public. The accountant must perform all checks correctly. A tax advisor (*belastingadviseur*) must confirm alleged statements of the tax inspector (*belastinginspecteur*) explicitly.

97 The only profession for which the Code provides a specific elaboration of the duty of care is that of the medical care provider. The article reads:

> 'Art. 7:453 – In providing the medical treatment, the care provider must observe the standards of a prudent care provider and, in doing so, he has to act in conformity with the responsibilities laid upon him by the professional standard for care providers.'

98 Although this article does not give much guidance in itself (the standard is not a formal standard), it has been submitted that the specific standards can be found in the standard contract drawn up by the Royal Dutch Society of Medicine and the National Patients Platform.[99] Interestingly, although this article reads as a

93 DSC 28 June 1991, NJ 1992/420 at 4.3.1. Yet a lawyer is not obligated to prevent a client from continuing with risky proceedings, see: Asser/Tjong Tjin Tai 7-IV 2014/201, citing DSC 2 February 2007, NJ 2007/92 (Juresta).

94 Asser/Tjong Tjin Tai 7-IV 2014/201, citing Court of Appeal Amsterdam 23 January 1997, NJ 2000/504.

95 Cf Asser/Tjong Tjin Tai 7-IV 2014/201 (translation and responsibility is my own): 'The public notary must perform all sorts of checks and acts in order to ensure that the deeds she must pass indeed achieve the intended legal results, such as checking the identity and authority to act of those appearing before him. (DSC 28 September 1990, NJ 1991/473 (Cezet); DSC 24 June 1985, NJ 1986/259), drafting the deed in a timely manner (DSC 2 February 1990, NJ 1990/795), follow specific instruction and ask for clarification if necessary (DSC 20 December 2002, NJ 2003/325 (Zürich LG), DSC 12 June 2009, NJ 2009/274), investigate the registers (DSC 14 June 2013, LJN BZ5712).' Cf *DT Boks*, Notariële aansprakelijkheid. Enige aspecten van civielrechtelijke aansprakelijkheid (diss 2002).

96 Asser/Tjong Tjin Tai 7-IV 2014/201, citing DSC 28 September 1990, NJ 1991/473 (*Cezet*); DSC 20 December 2002, NJ 2003/325 (*Zürich LG*); DSC 14 June 2013, NJ 2013/340.

97 Asser/Tjong Tjin Tai 7-IV 2014/201, citing DSC 15 November 1996, NJ 1997/152 (*Leutscher/Banco de Jerez*).

98 Asser/Tjong Tjin Tai 7-IV 2014/201, citing DSC 8 November 1991, NJ 1992/134 (*Prins/Van Leeuwen*).

99 *E Hondius/A van Hooft*, The new Dutch law on medical services, Netherlands International Law Review (NILR) XLII (1996) 6.

duty of care, it truly is contractual. The main argument in favour of this choice is that of enlarged self-determination, but there are drawbacks in cases where the patient cannot contract, either because she is unable to do so (eg comatose) or because she is a child and her parents contract.[100]

3) *Third Parties*

A service provider may also owe a duty of care towards third parties. In that case, the tortious norm of art 6:162 Dutch CC is determined by the standard of care stipulated in art 7:401 Dutch CC (or art 7:453 Dutch CC), ie that of a prudent service provider. It will depend on the specific circumstances whether the standard of care of a prudent service provider also entails caring for the interests of third parties. Examples in case law include: public notaries (*notarissen*) towards parties that have some interest in the deed; accountants towards anyone who may be expected to rely on their accounts; and medical care providers towards the father and child in extreme wrongful birth cases.[101] 99

4) *Exclusion Clauses*

Liability for breach of contract can generally be excluded. In certain circumstances, excluding liability for failing to observe the standard of care stipulated by art 7:401 Dutch CC can be invalid due to this being contrary to the standards of reasonableness and fairness (cf art 6:248 Dutch CC). The duty of care of medical care providers cannot be excluded (art 7:463 Dutch CC). Advocates (*advocaten*) can only exclude liability for damages over and above their non-insured own risk (art 5 Decree on administration and financial integrity). Other regulations may provide for similar rules. 100

As submitted in sec III above, an exclusion clause can normally only be invoked against third parties if it would be unreasonable *not* to do so. The reasons for extension must be found in the specific circumstances of the case.[102] It is impossible to give a general catalogue of exclusion clauses for professional liability that can be invoked against third parties, but it can be submitted that there are no reasons to assume that these cases will not be determined along similar lines. Relevant circumstances can be: the conduct of the 101

100 Ibid, 2.

101 DSC 29 May 1998, NJ 1999/287 (*Caravanpark*); DSC 13 October 2006, NJ 2008/528 (*Deloitte & Touche/Vie d'Or*); DSC 18 March 2005, NJ 2006/606 (*Baby Kelly*). Cf Asser/Tjong Tjin Tai 7-IV 2014/199 & 204; *WT Nuninga*, Wrongful testing and its lively consequences (2014) 16(1) European Journal of Law Reform (EJLR) 178 f.

102 DSC 20 June 1986, NJ 198/35 (*Citronas*) in which the Dutch Supreme Court cites DSC 7 March 1969, NJ 1969/249 (*Gegaste Uien*) and DSC 12 January 1979, NJ 1979/362 (*Securicor*); see also DSC 21 January 2000, NJ 2000/553 (*ODS/CPS*).

third party (ie whether the third party has given the contractual party reason to believe that the exclusion clause could also be invoked against her); the special nature of the relation between the three parties; and the special nature of the agreement.[103]

CASES

102 In discussing the cases, these general notions about tortious and contractual liability under Dutch law must be kept in mind.

103 Under Dutch tort law, liability ensues if (i) there is an unlawful act (art 6:162(1) and (2) Dutch CC) that (ii) can be attributed to the tortfeasor (art 6:162(1) and (3) Dutch CC), and (iii) causes (arts 6:162(1) and 6:98 Dutch CC) (iv) damage (art 6:162(1) and sec 6.1.10 Dutch CC), and (v) the norm was intended to (a) protect the injured party (art 6:162(1) Dutch CC), and (b) protect against the damage as it ensued (art 6:163 Dutch CC). These five requirements are cumulative. The fifth requirement will hereinafter be referred to as tortious relativity. The first strand will be referred to as personal relativity, and the second as relativity of damage.

104 Under Dutch contract law, liability ensues if there is an obligation (*verbintenis*) that is not complied with (art 6:74 Dutch CC). Every failure in compliance gives rise to liability, provided (i) the defect can be attributed to the debtor (arts 6:74(1) and 6:75 Dutch CC), and (ii) the debtor is in default (*verzuim*) or can no longer perform (art 6:81 Dutch CC). Obligations arise if a party has expressed a willingness to so be bound (art 3:33). A contract gives rise to two or more obligations (art 6:213 Dutch CC).

105 In the discussion below, only those aspects relevant to the particular case will be discussed.

CASE 1. THE UNATTRACTIVE SHOPPING MALL

106 Under Dutch contract law, a contract concluded for the benefit of the third party normally does not allow the third party to sue for non-performance. Nevertheless, it could be argued that the clause allowing for subletting can be construed as a third party clause, allowing a potential subletter to rely on the *entire* contract once she accepts this clause (cf art 6:253(1) Dutch CC). C's contract with Z could then be constructed as an acceptance of this clause,

103 Cf DSC 21 January 2000, NJ 2000/553 (*ODS/CPS*).

as the acceptance of a so-called third party clause only has to be addressed to one of the parties (art 6:253(3) Dutch CC). This allows C to rely on the contract between Z and D directly (art 6:253(1) Dutch CC). It should be emphasised that the construction of the subletting clause advocated above is not straightforward. The court would have to determine whether that explanation would be what both parties could, given the circumstances, reasonably expect the clause to entail.[104] This cannot be determined on the limited facts of this case. If it is to be construed as such, however, it is clear that D's failure to keep the mall clean and attractive will be a breach of that clause and allow C to claim. As for the amount of damages, it would appear that C could claim for loss of profit (art 6:96(1) Dutch CC).

Alternatively, it is worth considering whether D's failure to act could give rise 107
to tortious liability. Under certain circumstances, non-performance without due regard for another person's legitimate interests is contrary to proper social conduct and, hence, unlawful.[105] Although it would appear that C had a legitimate interest in the proper performance of the contract, much would depend on the specific circumstances. The fact that D allowed subletting supports this suggestion. Nevertheless, whether this would be enough to render D's conduct unlawful against C depends on the specific circumstances of the case. If it were, the other requirements for liability would pose no difficulty. As for the amount of damages, it would appear that C could claim for loss of profit (art 6:96(1) Dutch CC).

CASE 2. THE IDLE LAWYER

Under Dutch contract law, a contract concluded for the benefit of a third 108
party normally does not allow the third party to sue for non-performance. Nevertheless, if a contract contains a so-called third party clause and the third party accepts this clause, the third party is allowed to sue for non-performance (art 6:253(1) Dutch CC). If the clause contains no obligation for the third party, it is accepted as soon as the third party is informed of the existence of the clause (art 6:253(4) Dutch CC). Whether a third party clause can be implied into this contract will depend on the specific circumstances of the case. The court would have to determine whether that explanation would be what both parties could,

---

[104] Cf DSC 13 March 1981, NJ 1981/635 (*Haviltex*) and arts 3:33–3:35 Dutch CC.

[105] Article 6:162(2) Dutch CC. Cf eg DSC 24 September 2004, Rechtspraak van de Week (RvdW) 2004, 108 (*Vleesmeesters/Alog*); DSC 12 October 1979, NJ 1980/117 (*Radio Modern/Edah*); DSC 24 February 1982, NJ 1983/367 (*Smael/Moszkowicz*); DSC 16 February 2007, NJ 2007/256 (*Tuin Beheer/Mr X*); DCS 20 January 2012, ECLI:NL:HR:2012:BT7496, NJ 2012/59; DCS 14 July 2017, ECLI:NL:HR:2017:1355, JA 2017, 140. See above no 74.

given the circumstances, reasonably expect the contract to contain.[106] If it is possible, though, C can sue D for breach of contract and claim damages directly as D can no longer correct his mistake (art 6:74 Dutch CC). The damages would simply be the £9,000 (art 6:95 Dutch CC).

109 Alternatively, it is worth considering whether D's failure to act could give rise to tortious liability. It would appear that D's conduct can be qualified as unlawful against C, as C had a legitimate interest in the proper performance of the contract and non-performance without due regard for C's legitimate interests is contrary to proper social conduct and, hence, unlawful.[107] The other requirements for tortious liability are not problematic in this case. The damages would simply be the £9,000 (art 6:95 Dutch CC).

CASE 3. THE DEFECTIVE HOUSE

110 If Z has acquired certain 'qualitative rights' related to her property, these rights are automatically transferred along with the property to C (art 6:251(1) Dutch CC). In order to establish whether C has a claim against D, it is worth inquiring whether Z obtained any qualitative rights upon construction.

111 A contractor is liable to the person that contracted for the construction if the defect that caused the house to collapse was 'hidden' upon completion (*oplevering*) and the contractor knew about the existence of the defect. Whether it qualifies as hidden depends on whether the expertise of Z would have allowed her to discover it. Assuming that Z did not have much building expertise, the defect qualifies as hidden. In literature it has been assumed that this automatically means D knew about this.[108] It should be noted, however, that this rests on a questionable interpretation of the preparatory materials.[109] Hence, although it is to be expected that a court will interpret 'known' as 'should have known', it must be emphasised that this is mere speculation.[110] Assuming that

---

106 Cf DSC 13 March 1981, NJ 1981/635 (*Haviltex*) and arts 3:33–3:35 Dutch CC.

107 Article 6:162(2) Dutch CC. Cf eg DSC 24 September 2004, RvdW 2004, 108 (*Vleesmeesters/Alog*); DSC 12 October 1979, NJ 1980/117 (*Radio Modern/Edah*); DSC 24 February 1982, NJ 1983/367 (*Smael/Moszkowicz*); DSC 16 February 2007, NJ 2007/256 (*Tuin Beheer/Mr X*); DCS 20 January 2012, ECLI:NL:HR:2012:BT7496, NJ 2012/59; DCS 14 July 2017, ECLI:NL:HR:2017:1355, JA 2017, 140. See above no 74.

108 Asser/Van den Berg 7-VI 2017/137; T&C Burgerlijk Wetboek, commentaar op artikel 762 Boek 7 BW.

109 Cf MvA, Kamerstukken II 1995/96, 23 095, no 5, 18 f. The only point of discussion was what qualifies as a hidden defect. The issue as to when the contractor 'knew' is simply not addressed.

110 As art 7:754 Dutch CC refers to both concepts, it would add to uniformity if this was copied. On the other hand, the fact that both are explicitly mentioned in art 7:754 Dutch CC and not in art 7:762 Dutch CC could be a contraindication.

the defect is indeed 'hidden', and that D was negligent in constructing the house, D remains liable for defects against Z (art 7:758(2)–(3) Dutch CC) and Z could bring a claim for breach of contract against D (arts 7:754 and 6:74 Dutch CC).[111]

For C the question now becomes whether the claim Z had would qualify as a qualitative right under art 6:251 Dutch CC. It must be submitted that they can, as they are so closely connected to Z's house that they only have a purpose in relation to that house (cf art 6:251(1) Dutch CC). This means that these rights are transferred along with the property, thus allowing C to bring the claim in contract, too. 112

Having established that these rights are transferred, the question becomes whether D can invoke the exclusion clause against C. It must be recalled that the exclusion clause was concluded with Z, not with C. Contractual relativity therefore prevents D from relying on it. Of course, under Dutch law exclusion clauses can be invoked against third parties if it would be unreasonable *not* to do so, but it cannot be imagined how it would be unreasonable in this case. After all, even for Z, who agreed to it, the clause was voidable. If liability ensues, therefore, the exclusion clause will not avail D. 113

Theoretically, it could be argued that D is liable to C in tort as well. It would appear that negligently constructing a house with hidden defects is unlawful against anyone occupying the house within a relatively short period, regardless of any contractual obligation. Whether it actually is will depend on all the circumstances of the case – and will therefore be largely decided at the discretion of the court. If unlawfulness towards C is established, the other requirements for liability will easily be met. Again, the exclusion clause will have no effect. 114

In both cases, the amount of compensation would be equal to the costs incurred to repair the damage to the house and the costs of the injury (art 6:95 Dutch CC). The court may need to estimate these costs in accordance with the nature of the specific injuries (art 6:97 Dutch CC). 115

CASE 4. APARTMENT IN FLAMES

If a landlord has knowledge or should have knowledge of a defect with the house, he is liable for damage caused by the defect (art 7:208 Dutch CC). In this case, therefore, it would appear that the failure to monitor gives rise to liability. This liability is contractual in nature as the obligation of art 7:208 Dutch CC is part of the special agreements section on rent agreements of the Dutch CC (sec 7.4 Dutch CC). The claim must therefore be brought on the basis 116

111 Cf MvT, Kamerstukken II 1992/93, 23 095, no 3, 23.

of art 6:74. Liability ensues without delay as the damage has already occurred and D can no longer repair the defect (cf art 6:81 Dutch CC). Damages will compensate all losses and costs incurred. Whether and to what extent these damages can be recovered will depend on the extent to which, at the time of the breach, they could reasonably have been expected to flow from the event.[112]

117 It would appear that C could, theoretically, also bring an action in tort. In theory, it is possible to construe a breach of art 7:208 Dutch CC as 'unlawful behaviour' in the sense of art 6:162(2) Dutch CC. Once this is accepted, the other requirements for tortious liability are easily established. Nevertheless, although there is no principle of *non cumul* and C could theoretically bring this action, it would appear that a court is likely to decide the case on the basis of contract law and either reject the tortious claim for lack of interest (as redress will already have been obtained) or grant the claim without awarding further compensation.

CASE 5. INJURED SKIER

118 If the cause for derailment is not entirely clear, it would appear that it is difficult for C to bring an action in tort. Under art 6:162 Dutch CC (unlawful act), C would have to prove that D1 has behaved unlawfully (ie contrary to law, proper social conduct, or custom). This may be difficult in itself to prove. Furthermore, the unlawful behaviour would need to be attributed to D1 (art 6:162(3) Dutch CC). If D1 can prove, for instance, that the ski lift was checked for defects frequently, the action may fail on this ground. It would appear that this is difficult to prove on the limited facts.

119 A more likely option would be to claim under art 6:174 Dutch CC. Under this provision, the possessor of immovable things (*opstallen*), which are not in a state that can be reasonably expected of them, can be liable if (i) the defects with the immovable things pose a risk of damage, and (ii) this risk materialises. This option may be preferred, as proving that the ski lift showed defects that could lead to derailment would suffice. An argument by D1 that she frequently checked the lifts would not release her of her liability. Nevertheless, as the cause is not entirely clear, the existence of a defect may be contested.

120 An action for breach of contract seems the most likely course of action by C. The obligation to keep C safe whilst in the park would qualify as an obligation of result. The fact that C is injured thus qualifies as a breach of contract (art 6:74 Dutch CC). Only if D1 can prove that this breach of contract cannot

---

[112] Asser/Hartkamp & Sieburgh 6-II 2013/69, citing DSC 1 July 1977, NJ 1978/84; DSC 13 November 1987, NJ 1988/210.

be attributed to her according to law, juridical act or social convention (art 6:75 Dutch CC) will she not be held liable. In this case, the burden of proof will be on D1.

Finally, the question is whether C can claim from D2. The insurance clause is somewhat opaque. 121

CASE 6. EXPLODING CAR

Assuming that C is a consumer (ie an individual purchasing products for herself, not as an entrepreneur; see art 7:5 Dutch CC), C could normally bring a claim for breach of contract on the basis of arts 7:24(1) and 6:74 Dutch CC against D1. Article 7:24 Dutch CC provides that a vendor in a consumer sale is liable for damage, other than damage recoverable under the product liability regime (see below), resulting from a non-conforming product. It is not difficult for C to establish that the car did not conform to what was to be expected. D1 will want to argue that the warranty has expired, thus phrasing the warranty as a de facto exclusion clause. In the context of a consumer sale, however, a warranty cannot have that effect (arts 7:6(1)[113] and 7:6a(1)[114] Dutch CC). Hence, C can recover compensation for all damage to the car and damage to other property that exceeds €500 (the first €500 will fall within the product liability regime). 122

C can claim damages in tort from D2 for (i) damage to other things (*zaken*) exceeding €500, and/or (ii) personal injury or death on the basis of art 6:185 ff Dutch CC (product liability). It is required that (i) the defect in the product was not impossible to detect, (ii) it is not established by D that the defect could not have existed upon production, or (iii) the product was produced in accordance with mandatory safety requirements (art 6:185(1) Dutch CC). After all, a car is a product (art 6:187 Dutch CC) and it is generally accepted that cars should not explode within three years, thus making the car defective (art 6:186 Dutch CC). C, on whom the burden of proof rests, can easily prove the existence of: (i) the defect, (ii) the damage, and (iii) the causal link between the two (art 6:188 Dutch CC). There are no indications of why the warranty concluded by D1 and C would work as an exclusion clause for D2. First, it was not concluded for D2's benefit, and secondly, even if it were, it would not be allowed to function as an exclusion clause on the basis of art 6:192(1) Dutch CC). 123

---

113 Rules on consumer sales (such as art 7:24 Dutch CC) cannot be deviated from to the detriment of the consumer.

114 Warranties in consumer sales cannot prejudice other rights of consumers.

CASE 7. RACING BOAT BURNING

124 First, it must be established whether contractual liability would ensue. It would appear that the contract between D and C is a normal sales contract (as opposed to a consumer sales contract) (art 7:1 Dutch CC). C could argue that the product was not in conformity with the contract as it was not suitable for 'normal use' (art 7:17 Dutch CC). It would appear that the ship was not suitable and thus liability would ensue. Case law teaches that the entire damage for which C is claiming compensation could be recovered on the basis of arts 6:74 and 6:98 Dutch CC.[115] The damage to the boat is evidently in a causal relationship with the non-conformity. As for the incurred costs, it could be argued that C would have had to pay for his repatriation expenses after the race either way, but in a similar case the DSC held that such costs were recoverable as they were made 'in vain' (*tevergeefs*).[116] The fact that they would have been made at the end of the race anyway does not alter this. All that is relevant, according to the DSC, is that costs were incurred 'in vain' due to the non-compliance.[117] In principle, therefore, C could claim compensation for the entire damage.

125 Having established liability in principle, it must now be inquired whether D's warranty could be construed as an exclusion clause. The court would have to determine whether that was what both parties could, given the circumstances, reasonably have expected the clause to entail.[118] It would appear that this is not very likely.

CASE 8. INSIDIOUS REPORT

126 C is essentially claiming compensation from D on the basis of tortious interference with a contract.[119] The report can be classified as an interference with a contractual obligation. The DSC has recognised that, under certain circumstances, an interference with a contract – leading to the lawful (rescission) or unlawful (breach) termination of a contract – can be unlawful.[120] In this case, the interference can be classified as unlawful. The fact that D knew,

---

115 Cf DSC 28 January 2005, NJ 2008/55.

116 Ibid, at 3.3.2.

117 Ibid, at 3.3.1–3.3.3.

118 Cf DSC 13 March 1981, NJ 1981/635 (*Haviltex*) and art 3:33–3:35 Dutch CC.

119 Liability for interference with a contract is generally believed to be tortious, see: *van Bochove* (fn 67) 35–38.

120 *Van Bochove* (fn 67) 45; *C Gielen*, Kort Begrip van het Intellectuele Eigendomsrecht (2011) 659 and citing case law. DSC 11 November 1937, NJ 1937/1096 (*Kolynos*); DSC 13 January 1961, NJ 1962/245 (*KIM/Sieverding*); DSC 12 January 1962, NJ 1962/246 (*Nibeja/Grundig*).

should have known or intended[121] for C to terminate the contract on the basis of D's information is of primary relevance.[122] Nevertheless, the DSC has made clear that this circumstance alone is insufficient for establishing liability. Other 'circumstances' are required. Circumstances that have been mentioned in case law and contribute to D's liability in this case are: (i) the fact that D's report was relied upon by C regarding the quality of Z's product, which can be classified either as incitement (leading to strongly increased culpability) or promotion (leading to slightly increased culpability) of termination;[123] (ii) the special relationship between D and C, which contributes to an assumption of influence'[124] and (iii) P's loss of her position as sole purchaser of Z's product, which is a serious detriment.[125] Attribution and personal relativity necessarily follow from this conclusion. Relativity of damage and a causal relationship exist, too, but require a little more detailed attention in the light of awarding damages.

The damages in this case are twofold. First, C's loss of the contract and the 127
loss of its position as sole purchaser qualify for compensation. Those damages are in a *conditio sine qua non* relationship with the interference and it would appear that this damage can be reasonably attributed considering the nature of the tort (intentional interference) and its nature (pecuniary loss).[126] Secondly, on the basis of art 6:104 Dutch CC, C may also claim the profits D already made from the contract. The causal relationship in this respect is also obvious. Furthermore, it is clear that the norm breached – ie the prohibition on competing unlawfully – aims to protect competitors (as D) against both types of damage. Finally, it should be emphasised that, however insidious the report is, damages cannot be exemplary or punitive in nature.[127]

CASE 9. CIRCULAR LETTER

In this case, the main question is whether statements made about competitors 128
in the course of business are unlawful. Under Dutch law, D has a duty of care

121 It is not clear whether D filed the report in order for P to terminate the contract. For that reason, both are mentioned.

122 Regarding the concept of 'knew or should have known', see DSC 26 January 2007, NJ 2007/78 (*Van de Ven/Sleegers*). Regarding the concept of 'intent', see *du Perron* (fn 56) 150; *van Bochove* (fn 67) 52. It is not necessary for the third party to benefit from the breach or termination: DSC 30 September 2005, NJ 2005/513 (*Melkquotum*).

123 *Van Bochove* (fn 67) 52 f.

124 DSC 3 January 1964, NJ 1965/16 (*Streefland/Van der Graaf*).

125 DSC 17 May 1985, NJ 1986/760 (*Curaçao/Boyé*); DSC 15 October 1999, NJ 2000/101 (*Driessen/Benegas*).

126 Cf Asser/Hartkamp & Sieburgh 6-II 2013/57.

127 Cf DCC 18 June 2010, RvdW 2010, 771 (*Doerga/Stichting Ymere*) at 3.6.

towards her competitor C when making statements about her and/or her services.[128] As the statements were not made upon request and were made in a public manner, the standard of care that D should have observed in making the statements was high.[129] Add to this the rule that false statements are generally unlawful,[130] and it would appear that D's statements are, without a doubt, unlawful.[131] The requirements of attribution and personal relativity necessarily follow.

129 It is difficult for C to prove what damage she suffered. There are two types of damage possible. First, if contracts were terminated, the loss suffered would qualify as pecuniary damage (art 6:106 Dutch CC). If C can prove a *conditio sine qua non* relationship between the termination and the statements, they are likely to be considered as having been caused by it (art 6:98 Dutch CC). The damage-based strand of relativity is not very problematic in this case either, as the norm prevents unlawfully caused loss of business. Secondly, C may have lost chances of concluding new contracts. In this case C is essentially alleging that she lost a chance. A loss of a chance can be recoverable under Dutch law.[132] This is only possible if the court finds that the claimant would have had a 'fair' (*redelijke*) chance of success but for the tortious act. It must be submitted that this will be hard to prove. The burden of proof is on C. It should be clear that, should C succeed, it is not the damage that could have ensued that is being recovered, but the value of the chance.[133] It will be up to the court to assess the damage (art 6:97 Dutch CC).[134] This gives the court considerable discretion. There are no judgments known in which the DSC has given guidelines as to how these damages ought to be determined.[135]

CASE 10. SHORTAGE OF SUPPLY

130 Under Dutch law, C's problem is prima facie a contract law problem. The alteration or 'new contract' appears to have been concluded under 'abuse

---

128 DSC 22 November 1934, NJ 1935/529, Weekblad voor het Recht (W) 12851 (*De Haan's Ochtendvoer*); DSC 4 January 1952, NJ 1952/158 (*Uitspannen*).

129 DSC 28 November 1941, NJ 1942/190 (*Gebroeders Pesie*).

130 DSC 24 December 1937, NJ 1941/660 (*Haka-Katten-Brood*).

131 This conclusion is confirmed by the more or less analogous case: DSC 4 January 1952, NJ 1952/158 (*Uitspannen*). Cf *Gielen* (fn 120) 660.

132 DSC 17 October 1997, NJ 1998/508 at 3.8; DSC 24 October 1997, NJ 1998/257 (*Baijings/Mr H*); DSC 19 January 2007, NJ 2007/63 at 3.4.3; DSC 16 February 2007, NJ 2007/256 at 3.3.a (*Tuin Beheer/Maatschap A*).

133 Asser/Hartkamp & Sieburgh 6-II 2013/79–80a.

134 DSC 12 December 2012, NJB 2013/147 (*Deloitte/H&H*) at 3.8. See also: art 6:97 Dutch CC.

135 A court could rely on an expert ruling to determine the extent of damages, see, for instance: Court of Appeal The Hague, 26 March 2013, ECLI:NL:GHDHA:2013:1494 at 34.

of circumstances' or 'undue influence' (art 3:44(1) and (4) Dutch CC),[136] as D deliberately used the circumstance that C was confronted with fewer suppliers to coerce an unconscionable bargain.[137] This means that the termination of the former contract and the conclusion of the new one – which appear to be one juridical act[138] – can be nullified, as a result of which the contract is voided and nullified *ab initio* (3:53 DCC). The result, of course, is that the former contract resurfaces. C can claim (i) recovery of payments already made under the new contract as payments not due (art 6:203 Dutch CC), and (ii) specific performance under the old contract for delivery at the old price (art 3:296 Dutch CC).

Theoretically, it is possible to try and construe these facts as amounting to a tortious act. That would, however, offer C no advantage as regards either the burden of proof – indeed it would be more difficult to prove, as the 'damage' would be a valid contract, which gives rise to the question of why it should be unlawful if the contract is not nullified – or the extent of damages. Furthermore mere abuse of circumstances does not qualify as a tort. Additional circumstances upon which the claim that D acted tortiously can be based are required. 131

CASE 11. INJURED ROCK STAR

In this answer, it will be assumed that D's behaviour is unlawful against X and can be attributed to her. There are two obstacles in establishing liability towards C. First, it must be submitted that the norm breached, ie causing an accident to X, was not intended to protect C. The personal strand of the doctrine of relativity thus prevents C from claiming damages. Secondly, it could be argued – although this is somewhat theoretical – that this damage is not caused by D in terms of art 6:98 Dutch CC as the nature of the norm prevents a court from 'reasonably attributing' this damage to the tortious act. It should be emphasised that a court is far more likely to apply the relativity doctrine 132

136 It would appear that the doctrine of duress (art 3:44(1) and (2) Dutch CC) is too strong for this case, as the loss of contract is the only threat involved. Cf *Hijma et al* (fn 45) 203 f.

137 Cf liability for informing improperly: DSC 18 June 1983, NJ 1983/723 (*Plas/Valburg*); DSC 23 October 1987, NJ 1988/1017 (*VSH/Shell*); DSC 14 June 1996, NJ 1997/481 (*MBO/De Ruiterij*); DSC 4 October 1996, NJ 1997/65 (*ABB/Staat*); DSC 12 August 2005, NJ 2005/467 (*CBB/JPO*); DSC 9 December 2011, NJ 2013/273 (*X/Y*); DSC 3 May 2013, NJ 2013/572 (*KLM (private procurement)*). Liability for breaking off negotiations: DSC 2 April 1993, NJ 1995/94 (*Cattier/Waanders*); DSC 25 January 2002, NJ 2003/31 (*Paalman/Lampenier*); DSC 5 June 2009, NJ 2012/182 (*Dexio*); DSC 5 June 2009, NJ 2012/184 (*Aegon*); DSC 5 June 2009, NJ 2012/183 (*Levob Bank*).

138 If one were to qualify them as two juridical acts, that would not change the analysis: in that case both juridical acts can be thought of as being performed as a result of abuse of circumstances. Subsequently, both can be nullified, thus achieving the same result.

and that, in any case, the second approach is effectively a reiteration of the first. In short, D's behaviour does not qualify as a tort against C.

133 The only damages C could possibly claim from D would be compensation for the damage that she incurred for the benefit of X, provided X would have been able to claim these damages had she incurred them herself (art 6:107 Dutch CC). Note, however, that art 6:107 Dutch CC also has a limiting effect: it not only *allows* C to claim these damages, it also *limits* the damage C can claim to those stipulated in the article.[139] Article 6:107 Dutch CC reads as follows:

> 'If someone has sustained physical or mental injuries as a result of an event for which another person is liable, then this other person must compensate not only the damage of the injured person, but also the costs which a third party has incurred on behalf of the injured person, insofar as the injured person, if he had incurred these costs himself, could have recovered them from the liable person. The pervious sentence does not affect costs which are incurred by virtue of insurance.'

The case at hand does not imply the existence of such cost.

CASE 12. EQUIPMENT DESTROYED

134 The case against D1 is a contractual case for non-performance. As it is no longer possible to perform adequately, C could normally claim damages directly (art 6:74 Dutch CC). It could be argued that since D1's non-performance was not the result of an error on his part, D1 escapes liability. Nevertheless, art 6:75 Dutch CC is not limited to a culpability assessment. Certain risks are attributed to the debtor regardless of culpability.[140] It would appear that since the delivery of equipment is the very thing that C and D1 contracted for and traffic accidents are normal and foreseeable risks of that business, this risk is attributable to D1 according to generally accepted principles or common opinion (*verkeersopvattingen*).[141]

135 The case against D2 is a tort case. It can be assumed that D2's behaviour was unlawful against X and can be attributed to her. There are two types of damage: (i) the damage to the equipment and (ii) the damage due to cancellation of the concert. The damage to the equipment is in a *conditio sine qua non* relationship with the unlawful act and can be reasonably attributed to it (arts 6:162(1) and art 6:98 Dutch CC). Furthermore, the norm was intended to protect

---

139 Cf DSC 9 October 2009, NJ 2010/387 (*Vilt*) at 3.5.

140 Cf *MM Olthof*, Commentaar op artikel 75 Boek 6 BW, in: JH Nieuwenhuis/CJJM Stolker/WL Val, T&C Burgerlijk Wetboek (2017); Asser/Hartkamp & Sieburgh 6-I 2016/353.

141 Cf Asser/Hartkamp & Sieburgh 6-I* 2012/354.

(i) the owner of the equipment against (ii) damage caused to it. If C is the owner, he can claim compensation for this damage from D2. The cancellation of the concert, however, is difficult. The damage is in a *conditio sine qua non* relationship with the unlawful act, but there are two obstacles in establishing liability for this damage. First, it must be submitted that the norm breached, ie causing an accident with D1, was not intended to protect C. The personal strand of the doctrine of relativity thus prevents C from claiming damages. Secondly, it could be argued – although this is somewhat theoretical – that this damage is not caused by D2 in terms of art 6:98 Dutch CC, as the nature of the norm prevents a court from 'reasonably attributing' this damage to the tortious act. It should be emphasised that a court is far more likely to apply the relativity doctrine and that, in any case, the second approach is essentially a reiteration of the first. C cannot claim these damages from D2.

CASE 13. SLIPPING ON A LETTUCE LEAF

It must first be examined whether the act is unlawful. Liability for dangerous 136
situations ensues if the damage is probable, foreseeable and substantial, whilst the burden to prevent it is smaller.[142] Several lower courts have held supermarkets liable for personal injuries for relatively trivial accidents, such as slipping on a wet doormat, tripping over an empty pallet, and being injured by broken glass on the floor (something that happened more often in that particular supermarket).[143] In a case that is highly similar to this one (ie slipping on a banana peel), however, the Common Court of Justice of the Netherlands Antilles and Aruba held that since the supermarket in question had sufficient safety measures in place to prevent accidents, liability was not established.[144] In respect of this case law, it would appear unlikely that liability will ensue. First, unlike the hazards in the lower instance case, slipping on a lettuce leaf is not a known hazard, which increases the burden of preventing it. Second, although there is no information on the degree of safety measures in this case, it would appear unlikely that the supermarket had so few safety measures in place that they were insufficient to prevent such a rare accident as slipping on a lettuce leaf.

---

142 Cf DSC 5 November 1965, NJ 1966/136 (*Kelderluik*), in which one can discern Justice Learned Hand's economic analysis of the tort of negligence in *United States v Carroll Towing Co* 159 Federal Reporter, Second Series (F 2d) 169 (2d Cir 1947) that liability ensues if PL>B.

143 District Court Eastern Brabant, 28 January 2014, Verkeersrecht (VR) 2014/89; District Court Gelderland 22 November 2013, ECLI:NL:RBGEL:2013:4727; Court of Appeal The Hague 6 November 2011, NJ 2009/102.

144 Common Court of Justice of the Netherlands Antilles and Aruba 19 June 2009, JA 2009/149 (*X/Publix*) at 2.4.

137 A 'contractual' claim would have to be based on pre-contractual liability, as entering and browsing a shop does not entail entering into a contract. Parties must observe the standards of reasonableness and fairness in their conduct with one another in the pre-contractual phase.[145] There are no reasons to assume, however, that the standard of care to be observed by negotiating parties includes ensuring that the other does not suffer physical injury. After all, the heightened standard of care in the pre-contractual phase relates to the conclusion (or non-conclusion) and/or the content of the contract.[146]

CASE 14. TEST DRIVE

138 C can claim compensation for the damage to the car in tort. The destruction of another person's property qualifies as either an infringement of another person's subjective right or as contrary to proper social conduct and is, therefore, unlawful (art 6:162(2) Dutch CC). The other requirements are clearly met. Damages would be determined in accordance with sec 6.1.10 Dutch CC.

139 Although C and D have not formally concluded a contract, it could be argued that this is an implied contract for a loan (*bruikleen*). Offer and acceptance may be implicit; all that is required is that a court is satisfied that the parties' wills coincided.[147] A contract for loan will entail a so-called 'obligation of result' (*resultaatsverplichting*) to return the car undamaged. Clearly D's returning the car damaged is a breach of that obligation and, since there are no justifications for the breach, will warrant damages (art 6:74 Dutch CC).

CASE 15. BREACH OF NEGOTIATIONS

140 Depending on the specific circumstance of the case, C may possibly claim damages from D in tort. The principle of freedom of contract governs Dutch law. Accordingly, in principle people are free to negotiate and enter into a contract with anyone and about anything, and they have the right to break off the

145 DSC 15 November 1957, NJ 1958/67 (*Baris/Riezenkamp*).

146 Cf DSC 2 April 1993, NJ 1995/94 (*Cattier/Waanders*); DSC 25 January 2002, NJ 2003/31 (*Paalman/Lampenier*); DSC 5 June 2009, NJ 2012/182 (*Dexio*); DSC 5 June 2009, NJ 2012/184 (*Aegon*); DSC 5 June 2009, NJ 2012/183 (*Levob Bank*); DSC 18 June 1983, NJ 1983/723 (*Plas/Valburg*); DSC 23 October 1987, NJ 1988/1017 (*VSH/Shell*); DSC 14 June 1996, NJ 1997/481 (*MBO/De Ruiterij*); DSC 4 October 1996, NJ 1997/65 (*ABB/Staat*); DSC 12 August 2005, NJ 2005/467 (*CBB/JPO*); DSC 9 December 2011, NJ 2013/273 (*X/Y*); DSC 3 May 2013, NJ 2013/572 (*KLM (private procurement)*).

147 Cf Asser/Hartkamp & Sieburgh 6-III 2014/189–190.

negotiations at any time. However, the freedom to break off negotiations once they have started and then to conclude a contract with a third party, as in this case, finds its limitations in other principles governing Dutch law. The Dutch judiciary has established an extensive practice of pre-contractual liability for discontinuance of negotiations.[148] The interests of the partner in the negotiations may, at a certain phase, weigh heavier than the principle of the freedom of the contract.[149]

In the case at hand it should first be determined whether the parties are still in the pre-contractual phase. According to Dutch law, the contractual phase may be reached even if not all points have been agreed upon. In such a case a contractual obligation to reach agreement on the points not yet settled rests on the parties and one speaks of a *pactum de contrahendo*. However, the case does not present enough facts to determine that the contractual phase had been reached. 141

Depending on the specific circumstances of the case, Dutch law may offer C the possibility to claim compensation for (i) the positive contractual interest (ie the profits not made due to the breach), and (ii) the negative contractual interest (ie the costs incurred in contracting and the damage caused due to the missed opportunity to conclude contracts with third parties). It would appear that the standard of care as regards the latter is a little lower than as regards the former. These will be dealt with in turn. 142

The key norm for establishing pre-contractual liability for positive contractual interest (which is also sufficient to establish liability for negative contractual interest) is whether the injured party could 'legitimately rely' on the other party to continue negotiations.[150] It could be argued that the agreement between D and C to continue negotiations on Friday could give rise to a legitimate interest on the part of C that a contract would come into existence. It should be noted, however, that much will depend on what has been said in the course of those negotiations and how far along the negotiations were. The DSC has urged lower courts to practice restraint in applying this remedy.[151] On these facts, no conclusive answer can be given. 143

As mentioned above, the liability regime for negative contractual interest is somewhat more relaxed. Even if C could not have legitimately relied on a contract coming into existence, D may be required to compensate C for the 144

---

148 DSC 18 June 1983, NJ 1983/723 (*Plas/Valburg*); DSC 23 October 1987, NJ 1988/1017 (*VSH/Shell*); DSC 14 June 1996, NJ 1997/481 (*MBO/De Ruiterij*); DSC 4 October 1996, NJ 1997/65 (*ABB/Staat*); DSC 12 August 2005, NJ 2005/467 (*CBB/JPO*); DSC 9 December 2011, NJ 2013/273 (*X/Y*); DSC 3 May 2013, NJ 2013/572 (*KLM (private procurement)*).

149 *M Ruygvoorn*, Afgebroken onderhandelingen en het gebruik van voorbehouden (diss 2009).

150 Ibid.

151 DSC 12 August 2005, NJ 2005/467 (*CBB/JPO*).

costs incurred. There is little guidance from practice, however, as to when exactly this liability will arise.[152] A catalogue of circumstances cannot be given.

145 As regards damages for the positive contractual interest, it must be submitted that there must be proof that it was plausible that a contract would have come into existence had the negotiations not been unlawfully breached.[153] This is fairly rare.[154] Damages for negative contractual interest (such as the costs incurred) are more easily established.[155]

CASE 16. NON-DISCLOSURE OF RELEVANT FACTS

146 A failure to provide information can, in principle, give rise to three strands of legal action. First, it would appear that the harvester provided did not conform to the harvester contracted for, as – given D's knowledge about the steep fields – C could have expected the harvester to be suitable for use on steep fields (art 7:17(2) Dutch CC). This would allow C to claim damages for non-performance (art 6:74 Dutch CC) or, if D can easily obtain a suitable harvester, claim replacement with a suitable harvester (art 7:21(1)(c) Dutch CC). Damages could equal the costs of the harvester and any damaged crops. Replacement costs would be borne by D.

147 Second, C could claim nullification of the contract on the ground that it was concluded on the basis of a fundamental mistake that D knew about. C would need to prove that the contract would not have been concluded if C had known about this mistake, and that D knew or should have known that C would not have contracted had she known about the reduced performance on steep hills (art 6:228(1)(b) Dutch CC). It would appear that, in this case, an error can be established, as D knew where C intended to use the harvester. The nullification will have a retroactive effect (art 3:53 Dutch CC) and C can claim his money back as payments not due (*onverschuldigde betaling*) (art 6:203 Dutch CC). Of course, C would be obligated to return the harvester to D as the property will be considered never to have been transferred in the first place.[156]

148 Additionally or alternatively, C may wish to claim damages from D in tort.[157] Had C, for instance, destroyed her crops due to the unsuitability of the

---

152 Cf Asser/Hartkamp & Sieburgh 6-III 2014/199.

153 DSC 23 October 1987, NJ 1988/1017 (*VSH/Shell*).

154 Cf Asser/Hartkamp & Sieburgh 6-III 2014/198.

155 Ibid.

156 One of the conditions for transfer is a valid *title* (in this case: the agreement) (art 3:84 Dutch CC). As the title will be considered never to have existed, the transfer never occurred.

157 Cf DSC 2 April 1993, NJ 1995/94 (*Cattier/Waanders*); DSC 25 January 2002, NJ 2003/31 (*Paalman/Lampenier*); DSC 5 June 2009, NJ 2012/182 (*Dexio*); DSC 5 June 2009, NJ 2012/184 (*Aegon*); DSC 5 June 2009, NJ 2012/183 (*Levob Bank*).

harvester (which was not the case here), C could claim those compensation for this damage from D in tort. These damages could be claimed regardless of whether C nullified the contract.[158] Furthermore, the negative contractual interest (costs incurred in contract and missed contracts with third parties) could be claimed, too, as C must be brought into the position she would have been had D provided correct information.[159]

---

158 Asser/Hartkamp & Sieburgh 6-III 2014/640.
159 Ibid, 641, citing DSC 3 April 1992, NJ 1992/396; DSC 9 June 1995, NJ 1995/692.

THE BORDERLINES OF TORT LAW IN NORWAY

Bjarte Askeland

QUESTIONS

I. Tracing the Borderlines . . . 385
A. Distinction between Tort and Contract . . . 385
B. Existence of a 'Grey Zone'? . . . 385
C. Common or Different Rules Regulating Tort and Contract . . . 386
D. Application of Common Rules in a Different Way . . . 386
II. Main Differences between Tortious and Contractual Liability . . . 386
A. Differences as Regards the Foundations of Liability . . . 386
1) Role of Intention . . . 387
2) Role of Wrongfulness and Fault and their Variations . . . 387
3) Role of Strict Liability . . . 388
B. Differences as Regards Causation . . . 389
C. Differences as Regards Remedies . . . 390
1) Degree of Certainty of the Damage . . . 390
2) Compensation for Non-Pecuniary Loss . . . 390
3) Compensation for Loss of Earnings and for Loss of Chance . . . 391
4) Restitutionary Damages . . . 392
5) Aggravated and Exemplary (or Punitive) Damages . . . 392
6) Other Remedies . . . 393
D. Differences as Regards Recoverability of 'Pure Economic Losses' . . . 393
E. Differences as Regards Liability for Others . . . 394
1) Liability for Auxiliaries and for Independent Contractors . . . 394
2) Liability of Representatives of Natural Persons . . . 396
3) Liability of the Auxiliary/Organ Itself . . . 397
F. Differences as Regards Liability in the Case of Multiple Tortfeasors/Breaching Parties . . . 399
G. Differences as Regards the Persons Who May be Protected . . . 400
H. Differences as Regards Defences . . . 400
I. Differences as Regards Limitation Periods . . . 401

J. Differences as Regards Proof ... 401
K. Reasons for the Differences ... 402
III. Limitation or Exclusion of Liability Arising from Tort and from Contract ... 402
A. Statutory Provisions Authorising a Limitation or Exclusion of Liability ... 402
B. Limitation or Exclusion of Contractual and Tortious Liability by Contract ... 404
1) Is it Possible to Limit or Exclude Contractual and Tortious Liability under a Contract? ... 404
2) To What Extent can a Contractual Exclusion Provide a Defence to a Third Party to the Contract? ... 404
IV. Non-Concurrence or Concurrence of Actions ... 405
A. Overview ... 405
1) Areas of Overlap between Tort and Contract ... 405
2) Approach to Non-Concurrence and Concurrence of Actions ... 405
B. Concurrence/Exclusion of Actions for the Protection against Personal Injury ... 405
C. Concurrence/Exclusion of Actions for the Protection of Property ... 405
D. Concurrence/Exclusion in the Case of Interference with Contractual Rights ... 406
1) Interference with a Contractual Relationship ... 406
2) Loss of Business due to Personal Injury to Someone Else's Employees or Clients or to Property Damage to the Entrepreneur ... 406
V. Specific Situations ... 408
A. Pre-Contractual Liability ... 408
B. Liability of Professionals ... 409

CASES

Case 1. The Unattractive Shopping Mall ... 410
Case 2. The Idle Lawyer ... 410
Case 3. The Defective House ... 411
Case 4. Apartment in Flames ... 411
Case 5. Injured Skier ... 412
Case 6. Exploding Car ... 413
Case 7. Racing Boat Burning ... 413
Case 8. Insidious Report ... 414
Case 9. Circular Letter ... 414
Case 10. Shortage of Supply ... 415

Case 11. Injured Rock Star 415
Case 12. Equipment Destroyed 416
Case 13. Slipping on a Lettuce Leaf........ 417
Case 14. Test Drive 417
Case 15. Breach of Negotiations 417
Case 16. Non-Disclosure of Relevant Facts 418

QUESTIONS

I. TRACING THE BORDERLINES

A. DISTINCTION BETWEEN TORT AND CONTRACT

The distinction between tort and contract is made firstly on recognising whether or not there is a binding contract between the tortfeasor (or his principal) and the victim. If not, the doctrine and principles of extra-contractual tort law are applied. However, there are certain areas where the rules of delict are applied even if there is a contract between the parties. In particular, there is a tradition for tort law reasoning whenever personal injuries are involved, regardless of the fact that the risk that led to the injury was caused by the contract and the fulfilment of contractual duties.[1] 1

B. EXISTENCE OF A 'GREY ZONE'?

Under Norwegian law, it is well recognised that there is a 'grey zone' between contract and tort. The older traditional doctrine referred to *culpa in contrahendo* as a situation that required special treatment.[2] As explained below in sec V.A, a modern version of the rules of liability within the grey area falls under the concept of 'pre-contractual liability'. The doctrine recognises that there is an area between contract and tort law, when the claimant may sue both in contract and in tort, even though neither of the approaches captures all the legal implications. This is, however, a minor problem to the parties involved and to the court. The rather pragmatic approach of the Norwegian legal doctrine allows a recognition of the fact that contractual relations, or something very near to a binding contract, may strengthen the grounds of liability in tort. It is also possible to take account of the contact between the parties in an overall judgement of whether liability should arise on the concrete merits of the case. 2

---

1 See, for example, the tradition in the area of injuries connected to medical treatment, *N Nygaard*, Skade og ansvar (6th edn 2007) 8, 470–473.

2 *P Augdahl*, Obligasjonsrettens alminnelige del (5th edn 1978) 251–252.

C. COMMON OR DIFFERENT RULES REGULATING TORT AND CONTRACT

3 It would be inaccurate to state that there are common rules governing the two areas. In both areas, one may establish a fact that fulfils the criteria of a legal basis of liability, economic loss and a causal link between the mentioned fact and the loss, but these rules are not considered common to tort and contract. The set of rules are similar, but they are perceived to be two separate regimes. Theorists maintain that the two sets of rules are 'parallel' and that they have 'many points of similarity'. Still, they emphasise the differences between the regimes.[3] The perception of two regimes is also reflected in the terminology on the subject. One speaks of 'compensation within a contract' and 'compensation outside a contract', referring to – in principle – two separate sets of compensation criteria.[4]

D. APPLICATION OF COMMON RULES IN A DIFFERENT WAY

4 As mentioned above, the rules are not actually common to tort and contract but are rather regimes with similarities. Hence the court operates with slightly different prerequisites, slightly different reasoning and slightly different outcomes of cases on each side of the borderline between contract and tort.

II. MAIN DIFFERENCES BETWEEN TORTIOUS AND CONTRACTUAL LIABILITY

A. DIFFERENCES AS REGARDS THE FOUNDATIONS OF LIABILITY

5 Generally the bases of liability are very much the same in the two disciplines.[5] However, some profound differences can be pointed out: whereas liability in tort law is based on prevention and deterrence, one must acknowledge another important intention behind the rules applied in contract law: the liability sanction is intended to *encourage* the contract debtor to fulfil his obligations.[6] Nygaard points out that compensation in contract is a *subsidiary* arrangement in order to fill the primary goal: performing the contract according to its content.[7]

---

3 See *Nygaard* (fn 1) 7 and *V Hagstrøm*, Obligasjonsrett (2nd edn 2011) 466.

4 See, for example, *Nygaard* (fn 1) 7 and *Hagstrøm* (fn 3) 466 f.

5 *Hagstrøm* (fn 3) 468.

6 *K Krüger*, Norsk Kontraktsrett (1989) 780; *Hagstrøm* (fn 3) 466 and *Nygaard* (fn 1) 7.

7 *Nygaard* (fn 1) 7.

As for delict, the goals of repairing the damage and prevention (deterrence) are considered the most important.[8]

1) *Role of Intention*

6 The role of intention is, for practical purposes, the same in both areas of law. In tort law, intent constitutes a reason for holding the tortfeasor liable for rather remote consequences of the damaging act.[9] The reasoning is that grave culpability, such as intent, should render a more extensive responsibility, also for more remote consequences of the damaging act. Hence one can speak of congruence or symmetry between the grounds of liability and the extension of liability.[10]

7 This way of reasoning will sometimes also arise in contract law. The principle of grading culpability and allowing it to be reflected in the question as to which consequences the tortfeasor should be liable for is embedded in the legislation relating to contracts. In fact, you can find this distinction and appreciation of the principle in positive statutory provisions. An example is the Norwegian Law of Sales (Kjøpsloven, kjl) §40.[11] If there is negligence involved on the part of the seller, liability will arise for *indirect* consequences of the breach of contract, see kjl §40 (3) cf §27. Otherwise, in the case of non-delivery that does not stem from negligence but rather because of mishaps within the seller's sphere (the impediment rule), the seller will be liable only for the *direct* loss, see kjl §40 (1) cf §27.

2) *Role of Wrongfulness and Fault and their Variations*

8 The role of fault is somewhat different in the two disciplines due to the fact that considerations of whether there is fault within contract law is very much tied to the obligations expressed or implied in the contract. Theorists emphasise that the *culpa* standard within contracts may contain a 'professional evaluation'.[12] It has also been held that there are objective standards regulating *culpa* or negligence in contract, based on the duties agreed upon when entering into the contract.[13] Thorson holds that the fact of entering into a contract implies that the tortfeasor knows more about the victim and the risks than is the case in extra-contractual relationships. Thus he maintains that this is the main

8 Ibid, 19 f. *P Lødrup* (with the assistance of *M Kjelland*), Lærebok i erstatningsrett (6th edn 2009) 108–118.
9 *Hagstrøm* (fn 3) 478, 550.
10 *Nygaard* (fn 1) 379 f.
11 Lov om kjøp 13 May 1988 no 27.
12 *Hagstrøm* (fn 3) 468 ff.
13 See ibid, 458.

reason for the difference in the application of the *culpa* norm.[14] In addition, there are many acts and codes of practice that indicate what can be considered as prudent behaviour in certain roles or functions that are characterised by a contractual relationship, typically attorneys, real estate brokers, accountants, entrepreneurs, etc. The hallmarks of good performance and prudent behaviour which have developed in such specialist fields leave, practically speaking, no excuses for not complying with the contractual duties, The expectations of professional behaviour, by the contractual parties and the established practice of good performance, all more or less tied to statutory provisions, make the *culpa* standard objective and rather strict.

9 In contrast, the consideration of whether there is fault outside a contract setting must be decided upon looser expectations of duty of care and other social and conventional expectations of a person acting in a function or acting with a mandate, with a certain purpose or pursuing a certain interest.[15] One might, somewhat crudely, say that the *culpa* standard for an average person is less strict and less clear outside the contract setting than within the contract setting.

3) Role of Strict Liability

10 In tort law, strict liability has developed over time for dangerous activities. It emerged in the second half of the 19th century in court practice. Strict liability is thus subject to uncodified rules based on court practice with the following content: an owner of property, machinery or equipment may be liable for the continuous, typical, extraordinary risks the said objects produce. In the course of the 20th century, strict liability was codified in many areas. We now have a series of statutory acts which contain such liability, amongst others the Motor Vehicle Insurance Act and the Act on Fun Fairs.[16]

11 As for contract law, strict liability has traditionally existed for certain situations, such as lack of money: a debtor can never be excused if he does not pay on time, regardless of the reason and regardless of whether there is fault on his part.[17] Strict liability could traditionally also be based on a guarantee from a vendor. Before 1988, strict liability arose for the damaging effects of sold goods. With the enactment of the Act of Sales and the Product Liability Act, the legal

---

14 *B Thorson*, Erstatningsrettslig vern for rene formuestap (2011) 235–241, 237.

15 The Norwegian *culpa* standard rests on a multi-faceted set of considerations displayed in practice and theory, see the elaboration in *Nygaard* (fn 1) 172–219 and *Lødrup* (fn 8) 127–190.

16 Bilansvarsloven 3 February 1961, bal. and Tivoliloven 7 June 1991 no 24, now Lov om Fornøyelsesinnretninger 22 May 2017 no 30.

17 For an elaboration of this rule, see *Augdahl* (fn 2) 269 ff, *Hagstrøm* (fn 3) 544 ff.

basis for liability was shifted to a more lenient or less strict liability rule.[18] For many acts within the field of contract law, liability is based on variations of the impediment rule of the United Nations Convention on Contracts for the International Sale of Goods (CISG). This has become the dominant liability rule within contract law.[19]

B. DIFFERENCES AS REGARDS CAUSATION

In principle, the same rules apply regarding factual causation. The but-for test is commonly used in both disciplines.[20] One difference is that the question of causality outside contract often refers to physical damage, whereas the question within contract often refers to pure economic loss. The former chain of causality will typically be linked to a negligent act of a tortfeasor, whereas the latter chain often features some kind of misinformation or unfulfilled expectations. The decisive rules are, however, very much the same. There has to be a basis of liability capturing a factual event that is *conditio sine qua non* for the damaging effect, and there has to be an adequate link between the damaging act and the damaging effect. 12

As for the scope of liability, there will, in principle, be a difference between delict and contract because the scope of liability in contract is affected by the content of the contract. The aim and the amount of money involved will be relevant to the normative process of limiting the extent of the recoverable damage. It is, however, emphasised by theorists that a disproportion between the amount of money involved in the contract and the award is not in itself sufficient to render the loss inadequate. In a case referred to in Rt 1972, 449, the contract amount was NOK 60,000, whereas the award was NOK 440,000. Thus the award was almost eight times the contract sum. Still, the question of adequacy turns on an overall weighing of factors, which also includes a consideration of reasonableness. This approach very much resembles the situation in tort law.[21] 13

As for the scope of liability in delict, the question turns on normal expectations for the tortfeasor at the point in time when the damaging act was committed. 14

---

18 See Kjøpsloven 13 May §27 1988 no 27 cf §40 and Produktansvarsloven 23 December 1988 no 104 §2-1.

19 See for example Avhendingslova 3 July 1992 no 93 §4-5 and Håndverkertjenesteloven 16 June 1989 no 63 §28.

20 See *Nygaard* (fn 1) 323 regarding delict and *Hagstrøm* (fn 3) 538 regarding contract. The reference to the but-for test is not made explicitly, rather implicitly, by reference to a principle of difference between the factual situation with the damage and the hypothetical situation that would have existed had the damaging event not happened.

21 This very point is made in *Hagstrøm* (fn 3) 547.

The question of adequacy is based on a test that, in principle, comprises two questions: was the damage *foreseeable* and was there a sufficiently *concrete and close* connection between the tortious act and the damage? This test is developed in cases on material damage to things.[22] It is, however, considered to be general.[23] It would be fair to say that the test must be supplemented by a consideration of reasonableness based on the concrete merits of the case.[24] One further element that may be considered is the question of whether or not, or to what degree, the victim had a possibility to protect himself. An important case in this respect is Rt 1973, 1268. A plane destroyed electricity cables supplying electricity to a large number of receivers, including a breeder of fish. Because of the lack of electricity, some fish died, for which the breeder claimed compensation. The Supreme Court found that there was not a sufficiently adequate causal link in this case. This reasoning included a statement on the fact that the owner of the fish could have protected himself by keeping a generator to produce electricity on his own.[25] The reasoning based on the possibility of self-protection has been emphasised in text books and doctrine.[26]

C. DIFFERENCES AS REGARDS REMEDIES

1) *Degree of Certainty of the Damage*

15 There are no articulated differences on this point. For both disciplines, the general principle of proof within civil law applies.[27] This means that the claimant has to prove that it is more likely than not that he will incur a loss. As regards damages in contract law, the question of proving a loss of profit is considered to be complicated.[28] Still, the regular rule on balance of probabilities applies.

2) *Compensation for Non-Pecuniary Loss*

16 As regards tort law, compensation for non-pecuniary loss depends on the existence of special legal bases for such compensation. It has been assumed for a long time that compensation for non-pecuniary loss will only be awarded where there is a statutory provision that so provides.[29]

22 See Rt 1955, 872 and Rt 1973, 1268.
23 *Nygaard* (fn 1) 367–371.
24 *Hagstrøm* (fn 3) 551 regarding contract law.
25 Rt 1973, 1268 at 1273.
26 See eg *Nygaard* (fn 1) 369.
27 For a thorough examination of the standards in this respect, see *M Strandberg*, Beviskrav i sivilie saker (2011).
28 *Hagstrøm* (fn 3) 563.
29 See, for example, *J Øvergaard*, Norsk erstatningsrett (1951) 251.

In contract law, such compensation depends on the wording of the contract. It is quite unusual for compensation clauses within contracts to cover non-pecuniary loss. The Package Travel Directive and the *Simone Leitner* case (ECJ C-168/2000) have been interpreted in such a manner that non-pecuniary loss must be covered in the case of breach of package travel contracts. Following this judgment, scholars maintain that the requisite of damage (Pakkereiseloven ("The Package Travel Act") 25 August 1995 no 52 §5-3 (*skade – "damage"*)) must include non-pecuniary loss.[30] 17

It follows from the above that there are distinct differences between the two areas of law regarding non-pecuniary loss. 18

3) Compensation for Loss of Earnings and for Loss of Chance

Compensation for loss of earnings is, in principle, regulated in the same manner in contract and delict. However, the question of adequate causation may lead to different results in the two disciplines of law. Whereas loss of earnings may be a foreseeable damage for a contracting party in breach of his contractual obligations, the loss of profit and earnings may not be so closely linked to a delictual act, unless the case concerns a personal injury which results in loss of capacity to work. 19

As for loss of a chance, this issue has not really been dealt with in court practice and has not been the subject of thorough analysis by scholars. Simonsen, however, in his 1997 doctoral thesis, addresses the question and concludes that there is no basis for such an assessment of damages within Norwegian tort law.[31] Strandberg reaches the same conclusion in his special work on compensation for personal injuries from 2005.[32] It follows from his presentation that the idea of loss of a chance appears to be somewhat alien to the Norwegian way of thinking.[33] Simonsen subsequently moves to a discussion of whether it is possible to import a doctrine of loss of a chance for certain areas of contract law, ie procurement law.[34] The approach shows that the idea of loss of a chance has no clear standing in Norwegian law regardless of whether the loss is within or outside contract. The subject has not been elaborated upon thoroughly in later theory; however it has been slightly touched upon. Hagstrøm maintains that the rule in art 4.4.3(2) UNIDROIT must apply in Norwegian law.[35] He has not, however, gained any support for his view by other leading scholars. 20

---

30 *E Monsen*, Rekkevidden av erstatningsrettslig vern for tap og ulempe som følge av formueskade, Jussens venner (JV) 2010, 1 ff.

31 *L Simonsen*, Prekontraktuelt ansvar (2007) 826–827.

32 *M Strandberg*, Skadelidtes hypotetiske inntekt (2005) 105–113.

33 This is emphasised by *Strandberg*, ibid, 110.

34 See *Simonsen* (fn 31) 828–834.

35 *Hagstrøm* (fn 3) 68.

4) *Restitutionary Damages*

21 Formally there is no rule on restitutionary damages within delictual tort law. The general rule is that the victim does not have a claim for the gains of the tortfeasor.[36]

22 There is, however, one case that granted an award to the claimant and it was apparently based on the concept of restitution: see the *Trollheimen* case, Rt 1981, 1215. An owner of reindeers had, without any legal basis or permit of any kind, allowed his animals to graze in Trollheimen (a large area of land in the mountains in the middle of Norway) for a number of years. The landowner claimed restitutionary damages based on the stipulated cost of renting a similar area for grazing. The Supreme Court merely referred to the compensation awarded to the landowner as 'compensation' (*erstatning*), but the economic reality was, as explained, something different. The material choice of restitutionary damages was, however, not specifically addressed or articulated in the premises of the decision. Still, it was very clear that the assessment of damages was in fact based upon a restitutionary approach.

23 As for contract law, the general rules are the same.[37]

24 There are, however, different statutory provisions scattered around in the private law area which provide that a claimant who has suffered an infringement can claim restitution of the gains that a perpetrator has made from the very infringement of the claimant's rights. The question of restitution of the gains first and foremost emerged in connection with the unlawful copying of trademarks and other kinds of illegitimate exploitations of another's rights or things. One scholar, Monsen, has, on the basis of these provisions, developed a general theory on the right to claim restitution, or more precisely disgorgement, of the gains in such cases.[38] The theory is primarily linked to Markedsføringsloven §8a cf 1 (an act on fair marketing and competition), but the approach and the principle also carries weight to a certain extent in general terms.

5) *Aggravated and Exemplary (or Punitive) Damages*

25 There is no actual tradition of punitive damages under Norwegian tort law. There are only certain elements of punitive damages detectable in some special legal provisions granting compensation for non-pecuniary loss in the case of personal injuries. The fact that it is possible and quite common to take into consideration

---

[36] *Nygaard* (fn 1) 70.

[37] See *Hagstrøm* (fn 3) 533 ff. The author presents the possible heads of damages after breach of contract, omitting to mention the gains of the tortfeasor.

[38] See *E Monsen*, Berikelseskrav (2007) 337–421.

the gravity of the damaging act when assessing non-pecuniary loss resembles the Anglo-American idea of punitive damages.[39]

As regards contract law, the need for punitive damages is met by the institute of 'fines per day'. If a contractual party fails to perform according to the contract, it is often agreed upon in the contract that the other party shall receive a certain amount of compensation per day. Such clauses are very common in standard contracts. There are also examples of statutory provisions prescribing such pecuniary sanctions.[40] 26

6) *Other Remedies*

As for delictual law, there is no right to compensation *in natura* and the claimant may also reject an offer of restitution in kind. Delictual tort law rules provide no legal basis for any duty to perform whatsoever.[41] 27

In contract law, the general rule is that a creditor may claim specific performance from the debtor of the natural good.[42] There are many provisions in several contract laws prescribing such duties.[43] 28

D. DIFFERENCES AS REGARDS RECOVERABILITY OF 'PURE ECONOMIC LOSSES'

There will, on average, be a greater possibility to recover pure economic loss in contract than in tort. In contract, the damage will be easier to explain as a breach of a contract which led the claimant to have certain expectations. For example, in general, it will be easier to prove loss of income from production if a term in the contract, such as the delivery of a machine which would subsequently be used to produce food, is breached. 29

In tort law, there is a need to explain why there is a compensable loss which may be difficult to formulate.[44] There is a long doctrinal development connected to the question of whether the basis of compensation for pure economic loss should be the same rules as those governing loss that stem from physical damage.[45] 30

39 For a more in-depth analysis, *B Askeland*, Punitive Damages in Scandinavia, in: H Koziol/ V Wilcox (eds), Punitive Damages: Common Law and Civil Law Perspectives (2009) 116–119.
40 See eg Bustadoppføringslova §17 cf §18.
41 See *Nygaard* (fn 1) 66.
42 See *Hagstrøm* (fn 3) 378.
43 See eg Kjøpsloven §23 and Avhendingslova §4-2.
44 See on this subject *Lødrup* (fn 8) 388 f, 394–397.
45 An informative and thorough elaboration of the developments in doctrine and in court practice is made by Bjarte Thorson in his doctoral thesis on the subject of pure economic loss, see *B Thorson*, Erstatningsrettslig vern for rene formuestap (2011) 35–64.

The majority of modern scholars now hold that there are profound differences and that it is actually problematic that the tort law doctrines have all been developed on the basis of physical damage, whereas nowadays the real problems concern pure economic loss. The question of compensation for pure economic loss divides itself into a number of very diverse problems of different areas of life.[46] A possible guideline for deciding these question may be the established more general boundaries of adequacy.[47] One problematic area has primarily been how to decide whether a frustrated expectation of receiving money should be considered a head of damage that should be compensated.[48] At the same time, scholars acknowledge that the question of compensation for pure economic loss to a great extent turns on the very question of the basis of liability and on questions of causation. A notable finding is, however, that the default rule in Norwegian law is not that the pure economic loss should not be compensated, rather the opposite.[49]

E. DIFFERENCES AS REGARDS LIABILITY FOR OTHERS[50]

1) *Liability for Auxiliaries and for Independent Contractors*

31 There is a cluster of rules stating that a principal should be responsible for tortious acts committed by auxiliaries. There are two main rules on the subject. Firstly, Skadeserstatningsloven (The Compensatory Damages Act), 13 June 1969, no. 26, (skl.) §2-1 reads that the employer, regardless of his own conduct, is liable whenever his employee causes damage in a culpable way within the scope of employment. The strict liability rule for the principal is justified by the fact that the employer and the employee have a close and lasting relationship with the purpose of supporting the interests of the principal. Hence, the rule only applies where there is a work relationship in the eyes of the law, for which there are certain guidelines in the preparatory works. For example, the degree of instructive competence on the part of the employer, the element of agreement on wages, the question of whose equipment is used, etc, will be relevant factors

---

46 An important doctrinal statement was made by Carsten Smith in 1961: *C Smith*, Solidaritet og regress i erstatningsretten (1961) 350. Paraphrased, he stated that the interests not connected to physical integrity were so diverse, and the rules of liability for violating such interests examined to such a minor degree that stating rules would be speculative. The statement was referred to in Thorson's doctoral thesis of 2011, see *Thorson* (fn 45) 24.

47 *Thorson* (fn 45) 265–318.

48 Important cases in this field are Rt 1951, 1132, Rt 2006, 1519 and Rt 2007, 425.

49 *Thorson* (fn 45) 321.

50 In the following part, the text is based on a part of the Norwegian report in the project 'Basic questions of tort law', see *B Askeland*, Norwegian Perspectives, in: H Koziol (ed), Basic Questions of Tort Law (2014) 99–161.

when deciding if there is a work relationship within the meaning of skl §2-1. In general, it is decisive whether the contract is aimed at producing a certain result or procuring a service over a period of time. The latter is a crucial feature of a work relationship within skl §2-1.[51] Unpaid services which take place in a very short period of time, for example a neighbour buying bread, are not regarded as qualifying.

A principal who engages a person or entity to perform some task as an independent contractor (not a servant) is not liable for any conduct of the independent contractor, provided that the task is not a part of a contractual obligation. Hence, in order to avoid liability for damage caused by his auxiliary, it may be vital for the principal to prove that the harm was caused outside the scope of employment or outside the scope of fulfilling a contractual obligation. 32

As for contract law, according to a general principle, a contracting party is identified with the people or entities he chooses to assist him in the activity of performing the contract obligations.[52] The justification for this rule is very much tied to the contractual obligation, the other party's expectations and the need for foreseeability.[53] 33

Hence, the main rule is that a principal is liable without fault whenever an auxiliary wrongfully causes damage to a contracting party in connection with his performance of a contractual duty.[54] The justification for this liability rule is simply that the contract must be fulfilled and for preventive reasons the contracting party must be liable for any error or fault committed by his helpers and/or personnel within his sphere.[55] 34

The contract therefore determines the boundaries of liability. The question of whether liability arises from a contract depends on the interpretation of the contract. When a subcontractor deliberately performs his duties in a manner that represents a breach of the contract, the question may be whether the contractor is liable even in such cases. The pyromania case Rt 2007, 1665 illustrates the difference between contract and delict very well. A security guard had the task of looking after some buildings. In order to get attention due to the fact that he discovered a fire, he deliberately set fire to one of the buildings. The owner of the builder sued his employer both in contract and on a delictual basis, the rule of employers' liability (skl. §2-1). The task of looking after the 35

51 Further on these guidelines, see *Nygaard* (fn 1) 224–227. See also the preparatory works of the Norwegian Act on Compensatory Damages (skl), Innstilling II fra komiteen til å utrede spørsmålet om barn og foreldres og arbeidsgiveres erstatningsansvar (1964) 27–28.

52 This is the equivalent of *Erfüllungsgehilfe* under German law; cf §278 BGB.

53 See *B Askeland*, Erstatningsrettslig identifikasjon (2002) 182.

54 See *Hagstrøm* (fn 3) 486 ff.

55 See on the subject *Askeland* (fn 53) 183 ff.

building put the pyromaniac in a position to carry out his misdeed. It is very interesting to note that the judges in this decision did not hold the security company liable as an employer, inferring that the pyromaniac act was outside the scope of employment. On the other hand, the company was held liable in contract. The decision shows that there is a different angle in the two disciplines when it comes to the attribution of fault of auxiliaries.

36 Doubtful questions may emerge whenever objects other than the objects central for the contractual performance are involved. Scholars have suggested that a first criterion could be whether the contract was a *conditio sine qua non* for the damage caused. This criterion may not, however, be precise enough and therefore leave too much responsibility with the principal. A suggestion has therefore been to say that a mishap in the performing of peripheral obligations of the contract would not lead to the establishment of liability.[56] The question has to be resolved on the concrete merits of the case.[57]

37 In many areas of private law, there are statutory provisions that prescribe liability for helpers based on the so-called impediment rule. The construction of the clauses are that a seller of a good or a service will be liable for the non-fulfilment of the contract clauses by one of his helpers or auxiliaries as long as the incident causing non-performance could be said to lie within the seller's sphere of control.[58] The construction is supplemented with a rule which states that the seller will only be acquitted if both the seller and his helper or auxiliary were confronted with an impediment outside their respective sphere of control.[59] This is a basis of liability that is slightly less strict than the model outlined above.[60]

2) Liability of Representatives of Natural Persons

38 A special rule on liability based on family relations is skl §1-2. This provision is relevant because it illustrates how family relations are dealt with when constructing liability rules within Norwegian law. Parents are liable regardless of fault for acts committed by their children that are deemed to be culpable – including negligent acts. Such acts are implicitly regarded as wrongful;

---

56 *E Selvig*, Husbondansvar (1968) 112; *Augdahl* (fn 2) 226.

57 An elaboration of these problems may be found in *Askeland* (fn 53) 214–233 and in *K Lilleholt*, Tingskade i kontrakt, in: K Krüger/K Lilleholt/G Holgersen (eds), Nybrott og odling, Festskrift til Nils Nygaard (2002) 171–180.

58 Kjøpsloven §27 (1).

59 Kjøpsloven §27 (2).

60 A presentation of the rule in the context of responsibility for auxiliaries is found in *Askeland* (fn 53) 178–249. The last part covers the question of liability for the fault of auxiliaries in the pre-contractual phase, cf 'pre-contractual liability', mentioned in section 1 above.

however, it is the *culpa* rule itself that is referred to in the wording of said provision. There is, however, a cap on the responsibility, as low as NOK 10,000. The rationale behind the rule is prevention and the need for the victim to have the damage compensated. Furthermore, reference is made to 'the general perception of justice' that parents out of decency would want to pay for the damage caused by their children.[61] It may be fair to add that the general tendency to identify children with parents, and vice versa, has also played a role. Under Norwegian law, several rules of identification are justified by referring to a 'psychological tendency to identify subjects with one another'.[62] One may assume that this social-psychological tendency is at play here, both in law and in the factual day-to-day acceptance of the rule in common cases.

As for contract law, the contracting party may be identified with his child based on the context and an interpretation of the wording of a statutory provision. For instance, a parent renting a house may be identified with the child in his house with regard to the contractual relation between the parent and the landlord.[63] Suppose that a child ruins the floor in a flat, which leads to the landlord having to repair it. The father of the child has entered into a rental contract and is, based on the contract, liable according to the law, regardless of his own fault. The practical effect of the contract is that the father is 'identified with' his child. In other words, the wrongful, damaging behaviour of the child is attributed to the father, being a party to the contract. 39

3) *Liability of the Auxiliary/Organ Itself*

The above-mentioned bases of liability include different variations of identification between a principal, for example, an employer, and an auxiliary who acts more or less on behalf of the principal. A sort of identification is also required where a physical person acts on behalf of a juridical person, cf what in German law is called '*Organhaftung*'. Under Norwegian law, the same institute is established, partly inspired by German law.[64] The idea that certain physical persons represent the juridical person or – so to speak – literally is the legal entity has not been expressed in any act; rather it is an uncodified general rule. This construction has limited practical significance because victims in 40

---

61 See Innstilling I, Om ny lov om erstatningsansvar for skade voldt av barn og ungdom (New act on ompensation for damage caused by children and youths) (1964) 17 f.

62 See *J Andenæs*, Identifikasjonsproblemet i erstatningsretten, Tidsskrift for Rettsvitenskap (TfR) (1943) 361–401, 482 and *Askeland* (fn 53) 60–66.

63 See Husleieloven §5–8.

64 The preparatory works of skl refer to German law and the '*Organtheorie*' of Gierke (*O von Gierke*, Die Genossenschaftstheorie und die deutsche Rechtsprechung (1875)); see Innstilling II om Det offentliges og andre arbeidsgiveres erstatningsansvar (The public authorities' and other employers' liability) 1964.

most cases will be better off suing on the basis of *respondeat superior*, skl §2-1. There are, however, certain rules whereby liability can only be established if the responsible subject in person committed the tortious act. This is the case of compensation of non-pecuniary loss for pain and suffering, cf skl §3-5. As mentioned above, this rule contains the prerequisites of intent or gross negligence. In some cases the victim is dependent on proving that the persons who are the organ of a legal entity, typically the management of a company, acted with gross negligence.

41 The question of which persons have to be considered to be organs, however, has traditionally been addressed by pointing to the highest levels of the company hierarchy. Hence, where damage is caused by the board and the chief executive in gross negligence, the company may be liable for the acts of its organs. Directors and managers at a lower level may also be considered to be organs, provided that they are the head of a division that is the origin of the damaging act. An interesting question is whether an accumulation of minor errors or minor negligence by persons at a sufficiently high level in the company may amount to gross negligence, rendering the company liable. This question was answered in the affirmative in a case from the district appeal court, RG 1995, 1298. The court found that as many as seven persons at the top level of a company had cumulatively caused the death of a truck driver whose wife was awarded compensation for bereavement, something that requires gross negligence by the responsible party in person. In my opinion, the idea of cumulative gross negligence contradicts the idea of an organ of the company. Furthermore, as long as the board of a company together may commit a tortious act as an organ of the company, there is no reason to establish liability based on the cumulative acts of another set of persons at the top level of the company.

42 Within contract law, the contract sometimes includes a waiver stating that the contracting party will not be held liable for damage caused by the grossly negligent conduct of his employees. The predominant opinion is that a contracting party, however, cannot validly present a waiver exempting him from the responsibility for his own grossly negligent conduct. Therefore, the other party in the contract may try to prove that the damage was caused by an organ of the contracting company.[65] An example is the case in Rt 1994, 426: a cargo controller decided that heavy rolls of papers should be stored in a special manner in the cargo hold before being shipped to a destination across the Atlantic. The storage was negligent and the rolls fell and were damaged during the journey overseas. The shipping company succeeded in being released from liability on the basis of a waiver for the grossly negligent acts of employees.

[65] See in particular *V Hagstrøm*, Om grensene for ansvarsfraskrivelse, særlig i næringsforhold, TfR (1996) 421–518.

The court found, however, that the cargo inspector could not be looked upon as an organ of the company, hence the company was acquitted. The case shows that the question of which physical persons are in positions that allow attribution of liability to the company to some extent must be discussed on the concrete merits of the case. In Rt 2012, 1062 a company was held liable based on the 'organ theory' where a manager at a lower level of the company hierarchy acted unlawfully; she was in charge of buying goods for sale in a company operating in the supermarket branch (Trumf AS). She had decided to buy and sell a child's chair that was an illegal copy of another trademark, and therefore the company was held liable for non-pecuniary damage according to Åndsverkloven (The Immaterial Works Act) §55.[66]

For practical purposes, one may hold that the limits of which personnel that may render a company liable is the same regardless of whether the act is committed within or outside a contract. In view of the fact that much of the doctrine relating to the delimitation of the organ is developed within contract law, yet at the same time with an eye to situations categorised as delictual torts, there are good reasons to perceive the delimitation as generally valid and therefore similar in the two categories. 43

F. DIFFERENCES AS REGARDS LIABILITY IN THE CASE OF MULTIPLE TORTFEASORS/BREACHING PARTIES

Outside contract there is a general rule regarding multiple tortfeasors, NCA §5-3. The rule prescribes that multiple tortfeasors are solidarily liable with a right to a proportional contribution based on the culpability and causality of each of the various liable parties. For a long time it has been held that this rule only applies outside contracts.[67] The theories of multiple tortfeasors have also been developed in extra-contractual contexts.[68] 44

In the law of obligations, a provision in the Act on Bonds (Gjeldsbrevloven) has been important.[69] §2 of said Act prescribes that if two or more person are debtors for the same claim, they are liable *in solidum*. There is also a provision stipulating a right of recourse between the parties. The provision's structure and content are very similar to the tort law rule in NCA §5-3. 45

---

66 Lov om Åndsverk 12 May 1961 no 2.

67 See *C Smith*, Solidaransvar og regress (1961) 349. This view is partly confirmed by the Supreme Court in Rt 2005, 870.

68 Significant works in this area are: *F Stang*, Skade voldt av flere (1919) *Smith* (fn 67). From more recent literature may be mentioned *B Askeland*, Tapsfordeling og regress (2006) 163–294 and *B Hagland*, Erstatningrettslig medvirkning (2012).

69 Gjeldbrevloven 17 February 1939 no 1.

46 The prevailing view has been that two or more tortfeasors or debtors may be liable *in solidum* regardless of whether the legal basis for the creditors' claim be in contract or not. In the mentioned case in Rt 2005, 870, the Supreme Court did not find it necessary to decide whether or not the rule in §5-3 applied because the result would be the same regardless of whether the parties were responsible on the basis of a contract or on a delictual basis. The background rule (a rule that applies unless otherwise agreed upon) is apparently that two subjects who are liable or debtors for the same claim are liable *in solidum*. Additionally, after having paid more than their share based on proportions of their contribution to the damage or claim, they will have a contribution claim against each other.

G. DIFFERENCES AS REGARDS THE PERSONS WHO MAY BE PROTECTED

47 Under tort law, every person or legal entity is protected against any kind of interference with their protected legal sphere. When it comes to consequential damage, the rules of adequacy put limits on how far third parties are protected. This question divides itself into a wide range of sectors. For instance, if a man dies, his dependants may have a claim for loss of financial support, whereas his employer as a main rule is not protected and will not be able to submit a claim.[70]

48 As for contract law, the only individuals protected by a contract are the contractual parties. This is a general principle in contract law.[71] It is, however, possible to engage in contracts for the protection of third parties, so-called '*tredjemannsavtale*' ('third party agreements'). This concept refers to a contract between A and B that generates benefits and corresponding rights for a third party C. There are many variations of such contracts and important in this respect are insurance contracts.[72]

H. DIFFERENCES AS REGARDS DEFENCES

49 As regards contributory negligence, a certain statutory provision (§5-1) in the Act on Compensatory Damages (Skadeserstatningsloven) specifically prescribes a proportional reduction of the claim according to the gravity of the negligence

---

70 See *Nygaard* (fn 1) 62; *Lødrup* (fn 8) 402 f and Rt 2004, 1816.

71 See for example *J Giertsen*, Avtaler [Contracts] (3rd edn 2014) 146.

72 For an overview of variations, see *K Lilleholt*, Kontraktsrett og obligasjonsrett (2017) 513–519 and *Krüger* (fn 6) 94–100.

in the claimant's contribution to the damage. This rule functions similarly to many rules in Europe and has approximately the same content as the provision contained in art 8:101 (1) of the Principles of European Tort Law. Scholars maintain that this rule also applies in contractual relationships.[73] The prevailing view is, therefore, apparently that there are no differences regarding the question of contributory negligence.

I. DIFFERENCES AS REGARDS LIMITATION PERIODS

For claims in delict and claims in contract, the limitation period is three years.[74] 50
In contract cases, this period commences at the point in time when the contract is binding whereas the starting point in delict is the point in time when the claimant knew or ought to have known that the damage occurred and who was responsible for it.[75]

The claim in tort will still be prescribed at the latest 20 years after the 51
damaging event has ended, see fel §9 (2). There is, however, an exception for personal injuries caused by activities bringing income and for injuries to persons under the age of 18. In such cases there is no upper limit, no so-called 'long stop'.

In contract the creditor is granted an extended period of one year in cases where 52
he could not or ought not to have known about the claim or the debtor, see fel §10 (1). The provision contains a long stop rule of 10 years, see fel §10 (4).

J. DIFFERENCES AS REGARDS PROOF

Both in tort and contract, the general rule of evidence within civil law applies. 53
The fact must be proved in the sense that the alleged fact must more likely than not have occurred. In tort law, this rule is abandoned in certain concrete situations where it is possible only for the alleged tortfeasor to prove that he was not responsible, whereas the claimant is not in a position to prove that the alleged tortfeasor actually caused the damage. An example is a case where a landlord had not cleared snow and ice away from a backyard in his building, used by his lodgers. One of the lodgers fell and injured himself on the slippery surface. It was not clear to the Supreme Court whether the maintenance of the backyard had been proper on the very afternoon that the lodger fell.

---

73 See, for example, *Hagstrøm* (fn 3) 584, *Krüger* (fn 6) 838.
74 See Foreldelsesloven (The Prescription of Claims Act) 18 May 1979 no 18 (fel) §3.
75 See fel §§3 and 9.

However, the Supreme Court found that the landlord himself had the burden of proving himself innocent on this point.[76]

54 Within contract law, there are several statutory provisions stating that the burden of proof is reversed. This is often a means of strengthening the thresholds of liability. The result and effect of the rules are that there is a presumption of culpability which applies unless otherwise proved.[77]

55 Contract areas where liability is based on *culpa* with a reversed burden of proof are, for example, the Act on Transporting Goods by Road.[78]

K. REASONS FOR THE DIFFERENCES

56 The differences are all due to profound differences in the function of tort and contract. Whereas tort law is an overall private law set of rules, which regulate the freedom to act and correspondingly protect the citizen from harm, contract law is very much a consequence of the idea of freedom of contract. The contractual party will always have the possibility to choose other solutions or at least to try to get the counterparty's acceptance of different terms. The fact that the party voluntarily entered into the contract makes it reasonable that the consequences of breach are more severe for him compared to the situation in tort law.

III. LIMITATION OR EXCLUSION OF LIABILITY ARISING FROM TORT AND FROM CONTRACT

A. STATUTORY PROVISIONS AUTHORISING A LIMITATION OR EXCLUSION OF LIABILITY

57 Limitations of the amounts awarded are contained in a number of acts governing liability in different areas of life. An example is the Act on Motor Vehicle Insurance[79] §9, which states that the maximum compensation amount in the case of damage to things following from one incident is NOK 10 million, ie €1.5 million. This is, however, not surprising given the fact that the provision is a part of an act on mandatory insurance. Apart from this provision, there are some statutory regulations on maximum awards in the Act on Freight by Sea[80]

---

76 See Rt 1960, 1201.

77 See on such clauses in *Hagstrøm* (fn 3) 476 ff.

78 Vegfraktavtaleloven 20 December 1974 no 68 §28.

79 Bilansvarsloven 3 February 1961, bal.

80 Lov om sjøfarten (sjøloven) 24 June 1994 no. 39.

§422 (175,000 SDR for each injured passenger), and in the Act on Carriage of Passengers by Air,[81] Luftfartloven §10-22 (100,000 SDR for each passenger). There are also similar maximum limits in other acts in special fields, such as the Produktansvarsloven (Product Liability Act) regarding liability stemming from the production or sale of medicines, and the Atomenergiloven (Act on Atomic Energy).[82]

The need for limitation rules of the kind mentioned above is affected by the fact that there is a general clause on reduction that may be applied both in delict and contract. Another defence is reduction. In tort law, there is a general reduction clause that revolves around the question of whether paying the claim would be unreasonably burdensome for the tortfeasor, ie skl. §5-2. 58

When this provision was enacted in 1985, the preparatory works in principle held the traditional view that there should be no reduction of compensation claims based on contract. However, the works pointed out certain situations where one might consider applying the reduction clause in spite of the contract between the victim and the alleged tortfeasor. One example was the situation that a person had taken care of a valuable painting for a friend, whereupon the caretaker, by an accidental fire, caused damage to the painting. In such cases, reduction might be possible after all, even though a contract existed between the tortfeasor and the victim. We may observe that the bailment for a friend is a typical situation on the borderline between contract and tort. 59

Since 1985, independently of the above-mentioned discussion in the preparatory works, a number of reduction clauses within certain areas of contract law have been enacted, such as the law of sales and the law of building of private houses.[83] A reduction clause may, however, also apply outside these areas following an important case in 2004, Rt 2004, 1887. A commune engaged an engineering firm to construct a breakwater in order to protect a factory from the sea. The engineering firm made huge mistakes in calculating how the sea would affect the breakwater in stormy weather. Because of this, the project was much more expensive than originally calculated – the commune claimed NOK 33,000,000, approximately €4,000,000. The engineering company was found liable. The award was, however, reduced by a third, based on the general reduction clause designed for delictual responsibility, skl. §5-2. Following this case, there is nothing preventing a tortfeasor from using the defence of the general reduction clause if facing claims in contract.[84] 60

---

81 Lov om luftfart 11 June 1993 no. 101.

82 See Produktansvarsloven 23 December 1988 no 104 §3-6 and Atomenergiloven 12 May 1972 §30.

83 See Kjøpsloven §70 (2) and Bustadoppføringslova §36 (3).

84 See on this effect *Hagstrøm* (fn 3) 558 f.

B. LIMITATION OR EXCLUSION OF CONTRACTUAL AND TORTIOUS LIABILITY BY CONTRACT

1) Is it Possible to Limit or Exclude Contractual and Tortious Liability under a Contract?

61 Exclusion of liability under contract has traditionally and commonly been used and it is an important instrument in contract. For example, 'back-to-back' clauses are rather common in contracts in the offshore industry. The main rule has traditionally been that there is a possibility for exclusion of the responsibility for *culpa* by employees, however not for grossly negligent or intentionally damaging acts performed *by the contracting party himself*. This stance has, however, been seriously questioned over recent decades and it is now held that this is merely a starting point for some contracts, namely those involved in typical business relationships.[85] All exclusions of liability are, however, at risk of being found void because of the fact that the courts are willing to use the general clause of revision of contracts on the basis of unreasonableness, see the Norwegian Act on Contracts (Avtaleloven, avtl) §36.[86] Revising the contract is most likely to occur when elements of unreasonableness emerge in contracts between a business and a consumer. Court practice has developed certain standards in order to deem whether or not an exclusion clause is valid, for instance in the area of contract between municipalities and citizens.[87]

2) To What Extent can a Contractual Exclusion Provide a Defence to a Third Party to the Contract?

62 The starting point for this question is that there is freedom of contract both for the alleged tortfeasor and the third party as a victim. The alleged tortfeasor may, however, not succeed in protecting himself from a claim from someone with whom he has not entered into any contract. Conversely, the third party will, in principle, be entitled to claim damages in tort regardless of what the tortfeasor agreed upon with another legal entity.

63 It is difficult to find a practical example where a third party may have a defence based on a contract that he is not a party to. Therefore it will, in principle,

---

[85] See *Nygaard* (fn 1) 310 and more thoroughly about the development and present state of law: *V Hagstrøm*, Om grensene for ansvarsfraskrivelse, særlig i næringsforhold, TfR (1996) 421–518.

[86] Lov omavslutning av avtaler, om fuldmagt og om ugyldige viljeserklæringer 31 May 1918 no 4.

[87] See for an instructive outline of the prevailing doctrine the case in Rt 2014, 656.

not make any difference whether the claim is based on contract or is tortious. Apart from these very general points of departure, the problem and related issues do not appear to have attracted any interest in Norwegian law.

IV. NON-CONCURRENCE OR CONCURRENCE OF ACTIONS

A. OVERVIEW

1) Areas of Overlap between Tort and Contract

Whenever a thing is damaged in the course of performing a contract, there is a possibility to sue the tortfeasor both in contract and on the basis of tort law. 64

In addition, whenever a *personal injury* occurs during the performance of a contract involving contact between the tortfeasor and the victim, there will be a possibility to sue on both legal bases. In fact, there is a tradition of applying extra-contractual liability rules in such cases even though the performance of a contract created the situation in which the damaging event took place.[88] 65

2) Approach to Non-Concurrence and Concurrence of Actions

The general stance under Norwegian law is that the concurrence of actions is accepted.[89] A victim has the right to choose to sue in contract or in torts or in both. The options are regarded as a part of the private law rights of the citizen. The general rule is thus that there is concurrence. 66

B. CONCURRENCE/EXCLUSION OF ACTIONS FOR THE PROTECTION AGAINST PERSONAL INJURY

Whenever a personal injury occurs during the performance of a contract involving contact between the tortfeasor and the victim, there will be a possibility to sue on both legal bases. In fact, there is, as mentioned above, a tradition of applying extra-contractual liability rules in such cases even though the performance of a contract created the situation in which the damaging event took place. 67

---

88 See *Nygaard* (fn 1) 7, 470–473.

89 Se on this: *A Tørum*, Direktekrav (2007) 144 ff and *B Askeland*, Skadelidtes valgrett Norsk Forsikringsforenings publikasjoner (2006) 6 f.

C. CONCURRENCE/EXCLUSION OF ACTIONS FOR THE PROTECTION OF PROPERTY

68 There are no bars to claiming damages both in tort and contract for the protection of property.

D. CONCURRENCE/EXCLUSION IN THE CASE OF INTERFERENCE WITH CONTRACTUAL RIGHTS

1) *Interference with a Contractual Relationship*

69 In general, a person may be held liable for interference with a contractual relationship between two other parties. There are several variations of this problem. At the core of the subject is the idea of 'good commercial practice' and different clauses that forbid unfair competition.[90] The general stance is that inducing a debtor to fail to fulfil his obligations to a creditor may constitute a basis of liability. A prevailing opinion has been that such acts may amount to negligence or fault, based on non-contractual liability. The factual act of inducing breach of contract may also be regarded as a violation of the general and partly codified rule of 'good commercial performance' under competition law. Scholars have maintained that the *culpa* rule and the rule on good performance must be harmonised, so that they actually prescribe the same standard of behaviour.[91] There are several cases showing that inducement to breach a contract may lead to the establishment of liability.[92] Under modern Norwegian law, the problem arises most often in the context of competition law, as a question of fair competition. A thorough analysis of the questions of whether different kinds of interference with contracts between other parties may constitute a breach of competition rules may be found in the mentioned work by Lunde.[93]

2) *Loss of Business due to Personal Injury to Someone Else's Employees or Clients or to Property Damage to the Entrepreneur*

70 As regards loss of business due to personal injury to someone else's employee, the question turns on the interpretation of the important decision in

---

90 See on the subject, *P Augdahl*, Den norske obligasjonsretts almindelige del (5th edn 1978) 410–412. *Hagstrøm* (fn 3); *T Lunde*, God forretningsskikk næringsdrivande imellom (2001) 411–456; *V Hagstrøm*, Fra erstatningsrettens grenseland: Ansvar for angrep på kontraktsforhold, in: Festskrift til Nils Nygaard (2002) 103–114.

91 See *Lunde* (fn 87) 415–416.

92 See Rt 1930, 761, Rt 1957, 426 and Rt 1993, 1464.

93 See *Lunde* (fn 87) 413–456.

Rt 2004, 1815. In this case, an important employee in a small limited company in the business of making signs for different purposes was injured in a traffic accident. The Supreme Court found that the company was not in a position to claim compensation from the traffic insurer for loss of income due to the injury of the important worker. At this point, the Supreme Court was divided in their view. Whereas three judges held that the damage was too remote for claiming damages, the two remaining judges found that it was unreasonable to refuse compensation to the company. An important argument for the majority of the court was that the employee might have been ill for many other reasons, and the fact that an employee was deprived of his working capacity was a risk that fell within the ordinary risks of the company's business. The risk should therefore not be shifted to the tortfeasor, in this case covered by the traffic insurer. The case has been criticised by scholars.[94]

In terms of loss of business due to damage to a client, there are good reasons to 71
believe that such loss will be found to be outside the scope of limitation based on arguments of adequacy. The case in Rt 2004, 1815, referred to above, may also provide guidelines in this kind of case. The client is more remote than an employee, even though the reasoning regarding the risk allocation is not valid in this situation. Still, the remoteness of the expectation of income or profit from a client makes it most probable that no damages will be awarded on the basis of the fact that a mere client relationship is affected by the alleged tortfeasor.

Damage to things that are subject to a contract between the claimant and the 72
victim as owner of the thing may lead to the establishment of liability depending on the concrete contractual relations. An important criterion is whether the interest of the contractual partner is sufficiently 'concrete and close' to be protected by the rules of liability. An important case in this respect historically is Rt 1955, 872: a ship lowered an anchor and damaged a cable so that a factory lost electricity and had to temporarily stop production. The interest of the factory was deemed to be sufficiently concrete and closely connected with the damage to the cable. Another important case that indicates the boundaries more precisely is Rt 1973, 1268: an airplane crashed into electricity cables, leaving a large number of electricity users with no electricity. The claimant was a fish farmer, who, due to the lack of electricity, suffered a loss stemming from the fact that a large number of (baby) fish died because the water was not sufficiently hot. In the action against the owner of the airplane, the State, the Supreme Court found that the risk of being ruined by a floodgate of claims in cable cases should speak for limiting the circle of compensable consequences. This was one of a few arguments that supported the decision not to pay compensation to the

---

[94] See *Nygaard* (fn 1) 376.

fish farmer. The loss of the fish farmer was found to be too *'fjernt og avledet'* ('remote and consequential') to qualify for damages. Somewhere in between the two cases the line is drawn when it comes to damage to property. In general one may hold that the damaged thing must be the object of the contract and it will speak for liability if the tortfeasor must know that the thing is partly exploited by a contractual party to the owner.[95]

V. SPECIFIC SITUATIONS

A. PRE-CONTRACTUAL LIABILITY

73 The discussion of pre-contractual liability has historically mainly focused on the view that *culpa in contrahendo* often made the contract void and that the award therefore should not be as if a binding and working contract had been concluded. Instead of granting compensation for the loss of profit gained from a binding contract, so-called *positiv kontraktsinteresse* ('the positive interest connected to the contract'), the award should be limited to covering expenses incurred in the confidence that a contract would be concluded, so-called *negative kontraktsinteresse* ('negative interest connected to the contract'). In modern doctrine, the same problems are referred to under the concept of 'pre-contractual liability' (*prekontraktuelt ansvar*).[96] The concept encompasses a number of situations where something goes wrong in the phase before a binding contract is concluded. At the heart of the concept lies *culpa in contrahendo*, but the concept captures more than just the chronological identification of the culpable incident.[97] There is a cluster of Norwegian Supreme Court cases from before the turn of the century that brought concrete solutions to concrete problems within the area.[98] There are also two modern cases worth mentioning. In the Nucleus case, Rt 2001, 1062, a party who had applied for a tender was granted compensation for being wrongfully neglected in the tender. The municipality had made significant mistakes in applying the rules

---

95 See on the general subject *Hagstrøm* (fn 3) 855–864, *Nygaard* (fn 1) 365–376, *Lødrup* (fn 8) 398–403 and *B Askeland*, Konkret og nærliggende interesse som avveiningskriterium ved erstatning for tredjemannsskader, JV (2001) 303 ff.

96 *Hagstrøm* (fn 3) 95–97. A thorough elaboration of many sides of the grey area is found in a doctoral thesis: *Simonsen* (fn 31).

97 See on the overlap and distinctions between *culpa in contrahendo* and pre-contractual liability, *Simonsen* (fn 31) 5.

98 Important cases are Rt 1967, 13, Rt 1970, 637 and Rt 1981, 462. A groundbreaking, identification, recognition and categorisation of the problems of pre-contractual liability was made by K Krüger in 1989, see *Krüger* (fn 6) 21–34.

prescribing the procedure of the tender and, therefore, the municipality had to pay compensation for loss of profit. In Rt 2007, 425, a gambler who failed to mark his bet correctly because of wrong information from the betting company was not granted any compensation for the loss of the amount he would have won had there not been any error on the part of the betting company. The very fact that no binding contract had been entered into was crucial to the reasoning of the Supreme Court.[99]

B. LIABILITY OF PROFESSIONALS

In many areas, Norwegian doctrine recognises the concept of 'professional liability'.[100] This is an expression meaning that there are quasi-stricter demands on the performance of a professional compared to the ordinary performance of everyday tasks.[101] The strict standard applies to various professionals who take on tasks, claiming to be a sort of expert or having special skills. This typically concerns lawyers, engineers, editors, surgeons and doctors. The strict standard partly follows from the contract: often the fee for performance of skilled professional tasks is relatively high. The employer pays for expensive services, and accordingly expects performance at a high level. At the same time, the mere role, for example of being a surgeon, carries with it expectations as regards the standard of performance. The skilled role has the effect that the strict demands on the professional apply even though the skilled expert may not be under any contractual relationship. For example, a doctor who helps a fellow passenger who falls ill during a flight must perform according to professional standards, even though his conduct must be characterised as the act of a good Samaritan. According to general rules of tort law, namely the *culpa* rule, a skilled person cannot rid himself of the expectations following from his skills, regardless of whether a contract is involved. 74

The heightened standard may have the consequence that the courts pay no heed to the fact that a tortfeasor acting in a 'skilled role' is inexperienced. An example is an attorney trainee who concluded an unfortunate settlement: see the case in Rt 1994, 1430. The fact that he was inexperienced did by no means exonerate him or his firm. Once he had taken on the task of being an attorney, he was judged by the standard of the professional role, with no regard to his lack of experience. 75

99 A closer examination of the case is made in *H Koziol/BC Steininger* (eds), European Tort Law 2007 (2008) 442 f.

100 Cf the Norwegian word '*profesjonsansvar*'.

101 See *Lødrup* (fn 8) 170–181.

CASES

CASE 1. THE UNATTRACTIVE SHOPPING MALL

76 C can claim compensation for his loss in torts. The owner of the mall has, on the basis of his contractual relationship to Z and others, a connection to the risk of losing income. This fact makes D responsible on the basis of the general uncodified *culpa* rule.[102] Taking all the circumstances into account, he should have acted in order to eliminate the risk. The risk that a failure to adequately maintain the shopping centre could be detrimental to the volume of sales in the shops was quite obvious to D. The fact that D must have been aware of the possibility that the store may be sublet, and in fact accepted this possibility in the contract with Z, also speaks for liability towards C.

77 C may also bring a claim in contract based on the special doctrine of direct claims.[103] This doctrine is based on a number of Supreme Court cases allowing claims backwards in the chain of contracts.[104] At the core of the doctrine is an uncodified rule on direct claims that applies whenever there is sufficient need for such a claim and it does not contradict the principles that may be inferred from several provisions that prescribe direct claims.[105] As for the situation in Case 1, it resembles, to a certain extent, the situation presupposed in the Act on Sales of Immovables (Avhendingslova, avhl) §4-16 and kjl §84, which both contain provisions prescribing direct claims.[106] In this author's opinion, there is a good chance that Norwegian courts would accept the direct claim and grant compensation.

CASE 2. THE IDLE LAWYER

78 This is a branch of contract with a foreseeable loss that has to be compensated on the basis of the contract. Due to the fact that the contractual relationship is between the solicitor D and W, the daughters cannot sue D in contract.

79 Under Norwegian law, the only possibility for the claimants would be to plead that the solicitor is liable in tort for the negligence shown in the delayed changing of the will. Thus, the daughters may file a claim in tort based on the fact that the lawyer acted culpably. He did not fulfil the duties that may be expected from

---

102 See *Nygaard* (fn 1) 182 ff.

103 See on this subject within Norwegian law, *Tørum* (fn 86).

104 See eg Rt 1981, 445.

105 For an elaboration of the principles and guidelines of argumentation for direct claims, see *Tørum* (fn 86) 293–338.

106 Lov om avhending av fast eigedom 3 July 1992 no 93 and Kjøpsloven 13 May 1988 no 27.

him based on his professional role. Although the lawyer and the daughters are not contractual partners, the situation and the risk connected to it must have seemed so clear to the lawyer that he had no justified reason not to perform. In the considerations of this question, it is very likely that the court will draw upon the ethical rules of lawyers, which have a special rule on the duty to serve the client in a timely manner: Advokatforskriften Chapter 12.[107] Although the daughters were not in a contractual relationship with the lawyer, the latter's duties within the contract to the client, based on the ethical rules, will have a bearing. The omission to arrange the will properly does not comply with the ethical standards and therefore the lawyer may be found to be liable. The fact that the lawyer knew the facts that made changing the will an urgent matter will speak against him. It can be claimed that he put the daughters' benefit from the will at risk due to his failure to act. Therefore, according to the culpability rule, he must react to this risk.

CASE 3. THE DEFECTIVE HOUSE

C can sue D in tort for redress of his personal injury. Regardless of the contents of the contract between D and Z, D has caused a risk connected to a building. When the risk results in damage, D should be liable based on the *culpa* rule. As for the damage to the building, there is no claim in tort. C bought a building with an inherent defect, and this contractual object defines his position only in contract, not in torts. 80

C will probably have no claim against D for the damage to the building on the basis of contract. This may be inferred from avhl §4-16. This provision reads that the buyer of a house has a direct claim against a former seller of the house, but only insofar as the seller has a claim against the former seller (his predecessor). Conversely, whenever there is an exclusion clause in the contract between the first seller and the first buyer, the clause also works against later buyers. 81

CASE 4. APARTMENT IN FLAMES

C has a claim in tort based on the regular, general *culpa* rule, provided that the defect in the circuit breaker was visible or otherwise detectable to D, in a manner that qualifies as negligence. The *culpa* rule and the other general rules on tort law are applicable to every victim that comes into the sphere of the risk. The fact that C has rented a flat does not make any difference on this point. 82

107 Administrative regulation of 20 December 1996 no 1161, cf Domstolsloven 13 August no 5 §218.

83 As for the contract between the tenant and the landlord, the Act on House Renting applies.[108] A special provision regarding the landlord's liability is found in §2-13, according to which the landlord is liable for any loss caused by breach of contract on the part of the landlord. The failure to supervise the circuit breaker will probably constitute sufficient breach. According to the preparatory works, the provision mainly refers to breaches of contract that do not result in personal injuries. The Norwegian tradition is, however, that claims of compensation for such damage may be based on contract. The landlord will not be liable for incidents beyond his control, cf the fact that §2-13 is a variation of the impediment rule in CISG.[109] Based on the facts of the case, the landlord was negligent in the supervision of the circuit breaker and, therefore, §2-13 will apply. According to this provision, even indirect loss may be covered whenever culpability is established. Damage to things is one type of indirect loss. Neither the provision nor the preparatory works mention anything about personal injuries. It would, however, contradict the Norwegian tradition to interpret the provision in the direction of excluding personal injuries. In the author's opinion, the wording of the Act on House Renting must be interpreted such that the provision allows for compensation also for personal injury in the special case at hand.

CASE 5. INJURED SKIER

84 D1 would be liable on the legal basis of the uncodified rule on strict liability, possibly in combination with elements of culpability on the part of D1. The fact that there is a contractual relationship between the tortfeasor and the victim will reinforce the grounds for liability. The question of strict liability is based on a variety of arguments that have developed in court practice. One such argument is the fact that the accident occurred while D1 was performing contractual duties in the course of his commercial business activity. The fact that D1 would have been able to take out insurance cover and thereby distribute the loss amongst all those using the ski lift is also an argument for liability that will be valid as a reason for holding him strictly liable.

85 The question of whether D2 is liable is a matter of interpretation of insurance clauses. Based on Norwegian traditions on the borderline between contract and tort, one would categorise the incident as a case of tortious liability and the insurance policy would cover the accident. It would be very unnatural to suggest that the fact that the victim had bought a ski pass took him outside the area

[108] Husleieloven 26 March no 17.

[109] See the UN Convention on International Sales of Goods §79.

covered by the insurance. The insurance will in general be taken out in order to cover damage occurring as a result of the commercial business.

CASE 6. EXPLODING CAR

To file claim in tort would be an unusual step, however it would be possible, taking into consideration that the ordinary requisites of liability are fulfilled by D2, who produced a defective good that caused C a loss. There is a causal connection between D2's defective production and C's loss. 86

C can sue both D1 and D2 in contract. According to a principle in contract law, one may file a claim with the seller's predecessor directly and gain the same legal position as the seller. As for this case, the kjl has a provision relating to such direct claims, §84. This provision applies. 87

There is a bar from claiming on the basis of breach of contract in kjl §32 (2). After two years the buyer can no longer claim that there has been a breach of a contract. There is an exception where the seller has shown gross negligence or has acted against good faith.[110] 88

If C is a consumer, he will, however, be able to claim compensation for a maximum period of five years from the date of the sale: see the special Act on Sales from Business Actors to Consumers (Forbrukerkjøpsloven, fbkjl).[111] 89

CASE 7. RACING BOAT BURNING

The question depends on whether C and D are consumers and whether the boat was mainly intended for leisure activities. If D is not considered to be a consumer, the regular kjl applies, according to which the provisional two-year limit will apply in the same way as in the case above. The warranty will apply so that C cannot file a claim against D. 90

If C is a consumer, he will still have a claim according to the five-year limit in fbkjl §27 cf §3.[112] Considering the character of the product, it is highly likely that the Consumer Sales Law will be applicable. It is, however, necessary that D is selling in the course of business and that C is considered to be a consumer. If so, the warranty of D will not be subject to the mandatory five-year limitation period, fbkjl §27. The warranty is therefore void according to fbkjl §3, which reads that 91

---

110 See *J Bergem/BE Konow/K Rognlien*, Kjøpsrett (2008) 181.

111 Lov om forbrukerkjøp 21 June 2002 no 34.

112 In §3 it is made clear that the terms may not be more disadvantageous to consumers than what follows from the statutory provisions.

the consumer may not be put in a weaker position than the Act prescribes. C may claim compensation for damage according to §33 first section and §34.

92 Again the tort law approach is highly unusual, but not inconceivable. The Product Liability Act[113] and the basis of liability in pal §2-1 do not apply because there is an exception in the Act concerning damage to the product itself, see pal §2-3 (3) a. There is also an exception in the case of a part of a product causing damage to a product into which the part of the product was incorporated. Whether a claim in tort can be filed is, therefore, dependent on whether it is possible to establish *culpa* on the part of D. Although *culpa* is established, it is very probable that the two-year period of warranty is perceived as a waiver clause also relevant to the damage which occurred as a result of a tort.

CASE 8. INSIDIOUS REPORT

93 This is a clear violation of the standards of good commercial practice, see the Norwegian Act on Marketing (Markedsføringsloven, mfl) §1.[114] D will be liable in tort on the basis of such a breach. The case exemplifies where the general *culpa* rule and the standard of good commercial practice concur, but also function as integrated and interconnected legal bases for liability. The case in Rt 1990, 607 may give some guidance. In this case, two employees in a computer company A, while still employed, established a competing company, B. As employees of A, they made contact with a seller of 'televideo-machines', which at the time (1983) was a novelty. They resigned from A and soon after began to buy and sell products acting for their newly established firm, B. The Supreme Court held that a general and uncodified duty of loyalty that supplemented the above-mentioned provision in mfl §1 existed. The provision and principle was a sufficient legal basis for compensation from both the employees and the company. The company was held liable for breach of good commercial practice, cf mfl §1.

94 The misinformation renders D liable to C for loss of profit. D's intentional misleading of C with the purpose of taking over a business partner supports a finding of liability despite the constraints of adequacy.

CASE 9. CIRCULAR LETTER

95 The conduct amounts to a violation of the standard of good commercial practice, cf mfl §1. C will be liable in tort for any loss caused by such conduct. The acts of

[113] Lov om produktansvar (pal.)23 December 1988 no. 104.

[114] Lov om kontroll med markedsføring ofg avtalevilkår 16 June 1972 no 47.

D are considered to be unfair competition, which render D liable for all losses caused to the claimant.

CASE 10. SHORTAGE OF SUPPLY

This question cannot be resolved by tort law. The solution to the question must be governed by contract law and the rules on revision of contracts, especially the general revision clause in avtl §36. The crucial question is whether the fact that D exploits the situation by increasing the price and demanding earlier payments is so unreasonable that the new contract must be considered to be void. In the mentioned provision, there are a number of guidelines for establishing unreasonableness, among others 'the position (strength or weaknesses) of the parties'. This speaks for revising the contract. Particularly the element of exploiting a monopoly situation may lead to the conclusion that the new contract terms are void. On the other hand, it is assumed that there is only a narrow possibility to revise contracts between business companies. In fact, to date there has been no example of a contract between business contract parties being revised.[115] Therefore in the author's opinion, the mere fact that C accepts the new terms puts him in a position where he cannot file any claims against D. 96

CASE 11. INJURED ROCK STAR

If a legal basis for liability on the part of D is presupposed, the question is whether a third party who has a loss that stems from his contractual relationship with the victim may have a claim against the tortfeasor. Such questions have traditionally been resolved by reference to the criterion of whether the third party has a 'concrete and close interest' connected to the damaged good. There is a string of Supreme Court cases giving guidelines to aid the understanding of this criterion.[116] Hence, the problems must be addressed on the concrete merits of the case in comparison to similar cases. The solution to the problem here probably turns on the interpretation of the case in Rt 2004, 1816. In this case, an employer was not awarded compensation for a loss stemming from the fact that a *key employee* was injured in a traffic accident. The Supreme Court found that employers in general assume the risk of their employees becoming ill or injured. Hence the loss on the part of the employer could not fall within the scope of liability of the tortfeasor. Thus the same reasoning would be appropriate in Case 11. C assumed the risk of X becoming ill. A part of the reasoning is 97

---

115 See on the subject *Giertsen* (fn 71) 130–131.

116 See the most important cases, Rt 1955, 859, Rt 1973, 1268 and Rt 2004, 1816.

that it is in general not foreseeable that a third party has a loss stemming from personal injuries. Theorists have suggested that the interest in the well-being of and the working capacity of an individual human being is exclusively held by the person herself.[117] This view applies both to the loss of profit and the cancellation costs. It would therefore be perfectly within the boundaries of the Norwegian legal method to resolve the case by acquitting D. A particular point is that the employee in the Norwegian case had a lasting and close connection to the employee that follows from a working contract, whereas the rock star has a loose and singular connection to the promoter C. This fact would not support holding D liable.

98 It should, however, be mentioned that there was a dissent in the case referred to, with a three to two majority decision. The decision has also been criticised by theorists. In this author's opinion, compensation should not be granted, this being justified by pointing to the reasoning above.

CASE 12. EQUIPMENT DESTROYED

99 The loss is even more remote in this case than in Case 11 above. The fact that the truck was transporting equipment to a comeback concert was in no way foreseeable to the bus driver. He can therefore not be responsible for the loss. The special circumstances regarding the use of the equipment in the truck are perceived as too remote consequences of the collision.

100 It does make a difference whether C is the owner of the equipment, because if C is the owner, he will have an extra-contractual (delictual) claim in tort against D2 for the damage to the equipment. This claim arises regardless of the contractual relationship between C and D1 and between D1 and D2.

101 C may also claim compensation for the damage to the equipment from D1 based on the transport contract pursuant to the Norwegian Act on Transporting Goods by Road §§27–28.[118] According to these provisions, D1 is liable for damage to the transported goods unless he can prove that the damage was caused by circumstances other than his negligence in performance of the contract, cf §28 first paragraph. As one can see, there is a reversal of the burden of proof. Based on the facts of the case, D1 may be able to prove that the damage was not caused by negligence on his part, hence C will not have a claim against D1.

---

117 See *H Andersson*, Trepartsrelationer i skadeståndsrätten (1997) 161 and 169. See also *Lødrup* (fn 8) 306–307.

118 See Vegfraktavtaleloven 20 December 1974 no 68.

CASE 13. SLIPPING ON A LETTUCE LEAF

Since the parties have not yet entered into a contract, there is no basis for liability in contract. The question will be whether there is a sufficient basis for liability in tort. The fact that the accident was caused by a danger on D's premises, a danger that at the same time was connected to the profit-making activity of D, speaks for strict liability. On the other hand, it is very hard to see that slipping on a lettuce leaf fulfils the criteria of strict liability, a 'continuous, typical and extraordinary risk' connected to the store. Based on a comparison to the case law on the subject, these criteria are not met. One must probably resort to the *culpa* rule. We know little about the reasons for the leaf lying on the floor. In general, slippery items on the floors of stores do not automatically lead to a finding of culpability. However, a Supreme Court case, Rt 1960, 1201, may support liability. A tenant fell in a backyard that was very slippery due to the presence of ice. The landlord could not prove that he had taken precautions to prevent damage, and was held liable for the loss stemming from personal injury. In general, the argument that risks connected to profit-making must be borne by the profit maker is widely supported under Norwegian law. Although it is mostly expressed in the context of strict liability, it may also have significant bearing on cases concerning the *culpa* rule. If there are reasons for the grocery shop having certain routines or measures in order to prevent potential customers from slipping, the situation may very well lead to the establishment of liability in tort. 102

CASE 14. TEST DRIVE

As long as D has not yet entered into a contract, the question must be resolved on the basis of tort law. The fact that the car is driven in a pre-contractual phase with the purpose of buying the car does not make any difference under the given circumstances. It seems clear that C will win the case and that D will have to pay damages to C. 103

CASE 15. BREACH OF NEGOTIATIONS

Insofar as C has incurred expenses in order to engage in the contract, he has a claim in tort based on the general *culpa* rule as applied in the pre-contractual phase.[119] If no expenses are incurred, there will be no claim. The duty that D has towards C is only a duty to negotiate. In such a case, there is a breach 104

119 See eg *Simonsen* (fn 31) 295 ff and 339–342.

of social conventions, and nothing more. This cannot constitute a basis for compensation.

105 The fact that the object of the contract is an antique which is not intended for production or sale makes it very difficult to establish any additional loss on the part of C. The loss of the non-pecuniary value of being able to enjoy the possession of this particular item does not fall within the concept of damage under Norwegian law.[120]

CASE 16. NON-DISCLOSURE OF RELEVANT FACTS

106 Within tort law, the fact that D knows about facts that suggest that C will incur a loss may, under special circumstances, call for activity on the part of D. Such a duty may partly be based on the fact that D has *tilknytning* (a connection) to the risk involved. In this case, D knows about special properties of the machine and at the same time he possesses information that makes it probable that C will engage in an activity that will lead to a poor performance. This is a factual situation where it seems natural that it can be resolved by rules of contract law, especially since the situation is regulated in kjl §17 b, see below. Once there is a contract between the victim and the tortfeasor, it seems somewhat inappropriate to apply tort law rules. This view is further supported by the fact that the 'damage' in the case is lost performance, something that may not easily be covered by the concept of damage in tort law.

107 D may, as suggested, be liable on the basis of contract. According to the provisions in kjl §17, a thing that is sold should fulfil a certain function which the seller must be aware of, except for cases where it is evident that the buyer did not rely on the information from the seller at this point. The wording of the provision leaves it somewhat uncertain as to whether the reduced performance might be considered a breach of contract. The circumstances described in the case, however, support considering the reduced performance as a breach of contract after all. A legal basis that may support this inference may be the principle of loyalty between contracting parties, which is positively expressed in several statutory provisions in the area of contract law, and even in case law. D had knowledge of information that would be useful for the buyer. D therefore ought to have discussed this prior to the closing of the sale. D's behaviour amounted to a breach of contract because of D's implied duty of loyalty towards C.

120 See eg *F Stang*, Erstatningsretten (2nd edn 1927) 304, 366.

THE BORDERLINES OF TORT LAW IN POLAND

Ewa BAGIŃSKA

QUESTIONS

I. Tracing the Borderlines ... 421
  A. Distinction between Tort and Contract ... 421
  B. Existence of a 'Grey Zone'? ... 422
  C. Common or Different Rules Regulating Tort and Contract ... 425
  D. Application of Common Rules in a Different Way ... 427
II. Main Differences between Tortious and Contractual Liability ... 427
  A. Differences as Regards the Foundations of Liability ... 427
    1) Role of Intention, Wrongfulness and Fault and their Variations ... 427
    2) Role of Strict Liability ... 430
  B. Differences as Regards Causation ... 430
  C. Differences as Regards Remedies ... 431
    1) Degree of Certainty of the Damage ... 431
    2) Compensation for Non-pecuniary Loss ... 431
    3) Compensation for Loss of Earnings and for Loss of Chance ... 432
    4) Restitutionary Damages ... 433
    5) Aggravated and Exemplary (or Punitive) Damages ... 434
    6) Other Remedies ... 435
  D. Differences as Regards Recoverability of 'Pure Economic Losses'? ... 437
  E. Differences as Regards Liability for Others ... 437
  F. Differences as Regards Liability in the Case of Multiple Tortfeasors/Breaching Parties ... 440
  G. Differences as Regards the Persons Who May be Protected ... 442
  H. Differences as Regards Defences ... 443
  I. Differences as Regards Limitation Periods ... 445
  J. Differences as Regards Proof ... 447
  K. Other Differences ... 448
  L. Reasons for the Differences ... 449

III. Limitation or Exclusion of Liability Arising from Tort and from Contract 449
A. Statutory Provisions Authorising a Limitation or Exclusion of Liability 449
B. Limitation or Exclusion of Contractual and Tortious Liability by Contract 451
1) Is it Possible to Limit or Exclude Contractual or Tortious Liability under a Contract? 451
2) To What Extent can a Contractual Exclusion Provide a Defence to a Third Party to the Contract? 452
IV. Non-Concurrence or Concurrence of Actions 452
A. Overview 452
B. Concurrence/Exclusion of Actions for the Protection Against Personal Injury 454
C. Concurrence/Exclusion of Actions for the Protection of Property 455
D. Concurrence/Exclusion in the Case of Interference with Contractual Rights 455
1) Interference with a Contractual Relationship 455
2) Loss of Business due to Personal Injury to Someone Else's Employees or Clients or to Property Damage to the Entrepreneur 457
V. Specific Situations 457
A. Pre-Contractual Liability 457
B. Liability of Professionals 459

CASES

Case 1. The Unattractive Shopping Mall 460
Case 2. The Idle Lawyer 460
Case 3. The Defective House 461
Case 4. Apartment in Flames 462
Case 5. Injured Skier 462
Case 6. Exploding Car 463
Case 7. Racing Boat Burning 463
Case 8. Insidious Report 464
Case 9. Circular Letter 464
Case 10. Shortage of Supply 464
Case 11. Injured Rock Star 465
Case 12. Equipment Destroyed 465
Case 13. Slipping on a Lettuce Leaf 465
Case 14. Test Drive 465
Case 15. Breach of Negotiations 466
Case 16. Non-Disclosure of Relevant Facts 466

QUESTIONS

I. TRACING THE BORDERLINES

A. DISTINCTION BETWEEN TORT AND CONTRACT

In Polish law, contractual and tortious liability are *clearly separated*, in written law, case law and scholarly writings. These two liability regimes are in many respects independent and distinct from one another, and yet they remain subject to some common rules and principles applicable to the law of obligations in general. 1

The separation of the two regimes has a long tradition in Polish civil law. The structure of the Polish law of obligations, and in particular the sources of obligations, have been shaped by the evolution of private law in Europe. The classification of sources of obligations made in the Institutes of Justinian into contracts, delicts, quasi-contract and quasi-delicts was commonly followed in Europe until the 19th century. Until 1795, Polish civil law was mainly based on case law and custom and under a very limited influence of Roman law.[1] After three partitions of the Republic of Poland by the Russian, Prussian and Austrian Empires in the 18th century, the Polish State ceased to exist for 123 years. During the time of partition, the entire Polish territory was under the influence of five legal systems: the Prussian Civil Code (replaced later by the German BGB), the Collection of Laws of the Russian Empire (Volume X on private law) of 1835, the Austrian Civil Code (ABGB), the Napoleonic Code, and Hungarian law (in the southern parts of Poland). All of the above were all official sources of law on the territory of Poland.[2] 2

In November 1918, when Poland regained its independence as a democratic state, substantial legal reforms were carried out. Instead of a synthesis of the systems already binding on the Polish territory, the Polish Codification Commission chose to follow modern legislative trends and experience of the Swiss legislator (the Swiss Code of Obligations) as well as the unification processes that were taking place at the supranational and international levels. In particular, when drafting a code of obligations, the Codification Commission abandoned the Justinian's classification of obligations and divided them into two categories: obligations resulting from acts of will (legal transactions, such as contracts and unilateral representations) and obligations arising from other conduct (lawful human acts, delicts, unjustified enrichment and other acts). 3

---

1 See *W Dajczak*, Historical development of private law in Poland, in: W Dajczak/AJ Szwarc/P Wiliński (eds), Handbook of Polish Law (2011) 50.

2 See *E Bagińska/M Tulibacka*, Tort Law in Poland, in: International Encyclopaedia of Laws (2014) nos 3–4; *Dajczak* (fn 1) 42–58.

4 Hence, the first Polish Code of Obligations (*kodeks zobowiązan* 1933) contained two sections in Chapter II entitled 'Creation of Obligations'. The first section contained provisions on contracts and unilateral representations (arts 29–114), while 'obligations arising from other conduct' comprised the following sources of obligations (in systematic order):

- *negotiorum gestio* – benevolent intervention in another's affairs without a mandate (arts 115–122);
- unjustified enrichment (arts 123–133);
- undue performance (arts 128–133); and
- delicts (illicit acts) (arts 134–167).

5 The rules on contractual liability were placed in Title IV on the extinguishing of obligations, and they regulated the mechanism of performing obligations from the point of view of sanctions that are imposed on the defaulted debtor.[3] The rules on damages, however, were included in the title on torts, and they were applicable to contractual liability absent any agreement or special provision to the contrary.

6 The Polish legislator codified the entire civil law in 1964. As far as the sources of obligations are concerned, the Civil Code of 1964 (*kodeks cywilny*, cc) followed more closely the structure of the BGB. As to the substance, the Civil Code was generally based on the Code of Obligations. The following sources of obligations have been distinguished:

- contracts (general provisions in arts 353–396);
- delicts (illicit acts) (arts 415–449(10]);
- unjustified enrichment (including undue performance) (arts 405–414);
- *negotiorum gestio* (arts 752–757); and
- remittance and securities (arts 921(1)–921(16)).

7 In contrast to the Code of Obligations, the Civil Code put some common rules on liability into the general part of obligations (see para 16 below), as well as modified the methods of repairing damage (art 159 co and art 363 cc).

B. EXISTENCE OF A 'GREY ZONE'?

8 There are a few instances and concepts that show a quite wide 'grey zone' between contracts and torts in Polish law.

---

[3] See *W Czachórski*, Odpowiedzialność kontraktowa i jej stosunek do odpowiedzialności deliktowej wg k.c. (1964) Nowe Prawo 951.

In addition to the Book on Obligations, liability in damages is also provided in other parts of the Civil Code, mainly in provisions that concern an exercise of some subjective rights (specifically, property rights).[4] These cases are not regarded as belonging to the realm of either *ex contractu* or *ex delicto*. The same applies to the liability for loss incurred in another's interest or in a common interest (rescue cases, art 438 cc[5]).[6] 9

Some authors consider a breach of legal (statutory) obligations as a source of a third kind of liability, thereby contesting the dichotomy between contractual and tortious liability. The concept of a third category (statutory) liability is applied in order to justify the conclusion that the liability is objective and not dependent on fault (this is a minority view, see also sec V.A.). The Civil Code provides for a compensatory sanction in art 387 §2 (impossibility of performance), art 103 §2 (apparent agency), art 390 §1 (promised/preliminary contract), and art 566 (seller's liability for defective things). This category of cases is sometimes referred to, under the influence of German legal theory, as liability arising from the reliance interest or liability for negative contractual interest. Other authors emphasise that because the liability arises in specific situations, damage resulting from lost confidence cannot be sought under the general rules.[7] 10

Although there is no written duty to act in good faith, the very idea is reflected in commonly accepted customs (good morals), which create a yardstick for the assessment of conduct by contractual parties, as well as in the concept of *culpa in contrahendo*. The latter concept, envisaged by several particular provisions, appears to enter and leave a grey zone, depending on interpretations of legislative changes. The Civil Code contains an explicit rule on the duty of good faith in the negotiation process. More generally, *culpa in contrahendo* is considered by a majority of scholars as leading to (or a type of) *tortious liability*.[8] As such, it is considered to require, by reference to a general clause of liability, proof of the defendant's fault. Hence, since 1933 the Polish approach has followed the French tradition. Although all approaches were presented in the early doctrine,[9] the dominant opinion has accepted the delictual character of liability. Recently, however, Kocot, in his monograph on this subject, argued that the particular 11

4 Arts 142, 149, 182 §1 cc.

5 'A person who acts out of duty or even voluntarily to avert the risk of damage to another or to avert a common danger, and suffers pecuniary loss, may demand redress for the loss sustained from the persons who benefited thereby in appropriate ratios.'

6 See *Z Radwański/A Olejniczak*, Zobowiązania – część ogólna (9th edn 2010) 86; *A Śmieja* in: A Olejniczak (ed), System Prawa Prywatnego, vol 6 (2nd edn 2014).

7 See *T Pajor*, Poland, in: VV Palmer/M Bussani (eds), Pure Economic Loss. New Horizons in Comparative Law (2008) 270.

8 *W Czachórski*, Zobowiązania. Zarys wykładu (8th edn 2002) 169.

9 *J Andrzejewski*, Odpowiedzialność przedkontraktowa (tzw. culpa in contrahendo) w kodeksie zobowiązań. Tradycja i inspiracja (2014) XXIII(4) Kwartalnik Prawa Prywatnego 955–972.

bases of liability discussed as *culpa in contrahendo* should be treated as autonomous institutions,[10] subject to autonomous interpretations. Thus, he has proposed a Polish 'third way' concept, calling it '*sui generis* liability' or '*ex culpae in contrahendo* liability'.

12 The duty to keep confidential all information which has been provided with a contractual reservation (art 72^1 §1 and §2 cc) also belongs to the grey area.[11]

13 Discrimination cases can fall within either tort or contract, depending on whether there is a pre-existing obligation between the parties. According to the Law on implementing some EU laws respecting equal treatment,[12] one can be held liable in damages for anti-discriminatory conduct (art 13) and a general reference is made to the principles in the Civil Code. In addition, art 15 introduces special prescription periods (three years *a tempore scientiae* and five years *a tempore facti*) and art 16 states that any claim for damages based on this Law is without prejudice to claims based on other statutory provisions. For example, in labour law, a ban on discrimination due to gender and the principle of equal treatment are stipulated in the Labour Code (art 18^{3a} §6 Labour Code). The law entitles the aggrieved employee to claim damages; however, also here the nature of the damages is not clear (whether they include only pecuniary loss or non-pecuniary loss or both). The dominant position is that the discriminatory conduct results in the contractual liability of the employer.[13]

14 Much more controversial is the nature of the liability of an employer for a violation of an individual's dignity and other personal rights, as well as the interests of its employees (this question pertains both to the direct and vicarious liability of the employer). Given that art 300 of the Labour Code refers to the Civil Code in matters not regulated by the former, a claim for compensation of non-pecuniary loss in cases of infringement of personal rights is governed by arts 24 and 448 cc (hence, a delictual basis). However, there is a developing tendency in the court practice to permit an employee to seek compensation of

---

10 See also *W Kocot*, Odpowiedzialność przedkontrakowa (2013) 66, 343. In English see *D Michoński*, Contractual or delictual? On the character of pre-contractual liability in selected European legal systems (2015) 20 Comparative Law Review 151.

11 See also *W Kocot*, Odpowiedzialność przedkontrakowa (2013) 66, 343. In English see *D Michoński*, Contractual or delictual? On the character of pre-contractual liability in selected European legal systems (2015) 20 Comparative Law Review 151. 1, the entitled party may demand from the other party the redress of the damage or the return of the profits obtained by that party.'

12 Act of 3 December 2010, Dz U 2010, no 254, item 1700.

13 See *M Szabłowska*, Kontraktowa odpowiedzialność pracodawcy za molestowanie seksualne w miejscu pracy lub w związku z pracą (2012/6) Monitor Prawa Pracy 292; *id*, Kontraktowa i deliktowa odpowiedzialność pracodawcy za naruszenie dóbr osobistych pracownika (2012/1) Przegląd Sądowy 42.

non-pecuniary loss from the employer *ex contractu* (art 448 cc in conjunction with art 300 Labour Code).[14]

Medical malpractice cases do not belong to the 'grey zone'. The liability of doctors will primarily be based on tort law. A patient who uses the public health care system does not conclude a contract with a physician or hospital. The liability can be governed by a contractual regime only if it derives from a contract for privately financed medical services concluded between the patient and a private hospital (or an individual practitioner).[15] Nevertheless, even in the case of privately contracted services, a doctor's negligent breach of contractual or statutory obligations may at the same time constitute a tort. The victim can choose between basing his/her claim in contract or in tort. Historical reasons can explain the preference for the tortious nature of a doctor's liability in damages. Until 2004 the Civil Code provided for the liability of the State for the fault of its functionaries, and medical professionals were regarded as functionaries. After World War II Polish courts held State-run health care institutions liable in tort for damage inflicted by a physician while carrying out the tasks entrusted to him/her. It was established that a hospital was liable not only for its own fault (so-called 'organisational fault'), but also for any fault of its physicians and medical staff, therapeutic and diagnostic acts included. 15

C. COMMON OR DIFFERENT RULES REGULATING TORT AND CONTRACT

These *common rules* are contained in Book 3 of the Civil Code ('Obligations') but placed in two different titles: Title III – 'General rules on contractual obligations'; and Title VI – 'Illicit Acts/Torts' (*czyny niedozwolone*). Title I, which regulates general matters within the area of obligations, applies to both. It contains provisions concerning: 16

- determination of extent of liability and compensation;
- adequate causation (art 361 §1);
- the principle of full compensation (art 361 §2);
- contributory negligence (art 362); and
- methods of repairing damage (art 363).

In common with other European jurisdictions, the main factual elements of tortious and contractual liability for damages in Polish law are the same. First of all, there must be an event triggering damage. Secondly, there must be 17

[14] See SN of 14 December 2010, I PK 95/10.
[15] It is typically a contract for the provision of medical services (art 750 cc).

damage, and thirdly, there has to be a causal link between the event and the damage. However, in the case of tortious liability, the liability may be based on three principles: fault, risk and equity, while in contract only on the first two. The principle of fault is the general basis both for liability for damage caused to anyone, and for a debtor's liability for the non-fulfilment of an obligation (see more details below sec II.A nos 32–38).

18 In the Civil Code, liability *ex contractu* is referred to as 'liability for damage resulting from non-performance or improper performance of an obligation' (art 471). Despite the term 'contractual liability', it is commonly understood that the said rules apply in the case of a breach of any obligation: a contract, a unilateral act of will, a legal provision (imposing the obligation regardless of any contractual relationship), a judicial decision or an administrative decision.[16]

19 The nature of the duty to redress damage is different in the two regimes. In liability *ex delicto*, the duty to compensate is *primary*, in the sense that, when a tort is committed, an obligation arises immediately – a duty to redress the damage. In liability *ex contractu*, on the other hand, the duty is *secondary* (consequential).[17] This is due to the fact that, according to the Polish system, a creditor is entitled to demand performance (in the common law meaning of 'specific performance') of a contractual obligation and this entitlement is seen as flowing from the very nature of an obligation.

20 It has been pointed out in legal literature that an insurer's liability does not fall into either of the discussed regimes. Rather this is a separate type of liability, so-called guarantee-distributive liability, where, in contrast to liability *ex contractu*, the duty to pay damages is of a primary character and, in contrast to liability *ex delicto*, the insurer instead of the tortfeasor is liable to pay indemnity.[18]

21 The *differences* between contractual and tortious liability for damage pertain to the following issues:

- unavailability of equity as a basis of liability in a contractual regime;
- basis of liability for acts of others;
- burden of proof of fault (which in tortious liability rests upon the claimant, and in contractual liability is shifted to the defendant);
- scope of recoverable damage (personal injury claims and in particular non-pecuniary damage only recoverable if sought in tort – see below on the concurrence of claims sec IV.A); and
- limitation periods.

16 See Radwański/Olejniczak (fn 6) 85.
17 Ibid.
18 Ibid, 86.

Some of the above differences are reduced by the fact that Polish law does not recognise the *non cumul* principle. Concurrence of bases of liability is permitted by art 443 cc. The claimant is hence free to choose the basis more favourable to him/her. 22

D. APPLICATION OF COMMON RULES IN A DIFFERENT WAY

The courts apply the common rules in the same way. A debatable issue concerns the method of repairing damage. Due to the fact that the general rule on the method of repairing the damage is to be found in the general part of obligations (art 363 §1 cc), it can be asserted that in both liability regimes, the injured party can choose the way in which the damage is to be redressed, either by restoration of the previous state of affairs or by the payment of an appropriate sum of money. If, however, restoration of the previous state of affairs is impossible or if it would entail undue hardship or excessive costs to the person liable, the injured person's claim shall be limited to a pecuniary payment (art 363 §1 cc). 23

However, legal scholarship questions the application of the method to restore the previous state of affairs in the contract regime. 24

II. MAIN DIFFERENCES BETWEEN TORTIOUS AND CONTRACTUAL LIABILITY

A. DIFFERENCES AS REGARDS THE FOUNDATIONS OF LIABILITY

1) *Role of Intention, Wrongfulness and Fault and their Variations*

As regards the foundations of liability, in general, fault liability and risk (strict) liability are two common foundations of liability for contracts and torts. 25

Polish tort law follows the 'general clause model', not the German 'protected interests model'. The general clause of art 415 establishes tortious liability based upon proven fault. It is supplemented by a number of separate provisions located in the Civil Code and in other pieces of legislation that regulate tortious liability in specified situations. While some of them are also based on fault, others are examples of strict liability, absolute liability, or liability based on equity. 26

The general clause of contractual liability is also fault-based, but the burden of proving a lack of fault has been shifted to the debtor (art 471). Hence, it is commonly said that art 471 establishes liability of a debtor based on presumed 27 fault: 'A debtor is obliged to remedy any damage arising from non-performance or improper performance of an obligation unless the non-performance or improper performance is due to circumstances for which the debtor is not liable.'

28 The idea that the conduct of the tortfeasor must be contrary to law (wrongful) has a counterpart in liability *ex contractu* in the requirement that the debtor has breached an existing obligation. An *additional* requirement to establish the fault of the debtor (lack of due diligence) is recognised by the prevailing *opinio iuris*. In Polish law, the type of fault does not determine the scope of compensation (see however nos 127–131). Any fault suffices to hold the defendant liable in tort, and he/she will be bound to pay compensation for proven damage.

29 The second general rule is that a debtor is liable, as for his/her own actions or omissions, for the actions and omissions of persons with the assistance of whom he/she performs the obligation, of the persons to whom he/she entrusts the performance of the obligation, and of his/her statutory representatives (art 474[19]). This is a basis of strict liability (see further remarks below nos 39–41).

30 The general provisions of Book 3 of the Civil Code ('Obligations') apply to contracts, torts and other types of obligations. As mentioned earlier, these common rules concern causation, scope and assessment of damages, reparation of damage other than personal injury, and contributory negligence.

31 The *principle of equity* (fairness) is only found in the realm of tort liability. The equity principle is regarded as subsidiary to fault or strict liability. The following three cases are based on principles of fairness (equity): public authority liability (art 417^2), liability for animals (art 431 §2), and personal liability of minors or incompetent persons (art 428). In these situations, the courts tend to relax the burden in respect of proving adequate causation, and to impose the obligation to redress harm (which is usually personal injury) on the defendant who neither committed a fault nor is strictly liable.

32 In Polish civil law, wrongfulness (unlawfulness) involves a breach of generally binding rules, and a contractual relationship is not subject to such general rules. The concept of unlawful conduct covers actions as well as omissions (provided that an obligation to act established by law or by general clauses was violated).

---

19 The debtor shall be liable for an act or omission of persons who assist him in performing the obligation, as well as for persons whom he entrusts with the performance of the obligation as if for his own act or omission. The above-mentioned provision shall also apply where the obligation is performed by the debtor's representative.

There is some disagreement among scholars concerning the relationship between the content of norms the breach of which can lead to tortious liability in a particular case and the conduct itself.[20] 33

In *contractual liability*, on the other hand, a debtor acts wrongfully if he/she breaches a contract by violating the creditors' rights under the contract. Sometimes, however, this is also called 'relative wrongfulness' (although this term in fact denotes something else).[21] In the Civil Code, the fault of a debtor is described in art 472: 'unless a special provision of the law or a legal act provides otherwise, a debtor is liable for failure to use due care'. The standard of care is generally addressed in art 355, which applies to both liability regimes. Accordingly, 'a person is obliged to display the diligence generally required in relations of a given type' (art 355 §1). Due diligence of the debtor within the scope of his/her economic activity shall be assessed with consideration to the professional nature of that activity (art 355 §2). This means that the duty of care required of a person engaged in a business or a profession is higher than the duty required of an ordinary person outside his/her profession.[22] 34

The objective standard is to be applied in instances of both contractual and delictual liability. Hence, the due care expected from a debtor and from a tortfeasor will be the same, unless of course it was modified in a contract. 35

Fault is defined as a subjective, improper nature of a person's conduct; improperness of behaviour relates to foreseeability and will.[23] It can thus be said that fault is an unacceptable attitude of a person who causes damage towards the specific conduct that harms interests protected by the law. It is not the result (damage) but the conduct which is taken into account in the determination of fault. The defendant is held to be 'at fault' because, in the particular circumstances, he/she failed to behave in a way he/she should have, and could have, behaved. Insane persons cannot of course be ascribed any fault. Absent any provisions in the rules on contracts, the rules on incapacitated persons (arts 425 and 426), to be found in the title on torts, will apply to these (rare) cases.[24] This is yet another example of common grounds for the assessment of a person's conduct. 36

---

20 This concerns the notion of 'conditional/relative unlawfulness' (literal translation of the notion of '*bezprawnosc wzgledna*'), which also exists in other legal systems, under a different name, for instance in Austria (the 'doctrine of the protective purpose of a provision'). The majority of scholars are of the opinion that unlawfulness in the context of tortious liability is only possible if the legal norm breached by the potential tortfeasor established rights for the group of persons to which the victim belongs. For instance: *B Lewaszkiewicz-Petrykowska*, Wina jako podstawa odpowiedzialności z tytułu czynów niedozwolonych (1969/2) Studia Prawno-Ekonomiczne 91 in the context of state liability *E Bagińska*, Odpowiedzialnosc odszkodowawcza za wykonywanie wladzy publicznej (2006) 397–401.

21 See *Radwański/Olejniczak* (fn 6) 318.

22 See SN of 20 May 1986, CRN III 82/86, OSN 8/1987, 125.

23 *Czachórski* (fn 8) 203.

24 SN of 22 October 1975, V PRN 4/75, OSN 5/1976, item 90.

37 As to fault, the role of *intention* is generally irrelevant for the duty to compensate to arise. In some types of contracts, however, intent in breaching a contract is an additional prerequisite for liability. In these cases the Polish legislator follows the Roman principle of *culpa lata dolo aequiparatur* and hence intent is equated with gross negligence (eg liability of carrier and freight forwarder).[25]

38 Intent becomes relevant when a debtor wishes to limit his/her contractual liability *ex ante* (art 473) – see below para 128.

2) Role of Strict Liability

39 In Poland, strict liability is known as 'liability based on risk'.[26] Polish law does not recognise only one single type of strict liability, but rather approaches the issue on a case-by-case basis. By using slightly different exoneration clauses and thus different levels of stringency, the law reflects the argument that various situations call for strict liability for different reasons.

40 In general, strict liability requires a specific norm to this effect. Hence, in the tort regime, strict liability attaches to dangerous activities or objects creating a risk of damage, for example premises and constructions, enterprises 'set in motion by natural powers', enterprises creating an aggravated risk of environmental damage, means of transport, dangerous products, nuclear installations, etc.[27] In the case of torts, strict liability prevails over fault rules (if both could be applied to the circumstances of a particular case).

41 As concerns the contractual regime, one should first of all note that a debtor can assume liability that is stricter than the default rules (ie presumed fault).[28] Hence, in the case of contracts, strict liability may be the result of the exercise of a party's will. The main role of statutory strict liability in contractual liability attaches to the debtor's liability for third persons (art 474) – see nos 74–75.

B. DIFFERENCES AS REGARDS CAUSATION

42 The causation requirement, based on the theory of adequate causation, is the same for both liability regimes. It is also interpreted in a similar way in court practice.[29]

25 Arts 757, 777, 788 §1, 791 §2, 801 §1, 849 §2, 852, 891 §1 cc.

26 Other notions used to describe it are: objective liability, liability without fault, or liability for result.

27 See *M Nesterowicz/E Bagińska*, Strict Liability in Poland, in: BA Koch/H Koziol (eds), Unification of Tort Law: Strict Liability (2002) 259–260.

28 Art 473: A debtor may, in a contract, assume liability for non-performance or for improper performance of an obligation resulting from the determined circumstances which, pursuant to the statute, he is not liable for.

29 See Radwański/Olejniczak (fn 6) 319.

Foreseeability is neither a prerequisite of causation, nor a limitation to the scope of liability. Contrary to the common law systems and some other European civil law systems, the foreseeability of damage has no influence on the extent of a debtor's liability in Polish law. 43

C. DIFFERENCES AS REGARDS REMEDIES

1) *Degree of Certainty of the Damage*

The same standard of proof of damage is applied to both torts and contracts. 44

2) *Compensation for Non-pecuniary Loss*

In general, pecuniary loss shall be compensated in every case, while non-pecuniary loss is compensable only when the law so permits. Pursuant to art 361 §2 cc, 'damage shall be fully compensated in the absence of contrary provisions of a contract or law'. 45

Contractual provisions deviating from the principle of full compensation are subject to the test of validity of legal transactions and must conform with the nature of contractual legal relations and with principles of justice. 46

Personal injury is regulated in more detail in the chapter on torts (arts 444–449 cc). Non-pecuniary loss arising from personal injury cases (pain and suffering), as well as from violations of personal interests, is covered by the claims listed in the mentioned provisions. 47

The following types of situations entitle the victim to claim compensation for non-pecuniary loss: 48

- bodily harm or health disorder (art 445 §1 cc);
- deprivation of liberty (art 445 §2 cc);
- sexual assault or misconduct (art 445 §2 cc);
- compensation awarded to the next of kin in the case of a victim's death (art 446 §3 cc); and
- infringement of personal rights (art 448 cc).

In addition, other non-financial wrongs (such as those originating in the violation of patients' rights or copyright infringements) are also reparable. The bases for such claims are found in separate statutes, which typically make reference to art 448 cc. Thus, compensating non-pecuniary loss belongs to the sphere of tortious liability by default. Even in the absence of a reference to tort rules, a court would still treat a claim for compensation of non-pecuniary loss as a tort claim. 49

50 A claim for compensation of non-pecuniary loss is not available under the contractual regime, although it should be mentioned that this approach is currently disputed among scholars. An exception is made as regards package travel contracts. Following the ECJ's *Leitner* case, the Supreme Court in its judgment of 9 November 2010 (III CZP 79/10) held that the legal basis of the tour operator's liability for loss of holidays was found in art 11a §1 of the Law on Travel Services (1997), which implements art 5 of Directive 90/314/EEC. According to the Supreme Court, art 11a §1 regulates the reparation of the entire damage suffered by a tourist and, hence, it includes both pecuniary and non-pecuniary losses. The Court rejected the theory recognising the right to holidays as a new personal right, as such recognition would be contrary to the provisions of the Civil Code.

51 Hence, personal injury (including non-pecuniary loss) stemming from a breach of a contract may be compensated when the violation concurrently constitutes a tort (concurrence of liabilities) – see sec IV.B.

3) Compensation for Loss of Earnings and for Loss of Chance

52 Loss of earnings consequent upon personal injury is recoverable *ex delicto* (see art 444 §1 cc). The same is true with respect to the loss of a chance. In general in Polish legal doctrine, the loss of a chance, the loss of expectations or *préjudice éventuel* are treated as one category and appear to be excluded from the scope of compensation. The law specifically provides cases where the loss of a chance may result in compensation. Article 444 §2 cc provides the victim of personal injury with the possibility to claim compensation for diminished future prospects. Further, according to art 446 §2, the family of a victim who died may claim compensation for their reduced standard of living. Within this category the courts award compensation for the lost chances to obtain certain financial means from the deceased, in addition to the pecuniary losses covered by an annuity (art 446 §2 cc).[30]

53 As regards the loss of the chance to obtain gains, a vast majority of legal scholars traditionally rejects such claims, albeit with various justifications. The key argument is that chances to obtain gains fall outside of the scope of normal causal consequences. The prevailing line of court practice follows the legal scholarship.[31] If a victim proves with a sufficiently high probability that he/she

[30] See *E Bagińska*, Causal Uncertainty and Proportional Liability in Poland, in: I Gilead/MD Green/BA Koch (eds), Proportional Liability: Analytical and Comparative Perspectives (2013) 253, nos 41–46.

[31] For instance: SN of 18 April 2002, II CKN 1216/00, OSNC 4/2003, item 58.

could have obtained the profits but for the damaging event, his/her loss will be compensated. However, if he/she fails to meet the heightened standard of proof, the court will likely classify the loss as potential damage or a loss of a chance, or loss of (subjective) expectations, and dismiss the case.[32] Typically, it is easier to prove such a loss *ex contractu* than *ex delicto*. Loss of healing (or 'loss of a chance of recovery') is either compensated under the heading of non-pecuniary loss or is included in the computation of an annuity (hence, into pecuniary damages).

4) *Restitutionary Damages*

Unjust enrichment (restitution) is generally regulated in Title V on 'Unjust Enrichment' of the Civil Code. Under the general rules of art 405, '[a]nyone who without legal grounds has gained a financial benefit at the expense of another person is obliged to hand over the benefit in kind, and if this is not possible, to return its value.' The Civil Code provides for *condictiones* in art 410. Due to their restricted scope, the courts apply the rules on restitution very rarely. This is partly due to the fact that the provisions of Title V do not prevail over the provisions on the duty to redress the damage (art 414). This means that the rule of art 414 cc allows for a concurrence between restitution and tort law regimes, but excludes it between restitution and contract law regimes. 54

Disgorgement of profits is not considered as a general remedy in Polish law, in particular it is unknown in tort and contract liability regimes. There must be a specific statutory entitlement to raise such a claim. Hence, under the Civil Code, disgorgement of profits (or gains) can be demanded in a few cases of pre-contractual liability, for example: 55

- if one party uses the classified information, which came to their knowledge during negotiations, for their own benefit (art 72^1 §2 cc);
- an entrepreneur whose right to a business name has been violated may demand: the removal of any consequences of the violation, a statement of appropriate content and form, compensation for pecuniary damage in accordance with general principles or that the disgorgement of profits by the perpetrator be released (art 43^{10} cc).

The disgorgement of profits as a remedy is an alternative to a claim for damages, and the choice between them rests on the claimant. 56

Interestingly, the disgorgement of profits as envisaged in the Act on Combatting Unfair Competition for torts of unfair competition has been combined with the 57

[32] See *Bagińska* (fn 30) no 46.

institute of unjust enrichment. In general, the Act entitles a claimant to seek the following pecuniary remedies:

- damages in accordance with the general principles of damages (ie an action based in tort);
- disgorgement of profits in accordance with the general rules (the only general rules on restitutionary damages are those applicable to unjust enrichment);
- an appropriate amount of money to be transferred to a determined social organisation the goal of which is to support Polish culture or related to the protection of national heritage – where the act of unfair competition was deliberate.

58 Consequently, the defendant will be released from the obligation to return the benefit or to reimburse its value if he/she has used it up or lost it in such a manner that he/she is no longer enriched, unless he/she should have taken into account the duty to return it when relinquishing the benefit or using it up (art 409).

59 Finally, disgorgement of profits is a universal remedy in the area of copyright law, patent law or trademark law. Polish law implemented the EC directives relating to intellectual property law[33] in such a way that a list of remedies, including injunctive remedies, is provided in the relevant statutes. Disgorgement of profits is available as a remedy in addition to a claim for damages. The latter is also construed in the alternative: for example, pursuant to the Copyright Law, a claimant may seek damages in accordance with the general rules (the Civil Code) or may demand a proper sum be paid to him/her (the double of an appropriate author's remuneration or a sum equal to the licence fee; in the case of an intentional violation triple damages have been held unconstitutional).[34]

5) *Aggravated and Exemplary (or Punitive) Damages*

60 Aggravated and exemplary damages are not allowed in Polish law.

61 Polish contract law permits penalty clauses ('liquidated damages clauses') with regard to non-performance or improper performance of a non-pecuniary

[33] The Act of 9 May 2007 (Dz U 2007, no 99, item 662) implemented Dir 93/83/EEC, Dir 93/98/EEC, Dir 96/9/EC and Dir 2004/48/EC.

[34] See art 79 of the Copyright Law (2004), art 287 of the Industrial Property Law (2000) and art 11 of the Law on the Protection of Databases (2001) See the Constitutional Tribunal judgment of 23 June 2015, SK 32/14, OTK ZU 6A/2015, item 84, as well as two opposing interpretations of the results of this judgement by the Supreme Court: SN of 10 November 2017, V CSK 41/14, OSNC 10/2018, item 101, and SN of 7 December 2017, V CSK 145/17, OSP 11/2018, item 111.

obligation. The law stipulates that the damage resulting from a breach shall be redressed by the payment of the stipulated liquidated damages. In the Code of Obligations of 1933, liquidated damages were referred to as 'contractual damages'; this notion emphasised both the compensatory role of liquidated damages and their main aim, which is the simplification of seeking redress should the non-performance of the obligation occur. The present regulation represents a slightly different legal form of liquidated damages, which are now called 'contractual penalties' (*kara umowna*) (art 483 cc).

Pursuant to the Supreme Court's opinion, although questioned in the doctrine, 62
the creditor's loss is not a prerequisite for a claim for liquidated damages. The creditor does not need to prove that he/she has suffered any damage as it is agreed that the parties introduce penalty clauses in order to guarantee the proper and timely performance of the contract.[35] On the other hand, the lack of damage or its actual scope should be taken into account when deciding on an ad hoc reduction of the liquidated damages. Given that the damage has occurred, the court may also use as a yardstick the hypothetical calculation of the scope of damages according to the general rules (arts 361, 363 cc).[36]

6) *Other Remedies*

As a rule, in Polish law specific performance is available alongside other 63
remedies. Because the law protects the creditor's interest, the latter can elect a suitable remedy in the event of the debtor's delay or default in performing his/her duties under a contract.

In particular, the creditor can demand so-called 'substitute performance', which 64
means that the creditor may perform the obligation by himself/herself on account of the debtor, with or without the consent of the court. The need to obtain the consent of a court is determined by the subject matter of performance. Consent is thus required for non-performance of an obligation to act, or to refrain from acting.

Injunctions are not regarded as a general remedy in Polish tort law. There are a 65
number of instances where a party can demand injunctive relief.

First of all, injunctive relief can be requested in the case of a violation of personal 66
interests under art 24 §1 cc. Article 24 provides that a person whose personal interest is threatened by the conduct of another can demand that the action ceases. If an infringement has already occurred, the victim may

[35] SN of 6 November 2003, III CZP 61/03, OSNC 5/2004, item 69.
[36] See Radwański/Olejniczak (fn 6) 366.

demand that its effects are rectified, which can entail in particular: a statement, compensation, or a sum of money paid to a social cause. Articles 445 and 448, which further specify conditions for assessing and awarding damages for non-pecuniary losses, also apply.

67 Secondly, the 'neighbourhood law' (nuisance law) prescribes a possibility to demand injunctive relief. However, the nature of liability in neighbourhood law is not entirely clear. There are many plausible arguments for qualifying the liability as delictual, as it is usually described in legal writings.[37] Pursuant to art 144 cc, the owner of immovable property should, when exercising his/her rights, refrain from activities which interfere with the use of the neighbouring immovable properties and which exceed normal use resulting from the socio-economic purpose of the immovable property and the local conditions. Owners as well as persons enjoying other proprietary rights can bring a claim based on this provision, which may lead to injunctive relief being granted. Conduct which disturbs the neighbouring land beyond acceptable local standards is illegal, and thus a claim for damages based on the general rules of the Civil Code can be filed. However, the illegality of an activity performed on neighbouring land would not be relevant for a tort action in damages based on art 435 cc (strict liability of an enterprise).

68 Further, the rule stipulated in art 439 cc should be mentioned here. According to this provision, a person who is directly exposed to the risk of damage resulting from the behaviour of another person, in particular due to a lack of proper supervision of the operation of an enterprise or business controlled by him/her, or of the condition of a building or any other installation possessed by him/her, may demand that that person undertake any measures necessary to avert the immediate danger, and, if necessary, also to give adequate security (eg to place a sum of money in the court deposit).

69 Another instance of judicial injunctions concerns cases of unfair competition, regulated by arts 18 and 19 of the Act on Combatting Unfair Competition of 16 April 1993.[38] Actions for injunctions can be sought in cases of many types of unfair practices specified in the Act, for example misleading or false indication of geographical origin, geographical indications, and information relating to the name or characteristics of goods or services. A court may order the unlawful act to be stopped, its effects be removed and that the competitor breaking the law make a single or multiple declaration of an appropriate form and content (in addition to monetary compensation). As a part of its interim ruling, the court may also place a ban on the sale of specific goods, their introduction into trade,

---

[37] See *W Katner*, Ochrona wlasnosci nieruchomosci przed naruszeniami posrednimi (1982) 130.

[38] Dz U 2003, no 153, at 1503 with amendments.

and advertising thereof. A temporary order may be requested from the court in whose district the unfair competitor's property is located.[39] Moreover, the Act does not prejudice claims under other legal provisions (such as the Civil Code, copyright law, patent law or trademark law).

D. DIFFERENCES AS REGARDS RECOVERABILITY OF 'PURE ECONOMIC LOSSES'?

Generally speaking, pure economic loss is not a distinct head of damage in Polish law and the courts do not recognise this concept. It is not seen as relevant in light of the wide scope of the provisions of the Civil Code concerning liability in tort. The common rules (art 361 §§1 and 2 cc) elucidate the principle of full compensation of damage falling within the limits of adequate causation.[40] 70

Hence, although pure economic loss is difficult to categorise in Polish law, it will be equally available on both contract and tort grounds. 71

In legal scholarship, on the other hand, pure economic loss is regarded as exclusively financial damage arising extra-contractually without any previous harm to the person or property of the claimant,[41] or as a type of pecuniary loss that occurs irrespective of an infringement of someone's rights.[42] The approach seems correct in light of comparative analysis of the concept of pure economic loss. Assuming that the definition is correct, the claim for pure economic loss will be available under tort law only to the indirect victim of the tort. In general, only persons who are directly injured (ie by a wrongful action directed against them) may claim compensation. Exceptions listed in the Civil Code concern personal injury and wrongful death. For example, if as a result of a bodily injury the victim died, the person obliged to redress the damage shall refund the costs of treatment and the funeral to the person who has incurred them. 72

E. DIFFERENCES AS REGARDS LIABILITY FOR OTHERS

There is a substantial difference between vicarious liability in tort and vicarious liability in contract, and this difference is due to the fact that the latter is stricter. 73

---

[39] See in general *J Szwaja* (ed), Ustawa o zwalczaniu nieuczciwej konkurencji. Komentarz (2001).

[40] SN of 21 January 2011, III CZP 116/10, OSNZD C/2011, item 54.

[41] See *Pajor* (fn 7) 258.

[42] Examples concern cases of unfair competition or sharing know-how.

74 A debtor is liable *ex contractu* for actions and omissions of persons with whose help he/she performs the obligation (subcontractors and assistants) as if for his/her own actions or omissions (art 474 first sentence). This rule also applies where the obligation is performed by the debtor's statutory representative (art 474 second sentence).

75 Hence, art 474 covers all four categories listed in the questionnaire (auxiliaries and independent contractors, legal representatives or organs of a company, representatives of natural persons, and the auxiliary/organ itself). The subcontractors and assistants do not have to be subordinate to the main contractor, and there is no requirement of dependency. The assessment of their conduct (breach of duty) is carried out according to the standard of due care required from the debtor as if he/she had performed the obligation personally. The liability is strict and may not be excluded by furnishing proof of lack of negligence in choosing the subcontractor (*culpa in eligendo*) or in supervising (*culpa in custodiendo*). In order to be exculpated, the debtor needs to prove that the persons who assisted in performing the obligation failed to perform due to circumstances beyond their control.

76 In the tort regime, the listed categories are treated differently.

77 In relation to liability for independent contractors, the possibility of raising independent contractor immunity as a defence is dependent on the determination of whether the case relates to liability for an independent contractor or for a servant (employer). In order to answer this question, one has to look at the scope of power of management and control over this person's activities.[43]

78 Article 429 cc provides that a person who entrusts an independent contractor with the performance of a task is liable for the damage he/she may cause while carrying it out. In contrast to employers' liability (art 430), however, this liability is based on fault. The defendant may escape liability if he/she refutes the presumption of *culpa in eligendo* in either of these two ways:

- he/she was not negligent in choosing the contractor;
- he/she entrusted the performance of the transaction to a person, enterprise or institution which performs such transactions within the scope of their professional activity.

79 The master is still personally liable for any other personal negligence. Should it be the case, both the principal and the independent contractor are jointly and severally liable for damage according to art 441 §1.

---

[43] See *M Nesterowicz/E Bagińska*, Liability for Damage Caused by Others under Polish Law, in: J Spier (ed), Unification of Tort Law: Liability for Damage Caused by Others (2003) 190–194.

On the other hand, a person who on his own account entrusts the performance of an act to a person who, during the performance of the act, is under his control and has a duty to follow instructions is liable for any damage caused by that person's fault in the course of performance (master–servant relationship, see art 430). 80

In relation to liability for liability of legal representatives of or organs of a company, there are two, very similar general clauses in the Civil Code: one relating to the tortious liability of physical persons (art 415 literally speaks of 'anyone') and one for legal persons (art 416). The latter concerns direct liability of legal persons for damage caused due to a fault of their 'organs'.[44] In practice this means that legal persons are liable for actions or omissions of physical persons representing their organs. This liability is limited, however, to (i) the conduct of persons who have been duly appointed as representing organs of a legal person, and (ii) only to those actions or omissions which remain within the persons' authority. If the act under scrutiny exceeds the limits set by statutes or other legal provisions, and its purpose is solely private (not linked with the activities of the corporation), liability under art 416 cc will be excluded. The legal person may, however, be liable for the fault in choosing the performer of the task (art 429 cc), and the physical persons creating the organ may be held liable on the grounds of art 415 cc, jointly and severally with the legal person (art 441cc). 81

The second prerequisite of the liability governed by art 416 cc is that the organ must be at fault. The fault of a one-person organ is assessed in the same manner as a natural person's fault. In the case of a collegiate organ, it should be established that some statutory duty was breached or that the act was otherwise wrongful (in breach of the principles of social cooperation[45] or general rules of conduct). No proof of individual fault is required. It suffices to establish subjective fault and wrongfulness of the organ's actions or omissions. The liability attaches to the legal person even if only one member of the organ was at fault (eg the head of the management board).[46] 82

As regards the organ's own liability, this is not admitted. Polish law follows the doctrine that legal persons act through their organs (art 39 cc). For instance, if the organ exceeded the scope of its authority and inflicted damage by concluding a contract, the liability attaches only to the natural person acting as an organ. 83

---

[44] In fact, art 415 cc has been applied more often to liability of legal persons than art 416 cc. The prerequisite of the legal person's liability pursuant to art 415 cc is typically their 'organisational' fault or negligent omission.

[45] SN of 21 December 1970, I CR 517/70, OSPiKA 1/1972, item 4.

[46] See Nesterowicz/Bagińska (fn 43) 186.

F. DIFFERENCES AS REGARDS LIABILITY IN THE CASE OF MULTIPLE TORTFEASORS/BREACHING PARTIES

84 The rules pertaining to joint and several obligations are contained in the general provisions on obligations, in arts 366–378 cc. A creditor may claim the entirety or some part of the obligation (performance) to be performed jointly by all obligors, by several of them or by each of them separately, and the satisfaction of the creditor by one obligor shall release the others (art 366 §1). All joint and several debtors remain obliged until the obligation towards the creditor has been fully satisfied. An obligation shall be joint and several where it results from a statute or from a juridical act. The liability of multiple breaching parties will hence be based on the rules of art 366 ff. The provisions in arts 366–378 cc have general application in any regime of liability.

85 The Civil Code *separately regulates the liability of multiple tortfeasors*. Article 441 §1 cc lays down a general rule of joint and several liability in all cases where more than one person is liable for the damage arising from a tort.[47] The basic requirement of art 441 §1 cc is the tortious infliction of damage. Secondly, the damage for which all the persons are liable must be one (indivisible) loss. The third requirement is a causal link between the damage and the event (tort), for which each of the joint tortfeasors bears liability. The causal link should be viewed in light of art 361 §1 cc.

86 Where multiple parties are responsible for the damage, it is irrelevant whether the actions of one party were direct or indirect or whether one party is more responsible or blameworthy than the other. As a principle, in cases where more than one person caused the damage, the degree of liability of individual persons is not to be identified or differentiated in the main lawsuit.[48]

87 Contribution claims are based on art 441 §§2 and 3 cc. If the damage resulted from acts or omissions of several persons, the person who redresses the damage may demand reimbursement of the appropriate part depending on the circumstances of the case, in particular the fault of the given person and the degree to which the latter contributed to the occurrence of the damage from the others (art 441 §2). Article 441 §2 cc controls the determination of contribution claims between tortfeasors who are liable on the same legal basis (eg fault liability). The scope of indemnity depends on the circumstances of the case, in particular on the degree to which each tortfeasor contributed to the injury. In a case where two persons may be held liable for damage on the basis

---

[47] See *M Nesterowicz/E Bagińska*, Multiple Tortfeasors under Polish Law, in: WVH Rogers (ed), Unification of Tort Law: Multiple Tortfeasors (2004) 151–155, 162.

[48] Ibid, 153, 156.

of strict liability (for creation of risk – arts 434 or 435 cc) and there is no ground to determine which person's activity was the actual cause of the damage, the Supreme Court holds the two persons jointly and severally liable (art 441 cc) because neither of them is able to prove any defence to strict liability.[49]

A person who redresses the damage for which he/she is liable in spite of the absence of fault has a right of recourse against the perpetrator if the damage occurred due to the latter's fault (art 441 §3 cc). 88

When the *liabilities in question are 'mixed'*, the Polish jurisprudence refers to a so-called *in solidum* obligation. This kind of obligation is not regulated in Polish law, even though the judicature has used the concept in several decisions since the Code of Obligations came into force in 1934. This type of obligation occurs when an injured person has two or more claims for damages that (i) are independent from each other, (ii) arise from different legal relations linking the victim with each obligor (in particular when one is liable in contract and another in tort), and (iii) where no legal basis exists for the obligors' joint and several liability. The separate claims are, however, connected in the way that they serve the same purpose of satisfying the creditor. Performance by one debtor will release the others because the damage to be repaired is considered as indivisible. 89

Case law is divided on the question of what provisions should be applicable to *in solidum* obligations. Pursuant to the Code of Obligations, the Supreme Court has held that the provisions on joint and several obligations are principally not applicable to an obligation of several debtors where the creditor was entitled to one performance, but the debtors are liable on different legal grounds (*in solidum* obligation). Nevertheless, the Court indicated that a claimant may demand payment from all the obligors and the payment by one of them will operate to extinguish the liability of the others.[50] Yet, in later case law, while interpreting the provisions of the Civil Code of 1964, the Supreme Court concluded that rules on joint and several liability should be applicable *per analogiam* to a situation where a claimant is entitled to one claim that he/she may enforce against two or more parties liable on different legal bases.[51] If the defendants are liable *in solidum*, the judgment against them will state so.[52] 90

As concerns the right to contribution between obligors liable *in solidum*, the law is quite vague. The dominant view in the jurisprudence allows for an application of the rule of art 441 §2 cc *per analogiam*.[53] However, this should 91

---

49 SN of 4 July 1985, IV CR 202/85, not published; SN of 24 February 1981, IV CR 17/81, OSPiKA 5–6/1982, item 64, cmt *J Skoczylas*.

50 SN of 14 November 1961, 3 CR 306/61, OSPiKA 9/1962, 255.

51 SN of 18 December 1968, 2 CR 409/68, OSN 11/1969, 207.

52 SN of 10 April 1974, I PR 66/74, OSN 3/1975, 45.

53 See *B Lewaszkiewicz-Petrykowska*, Wyrządzenie szkody przez kilka osób (1978) 180 f.

be distinguished from the case of the concurrent liability of an insurer and tortfeasor, in particular when the victim may bring an *actio directa* against the insurer. By virtue of art 828 §1cc, 'unless otherwise agreed, as of the day the insurer pays the compensation, the policyholder's claim against the third party liable for the damage is transferred by force of law to the insurer up to the amount of the compensation paid'. If the insurer has covered only a part of the damage, the insuring party shall be entitled to priority in satisfaction as to the remaining part of it before the insurer's claim'. The insurer has a right to a contribution (*sensu largo*) vis-à-vis the wrongdoer (subrogation of a creditor, *cessio legis* – see art 518 §1 point 4 cc).

G. DIFFERENCES AS REGARDS THE PERSONS WHO MAY BE PROTECTED

92 It does not require any elaboration that tort law rules protect everyone and that a contractual obligation is effective only *inter partes* (subject to certain exceptions). In general, under Polish law, only persons who are directly injured (ie by a wrongful action directed against them) may claim compensation. As Pajor rightly pointed out, the boundaries of tortious liability are defined not only through interpretation of prerequisites of art 415 cc, but also of art 446 cc.[54] The latter rule provides for claims of victims *par ricochet* in personal injury cases only. Secondary victims are entitled to demand compensation for their own losses only in the case of death of the primary victim (art 446 §§2–4 cc).

93 The privity rule is of course a general rule in contracts, but the concept of 'contracts with protective effects' is not recognised in Polish law. Scholars agree that a creditor–debtor relationship and, consequently, all claims resulting therefrom, are only relevant between the specific creditor and debtor. This relationship does not normally entail any duties *erga omnes*. Hence, in general, third parties cannot claim recovery *ex contractu*, unless they can prove that the contract was entered into for the benefit of a third party (art 393 cc[55]).[56] However, if the breach amounts to a tort directed against the general interest

---

54 See *Pajor* (fn 7) 279.

55 Art 393 reads: '§1. If it has been reserved in a contract that the debtor would render performance for the benefit of a third party, this party, unless the contract provided otherwise, may demand directly from the debtor that the performance be rendered. §2. A reservation regarding the duty to render performance for the benefit of a third party may not be revoked or amended if the third party has declared to either of the parties that he would like to make use of the reservation. §3. The debtor may raise defences arising from the contract against a third party as well.'

56 See *Radwański/Olejniczak* (fn 6) 318.

and therefore against that of third parties, the latter could sue under tort rules as long as they can establish adequate causation between the conduct and the ensuing loss.[57]

This approach has been taken in at least two situations. The first concerned an employer's liability for injuries sustained by his employees because of defective machines or tools that failed to work. The second category of cases embraces distant, indirect victims. For example, when due to medical malpractice, an artist failed to appear at a recital, we can speak of a loss incurred not only by the artist but also by the organisers of the recital. Here, the key question is to whom the defendant's conduct was directed. Taken from this perspective, the problem seems to be one of proximate cause or of adequate causation. In the given example, the organisers of the concert will be unable to recover from the physician.[58] 94

In recent years, the privity debate has returned, as third parties tend to bring claims for pure economic loss in the case of improper performance of a contract for financial services between a company and its auditor. As regards this category of claimants (as opposed to claims sought by the contracting party), no court decisions can be reported from Poland. So far, the recognition of liability of auditors or banks for pure economic loss derives from the *tortious* consequences of the breach of an existing contract. The limits that are put on the reparable loss require an analysis of the duties violated by the professional. Liability is likely to be established if the duties were general and binding on the actor regardless of any contractual bond, and where the actor was aware that the breach of such duties will likely cause damage to certain third persons.[59] 95

H. DIFFERENCES AS REGARDS DEFENCES

As far as general defences to a debtor's liability are concerned, we should recall art 471 cc on the liability of a debtor for breach of contract. In order to be relieved of liability, the debtor has to prove an exculpating event: he has to prove that the violation of the obligation was due to circumstances beyond his control, including but not limited to force majeure. Force majeure is also an exonerating fact that excludes tortious liability. Force majeure is understood in both regimes to mean an extraneous and extraordinary event, the effects of which could neither have been foreseen nor prevented. The foreseeability of an event should 96

57 See *W Wagner* in: D Lasok (ed), Obligations in Polish Law, vol II (1974) 12.
58 See *Wagner* (fn 57) 12 f; *A Ohanowicz*, Obligations. General Part (1958) 930.
59 See also *Pajor* (fn 7) 272 f.

be seen objectively as the ability to foresee a concrete situation and outcome of force majeure. The anticipation of the phenomenon as such (eg the arrival of a tornado or flood) does not permit the conclusion of force majeure, unless its consequences could not have been foreseen or avoided.

97 The defences not explicitly regulated in the Civil Code, such as the assumption of risk and consent, are equally applicable to contracts and torts. The defences of necessity as well as self-help and self-defence are situated in the title on torts. If damage is caused in a state of necessity or as the consequence of self-defence, the element of wrongfulness of conduct is lacking, which excuses the actor from tortious liability. In the absence of similar rules in general contract law, the said defences are interpreted as applicable to contract cases as well. The list of defences include:

- self-defence – art 423 cc stipules that a person who acts in self-defence to resist a direct and unlawful attack on any of his/her interests or those of another person shall not be liable for the damage caused to the assailant. The rule covers both personal and proprietary interests;
- a person who destroys or damages another person's thing or kills or injures another person's animal in order to avert danger directly threatened by the thing or animal to himself or others is not liable for the resulting damage. Liability can be avoided if the person in question did not cause the danger himself/herself, if the danger could not otherwise have been averted, and if the interest preserved was clearly more important than the interest violated (art 424 cc). Contrary to art 423 cc, this rule also covers sources of danger other than human behaviour (ie a threat must come from a thing or an animal).

98 An owner cannot object to the use and even damage or destruction of a thing by another person if it is necessary to avert danger directly threatening the personal interests of that person or a third party. However, the actor will have to remedy any resulting damage to the owner pursuant to art 142 §1 cc. This rule of reparation also applies in the case of danger threatening property rights unless the threatened damage is clearly and disproportionately smaller than the loss which the owner could suffer as a result of the thing being used, damaged or destroyed.[60]

99 Furthermore, there are no major differences between the regimes as regards contributory negligence. According to art 362 cc, if the injured person contributed to the occurrence or increase of the damage, the obligation to redress it shall be

[60] *Wagner* (fn 57) 193.

correspondingly reduced according to the circumstances, and in particular the degree of fault of both parties.

I. DIFFERENCES AS REGARDS LIMITATION PERIODS

There are *important differences* in this respect. In Polish law, prescription of claims does not result in the termination of a right. Hence, the duty to perform on the part of the debtor becomes a natural obligation. If it is fulfilled, even accidentally, no restitution is possible (art 411 point 3 cc). The general rules on prescription (limitation) of claims are contained in the general part of the Civil Code (in arts 117–123 cc). 100

The right (claim) survives the lapse of time, but the debtor, when sued, may raise a defence of limitation of action and the court will, in principle, dismiss the claim (ie the claim is time-barred). Should the debtor not raise this defence, the court,in principle, will enforce the claim.[61] The latest revision of the civil code (2018) reintroduced the ex officio operation of prescription rules for claims against consumers (by which claims we understand contractual claims).[62] The legislator has also shortened the general prescription period of ten years to six years. According to the new rule "After the lapse of prescription period the creditor cannot demand payment of the claim against a consumer" (Art 117§2^1 cc). With a view to enhancing the protection of consumers, the nature of the prescription which runs in favour of the consumer has been changed in the way that the obligation turns into a natural obligation by operation of law as soon as the prescription time lapses, and regardless of whether the consumer has raised the plea of prescription. This strict rule has been mitigated by the new competence of a court not to take the prescription into account when justice so requires. 101

As to the length of the limitation periods, unless a specific regulation provides otherwise, the general limitation period for pecuniary claims (all except tort claims) is six years and for claims concerning periodical performances as well as claims connected with conducting business activity the limitation period is three years. Limitations periods cannot be shortened or extended by parties. However, several examples of shorter periods are to be found in the regulation of particular nominate contracts. 102

---

61 Ibid, 40 f.

62 The act of 13 April 2018 on the revision of the civil code, Dz.U. 2018, item 1104. In force as of 9 July 2018.

103 With regard to contractual claims, art 120 §1 cc, which stipulates that the limitation period begins to run on the day the claim accrues. The period may be suspended (art 121[63]) or interrupted (art 124[64]), in which case it runs anew once the ground for interruption ceases. This is a rule of accrual for contractual claims for compensation of damage. Until the damage occurs, a prescription period does not start.

104 Separate rules on the commencement of the prescription period exist for *tort claims*. They were modified in 2007 by the Act of 16 February 2007 on the Revision of the Civil Code.[65]

105 A claim for redress of damage caused by a tort shall be barred after a period of *three* years from the date on which the injured person learned or should have learned about it and about the person obliged to redress it. However, the longstop is 10 years from the date on which the event causing damage occurred (art 442[1] §1 cc).[66]

106 Pursuant to art 442[1] §2 cc, if damage resulted from a crime or misdemeanour, compensation claims are barred after a period of *20* years from the date when the crime or misdemeanour was committed, regardless of when the person who suffered the damage learned about it and about the person obliged to redress it. It should be remembered that a civil court can decide about the criminal nature of the actor's conduct. No criminal court verdict is required.

107 Special rules relate firstly to *personal injury claims*, which cannot expire before the lapse of three years from the day on which the injured person learned about the injury and about the person obliged to redress it (art 442[1] §3 cc). This rule means that, regardless of the lapse of time *a tempore facti*, whether 10 or 20 years, a claim arising from personal injury will not be time-barred for three years from *tempore scientiae*. Hence, the longstop of 10 years is 'suspended' in personal injury cases. Nevertheless, the periods running *a tempore facti* may

---

63 Art 121 cc: 'A limitations period does not start and, if started, is suspended: (1) for claims by children against parents – for the duration of the parental authority; (2) for claims by persons who do not have full capacity for legal acts against persons exercising guardianship or curatorship – for the time during which the guardianship or curatorship is exercised; (3) for claims brought by one spouse against the other – for the duration of the marriage; (4) for any claims if, due to force majeure, the entitled person cannot bring before a court or other authority set up to hear cases of a given type – for the duration of the impediment.'

64 Art 123 cc: '§1. The running of the limitations period is interrupted: (1) by any action before a court or other authority appointed to hear cases or enforce claims of a given type or before an arbitration tribunal taken directly to either assert or establish, or satisfy or secure a claim; (2) by recognition of a claim by the person against whom the claim is made; (3) by commencement of mediation.'

65 Dz U 2007, no 80, item 538, reported by *E Bagińska* in: H Koziol/BC Steininger (eds), European Tort Law 2007 (2008) 451, nos 1–5.

66 SN of 17 February 1982, OSNC 1983 item 8.

remain more convenient for the injured party as regards evidentiary burdens. Secondly, claims brought by *minors* for redress of personal injury may not expire earlier than two years from the day on which they reached maturity.

The above-mentioned revision of the civil code in 2018 also added a rule that in any case a prescription period longer than two years ends on the last day of a calendar year. Hence, the legislator introduced a new type of extension of a prescription period, but it remains unclear whether this new rule (placed in the general part of the civil code) should be applied to tort claims, all of which prescribe in a period longer than two years. It will definitely apply to contractual claims. If we allowed an interpretation according to which art 118 cc applies to tort claims, then the extension rules concerning personal injury claims would become meaningless. 108

A special rule on prescription concerning product liability claims is contained in art 449^8 cc. It must be construed in conformity with the Product Liability Directive 85/374/EEC.[67] Product liability claims prescribe upon three years from the discovery of the damage and the person liable, but no longer than 10 years from putting the product into circulation. 109

Article 442 §2 covers claims raised against a person who is vicariously liable for a *criminal act* (such as an offence) of its servant.[68] In the case of vicarious liability, the nature of the event triggering liability of both the servant and the master permits and requires the application of the same prescription period to all claims for redress. As long as the damage arises from an offence, it is irrelevant whether the claimant directs his/her claims against the perpetrator himself or (also) against other persons answerable in tort for the damage.[69] The source of the damage, ie a criminal act, is a decisive factor. On the other hand, there are also a number of judgments in which the Supreme Court has held that different limitation periods might apply to the same claim brought against different wrongdoers who are jointly and severally liable for the same damage.[70] 110

J. DIFFERENCES AS REGARDS PROOF

According to art 6 cc, '[t]he burden of proof relating to a fact rests on the person who attributes legal consequences to that fact'. The answer to the question of 111

---

67 Directive of 25 July 1985 on the approximation of the laws, regulations and administrative provisions of the Member States concerning liability for defective products, OJ L 85, 210, 29–33.

68 SN of 19 November 2009, IV CSK 257/09, OSP 7–8/2010, item 79.

69 See SN of 29 October 1962, 2 CR 1064/61, OSNC 9/1963, item 211; SN of 16 January 2008, IV CSK 380/07, OSNC ZD, D/2008, item 102.

70 SN of 11 February 2003, V CKN 1664/00, OSNC 5/2004, item 75.

who bears the burden of proof of fault depends on the ground for liability. In the contractual regime, the debtor's fault is presumed (art 471 cc). In tort law the burden of proving fault is, in some situations, shifted through a presumption of fault, for example in cases of vicarious liability for independent contractors (eg art 429 cc) and liability for minors and incapable persons (art 427 cc).

112 As regards the standard of proof generally, courts require 'a probability bordering on certainty' of facts establishing liability, which means that a judge must be convinced beyond reasonable doubt.

113 Finally, when awarding damages for harm, a Polish court has some freedom in determining the amount of damages. By virtue of art 322 Code of Civil Procedure (ccp), '[i]f in the case of claim for damages … a court shall deem that it is not possible or extremely difficult to prove accurately the amount of the claim, the court may adjudicate a relevant amount of money in accordance with its evaluation, based on the consideration of all circumstances of the case.'

K. OTHER DIFFERENCES

114 The Civil Code describes anyone below the age of 13 as 'not liable for damage caused' (art 426). Article 426 concerns delictual capacity as it is placed in the chapter on torts. However, the same age is the age limit for contractual capacity. The majority of scholars are of the view that art 426 only relieves minors below the age of 13 of fault liability, but not of strict liability or liability based on equity.[71]

115 Minors between the ages of 13 and 18 enjoy a reduced contractual capacity (arts 14 and 18 cc), while minors below the age of 13 have no capacity. They can enter into contracts concerning insignificant, current matters of everyday life; such a contract becomes valid upon its performance, unless it results in a gross detriment to a person incapable of juridical acts.

116 In contrast to contractual claims, claims *ex delicto*, stemming from a personal injury (specified in arts 444–448) cannot be assigned, unless they are already enforceable and have been recognised either in writing or by a final decision. Delictual claims involving property damage can be transferred in accordance with general rules (the rule is the transferability of pecuniary claims).

117 As to the issue of succession, there are a number of special rules concerning the succession of contractual claims. In the realm of torts, in principle all claims for personal injuries become extinct upon the death of the injured person. The courts have created some exceptions to the general rule.

[71] *Z Banaszczyk*, O odpowiedzialności deliktowej osoby małoletniej za czyn własny na zasadzie winy, in: M Pyziak-Szafnicka (ed), Odpowiedzialnosc cywilna. Księga pamiątkowa ku czci Profesora Adama Szpunara (2004) 103.

A claim for non-pecuniary loss, as a subjective right linked with the injured person, expires with her death and is not transmitted to her estate. However, an exception to the rule stems from art 445 §3 cc. Accordingly, a claim for compensation of non-pecuniary harm shall pass to the heirs of the deceased only if the claim was acknowledged in writing or the action was commenced when the deceased was still alive. 118

The plaintiff may always sue the tortfeasor (*ex delicto*) or the debtor (*ex contractu*) in the place of their residence (*actor sequitur forum rei*). The alternative jurisdiction is as follows: 119

- according to art 35 ccp, a claim arising from a tort may be brought before the court of the place of the event that caused the harm;
- a contractual claim can be brought before the court of the place of the performance of the contract (art 34 ccp).

L. REASONS FOR THE DIFFERENCES

The general reasons for the differences between tort liability and contract liability can be found in the historical evolution of Polish civil law (above nos 3–4). Contract law has developed as a part of the law of obligations. Following the German legal tradition, Polish contract law is based on the concept of an act of will (legal transaction), which is broader that the concept of contract.[72] Something that is not based on a legal transaction is not a contract. Hence, according to some authors, the contract/tort divide is not exclusionary but there is a third category of civil liability. 120

III. LIMITATION OR EXCLUSION OF LIABILITY ARISING FROM TORT AND FROM CONTRACT

A. STATUTORY PROVISIONS AUTHORISING A LIMITATION OR EXCLUSION OF LIABILITY

The Civil Code permits the parties to *exclude* the possibility of tort liability, which in 1964 was regarded as a novelty,[73] and was even called a legislative 121

72 The defects in representations, formation of contract, agency (representation) are governed by the rules of the General Part of the Civil Code.

73 See *S Garlicki*, Czyny niedozwolone w kodeksie cywilnym (1965) Nowe Prawo 1395.

experiment.[74] It is important to point out that, while the Civil Code allows contractual parties to circumvent the choice of liability (art 443 applies 'unless the contract between the parties stipulates otherwise), at least in relations between them, such contractual clauses must comply with the law and with the principles of community life.[75]

122 Pursuant to art 437 cc, the liability defined in art 435 (the liability of an enterprise set in operation by natural forces) and in art 436 (road traffic accidents) may not be excluded or limited in advance.

123 Amongst the most important statutory rules, art 440 cc should be seen as the basis for an ad hoc reduction of the liability of a tortfeasor. Pursuant to art 440, in relations between natural persons, the scope of the duty to redress damage may be limited according to the circumstances of the case if, having regard to the financial circumstances of the injured person or those of the person liable for the damage, the principles of community life (principles of fairness) require such limitation. This rule is interpreted strictly and applied rarely by the courts as it only concerns physical persons (typically uninsured). The judge may reduce the award taking into account all factors, including the economic position of the parties and the degree of the tortfeasor's fault.[76] The said legal rule does not permit a total release of the liable person from the legal obligation to repair damage.[77] Moreover, principles of fairness do not support a reduction of damages where the breach of duty was so grave as to constitute a criminal offence and where it caused personal injury.

124 The competence of the parties to limit liability under a contract stems from the principle of freedom of contract and is reflected in art 472 cc ('a debtor is liable for failure to show due diligence unless otherwise agreed in a contract or provided by law').

125 An example of a statutory limitation of liability arises in the case of a donation contract. The donating party shall be obliged to redress the damage resulting from the non-performance or improper performance of the obligation if the damage was inflicted intentionally or by gross negligence (art 891 §1 cc). If the thing donated has defects, the donating party shall be liable for the damage which he/she has inflicted upon the benefiting party by not having notified him/her in due time of the defect, despite having known of it. Liability does not arise if the benefiting party might have noticed the defect with ease (art 892 cc).

---

74 See *Czachórski* (fn 3) 951.

75 See *Czachórski* (fn 8) 273.

76 There are some limitations to the rule. It will not be applied in cases of intentional fault, gross negligence or personal injury, since then the reduction would be contrary to the principle of fairness. See: *M Nesterowicz et al*, Kodeks cywilny z komentarzem [The Civil Code with a commentary], vol 1 (1989) 438.

77 Eg SN of 26 January 2011, IV CSK 308/10, OSP 11/2011, item 112.

Caps on liability are alien to the Polish civil law tradition but they have normally been introduced because international conventions and/or EU directives so require. Therefore, statutory limits regarding property damage are to be found in product liability rules, air law, intellectual property law and in the rules on the statutory liability of hotel keepers (art 849 §1 cc). 126

B. LIMITATION OR EXCLUSION OF CONTRACTUAL AND TORTIOUS LIABILITY BY CONTRACT

1) *Is it Possible to Limit or Exclude Contractual or Tortious Liability under a Contract?*

Polish law respects the principle of freedom of contract, provided that the contents and aims of the contract do not contravene the very nature of the contract, the law, or the principles of community life (art 353^1 cc). These general criteria allow the courts to control and disregard a contractual or tortious limitation of liability. The most common way to limit contractual liability is by means of a clause on liquidated damages. The liquidated damages are due to the creditor to an amount reserved in the contract regardless of the extent of the damage suffered. In Polish law, the creditor cannot demand damages exceeding the amount of liquidated damages, unless the parties have decided otherwise. However, if the obligation has been performed to a significant extent, or where liquidated damages are grossly excessive, the debtor may demand a reduction thereof (art 484 §2 cc). The rules on liquidated damages apply accordingly to a case where a specific statutory provision stipulates the duty of the debtor to pay the creditor a specified sum for non-performance or unsatisfactory performance of the non-pecuniary obligation (in the absence of a contractual stipulation).[78] 127

Pursuant to art 473 §2 cc, a reservation that the debtor will not be liable for damage that he/she inflicts on the creditor intentionally shall be invalid. This rule also applies to the limitation of tortious liability (to a certain degree of fault). Intentional fault is described in the doctrine in an identical way as the same notion in criminal law: as a situation when the perpetrator foresees the possibility of a negative outcome of his/her conduct (damage) and either directly wishes for this outcome (*dolus directus*) or simply accepts that it may occur (*dolus eventualis*).[79] 128

In addition, in transactions with consumers, any contractual limitation or exclusion of compensation due to a failure to perform a contract or infliction of personal injury is unfair (art 385^3 points 1 and 2 cc) and, therefore, not binding. 129

---

78 See art 485 cc.

79 See *A Szpunar*, Czyny niedozwolone w kodeksie cywilnym (1970) XV Studia Cywilistyczne 53.

In consumer contracts, such limitations or exclusions would also now come under scrutiny due to the provisions of the Unfair Contract Terms Directive.[80]

130 An exclusion or limitation of tort liability for personal injury is void because it violates the law and the principles of community life.

2) *To What Extent can a Contractual Exclusion Provide a Defence to a Third Party to the Contract?*

131 Only the parties to a contract may limit or exclude their liability by a contractual clause. Such a caveat is ineffective vis-à-vis a third party and it may not influence the application of a proper legal basis of claims brought by the third party based on tort law.[81] In one case, a doctor and a hospital had entered into a contract to perform medical services (hence not a contract of employment), in which the parties agreed that the doctor, as an independent contractor, would be solely liable for damage caused to patients in connection with her services performed in the hospital. The lower courts found the hospital liable on the basis of art 430 cc (vicarious liability), and held both defendants jointly and severally liable. On the question of application of art 429 cc, the Court held that a caveat in the contract between the doctor and the hospital is ineffective and it may not influence the application of a proper legal basis of claims brought by third persons based on tort law.

132 In general, a third party cannot bring a claim based on a contract concluded between other parties, unless the contract is for the benefit of that party (art 393 cc). In such a case, the debtor may raise defences arising from the contract against a third party.

IV. NON-CONCURRENCE OR CONCURRENCE OF ACTIONS

A. OVERVIEW

133 The Code of Obligations (1933) was silent on the issue of concurrence of actions. The concept of concurrence of liabilities was advocated by legal scholars[82] and followed by the judiciary even before the enactment of the 1964 Civil Code. In a decision from 26 October 1956 (based on the Code of Obligations), the Supreme

---

[80] Directive of 5 April 1993 on unfair terms in consumer contracts, OJ L95/29–34.

[81] See judgment SN of 26 January 2011, IV CSK 308/10, OSP 11/2011, item 112 (with regard to the contract between the doctor and the hospital).

[82] See *W Czachórski*, Zbieg odpowiedzialności cywilnej według kodeksu zobowiązań, PWN 1960; *A Ohanowicz*, PWN 1963.

Court confirmed that in cases of breaches of contracts, a claimant might use either tortious or contractual liability as a legal basis for their claims.[83] For example, the delivery of a defective product by a seller is, first of all, a violation of an obligation resulting from the contract. However, at the same time, it may constitute a tort if it amounts to an 'infringement of a legal provision of a general binding force or principles of community life'. Following these decisions, courts began to apply tort law to product liability cases.[84]

The Supreme Court also held that 'the concurrent causes of liability arises in a situation where the debtor not only fails to perform or improperly performs his contractual obligations, but at the same time he breaches a legal rule by which he is bound regardless of the legal relationship between the parties. The conduct of the debtor is then deemed a delict (tort)'.[85] 134

Presently, pursuant to art 443 cc, the fact that an act or omission from which the damage arose constituted the non-performance or the improper performance of a pre-existing obligation does not preclude a claim for damages in tort, unless the pre-existing obligation provides otherwise. 135

The concurrence of liabilities is only allowed between the parties to a contract and provided that the debtor is liable in contract. Hence, there may be no concurrence with respect to a third party, who remains outside of the contractual bond, because the third party may only be held liable in tort. 136

When the debtor's breach of contract amounts to a tort, the creditor can bring two types of claims: (i) *ex contractu*, and (ii) *ex delicto*. The injured party (the creditor) may choose to base its action on either contract or tort. Typically, depending on the situation, one of the causes may be more favourable to the injured. However, a court is only bound by the factual basis of the claim, and not bound by the legal basis provided for by the plaintiff. Thus, it should take into consideration *ex officio* the possibility that the tort regime may be applied to a claim for non-pecuniary loss. 137

This concurrence has created some dispute in legal doctrine. I share the view that the plaintiff may bring different claims based on different legal bases, but the court must apply the whole set of rules of a given regime of liability to a claim based on this regime (burden of proof of fault, prescription, scope of damage).[86] One may not create a mixed contractual-tortious regime for a single claim.[87] 138

---

83 SN of 26 October 1956, OSN 1958, item 1.

84 For a detailed analysis see: *M Tulibacka*, Product Liability Law in Transition. A Central European Perspective (2009) 178, 189, and 199–201.

85 SN of 28 April 1964, II CR 540/63, OSPiKA 1965, 197.

86 See *Wagner* (fn 57) 10 f; *Czachórski* (fn 3) 949.

87 See *A Ohanowicz*, Zbieg norm w polskim prawie cywilnym (1963) 118; *M Nesterowicz*, Comment to SN 17 December 2004, II CK 300/04, OSP 2/2006, item 20, 95.

139 Hence, this is an 'option' approach, or – according to some authors – an 'accumulation' approach. The view supporting the precedence of contractual liability over tortious liability is rare. The precedence of contractual liability is accepted, however, in cases where the statutory limitations to the debtor's contractual liability, or the limitation of the scope of damages in certain contracts (in a contract of carriage, art 777 §1; a contract of forwarding, art 801 §3 cc;[88] a hotel keeper's liability, art 849 §2 cc) would be circumvented by the choice of tort liability under art 443 cc.[89]

140 Moreover, the concurrence of actions in the area of product liability is regulated in art 449^{10} cc. Accordingly, the provisions on liability for damage caused by a dangerous product do not exclude liability for damage based on general rules, for damage arising from non-performance or improper performance of an obligation or liability under implied warranty for defects and quality guarantee.

B. CONCURRENCE/EXCLUSION OF ACTIONS FOR THE PROTECTION AGAINST PERSONAL INJURY

141 Courts have established that inflicting bodily injury upon a person always constitutes a tort. If it is caused by a failure to perform or an improper performance of an existing obligation, the wrongdoer may be liable either *ex contractu* or *ex delicto*.

142 The practical implications of the concurrence approach to the relationship between tortious and contractual liability are significant in some areas, including medical liability, travel law and product liability.

143 First, liability of a privately contracted physician is contractual (art 471 cc), but it can be tortious if personal injury occurs (art 415 cc). The victim can choose to base her claim in either contract or tort. Hence, the source of civil liability of a physician may be either a tort or a contract between the former and the patient, or a contract between a patient and a medical care establishment.

144 Secondly, when a travel agency breaches a contract of travel, it is liable to the client in contract as well as in tort if a tourist suffers personal injury (eg when he contracts food poisoning in a hotel restaurant, or when he breaks his leg on a hotel staircase).

---

88 Both provisions refer to the limitation of liability of the carrier (for carry-on luggage) and the forwarding agent (for money, valuables and securities) to the cases of intentional fault or gross negligence.

89 *Śmieja* (fn 6) 694; *G Bieniek*, Commentary on the Civil Code, vol I (2002) 727.

As the tort regime is the only ground upon which compensation of non-pecuniary loss can be sought (art 445 or art 446 §4 in the case of wrongful death), the courts have played a primary role in 'dressing' contractual breaches for torts. For example, the Supreme Court held that a seller of a defective orthopaedic device committed a tort when he failed to repair the device in due time and the subsequent attempts to repair the device failed to ensure the required quality, which resulted in the increased physical effort and suffering of the disabled user.[90] 145

C. CONCURRENCE/EXCLUSION OF ACTIONS FOR THE PROTECTION OF PROPERTY

The concurrence of actions in tort and in contract is also possible with regard to property damage. For example, the Supreme Court has repeatedly held that a breach of the duty to safeguard deposits constitutes a bank's own fault leading to its liability in tort (art 415 cc).[91] The concurrence of liabilities has often been applied to the liability of professionals (public notaries, advocates, authorised dealers, accountants, etc). 146

D. CONCURRENCE/EXCLUSION IN THE CASE OF INTERFERENCE WITH CONTRACTUAL RIGHTS

1) *Interference with a Contractual Relationship*

In the general law of torts, there is no explicit provision with regard to interference with a contractual relationship. Hence, the plaintiff must use the general clause of liability. However, doctrinal views are divided. Some authors consider interference with a contractual relation to always be a tort (against the creditor whose legitimate expectations may not be fulfilled at all or may be fulfilled to a lesser extent).[92] These views are, however, only held by a minority because Polish law rather strictly respects the rule of privity of contract. The majority of scholars criticise this approach by pointing out that a creditor–debtor relationship, and all the claims resulting from it, are only relevant between the specific creditor and debtor. This relationship does not normally entail any obligations *erga omnes*. Further, Polish civil law rarely refers to the general concept of duty of care, more specifically to the duty to prevent harm caused to anyone. Thus, 147

---

[90] SN of 17 December 2004, II CK 300/04, OSP 2/2006, item 20.

[91] SN of 20 May 2005, III CK 661/04, Prawo Bankowe 10/2005, 11; SN of 19 November 2009, IV CSK 257/09, OSP 7–8/2010, item 79.

[92] *A Kubas*, Rozszerzona skuteczność wierzytelności (1969) XIII–XIV Studia Cywilistyczne 215 ff.

any interference with a contractual relationship is not in itself a tort. Another argument supporting this point of view is that, normally, an interference with a contractual relationship does not meet the requirement of unlawfulness.[93] As mentioned above, unlawfulness means breaching generally binding rules, and a contractual relationship does not entail such rules.

148 While the majority of writers agree that an interference with a contractual relationship is not automatically a tort, they do not exclude the possibility that it might be a tort if certain conditions are met. The person interfering must show an intention to harm the interests of the creditor, and such an intention to harm is contrary to the principles of community life (thus it is unlawful).[94] Further, taking into account the need for an express intention to cause harm, the requirement of fault, which is generally present in tortious liability, must be qualified here: only intentional fault can lead to liability in such cases. It is also argued that the intention to harm a creditor's interests must be the main or the sole purpose of the conduct in question. If the main aim was rather to benefit the person interfering, in the context of ordinary market competition, there is no tort.[95]

149 In business relations, an interference with contractual relationships of others is a specific tort of unfair competition (*czyn nieuczciwej konkurencji*). Pursuant to the general clause (under art 3 of the Act of 1993 on Combatting Unfair Competition[96]), a tort of unfair competition refers to conduct of a businessperson which is contrary to law or to the rules of proper conduct if it endangers or violates interests of another businessperson or interests of a client. Specific torts of unfair competition are regulated in the subsequent sections of the Act on Combatting Unfair Competition. The regulation is regarded as *lex specialis* to the Civil Code tort law rules.

150 Interferences with contractual relations are governed by art 12 of the Act on Combatting Unfair Competition. The forbidden conduct may take the form of instigating a client or a third person to breach the contract with a competitor or to terminate such a contract in order to gain benefits (for the instigator or a third person) or to cause (business) loss to the competitor.

151 A tort of unfair competition gives rise to a variety of claims under the Act on Combatting Unfair Competition (in particular an action for cessation of the conduct). The court may rule that the unlawful conduct be stopped, its effects be removed and that the competitor breaking the law must make a single or multiple declaration in an appropriate form and with appropriate contents. It

---

93 Sometimes, however, it is called 'relative wrongfulness'. The debtor acts wrongfully if in breach of contract: by violating the creditors' rights under the contract.

94 *P Machnikowski* in: A Olejniczak (ed), System Prawa Prywatnego, vol 6 (2nd edn 2014) 387.

95 Ibid.

96 Dz U 2003, no 153, at 1503 with later amendments.

may also award an appropriate amount of money to be paid to a social cause relating to the Polish culture or the protection of national heritage as pecuniary compensation for a negligent infringement of fair competition.

2) Loss of Business due to Personal Injury to Someone Else's Employees or Clients or to Property Damage to the Entrepreneur

Such damage would be considered as indirect, or alternatively, the injured person would be considered as an indirect victim of a tort. In Poland, such a loss would not be compensated. 152

Since 1933, the traditional approach of both the Polish legislator and courts has been based on the presumption that only persons who are directly injured (ie by the wrongful action directed against them) may claim compensation. The loss suffered by an indirect victim is distinguished from the harm of the directly injured. Exceptions to this rule have been gradually introduced into the Civil Code, but in all instances they concern cases of personal injury and/or violation of personal interests. The exceptions are contained in art 446 cc, which in its four paragraphs also indicates the category of entitled claimants (hence, a person who suffered funeral expenses, the next of kin, a relative to whom the deceased provided support). Currently, however, both courts and jurisprudence advocate that the exception is the rule and all persons, whether direct or indirect victims, should be entitled to compensation of damage arising from a tort.[97] 153

V. SPECIFIC SITUATIONS

A. PRE-CONTRACTUAL LIABILITY

Until the Act of 14 February 2003,[98] *culpa in contrahendo* was not regulated by the Civil Code in general. There were provisions concerning specific conditions where such liability would be possible, such as the following: 154

- if a party knew of the impossibility of performance at the time of concluding the contract (art 387 §2);
- if a party whose profession it is to accept commissions to perform tasks does not wish to perform a certain task and yet gives the impression that he does wish to do so (art 736);

[97] See *E Bagińska*, Dopuszczalność dochodzenia przez osoby bliskie zadośćuczynienia w związku z doznaniem poważnej szkody na osobie przez bezpośrednio poszkodowanego (2016/2) Kwartalnik SSP 'Iustitia' 69.

[98] Act of 14 February 2003, Dz U 2003, no 48, item 408, in force since 25 September 2003.

- if a person who concludes a contract as an attorney-in-fact (apparent agent) but is in fact not entitled to do so or where he goes beyond the scope of power of attorney and the person on behalf of whom it was concluded does not confirm the contract, the contract is invalid and the apparent agent shall be obliged to return what he received from the other party (in the course of performance), as well as to redress the damage which the other party incurred (limited to the negative contractual interest) (art 103 §2);
- if the party obliged to conclude a promised contract evades its conclusion, the other party may demand the redress of damage which it incurred by expecting the conclusion of the promised contract. The parties may otherwise specify the scope of the damages in the preliminary contract (art 390 §1).

155 In 2003, the new art 72 §2[99] and art 72^1 §1 and §2[100] cc gave rise to heated discussions which challenged the traditional view of *culpa in contrahendo*. Article 72 §2 cc specifies that a party who commenced or preceded with negotiations in violation of the principle of proper conduct, especially when there was no intention to conclude a contract, is liable to the other party for losses sustained because the latter expected that the contract would be concluded.

156 It is unclear whether fault is still the necessary requirement to establish the liability of those whose conduct during contractual negotiations caused losses to the other party. According to some authors, liability has 'lost' its tortious nature. The provision is not placed in the Title of the Code concerning tort liability, or in Book 3 ('Obligations'), but in Book 1 ('General Provisions'). This emphasises its distinct character. Further, it is neither fault nor strict liability. It is dependent upon a party negotiating in a manner which breaches the rules of proper conduct, but the relations of this requirement to notions such as wrongfulness or to the duty to act honestly or the *neminem laedere* duty is also unclear.

157 However, the new interpretation has not replaced the traditional view of the delictual nature of liability for *culpa in contrahendo*, which appears to prevail in the doctrine.[101]

---

99 A party which enters into or conducts negotiations in breach of good practices, in particular with no intention of concluding the contract, is obliged to remedy any damage which the other party suffered as a result of his reliance on the conclusion of the contract.

100 '§1. If, during negotiations, a party made information available with a reservation of confidentiality, the other party cannot disclose it nor hand it over to other persons nor use the information for its own purposes unless the parties agreed otherwise. §2. In the case of non-performance or improper performance of the obligations referred to in §1, the entitled party may demand from the other party the redress of the damage or the return of the profits obtained by that party.

101 See *AM Zachariasiewicz*, Culpa in contrahendo in Polish law, in: B Heiderhoff/G Zmij (eds), Tort Law in Poland, Germany and Europe (2009) 133, 138.

The scope of reparable damage is limited to what scholars refer to as the 'negative interest of the contract'. Thus, a person who was under the impression that the contract would be concluded can recover costs incurred during negotiations, for instance costs of telephone calls, travel, preparation of contractual documents, legal assistance and translation, and any official charges incurred in preparation of the transaction. While the 'positive interest of the contract' includes everything the victim would have obtained if the contract had been performed properly, the negative interest focuses on the fact that the contract was not concluded at all, and thus it is considered that compensation of the latter is not always very high. There is no consensus among scholars and the judiciary as to whether the compensation ought also to cover the potential profits and other benefits which would have followed a contract potentially concluded with someone else. However, if there is sufficient proof that another contract would have been concluded (such as an offer from another potential contracting party), there seem to be no obstacles to compensating profits and benefits which would thus have been obtained.[102] 158

B. LIABILITY OF PROFESSIONALS

As mentioned above in nos 35–37, in Polish law the standard of care is addressed in art 355 cc. Pursuant to the above provision, the level of care required of a person engaged in a business, such as a physician, a banker or a broker, is higher than what is required of an ordinary person outside the profession.[103] The standard against which a professional tortfeasor's conduct is measured is objective. The standard of conduct is the same for both contractual and tortious liability. 159

Liability for professional negligence vis-à-vis a client is typically based on a breach of a contract for services. However, a breach of professional standards envisaged in the statutes and deontological rules may, under the given circumstances, create a tort (toward the client) and justify a claim *ex delicto*.[104] The courts have tended to establish the tortious liability of a professional based on the general clause of liability for fault (art 415 cc). This requires an analysis of the nature of the duty breached by the professional. It is, however, debatable whether professional diligence should be treated as a part of unlawfulness or as a part of subjective fault. Both the objective standard of care and the professional character of a given 160

---

102 *M Kalinski* in: A Olejniczak (ed), System Prawa Prywatnego: Prawo Zobowiązań. Część Ogólna, vol 6 (2009) 109.

103 SN of 20 May 1986, CRN III 82/86, OSN 8/1987, item 125.

104 SN of 1 December 2006, I CSK 315/06, OSN 11/2007, item 169.

activity allow the conclusion that the negligence of a professional is established through the sole breach of his duty.[105]

161 The obligations (duties) of professionals stem from a contract, mandatory legal rules, life experience and common sense, as well as from deontological norms (professional standards, usually incorporated in codes of ethics). If the allegedly negligent conduct violated the above duties, which bind a professional independently from any contractual relationship, then courts usually establish tortious liability.

162 For example, the court developed a bank's general duty of care towards its depositors to ensure safety of money deposits. This duty is currently enshrined in art 50 §2 of the Banking Law. In practice, the scope of this duty goes beyond contractual obligations and banking laws. According to court practice and legal scholarship, the bank's duty exists both in the pre-contractual and post-contractual phase of a legal relationship with the client.

CASES

CASE 1. THE UNATTRACTIVE SHOPPING MALL

163 C is not in privity with D, hence he cannot sue D for a breach of contract as Polish law does not follow the doctrine of protective purpose of a contract. This notwithstanding, it could be argued that D was aware that a failure to meet his duties under the contract would have a detrimental impact on subtenants, who are technically third parties to the contract between C and D. Hence, the conduct of D was directed towards the interests of subtenants as well. However, tortious liability can be established only if the failure to keep the place clean and attractive violates generally binding legal rules or accepted norms of conduct (principles of community life). Here, it simply violated contractual obligations. C's claim will thus fail.

CASE 2. THE IDLE LAWYER

164 Under Polish law, this case concerns the liability of a notary (as a rule, a will takes the form of a notarial deed unless it is handwritten). Article 49 of the Notaries Act[106] provides that: 'A notary is liable for damage inflicted when performing notarial activities based on principles specified in the Civil Code, taking into

[105] SN of 1 December 2006, I CSK 315/06, OSN 11/2007, item 169.

[106] Act of 14 February 1991 (Prawo o notariacie), Dz U 2008, no 189, item 1158 with amendments.

account the level of care a notary is obliged to observe when performing such activities.' The provision does not determine whether a notary bears contractual or tortious liability. As a consequence, a controversy has arisen in legal writings and in judicial decisions as to the appropriate regime of a notary's liability. I support the viewpoint that a notary is liable in tort, because the duties of a notary arise from law and are binding towards all persons (both parties to a notarial activity and third parties). Moreover, a notary's liability is strongly connected with public functions. According to art 80 §2 of the Notaries Act, a notary is obliged to duly safeguard rights and just interests of parties and other persons in relation to whom his notarial activity may have legal effects. The liability of notaries towards clients and third parties is thus based on fault (art 415 cc). In addition to typical requirements of tort liability, the victim must prove a connection between the tort of a notary and the infringement of his professional (statutory) obligations. This approach is well established in legal scholarship and judicial decisions.[107] However, the view that favours contractual liability of notaries is less convincing.[108]

In recent practice, the courts have increasingly used the label 'professional tort of the notary'. For example, in the judgment of 8 December 2004[109] the Supreme Court held that the failure to provide information concerning all the consequences of statements made by clients is in violation of a general duty of a notary envisaged in art 80 §3 of the Notaries Act, and constitutes 'a professional tort of the notary'. 165

CASE 3. THE DEFECTIVE HOUSE

Pursuant to art 434 cc, an independent possessor of a building is liable for damage caused by the collapse of the building or the detachment of a part thereof, as long as the collapse or the detachment occurred as a consequence of either the absence of proper maintenance of the building or a defect in its construction. Here, however, the possessor (C) is the one who suffered personal injury. C can thus sue Z as his seller for a defective house (five years' warranty liability for defects in buildings[110]). Under the warranty regime, C does not have to prove Z's fault; an alternative route would be to file a claim based on the improper 166

107 See *B Lewaszkiewicz-Petrykowska*, Uwagi o zasadach rzadzacych cywilna odpowiedzialnoscia notariusza, PS no 2/1995, 29 ff. For jurisprudence, see decisions of the Supreme Court: SN of 30 May 2000, IV CKN 36/00, OSNC 2000, no 12, item 223; SN of 12 June 2002, III CKN 694/00, OSN 2003, no 9, item 124; SN of 9 May 2008, III CSK 366/07, unpublished; SN of 15 April 2010, II CSK 544/09, OSN ZD, no D/2010, item 113.

108 See *M Kolasinski*, Odpowiedzialnosc cywilna notariusza (2005) 164 ff.

109 I CK 303/04, unpublished.

110 Art 568 (as changed in 2014); before 25 December 2014, the statutory warranty lasted for three years in cases of buildings and one year for movables (currently two years).

performance of a sales contract, but then the seller can rebut the presumption of fault (given that Z did not know of D's negligence).

167 The fact that C suffered personal injury will facilitate the finding of a tort committed by D. D's fault will be the most difficult element to prove. C has to prove that D failed to observe the mandatory rules of professional conduct, the deontological norms binding in the construction business, generally binding legal rules or accepted norms of conduct (principles of community life). All those norms apply *erga omnes*.

168 The contractual stipulation is not valid towards Z. In a case from 26 January 2011,[111] the Supreme Court held that a caveat in the contract on provision of medical services similar to that in the case scenario was ineffective and could not have any impact on the application of a proper legal basis to claims of third persons based on tort law.

CASE 4. APARTMENT IN FLAMES

169 The landlord is responsible for maintaining the rented apartment in a safe condition. The breach of contractual duties has caused a personal injury. This is a typical scenario where the concurrence of liabilities will arise. In order to seek compensation for non-pecuniary loss and other claims (for cost of treatment, annuities, etc) V has to resort to the tort regime, which is more favourable to the victim, as the fault can be established (the burden of proof is on C, if he chooses to file a claim in tort: art 415cc).

CASE 5. INJURED SKIER

170 Here, again, the fact that C suffered personal injury will facilitate the finding of a tort committed by D1. The prima facie basis for liability is art 435 cc – strict liability of an enterprise 'set in operation by natural forces'. It appears that the insurance policy does not cover strict liability, but only liability for fault in the operation of the resort. Hence, it should be noted that strict liability and fault liability bases for the claim can concur in a given case. It is not entirely excluded that a Polish court will find that the general clause of art 415 cc applies to the facts. In the Supreme Court decision of 2 December 2003, the Court established the liability of restaurant owners for injuries caused to customers. The Court held that the obligation to ensure the protection of the health and life of customers does not only arise from legislation, but also from principles of community life,

[111] IV CSK 308/10, OSP 11/2011, item 112.

and the professional nature of the defendants' activity.[112] In the Court's view, the general duty not to cause damage to anyone (the so-called *neminem laedere* rule) requires that all necessary action be taken in order to avoid damage to persons or things. Failure to do so can be wrongful, depending on the circumstances. In the light of the case law, C has good chances of success in the suit against D1 and D2.

CASE 6. EXPLODING CAR

The existence of strict liability for products does not exclude liability for damage (here: to the product itself) based on general principles (art 449^{10} cc). Liability in tort for losses stemming from the accident is independent of the seller's liability for defects (which in this case is time-barred). 171

In Poland, judgments involving defective cars introduced the idea of sellers being held liable in tort to injured buyers,[113] which later developed into producer's liability based on 'objectivised fault' for defects (art 415 cc). More specifically, the Supreme Court found that selling a motor vehicle with technical defects capable of causing an accident was not only a breach of contract but also a breach of the duty not to endanger human life and health.[114] In another case, the Court ruled that supplying a defective product was not only a breach of contract, but could also be a tort provided it constituted a breach of a provision of law or the principles of community life (including the principles of public safety and protection of human life and health). 172

CASE 7. RACING BOAT BURNING

It is doubtful whether installing special electronic equipment violates generally binding legal rules, accepted norms of conduct (principles of community life), or the mandatory rules of professional conduct (given that D is a professional). Therefore, it is unlikely that D committed a tort. 173

D's 'general' contractual liability for losses stemming from the accident caused by a defective boat is independent of his strict liability for defects (under warranty). Although the warranty liability has expired, the seller can still answer for improper performance of the contract of sale, as the prescription period of six years (art 118 cc) runs from the day of the conclusion of the contract. A claim based on the improper performance of a sales contract is favourable to C as D will not be able to rebut the presumption of fault (art 471 cc). 174

---

112 III CK 430/03, OSNC 2005, no 1, at 60 and 64.
113 II CR 96/62, at 40, 41, PSN, II CR 540/63, OSN 1965/32.
114 II CR 96/62, at 44.

CASE 8. INSIDIOUS REPORT

175 This case will be decided by reference to the rules on unfair competition. Interferences with contractual relations are regulated in art 12 of the Act on Combatting Unfair Competition. The prohibited conduct may take the form of encouraging a client or a third person to breach a contract with a competitor or to terminate such a contract, in order to gain benefits (for the instigator or a third person) or to cause the competitor a (business) loss.

176 C can also claim damages for the intentional breach of duties under the contract of employment.

CASE 9. CIRCULAR LETTER

177 This case will be decided by reference to the rules on unfair competition. The circulation of the letter, in particular in the part requesting customers to refrain from dealing with C, can be considered as a specific (named) tort of unfair competition. Pursuant to art 14 §1 of the Act on Combatting Unfair Competition, 'disseminating untrue or misleading information about oneself or another entrepreneur or undertaking in order to yield benefits or bring detriment' is a tort of unfair competition. C may also allege protection under the general clause on unfair competition which defines the act (tort) of unfair competition as an activity contrary to the law or good practices, which threatens or infringes the interest of another entrepreneur or customer (art 3 §1 of the Act on Combatting Unfair Competition).

178 Alternatively, C can sue D for injury to his reputation in accordance with the general principles on protection of personal rights: arts 24 and 448 cc.

CASE 10. SHORTAGE OF SUPPLY

179 This case is governed by the rules on unfair competition. The general clause on unfair competition will apply to the facts. The rule on contractual exploitation appears equally unlikely to be applied due to the lack of a gross imbalance between the performances of both parties.[115]

---

115 Article 388 '§1 cc: If one of the parties, taking advantage of the forced circumstances, infirmity or inexperience of the other party, in exchange for his performance accepts or stipulates for himself or for a third party the performance whose value at the moment of the conclusion of the contract grossly exceeds the value of his own performance, the other party may demand a reduction in his performance or an increase in the performance due to him, and where

CASE 11. INJURED ROCK STAR

C is an indirect victim of D's tort. He is not entitled to damages, because the rule related to indirect victims is clear: only the closest person can claim damages in the case of the victim's death (art 446 cc). The key question is to whom the defendant's conduct was directed (here: to X). Taken from this perspective, the problem is also one of adequate causation. In the given example, according to the majority opinion, D will not be liable towards C. 180

CASE 12. EQUIPMENT DESTROYED

As in the preceding case, a tort action against D2 will turn on the question of adequate causation (D2's insurer can be sued directly) or the problem of the direct/indirect victim. The answer by a Polish court is rather speculative, but probably negative, as there is only an adequate causal link between the loss or damage to the cargo and the accident involving the truck. It is irrelevant who the owner of the equipment is; its loss will have to be redressed. The profits that have been lost because of the cancellation of the concert will be regarded as too remote to be compensated. 181

One could try to argue that C should first sue D1, who in turn can sue D2 in recourse. However, this will not be successful either because D1 will easily be relieved of contractual liability as he was not at fault (D2 caused the accident). 182

CASE 13. SLIPPING ON A LETTUCE LEAF

C can sue D in tort. The shop owner has a duty to ensure that its premises are safe because they are open to the public. The violation of this duty is often equated with the breach of the general duty not to put others at risk of inflicting harm, which can be rooted in the principles of good morals. Such a violation justifies liability pursuant to art 415 cc. 183

CASE 14. TEST DRIVE

C's claim will be grounded in tort law (negligent driving), as there is no contract. There is no rule stipulating pre-contractual liability in this case either. 184

---

both are excessively difficult, he may demand invalidation of the contract. §2. The above entitlements shall expire upon the lapse of two years from the day of the conclusion of the contract.'

185 As C is insured under the compulsory third party motor insurance, the relevant provisions of insurance law should be consulted. Article 38 §1 of the Law on Compulsory Insurance[116] contains certain exclusions that apply to damage to property. Among others, the insurer is not obliged to pay for any damage to property sustained by the possessor of a vehicle because of the driver's negligent conduct.

CASE 15. BREACH OF NEGOTIATIONS

186 Article 72 §2 cc specifies that a party who commenced or proceeded with negotiations in violation of the principle of proper conduct, especially when there was no intention to conclude a contract, 'is liable to the other party for losses sustained because the latter expected that the contract would be concluded'. It appears that this liability has 'lost' its tortious nature. The scope of recoverable compensation is limited to what scholars refer to as the 'negative interest of the contract'.

CASE 16. NON-DISCLOSURE OF RELEVANT FACTS

187 D as a seller must fulfil a great number of information duties. The fact that D knew of the prospective use of the machine by C relates to his good faith; however, the machine is not defective, so D did not conceal any defect. There is no specific entitlement to damages in Polish law.

[116] Act of 22 May 2003 on compulsory insurance, the Insurance Guarantee Fund and Polish Bureau of Traffic Insurers, Dz U 2003, no 124, item 1152.

THE BORDERLINES OF TORT LAW IN SOUTH AFRICA

Johann NEETHLING

QUESTIONS

I. Tracing the Borderlines 469
II. Main Differences between Tortious and Contractual Liability. 470
  A. Differences as Regards the Foundations of Liability 470
  B. Differences as Regards Causation. 472
  C. Differences as Regards Remedies 472
    1) Degree of Certainty of the Damage 473
    2) Compensation for Non-Pecuniary Loss 473
    3) Compensation for Loss of Earnings and for Loss of Chance 473
    4) Restitutionary Damages. 474
    5) Aggravated and Exemplary (or Punitive) Damages. 474
    6) Other Remedies. 475
  D. Differences as Regards Recoverability of 'Pure Economic Losses'. . . . 476
  E. Differences as Regards Liability for Others. 477
    1) Liability for Auxiliaries and Independent Contractors 477
    2) Liability for Legal Representatives or Organs of a Company 477
    3) Liability of Representatives of Natural Persons. 478
    4) Liability of the Auxiliary/Organ Itself 478
  F. Differences as Regards Liability in the Case of Multiple Tortfeasors/Breaching Parties. 478
  G. Differences as Regards the Persons Who May be Protected. 479
  H. Differences as Regards Defences 481
  I. Differences as Regards Limitation Periods 482
  J. Differences as Regards Proof 483
  K. Other Differences 483
    1) Time for Computation of Damage 483
    2) Capacity of Persons. 484
    3) Jurisdiction of Courts. 484
    4) Rules on Conflict of Laws 484

5) Transmissibility of Claims 484
6) Values Underlying Contract and Delict 485
L. Reasons for the Differences 485
III. Limitation or Exclusion of Liability Arising from Tort and Contract 485
A. Statutory Provisions Authorising a Limitation or Exclusion of Liability 485
B. Limitation or Exclusion of Contractual and Tortious Liability by Contract 486
IV. Non-Concurrence or Concurrence of Actions 488
A. Overview 488
B. Concurrence/Exclusion of Actions for the Protection against Personal Injury 490
C. Concurrence/Exclusion of Actions for the Protection of Property 491
D. Concurrence/Exclusion in the Case of Interference with Contractual Rights 492
1) Interference with a Contractual Relationship 492
2) Loss of Business due to Personal Injury to Someone Else's Employees or Clients or to Property Damage to the Entrepreneur 493
V. Specific Situations 494
A. Pre-Contractual Liability 494
B. Liability of Professionals 495

CASES

Case 1. The Unattractive Shopping Mall 495
Case 2. The Idle Lawyer 496
Case 3. The Defective House 497
Case 4. Apartment in Flames 498
Case 5. Injured Skier 498
Case 6. Exploding Car 499
Case 7. Racing Boat Burning 500
Case 8. Insidious Report 501
Case 9. Circular Letter 502
Case 10. Shortage of Supply 502
Case 11. Injured Rock Star 503
Case 12. Equipment Destroyed 504
Case 13. Slipping on a Lettuce Leaf 504
Case 14. Test Drive 505
Case 15. Breach of Negotiations 505
Case 16. Non-Disclosure of Relevant Facts 505

QUESTIONS

I. TRACING THE BORDERLINES

South African law does make a clear distinction between tort (delict) and contract mainly because there are various material differences between these two legal phenomena. These differences are, for historical, systematic and practical reasons, also supported by the fact that breach of contract is not formally treated as part of the law of delict but is considered to be part of the law of contract. The law of contract provides specific rules for breach of contract that are not applicable to a delict.[1] This accordingly necessitates its treatment as a separate and independent form of wrongful conduct. The distinction between delict and breach of contract is clearly apparent from the fact that one and the same act may render the wrongdoer liable *ex contractu* as well as *ex delicto*.[2] 1

Examples of the recognition of a 'grey zone' between contract law and the law of delict are scarce. Our law of contract does not recognise the application of *culpa in contrahendo* (negligence in the conclusion of a contract). However, in some instances delictual and contractual principles overlap. One example is pre-contractual delictual liability, where the courts intimated that principles and terminology of contract law should preferably be avoided, unless it is possible to reconcile such principles with applicable delictual principles. Other examples of such overlap occur in instances of professional liability where a duty to act with reasonable care and skill as an implied term of the contract can also give rise to a delictual duty with a similar content; or in the case of the direct liability of mandators, there does not seem to be a difference between 'tort cases' and 'contract cases'.[3] 2

As is clear from the above, in principle different rules regulate tort and contract, but where these rules overlap, courts seem to apply them basically similarly. 3

---

1 *JC van der Walt/JR Midgley*, Principles of Delict (4th edn 2016) 5.

2 See below nos 50–55 on the concurrence of delictual actions and the contractual action.

3 As to pre-contractual delictual liability (see below no 60) this appears to be the case in respect of the two principles traditionally belonging to the inquiry into an actionable misrepresentation in the case of cancellation of a contract, but employed in this field by Conradie JA in *ABSA Bank Ltd v Fouche* 2003 1 SA 176 (SCA) 181, 185. The two principles require a misrepresentation to be material, and to induce the plaintiff to conclude a contract: 'Materiality' can be applied meaningfully in respect of delictual wrongfulness while 'inducement' clearly concerns factual causation, viz whether the misrepresentation caused the relevant conclusion of a contract (*Bayer South Africa (Pty) Ltd v Frost* 1991 4 SA 559 (A) 575; *Fouche* (supra) 188 f; *Standard Bank of South Africa Ltd v OK Bazaars (1929) Ltd* 2000 4 SA 382 (W) 398–400). As to professional liability or the direct liability of mandators, see below nos 61, 21.

II. MAIN DIFFERENCES BETWEEN TORTIOUS AND CONTRACTUAL LIABILITY

A. DIFFERENCES AS REGARDS THE FOUNDATIONS OF LIABILITY

4 A delict is the act of a person that in a wrongful and culpable way causes harm to another.[4] Wrongfulness inter alia lies in the infringement of a right or the breach of a legal duty,[5] while fault consists of intent or negligence.[6] Similarly, breach of contract is an act by a person (contracting party) which in a wrongful and culpable way[7] causes damage to another (contracting party).[8] Wrongfulness lies

---

[4] See *J Neethling/JM Potgieter*, Neethling-Potgieter-Visser Law of Delict (7th edn 2015) 4; cf *M Loubser/R Midgley* (eds), The Law of Delict in South Africa (3rd edn 2017) 7 f; *NJ van der Merwe/PJJ Olivier*, Die Onregmatige Daad in die Suid-Afrikaanse Reg (6th edn 1989) 1; *PQR Boberg*, The Law of Delict: Vol I Aquilian Liability (1984) 1; *Van der Walt/Midgley* (fn 1) 1–2. Exceptions, however, exist because relations in life simply refuse to be regulated by inflexible rules. One of the most important developments which has taken place in the field of delictual liability during the past eight to 10 decades is the formation and recognition of instances of liability without fault (strict liability) as distinct from traditional liability where fault is an essential requirement (see *Neethling/Potgieter* (supra) 379 f; *Loubser/Midgley* (supra) 457 f; *J Neethling*, South Africa, in: B Koch/H Koziol (eds), Unification of Tort Law: Strict Liability (2002) 269 f).

[5] *Neethling/Potgieter* (fn 4) 33 f, 47, 51 f, 55 f; *Loubser/Midgley* (fn 4) 184 f.

[6] Three forms of intent are recognised, viz *dolus directus, dolus indirectus* and *dolus eventualis*, while negligence is judged by the standard of the reasonable person: whether damage was reasonably foreseeable and preventable (see *Neethling/Potgieter* (fn 4) 129 f; *Loubser/Midgley* (fn 4) 145 f).

[7] Although intention is not a requirement for breach of contract, it can of course be committed intentionally (see *Country Cloud Trading CC v MEC, Department of Infrastructure Development* 2014 2 SA 214 (SCA) 223 f for a recent example of a breach committed with *dolus eventualis*).

[8] *Van der Walt/Midgley* (fn 1) 5; *BC Stoop, Qui habet commoda ferre debet onera* (You cannot have your cake and eat it). The relevance of fault in breach of contract [1998] Journal of Contemporary Roman-Dutch Law (Tydskrif vir Hedendaagse Romeins-Hollandse Reg, THRHR) 1, 10; *Neethling/Potgieter* (fn 4) 6. In the field of labour law (breach of the contract of service) a different regime applies. The Labour Relations Act 66 of 1995 protects the rights allocated to employees not be unfairly dismissed and limits 'fair' dismissals to three grounds, one of which is misconduct by the employee. In this regard there is a distinction between so-called 'fault' and 'no fault' dismissals. 'Fault' in itself could be either 'intent' or even 'gross negligence' on the side of the employee, depending on the type of misconduct (see *J Grogan*, Dismissal (2010) 78 f; *JV du Plessis/MA Fouche*, Practical Guide to Labour Law (7th edn 2012) 288). Each case should be judged on its own merits pertaining to the element of fault and the type of dismissal at hand. Employees could also resign due to the actions or omission of their employers, the so-called 'constructive dismissals' where the working environment had been made intolerable and the employee then resigns. The ultimate reason for dismissals for misconduct is a mere reasoning that it would not be in the interest of an employer to retain the services of an employee who cannot (an absence of intent) or will not (intent present) do their work properly (see *Grogan* (supra) 80, 82).

in breach of a duty imposed by the contract.[9] Although both delict and breach of contract may involve breach of a duty, it has been alleged that the origin of the duties differs in each case: a delict consists in the breach of a duty imposed by law whereas breach of contract comprises the breach of a duty voluntarily assumed.[10] This distinction may have merits but there are also objections. One is that it describes a delict solely in terms of a breach of a duty, without including the infringement of a right or legally protected interest.[11] Another is that although a contractual duty may flow from the will of the parties (such as the duty to pay compensation for breach of contract), that duty is in reality imposed by law as a consequence of the unlawful breach of the contract.[12]

It is controversial whether fault (intention or negligence) is a prerequisite for a 5
breach of contract. In *Administrator, Natal v Edouard*[13] it was clearly stated 'fault is not a requirement for a claim for damages based upon a breach of contract'. In contradistinction, Hutchison and Pretorius[14] maintain that the statement in *Edouard* is 'a sweeping generalisation' and that fault is indeed required for most forms of breach of contract apart from repudiation[15] and in certain instances of positive malperformance.[16] In these cases liability therefore seems to be strict.[17] It has been suggested that the reasonable person test for negligence should apply in all cases of a breach of contract.[18]

In light of the above, there is apparently no difference in principle between a 6
delict and breach of contract as both are concerned with conduct that wrongfully and culpably causes damage to another.[19] However, as will be clear from the

---

9 Cf *D Hutchison/C-J Pretorius* (eds), The Law of Contract in South Africa (2009) 8 f.

10 See *RG McKerron*, The Law of Delict (7th edn 1971) 2 f; see also *Freddy Hirsch Group (Pty) Ltd v Chickenland (Pty) Ltd* 2011 4 SA 276 (SCA) 292; cf *Neethling/Potgieter* (fn 4) 6 fn 24; *Van der Walt/Midgley* (fn 1) 5; *Loubser/Midgley* (fn 4) 191; *JM Burchell*, Principles of Delict (1993) 3; *Hutchison/Pretorius* (fn 9) 8.

11 See *Burchell* (fn 10) 3.

12 See *Hutchison/Pretorius* (fn 9) 8 f. They conclude: 'There is accordingly a close similarity between a breach of contract and a delict.'

13 1990 3 SA 581 (A) 597; cf also *Loubser/Midgley* (fn 4) 233 ; *Van der Walt/Midgley* (fn 1) 5.

14 *Hutchison/Pretorius* (fn 9) 276 f, 278; see also *Stoop* (fn 8) 10 and the sources referred to by him in fn 64.

15 The intention to repudiate is judged objectively by means of a reasonable person test (*Hutchison/Pretorius* (fn 9) 295); see eg *Van Rooyen v Minister van Openbare Werke* 1978 2 SA 835 (A) 845 f; *OK Baaars (1929) Ltd v Grosvenor Buildings (Pty) Ltd* 1993 3 SA 471 (A) 480 f (subjective intention to end the contract not required).

16 The absence of fault is for example no excuse for malperformance where a party had guaranteed or warranted his performance (see *Hutchison/Pretorius* (fn 9) 293; *Loubser/Midgley* (fn 4) 233).

17 As to strict liability in delict, see above fn 4.

18 *A van Aswegen*, Die Sameloop van Eise om Skadevergoeding uit Kontrakbreuk en Delik (1991) 194; see however *Stoop* (fn 8) 11.

19 Cf *Lillicrap, Wassenaar and Partners v Pilkington Brothers (SA) (Pty) Ltd* 1985 1 SA 475 (A) 495 f and the authority cited there.

discussion below, there are various material differences between these two legal phenomena. Thus, despite the apparent similarity between a delict and breach of contract, these concepts may not be treated identically. At most, it can be said that both are species of the genus 'wrongful conduct' in private law.[20]

B. DIFFERENCES AS REGARDS CAUSATION

7 The enquiry into causation in the law of contract is essentially the same as that in the law of delict.[21] A distinction is made between factual and legal causation. Factual causation is established by means of the but-for or *conditio sine qua non* test.[22] But the scope of liability (legal causation) may differ because different measures limiting liability apply. Legal causation in the law of delict is not determined by a single yardstick (for example, reasonable foreseeability or direct consequences), but a flexible approach is adopted.[23] On the other hand, in the law of contract, a 'dichotomous orthodox approach' is followed. This entails that general damage flowing from a breach of contract is not too remote while special damage is presumed to be too remote. Generally, damage that is foreseeable or reasonably foreseeable will not be too remote and it thus seems that foreseeability is accepted as the only criterion for the limitation of contractual liability.[24] The scope of liability may thus differ if the law of delict should employ a different yardstick than the law of contract.

C. DIFFERENCES AS REGARDS REMEDIES

8 Breach of contract is only constituted by the non-fulfilment by a contractual party of a contractual personal right (claim) or an obligation to perform. Accordingly, the primary remedy for breach of contract is directed at enforcement, fulfilment or execution of the contract; a claim for damages as a remedy only plays a secondary part.[25] By contrast, a delict is constituted by the infringement of any

---

20 See *Neethling/Potgieter* (fn 4) 6.

21 See *Hutchison/Pretorius* (fn 9) 334.

22 As to delict see *Neethling/Potgieter* (fn 4) 184 f; *Loubser/Midgley* (fn 4) 101 f; as to breach of contract see *Hutchison/Pretorius* (fn 9) 335.

23 This approach is based on policy considerations, reasonableness, fairness and justice, while the traditional criteria for legal causation (such as adequate causation, direct consequences and reasonable foreseeability) may still play a subsidiary part (see *Neethling/Potgieter* (fn 4) 206 f; *Loubser/Midgley* (fn 4) 123 f). It has been submitted that this test might also profitably be employed in the law of contract (see *Thoroughbred Breeders' Association of South Africa v Price Waterhouse* 2001 4 SA 551 (SCA) 582 f), but this has not yet happened.

24 See *Van Aswegen* (fn 18) 328–330; cf *Hutchison/Pretorius* (fn 9) 335–338.

25 See *Hutchison/Pretorius* (fn 9) 308 f for an overview of contractual remedies at the disposal of the plaintiff.

legally recognised interest or breach of a legal duty to prevent harm, excluding the non-fulfilment of a duty to perform by a contractual party. Consequently, the delictual remedies[26] are primarily directed at compensation (damages or satisfaction), and not at fulfilment.[27]

1) *Degree of Certainty of the Damage*

In general, there does not seem to be any difference in contract or delict as to 9
the degree of certainty of the damage. The plaintiff must prove on a balance of probability that he has suffered damage and what the extent of such damage is.[28] Because it may sometimes be very difficult to determine the exact extent of the loss, there are practical guidelines (for example, in the case of future loss, the taking into consideration of certain probable events) which are of assistance in estimating the damage in question. In general, the plaintiff is required to tender the best possible evidence in respect of the extent of his loss, even though calculating the loss on such evidence may in fact be a difficult task.[29]

2) *Compensation for Non-Pecuniary Loss*

In delict, patrimonial as well as non-patrimonial damages may be claimed,[30] 10
while the latter may not be recovered for breach of contract.[31]

3) *Compensation for Loss of Earnings and for Loss of Chance*

In delict a distinction is made between loss of earnings up to the date of the trial, 11
and loss of future earnings or earning capacity. As to the former, the plaintiff is entitled to damages representing the income he would have earned but for the delict causing his inability to earn. The amount is normally not difficult to calculate. However, in the case of loss of future earnings or earning capacity, the calculation is, because of uncertainty in predicting the future, much more problematic, and is therefore based on the court's discretion to award a

26 See for an overview *Neethling/Potgieter* (fn 4) 221 f, 267 f; *Loubser/Midgley* (fn 4) 485 f.

27 See *Van Aswegen* (fn 18) 303 f; *Neethling/Potgieter* (fn 4) 6; *Loubser/Midgley* (fn 4) 232; *Van der Walt/Midgley* (fn 1) 5.

28 See *JM Potgieter/L Steynberg/TB Floyd*, Visser & Potgieter Law of Damages (3rd edn 2012) 563 f.

29 Cf *Neethling/Potgieter* (fn 4) 250; *Hutchison/Pretorius* (fn 9) 332.

30 In delict, the Aquilian action must be used to claim patrimonial damages while for non-patrimonial damages the *actio iniuriarum* and the action for pain and suffering must be instituted (see *Neethling/Potgieter* (fn 4) 5).

31 *Administrator, Natal v Edouard* 1990 3 SA 581 (A) 595 f; see also *Van der Walt/Midgley* (fn 1) 5; *Loubser/Midgley* (fn 4) 233; *Neethling/Potgieter* (fn 4) 6 fn 26; *Hutchison/Pretorius* (fn 9) 332.

reasonable and fair amount of damages.[32] On the other hand, in contract, breach of an employment contract terminating the contract entitles the plaintiff to the sum due to him for the unexpired period of the contract less any sum he earned or could reasonably have earned during this period.[33]

12 As far as damages for loss of a chance is concerned, there does not seem to be any fundamental difference between delict and breach of contract. Loss of a chance is regarded as a form of prospective loss which is damage which will, with a sufficient degree of probability, materialise after the delict or breach of contract.[34]

4) Restitutionary Damages

13 In delict the measure of damage is referred to as negative interest (*interesse*) because damage is calculated with reference to the plaintiff's position but for the delict. In contract the measure of damage is indicated as positive interest (*interesse*) since damage is calculated with reference to the position the plaintiff would have occupied had proper performance in terms of the contract taken place. Contractual negative interest, also referred to as restitutionary damages,[35] is calculated with reference to the position the plaintiff would have occupied had the contract not been concluded.[36] It has been submitted that positive interest in contract does not differ fundamentally from negative interest in delict since contractual positive interest may also be defined with reference to the position the plaintiff would have been in if the breach of contract had not occurred.[37]

14 The term restitutionary damages may also refer to damages for the gain or profit that the defendant has made as a result of the breach of contract or tort. In South African law, following English law, a court may order a defendant, especially as to the passing-off action, to render an account of profits. However the position in this regard is uncertain.[38]

5) Aggravated and Exemplary (or Punitive) Damages

15 Delictual remedies are compensatory in character, compensating or indemnifying the aggrieved party for the harm the wrongdoer has caused.

---

32 See *Potgieter/Steynberg/Floyd* (fn 28) 462 f; *Loubser/Midgley* (fn 4) 491–492.

33 See *Potgieter/Steynberg/Floyd* (fn 28) 402–404.

34 See *Potgieter/Steynberg/Floyd* (fn 28) 135; *J Neethling*, Causal uncertainty and proportional liability in South Africa, in: I Gilead/MD Green/BA Koch (eds), Proportional Liability: Analytical and Comparative Perspectives (2013) 288, 292 f.

35 See *Potgieter/Steynberg/Floyd* (fn 28) 81 fn 76, 90, 202, 380, 430.

36 See *Potgieter/Steynberg/Floyd* (fn 28) 80 f; *Hutchison/Pretorius* (fn 9) 328 f.

37 See *Potgieter/Steynberg/Floyd* (fn 28) 81; see also *Van Aswegen* (fn 18) 315 f who states inter alia that negative interest in contract is encountered only in two instances, viz misrepresentation inducing a contract and as an alternative measure of contractual damage.

38 *J Neethling*, Van Heerden-Neethling Unlawful Competition (2nd edn 2008) 82–84.

The function of the law of delict is not aimed at punishing the perpetrator.[39] Since a penalty clause may be applicable for breach of contract, contractual liability can be extended much wider than delictual liability.[40] Nevertheless, the penalties in terms of the Conventional Penalties Act 15 of 1962[41] are also primarily aimed at compensation and not at punishment. In terms of the Act, such penalties are enforceable, but – and this is important – subject to a reduction by the court to such an extent as it may consider equitable in the circumstances if it appears that the penalty is out of proportion to the prejudice suffered by the creditor. The penalty may nevertheless be more than the creditor's actual patrimonial loss because prejudice is clearly much wider than such loss.[42]

6) *Other Remedies*

There is no difference as far as an interdict (injunction) is concerned. This remedy is aimed at preventing impending wrongful conduct – a delict or breach of contract – or the continuation thereof.[43] The primary remedy for breach of contract is specific performance.[44] Although delictual remedies are primarily aimed at damages, restoration in kind is available in some cases.[45] 16

---

39 See *Van der Merwe/Olivier* (fn 4) 1–2; *Van der Walt/Midgley* (fn 1) 4; cf *Burchell* (fn 10) 2; see also eg *Argus Printing and Publishing Co Ltd v Esselen's Estate* 1994 2 SA 1 (A) 29–30; *Dikoko v Mokhatla* 2006 6 SA 235 (CC) 263; *Mogale v Seima* 2008 5 SA 637 (SCA) 641 f; *Seymour v Minister of Safety and Security* 2006 5 SA 495 (W) 500; *Fose v Minister of Safety and Security* 1997 3 SA 786 (CC) 823–828. However, according to Roman-Dutch law and some (particularly earlier) case law (see eg *Masawi v Chabata* 1991 4 SA 764 (ZH) 772; *Salzmann v Holmes* 1914 AD 471, 480, 483) the *actio iniuriarum* may in certain cases be used to claim punitive damages from the wrongdoer. See for a full discussion *J Neethling*, Punitive damages in South Africa, in: H Koziol/V Wilcox (eds), Punitive Damages: Common Law and Civil Law Perspectives (2009) 122 f; *J Neethling*, The law of delict and punitive damages (2008) Obiter 238 f; *Neethling/Potgieter* (fn 4) 7 fn 30. In the field of labour law, compensation for an unfair labour practice includes punitive damages. In *Viljoen v Nketoana Municipality* 2003 24 ILJ (LC) para 35 the court put it as follows: 'An award of compensation in terms of s194 (1) [of the Labour Relations Act 66 of 1995] is ... a combination of *solatium* for the employee and punishment against an employer for unfair treatment in the employment context'. See also *Gimini Indent Agencies CC t/a S & A Marketing v Commission for Conciliation, Mediation and Arbitration* (1999) 20 ILJ 2872 (AH) para 18.

40 See *Van Aswegen* (fn 18) 361 f.

41 See for a discussion of the Act, *Potgieter/Steynberg/Floyd* (fn 28) 387 f; *Hutchison/Pretorius* (fn 9) 339–343.

42 See also *Neethling* in: Koziol/Wilcox (fn 39) 135 f.

43 See *Neethling/Potgieter* (fn 4) 269 f; *Hutchison/Pretorius* (fn 9) 344 f.

44 *Hutchison/Pretorius* (fn 9) 319–322.

45 See *Potgieter/Steynberg/Floyd* (fn 28) 186 f. Examples of such cases are the erection of shacks which have been unlawfully removed (*Vena v George Municipality* 1987 4 SA 29 (C) 52), the release of a person unlawfully detained, and a retraction and apology in instances of defamation (the *amende honourable*) (see eg *Mineworkers Investment Co (Pty) Ltd v Modibane* 2002 6 SA 512 (W) 521 f; *Dikoko v Mokhatla* 2006 6 SA 235 (CC) 258–261, 274–276; *Isparta v Richter* 2013 6 SA 529 (GNP) 538 f; *University of Pretoria v South Africans*

D. DIFFERENCES AS REGARDS RECOVERABILITY OF 'PURE ECONOMIC LOSSES'

17 The recoverability of pure economic loss is recognised in principle in both contract and delict.[46] Problems were, however, encountered as to the availability of a delictual action for pure economic loss alongside an action in contract.[47]

18 As to product liability in delict, the Consumer Protection Act 68 of 2008 makes provision for strict liability for harm caused by defective products but limits harm to death, injury or illness of a natural person, damage to property, and economic loss resulting from these instances of harm.[48] Pure economic loss is thus not covered by the Act.[49] An important implication of this is that the common law on product liability for such loss, which is based on fault, is then applicable.[50]

19 The position with respect to state liability for pure economic loss should also be mentioned.[51] Here the court has to exercise a value judgement in light of our constitutional *boni mores* to ascertain whether there was a legal duty on the state to act positively to avoid the pure economic loss. But the general approach of our law in this regard remains conservative.[52] This is particularly apposite in instances of protection against unjust administrative action by the state. Although organs of state and administrators have no delictual immunity, in the absence of *mala fides* mere negligent statutory breach and consequent economic loss is not sufficient to hold state officials delictually liable for the improper performance of an administrative function.[53]

---

for the Abolition of Vivisection 2007 3 SA 395 (O); cf also *Le Roux v Dey* 2011 3 SA 274 (CC) 322, 333 f; *Media 24 Ltd v SA Taxi Securitisation* 2011 5 SA 329 (SCA) 350 f; *Neethling/Potgieter* (fn 4) 268 fn 18).

46 See as to delict *Neethling/Potgieter* (fn 4) 305 f; *Loubser/Midgley* (fn 4) 274 f.

47 See the discussion in no 50 below.

48 Sec 65(1), (5).

49 See *J Neethling/JM Potgieter*, The continued importance of common law product liability *ex delicto* [2014] THRHR 506–508; *contra*, however, *M Loubser/E Reid*, Product Liability in South Africa (2012) 93. See for a discussion of sec 61(5) *Loubser/Midgley* (fn 4) *573*; *Loubser/Reid* (supra) 93–100; *J Neethling*, Strikte aanspreeklikheid vir defekte produkte [2011] Journal of South African Law (Tydskrif vir die Suid-Afrikaanse Reg, TSAR) 813.

50 As was the case in *Freddy Hirsch Group (Pty) Ltd v Chickenland (Pty) Ltd* 2011 4 SA 276 (SCA).

51 See *J Neethling*, State (public authority) liability *ex delicto* (2) [2013] THRHR 118–121.

52 See eg *Steenkamp NO v Provincial Tender Board, Eastern Cape* 2007 3 SA 121 (CC) 133–144.

53 See eg *Steenkamp NO v Provincial Tender Board, Eastern Cape* 2007 3 SA 121 (CC) 144 (2006 3 SA 151 (SCA) 162 f 169); *South African Post Office v De Lacy* 2009 5 SA 255 (SCA) 256–258; *Minister of Finance v Gore NO* 2007 1 SA 111 (SCA) 139.

E. DIFFERENCES AS REGARDS LIABILITY FOR OTHERS

1) *Liability for Auxiliaries and Independent Contractors*

In this regard vicarious liability may differ insofar as it may be more extensive in the case of delict than for breach of contract. For example, in the employer–employee relationship, the employer is vicariously liable for the delict of his employee if the latter acted within the scope of his employment.[54] On the other hand, the employer can only be liable for breach of contract by his employee if the latter acted in the execution of the employer's (as contracting party) obligations in terms of the contract.[55] In *Weinberg v Olivier*,[56] the court spoke of 'delegation of the performance of the obligation'. This will, for example, be the case where a person breached a contract of service with the responsible contracting party in the execution of his obligations as an employee.[57] 20

Under South African law mandators are not vicariously liable for the delicts of their independent contractors.[58] There does not seem to be a difference between 'tort cases' and 'contract cases' in this respect. The principles applied in a tort case[59] were indeed extended to a contract case in which the damage was not caused by the mandatary but by a further subcontractor employed by the mandatary.[60] 21

2) *Liability for Legal Representatives or Organs of a Company*

This position is the same as that of the vicarious liability of employers for employees, but a distinction should be made between a company's vicarious and direct liability. A company is not different from a natural person with regard to its vicarious liability for the delicts of its employees (such as its CEO). In this respect the same legal principles apply to both companies and natural persons.[61] However, a company is directly, and not vicariously, liable for the delicts of persons in control of the company – its so-called 'directing mind' 22

---

54 *Neethling/Potgieter* (fn 4) 365 f; *Loubser/Midgley* (fn 4) 467 f; *J Neethling*, Liability for damage caused by others under South African law, in: J Spier (ed), Unification of Tort Law: Liability for Damage Caused by Others (2003) 222.

55 *Van Aswegen* (fn 18) 341–343; *Loubser/Midgley* (fn 4) 233.

56 1943 AD 181.

57 See *Van Aswegen* (fn 18) 341–343; *Hutchison/Pretorius* (fn 9) 218 f. But the parties may agree that their liability should be joint and several (*Hutchison/Pretorius* (fn 9) 219).

58 See *Neethling* (fn 54) 225; *Neethling/Potgieter* (fn 4) 391 fn 126.

59 See eg *Langley Fox Building Partnership (Pty) Ltd v De Valence* 1991 1 SA 1 (A).

60 See *De Jager v Taaf Hamman Holdings (Edms) Bpk* 1993 1 SA 281(O) 291 f; *Neethling* (fn 54) 225.

61 See *Neethling* (fn 54) 219.

or *alter ego*.[62] It seems that directors of a company will normally qualify as its directing mind.[63]

3) *Liability of Representatives of Natural Persons*

23 There is no vicarious liability of, for example, parents for the delicts of their children.[64] A parent may of course be directly liable for a delict of her child. This will be the case where the parent was under a legal duty to prevent the child from committing the delict, and negligently failed to do this.[65]

4) *Liability of the Auxiliary/Organ Itself*

24 The employer's liability does not insulate the employee from personal liability for his delict. In principle the victim may choose to sue the employee alone. Due to the fact that the employee is also delictually liable, the employer and employee are regarded as joint wrongdoers as against the victim. However, clearly a right of recourse is only available to the employer.[66]

F. DIFFERENCES AS REGARDS LIABILITY IN THE CASE OF MULTIPLE TORTFEASORS/BREACHING PARTIES

25 The liability of joint delictual wrongdoers differs from that of joint parties to a contract. In the law of contract, the general rule is that if more than one contracting party is liable for the same performance, then, in the case of a breach of contract, each of them is only liable for his pro rata share of the performance.[67] In the law of delict, on the other hand, joint wrongdoers are jointly and severally liable for the full damage.[68] Liability *ex delicto* may thus be wider than liability *ex contractu*.[69]

---

62 See *Neethling* (fn 54) 219 f; cf also eg *Barkett v SA National Trust & Assurance Co Ltd* 1951 2 SA 353 (A) 362.

63 See *Neethling* (fn 54) 220; *Neethling/Potgieter* (fn 4) 390 fn 114.

64 *De Beer v Sergeant* 1976 1 SA 246 (T); see *Neethling* (fn 54) 220.

65 *De Beer v Sergeant* 1976 1 SA 246 (T) 251; *Neethling* (fn 54) 220; *Neethling/Potgieter* (fn 4) 70 fn 228.

66 *Botes v Van Deventer* 1966 3 SA 182 (A) 205 f; *Neethling* (fn 54) 224; *Neethling/Potgieter* (fn 4) 393.

67 However, where the contractual debt is indivisible, all the contractual parties can be jointly sued for the debt (*Van Aswegen* (fn 18) 339).

68 *Neethling/Potgieter* (fn 4) 279 f; *Loubser/Midgley* (fn 4) 535–540.

69 See *Van Aswegen* (fn 18) 338–341.

G. DIFFERENCES AS REGARDS THE PERSONS WHO MAY BE PROTECTED

In delict not only the primary victims, but also secondary victims may be protected. Clear examples are the action of dependants where they may claim for loss of support as a result of the wrongful, culpable death or injury of their breadwinner.[70] Persons (such as breadwinners) who have a legal duty to support dependants may also institute a delictual action against a wrongdoer who wrongfully and negligently injures a dependant, causing an increase of said duty (eg medical expenses).[71] Should an heir or a member of a deceased's immediate family (such as his spouse, parent or child) meet the funeral expenses, the former may recover his expenses from the wrongdoer.[72] Compensation for emotional shock may be claimed by secondary victims[73] who, for example, were informed of the death or injury of a close relative;[74] or who personally witnessed the death or injury of someone with whom they had a close relationship.[75] However, persons who stand or stood in a contractual relationship to an injured or deceased person may in principle not claim for the loss they suffered where the injury or death constituted a negligent (as opposed to intentional) interference with the contractual relationship. This is dictated by legal policy because the opposite view may lead to an 'unmanageable situation'.[76] 26

70 See *Neethling/Potgieter* (fn 4) 292 f; *Loubser/Midgley* (fn 4) 346–354 ; *J Neethling*, Action of dependants in South African law: Direct or indirect?, in: H Koziol/J Spier (eds), Liber Amicorum: Pierre Widmer (2003) 253 f. It is however controversial whether the dependant's action is based on a delict committed against the breadwinner or against the dependants themselves. It is also controversial whether the breadwinner may claim for loss of support if the breadwinner was merely injured (see *Neethling/Potgieter* (fn 4) 292 f, 299 f; *Brooks v Minister of Safety and Security* 2009 2 SA 94 (SCA) 99 f).

71 *Neethling/Potgieter* (fn 4) 291; *Loubser/Midgley* (fn 4) 344 f.

72 *Neethling/Potgieter* (fn 4) 290; *Loubser/Midgley* (fn 4) 361.

73 *Neethling/Potgieter* (fn 4) 300 f; *Loubser/Midgley* (fn 4) 361 f.

74 The so-called 'hearsay cases': see eg *Barnard v Santam Bpk* 1999 1 SA 202 (SCA) 209.

75 See *Road Accident Fund v Sauls* 2002 2 SA 55 (SCA) 62 f where the court said: 'It is not justifiable to limit the sort of claim now under consideration ... to a defined relationship between primary and secondary victims, such as parent and child, husband and wife, etc. Of course, in determining limitations a court will take into consideration the relationship between primary and secondary victims. The question is one of legal policy, reasonableness, fairness and justice, ie was the relationship between the primary and secondary victims such that the claim should be allowed, taking all facts into consideration.'

76 *Union Government v Ocean Accident and Guarantee Corporation Ltd* 1956 1 SA 577 (A) 585 f. Cf *Loubser/Midgley* (fn 4) 281 f /. Exceptions are nevertheless recognised: if same-sex partners had a permanent life relationship similar to a marriage, during which the now deceased person undertook a contractual duty of support, the action of dependants is available to the surviving partner (*Du Plessis v Road Accident Fund* 2004 1 SA 359 (SCA)). This approach now also applies to a heterosexual life partnership akin to marriage, eg where the life partners agreed to get married, had already undertaken reciprocal duties of support and had executed a family will as evidence of their commitment to each other (*Paixão v Road Accident Fund* 2012 6 SA 377 (SCA) 390 f). See further *Neethling/Potgieter* (fn 4) 296 f.

27 The courts are, however, reluctant to protect secondary victims of breach of contract. In *Country Cloud Trading CC v MEC, Department of Infrastructure Development*,[77] the court had to decide whether delictual liability should be extended to a contracting party for damage suffered by a stranger to the contract (third party plaintiff) resulting from the intentional repudiation of the contract by that contracting party. It held that the plaintiff's claim could not succeed,[78] mainly for the following reasons: imposition of liability could lead to indeterminate liability, and the plaintiff was not 'vulnerable to the risk of harm', which signifies that the plaintiff could reasonably have avoided the harm suffered by other means. The ability or otherwise of a plaintiff to protect himself against damage plays an important part in ascertaining liability for pure economic loss.[79] Where he is unable to protect himself against the loss, this will support a conclusion that the defendant is liable;[80] vice versa, where the plaintiff can protect himself against such loss, for example by obtaining insurance cover,[81] or, in a contractual 'setting' by contractual provisions,[82] or by other reasonable means avoid making himself 'vulnerable' to the risk of loss,[83] the opposite conclusion may be reached.

28 Where a contract for the benefit of a third party (*stipulatio alteri*) has been concluded, under certain circumstances the contract will be enforceable by the third party.[84] Contractual terms may also play a role in determining delictual wrongfulness as against a third party, particularly in instances of liability for omissions or pure economic loss, that is, with regard to the existence of a legal

---

77 2014 2 SA 214 (SCA), confirmed on appeal by the Constitutional Court (*Country Cloud Trading CC v MEC, Department of Infrastructure Development, Gauteng* 2015 1 SA 1 (SCA)); see *J Neethling/JM Potgieter*, Breach of contract and liability to third parties [2015] THRHR 711 f.

78 2014 2 SA 214 (SCA) 225–227. In *AB Ventures Ltd v Siemens Ltd* 2011 4 SA 614 (SCA) the court also dismissed the claim by a third party who allegedly suffered damage as a result of a negligent breach of contract. See *J Neethling*, Delikseis deur derde party weens kontrakbreuk [2015] TSAR 188 f.

79 *Neethling/Potgieter* (fn 4) 312.

80 *Indac Electronics (Pty) Ltd v Volkskas Bank Ltd* 1992 1 SA 783 (A) 799; *Freddy Hirsch Group (Pty) Ltd v Chickenland (Pty) Ltd* 2011 4 SA 276 (SCA) 296.

81 *Indac Electronics (Pty) Ltd v Volkskas Bank Ltd* 1992 1 SA 783 (A) 799; *Freddy Hirsch Group (Pty) Ltd v Chickenland (Pty) Ltd* 2011 4 SA 276 (SCA) 296.

82 See eg *Trustees, Two Oceans Aquarium Trust v Kantey & Templer (Pty) Ltd* 2006 3 SA 138 (SCA) 149; *Fourway Haulage SA (Pty) Ltd v SA National Roads Agency Ltd* 2009 2 SA 150 (SCA) 162; *Mediterranean Shipping Co (Pty) Ltd v Tebe Trading (Pty) Ltd* [2007] 2 All SA 489 (SCA) 495; *Delphisure Group Insurance Brokers Cape (Pty) Ltd v Dippenaar* 2010 5 SA 499 (SCA) 508 f.

83 *Cape Empowerment Trust Limited v Fisher Hoffman Sithole* 2013 5 SA 183 (SCA) 194 f. In this case, the court held that if the plaintiff could reasonably have avoided damage by other means and consequently could have made himself non-vulnerable to loss, but did not do so, this would be an important indicator that the defendant did not act wrongfully. See also *Country Cloud Trading CC v MEC, Department of Infrastructure Development* 2014 2 SA 214 (SCA) 226 f; *Delphisure Group Insurance Brokers Cape (Pty) Ltd v Dippenaar* 2010 5 SA 499 (SCA) 509.

84 See *Hutchison/Pretorius* (fn 9) 224–228.

duty to prevent damage. Where there was a contractual undertaking for the safety of a third party, such undertaking may be indicative of a delictual legal duty to prevent harm to that party.[85] This explains why, for example, an appointed life-saver has a legal duty to rescue swimmers at a swimming pool or a beach.[86]

The action of the disappointed beneficiary[87] should also be mentioned here. 29
According to *BOE Bank Ltd v Ries*[88] a prejudiced beneficiary will succeed if his claim complies with all the ordinary requirements of a delict. The following factors are strongly indicative of a legal duty to prevent prejudice to the beneficiary: the existence of a valid (professional) contract between the defendant and the testator placing a duty on the defendant to act with the necessary care (professional skill) to ensure that a particular (testamentary) benefit will accrue to the beneficiary;[89] and the existence of a delictual legal duty on the defendant to refrain from wrongful conduct (such as misrepresentation) against the testator which could deprive the beneficiary of a particular benefit.[90]

H. DIFFERENCES AS REGARDS DEFENCES

Contributory negligence may only be raised against a delictual claim. The 30
Apportionment of Damages Act 34 of 1956 applies only to delictual claims, and not to damage suffered as a result of breach of contract.[91] The main reason for this is that the Act was historically not intended to apply to claims for breach of contract, but only to amend the law of delict. In certain circumstances, it may thus be to the advantage of a contributorily negligent plaintiff to institute a contractual action.[92] However, a strong case can be made out in favour of intervention by the legislature to provide for cases where a defendant's breach of contract is described in terms of his negligence, while the plaintiff by his own negligence contributed to the damage.

---

85 *Boberg* (fn 4) 212, 225, 260. The assumption of contractual obligations may thus be indicative of a delictual legal duty as against non-contracting parties (see *Chartaprops 16 (Pty) Ltd v Silberman* 2009 1 SA 265 (SCA) 276; *Longueira v Securitas of South Africa (Pty) Ltd* 1998 4 SA 258 (W) 263). See also below no 48.

86 *Neethling/Potgieter* (fn 4) 71.

87 See *Aucamp v University of Stellenbosch* 2002 4 SA 544 (C) 565 f, 569–574 for details.

88 2002 2 SA 39 (SCA) 46.

89 See *BOE Bank Ltd v Ries* 2002 2 SA 39 (SCA) 47 48, 49 f.

90 *Aucamp v University of Stellenbosch* 2002 4 SA 544 (C) 566–568. In this case a testator lost his membership of a group insurance scheme as a result of a negligent misrepresentation of his employer (the defendant). Consequently the plaintiffs (his wife and children) could not claim death benefits in terms of the scheme.

91 See *Thoroughbred Breeders' Association of South Africa v Price Waterhouse* 2001 4 SA 551 (SCA) 590 f; see also *Loubser/Midgley* (fn 4) 233 ; *Hutchison/Pretorius* (fn 9) 338; *Neethling/Potgieter* (fn 4) 176.

92 See *Van Aswegen* (fn 18) 356–358.

31 In this regard a distinction is made between the plaintiff's negligent conduct before the damage-causing event and such conduct after the event. Only the former is relevant as contributory negligence for the purposes of apportionment of damages, while the latter must be taken into account when determining legal causation and may thus exclude the defendant's liability for harmful consequences that are too remote.[93]

32 *Volenti non fit iniuria* is generally recognised as a defence against a delictual claim.[94] Consent to injury is a unilateral act. In other words, the existence of a contract between the injured party and the actor is unnecessary to relieve the actor of liability. Because consent is a unilateral act, it may be unilaterally revoked by the consenting party at any stage preceding the actor's conduct.[95] As with consent, a unilateral waiver of this right by an injured party to institute a delictual action may also extinguish the (possible) liability of a wrongdoer. Such a *pactum de non petendo in anticipando*[96] must be distinguished from consent to harm which, as said, does not entail a contract between the injured party and the actor. Although the effect of a *pactum* and consent are the same – in each case the actor is not held liable – the reasons for the actor not being held liable are different. In the case of a *pactum*, the actor commits a delict but the prejudiced person undertakes not to hold the actor liable. Wrongfulness is thus not excluded, as is the case with consent; only the resultant action is.[97] However, and this is important, a unilateral waiver of a contractual right to performance cannot extinguish the other contracting party's obligation to perform. For this purpose an agreement between the parties to the contract is required.[98]

I. DIFFERENCES AS REGARDS LIMITATION PERIODS

33 The prescription rules for delict and breach of contract are very similar. According to the Prescription Act 68 of 1969,[99] a debt prescribes (and the claim based on it is thus also extinguished) three years after it originated.[100] Debt includes any liability that originates from inter alia delict or contract and prescription

---

93 See *Gibson v Berkowitz* 1996 4 SA 1029 (W) 1051 f; *Neethling/Potgieter* (fn 4) 176 f.

94 See *Neethling/Potgieter* (fn 4) 108 f; *Loubser/Midgley* (fn 4) 204 f.

95 *Van der Merwe/Olivier* (fn 4) 92; *Van der Walt/Midgley* (fn 1) 214; *Neethling/Potgieter* (fn 4) 109 f.

96 *Neethling/Potgieter* (fn 4) 114; *Van Aswegen* (fn 18) 351 f; *Loubser/Midgley* (fn 4) 212 f.

97 *J Neethling/JM Potgieter*, Borderline between the law of contract and the law of delict [2012] THRHR 111.

98 See *Van Aswegen* (fn 18) 343–351.

99 See generally *Van der Merwe/Olivier* (fn 4) 283–291; *Loubser/Midgley* (fn 4) 248 f; *Hutchison/Pretorius* (fn 9) 385–387; *Neethling/Potgieter* (fn 4) 278.

100 There are other Acts which lay down specific periods of prescription or extinction, eg with regard to 'third party' claims under the Road Accidents Fund Act 56 of 1996 sec 23, the period is two (or three) years; that for claims under the Apportionment of Damages Act 34

commences to run as soon as the debt is due. This arises from a delict the moment all the elements of a delict are present, and from breach of contract the moment the breach becomes enforceable, provided also that the creditor has knowledge (or ought reasonably to know) of the identity of the wrongdoer and the facts from which the debt arises. But the creditor shall be deemed to have such knowledge if he could have acquired it by reasonable care.[101] The ending of prescription may be suspended[102] or interrupted.[103]

J. DIFFERENCES AS REGARDS PROOF

The standard of proof for both delict[104] and breach of contract is that the plaintiff must prove the relevant cause of action on a preponderance or balance of probability. But the onus of proof may differ in respect of contractual and delictual claims. In delictual actions, the onus is on the plaintiff to prove negligence on the part of the defendant.[105] On the other hand, where a claim is instituted against a person for breach of contract where fault is required, the onus is on the defendant to show that he was not negligent.[106] This also applies to a claim for damage to property against the person who was in possession of the property in terms of lease, *depositum*, *commodatum*, pledge or *locatio conductio*.[107] 34

K. OTHER DIFFERENCES

1) *Time for Computation of Damage*

The time for the computation of the extent of damage in the two instances differs. In the law of delict, the extent of the damage is usually measured with reference 35

---

of 1956 sec 2, 12 months; as well as that for claims under the Compensation for Occupational Injuries and Diseases Act 130 of 1993 sec 43 (see further *Potgieter/Steynberg/Floyd* (fn 28) 346–348; *Loubser/Midgley* (fn 4) 258 5 f). With regard to the recovery of debts from organs of the state, the Institution of Legal Proceedings against Certain Organs of State Act 40 of 2002 has been brought in line with the provisions of the Prescription Act 68 of 1969.

101 See sec 12 of the Act.

102 Sec 13 of the Act. The ending of prescription will be delayed under certain circumstances, eg where the debtor is outside the country, or the creditor is a minor or mentally ill (see *Loubser/Midgley* (fn 4) 252 f; *Hutchison/Pretorius* (fn 9) 386 f).

103 Secs 14 and 15 of the Act. Prescription will be interrupted by an acknowledgement of liability by the debtor or by the serving on the debtor of any process whereby the creditor claims payment from the debtor (see *Loubser/Midgley* (fn 4) 254 f; *Hutchison/Pretorius* (fn 9) 386).

104 See *Neethling* (fn 34) 283 fn 1.

105 See *Neethling/Potgieter* (fn 4) 160–162; *Loubser/Midgley* (fn 4) 233.

106 See *Van Aswegen* (fn 18) 380 f fn 309, 372 f; *Loubser/Midgley* (fn 4) 233.

107 *Van der Walt/Midgley* (fn 1) 81 f; *Manley van Niekerk (Pty) Ltd v Assegai Safasis and Film Productions (Pty) Ltd* 1977 2 SA 416 (A) 422 f.

to the date of the commission of the delict. In the law of contract, on the other hand, the extent of the damage is usually measured with reference to the time of the conclusion of the contract (and not the breach thereof). Obviously these two calculations may differ. The contractual position is subject to criticism since damage is caused by a breach of the contract and not by the conclusion thereof.[108]

2) Capacity of Persons

36 The requirements for the capacity of persons for the two types of liability are such that, in a given case, a person may 'qualify' for delictual liability but not for liability for breach of contract. To illustrate, reference may be made to the position of the minor. Although he may conclude a valid contract without assistance, he cannot be sued for 'breach of contract' since this involves an unenforceable natural obligation.[109] He may nevertheless qualify as a delictual wrongdoer and be sued as such.[110]

3) Jurisdiction of Courts

37 Different courts may have jurisdiction in claims for delict and breach of contract respectively. The court that has jurisdiction on the ground of delict may, for example, be convenient and advantageous to the plaintiff.[111]

4) Rules on Conflict of Laws

38 The rules of private international law or conflict of laws differ in respect of delictual and contractual claims. As a rule, the law of the place where the delict was committed (*lex loci delicti*) applies to delictual actions, while with regard to contractual actions, the law of the place where the contact was concluded (not breached) (*lex loci contractus*) is applicable.[112]

5) Transmissibility of Claims

39 A contractual claim is actively transmissible,[113] while a delictual claim for non-patrimonial damages (such as compensation for pain and suffering under the action for pain and suffering, or satisfaction for insult or defamation under the

108 See *Van Aswegen* (fn 18) 330–332; *Loubser/Midgley* (fn 4) 233.
109 See *Hutchison/Pretorius* (fn 9) 151 f.
110 See *Van Aswegen* (fn 18) 333–338; *Neethling/Potgieter* (fn 4) 276.
111 See *Van Aswegen* (fn 18) 373–378, 379; *Loubser/Midgley* (fn 4) 233.
112 See *Van Aswegen* (fn 18) 379; *Loubser/Midgley* (fn 4) 233.
113 *Administrator, Natal v Edouard* 1990 3 SA 581 (A) 597.

actio iniuriarum) is only actively transmissible after *litis contestatio*. The claim therefore lapses if the plaintiff or the defendant dies before *litis contestatio*.[114]

6) *Values Underlying Contract and Delict*

There is an important difference between the values that underlie contract 40
and delict. Whereas the law of contract largely deals with voluntarily assumed obligations, the law of delict imposes obligations in accordance with the general societal norm of reasonableness or the *boni mores*.[115]

L. REASONS FOR THE DIFFERENCES

The differences are, for historical, systematic and practical reasons, as a premise 41
based on the reality that the law of contract largely deals with voluntarily assumed obligations, while the law of delict imposes obligations laid down by law. Accordingly, the law of contract provides specific rules for breach of contract that are not applicable to a delict.

III. LIMITATION OR EXCLUSION OF LIABILITY ARISING FROM TORT AND CONTRACT

A. STATUTORY PROVISIONS AUTHORISING A LIMITATION OR EXCLUSION OF LIABILITY

Statutory vicarious liability is created by the South African Schools Act 84 of 42
1996, which provides that the state is exclusively liable for damage caused by any delict (eg by teachers or learners) that is associated with an educational activity of a public school.[116] However, the state is not liable for claims based on breach of contract against the school.[117]

---

114 *Van der Walt/Midgley* (fn 1) 5; *Loubser/Midgley* (fn 4) 233 ; *Neethling/Potgieter* (fn 4) 267; contra *Nkala v Harmony Gold Mining Company Ltd* (Treatment Action Campaign NPC as amicus curiae) 2016 5 SA 240 (GJ) as to a class action for damages for bodily injuries and the transmissibility of a claim for general damages.

115 See *Loubser/Midgley* (fn 4) 233.

116 Sec 60(1); see *Louw v LUR vir Onderwys en Kultuur, Vrystaat* 2005 6 SA 78 (O) 85; confirmed in 2006 1 SA 192 (SCA); *PJ Visser*, Staatsaanspreeklikheid weens nalatige optrede deur personeellid in diens van openbare skool [2006] THRHR 523 f.

117 See *Bastian Financial Services (Pty) Ltd v General Hendrik Schoeman Primary School* 2008 5 SA 1 (SCA) 12 f. This conclusion is, according to the court, supported by sec 20(10) of the Act, which provides that the state is not liable for any act at a public school that flows from its contractual responsibilities as employer against its staff (see further *Louw v LUR vir Onderwys en Kultuur, Vrystaat* 2006 1 SA 192 (SCA) 195–197; cf *Visser* (fn 116) 523 f).

43 In instances where strict liability has been imposed by legislation, the extent of the liability is often curtailed by fixing maximum amounts of compensation.[118] For example, in terms of the National Nuclear Regulator Act 47 of 1999,[119] the strict liability[120] for nuclear damage by any holder of a nuclear installation licence is limited, for each nuclear accident, to the amounts determined in accordance with the Act. This relates to the level of financial security to be provided by such holders. However, the maximum amount(s) may be raised by Parliament providing for appropriate funds to cover the compensation for claims exceeding the maximum amount(s).

44 In terms of the Compensation for Occupational Injuries and Diseases Act 130 of 1993,[121] the Road Accident Fund Act 56 of 1996[122] and the Labour Relations Act 66 of 1995[123] the amount of damages as well as the type of damage in respect of which damages may be recovered, are limited or excluded.[124] In the case of the first Act, the liability of the employer is excluded and replaced with a claim against the Director-General, while in the case of the second Act, motor accident victims of negligent driving must claim against the Fund, and only when the Fund is unable to pay any compensation, from the negligent driver.

B. LIMITATION OR EXCLUSION OF CONTRACTUAL AND TORTIOUS LIABILITY BY CONTRACT

45 An important factor present in contract and absent in delict is the competence of the parties to regulate, limit or expand by arrangement among themselves the consequences of any prospective breach. A contract, it has been said, is the ultimate limiting device.[125] The parties to a contract may restrict their liability – contractual as well as delictual – through an exclusionary (exemption) clause.[126] Liability for damage caused by intentional conduct may, however, not be excluded

---

118 See *Neethling/Potgieter* (fn 4) 381.

119 Secs 29, 30, 33.

120 See *Neethling/Potgieter* (fn 4) 400 f.

121 Secs 22(3), 35(1). An employee may claim only for patrimonial loss (not for non-patrimonial damage: pain and suffering) and the extent of the claim is also limited.

122 Secs 17(1), 18, 21. A motor accident victim may not claim for property damage but only for other patrimonial damage (such as medical expenses, loss of income or support and funeral expenses), as well as non-patrimonial damage. The maximum amount of damages is limited depending on the type of damage.

123 Sec 194 places a maximum limit on the compensation that the court may award to an employee for unfair dismissal (breach of contract).

124 See *Potgieter/Steynberg/Floyd* (fn 28) 330–333.

125 *Freddy Hirsch Group (Pty) Ltd v Chickenland (Pty) Ltd* 2011 4 SA 276 (SCA) 292.

126 See in this regard *Van der Walt/Midgley* (fn 1) 62; *Neethling/Potgieter* (fn 4) 277 f; *Van Aswegen* (fn 18) 352 f; *Loubser/Midgley* (fn 4) 231–240.

in this manner. After initial uncertainty as to whether gross negligence should be treated in the same way as intent, it was held that the exclusion of liability for gross negligence is permissible.[127] However, the Consumer Protection Act 68 of 2008 prohibits exemption of liability for gross negligence vis-à-vis consumers.[128]

The precise restriction on the wrongdoer's liability will depend on the interpretation of the clause concerned.[129] The courts follow a strict and limiting approach: the exclusion of liability must be formulated clearly and unambiguously ('plainly') to be enforceable.[130] A contract will not be enforceable if it is against public policy.[131] The interpretation will naturally influence the question of what remedies the prejudiced party has at his disposal. A contractual term excluding or limiting liability may therefore, depending on the interpretation thereof, apply only to contractual liability. The party committing breach of contract may therefore still be delictually liable.[132] Up to now no distinction has been made between personal injury and property damage. However, *Johannesburg Country Club v Stott*[133] left open the question of whether exclusion of liability for damages in the case of *negligent homicide* conflicted with the high value placed on the inviolability of human life by the Bill of Rights. 46

The Consumer Protection Act 68 of 2008 prevents the contractual exclusion of the various consumer rights protected by the Act. Proper notice must be given to consumers of any other proposed exemption from liability, and the courts are 47

---

127 *Government of the Republic of South Africa v Fibre Spinners & Weavers (Pty) Ltd* 1978 2 SA 794 (A) 807; see also *First National Bank of SA Ltd v Rosenblum* 2001 4 SA 189 (SCA) 201; cf *Afrox Healthcare Bpk v Strydom* 2002 6 SA 21 (SCA) 35; *Van Aswegen* (fn 18) 355.

128 Sec 51(1)(c)(i); see *Loubser/Reid* (fn 49) 37; *Hutchison/Pretorius* (fn 9) 236.

129 See *Neethling/Potgieter* (fn 4) 277 fn 101; cf *Van der Walt/Midgley* (fn 1) 62.

130 See eg *First National Bank of SA Ltd v Rosenblum* 2001 4 SA 189 (SCA) 195 f; *Durban's Water Wonderland (Pty) Ltd v Botha* 1999 1 SA 982 (SCA) 989; *Johannesburg Country Club v Stott* 2004 5 SA 511 (SCA) 516 f; *Afrox v Healthcare Bpk v Strydom* 2002 6 SA 21 (SCA) 34; *Van der Westhuizen v Arnold* 2002 6 SA 453 (SCA) 468 f; *Masstores (Pty) Ltd v Murray & Roberts Construction (Pty) Ltd* 2008 6 SA 654 (SCA) 662 f; *Drifters Adventure Tours CC v Hircock* 2007 2 SA 83 (SCA) 87; *Walker v Redhouse* [2007] 4 All SA 1217 (SCA) 1221; *ER24 Holdings v Smith NO* [2007] 4 All SA 679 (SCA) 683. In *Swinburne v Newbee Investments (Pty) Ltd* 2010 5 SA 296 (KZD) 307 f the court pointed out that if the language of a disclaimer or exemption clause is such that it exempts the proferens from liability in express and unambiguous terms, effect is to be given to that meaning, but, if there is ambiguity in the language, it is to be construed against the proferens. The opinion of a reasonable person is important in the interpretation of an exclusion clause.

131 In *Freddy Hirsch Group (Pty) Ltd v Chickenland (Pty) Ltd* 2011 4 SA 276 (SCA) 285–287 the court held that the exclusion clause that purported to exclude all statutory and common law terms, warranties or representations as to the quality or fitness of foodstuff was contrary to public policy and unenforceable. See also *Loubser/Reid* (fn 49) 35.

132 See *Van Aswegen* (fn 18) 358 f.

133 2004 5 SA 511 (SCA) 518 f; see also *Afrox Healthcare Bpk v Strydom* 2002 6 SA 21 (SCA); cf *Loubser/Midgley* (fn 4) 244 –247.

given extensive powers to correct 'prohibited conduct, unfairness, injustice or unconscionability'.[134]

48 It is controversial whether contracting parties may exclude delictual liability towards third parties[135] since there are two opposing decisions in the Supreme Court of Appeal: *Viv's Tippers v Pha Phama Staff Services*[136] and *Chartaprops 16 (Pty) Ltd v Silberman.*[137] The viewpoint in *Viv's Tippers* supporting such exclusion of liability should not be followed because it seems unfair and unreasonable to apply the exclusion-of-liability terms directly to possible delictual claims of non-contracting persons.[138] But this does not mean that the terms of a contract are irrelevant as regards delictual wrongfulness. The assumption of contractual obligations may indeed be indicative of a legal duty as against non-contracting parties. Whether it does so in a particular case is a matter that will be determined by legal and public policy.[139]

49 The question *whether* a contractual exclusion may provide a defence to a third party to the contract is a matter, as far as could be ascertained, that has not been dealt with in our law.

IV. NON-CONCURRENCE OR CONCURRENCE OF ACTIONS

A. OVERVIEW

50 As a rule a delictual remedy and a contractual action can concur only in circumstances where breach of contract simultaneously also constitutes a delict against the wronged contracting party.[140] This will first of all be the case

---

134 See secs 51 and 52 of the Act; *Loubser/Reid* (fn 49) 37; *Hutchison/Pretorius* (fn 9) 54. The National Credit Act 34 of 2005 secs 90(1) and (2)(c) also prohibit the exclusion in a credit agreement of common law rights that would otherwise be applicable (see *Hutchison/Pretorius* (fn 9) 236).

135 Eg a contract between a security firm and the owner of parking facilities excluding delictual liability of the firm as against the owner of a vehicle stolen from the facility, or between a shop owner and a cleaning company excluding liability of the company towards clients who injure themselves slipping on a dirty floor in the shop.

136 2010 4 SA 455 (SCA); see *J Neethling*, Delictual liability of a security firm for the theft of a vehicle guarded by its employee [2011] THRHR 169 f.

137 2009 1 SA 265 (SCA) 285 f.

138 See also *Compass Motors Industries (Pty) Ltd v Callguard (Pty) Ltd* 1990 2 SA 520 (W) 529; *Neethling/Potgieter* (fn 97) 108 f.

139 *Chartaprops 16 (Pty) Ltd v Silberman* 2009 1 SA 265 (SCA) 276; *Longueira v Securitas of South Africa (Pty) Ltd* 1998 4 SA 258 (W) 263.

140 See *Neethling/Potgieter* (fn 4) 273–275; cf *Van der Walt/Midgley* (fn 1) 57–59; *Loubser/Midgley* (fn 4) 235–240 ; *Hutchison/Pretorius* (fn 9) 9.

if the conduct complained of, apart from constituting breach of contract, also wrongfully and culpably infringes a legally recognised interest which exists independently of the contract, such as property or a personality interest.[141] However, the courts were reluctant to construe an interest that could exist independently of the contract in instances of pure economic loss.[142] Where professional services were negligently supplied pursuant to an agreement (such as with attorneys, auditors and architects) the prejudiced person would normally only have the contractual action at his disposal.[143] In *Pinshaw v Nexus Securities (Pty) Ltd*,[144] a different approach was followed. The court held that this viewpoint was not applicable to quasi-professional contracts (eg contracts with persons providing financial services and presenting themselves as experts), and that the Aquilian action for pure economic loss may be concurrent with the contractual action in such instances. Van der Walt and Midgley[145] agree with this approach but go one step further. They are of the opinion that independent delictual liability is possible in instances of pure economic loss where the delictual claim is not based solely on breach of contract. In *Holtzhausen v ABSA Bank Ltd*,[146] the court followed this approach. It found that the plaintiff's delictual claim did not depend upon a breach of a contractual duty but rather upon general delictual principles concerning negligent misrepresentation.

Nevertheless, in *Lillicrap, Wassenaar and Partners v Pilkington Brothers (SA) (Pty) Ltd*[147] the court warned that Aquilian liability should not readily be extended to pure economic loss in a contractual context, primarily because the position of the parties had been determined by contractual provisions which they themselves had preferred and which they had expected to be applicable. Moreover, the court emphasised that extension of liability under the Aquilian action would not be 51

141 See eg *Lillicrap, Wassenaar and Partners v Pilkington Brothers (SA) (Pty) Ltd* 1985 1 SA 475 (A) 496, 499; *Mukheiber v Raath* 1999 3 SA 1065 (SCA) 1069.

142 Cf *Lillicrap, Wassenaar and Partners v Pilkington Brothers (SA) (Pty) Ltd* 1985 1 SA 475 (A) 499 f; *Erasmus v Inch* 1997 4 SA 584 (W) 594 f; *Bayer South Africa (Pty) Ltd v Frost* 1991 4 SA 559 (A) 570.

143 Cf *Lillicrap, Wassenaar and Partners v Pilkington Brothers (SA) (Pty) Ltd* 1985 1 SA 475 (A) 500; *Erasmus v Inch* 1997 4 SA 584 (W) 592–595; *Van der Walt/Midgley* (fn 1) 58.

144 2002 2 SA 510 (C) 518 f, 534–536; however, see *Alfa Laval Agri (Pty) Ltd v Ferreira* 2004 2 SA 68 (O) 77 f.

145 (fn 1) 58.

146 2008 5 SA 630 (SCA) 633; see also *J Neethling*, Sameloop van die Aquiliese en kontraksaksie by suiwer ekonomiese verlies [2009] TSAR 573 f; *Neethling/Potgieter* (fn 97) 107 f; *J Neethling/JM Potgieter*, Concurrence of contractual and Aquilian claims: recent cases [2014] THRHR 287 f; cf *Media 24 Ltd v Grobler* 2005 6 SA 328 (SCA) 350 f; *Freddy Hirsch Group (Pty) Ltd v Chickenland (Pty) Ltd* 2011 4 SA 276 (SCA) 292; *Nashua Mobile (Pty) Ltd v GC Pale CC t/a Invasive Plant Solutions* 2012 1 SA 615 (GSJ); *NSC Carriers & Forwarding CC v Hyprop Investments Ltd* 2013 1 SA 340 (GSJ); *Nortje v Fakie* 2013 1 SA 577 (KZP); *Living Hands (Pty) Ltd v Ditz* 2013 2 SA 368 (GSJ).

147 1985 1 SA 475 (A) 500; see also *Alfa Laval Agri (Pty) Ltd v Ferreira* 2004 2 SA 68 (O) 76.

allowed in the field of contract law if the prejudiced party disposes of adequate contractual remedies. In *Trustees, Two Oceans Aquarium Trust v Kantey & Templer*,[148] the court confirmed the approach in *Lillicrap* and reiterated that if the prejudiced party had adequate contractual remedies at his disposal, there is no policy imperative for the law to superimpose a further remedy. But the court went a step further by finding that no reason exists why Aquilian liability should be extended to rescue a plaintiff who was in the position to avoid the risk of harm by contractual means, but who failed to do so.[149] It is submitted that where a delictual action has not expressly been excluded in a contract, the law should be loath not to allow the Aquilian action for an independent delict in a contractual setting.[150]

52 In *AB Ventures Ltd v Siemens Ltd*,[151] the court, despite the absence of a concurrence of actions (since there was no contract between the plaintiff and the defendant), found that such absence did not constitute a difference in principle from the above cases where such concurrence was indeed present. The court therefore denied a delictual claim because, in its view, the plaintiff could have protected itself in its contract with a third party, but failed to do so.[152]

53 The approach in our law in instances where a delictual remedy and a contractual action indeed concur (that is, in circumstances where breach of contract simultaneously also constitutes a delict against the wronged contracting party) is that the injured person can then choose whether he wants to claim *ex contractu* or *ex lege Aquilia*,[153] or he can institute the remedies in the alternative.[154] Van der Walt and Midgley[155] also mention the possibility that the two remedies may be instituted cumulatively provided that the plaintiff may not recover more than his actual loss.

B. CONCURRENCE/EXCLUSION OF ACTIONS FOR THE PROTECTION AGAINST PERSONAL INJURY

54 The delictual actions for pain and suffering and consequential patrimonial loss (as a result of personal injury), and the contractual action concur in circumstances

148 2006 3 SA 138 (SCA) 145 f.

149 Cf further *Mediterranean Shipping Co (Pty) Ltd v Tebe Trading (Pty) Ltd* [2007] 2 All SA 489 (SCA) 495.

150 See *Neethling/Potgieter* (fn 146) 295 f.

151 2011 4 SA 614 (SCA).

152 See *Neethling/Potgieter* (fn 97) 114–116 for criticism.

153 See eg *Lillicrap, Wassenaar and Partners v Pilkington Brothers (SA) (Pty) Ltd* 1985 1 SA 475 (A) 496, 499; *Van Wyk v Lewis* 1924 AD 438.

154 Eg *Greenfield Engineering Works (Pty) Ltd v NKR Construction (Pty) Ltd* 1978 4 SA 901 (N); *Wellworths Bazaars Ltd v Chandlers Ltd* 1948 3 SA 348 (W).

155 *Van der Walt/Midgley* (fn 1) 81.

where breach of contract also results in a wrongful and culpable infringement of the physical-mental integrity of the wronged contracting party. An example of this situation is where a patient is operated on in terms of a contract by a surgeon who performs the operation negligently and the patient's health suffers a setback. The patient then has a contractual action for patrimonial damages, as well as an action for pain and suffering for compensation.[156] Since two independent actions are involved, each with its own requirements and purpose, they may co-exist and be instituted simultaneously.[157] This viewpoint is also apparent from the decision in *Administrator, Natal v Edouard*.[158] The court held that compensation for pain and suffering experienced as a result of breach of contract cannot be claimed with the contractual action; for this purpose the delictual action for pain and suffering must be employed.[159] The general principles applicable to the exclusion of actions are also applicable here.[160]

C. CONCURRENCE/EXCLUSION OF ACTIONS FOR THE PROTECTION OF PROPERTY

As said, a concurrence of the delictual and contractual action is present if the 55
conduct complained of, apart from breach of contract, also wrongfully and culpably infringes a legally recognised interest which exists independently of the contract, and this is the case with damage to property.[161] Examples from case law are the following: in a contract of lease, the lessor can claim for damage to the leased property either in contract or in delict;[162] in a building contract between a builder and the building owner of property, the builder can also be liable in delict to the owner for building an unsafe structure;[163] and in a contract

156 See *Van Wyk v Lewis* 1924 AD 438; *Neethling/Potgieter* (fn 4) 258. This approach is eg also in principle applicable where a horse which was leased by its owner to the plaintiff, bolted as a result of negligence on the part of the owner's employees, and seriously injured the plaintiff's daughter (cf *Lawrence v Kondotel Inns (Pty) Ltd* 1989 1 SA 44 (D) 52 f).

157 See *Van der Merwe/Olivier* (fn 4) 476 f.

158 1990 3 SA 581 (A) 596 f; *Edouard v Administrator, Natal* 1989 2 SA 368 (D) 392 f; cf also *Van der Merwe/Olivier* (fn 4) 476 f discussion of *Van Wyk v Lewis* 1924 AD 438.

159 In this case the Appellate Division decided that the failure of a provincial hospital to sterilise a married woman for socio-economic reasons in terms of a contract, constituted a breach of contract. According to the court, this omission founded an action for damages for the loss she and her husband suffered as a result of the maintenance of a child who was born because of the omission. However, the breach of contract does not also found a claim for non-patrimonial damages for the pain, suffering, inconvenience and loss of amenities of life which the woman experienced as a result of her pregnancy and the birth of the child.

160 See above no 45 f.

161 See above no 50; see also *Loubser/Midgley* (fn 4) 235 f.

162 See *Lillicrap, Wassenaar and Partners v Pilkington Brothers (SA) (Pty) Ltd* 1985 1 SA 475 (A) 496.

163 *SM Goldstein & Co (Pty) Ltd v Cathkin Park Hotel (Pty) Ltd* 2000 4 SA 1019 (SCA) 1024; cf *Cathkin Park Hotel v JD Makesch Architects* 1993 2 SA 98 (W) 101–103.

between a security firm and the owner of a house, the firm can in principle be liable *ex contractu* and *ex delicto* for theft of property from the house.[164] As with protection against personal injury, the general principles applicable to the exclusion of actions are also applicable here.[165]

D. CONCURRENCE/EXCLUSION IN THE CASE OF INTERFERENCE WITH CONTRACTUAL RIGHTS

1) *Interference with a Contractual Relationship*

56 Under South African law, most of the decisions[166] deal with intentional interference with a contractual relationship by a third party causing one of the contracting parties to commit a breach of contract (inducement to breach of contract).[167] Examples are enticing another person's employees to breach of contract,[168] or instigating such persons to terminate their contracts of service unlawfully.[169] Interference with the contractual relationships of a competitor occurs frequently.[170] For example, A acts unlawfully towards his rival B if he entices away B's customers, suppliers, credit grantors, etc by inducing them to commit breach of contract;[171] or where he bribes B's employee in order to

---

164 Cf *Imvula Quality Protection (Pty) Ltd v Loureiro* 2013 3 SA 407 (SCA).

165 See above no 45 f.

166 In *Atlas Organic Fertilizers (Pty) Ltd v Pikkewyn Ghwano (Pty) Ltd* 1981 2 SA 173 (T) 202 the court stated: 'A delictual remedy is available to a party to a contract who complains that a third party has intentionally and without lawful justification induced another party to the contract to commit a breach thereof'; see also *Genwest Batteries (Pty) Ltd v Van der Heyden* 1991 1 SA 727 (T) 729; *Aetiology Today CC t/a Somerset School v Van Aswegen* 1992 1 SA 807 (W) 820; *Dun and Bradstreet (Pty) Ltd v SA Merchants Combined Credit Bureau (Cape) (Pty) Ltd* 1968 1 SA 209 (C) 215; cf *Country Cloud Trading CC v MEC, Department of Infrastructure Development, Gauteng* 2015 1 SA 1 (CC) para 29 f; *Minister for Safety and Security v Scott* [2014] 3 All SA 306; see in general *Neethling/Potgieter* (fn 4) 323–327; *Loubser/Midgley* (fn 4) 284 –291; *Neethling* (fn 38) 245–247.

167 However, interference with a contractual relationship may also be present where the third party's conduct resulted in a contracting party not obtaining the performance to which it was entitled (see *Neethling/Potgieter* (fn 4) 324). In *Pick 'n Pay Retailers (Pty) Ltd v Liberty Group Ltd* 2015 4 SA 241 (GP), *Masstores (Pty) Ltd v Pick 'n Pay Retailers (Pty) Ltd* 2016 2 SA 586 (SCA) and *Shoprite Checkers (Pty) Ltd v Masstores (Pty) Ltd* [2016] 3 All SA 926 (ECG) the courts supported this approach with regard to interference with an exclusive trade agreement; but in *Masstores (Pty) Ltd v Pick 'n Pay Retailers (Pty) Ltd* 2017 1 SA 613 (CC) the Constitutional Court did not agree and set aside the decisions of the courts below because it would interfere with the principle of free competition.

168 Cf *Jansen v Pienaar* (1881) 1 SC 276; *Atlas Organic Fertilizers (Pty) Ltd v Pikkewyn Ghwano (Pty) Ltd* 1981 2 SA 173 (T) 202 f.

169 Cf *Atlas Organic Fertilizers (Pty) Ltd v Pikkewyn Ghwano (Pty) Ltd* 1981 2 SA 173 (T) 200; *New Kleinfontein Co Ltd v Superintendent of Labourers* 1906 TS 241.

170 See *Neethling* (fn 38) 246 f.

171 *Neethling* (fn 38) 246.

acquire B's trade secrets;[172] or where he incites a salesperson of B to sell A's competitive product in conflict with the terms of his contract of service;[173] or where he instigates an employee of B to terminate his contract of employment unlawfully with the aim of employing him;[174] or where he solicits his rival's (B) personnel to subvert or disrupt B's business from within (that is, while they were still in his employ and thus inducing breach of their employment contract);[175] or even where A intentionally assists or supports a person to breach his contract with a competitor.[176]

In these cases, there is, however, not a true concurrence of actions since the third party will be sued *ex delicto* for the interference with the contractual relationship, while the contractual party will be sued for breach of contract. 57

2) *Loss of Business due to Personal Injury to Someone Else's Employees or Clients or to Property Damage to the Entrepreneur*

An entrepreneur who stands in a contractual relationship to the injured employee or client may in principle not claim for the loss of business where the injury constituted a negligent interference with the contractual relationship.[177] This is dictated by legal policy. According to the Appellate Division in *Union Government v Ocean Accident and Guarantee Corporation Ltd*,[178] the opposite view may lead to an 'unmanageable situation'.[179] However, nowadays there seems to be a change of attitude by the Supreme Court of Appeal since it held that any negligent conduct by a third party which causes the infringement of a contractual personal right may, in principle, found the Aquilian action.[180] 58

---

172 The employee's revelation of the trade secrets to A constitutes breach of his contract with B (see *Neethling* (fn 38) 223 ff).

173 See *Atlas Organic Fertilizers (Pty) Ltd v Pikkewyn Ghwano (Pty) Ltd* 1981 2 SA 173 (T) 202 f.

174 Cf *Atlas Organic Fertilizers (Pty) Ltd v Pikkewyn Ghwano (Pty) Ltd* 1981 2 SA 173 (T) 200.

175 *Hushon SA (Pty) Ltd v Pictech (Pty) Ltd* 1997 4 SA 399 (SCA).

176 *Genwest Batteries (Pty) Ltd v Van der Heyden* 1991 1 SA 727 (T) 728 f.

177 Intentional interference is, however, in principle actionable (see *Neethling/Potgieter* (fn 4) 323–327; *Loubser/Midgley* (fn 4) 284 –293 39; *Neethling* (fn 38) 245–247).

178 1956 1 SA 577 (A) 585 f. Cf *Loubser/Midgley* (fn 4) 281 f.

179 The court stated: 'It is easy to imagine the absurdities that would arise if all persons contractually linked to the injured [or deceased] person could sue the careless injurer for the loss suffered by them. The case was put to us of the injured building contractor who in consequence of his injury has to discontinue his contract, so that his employees and the building owner and the architect and his sub-contractors and their employees are all put to some loss. Insurance companies would also be a wide class of plaintiffs who could bring actions when persons insured by them were negligently injured or, presumably, killed, if the extension of liability contended for were recognised. In fact it would be a rare accident that did not give occasion for a crop of actions at the suit of persons who had made contracts with the injured party.'

180 See *Minister for Safety and Security v Scott* [2014] 3 All SA 306 paras 31 f, 36; *J Neethling/JM Potgieter*, Delictual liability for negligent interference with a contractual relationship [2015]

The fear of unlimited liability may be allayed by the correct application of all the elements of a delict.

59 Furthermore, an entrepreneur may claim for loss of business due to damage to his property, for example by destroying his advertising posters, by damaging his delivery vehicles,[181] or by burning down his factory building.[182]

V. SPECIFIC SITUATIONS

A. PRE-CONTRACTUAL LIABILITY

60 Pre-contractual liability *ex delicto* can arise where a party to a potential contract commits a delict in the pre-contractual phase, or even where a third party frustrates the conclusion of a contract.[183] This is clearly not a concurrence of delict and contract because the delict occurs before the contract is concluded and there is therefore no question of a breach of contract.[184] An example is where a party to a potential contract induces the other party by a negligent misrepresentation to enter the contract.[185] Traditionally the courts were opposed to the granting of a delictual action in this situation.[186] A change in the attitude of the courts[187] was, however, confirmed by the Appellate Division in *Bayer South Africa (Pty) Ltd v Frost*.[188] Corbett CJ found[189] that there is, in principle, no good reason why in the recognition of a delictual action for negligent misrepresentation any distinction should be made between a misrepresentation which induces a contract and one made outside the contractual sphere. A negligent misrepresentation may, therefore, depending on the circumstances and provided that all the requirements for delictual liability are present,[190] give

THRHR 856 f. Cf also *Dantex Investment Holdings (Pty) Ltd v Brenner* 1989 1 SA 390 (A) 395; *Amod v Multilateral Motor Vehicle Accidents Fund (Commissioner for Gender Equality Intervening)* 1999 4 SA 1319 (SCA) 1326 1331; *Du Plessis v Road Accident Fund* 2004 1 SA 359 (SCA).

181 Cf *Modimogale v Zweni* 1990 4 SA 122 (B).

182 See *Neethling* (fn 38) 302 f.

183 *Makulu Plastics & Packaging CC v Born Free Investments 128 (Pty) Ltd* 2013 1 SA 377 (GSJ) 381–383.

184 See *Loubser/Midgley* (fn 4) 234.

185 *Loubser/Midgley* (fn 4) 234.

186 See eg *Hamman v Moolman* 1968 4 SA 340 (A); *Du Plessis v Semmelink* 1976 2 SA 500 (T).

187 See eg *Kern Trust (Edms) Bpk v Hurter* 1981 3 SA 607 (C).

188 1991 4 SA 559 (A); see also *ABSA Bank Ltd v Fouche* 2003 1 SA 176 (SCA) 180, 185; *OK Bazaars (1929) Ltd v Standard Bank of South Africa Ltd* 2002 3 SA 688 (SCA) 695; *Thatcher v Katz* 2006 6 SA 407 (C) 411; cf also *McCann v Goodall Group Operations (Pty) Ltd* 1995 2 SA 718 (C) 721.

189 See *Bayer South Africa (Pty) Ltd v Frost* 1991 4 SA 559 (A) 568, 570.

190 In this regard Corbett CJ (ibid) remarked that each case must be decided in light of the ordinary delictual principles for negligent misrepresentation. Principles and terminology

rise to a delictual claim for damages, even though the misrepresentation induced the plaintiff to conclude a contract with the party who made it.[191]

B. LIABILITY OF PROFESSIONALS

The liability of professionals (experts) is based on ordinary principles of delict,[192] 61
but in the case of an expert the test for negligence in respect of the exercise of the expert activity is the test of the so-called reasonable expert; in other words, the reasonable dentist, reasonable medical doctor, reasonable attorney, reasonable banker, reasonable auditor or accountant, reasonable engineer and architect, etc. The relationship between a professional and his client (patient) is usually but not necessarily a contractual one.[193] Where such a relationship exists, and the professional negligently causes personal injury (eg medical doctor), property damage (eg engineer) or even pure economic loss (eg banker) to a client, the latter may sue the professional *ex contractu* for breach of contract as well as *ex delicto* provided that all the elements of a delict are present.[194] In these cases, a duty to act with reasonable care and skill as an implied term of the contract can also give rise to a delictual duty with a similar content.[195]

CASES

CASE 1. THE UNATTRACTIVE SHOPPING MALL

C may not bring a claim in contract against D simply for the reason that there 62
is no contractual relationship between the two parties. C's only hope of success is a claim in delict for pure economic loss (lost earnings) against D, based on the latter's breach of his contractual obligation to Z (and other tenants) to keep the shopping mall clean and attractive. In principle South African law is not opposed to such a claim, provided that all the requirements for delictual liability, especially wrongfulness, have been met.[196] As to wrongfulness, the yardstick that must be applied is the general criterion of reasonableness

---

of contract law should preferably be avoided, unless it is possible to reconcile such principles with applicable delictual principles (see further *Neethling/Potgieter* (fn 4) 323 fn 261; above fn 3).

191 See also *Loubser/Midgley* (fn 4) 234.

192 See *Loubser/Midgley* (fn 4) 325 f; cf *Neethling/Potgieter* (fn 4) 145–147.

193 See *Louber/Midgley* (fn 4) 327, 331, 333, 336, 340 2.

194 As explained above nos 50–53.

195 See *Louber/Midgley* (fn 4) 325 70.

196 See *Country Cloud Trading CC v MEC, Department of Infrastructure Developmen* 2014 2 SA 214 (SCA); 2015 1 SA 1 (CC); above no 27.

or *boni mores*,[197] which requires the court to exercise a value judgement embracing all relevant facts and involving considerations of policy.[198]

63 The crucial question in this case is whether there were policy considerations that positively point to the extension of delictual liability to the present situation, but this does not seem to be so. First of all, D did not know or subjectively foresee that his failure would cause damage to C, since D was not informed about Z's subletting to C.[199] This factor is often an important, even a decisive factor in the determination of wrongfulness in instances of pure economic loss.[200] Secondly, the imposition of liability could lead to indeterminate liability since all the other tenants in the shopping mall would then also be able to claim.[201] Thirdly, C was not 'vulnerable to the risk of harm', which signifies that he could reasonably have avoided the harm suffered by other means. The ability or otherwise of a plaintiff to protect himself against damage nowadays also plays an important role in ascertaining liability for pure economic loss.[202] In this case C could have protected himself against his loss in his contract with Z.[203] Consequently C's claim against D *ex delicto* would probably also fail.

CASE 2. THE IDLE LAWYER

64 This case concerns the action of the disappointed beneficiary.[204] As with the previous case, W's daughters will not have a contractual claim against D.

197 See eg *Hirschowitz Flionis v Bartlett* 2006 3 SA 575 (SCA) 588, 589; *Santam Bpk v Henery* 1999 3 SA 421 (SCA) 430.

198 See eg *Indac Electronics (Pty) Ltd v Volkskas Bank Ltd* 1992 1 SA 783 (A) 797; *Steenkamp NO v Provincial Tender Board, Eastern Cape* 2007 3 SA 121 (CC) 139; *Mediterranean Shipping Co (Pty) Ltd v Tebe Trading (Pty) Ltd* [2007] 2 All SA 489 (SCA) 494; *Fourway Haulage SA (Pty) Ltd v SA National Roads Agency Ltd* 2009 2 SA 150 (SCA) 156; *BOE Bank Ltd v Ries* 2002 2 SA 39 (SCA) 46 f.

199 See eg *Coronation Brick (Pty) Ltd v Strachan Construction Co (Pty) Ltd* 1982 4 SA 371 (D) 386; *BOE Bank Ltd v Ries* 2002 2 SA 39 (SCA) 49; *Neethling/Potgieter* (fn 4) 309.

200 See eg *BOE Bank Ltd v Ries* 2002 2 SA 39 (SCA) 49; *Neethling/Potgieter* (fn 4) 309 fn 169.

201 See eg *Greenfield Engineering Works (Pty) Ltd v NKR Construction (Pty) Ltd* 1978 4 SA 901 (N) 916 f; *Neethling/Potgieter* (fn 4) 311. In *Fourway Haulage SA (Pty) Ltd v SA National Roads Agency Ltd* 2009 2 SA 150 (SCA) 161 the court stated 'that liability will more readily be imposed for a single loss of a single identifiable plaintiff occurring but once and which is unlikely to bring in its train a multiplicity of actions'.

202 *Neethling/Potgieter* (fn 4) 312.

203 See *AB Ventures Ltd v Siemens Ltd* 2011 4 SA 614 (SCA) where the court denied a delictual claim because in its view the plaintiff could have protected itself in its contract with a third party, but failed to do so. Cf also eg *Trustees, Two Oceans Aquarium Trust v Kantey & Templer (Pty) Ltd* 2006 3 SA 138 (SCA) 149; *Fourway Haulage SA (Pty) Ltd v SA National Roads Agency Ltd* 2009 2 SA 150 (SCA) 162; *Mediterranean Shipping Co (Pty) Ltd v Tebe Trading (Pty) Ltd* [2007] 2 All SA 489 (SCA) 495; *Delphisure Group Insurance Brokers Cape (Pty) Ltd v Dippenaar* 2010 5 SA 499 (SCA) 508 f; *Neethling/Potgieter* (fn 4) 27 fn 87.

204 See above no 29.

However, as a result of the negligent non-compliance by D with the obligation arising from the contractual relationship between D and W, the daughters suffer damage in the form of pure economic loss. Any claim that they might have against him will therefore have to be delictual. The prejudiced beneficiaries will only succeed if their claim complies with all the ordinary requirements of a delict.[205] As with other cases of pure economic loss, the requirement of wrongfulness is of particular importance and will be based on the breach of a legal duty that D had to prevent damage to the beneficiaries.[206]

To ascertain whether such a duty existed, again the *boni mores* yardstick should be employed,[207] where the following factors may be strongly indicative of said duty:[208] the existence of the valid (professional) contract between D (as solicitor) and W (the testator) placing a duty on the defendant to act with the necessary care (professional skill) to ensure that a particular (testamentary) benefit will accrue to the beneficiaries;[209] D's knowledge that the beneficiaries would suffer loss as a result of his negligent omission;[210] practical steps could have been taken by D to prevent the economic loss by changing the will, having regard to the reasonableness of expenses involved and the relative ease with which the steps could have been taken;[211] and the absence of indeterminate liability since liability will be imposed for fixed losses of two identifiable plaintiffs occurring but once.[212] In light of these factors the daughters should succeed with their claim for £9,000 each. 65

CASE 3. THE DEFECTIVE HOUSE

Since there is no contractual relationship between D and C, C may not sue D *ex contractu* for the harm he suffered. However, D will have a delictual claim, both for compensation for his bodily injuries and for damages for the damage to his house, caused by the defect as a result of D's negligence. The exclusion clause in the contract between D and Z is not applicable to C as non-contracting third party.[213] The fact that C's claim arose five years after the house was built 66

205 *BOE Bank Ltd v Ries* 2002 2 SA 39 (SCA) 46.

206 See *Aucamp v University of Stellenbosch* 2002 4 SA 544 (C) 565–567; see also *J Neethling/ JM Potgieter*, Die hoogste hof van appèl gee hoop vir die teleurgestelde begunstigde ('disappointed beneficiary') [2002] THRHR 477 f.

207 See eg *Minister for Safety and Security v Scott* [2014] 3 All SA 306 para 32; *Neethling/Potgieter* (fn 4) 307 f.

208 See *Neethling/Potgieter* (fn 4) 313.

209 *Neethling/Potgieter* (fn 4) 313; *BOE Bank Ltd v Ries* 2002 2 SA 39 (SCA) 47.

210 Cf above no 62 f.

211 Cf eg *Hirschowitz Flionis v Bartlett* 2006 3 SA 575 (SCA) 589; *Neethling/Potgieter* (fn 4) 310.

212 Cf above no 63.

213 Cf above nos 45 f, 48.

by D also does not affect its validity since the prescription of his claim only commences to run the moment all the elements of a delict are present, and C has knowledge of the identity of the wrongdoer (D) and the facts from which the delict arises.[214] C should therefore succeed *ex delicto*.

CASE 4. APARTMENT IN FLAMES

67 As indicated,[215] the delictual actions for pain and suffering and the Aquilian action for consequential patrimonial loss (as a result of personal injury), and the contractual action concur in circumstances where breach of contract also results in a wrongful and culpable infringement of the physical-mental integrity of the wronged contracting party. In this case, C may thus claim patrimonial damages (eg for medical expenses) resulting from her physical injuries caused by the negligent landlord's breach of the contract of lease, either *ex contractu* or with the Aquilian action, from D.[216] However, C may not claim compensation for pain and suffering experienced as a result of D's breach of contract with the contractual action; for this purpose the delictual action for pain and suffering must be employed.[217]

CASE 5. INJURED SKIER

68 As with the previous case, a concurrence of the delictual actions for pain and suffering and the Aquilian action for patrimonial damages, and the contractual action for patrimonial damages seems to be at hand. It is assumed that D1 will be contractually liable against C for breach of contract by not maintaining the ski lift in a safe operating condition. As to delictual liability, it will be difficult to prove negligence on D1's side because the reasons why the ski lift derailed and fell were not fully clarified. It is submitted that the application of the maxim *res ipsa loquitur* may solve the issue. This phrase normally refers to a situation where the facts of the matter are such as to give rise to an inference of negligent conduct[218] and finds application 'where the only known facts, relating to negligence, consist of the occurrence itself'.[219] This phrase may thus be applied where, as in the present case, the ski lift derailed and fell because this event will not usually occur

214 Cf above no 33 on the Prescription Act 68 of 1969.
215 Above no 54.
216 Cf above no 55.
217 See *Administrator, Natal v Edouard* 1990 3 SA 581 (A) 596 f.
218 *Boberg* (fn 4) 377 f; *Neethling/Potgieter* (fn 4) 161 f.
219 *Sardi v Standard & General Insurance Co Ltd* 1977 3 SA 776 (A) 778.

without accompanying negligence.[220] However, D1 may still submit evidence to show that the occurrence in question bears no relation to any negligent conduct on his part.[221] Where this is not possible, C will be able to claim patrimonial damages as well as compensation for pain and suffering for his personal injuries *ex delicto* from D1.

69 As far as C's claim against D2 is concerned, D2's defence that this was a case of contractual liability which was not covered under D1's policy can only succeed if D1 did not commit a delict (tort) against C. However, as indicated, in light of the application of the maxim *res ipsa loquitur* a strong case can be made that D1 indeed caused C's injuries negligently and will therefore be delictually liable. Consequently, C may be able to claim from D2 patrimonial damages and compensation for pain and suffering up to the amount of €900,000.

CASE 6. EXPLODING CAR

70 It is clear that C does not have a claim for breach of contract against D1 or D2 as the warranty against all defects expired after two years. C will therefore have to claim *ex delicto* against both defendants for the damage caused by the defect. Product liability for defective products can, in South African law, be based on two grounds. First of all, the common law of product liability is based on the Aquilian action and its ordinary requirements must thus be satisfied. Accordingly, all the elements of a delict, that is conduct, wrongfulness, fault, causation and damage must be present for delictual liability to ensue.[222] Secondly, product liability can be based on sec 61 of the Consumer Protection Act 68 of 2008 which introduced strict liability by providing that inter alia the manufacturer or retailer of goods is liable for harm caused to consumers by defective goods, irrespective of the presence or absence of negligence.[223]

71 As to common law liability, it will be difficult to prove causation and negligence on D1's part. It stands to reason that D1 was not responsible for the defect that destroyed the car (absence of factual causation). However, if D1 knew about the defect or could reasonably have discovered it, his negligent conduct contributed

220 *Neethling/Potgieter* (fn 4) 161.

221 See in general *Pringle v Administrator Transvaal* 1990 2 SA 379 (W); *Bayer South Africa (Pty) Ltd v Viljoen* 1990 2 SA 647 (A).

222 See eg *Wagener and Cuttings v Pharmacare Ltd* 2003 4 SA 285 (SCA) 300; *Ciba-Geigy (Pty) Ltd v Lushof Farms (Pty) Ltd* 2002 2 SA 447 (SCA) 470 f; *Freddy Hirsch Group (Pty) Ltd v Chickenland (Pty) Ltd* 2011 4 SA 276 (SCA) 293. See also *Loubser/Reid* (fn 49) 39 f; *Neethling/Potgieter* (fn 4) 335 f.

223 See *Loubser/Reid* (fn 49) 56 f; *Neethling/Potgieter* (fn 4) 399 f.

to C's damage and he may be liable *ex delicto*.[224] Be that as it may, C's chances of success seem to be slim. On the other hand, C may succeed with the Aquilian action against D2. As was stated in *Ciba-Geigy (Pty) Ltd v Lushof Farms (Pty) Ltd*,[225] it 'is actually self-evident that, according to the legal convictions of the community, a manufacturer acts incorrectly and therefore wrongfully if he makes a product commercially available which in the course of its designated use, and due to a defect, causes damage to the consumer thereof'. The only remaining matter is whether D2 caused the defect negligently.[226] Since it is normally very difficult for the prejudiced party to prove this, his onus should be alleviated by a specific application of the doctrine of *res ipsa loquitur*.[227] It is submitted that the *res ipsa loquitur* inference of negligence should at least be made where a consumer proves that he was prejudiced by a defective product and that the product was in that state when the manufacturer abandoned his control over it. Seen thus, C should succeed against D2 with the Aquilian action.

72 As to liability under the Consumer Protection Act, C should be able to claim compensation for his full damage from D2 since the destruction of his car was caused by the car's defective fuel line. The negligence or otherwise of D2 is irrelevant because his liability is strict. Although the Act also makes provision for the strict product liability of D1 as a retailer of new cars, he may have a defence in terms of sec 61(4) which provides that he may escape liability if it was unreasonable to expect him (as a retailer) to have discovered the defect,[228] and this seems to be the case here.

CASE 7. RACING BOAT BURNING

73 As in the previous case, C does not have a claim for breach of contract against D since the warranty against all defects expired after two years. The common law implied warranty against latent defects will also not be of assistance to C since consequential damages may only be claimed in special cases not applicable

224 Cf *A Gibb and Son (Pty) Ltd v Taylor and Mitchell Timber Supply Co (Pty) Ltd* 1975 2 SA 457 (W) 464.

225 2002 2 SA 447 (SCA) 470 (translation); cf *Freddy Hirsch Group (Pty) Ltd v Chickenland (Pty) Ltd* 2011 4 SA 276 (SCA) 294 f; see also *Loubser/Midgley* (fn 4) 305 f.

226 See *Neethling/Potgieter* (fn 4) 337 f; cf also *Combrinck Chiropraktiese Kliniek (Edms) Bpk v Datsun Motor Vehicle Distributors (Pty) Ltd* 1972 4 SA 185 (T) 190); *Bayer South Africa (Pty) Ltd v Viljoen* 1990 2 SA 647 (A) 661 f.

227 See *Neethling/Potgieter* (fn 4) 338 f; cf above no 68 f.

228 See *Loubser/Reid* (fn 49) 133. They are critical of the defence. According to them this section offers retailers a means of escaping strict liability in all situations where they can establish that their conduct was reasonable and therefore blameless, which is something akin to readmitting fault-based liability through the back door.

in casu.[229] C will therefore have to claim *ex delicto* against D for the damage caused by the defect. Since D is not the manufacturer, importer, distributor or retailer of the defective navigation equipment, the strict liability of the Consumer Protection Act will not be applicable to him.[230] Accordingly, C must base his claim on the common law Aquilian action. Since the requirements of an act, wrongfulness and factual causation present no problems, C will have to prove, firstly, that D was negligent in adding the defective equipment, that is, that he should reasonably have foreseen that the equipment was defective and that it could cause damage to the boat, and that he should have taken reasonable steps to prevent it.[231] In this regard the application of the doctrine of *res ipsa loquitur* may be of assistance to C.[232] It is submitted that the *res ipsa loquitur* inference of negligence should be made where C proves that he was prejudiced by a defective product and that the product was in that state when D abandoned his control over it. Secondly, C must also prove legal causation, that is that the remote consequence of repatriation expenses should reasonably be imputed to D.[233]

CASE 8. INSIDIOUS REPORT

C can sue D in contract as well as in delict. It is clear that D, by filing the 74
disparaging report on company Z which led C to terminate its contract with Z, was as an employee disrupting D's company from within, so that he, while still in the employment in C, could set up his own company and conclude a similar contract with Z. D's subversive conduct, while in the employment of C, undoubtedly constitutes a breach of his employment contract with C for which he has the ordinary contractual remedies at his disposal.[234] The question arises whether the conduct complained of also constitutes unlawful competition as a delictual cause of action. As said,[235] this will only be the case if, apart from breach of contract, the conduct also wrongfully and culpably infringes a legally protected interest which exists independently of the contract. In South African law, the goodwill of a business has been recognised as such an interest,[236] and infringement of goodwill will be wrongful if it is in conflict with the competition principle or the *boni mores* yardstick.[237] Whether this is the case will naturally depend on the

229 See *Loubser/Reid* (fn 49) 27.
230 Cf above nos 70, 72.
231 See *Neethling/Potgieter* (fn 4) 137 f.
232 See *Neethling/Potgieter* (fn 4) 338 f; cf above nos 68 f, 71.
233 See *Neethling/Potgieter* (fn 4) 200–203.
234 See *Neethling* (fn 38) 251.
235 Above nos 48, 50.
236 See *Neethling* (fn 38) 106 f.
237 See *Neethling* (fn 38) 123 f as to these criteria for wrongfulness; see also *Masstores (Pty) Ltd v Pick 'n Pay Retailers (Pty) Ltd* 2017 1 SA 613 (CC) where the competition principle was

relevant circumstances. It almost stands to reason that D's subversive conduct with the aim of setting up a competing business with his employer will be branded as wrongful and also ground a delictual action against D.[238]

CASE 9. CIRCULAR LETTER

75 C's claim cannot be based on breach of contract. He must therefore sue D *ex delicto*. If D's defamatory statements about C cannot be justified by any recognised ground of justification, such as that the statements are true and in the public interest or constitutes fair comment on matters that are true and in the public interest,[239] C can institute an *actio iuiuriarum* to claim *solatium* (satisfaction) for the intentional infringement of his right to a good name (*fama*). He can also claim damages for his patrimonial loss as a result of customers refraining from dealing with him, simultaneously infringing the goodwill of his new company Z.[240]

CASE 10. SHORTAGE OF SUPPLY

76 D's threat to discontinue the distribution of parts to C if C does not comply with D's demands may constitute duress (improper pressure)[241] since it forced C to accept the new conditions. Generally persons are free to decide with whom they want to contract.[242] But if the decision was obtained by improper means, the contract is voidable at the option of C and he may in a proper case also claim damages since duress is a delict giving rise to the Aquilian action.[243] However,

---

recognised and applied for the first time by our highest court to ascertain the unlawfulness of competition.

238 An analogous case can be found in *Hushon SA (Pty) Ltd v Pictech (Pty) Ltd* 1997 4 SA 399 (SCA). A was an importer of certain air-conditioning equipment from Korea. B was engaged in a similar business but it imported its equipment from Japan. The managing director of B conceived a scheme whereby certain key personnel of A (his director and sales manager) were encouraged to feed disinformation to A's Korean supplier about A's capabilities for dealing adequately in the supplier's products. The aim of the scheme was to undermine the supplier's confidence in A and eventually eliminating A as a competitor, in order to secure an advantage for a company of B and in this way to protect the interests of B and its Japanese supplier. Nienaber JA (406) did not hesitate to condemn B and its co-conspirators' conduct in their plot to assassinate A commercially, and to find all of them jointly and severally liable for the loss that A suffered as a result of the conspiracy.

239 See *Neethling/Potgieter* (fn 4) 351 f, 357 f.

240 See *Neethling/Potgieter* (fn 4) 342; *Neethling* (fn 38) 268 f; cf *Media 24 Ltd v SA Taxi Securitization* 2011 5 SA 329 (SCA).

241 See *Hutchison/Pretorius* (fn 9) 136 f.

242 *Times Media Ltd v SABC* 1990 4 SA 604 (W) 607; *Neethling* (fn 38) 287.

243 *Hutchison/Pretorius* (fn 9) 137, 140.

as pointed out by Hutchison and Pretorius,[244] it is an open question whether a threat to the purely economic interests of the other party (as in the present case with C) can constitute actionable duress in South African law. Although such economic duress may be found to exist in appropriate cases, in *Medscheme Holdings (Pty) (Ltd) v Bhamjee*[245] the court held that such cases are likely to be rare, and explained:

> 'For it is not unlawful, in general, to cause economic harm, or even to cause economic ruin, to another, nor can it generally be unconscionable to do so in a competitive economy. In commercial bargaining the exercise of free will (if that can ever exist in any pure form of the term) is always fettered to some degree by the expectation of gain or the fear of loss ... [H]ard bargaining is not the equivalent of duress, and that is so even where the bargain is the product of an imbalance in bargaining power. Something more ... would need to exist for economic bargaining to be illegitimate or unconscionable and thus to constitute duress.'

Seen in this light, C's chances of success are slight.

CASE 11. INJURED ROCK STAR

As said,[246] it has for a long time been accepted as trite law that a person (entrepreneur) who stands in a contractual relationship to an injured person (client) may, for fear of opening the door for unlimited liability, not claim for the loss of business where the injury constituted a negligent interference with the contractual relationship. However, in *Minister for Safety and Security v Scott*[247] the court accepted that any negligent conduct by a third party which causes the infringement of a contractual personal right may, in principle, found the Aquilian action. The fear of unlimited liability can be allayed by the correct application of all the elements of a delict. The requirement of wrongfulness, especially, plays an important part since prejudice almost always, as in the present case, takes the form of pure economic loss.[248] The *boni mores* yardstick, informed by policy considerations, should be applied. In this regard, the wrongdoer's subjective knowledge that the plaintiff will be prejudiced[249] will be of paramount importance in establishing wrongfulness.[250] In light of this, C's action against 77

244 *Hutchison/Pretorius* (fn 9) 139.
245 2005 5 SA 339 (SCA) 346.
246 See above no 56.
247 [2014] 3 All SA 306 paras 31 f, 36.
248 Although in the present case the patrimonial loss involved was indeed the result of personal injuries it did not concern the *plaintiff's* injuries (see *Neethling/Potgieter* (fn 4) 306 fn 150).
249 See *Lanco Engineering CC v Aris Box Manufacturers (Pty) Ltd* 1993 4 SA 378 (D) 388 f.
250 See *Neethling/Potgieter* (fn 4) 309–313.

D will probably fail for lack of wrongfulness because D did not foresee that C would suffer economic loss as a result of the rock star's injuries.

CASE 12. EQUIPMENT DESTROYED

78 As with the previous case, in this case there was also a negligent interference with the contractual relationship between C and D1 by D2, but the difference between the two cases is that C suffered property damage (destruction of equipment) with consequential financial loss (cancellation of concert) and not pure economic loss. C may claim damages for his total loss from D2 who caused the accident since all the requirements of the Aquilian action have been met. C will, however, not be able to claim damages from D1, neither for breach of their contract of lease since the accident was caused by D2, thereby rendering delivery of the equipment impossible,[251] nor *ex delicto* since D1 did not cause the accident.

CASE 13. SLIPPING ON A LETTUCE LEAF

79 There is no question of liability in contract simply because no contract was concluded. This situation may qualify as liability *ex delicto* if D, as party to a potential contract with C, commits a delict in the pre-contractual phase (before C bought anything).[252] The question is therefore simply whether D was negligent with regard to C's slipping on the lettuce leaf and breaking her leg. In *Gordon v Da Mata*[253] the court answered the question in the affirmative. Here the plaintiff slipped on a cabbage leaf on the floor of the defendant's greengrocery. The cabbage leaf had fallen on the floor while the defendant's assistant was slashing off cabbage leaves. The court held that a reasonable person would definitely have taken steps to prevent leaves from falling onto the floor by collecting them in a receptacle because this would not have required much trouble or high cost.[254] C should therefore succeed with her claim in tort.

---

251 See *Hutchison/Pretorius* (fn 9) 301 f.

252 Cf above no 60.

253 1969 3 SA 285 (A).

254 Cf however *City of Salisbury v King* 1970 2 SA 528 (RA) where the court had to decide whether it was negligent to leave potentially slippery vegetable matter lying on a market floor. The plaintiff slipped on a piece of vegetable on the floor of a large market while the sale of vegetables was in progress. The court held that the mere presence of vegetable matter on a market floor did not in itself indicate negligent conduct; it would be unreasonable, expensive and unrealistic to expect the immediate removal of vegetable matter as it fell onto the floor.

CASE 14. TEST DRIVE

As with the previous case no contract has been concluded as the parties were still negotiating. There is thus no question of liability in contract. This situation may, however, qualify as a pre-contractual situation where liability *ex delicto* will apply if D, as party to a potential contract with C, commits a delict in the pre-contractual phase (before the negotiations concerning the car were finalised).[255] The question is therefore whether D was negligent with regard to the smashing of the car against the tree. If so, C can sue D *ex delicto* for damages. 80

CASE 15. BREACH OF NEGOTIATIONS

Persons entering into negotiations to conclude a contract are generally free to terminate the negotiations at any time. But where a party, such as D *in casu*, creates an expectation that a contract may eventually be concluded, the breaking off of negotiations may have legal consequences.[256] In South African law, the courts have accepted that the principle of *bona fides* is applicable to pre-contractual negotiations, that is, 'it applies to the very process of reaching *consensus*'.[257] However, according to Hutchison and Pretorius,[258] generally a party breaking off negotiations will not incur delictual liability since the other party relying on a representation that the contract will be concluded – in this case that D will continue negotiations – usually takes a calculated risk that this will not eventuate.[259] For this reason C's claim against D will probably fail. 81

CASE 16. NON-DISCLOSURE OF RELEVANT FACTS

This is a clear case of pre-contractual liability *ex delicto* where a party to a potential contract induces the other party by a negligent misrepresentation to enter into the contract and thus commits a delict in the pre-contractual phase.[260] It stands to reason that all the requirements of a delict have to be met.[261] *In casu* there was an act in the form of an omission which comprised of the non-disclosure of information about the machine's reduced performance 82

---

255 Cf above no 60.

256 See *Hutchison/Pretorius* (fn 9) 61 f.

257 See *Savage and Lovemore Mining (Pty) Ltd v International Shipping Co (Pty) Ltd* 19872 SA 149 (W) 198; *Hutchison/Pretorius* (fn 9) 62.

258 *Hutchison/Pretorius* (fn 9) 62.

259 Cf *Murray v McLean* 1970 1 SA 133 (R) 137 f.

260 See above no 60.

261 See *Bayer South Africa (Pty) Ltd v Frost* 1991 4 SA 559 (A); *Loubser/Midgley* (fn 4) 234.

when used on steep fields.[262] Wrongfulness depends on whether there was a legal duty to furnish the correct information in the particular circumstances, and this is ascertained with reference to the reasonableness or *boni mores* criterion.[263] It has been held that where a person has specific information in his exclusive possession by reason of his particular occupation, there is a legal duty on him to convey that information.[264] In *Bayer South Africa (Pty) Ltd v Frost*,[265] the court took into account that the misrepresentation in that case 'related to technical matters concerning a new product about which [plaintiff] as a lay customer would necessarily be ignorant and [defendant] as the distributor would, or should, be knowledgeable'. Accordingly, D had a legal duty to disclose full information about the harvester to C and acted wrongfully by failing to do so. Apart from contractual remedies,[266] C should therefore succeed *ex delicto* in his claim against D (assuming that negligence and causation were also present).

262 See *McCann v Goodall Group Operations (Pty) Ltd* 1995 2 SA 718 (C) 721, 726; *Bowley Steels (Pty) Ltd v Dalian Engineering (Pty) Ltd* 1996 2 SA 393 (T).

263 See eg *Siman and Co (Pty) Ltd v Barclays National Bank Ltd* 1984 2 SA 888 (A) 913 f; *Lillicrap, Wassenaar and Partners v Pilkington Brothers (SA) (Pty) Ltd* 1985 1 SA 475 (A) 498; *McCann v Goodall Group Operations (Pty) Ltd* 1995 2 SA 718 (C) 722 f.

264 See *Neethling/Potgieter* (fn 4) 317. Besides, where there is a contractual relationship between the parties, such persons have a duty *inter partes* to furnish correct information concerning a matter arising from the contract and relating to its implementation. In *McCann v Goodall Group Operations (Pty) Ltd* 1995 2 SA 718 (C) 726 the court held that a delictual duty to disclose the full particulars arises inter alia where the defendant 'has knowledge of certain unusual characteristics relating to or circumstances surrounding the transaction'.

265 1991 4 SA 559 (A) 575.

266 See *Hutchison/Pretorius* (fn 9) 122 f.

THE BORDERLINES OF TORT LAW IN SPAIN

Miquel MARTÍN-CASALS and Albert RUDA-GONZÁLEZ*

QUESTIONS

I. Tracing the Borderlines 509
  A. Distinction between Tort and Contract 509
  B. Existence of a 'Grey Zone' in Between? 511
  C. Common or Different Rules Regulating Tort and Contract 513
  D. Application of Common Rules in a Different Way 514
II. Main Differences between Tortious and Contractual Liability 515
  A. Differences as Regards the Foundations of Liability 515
  B. Differences as Regards Causation 520
  C. Differences as Regards Remedies 521
    1) Degree of Certainty of the Damage 521
    2) Compensation for Non-Pecuniary Loss 522
    3) Compensation for Loss of Earnings and for Loss of Chance 523
    4) Restitutionary Damages 524
    5) Aggravated and Exemplary (or Punitive) Damages 525
    6) Other Remedies 526
  D. Differences as Regards Recoverability of 'Pure Economic Losses' 528
  E. Differences as Regards Liability for Others 528
  F. Differences as Regards Liability in the Case of Multiple Tortfeasors/ Breaching Parties 530
  G. Differences as Regards the Persons Who May be Protected 531
  H. Differences as Regards Defences 535
  I. Differences as Regards Limitation Periods 537
  J. Differences as Regards Proof 538
  K. Other Differences 539
      1) Private International Law 539

* This contribution has been written in the framework of the research project DER2016-77229-R (Spanish Ministry of Economy and Competitiveness) of which the authors are co-directors.

2) Rules of Jurisdiction 540
3) Capacity 540
L. Reasons for the Differences 541
III. Limitation or Exclusion of Liability Arising from Tort and from Contract 542
A. Statutory Provisions Authorising a Limitation or Exclusion of Liability 542
B. Limitation or Exclusion of Contractual and Tortious Liability by Contract 543
1) Is it Possible to Limit or Exclude Contractual and Tortious Liability under a Contract? 543
2) To What Extent Can a Contractual Exclusion Provide a Defence to a Third Party to the Contract? 545
IV. Non-Concurrence or Concurrence of Actions 545
A. Overview 545
1) Areas of Overlap between Tort and Contract 545
2) Approach to Non-Concurrence and Concurrence of Actions 547
B. Concurrence/Exclusion of Actions for the Protection Against Personal Injury 550
C. Concurrence/Exclusion of Actions for the Protection of Property 550
D. Concurrence/Exclusion in the Case of Interference with Contractual Rights 550
1) Interference with a Contractual Relationship 550
2) Loss of Business due to Personal Injury to Someone Else's Employees or Clients or to Property Damage to the Entrepreneur 550
V. Specific Situations 552
A. Pre-Contractual Liability 552
B. Liability of Professionals 555

CASES

Case 1. The Unattractive Shopping Mall 557
Case 2. The Idle Lawyer 558
Case 3. The Defective House 559
Case 4. Apartment in Flames 559
Case 5. Injured Skier 560
Case 6. Exploding Car 560
Case 7. Racing Boat Burning 561
Case 8. Insidious Report 562
Case 9. Circular Letter 563

Case 10. Shortage of Supply 563
Case 11. Injured Rock Star 564
Case 12. Equipment Destroyed 564
Case 13. Slipping on a Lettuce Leaf 565
Case 14. Test Drive 565
Case 15. Breach of Negotiations 566
Case 16. Non-Disclosure of Relevant Facts 566

QUESTIONS

I. TRACING THE BORDERLINES

A. DISTINCTION BETWEEN TORT AND CONTRACT

The Spanish Civil Code (CC) has followed the Franco-Italian model with regard to the classification of the so-called 'sources' of obligations, a model which in its turn has its origin in the Institutes of Justinian (I. 3, 13, 2). As is well known, the latter arranged obligations in four classes, namely contractual, quasi-contractual, delictual, and quasi-delictual. The Civil Code devotes its Book 4 to the rules on 'Obligations and Contracts'. Title I of that Book starts with a set of 'General Provisions', among which a rule on 'sources of obligations' is included (art 1089), according to which, 'Obligations arise from the law, from contracts and quasi-contracts and from unlawful acts or omissions or those in which there is any kind of fault or negligence'.[1] A similar rule can be found in the private law of the regional civil law of Navarre (art 488 of the 'Compilation').[2] 1

Contract as such is not defined by the Civil Code; however, it is provided that 'contract exists from the time where one or several persons consent to bind themselves vis-à-vis another or others to give something or to provide a service' (art 1254). Therefore, the essence of contract is that the parties bind themselves (see also art 1258) and they may thus enforce such agreement as if it was law *inter partes* (art 1901). The contract is thus *lex contractus* (as the Decision of the Supreme Court (Sentencia del Tribunal Supremo, STS) 17.10.2001 (RJ 2001, 8641) puts it). By contrast, obligations arising from tort are subject to the tort law provisions in the Civil Code itself (arts 1902–1910). Tort is also devoid of statutory definition, however the general rule is that whoever causes damage to another in a negligent way is bound to compensate him (art 1902). 2

---

1 Unless otherwise stated, the official translation by the Spanish Ministry of Justice is used in this report. See <www.mjusticia.gob.es/cs/Satellite/es/1288774502225/ListaPublicaciones.html?param1=1288775993122>.

2 *Ley 1/1973, de 1 de marzo, por la que se aprueba la Compilación del Derecho Civil Foral de Navarra* (Boletín Oficial del Estado (BOE) no 57, 7.3.1973).

3 The Spanish Civil Code tackles both kinds of liability in a separate way. Contract law rules are provided for in Book 4, Title II ('On contracts', ie arts 1254–1886), whereas tort law rules are included in Chapter II ('On the obligations which arise from fault or negligence') of Title XVI ('On the obligations which are created without an agreement') of the same Book (arts 1902–1910). Nevertheless, since both tort and contract are among the so-called sources of the obligations (pursuant to art 1089 CC), some rules seem to be common to both of them, in particular the chapter 'On obligations' (Book 4, Title I, ie arts 1088–1253). Nonetheless, art 1093 CC provides that obligations arising from negligent acts or omissions which are not punished by the law will be governed by the tort law provisions in the same Civil Code (arts 1902–1910). As a result, the provisions on the nature and effects of the obligations will not, as a rule, govern tort liability – except for the case where the tortfeasor breaches his duty to compensate for damage caused.[3]

4 Therefore the reason why Spanish law distinguishes between tort and contract is twofold: (a) mere historical tradition, since such a distinction could already be found in other legal systems which had a strong influence on the Spanish codification of private law; and (b) the distinction allows the legislature to shape the statutory rules regarding each of the sources of the obligations, by keeping those general rules applicable to all of them in one place, and then adding specific sets of rules for each of them in the other. Nevertheless, the elaboration of a general theory on the law of obligations has brought with it the idea that the principles which govern liability of the debtor are the same irrespective of whether the obligation derives from contract or tort. In that vein, some legal scholars have advocated in favour of a unification of both liability regimes.[4] Such a proposal has been opposed by others who stress the different function of contract – ie the distribution of risks between the parties – in contrast to tort.[5]

5 A parallel may be drawn with the statutory regime on the liability of public authorities. Again, a distinction is made between contract and tort. The rules on the former are laid down in the Act on the Contracts of the Public Sector

---

3 See *LF Reglero Campos/F Peña López*, Capítulo I: Conceptos generales y elementos de delimitación, in: LF Reglero Campos/JM Busto Lago (eds), Tratado de responsabilidad civil (5th edn 2014) 65–263, at 160.

4 See *M Espinosa de Rueda Jover*, Aspectos de la responsabilidad civil, con especial referencia al daño moral, Anales de Derecho 1986, no 9, 41–68, 48 and *M Yzquierdo Tolsada*, La zona fronteriza entre la responsabilidad contractual y la aquiliana. Razones para una moderada unificación, Revista Crítica de Derecho Inmobiliario (RCDI) 1991, vol 603, 443–489, at 448 ff.

5 See *FA Pantaleón Prieto*, El sistema de responsabilidad contractual (materiales para un debate), Anuario de Derecho Civil (ADC) 1991, 1019–1092, at 1020.

(LCSP).[6] By contrast, the liability of public authorities in tort is governed by the Act on the Legal Regime of the Public Sector (LRJAP),[7] arts 32–36.

B. EXISTENCE OF A 'GREY ZONE' IN BETWEEN?

In principle, liability is contractual whenever damage derives from a violation of the contractual relationship between the parties, whereas it is tortious whenever – even though a previous contractual relationship may exist between the same – damage has not been caused 'within the strict orbit of what was agreed upon' (*la estricta órbita de lo pactado*). This is so when damage is considered to be 'foreign' or 'alien' to the nature of that legal transaction (among others, STS 4.3.2009 (RJ 2009, 1873)). So, for instance, compensation for damage allegedly derived from consumption or addiction to tobacco cannot be claimed in contract against the manufacturer, since the contractual relationship exists only as regards the sellers (STS 22.12.2009 (RJ 2009, 162)).[8] However, as these decisions acknowledge, it cannot be excluded that there are 'mixed areas' in between. 6

This is the case firstly where there is a breach of contract as regards legally protected goods of special importance, such as life or physical integrity. These may be deemed to be the object of a general duty of protection, which case law expresses by way of the so-called principle of 'unity of the civil fault' (*unidad de culpa civil*).[9] However, this approach neglects the fact that the relevant aspect is whether the damage derives from the breach of contract or not.[10] 7

A second grey area may be found in cases where a duty of protection or safety is infringed, in particular in the case of the performance of a transport contract. However, the prevailing opinion holds that such a duty is accessory to the main obligation in the contract (transporting the person or thing) and, therefore, liability is contractual.[11] Such obligations may be derived from the general duty of good faith in contract (art 1258 CC). A similar reasoning may exist with regard 8

---

6 *Ley 9/2017, de 8 de noviembre, de Contratos del Sector Público, por la que se transponen al ordenamiento jurídico español las Directivas del Parlamento Europeo y del Consejo 2014/23/UE y 2014/24/UE, de 26 de febrero de 2014* (BOE no 272, 9.11.2017), which supersedes the previous *Real Decreto Legislativo 3/2011, de 14 de noviembre, por el que se aprueba el texto refundido de la Ley de Contratos del Sector Público* (BOE no 276, 16.11.2011).

7 *Ley 40/2015, de 1 de octubre, de Régimen Jurídico del Sector Público* (BOE no 236, 2.10.2015).

8 The claim in tort was already time-barred so the court finally dismissed it.

9 On which see sec IV.A.2 below.

10 See *M Yzquierdo Tolsada*, Sistema de responsabilidad civil, contractual y extracontractual (2001) 96.

11 See *JJ Blanco Gómez*, La concurrencia de responsabilidad civil contractual y extracontractual en un mismo hecho dañoso. Problemática en derecho sustantivo español (1996) 131.

to damage suffered by a worker, which would be governed by contractual liability on the same tenet.[12] Nonetheless, there is some disagreement as regards case law, even between Chambers of the same Supreme Court – the Civil Chamber being in favour of the tortious nature of the claim, and the Social Chamber of its contractual nature. This has important consequences as regards the possibility to cumulate – Civil Chamber – or not – Social Chamber – the compensation award in tort with the amounts to be paid by social security by reason of the work accident.[13]

9 There are many other grey areas in which case law has stated that liability is contractual. In general, a mere pre-existing relationship between the parties in the accident may be a sufficient basis in order to deem the case to be governed by contract law. A remarkable case is damage caused within the framework of the relationship between co-owners – in spite of the fact that co-ownership is a property rights' situation (art 392 ff CC). Similarly, a relationship governed by public law, according to which one of the parties is bound to carry out certain public services, may again be sufficient for contract law to be applicable (as in STS 26.1.1984 (RJ 1984, 386): liability of the company responsible for managing the local sewage system for damage caused by a filtering of faecal waters). Legal scholarship has also suggested that liability derived from a quasi-contract such as *negotiorum gestio* is contractual,[14] although opinions to the contrary are not lacking.[15] A matter of further discussion is whether liability derived from mere social contact is contractual or tortious. As regards post-contractual liability, it is seen as an extension of contractual liability itself, and therefore deemed to be contractual.[16] A legal opinion makes a distinction depending on whether the contractual relationship has been extinguished or not. So, for instance, if an editor prints more book copies than agreed under the publishing contract, liability is contractual if printing occurred during the contract execution – as seems to have been the case in STS 14.10.1983 (RJ 1983, 5326) – and tortious in the opposite case.[17]

10 Another area where the contractual or tortious nature of the claim has been discussed is *culpa in contrahendo*, to be dealt with later.[18]

---

12 See ibid, 140 with further references.

13 See *F Gómez Pomar*, Responsabilidad extracontractual y otras fuentes de reparación de daños: 'Collateral Source Rule' y afines, InDret <www.indret.com> 2000, 1–10, at 5 ff, and *G Moliner Tamborero*, La responsabilidad civil derivada de accidente de trabajo: culpa contractual o culpa extracontractual, in: JA Moreno Martínez (ed), La responsabilidad civil y su problemática actual (2007) 689–716, at 698 and 706.

14 See *S Cavanillas Múgica/I Tapia Fernández*, La concurrencia de responsabilidad contractual y extracontractual: tratamiento sustantivo y procesal (1992) 9 with further references.

15 See *Yzquierdo* (fn 4) 458.

16 See ibid, 462.

17 See *R Bercovitz Rodríguez-Cano*, Comentario a la sentencia de 14 de octubre de 1983, Cuadernos Civitas de Jurisprudencia Civil (CCJC) 1983, vol 3, 993–1000, at 1000.

18 See sec V.1 below.

C. COMMON OR DIFFERENT RULES REGULATING TORT AND CONTRACT

As has been pointed out, both tort and contract are governed by the general rules 'On obligations' laid down in Book 4, Title I of the Civil Code. However, many of them will only be applicable to contract. This seems clear with regard to rules on conditions (arts 1113–1125) or terminus (arts 1125–1130), remedies in the case of bilateral contracts (art 1124 CC), so-called 'alternative obligations' – where the choice between one of several obligations is left to the debtor's choice (art 1131) – or rules on liquidation of damages (*cláusula penal*), whereby the parties provide in advance the compensation for contractual breach (arts 1152–1155). By contrast, rules on divisible or indivisible obligations (arts 1149–1151), extinction of the obligations (arts 1156–1213) and proof of the obligations (arts 1216–1230) seem applicable irrespective of whether the obligation arises from tort or contract. Most importantly, there is a Chapter 'On the nature and effects of the obligations' (Chapter II, Title I, Book 4), which lays down very general rules, also applicable to both – including the definition of fault (art 1104), the defence of force majeure or unforeseeable circumstances (art 1105), compensable damage (actual loss and loss of earnings, art 1106), delay (art 1108) and payment of interest (art 1109), payment (art 1110), the action of subrogation (art 1111) and transmissibility of the obligation (art 1112). 11

Apart from that, the Civil Code provides that civil obligations deriving from crimes or misdemeanours will be governed by the Criminal Code (CP)[19] (art 1092 CC). In practice, it is usual to refer to this set of provisions as governing so-called *ex delicto* liability (arts 109–122). Since the Civil Code refers to 'civil obligations', it may be construed that *ex delicto* liability embraces both damage caused by tort (eg attempted murder) and by contract (eg fraud by means of a sales contract). Certainly, art 1093 CC provides – as was already pointed out – that obligations deriving from negligent acts or omissions which are not punished by the law will be governed by the tort law provisions in the same Civil Code (arts 1902–1910). A systematic construction of arts 1092 and 1093 would suggest that *ex delicto* liability refers only to tort. Nevertheless, the fact is that the *ex delicto* liability rules of the Criminal Code are broad and generic enough to embrace both tort and contract. For instance, restitution is included among the legal effects of crime, as if it were a manifestation of liability *ex delicto* (art 110 CP). Restitution may be requested not only in cases where the victim suffers a tort (eg a theft) but also where she was involved in a contract which 12

[19] *Ley Orgánica 10/1995, de 23 de noviembre, del Código Penal* (BOE no 281, 24.11.1995). Similarly, tort liability of the personnel of a public authority is governed by the same statutory rules (pursuant to art 146.1 LRJAP).

was later nullified on the basis on invalidity, due to the commission of a crime (eg fraud). In this regard, the labels of 'criminalised legal transactions' (*negocios jurídicos criminalizados*) or 'criminalised contracts' (*contratos criminalizados*) have been indistinctly used to refer to those contracts where, behind the formal appearance of a valid contract, a real criminal intention of one of the parties – eg fooling the counterparty – is hiding (eg STS Criminal Chamber 6.3.2014 (RJ 2014, 2017), 19.5.2014 (RJ 2014, 2753) and 1.7.2014 (RJ 2014, 3675)). Therefore, restitution is not always a legal effect of the criminal deed, but may derive from a crime committed by means of an illicit contract.[20] Nevertheless, the illicit nature of such a contract will generally entail its invalidity, so liability will be based in tort. Moreover, restitution is not – strictly speaking – a legal effect of liability but a remedy to protect the holder of a real right – or the mere possession – over the thing which has to be returned.[21]

D. APPLICATION OF COMMON RULES IN A DIFFERENT WAY

13 In principle, rules which are common to tort and contract should be construed in the same way, due to the principle of unity of the legal system. However, there may be some differences due to the different context in which those provisions may be applied.

14 One example is the general rule in art 1107 CC. It provides that the debtor in good faith will only be liable for foreseen or foreseeable damage, and which is a necessary consequence of the breach. By contrast, the debtor who breaches the contract in an intentional or wilful manner is liable for every single damage event resulting from the breach. 'Intent' (*dolo*) in this context means that the party in breach not only wanted to breach the contract but also knew that his failure to perform was not justified (STS 17.3.2011 (RJ 2011, 2881)). Therefore the breach has to be conscious and voluntary (which excludes breach in gross negligence).[22] As to 'good faith', it has sometimes been construed to be broader than fault (STS 31.7.2007 (RJ 2007, 5093)). Therefore, for instance, a debtor who could not foresee the probability of a crisis in the real estate market is deemed to be in good faith (STS 10.2.2014 (RJ 2014, 1006)). However, other decisions have construed 'good faith' as meaning negligence (STS 19.2.2014 (RJ 2014, 1129)). The moment which is taken into account to decide whether damage was

---

[20] In legal scholarship *I Nadal Gómez*, El ejercicio de acciones civiles en el proceso penal (2002) 113, 137 and 148.

[21] As *R Juan Sánchez*, La responsabilidad civil en el proceso penal, La Ley 2004, 46 and 137, observes.

[22] See *Pantaleón* (fn 5), ADC 1991, 1019, 1034.

foreseeable is the one in which the obligation was created (art 1107 I). The rule makes sense in contract, since contract is a way for the parties to allocate risks among themselves. This is an argument for excluding tort from the scope of the application of the rule.[23]

However, it is also true that the provision is located among general rules 'On obligations' and, as a result, embraces every kind of obligation, irrespective of its source (STS 20.6.1989 (RJ 1989, 4702)). Case law has therefore discussed whether damage was a foreseeable result of the accident, especially in cases of damage caused by the misbehaviour of visitors at a disco (STS 2.10.1997 (RJ 1997, 6964)). It is therefore surprising that the Spanish Supreme Court has stated that art 1107 CC can be extended to tort (STS 15.6.2010 (RJ 2010, 5151)). Some court decisions in tort cases have construed art 1107 CC as a rule which limits liability for damage, by excluding compensation for damage which was not connected to the damaging event (STS 2.3.2006 (RJ 2006, 919)). A scholarly opinion has suggested a different interpretation of art 1107 CC along the lines of economic analysis of law, according to which the provision is an instrument to create incentives to communication of private contractual information between parties.[24] 15

II. MAIN DIFFERENCES BETWEEN TORTIOUS AND CONTRACTUAL LIABILITY

A. DIFFERENCES AS REGARDS THE FOUNDATIONS OF LIABILITY

As has been mentioned, the Civil Code tackles both kinds of liability in a separate way and this is a reflection of a fundamental difference between them. Certainly, in both cases, the trigger of liability is the causation of damage by one person to another. However, in the case of contract, damage results from the violation of an agreement between the parties. Therefore, breach consists in a departure from the principle that promises should be kept (*pacta sunt servanda*, art 1091 CC). On the contrary, liability in tort is independent of any such agreement or any previous relationship between the parties. The foundation of liability is 16

---

23 See *Pantaleón* (fn 5) 1031; *CI Asúa González*, La culpa 'in contrahendo' tratamiento en el Derecho alemán y presencia en otros ordenamientos (1989) 289, and *Yzquierdo* (fn 10) 81.

24 See *F Gómez Pomar*, Previsión de daños, incumplimiento e indemnización (2002) 266. According to the same, 'intent' pursuant to art 1107 CC means deceptive, opportunistic or malicious conducts (at 275).

thus usually found in the principle that nobody should harm another (*neminem laedere*). It has also been pointed out that contractual liability is a particular species or manifestation of this general duty not to harm others.[25]

17 As a general rule, tort requires a subjective element for liability to be established. Liability is, therefore, 'subjective' or fault-based (art 1902 CC). Fault (*culpa o negligencia*) is a broad concept which is commonly construed as also including intent (*dolo*). Regarding contract, the Civil Code provides that those who act with any kind of 'intent, negligence or default' (*dolo, culpa o morosidad*) will be liable for damage derived from the infringement of their obligations. Nonetheless, the Code also includes the case of those who 'in any way infringe the wording of the same' (art 1101). There is, therefore, ground for discussing whether contract-based liability is based on fault only – as the prevailing opinion holds – or if it is strict in nature.[26]

18 Apart from this, there are some special liability rules regarding contract which require fault on an explicit basis, as is the case with some rules in the Code of Commerce (*Código de comercio*, Ccom)[27] regarding the liability of the captain of a vessel for damage (art 618). By contrast, contractual liability is strict in other situations, for example in the case of liability of innkeepers or restaurateurs for damage to any personal effects brought by travellers in inns and restaurants (art 1783 CC).

19 In this regard, the distinction – inspired by French law – between *obligaciones de medios* and *obligaciones de resultado* has been traditionally used by Spanish case law as regards contract. Therefore, if the debtor was obliged to attain a certain result – as in the case of a contract of works (*arrendamiento de obra*, art 1588 CC) – she will be held liable for failing to do so, regardless of fault. According to some legal scholars, fault will then be presumed.[28] However, if the debtor was merely obliged to carry out a certain activity, she will be held liable if she behaved in a negligent way only – as in the case of the agent (art 1726).[29]

20 This distinction between obligations of means and obligations of result has also been used by case law in tort law cases, in particular where the liability of professionals was at stake. For instance, there has been much debate on whether a physician owes a duty of result or is only bound to carry out a certain activity.

25 Among others see *JL Lacruz Berdejo/F Rivero Hernández*, Elementos de Derecho Civil, vol II-1 Derecho de Obligaciones. Teoría del Contrato (2004) 165.

26 See *L Díez-Picazo*, Fundamentos del Derecho civil patrimonial, vol II (5th edn 1996) 577; similarly, *G Díez-Picazo Giménez*, La mora y la responsabilidad contractual (1996) 366.

27 *Real Decreto de 22 de agosto de 1885 por el que se publica el Código de Comercio* (BOE no 289, 16.10.1885).

28 So for instance *Lacruz/Rivero* (fn 25) 172.

29 This is consistent with the fact that agency is usually gratuitous in nature (art 1711 CC). See *Díez-Picazo* (fn 26) 583.

In this vein, a distinction has been drawn between curative medicine – where the physician aims at healing the patient, but is not bound to reach any specific result – and voluntary medicine – where the patient is a healthy person who wants his/her physical or aesthetic appearance to be changed by the doctor. This is the case of aesthetic surgery (STS 22.7.2003 (RJ 2003, 5391)) or odontology (STS 28.6.1999 (RJ 1999, 4894) and 7.2.1990 (RJ 1990, 668)), and surgery which seeks the transformation of a biological function of the patient, such as sexual activities (as in the case of vasectomies: STS 26.7.2006 (RJ 2006, 6127), 11.2.1997 (RJ 1997, 940) and 25.4.1994 (RJ 1994, 3073)). In the latter case (promise of a result), it has been suggested that protection of the victim prompts a flexible approach as to the fault requirement, and, accordingly, the doctor could be held liable as if she were acting in the framework of a works contract.[30] Nevertheless, the distinction itself has been the object of harsh criticism, including the argument that it is unclear and that any obligation may be considered as one of means or one of result, depending on the point of view from which it is seen.[31] Moreover, the behaviour of the physician who promises a result which is not in his power to attain may be deemed deceptive and therefore such physician may be held liable – in tort – for a violation of a pre-contractual duty to inform.[32] A shift may be perceived in case law, which has abandoned the – outdated, according to STS 19.7.2013 (RJ 2013, 5004) – distinction for the time being (see also STS 28.6.2013 (RJ 2013, 4986) and 22.11.2007 (RJ 2007, 8651)).[33]

As regards intent, case law has pointed out that it does not give rise to a separate claim, but works as an element which triggers an aggravated liability of the party who behaved in an intentional manner both in contract and in tort (STS 25.2.2013 (RJ 2013, 7413) and 7.6.2013 (RJ 2013, 8385)). This is, however, an excessive generalisation, since the role of intent is different in each of them. In tort, the liable person has to compensate for damage caused. However, in contract, a distinction applies depending on whether the debtor breached the contract in good faith (*de buena fe*, ie with no intent) or in an intentional manner (art 1107 CC), as has already been seen.[34] The prevailing opinion is against applying such a distinction to tort. Therefore, the debtor who behaved without intent is treated in a more benign way, whereas the debtor who acted with malice 21

30 See *JA Seijas Quintana*, Responsabilidad civil médica: ¿Obligación de medios; obligación de resultados?, Revista de la Asociación de Abogados Especializados en Responsabilidad Civil y Seguros (RAAERCS) 2009, no 29, 9–22, at 10.

31 See *A Cabanillas Sánchez*, Las obligaciones de actividad y de resultado (1993) 20.

32 See *E Llamas Pombo*, Doctrina general de la llamada culpa médica, in: D Bello Janeiro/C Maluquer de Motes i Bernet (eds), Estudios acerca de la responsabilidad civil y su seguro (2005) 231–276, at 246.

33 However in its defense see *C Crespo Mora*, Las obligaciones de medios y de resultado de los prestadores de servicios en el DCFR, InDret <www.indret.com> 2013, 1–45, at 5 ff.

34 See no 14 above.

is liable to the same extent as a wrongdoer in tort. From this perspective, in the case of intentional damage, contract and tort are the same.[35]

22 Another difference is that if the tortfeasor behaved in an intentional way and he/she is a civil servant, the State – which will be held liable for his/her act – has a recourse claim against the tortfeasor (pursuant to art 36.2 LRJSP). Such intent – or gross negligence – has to be established, so the mere fact that the public authority at stake had been held liable by a previous decision for the same facts is not sufficient to hold the civil servant liable on such a basis (Superior Court of Justice (Tribunal Superior de Justicia, TSJ) of Aragón 8.10.2013 (JUR 2014, 15564)). The recourse claim itself is not based in tort but in the violation of pre-existing duties of the civil servant towards the State and is therefore deemed to be contractual.[36]

23 Moreover, in the case of contractual liability for fault, the judge is statutorily allowed to reduce the debtor's liability depending on the case (art 1103 CC). Although the provision is worded in such a way that a reduction may be applicable 'to every kind of obligations', legal scholarship has suggested that it is only so in the case of damage caused by a contractual breach which, although foreseeable as such, was not foreseeable as regards its amount.[37] However, Spanish courts have made ample use of that judicial power, including tort cases.[38] Accordingly, art 1103 CC has been repeatedly mentioned as a legal ground for a reduction of damages in the case of contributory negligence of others,[39] even though this is not what the provision is about. At any rate, the judge may not use that power in the case of an intentional breach of contract (since liability for intentionally inflicted damage may be claimed 'in every kind of obligation' pursuant to art 1102 CC (STS 19.2.2014 (RJ 2014, 1129)). Gross negligence (*culpa grave*) is equated with intent.[40]

24 As regards wrongfulness, the general clause of fault-based liability does not refer to it as a separate condition of liability. According to many authors, wrongfulness consists in the violation of the general principle that nobody should harm others, which has been already mentioned. Other scholars have objected that wrongfulness lacks a separate entity as a liability condition.[41]

---

35 See *R de Ángel Yágüez*, Tratado de responsabilidad civil (1993) 810.

36 See *F Peña López*, La vía de regreso frente al personal al servicio de las Administraciones Públicas, in: D Bello Janeiro/C Maluquer de Motes i Bernet (eds), Estudios acerca de la responsabilidad civil y su seguro (2005) 289–335, at 297.

37 See *Pantaleón* (fn 5) 1019–1092, at 1037 ff. Therefore, it is not applicable to tort (ibid, 1042).

38 Eg STS 20.6.1989 (RJ 1989, 4702) and 19.6.1996 (RJ 1996, 5803).

39 Eg STS 7.11.2000 (RJ 2000, 9911) and 22.4.2013 (RJ 2013, 3690).

40 STS 6.5.2002 (RJ 2002, 3675) and 23.10.2012 (RJ 2012, 1542).

41 See *F Pantaleón Prieto*, Artículo 1902, in: A Cabanillas Sánchez et al (eds), Comentario del Código Civil (1991) 1995; *id*, Responsabilidad extracontractual, in: Enciclopedia Jurídica Básica, IV (1995) 5942–5948, at 5946.

As has been mentioned, the difference in the case of contracts lies in the fact that damage triggering contractual liability is a breach of the contractual promise.

The standard of care is approximately the same both in contract and tort, since fault is defined in the general set of rules on obligations.[42] According to art 1104 CC, fault is the failure to behave with the care which is required by the nature of the obligation, taking the circumstances of persons, time and place into account. The standard of care per default is the objective one of the reasonable man or *buen padre de familia* (akin to the Roman *bonus pater familias*). However, with regard to contract law, these circumstances play a secondary role, since the care to be adopted by the debtor will be determined by the nature of the contractual obligation. Therefore, the debtor will have to behave with all the care required in order to perform his obligation, regardless of what this is. Moreover, courts have usually stressed the rigour of care required in tort, thereby stating that if damage occurred, it must have been due to the negligent behaviour of the defendant – which draws fault liability very close to strict liability.[43] Nevertheless, this may not make a great difference since, also in the case of contracts, liability of the debtor has come close to strict liability.[44] 25

Additionally, the Civil Code gives the parties the possibility to lower the level of care required, establish an increased standard of care (art 1104 para 2 CC), as in the case of professionals, or either a subjective criterion (*culpa in concreto*, or *diligentia quam in suis*). The liability of professionals will thus be assessed against the rules of the profession (*lex artis ad hoc*).[45] As regards the case where the conclusion of a contract harms the interests of a third person – with whom one of the contracting parties is already contractually bound – the applicable standard of care is also professional in nature.[46] In the case of agents, the judge may assess fault in a more or less rigorous manner depending on whether the agency (*mandato*) was remunerated or not (art 1726 CC). 26

The parties to a contract may not exclude liability for damage caused with intent (art 1102 CC) or for gross negligence (*culpa grave*).[47] As will be seen later in greater detail, this kind of agreement may not be possible with regard to tort liability, where the parties involved may not have had any previous contact before damage occurred.[48] 27

---

42 See sec I.C above.

43 See *M Martín-Casals/J Ribot Igualada/J Solé Feliu*, Spain, in: BA Koch/H Koziol (eds), Unification of Tort Law: Strict Liability (2002) 281–321, at 291 no 40.

44 See *L Puig Ferriol*, La concurrencia de responsabilidad contractual y extracontractual, in: JA Moreno Martínez (ed), La responsabilidad civil y su problemática actual (2007) 885–909, at 890.

45 Among others see STS 30.12.2004 (RJ 2005, 516) and 8.9.1998 (RJ 1998, 7548).

46 See *Á Fernández Arévalo*, La lesión extracontractual del Crédito (1996) 341 ff. See also sec IV.1.1 below.

47 Instead of many, see *Lacruz/Rivero* (fn 25) 173.

48 See sec III.B.1 below.

28 As to the role of strict liability, the Civil Code provides several instances of strict liability in tort, to which a plethora of so-called special statutes – ie statutes outside the Civil Code – can be added. As regards the first group, it includes liability of the possessor of an animal (art 1905 CC), liability for excessive fumes (art 1908.2 CC) and the fall of trees (art 1908.3 CC), and liability of the head of the family for damage caused by things that are thrown away or fall from a dwelling (art 1910 CC), as well as, according to some legal writers, liability of the owner of a building for damage caused by its collapse if it was due to a lack of repairs (art 1907 CC).[49] Outside the Code, there are many strict liability rules, for example with regard to nuclear liability (Nuclear Damage Liability Act (LRCDN)),[50] environmental damage (Environmental Liability Act (LRM)),[51] traffic accidents, hunting (art 33.1 and 5 Hunting Act (LC)),[52] product liability, etc. It has already been mentioned that liability in contract comes close to strict liability.

B. DIFFERENCES AS REGARDS CAUSATION

29 As mentioned above, the extent of liability in contract and in tort is different on the basis of art 1107 CC. This raises the issue of foreseeability of damage, since the debtor in good faith will only be held liable for damage which is a necessary consequence of the breach and was foreseeable. 'Necessary consequence' is construed in a similar sense to the expression 'direct and immediate consequence' of the French (art 1151) and Italian (art 1223) Civil Codes.[53] The expression is understood as including not only intrinsic damage or *damage propter rem ipsam habitam*. Having said that, it remains unclear what other damage may be attributed to the debtor in breach. The judge may exclude damage which is too remote. In the case of a debtor in good faith, such damage may occur without her liability on the basis that it was unforeseeable at the moment of contracting.[54]

30 In addition, causation is usually not a major hurdle in cases of contractual liability. Sometimes the legal analysis focuses on other conditions of liability, in particular fault. Therefore, it seems that causation has been analysed more in the context of tort. Obviously there are also contract law cases where causation issues arise – in particular those relating to medical malpractice – but the analysis of

---

49 For further details, see *Martín-Casals/Igualada/Solé Feliu* (fn 43) 289 no 32.

50 *Ley 12/2011, de 27 de mayo, sobre responsabilidad civil por daños nucleares o producidos por materiales radiactivos* (BOE no 127, 28.5.2011).

51 *Ley 26/2007, de 23 de octubre, de Responsabilidad Medioambiental* (BOE no 255, 24.10.2007).

52 *Ley 1/1970, de 4 de abril, de Caza* (BOE no 82, 6.4.1970).

53 See *Lacruz/Rivero* (fn 25) 207.

54 Again, *Lacruz/Rivero* (fn 25) 207.

causation seems to be more or less the same. In general, a distinction is drawn between causation in fact (*conditio sine qua non*) and legal causation or the scope of liability (following the German doctrine on *objektive Zurechnung*).[55] Legal scholars who support this basic distinction apply it both in tort and contract.[56] Such a distinction, which has brought much clarity to the legal analysis, has, however, recently been objected to by a scholarly opinion.[57]

There are, however, some qualifications to the general rule, for instance in the case of a contract of deposit: whenever the depositary used the thing deposited without the depositor's express consent, he will be 'liable for any damage' (pursuant to art 1767 CC) – therefore even for damage which is not causally linked to such a use.[58] Similarly, in the case of a commodate (*comodato*) – ie a gratuitous loan of a thing for a certain time period – the borrower will be liable for damage consisting in the loss of a thing under certain circumstances, even though the loss may have resulted from a fortuitous event (art 1744 CC). Therefore, it is not required that damage is causally linked to the conduct of the borrower.[59] 31

C. DIFFERENCES AS REGARDS REMEDIES

1) *Degree of Certainty of the Damage*

For liability to be established either in contract or in tort, damage has to be certain. The degree of certainty to be attained by the plaintiff is unclear. The courts may disregard claims where damage seems purely hypothetical or based on mere assumptions or 'dreams of fortune' and this is valid both in tort[60] and in contract.[61] Therefore, proof of the loss of earnings (*lucro cesante*) may be more difficult in both areas of law in comparison to proof of positive damage 32

55 See *FA Pantaleón Prieto*, Causalidad e imputación objetiva: criterios de impuración, in: Asociación de Profesores de Derecho Civil (ed), Centenario del Código Civil II (1990) 1561–1591; *P Salvador-Coderch/N Garoupa/C Gómez-Ligüerre*, Scope of liability: the vanishing distinction between negligence and strict liability, European Journal of Law and Economics 2009, no 28, 257–287.

56 See *FA Pantaleón Prieto*, Responsabilidad contractual, in: Enciclopedia Jurídica Básica, IV (1995) 5922–5926, at 5925; *id* (fn 5) at 1036.

57 See *M García-Ripoll Montijano*, Ilicitud, culpa y estado de necesidad (2006) and *F Peña López*, Dogma y realidad del derecho de daños: imputación objetiva, causalidad y culpa en el sistema español y en los PETL (2011) passim.

58 See *Díez-Picazo* (fn 26) 582.

59 Ibid, 583.

60 Thus, SSTS 5.11.1998 (RJ 1998, 8404), 14.7.2003 (RJ 2003, 4629), and 14.3.2005 (RJ 2005, 2236).

61 For instance, SSTS 20.7.2011 (RJ 2011, 7379), 9.4.2012 (RJ 2012, 8986) and 26.9.2013 (RJ 2013, 7047).

(*daño emergente*). Future damage is compensable if it is certain. According to case law, for future losses of earnings, a reasonable degree of verisimilitude has to be attained, according to an assessment of 'objectivable' probabilities (STS 16.12.2009 (RJ 2010, 859) and 18.11.2013 (RJ 2014, 2388)).

33 Proof of damage has been eased in tort in a number of ways which do not seem to exist in contract. First, the doctrine of 'damage *in re ipsa*' states that in some situations the mere occurrence of a certain situation of fact amounts to damage. However, doubts may exist as to whether there is 'damage *in re ipsa*' in a particular case (as pointed out by the Decision of the Judge of Commercial Affairs (Sentencia Juzgado de lo Mercantil, SJMErc) no 1 Granada 30.11.2012 (AC 2013, 1605)). Therefore, a second possibility that has been raised is to statutorily provide that a certain level of compensation will be awarded to the victim, who nevertheless retains the possibility to prove that damage was greater. An example can be found in the protection of trademarks (art 43.5 Trademark Act (LM)).[62] The rule lacks a punitive nature and finds its justification in the usual evidentiary hurdles faced by the right holder in such cases instead.[63] Some courts have applied such a rule as a last resort device, ie if it is not possible to prove damage otherwise (Decision of the Court of Appeal (Sentencia de la Audiencia Provincial, SAP) Barcelona, 15th Section, 28.5.2014 (AC 2014, 1032)). The Supreme Court has made clear that such compensation is to be paid 'at any rate and with no evidence needed at all' – thus leaving the possibility of requesting a higher compensation award unaffected if proved (STS 9.12.2009 (RJ 2009, 2074))[64] – although it is debatable whether that includes the case where the claimant failed to request any compensation (STS 9.12.2010 (RJ 2011, 1414)).[65] By contrast, there are no similar rules in contract law.

2) *Compensation for Non-Pecuniary Loss*

34 As a general rule, non-pecuniary loss is compensable both in tort and in contract. In spite of some oscillations in case law, nowadays it is generally acknowledged that there should be no differences in this regard between the two liability regimes.[66] Some particularities exist with regard to the former, in particular in the case of product liability due to the influence of the EU Directive. The Product Liability Act[67] of 1994, which transposed the Directive into Spanish law, had

---

62 *Ley 17/2001, de 7 de diciembre, de marcas* (BOE no 294, 8.12.2001).

63 As *P del Olmo*, Punitive Damages in Spain, in: H Koziol/V Wilcox, Punitive Damages: Common Law and Civil Perspectives (2009) 148 no 25, points out.

64 In a similar vein, see STS 25.10.2012 (RJ 2012, 10130).

65 Similarly see SJMErc no 1 Pamplona, 8.4.2014 (AC 2014, 610).

66 So for instance *Yzquierdo* (fn 10) 83.

67 *Ley 22/1994, de 6 de julio, de Responsabilidad civil por daños causados por productos defectuosos* (BOE no 161, 7.7.1994).

excluded liability for non-pecuniary loss, with the result that it would have to be compensated under the general tort liability rules (pursuant to its art 10.2). Strangely enough, the Government included the product liability statutory regime in a consolidated text on consumer protection and, in doing so, the exclusion of liability for non-pecuniary loss simply disappeared (cf art 128 of the Act on the Consumers and Users (TRLGDCU)).[68] As a result, it seems unclear whether: (a) non-pecuniary loss caused by a defective product is compensable under the new statutory regime, as the wording of the Act seems to suggest, or (b) this entails a change with regard to previous law which the Government was actually not legally entitled to do (ie the Government overstepped its mandate or behaved *ultra vires*). Therefore, should this second opinion be followed, the previous criterion – ie exclusion of non-pecuniary loss under the Directive – should be followed in spite of the literal wording of the consolidated Act.[69]

Furthermore, non-pecuniary loss will not be compensable in some cases in tort. In particular, if damage derives from the violation of a trademark right, in order to establish the compensation award, the victim may choose between (a) the 'negative economic consequences, including the benefits which she would have obtained through the use of the trademark but for the violation, and the benefit obtained by the infringer as a result of the violation' and (b) 'the amount which the infringer would have had to pay in exchange for a licence which would have authorised him to use the trademark according to the law' (art 43.2 LM). The importance of such a choice is paramount as regards non-pecuniary loss, since such damage may only be compensated if the victim opts for the first possibility (eg SAP La Rioja, 1st Section, 7.9.2012 (AC 2013, 307)). Moreover, non-pecuniary loss cannot be established on the basis of the above-mentioned doctrine of 'damage *in re ipsa*', but has to be proved by the claimant trademark holder (STS 18.2.1999 (RJ 1999, 660) and SAP Barcelona, 15th Section, 25.7.2012 (AC 2013, 299)). 35

3) Compensation for Loss of Earnings and for Loss of Chance

Loss of earnings and loss of a chance are compensable under both contract and tort. It seems there are very few differences, if any, in this regard, at least at the present moment. As regards loss of earnings, the new *baremo* or compensation scheme offers an actuarial assessment for loss of earnings in the case of traffic 36

---

[68] *Real Decreto Legislativo 1/2007, de 16 de noviembre, por el que se aprueba el texto refundido de la Ley General para la Defensa de los Consumidores y Usuarios y otras leyes complementarias* (BOE no 287, 30.11.2007).

[69] See *J Solé Feliu*, Comentario a la Sentencia de 28 de mayo de 2012, Responsabilidad civil del fabricante por los daños causados por el medicamento Agreal, Cuadernos Civitas de Jurisprudencia Civil 2013, no 91, 265–286.

accidents, which is also being used by the courts in other areas. As regards compensation for loss of a chance, it must be noted that, when it was first accepted by case law, loss of a chance included non-pecuniary loss only, so pecuniary damage was left uncompensated. Currently loss of a chance includes both and in practice mainly refers to cases of losing the chance of bringing or continuing a claim due to a lawyer's negligence and to losing the chance of healing or survival due to medical negligence. A particular situation may arise when damage results from the annulment of a void contract. In that case, it has been suggested that compensation has to be paid for the costs of concluding the contract which has been declared void or the higher cost of concluding a new one. Moreover, the damages award should include an amount for damage consisting in the loss of a chance to conclude a contract, which the victim has lost as a result of having trusted in the validity of the subsequently annulled contract.[70]

4) *Restitutionary Damages*

37 Restitutionary damages as such do not exist under Spanish law. It may happen that a party in breach of a contract is enriched thanks to such a breach, for instance where the breach is induced by a third party. In these cases, the victim may file a claim against the breach's inducer. However, the claim is for damage compensation, not disgorgement of benefits obtained. As regards disgorgement, there is disagreement between those according to whom no principle makes the debtor liable to disgorge the benefit obtained[71] and those according to whom the creditor is entitled to the so-called *commodum ex negotiatione* (art 1186 CC). From the latter perspective, if the debtor breaches his promise by transferring to a third person the thing he owed to the creditor, the latter will be entitled to what the debtor may receive in exchange.[72]

38 With regard to tort, there are some instances where a statute takes the benefits obtained by the tortfeasor into account when establishing the damages award. The most prominent case is compensation for infringement of intellectual property rights, according to the German doctrine on the *dreifache Schadensberechnung* as adopted by the Intellectual Property Act (art 140).[73] Such a solution has

[70] See *MP García Rubio*, La responsabilidad precontractual en el Derecho español (1991) 213 and 241 and *S Gaspar Lera*, Formación de la voluntad contractual, vicios del consentimiento y remedios, in: MA Parra Lucán (ed), Negociación y perfección de los contratos (2014) 269–315, at 306.

[71] See *Á Carrasco Perera*, Art. 1107 CC, in: M Albaladejo (ed), Comentarios al Código Civil y Compilaciones Forales, vol XV-1 (1989) 668.

[72] Whose value may exceed that of the thing originally promised to the affected creditor. See *Pantaleón* (fn 5) 1022.

[73] *Real Decreto Legislativo 1/1996, de 12 de abril, por el que se aprueba el Texto Refundido de la Ley de Propiedad Intelectual, regularizando, aclarando y armonizando las disposiciones legales vigentes sobre la materia* (BOE no 97, 22.4.1996).

been harshly criticised by legal scholarship, according to which, the legislature intermingles tort and unjust enrichment instead of keeping them separate.[74] This later approach was introduced by a legislative reform in the case of interference with the right of honour, privacy and one's own image (art 9.2.c Organic Act 5/1982 (LPCDH)).[75] A general remedy allowing the victim to disgorge benefits is lacking under Spanish law, although legal scholars have made some proposals to that end.[76] This is in contrast with the rule which allows confiscation of profits in the case of liability *ex delicto* (art 127.1 CP). At any rate, such a remedy cannot consist in punitive damages,[77] as will now be seen.

5) *Aggravated and Exemplary (or Punitive) Damages*

Punitive damages cannot be awarded under Spanish law. They are contrary to the most fundamental principles of the Spanish legal system (see STS 19.12.2005 (RJ 2006, 295) and 12.1.2009 (RJ 2009, 544)), and in particular to the requirement that punishments are statutorily established in accordance with the principle of legality (art 25 Spanish Constitution, CE). However, there are some special rules which have sometimes been seen through the lens of punitive damages. A first example consists in the rules which entitle the victim of a tort to disgorge the benefits obtained by the tortfeasor.[78] Nevertheless, it has also been pointed out – and rightfully so – that disgorgement and punitive damages are different.[79] Another example is the social security surcharges that an entrepreneur will have to pay after having been held liable of a labour accident.[80] Such surcharges, which range from 30% to 50%, may be imposed on the entrepreneur in cases where the accident resulted from a lack of compliance with the regulatory requirements as to safety or hygiene at work (pursuant to art 164 of the General Social Security Act).[81] 39

---

74 So *Pantaleón* (fn 5) 5944.

75 *Ley Orgánica 1/1982, de 5 de mayo, de protección civil del derecho al honor, a la intimidad personal y familiar, y a la propia imagen* (BOE no 115, 14.5.1982).

76 See *M Martín-Casals/A Ruda*, El mal samarità. L'absorció de beneficis per la gestió impròpia de negocis aliens, in: Universitat de Girona (ed), Institut de dret privat europeu i comparat, Contractes, responsabilitat extracontractual i altres fonts de les obligacions al Codi Civil de Catalunya, Documenta Universitaria 2012, 503–553, 540 ff.

77 See *M Martín-Casals*, La 'modernización' del Derecho de la responsabilidad extracontractual, in: Asociación de Profesores de Derecho Civil (ed), Cuestiones actuales en materia de responsabilidad civil (2011) 11–111, at 26.

78 See *JM Busto Lago/F Peña López*, Enriquecimiento injusto y responsabilidad civil extracontractual, Anuario da Facultade de Dereito da Universidade da Coruña, 1997, no 1, 141–166, at 159 f and *R Bercovitz Rodríguez-Cano*, La dignidad de las víctimas de delitos, Aranzadi Civil 2010, no 6.

79 See *R de Ángel Yágüez*, La responsabilidad civil. Cuestiones previas de delimitación, in: I Sierra Gil de la Cuesta (ed), Tratado de responsabilidad civil, I (2nd edn 2008) 3–123, at 104.

80 For further details see *del Olmo* (fn 63) 148 no 26 ff.

81 *Real Decreto Legislativo 8/2015, de 30 de octubre, por el que se aprueba el Texto Refundido de la Ley General de la Seguridad Social* (BOE no 261, 31.10.2015).

40 Penalty clauses are accepted under contract law, although the judge is allowed to moderate them if the party in breach has at least started to perform the obligations of the contract (pursuant to art 1154 CC; unlike under art 56 of the Ccom, which does not provide for such a possibility).[82] Such moderation is not possible in the case of partial breach where the parties establish the penalty clause in consideration of that particular case of partial breach (STS 30.4.2013 (RJ 2013, 4609)). As regards consumer contracts, those clauses which impose on the consumer or user in breach a duty to pay a disproportionately high degree of compensation are void (art 85.6 TRLGDCU). With regard to contracts in the public sector, the contracts may provide penalty clauses within certain limits. In particular, such penalties have to be proportionate to the seriousness of the breach and not exceed 10% of the budget laid down in the public contract (art 192.1 LCSP).

6) Other Remedies

41 Specific performance is a contractual remedy. The Civil Code gives the creditor the choice between it and discharge because of breach, plus compensation in either case (art 1124 para 2 CC). The court may give the debtor an additional period to perform if some circumstance justifies such an extension (art 1124 para 3; similarly, art 223 LCSP). The party in breach is bound to compensate the other for damage resulting from such a breach (art 225.2 and 3 LCSP). With regard to tort law, there are no provisions on the form of compensation. The liable person may compensate the victim in kind (*reparación en natura*) or through a monetary equivalent (*indemnización pecuniaria*). In the case of liability *ex delicto*, the court may choose – provided that the culprit agrees – a punishment consisting in the culprit working 'for the benefit of the community', which may consist, inter alia, in the restoration of damage caused (art 49 CP). There is therefore an intertwining in this context between liability in tort and criminal liability.[83]

42 Injunctions are provided for by some special statutes, or example regarding consumers and users (art 53 TRLGDCU), environmental liability (art 17 LRM), intellectual property (art 139 LPI), interference with the right to honour, privacy or one's own image (art 9.2.a and b LPCDH). However injunctions are not, strictly speaking, a tort law remedy from the Spanish perspective, but a sort of precautionary measure to prevent damage from occurring or becoming worse. Therefore, inhibitory actions (*acción negatoria*), recovery of the thing (*acción*

[82] See *J Gómez Calero*, Contratos mercantiles con cláusula penal (1983) 45 and 93.

[83] See *B Mapelli Caffarena*, Las consecuencias jurídicas del delito (4th edn 2005) 403.

reivindicatoria), etc do not presuppose fault on the side of the defendant or even damage.[84] Therefore, for instance, legal scholarship has advocated an extension of precautionary protection of the victims of certain torts, such as so-called 'domestic violence'.[85] In recent times, injunctions have been used against innocent intermediaries as a means to stop third-party copyright infringement.[86] In contract, such precautions are usually taken on request by the creditor, who fears that the debtor may not fulfil his obligations (art 1503 CC).

Moreover some special regimes provide specific additional remedies, such as 43 publication of a decision in the case of violation of the right to honour, privacy or one's own image (art 9.2.a LPCDH and art 216 CP), or a right of trademark (art 41.1.e LM); a crime against the intellectual property right (art 272 CP), the market or consumers (art 288 CP);[87] cancellation and rectification in the case of violation of the right to personal data protection (arts 14 and 15 Personal Data Protection Act (LOPD));[88] or restoration of the damaged environment (art 339 CP). Publication of the court decision does not have a compensatory nature but merely aims at removing the effects of the damaging event (STS 17.10.2012 (RJ 2012, 9718)).

The victim may also request restitution, either according to the Civil Code (eg 44 in case a contract is invalidated, art 1294 CC) or the Criminal Code (if *ex delicto* liability arises, pursuant to art 110 CP). Although the Criminal Code deals with restitution as if it were an effect of liability, legal scholarship makes clear that both claims are separate and different, so restitution should not be confused with compensation (pursuant to art 1902 CC). Therefore, if the claimant requests compensation but does not include restitution in his claim, the judge may award the former but will not be allowed to award the latter.[89] A right to restitution is also a legal effect of invalidity of contracts (art 1303 CC). If the thing to be returned under the duty to restitution is in possession of a third party, the victim will have to bring her to court as well – in addition to the contractual counterparty – so the contract can be judicially declared void as against such third party and she may defend herself if needed.[90] An example is a Decision

---

84 See *Pantaleón* (fn 5) at 5943.

85 See *MP García Aburuza*, La violencia doméstica desde el ámbito civil, Revista Aranzadi Doctrinal 2010, no 11, fn 15 and accompanying text.

86 See *M Husovec/M Peguera*, Much Ado About Little: Privately Litigated Internet Disconnection Injunctions, International Review of Intellectual Property and Competition Law (IIC), 2015, no 46(1), 10–37 and <http://papers.ssrn.com/sol3/papers.cfm?abstract_id=2465616> at 11.

87 Such publication is an additional punishment (*Juan* (fn 21) 228 ff).

88 *Ley Orgánica 3/2018, de 5 de diciembre, de protección de datos personales y garantía de los derechos digitales* (BOE no 294, 6.12.2018).

89 See *Nadal* (fn 20) 19 and 22.

90 See *J Delgado Echeverría/MÁ Parra Lucán*, Las nulidades de los contratos: en la teoría y en la práctica (2005) 328 and 332 and *Nadal* (fn 20) 180.

of the Constitutional Court (Sentencia del Tribunal Constitucional (STC) 278/1994, of 17.10.1994),[91] which declared the obligation of a municipality to give back a piece of land it had received from an individual, as a result of the nullity of the contract on the basis of fraud by another person. The municipality was, as a result, entitled to compensation, the amount of which was equivalent to the price it paid for the land.[92]

D. DIFFERENCES AS REGARDS RECOVERABILITY OF 'PURE ECONOMIC LOSSES'

45 Pure economic losses do not constitute a separate category of damage under Spanish law. Under Spanish law, every kind of damage may be compensated according to the general clause of liability in tort (art 1902 CC). However, this does not necessarily mean that every instance of pure economic loss is compensated with no qualifications of any kind. The fact is that Spanish law makes use of concepts other than the typology of damage, such as the requirement of certainty of damage, or causation (for damage may be deemed too remote).[93] For the same reason, there are no relevant differences in comparison with contract.

E. DIFFERENCES AS REGARDS LIABILITY FOR OTHERS

46 Spanish law knows several cases of liability for the acts of others, namely liability of parents for their children (art 1903 para 2 CC), of a guardian for the minors or disabled persons under their charge and who live with them (art 1903 para 3 CC), of a principal of an establishment or enterprise for the acts of their dependents (art 1903 para 4), and of directors of centres of non-higher education for the acts of minor students (art 1903 para 5 CC). Liability is based in all these cases on the fault of the liable person, who may escape liability if he/she proves that he/she behaved with the care required to prevent damage from happening (art 1903 para 6 CC). The rationale of the rule is commonly regarded to be the fault

---

[91] It can be found at <http://hj.tribunalconstitucional.es/HJ/es-ES/Resolucion/Show/SENTENCIA/1994/278>.

[92] It has been suggested that such amount may be lower than the cost of removing the waste which had been kept on the piece of land, since the municipality had acquired it to use it as a waste disposal facility. See *MÁ Parra Lucán*, El tercero obligado a restituir la cosa. Acción civil en el proceso penal: declaración de nulidad de titulo por la jurisdicción penal e indemnización de daños (A propósito de la STC 278/1994, de 17 de octubre), Derecho privado y Constitución (DPyC) 1995, no 5, 307–328, at 314.

[93] See *M Martín-Casals/J Ribot Igualada*, Pure economic loss: la indemnización de los daños patrimoniales puros, in: S Cámara Lapuente (ed), Derecho privado europeo (2003) 883–920, at 885 ff.

in the selection (*culpa in eligendo*) or supervision (*culpa in vigilando*) of the persons for whose acts another is liable – or, according to a minority opinion, a responsibility intrinsic to the parental authority, in the case of liability of the parents for acts of their children.[94] However, it is very difficult in practice to rebut the presumption of fault and, therefore, liability comes very close to vicarious liability. The Criminal Code (CP) provides similar rules with regard to liability in tort when the fact amounts to a crime or misdemeanour (arts 120 and 121). The latter regime applies only in the case of subsidiary liability of a public administration due to a criminal deed by a public official (see STS 30.1.1995 (RJ 1996, 189)).

There are no general rules comparable in contract, but only particular applications of the same idea in the rules devoted to particular contracts (eg art 1564 with regard to the contract of services). The *culpa in eligendo/vigilando* rationale may be equally valid in this context.[95] Nevertheless, it has been pointed out that, both in contract and in tort, the possibilities for the principal to escape liability on the basis of careful conduct are very scarce.[96] Moreover, in contract, the fact of whether or not the agent is dependent on the principal is not that relevant – in contrast to tort, pursuant to art 1903 para 4 CC. In this regard, the key issue is that the debtor may fail to perform what was due regardless of whether it was he personally or a collaborator of his who caused damage.[97] Additionally, in the case of a works contract, liability of the contractor is subjected to more rigorous rules, as has already been pointed out.[98] Indeed, the contractor is liable for the work performed by any persons hired to perform it (art 1596 CC). This is an instance in which the strict nature of the contractor's liability may be perceived.[99] Moreover, there are restrictions n the possibility to subcontract the works in order to preserve health and safety of the workers.[100] Restrictions also apply to subcontracts in the public sector (arts 227 and 228 LCSP). 47

As for the independent contractor, from a contract law perspective, the debtor will be liable for what he/she promised independent from the fact that the first was hired. However, from a tort law perspective, only the independent contractor will be liable. 48

---

94 See *A Paños Pérez*, La responsabilidad civil de los padres por los daños causados por menores e incapacitados (2010) 49 with further references.

95 See *Lacruz/Rivero* (fn 25) 172. Cf *Pantaleón* (fn 5) 1058 and 1069, for whom it is sufficient that breach is attributable 'on a subjective basis' to the debtor, even in the absence of fault on his side.

96 See *Yzquierdo* (fn 10) 82.

97 See *Blanco* (fn 11) 137.

98 See sec II.A.3 above.

99 See *Díez-Picazo* (fn 26) 584.

100 See *Ley 32/2006, de 18 de octubre, reguladora de la subcontratación en el sector de la construcción* (BOE no 250, 19.10.2006).

49 With reference to the liability for legal representatives or organs of a company, leaving aside the cases which have already been commented upon, it is generally considered that liability may be established both in contract and in tort. In the case of the organs of a company, it is the company itself which is party to the contract and therefore liable for damage caused. Also from a tort law perspective, the organs lack legal personality and, therefore, it is also the company which will be held accountable for damage caused.

F. DIFFERENCES AS REGARDS LIABILITY IN THE CASE OF MULTIPLE TORTFEASORS/BREACHING PARTIES

50 One of the most salient differences between contract and tort relates to the situation of multiple tortfeasors. As a rule, the Civil Code provides that obligations will only be joint and several on the condition that the obligation so provides (art 1137 CC). Therefore, the general rule is that a plurality of obligations are separate and dealt with as independent obligations, where every single debtor owes a separate debt (art 1138 CC). The system is thus one of several (*parciariedad*), not solidary (*solidaridad*), obligations. However, case law has – in order to improve the protection of victims – construed the provision above-mentioned as valid with regard to contractual obligations only. It derives from this that obligations created from other sources – including tort – are therefore not several but solidary. In this context, many decisions refer to the expressions of 'obligations *in solidum*' or *solidaridad impropia*, in particular in situations where it is clear that several persons caused damage but it is unclear to what proportion.[101] Such a solution is commonly adopted as regards building construction defects, where it is usually very difficult to ascertain the proportion to which the participants in the construction process contributed to causing the defects, or which of them was the one who actually caused them.[102] Moreover, it seems that case law is more prone to establish liability on a solidary basis in cases where multiple tortfeasors behave in a joint and intentional manner so as to cause damage.[103] As a result of such a flexible application of solidary liability in tort, there are almost no differences between it and contract in this regard.[104]

51 Furthermore, it must be noted that some contractual obligations are deemed indivisible (eg the obligations to deliver a certain thing or those which are not susceptible to partial performance, art 1151 CC), and therefore have to be

---

101 See *J Solé Feliu*, La responsabilidad extracontractual del principal por hechos de sus auxiliares: principios y tendencias (2012).

102 See eg STS 3.10.1996 (RJ 1996, 7006), 15.12.2000 (RJ 2000, 10445) and 8.2.2001 (RJ 2001, 2047).

103 See *Puig* (fn 44) 906 with further references.

104 See *Yzquierdo* (fn 10) 82.

performed by all the debtors together (*obligaciones mancomunadas*, art 1139 CC). Should one of the debtors fail to perform, all of them would be in breach since one alone cannot – because of the indivisibility of the obligation – perform his/her obligation without the others (art 1150 CC).

G. DIFFERENCES AS REGARDS THE PERSONS WHO MAY BE PROTECTED

From a Spanish perspective, this question makes sense with regard to contract only because every person is entitled to compensation if he/she suffers damage falling within a tort law rule (art 1902 CC being the rule by default, as has been mentioned earlier). In contrast to this, only the creditor will be entitled to request damages for the breach of contract (pursuant to art 1124 para 2 CC), since the contract is effective between the parties – and their heirs – only (art 1257 para 1 CC), according to the principle of privity of contract (*relatividad de los contratos*). In the case of stipulation in favour of a third party (art 1257 para 2 CC), these individuals may claim compensation from the promisor for his/her breach of contract (however not an action in discharge).[105] 52

A contract with protective effects for third persons does not exist under Spanish law. Certainly, particular statutes provide a direct action (*acción directa*) that allows an extension of liability as regards third parties. This is the case regarding the collapse of buildings (art 1591 CC) and the possibility for the workers and providers of construction materials to file a direct claim not only against the contractor who is the other party to the contract, but also against the owner of the works, with whom they have not contracted (art 1597 CC). Nevertheless, it is generally admitted that such action cannot – in contrast to the French *action directe* – be extended beyond cases other than those expressly provided for by the statutes at stake.[106] The reason is the principle of privity (*relatividad*) of contract (art 1257 CC).[107] Therefore, any extension of the obligational effects of a legal relationship as regards a third party is exceptional and requires a previous statutory provision authorising it.[108] Accordingly, for instance, a subcontractor of one of the parties in a contract has no action in contract against the other party in the first contract (STS 3.12.1990 (RJ 1990, 9543)). By contrast, the victim has a direct action against the liability insurer of the tortfeasor 53

105 See *Lacruz/Rivero* (fn 25) 524.

106 See *Martín-Casals/Ribot/Solé* (fn 43) 288 no 30.

107 See *A López Frías*, Contratos conexos: estudio de supuestos concretos y ensayo de una construcción doctrinal (1994) 306.

108 See *LF Ragel Sánchez*, Protección del tercero frente a la actuación jurídica ajena: la inoponibilidad (1994) 50.

(art 76 Insurance Contract Act (LCS)).[109] Such an action is not based upon the insurance contract – although its existence is required – but upon the law. Therefore, (a) the insurer cannot escape liability on the basis of the lack of payment of the insurance premium by the insured person, and (b) even the Public Prosecutor may file such a direct action in a criminal procedure.[110]

54 As regards chains of contracts, they have attracted considerable attention after the infamous *English Opening School* case, in which a large language school left thousands of students in the lurch without previous notice, after they had, most times inadvertently, concluded loan contracts with a third company.[111] Chains of contracts are grouped into the broader category of 'connected contracts' (*contratos conexos*), ie contracts in which there is a functional connection between the plurality of contracts agreed upon by the parties.[112] The legal effect of such a connection is that inefficacy of one of the connected contracts propagates to the others, as stated by case law.[113] At present, such contracts are statutorily tackled from the perspective of consumers' protection. So-called 'linked credit agreements' have actually become one of the most conflict-ridden issues in consumer credit in Spain.[114] Consumers enjoy particular protection in cases where they have concluded two contracts (credit and sales) with two different entrepreneurs (lender and seller) and one of them breaches the contract.

55 The Consumer Credit Contracts Act[115] (LCCC) provides that a chain of contracts (*contratos vinculados*) exists whenever (a) the credit is used on a sole basis to finance a contract related to the provision of specific goods or the provision of specific services, and (b) the two contracts constitute a commercial unit from an objective perspective (art 29.1). Such a 'commercial unit' exists whenever the provider takes part in the preparation or conclusion of the credit contract, so both contracts may be considered, from an objective point of view, as a single economic transaction, in which the provider collaborates with the lender.[116]

---

109 *Ley 50/1980, de 8 de octubre, de Contrato de Seguro* (BOE no 250, 17.10.1980).

110 See *Juan* (fn 21) 358 ff.

111 See *MJ Marín López*, La protección jurídica de los alumnos de English Opening School, Actualidad Jurídica Aranzadi 2002, no 548, and *C González González*, Estudiantes de inglés: ¡no pago sin mi curso!, Revista Aranzadi Doctrinal 2011, no 6.

112 See *López Frías* (fn 107) 282; similarly, *S Navas Navarro*, Notas sobre la financiación por un tercero y el crédito al consumo (Los derechos ejercitables por el consumidor frente al financiador en los contratos vinculados, art. 15 Ley 7/1995, de 23 de marzo, de crédito al consumo), Estudios sobre consumo 2000, no 53, 33–46, at 38.

113 See *López Frías* (fn 107) 297 with further references.

114 They also pose problems from the perspective of antitrust law. In this context, a chain of contracts consists in the sale of a product which is subordinated to the compulsory acquisition of a different product (so-called 'tied product'). See *C Herrero Suárez*, Los contratos vinculados (Tying agreements) en el derecho de la competencia (2006) 27 and 32.

115 *Ley 16/2011, de 24 de junio, de contratos de crédito al consumo* (BOE no 151, 25.6.2011).

116 See *MJ Marín López*, Contratos vinculados y cierre del negocio, Revista CESCO de Derecho de Consumo 2012, no 4, 160–184 <www.uclm.es/profesorado/mjmarin/invest_art_56.pdf> 167.

However – and in contrast with previous law[117] – it is now not required for a chain of contracts to exist that the parties are bound by on an exclusive basis[118] – in fact, such exclusivity seriously curtailed the freedom of the consumer, who was deprived of the possibility of contracting with a lender of his choice (eg STS 1.2.2011 (RJ 2011, 1813) and 4.2.2013 (RJ 2013, 1842)). The gravity of the social reality forced the intervention of the legislature to eliminate the exclusivity requirement with regard to contracts in which a continuous provision of services had been agreed upon.[119] Moreover, the present statutory regime lays down a presumption that the lender and the provider have agreed upon a remuneration to be paid by the latter to the former, so the loan cannot be deemed gratuitous – and therefore the contract cannot be excluded from the scope of application of the LCCC (art 3 f).[120] Nonetheless, the mere fact that the destination of the money is mentioned in the credit contract does not necessarily mean that the contracts are deemed to be a chain.[121]

In case of breach of the provider, the consumer may exert against the lender the same rights he has against the provider (art 29.3). The Act does not specify upon which rights the consumer may ground a claim. However, it seems that these include: (a) the right to suspend payment to the lender; (b) the right to a reduction in the amount of the loan; (c) the right to request performance of the contract; and (d) the right to reimbursement of the price of acquisition.[122] However, the consumer is not entitled to request compensation from the lender for damage deriving from the provider's breach, since – it is argued – the compensation claim does not ensue from the contract or the contract's breach, but from the negligent causation of damage.[123] Apart from that, if for any reason 56

See also *J Vicente Gavidia Sánchez*, El crédito al consumo: (cesión y contratos vinculados) (1996) 69 ff.

117 Cf *Ley 7/1995, de 23 de marzo, de crédito al consumo* (BOE no 72, 25.3.1995) (arts 14 and 15.1).

118 Such a requirement had given rise to a considerable amount of litigation. See *MJ Marín López*, Interpretación y prueba del 'acuerdo previo, concertado en exclusiva', entre prestamista y proveedor (art. 15.1.b de la Ley de Crédito al Consumo): doctrina de las Audiencias Provinciales, Revista Doctrinal Aranzadi Civil-Mercantil 2008, no 18.

119 Art 134 of the *Ley 62/2003, de 30 de diciembre, de medidas fiscales, administrativas y del orden social* (BOE no 313, 31.12.2003) thus modified art 15 of the 1995 Act. It must be borne in mind that the banks had insisted that the students pay for the language courses they did actually not attend, denying that there was any relationship of exclusivity between them and the schools. See *MJ Marín López*, Crédito al consumo y contratos vinculados. Estudio jurisprudencial (2010) 19.

120 This is also an improvement in comparison with the previous statutory regime. See *MP Álvarez Olalla*, Novedades en la Ley de Contratos de Crédito al Consumo, Revista Doctrinal Aranzadi Civil-Mercantil 2011, no 7.

121 See *A Díaz Martínez*, La nueva regulación de los contratos vinculados en la Ley 16/2001, de 24 de junio, de contratos de crédito al consumo, Boletín del Ministerio de Justicia 2013, no 2155, 1–32, at 6.

122 See *Marín López* (fn 116) 171.

123 Again, see ibid, 171.

the contract between the provider and the consumer lacks any effects – such as in case of discharge for non-performance, right of withdrawal, nullity, etc – the contract between the consumer and the lender will also be ineffective. Therefore the consumer may claim that the latter contract is declared to be discharged (arts 26.2 and 29.2 LCCC). A similar rule is provided in the statutory regime on so-called 'time sharing' (art 15.2 Time Sharing Act).[124]

57 In the absence of a clear statutory solution as regards the moment from which the contract loses its effects, most courts state that inefficacy lacks a retroactive nature, and therefore the lender is bound to give back the money paid by the consumer since the non-performance of the contract by the provider (eg from the moment when a language school finally closed its doors, STS 22.2.2011 (RJ 2011, 2470)). As a result, if the consumer totally failed to receive the teaching promised to him under the contract, he may recover the entire amount paid by him.[125]

58 With regard to public contracts, the person who concludes a contract with the public authority is obliged to compensate any third parties for damage resulting from the operations required by the execution of the contract (art 214.1 LCSP). However the public authority itself may be held liable instead, provided that damage results from an order issued by the same (art 214.2 1st part LCSP). The public authority will also be liable for damage caused to third parties as a result of defects in the project prepared by the same public authority (art 214.2 2nd part LCSP). In the case of a services contract (art 301 LCSP), it is expressly provided that the contractor will be responsible for the technical quality of the works and services he/she carries out, and therefore obliged to compensate the public administration and any third parties for damage derived from omissions, errors, inadequate methods or incorrect conclusions in the execution of the contract (art 305.2 LCSP). Furthermore, the contractor will be liable towards the public administration or third parties for damage resulting from any defects or technical insufficiencies of a works project, as well as for any material errors, omissions or violations of statutory or regulatory provisions attributable to the same (art 312.1 LCSP). However, in the case of damage caused to third parties, the contractor will be liable to compensate only half of the damage; the other half will be compensated by the public administration (art 312.2 LCSP).

---

124 *Ley 4/2012, de 6 de julio, de contratos de aprovechamiento por turno de bienes de uso turístico, de adquisición de productos vacacionales de larga duración, de reventa y de intercambio y normas tributarias* (BOE no 162, 7.7.2012).

125 See *Marín López* (fn 116) 183.

H. DIFFERENCES AS REGARDS DEFENCES

The debtor will be freed from his/her contractual obligation if performance becomes impossible – for example, the thing is destroyed or lost – without his/her fault and before he/she has incurred a delay (*mora*) (art 1182 CC). The same occurs if an obligation to do something becomes impossible in a physical or legal sense (art 1184 CC). As a general rule, which embraces any kind of obligation, nobody can be held liable for unforeseen or unavoidable events (art 1105 CC). Therefore there is no liability in the case of force majeure or unforeseen circumstances (*caso fortuito*) which cannot be attributed to the defendant.[126] 59

The act of a third party will usually be treated as force majeure from the point of view of the defendant (therefore, it is that party who may be sued if the required conditions concur). From this point of view, there are no remarkable differences between contract and tort. However, it must be noted that some special statutes lay down a separate set of rules on defences. For instance, the act of a third party is not a defence in the case of nuclear liability (although the operator will have a claim against the person who intentionally caused damage, art 8 LRCDN). As regards environmental liability, instead of using the concept of force majeure, the statute lays down particular instances of irresistible events which exclude liability (eg armed conflicts, hostilities, civil war, insurrections, etc, art 3.4 LRM; similarly, art 17.3 LRCDN). Legal scholarship has suggested that force majeure should actually not be a defence with regard to nuclear liability.[127] The statutory regime on public contracts makes clear what constitutes force majeure: (a) fire caused by atmospheric electricity; (b) natural events of a catastrophic nature (such as tidal waves, earthquakes, volcanic eruptions, movements of the soil, sea storms, floods or similar events); and (c) destruction caused in a violent manner in times of war, looting, or serious alterations of the public order (art 231 LCSP). 60

As to contributory negligence, there are some differences as regards its treatment in contract and tort, due to the different contexts in which it may take place. As regards contract, the basic assumption is that the creditor has to collaborate with the debtor so the latter can perform the obligation. Where the creditor refuses to collaborate, this may amount to a situation abstractly called 'delay of the creditor' (*mora del acreedor*). Should that happen, the creditor would bear the risk that the obligation becomes impossible (art 1185 CC), which would be 61

[126] In the same vein, art 614 Ccom on liability of the captain for breach of a travel contract; similarly, art 620 I Ccom. A special regime refers to contracts in the public sector, since the contractor will be entitled to compensation for damage caused by force majeure unless there was negligent conduct on his/her side (art 231.1 LCSP).

[127] See *F Bonet Ramón/FV Bonet Bonet*, Responsabilidad civil nuclear, in: Estudios de Derecho Civil en honor al profesor Castán Tobeñas, vol 5 (1969) 51–156, at 124.

so, for instance, in the above-mentioned case of the borrower under commodate (art 1744 CC).[128] However, his liability is limited to the value of the thing at stake; therefore it does not embrace any other consequential damage suffered by the lender under commodate.[129]

62 Moreover, the debtor may discharge his obligation by delivering the promised thing to the judge (*consignación*), provided that the creditor refuses to accept it without justification (art 1176 CC). The creditor may come to be in such a situation even where he acts without any fault, provided that he fails to collaborate in the debtor's performance, so through the delivery the debtor will not be deemed to have breached the contract.[130]

63 As regards tort, the starting point is that the victim does not, strictly speaking, have a duty not to be negligent towards herself. However, the compensation award may be reduced or even excluded whenever the victim contributed to causing her own damage. For instance, as regards tort, it has been pointed out that art 1902 CC does not mention contributory negligence, but that there was actually no need to do so.[131] It is in the strict liability regimes concerning tort where there is usually such a reference, so almost every strict liability rule is accompanied by a contributory negligence defence (art 33.5 LC, 145 TRLGDCU, etc). Moreover, the *ex delicto* liability regime provides that where the victim contributed to causing damage, the courts may reduce the compensation amount (art 114 CP). In some cases, only gross negligence or intent of the victim will be taken into account (as in the case of nuclear liability, pursuant to art 17.2 LRCDN),[132] therefore it will be more difficult for the liable person to escape liability on the basis of contributory negligence. Similarly, as regards workers' compensation, if the accident at work is due to the 'intent or gross negligence' of the worker who suffered the accident, it will not be considered to be a 'work accident' (art 156.4.b Social Security Act (LGSS)).[133]

64 Apart from this, as has been partly pointed out, contributory negligence is a defence in tort regardless of whether the liability rule is strict or fault-based. So, for instance, in the case of traffic liability accidents, the special statutory regime

---

128 See sec II.B above.

129 See *Díez-Picazo* (fn 26) 583.

130 See *Lacruz/Rivero* (fn 25) 183.

131 See *F Peña López*, Lección 4ª. El nexo causal, in: JM Busto Lago/LF Reglero Campos (eds), Lecciones de responsabilidad civil (2nd edn 2013) 105–135, at 126.

132 This is in contrast with the previous statutory regime, on which see *Bonet/Bonet* (fn 127) 131. Previously, mere negligent behaviour of the victim was enough to reduce or even exclude liability.

133 *Real Decreto Legislativo 8/2015, de 30 de octubre, por el que se aprueba el Texto Refundido de la Ley General de la Seguridad Social* (BOE no 261, 31.10.2015).

(Motor Vehicle Accident Liability Act (LRCSCVM))[134] lays down a strict liability rule for personal injury caused by 'facts of the traffic' (*hechos de la circulación*). Such a liability rule is explicitly based on the idea of 'risk created by driving' (art 1.1 I) and is therefore independent from any fault of the driver. However, contributory negligence of the victim is a defence (art 1.1 II). According to the wording of the provision, the driver will be exempted from liability if damage is due to the contributory negligence of the victim 'on a sole and exclusive basis' (*debidos únicamente a la culpa exclusive del perjudicado*). The provision also allows a reduction of liability up to a maximum of 75% if contributory negligence only contributes to the production of damage and provides for specific rules for the protection of children under the age of 14 and other vulnerable persons in the case of personal injury (art 1 II).

I. DIFFERENCES AS REGARDS LIMITATION PERIODS

There are separate prescription periods for claims in tort and in contract. The former are shorter periods (one year under the Spanish Civil Code (art 1968 CC), three under the Catalan Civil Code (art 121-21.d CCCat)).[135] The *dies a quo* depends on a subjective element as does the knowledge of the victim (*desde que lo supo el agraviado*, art 1968.2 CC; similarly, art 121-23 CCCat). Therefore, the time period starts to run when the victim knows she suffers damage and whom she may file the claim against. By contrast, claims in contract are governed by the general limitation period of five years under Spanish law (art 1964 CC) or 10 years under Catalan law (art 121-20 CCCat). Therefore, prescription is one of the most important differences between contract and tort. However, it has been suggested that in practice the differences are minimal due to the stance adopted by case law as to the *dies a quo*, which, as has been pointed out, takes the knowledge of the victim as the triggering event.[136] 65

Some special tort law statutes provide different limitation periods (eg three years in the case of product liability (art 143 TRLGDCU) and nuclear liability (art 15.2 LRCDN)). In the case of environmental damage, the public authority has five years to recover the costs of the measures adopted to prevent, avoid or repair 66

---

134 *Real Decreto Legislativo 8/2004, de 29 de octubre, por el que se aprueba el texto refundido de la Ley sobre responsabilidad civil y seguro en la circulación de vehículos a motor* (BOE no 267, 5.11.2004), as amended by the *Ley 35/2015, de 22 de septiembre, de reforma del sistema para la valoración de los daños y perjuicios causados a las personas en accidentes de circulación* (BOE no 228, 23.9.2015).

135 *Ley 29/2002, de 30 de diciembre, primera Ley del Código civil de Cataluña* (BOE no 32, 6.2.2003).

136 See *Puig* (fn 44) 890.

damage (art 48.2 LRM). Some of these statutes also lay down a second, absolute, period, after which no claim may be filed (10 years since the product was put into circulation (art 144 TRLGDCU); 30 years since the nuclear accident in the case of damage to persons (art 15.1.a LRCDN), and 10 years in all other cases (art 15.1.b LRCDN)). Catalan law also provides a long-stop period of 30 years since the right to claim was born, regardless of whether or not the interested party knew about the claim being born (art 121-24 CCCat). As regards liability *ex delicto*, the criterion adopted by case law is that the prescription period is not one year (pursuant to art 1902 CC) but rather the general limitation period of five years (pursuant to art 1964 CC). Such a difference has been justified on the basis that the claim in tort and the claim in liability *ex delicto* are different in nature.[137] The result is that liability in contract and *ex delicto* liability share the same limitation period, whereas so-called 'pure tort liability' – ie liability in tort where the deed does not amount to a crime or misdemeanour – is subject to a notably shorter period.[138]

67 Usually interruption of the limitation period is governed by the general rules of the Civil Code (art 1973 ff CC), to which some special statutes expressly refer (eg art 143.2 TRLGDCU). Exceptionally, the special statute lays down a separate regime on interruption. This is the case of environmental liability, which may be explained due to the public nature of the recovery costs mechanism provided for by the Act (art 48.3 LRM) and the procedural particularities that this entails.

68 Limitation cannot be suspended but only interrupted under the Spanish Civil Code. However, the Catalan Civil Code provides that limitation may be suspended in the case of force majeure (art 121-15 CCCat), for some personal or family reasons (art 121-16 CCCat) or during the time the estate of a deceased person is unclaimed (*herència jacent*, art 121-17 CCCat).

J. DIFFERENCES AS REGARDS PROOF

69 Proof is governed by procedural rules which are common to contract and tort. The claimant, as a rule, bears the burden of proving the elements which give ground to the claim, and the defendant those which oppose it (art 217 Act on Civil Procedure (LEC)).[139] Therefore the victim of wrongdoing will usually have to bring evidence as to damage, causation, and fault – as regards the latter, provided that it is required by the tort law rule (STS 21.6.2007 (RJ 2007, 3783)). The courts may shift the evidentiary burden of proof of fault under very specific

137 See *Nadal* (fn 20) 89. However this is a much debated issue. Also see *Juan* (fn 21) 51 ff.

138 Such a regime has been harshly criticised by legal scholarship. Among others see *Yzquierdo* (fn 10) 73 and *Pantaleón* (fn 5) 5944.

139 *Ley 1/2000, de 7 de enero, de Enjuiciamiento Civil* (BOE no 7, 8.1.2000).

circumstances, where the activity is a very risky one. However, it seems that the courts have adopted a more restrictive stance to this regard – in contrast to previous case law, which had systematically shifted the legal burden of proof of fault.[140]

70 On the contrary, in contract it is usually sufficient for the creditor to prove breach and damage, so the debtor will have to prove that a defence exists in order to escape liability for such breach. This is in line with the traditional view, according to which contractual liability is based on fault. However, as pointed out above, such a view is challenged on two counts: (a) first, it has been suggested that there is little or no difference in this regard between contract and tort since, due to the application of the rules on the burden of proof, the creditor will usually bear the burden of proving fault;[141] and (b) second, some legal scholars have pointed out that the debtor does not escape liability by proving he was careful, but by proving that the breach was caused by a supervening impossibility which was not attributable to him only.[142]

71 In the case of informed consent, it is the person obliged to inform who has to prove that he actually informed the other party (STS 29.10.2004 (RJ 2004, 7218)). The reversal of the burden of proof of fault is not allowed in the case of contractual liability. Case law had even stated that there was a presumption that the debtor had acted without negligence (in a case of professional liability of a lawyer, STS 21.6.2007 (RJ 2007, 3783)). However, in the case of a contract of deposit, whenever the thing deposited was delivered closed and sealed, the depositary will be liable for damage if the seal or lock was forced as a result of his negligence (art 1769 I CC). Such negligence will be presumed on a rebuttable basis (pursuant to art 1769 II CC).

K. OTHER DIFFERENCES

72 There are differences in other fields.

1) Private International Law

73 Contractual obligations are governed by the law to which the parties have expressly submitted, provided it has a connection with the business or interest at stake; subsidiarily, the law common to both parties; if there is none, the law of the

140 See *Martín-Casals/Ribot/Solé* (fn 43) 283 no 9 ff.

141 This was already held by *J Castán Tobeñas/G García Cantero*, Derecho civil español, común y foral, vol III, Derecho de obligaciones (14th edn 1986) 223.

142 See *F Jordano Fraga*, La responsabilidad contractual (1987) 227 ff, followed by *Díez-Picazo* (fn 26) 577 ff; similarly, see *Díez-Picazo Giménez* (fn 26) 363 f.

place of common usual residence, and lastly, the law of the place of conclusion of the contract (*lex loci contractus*, art 10.5 CC). Tort law claims will be governed by the law of the place where the tortious acts or omissions occurred (*lex loci delicti commissi*, art 10.9 para 1 CC).

2) *Rules of Jurisdiction*

74 As a general rule, territorial jurisdiction corresponds to the court of the domicile of the defendant (art 50 LEC).[143] This is also the case if the claim is grounded upon the infringement of the rights to honour, privacy and one's own image, as well as other fundamental rights (art 52.1.6 LEC). In the case of compensation claims for damage caused by motor vehicle accidents, the court with jurisdiction will be that of the place where the damage was caused (art 52.1.9 LEC). There are other special criteria for cases of intellectual property or injunctions filed to protect the collective or diffuse interests of consumers, among others. A problem may arise where the claimant has to file a claim in contract against a public authority and in tort against a public servant (eg the mayor), since different courts deal with public law claims and private law claims. A solution may be to file both claims before a civil court, on the basis – pursuant to art 9.2 of the Organic Act on the Judicial Power (LOPJ)[144] – that the civil jurisdiction has an 'attracting force' (*vis atractiva*) as regards issues which are not attributed to any other jurisdiction (so eg SAP Zamora 7.5.1999 (AC 1999, 6074)).

3) *Capacity*

75 A person has capacity to conclude a contract if he/she (a) is over 18, or (b) is a minor who has been emancipated, and (c) has not been judicially declared to be disabled (art 1263 CC). Therefore, only a person who has 'capacity to conduct himself/herself' (*capacidad de obrar*) may validly enter into a contract. By contrast, the rule in tort is that the tortfeasor must have tortious capacity (*capacidad de culpa civil*), ie he/she must be able to understand the relevance of his/her acts and the capacity to act accordingly in order to be held liable for the damage caused.[145] However, other persons may be held liable for such damage (pursuant to art 1903 CC), as explained above.[146] In spite of the apparent

[143] On international aspects see *A Crespo Hernández*, Delimitación entre materia contractual y extracontractual en el Convenio de Bruselas: implicaciones en orden a la determinación de la competencia judicial internacional: Comentario a la sentencia del TJCE de 27 de octubre de 1998 (La Ley, 1998, 9964), Diario La Ley 1998, no 6, 2178–2181.

[144] *Ley Orgánica 6/1985, de 1 de julio, del Poder Judicial* (BOE no 157, 2.7.1985).

[145] See *Yzquierdo* (fn 10) 82.

[146] See sec II.E.4 above.

contrast between contract and tort, it has been suggested that there is little or no difference.[147]

76 As regards public contracts, there are special duties affecting public authorities in the case of conclusion of a contract. In particular, the public authority is obliged to appoint a 'responsible person' who will have to supervise the execution of the contract and ensure that the contract is performed (art 52 LCSP). The persons who conclude a public sector contract with a public authority are also required to meet certain requirements as to solvency and capacity (art 54 ff LCSP).

L. REASONS FOR THE DIFFERENCES

77 The most obvious reason is that the Spanish Civil Code distinguishes between contract and tort as two separate sources of obligations (art 1088 CC), each governed by a separate set of rules – even if some of them are common, as has been shown above. From a general perspective, contract and tort liabilities are different in that the first require the breach of a pre-existing obligation, which was agreed upon by the parties (the contract has the effect of an act between the parties, according to the Civil Code (art 1091)), whereas in tort there is no previous obligation to that which arises from inflicting harm upon another (unless one uses the concept of obligation in a very broad sense so as to include the duty not to harm others). This basic difference means that the parties in a contract have the possibility to foresee the consequences of a breach and to lay down rules accordingly, by making use of the autonomy that the legal system gives them (art 1255 CC). This self-regulation is obviously not possible where a previous agreement between the parties does not exist or – should it exist – has no relationship to the particular damage caused.

78 Interestingly, the Proposal for a Modernisation of the Civil Code on Obligations and Contracts, drafted by the General Codification Commission in 2009 (PMCC),[148] focused on obligations in general and contracts (both in general and in particular), but no attempt was made to modernise the law of tort. The Proposal maintains the distinction between the 'obligations which are born in a contract' and those which derive from 'damage for which one must be liable extra-contractually' (art 1092 para 1). A section is added on the compensation of damage (*De la indemnización de daños y perjuicios*), but it is restricted to

---

147 See *JM Miquel González*, La responsabilidad contractual y extracontractual: distinción y consecuencias, Cuadernos de Derecho Judicial 1993, no 19, 59–78, at 61 ff; he is followed by *Puig* (fn 44) 891.

148 Comisión General de Codificación (Sección de Derecho civil), *Propuesta de modernización del Código Civil en materia de obligaciones y contratos*, Madrid, Ministerio de Justicia, 2009.

contracts, since its first provision establishes that 'the creditor has the right to be compensated for damage which the breach causes him' (art 1205 para 1).

III. LIMITATION OR EXCLUSION OF LIABILITY ARISING FROM TORT AND FROM CONTRACT

A. STATUTORY PROVISIONS AUTHORISING A LIMITATION OR EXCLUSION OF LIABILITY

79 As has already been mentioned, the general rule under Spanish law is that courts are allowed to reduce the damages award in the case of fault-based liability 'depending on the circumstances' (art 1103 CC).[149] Case law describes such a rule as an exception to the principle of full compensation, an exception which is based on equity and is justified by the lack of proportion between damage caused and the negligent behaviour of its author, even if there is no contributory negligence on the part of the victim (STS 19.2.2014 (RJ 2014, 1129)). The judge may reduce liability even *ex officio*, ie on his/her sole initiative (STS 20.6.1989 (RJ 1989, 4702)). Moreover, the reduction is discretionary, ie it is not required for liability to be reduced that any other co-causes or contributory activities from other persons are proved (again, STS 20.6.1989 and also STS 20.4.2011 (RJ 2011, 3597)). Due to this discretion, the Supreme Court is not allowed to review the way the lower court used such power on appeal (among many others, STS 30.11.2007 (RJ 2007, 8656) and 19.5.2010 (RJ 2010, 3704)). Nevertheless, case law has left the possibility open for such a review where the lower court either (a) applied its discretionary power in an irrational or disproportionate manner (for which the contribution of one of the contractual parties to causing the damage may be taken into account, as in STS 18.7.2013 (RJ 2013, 5532)), or (b) failed to even discuss the possibility of applying it, even though such a possibility was actually 'imposed on a logical and compulsory basis by the exceptional circumstances of the particular case' (as was decided by STS 19.6.1996 (RJ 1996, 5803)). Another decision states that the manner in which the judicial power is used is not reviewable, but the decision itself as to whether to use such a power or not is (STS 23.10.2012 (RJ 2012, 1542)).

80 A particular application of the reduction of the compensation award on the basis of equity may be found in the statutory regime on the criminal liability of minors.[150] This regime includes both criminal and tort liability of minors (ie persons between 14 and 18 years old, pursuant to art 1.1 Act on the Criminal

---

[149] See sec II.A.3 above.

[150] See also sec II.E.4 above.

Liability of Minors (LORPM)).[151] According to the special Act, when the liable person is younger than 18, his/her parents, custodians, fostering custodian (*acogedor*) or keeper – statutorily or in fact – will be held solidarily liable together with the minor. However, if such persons 'did not favour the minor's conduct either with intent or gross negligence, their liability may be reduced by the judge according to the case' (art 61 LORPM). Therefore, only if the guardians succeed in proving that they acted with only slight negligence may the court reduce their liability – not that of the minor himself/herself (art 61.3 if LORPM). This draws liability of the guardians close to strict liability,[152] and for this reason this special liability regime has been criticised as rather harsh.[153]

Apart from this, mention has already been made of the judicial power to moderate the liquidation of damages pursuant to art 1154 CC.[154] 81

The Code of Commerce provides a way to escape liability in the case of damage caused by vessels. In particular, the shipowner (*naviero*) and the ship's co-owners will be exonerated from liability for damage caused by the captain in connection with the cargo of the vessel provided that they abandon ownership on the ship (arts 587 and 590 Ccom). 82

B. LIMITATION OR EXCLUSION OF CONTRACTUAL AND TORTIOUS LIABILITY BY CONTRACT

1) *Is it Possible to Limit or Exclude Contractual and Tortious Liability under a Contract?*

As has already been partially mentioned, the parties may, based on their contractual freedom (art 1255 CC), lay down the rules which will govern liability in case it arises. The only limit is that liability for intentionally caused damage may not be excluded in advance (art 1102 CC and, with regard to the sales contract, art 1476 CC). Moreover, and in spite of the fact that the Civil Code does not distinguish as a general rule among degrees of negligence,[155] it is construed that gross negligence equates to intent in this regard and therefore liability for serious fault (*culpa grave*) may also not be excluded.[156] Nonetheless, according 83

---

151 *Ley Orgánica 5/2000, de 12 de enero, reguladora de la responsabilidad penal de los menores* (BOE no 11, 13.1.2000).

152 As *MR Ornosa Fernández*, Derecho penal de menores (2011) 445, observes.

153 See eg *ML Atienza Navarro*, La responsabilidad civil por los hechos dañosos de los alumnos menores de edad (2000) 152 and *S de Salas Murillo*, Responsabilidad civil e incapacidad (2003) 106 f, 153.

154 See sec II.C.5.

155 See *Pantaleón* (fn 5) 5943.

156 See sec II.A.3 above.

to legal scholarship, it is possible to exclude or limit liability for damage caused intentionally by auxiliaries in the performance of their obligations.[157]

84 Clauses excluding tort liability in advance are problematical on many counts: (a) they are not explicitly provided for by the legislature; (b) exclusion of liability is an exception to the general rule that the tortfeasor has to compensate for damage caused, and such an exception can, therefore, not be construed extensively; (c) no application on the basis of analogy seems possible with regard to the rules in contract, since there is actually no analogy between contract and tort; and (d) if the general rule of tort liability for fault (art 1902 CC) is of an imperative or mandatory nature, no voluntary derogation by the parties can be admitted.[158] And obviously, the tortfeasor and the victim may not have had the opportunity to agree upon such clauses before damage was caused. Nevertheless, a legal opinion holds that such clauses may be valid and that the issue is under which conditions or with what limits and in particular with the limit of *ordre public*.[159] In a similar vein, it is suggested that there are no differences in this regard between tort and contract, so limitation and exclusion contracts are valid in the first under the same conditions as the second.[160] As regards *ordre public*, it prevents some clauses from being validly agreed upon, such as those which (a) negatively affect the protection of the physical or moral integrity of the person, (b) impinge upon other fundamental rights, (c) violate human dignity, (d) exclude liability for damage caused with intent or gross negligence, or (e) imply a position of abuse of a dominant position.[161]

85 Limitation or exclusion clauses may be abusive under certain circumstances. In particular, it is abusive that the consumer remains unconditionally bound to perform the contract even though the entrepreneur has failed to fulfil his obligations (art 85.5 TRLGDCU). Moreover, the clause may be deemed abusive if it excludes or limits the legal rights of the consumer or user in the case of total or partial breach or defective performance by the entrepreneur (art 86.1 I TRLGDCU), in particular, clauses which restrict the consumer's or user's right to compensation for damage caused by lack of conformity of the goods or services with the contract (art 86.1 II TRLGDCU). Apart from that, the following clauses will be deemed abusive: (a) the exclusion or limitation of liability of the entrepreneur as regards performance of the contract, 'for damage or for death

157 See *Pantaleón* (fn 5) 5926.

158 See *N Álvarez Lata*, Cláusulas restrictivas de responsabilidad civil (1998) 103–116. Also see, on the limits of analogical reasoning, *F de Castro y Bravo*, Derecho civil de España (2008) 539.

159 So *Yzquierdo* (fn 10) 371.

160 See *García Rubio* (fn 70) 258.

161 See *MC Luque Jiménez*, Las cláusulas limitativas y exoneradoras de responsabilidad civil, Revista de responsabilidad civil, circulación y seguro (RRCCS) 2009, no 4, 7–24, at 12 and *García Rubio* (fn 70) 260 f.

or for personal injury caused to the consumer and user by an action or omission of the first' (art 86.2 TRLGDCU); (b) the imposition of any other waiver or limitation of the consumer's or user's rights (art 86.7 TRLGDCU); and (c) the imposition of the burden of proof to the detriment of the consumer or user in cases in which the other party should otherwise bear it (art 88.2 TRLGDCU). Legal scholarship deems a clause on exclusion or limitation of liability for slight negligence invalid as abusive when included in standard terms.[162]

2) *To What Extent Can a Contractual Exclusion Provide a Defence to a Third Party to the Contract?*

86 As has been noted, the principle of privity of contracts (art 1257 CC) entails that they bind the parties only, not any third parties. Therefore, the defence provided to a third party will only be effective against the claimant if the first was a contractual party. Agreements between the parties are ineffective against a victim who is not a party of the same.[163] However, the parties may file actions in recourse or in contribution against each other because of such agreements.

IV. NON-CONCURRENCE OR CONCURRENCE OF ACTIONS

A. OVERVIEW

1) *Areas of Overlap between Tort and Contract*

87 There may be several areas in which tort and contract may overlap. The first refers to the situation where there is a contract between the parties but it is not clear whether damage results from a breach of the contract or from a general duty not to harm.[164] Another recurring scenario is medical malpractice, as will be seen below.[165]

88 Other situations in which an overlap between contract and tort may occur may be cases where the keeper of a thing loses or causes damage to the thing which had been delivered to him in custody, or damage to the lessee of a thing which occurs due to the poor condition in which the lessor-owner keeps it.[166] Apart from this, case law has admitted that liability in contract and in tort may concur

162 See *Luque* (fn 161) 13 and *Pantaleón* (fn 5) 5926.
163 See *Yzquierdo* (fn 10) 371.
164 See sec IV.2.
165 See sec V.2.
166 Both examples are taken from *H Campuzano Tomé*, Nociones generales sobre responsabilidad civil (1997) 27.

in the case of damage caused in the course of transportation of a thing: for instance, the transporting company – with which the claimant concluded the transport contract – may be held liable in contract on a solidary basis with the persons who materially carried out the transportation – who are held liable in tort, absent a contractual relationship with the claimant (STS 9.1.1985 (RJ 1985, 167)). Such a solution has been labelled as dubious and unnecessary by legal scholarship.[167]

89 A different possible scenario in which the contract–tort interplay may become relevant is the situation where the conduct of a third party has an impact on the contract concluded by different persons. One example is the unauthorised publication of pictures of a celebrity wedding, thereby interfering with the exclusive licence to publish pictures contracted between the celebrities at stake and a specific publisher (as in the well-known case of *Douglas v Hello! Ltd* (2005) EWCA Civ 595). It has been suggested that grounding a tort claim on the violation of the rights to privacy and one's own image is inadequate, since what is really at stake is the protection of business. Therefore, liability in these cases should be based on contract.[168] However, such a solution is unsatisfactory, since the publisher of the unauthorised pictures was not a party in the original contract. Therefore, this is at most an instance of tortious interference with a contract.

90 A different scenario derives from the violation of a clause of exclusivity included in a contract. For instance, a well-known singer fails to fulfil an obligation towards a recording company and records a disc with a different company (STS 23.3.1921).[169] It was then held that the musician is liable in contract and the third company in tort, but liability is separate, not solidary (pursuant to art 1137 CC).[170] By contrast, in a similar case where the party in breach was a writer, the Supreme Court held that both she and the other publishing company were liable – the first in contract and the second in tort – on a solidary basis (STS 4.5.1973 (RJ 1973, 2291)). Legal scholarship has criticised the latter solution, since solidarity may only be applied provided that both liabilities derive from a single source or cause, which does not exist where one of the defendants is liable in tort and the other in contract.[171] Moreover it has been suggested that the third party who contributes in a decisive manner to harming the conflicting

---

[167] See *De Ángel* (fn 35) 29.

[168] See *M Ángel Rodríguez*, El derecho fundamental a la intimidad personal y las exclusivas periodísticas, Actualidad Jurídica Aranzadi (AJA) 2004, no 613.

[169] Gaceta de Madrid no 337, 3.12.1921, 228–233.

[170] On which see sec II.F above. On the applicable standard of care in these cases, see sec II.A above.

[171] See *Puig* (fn 44) 901.

interest of the other contracting party may be held liable in contract, not in tort – provided that the first knew about the previous contract.[172] Accordingly, if the party which was already contractually bound misleadingly expressed in the second contract that she was free of any previous obligation, the third party who ignored the fact that such previous obligation did actually exist is not liable (STS 20.3.1995 (RJ 1995, 1965)). The alternative view suggests that the general rule of liability in tort is broad enough so as to include the protection of personal rights, so the third party could be held liable in tort.[173]

Another situation in which tort and contract may overlap results from the allocation of liability with regard to the third party who actually caused damage. As has been pointed out, the operator of a nuclear facility may be declared liable even if damage was caused by a third party. The mere fact that the operator has been declared liable does not prevent the third party at stake from being declared liable for the same damage (art 53.1 Nuclear Energy Act (LEN)).[174] However, the operator will have a recourse action against the third party, on the condition that it was so provided on an explicit basis in the contract between both (art 53.2 LEN). Similarly, in the context of liability for construction defects, the developer is liable on a solidary basis for any material damage resulting from constructive defects (art 17.3 para 2 LOE). Therefore, the developer fulfils the function of guaranteeing that the construction works are carried out properly and with no defects. Nevertheless, he may have a claim in contribution against the other persons who intervened in the construction, and such claims may or may not be based on contract, depending on the circumstances. 91

2) *Approach to Non-Concurrence and Concurrence of Actions*

The situation under Spanish law is anything but clear. Case law is extremely confusing and disagreement exists between supporters of opposing points of view in legal scholarship.[175] Indeed, problems have arisen in situations where the claimant fails to choose the proper basis of the liability claim. For instance, the defendant was found liable in tort, but the claimant grounded the claim in contract, or vice versa. In such scenarios, the question is whether the court may change the basis of the claim and back up its decision on a legal ground not chosen by the claimant – or even worse, whether the court may reject the claim without any further examination of the merits of the case. If the court were not 92

172 See *Puig* (fn 44) 904. The author puts this in connection with the need to protect rights previously acquired by other persons as a general rule – on which see *LF Ragel Sánchez*, Protección del tercero frente a la actuación jurídica ajena: la inoponibilidad (1994) 107 ff.

173 See *Cavanillas/Tapia* (fn 14) 7.

174 *Ley 25/1964, de 29 de abril, de energía nuclear* (BOE no 107, 4.5.1964).

175 See *Cavanillas/Tapia* (fn 14) 209 ff.

allowed to change the claim's legal basis, then the decision would be invalid on the basis of a lack of congruence (ie the reasoning of the decision would not match the legal grounds provided by the claimant). In that hypothesis, the decision would be ill grounded on the basis of 'incongruence *extra petitum*'. According to procedural legislation, the court may not depart from the 'cause of the claim' (*causa petendi*) by resorting to foundations either in fact or in law which are different to those alleged by the parties. However, it is entitled to resolve the case on the basis of rules applicable to the case even though they may not have been mentioned by the parties (art 218.1 II LEC). Therefore there is no incongruence (*incongruencia*) if the court grounds its decision on legal considerations different to those alleged by the parties.[176]

93 Case law has stated that there is no incongruence if the claimant grounds its claim on liability *ex delicto* under the Criminal Code but the court resolves the case on the basis of contractual liability rules (so, for instance, in a case of breach of contract by the agent, STS 14.1.2013 (RJ 2014, 1842)). It is interesting to note that, in spite of the duality of liability regimes (one in the Civil Code and another in the Criminal Code), it is usually understood that the liability claim is one and the same – the only difference being that it may be filed before a civil law court or a criminal law court. However, some legal scholars and most court decisions start from the assumption that the *ex delicto* liability claim and the claim in tort under art 1902 CC are different, inasmuch as the legal effects in both cases are also different.[177] Should that second position be adopted, the court would not be allowed to decide on a basis other than that chosen by the claimant, since otherwise a situation of inability to defend oneself (so-called *indefensión*) would arise (thereby infringing a fundamental right of the defendant, as enshrined in art 24 CE). A majority of decisions therefore adopt the stance that both claims are different, especially in those cases where this is more favourable to the victim of the criminal deed.[178]

94 By contrast, if the claim is based on contractual liability, the court may not decide on the basis of tort. So, for instance, if an architect is sued because of an alleged defect in the works' supervision, such a claim is autonomous and independent from any liability based on the above-mentioned art 1591 CC. As the Supreme Court has put it, both liability regimes are different as regards the statutory regime and contents, mainly from the perspective of the regulation of interests agreed upon by the contractual parties, as well as with regard to the standard of care or the allocation of risks between the parties. As a result, both an automatic accumulation of actions and an application *ex officio* on the basis of

176 See *Juan* (fn 21) 385.
177 Instead of many, see *Nadal* (fn 20) 58–60 and 79.
178 See *Nadal* (fn 20) 68.

the *iura novit curia* principle are excluded (STS 23.4.2014 (RJ 2014, 3849)). This entails an abandonment of the doctrine which has been traditionally followed by Spanish courts, namely the so-called 'unity of civil fault' (among many others, STS 29.11.1994 (RJ 1994, 9165) and 29.10.2008 (RJ 2008, 5801)). According to such doctrine, fault in contract and in tort is essentially the same, so the claimant may (a) choose between one and the other, (b) claim in one and subsidiarily in the other, or (c) cumulate both claims. In this third case, the claimant would furnish the court with the facts of the case and the court would then place them either in tort or in contract. For this to happen, it is required that (a) the claimant has chosen a legal qualification of the facts which is wrong or imprecise, and (b) the other party is not negatively affected as regards the right to a fair trial and thus not deprived of the possibility to defend herself (STS 18.6.2008 (RJ 2008, 4470)). No such impossibility would exist where the claimant has sufficiently described the facts of the case as well as damage alleged, even though she may have erred as to the legal qualification of liability.[179]

A court may thus find that a bank is liable in tort – even though the customer's 95
claim was grounded upon contract – for having intentionally executed a loan in spite of the fact that the debtor had already discharged his obligation by lodging the money before the court and was therefore no longer obliged to pay (STS 7.6.2013 (RJ 2013, 8385)). On the same tenet, a court is not allowed to simply dismiss the claim on the mere basis that the claimant failed to choose the right cause of action. So, for instance, in the case where a car was stolen from a hotel car park, the liability claim filed by the customer who had a contract with the hotel cannot be dismissed on the mere basis that it was grounded in tort instead of in contract – but the court is nevertheless bound to decide in contract (STS 1.2.1994 (RJ 1994, 854)). However, it seems very difficult to draw clear lines in this area and sometimes the courts have adopted a more cautious stand. So, for instance, if the claimant has filed a claim in contract against a professional society for having advised him negligently with regard to taxation issues, the claimant cannot request on the same basis that the professional who carried out the advising activity is declared liable in tort, even though the professional at stake may be a manager and partner of the society (STS 30.5.2014 (RJ 2014, 4217)).

In the case of *culpa in contrahendo*, the claimant may accumulate both claims 96
or she may request a generic liability so the judge will decide on which basis to decide; or the judge may even rectify the incorrect choice of the claimant. Therefore, there is a concurrence of rules.[180]

---

179 See *De Ángel* (fn 35) 49; similarly *Blanco* (fn 11) 144.

180 See *E Vázquez de Castro*, Ilicitud contractual: supuestos y efectos (2003) 541.

B. CONCURRENCE/EXCLUSION OF ACTIONS FOR THE PROTECTION AGAINST PERSONAL INJURY

97 As has been pointed out above, the principle of 'unity of the civil fault' allows the victim to file a claim either in contract or in tort where personal injury is caused both in breach of contract and in the case of a breach of a general duty of protection.[181]

C. CONCURRENCE/EXCLUSION OF ACTIONS FOR THE PROTECTION OF PROPERTY

98 The owner and the holders of an interest in legal interests in things (so-called *derechos reales*) are protected by property law rules. If their possession is interfered with by another, they may thus request summary protection from the judge to prevent dispossession from occurring or to recover possession if they have already been dispossessed (art 250.4 LEC). Other actions may be available, including recovery of ownership (*acción reivindicatoria*, art 348 CC) and anticipatory actions (*acción negatoria*), inter alia. There are no special rules on concurrence or exclusion of actions in the tort/contract issue so the general criteria would apply.

D. CONCURRENCE/EXCLUSION IN THE CASE OF INTERFERENCE WITH CONTRACTUAL RIGHTS

1) Interference with a Contractual Relationship

99 Interference with a contractual relationship may amount to wrongful behaviour for which the tortfeasor may be held liable. Liability in contract is excluded due to the privity of contract (art 1257 CC).

2) Loss of Business due to Personal Injury to Someone Else's Employees or Clients or to Property Damage to the Entrepreneur

100 Compensation of pure economic losses resulting from personal injury or death of primary victims, ie of persons other than the plaintiff (or secondary victim), are confined – in the case of death and sometimes also in the case of very serious personal injury – to relatives and close persons. As regards employers, Spanish

[181] See secs II and IV.A.2 above.

legal writing, following Italian scholarship, has raised the question of whether damages should be awarded at least in those cases in which the contract required personal performance or when the plaintiff could prove consequential damage (eg for the costs incurred to replace the injured or dead debtor, or because performance could not be carried out within the period established in the contract as essential).[182] However, case law has basically referred to compensation in the case of public authorities as the employer of traffic policemen who were injured in traffic accidents. In these cases, civil courts have repeatedly ruled against compensation, arguing that the State failed to prove that it had incurred extra expenses to cover the functions undertaken by the police officer who was injured and that it did not prove the amount of these expenses which, therefore, would mean that it had not complied with the requirement of proving the damage sustained.[183] The Criminal Chamber of the Supreme Court, which had previously adopted a different criterion,[184] has eventually adopted the same.[185] A sector of legal scholarship, however, has been very critical of cases rejecting compensation and has argued that, although this position could be explained according to the so-called 'theory of the difference' (*Differenztheorie*), it does not fit within the concept of damage generally accepted in Spanish tort law.[186]

Cases giving rise to loss of business due to property damage usually refer 101
to interference with resources, which are either means of communication (channels, roads, bridges, etc), transmitters of energy or telecommunications. Decisions that deal with these sorts of cases, where third parties negligently interrupt the electricity supply or block communications by road, railway or other means, resulting in a claim filed by persons other than the owners or operators of the means of communication or resources, are very uncommon in Spanish law.[187] Whether or not liability arises usually depends on whether the court considers that a causal link between the defendant's act and the pure economic loss suffered by the plaintiff has been proven (as in STS 30.5.1986 (RJ 1986, 2918), with regard to the physical harm caused to a factory that provoked

---

182 See *Á Fernández Arevalo*, La lesión extracontractual del crédito (1996) 155–194.

183 So in STS 29.9.1986 (RJ 1986, 4922) and, among many others, SSTS 14.2.1980 (RJ 1980, 516), 14.4.1981 (RJ 1981, 1539) and 25.6.1983 (RJ 1983, 3685).

184 SSTS 2ª 13.12.1983 (RJ 1983, 6522), 2.12.1988 (RJ 1988, 9358), 12.6.1989 (RJ 1989, 5094), 11.12.1989 (RJ 1989, 9527) and 10.5.1990 (RJ 1990, 3894).

185 In SSTS 2ª 13.5.1999 (RJ 1999, 3812) and 9.6.1999 (RJ 1999, 3882).

186 See *Fernández Arevalo* (fn 182) 184, fn 31 and further references there.

187 Although there are many decisions in which telephone, electric or railway companies file a claim for compensation for damage caused as the result of cables being broken, especially against building and excavating companies, these are not cases of pure economic loss but of economic loss consequential upon a physical injury. See *F Gómez Pomar*, Comentario a la sentencia de 29 de diciembre de 2001, CCJC 2002, vol 57, 559–581. The same applies when the breaking of the cable causes a surge of power which damages a machine or electrical devices (see SAP Coruña 20.11.1998 (AC 1998/2204)).

a temporary dismissal of workers) or not (as in STS 28.2.1983 (RJ 1983,1079), concerning the destruction of rented premises which caused the termination of the lease, where the Supreme Court held that the causal link had not been proven). Finally, as regards transferred loss, which is treated mainly in relation to the transfer of risks, among others, in contracts of sale (art 1452 CC) and with regard to bequests (art 882 CC), the prevailing legal opinion considers that the person who, although not being the owner of the property lost, suffers the damage can claim for compensation.[188]

V. SPECIFIC SITUATIONS

A. PRE-CONTRACTUAL LIABILITY

102 The Spanish Civil Code does not make any reference to the situation where one party causes damage to another through his malicious or incorrect behaviour in the course of contractual negotiations. In fact, it does not create any duties for the parties during the pre-contractual stage. Indeed, the broad scope of the general rule of liability for tort (art 1902 CC) likely makes it unnecessary to resort to the idea of duties of protection at the pre-contractual level.[189] However, it makes some indirect references to that stage when dealing with defects in consent such as error (art 1262 ff CC) or liability of the seller for defects or hidden charges of the thing sold (art 1484 CC). The exercise of the remedies provided for in those rules requires that a contract has been concluded and that the defect existed already at the pre-contractual stage.[190] Moreover, a party may incur liability if (a) it involves the other in useless contractual negotiations, (b) it leads the other to conclude an invalid contract or a contract lacking efficacy, or (c) the other party suffers damage during the pre-contractual negotiations with the result that the contract is ultimately not concluded. No liability arises, though, if negotiations were not broken by the malicious conduct of any of the parties and the essential contents of the agreement had not yet been agreed upon (SAP Madrid 13.9.2000 (JUR 2000, 279377)). So, for instance, if the parties fail to obtain the necessary administrative authorisation but the defendant has done everything that was required of him to obtain them, there is no *culpa in contrahendo* (STS 6.5.2013 (RJ 2013, 4945)). Liability is also excluded where a breaking off of the negotiations was not done arbitrarily by one of the parties,

188 *Fernández Arevalo* (fn 182) 55–111 and further references therein.

189 See *P Valés Duque*, La responsabilidad precontractual o *culpa in contrahendo*, in: S Fernández Campo et al, Libro-Homenaje al profesor Manuel Amorós Guardiola, vol 1 (2006) 713–748, at 730.

190 See *JC Menéndez Mato*, La oferta contractual (1998) 26.

but was a commercial strategy of the alleged victim (SAP Valladolid 9.11.1998 (AC 1998, 8974)).[191] The freedom of the parties to withdraw from contractual negotiations does not exonerate them from liability if such a withdrawal harms the legitimate interests of the counterparty.[192] Contractual freedom is therefore not absolute since it has to be exercised in a legitimate manner.[193]

Both case law and legal scholarship are divided as to whether the case of *culpa in contrahendo* should be considered an instance of contractual liability or tort liability. The prevailing scholarly opinion holds that since no contract has yet been concluded between the parties, damage is governed by the rules on tort (art 1902 ff CC).[194] The leading case was decided by STS 16.5.1988 (RJ 1988, 4308), in which a bank clerk incurred some expenses after having been offered a new workplace in Miami by the same bank (see also STS 30.1.2008 (RJ 2008, 340)). It may be noted that some court decisions – and legal scholars – ground liability for *culpa in contrahendo* upon the general doctrine on the abuse of rights (pursuant to art 7 CC);[195] however, that leaves the fact that it is governed by art 1902 CC unchanged (STS 16.12.1999 (RJ 1999, 8978)). With regard to contracts in the public sector, it seems that *culpa in contrahendo* is dealt with as an instance of tort liability (arts 47.3 and 48 LCSP). 103

For liability *in contrahendo* to arise, certain conditions must concur, namely: (a) the creation of a situation of trust in the other party, so she could reasonably believe that negotiations would come to a good end; (b) a failure of the liable party to act in a trustworthy manner, breaching those negotiations without any justification; (c) damage to the victim; and (d) a causal link between the trust and damage (STS 14.6.1999 (RJ 1999, 4105) and 15.6.2009 (RJ 2009, 3394)). Moreover, *culpa in contrahendo* is different from the breach of a so-called 'preparatory contract' (*precontrato*), the breach of which gives rise to contractual liability.[196] However, it has also been pointed out that the case of *culpa in contrahendo* is far more specific than the general situation taken into account by 104

---

191 The claimant had requested the counterparty provide a security before entering into the contract, and the latter refused at a moment in which the former had already incurred some expenses.

192 See *Asúa González* (fn 23) 251.

193 See *E Vázquez de Castro*, Determinación del contenido del contrato: presupuesto y límites de la libertad contractual (2002) 72 and *A Manzanares Secades*, La responsabilidad precontractual en la hipótesis de ruptura injustificada de las negociaciones preliminares, ADC 1984, 687–748, at 688.

194 Among others see *Ál Carrasco Perera*, Art. 1101 CC, in: M Albaladejo (ed), Comentarios al Código Civil y Compilaciones Forales, vol XV-1 (1989) 429 and *J Espinoza Espinoza*, La responsabilidad civil precontractual, Revista general de legislación y jurisprudencia (2014) 2, 207–260, at 250.

195 See *García Rubio* (fn 70) 131 with further references.

196 See *Yzquierdo* (fn 10) 89; cf *García Rubio* (fn 70) 125.

the general clause of liability for fault under art 1902 CC. In particular, *culpa in contrahendo* is thought to arise from a violation of the duty of good faith (a duty which is laid down in art 1258 CC in connection with contract and art 7.1 CC in connection with the exercise of rights).[197] Some case law seems to go in the direction of an analogous application of the rule of art 1258 CC (STS 17.9.2013 (RJ 2013, 6826)) or stresses that the breaking off of negotiations has to occur in bad faith, or at least negligently, for liability to arise (STS 14.12.2012 (RJ 2012, 376)). Therefore intent is not necessary to establish such liability.[198] It has been suggested that art 1902 provides too general a basis in order to establish when liability *in contrahendo* will exist. Therefore, it is not entirely clear when the breaking off of negotiations is justified or not unless further criteria are provided by the courts.[199] Moreover, the Spanish courts (as happened in STS 16.5.1988, already referred to) have resorted to *culpa in contrahendo* even in situations where there was a pre-existing contractual relationship between the parties.

105 Arguments used to support the contractual nature of liability for *culpa in contrahendo* are: (a) a duty the violation of which gives rise to liability is one which binds the parties only; (b) liability *in contrahendo* includes not only liability for breach but also pre-contractual liability and liability due to the infringement of a duty of protection; and (c) liability *in contrahendo* requires that a violation of the duty of good faith has occurred.[200] For instance, annulment on the basis of malice is dealt with by contract law rules (art 1269 CC). The case where a seller fails to tell the truth to the buyer and therefore makes the contract voidable is dealt with from that perspective (eg STS 26.10.1981 (RJ 1981, 4001)). Arguments against the contractual nature of liability *in contrahendo* are: (a) that the contents of the conduct to be carried out are too uncertain at the pre-contractual stage;[201] (b) equating the breaking off of negotiations to a breach of contract would entail a violation of the principle of contractual freedom (art 1255 CC);[202] and (c) the range of the general rule of tort liability makes it unnecessary to resort to contract rules at this stage.[203]

---

197 Instead of many see *M Alonso Pérez*, La responsabilidad precontractual, RCDI 1971, 857–922, at 869 and *CI Asúa González*, Responsabilidad en la formación del contrato (responsabilidad precontractual), in: MA Parra Lucán (ed), Negociación y perfección de los contratos (2014) 139–168, at 141 ff.

198 See *Asúa González* (fn 23) 280.

199 See *Á Carrasco Perera*, Cartas de intenciones, precontratos, responsabilidad in contrahendo y obligatoriedad de los tratos en la jurisprudencia española, Revista Doctrinal Aranzadi Civil-Mercantil 2005, no 21 (digital version without page numbers).

200 In this vein see *Carrasco* (fn 194) 429; *Jordano* (fn 142) 32 fn 21.

201 See *Asúa González* (fn 23) 259.

202 See *Carrasco* (fn 194) 429 f and *Yzquierdo* (fn 10) 89.

203 See *Asúa González* (fn 197) 145 and *García Rubio* (fn 70) 58.

An intermediate position is held by those for whom *culpa in contrahendo* is a third category, separate from both tort and contract[204] and based on a duty of 'good faith *in contrahendo*', identical to that existing under contract pursuant to art 1258 CC. This seems close to the stance adopted by the Rome II Regulation,[205] according to which *culpa in contrahendo* derives from an act 'other than tort/ delict' (Recital 29); however, it is also deemed 'non-contractual' (arts 2.1 and 12). 106

As regards compensation, the prevailing opinion holds that compensation should be established with regard to the negative interest or 'reliance interest' – therefore not with regard to the positive interest or 'expectation interest'.[206] Therefore, the aim of damages is to leave the victim as if she had not suffered any damage. However, it has been suggested that the latter would be compensated in case of intent *in contrahendo*,[207] as in the case where the party who refused to fulfil a formal requirement later wilfully claims that the contract should be declared void for lack of form.[208] The legislature has not had to deal with such situations except for consumer credit contracts – where a special regime is laid down to protect consumers. It provides that in addition to restitution after the credit granted for the acquisition of certain assets has been declared void, the lender or entrepreneur to which nullity cannot be attributed is entitled to (a) a reduction of 10% of the instalments paid, in compensation for the fact that the buyer has possessed the things; (b) an amount equal to the initial outlay (*desembolso inicial*) for the commercial depreciation of the object.[209] Moreover, the seller may require adequate compensation for the deterioration of the thing sold (art 23 LCCC).[210] 107

B. LIABILITY OF PROFESSIONALS

As regards professionals, there has been a trend in case law to hold them liable on almost strict liability basis, in particular as regards the construction sector. Such a trend has, however, not extended to health professionals.[211] Private 108

204 See *Alonso* (fn 197) 859 ff.

205 Regulation (EC) No 864/2007 of the European Parliament and of the Council of 11 July 2007 on the law applicable to non-contractual obligations (Rome II) [2007] OJ L199/40.

206 Instead of many, see *Vázquez de Castro* (fn 180) 543.

207 See *Valés* (fn 189) 739.

208 See *García Rubio* (fn 70) 140.

209 When this amount is higher than one-fifth of the selling price, the deduction is reduced to the latter.

210 *Ley 16/2011, de 24 de junio, de contratos de crédito al consumo* (BOE no 151, 25.6.2011). The rule could already be found in the previous statutory regime, see art 9 of the *Ley 7/1995, de 23 de marzo, de crédito al consumo* (BOE no 72, 25.3.1995).

211 See *Pantaleón* (fn 5) 5948.

doctors are bound to their patients by a contract, but most medical services in Spain are provided by the public health system. Therefore the victim does not have any contractual relationship with the physicians or the health system as such. Problems of delimitation may therefore arise. In particular, the significant difference as regards the prescription period[212] invites victims to advocate the contractual nature of a legal relationship in order to avoid the one-year period prescription in tort – thereby giving rise to a 'pseudo-contractual relationship'[213] – or vice versa, the parties may stress the alleged tortious nature of the case in order to avoid any problems in contract.[214] So, for instance, liability is tortious if damage ensues from the doctor's refusal to conclude a contract, the contract between patient and doctor is void (after nullity has been judicially declared), damage is caused to a person other than the patient, or the doctor treats someone he found in an emergency in the street.[215] The reasons for dealing with claims against public and private hospitals or doctors in a different way have been contested on the basis that the liability problem is the same in both areas.[216]

109 As regards professionals in the construction sector, mentioned above, this is an area where a certain overlap between tort and contract may occur.[217] Although the Act on Edification (LOE)[218] was passed in 1999, art 1591 CC was not superseded by it, at least in an explicit way.[219] The latter establishes the liability of the contractor of a building for damage derived from its collapse (*ruina*), provided that the damage occurred within 10 years from completion of the construction. Case law has stated that the claim under art 1591 CC is compatible with a claim for contractual breach (STS 21.3.1996 (RJ 1996, 2233)). If the claimants sue on the basis of a contractual breach under art 1101 CC, the court may not hold the architect liable under art 1591 CC, since that amounts to a change in the 'cause of the claim' or *causa petendi* (STS 17.10.2001 (RJ 2001, 8641)). It is established case law that the acquirers (and sub-acquirers) of apartments or commercial premises, etc, in a building also have legal standing to claim liability under art 1591 CC. Case law usually refers to art 1591 CC

---

212 As already noted, see sec II.I above.

213 As *A Domínguez Luelmo*, El ejercicio ante los tribunales de las acciones de responsabilidad civil contractual y extracontractual: análisis de sus fronteras, in: Asociación de Profesores de Derecho Civil (ed), Cuestiones actuales en materia de responsabilidad civil (2011) 113–312, at 120, puts it.

214 As pointed out by *Yzquierdo* (fn 10) 85.

215 See *Llamas* (fn 32) 240 f.

216 See *Blanco* (fn 11) 133.

217 See sec I.B above.

218 *Ley 38/1999, de 5 de noviembre, de Ordenación de la Edificación* (BOE no 266, 6.11.1999).

219 However, in favour of deeming it superseded by the 1999 Act, see *Á Carrasco Perera*, La insistente recurrencia de un falso problema: ¿está derogado el art. 1591 Código Civil?, AJA 2000, no 454.

as an instance of 'statutorily established liability' (*responsabilidad ex lege*) (eg STS 30.9.1991 (RJ 1991, 6075)). This is clear when the claimant raises the issue of the construction defects before the edifice has been handed over to him, ie when the contract has not been performed yet. In such a situation, case law states that liability cannot be grounded upon art 1591 CC but at any rate upon the contract (STS 7.5.2001 (RJ 2001, 6897)). According to legal scholarship, art 1591 should be considered as a tort liability rule despite it being systematically included among the rules governing contracts of works.[220]

The Edification Act provides a further example of overlap between tort and contract, in line with the preceding case law. Pursuant to art 17.7 of the Act, persons who intervene in the construction process will be liable as regards the owners and third party acquirers, 'without affecting their contractual liabilities' (see STS 2.10.2003 (RJ 2003, 6451), 28.2.2011 (RJ 2011, 455) and 21.10.2011 (RJ 2012, 1122), among others). As regards contracts in the public sector, the contractor will be liable for the collapse of the works after the expiration of the guarantee time period if the collapse is due to a breach of contract by the contractor, provided that damage is evident within 15 years from the moment in which the works were handed over to the other party (art 244 LCSP). The rule is included among the remedies for breach of contracts of works. 110

CASES

CASE 1. THE UNATTRACTIVE SHOPPING MALL

The lessor is bound as regards the lessee to preserve the facilities in proper condition (arts 21 and 30 of the Law on the lease of urban apartments (LAU)).[221] The lessee may undertake the necessary repairs in case of an emergency (art 21.4 LAU) and discharge the contract if the lessor fails to fulfil his obligation (art 27.3.a LAU). Since the thing leased is not an apartment – in which case the rule would be different – but commercial premises, the lessee may sublet the store without the consent of the lessor, although the former must inform the latter within one month (art 32.1 and 4 LAU). The sub-lessee may not file a claim against the lessor D in contract because of privity of contract (art 1255 CC). Nonetheless, it is noteworthy that, by way of exception, privity does not prevent 111

[220] See *JL Lacruz Berdejo/F Rivero Hernández*, Elementos de Derecho Civil, vol II-2, Derecho de obligaciones. Contratos y cuasicontratos. Delito y cuasidelito (5th edn 2013) 189.

[221] *Ley 29/1994, de 24 de noviembre, de Arrendamientos Urbanos* (BOE no 282, 25.11.1994).

the sub-lessee from being obliged to pay the rent also to D (pursuant to art 1552 CC).[222] By contrast, the sub-lessee may file the claim in tort. However, since this is a pure economic loss, the courts may be reluctant to award him any damages, probably due to lack of causation, as explained above.[223]

CASE 2. THE IDLE LAWYER

112 A later will would have revoked the previous one (art 739 CC); however, the merely verbal request to the solicitor (or notary, under Spanish law) lacks any revocation effect since it lacked the formalities required by the law (art 738 CC). The notary may be liable if he caused damage intentionally, or in an inexcusably negligent manner or due to ignorance (art 146 of the Notaries Regulation).[224] The Civil Code makes a specific reference to liability in the case where a will is declared void because of a lack of formal legal requirements due to his malice or inexcusable negligence or ignorance (arts 705 and 715 CC).[225] Such liability is contractual as regards the client of the notary and tortious as regards third parties (STS 6.5.1994 (RJ 1994, 3718)). Therefore, if a notary delayed the elaboration of a will, he could be held liable in tort provided that damage was caused in any of the ways mentioned. If, as in the hypothetical above, the claimants had requested a lawyer manage this issue and his delay caused them damage, they may sue him either in contract or in tort. In a similar case, the claim against the notary and the lawyer was dismissed on the grounds of lack of negligence, in view of the short period of time which had elapsed since the claimants had requested the lawyer intervene and the sudden, totally unexpected and surprising death of the testator (only six days).[226]

---

222 See *L Puente de Pinedo*, Artículo 1552, in: A Domínguez Luelmo (ed), Comentarios al Código Civil (2010) 1700.

223 See no 100 above.

224 *Decreto de 2 de junio de 1944, por el que se aprueba con carácter definitivo el Reglamento de la organización y régimen del Notariado* (BOE no 189, 7.7.1944).

225 This was the case eg of SAP Madrid 5.9.1997 (AC 1997, 2241). In other cases, the claim was dismissed because of lack of causation between damage and a very minor error by the notary (SAP Las Palmas 8.4.2009 (AC 2009, 1680)). The victim may also sue the court's attorney (*procurador*) who caused the first damage (consisting in receiving a lesser share of the deceased's estate) due to a failure to deliver a court's document to the lawyer (SAP Burgos 30.10.2004 (JUR 2004, 56834), according to which the claim can be grounded on the contract of mandate between the victim and the attorney).

226 SAP Navarra 13.11.2011 (AC 2001, 238). The lawyer had asked the notary to prepare a new will on the day after he received the claimants' request and there was no real indication as to an emergency situation.

CASE 3. THE DEFECTIVE HOUSE

As explained above, the exclusion of liability agreed upon by D and Z has no effects as regards the subsequent acquirer of the house on the basis of privity of contract (art 1255 CC). Therefore, the claim filed by Z against D will have to be based in tort. Such liability is governed by special rules applicable to damage caused by agents in the so-called 'building process' (*proceso de la edificación*).[227] According to them, those agents – ie the developer, the constructor, etc – are liable for material damage to the building due to the defects of its structural elements for a period of 10 years (art 17.1.a LOE), and a period of three years in the case of defects of other elements (art 17.1.b LOE). Therefore, personal injury falls outside the scope of this regime and will be governed by the general rules (art 1902 CC). Since the statutory period starts to run from the moment in which the works were finished and handed over to the other party (art 17.1 LOE), the case will certainly fall outside the special rules. Additionally, the LOE provides that its liability regime is laid down 'without prejudice of the liability in contract' (art 17.1 LOE). In the case at stake, the sub-acquirers will probably not make use of the possibility – provided by case law, as may be recalled – to put themselves in the position of the commissioner of the house (Z), due to the existence of the exclusion clause. As a result, C may base his claim on the rule of art 1591 CC on the collapse of buildings, which (a) covers all damage – not restricted to damage to the building – and (b) lays down a general period of 10 years since the construction took place, a period within which the defects may become evident. 113

CASE 4. APARTMENT IN FLAMES

The landlord is obliged in contract to carry out the necessary repairs in order to preserve the apartment in a suitable condition of habitability, except where the deterioration of such condition is caused by the tenant (art 21.1 LAU). According to the Civil Code, it is presumed that the deterioration is caused by the tenant unless proved otherwise (art 1563). Since in the case under discussion fault on the side of the landlord has been established, the failure to fulfil the preservation duty makes the same contractually liable for damage deriving from deterioration. However, taking into account that the victim suffers personal injury as a result of a breach of contract and of a general duty of protection, the above-mentioned case law doctrine on the 'unity of civil fault' would mean that a claim could be filed either in tort or in contract, or both.[228] 114

---

227 See no 109 ff above.

228 See nos 7 and 97 above.

CASE 5. INJURED SKIER

115 The hypothetical fits within the facts of a case decided by the Spanish Supreme Court (STS 10.6.1991 (RJ 1991, 4434)).[229] The victim was insured against damage but insurance included tort liability only. However, the court did not have any qualms about holding that liability was tortious – with the result that the insurer could be forced to pay – even though damage resulted from the malfunctioning of a ski-tow of the ski resort with which the victim was contractually bound by way of the usual ski pass.

CASE 6. EXPLODING CAR

116 The Spanish Civil Code lays down a special regime on liability of the seller along the lines of the Roman *aedilitian remedies*. The seller is thus liable whenever the thing sold has a latent defect (arts 1461, 1474.2 and 1484 CC), even if he ignored such a defect – unless agreed otherwise (art 1485 CC). However, the action must be filed within six months from the delivery of the thing (art 1490 CC), so these remedies will not be available to C.[230] The same will also not be able to file a claim for lack of conformity under the statutory regime on consumer protection (art 114 Consumer Protection Act (TRLGDCU)),[231] since the two-year period since delivery, provided for by these rules (art 123), has also lapsed. The possibility remains to file a claim for breach of contract under the general regime on lack of performance, requesting the contract to be discharged plus compensation for damage suffered (art 1124 CC),[232] for which there is a longer prescription period (five years, art 1964 CC). The seller D1 may thus be held liable, although he may file a recourse action against the producer D2 (STS 8.10.2010 (RJ 2010, 7450)).[233] C cannot sue D2 in contract due to privity (art 1255 CC and STS 14.11.1984 (RJ 1984, 5554)).

---

229 Commented upon by *M Martínez Martín*, CCJC 1991, vol 27, 777–791.

230 The applicable time period is even shorter (30 days) in the case of a commercial sale (art 342 Ccom).

231 The latter – providing an action to correct the defect, or subsidiarily reducing the price or discharging the contract (art 118 TRLGDCU) – is incompatible with the exercise of the *aedilitian* remedies (art 117 TRLGDCU), so if both had been available, he would have had to choose between one of the sets of remedies. In recent case law see SAP Barcelona 12.6.2014 (AC 2014, 1689).

232 According to the prevailing opinion, the *aedilitian* remedies are compatible with the general remedies for breach. However, the relationship between both has been the matter of some discussion. See *F Gómez Pomar*, El incumplimiento contractual en Derecho español, InDret <www.indret.com> 2007, 1–49, at 13.

233 This decision held both the producer and the seller liable on a solidary basis for some defective air conditioning units because 'there is an intimate connection between their obligations

The claimant could additionally sue D2 in tort. Since damage is caused to the product itself, it is excluded from the product liability regime (art 142 TRLGDCU), but the action has to be filed within three years from the occurrence of damage (art 143.1 TRLGDCU). As is known, such an exclusion is grounded upon the idea – held by the drafters of the EU Product Liability Directive – that damage to the product itself should remain a matter of contract law.[234] According to the Supreme Court, in such a case the claimant must ground his claim on the rules on the contract of sale (STS 8.10.2010, mentioned above). If C wants to sue in tort, he will have to resort to the general rule of art 1902 CC, which requires that fault is established. For that reason, the franchise provided by the Spanish product liability regime – according to which there must be a deduction of €500 (art 141.a TRLGDCU) – is not applicable where damage affects the product itself and compensation of such damage is grounded upon a different legal basis (as in the case of SAP Palencia 22.1.2001 (AC 2001, 241)). In the Spanish case law, a claim in a case similar to the one under discussion failed because the claimant failed to establish that damage to the vehicle was the result of an original defect of the same (SAP Madrid 8.11.2007 (JUR 2008, 45612)), whereas in a different case the causal link was established on the basis of a proof by presumptions and the manufacturer was held liable on the basis of art 1902 CC, which had already been used by the claimant as a basis of his claim (SAP Barcelona 21.4.2005 (JUR 2005, 112401)).[235] 117

CASE 7. RACING BOAT BURNING

As in the previous case, the *aedilitian* remedy against the seller is time-barred (as occurred in SAP Málaga, 30.6.2005 (JUR 2005, 240171), also in a boat case).[236] However, the buyer could sue D for breach of the contract of sales or, if this is the case, of works (as in SAP Girona 25.2.2009 (AC 2009, 1249), where a defective swimming pool pump damaged itself). C could also bring the manufacturer to court in tort on the basis of art 1902 CC (if the first establishes fault) or on the basis of product liability rules (except for damage to the product itself, art 142 TRLGDCU). Therefore, the manufacturer would be liable for damage caused, 118

and, even though the source of the obligations is not exactly the same, the aim of liability as regards the acquirer is'.

234 In legal scholarship see, among others, *MA Parra Lucán*, La protección del consumidor frente a daños (2011) 207.

235 By contrast, where the claimant relies on the product liability regime only, the claim is doomed to fail (eg SAP Barcelona 8.2.2001 (AC 2001, 2013)).

236 Nonetheless, in that case the court excluded that the installation of a new engine by the seller had any influence on the boat sinking, which was actually caused – it was concluded – by a manufacturing defect. The court finally found against the manufacturer on the basis of the liability rules on damage to consumers (the equivalent to the current art 147 ff TRLGDCU).

including damage to the thing to which the defective equipment was attached (as in the case decided by SAP Baleares 28.6.2010 (JUR 2010, 304375)). For instance, the manufacturer of a defective part may be held liable for damage to the car involved in an accident caused by such a defect (as in SAP Zaragoza 10.2.2004 (JUR 2004, 92259)).

CASE 8. INSIDIOUS REPORT

119 It is apparent that the employee has denigrated his employer in order to promote his own company, which amounts to unfair competition (arts 1 and 2 of the Unfair Competition Act (LCD)).[237] His disparaging report violates the duty of good faith which the employee is expected to observe in the framework of his labour contract (art 5.a of the Workers' Statute (ET)),[238] so the act as such amounts to untrue or disloyal behaviour forbidden by the law (art 4.1 LCD). The employee may also have violated an agreement of non-concurrence, which is valid pursuant to Spanish law within certain limits (art 21 ET). The company may thus file a claim for compensation of damage derived from a breach of contract, since the employee is also bound to act according to the principle of good faith (art 1258 CC). Apart from that, since the report contained some false information which may mislead the addressee, this may also amount to a so-called 'deceptive act' (*acto de engaño*) (art 5 LCD) or a 'denigration act', ie an act which disseminates statements on the activity, the services, the establishment or the commercial relationships of a third party which are adequate to diminish its goodwill on the market (art 9 LCD). As a result, the company may file a claim on the basis of the LCD to request a declaration of unfairness, cessation of the unfair conduct or prohibition of its being repeated in the future, removal of that conduct's effects, rectification of the misleading, incorrect or false information, compensation for damage caused (provided that there is fault or intent) and the disgorgement of the defendant's unjust enrichment (art 32 LCD). The prescription period applicable to these actions is one year since the moment when they could be filed (art 35 LCD). This is an instance of liability derived from the infringement of an act, and therefore it is not based on the infringement of a contract. Therefore, the victim may recover compensation for non-pecuniary loss (immaterial damage derived from the denigration) as well as for economic losses. The latter claim, however, may fail due to a lack of proof of causation (as occurred in a very similar case decided in STS 11.6.2006 (RJ 2006, 4977)).

---

237 *Ley 3/1991, de 10 de enero, de competencia desleal* (BOE no 10, 11.1.1991).

238 *Real Decreto Legislativo 2/2015, de 23 de octubre, por el que se aprueba el texto refundido de la Ley del Estatuto de los Trabajadores* (BOE no 255, 24.10.2015).

CASE 9. CIRCULAR LETTER

Usually compensation claims for violation of the right to honour are based on a special statute, the LPCDH mentioned above.[239] D may claim he has criticised C based on his freedom of expression (art 20.1 CE), however such freedom is limited by C's right to honour (art 20.4 CE). Therefore, D may incur liability (pursuant to art 9 LPCDH) if his comments are not true, do not serve the public interest, or are offensive. The limitation period applicable to the claim is four years from the moment when C could file it (art 9.5 LPCDH). 120

Leaving that aside, the parties may have agreed upon a contractual restriction of competition between them (pursuant to art 20 of the Act on Agency (LA)).[240] Accordingly, the agent may not carry out the same professional activity after the agency contract has expired (art 20.1), with a maximum duration of two years since the contract's extinction (art 20.2). Obviously, the failure to adhere to that agreement makes C contractually liable for any damage caused. The prescription period applicable to claims derived from the agency contract is governed by the Commercial Code (pursuant to art 4 LA); however, due to the lack of a specific period, the general five-year prescription period of the Civil Code (art 1964) is applicable (pursuant to art 943 Ccom). 121

D may bring C to court for professional intrusion, which is a crime under Spanish law (art 403 CP). Should C be held criminally accountable, he would also have to compensate for damage caused pursuant to the provisions of the Criminal Code (art 119 ff).[241] C's gains would then be confiscated too (art 127.1 CP).[242] 122

The agent may be entitled to a compensation for the clientele kept by D (art 29 LA). However, such right is excluded if the agency contract was extinguished because of the agent having breached statutory or contractual obligations (art 30.a LA). 123

CASE 10. SHORTAGE OF SUPPLY

D is abusing its dominance in the market, thereby infringing competition law rules (art 2 of the Competition Act (LDC)).[243] In particular, D has abused his position by imposing a price and other commercial terms in an unfair way upon 124

239 See fn 76 and accompanying text above.

240 *Ley 12/1992, de 27 de mayo, sobre Contrato de Agencia* (BOE no 129, 29.5.1992).

241 See fn 20 and accompanying text above.

242 See no 38 above.

243 *Ley 15/2007, de 3 de julio, de defensa de la competencia* (BOE no 159, 4.7.2007).

the counterparty (art 2.1 LDC). Such conduct amounts to a serious infraction of the Act, which may give rise to the imposition of a fine by the public authorities (art 61.3.b LDC). That special statutory regime does not provide any rule on civil liability although this changed after Directive 2014/104/EU[244] was transposed into Spanish law.[245] According to the resulting statutory regime, the infringer may be held liable for the infringement of competition law (new art 71 LCD). According to the general rules on contract, any agreement which contravenes the rules on competition may be deemed illegal (arts 1272 III and 1275 CC) and therefore radically void (art 1306.2 CC). As a result, no contractual liability may arise from an agreement which infringes antitrust law; liability should be based on tort instead (art 1902 CC).[246]

CASE 11. INJURED ROCK STAR

125 As pointed out above,[247] claims for pure economic loss derived from a third party's interference with a contract may fail under Spanish law due to a lack of causation or of damage. So, for instance, in a case where the claimant had alleged that an erroneous weather forecast had been broadcast by the defendant (a public TV channel), thereby causing a reduction in the revenue of a concert, the Supreme Court considered that damage had not been established and that the fact that few people attended the concert may have been caused by other factors (STS 19.10.1992 (RJ 1991, 8081)).

CASE 12. EQUIPMENT DESTROYED

126 See the answer to the previous case.

---

244 Directive 2014/104/EU of the European Parliament and of the Council of 26 November 2014 on certain rules governing actions for damages under national law for infringements of the competition law [2014] OJ L349/1.

245 See *Real Decreto-ley 9/2017, de 26 de mayo, por el que se transponen directivas de la Unión Europea en los ámbitos financiero, mercantil y sanitario, y sobre el desplazamiento de trabajadores* (BOE no 126, 27.5.2017). In legal scholarship, see *C Oró Martínez*, Las reclamaciones por daños derivados de una infracción del Derecho de la competencia de la UE: primeras observaciones sobre la Directiva 2014/14/UE, La Ley Unión Europea 2015, no 22, 28–34.

246 See *F Peña López*, La responsabilidad civil y la nulidad derivadas de la realización de un ilícito antitrust (2000) 215–217.

247 See no 101 above. See also, in a sense coincident with the text and related to a similar hypothetical, *MÁ Parra Lucán*, Daños puramente económicos. Informe español, Actualidad Civil 2006, no 3, 268–283, at 'Case 2'.

CASE 13. SLIPPING ON A LETTUCE LEAF

This would probably be dealt with as a case of pre-contractual liability under Spanish law. According to some legal scholars, the seller has a kind of 'obligation of safety' as regards potential customers. However, this does not make any difference as regards the practical solution, since a specific rule for the pre-contractual setting is lacking and the situation would thus fall under tort.[248] In fact, the scope of the general rule of liability in tort makes it unnecessary to resort to the idea of an obligation of safety to hold the potential seller liable.[249] 127

CASE 14. TEST DRIVE

Since there is no contract between the parties, liability is tortious and will be governed by the statutory regime on motor vehicle accidents (art 1 LRCSCVM). This act includes both personal injury and damage to property within its scope of application. Therefore, both C – for damage to the car – as well as the owner of the tree may sue the driver D under that liability regime. Nevertheless, for liability for damage to property to be established, it is required that the driver has behaved in a negligent way (art 1.1 III LRCSCVM). For liability to be based in contract, it has to be proven that the parties agreed upon a specific contract, eg a 'loan of use' or commodate (*comodato*). In that case, the commodatary (C) would be liable for fault (pursuant to art 1746 CC; eg SAP Málaga 27.3.2006 (JUR 2006, 215886)). Case law has stated that the seller D is not entitled to retain possession of the car which is eventually sold to C on the mere basis that the latter has damaged the 'courtesy car' which was delivered on commodate to him in the interim period (SAP Málaga 29.4.2004 (JUR 2004, 200189) and SAP A Coruña 30.6.2014 (JUR 2014, 219190)). The owner of the tree may also sue D, who will, as a rule, be the holder of the compulsory insurance, and who may be held liable on the basis of his own fault (art 1902 CC) or on an analogous basis, with regard to the liability for others (art 1903 CC) according to case law.[250] 128

---

248 See *Carrasco* (fn 194) 433 with further references.

249 See sec I.B above.

250 However, such a solution has been criticised by legal scholarship, eg *E Corral García*, La responsabilidad extracontractual indirecta del propietario de un vehículo por los daños causados por un conductor autorizado, Revista General de Derecho 1995, no 612, 9573–9592. This author nevertheless would make the owner pay on the basis of the creation of a risk (at 9587). Cf *E Roca Trias*, La responsabilidad del propietario de vehículos, Revista Jurídica de Catalunya 1995, no 1, 135–150, at 150, according to whom the owner is liable based on the analogous application of liability for animals (art 1905 CC).

CASE 15. BREACH OF NEGOTIATIONS

129 The general principle of good faith (pursuant to art 7.1 CC) means that the parties have to behave according to good faith not only during the contract (as provided by art 1258 CC), but also in the previous and the later stages.[251] During the pre-contractual stage, there is certainly no truly legal relationship between the parties, but there is obviously a social relationship or a 'social contact' from which certain duties derive, including the one to negotiate in good faith.[252] Therefore, antique dealer D is free to accept the new offer. Nevertheless, if the new customer X does not request an immediate reply, D must tell the other party C so the latter has the opportunity to say whether she would like to conclude the contract or not.[253] As has been explained above, the lack of a general rule on *culpa in contrahendo* means that this case may be resolved through the application of the general rules on tort (art 1902 CC).[254] Concerning the procedural aspects, case law has stated that the fact that the claimant filed his action in contract does not prevent the court from deciding on the basis of *culpa in contrahendo* (STS 16.5.1988, (RJ 1988, 4308)).[255] However, the court may not establish liability *in contrahendo* if the claimant requested that the contract be declared valid and subsequently fulfilled by the debtor (STS 2.6.2000 (RJ 2000, 5092)).

CASE 16. NON-DISCLOSURE OF RELEVANT FACTS

130 The case may be treated as an instance of so-called negative intent or malicious reticence (*reticencia dolosa*), whereby one of the parties intentionally keeps silent about some information knowing that the ignorance of the counterparty is key to the conclusion of the contract. According to case law, malicious reticence determines that the contract is annullable on the basis of deception (art 1269 CC), provided that a statute, usage or good faith imposed upon the seller an obligation to inform the buyer and the first remains silent. Therefore the key is

---

[251] See *S Hidalgo García*, Artículo 1258, in: A Domínguez Luelmo (ed), Comentarios al Código Civil (2010) 1374.

[252] See *L Díez-Picazo*, Fundamentos del Derecho civil patrimonial, vol I, Introducción. Teoría del contrato (6th edn 2007) 311.

[253] So, relying on Italian legal scholarship, *Manzanares* (fn 193) 694.

[254] See fn 194 and accompanying text above.

[255] See no 103 above. The case concerned a bank clerk to whom a change of workplace to Miami had been offered.

whether the seller failed to honour a duty to inform or not.[256] The victim may request the contract be annulled within four years from the moment when the contract was performed (art 1301 CC). The buyer may also use the remedies of the contract of sale (*aedilitian* actions) or claim compensation for damage suffered (expectation damages, probably including the ruined crop).[257]

[256] See *Díez-Picazo* (fn 252) 202 and *J Ribot Igualada*, Artículo 1269, in: A Domínguez Luelmo (ed), Comentarios al Código Civil (2010) 1393.

[257] See *F Herranz*, Spain, in: J Cartwright/M Hesselink (eds), Precontractual Liability in European Private Law (2008) 391.

THE BORDERLINES OF TORT LAW IN SWITZERLAND

Pierre WIDMER, Bénédict WINIGER and Caroline DURET

QUESTIONS

I. Tracing the Borderlines 572
A. Distinction between Tort and Contract 572
B. Existence of a 'Grey Zone'? 573
C. Common or Different Rules Regulating Contract and Tort. 573
D. Application of Common Rules in a Different Way 574
II. Main Differences between Tortious and Contractual Liability 574
A. Differences as Regards the Foundations of Liability 574
1) Role of Intention 574
2) Role of Wrongfulness and Fault and their Variations 574
3) Role of Strict Liability. 575
B. Differences as Regards Causation. 576
C. Differences as Regards Remedies 576
1) Degree of Certainty of the Damage 576
2) Compensation for Non-Pecuniary Loss 577
3) Compensation for Loss of Earnings and for Loss of Chance 577
4) Restitutionary Damages 577
5) Aggravated and Exemplary (or Punitive) Damages. 578
6) Other Remedies. 578
D. Differences as Regards Recoverability of 'Pure Economic Losses'. . . . 579
E. Differences as Regards Liability for Others. 579
1) Liability for Auxiliaries and for Independent Contractors 579
2) Liability for Legal Representatives or Organs of a Company. 580
3) Liability of Representatives of Natural Persons. 581
4) Liability of the Auxiliary/Organ Itself 582
F. Differences as Regards Liability in the Case of Multiple Tortfeasors/Breaching Parties. 582
G. Differences as Regards the Persons Who May be Protected. 582
H. Differences as Regards Defences 583

I. Differences as Regards Limitation Periods 583
J. Differences as Regards Proof................................ 584
K. Other Differences 585
L. Reasons for the Differences 585
III. Limitation or Exclusion of Liability Arising from Contract and from Tort.. 585
A. Statutory Provisions Authorising a Limitation or Exclusion of Liability 585
B. Limitation or Exclusion of Contractual and Tortious Liability by Contract.. 586
IV. Non-Concurrence or Concurrence of Actions 587

CASES

Case 1. The Unattractive Shopping Mall 587
A. Tort: Liability of the Property Owner (Art 58 SCO) 587
B. Liability Based on the Breach of Contractual Obligations of a Lease Contract (Arts 97 and 253 ff SCO).................. 590
C. Solution.. 591
Case 2. The Idle Lawyer 591
A. Liability Based on Tort (Art 41 SCO)?........................ 591
B. Liability Based on the Breach of an Agency Contract (Arts 97 and 394 ff SCO)? 592
C. Solution.. 593
Case 3. The Defective House 593
A. Liability Based on Tort (Art 41 SCO)?........................ 593
B. Contractual Liability (Art 97 SCO) 594
C. Solution.. 594
Case 4. Apartment in Flames... 595
A. Tort: Liability of the Property Owner (Art 58 SCO) 595
B. Liability Based on the Breach of Contractual Obligations of a Lease Contract (Arts 97 and 253 ff SCO).................. 595
C. Solution.. 596
Case 5. Injured skier 597
A. Claim against D1.. 597
1) Tort: Liability of the Property Owner (Art 58 SCO) 597
2) Liability Based on the Breach of Contractual Obligations of a Transport Contract (Art 49 Para 1 LTV) 597
B. Claim against D2.. 598
C. Solution.. 598
Case 6. Exploding Car... 598
A. Liability for Defective Products According to Swiss Law (LRFP) 599

B. Liability Based on Tort (Art 41 SCO)? . . . 600
C. Liability Based on the Breach of a Sales Contract (Arts 97 and 184 ff SCO)? . . . 600
D. Solution . . . 601
Case 7. Racing Boat Burning . . . 602
A. Liability Based on Tort (Art 41 SCO)? . . . 602
B. Liability Based on the Breach of a Sales Contract? (Arts 97 and 184 ff SCO) . . . 602
C. Solution . . . 602
Case 8. Insidious Report . . . 603
A. Liability Based on Tort (Art 41 SCO)? . . . 603
B. Liability Based on the Breach of an Employment Contract (Arts 97 and 319 ff SCO)? . . . 603
C. Solution . . . 604
Case 9. Circular Letter . . . 604
A. Liability Based on Tort (Art 41 SCO)? . . . 604
B. Liability Based on the Breach of a Contract? (Art 97 SCO) . . . 604
C. Solution . . . 605
Case 10. Shortage of Supply . . . 605
A. Liability Based on Tort (Art 41 SCO)? . . . 605
B. Liability Based on the Breach of a Sales Contract? (Arts 97 and 184 ff SCO) . . . 606
C. Solution . . . 606
Case 11. Injured Rock Star . . . 606
A. Tort: General Principle, *Reflexschaden* . . . 606
B. Contractual Liability (Art 97 SCO) . . . 607
C. Solution . . . 607
Case 12. Equipment Destroyed . . . 607
A. Claim against D1 . . . 607
1) Tort Liability (Art 41 SCO) . . . 607
2) Liability Based on the Breach of Contractual Obligations of a Transport Contract (Arts 97 SCO, 440 ff SCO) . . . 608
B. Claim against D2 . . . 608
1) Tort: General Principle, Purely Economic Damage and Indirect Damage . . . 608
C. Contractual Liability (Art 97 SCO) . . . 609
D. Solution . . . 609
Case 13. Slipping on a Lettuce Leaf . . . 609
A. Tort: General Principles (Art 41 SCO) and the *Gefahrensatz* . . . 609
B. Liability Based on the Breach of a Sales Contract? (Arts 97 and 184 ff SCO) . . . 610
C. Solution . . . 611

Case 14. Test Drive 611
A. Liability Based on Tort (Art 41 SCO and the LCR)? 611
B. Liability Based on a Sale on Approval (Arts 223 ff SCO) and on the Loan Contract (Arts 305 ff SCO) 612
C. Solution. 612
Case 15. Breach of Negotiations 613
Case 16. Non-Disclosure of Relevant Facts 614
A. Liability Based on Tort (Art 41 SCO)?........................ 614
B. Liability Based on the Breach of a Sales Contract? (Arts 97 and 184 ff SCO) 615
C. Solution. 615

QUESTIONS

I. TRACING THE BORDERLINES

A. DISTINCTION BETWEEN TORT AND CONTRACT

1 In the Swiss Code of Obligations (SCO; Classified compilation – *Recueil systématique du droit fédéral*, RS 220), Swiss law distinguishes three main sources for the establishment of an obligation: (1) contract (arts 1–40 SCO); (2) tort (arts 41–61 SCO); and (3) unjust enrichment (arts 62–67 SCO). Further, in Section 2 of Title 2, entitled 'The Consequences of Non-Performance of Obligations', art 97 SCO establishes the liability of the obligor failing to properly discharge his obligation by stating that he has to compensate 'the resulting loss or damage, unless he can prove that he was not at fault'. This very broad wording is generally seen as covering typical non-performance (complete failure or delay) as well as the so-called 'positive breach of contract', ie the fact that improper performance by the obligor causes damage by infringing rights (bodily integrity, property) of the obligee. There is also a discussion about the possibility to adopt the concept – developed by the German doctrine – of the so-called 'contract with protective effects for third parties' (*Vertrag mit Schutzwirkung zugunsten Dritter*) in Swiss law; this would mean that the duty to perform properly would also work in favour of a certain (limited) circle of 'innocent by-standers'.

2 Furthermore, art 99 para 3 SCO prescribes that 'the provisions governing liability in tort apply mutatis mutandis to a breach of contract' if one of the parties is at fault, which obviously means that contractual liability is a different category to liability in tort. A glaring difference when comparing art 97 with art 41 SCO (general clause for liability in tort) is that, in the contractual context,

the burden of proof relating to fault is reversed (in fact, this difference is more apparent than real, see below no 49; for further – seeming – differences, see nos 26 f and nos 39 ff).

B. EXISTENCE OF A 'GREY ZONE'?

The system does not explicitly 'recognise' a grey zone. However, the jurisprudence admits the concept of '*culpa in contrahendo*' and – more recently – that of 'liability based on confidence' (*Vertrauenshaftung*), which is to a certain extent a generalisation of the basic idea governing *culpa in contrahendo.* Liability based on confidence is admitted if a third party has provoked, by an act or an omission, legitimate reliance towards the victim and if the disappointment of this reliance causes damage to the victim. This concept was developed by the Supreme Court in the Swissair case,[1] where Swissair knowingly tolerated that the economically independent company X stated in its advertising that Swissair was 'behind' X and where X's bankruptcy later caused damage to the victim. In other words, a party is answerable for frustrating the legitimate reliance it created on the other party. The grey zone is characterised by the fact that the jurisprudence hesitates between delict and contract in applying certain modalities, in particular with regard to time limits. Another phenomenon to be classified in the 'grey zone' is the already mentioned concept of 'contract with protective effects for third parties' which would lead to a breach of the privacy of contract. 3

C. COMMON OR DIFFERENT RULES REGULATING CONTRACT AND TORT

As already shown in sec I.A, there is a regulation by reference in art 99 para 3 SCO which declares that 'the provisions governing liability in tort apply mutatis mutandis to a breach of contract', provided that one of the parties is at fault. In other words, we have in principle separated the rules on contractual and on delictual liability. However, there is one exception: if in contractual liability a party is at fault, the rules of delictual liability (which is based on fault) are applied. This solution has a considerable advantage: it prevented the legislator from developing in parallel contractual and delictual rules for fault-based liability. Thus, the rules of arts 41 ff SCO can be considered as a kind of general part of the law regulating the compensation of losses. 4

---

1 Official Compendium of Decisions of the Federal Supreme Court (Recueil officiel des arrêts du Tribunal fédéral, ATF) 120 II 331.

D. APPLICATION OF COMMON RULES IN A DIFFERENT WAY

5 Courts certainly tend to evaluate the duties of an obligor with more rigour than those of a purely casual wrongdoer. This affects the strictness in assessing the degree of fault in particular. Contrary to Austrian law (§1299 ABGB), the Swiss system has no particular provision on the liability of specialists; in fact, however, duties of care of people alleging to have special skills are treated according to the appearance they arouse in their partners. This may also be considered as a type of 'liability based on confidence' (see no 3).

II. MAIN DIFFERENCES BETWEEN TORTIOUS AND CONTRACTUAL LIABILITY

A. DIFFERENCES AS REGARDS THE FOUNDATIONS OF LIABILITY

1) *Role of Intention*

6 Intent (malice) is considered to be the highest degree of fault.[2] As Swiss law permits the degree of fault to be taken into account, liability could be assessed with more rigour than if damage had been caused by mere negligence. In particular, contributory negligence of the victim could partly be reduced by the wrongdoer's intent.[3] It may also have an influence on the assessment of the causal link and its directness. We are not aware, however, if these elements would be evaluated in a substantially different way depending on whether the liability is contractual or delictual.

2) *Role of Wrongfulness and Fault and their Variations*

7 As far as wrongfulness is concerned, the difference may be seen in the fact that the contingency of infringements is widened by the specific obligations and duties implied in the contract. Such obligations and duties supplement those which the contracting partners owe each other independently of any contractual relationship. You could also say that unlawfulness as it is understood in tort is enlarged in the field of contract by the possible violations of the specific law of the

---

2 *K Oftinger/EW Stark*, Schweizerisches Haftpflichtrecht II/1 (4th edn 1987) §16 nos 22 ff; *W Fellmann/A Kottmann*, Schweizerisches Haftpflichtrecht I (2012) nos 559 ff; *R Brehm*, Berner Kommentar zum schweizerischen Privatrecht, Art 41–61 OR (in the following: BK-*Brehm*) (4th edn 2013) art 41 OR nos 192 ff.

3 On contributory negligence see especially ATF 128 II 49.

contracting parties, ie by any breach of contract. To the extent that one admits the dichotomy of wrongfulness of result (*Erfolgsunrecht*) and wrongfulness of behaviour (*Verhaltensunrecht*), it could be said that wrongfulness of result – ie wrongfulness deduced from the infringement of a strongly protected interest (life, bodily and mental integrity, personality rights) – occurs in the delictual as well as in the contractual context and is identical in both fields, whilst wrongfulness arising from a breach of contract is always and by definition a form of wrongfulness of behaviour.

Fault is also fundamentally a unitary concept. So-called 'contractual fault' is not different in comparison with fault in the field of tort. Simply – and in parallel to what was just said regarding wrongfulness – the contractual context sets forth specific duties, the violation of which is considered as a fault. 8

It is frequently admitted[4] that the standard of care is judged in a stricter and more objective way in the context of contract than in that of tort. This attitude in doctrine and jurisprudence has no clear-cut legal basis; it is deduced from the mere fact that the obligor has engaged in a particular relationship with the obligee and has explicitly promised a certain performance, but implicitly has also committed to achieve such performance without causing damage to the obligor's interests.[5] It is true however that there is a rather sensible tendency to strengthen the requirements vis-à-vis the obligee and to appreciate them in a more objective way, ie in a way fostering the (average) obligor's interests. This tendency is manifestly corroborated by the reversal of the burden of proof that prevails in the contractual context (see below nos 49 f). 9

In the frame of some specific contracts, the responsibility of the obligor is even 'strict', ie independent of fault (eg the liability of the vendor in a sales contract). 10

3) *Role of Strict Liability*

Apart from the situation where a particular contractual regime establishes strict liability (as mentioned above no 10), the cases where the law provides for strict liability (mainly in relation with typical and particularly elevated risks, but also in the sphere of liability for others and especially enterprise liability) have the effect that the *difference between tortious and contractual liability is* 11

---

4 See *P Gauch/WR Schluep/J Schmid/S Emmenegger*, Schweizerisches Obligationenrecht, Allgemeiner Teil II (10th edn 2014) no 2981 passim and concerning the burden of proof.

5 As said at the beginning, contractual liability is in general stricter than tort liability. For example, according to art 103 of the SCO, if the contractual debtor is late in the execution of his obligations, he is liable for hazard (notably *E Bucher*, Schweizerisches Obligationenrecht. Allgemeiner Teil (2nd edn 1988) 360 ff), while in tort law hazard can be invoked by the tortfeasor as a motive for reduction of liability.

completely removed. The explanation for this phenomenon lies in the fact that, where the liability is no longer attached to human conduct (and contractual liability is exclusively attached to human conduct), but to a more or less clearly and objectively defined situation of risk, it becomes totally irrelevant whether or not the person responsible for this risk stood in a contractual relationship with the victim(s).[6] The most illustrative example of this effect is product liability: the producer (manufacturer, importer or supplier) is liable towards the person injured by a defective product, regardless of whether he was simultaneously the vendor of the product and whether the victim was his (direct) customer and contractual partner. Similarly, if I hit somebody with my motor vehicle, it is not of the slightest importance if the injured person is my tenant or my landlord, my charlady, my barber or family doctor.

B. DIFFERENCES AS REGARDS CAUSATION

12 There is *no significant difference in the concept of causation*, whether it is used in the delictual or the contractual context. In both fields of application, mechanical causation (natural causation) is not sufficient. What is determinant is the (adequate) causal link existing between the conduct (action or omission) of the wrongdoer/debtor – which is qualified as a violation of a general or of a contractual duty – and the injury which entails a patrimonial or a non-pecuniary loss. It may be, however, that the specific object of a contract creates a framework which facilitates the assumption of a causal relation between the debtor's conduct and the damaging event; take as an example a contract involving medical care in the case of bodily injury, or another one necessitating an interference with property where damage to things is at stake.

13 Foreseeability may of course also be influenced by the specific nature of the contract and will potentially perhaps be judged in a more severe way when a contractual relationship typically holds inherent risks.[7]

C. DIFFERENCES AS REGARDS REMEDIES

1) *Degree of Certainty of the Damage*

14 Damage has to be proven with the *greatest possible certainty* by the person who claims compensation. This principle, laid down in art 42 para 1 SCO

---

[6] See *P Widmer/F Krauskopf*, Privatrechtliche Haftung, in: S Weber/P Münch (eds), Haftung und Versicherung, Handbücher für die Anwaltspraxis (2015) 18 ff, nos 2.31 ff (part 2.36).

[7] On foreseeability (and adequacy) in tort see *M Jaun*, Haftung für Sorgfaltspflichtverletzung (2007) 334 ff.

(in consonance with the general norm on proof in art 8 Swiss Civil Code, SCC, RS 210) is valid in tort and in the sphere of contract as well. This also follows from art 99 para 3 SCO, according to which: 'the provisions governing liability in tort apply mutatis mutandis to a breach of contract'.

However, para 2 of art 42 SCO somewhat loosens the rigidity of the general principle by stating that: 'Where the exact value of the loss or damage cannot be quantified, the court shall estimate the value at its discretion in the light of the normal course of events and the steps taken by the injured party.' 15

2) *Compensation for Non-Pecuniary Loss*

In both categories, compensation for non-pecuniary loss will be awarded if the harm amounts to a serious violation of personality rights of the victim (arts 47 and 49 SCO). 16

3) *Compensation for Loss of Earnings and for Loss of Chance*

Compensation for loss of earnings (*lucrum cessans*) is normally awarded in both categories. Here again, the specific nature of the contract and the fact that the obligee uses the object of the contract for business purposes may be taken into consideration when determining the extent of compensation.[8] 17

Loss of chance has, to date, not been recognised as compensable damage by Swiss courts.[9] In doctrine there is however strong support for the acceptance of this type of loss,[10] and the proponents of such recognition would not, as far as we can see, make a difference between tort and contract. 18

4) *Restitutionary Damages*

Restitutionary damages, in the sense of compensation or reimbursement for profits realised as a result of a delict or a breach of contract, are not explicitly provided for in Swiss law. This should still be integrated in a future law reform. In the meanwhile, a certain skimming of profits may be accomplished by applying the rules on *negotiorum gestio* (agency without authorisation; arts 420 and 423 SCO).[11] 19

---

8 Notably *I Schwenzer*, Schweizerisches Obligationenrecht, Allgemeiner Teil (7th edn 2016) no 14.13; *Bucher* (fn 5) 343 f; BK-*Brehm* (fn 2) art 41 OR nos 70 ff.

9 ATF 133 III 462, 471.

10 Pro: BK-*Brehm* (fn 2) art 42 OR no 56 (with lit); *C Müller*, La perte d'une chance, Etude comparative en vue de son indemnisation en droit suisse, notamment dans la responsabilité médicale (2002) no 323; contra: *Schwenzer* (fn 8) no 14.12a.

11 See notably ATF 133 III 153.

20 Restoration in kind is possible in both categories. Article 43 para 1 SCO, according to which the judge has to choose the best form of compensation (which implicitly means that restoration in kind and payment of damages are equivalent), is applicable in the context of tort as well as in that of contract: 'The court determines the form and extent of the compensation provided for loss or damage incurred, with due regard to the circumstances and the degree of culpability.'

21 In practice, however, compensation in money prevails, even if, ultimately, the courts tend to pay more attention to the request of the injured party.

5) Aggravated and Exemplary (or Punitive) Damages

22 Aggravated and punitive damages are excluded in both tort and contractual liability. Full compensation of the properly calculated damage is considered as the sum available at the most, and an additional award could even be considered as violating the public order (principle of the 'interdiction of enrichment', *Bereicherungsverbot*). In doctrine, there are some voices pleading for a more flexible position on this issue.[12] Furthermore, in a case of a moral tort, the Supreme Court granted the victim damages amounting to the presumed benefit the tortfeasor had made by publishing disparaging articles on the victim in his newspaper.[13]

6) Other Remedies

23 Specific performance is of course a typical remedy in the field of contract. Unlike in the common law, it is considered to be a proper way to subsequently perform, as far as it is still possible and not too cumbersome for the obligee (arts 107 and 108 SCO).

24 In the field of tort, restoration in kind (above no 20) is a closely related concept.

25 Injunctions (such as prohibiting a threatening infringement, ordering the cessation of an existing infringement or declaring unlawful a lasting infringement) are usually not considered as remedies belonging to tort law (*Schadenersatzrecht*). They may, however, be used as an alternative or a complement to monetary compensation in the case of non-pecuniary losses as envisaged in art 49 para 2 SCO: 'The court may order that satisfaction be provided in another manner instead of or in addition to monetary compensation.'

---

12 Clearly against punitive damages ATF 122 III 463, 467; BK-*Brehm* (fn 2) art 42 OR no 15; rather in favour *Schwenzer* (fn 8) no 14.12b; *P Hachem* in: S Wolf/M Mona/M Hürzeler (eds), Prävention im Recht (2008) 210 f.

13 ATF 133 III 153.

D. DIFFERENCES AS REGARDS RECOVERABILITY OF 'PURE ECONOMIC LOSSES'

Presently, recoverability of pure economic losses is one of the main differences between contract and tort. While pure economic loss is in principle always recoverable on the basis of contractual liability (insofar as the loss is a result of the breach of contract), it is, on the other hand, in principle excluded from recoverability in the field of tort. At least, this is or was the predominant opinion in Swiss law to date. This restrictive attitude in tort law has its justification in the doctrine of 'objective unlawfulness' related to the result of the interference (*Erfolgsunrecht*), according to which – apart from so-called absolutely protected rights (such as bodily integrity, personality and property) – mere patrimonial interests are only protected if there is a specific norm which ensures such protection. 26

There is, however, a recent and increasingly strong trend in doctrine to adhere to the 'subjective theory' of unlawfulness, where the focus lies on the behaviour (violation of a duty, *Handlungsunrecht*) of the tortfeasor. The aim of this new trend is precisely to include 'pure economic loss' into the sphere of principally recoverable loss in the field of tort liability too. In a project aiming at a comprehensive reform of the General Part of the Swiss Code of Obligations (OR/SCO 2020), it was even proposed to completely abandon the requirement of unlawfulness, or rather to integrate it into the concept of fault.[14] If this approach had been accepted, the difference between contract and tort would be reduced to quite a large extent.[15] However, this project was recently rejected by the Swiss Government. 27

E. DIFFERENCES AS REGARDS LIABILITY FOR OTHERS

1) Liability for Auxiliaries and for Independent Contractors

Liability for auxiliaries is one of the salient differences between the two categories. In the field of extra-contractual liability, the responsibility of the principal is – according to art 55 SCO – a personal liability of the employer for his failure to select, instruct and properly supervise his employees, but with a reversed burden of proof. Under the law in action, ie the rules developed by jurisprudence (ATF 110 II 456) and doctrine, this responsibility of the employer has been 28

[14] *C Huguenin/RM Hilty* (eds), Schweizer Obligationenrecht 2020, Entwurf für einen neuen allgemeinen Teil (2013) art 46 ff.

[15] *P Widmer*, Switzerland, in: H Koziol (ed), Unification of Tort Law: Wrongfuless (1998) 117 ff (with lit); BK-*Brehm* (fn 2) art 41 OR nos 38 ff; a resumé of the discussion in *Fellmann/Kottmann* (fn 2) nos 306 ff, nos 334 ff; also *Schwenzer* (fn 8) nos 50.28 ff.

transformed into a quasi-strict liability of the enterprise (or the entrepreneur) for defective organisation. This means in essence that the (counter-)proof of proper diligence provided by the Code is, in practice, very hard to adduce. On the other hand, it is clear in the extra-contractual context that the independent contractor cannot be regarded as an auxiliary, but is himself a principal who can be rendered liable for losses caused by his employees or agents.

29 In the area of contract, the obligor is in principle liable for damage caused by his agents as if he had acted himself (art 101 SCO).[16] This means that liability for auxiliaries in this context is still based on (very much objectivised) fault, but evaluated according to the standard of conduct that would apply to the principal himself had he performed personally (so-called 'hypothetical reproach'). The burden of proof relating to this fault is reversed – as always in contractual liability – to the detriment of the obligor (art 97 SCO).

30 In reality, there is not a great difference between the two regimes in terms of severity. In particular, the doctrine of the 'hypothetical reproach' works only in one direction: the principal cannot escape liability by showing that his personal skills are less developed than those of his agent. This means that, for the establishment of the required standard of conduct, the particular competences of the employee are imputable to the employer.[17]

31 The major difference, compared to liability in tort, remains the treatment of the independent contractor: if the obligor has engaged an independent contractor to realise the promised performance, he is liable for deficiencies of this person in the same way as he would be for a (subordinated) auxiliary. Only in the frame of an agency contract (arts 394 ff SCO) may the liability of the principal for a representative be somewhat mitigated insofar as he is then only responsible for the careful selection and instruction of the third party if the delegation of the business to this third party was authorised by the contract (arts 398 and 399 SCO).

2) *Liability for Legal Representatives or Organs of a Company*

32 Regarding the liability of organs of associations and/or companies (legal entities in general), art 55 SCC declares that:

> '1 The governing bodies express the will of the legal entity.
> 2 They bind the legal entity by concluding transactions and by their other actions.
> 3 The governing officers are also personally liable for their wrongful acts.'

---

16 Notably: ATF 92 II 19; 117 II 337; *Bucher* (fn 5) 350 ff.

17 ATF 130 III 591.

It follows from this provision that, in the first place, it is the company itself which is liable as a contract partner as well as a person responsible in tort. According to para 3, the organs or governing officers as individuals are 'also personally liable for their wrongful acts'. This means that – where tortious liability is at stake (possibly also in concurrence with contractual liability) – the organs/officers will be solidarily (jointly and severally) liable with the company itself, provided that they are at fault. The nature of the responsibility of the legal entity itself is controversial: some consider it a kind of vicarious liability which presupposes wrongful and faulty behaviour of one or more organs – behaviour that will be imputed to the legal entity as such; others – following the theory of 'real corporate personality' (Gierke)[18] – regard it as authentic and direct strict liability borne by the legal entity (by definition lacking delictual capacity) itself. 33

Normally liability insurance taken out by the enterprise covers both the responsibility of the company as well as that of the single organs/officers. 34

3) *Liability of Representatives of Natural Persons*

The so-called 'head of the family' (normally the parents) is liable for damage caused by members of his/her household who are minors or who suffer from mental disability or illness or are otherwise subject to a general guardianship, unless he/she shows that his/her supervision of the household was as diligent as would normally be expected in the circumstances prevailing (art 333 SCC). This form of liability in tort is generally considered to be strict, even if the criteria for the evaluation of due care in supervision are somewhat lenient. 35

In the field of contract, the parents – provided they have parental care – are vested with the power to represent their children; where one of two parents acts alone, it is presumed that he/she does so with the other's consent (art 304 paras 1 and 2 SCC). As representatives of their children, the parents are prevented from certain conduct, such as providing financial guarantees, establishing foundations or making gifts (art 304 para 3 SCC). However, the child him/herself may, insofar as he/she enjoys capacity of judgement, establish rights and obligations concerning his/her personal affairs and exercise strictly personal rights in the sense of the law of persons; for such commitments, the child is liable with all his/her assets (art 305 SCC). Similar rules are applicable *mutatis mutandis* to the cases of representative guardianship in the frame of the law of adults' protection (art 394 SCC) 36

In the frame of the recently revised regulation regarding the 'Protection of Adults' (former tutelage or guardianship), liability in the case of damage caused in the 37

---

18 *O Gierke*, Deutsches Privatrecht, zweiter Band, Sachenrecht (1905), pp. 375 ss.

course of an activity related to adult protection measures is a public authority liability incumbent on the competent canton and independent of any fault of the agent. As State liability, it is also primary and exclusive in nature, ie the injured person can only sue the canton as (public) legal entity and not the individual civil servant. The canton may then exercise a right of recourse according to its applicable cantonal law (arts 454 ff SCC).

4) *Liability of the Auxiliary/Organ Itself*

38 See no 32 ff above.

F. DIFFERENCES AS REGARDS LIABILITY IN THE CASE OF MULTIPLE TORTFEASORS/BREACHING PARTIES

39 The rules of joint and several (solidary) liability apply to extra-contractual as well as to contractual tortfeasors/obligors. As will be explained in sec IV, the general principle is the concurrence of actions, also between contract and tort, to the extent that the damage and the person(s) liable are identical under both regimes (arts 50, 51 and 143 ff SCO).

40 There is, however, a (controversial) distinction between contract and tort as far as the internal relationship between several tortfeasors is concerned. Article 51 para 2 SCO introduces a problematic hierarchy between the solidary liable persons, according to which: 'compensation is provided first by those who are liable in tort and last by those who are deemed liable by statutory provision without being at fault or in breach of contractual obligation.'

41 This provision is normally interpreted in the sense that a person liable in tort and for fault has no right of recourse against his fellow debtors if their liability is based 'only' on contract or results from a strict liability regime. The justification of this strange regime, still upheld by the Federal Tribunal,[19] is challenged by the prevailing doctrine.

G. DIFFERENCES AS REGARDS THE PERSONS WHO MAY BE PROTECTED

42 Generally speaking, the privity of contract is largely upheld, so that the liability of the obligor protects only the obligee. There have been some timid attempts to admit the concept of 'contract with protective effect for third parties' but it cannot be said that the idea has met with great success.

---

[19] ATF 137 III 352 consideration (c.) 4.1, 353 (with lit).

As has already been shown above (no 11), the distinction between contract and tort disappears when a type of strict liability is applicable. Product liability is particularly instructive in this context again, because it allows – independently from any contractual consideration – a claim to be lodged against a member in the distribution chain (importer, supplier) if the effective producer cannot be established. 43

H. DIFFERENCES AS REGARDS DEFENCES

In principle, there is no difference between extra-contractual and contractual liability as far as defences in general are concerned. In both domains, responsibility is in principle based on fault (arts 41 ff and 97 SCO); absent such a fault, the actor is not liable. A uniform application to both categories also takes place for those defences which relate to causation, ie force majeure, hazard,[20] intervention of a third party and contributory negligence of the victim itself. Of course, to the extent to which fault plays a role, it is possible that an external cause will be judged somewhat differently in a contractual context (see above no 8). 44

A more differentiated approach may be taken where the defence relates to unlawfulness or breach of a contractual duty, ie where it has its basis in a ground of justification. The classical motives (legitimate self-defence, state of necessity, consent of the victim, lawful authority or a preponderant public or private interest) are largely identical, but they may be subject to more nuances according to the specific contractual circumstances and agreements. 45

It is also worthwhile remembering that all these defences do not only work as an 'all or nothing' system, but can also lead to partial exoneration, depending on their weight and gravity (see arts 7:101 and 7:102 PETL: 'Liability can be excluded if *and to the extent* ...'; see also arts 43 and 44 SCO).[21] 46

I. DIFFERENCES AS REGARDS LIMITATION PERIODS

It is certainly the divergence in the ruling on limitation periods (prescription) which has the greatest practical impact on the difference between contractual and extra-contractual liability. Liability in tort is governed by a regime of 47

---

[20] BK-*Brehm* (fn 2) art 41 OR no 142, art 43 no 52; *Fellmann/Kottmann* (fn 2) no 460, nos 476 ff.

[21] See *P Widmer/B Winiger*, Causal Uncertainty and Proportional Liability in Switzerland, in: I Gilead/MD Green/BA Koch (eds), Proportional Liability: Analytical and Comparative Perspectives (2013) 323, 324 no 3, 328 nos 11 ff; BK-*Brehm* (fn 2) art 43 OR nos 23 ff; *Fellmann/Kottmann* (fn 2) nos 2418 ff.

very short so-called 'simple' periods of one or two years, which are normally extended by a longer period of so-called 'absolute prescription' (art 60 SCO).[22] With regard to the short 'simple' prescription period, the *dies a quo* is determined by subjective elements; it begins to run from the day 'on which the injured party became aware of the loss or damage and of the identity of the person liable'. The 'absolute prescription period', on the other hand, which has a subsidiary function for cases where the conditions of simple prescription are not fulfilled, lasts for 10 years, but it begins to run from an objectively determined starting point, namely 'the date on which the loss was caused' (in the German version 'the date on which the damaging act took place'). It is controversial whether this formulation means the very day on which the act that caused the damage was performed or if it could also be understood in the sense that the date when the damage occurred or was (or could have been) perceived is determinant. This uncertainty is one of the reasons why the law of prescription is currently under revision,[23] the main reason being the unsatisfactory situation which has arisen because of 'asbestos cases', where the injury frequently appeared after more than 10 years from the date when the victim came into contact with the toxic substance.[24]

48 As far as contract is concerned, the limitation (normal) period is a unique one of 10 years, and the *dies a quo* is the day on which 'the debt is due' (arts 127 ff SCO). In conjunction with the fact that Swiss law admits the concurrence of contractual and extra-contractual actions in compensation, this leads to the result that – in cases where both foundations of the claim can be invoked – the claimant will shift to the contractual path once the limitation period under tort law has expired.

J. DIFFERENCES AS REGARDS PROOF

49 As regards the burden of proof, we have already mentioned (above answer to question 1.1) that – in respect of fault – there is a reversal of this burden to the advantage of the claimant when he proceeds on a contractual basis (art 97 SCO). This finding however has to be relativised: fault as such is not an object to be proved, as it is not a fact but a value judgement. What can be proved is the conduct of the tortfeasor and the standard of conduct imposed upon him.

---

22 BK-*Brehm* (fn 2) art 60 OR nos 7 ff; *Fellmann/Kottmann* (fn 2) nos 3027 ff, nos 3037 ff, nos 3041 ff.

23 On this revision, see: Forum: Révision du droit de la prescription (with contributions by *F Werro et al*) HAVE/REAS 1/2012, 70 ff; *P Widmer*, Le dies a (quipro) quo dans la prescription subsidiaire, HAVE/REAS 1/2014, 69 ff.

24 See also: *P Loser*, Die Vertrauenshaftung im schweizerischen Schuldrecht (2006) nos 1124 ff; *B Chappuis*, Le moment du dommage (2007) nos 832 ff.

The proof of these two elements also serves as a basis for the estimation of whether or not the person in question has violated a statutory or a contractual norm (unlawfulness/breach of contract). In both cases (contract and tort), the claimant has to prove the standard of conduct applicable to the specific case, the violation of the standard, as well as his loss and the causal link between his loss and the behaviour of the (potential) tortfeasor.[25]

The standard of proof in itself does not vary depending on whether the claim is based on contract or tort. In fact, however, the reversal of the burden of proof relating to fault also tends to influence the standard of proof. In principle, the court has to be convinced of the facts put forward by the claimant. According to art 42 para 2 SCO, 'Where the exact value of the loss or damage cannot be quantified, the court shall estimate the value at its discretion in the light of the normal course of events'. Based on the provision of art 99 para 3 SCO (quoted in no 4 above), this possibility can also be used in the contractual context. 50

K. OTHER DIFFERENCES

Apart from those just mentioned – briefly summed up: burden of proof, liability for auxiliaries and independent contractors, and limitation periods – there are *no essential differences*. And even those which do exist or apparently exist are not beyond question as regards their justification. To the extent to which a concurrence of actions is possible between contract and tort, it seems difficult to explain why their modalities should differ from each other. 51

L. REASONS FOR THE DIFFERENCES

See no 51 above. 52

III. LIMITATION OR EXCLUSION OF LIABILITY ARISING FROM CONTRACT AND FROM TORT

A. STATUTORY PROVISIONS AUTHORISING A LIMITATION OR EXCLUSION OF LIABILITY

Swiss law allows – with certain restrictions – agreements including an exclusion or limitation of liability. According to art 100 SCO, such a contractual 53

25 See *Gauch/Schluep/Emmenegger* (fn 4) no 2998.

agreement is valid in relation to liability for slight negligence; it would be void if it purported to exclude or limit liability 'for unlawful intent or gross negligence'.[26] The parties can also consent to more strict conditions of liability.[27] In several special acts instituting a type of strict liability (eg motor vehicles, product liability, etc), contractual clauses limiting or excluding liability are totally prohibited.

54 Curiously enough, the regime is less strict in the field of liability for auxiliaries. Article 101 para 2 SCO provides that such liability 'may be limited or excluded by prior agreement'. In this case, there is no restriction depending on the degree of fault (either of the auxiliary or the principal).[28]

55 Further restrictions are envisaged at the court's discretion where the party which renounces the right to claim compensation was at the other party's service (or otherwise dependent on him or her), or, as well in art 100 as in art 101 SCO, where the liability arises 'in connection with commercial activities conducted under official licence' (eg banking activities).

56 In doctrine, a rather strong tendency advocates a complete interdiction of exoneration clauses in relation to bodily injury. Moreover, the revised act on unfair competition gives a possibility to have unfair clauses in general conditions declared void by a court.

B. LIMITATION OR EXCLUSION OF CONTRACTUAL AND TORTIOUS LIABILITY BY CONTRACT

57 It is generally admitted that exoneration clauses which are valid in consideration of the restrictions just mentioned produce their effects in contractual as well as in extra-contractual liability (provided again that the two types of action concur in the given case).

58 For contractual clauses limiting liability, see the explanations in nos 53 ff.

---

26 *L Thévenoz* in: L Thévenoz/F Werro (eds), Commentaire romand, Code des obligations I, Art 1–529 CO (in the following: CR CO I-*Author*) (2nd edn 2012) art 100 CO no 15, for different forms of clauses art 100 no 6; *Schwenzer* (fn 8) nos 24.04 ff; *W Wiegand* in: H Honsell/NP Vogt/W Wiegand (eds), Basler Kommentar, Obligationenrecht I, Art 1–529 OR (in the following: BSK OR I-*Author*) (6th edn 2015) art 100 OR no 6.

27 CR CO I-*Thévenoz* (fn 26) art 100 CO no 7.

28 CR CO I-*Thévenoz* (fn 26) art 101 CO nos 37 f; BSK OR I-*Wiegand* (fn 26) art 101 OR nos 16 ff; *Gauch/Schluep/Emmenegger* (fn 4) nos 3054 ff.

IV. NON-CONCURRENCE OR CONCURRENCE OF ACTIONS[29]

According to Swiss civil law, if the tortfeasor violates a contractual obligation and acts unlawfully, the victim has, in principle, the possibility to invoke together both contractual and tort grounds for liability.[30] The principle is therefore an accumulation of titles but an optional choice can be made between both types of liability, in the sense that the fulfilment of the pretension based on one of both titles extinguishes also the concurring pretension based on the other title. According to the majority view, concurrence also occurs where a type of strict liability is applicable to damage representing simultaneously a violation of contractual obligations. There are no exclusions whatsoever as regards the type of injury or any other distinguishing features.[31] 59

CASES

CASE 1. THE UNATTRACTIVE SHOPPING MALL

A. TORT: LIABILITY OF THE PROPERTY OWNER (ART 58 SCO)

The general conditions of liability based on tort are regulated in the general clause of extra-contractual responsibility of art 41 SCO: 60

> '1 Any person who unlawfully causes loss or damage to another, whether wilfully or negligently, is obliged to provide compensation.'

According to art 41 SCO, the five conditions founding the liability based on tort are:[32] 61

- damage;
- a damaging act;

---

29 We would like to thank Roger Gulka for his valuable assistance.

30 'Wenn der Schädiger durch sein Verhalten gleichzeitig eine vertragliche Pflicht verletzt und eine unerlaubte Handlung begeht, kann sich der Geschädigte nebeneinander auf beide Haftungsgründe berufen' (ATF 113 II 246 c. 3); ATF 112 II 142 c. 3b; ATF 99 II 321 c. 5.

31 *Widmer/Krauskopf* (fn 6) 21 f, no 2.36 and fn 40 ibid.

32 *V Roberto*, Haftpflichtrecht (2013) no 03.05; *C Müller*, La responsabilité civile extracontractuelle (2013) no 72; *id* in: A Furrer/AK Schnyder (eds), Handkommentar zum Schweizer Privatrecht, Art 1–183 OR (in the following: CHK-*Author*) (3rd edn 2016) art 41 OR no 5; *Oftinger/Stark* (fn 2) §16 nos 17 ff; CR CO I-*Werro* (fn 26) art 41 CO no 6; *A Koller*, Schweizerisches Obligationenrecht, Allgemeiner Teil, OR AT, Handbuch des allgemeinen Schuldrechts (4th edn 2017) 2.114; *P Engel*, Traité des obligations en droit suisse (2nd edn 1997) 447; Arrêt du Tribunal fédéral (Decision of the Federal Supreme Court) 6B_1117/2013 du 6 mai 2014 c. 2.

- a causal link between the action of the tortfeasor and the damage;
- unlawfulness; and
- fault (cf Case 3).

62 Article 41 SCO sets out a responsibility based on fault (*Verschuldenshaftung, responsabilité fondée sur la faute*), which can be opposed to a causal responsibility (*Kausalhaftung, responsabilité causale*), where the condition of fault is no longer required.[33] The general rule of art 41 SCO is applied if the specific conditions for another type of responsibility are not fulfilled.[34]

63 *In casu*, art 58 SCO, as regards the liability of the property owner, is relevant.

> '1 The owner of a building or any other structure is liable for any damage caused by defects in its construction or design or by inadequate maintenance.
> 2 He has a right of recourse against persons liable to him in this regard.'

64 The conditions of art 58 SCO are: (i) the presence of a building or any other structure; (ii) a defect; (iii) damage; (iv) a causal link between the defect of the structure and the damage; and (v) unlawfulness.[35]

65 In Swiss law, two causal links have to be established: natural causality and adequate causality. Regarding the former, a fact is the natural cause of a result if it constitutes a *conditio sine qua non*, which means that if the defect had not existed, the damage would not have occurred. Regarding the latter, the jurisprudence acknowledges that adequate causality is established if the cause of the damage is, according to the ordinary course of life and the general experience of life, suitable to cause an effect such as the one that occurred in a way that this result seems to be generally favoured by the fact in question.[36]

66 Damage is described as an involuntary diminution of one's net patrimony[37] due to the infringement of an absolute subjective right (physical integrity, life, honour) or to an object; it can also be the suffering endured by a victim in

---

[33] *Müller*, Responsabilité (fn 32) no 15; CHK-*Müller* (fn 32) art 41 OR no 5; *Engel* (fn 32) 531.

[34] *Müller*, Responsabilité (fn 32) no 11; CR CO I-*Werro* (fn 26) art 41 CO no 1; *Engel* (fn 32) 531.

[35] On the link between the defective structure and unlawfulness: Arrêt du Tribunal fédéral 4C.45/2005 du 18 mai 2005 c. 4.2.1; *Müller*, Responsabilité (fn 32) nos 153 f; CR CO I-*Werro* (fn 26) art 58 CO no 16; certain authors do not even mention unlawfulness: *Engel* (fn 32) 545; BK-*Brehm* (fn 2) art 58 OR 845 ff.

[36] Arrêt du Tribunal fédéral 4A_59/2009 du 7 septembre 2009 c. 6.2; ATF 129 II 312 c. 3.3; ATF 112 II 439 – JdT 1987 I 392; ATF 81 II 445 – JdT 1956 I 265; ATF 83 II 411 – JdT 1958 I 419; ATF 87 II 127 – JdT 1961 I 544; *Müller*, Responsabilité (fn 32) nos 207 ff; *Engel* (fn 32) 482 ff.

[37] ATF 127 III 543 c. 2b; ATF 129 III 18 c. 2.4; ATF 133 III 462 c. 4.4.2; ATF 115 II 474; ATF 116 II 441; ATF 127 III 73 c. 4a.

the case of physical suffering (art 47 SCO) or in the case of a breach of one's personal rights (art 49 SCO).[38] Following the theory of difference (*théorie de la différence, Differenztheorie*), the damage is defined by the difference between the patrimony of the victim and what it would have been if the damaging act had not occurred.[39] It can present itself in the form of a diminution of assets, of an increase of liabilities, of a non-augmentation of assets or of the non-diminution of liabilities.[40] The damage can take several forms, such as effective loss[41] (*damnum emergens*) or loss of profits[42] (*lucrum cessans*).

The damaging act can take the form of an action, but also of an omission to act.[43] 67

C's damage consists in a shortfall (*lucrum cessans*) due to the diminution of his sales of shoes. If the victim loses a profit which can be considered as usual, or that he likely should have gained following the ordinary course of events, the damage is a shortfall (*manque à gagner, entgangener Gewinn*).[44] The Swiss Supreme Court considers this type of damage as a 'purely economic damage' (*dommage purement économique, reiner Vermögensschaden*), which means that a prejudice appeared without touching the physical integrity of a person or without the damage, destruction or loss of an object.[45] This kind of damage is not reparable, unless it is the consequence of an unlawful act causing physical damage or moral harm to the victim or if a rule the aim of which is to protect the victim's patrimony exists.[46] 68

The Swiss Supreme Court supports the theory of objective unlawfulness (*théorie objective de l'illicéité, objective, Widerrechtlichkeitstheorie*), which 69

---

38 ATF 116 II 441 c. 3a/aa – JdT 1991 I 166.

39 ATF 133 III 462 c. 4.4.2; ATF 129 III 18 c. 2.4; ATF 132 III 359 c. 4; ATF 129 III 331 c. 2.1; ATF 128 III 22 c. 2e/aa; ATF 127 III 73 c. 4a; ATF 127 III 543 c. 2b; BK-*Brehm* (fn 2) art 41 OR no 70b; BSK OR I-*Kessler* (fn 26) art 41 OR no 3.

40 ATF 129 III 18 c. 2.4; ATF 133 III 462 c. 4.4.2; ATF 132 III 359 c. 4; ATF 128 III 22 c. 2e/aa, ATF 128 III 180 c. 2d; ATF 127 III 543 c. 2b; ATF 129 III 331 c. 2.1; ATF 127 III 73 c. 4a; BK-*Brehm* (fn 2) art 41 OR no 70b; BSK OR I-*Kessler* (fn 26) art 41 OR no 3.

41 This is the case when the damage event has to effect a decrease in net patrimony (BSK OR I-*Kessler* (fn 26) art 41 OR no 3; *Müller*, Responsabilité (fn 32) no 104).

42 If the damage act deprives the victim of the possibility of increasing his patrimony (BSK OR I-*Kessler* (fn 26) art 41 OR no 3; *Müller*, Responsabilité (fn 32) no 104).

43 ATF 121 III 358; BK-*Brehm* (fn 2) art 41 OR no 108; *Müller*, Responsabilité (fn 32) no 211; *Oftinger/Stark* (fn 2) §16 no 106; BSK OR I-*Kessler* (fn 26) art 41 OR no 18; *Engel* (fn 32) 453; *H Rey*, Ausservertragliches Haftpflichtrecht (4th edn 2008) no 591; *Roberto* (fn 32) no 06.09.

44 ATF 90 II 417 c. 3; ATF 82 II 401.

45 Arrêt du Tribunal fédéral 4A_653/2010 du 24 juin 2011 c. 3 – JdT 2012 I 270; ATF 133 III 323 c. 5.1; ATF 118 II 176 c. 4b; BSK OR I-*Kessler* (fn 26) art 41 OR no 13; BK-*Brehm* (fn 2) art 41 OR no 85; CR CO I-*Werro* (fn 26) art 41 CO no 20; *A Guyaz/M Vautier Eigenmann*, Le dommage purement économique, in: F Werro/P Pichonnaz (eds), Le dommage dans tous ses états, Colloque du droit de la responsabilité civile 2013, Université de Fribourg (2013) 195, 197.

46 ATF 133 III 323 c. 5.1; ATF 132 III 122 c. 4.1; BK-*Brehm* (fn 2) art 41 OR nos 38d ff; CR CO I-*Werro* (fn 26) art 41 CO no 20.

considers that the damaging action or omission is unlawful if it infringes a juridical rule; the damaging act must either violate an absolute right of the victim such as physical integrity or property (*illicéité de résultat, Erfolgsunrecht*), or violate any norm of the entire legal order (*illicéité de comportement, Verhaltensunrecht*).[47]

70 In the case of purely economic damage, the Swiss jurisprudence admits an additional condition to objective unlawfulness, as it must result from the violation of a behaviour norm (*norme de comportement, Schutznorm*),[48] destined to protect the rights of the victim affected by the damaging act; these norms can be taken from the entire Swiss legal order, whether they come from administrative, private or criminal law, whether they are written or unwritten, of federal or cantonal law.[49] *In casu*, C is not protected by such a specific (non-contractual) norm and cannot claim damages on a tort basis.

B. LIABILITY BASED ON THE BREACH OF CONTRACTUAL OBLIGATIONS OF A LEASE CONTRACT (ARTS 97 AND 253 FF SCO)

71 The contract is ruled by arts 253 ff SCO, subletting is authorised by art 262 SCO unless the landlord opposes it under certain conditions. The tenant must inform the landlord of the conditions of the contract (art 262 para 2 lit a SCO), the terms and conditions of the sub-lease cannot be unfair in comparison with those of the principal lease (art 262 para 2 lit b SCO) and the subletting must not give rise to major disadvantages for the landlord (art 262 para 2 lit c SCO). If the tenant sublets the property without informing the landlord, the subletting can still be valid if it respects the conditions of art 262 para 2 lit b and c SCO.[50] In the authors' opinion, the subletting is valid, despite Z violating a term of the contract.

72 C has signed a contract with Z and has no contractual link with the landlord D,[51] even if sometimes the law recognises a legal relationship between the two.[52]

---

47 Arrêt du Tribunal fédéral 4A_59/2009 du 7 septembre 2009 c. 6.2; ATF 133 III 323 c. 5.1; ATF 132 III 122 c. 4.1; ATF 123 III 312; ATF 122 III 309; 119 II 127; BSK OR I-*Kessler* (fn 26) art 41 OR no 31; *Oftinger/Stark* (fn 2) §16 no 43; BK-*Brehm* (fn 2) art 41 OR no 33c; *Engel* (fn 32) 449; *Müller*, Responsabilité (fn 31) no 158.

48 ATF 138 III 276 – JdT 2012 I 270; ATF 112 II 118 c. 5e; ATF 119 II 127 c. 3 – JdT 1994 I 298; ATF 125 III 86 c. 3b – JdT 2001 I 73; ATF 132 III 122 c. 4.1; ATF 129 IV 322 c. 2.2.2; 124 III 297 c. 5b; ATF 115 II 18 c. 3a; ATF 109 II 124 c. 2a; ATF 94 I 642 c. 5.

49 Arrêt du Tribunal fédéral 4A_653/2010 du 24 juin 2011 c. 3; ATF 133 III 323 c. 5.1; ATF 90 II 279 c. 4; ATF 88 II 281; ATF 78 II 422 c. 2a; CR CO I-*Werro* (fn 26) art 41 CO no 76.

50 *D Lachat*, Le bail à loyer (2nd edn 2008) 574 no 2.2.10.

51 Ibid, 579, §2.4.1.

52 Ibid, 579, §2.4.2.

C can however file a claim against Z who takes responsibility for the landlord's deficiencies, as the latter is considered by the jurisprudence and the doctrine as an auxiliary of Z, according to art 101 SCO.[53]

C. SOLUTION

If C wishes to claim damages based on the contract, he must file a claim against Z, as the latter is responsible for D's actions. 73

CASE 2. THE IDLE LAWYER

In Swiss law the conditions for disinheritance are extremely strict (arts 477 ff SCC, notably grave crimes against the *de cujus*, etc). The most common means to fight such a disposition would be to contest the validity of the will itself or to require its modification.[54] The daughters would in principle have two possibilities: seek to be restored to their legal inheritance rights (*réserve héréditaire, Pflichtteil*), or seek an amount equal to that which they would have received in accordance with W's wishes, as conveyed to his lawyer. If the daughters can prove that W did change his mind, it is not excluded that the judge would restore them to their legal inheritance rights by partially annulling the will or, most probably, modifying it and allocating £9,000 to each of them. The claim should be filed against the other heirs. 74

A. LIABILITY BASED ON TORT (ART 41 SCO)?

In this case the general clause of extra-contractual liability of art 41 SCO will be applicable. The five conditions previously mentioned (Case 1) must be fulfilled: damage, a damaging act, a natural and adequate causal link between the two, unlawfulness, and fault. 75

By not fulfilling his contractual obligations towards W, D caused damage to W's two daughters, as they did not receive the part of the estate their father wanted them to have. The damage is purely economic; a behavioural norm has to be violated in order the unlawfulness of D's actions to be recognised (cf Case 1). 76

---

[53] ATF 119 II 337 c. 3c/aa; *Lachat* (fn 50) 581 no 2.4.5.

[54] Eg ATF 5A_89/2011.

77 According to art 394 para 1 SCO, the agent undertakes to conduct certain business or provide certain services in accordance with the terms of the contract. The agent is liable to the principle for the diligent and faithful performance of the business entrusted to him (art 398 para 2 SCO). The agent has an obligation of means,[55] which D clearly did not fulfil by failing to draft W's will in a reasonable time frame.

78 According to tort law, the daughters could only file a claim in tort if the lawyer had violated a rule protecting them. *In casu*, they cannot invoke contractual norms protecting the *de cujus* (principle of the relative effect of contracts); the authors are not aware of other norms the violation of which they could base their claim on.

79 Nevertheless, one could try to plead that a lawyer or a notary (often mandated to prepare wills) functions as a public officer and engages with third parties on the ground of good faith. However, the chance of winning with such an argument seems to the authors to be rather slim.

B. LIABILITY BASED ON THE BREACH OF AN AGENCY CONTRACT (ARTS 97 AND 394 FF SCO)?

80 The two daughters did not have any contractual relation with the notary, only W and D were linked by a contract.

81 The Swiss Supreme Court has already examined the possibility to apply the German concept of *Vertrag mit Schutzwirkung zugunsten Dritter*, concerning situations where the execution of a contract provides advantages or disadvantages for a third party to whom the debtor would be liable too; this concept has so far been rejected, one of the controversies being the breaching of the principle of the relativity of conventions.[56] The Swiss Supreme Court is generally unwilling to breach this principle.[57]

---

55 ATF 115 II 50.

56 ATF 130 III 345 c. 1 – JdT 2004 I 207; Arrêt du Tribunal fédéral 4A_226/2010 du 28 juillet 2010, for a comment on this decision, cf *P Pichonnaz*, La relation entre maître d'ouvrage et sous-traitant – Le problème de la réparation directe du dommage subi par le maître – TF (BGer) 4A_226/2010 (28 juillet 2010) – italien, BR/DC 2011, 74; Arrêt du Tribunal fédéral 4C.194/1999 du 18 janvier 2000; ATF 121 III 310 c. 4a-c – JdT 1996 I 364; ATF 120 II 112 c. 3b – JdT 1995 I 202; ATF 117 II 315 c. 5 – JdT 1993 II 152; *N Kuonen*, La responsabilité précontractuelle: Analyse historique, étude de la phase précontractuelle et des instruments précontractuels, théorie générale en droit suisse (2007) no 1250; *F Bianchi*/JT *Michel*, Contrat d'entreprise, in: Not@lex 2012 vol 1, 31.

57 For a comparative summary on this matter, see: *P Gilliéron*, Les dommages-intérêts contractuels, CEDIDAC – Centre du droit de l'entreprise de l'Université de Lausanne, vol 88 (2011) 26 ff.

According to art 560 SCC, on the death of the deceased, the estate in its entirety vests by operation of law in the heirs (art 560 para 1 SCO); subject to the statutory exceptions, the deceased's claims, rights of ownership, limited rights in rem and rights of possession automatically pass to the heirs and the debts of the deceased become the personal debts of the heirs (art 560 para 2 SCO). The heirs are subrogated to the deceased in all the patrimonial rights and obligations; they can claim information and accounts relative to contractual relations, as long as the contractual relations were not strictly personal.[58] The heirs are entitled to act to defend the patrimony of the succession[59] (see also art 405 SCO on the rights of heirs in the contract of mandate). In the present case, the daughters would have to prove that D's actions caused damage to W. 82

At this point, different arguments could be raised, leading to different outcomes. Either, firstly, the two sisters have been disinherited and the judge refuses to annul the will. In this case they would not have a contractual claim. Or, secondly, the judge annuls the will. In this case, the daughters are restored in their legal inheritance rights, inherit according to the law and are subrogated to W's patrimonial rights and obligations towards the lawyer. They have a contractual claim against the lawyer and can recover the expenses they incurred for the trial and all other damage they suffered. Or, finally, the judge modifies the will according to W's wishes but does not restore the daughters to their position as legal heirs, in which case the daughters have no contractual claim. 83

C. SOLUTION

The daughters cannot file a claim in tort. They have a contractual claim if they are restored to their position as legal heirs. 84

CASE 3. THE DEFECTIVE HOUSE

A. LIABILITY BASED ON TORT (ART 41 SCO)?

In this case, the general clause of extra-contractual responsibility of art 41 SCO will be applicable. The five conditions previously mentioned (cf Case 1) must 85

---

58 ATF 136 III 461 – JdT 2010 I 432 c. 4; Arrêt du Tribunal fédéral 5C_8/2007 du 10 septembre 2007 – SJ 2008 I 98 c. 2.5; ATF 89 II 87 c. 6.

59 *J Guinand/M Stettler/A Leuba*, Droit des successions (art 457–640 CC) (6th edn 2005) 219, no 449; *P Piotet*, Traité de droit privé suisse, Tome IV – Droit successoral (2nd edn 1988) 513.

therefore be fulfilled: damage, a damaging act, a natural and adequate causal link between the two, unlawfulness, and fault.

86 Fault can be defined as blameworthy behaviour of the tortfeasor.[60] There are two aspects to the notion of fault: the first relates to the capacity of discernment of the tortfeasor;[61] the other is related to the author's intention or negligence.[62] In order to analyse the negligence of the author (which supposes that he could have anticipated the damageable act[63]), his knowledge and education have to be taken into consideration.[64] Because of a lack of specific technological knowledge, the tortfeasor's intention or negligence cannot be held: as a result, in these circumstances, it leads to the exclusion of fault.[65] *In casu*, we have to admit that D had the necessary technological knowledge. The wording of the case leads us to believe that D is responsible for an unlawful act (bodily injury, material damage to the house) due to his negligent behaviour, which is therefore a fault.

87 The main question in this case is to assess whether the clause excluding liability is applicable to C. According to art 100 SCO, any agreement purporting to exclude liability for unlawful intent or gross negligence in advance is void. An analysis of the clause of the contract and the degree of negligence of D could be made in order to examine if it was applicable to Z. Nonetheless, a contractual clause restricting liability (usually for tort) is inapplicable to third parties who did not agree to it.[66] Therefore, D cannot invoke this clause against C.

B. CONTRACTUAL LIABILITY (ART 97 SCO)

88 D and C have no contractual relationship. Therefore, C cannot invoke the violation of any contractual obligations towards D.

C. SOLUTION

89 D is responsible in tort: the clause of exclusion of responsibility has zero effect on C.

---

60 *H Honsell/B Isenring/MA Kessler*, Schweizerisches Haftpflichtrecht (5th edn 2013) 76, no 2; *K Oftinger/EW Stark*, Schweizerisches Haftpflichtrecht I (5th edn 1995) §5 no 13.

61 *Honsell/Isenring/Kessler* (fn 60) 77, no 4; BSK OR I-*Kessler* (fn 26) art 41 OR no 52.

62 *Honsell/Isenring/Kessler* (fn 60) 77, no 4; BSK OR I-*Kessler* (fn 26) art 41 OR no 45 and no 48.

63 ATF 99 II 176 – JdT 1974 I 71 c. 1.

64 CR CO I-*Werro* (fn 26) art 41 CO no 56.

65 ATF 114 II 376 – JdT 1988 I 686 c. 2.

66 CR CO I-*Thévenoz* (fn 26) art 100 CO no 13b; *M Hochstrasser*, Freizeichnung zugunsten und zulasten Dritter (2006) no 488.

CASE 4. APARTMENT IN FLAMES

Already in 1934, the Swiss Supreme Court ruled[67] that, in the case of a damage caused by a poorly maintained building or other structure, the liability of the owner could not only be engaged for a tort but also for a breach of the lease contract. The harmed tenant can therefore invoke both types of liabilities. 90

A. TORT: LIABILITY OF THE PROPERTY OWNER (ART 58 SCO)

If C wants to file an action based on tort, she would have to try invoking the liability of the property owner of art 58 SCO for defects in its construction or design or by inadequate maintenance. The conditions mentioned above must be fulfilled (cf Case 1). A circuit breaker can be considered as a structure, a notion defined as a material object, crafted or designed by man, having a direct or indirect link with the soil it is attached to.[68] The Swiss jurisprudence has, for example, already recognised pipes[69] or washing machines[70] as structures. 91

In casu, the circuit breaker is clearly defective as it caused a fire. C is a victim of damage which was caused due to the defective structure. The causal link can be established. The conditions of art 58 SCO are fulfilled. Therefore, C can claim damages. In the unlikely hypothesis that the Court would not consider the circuit breaker as a structure according to art 58 SCO, the general clause of art 41 SCO would have to be invoked by C, but she would have to prove that the landlord D committed a fault. 92

B. LIABILITY BASED ON THE BREACH OF CONTRACTUAL OBLIGATIONS OF A LEASE CONTRACT (ARTS 97 AND 253 FF SCO)

Article 97 para 1 SCO is the Swiss legal basis to found a claim for damages in the case of the violation or poor execution of obligations based on a contract:[71] 93

---

67 See ATF 60 II 341 – JdT 1935 I 238.

68 ATF 130 III 736 – JdT 2006 I 78; BK-*Brehm* (fn 2) art 58 OR no 26; *Engel* (fn 32) 547 f; CHK-*Müller* (fn 32) art 58 OR no 3.

69 See art 676 SCC; ATF 121 III 448 c. 3c; CHK-*Müller* (fn 32) art 58 OR no 3 and no 7.

70 *Engel* (fn 32) 549; for washing machines, see ATF 90 II 227 – JdT 1964 I 34 – SJ 1965 193; for the bath heater, see ATF 57 II 106 – JdT 1931 I 338; for bathroom accessories in general, see ATF 117 II 47.

71 CR CO I-*Thévenoz* (fn 26) art 97 CO no 2.

> '1 An obligor who fails to discharge an obligation at all or as required must make amends for the resulting loss or damage unless he can prove that he was not at fault.'

It states the general conditions of contractual liability:[72]

- damage,
- a breach of a contractual obligation and,
- a causal link between the two,
- fault is presumed, but the defendant has the possibility to prove that he was not at fault.

94 C and the landlord D are linked by a lease contract they signed (arts 253 ff SCO).

95 The landlord is required to make the object available on the agreed date in a condition fit for its designated use and to maintain it in that condition (art 256 para 1 SCO). An object is defective if its real condition does not comply with the condition required for its designated use and thus the object is defective if it lacks a quality the landlord promised in the contract or a quality the tenant could legitimately expect.[73] The tenant must, however, remedy defects which can be dealt with, such as minor cleaning or repairs as part of regular maintenance (art 259 SCO). If more serious defects are present, the tenant can seek damages, unless the owner can prove that he was not at fault (art 259a para 1 lit c and art 259e SCO).[74] *In casu*, if the circuit breaker is considered as a medium or a major defect (art 259 SCO *a contrario*), we can consider that the conditions of contractual responsibility are fulfilled. The owner being at fault, he will not be able to reverse the presumption of fault.

C. SOLUTION

96 D's contractual and extra-contractual liabilities can be invoked. Fault not being required according to art. 58 SCO D cannot exculpate himself by proving that he is not at fault. Consequently, this extra-contractual action is more favourable to C.

---

72 Ibid, art 97 p 737, §3.

73 ATF 135 III 345 c. 3.2; Arrêt du Tribunal fédéral 4C.97/2003 du 28 octobre 2003 c. 3.1; CR CO I-*Lachat* (fn 26) art 258 CO no 1.

74 Arrêt du Tribunal fédéral 4C.97/2003 du 28 octobre 2003 c. 3.2.

CASE 5. INJURED SKIER

A. CLAIM AGAINST D1

1) *Tort: Liability of the Property Owner (Art 58 SCO)*

In casu, art 58 SCO relative to defective structures is applicable and the conditions mentioned above (cf Case 1) must be fulfilled; however, art 58 SCO does not require fault. 97

The jurisprudence has explicitly considered a ski lift as a structure.[75] Due to a construction defect, or poor maintenance, the ski lift would be considered as defective by a law court. Following the wording of the case, C has suffered physical damage. The natural and adequate causal link appears to be established between the defect of the structure and the damage caused to C. 98

We can conclude that the conditions of art 58 SCO are established. This case involves a defective structure which, due to its inadequate construction or maintenance, caused a derailment and a cable fall resulting in physical damage/injury to P. Being the owner of the ski resort, D would be held liable according to art 58 SCO and would have to pay damages. 99

2) *Liability Based on the Breach of Contractual Obligations of a Transport Contract (Art 49 Para 1 LTV)*

In Swiss law, the contract between the passenger C and the company owner D1 is ruled by a recent *lex specialis*: the federal act on the transport of passengers[76] (LTV). We can posit that the ski lift is a means of transport, which conveys passengers on a cableway (art 1 para 2 LTV). The company owner, D1, has the contractual obligation to transport the counterparty from one station to another (art 19 para 1 LTV). According to art 42 LTV, the company is liable for the damage caused by the employees in the execution of the transport, in the performance of their service; the subcontractors and their employees are assimilated to such persons. 100

Article 42 LTV transposes the rule of art 101 para 1 SCO, which institutes contractor's liability if his associates or subcontractors cause damage 101

---

75 ATF 60 II 218; Arrêt non publié du Tribunal fédéral 4C.301/1988 du 17 février 1989 (cited by BK-*Brehm* (fn 2) art 58 OR no 45); PKG (Praxis des Kantonsgerichts; Practice of the Grison Cantonal Court) 1988 48 ff, c. 3 du 4 juillet 1988.

76 RS 745.1: Loi sur le transport de voyageurs / Personenbeförderungsgesetz / Legge sul trasporto di viaggiatori.

when executing their task (*responsabilité pour le fait des auxiliaires, Hilfspersonenhaftung*).[77] D1 would still be held liable if one of his employees or associates was responsible for the damage, unless he proves that they took enough care according to the claimant's expectations towards an execution by the employer himself. We can add that art 55 SCO (employers' liability) concerns tort liability while art 101 SCO relates to contractual liability.

102 *In casu*, the execution of the task to transport C up the mountain was not realised, because of the ski lift derailment and cable fall. There is damage and the natural and adequate causal links have been established.

B. CLAIM AGAINST D2

103 In Swiss law, the hypothesis of C directly filing a claim against D2 is not conceivable. The reason is that there is neither a relationship in contract or in tort between them; moreover, the latter did not cause the damage to C.

104 The situation would be different if we admitted that, on the basis of the contract, D1 had to be subrogated by D2. In this case, C would invoke towards D2 all the arguments he had towards D1. As a result, D2 would be obliged to pay damages.

C. SOLUTION

105 D1 is liable in tort according to art 58 SCO and also for a violation of the transport contract that caused damage (art 42 LTV). In the case of a (contractual) subrogation of D1 by D2, C can directly file a claim against D2 and the insurer D2 will have to compensate the damage.

CASE 6. EXPLODING CAR

106 C wants to file two actions, one against the car seller D1 and the other against the car manufacturer D2. Concerning the manufacturer, C has to examine whether the law concerning the liability for defective products applies (nos 107 ff).[78] He has to examine whether liability could be based on tort (art 41 SCO)

---

77 CHK-*Furrer/Wey* (fn 32) art 101 OR nos 1 ff and no 13; CR CO I-*Thévenoz* (fn 26) art 101 CO no 1 and no 3.

78 RS 221.112.944: Loi fédérale sur la responsabilité du fait des produits / Bundesgesetz über die Produktehaftpflicht / Legge federale sulla responsabilità per danno da prodotti.

(nos 112 f). Furthermore, he has to examine whether he can invoke D1's liability based on the sales contract (nos 115 ff).

A. LIABILITY FOR DEFECTIVE PRODUCTS ACCORDING TO SWISS LAW (LRFP)

Swiss legislation on liability for defective products is largely inspired by European legislation.[79] The LRFP establishes a causal liability (ie without consideration of the fault criterion) only based on the defect of the product.[80] The objective of this law is to protect the consumer against damage caused to his health or property by a defective product.[81] 107

The 'producer' (art 2 para 1 LRFP) of a finished product, of any raw material or of a component part is responsible for any physical harm or material damage to an item principally reserved for personal usage (art 1 para 1 LRFP). However, the producer is not responsible for damage caused to the defective product itself (art 1 para 2 LRFP). In addition to the conditions of having a product, a producer and damage, a defect and a causal link between the defect and the damage are also required to establish liability. 108

According to art 4 LRFP, a product is defective when it does not provide the safety which a person is entitled to expect, taking all circumstances into account, including the use to which it could reasonably be expected that the product would be put. The Swiss Supreme Court points out that the defect is determined by the lack of security – because a basic security is expected by the consumer – and not by the product's inaptitude to be used.[82] Moreover, the LRFP is not applicable if the consumer uses the product in a manner for which it was not intended.[83] 109

Knowing the producer is not responsible for the damage caused to the defective product itself (art 1 para 2 LRFP), D2's liability according to the LRFP will not be engaged.[84] If C had been himself injured, or if other belongings had been damaged, he could have invoked the LRFP only for this damage, not for the car itself. To claim damages for the destroyed car, C would have to file an action against the seller, based on the sales contract (nos 115 ff).[85] 110

---

79 ATF 133 III 81 c. 3; ATF 137 III 226 c. 2.2; *S Marchand*, Droit de la consommation (2012) 104.

80 ATF 133 III 81 c. 3.

81 ATF 137 III 226 c. 3.2.

82 ATF 133 III 81 c. 3.1; ATF 137 III 226 c. 3.2.

83 ATF 133 III 81 c. 3.1.

84 Art 1 §2 LRFP; *Marchand* (fn 79) 108.

85 Ibid.

111 The situation might be different if the element having caused the damage were clearly separated from the rest of the car (eg battery, radio etc). If this element were produced by a third party, one might argue that the LRFP would partly be applicable and C could file a claim against the producer of the battery etc, in order to obtain damages for the patrimonial diminution resulting of the personal injury and property damage (but not for the battery itself).

B. LIABILITY BASED ON TORT (ART 41 SCO)?

112 In this case, the general clause of extra-contractual responsibility of art 41 SCO is applicable. The five conditions previously mentioned (cf Case 1) must be fulfilled: damage, a damaging act, a natural and adequate causal link between the two, unlawfulness, and fault. Two conditions, unlawfulness and fault, will be considered here, while the others can be considered as established.

113 *In casu*, C's property has been destroyed, and the right to property, as all rights in rem, is an absolute right enforceable against all.[86] Therefore, the destruction of the car is unlawful.

114 C's difficulties would arise when he would have to prove the fault of D1 and D2. However, if C can prove that there was a design or construction error that either D1 or D2 should have noticed, considering their knowledge in car construction, the condition of fault would be fulfilled and their liability for tort would be engaged. As D1 and D2 are employers, they are vicariously liable for their auxiliaries according to art. 55 SCO. But this disposition offers them the possibility to prove that they have satisfied their obligations in eligendo, instruendo and custodiendo. If they can bring this proof, they will not be held liable.

C. LIABILITY BASED ON THE BREACH OF A SALES CONTRACT (ARTS 97 AND 184 FF SCO)?

115 The seller is in principle liable to the buyer for any breach of warranty of quality and for defects that would materially or legally negate or substantially reduce the value of the object or its fitness for the designated purpose; the seller is liable even if he was not aware of the defects (art 197 SCO). However, the seller is not liable for the defects the buyer knows about or should have known

86 *P-H Steinauer*, Les droits réels I (5th edn 2012) no 23.

about unless the buyer assured him they did not exist at the moment of the conclusion of the contract[87] (art 200 SCO).

116 Once the buyer has bought and entered into possession of the object of sale, he has the obligation to inspect its condition as soon as feasible in the normal course of business and, if he discovers defects for which the seller is liable under warranty, must notify them to him without delay (art 201 para 1 SCO). By failing to do so, the object is deemed accepted with its defects (art 201 para 2 SCO). If the defects appear subsequently, the seller must be notified immediately (art 201 para 3 SCO). The buyer is not obliged[88] to ask an expert to look for hidden defects that usual verification would not reveal.[89]

117 In claims for breach of warranty of quality and fitness, the buyer may sue either to rescind the contract of sale for breach of warranty (art 208 SCO) or to have the sale price reduced by way of compensation for the decrease in the object's value (art 205 para 1 SCO). The buyer can also have the object replaced (art 206 SCO). The time limit to invoke such actions in warranty is fixed by law and limited to two years (art 210 para 1 SCO) unless the seller proves that the buyer wilfully misled him (art 210 para 6 SCO).

118 If the buyer desires to rescind the contract, art 208 para 3 SCO allows him to claim damages. If he prefers the other possible courses of action, he can claim damages on the basis of art 97 SCO,[90] but only if he fulfilled his obligations regarding verification and time limit of art 210 para 1 SCO, therefore reducing the scope of art 97 SCO significantly.[91] *In casu*, even if C fulfilled all his obligations of verification, he cannot invoke any of the warranty actions due to the expiration of the time limit of art 210 para 1 SCO, unless he can prove that the buyer wilfully misled him.

D. SOLUTION

119 C can invoke the LRFP if D1 is not the manufacturer of the fuel line; his claim could cover all the damage except that to the fuel line. He can invoke art 41 SCO

[87] ATF 117 II 259 c. 1.
[88] ATF 131 III 145 c. 6.3.
[89] ATF 76 II 221 c. 2.
[90] The Swiss Supreme Court refuses the application by analogy of 208 para 3 SCO: ATF 133 III 335 – JdT 2010 I 223 c. 2.4.1; ATF 63 II 401 c. 2 – JdT 1938 I 307; ATF 107 II 161 c. 7a – JdT 1981 I 582.
[91] Arrêt du Tribunal fédéral 4C.200/2006 du 20 septembre 2006 c. 3.1; ATF 96 II 181 c. 3a; ATF 58 II 207 c. 2 – JdT 1933 I 55; ATF 63 II 401 c. 3 – JdT 1938 I 306; ATF 90 II 86 c. 1 – JdT 1964 I 560; ATF 133 III 335 – JdT 2010 I 223 c. 2.4.1 (the Swiss Supreme Court confirms its jurisprudence in this sentence); CR CO I-*Venturi/Zen-Ruffinen* (fn 26) art 197–210 CO no 18 and art 210 CO no 2; BSK OR I-*Honsell* (fn 26) art 210 OR no 3.

only if he can prove the fault of either D1 or D2, but he will be unable to file a claim based on the sales contract, as the warranty period has expired.

CASE 7. RACING BOAT BURNING

A. LIABILITY BASED ON TORT (ART 41 SCO)?

120 For this case, we can refer to the previous one (Case 6). The five conditions of art 41 SCO must be fulfilled: damage, a damaging act, a natural and adequate causal link between the two, unlawfulness, and fault.

121 Adequate causality would *in casu* be slightly more difficult to establish than in the previous case. However, as the Swiss Supreme Court considers that, in order to establish an adequate causal link, the result does not have to necessarily happen regularly or frequently – even extraordinary consequences can constitute an adequate consequence of the cause[92] – we can admit that a court would accept its existence in our case.

122 The condition of fault is also a problematic question that depends on elements that are not described in this hypothetical. If C can prove D's fault, the latter's liability is engaged.

B. LIABILITY BASED ON THE BREACH OF A SALES CONTRACT? (ARTS 97 AND 184 FF SCO)

123 The resolution of this aspect of the case is exactly identical to that in the previous case.

C. SOLUTION

124 C does not intend to file a claim against the producer of the electronic equipment, but he could invoke the LRFP if he wanted to do so; he could seek compensation for the damage caused to the boat and the travel expenses incurred, but not for the electronic equipment added by D. For all other considerations, they are identical to those in the previous case.

---

92 Arrêt du Tribunal fédéral 4A_45/2009 du 25 mars 2009 c. 3.4.1; Arrêt du Tribunal fédéral 5C.88/2004 du 26 octobre 2004 c. 4.1; Arrêt du Tribunal fédéral 5C.125/2003 du 31 octobre 2003 c. 4.2 – SJ 2004 I 407; ATF 119 Ib 334 c. 5c; ATF 96 II 392 c. 2; BK-*Brehm* (fn 2) art 41 OR nos 124 ff; BSK OR I-*Kessler* (fn 26) art 41 OR no 17; CR CO I-*Werro* (fn 26) art 41 CO no 43.

CASE 8. INSIDIOUS REPORT

A. LIABILITY BASED ON TORT (ART 41 SCO)?

In this case, the general clause of extra-contractual responsibility of art 41 SCO is applicable. The five conditions previously mentioned (cf Case 1) must be fulfilled: damage, a damaging act, a natural and adequate causal link between the two, unlawfulness, and fault. *In casu*, all the conditions are fulfilled, but knowing that the damage is purely economic, the violation of a behaviour norm is a prerequisite in order to recognise the unlawfulness of D's actions (cf Case 1). 125

By betraying his employer, D violated rules of the SCO on the loyalty due by an employee to his employer (art 321a para 1 and 3 SCO). A violator of such rules could also be found guilty of criminal mismanagement according to art 158 of the Swiss Criminal Code (CPS).[93] Moreover, D's behaviour also violates rules from the Law on Unfair Competition (LCD),[94] such as the general clause of art 2 LCD, which considers as disloyal and unlawful all commercial behaviour or practices which are misleading or which contravene the rules of good faith and which have an influence on the relations between competitors or between suppliers and clients. Article 9 para 3 LCD establishes the link between a violation of the LCD and the general dispositions for tort of arts 41 ff SCO. 126

The natural and adequate causal links can be established. The fault is clearly established as D, without any doubt, acted intentionally. Therefore, the conditions of art 41 SCO are fulfilled. 127

B. LIABILITY BASED ON THE BREACH OF AN EMPLOYMENT CONTRACT (ARTS 97 AND 319 FF SCO)?

For the application of the general clause of responsibility of art 97 SCO a violation of the employment contract between C and D must be established (arts 319 ff SCO). 128

In casu, we have previously explained that D violated his obligations of loyalty towards C (art 321a para 1 and 3 SCO). 129

According to art 321e para 1 SCO, the employee is liable for any loss or damage he causes to the employer, whether wilfully or by negligence. For the application of art 97 para 1 SCO, the Swiss Supreme Court demands that the employer 130

93 RS 311.0: Code pénal suisse / Schweizerisches Strafgesetzbuch / Codice penale svizzero.

94 RS 241: Loi sur la concurrence déloyale / Bundesgesetz gegen den unlauteren Wettbewerb / Legge federale contro la concorrenza sleale.

proves the damage, its amount, the employee's violation and the causal link between the violation and the damage,[95] or that the employee proves his absence of fault.[96]

C. SOLUTION

131 C is liable according to art 41 SCO, as he violated a rule of behaviour protecting the victim of the purely economic damage and, according to art 321e SCO, for a breach of the labour contract.

CASE 9. CIRCULAR LETTER

A. LIABILITY BASED ON TORT (ART 41 SCO)?

132 In this case, the general clause of extra-contractual responsibility of art 41 SCO is applicable. The five conditions previously mentioned (cf Case 1) must be fulfilled: damage, a damaging act, a natural and adequate causal link between the two, unlawfulness, and fault. *In casu*, all the conditions are fulfilled, but knowing that the damage is purely economic, the violation of a behaviour norm is a prerequisite in order to recognise the unlawfulness of D's actions (cf Case 1).

133 If D's allegations are lies, this would constitute a violation of art 3 para 1 lit a LCD, which considers as disloyal the fact of denigrating somebody, his services, his achievements, his tariffs or business by imprecise, fallacious or gratuitously offensive allegations. This behaviour can constitute a criminal offence according to art 23 para 1 LCD. It could also constitute defamation (art 173 CPS).

134 If D's allegations are true, the violation of the LCD is less evident. The general clause of art 2 LCD could be invoked if C proves that D acted against good faith. The possibility to invoke art 173 CPS remains open.

B. LIABILITY BASED ON THE BREACH OF A CONTRACT? (ART 97 SCO)

135 In order to claim damages for a breach of contractual obligations, the two parties must be linked by a contract. *In casu*, C was linked to D by a commercial

---

95 ATF 97 II 142 c. 5b.

96 CR CO I-*Aubert* (fn 26) art 321e CO no 4.

agency contract (art 418a ff SCO). However, this contract was terminated. In certain situations, obligations can remain after the termination of the contract (cf arts 340 ff SCO *cum* 418d para 2 SCO),[97] but they do not apply in our situation. Therefore, C cannot found his claim on any contract.

C. SOLUTION

C can invoke art 41 SCO with a high chance of success, but the contract being terminated, no claim based on art 97 SCO can be invoked. 136

CASE 10. SHORTAGE OF SUPPLY

A. LIABILITY BASED ON TORT (ART 41 SCO)?

In this case, the general clause of extra-contractual responsibility of art 41 SCO is applicable. The five conditions previously mentioned (cf Case 1) must therefore be fulfilled: damage, a damaging act, a natural and adequate causal link between the two, unlawfulness, and fault. *In casu*, four conditions are fulfilled, but knowing that the damage is purely economic, the violation of a behaviour norm is a prerequisite in order to recognise the unlawfulness of D's actions. 137

We can think about the dispositions of the Swiss Cartel Act (LCart).[98] Article 7 para 1 LCart forbids dominant undertakings from abusing their position in the market, thus disadvantaging their trading partners by, for example, imposing unfair prices or other unfair conditions of trade (art 7 para 2 lit c LCart). The Swiss Supreme Court judged that the term 'imposition' supposes that the commercial partner can neither avoid nor oppose the economic pressure resulting from the dominant position,[99] typically by imposing unfair prices or unequal commercial conditions.[100] Article 12 para 1 lit b LCart establishes the link between a violation of the LCart and the general dispositions for tort of arts 41 ff SCO. 138

---

97 They have to be drafted in the contract, cf *S Marchand*, Clauses contractuelles – Du bon usage de la liberté contractuelle (2008) 248 f.

98 RS 251: Loi fédérale sur les cartels et autres restrictions à la concurrence / Bundesgesetz über Kartelle und andere Wettbewerbsbeschränkungen / Legge federale sui cartelli e altre limitazioni della concorrenza.

99 ATF 137 II 199 – JdT 2011 I 157 c. 4.3.5; *J Xoudis*, Droit de la concurrence, JdT 2012 I 107, p 115.

100 *B Merkt*, Abus de position dominante: développements récents de la pratique, in: I Hochreutener/W Stoffel/M Amstutz (eds), Pratique du droit de la concurrence (2013) 64.

139 D would therefore be liable for his actions, as the company has abused its dominant position in the market.

B. LIABILITY BASED ON THE BREACH OF A SALES CONTRACT? (ARTS 97 AND 184 FF SCO)

140 If C and D sign a new contract for every shipment, then there cannot be any violation of contractual obligations, as every new sale is the result of different negotiations.

141 If the sales contract is a long-term contract, which means that D has to deliver components to C for a certain period and for a certain price, by threatening C with stopping the deliveries, D breaches his contractual obligations. According to art 184 SCO, D is obliged to deliver the item sold and transfer ownership of it to the buyer in return for the sale price, which the buyer undertakes to pay to the seller. C can file an action against D for damages according to art 97 SCO.

C. SOLUTION

142 C can invoke D's liability in tort (art 41 SCO); he can also sue D for breach of the contract (art 97 SCO), provided that it is a long-term contract.

CASE 11. INJURED ROCK STAR

A. TORT: GENERAL PRINCIPLE, *REFLEXSCHADEN*

143 The general clause of extra-contractual responsibility of art 41 SCO is applicable. The five conditions previously mentioned (cf Case 1) must therefore be fulfilled, in this case, the analysis of the condition of damage will be the focus of our attention.

144 In addition to what we have previously mentioned (cf Case 1) about damage, the Swiss legal order distinguishes between two other sorts of damage: direct or personal damage (*dommage propre/dommage direct, Eigenschaden/Direktschaden*) and indirect or reflexive damage (*dommage réfléchi/dommage par ricochet, Reflexschaden/Indirektschaden*). The first affects the victim personally and directly.[101] The second indirectly affects a third person through

---

101 BK-*Brehm* (fn 2) art 41 OR no 17; *Müller* Responsabilité (fn 32) no 99.

the direct damage suffered by victim of the damaging act.[102] In principle, the jurisprudence does not acknowledge reparation for reflex damage,[103] unless the rule violated protects both victims: the victim suffering a direct damage as well as the reflex victim.[104] Indeed, if there is a protective rule, the Supreme Court will consider it not as a reflex but a direct victim[105] and, therefore, the damage would be compensable.

C suffers a prejudice due to the effective loss and the loss of profits 145
following the cancellation of the concert. However, the direct victim of the accident is X, therefore C's damage is only reflexive and cannot be compensated. This case is in fact a classic illustration of this type of situation in doctrine.[106]

B. CONTRACTUAL LIABILITY (ART 97 SCO)

C and D are not linked by any contract and therefore it is impossible to invoke 146
art 97 SCO.

C. SOLUTION

C has no possibility to claim any damages from D, as he is only a reflex victim 147
of the car accident and not a direct one.

CASE 12. EQUIPMENT DESTROYED

A. CLAIM AGAINST D1

1) Tort Liability (Art 41 SCO)

D1 is not the author of the damaging act; therefore, there cannot be any claim 148
against him in tort.

---

102 BK-*Brehm* (fn 2) art 41 OR no 20 and no 74a; *Müller*, Responsabilité (fn 32) nos 99 f; CR CO I-*Werro* (fn 26) art 41 CO no 14.

103 ATF 82 II 36 c. 4a; ATF 104 II 95 c. 2a – JdT 1978 I 557; ATF 126 III 521 c. 2a – JdT 2001 I 506; ATF 102 II 85 c. 6c – JdT 1976 I 614; BK-*Brehm* (fn 2) art 41 OR no 20 and no 74a; BSK OR I-*Kessler* (fn 26) art 41 OR no 8; CR CO I-*Werro* (fn 26) art 41 CO no 14; *Rey* (fn 43) no 356.

104 ATF 102 II 85 c. 4b; ATF 101 Ib 252 c. 2d; BK-*Brehm* (fn 2) art 41 OR no 20 and no 74a; BSK OR I-*Kessler* (fn 26) art 41 OR no 8; CR CO I-*Werro* (fn 26) art 41 CO no 14; *Rey* (fn 43) no 356 and nos 360 ff.

105 ATF 102 II 85 c. 4b; ATF 101 Ib 252 c. 2d; BK-*Brehm* (fn 2) art 41 OR nos 23 ff; BSK OR I-*Kessler* (fn 26) art 41 OR no 8; CR CO I-*Werro* (fn 26) art 41 CO no 14.

106 *Müller*, Responsabilité (fn 32) no 100; CR CO I-*Werro* (fn 26) art 41 CO no 14; *Engel* (fn 32) 476; *Rey* (fn 43) no 355.

2) *Liability Based on the Breach of Contractual Obligations of a Transport Contract (Arts 97 SCO, 440 ff SCO)*

149 The general clause of responsibility of art 97 SCO can be applied. However, D1 will not be held liable if he can prove that he was not at fault. In particular, according to the dispositions on the transport contract (art 440 ff, 447 ff SCO), the transporter is liable for the loss of the transported goods, except he proves that he was not at fault or that the damage would also have occurred to a diligent transporter.

150 *In casu*, we suppose that D1 was not at fault, given the accident has been caused by D2. Consequently, C's contractual action against D1 seems to be compromised.

B. CLAIM AGAINST D2

1) *Tort: General Principle, Purely Economic Damage and Indirect Damage*

151 If the equipment did not belong to C and if D2 is the owner of his vehicle, the general clause of extra-contractual responsibility of art 41 SCO will not be applicable. The Swiss legislation on road traffic (LCR)[107] provides for a causal responsibility (liability established regardless of the fault criterion) of the holder of the car (art 58 para 1 LCR); therefore we must examine the same conditions of art 41 SCO previously referred to (cf Case 1), except for fault. If all the requirements of the LCR are fulfilled, D2 would be liable towards C for loss of profits and other expenses due to the cancelled concert.

152 If the equipment belongs to C and if D2 is the owner of his vehicle, D2 would be liable in addition for the loss of the equipment. In other words, the accident was caused by D2 destroying at the same time C's equipment, D1's truck and causing the cancellation of the concert. On the one hand, D2 has to pay damages for loss of property-value (C's equipment and D1's truck). On the other hand, if we consider the loss of profits due to the cancelled concert, the damage is material and represents a pure economic loss. Concerning the purely economic damage, a norm protecting C's and D1's legally protected interests has to be violated in order to establish the unlawfulness of D2's actions. By destroying C's electronic equipment, D2 acted unlawfully by violating arts 641 SCC, 144 CPS (criminal rule protecting property) and art. 58 para 1 LCR.

153 The notion of fault only comes into consideration if the author of the accident can prove that the victim was at fault (cf art 59 LCR). *In casu*, the necessary

107 RS 741.01: Loi fédérale sur la circulation routière / Strassenverkehrsgesetz / Legge federale sulla circolazione stradale.

information is not given, but the authors consider that D2 is entirely responsible for the accident.

C. CONTRACTUAL LIABILITY (ART 97 SCO)

C cannot invoke against D2 any claim in contractual liability, because there is no contractual relationship between the two of them. 154

D. SOLUTION

In conclusion, C can only file a claim in tort against D2 for the equipment destroyed and the economic damage resulting, directly or indirectly. 155

CASE 13. SLIPPING ON A LETTUCE LEAF

A. TORT: GENERAL PRINCIPLES (ART 41 SCO) AND THE *GEFAHRENSATZ*

In this case, the general clause of extra-contractual responsibility of art 41 SCO is applicable. The five conditions previously mentioned (cf Case 1) must therefore be fulfilled: damage, a damaging act, a natural and adequate causal link between the two, unlawfulness, and fault. 156

C is victim of a physical harm because her leg broke. The damaging act can take the form of an action, but also of an omission to act (cf Case 1). 157

The natural and adequate causal links between the presence of the lettuce leaf and the accident can be established. 158

The dangerous situation generated by the presence of this lettuce leaf on the floor can be related to the praetorian notion of *Gefahrensatz*, which implies that the person who creates or maintains a dangerous situation has to take appropriate measures to avoid that this danger materialises in the form of a prejudice to others.[108] 159

The qualification of the *Gefahrensatz* as an unlawful or faulty omission is unclear in the Swiss doctrine and jurisprudence.[109] We consider that the concept of 160

---

108 ATF 82 II 28; ATF 90 II 89; ATF 93 II 92; ATF 95 II 96; ATF 96 II 112; ATF 98 II 48; ATF 126 II 113 c. 2a/aa; *Oftinger/Stark* (fn 2) §16 no 26; BK-*Brehm* (fn 2) art 41 OR no 44; BSK OR I-*Kessler* (fn 26) art 41 OR no 19a; *Müller*, Responsabilité (fn 32) no 169 and no 241; *Engel* (fn 32) 450 f.

109 Certain authors and court decisions place the *Gefahrensatz* with unlawfulness, such as: *Engel* (fn 32) 450 f; BK-*Brehm* (fn 2) art 41 OR nos 44–44b; BSK OR I-*Kessler* (fn 26) art

Gefahrensatz contains the elements of both unlawfulness and fault. As a norm enjoining the initiator of the danger to act, its violation is unlawful (*illicéité de comportement*). Unlawfulness also consists in the infringement of C's absolute right to physical integrity (*illicéité de résultat*). Moreover, the *Gefahrensatz* cannot be detached from fault, as the initiator of the danger can be reproached for not having taken the necessary protective measures, due to negligence or intention, to protect any third person from a risk he should and could have confined.

161 It is important however to state that the notion of *Gefahrensatz*, for it to make sense, can be invoked only if the peril created or maintained reaches a certain level of dangerousness,[110] otherwise anything anywhere could potentially be dangerous, from hitting oneself on a door knob to a paper cut. The degree of dangerousness cannot be determined by a general rule, but must be decided by the judge for every specific case.[111] Moreover, the initiator of the danger is not obliged to take excessive or overly expensive safety measures, regarding the specific circumstances.[112]

162 *In casu*, the solution would depend on many elements that are not stated in the hypothetical. However, it seems unlikely that a Swiss court would not hold the store D liable in this case.

B. LIABILITY BASED ON THE BREACH OF A SALES CONTRACT? (ARTS 97 AND 184 FF SCO)

163 As he had not bought anything in the shop D, C did not enter into a contractual relationship with the store under the form of a sales contract according to art 184 SCO. The question of whether a pre-contractual relationship exists between D and C could be asked.

164 However, the Swiss Supreme Court has ruled that, regardless of whether the liability is contractual or extra-contractual in nature, it changes

41 OR no 19a and no 38; *Schwenzer* (fn 8) no 50.33; ATF 93 II 89 – JdT 1968 I 322 c. 3; ATF 93 II 329 – JdT 1969 I 130 c. 5; ATF 95 II 93 c. I.2; ATF 106 IV 80 c. 4a; ATF 116 Ia 162. Others place the *Gefahrensatz* with the fault: *Oftinger/Stark* (fn 2) §16 nos 26 ff; *Rey* (fn 43) nos 866 ff; ATF 71 II 107 – JdT 1945 I 446 c. 2; ATF 79 II 66 – JdT 1954 I 86; ATF 80 II 247 – JdT 1955 I 316. Finally, certain authors place the *Gefahrensatz* with the fault and unlawfulness: *Müller*, Responsabilité (fn 32) no 169 and no 241; ATF 124 III 297 c. 5b (in this case, both unlawfulness and fault are analysed, but the Supreme Court insists more on the aspects linked with the fault); ATF 57 II 165; ATF 116 II 138.

110 *Oftinger/Stark* (fn 2) §16 no 28.

111 Ibid, §16 no 28.

112 For example, the exploitant of a ski resort is not obliged to put protective cushions on all trees of the forest, but only on the pillars of the teleski he exploits and that can represent a certain danger (ATF 126 III 113 c. 2a/aa).

nothing as regards the obligations of securing any dangers created (*Verkehrssicherungspflicht*). From this perspective, D is under an obligation to take precautionary measures independently of the existence of a contract.

C. SOLUTION

It seems likely that a Swiss court would consider the store D as liable under tort. 165

CASE 14. TEST DRIVE

A. LIABILITY BASED ON TORT (ART 41 SCO AND THE LCR)?

The Swiss legislation on road traffic (LCR)[113] provides for the liability of the 166 holder (*détenteur*, *Halter*) of a vehicle (art 58 para 1 LCR). The holder of a vehicle is the person effectively and permanently possessing the power to dispose of the vehicle and who uses it in his own interest.[114] *In casu*, C is the holder of the car; this condition is not altered if the holder voluntarily lends the vehicle to a third party for a short time.[115] The holder answers for the fault of the driver as if it were his own (art 58 para 4 LCR). This means that C is by definition liable for the damage caused by the accident or the car of which he is the holder.[116] C therefore is liable for the damage to the tree.

The liability of the driver himself, who is *in casu* not the holder, is ruled by the 167 general rules of extra-contractual liability of arts 41 ff SCO.[117] For the damage to the car, C will have to invoke D's liability in tort. As for the damage to the tree, the owner of the tree has the possibility to invoke art 58 para 4 LCR against C and art 41 para 1 SCO against D; the two are jointly liable according to art 60 para 1 LCR.[118]

---

113 RS 741.01: Loi fédérale sur la circulation routièr / Strassenverkehrsgesetz / Legge federale sulla circolazione stradale.

114 See art 78 §1 Ordonnance réglant l'admission à la circulation routière (OAC, RS 741.51); *Y Jeanneret*, Les dispositions pénales de la Loi sur la circulation routière (LCR) (2007) 3 no 4; ATF 63 II 209 – JdT 1938 I 159; ATF 129 III 102 – JdT 2003 I 500; ATF 129 III 410 c. 4 – JdT 2003 I 353; ATF 117 II 609 – JdT 1992 I 727; ATF 101 II 133; ATF 99 II 315 – JdT 1974 I 458; ATF 70 II 179.

115 *Jeanneret* (fn 114) 3 no 4; ATF 129 III 410 – JdT 2003 I 353; ATF 129 III 102; ATF 70 II 179 c. 1 – JdT 1944 I 459.

116 ATF 117 II 101 – JdT 1991 I 712; *R Brehm*, La responsabilité civile automobile (2nd edn 2010) nos 119 ff and no 143.

117 *Brehm* (fn 116) no 122.

118 *Brehm* (fn 116) no 143.

168 *In casu*, all the conditions of art 41 para 1 SCO would certainly be fulfilled, and D would be liable in tort towards C (and solidarily liable with C towards the tree owner).

B. LIABILITY BASED ON A SALE ON APPROVAL (ARTS 223 FF SCO) AND ON THE LOAN CONTRACT (ARTS 305 FF SCO)

169 Swiss law recognises the contract for sale on approval (arts 223 ff SCO), submitted to a condition, by definition in this context as well as potestative as suspensive, which is the acceptance of the buyer.[119] Decisions based on art 223 SCO can be counted on the fingers of a butcher's hand. In a very similar case judged in Geneva,[120] the Court of Justice of Geneva explained that the buyer must not act against the rules of good faith in order to prevent the suspensive and potestative condition from arising; the buyer who decides not to buy the object is obliged to return in the same condition as it was when it was given to him, as in a loan of use contract (arts 305 ff SCO).

170 The borrower has the obligation to return the object in the condition in which he received it, besides the normal wear caused by the authorised use of the object; if the object has deteriorated, his liability is contractual.[121] D damaged C's car and it is assumed that he did not conclude the sale, therefore he did not return the car in good condition. D has violated his contractual obligations and C can therefore claim damages based on the general clause of art 97 para 1 SCO.[122]

C. SOLUTION

171 D would be liable in tort for the damage to C, and he would be liable together with C towards the tree owner. Further D is liable towards C based on the breach of his extra-contractual obligations, and based on the contractual obligations of a loan for use.

---

119 BSK OR I-*Giger* (fn 26) arts 223–225 OR no 11; CR CO I-*Venturi/Zen-Ruffinen* (fn 26) art 223 CO no 1; ATF 55 II 39.

120 Perren contre Blanc et Paiche S.A. (3 décembre 1963), SJ 1961 185.

121 Perren contre Blanc et Paiche S.A. (3 décembre 1963), SJ 1961 185; BSK OR I-*Schärer/Maurenbrecher* (fn 26) art 305 OR no 14.

122 BSK OR I-*Schärer/Maurenbrecher* (fn 26) art 305 OR no 14 and art 307 OR no 5; CR CO I-*Bovet/Richa* (fn 26) art 306 CO no 6 and no 7; Perren contre Blanc et Paiche S.A. (3 décembre 1963), SJ 1961 185.

CASE 15. BREACH OF NEGOTIATIONS

172 The problem D has is that C did not commit any unlawful act, and he also did not breach a contract knowing that no contract had been concluded. Therefore, we are in the case of a pre-contractual liability, known also as *culpa in contrahendo*.

173 After many tergiversations, the Swiss Supreme Court has established an analogy between *culpa in contrahendo* and liability based on trust (*responsabilité fondée sur la confiance*, *Vertrauenshaftung*), which is neither contractual nor extra-contractual.[123] In the absence of an agreement or contract, liability based on trust and on the principle of good faith (art 2 SCC) supposes that the parties are in a 'particular juridical relation' (*relation juridique particulière*, *rechtliche Sonderverbindung*) creating a situation of confidence worthy of protection.[124] Unlawfulness results in the fact that the confidence given has been deceived.[125] To resume, the conditions for liability based on trust are the existence of a particular juridical relation, the breach of confidence contrary to the rules of good faith, and of course the presence of damage, a natural and an adequate causal link between the damage and the behaviour breaching the good faith.[126]

174 According to the Swiss Supreme Court, a particular juridical relation arises from the conscious or legally attributable behaviour of the tortfeasor; an accidental and unwanted meeting, as occurs in the case of extra-contractual liability, does not create such a situation.[127] The Swiss Supreme Court admits in its jurisprudence that parties negotiating a contract are in a particular juridical relation.[128]

175 Liability resulting from *culpa in contrahendo* relies on the idea that, during the negotiations, the parties must act according to the rules of good faith. There is no obligation to conclude a contract following the negotiations; however,

---

123 ATF 130 III 345 – JdT 2004 I 207 c. 2.1; ATF 121 III 350 c. 6c; ATF 120 II 331 – JdT 1995 I 359 c. 5a; CR CO I-*Thévenoz* (fn 26) arts 97–109 CO no 19; BSK OR I-*Wiegand* (fn 26) arts 97–109 OR no 11.

124 ATF 121 III 350 c. 6c; ATF 130 III 345 – JdT 2004 I 207 c. 2.2; ATF 120 II 331 c. 5a – JdT 1995 I 363; ATF 124 III 297 c. 6a – JdT 1999 I 274; 121 III 350 c. 6c; ATF 120 II 331 c. 5a – JdT 1995 I 364; Arrêt du Tribunal fédéral 4C.299/1998 du 7 janvier 1999 c. 4a – SJ 2000 I 537; Arrêt du Tribunal fédéral 4C.280/1999 du 28 janvier 2000 c. 3a – SJ 2000 I 554; CR CO I-*Thévenoz* (fn 26) arts 97–109 CO no 20.

125 ATF 121 III 350 c. 6c; CR CO I-*Thévenoz* (fn 26) arts 97–109 CO no 22 f.

126 CR CO I-*Thévenoz* (fn 26) arts 97–109 CO nos 22e ff; *Kuonen* (fn 56) nos 1429 ff.

127 ATF 130 III 345 – JdT 2004 I 207 c. 2.2; ATF 128 III 324 c. 2.2 – SJ 2003 I 52; Arrêt du Tribunal fédéral 4C.280/1999 du 28 janvier 2000 c. 3a – SJ 2000 554 f.

128 CR CO I-*Morin* (fn 26) art 1 CO no 130; ATF 120 II 331 c. 5a – JdT 1995 I 359; ATF 121 III 350 c. 6c; ATF 130 III 345 c. 2.2 – JdT 2004 I 207; ATF 134 III 390 c. 4.3.2 – SJ 2008 I 361.

reciprocal duties are imposed. In particular, each party must negotiate respecting the principle of good faith in accordance with its real intentions and inform the other, to a certain extent, of the circumstances likely to influence his decision to conclude the contract.[129] *Culpa in contrahendo* does not require an intentional fault; the obligations to inform depend on the nature of the contract, on the progress of the negotiations or on the intentions of the parties.[130]

176 The obligation to negotiate seriously forbids the parties from engaging in or continuing negotiations without any intention to conclude the contract.[131]

177 *In casu*, D clearly deceived C's confidence, by selling the antique to X behind his back. Both parties had entered into negotiations that were left on hold for a few days, but were supposed to continue once D had returned from his business trip. By having agreed to continue the negotiations, C and D were in a pre-contractual relation and D breached his obligation to behave in good faith by not acting in the way he had promised. As there is no information about a specific damage, we assume that C suffered legally relevant damage.

178 *Solution:* C will have to prove the damage, the causal link between the breach of the contractual obligations and the damage as well as D's fault. D would then have to pay damages to C.

CASE 16. NON-DISCLOSURE OF RELEVANT FACTS

A. LIABILITY BASED ON TORT (ART 41 SCO)?

179 In this case, the general clause of extra-contractual responsibility of art 41 SCO is applicable. The five conditions previously mentioned (cf Case 1) must therefore be fulfilled: damage, a damaging act, a natural and adequate causal link between the two, unlawfulness, and fault. *In casu*, all the conditions are fulfilled, but knowing that the damage is purely economic, a behaviour norm has to have been violated in order to establish the unlawfulness of D's actions.

180 Article 28 SCO forbids a party from acting fraudulently towards another. Fraudulent behaviour violates the principle of good faith.[132] Such conduct occurs when the author either deliberately affirms false facts or dissimulates true facts, therefore causing the mistake from which the victim suffers[133] as it

---

129 ATF 105 II 75 – JdT 1980 I 66 c. 2a; ATF 102 II 84 – JdT 1977 I 213; ATF 92 II 333 c. 3b – JdT 1968 I 38; ATF 90 II 455 c. 4 – JdT 1965 I 280.

130 ATF 105 II 75 – JdT 1980 I 66 c. 2a.

131 ATF 77 II 135; ATF 121 III 350 c. 6c and d – SJ 2002 I 164 c. 3a; CR CO I-*Morin* (fn 26) art 1 CO no 132; *Kuonen* (fn 56) no 1485.

132 CR CO I-*Schmidlin* (fn 26) art 28 CO no 4.

133 ATF 132 II 161; ATF 39 II 271; CR CO I-*Schmidlin* (fn 26) art 28 CO no 5.

influenced him in signing a contract.[134] In the case of passive fraud, the author deliberately withholds information that would have led the other party not to sign the contract; even if the victim behaved negligently, the author should not take any benefit from this circumstance of weakness.[135] *In casu*, D withheld information that he should have given to C and thus he deliberately acted in bad faith. Even if D had not known about the C's sloped ground, this information is sufficiently important to be disclosed by any means.

B. LIABILITY BASED ON THE BREACH OF A SALES CONTRACT? (ARTS 97 AND 184 FF SCO)

The buyer has the obligation to verify the object he buys (cf Case 6), but if 181 the seller has wilfully misled the buyer, liability for breach of warranty is not limited by any failure on the buyer's part to give prompt notice of defects (art 203 SCO).

The seller behaves fraudulently if he intentionally gives false indications on the 182 quality of the object or intentionally does not reveal hidden defects of the object that the buyer could not detect;[136] the buyer has to prove the fraud.[137]

Swiss law provides time limits for actions in warranty (art 210 para 1 SCO) 183 unless the seller wilfully misled the buyer (art 210 para 6 SCO).

It is irrelevant if C respected all the legal obligations of verification and 184 notification of the damage, as D behaved fraudulently. He will be able to either rescind the contract (arts 205 and 208 SCO), seek a reduction of the price (art 205 SCO), have the machine replaced (art 206 SCO) and/or obtain damages for poor execution of the contract (art 97 SCO or 208 para 3 SCO).

C. SOLUTION

C can invoke D's extra-contractual liability for his faulty behaviour; he can 185 also invoke the actions on warranty to claim reparation, a replacement of the machine or a reduction of the price.

---

134 ATF 136 III 528 – SJ 2003 I 267.

135 ATF 116 II 431 – JdT 1991 I 45; CR CO I-*Schmidlin* (fn 26) art 28 CO no 9; BSK OR I-*Schwenzer* (fn 26) art 28 OR no 8.

136 ATF 131 III 145 – JdT 2007 I 261 c. 8.1; ATF 66 II 132 c. 6 – JdT 1940 I 554.

137 ATF 131 III 145 – JdT 2007 I 261 c. 8.1.

THE BORDERLINES OF TORT LAW IN THE UNITED STATES

W Jonathan Cardi and Michael D Green*

QUESTIONS

I. Tracing the Borderlines 619
II. Main Differences between Tortious and Contractual Liability 620
A. Differences as Regards the Foundations of Liability 620
B. Differences as Regards Causation 621
C. Differences as Regards Remedies 625
1) Standard of Proof 625
2) Consequential Damages 626
3) Non-Pecuniary Loss 627
4) Loss of Earnings and Loss of Chance 627
5) Restitution 629
6) Punitive Damages 631
7) Specific Performance and Injunctions 632
D. Differences as Regards 'Pure Economic Losses' 633
E. Differences as Regards Liability for Others 634
F. Differences as Regards Liability in the Case of Multiple Tortfeasors/Breaching Parties 635
G. Differences as Regards the Persons Who May be Protected 637
H. Differences as Regards Defenses 639
I. Differences as Regards Limitation Periods 642
J. Differences as Regards Proof 644
K. Other Differences 646
L. Reasons for the Differences 647

* The authors of this contribution would like to thank Professors Tim Davis, Wake Forest University School of Law, and Vincent Cardi, West Virginia University College of Law, for their helpful comments and advice, and Kelsey Kolb for her superb research assistance.

III. Limitation or Exclusion of Liability Arising from Tort and from Contract 648
A. Statutory Provisions Authorising a Limitation or Exclusion of Liability 648
B. Limitation or Exclusion of Contractual and Tortious Liability by Contract 649
1) Is it Possible to Limit or Exclude Contractual and Tortious Liability under a Contract? 649
2) Do Contractual Limitations and Exclusions Apply to Third Parties? 651
IV. Non-Concurrence or Concurrence of Actions 652
A. Overview 652
B. Concurrence/Exclusion of Actions for the Protection against Personal Injury and of Property 656
C. Concurrence/Exclusion in the Case of Interference with Contractual Rights 657
1) Interference with a Contractual Relationship 657
2) Loss of Business due to Personal Injury to Someone Else's Employees or Clients or to Property Damage to the Entrepreneur 657
V. Specific Situations 657
A. Pre-Contractual Liability 657
B. Liability of Professionals 658

CASES

Case 1. The Unattractive Shopping Mall 659
Case 2. The Idle Lawyer 659
Case 3. The Defective House 660
Case 4. Apartment in Flames 661
Case 5. Injured Skier 661
Case 6. Exploding Car 662
Case 7. Racing Boat Burning 662
Case 8. Insidious Report 663
Case 9. Circular Letter 664
Case 10. Shortage of Supply 664
Case 11. Injured Rock Star 665
Case 12. Equipment Destroyed 665
Case 13. Slipping on a Lettuce Leaf 666
Case 14. Test Drive 666
Case 15. Breach of Negotiations 666
Case 16. Non-Disclosure of Relevant Facts 666

In the United States, both tort and contract law are generally matters of state rather than federal law. While there is a common core to both tort and contract doctrines in the US, one can find variation – sometimes narrow but sometimes broad – across the 51 independent state jurisdictions.[1] In this United States country report, we attempt to provide a synthesis of state law while also trying to point out states whose laws deviate significantly from the synthesis. 1

QUESTIONS

I. TRACING THE BORDERLINES

The bases for liability in tort and contract are thought of as distinct in the US.[2] The phrase 'law of obligations' is largely unknown in the United States. Contractual obligations are derived from the agreement of the parties to a contract that sets forth the bilateral obligations of the parties. By contrast, tort duties are imposed on parties by operation of law.[3] This clean conceptual separation can break down in a number of contexts in which a tort occurs in a relationship where there is also a contract or potential contract between the parties, and where a contract is meant to benefit a third party. Medical and other professional malpractice, 2

1 In some areas, variation has been narrowed by uniform state laws that are promulgated by an organization now known as the Uniform Law Commission. The Commission drafts model uniform state laws that individual states may decide to enact as positive law. Probably the most successful such effort is the Uniform Commercial Code, which was prepared in collaboration with the American Law Institute and has been adopted in all 50 US states, although art 2, governing the sale of goods, has not been enacted in one state, Louisiana. *H Gabriel*, The Revision of the Uniform Commercial Code – How Successful Has It Been? (2001) 52 Hastings Law Journal (Hastings LJ) 653 (commercial law is primarily uniform throughout the United States because of the existence and passage of the Uniform Commercial Code (UCC) in all of the states and the District of Columbia).

2 Two prominent scholars recently catalogued a number of differences: '[T]ort law has a substantial causation requirement, but causation is seldom an issue in contract. Tort law recognizes claims for punitive damages; contract law by and large does not. Contract law limits the magnitude of recovery through doctrines like foreseeability and certainty; tort law mainly employs proximate cause and duty of care, which limit liability in a different way. And the list continues: economic harm (common in contract but not in tort), non-pecuniary losses (common in tort but much less in contract), comparative fault (applied as a defense in tort but not in contract), and mitigation of damages (common in contract, not in tort).' *O Ben-Shahar/A Porat*, Foreword: Fault in American Contract Law (2009) 107 Michigan Law Review (Mich L Rev) 1341, 1341.

3 Some law and economics scholars have developed a unified model of contract and tort whose premise is that in both the parties are incentivized to act to avoid losses greater than the gains from acting otherwise. See *Ben-Shahar/Porat* (fn 2) 1341.

products liability, landlords' obligations for defects in rented premises,[4] implied warranties and other terms in contracts, and contractual waivers of tort liability are among the instances in which this occurs.

3 A court's characterization of an action as tort or contract matters for several reasons. Statutes of limitations typically limit tort actions to two years from the date of discovery of injury; contract actions typically are given four years from the date of material breach. Insurance contracts and principles of governmental immunity sometimes turn on the nature of the claim. The standard for liability is also quite different – to prevail in the typical tort case, a plaintiff must prove negligence; breach of contract requires no such proof, but merely that the defendant breached the agreed-upon terms. In addition, the applicable damages rules are different – rules regarding mitigation, scope of liability (proximate cause), non-pecuniary losses, and punitive damages are much more permissive in the tort context than in contract. Indeed, even some rules that tort and contract actions share – eg causation – are applied differently in sometimes outcome-determinative ways. Finally, defenses to tort and contract actions are often distinct – eg the tort defense of comparative fault is not typically an available defense in contract actions (with the possible exception of warranty claims). Each of these differences is elucidated in detail below.

II. MAIN DIFFERENCES BETWEEN TORTIOUS AND CONTRACTUAL LIABILITY

A. DIFFERENCES AS REGARDS THE FOUNDATIONS OF LIABILITY

4 The main basis for liability in tort is negligence, a form of fault that entails failure to exercise reasonable care. For historical reasons, there are a number of specific torts where intent to do harm (different types of harm for different intentional torts) is an element. As well, there are a few pockets of strict liability, in which fault is not required but typically some additional element is required. That is to say, there are no 'absolute liability' torts in which only causation is required. Abnormally dangerous activity, keeping of wild or dangerous animals, and products liability are the most prominent areas in which strict liability has been imposed in the US.

5 Breach of contract does not require fault. Simply failing to fulfil a promise made in the contract, regardless of whether the breach is intentional, careless, or innocent,

[4] See *MT Lonegrass*, Convergence in Contort: Landlord Liability for Defective Premises in Comparative Perspective (2010) 85 Tulane Law Review (Tul L Rev) 413, 417.

is sufficient to impose liability based on breach of contract. Indeed, this principle is so well settled and accepted that one cannot easily find it expressed in governing case law or secondary sources.[5] Having said that, there are some contractual doctrines that might be understood to ameliorate the harshness of contractual strict liability. Various excuses, including impracticability, impossibility, and frustration of purpose forgive non-performance when significant unanticipated events dramatically affect the difficulty of performance.[6] And the withholding of excuse to forgive non-performance when impossibility is the fault of the non-performer[7] reveals additional considerations of wrongdoing in contract law.[8]

B. DIFFERENCES AS REGARDS CAUSATION

6 Cause in fact and scope of liability (proximate cause) play robust roles in tort law. With the exception of torts that do not require the plaintiff to demonstrate that she suffered harm (eg trespass to property), the plaintiff must prove that her harm was caused by the tortious conduct of the defendant.[9] Two standards are employed to determine factual cause in the United States. The first, and majority, rule is to inquire whether the defendant's tortious conduct was a 'substantial factor' in the plaintiff's harm. Many courts employing this standard will recognize that conduct cannot be a substantial factor unless it is also a but-for cause of the harm, but there are repeated instances in which courts neglect that requirement, resulting in a standard that is largely meaningless and leaves great discretion to the fact finder.[10] The second factual cause test is the

5 But see *DB Dobbs et al*, The Law of Torts, vol 1 (2nd edn 2011) §5 no 8 ('Contract law is at least formally strict liability law'); *EA Farnsworth*, Contracts (4th edn 2004) §8.8 no 535 ('This is true even if [the failure to fulfill a promise] is insubstantial, even if it is neither willful nor negligent, and even if the [defendant] is unaware of it.); ibid, §12.8 no 61 ('[C]ontract law is, in its essential design, a law of strict liability').

6 See *RA Hillman*, Principles of Contract Law (3rd edn 2014) 354–365; see also Restatement (Second) of Contracts §262 (1981) (performance excused when contract requires personal performance of individual who dies or is incapacitated before performance is completed).

7 *Farnsworth* (fn 5) §9.6 no 632 f.

8 For a variety of perspectives on this dichotomy between tort and contract law, see *Ben-Shahar/Porat* (fn 2) 1341.

9 See Restatement (Third) of Torts: Liability for Physical and Emotional Harm §26 (2010).

10 One commentator observes regarding the substantial factor test: 'The substantial factor test is not so much a test as an incantation. It points neither to any reasoning nor to any facts that will assist courts or lawyers in resolving the question of causation. Put differently, the substantial factor test requires no particular mental operation. It invites the jury's intuition.' *Dobbs et al* (fn 5) §189 no 634 (footnotes omitted). For courts using substantial factor to require more than but-for cause, see *Bostic v Georgia-Pacific Corp*, 439 South Western Reporter, Third Series (SW 3d) 332, 342 (Tex 2014); *Shyface v Sec'y of HHS*, 165 Federal Reporter, Third Series (F 3d) 1344, 1352–1353 (Fed Cir 1999); *Challis Irrigation Co v State*, 689 Pacific Reporter, Second Series (P 2d) 230, 235 (Idaho Ct App 1984); see also *Culver v Bennett*, 588 Atlantic Reporter, Second Series (A 2d) 1094 (Del 1991); *Ten Hagen v DeNooy*, 563 North Western

but-for requirement, which means that the conduct must be a necessary (but not necessarily sufficient) condition for the plaintiff's harm.[11]

7 Scope of liability plays an important role in limiting the liability of some tort defendants. Because a defendant's negligence may have continuing effects that result in a variety of harms removed from the foreseeable risks that made the defendant negligent, courts have used this element (often termed 'proximate cause') to permit a defendant whose tortious conduct was a factual cause of a plaintiff's harm to avoid liability.[12] Some intervening causes, ie other causally relevant conduct that occurred after the defendant's negligent conduct, especially if found unforeseeable, are deemed to obviate a defendant's tortious conduct as a proximate cause of harm.[13] The Third Restatement of Torts takes the position that superseding cause limitations are merely a stylized version of the rule that a defendant's liability is limited to harms that result from the risks that made the defendant's conduct tortious.[14] However, a number of courts continue to focus on the foreseeability of the superseding cause rather than the foreseeability of the type of harm that occurs, resulting in superseding causes playing a more robust rule in exonerating defendants of tort liability.[15]

8 Contract also has a factual cause requirement, although it requires attention much less frequently than in tort.[16] One scours contract cases and commentaries for discussion of causation, unlike the situation in tort law. A random survey of six contracts casebooks reveals no chapters or sections devoted to causation and no entries in their indices for causation or related terms such as proximate cause or factual cause. By contrast, one could not find a torts casebook that does not have a chapter (or more) devoted to the subject.

9 The basic causal inquiry in contract is whether the defendant's breach caused the plaintiff to lose out on the benefit it was to gain by the other's performance.[17]

Reporter, Second Series (NW 2d) 4 (Iowa 1997). For courts using substantial factor to mean something less than but-for cause, see, eg, *Mayhue v Sparkman*, 653 North Eastern Reporter, Second Series (NE 2d) 1384 (Ind 1995); *Roberson v Counselman*, 686 P 2d 149 (Kan 1984); *Hake v Manchester Twp*, 486 A 2d 836 (NJ 1985).

11 See Restatement (Third) of Torts: Liability for Physical and Emotional Harm §26 (2010).

12 See, eg, *Pittway Corp v Collins*, 973 A 2d 771, 787 (Md 2009) ('Legal causation is a policy-oriented doctrine designed to be a method for limiting liability after cause-in-fact has been established').

13 See Restatement (Third) of Torts: Liability for Physical and Emotional Harm §34 & cmt a (2010).

14 Ibid, §34 (2010).

15 Eg, *Latzel v Bartek*, 846 NW 2d 153 (Neb 2014).

16 See *Ben-Shahar/Porat* (fn 2) 1341 ('causation is seldom an issue in contract'); *Farnsworth* (fn 5) §12.1 no 731, fn 9 ('Although the same problems of multiple cause and of intervening cause that enliven the law of torts also arise in connection with contract damages, they are less important than in the law of torts').

17 All factual causation inquiries require framing: the outcome of interest must be specified and the act, conduct or phenomenon of interest also must be identified. Only then can we ask if

Causation becomes knotty when there are a number of independent potential causes of harm,[18] and it is difficult to determine which one of those causes was responsible. Thus, in a toxic tort case, there are many causes of leukemia, including non-environmental ones, and it is difficult in an individual case to determine which one is responsible for the claimant's disease. By contrast, in contract cases, there are rarely other potential causes of the claimant's failing to obtain the benefit of the bargain. In most contract cases that inquiry is readily and uncontroversially resolved, obviating the necessity to adjudicate the matter of causation. Thus, contract law imposes a similar factual causation requirement but one that more frequently does not require attention because of the contractual context that frames the causal inquiry.[19]

Not surprisingly, consequential damages[20] in the form of lost profits often 10
require attention to causation because there are a number of independent causes that may produce diminished profits, including the defendant's breach. When courts do address causation in contracts cases, they appear to use the same terminology as is employed in torts cases.[21] Thus, in one case, a bank breached its contract to provide a safe deposit box to a husband and wife jointly by permitting the daughter of the husband access to the safe deposit box without obtaining written permission of both holders, as the agreement required. The wife sued for the value of securities that were removed by the daughter and sold

---

the act of interest caused the specified outcome. See *DW Robertson*, The Common Sense of Cause in Fact (1997) 75 Texas Law Review (Tex L Rev) 1765.

18 The reader should appreciate that there are always multiple causes of any outcome. We distinguish a single causal chain that contains all of those multiple causes necessary for the outcome from multiple distinct causal chains each of which is independently sufficient to cause the outcome of interest. The latter is what is meant by 'independent potential causes of harm' in the text.

19 In tort law, the inquiry is framed by plaintiff's harm and defendant's tortious conduct. In contract, the causal inquiry is framed by a defendant's breach and a plaintiff's losing the benefit it would receive had the defendant performed.

20 The distinction between direct and consequential damages for breach of contract has been described as: 'Direct economic loss may be said to encompass damage based on insufficient product value; thus, direct economic loss may be "out of pocket" the difference in value between what is given and received or "loss of bargain" the difference between the value of what is received and its value as represented. Direct economic loss also may be measured by costs of replacement and repair. Consequential economic loss includes all indirect loss, such as loss of profits resulting from inability to make use of the defective product.' Note, Economic Loss in Products Liability Jurisprudence (1966) 66 Columbia Law Review (Colum L Rev) 917, 918.

21 See *Reiman Associates, Inc v R/A Advertising, Inc*, 306 NW 2d 292 (Wis Ct App 1981) (employing substantial factor to determine causation in contract case and quoting from a tort case for support); *Cedar Hills Properties Corp v Eastern Federal Corp*, 575 Southern Reporter, Second Series (So 2d) 673 (Fla Dist Ct App 1991) (employing substantial factor and quoting Corbin on Contract, a leading contracts treatise, in support); *Kopper Glo Fuel, Inc v Island Lake Coal Co*, 436 Federal Supplement (F Supp) 91 (ED Tenn 1977) (employing 'proximate cause' to mean factual cause).

for the benefit of the husband. Factual cause existed only because the husband's terminal illness would not have permitted him to personally gain access to the box.[22] The court displayed similar muddled usage of causal terms as one might find in torts cases:

> 'Because the breach was a substantial factor contributing to [plaintiff's] loss, *Fowler v Campbell* guides our analysis of [plaintiff's] claim. Fowler provides: "[i]n order to recover on a breach of contract claim, the alleged breach must be a cause in fact of the plaintiff's loss." Evidence adduced at trial supports the trial court's determination that the Bank's breach of contract was a cause in fact of [plaintiff's] loss. The Bank argues that Harold's subsequent endorsement of the certificates and distribution to other family members is the true cause of [plaintiff's] loss. This, however, is not determinative of the outcome here. "For a cause in fact to be a legal cause, it must have been a substantial factor in bringing about the harm." *Fowler*. "The test of causation in common law contract actions is not whether the breach was the only cause, but whether the breach was a substantial factor in bringing about the harm." *Id.* While Harold's subsequent endorsement and distribution of proceeds from the certificates to his daughter, Deborah Hopkins, and her children may have contributed to [plaintiff's] loss, Indiana does not recognize comparative causation in breach of contract claims. The trial court properly concluded that the Bank's breach of contract was a substantial factor in bringing about [plaintiff's] damages.'[23]

11 With regard to scope of liability, contract does not generally employ terms such as proximate cause,[24] legal cause, or scope of liability. Yet it does appear to have some doctrines that are analogous or at least similar to these concepts in tort law. In the realm of superseding causes, impossibility, impracticability, and frustration of purpose all entail unusual or unforeseeable events that are the basis for exonerating a party's contract breach.[25] While such events may be unforeseeable, they occur before the defendant's breach – indeed they are a cause of the breach – and they do not result in harm different from the type of harm we might expect a defendant's breach to cause.[26]

---

22 *Parke State Bank v Akers*, 659 NE 2d 1031 (Ind 1995).

23 Ibid, 1034 (citations omitted); see also *Cedar Hills Properties Corp v Eastern Federal Corp*, 575 So 2d 673, 677 (Fla Dist Ct App 1991) (confusing multiple independent sufficient causes and multiple necessary causes).

24 Save to mean factual causation.

25 See *R VerSteeg*, Perspectives on Foreseeability in the Law of Contracts and Torts: The Relationship Between 'Intervening Causes' and 'Impossibility' (2011) 2011 Michigan State Law Review (Mich St L Rev) 1497; *R Chester/SE Alumbaugh*, Functionalizing First-Year Legal Education: Toward A New Pedagogical Jurisprudence (1991) 25 University of California Davis Law Review (UC Davis L Rev) 21, 58.

26 Thus, contrary to Professor VerSteeg, these doctrines are not 'actually one and the same'. *VerSteeg* (fn 25) 1509.

C. DIFFERENCES AS REGARDS REMEDIES

The basic theories of remedial awards in tort and contract are different. Tort law provides compensation designed to restore the claimant to the position she was in before being injured. When the harm is pecuniary, that goal is more or less attainable.[27] By contrast, contract law attempts through its remedial award to put the claimant in the position she would have been in if the other party had performed as required in the contract; this is often referred to as 'expectation damages.'[28] That loss is measured as of the time that performance should have occurred; to the extent that market changes reduce the benefit of performance, the claimant's recoverable damages reflect that risk. An alternative to expectation damages, sometimes employed in contract, especially when the claimant is unable adequately to prove expectation damages such as lost profits, is 'reliance damages.' Under this theory, a claimant can recover costs incurred in reliance on the promises made by the breaching party in the contract.[29] 12

1) Standard of Proof

With regard to the standard of proof that the claimant has suffered loss, the preponderance of the evidence standard is employed in tort law and sometimes in contract. However, a number of jurisdictions have a higher standard for some contract issues – reasonable certainty – which seems to be employed especially with regard to consequential damages.[30] When the evidence of the existence of loss fails to meet this threshold and is uncertain or speculative, the only damages permitted are nominal.[31] However, most US courts do not demand the same rigor in proving the *amount* of loss as opposed to the existence of such. '[W]hen the existence of damage is certain, and the only uncertainty is as to its amount, the plaintiff will not be denied a recovery of substantial damages.'[32] 13

---

27 Under American law, the parties bear their own attorney's fees so a successful claimant does not receive the full measure of damages determined by the fact finder. The considerably larger awards for non-pecuniary damages in the United States compared to other western countries may at least partially be explained by this fact.

28 See Restatement (Second) of Contracts §344 (1981).

29 See *Farnsworth* (fn 5) §12.16 no 805 f.

30 See *JM Perillo*, Calamari and Perillo on Contracts (6th edn 2009) §14.8 no 497; *Ind & Mich Elec v Terre Haute Indus*, 507 NE 2d 588, 601 (Ind Ct App 1987). Tort law has long employed the substantial factor standard for causation. Its use has been roundly criticized by commentators and the Third Restatement. See Restatement (Third) of Torts: Liability for Physical and Emotional Harm §26 cmt j & rptrs note to cmt j (2010) note 10 supra.

31 See, eg, *Contemporary Mission, Inc v Famous Music Corp*, 557 F 2d 918, 926 (2d Cir 1977).

32 Ibid.

2) *Consequential Damages*

14 Recovery for consequential damages in the US has been highly influenced by the well-known English case of *Hadley v Baxendale*.[33] The plaintiff in *Hadley* sought to recover for lost profits when the defendant delayed shipping a broken machine shaft to a third party who was to construct a replacement. The plaintiff's grist mill was shut down for the length of the delay because he did not have a backup shaft. The appeals court overturned the jury's award of lost profits, after distinguishing between what are known today as general damages – those that ordinarily arise from contract breaches, such as the loss of the benefit of the bargain – and consequential damages. Recovery of the former requires no special showing, but the *Hadley* court insisted that consequential damages could only be recovered through proof that the parties contemplated such damages as a probable result of breach and that they contemplated such damages at the time of contracting. Thus, a high standard of foreseeability of the type of harm by the party who is to be charged with such consequential damages must exist.[34] The *Hadley* limitation on recoverable damages was designed to facilitate increasing commercial activity in the early stages of the industrial revolution.

15 Tort law, unlike contract law, routinely permits recovery of consequential damages – when an injured victim suffers lost wages as a result of physical injury, no foreseeability inquiry is required, although one would ordinarily expect that serious physical injury would result in such a loss.

> 'Damages awarded in a negligence action may differ from the damages awarded for a breach of contract claim arising from the same set of facts. "We have said that tort damages are not limited by the reasonable contemplations of the parties. Instead, the amount of direct injury is compensated, whether its extent was contemplated or not."'[35]

16 Under the proximate cause/scope of liability rubric, defendants may be absolved of liability for certain harms. This limitation on liability is often expressed in foreseeability terms: a defendant is not subject to liability for harms of a type that are unforeseeable at the time of the defendant's breach of duty. Note that the time for assessing foreseeability is different from contract.[36] More importantly, this limitation on liability is born of a combination of necessity and fairness,

---

33 156 English Reports (Eng Rep) 145 (1854).

34 See Restatement (Second) of Contracts §351(1981) ('Damages are not recoverable for loss that the party in breach did not have reason to foresee as a probable result of the breach when the contract was made').

35 *RET Corp v Frank Paxton Co*, 329 NW 2d 416, 420 (Iowa 1983).

36 For an argument that the foreseeability standard of *Hadley v Baxendale* be replaced with the tort doctrine of proximate cause, see *MA Eisenberg*, The Principle of *Hadley v Baxendale* (1992) 80 California Law Review (Calif L Rev) 563.

rather than commercial encouragement. Causal chains can run a long way, and some limit on consequences is required. Moreover, it seems fair to limit a tortfeasor's liability to harm resulting only from the foreseeable risks that made the tortfeasor negligent.[37]

3) *Non-Pecuniary Loss*

Non-pecuniary loss is routinely recoverable in tort when it is consequential to physical injury. Recovery for stand-alone emotional distress has expanded somewhat in the US in recent decades but still remains quite constrained.[38] The foreseeability rule of *Hadley v Baxendale* would render much non-pecuniary loss unrecoverable in contract cases. But the bar to non-pecuniary damages in contract seems to rest on a broader footing than just unforeseeability, although it is not entirely impermeable. The Second Restatement of Contracts provides: 'Recovery for emotional disturbance will be excluded unless the breach also caused bodily harm or the contract or the breach is of such a kind that serious emotional disturbance was a particularly likely result.'[39] Contracts that have been recognized as likely to result in emotional harm include those involving the handling and disposal of human remains and hotel and transportation contracts when the provider wrongly expels the guest or passenger.[40] 17

Thus, there may be less difference in this respect between tort and contract than initially meets the eye. Both permit recovery for emotional harm that is consequential to personal injury. Neither permits recovery ordinarily for emotional harm consequential to property damage. Yet both find exceptions for contracts or torts that are particularly likely to cause such loss when breached. The standard for recovery of stand-alone emotional harm in the Third Restatement of Torts is quite similar to §353 of the Second Restatement of Contracts, permitting recovery in 'specified categories activities, undertakings, or relationships in which negligent conduct is especially likely to cause emotional harm.'[41] 18

4) *Loss of Earnings and Loss of Chance*

Where breach of a contract results in a party not being paid for services provided, damages for the lost earnings are recoverable. However, lost earnings that are 19

---

37 Restatement (Third) of Torts: Liability for Physical and Emotional Harm §29 cmt e (2010).

38 See ibid, §§45–48 & Scope Note (2012) (explaining the expansion of recovery for stand-alone emotional distress and the instances in which it is currently recoverable).

39 Restatement (Second) of Contracts §353 (1981).

40 See *Perillo* (fn 30) §14.5 no 495.

41 Restatement (Third) of Torts: Liability for Physical and Emotional Harm §47(b) (2012). The Third Restatement also provides for recovery for stand-alone emotional harm when the victim is in the zone of physical danger and when a bystander observes the tortfeasor cause serious bodily harm to a close family member.

consequential to the breach are more carefully regulated by courts and subject both to the foreseeability limitation of *Hadley v Baxendale* and the reasonable certainty standard of proof with regard to the existence of such lost profits. However, when these requirements are satisfied, lost profits may be recovered.[42]

20 Some states have adopted a rule that bars the recovery of lost profits when the plaintiff is a new business on the rationale that many new businesses are unsuccessful, and thus the existence of lost profits is too speculative to permit their recovery.[43] However, there is a distinct trend away from a rigid rule precluding new businesses from recovering lost profits and instead permitting them to attempt to prove, with the requisite certainty, that the business would have been successful and earned profits.[44]

21 Tort law routinely permits recovery of lost earnings that are consequential to personal injury or property damage.[45] If an individual tortiously destroys a customized truck that cannot be replaced for a period of time, the owner is entitled to recover lost profits for the period required to replace the truck. However, lost profits alone – which constitute economic loss – are recoverable only on a very limited basis in tort law.[46]

22 When a party is unable to prove with the requisite degree of certainty that it was deprived of the opportunity to avoid a loss or obtain a gain because of the tortious conduct or breach of contract of the defendant, two legal responses are possible. One is to deny recovery on the simple basis that the plaintiff has failed to meet its burden of proof. The other is to recognize the lost chance or opportunity as cognizable harm itself and permit recovery for that harm. The value of the lost chance can be calculated by determining damages for the chance or opportunity and discounting it by the likelihood the defendant caused such loss.[47] Thus, if a doctor's negligent failure to diagnose a patient's cancer results in reducing his chance to be cured and survive from 20% to 0%, the plaintiff would recover 20% of the damages that would be awarded for wrongful death.[48] Most contemporary US court decisions in tort recognize lost chance, albeit in a limited context: medical malpractice that results in the patient failing to obtain

---

42 See *Lewis v Mobil Oil Corp*, 438 Federal Reporter, Second Series (F 2d) 500 (8th Cir 1971).

43 See *In re Merritt Logan, Inc*, 901 F 2d 349, 356 (3d Cir 1990); *Perillo* (fn 30) §14.8 no 499.

44 See *Humetrix, Inc, v Gemplus SCA*, 268 F 3d 910, 920 (9th Cir 2001).

45 See, eg, *Ameristar Jet Charter, Inc v Dodson Int'l Parts, Inc*, 155 SW 3d 50, 54 (Mo 2005) ('In many contract and tort cases involving damage to persons, property or businesses, a party requests damages for loss of business profits').

46 See below nos 37–39.

47 'The lost opportunity may be thought of as the adverse outcome discounted by the difference between the ex ante probability of the outcome in light of the defendant's negligence and the probability of the outcome absent the defendant's negligence.' Restatement (Third) of Torts: Liability for Physical and Emotional Harm §26 cmt n (2010).

48 See *MD Green*, Causal Uncertainty and Proportional Liability in the US, in: I Gilead et al (eds), Proportional Liability: Analytical and Comparative Perspectives (2013) 362–365.

the benefit that proper medical care would have provided.[49] Often these cases involve delays in diagnosis that reduce the chance that the patient will obtain a successful outcome.[50]

Limited recognition of recovery for a lost chance exists in contract law, albeit with a very different line drawn between those lost opportunities that are recognized as harms and those that are not. The seminal case is from England and involved a beauty contest in which the plaintiff was one of 50 semi-finalists, of whom 12 would win a cash prize.[51] The plaintiff was awarded £100, about 25% of the smallest prize, which was affirmed by the appellate court.[52] The Second Restatement of Contracts accepted this principle but limited it to aleatory contracts – those in which obtaining the benefit of the chance is conditioned on an event that neither party controls.[53] Thus, contests, such as the beauty contest in *Chaplin*, are one of a small category of contract cases in which a lost opportunity is recognized as an item of harm for which recovery can be had. 23

5) *Restitution*[54]

The term 'restitution,' in American law, most often refers to an independent cause of action seeking damages for unjust enrichment – an action that is available under facts that also might support an action in tort or in contract. In this section, we use the term instead to refer not to this cause of action, but to a means of measuring damages according to the defendant's wrongful gain, rather than the plaintiff's loss. 24

Restitution damages, while also available in tort scenarios, are more commonly employed in contract law and quasi-contract circumstances.[55] The premise for restitution is that a wrongdoer should not benefit from ill-gotten gains. The remedy is to remove those gains from the wrongdoer and use them to compensate the injured party. Thus, rather than honoring the injured party's expectation of 25

---

49 One commentator explained the potential breadth of full-throated recognition of lost chance: 'all cases of causal uncertainty may potentially be converted into loss of chance cases by … a redescription of the harm.' *Vaughan Black*, Not a Chance: Comments on Waddams, The Valuation of Chances (1998) 30 Canadian Business Law Journal (Canadian Bus LJ) 96, 98.

50 *Green* (fn 48) 364.

51 *Chaplin v Hicks* [1911] 2 King's Bench (KB) 786.

52 *Perillo* (fn 30) §14.10 no 502.

53 The Second Restatement provides: 'If a breach is of a promise conditioned on a fortuitous event and it is uncertain whether the event would have occurred had there been no breach, the injured party may recover damages based on the value of the conditional right at the time of breach.' Restatement (Second) of Contracts §348(3) (1981).

54 This section is drawn in part from *Farnsworth* (fn 5) §12.19–20 nos 820–827; *Perillo* (fn 30) §14.10 no 502.

55 Restitution is employed when, for a variety of reasons, a valid enforceable contract has not been formed but the parties have proceeded in some respect as if there were. Thus, where an agreement is too indefinite to form an enforceable contract, if one party's performance has

gain, restitution attempts to put the breaching party in the same position that would have existed had it not breached the contract.

26 In contract, some total breaches[56] will result in the expectation loss to the injured party being greater than the benefit obtained by the breaching party. In such cases, because expectation damages will be more than the amount required to deprive the breaching party of its gain, the injured party will prefer expectation damages to restitution, and there is no need to consider restitution.

27 However, in circumstances where contract damages favor the breaching party, restitution is a preferable remedy for the injured party. Thus, in *Bush v Canfield*,[57] the parties agreed to a sale of flour for $14,000, for which the buyer made a partial payment of $5,000. The seller breached even though the price of flour declined so that the value of the flour was $11,000. The buyer sought return of its deposit and the seller contended the plaintiff should recover only $2,000 because if the contract had been completed, the buyer would have suffered a loss of $3,000. Invoking the principle of unjust enrichment, the court ruled for the buyer: 'The defendant has violated his contract; and it is not for him to say, that if he had fulfilled it, the plaintiffs would have sustained a great loss, and that this ought to be deducted from the money advanced.'[58] Circumstances such as *Bush v Canfield* are relatively rare, as the defendant would have been better off to perform the contract, which had become favorable to the defendant because of the reduction in the price of flour. Restitution is not limited to monetary awards; specific restitution may require the return of property or other action by the defendant – this form of restitution takes the form of an action for replevin.[59]

28 Restitution is ordinarily limited to circumstances where the benefit to the breaching party is unjust and at the expense of the injured party – this is not necessarily the same thing as the benefit being a result of the breach itself.[60] This exception preserves efficient breach, which occurs when the breaching party's services or goods become more valuable than they would be if used to perform the contract. The breaching party compensates the injured party accordingly based on expectation damages, and the higher value of the breaching party's performance is realized. Although the benefit to the breaching party was a result of the breach, a court might hold that the benefit is not unjustly retained.

---

benefited the other, restitution will be awarded. See Restatement (Third) of Restitution and Unjust Enrichment §31 (2011).

56 Restitution is unavailable for partial breaches.

57 2 Connecticut Reports (Conn) 485, 488 (1818).

58 Ibid, 488.

59 See, eg, *Wallace v Cox*, 142 NW 578 (Neb 1912).

60 See Restatement (Second) of Contracts §370 cmt a (1981).

Restitution is even more rarely invoked in tort perhaps because the gain to defendants of causing harm is rarely greater than the loss imposed on the plaintiff. That is true by definition for negligence should a court pursue an analysis derived from the famous *Carroll Towing*[61] case, which requires that the expected value of harm be greater than the burden of precaution (or gain obtained by avoiding taking the precaution) that the defendant would have had to bear. 29

Breach of fiduciary duty is one area in which restitutionary principles may be employed. Although fiduciary duties generally arise out of contract, some areas, such as professional malpractice, are addressed as tort matters. When a fiduciary, for example a lawyer, misappropriates a financial opportunity of one to whom the duty is owed, restitution is available.[62] Other areas of tort law where a victim may elect restitution over compensatory damages is when property of another is taken, through fraud or conversion, and put to use for the benefit of the defendant and tortious interference with contract.[63] 30

6) *Punitive Damages*

Punitive damages, like damages for emotional harm, are generally available in tort cases if the defendant has acted with the requisite culpability, anywhere from gross negligence to recklessness to wanton, willful, or oppressive conduct, depending on the jurisdiction. Judicial and legislative reform in the past several decades has limited the availability of punitive damages. Some jurisdictions have abolished them, some have made the standard of proof more rigorous, requiring clear and convincing evidence of the requisite culpability, and some have limited their amount.[64] US Supreme Court decisions, based on constitutional due process provisions, have imposed careful judicial review of jury awards of punitive damages and more careful instructions to juries of the basis for making such awards and the determination of the appropriate amount of damages.[65] They have also limited the amount of punitive damages to no more than nine times the compensatory damages for state law claims and no more than 100% of compensatory damages for federal law claims.[66] 31

---

61 *United States v Carroll Towing Co*, 159 F 2d 169 (2d Cir 1947). Judge Hand expressed this concept algebraically as P X L > B, where the product of P, the probability of harm occurring, and L, the magnitude of loss, constituting the expected value of harm, is compared to B, the burden of preventing the expected loss of harm.

62 Eg, *Verenes v Alvanos*, 690 South Eastern Reporter, Second Series (SE 2d) 771 (SC 2010).

63 See *DB Dobbs*, Law of Remedies (2nd edn 1993) §4.1(1) no 367 f.

64 See *MA Franklin et al*, Tort Law and Alternatives (9th edn 2011) 775.

65 See *State Farm Mutual Auto Ins Co v Campbell*, 538 United States Supreme Court Reports (US) 408 (2003).

66 See *Exxon Shipping Co v Baker*, 554 US 471 (2008).

32 Punitive damages are ordinarily unavailable in contract actions.[67] The limited instances in which punitive damages are awarded in the contract context are when one party commits an independent tort of sufficient reprehensibility (and then the award of punitive damages is for the commission of a tort not breach of a contract), malicious violation of a fiduciary duty, and against insurance companies for bad faith failure to settle claims or breach of the insurer's duty of good faith in first-party claim processing.

7) Specific Performance and Injunctions

33 An injunction is a remedy more common in contract than in tort. In the typical tort case, the parties have no knowledge that tortious behavior is imminent. Injunctive relief is thus uncommon in tort, with some exceptions: when the tort is continuing, such as nuisance, trespass (of real or personal property), or defamation, and in the context of statutory and constitutional torts. One other area in which courts have employed injunctions in tort cases is as a method of providing medical monitoring (where that claim is recognized) by imposing requirements on the defendant periodically to fund medical surveillance for a plaintiff who was exposed to a toxic substance that increased her risk of disease.[68] Note that in order to obtain an injunction, a plaintiff must prove that money damages would be inadequate, another hurdle sometimes difficult to clear in the tort context.

34 Specific performance is simply a term referring to an injunction enforcing fulfilment of a contractual promise. In contract actions, specific performance is only available in limited situations – there is an obvious difficulty in requiring an individual or firm to do something it does not want to do and to monitor that performance for acceptability. Because specific performance is an equitable remedy, the plaintiff who seeks it must demonstrate that available relief at law – monetary relief – is inadequate to rectify the defendant's breach. Other equitable considerations, such as unclean hands or delay by the plaintiff, may result in denying specific performance. Money damages are most likely to be inadequate when there are personal reasons for the plaintiff's seeking performance. Thus, a person who entered a contract to purchase her childhood home could validly claim that damages would be an inadequate remedy, and specific performance is required for her to enjoy the benefit of the bargain she made. A strategic difference that exists in the US where civil juries are the norm is that there is no right to a jury in cases in equity, including requests for specific performance.[69]

---

67 See *Perillo* (fn 30) §14.3 no 488.

68 See *Friends for All Children, Inc v Lockheed Aircraft Corp*, 746 F 2d 816 (DC Cir 1984).

69 Other strategic differences are explained in *Dobbs* (fn 63) §12.8(1) no 805 f.

D. DIFFERENCES AS REGARDS 'PURE ECONOMIC LOSSES'

Typically, breach of contract results in economic harm to the other party. There are no restrictions in the US on recovery for economic loss when breach of a contract causes financial loss. 35

Recovery for pure economic loss is far more restrictive in tort. There are two reasons for this limitation. First, tort law ordinarily defers to contract where there is a contract between the parties. Private arrangements to which the parties have agreed better further freedom and are more likely to reflect the needs of the parties than are rules imposed by law, such as tort law. Second, economic loss ripples through the economy with almost no stopping point. To take the Gulf Coast oil spill in 2010 as an example, fishermen suffered economic loss due to their inability to fish, frozen fish manufacturers in the Midwest suffered economic loss when they could not supply their needs from those fishermen, employees of the frozen fish manufacturer suffered economic loss when they were laid off due to reduced production, restaurants in the town suffered economic loss because of the reduced income of those employees, and so on. 36

The 'economic loss rule' is a relatively recent development in the US and arose during the growth and development of strict products' liability in the latter half of the 20th century. Courts appreciated that when the victim suffers neither personal injury nor property damage and was only harmed because the product failed to perform as it should have, contract and warranty rules[70] should govern such disputes. In that narrow context, the economic loss rule is well established,[71] although there are sometimes difficulties of categorization when a component in a larger product fails and causes harm to the product.[72] 37

But the economic loss rule has come to mean more.[73] Unlike personal injury and property damage for which there is a default duty of reasonable care to avoid such harm, there is no general duty in tort law to avoid causing pure economic loss. A contractor who negligently constructs a building on a busy city block is not subject to liability to the other businesses on the block if the contractor's building collapses, necessitating closure of the street that forces those businesses to close and lose profits.[74] Note that this is true despite the fact that there is no contractual relationship between the business owners and 38

70 Those rules are particularly well settled because of the success of the Uniform Commercial Code, which has been adopted in every jurisdiction in the US.

71 See *East R Steamship Corp v Transamerica Delaval Inc*, 476 US 858 (1986).

72 See, eg, *Jimenez v Superior Court*, 58 P 3d 450 (Cal 2002).

73 See Restatement (Third) of Torts: Liability for Economic Harm §1 cmt b (Tent Draft No 1, 2012).

74 See *532 Madison Ave Gourmet Foods, Inc v Finlandia Center, Inc*, 750 NE 2d 1097 (NY 2001).

the contractor.[75] There are some specific areas in which such a duty exists, but these are carefully circumscribed areas such as negligent misrepresentation in the course of one's business or trade.[76] Beyond unintentionally causing economic harm, tort law similarly carves out certain areas where intentionally causing economic harm subjects the actor to liability – fraud and interference with contractual relations are two such – but there is no general bar to intentionally causing economic harm. Thus, ruthless but lawful competition may be substantially certain to cause economic harm yet there is no liability for such conduct.

E. DIFFERENCES AS REGARDS LIABILITY FOR OTHERS

39 Employers are liable for the torts of their employees (including officers of the company) committed within the scope of employment.[77] By contrast, they generally are not liable for the torts of their independent contractors subject to a number of exceptions.[78]

40 Contract has no notion of 'vicarious liability.' A party who makes a promise in the context of an enforceable contract is liable for failing to perform that promise, regardless of whether the reason relates to another individual, whether employee, independent contractor, or volunteer, or to the conduct of the party entering into the contract. One area in which 'vicarious liability' might be thought to apply to contract breaches involves a co-venturer who is liable for breach of a contract entered into by and in the course of the joint venture, regardless of which of the co-venturers is responsible for the breach.[79]

41 Parents in the United States are generally not vicariously liable for the torts of their children, although they may be liable in their own right if negligent with

---

[75] See, eg, *Rardin v T & D Mach Handling, Inc*, 890 F 2d 24 (7th Cir 1989) (purchaser of printing press could not recover in tort for lost profits due to negligent handling of press by a moving contractor hired by the seller).

[76] See Restatement (Third) of Torts: Liability for Economic Harm §5 (Tent Draft No 1, 2012).

[77] We do not delve into the difficulties of determining when an employee is acting within the scope of employment, an issue that is particularly salient when an employee commits an intentional tort. See generally Note, *MJ Sartor*, Respondeat Superior, Intentional Torts, and Clergy Sexual Misconduct: The Implications of *Fearing v Bucher* (2005) 62 Washington & Lee Law Review (Wash & Lee L Rev) 687, 700–710.

[78] Those exceptions are detailed in Restatement (Third) of Torts: Liability for Physical and Emotional Harm §§57–65 (2012). Sometimes courts impose vicarious liability on those employing independent contractors under the rubric of 'non-delegable duty,' which means that the employer is subject to liability if it or anyone it hires commits a tort for which there is a non-delegable duty. See ibid, §55 cmt d.

[79] See, eg, *Radaker v Scott*, 855 P 2d 1037, 1041 (Nev 1993) ('All members of a joint venture are jointly and severally liable to third persons for wrongful acts committed in furtherance of the joint enterprise'); *Wales v Wales*, 662 NW 2d 371 (Iowa Ct App 2003).

respect to the supervision of their minor children who pose risks to others.[80] Some states have enacted statutes making parents vicariously liable for certain acts, such as vandalism, by their children, typically with a cap on the total amount of damages for which they can be held liable.[81]

The employee who commits a tort in the scope of employment is liable along with the employer for harm caused. Technically, the employer who is vicariously liable is entitled to indemnity from the employee, who has acted tortiously. As an empirical matter, employers almost never seek indemnity from their employees for a variety of reasons, including that often the employee will not have insurance or the personal resources to pay any such claim.[82] 42

We close by observing that some torts are attributed to the principal rather than an individual agent within the principal. The best example of this is products' liability. It is the product manufacturer – not the employee who negligently designs the product – who is liable for defective design. Although in theory the employee might be sued outside of the product liability realm for her negligence in designing the product, such suits are almost never brought. 43

F. DIFFERENCES AS REGARDS LIABILITY IN THE CASE OF MULTIPLE TORTFEASORS/BREACHING PARTIES

Joint and several liability is no longer the majority rule for multiple parties held liable in tort cases in the US; indeed, because of the fragmentation among states in reforming this area, there is no majority rule. The Third Restatement of Torts, reflecting this variation, has five different tracks that conform to different approaches extant in the United States.[83] 44

It would do well to note that joint and several liability has two major effects. First, it imposes the risk that one or more joint tortfeasors will be insolvent on the other tortfeasors rather than on the plaintiff.[84] Second, it places the burden of joining other tortfeasors and pursuing them for their proportionate share on the defendant rather than the plaintiff, who can recover her entire damages from any one defendant.[85] 45

---

80 See Restatement (Third) of Torts: Liability for Physical and Emotional Harm §41(b) (2012).

81 See *Franklin et al* (fn 64) 57.

82 The other reasons are explored in *G Schwartz*, The Hidden and Fundamental Issue of Employer Vicarious Liability (1996) 69 Southern California Law Review (S Cal L Rev) 1739.

83 See Restatement (Third) of Torts: Apportionment of Liability §17 cmt a (2000). A bit out-of-date tables reflecting the rules in each state in the United States can be found in the Third Restatement at reporters note to §17 cmt a.

84 Ibid, §10 cmt a.

85 Ibid, §10 cmt b. While this is true in theory, in practice most plaintiffs sue all solvent tortfeasors because they can recover from each of them in settlement. Trials in civil cases

46 Two forces resulted in the modification of joint and several liability in the US beginning in the second half of the 20th century. Comparative fault was widely adopted and the rationale for joint and several liability – that as between culpable defendants and an innocent plaintiff the risk of insolvency should be placed on the culpable defendants – was compromised.[86] Plaintiffs whose fault contributed to their own harm could recover partial damages with the advent of comparative fault. In addition, the 1970s saw the beginning and growth of 'tort reform,' legislative efforts, driven by politics, that largely cut back on tort liability, including modification of joint and several liability.[87]

47 Today, in the US, both pure joint and several liability and pure several liability are reflected in the law among various jurisdictions, as well as three different hybrid approaches. Under pure several liability, each defendant is only liable for its apportioned share of comparative fault, and, in some jurisdictions, apportionment can be made to non-parties. One of three hybrids employs proportional liability when one or more defendants is insolvent; the share of the insolvent defendant is reallocated to the remaining parties in proportion to their comparative fault. Another hybrid employs joint and several liability for pecuniary loss and several liability for non-economic loss. The third hybrid uses joint and several liability for defendants whose comparative fault is above a threshold, often 50%, while limiting the liability of all under the threshold to several liability. Even with these five different schemes, there is additional variation, as some states combine two forms of hybrid liability and others use different schemes for different types of torts.[88]

48 Multiple parties, of course, occur much less frequently in the contract arena.[89] However, when multiple parties promise to perform the same obligation, whether

---

have become extremely rare, around 1–2% of all cases filed. See <http://www.abanct.org/litigation/vanishingtrial> (American Bar Association research revealing that the percentage of federal civil cases going to trial was 1.8% in 2002); *M Galanter*, The Vanishing Trial: An Examination of Trials and Related Matters in Federal and State Courts (2004) 1 Journal of Empirical Legal Studies (JELS) 459, 512.

86 See, eg, *Brown v Keill*, 580 P 2d 867, 874 (Kan 1978); *RN Pearson*, Apportionment of Losses Under Comparative Fault Laws – An Analysis of the Alternatives (1980) 40 Louisiana Law Review (La L Rev) 343, 362 ('When the plaintiff himself has been negligent, the logical support for joint and several liability evaporates'); *CA Mutter*, Moving to Comparative Negligence in an Era of Tort Reform: Decisions for Tennessee (1990) 57 Tennessee Law Review (Tenn L Rev) 199, 306 f.

87 On tort reform generally in the US, the American Tort Reform Association (funded by defense interests) catalogues tort reform throughout the US on a state-by-state basis on its website. See <http://www.atra.org/>.

88 See Restatement (Third) of Torts: Apportionment of Liability Topic 2 (2000).

89 See, eg, *InvestIN com Corp v Europa Intern, Ltd*, 293 SW 3d 819, 829 (Tex App 2009) (reversing the entry of a joint and several judgment against defendant company and its president; agreement neither explicitly nor implicitly imposed joint and several obligations on president).

they are joint,[90] joint and several, or several promisors depends, unlike in tort law, on what the parties to the contract intend.[91] Historically, the default rule (in the absence of specification in the contract) was that multiple promises to perform the same obligation created a joint obligation, but that rule has been modified in most states to provide a default of joint and several liability.[92] Our research has revealed almost no pure several liability being imposed by contemporary courts in contract cases. Thus, by contrast with torts, joint and several liability appears to be the dominant form of liability for multiple promisors of the same promise. This makes sense, as the promisee has been 'wronged' by the breach of the multiple promisors and, as in pre-comparative fault days, is not a wrongdoer.

G. DIFFERENCES AS REGARDS THE PERSONS WHO MAY BE PROTECTED

While both tort and contract law once had strict 'privity of contract' requirements, 49
the famous case of *MacPherson v Buick Motor Co*,[93] in 1916, began the cleavage of tort and contract with regard to privity, thereby enabling the development of product liability. Today, privity plays almost no role in tort suits across all US jurisdictions. By contrast, only the party to a contract or, in the case of third-party beneficiaries,[94] such a beneficiary, can sue to enforce a contract or for economic loss (we address personal injury and property damage below) arising from breach of the contract.

In the case of products that cause personal injury or property damage, warranty 50
law has made considerable accommodation of tort law principles.[95] The sale

90 Joint promisors must be sued in the same suit by a promisee. This joinder requirement, quite archaic, has been reformed in many states to modify the compulsory joinder requirement, especially when one of the joint promisors is insolvent or beyond the jurisdiction of the forum. See, eg, New York Civil Practice Law and Rules (NY CPLR) §1501 (McKinney); see also Restatement (Second) of Contracts §290 & Statutory Note to Ch 13 (1981).

91 Restatement (Second) of Contracts §289(2) (1981).

92 See, eg, Delaware Code Annotated (Del Code Ann) tit 6, §2701 ('[a]n obligation or written contract of several persons shall be joint and several, unless otherwise expressed'); Restatement (Second) of Contracts §289(3) (1981).

93 111 NE 1050 (NY 1916).

94 The seminal case recognizing the right of third-party beneficiaries in the US is *Lawrence v Fox*, 20 NY 268 (1859). On third-party beneficiaries generally, see *Perillo* (fn 30) §§17.2–14 nos 578–600.

95 The drafters of the initial UCC, who worked from 1942 to 1952, when the first version was published, focused on commercial transactions, although late in the drafting day they made accommodation for personal injury and property damage arising from breach of warranty. One commentator has been critical of that effort because of the substantial difference between the commercial and physical injury context. See *M Franklin*, When Worlds Collide: Liability Theories and Disclaimers in Defective-Product Cases (1966) 18 Stanford Law Review (Stan L Rev) 974.

of goods is governed in the US by the Uniform Commercial Code (UCC), a joint product of the American Law Institute and the National Conference of Commissioners on Uniform State Laws.[96] As previously mentioned, the UCC has been enacted in virtually every state,[97] although there are some minor variations in the versions enacted from state to state. The UCC provides for two warranties that are created only by the parties: express warranties[98] and implied warranties of fitness for a particular purpose.[99] In addition, the implied warranty of merchantability[100] is imposed on every sale of goods governed by the UCC.[101]

51 Privity for personal injury or property damage arising from breach of warranty is a bit complicated. First, we must distinguish between what is known as vertical privity and horizontal privity. Vertical privity refers to those entities in the chain of distribution from raw material supplier to component part manufacturer through retailer. Whether an injured person must sue only the retailer or may sue others in the chain of distribution is a matter of vertical privity. By contrast, horizontal privity addresses who, besides the initial consuming purchaser, may sue. Thus, whether the spouse of a consumer who purchased botulism-contaminated soup can sue the retailer is a matter of horizontal privity, while whether the consumer can sue the manufacturer of the soup is a matter of vertical privity. Because of controversy over the extent to which privity limitations should be relaxed for breach of warranty, the UCC avoided addressing vertical privity,[102] leaving the matter to individual state law, and provided three alternatives for horizontal privity from which states that enacted the UCC could choose.[103]

52 The first, and most restrictive, version limits horizontal privity to a 'natural person who is in the family or household of his buyer or who is a guest in his home if it is reasonable to expect that such person may use, consume or be affected by the goods and who is injured in person.'[104] This version excludes employees who are injured in the workplace by machinery or other goods (workers' compensation in the US bars tort suits against the employer but not suits against third parties).

---

96 The UCC can be found online at the Legal Information Institute at Cornell University School of Law, <http://www.law.cornell.edu/ucc>.

97 See above fn 1.

98 See UCC §2-313.

99 The latter warranty is implied but only based on the actions of the parties. Its creation requires a particular purpose of the buyer known by the seller and the buyer's reliance on the seller's expertise in recommending suitable goods. See UCC §2-315.

100 See UCC §2-314.

101 The UCC does not prohibit disclaimers of the implied warranty of merchantability, rather imposing rules on the form and content of any such disclaimer: UCC §2-316(2) & (3). The UCC also regulates limitations on remedies: UCC §2-719.

102 See UCC §2-318 cmt 3 ('the section … is neutral and is not intended to enlarge or restrict the developing case law on whether the seller's warranties, given by his buyer who resell, extend to other persons in the distribution chain').

103 UCC §2-318.

104 Ibid, Alt A.

Alternative B extends warranty protection to all individuals suffering personal injury who might be expected to be affected by the goods. Alternative C, the most liberal, includes property damage and, concomitantly, extended protection beyond individuals to legal entities such as corporations.

The term 'chain of contracts' is used in US jurisprudence to mean the parties are in vertical privity, as explained above. The concept is used in a wide variety of contexts often having nothing to do with those protected by a contract. Thus, for example, in constructions contracts, often whether a subcontractor or other person can impose a mechanics' lien on the constructed property depends on whether the claimant is in a chain of contracts with the owner.[105] Another context in which the concept has been used is to expand the limitations imposed by the economic loss rule, which limits tort law from providing a remedy for economic loss when the parties are in a contractual relation. Some courts have employed the concept of chain of contracts to limit tort liability even when the parties do not have a direct contractual relationship.[106] Another area in which chain of contracts has played a role is in the area of 'statutory employers,' ie those who are not formally the employer of an employee working on a job, but who, because of their contractual relationship with the formal employer, are protected by the exclusive remedy bar against bringing a tort claim against an employer by an occupationally injured employee.[107] 53

H. DIFFERENCES AS REGARDS DEFENSES

There are a variety of defenses found only in either tort or contract because they are peculiar to the context in which those two fields operate. Thus, the statute of frauds mandates that certain contracts must be in writing to be enforceable and is treated by courts as an affirmative defense.[108] Obviously, there is no 54

---

105 See, eg, *Benning Const Co v Dykes Paving & Const Co, Inc*, 426 SE 2d 564, 566 (Ga 1993) ('"subcontractor" will be construed to mean one who, pursuant to a contract with the prime contractor or in a direct chain of contracts leading to the prime contractor, performed services or procured another to perform services in furtherance of the goals of the prime contractor'). See generally *LF Elmore/JW Ralls/LE Catoe* (eds), Fundamentals of Construction Law (2nd edn 2013) 4 f.

106 See, eg, *Indianapolis-Marion Cnty Pub Library v Charlier Clark & Linard, PC*, 929 NE 2d 722, 740 (Ind 2010) ('We hold instead that there is no liability in tort to the owner of a major construction project for pure economic loss caused unintentionally by contractors, subcontractors, engineers, design professionals, or others engaged in the project with whom the project owner, whether or not technically in privity of contract, is connected through a network or chain of contracts'); *Rollander Enterprises, Inc v HC Nutting Co*, 950 NE 2d 850 (Ind Ct App 2011).

107 See, eg, *Annett Holdings, Inc v Kum & Go, LC*, 801 NW 2d 499, 504–505 (Iowa 2011).

108 See *Smestad v Harris*, 796 NW 2d 662 (ND 2011); *First Nat'l Bank in Dallas v Zimmerman*, 442 SW 2d 674 (Tex 1969).

analogous defense in tort law because, except for defamation and privacy, there is no writing that reflects a tort. Similarly, assumption of risk is a defense in tort law[109] but there is no comparable defense in contract law. Statutes of limitations are common to tort and contract, and those are addressed in the next section.[110]

55 One major area of overlap concerns a plaintiff's risky conduct that contributes to his harm. Both tort law in product liability and contract law in breach of warranty[111] are confronted with this issue. The US has adopted comparative fault and, although early strict product liability cases limited the use of negligence by a plaintiff,[112] today it is widely accepted as a defense reducing recovery in product liability cases[113] despite the objection that a plaintiff's fault cannot be compared with a strictly liable defendant who sells a defective product.[114]

56 By contrast, there is no uniform treatment of plaintiff conduct among courts in the US in contract cases, probably because the UCC does not squarely address the problem. A product liability text[115] explains:

> 'The Uniform Commercial Code does not expressly cover contributory or comparative negligence, but some of its provisions and official comments tangentially address the plaintiff's conduct under the guise of proximate causation. Comment 13 to §2–314 (which deals with an implied warranty of merchantability) provides that "[a]ction by the buyer following an examination of the goods which ought to have indicated the defect complained of can be shown as a matter bearing on whether the breach itself was the cause of the injury."'

57 UCC §2-316(3)(b), which deals with disclaimers, provides that when a buyer has inspected goods or refuses to inspect them, no implied warranty exists with regard to defects that the inspection should have revealed. Comment 8 to §2-316 elaborates: '[I]f the buyer discovers the defect and uses the goods anyway, or if he unreasonably fails to examine the goods before he uses them, resulting injuries may be found to result from his own action rather than proximately from the breach of warranty.'

---

109 Historically, implied assumption of risk was a complete defense to recovery, but more recently most courts have merged assumption of risk with comparative fault. See *Dobbs et al* (fn 5) §§235–238 nos 841–861.

110 See nos 62–67 below.

111 See text accompanying fns 93–103.

112 Restatement (Second) of Torts §402A cmt n (1965); *McCown v International Harvester Co*, 342 A 2d 381 (Pa 1975).

113 See Restatement (Third) of Torts: Apportionment of Liability §1 rptrs note to cmt b (2000).

114 See ibid, §8 cmt a (2000) (explaining that even when theories of liability are incommensurate '"Assigning shares of responsibility" may be a less confusing phrase because it suggests that the factfinder, after considering the relevant factors, *assigns* shares of responsibility rather than *compares* incommensurate quantities'); *Daly v General Motors Corp*, 575 P 2d 1162 (Cal 1978).

115 *DA Fischer et al*, Products Liability: Cases and Materials (5th edn 2014) 714 f.

UCC §2-715(2)(b) provides that the plaintiff can recover consequential damages for breach of warranty, including 'injury to person or property proximately resulting from any breach of warranty.' Comment 5 to §2-715 provides that: 58

> '[w]here the injury involved follows the use of goods without discovery of the defect causing the damage, the question of "proximate" cause turns on whether it was reasonable for the buyer to use the goods without such inspection as would have revealed the defects. If it was not reasonable for him to do so, or if he did in fact discover the defect prior to his use, the injury would not proximately result from the breach of warranty.

Often without referring to these Code provisions, several early opinions held that a plaintiff's negligence constitutes a defense in an action for breach of warranty. For example, in *Signal Oil and Gas Co v Universal Oil Products*,[116] the court held that a plaintiff's negligence constitutes a comparative defense (and consequently reduces rather than bars the plaintiff's recovery) in an action for breach of an implied warranty of merchantability. In *Erdman v Johnson Bros. Radio & Television Co*,[117] the court held that the plaintiff's contributory negligence is a complete bar to recovery for breach of an implied warranty of merchantability. The plaintiff in *Erdman* apparently was actually aware of the defect, so the court may have been applying a more limited defense of assumption of risk.[118] 59

Other courts, however, have held that a plaintiff's negligence is not a defense to an action for breach of warranty (at least where the plaintiff was not actually aware of the defect). Sometimes these cases turn on the particular language of a state's comparative responsibility statute.[119] When comparative responsibility statutes use broader language, courts may apply comparative responsibility principles to breach of warranty claims.[120] The situation in some states remains confused.[121] 60

Courts seem to be most reluctant to apply comparative principles to breaches of express warranties.[122] This is especially true in the case when the plaintiff's 61

---

[116] 572 SW 2d 320 (Tex 1978).

[117] 271 A 2d 744 (Md 1970).

[118] See also *Torres v Northwest Engineering Co*, 949 P 2d 1004 (Haw 1997) (express warranty claim governed by pure comparative negligence principles where the plaintiff was killed when the defendant's crane toppled over) and *JCW Electronics, Inc v Garza*, 257 SW 3d 701 (Tex 2008) (one who seeks damages for death or personal injury pursuant to a breach of implied warranty claim under art 2 of the Uniform Commercial Code seeks damages in tort and is accordingly subject to the comparative responsibility scheme set forth in the state comparative responsibility statute).

[119] See, eg, *Phillips v Duro-Last Roofing, Inc*, 806 P 2d 834, 837 (Wyo 1991) (noting the statute referred only to 'negligence').

[120] See *Montag v Honda Motor Co, Ltd*, 75 F 3d 1414, 1419 (10th Cir 1996).

[121] See *Carter v Brighton Ford, Inc*, 251 P 3d 1179 (Colo Ct App 2010).

[122] See, eg, *Holt v Stihl*, Inc, 449 F Supp 693 (ED Tenn 1977) and *Shaffer v Debbas*, 21 California Reporter (Cal Rptr) 2d 110, 114 (App 1993).

'misconduct' is to have simply relied on the truthfulness of the defendant's representation concerning the product.[123]

I. DIFFERENCES AS REGARDS LIMITATION PERIODS

62 Statutes of limitations are affirmative defenses in both tort and contract law. In tort law, different limitations periods may exist (within the same jurisdiction) depending on the type of tort or whether the action is brought as a wrongful death or survival action.[124] Similarly, in contract law, the applicable limitations period for breach of warranty in the sale of goods may be different from the period for other contracts. Because contracts for the sale of goods are governed by the UCC, which provides its own statute of limitations for warranty claims of four years from tender of delivery, most states have a four-year statute of limitations for such claims. By contrast, other breach of contract claims are often subject to different limitations periods.[125] In general, statutory periods for contract claims are longer than for tort claims for the good reason that evidence for contract claims tends to be in writing and not subject to deterioration in the way that testimonial evidence in tort actions often is.

63 Thus, in some states, different periods may apply in a suit based on personal injury that asserts a warranty claim and a tort claim.[126] However, some states, either by statute or court decision, have provisions that provide a uniform statute of limitations for suits based on personal injuries, regardless of the theory of liability asserted.[127]

---

123 See *Hensley v Sherman Car Wash Equipment Co*, 520 P 2d 146 (Colo Ct App 1974).

124 Thus, eg, in North Carolina, the statute of limitations for defamation is one year (NCGSA §1-54), while the period is three years for wrongful death suits (ibid, §1-53), and it is five years for suits against railroads for causing property damage in the process of road construction (ibid, §1-51).

125 Thus, in Iowa, the statute of limitations for written contracts is 10 years (Iowa Code §614.1.5), while the period is five years for oral contracts (ibid, §614.1.4), and four years for breach of warranty in the sale of goods (ibid, §554.2725).

126 Because a claim accrues at different times in tort and warranty claims, one or the other may provide the longer period depending on when tender of delivery (accrual for warranty purposes) occurred in relation to the plaintiff suffering injury (accrual for tort purposes). Thus, if the plaintiff suffers injury five years after tender of delivery, say two years, this would permit a tort claim, while a longer warranty period of four years would bar the warranty claim. See, eg, *Salvador v I H English of Philadelphia, Inc*, 307 A 2d 398, 403 (Pa Super Ct 1973), aff'd sub nom, *Salvador v Atl Steel Boiler Co*, 319 A 2d 903 (Pa 1974) (plaintiff could pursue warranty claim even though tort claim was barred by statute of limitations).

127 Eg, Iowa Code §614.1.2 (claims 'founded on injuries to the person or reputation … whether based on contract or tort … within two years').

Accrual of both a tort and contract claim is ordinarily when the last required element of the claim occurs[128] – in tort, injury to the plaintiff,[129] and in contract, breach by the defendant.[130] A variety of exceptions exist that extend accrual to a later time. Thus, when the defendant fraudulently conceals her wrongdoing, as when a doctor denies that malpractice is the reason for plaintiff's physical difficulties, accrual is suspended for the period when the fraud prevents the plaintiff from discovering the source of his harm. 64

Perhaps the most important and most significant exception to accrual-at-injury is the discovery rule, which delays accrual when the plaintiff is unaware of the existence of injury and, in some cases and jurisdictions, is also unaware of the cause of the injury and the defendant's wrongdoing in causing the injury.[131] This discovery exception is critical in toxic tort cases in which the defendant's wrongdoing – failure to warn of the dangers of exposure to a chemical – may occur at the outset of exposure but the disease does not manifest itself for many years or even decades. Even after manifestation, the plaintiff may not know that chemical exposure was the cause of the disease or that the defendant's warning failure to the plaintiff's employer was the reason for the exposure.[132] The discovery rule is also employed, when the facts support it, in contract actions.[133] 65

In addition to delayed accrual, other doctrines suspend the running of the statute-of-limitations clock. Thus, many jurisdictions toll the statute of limitations for children during the period of minority because they are disabled from bringing suit themselves.[134] Some jurisdictions suspend the statute running when the victim is under other disabilities that would prevent or make more difficult suit, such as a mental disability, incarceration or service in the military.[135] Tort reform legislation in many states has often cut back on these tolling doctrines, 66

---

128 See *Neel v Magana, Olney, Levy, Cathcart & Gelfand*, 491 P 2d 421 (Cal 1971).

129 Some exceptions exist and instead start accrual at the time of the defendant's wrongful act. See *Dobbs et al* (fn 5) §241 no 876 f.

130 See *Ehrenhaft v Malcolm Price, Inc*, 483 A 2d 1192, 1198 (DC 1984) ('it is well settled that in a contract action, the statute of limitations begins to run "from the date a contract is breached"').

131 See *Fischer et al* (fn 115) 769–777.

132 See generally *Dobbs et al* (fn 5) §243 nos 877–884. The difficulties of delay resulting from latent disease and the fact that evidence on a critical aspect of such cases – causation – actually improves with the passage of time led one commentator to advocate the abolition of all statutes of limitations in toxic tort cases. See *MD Green*, The Paradox of Statutes of Limitations in Insidious Disease Litigation (1989) 76 Calif L Rev 965.

133 See *Ehrenhaft v Malcolm Price, Inc*, 483 A 2d 1192, 1203 (DC 1984) ('We therefore hold that in an action based upon tort and contract claims arising out of allegedly deficient design and construction of an addition to a house, the cause of action does not accrue until the plaintiff knows, or in the exercise of reasonable diligence should know, of the injury').

134 While children may not unilaterally bring suit, statutory provisions authorize appointment of guardians to prosecute tort claims on behalf of minors.

135 See *Dobbs et al* (fn 5) §246 no 895 f.

particularly in the area of medical malpractice.[136] These tolling doctrines are generally applicable and apply in both tort and contract actions.

67 Enacted in the midst of widespread adoption of strict product liability, statutes of repose are similar in some respects to statutes of limitation but deserve separate mention. Statutes of repose are like limitation periods in that they cut off claims that are of a specified age. They are different in that they begin to run not when the last element of the claim has occurred but when the defendant's tortious conduct is completed, which for product liability claims occurs when the defendant sells the product.[137] They are also different in that their purpose is to provide repose to those who might otherwise be held liable within a reasonable period – usually a longer one, 8–12 years, than for limitation periods.[138] Unlike statutes of limitations, statutes of repose can bar a claim before it accrues, for example long-latency toxic harm claims.[139]

68 In addition to product liability claims, statutes of repose exist for other defendants who were thought to be overburdened by lawsuits during the tort reform efforts that began in the 1970s and include health care professionals and governmental agencies. Builders and architects are also common beneficiaries of statutes of repose regardless of whether the claims against them are in contract or tort.[140]

69 Tort liability may also arise from the same factual behavior that also constitutes a crime. However, the statute of limitations is unaffected by whether the facts also constitute a crime. Many US jurisdictions do have provisions that provide the judge in a criminal case authority to order restitution to the victim.[141] In such case, the applicable statute of limitations would simply be the one for the criminal offense with which the defendant is charged.

J. DIFFERENCES AS REGARDS PROOF

70 Because of the existence of jury trials, the burden of proof in the US consists of two components: the burden of production and the burden of persuasion. The former, a matter of law for the court, requires the court to determine if the

---

[136] See, eg, Arkansas Code Annotated (Ark Code Ann) §16-114-203(c) (reducing the period of minority during which the statute of limitations is tolled from 18 to 9 years in medical malpractice actions).

[137] See, eg, *Heath v Sears Roebuck & Co*, 464 A 2d 288 (NH 1983).

[138] See generally *Dobbs et al* (fn 5) §§244 nos 884–890.

[139] See *CTS Corp v Waldburger*, 134 Supreme Court Reporter (S Ct) 2175, 2182 (2014) ('The statute of repose limit is "not related to the accrual of any cause of action; the injury need not have occurred, much less have been discovered"').

[140] See, eg, Cal Civ Proc Code §337.15 (providing a 10-year statute of repose for real estate developers, builders, and architects).

[141] Eg, 18 United States Code (USC) §3663.

party with the burden of proof has introduced sufficient evidence to permit a reasonable jury to find in its favor. Thus, consider a pedestrian who is injured in a collision with a green car that runs a red light and speeds off after colliding with the plaintiff. If a plaintiff sued an owner of a green car but had no additional evidence that it was the defendant's green car that hit him, the court would rule the plaintiff failed to introduce sufficient evidence to permit a jury to find it was the defendant who ran the red light and injured the plaintiff and grant judgment as a matter of law for the defendant.

By contrast, the burden of persuasion is a matter applicable to the jury and is explained to it during the instruction phase of a trial. The jury must find that the evidence in support of the party with the burden of proof exceeds the standard of proof to render a verdict for that party. If the evidence is only equal to or below the applicable standard of proof, the party with the burden of persuasion has failed to satisfy it, and the verdict must be for the other party. The standard of proof in civil cases is ordinarily a preponderance of the evidence, which is often described as more likely than not.[142] In a variety of contexts that are disfavored – the award of punitive damages, claims of fraud, oral contract of devise – the standard of proof may be heightened.[143] 71

In a number of legal areas in which the best evidence is statistical, ie epidemiology in toxic tort cases to prove causation, courts have accepted the idea that general statistical evidence that supports a conclusion that the probability of that element existing is slightly greater than 50% is sufficient for the jury to make such a finding.[144] As mentioned previously, some courts require a higher standard of proof with regard to consequential damages in contract cases.[145] In addition, the existence and terms of an oral contract must be proved to a higher standard, often described as by clear and convincing evidence.[146] 72

These principles are equally applicable in tort and contract actions. In both, the burden of proof on the elements of a prima facie claim is on the plaintiff. The 73

---

142 See *MD Green*, Causal Uncertainty and Proportional Liability in the US, in: I Gilead et al (eds), Proportional Liability: Analytical and Comparative Perspectives (2013) 343.

143 See below text accompanying fn 145 f.

144 See, eg, *In re Joint E & S Dist Asbestos Litig*, 52 F 3d 1124, 1128 (2d Cir 1995) ('epidemiological evidence is indispensable in toxic and carcinogenic tort actions where direct proof of causation is lacking'). Courts have also ungrudgingly accepted use of statistical evidence in one aspect of employment discrimination know as disparate impact, ie use of an employment test or requirement that has a disparate impact on a protected class. See *Int'l Bhd of Teamsters v United States*, 431 United States Supreme Court Reports (US) 324, 339 (1977) ('our cases make it unmistakably clear that "(s)tatistical analyses have served and will continue to serve an important role" in cases in which the existence of discrimination is a disputed issue').

145 See no 13 above.

146 See, eg, *King v Richards*, 584 P 2d 50, 51 (Alaska 1978).

defendant, however, bears the burden of proof on items that are deemed to be affirmative defenses.

74 Along with these formal principles, courts have a variety of devices to adapt the burden of proof to considerations of policy or difficulties of proof. With regard to the burden of production and the sufficiency of the evidence, courts may adjust what constitutes sufficient evidence based on the difficulty of obtaining that evidence. Thus, in toxic torts where experience does not permit making causal attributions, courts have accepted statistical evidence that historically was rejected as proof.[147] In the area of alternative liability, courts have shifted the burden of proof to identify the wrongdoer when two tortfeasors each act in a way that could have caused the plaintiff's harm but only one actually did (the 'two hunters' hypothetical).[148] The policy that as between the two culpable defendants and an innocent (in the time of contributory negligence) plaintiff, the culpable parties should bear the burden of a lack of evidence justifies such a shift in the burden of proof. Similarly, in contract, the burden of proof has been shifted on an issue when common sense or policy suggests that such a shift would be appropriate.[149]

K. OTHER DIFFERENCES

75 One other difference between tort and contract relates to the unique procedural practice of affording a right to jury trial in civil cases in the United States. That right is circumscribed officially by the rule that the jury is to decide facts while the court is to decide law,[150] which leaves a great deal of discretion when the issue is a mixed question of law and fact, such as negligence. Tort law has been inclined to leave more decision making to the jury in the belief that the common sense of the community can usefully be brought to bear on the question of whether reasonable care was exercised and whether it is fair that the harm suffered by

[147] See, eg, *Smith v Rapid Transit, Inc*, 58 NE 2d 754 (Mass 1945); *SC Gold*, The 'Reshapement' of the False Negative Asymmetry in Toxic Tort Causation (2011) 37 William Mitchell Law Review (Wm Mitchell L Rev) 1507, 1542 (explaining courts' historical reluctance to accept 'naked statistical evidence' and increased willingness to accept such evidence in contemporary litigation).

[148] See *Summers v Tice*, 199 P 2d 1 (Cal 1948); Restatement (Third) of Torts: Liability for Physical and Emotional Harm §28 cmt f (2010).

[149] See, eg, Minnesota Statutes (Minn Stat) §514.02 (shifting the burden of proof to a party in a construction contract who received payment to prove the reason for such payment where party had notice that a creditor claimed payment remained due); *SI Becher*, A 'Fair Contracts' Approval Mechanism: Reconciling Consumer Contracts and Conventional Contract Law (2009) 42 University of Michigan Journal of Law Reform (U Mich JL Reform) 747, 780 (advocating shifting or lowering the burden of proof for consumer contracts in which the seller did not obtain approval from a proposed independent certifying entity).

[150] The jury's role has been limited in a variety of other formal and covert ways.

the plaintiff be within the scope of the defendant's liability. By contrast, contract law has deemed more questions as matters of law for the court[151] in the belief that providing rules of law in the commercial context will provide stability and efficiency for those entering into contractual arrangements.

One court, in a breach of employment contract case, remarked on the adoption of a presumption that employment contracts are at will, thereby requiring a discharged employee suing for breach to prove the existence in the contract of a term for employment. The court's comment illustrates the impact of the jury on the substantive law: 76

> 'We note that a jury is much more likely to be composed of employees as opposed to employers. We hope that it does not exhibit too cynical a view of humanity for us to be concerned that this might affect more than an occasional verdict. The law is replete with procedural rules designed to guard against the danger of prejudicial jury verdicts. The at-will presumption is such a rule. However, the presumption can be rebutted by clear evidence that the parties intended a contrary result. This is a sufficient safeguard. It balances the need to protect against prejudicial verdicts with the legal system's obligation to enforce the individual parties' expectations.'[152]

However, the court failed to appreciate that the 'presumption' it described had no effect. The burden of proof of the existence and terms of an agreement are on the party seeking to enforce it.[153] Thus, even in the absence of a presumption, a party contending that an employment contract contained a provision that specified a term for the contract would have the burden of proof. A presumption does no more than shift the burden of proof from the party that would ordinarily have it to the opposing party. 77

L. REASONS FOR THE DIFFERENCES

No doubt some of the differences identified are largely the result of historical artifact.[154] Since the mid- to late 19th century when tort law became an independent body of law in the United States, contract and tort have developed separately through the common law system, which is often labyrinthine as it responds to many different influences. 78

---

151 Eg, the interpretation of contractual language. See *Brisbane Lodging, LP v Webcor Builders, Inc*, 216 California Appellate Reports, Fourth Series (Cal App 4th) 1249, 1253 (2013).

152 *Greene v Oliver Realty, Inc*, 526 A 2d 1192, 1198 (Pa Super Ct 1987).

153 See *Compass Tech, Inc, v Tseng Laboratories, Inc*, 71 F 3d 1125, 1133 (3d Cir 1995); *Bedrock Stone & Stuff, Inc v Manufacturers & Traders Trust Co*, 2006 Westlaw (WL) 890993 (ED Pa 2006).

154 For examination of the history of English law that made the distinction between tort and contract, see *R Kreitner*, Fault at the Contract-Tort Interface (2009) 107 Mich L Rev 1.

79 No doubt some differences reflect that contract involves voluntary agreements of the parties while tort consists of rules crafted for appropriate behavior that risks harm to strangers. 'Freedom of contract' is a common phrase meant to convey that parties to a contract should be free to arrange their affairs as they see fit. While this simplistic version of contracts has required significant adjustment, the rhetoric of freedom remains a powerful influence.[155] By contrast, tort law regulates conduct that poses risks to strangers where voluntary arrangement is virtually impossible.[156] (To be sure, tort law, by imposing standards of conduct, also affects one's freedoms.) In such circumstances, common law judges feel more free to craft rules that they believe will best serve society – not just the parties to the accident but others whose interests may be affected by the rule of tort law. *MacPherson v Buick Motor Co*,[157] a case credited with beginning the modern product liability movement by removing the requirement of privity of contract for tort suits, famously declared:

> 'We have put aside the notion that the duty to safeguard life and limb, when the consequences of negligence may be foreseen, grows out of contract and nothing else. We have put the source of the obligation where it ought to be. We have put its source in the law.'[158]

III. LIMITATION OR EXCLUSION OF LIABILITY ARISING FROM TORT AND FROM CONTRACT

A. STATUTORY PROVISIONS AUTHORISING A LIMITATION OR EXCLUSION OF LIABILITY

80 Among 51 state jurisdictions, a wide variety of statutes limit or exclude liability for either contract or tort in particular contexts. For example, some statutes limit liability in the context of bankruptcy[159] or shield corporate owners or investors from liability.[160] The Federal Tort Claims Act limits the tortious liability of the

---

155 An example of a court deferring to the parties' arrangement is Brisbane Lodging, *LP v Webcor Builders, Inc*, 216 Cal App 4th 1249 (2013). In a construction contract, the parties provided that claims would accrue upon substantial completion of the project, which rendered null the delayed discovery rule, which otherwise would have resulted in the claim being timely. The court held the parties' modification of accrual should be given effect, relying on 'public policy principles applicable to the freedom to contract.' Ibid, 1253.

156 There are some exceptions. Product liability, for example, includes both those in privity with sellers and third-party 'strangers' to those contractual relationships.

157 111 NE 1050 (NY 1916).

158 Ibid, 1051.

159 11 USCA §502(b)(7) (2014) (limiting the liability of a debtor-employer, in bankruptcy proceedings, on employment contracts, to one year's worth of compensation).

160 Eg Del Code Ann tit 6, §18-101 ff (West 2014) (allowing companies to be structured in a way that protects investors in the company; allowing liability – in contract or tort – only up to the amount they have invested).

government and government officials, and many state statutes do the same with regard to state and local governments.[161] Other statutes cover narrow issues – for example, the National Childhood Vaccine Injury Act of 1986, which bars tort suits and sets up a national compensation system for vaccine-related injuries.[162] Finally, there exist many state statutes enacted as part of the tort reform movement,[163] with targeted provisions – for instance, setting caps on damages[164] – the primary aim of which is ultimately to limit liability.

B. LIMITATION OR EXCLUSION OF CONTRACTUAL AND TORTIOUS LIABILITY BY CONTRACT

1) *Is it Possible to Limit or Exclude Contractual and Tortious Liability under a Contract?*

Contractual and tortious liability may be limited, or in the torts context excluded, by contract. There are four general types of limitations and exclusions: Typically with respect to breach of contract claims, parties may create a 'limitation of liability' or 'liquidated damages' clause, which 'guarantees only that a party will not be held liable for damages above a specified ceiling.'[165] A party may eliminate its liability to another in tort via an 'exculpatory clause.'[166] Parties may also agree to indemnity provisions, which require one party to discharge the liability of the other.[167] Finally, parties to a contract may agree to take disputes to an arbitrator, rather than a court of law. 81

In tort cases, '[a] promise not to sue or an agreement exempting one from liability for future damage caused by the latter's simple negligence will generally be upheld.'[168] Contractual limitations on liability for recklessness or intentional torts, however, are typically held to be invalid as a matter of law. Even disclaimers of negligence might, in a particular case, be void for reasons of public policy. Courts consider a number of factors in ruling on the validity of an exculpatory agreement – for example, the relationship of the parties, whether the party seeking enforcement is charged with a duty of public service, and the disparity of 82

161 See 28 USCA §1346(b) (2014).

162 42 USCA §300aa-15 (2014).

163 State tort reform legislation is catalogued by the American Tort Reform Association. See < http://www.atra.org/>.

164 See, eg, Texas Civil Practice and Remedies Code Annotated (Tex Civ Prac & Rem Code Ann) §74.301 (West 2013).

165 *SH Williams*, Consumers and Remedies: Do Limitation of Liability Clauses Do More Harm than Good? (2014) 65 South Carolina Law Review (SC L Rev) 663, 665 (emphasis added).

166 Ibid.

167 23 Williston on Contracts (4th edn) §61:59.

168 8 Williston on Contracts (4th edn) §19:25.

bargaining power between the parties.[169] Such rulings are particularly common in the following circumstances: where products' manufacturers and distributors attempt to avoid liability for 'personal injur[ies] resulting from dangerous products'; where hospitals require patients to release all negligence claims ('partly because ... patients [do] not acquiesce voluntarily and partly because medical services were themselves so important'); where medical researchers disclaim liability for harm to their human subjects; where public agencies, caregivers such as public schools, or businesses affecting a public interest disclaim negligence liability; where employers ask employees to release all potential liability in an employment contract; where parents release their children's future claims for an injury that occurs during the commission of a commercial activity.[170] A statutory liability scheme might also influence the enforceability of releases. A statute might, for example, prescribe safety standards for a particular industry. If a waiver purports to release an industry member from liability for violating such standards, the clause will not be enforced.[171]

83 The ability of a party to a contract to disclaim liability for breach of that contract is more limited. Indemnification agreements covering liability for breach of contract actions are generally enforceable.[172] Similarly, a party to a contract may assign its duties and liabilities under a contract to a third party, with the assent of the other contracting party.[173] The courts prohibit parties, however, from entering into a contract where one party has no course of redress – put differently, A may not enter into a contract with B if A is not actually bound to any promise.[174] In the seminal case of *Miami Coca-Cola Bottling Co v Orange Crush Co*,[175] the plaintiff company sought specific performance of an agreement that, by its terms, could be cancelled at any time by the plaintiff. The Fifth Circuit held that 'the contract was void for lack of mutuality[;] ... the appellant did not promise to do anything, and could at any time cancel the contract.'[176] As Williston, a famous authority on contracts, explained: '[t]he general rule of law is ... that where the consideration for the promise of one party is the promise of the other party there must be absolute mutuality of engagement, so that each party has the right to hold the other to a positive agreement. Both parties must be bound or neither is bound.'

---

[169] Restatement (Second) of Torts §496B cmts e–j (1965).
[170] See *Dobbs et al* (fn 5) §234.
[171] Ibid.
[172] See, eg, Del Code Ann tit 8, §145 (West 2014) (allowing corporations to indemnify its officers for any liability they may incur in the execution of their duties).
[173] See Limits on Delegation, 29 Williston on Contracts (4th edn) §74:27 ('No one can assign his liabilities under a contract without the consent of the party to whom he is liable').
[174] See Mutuality of Obligation and Mutuality of Remedy Distinguished, 25 Williston on Contracts (4th edn) §67:42.
[175] 296 F 693 (5th Cir 1924).
[176] Ibid, 704.

Parties to a contract may, however, limit the damages to be paid upon breach by use of a 'liquidated damages clause.' Under the UCC §2-718(1): 84

> '[d]amages for breach by either party may be liquidated in the agreement but only at an amount which is reasonable in the light of the anticipated … harm caused by the breach, the difficulties of proof of loss, and the inconvenience or nonfeasibility of otherwise obtaining an adequate remedy. A term fixing unreasonably large liquidated damages is void as a penalty.
>
> Such limitations on the amount of liability are not common in the torts realm, although to the extent they exist, their enforceability turns on public policy as do complete exclusions of liability.'

Arbitration agreements are enforceable with regard to both tort and contract claims.[177] Although initially disfavored by the courts, arbitration clauses are now looked upon as a favorable alternative to litigation and are thus granted an expansive deference.[178] Indeed, the Federal Arbitration Act (FAA) merely requires that arbitration clauses satisfy general contract requirements to be valid and enforceable.[179] Pursuant to the FAA, courts regularly stay proceedings in their court and require the parties to proceed with arbitration.[180] 85

2) *Do Contractual Limitations and Exclusions Apply to Third Parties?*

A third-party beneficiary may enforce the duties of a promisor and is entitled to receive the benefits of the contract if she is an *intended* beneficiary.[181] Courts 86

177 See 21 Williston on Contracts §57:31 (4th edn) ('Claims arising out of *torts* and nuisances may be submitted to arbitration' (emphasis added)); ibid, §57:1 ('[Arbitration] may be used to describe the process by which international disputes, industrial disputes, commercial disputes or other disputes, whether resulting from an alleged *breach of contract* or otherwise, are resolved' (emphasis added)).

178 See ibid, §57:1 ('[A]rbitration is today favored as an alternative to litigation. … An arbitration agreement or clause may be broad or narrow, mandating either that the parties resolve every dispute through arbitration or directing that only certain, specific issues are to be resolved in that manner').

179 9 USCA §2 ('A written provision in any … contract evidencing a transaction involving commerce to settle by arbitration a controversy thereafter arising out of such contract … shall be valid, irrevocable, and enforceable, save upon such grounds as exist at law or in equity *for the revocation of any contract*' (emphasis added)); see also Cumulative Supplement, 21 Williston on Contracts §57:3 (4th edn) ('Although Federal Arbitration Act (FAA) generally requires application of ordinary state-law principles governing formation of contracts when determining questions of arbitrability, it also establishes liberal federal policy favoring arbitration, which controls despite any contrary state substantive or procedural policies').

180 See, eg, *Durkin v CIGNA Prop & Cas Corp*, 942 F Supp 481, 489 (D Kan 1996).

181 Restatement (Second) of Contracts §304 (1981) ('A promise in a contract creates a duty in the promisor to any *intended* beneficiary to perform the promise, and the intended beneficiary may enforce the duty' (emphasis added)); ibid, §315 (1981) ('An *incidental* beneficiary

generally hold that this rule extends to waivers or limitations of liability. Thus, where a promisor sues an intended beneficiary, the beneficiary is able to avail itself of the exclusion or limitation of liability.[182] The more difficult question is whether the parties to the contract may avail themselves of an exculpatory or limitations clause in defending a suit brought by the third-party beneficiary. After all, the beneficiary did not bargain for the clause and thus arguably should not be barred from suing to enforce the contract. Where a parent has waived tort liability on behalf of a child participating in a recreational activity, for example, courts overwhelmingly hold the waiver to be invalid.[183] Nevertheless, courts sometimes enforce waivers of liability against intended beneficiaries, particularly in the context of subcontractors.[184]

IV. NON-CONCURRENCE OR CONCURRENCE OF ACTIONS

A. OVERVIEW

87 As a general matter, the fact that parties have a contractual relationship with one another does not preclude one party from suing the other in tort. A particular act might constitute both a tort and a breach of contract, and the harmed person may sue pursuant to both tort and contract law.[185] To say that a plaintiff may sue in both does not, of course, mean that the plaintiff may collect more than her total damages. Rather, should the plaintiff succeed in both actions, then the full panoply of damages for both causes of action will be allowed, limited of course by the types and amounts of harm the plaintiff in fact suffered. A number of doctrines, however, limit the availability of dual claims in tort and contract in some structured ways, and in other ways that are less predictable.

88 The most significant limitation is the economic loss rule, which (as described above[186]) negates a negligence duty of reasonable care in cases where the

acquires by virtue of the promise no right against the promisor or the promisee' (emphasis added)).

182 See, eg, *Miller v Chesterfield Village GP, LLC*, 232 SW 3d 683 (Mo 2007) (denying applicability of liability waiver to a third party, sued in tort, who did not amount to a third party beneficiary); *Appalachian Ins Co v McDonnell Douglas Corp*, 214 Cal App 3d 1 (1989) (enforcing waiver in tort suit against intended beneficiary subcontractors).

183 *Hojnowski v Vans Skate Park*, 901 S 2d 381, 388 (NJ 2006).

184 See, eg, *Buttonwood Co, Inc v E Clifford Durrell & Sons, Inc*, 1997 WL 1433767 (Pa Com Pl 1997) ('Such exculpatory clauses in contracts have been held to be dispositive by the courts in this Commonwealth for rejecting third-party beneficiary claims asserted by subcontractors for unpaid materials or services').

185 See, eg, *Peitzman v City of Illmo*, 141 F 2d 956 (8th Cir 1944).

186 See no 37 f above.

plaintiff has suffered solely financial injuries. In most cases involving contract-related wrongdoing, the plaintiff's harm is purely economic. Thus, even where a tort duty might otherwise apply, a plaintiff's recovery of pure economic losses is limited to an action for breach of contract. There are several exceptions to the economic loss rule, however, some of which often arise in the context of contractual relations – for example, professional malpractice, fraud, wrongful discharge, defamation, tortious interference with contract, and certain claims for bad faith breach of insurance[187] or property rental contracts.[188] In these types of cases, a plaintiff may sue in tort instead of, or in addition to, contract.[189] Many of these scenarios are discussed in further detail later in this US report.

In light of the economic loss rule, the question of potentially overlapping tort 89
and contract claims is largely reduced to cases in which one party to a contract causes physical harm or property damage to the other contracting party or to a third-party beneficiary. In a few narrow areas, courts are fairly clear that plaintiffs are entitled to recover pursuant to tort law – namely, professional malpractice and a landowner's duty to repair.[190] Outside of these scenarios, this area of law is extraordinarily opaque and is governed by a patchwork of concepts that, as applied, appear at best unprincipled, and at worst internally inconsistent. The concepts are as follows:

(i) Determining the interest at stake. Under the Uniform Commercial Code, 90
which governs contracts for the sale of goods, recovery for a breach of contract can include damages for personal injury if such damages are contemplated at the time of contracting by the parties.[191] Courts sometimes hold similarly with regard to contracts for services.[192] Nonetheless, citing the nature of the harm, courts often characterize such actions as tort claims, ignoring or expressly dismissing the contract claim.[193] Other courts disallow a claim either in tort or

---

187 See *Freeman & Mills, Inc v Belcher Oil Co*, 900 P 2d 669 (Cal 1995).

188 *Dobbs et al* (fn 5) §453 no 1290.

189 Although this is the majority approach, not all jurisdictions agree. See, eg, *Brockmeyer v Dun & Bradstreet*, 335 NW 2d 834 (Wis 1983) (limiting wrongful discharge claims to contract).

190 See Restatement (Second) of Torts §§357, 375 (1965).

191 See UCC §2-715(b).

192 See, eg, *Murphy v Implicito*, 920 A 2d 678 (NJ 2007) ('We have previously indicated that no material difference exists between different types of claims seeking relief for conduct proximately causing personal injuries, irrespective of whether the act forming the basis for the cause of action is a breach of a duty defined by contract law or a breach of a duty defined by tort law') (citing *Dunn v Praiss*, 638 A 2d 875 (NJ App Div 1994), rev'd on other grounds, 656 A 2d 413 [NJ 1995]).

193 See, eg, *Delfuoco v K-Mart Corp*, 2000 WL 35504903, at *1 (Mass Super Ct 2000) ('[I]f recovery is sought for the cost of completing performance of a contract or remedying defects in performance, the applicable statute is six years. If, on the other hand, the damages sought are for personal injuries, the two-year [tort] statute of limitations is applicable'); *Murray v University of Pennsylvania Hosp*, 490 A2 d 839, 841–42 (Pa 1985) (disallowing contract action because plaintiff claimed damages for physical injury).

contract on grounds that one or the other is really the 'gist of the action.'[194] Still others enforce a preference for contract, but will allow a tort claim in light of a 'significant public interest.'[195] In summary, one might characterize these types of cases – that is, claims for personal injuries or property damage resulting from contract-related wrongdoing – as limiting a plaintiff to either a tort or contract claim according to the nature of the interest at stake. The reasoning in such cases often strikes one as opaque. As one commentator has written:

> 'In sum, one cannot help but be amazed by the volume of conflicting and contradictory precedent governing the matter of distinguishing tort from contact theory in cases involving the rendering of services. Some courts are so completely befuddled by the illogical distinctions swirling around them that they cannot keep the supposed taxa distinct and in the final analysis misapply the putative taxonomic rules of recovery without any legitimate basis for deviation owing seemingly to pure confusion.'[196]

91 *(ii) The independent duty doctrine.* Many states have adopted the 'independent duty doctrine,' which provides that as between parties to a contract, 'tort liability requires a breach of a legal duty independent of contract.'[197] Such a duty must arise 'from extraneous circumstances, not constituting elements of the contract,'[198] or as some courts express the rule, where 'a duty [would be] owed even if no contract existed.'[199] One example of this distinction tracks the

---

194 *Ginley v EB Mahoney Builders, Inc*, 2005 WL 27534 (ED Pa 2005). For other examples of courts using 'nature of the inquiry' type reasoning, see, eg, *Sommer v Federal Signal Corp*, 593 NE 2d 1365 (NY 1992) (considering 'the nature of the injury, the manner in which the injury occurred and the resulting harm' and deciding that 'where the plaintiff is essentially seeking enforcement of the bargain, the action should proceed under a contract theory'); *Bryan's Quality Plus, LLC v Shaffer Builders, Inc*, 2008 WL 3523935 (ED Pa 2008) (denying plaintiff's fraud claims because they resembled related contract claims); *Erickson v YMCA of Nyack*, 108 AD 2d 720 (NY Sup Ct App Div 1985) (dismissing contract action because the 'essence' of the plaintiff's claim was tort).

195 See, eg, *Trustees of Columbia U in City of New York v Gwathmey Siegel and Assoc Architects*, 601 New York Supplement, Second Series (NY S 2d) 116 (App Div 1993) (recognizing that 'separate tort liability can arise independently of the contractual relationship between the parties where the nature of the performance called for is affected with a significant public interest and a failure to perform the service carefully and competently can have catastrophic consequences'); *Erlich v Menezes*, 981 P 2d 978 (Cal 1999) (same).

196 *J Lavitt*, Leaving Contemporary Legal Taxonomy (2012) 90 Denver University Law Review (Denver U L Rev) 213, 234.

197 See, eg, *Kreisers Inc v First Dakota Title Ltd Partnership*, 852 NW 2d 413, 419 (SD 2014).

198 Ibid.

199 *Sutton Funding, LLC v Herres*, 936 NE 2d 574 (Ohio Ct App 2010). Another common statement of this rule is as follows: courts will 'foreclose tort claims (1) arising solely from the contractual relationship between the parties; (2) when the alleged duties breached were grounded in the contract itself; (3) where any liability stems from the contract; and (4) when the tort claim essentially duplicates a breach of contract claim or where the success of the tort claim is dependent on the success of a breach of contract claim.' 2 Standard Pennsylvania Practice 2d §6:13.

European doctrine of *culpa in contrahendo*. Courts are more likely to hold that a tort duty exists independent of the contract in cases where wrongful conduct occurred before a contract was signed – for example, fraud in the inducement of a contract or during contract negotiations – than during the contractual term.[200]

Application of the independent duty rule often appears arbitrary and perhaps even outcome-driven. For example, consider a case in which a medical supply company sued a property title company for professional negligence, which negligence resulted in the plaintiff being subject to additional tax liabilities.[201] Although the defendant's negligent act was clearly in the performance of its contractual duties, the court held that a tort duty arose not from the contract itself, but from the defendant's pre-contractual advertisements that it could handle the transactions ultimately covered by the contract. This reasoning reaches mightily for an extra-contractual hook for a negligence duty; but in other cases, courts stretch their reasoning in the opposite direction. Thus, the doctrine seems ultimately malleable, an instability complicated by (iii) below. Nevertheless, many courts and secondary sources consistently cite the independent duty as being central to doctrine governing the tort–contract borderline.[202] 92

(iii) A tort duty may arise from a contractual promise. In direct contradiction to (ii), many courts hold that an independent tort duty may arise from an enforceable contractual promise.[203] This is true both with respect to the promisee and also to a third-party beneficiary.[204] Such a duty might arise from a bargained-for exchange or in the context of a gratuitous promise with detrimental reliance (promissory estoppel).[205] It is hard to know what to make of this common practice, particularly in light of the independent duty rule; nonetheless, this doctrine lives side by side with that rule in many jurisdictions and is an important part of the tort–contract landscape. 93

(iv) Teleological reasoning. As a final twist in this contorted area of law, there is some evidence that the reason a court is being asked to decide between tort and contract affects the court's ultimate answer to the question. If, for example, it is for purposes of determining the availability of punitive damages, courts seem more likely to determine that the applicable law is contract, in which case recovery 94

---

200 See, eg, *Formosa Plastics Corp USA v Presidio Engineers and Contractors, Inc*, 960 SW 2d 41 (Tex 1998) (upholding tort claim for fraudulent inducement although such claims would be limited to contract if occurring during the term of the contract); *International Star Registry of Ill v Omnipoint Marketing, LLC*, 510 F Supp 2d 1015 (SD Fla 2007) (same).

201 *Kreisers*, 852 NW 2d, at 414.

202 See, eg, *Dobbs et al* (fn 5) §615.

203 See, eg, *Nazami v Patrons Mut Ins Co*, 910 A 2d 209 (Conn 2006).

204 *Dobbs et al* (fn 5) §321.

205 See, eg, *Mixon v Dobbs Houses, Inc*, 254 SE 2d 864 (Ga 1979) (imposing tort duty on defendant, who promised plaintiff that he would notify him should his pregnant wife call with the news that she was in labor); Restatement (Second) of Torts §§323, 324A (1965).

of punitive damages is prohibited.[206] If, on the other hand, it is for statute of limitations purposes, courts have been more equivocal, often characterizing a plaintiff's claim as sounding in tort and therefore barring claims made later than two years after discovery of the injury.[207]

95 The following are a few hypotheticals, the answers to which would vary considerably among jurisdictions due to the unpredictable application of the tests described above:

96 P and D contract for P's purchase of five new bulletproof vests for its security guards. D fails to deliver the vests as agreed, and one of the security guards is shot that very day.

97 P purchases a home alarm system from D. The system is designed so that when the alarm is tripped, D's central office contacts local police and sends them to the house. A burglar enters P's home and sets off the alarm. Although the alarm sounds, D negligently fails to contact the police. P's property is stolen by the burglar.

98 P hires D, a plumber, to fix a leak in her faucet. D negligently makes the leak worse, and the resulting flood of water causes an electric short in the toaster oven, which leads to a fire, destroying the house.[208]

B. CONCURRENCE/EXCLUSION OF ACTIONS FOR THE PROTECTION AGANST PERSONAL INJURY AND OF PROPERTY

99 This subject is covered sufficiently in the overview above. There is no difference between courts' treatment of cases involving personal injury and property harm.

---

206 See, eg, *Road & Highway Builders v N Nev Rebar*, 284 P 3d 377 (Nev 2012) (reversing an award of punitive damages because 'breach of contract claim should prevail over tort claims'); *Dunn Const Co v Cloney*, 682 SE 2d 943 (Va 2009) (disallowing punitive damages claim for fraud, limiting suit to contract claim). Courts do not always hold thus, however. Where a court finds that fraud (eg) rises 'to the level of an independent tort,' courts will allow the tort action, accompanied by punitive damages. See, eg, *Woodkrest Custom Homes Inc v Cooper*, 108 So 3d 460 (Miss Ct App 2013).

207 *Dobbs et al* (fn 5) §320 no 869, fn 18 ('For statute of limitations purposes, personal injury actions are likely to be characterized as tort, even if they depend upon a contractual relationship'); YMCA of Nyack, 108 New York Supreme Court Appellate Division Reports, Second Series (AD 2d) 720 (NY Sup Ct App Div 1985) (dismissing contract action because 'essence' of plaintiff's claim was tort).

208 Cf *Matarazzo v Millers Mutual Group, Inc*, 927 A 2d 689 (Pa 2007) (holding that homeowners' suit against municipal authority – alleging that the authority failed to fulfill its promise to turn off the water to the plaintiffs' vacant house, which resulted in the freezing and breaking of their pipes and flooding of their home – sounded in tort, not contract, for purposes of determining governmental immunity).

C. CONCURRENCE/EXCLUSION IN THE CASE OF INTERFERENCE WITH CONTRACTUAL RIGHTS

1) *Interference with a Contractual Relationship*

A suit against a third party for interference with a contract is a matter for tort law, not contract. Tortious interference is available where a defendant 'intentionally and improperly interferes with the performance of a contract … between another and a third person, by preventing the other from performing the contract or causing his performance to be more expensive or burdensome'.[209] Of course, if a party to the contract was induced by a third person to breach the contract, then the non-breaching party would have a contract action against the breaching party as well as a tort suit against the third party who interfered. 100

2) *Loss of Business due to Personal Injury to Someone Else's Employees or Clients or to Property Damage to the Entrepreneur*

Recovery in tort for lost revenues stemming from personal injury or property damage to others is barred by the economic loss rule. A plaintiff's only common law recovery in such cases would be pursuant to contract or, in a rare instance, restitution. 101

V. SPECIFIC SITUATIONS

A. PRE-CONTRACTUAL LIABILITY

Where parties never arrive at a contractual agreement at all, there can be no claim for breach of contract, and thus no concurrence problem exists. In such case, a plaintiff must sue under tort or pursuant to promissory estoppel, a claim that is not easily characterized as either tort or contract.[210] Where a contract does exist 102

---

209 Restatement (Second) of Torts §766A (1979).

210 See, eg, *Seltzer v Dunkin' Donuts, Inc*, 2011 WL 1532398 at *6 no 17 (ED Pa 2011) ('[W] hile promissory estoppel has sometimes been said to reside between tort and contract, the Pennsylvania Supreme Court has made it clear that "promissory estoppel … sounds in contract law"'); *OC Snyder*, Promissory Estoppel as Tort (1949) 35 Iowa Law Review (Iowa L Rev) 28, 45 ('No complete identification of the doctrine of promissory estoppel can be made: in the generalization of the doctrine, some "re-uniting of tort and contract principles" appears and this makes it hard to categorize the principle of promissory estoppel as one of "tort" or "contract"'); *EM Holmes*, Restatement of Promissory Estoppel (1996) 32 Willamette Law Review (Willamette L Rev) 263 ('Promissory estoppel does not languish in the contract/ tort shadowland but rests, stably rooted in equity, in [13] jurisdictions').

between the parties, but where the alleged tortious conduct occurred before the contract was formed, courts are nonetheless more likely to limit recovery to tort or promissory estoppel. This is because courts often hold that a tort duty exists independent of the contract in cases where the wrongful conduct occurred before a contract was signed as opposed to during the contractual term.[211]

B. LIABILITY OF PROFESSIONALS

103 The liability of professionals is another area in which courts among various jurisdictions take vastly different approaches. In the health care context, for example, where plaintiffs are typically seeking recovery for personal injuries, some courts limit recovery to tort, specifically a claim for medical malpractice.[212] These courts disallow claims for breach of contract except where a doctor has made express warranties, covenanting to cure the plaintiff pursuant to a specific treatment plan.[213] In other jurisdictions, a plaintiff may sue in both tort and contract for medical injuries.[214]

104 Because other types of professional liability cases typically involve pure economic loss, most courts leave such suits to contract law due to the economic loss rule,[215] with some significant exceptions – financial service professionals like lawyers and accountants are subject to professional malpractice suits in tort despite the rule.[216] Courts do not often offer convincing justifications for distinguishing between professions in this regard – explanations typically focus on the fact that non-financial service professionals offer a material service, rather than a purely financial one.[217] With regard to legal malpractice in particular, there is a split among jurisdictions on the matter of concurrence of tort and contract actions. Like medical malpractice, some courts do not allow breach of contract actions in attorney malpractice suits, except where the lawyer failed to deliver on a promise

211 See no 91 above.

212 See, eg, *Ley v St Louis County*, 809 SW 2d 734, 737 (Mo Ct App 1991) (holding that plaintiffs cannot recover for medical malpractice under a breach of contract theory).

213 Eg, *Gage v Morse*, 933 SW 2d 410, 420 (Mo Ct App 1996).

214 See, eg, *Sullivan v O'Connor*, 296 NE 2d 183, 188–89 (Mass 1973) (upholding jury verdict against defendant doctor on breach of contract claim, but for the defendant on tort claim, and even upholding award for pain and suffering damages pursuant to contract claim).

215 See, eg, 2314 *Lincoln Park West Condominium Assoc v Mann, Gin, Ebel & Frazier, Ltd*, 555 NE 2d 346 (Ill 1990) (barring tort claims against architects in claims for purely economic losses).

216 See, eg, *Congregation of the Passion, Holy Cross Province v Touche Ross & Co*, 636 NE 2d 503 (Ill 1994) (denying application of the economic loss rule to bar tort suits for accountant malpractice – distinguishing such claims from suits against architects, in which the economic loss rule does bar claims for purely economic losses).

217 Ibid, 527 (dissenting on the grounds that this distinction between accountant and architectural services does not justify the difference in tort liability).

expressly stated in the contract.[218] Other professionals, such as architects, are subject to all of the various ambiguities described in sec IV.A.[219]

CASES

CASE 1. THE UNATTRACTIVE SHOPPING MALL

The economic loss rule would ordinarily bar a tort claim by C against D. However, a claim for nuisance, which protects the enjoyment and use of real property, might be available against the landlord. In the context of personal injury claims, landlords are often held liable to tenants for nuisance.[220] Jurisdictions are split, however, as to whether a plaintiff might recover in nuisance for pure economic harm[221] – a search for such claims in the commercial leasing context produced no results. Furthermore, because C and D are not in privity, C would not have an action in contract against D. Nor do courts treat sub-lessees as third-party beneficiaries. Finally, consequential damages are rare in breach of lease cases, particularly lost profits.[222] 105

CASE 2. THE IDLE LAWYER

As explained above, there is a split among jurisdictions on whether both a tort and contract claim can be brought for legal malpractice. Some courts do not allow breach of contract actions in attorney malpractice suits, except where the lawyer failed to deliver on a promise expressly stated in the contract with the client. The facts here do not specify on this account. In other courts, the daughters would 106

---

218 Compare, eg, *Bishop v Owens*, 272 P 3d 1247, 1251–53 (Idaho 2011) (denying breach of contract liability, where the contract stated that '[a]ttorneys shall represent Client in said matter and do all things necessary, appropriate, or advisable, in regard thereto,' on the grounds that such a promise is not materially different from the standard applied in the tort malpractice claim) with *Johnson v Jones*, 652 P 2d 650, 654 f (Idaho 1982) (holding that a breach of contract claim would arise only if the attorney did not do what she promised to do in the contract – eg, failing to draw up a contract of sale).

219 See Limitations on Tort Damages – Contract Constraint, 6 Bruner & O'Connor Construction Law §19:9 (2014).

220 See, eg, *Nida v Spurgeon*, 998 NE 2d 938 (Ill App Ct 2013) (noting that a tenant may sue a landlord for injuries stemming from a condition that constitutes a nuisance).

221 Compare, eg, *Duquesne Light Co v Pennsylvania Am Water Co*, 850 A 2d 701 (Pa 2004) (barring nuisance claim for purely economic harm) with *The Stop and Shop Companies, Inc v Fisher*, 444 NE 2d 368 (Mass 2006) (allowing nuisance claim for loss of business despite the fact that federal courts apparently hold contra).

222 The authors wish to thank their colleague, and property law expert, Tanya Marsh for her insights on this case.

be allowed to bring both contract and tort actions and recover damages under either theory. Among those states that do permit contract actions, a number of courts employ a third-party beneficiary analysis to permit claims by disappointed beneficiaries against the lawyer hired to draft a will.[223] As a general matter, legal malpractice is typically addressed as a matter of tort law. In the context of this case specifically, since the seminal case of *Biakanja v Irving*,[224] in California in 1958, most US courts have permitted tort actions for malpractice in drafting a will despite a lack of privity between the disappointed beneficiaries and the attorney.[225] However, when the devisee's testamentary intent to benefit the disappointed beneficiaries is not revealed in the will, a number of jurisdictions deny such claims.[226]

CASE 3. THE DEFECTIVE HOUSE

107 Warranties of merchantability (or habitability, in this context) apply in most states to the sale of new houses.[227] Jurisdictions are split as to whether such

---

223 See, eg, *Garcia v Borelli*, 180 California Reporter (Cal Rptr) 768, 772 (Ct App 1982) ('It is settled that intended beneficiaries of a will who lose their testamentary rights because of failure of the attorney who drew the will to properly fulfill his obligations under his contract with the testator may recover damages as third party beneficiaries'); see generally *JM Feinman*, Liability of Lawyers and Accountants to Non-Clients: Negligence and Negligent Misrepresentation (2015) 67 Rutgers University Law Review (Rutgers UL Rev) 127, 158 f.

224 320 P 2d 16 (Cal 1958).

225 See, eg, *Passell v Watts*, 794 So 2d 651, 652 (Fla Dist Ct App 2001) ('Intended third-party beneficiaries of testamentary documents have standing to bring an action for legal malpractice if they are able to show that the testator's intent as expressed in the will is frustrated by the negligence of the testator's attorney') (internal quotation marks and citations omitted); *Leyba v Whitley*, 907 P 2d 172, 177 (1995) ('Even if an intended third-party beneficiary is not strictly in privity, we join those jurisdictions that have rejected any stringent privity test as the touchstone of an attorney's duty to a nonclient'); *Simpson v Calivas*, 650 A 2d 318, 322 (NH 1994) ('We agree that although there is no privity between a drafting attorney and an intended beneficiary, the obvious foreseeability of injury to the beneficiary demands an exception to the privity rule'); *Auric v Continental Cas Co*, 331 NW 2d 325, 327 (Wis 1983) ('We conclude that a beneficiary of a will may maintain an action against an attorney who negligently drafted or supervised the execution of the will even though the beneficiary is not in privity with that attorney'). But see *Robinson v Benton*, 842 So 2d 631, 634 (Ala 2002) ('an intended beneficiary has no standing to bring a legal-malpractice action against an attorney because there is no privity between the beneficiary and attorney, and in the absence of privity, the attorney owes no duty to the beneficiary'); *Noble v Bruce*, 709 A 2d 1264, 1275 (Md 1998); *Maneri v Amodeo*, 238 NY S 2d 302 (NY Sup Ct App Div 1963).

226 See, eg, *Hall v Kalfayan*, 118 Cal Rptr 3d 629, 634 (Ct App 2010); *Kinney v Shinholser*, 663 So 2d 643, 645 (Fla Dist Ct App 1995); *Espinosa v Sparber, Shevin, Shapo, Rosen & Heilbronner*, 612 So 2d 1378, 1380 (Fla 1993); *Schreiner v Scoville*, 410 NW 2d 679 (Iowa 1987); *Mieras v DeBona*, 550 NW 2d 202, 214 f (Mich 1996); *Harrison v Lovas*, 234 P 3d 76, 78 (Mont 2010) (trust documents).

227 25 American Law Reports, Third Series (ALR 3d) 383 ('Many cases involving the construction and sale of a new dwelling have held the builder or other vendor liable for loss or injury

warranties extend to a subsequent purchaser.[228] Thus, in most states, because C and D are not in contractual privity, C would not be able to sue D for breach of contract. If this hypothetical involved the sale of goods, rather than a house, jurisdictions are also split as to whether privity is required, although most have abolished the requirement of vertical privity.[229] Similarly, jurisdictions are split on whether C may sue D for the tort of negligence.[230] Although most jurisdictions appear to allow such suits for personal injury, a few jurisdictions disallow suit for harm done to the house itself.[231] In addition, a number of states have passed statutes voiding contractual provisions that would limit a homeowner's recovery for construction defects.[232] Finally, it is worth noting that states often treat commercial real estate differently, denying liability pursuant to the economic loss doctrine.

CASE 4. APARTMENT IN FLAMES

A landlord's negligent failure to maintain or repair dangerous conditions is one 108
of the areas in which US courts allow actions in both contract and tort.[233] Some such courts assign property damage to contract recovery and personal injury to tort. Others simply allow the plaintiff to recover all damages pursuant to a tort claim.

CASE 5. INJURED SKIER

C would be able to pursue a tort action because the tort duty is unrelated to 109
the contract and arises as a result of D1's obligations to those on its premises and due to its active risk-creating operations (running a ski lift) on the property. It is also possible that D1 could be liable for breach of contract, as D1's contractual promise of a ride to the top of the mountain was broken. It is

sustained because of defects in the physical condition of the dwelling. The basis for liability of the builder or other vendor has been varied, ranging from the general area of tort, to warranty principles, to breach of the contract of sale'); 10 ALR 4th 385 ('[C]ourts have resisted extending an express warranty given by the builder to the original purchaser so as to permit subsequent purchasers to bring suit on the basis of contracts to which they were not parties').

228 *Speight v Walters Development Co, Ltd*, 744 NW 2d 108, 111–113 (Iowa 1996) (citing cases on both sides of the issue).

229 *M Shapo*, Shapo on the Law of Products Liability (2014) §16.01.

230 *Cosmopolitan Homes, Inc v Weller*, 663 P 2d 1041, 1044–45 (Colo 1983) (citing cases in support of such actions and those disallowing them due to the economic loss rule).

231 Ibid.

232 Eg CRS 13-20-806(7).

233 Restatement (Second) of Torts §375 (1965).

unusual for such a case to proceed in contract, however, where the plaintiff's damages are for personal injury, both because tort law typically prevails and because consequential damages for personal injury are uncommon in such a scenario. In addition, were the plaintiff seeking to proceed in contract to avoid the tort statute of limitations, a court might well deny the plaintiff's claim, for the reasons described in sec IV.A above. Because C's claim would likely sound in tort, D2 would be ordered to pay the plaintiff's judgment.

110 In most US jurisdictions, C would not be permitted to join D2 in any underlying tort or contract action against D1. The rule against direct actions is a consequence of the US commitment to jury trials and concern that the existence of liability insurance would bias a lay jury in its determination of whether liability exists.

CASE 6. EXPLODING CAR

111 In most US jurisdictions, C would not have a tort claim against D1 (whom we assume is a dealer in cars) or D2 because of the 'economic loss rule' that developed with the adoption of strict product liability. When the only harm is the deficiency in the product or its performance, the economic loss rule displaces tort and leaves buyers only to their contractual remedies.[234] While some courts made exceptions to this economic loss rule when the misperformance of the product occurred in a 'tort-like' accident,[235] most courts adhere to limiting the buyer's remedy to contract so long as nothing other than the good itself is harmed. C would likely have a contract claim against both D1 and D2[236] for breach of implied warranty of merchantability – although the express warranty lasted only two years, an implied warranty of merchantability exists by operation of law and can only be disclaimed by express and conspicuous language in the contract.[237] The statute of limitations in the case of the sale of goods, which is four years from tender of delivery, would not bar this warranty claim.

CASE 7. RACING BOAT BURNING

112 A plaintiff has no tort claim for a defective product that causes damage only to the product itself. This is a manifestation of the economic loss rule. Thus, the

234 Restatement (Third) of Torts: Liability for Economic Harm §3 & cmt a (Tent Draft No 1, 2012); *East River SS v Transamerica Delaval*, 476 US 858 (1986).

235 Eg, *Lloyd v General Motors Corp*, 916 A 2d 257 (Md 2007).

236 Most courts in the US do not require vertical privity for breach of warranty in the sale of goods.

237 UCC §2-316.

success of a tort claim in this case would turn on whether the boat is separable from the electronic equipment. Had the boat burned while owned by D, D might have had a viable tort claim against the manufacturer of the electronic equipment. Where a component has been integrated into a larger product before sale to the consumer, courts have held that the products have merged, and the tort claim therefore fails.[238] C might have a tort claim against the manufacturer of the electronic equipment, although proving that the defect existed at the time of manufacture may be difficult. Assuming that D is a casual seller, D also will not be liable to C in contract – the implied warranty of merchantability does not apply to non-merchant sellers of used goods and the statute of limitations has expired for the express warranty provided by D.[239] Were C to establish a breach of warranty, recovery of repatriation costs would depend upon the foreseeability doctrine of *Hadley v Baxendale*, described in sec I.C above.

CASE 8. INSIDIOUS REPORT

C would potentially be able to bring concurrent actions in tort and in contract. In tort, C would sue for tortious interference with contract and for fraud,[240] both of which are exceptions to the economic loss rule. Unless the employment contract otherwise provides, C would also have a viable action for breach of D's contract duty to C to perform in good faith and in C's interests. Whether a court would allow C to pursue actions for either tort or contract or both concurrently would depend upon the jurisdiction's application of the various doctrines described in sec IV.1. In this case, it seems likely that a tort duty would exist independent of the employment contract and thus that a tort suit would be allowed. Whether C would be allowed to bring an action instead, or concurrently, for breach of contract (for example if the tort's statute of limitations had run) is difficult to predict, although this case seems to lend C particularly compelling arguments that both claims are independently supported and that neither is the sole 'gist' of the action. 113

In addition to tort and contract claims, every state in the US has enacted a statute prohibiting unfair trade and consumer practices. Their gist is to protect consumers and businesses from fraudulent, misleading, or deceptive trade practices. These statutes typically provide, contrary to the usual US rule, that successful plaintiffs may recover attorney's fees from the defendant. These 114

238 See *E River SS Corp v Transamerica Delaval, Inc*, 476 US 858, 867 (1986); *Fischer et al* (fn 115) 652 f.

239 UCC §§2-314, 2-104.

240 Fraud is established where there has been (1) an intentional misrepresentation (2) of fact (3) that proximately causes harm and (4) is material, (5) intended to induce and (6) does induce reliance by the plaintiff, (7) which is reasonable or 'justifiable.' *Dobbs et al* (fn 5) §664.

statutory claims are asserted along with any tort or contract claims the victim may have. False disparagement of a competitor's products is recognized as a violation of these statutes.[241] Some statutes expressly prohibit disparagement through false or misleading statements of facts.[242]

CASE 9. CIRCULAR LETTER

115 C has no contract claim against D because none of the acts by D implicate obligations it would have pursuant to the agency agreement with C.[243] C's company, Z, would have viable tort claims for tortious interference with prospective contractual relations and C for defamation.[244] Because C has no contract claim against D, no concurrence issue exists.

116 In addition to tort claims, Z may have a claim based on the state's unfair trade and consumer practices statute. Both the tort and statutory claim could be asserted against D.

CASE 10. SHORTAGE OF SUPPLY

117 Assuming that C had a long-term contract with D requiring D to supply parts to C, C would likely have a viable contract action to invalidate the modification and claim breach of contract. Because this hypothetical involves a contract for the sale of goods, it is governed by the Uniform Commercial Code. Although the UCC allows modifications of contracts without requiring additional consideration,[245] C can likely invalidate the modification under a claim of duress because C's assent resulted from D's improper threat. Furthermore, D's conduct might be a breach of the pre-existing contract obligation of good faith and fair dealing, thus providing an additional basis for C's breach of contract claim.

---

241 Eg, *Nelson v State Farm Mut Auto Ins Co*, 988 F Supp 527, 530 (ED Pa 1997); see generally *HD Nims*, Unfair Competition by False Statements or Disparagement (1933–1934) 19 Cornell Law Quarterly (Cornell LQ) 63.

242 Eg, Tex Code Ann, Bus & Com §17.46(8).

243 If the employment contract included a non-competition clause, however, then D might have an action for breach of contract against P.

244 See 44 Causes of Action 2d 339 (2010) ('To establish a prima facie case in an action for defamation involving the plaintiff's profession, trade, or business, the plaintiff must generally prove that (1) the defendant made a defamatory statement concerning the plaintiff; (2) the defendant published the defamatory statement by communicating it to a third person; (3) the defamatory statement was false; and (4) the defendant acted with the degree of fault required in the circumstances of the case').

245 UCC §2-209.

Tort claims are less likely to succeed, and thus the overlapping claims' issue is unlikely to arise in this context. Although for a short period of history some courts recognized a tort claim for 'bad faith breach of contract,' courts have since abrogated such actions outside the context of insurance[246] and property rental contracts.[247] P might instead try a claim for 'economic duress.' Economic duress is actionable when 'economic (or emotional) threats are … used to extract some concession or transaction … when the victim, without reasonable alternative, gives up something of value in response to the threat.'[248] Such claims are not easily won, however, as 'courts have generally favored freedom of contract and have been reluctant to supervise fairness of agreements except in extreme cases.'[249] 118

CASE 11. INJURED ROCK STAR

C's potential tort claims against D are barred by the economic loss rule. Furthermore, C cannot sue D for breach of contract because, as explained in sec II.C.2 above, only parties to a contract or intended beneficiaries have the right to enforce a contract. (Although not particularly relevant to this project, X would likely be excused from the contract with C. As the Restatement of Contracts states: 'If the existence of a particular person is necessary for the performance of a duty, his death or such incapacity as makes performance impracticable is an event the non-occurrence of which was a basic assumption on which the contract was made.'[250]) 119

CASE 12. EQUIPMENT DESTROYED

Presuming that D1 did not act negligently in any way, C does not have a tort claim against D1, and thus there is no potential for overlapping tort/contract claims. C's contract claim against D1 depends on the specific terms of the contract, particularly who bears the risk that D1 will not be able to perform. Although strict liability governs breaches of warranty in the US, the doctrine of impossibility (including failure to deliver due to the negligence of a third party) softens that strict liability and might serve to excuse performance. 120

---

246 See *Freeman & Mills, Inc v Belcher Oil Co*, 900 P 2d 669 (Cal 1995).

247 *Dobbs et al* (fn 5) §453 no 1290.

248 Ibid, §707.

249 Ibid.

250 See Restatement (Second) of Contracts §262 (1981).

121 As in the prior hypothetical, C would have no contract action against D2 because D2 was not a party to the contract – thus, no tort/contract concurrence issue exists. Assuming that C owned the equipment and that the equipment was damaged, C would have a viable tort cause of action for damage to the equipment itself. Loss of profits from the concert, although economic damages, would also potentially be recoverable (subject to proximate cause limitations) as they derive from the property damage. If the property was not damaged, then C's tort claim would be barred by the economic loss rule.

CASE 13. SLIPPING ON A LETTUCE LEAF

122 C's only claim in this hypothetical is in tort. There is no argument for breach of contract or even promissory estoppel. No contract between C and D ever existed nor did D make any promise on which C relied or which caused harm to P.

CASE 14. TEST DRIVE

123 C's suit against D will be solely for negligence, unless C and D had a contract (express or implied) covering the test drive, as many car dealerships do. In that case, C may sue for both tort and contract, subject to the potential limitations described in sec IV.1.

CASE 15. BREACH OF NEGOTIATIONS

124 Although, with additional facts, D might be liable for fraud or pursuant to the doctrine of promissory estoppel, C does not have a viable action for breach of contract, as there was no consideration for D's promise. Critical to D's fraud claim would be whether: (1) D did not intend at the time she made the promise to wait until Friday to comply with that promise; and (2) C could establish justifiable reliance on D's promise; and (3) C suffered harm as a result of relying on D's promise.

CASE 16. NON-DISCLOSURE OF RELEVANT FACTS

125 C can make concurrent arguments for breach of contract, breach of warranty, and the tort of fraud (specifically, fraudulent non-disclosure), although C's

claims are by no means certain to succeed under the elements of those claims.[251] C's contract claim would likely be unsuccessful since D made no promise with regard to the suitability of X machine on sloped terrain. C's warranty claim would be unsuccessful because no warranty would have been breached (the most likely one, implied merchantability, would not extend to use on a steep slope) and independently as well if D were not in the business of selling machinery. With regard to the question of concurrence, concurring actions would likely be allowed for two reasons: fraud is an exception to the economic loss rule, and D's alleged fraudulent non-disclosure occurred before the contract was formed, thus likely satisfying the independent duty rule.

---

251 Cf *Omega Engineering Inc v Eastman Kodak Co*, 908 F Supp 1084 (Conn 1995) (holding such concurring claims viable in context of sale of underperforming batteries).

THE BORDERLINES OF TORT LAW

Economic Perspectives

Michael Faure and Wenqing Liao

I. Introduction 670
II. Tracing the Borderlines. 671
  A. Torts: Internalising Externalities 671
  B. Contracts: Facilitating Cooperation Through Credible Commitments 672
  C. A Borderline: The Coase Theorem 674
  D. Policy Consequences. 675
III. Main Differences between Tortious and Contractual Liability. 676
  A. Differences as Regards the Foundations of Liability. 676
  B. Differences as Regards Foreseeability 678
  C. Differences as Regards Remedies. 680
    1) Principal Remedies 680
    2) Specific Performance. 681
    3) Compensation for Non-Pecuniary Loss 682
    4) Punitive Damages 685
    5) Liquidated Damages 692
  D. Differences as Regards 'Pure Economic Losses'. 695
  E. Differences as Regards Defences 696
    1) In the Tort Case 696
    2) In the Contract Case 697
IV. Limitation or Exclusion of Liability Arising from Tort and from Contract. 701
  A. By Statute or Courts. 701
  B. Limitation of Liability by Contract 702
V. Non-Concurrence of Actions. 704
VI. Specific Situations of Overlap between Contract and Tort 704
  A. Pre-Contractual Liability 704
  B. Professional Liability. 705
VII. Conclusion 707

I. INTRODUCTION

1 The questionnaire which constitutes the basis for this project rightly asks the question to what extent the traditionally different treatment of tortious and contractual liability is still justified today. This chapter will address that question from the perspective of economic analysis of law. As a principal matter, tort and contract indeed have, at least from an economic perspective, a different basis. The most important distinction which will crucially influence the way in which tortious and contractual liabilities are regulated is that, to an important extent, contracts can be freely negotiated between consenting parties and hence the contents of contractual liability can be determined by the parties through the conditions of the contract. The story is principally a different one in a tort context where the victim usually is a third party who does not stand in a contractual relationship to the tortfeasor. However, the point mentioned in the questionnaire, being that the boundaries between the two areas may increasingly become blurred, can to some extent be recognised from an economic perspective as well.

2 This chapter, dealing with the borderlines between contract and tort, will attempt to identify the main differences between contracts and torts from an economic perspective and will consequently focus on the different ways in which contractual and tortious liabilities are regulated. This chapter will to the extent possible follow the questions mentioned in the questionnaire, although they may not all be addressed since not all of them have economic relevance or are discussed in the relevant economic literature.

3 The remainder of this chapter will be structured as follows: first the borderlines will be traced by explaining the main differences between contracts and torts (sec II); next the differences between tortious and contractual liability will be discussed (sec III) as well as the possibility to limit liability (sec IV). The question whether contractual and tortious liability can be cumulated will be addressed in sec V and specific situations of pre-contractual and professional liability will be dealt with in sec VI.

4 It should be stressed that many of the aspects, more particularly those related to the main differences between tortious and contractual liability (sec III) could require a very detailed discussion. Some aspects have to some extent been discussed in other contributions to projects of the European Group on Tort Law (EGTL); those analyses will not be repeated here; it will suffice to summarise the main results of the literature.

II. TRACING THE BORDERLINES[1]

A first question that arises is what the different aims are of contracts and torts and consequently whether, from an economic perspective, there is a need to regulate contracts or torts differently. We will address this question by briefly addressing the economic function of tort law (sec II.A) and of contract law (sec II.B). We will then indicate that there can be 'grey zones' as well since externalities (the existence of which is the main economic reason for tort law) can sometimes be internalised via contracts, as has been identified by Coase (sec II.C). That points to different reasons for the regulator to intervene in torts rather than in contracts and hence for different economic foundations for tortious versus contractual liability (sec II.D). 5

A. TORTS: INTERNALISING EXTERNALITIES

Some activities in society can cause side effects that are not felt by the decision maker himself but by third parties. These side effects can be positive (positive externalities) but could also be negative (externalities). The starting point for the economic analysis of torts is that a decision maker will in principle not take into account the external costs of his activity in his decision making process. One could think of a firm producing pharmaceuticals, causing pollution of the waste water that results from the production activities. In this example, the pollution will constitute the negative externality since it is not taken into account in decisions on the production level and investments in measures to avoid pollution, such as the instalment of a water treatment plant. 6

Victims of the externality may, for example, be the downstream fishermen in another country who hence have no chances to negotiate with the pharmaceutical company in order to achieve a reduction of the harm. Voluntary transactions will in this case, differently than in a contractual setting, not be possible. 7

The economic problem caused by the externality is that it constitutes a market failure. It constitutes a market failure since the relative price of the harm will not be reflected in the prices charged by the pharmaceutical company, as a result of which an inefficient care level (prevention of harm) and an inefficient activity level (output of pharmaceuticals) will follow. The main goal of tort law is therefore to expose the pharmaceutical company (in this example) 8

1 This corresponds to question I.A of the questionnaire.

to the social costs of its activity, in other words to force it to internalise the externality. Tort law is needed because in most tort cases (differently than in a contractual setting) voluntary transactions (for example, between car drivers and pedestrians) are impossible. In the words of Cooter and Ulen: 'The economic essence of tort law is its use of liability to internalise externalities created by high transaction costs.'[2]

9 To reiterate: torts create an externality which in economic terms can be considered as a market failure. That market failure has to be corrected by exposing the tortfeasor via liability rules to the accident costs since voluntary negotiations cannot lead to such an internalisation of the externality.[3]

B. CONTRACTS: FACILITATING COOPERATION THROUGH CREDIBLE COMMITMENTS

10 The goals of contract law are different to the goals of tort law, more particularly since in this case a voluntary transaction is possible. In the words of Cooter and Ulen, 'Contract law facilitates cooperation among people by enabling them to make credible commitments.'[4]

11 Shavell provides reasons why contracts are made in the first place:

(1) for a future provision of goods and services;[5]
(2) contracts can be made for the reallocation or sharing or risks;
(3) contracts take place because of differences in beliefs (eg concerning future prices); and
(4) contracts can be made to alter the timing of consumption.

12 He equally provides reasons why contract enforcement (and thus contract law) is desirable:[6]

(1) without contract enforcement, a party would be able to appropriate funds that had been paid for contract performance, rendering the contract unworkable;
(2) without enforcement, a party might not deliver a promised good or perform a promised service;

---

2 *R Cooter/T Ulen*, Law & Economics (5th edn 2008) 325.
3 Below we will discuss the hypothesis of the Coase theorem where internalising the externality via contracts can take place, more particularly in a low transaction cost setting.
4 *Cooter/Ulen* (fn 2) 324.
5 *S Shavell*, Foundations of Economic Analysis of Law (2004) 296.
6 *Shavell* (fn 5) 297 f.

(3) without enforcement, the price cannot be fixed in advance and problems like a so-called price holdup or opportunistic bargaining about the price of the transaction might reduce the value of the contract.

In sum, economic theory assumes that parties cooperate via contracting in order to reach a utility-maximising exchange. 13

A contract is in fact a simple exchange: Wenqing could sell an aquarium to Michael for a price of, say, €200.[7] The contract can be Pareto efficient for the simple reason that Wenqing did not value the aquarium that highly. She did not need it anymore and only valued it at €100, whereas Michael, a great fish lover, attaches a utility to it of much more than €200, for example €300. In the reality of contract law, things become more complicated since the exchange could not take place at exactly the same moment, but there may be a difference in time. Wenqing could, for example, not deliver the aquarium at the moment that Michael pays the money, but she could promise Michael to sell him the aquarium and Michael could pay when he received the aquarium or at a later moment. It is precisely this passage of time that may create all kind of impediments: for example, because after they concluded the contract and Wenqing promised to deliver Michael the aquarium, the circumstances could have changed. For example, Wenqing may have found a third person who would be willing to pay a higher price (say €400) than Michael, or Michael may receive the aquarium and not pay, for example because he became insolvent. 14

This simple example shows that contracts generally increase the expected utility of parties and hence social welfare. Differently than in tort law, parties will, via private bargaining, automatically reach welfare-increasing solutions in contracts. The main goal of law is therefore to enforce the contract that parties have voluntarily negotiated. The simple example also shows that the situation where the execution of a promise (eg delivery of a good or performance of a service) takes place immediately at the same moment when the other also performs his duty (eg to pay a price) usually does not give rise to much debate. Problems (and hence the need for contract law) often arise because there is a lapse of time between the conclusion of the contract (when the promise is made) and the execution. Given the existence of transaction costs, contracting parties are unable to draft a fully complete contract which has included all the potential risks arising after the conclusion of the contract. This creates possibilities for opportunism and contract gaps. Thus, the main goals of contract law are then (in principle) to make sure that parties stick to the promise they originally made in their contract and to provide default rules filling the contract gaps that are intentionally or unintentionally left by the parties. 15

---

7 The example is borrowed from *A Ogus/M Faure*, Economie du droit: le cas français (2002) 96.

C. A BORDERLINE: THE COASE THEOREM

16 Above it was held that the main function of contract law is to enforce transactions voluntarily agreed between parties that are assumed to be welfare-maximising, whereas tort law is necessary to internalise negative externalities. There is in a way a borderline between contract and tort when one addresses the situation where negotiations would be possible concerning the internalisation of an externality.

17 This can be illustrated with a simple example. Assume that a factory is emitting smoke, causing harm of €200 to each of three victims living in its neighbourhood. Assume furthermore that the emissions are only causing harm to the three victims and to no one else.[8] Assume further that there is no feasible way in which the victims could prevent this harm from occurring. The factory, on the other hand, could eliminate all the emissions by installing a filter, which costs €300. The first question to be answered in this straightforward example is what the optimal result will be: installation of the filter or not. Since a total cost of €600 can be avoided by investing just €300, the optimal solution is obviously that the filter should be installed. The other possible solution would be a relocation of the victims, which will not be cost-efficient if the relocation costs for the three victims would be substantially higher than €300.

18 The question then arises whether the optimal solution will follow – in this case, whether the filter will be installed. Coase holds that, if the transaction costs are zero, an optimal allocation of resources will always take place, irrespective of the contents of the governing legal rule. This is usually known as the Coase theorem. The optimal allocation of resources in this example is obviously the installation of the filter. Taking up the example, we can easily demonstrate that the Coase theorem applies to this case: the filter will indeed be installed no matter what the content of the legal rule is. If the law holds the factory liable to pay compensation to the victims, the installation of the filter is obviously in the interest of the factory. By installing the filter which costs just €300, the factory can avoid having to pay compensation to the victims (of €600). Under this legal regime, which one could for now call a 'polluter pays' regime, the optimal result will therefore follow. The same is, however, true if the factory is not liable and victims bear their own damage; a 'right to pollute' regime. Given the assumption of zero transaction costs, the victims will get together and negotiate with the factory to convince it to install the filter. By paying the factory the price of the filter, the victims still are better off since the total costs of the damage are considerably larger than the costs of the filter. Hence, in both

---

[8] Hence, in this example we disregard the fact that the emissions will obviously also cause harm to the environment as such.

cases, the 'polluter pays' rule or the 'right to pollute' rule, the efficient outcome will follow.

This has become known as the Coase theorem.[9] An important policy consequence of this Coase theorem is that, when its conditions are fulfilled, the internalisation of the externality can take place even in the absence of legal rules. In that sense, contract and tort are blurred because it is through bargaining that the optimal result will follow. However, one has to bear in mind that this Coasian bargaining obviously only works under the assumption of zero transaction costs, where a bargain between a potential victim and a potential wrongdoer is hence possible. As was explained above, if these conditions are no longer fulfilled, legal rules have to intervene to force the wrongdoer to internalise the externality. One of those legal rules can be tort law. Whether bargaining is possible may to a large extent depend upon the specific context. In some small-scale pollution cases, for example where a factory causes nuisance and the effects of the nuisance are limited to a few victims, Coasian bargaining may be possible. However, in the scenario when the number of bargainers is uncertain, for example between drivers and pedestrians, transaction costs would be prohibitive. In the words of Cooter and Ulen: 19

> 'Every driver cannot negotiate with every other driver and agree among themselves concerning how to allocate the costs of future accidents. Nor can every driver enter into a contract with every other motorist or pedestrian who might get hit by his car. Motorists cannot conclude a series of private agreements to take socially efficient care.'[10]

D. POLICY CONSEQUENCES

These different foundations of contract and tort obviously have consequences for tortious and contractual liability, as will be discussed below. There is equally an important consequence as far as the question of what the precise task of the law (legislator) would be with respect to either contract or tort is concerned. 20

As was mentioned above,[11] from an economic perspective, the main task of law with respect to contracts is, generally, to enforce a contract that has been validly concluded between parties. The fundamental rule in contract law, also from an economic perspective, is that the lawmaker (and hence the judge) will recognise the contents of the contract as it has been concluded between parties. This is the principle of mutual assent.[12] As a consequence, from an economic perspective, there are few reasons to intervene in the contents of a contract, except if there 21

9 *RA Coase*, The Problem of Social Cost (1960) 3 Journal of Law and Economics 1–44.

10 *Cooter/Ulen* (fn 2) 324.

11 With reference to *Shavell* (fn 5) 296.

12 *Shavell* (fn 5) 327.

were fraud, mistake, duress or insufficient disclosure of information.[13] This explains why most contract law rules are default rules rather than being mandatory in nature. Courts will hence have to assess contract formation, to verify whether a contract has been validly concluded. In some other cases, courts also have the task of interpreting contracts or filling in gaps that were left by the contracting parties.[14] The measure to be applied by the courts is that the court will seek to enhance the welfare of the parties to the contract and (to the extent that other parties are affected) social welfare as well.[15] As a general rule, contract law therefore accepts the contents of the contract as concluded between the parties and, if the contract is held valid, the main task of the law (and hence of the court) is to enforce it. The contract, as indicated, primarily concerns the interest and wealth of the contracting parties, although third parties can be affected by a contract as well.

22 The situation in tort different. As torts may cause negative externalities they can lead to a market failure and therefore to a welfare loss. Compared to contracts, which are for the increase of private welfare, tort law, from an economic perspective, is aimed at adjusting a potential wrongdoer's motivation in order to internalise the externalities of their wrongdoing and, as a result, reducing social cost. That makes the importance of law to regulate torts even more important.

III. MAIN DIFFERENCES BETWEEN TORTIOUS AND CONTRACTUAL LIABILITY

A. DIFFERENCES AS REGARDS THE FOUNDATIONS OF LIABILITY

23 The foundations of liability in tort have, from an economic perspective, been widely studied in earlier projects for the EGTL.[16] The main division in tort law is that between strict liability and negligence, the main difference between both rules being that strict liability holds the tortfeasor liable as soon as his behaviour caused the damage whereas, under negligence, it is required that his behaviour fell short of a particular standard of care (and is thus considered a fault or negligence). The literature generally holds that, in so-called unilateral accidents (where only one party, the injurer, contributes to the accident risk), both strict liability and negligence provide incentives for optimal care, but only

---

13 Ibid, 329–337.

14 Ibid, 299–304.

15 Ibid, 294.

16 See for the economic analysis of fault, *M Faure*, Fault. Economic Analysis, in: P Widmer (ed), Unification of Tort Law: Fault (2004) 311–330 and for strict liability, *M Faure*, Strict Liability, Economic Analysis, in: BA Koch/H Koziol (eds), Strict Liability (2002) 361–394.

strict liability provides incentives to follow an optimal activity level.[17] In a bilateral accident situation (where also the victim can influence the accident risk), it is important to add a defence to take into account the victim's behaviour as well, especially to the strict liability rule.[18] When both optimal care and an optimal activity level need to be reached in a bilateral accident situation, there is no first best solution. The problem is that strict liability with a contributory negligence defence leads to both optimal care and an optimal activity level for the injurer, but not for the victim,[19] but the opposite is true with negligence: that rule leads to both optimal care and activity levels for the victim (being exposed to the residual losses), but not for the injurer.[20] That is why it is generally held that strict liability is more appropriate when it is important to control the activity of the injurer. This is generally considered to be the case in so-called ultra-hazardous activities.[21] Moreover, intent will also play a role in tort liability since,[22] from an economic perspective, intent substantially increases the probability of an accident. Intent may therefore be a reason to impose damages in tort that are higher than the harm suffered by the victim, in other words punitive damages.[23]

The situation with respect to contractual liability is different in the sense that 24
the distinctions central to tort law (between strict liability, negligence or intent) do not play a role in contract law. From an economic perspective, 'a party will be assumed to commit breach if his position after breach and payment of damages would be better than if he performed'.[24] This is the basis of the notion of 'efficient breach'. From an economic perspective, the reasons for breach are irrelevant. The basic measure of damages, expectation damages, will put the victim of the breach in the position that he would have enjoyed had the contract been carried out. Thus, if a seller would be better off by breaching instead of by performing from an economic perspective he can breach, pay expectation damages to the buyer and both can be mutually better off. The following example can illustrate this.

17 *S Shavell*, Strict Liability versus Negligence (1980) 9 Journal of Legal Studies 1–25 and *HB Schäfer/F Müller-Langer*, Strict Liability versus Negligence, in: M Faure (ed), Tort Law and Economics (2009) 3–45.

18 *M Artigoti Golobardes/F Gómez Pomar*, Contributory and Comparative Negligence in the Law and Economics Literature, in: M Faure (ed), Tort Law and Economics (2009) 46–79.

19 Since the contributory negligence standard only takes into account care levels and not optimal activity levels for the victim.

20 Since the due care standard verified by the judge will only verify efficient care, but not optimal activity levels of the injurer.

21 *Shavell* (fn 5) 208–212.

22 On the economic analysis of intent in torts, see *W Landes/R Posner*, An Economic Theory of Intentional Torts (1981) International Review of Law and Economics 127.

23 *Shavell* (fn 5) 243–247. We will come back to the economic foundations for punitive damages in contract and tort below in sec III.C.4.

24 Ibid, 343.

25 Suppose Yleen agrees to deliver 100,000 custom-ground widgets at 10 per piece to Xavia for use in her boiler factory. Xavia expects that the piece value of the widget is 14. After Yleen has delivered 10,000, Zamira comes to Yleen and explains that she desperately needs 25,000 widgets at once and she would offer 15 per piece for them. In this case, by transferring 25,000 widgets to the second buyer Zamira, Yleen will earn an extra profit of 125,000 (25,000*15 – 25,000*10). At the same time, the first buyer Xavia is going to lose an expected profit of 100,000 (25,000*(14 – 10)). If the condition of full compensation is held, Yleen will still earn a profit of 25,000 (125,000 – 100,000) even after reimbursing Xavia for his loss. In the end, this breach leads to a Pareto superior result since it makes both the seller (Yleen) and the second buyer (Zamira) better off without making the first buyer (Xavia) worse off.

26 For economists, breach of contract is hence value neutral and the reasons for breach are irrelevant. Even stronger: efficient breach (breach because the seller would be worse off with performance) is often intentional. Shavell notes that this contrasts with the view of most legal scholars who view breach as a morally bad act. He stresses, however, that there is nothing immoral about the behaviour of the breaching party. It is simply a consequence of the fact that *ex ante*, when the contract was made, both parties would prefer the expectation damages to any other damage measure.[25] Here again there is an important difference between contract and torts since the efficient measure of damages would not depend upon the motive (intent or not) or the particular behaviour (fault or not) of the breaching party. In that sense one could argue that contractual liability is 'strict' and applies as soon as a contractual obligation has been breached and no valid defence for the breach can be advanced.

B. DIFFERENCES AS REGARDS FORESEEABILITY

27 For the economic analysis of tort law, foreseeability is a crucial element and a foundation for tort liability. The reason is that liability is considered as an instrument to provide incentives for prevention to potential tortfeasors. The idea of being exposed to liability is supposed to have a beneficial effect on the behaviour of the potential tortfeasor, ie to lead to a behavioural change in order to avoid liability (under negligence) or to take an optimal care and activity level (under strict liability). A basic prerequisite for the economic analysis of tort is therefore that a potential tortfeasor has possibilities to know the contents of the rules and (under negligence) the standard of care on the basis of which he can adapt his behaviour. That is why a retrospective liability does not, in principle,

---

[25] See ibid, 345–348 and 354 f.

serve any purpose as far as the prevention of accidents is concerned.[26] If suddenly a certain type of behaviour were to be considered as leading to liability *ex post* whereas this was not the case *ex ante*, a finding of liability would never affect the incentives for that particular tortfeasor for the future.[27]

An interesting issue discussed in the literature is whether the foreseeability should affect the objective probability or rather the subjective probability as perceived by the injurer. In some cases the subjective probability may be lower than the objective probability and will therefore not produce sufficient *ex ante* behavioural effects. The question arises as to whether, for those low-probability accidents of which the probability is likely to be underestimated by injurers, liability should be excluded. Ben-Shahar indicates that even though there may not be an influence on the level of care, liability for unforeseen harms may have the desirable effect of reducing the activity level.[28] Moreover, the effect of liability also for unforeseen consequences may be that it provides incentives to acquire accurate information *ex ante* and thus to anticipate these unforeseen harms.[29] It is therefore suggested that the unforeseeability doctrine in tort should be replaced by a doctrine of 'expensive foreseeability': only risks that are too costly to anticipate and foresee should be excluded from the scope of liability.[30] 28

Foreseeability equally plays an important role in contract law. It leads to the rule that the breaching party should only be held to compensate for consequential harms that are normal and which arise 'in the natural course of things'. It is the famous English case of *Hadley v Baxendale* which constitutes the starting point.[31] In this case, the English court held that the promisor is only liable for losses that he did foresee or could be expected to have foreseen when the contract was concluded as a possible consequence of his breach. Foreseeability in contract law provides a crucial prerequisite for rational behaviour. A promisee is encouraged to base his decision making on a reasonable prediction of his potential liability since he is not liable for the losses that are unpredictable and too remote. In this respect, the foreseeability rule functions similarly in contract and tort. More importantly, foreseeability also works as a supplement to market regimes by facilitating risk allocation and information exchange in transactions. A promisee is induced to disclose information regarding his 29

---

26 *M Faure/P Fenn*, Retroactive Liability and the Insurability of Long-Tail Risks (1999) 9 International Review of Law and Economics 487–500.

27 *M Faure*, Environmental Liability, in: M Faure (ed), Tort Law and Economics (2009) 261.

28 *O Ben-Shahar*, Causation and Foreseeability, in: M Faure (ed), Tort Law and Economics (2009) 100–102.

29 *S Shavell*, Liability and the Incentives to Obtain Information about Risk (1992) 21 Journal of Legal Studies 257–270 and *O Ben-Shahar*, Should Products Liability be Based on Hindsight? (1999) 14 Journal of Law, Economics and Organisation 325–357.

30 *Ben-Shahar* (fn 28) 101.

31 For an analysis of foreseeability in contract law, see *Ben-Shahar* (fn 28) 102–104.

expected loss at the stage of contract formation if he prefers to allocate the risk to the promisor and he would like to pay for this. Otherwise, the promisee himself shall take precautions against the risk.[32] As a result, a risk-averse promisee has to disclose as much information regarding the risk of non-performance as possible in order to enlarge the magnitude of damages; or he has to pay the debtor to assume liability for unforeseen consequences.[33]

30 An important feature of the foreseeability rule in contract law is that parties are free to opt it out from their contract and in practice they frequently do so.[34] It is always the case that the foreseeability rule is excluded and the debtor is exposed to liability for unforeseen losses, if the promisee is risk-averse and places a high value on performance.[35] As a result, the promisee is induced to increase the precaution costs in order to limit his expected liability.

C. DIFFERENCES AS REGARDS REMEDIES

1) *Principal Remedies*

31 The principal remedy in a tort case is compensation of the victim. This hence includes monetary compensation and (in principle) no other direct forms of redress. The goal of the remedy in tort is to bring the victim back to his original utility curve by repairing the material damage (or curing the injuries) at the expense of the tortfeasor.[36] Repair could also be an appropriate remedy as well as replacement. If that is, however, not possible, the tortfeasor should pay an amount of money to bring the victim back to his original position.[37] This, in principle, requires a full compensation of the victim.

32 In contract law, it is assumed that parties would *ex ante* wish a high sanction for any violation of terms in order to induce compliance. The sanction would thus only serve adherence to the contract.[38] Different from the remedies in tort, contract remedies are supposed to entitle a victim to his expected gains from the performance of a contract. This could be achieved by a damages payment imposed on the breaching party and in some legal systems this is primarily

---

32 *RA Posner*, Economic Analysis of Law (7th edn 2007) 126.

33 *R Cooter/T Ulen*, Law & Economics (7th edn 2011) 337.

34 *EA Posner*, Contract Remedies: Foreseeability, Precaution, Causation and Mitigation, in: B Bouckaert/De G Geest (eds), Encyclopedia of Law and Economics (2000) 164.

35 The opposite of 'a high value creditor' is 'a low value creditor'. A high value creditor will suffer a larger loss in the case of breach of a contract. In contrast, a low value creditor suffers a smaller loss in the case of a breach. See *Posner* (fn 34) 165 f.

36 *L Visscher*, Tort Damages, in: M Faure (ed), Tort Law and Economics (2009) 156.

37 Ibid.

38 *Shavell* (fn 5) 343.

undertaken by contract damages. A basic measure of damages is the measure of expectation damages. This is the amount that, if paid, will put the victim of the breach in the position he would have been in had the contract been carried out.[39] Expectation damages, in law and economics theory, are justified in order to induce an efficient level of performance of a contract. The following example shows how a debtor acts under expectation damages.

Suppose Yleen agrees to produce a car and sell it to Xavia at a price of €10,000. 33
Suppose at the time when Yleen and Xavia enter into the contract, Yleen estimates that the production cost of the car will be €5,000 but Xavia estimates he can resell the car for €15,000. Assume that Xavia is able to obtain ideal expectation damages (€5,000) when Yleen fails to produce the car. In this case, Yleen will anyhow perform the production as long as the production cost does not exceed €15,000 in order to avoid payment of damages. Even if the production cost reaches €14,000, Yleen will still choose to perform the production since it creates a higher surplus for Yleen than non-performance.[40] In contrast, only if the production cost is higher than €15,000 will Y prefer non-performance instead of performance.

As is shown in the above example, the availability of expectation damages ensures 34
the buyer will receive the performance or the equivalence of the performance. From the perspective of a seller, expectation damages provide him with an opportunity to commit a breach when it would be very expensive for him to perform. The expectation measure of damages is the measure that parties choose in a mutually optimal completely specified contract.[41]

2) *Specific Performance*

As was already indicated, under tort law, the crucial point from an economic 35
perspective is to force the tortfeasor to bring the victim back to his original utility curve by repairing the material damage.[42] Repair or replacement can hence also be a remedy in a tort case (although usually monetary damages will be sought). In that sense 'specific performance' (although not qualified as such in the tort case) could also be a remedy in tort. In practice in most tort cases, victims will seek monetary compensation from the tortfeasor.

The question under what circumstances a victim of breach can seek specific 36
performance in a contract case is a much debated one on which the solutions between legal systems also differ. Specific performance in contract law is enforced

39 Ibid.

40 The net profit that Yleen will obtain from producing the car is 4,000, while the net profit from non-performance is −5,000.

41 *Shavell* (fn 5) 345.

42 *Visscher* (fn 36) 156.

in a way that a breaching party is compelled to literally perform the contract as required. In some legal systems, a breaching party would be ordered to take some substitutive steps, such as curing the defects or delivering a replacement, in order to make the other party obtain what he expects from the contract.[43] From an economic perspective, it is generally held that specific performance is desirable for completely specified contracts, but not for incomplete contracts.[44] Specific performance defers from expectation damages in that it forces a promisor to always comply with the contract unless the promisee permits him to do otherwise. Contract scholars who disfavour specific performance as the default contract remedy point out that this remedy has a danger of causing excessive performance, even when the costs of performance outweigh the value of it.[45] Besides, enforcement of specific performance may lead to high administrative costs and this is particularly the case for contracts involving duties to perform some acts.[46]

37 The high costs involved in specific performance render this remedy less welcome by courts in practice. For example, Lando and Rose observed that specific performance is in fact a rare remedy even in the civil law system in which specific performance is considered to be the primary contract remedy.[47] Instead, a cover purchase is found to be more acceptable by courts in both common law and civil law. That is, the court will allow an aggrieved promisee to make an alternative transaction and recover the price difference between the alternative contract and the original one.[48]

3) *Compensation for Non-Pecuniary Loss*

38 In the tort case, arguments go in two different directions. From the point of accident prevention, a tortfeasor should in principle be held to provide full compensation to the victim to give him optimal incentives for accident prevention.[49] Precisely because it is important to hold the injurer to an optimal level of prevention he should be held to compensate the full loss of the victim,

---

43 See Principles of European Contract Law, art 9:102 (1); BGB §437; Code Civil, art 1644.

44 *Shavell* (fn 5) 312 f.

45 See eg *RL Birmingham*, Damage Measures and Economic Rationality: The Geometry of Contract Law (1969) Duke Law Journal 70; *R Cooter/MA Eisenberg*, Damages for Breach of Contract (1985) 73 California Law Review 1463 f; *R Cooter*, Unity in Tort, Contract, and Property: The Model of Precaution (1985) 73 California Law Review 11–19, 29–37; *S Shavell*, Damage Measures for Breach of Contract (1980) 11 Bell Journal of Economics 470.

46 *A Schwartz*, The Case for Specific Performance (1979) 89 Yale Law Journal 277.

47 *H Lando/C Rose*, On the enforcement of specific performance in Civil Law countries (2004) 24 International Review of Law and Economics 481–484.

48 Ibid, 484.

49 See *M Adams*, Warum kein Ersatz von nicht Vermögensschäden, in: C Ott/HB Schäfer (eds), Allokationseffizienz in der Rechtsordnung (1989) 213.

which should therefore in principle include non-pecuniary losses.[50] There may, however, according to Adams, be a reason to be reluctant with the compensation of non-pecuniary loss in the case of so-called bilateral accidents.[51] Bilateral accidents are those where the victim also has to take efficient care and an efficient activity level. Often victims take preventive measures that cannot be observed. Not providing full compensation of non-pecuniary loss would, in bilateral accident cases, therefore be an element of risk reduction on the side of the victim.

Also from the loss-spreading angle, the need to compensate non-pecuniary losses is debated. Adams holds that non-pecuniary losses do not create a demand for extra money.[52] Usually victims do not *ex ante* have a demand for insurance against *ex post* non-pecuniary losses.[53] Paying a premium today would lead to a reduction in the victim's wealth to cover a loss which does not bring about a demand for additional money.[54] The argument that potential victims would *ex ante* not demand insurance against non-pecuniary losses therefore also casts doubt on the argument that non-pecuniary losses would have to be compensated from a loss-spreading perspective. However, Croley and Hanson argue that the mere fact that no insurance against non-pecuniary losses is purchased would not be an argument against compensating non-pecuniary losses.[55] Compensation for non-pecuniary damage hence remains a debated issue from an economics perspective, at least in tort law.[56] 39

In the contract case the compensation of non-pecuniary losses is also debated. 40
A classic example constitutes the situation whereby a consumer asks someone to develop a roll of film with photos, which subjectively have a very high value for the particular consumer. When the transaction costs are not too high (compared to the value of the service), parties could agree that, if something were to go wrong during the development of the photos, the consumer would also receive compensation for non-pecuniary loss. Such an agreement will obviously be translated by the provider of the service in the price which will be charged for the development of the film. This shows that, in principle, in a contract situation,

50 See *M Faure*, Compensation of Non-Pecuniary Loss: An Economic Perspective, in: U Magnus/J Spier (eds), European Tort Law. Liber Amicorum for Helmut Koziol (2000) 143–159.

51 *Adams* (fn 49) 214.

52 Ibid, 215.

53 Ibid, 216.

54 See *C Ott/HB Schäfer*, Schmerzensgeld bei Körperverletzungen: Eine ökonomische Analyse, Juristenzeitung 45 (1990) 563–573.

55 See *S Croley/JD Hanson*, The Non-Pecuniary Costs of Accidents: Pain-and-Suffering. Damages in Tort Law (1995) 108 Harvard Law Review 1785.

56 For details, see *Visscher* (fn 36) 163–165; see also *V Karapanou/L Visscher*, Towards a Better Assessment of Pain and Suffering Damages (2010) 1(1) Journal of European Tort Law 48–74.

parties can *ex ante* agree whether non-pecuniary loss will be compensated or not, provided that the administrative costs make such an *ex ante* agreement possible. The (implicit) agreement on that point can then be signalled via the price mechanism.[57]

41 In general, however, no compensation will be awarded for non-pecuniary loss in the contract case for the simple reason that the damage is too subjective and therefore too diverse. If all consumers of photo-development services were always entitled to compensation for non-pecuniary loss, this would inevitably lead to a substantial increase in the price for the development of films. This price increase might be socially undesirable, since many consumers might not be willing to pay the increased price for an additional protection for which they have no demand. Hence, if the law forced all producers of those services to compensate non-pecuniary losses, this would lead to a negative redistribution since all consumers would have to pay a higher price for an additional protection which only benefits the few, being those who *ex ante* expect a subjectively high non-pecuniary loss and are therefore willing to pay the higher price. Precisely this subjective and diverse character of non-pecuniary loss in this example is the economic reason why non-pecuniary loss will in those cases in principle not be compensated.

42 Obviously other agreements are always possible if the particular consumer expects *ex ante* to have a potentially high non-pecuniary loss. In that case, he can reach a separate agreement with the producer or provider of the service.[58] Again, if case law allowed for compensation of non-pecuniary loss in those cases (which is the case in some countries), this would lead to a price increase for all consumers, whereas only the few who need this additional protection may benefit. A good example is the situation of interruption of the provision of electricity. Usually standard form contracts exclude compensation for non-pecuniary loss in such cases, which makes economic sense. If the electricity provider were forced to compensate the losses of, for example, those who possess 30 aquariums in their cellar and hence suffer a relatively large loss, this would lead to a price increase for all consumers, whereby only the aquarium lover in this example would benefit.

43 From an economic point of view, it would be better to avoid this negative redistribution by allowing the consumer either to agree on a specific higher amount of compensation with the producer of the service[59] or to allow the consumer to conclude first party insurance, taking into account his personal

---

57 This point was also made by Faure, see *id*, Interdependencies between Tort Law and Insurance (1997) 2(2) Risk Decision and Policy 193–210.

58 *P Von Randow*, Kommentar, in: C Ott/HB Schäfer (eds), Allokationseffizienz in der Rechtsordnung (1989) 218–222.

59 If those negotiations are possible, given the administrative cost involved.

demand for additional protection. This point, that full compensation in contractual relations is, given the diversity of the loss, usually inefficient, has been systematically developed by Rea.[60]

4) Punitive Damages

The imposition of punitive damages in private law has been a subject of debate for a long time. In contrast to public law, for which the sanctions are merely act-based,[61] private law in traditional theory is supported by so-called 'harm-based' sanctions, which aim to optimally allocate the cost of harm after the harm has taken place. The traditional goals implied in the damage rules are formulated as two principles: the compensation principle and the marginal costs principle.[62] To be precise, the law should fully compensate the victim for his suffering and minimise total social costs by balancing 'the incremental benefit of each precautionary activity to its incremental cost'.[63] In this sense, the traditional tort law story favours the compensation rule, implying that damages paid by an injurer should in theory be equal to the harm caused by his behaviour. According to this rule, a potential injurer is thus made to internalise the cost of harm caused by his behaviour. A direct result is that a potential injurer will take proper measures to prevent the harm (level of care) and reduce the magnitude of participating in risky activities (activity level) under the threat of being held liable.[64] For instance, if the level of liability for a risky action is €1,000, which equals the magnitude of the potential harm caused by this action, a firm might pay up to €1,000 to prevent the risk or it will only engage in this activity when the potential benefit from it is higher than €1,000. 44

The traditional story of compensatory damages, however, only works in the situation when the injurer is found liable without doubt and the harm caused by his activity is definite. Academic studies have summarised some scenarios where compensatory damages cannot reach the expected goal and hence they propose a rule of punitive damages. For instance, according to Polinsky and Shavell, 'punitive damages ordinarily should be awarded if, and only if, an 45

---

60 *S Rea*, Non-pecuniary loss and breach of contract (1982) 11 Journal of Legal Studies 35–53.

61 In the area of public law, for instance criminal law or administrative law, the legal sanction is mostly placed on wrongful actions. The purpose is to punish and to prevent wrongful acts.

62 See on compensation as the principal remedy in the tort case above sec III.C.1.

63 *R Cooter*, Unity in Tort, Contract, and Property: The Model of Precaution (1985) 73 California Law Review 1. (These principles are based on common law rules. As is indicated by Prof Cooter, 'Much of the common law is concerned with allocating the costs of harm, such as the harm caused by accidents, nuisances, breaches of contract, or governmental takings of private property'.)

64 *Shavell* (fn 17) 1 f. (In tort law theory, the 'level of care' denotes the level of precaution that will be undertaken by a potential injurer for a potential victim. The 'activity level', indicates a party's magnitude of engaging in particular activities.)

injurer has a chance of escaping liability for the harm he causes.'[65] In real life, the difficulty of identifying the injurer, the complexity of the rules of evidence,[66] as well as the high cost of litigation, all increase the chance that an injurer may escape liability for harms for which he should take responsibility. Take a slander case as an example. In order to obtain an appropriate amount of compensation, a victim has to prove who is responsible for dispersing the slander and the amount of harm suffered by him. However, in many cases involving slander on the electronic highway, identifying the injurer and measuring the harm might be costly and time-consuming or sometimes impossible. Moreover, in some cases, injurers might intentionally take some steps to avoid detection and liability, such as running away from an automobile accident. If the injurer deliberately tries to hide the fact of infringements, the possibility of holding him liable is even lower. Even if a victim has already identified the injurer and could demonstrate his loss, the high cost involved in litigation may still reduce his willingness to sue and this also increases the possibility that an injurer may escape liability for the harm caused by him.[67] As a result, the problem of under-deterrence is apparent. That is, compensatory damages that are equal to a victim's loss cannot provide potential injurers with sufficient incentives to take a proper level of care and a reasonable activity level. Actors are likely to take insufficient precautions against the potential harm or increasingly engage in a particular behaviour. Moreover, a systematic under-compensation problem is created because victims can hardly obtain sufficient damages that can fully cover the harm caused by the injurers. To the above problem, a possible solution is offsetting the low possibility of detection by increasing the amount of damages. To summarise, it is suggested that judges should grant punitive damages for the purpose of overcoming both the under-deterrence problem and the under-compensation problem that are caused by the traditional damage rule.[68]

46 Another approach to understanding the theory of punitive damages is to consider deterrence as the main reason for introducing punitive damages by tort law. Louis Visscher analyses four concrete scenarios in which traditional compensatory damages cannot work well. As suggested, traditional compensatory damages might be problematic if:[69] (1) there is a chance that an

65 *AM Polinsky/S Shavell*, Punitive Damages: An Economic Analysis (1998) 11 Harvard Law Review 874.

66 Normally, a plaintiff in a tort case has to prove the magnitude of the harm suffered by himself, the person who should be held responsible for the harm as well as the causal relationship between the harm and the defendant's behaviour. In many cases, more particularly in a negligence setting a plaintiff has to prove the injurer's fault as well.

67 *Polinsky/Shavell* (fn 65) 888.

68 Ibid, 936.

69 *LT Visscher*, Economic Analysis of Punitive Damages, in: H Koziol/V Wilcox (eds), Punitive Damages: Common Law and Civil Law Perspectives (2009) 219.

injurer would escape liability for the harm he has caused; or (2) it is difficult to assess the victim's losses, such as non-monetary losses; or (3) the cost or benefit of the behaviour is socially illicit, for example the injurer experiences joy by intentionally causing harm to the victim; or (4) the transaction cost is low, so that the injurer should be induced to seek a voluntary transfer of entitlement from the victim by a property rule rather than by a liability rule.[70] However, the second scenario itself cannot be a good justification for granting punitive damages, according to Visscher. The risk of under-compensation always arises when it is difficult to accurately assess the victim's losses, such as with non-monetary losses. If there is a high chance that some non-monetary losses will be excluded from compensatory damages, such losses might also be excluded from punitive damages since punitive damages cannot be assessed as accurately as compensatory damages.[71] Besides, there is also a risk that the court might overestimate rather than underestimate the amount of damages when non-monetary losses are involved. In this case, it is hardly convincing to grant the victim an amount of damages that exceeds his true loss. For losses that are difficult to estimate, merely enhancing the amount of damages will not really solve the problem. In this sense, punitive damages might not work better than compensatory damages in solving the difficulty of loss-assessment.[72] However, the main problem for traditional compensatory damages in the other three aforementioned scenarios is the damages. Damages grounded on the victim's loss are insufficient to induce economically desirable behaviour, such as a reasonable level of care, or an activity level in the case of contract law, which refers to the desirable number of voluntary transactions. Under-compensation could inefficiently lower the number of transactions and hence reduce activity levels. In the third scenario, if the benefit or cost of an act is deemed to be socially illicit, such an act (an assault) should not be performed at all. If the

70 *G Calabresi/AD Melamed*, Property Rules, Liability Rules, and Inalienability: One View of the Cathedral (1972) 85 Harvard Law Review 1090–1093, 1105–1010. (A property rule protection makes the permission of an entitlement's owner a necessary condition for transfer of this entitlement. In that case, another person can only take the entitlement from the holder when the holder agrees (for instance, the owner sells it). If another party acquires an entitlement without the owner's permission, the law will impose a specific sanction on him, which is normally represented as an injunction, a fine or imprisonment. In contrast, a liability rule protection only requires the infringer of the entitlement to pay the owner monetary compensation. The sum of compensation will be decided by a third party, typically a court.)

71 *Polinsky/Shavell* (fn 65) 940 f.

72 Some people might suggest solving the difficulty of assessing non-monetary losses by basing punitive damages upon the injurer's gain rather than the victim's loss. See eg *AM Polinsky/S Shavell*, Should Liability be Based on the Harm to the Victim or the Gain to the Injurer? (1994) 10 Journal of Law Economics and Organization 434; (Polinsky/Shavell (ibid) explain that the probable reason for awarding gain-based damages is that 'an injurer's gain is easier to calculate than the victim's loss'. But gain-based damages are still problematic if the estimation of the gain is inaccurate and hence there is still a risk of underestimating the gain.) See also *Visscher* (fn 69) 226.

damages that an injurer has to pay only equal the amount of losses to the victim, the injurer will still commit such an act as long as it creates higher gains than losses. In the last scenario where transaction costs are low, it is assumed that parties will prefer voluntary transactions over involuntary transactions, since voluntary transactions based on mutual consent will finally increase social welfare. According to economic theory, under the traditional damage rule, entitlements could be transferred without the owner's consent as long as the injurer is able to pay damages to compensate the owner's losses.[73] In this sense, people may not choose voluntary transactions, even if transaction costs are low. In contrast, the only way of transferring an entitlement under the protection of property rule is by mutual agreement. In other words, a property rule requires people to negotiate for trade, which hinders the transfer of the entitlement without the owner's consent. Therefore, Visscher recommends that punitive damages should be granted for motivating voluntary transactions in the case of low transaction costs.[74]

47 What could the economic justifications to award punitive damages in contract law be? In US law, punitive damages are apparently awarded for breaches that are considered 'willful, bad faith of fraudulent'.[75]

48 An idea is to focus on the subjective intention of the breacher and it is held that punitive damages should be designed in order to deter breaches that are committed wilfully or intentionally. For instance, William S Dodge distinguishes wilful breaches from involuntary breaches.[76] According to Dodge, involuntary breaches are referred to as breaches in good faith, in the case where 'some defense like impossibility excused performance, even though a court later determined that the requirements for the defense has not been met, because the promisor would not think at the time that she was voluntarily breaching the contract.'[77] In comparison, wilful breaches are labelled as deliberate breaches. Wilful breaches include any breaches that are committed with the intention of voluntarily breaching the contract. A typical case of wilful breaches, according to Dodge, are opportunistic breaches that 'a party attempts to get more than he bargained for at the expense of the non-breaching party',[78] such as a refusal to pay in bad faith after the other party has performed or appropriation of the other party's property through fraud. Moreover, other breaches under the

---

73 See *Visscher* (fn 69) 227–229.

74 Ibid.

75 See *R Craswell*, When is a Willful Breach 'Willful'? The Link between Definitions and Damages (2009) 107 Michigan Law Review 1501.

76 *WS Dodge*, The Case for Punitive Damages in Contracts (1999) 48 Duke Law Journal 651–654.

77 Ibid, 652.

78 Ibid.

subjective status of being called deliberate are also wilful. For instance, if a potential breacher decides not to perform because a better opportunity arises after the contract has been concluded or because performance has simply become more costly than anticipated, the breach is deemed as willul because the breacher knows that he is not going to perform without being excused. After distinguishing between involuntary breaches and wilful breaches, Dodge points out that wilfulness of a breach is the pre-condition for awarding punitive damages and suggests making punitive damages the default rule for wilful breach. Dodge summarises three major reasons for selecting punitive damages as the default rule. Firstly, punitive damages should be used to solve the under-compensation and under-deterrence problem of compensatory damages in dealing with opportunistic breach.[79] Secondly, the purpose of applying punitive damages to wilful breaches other than opportunistic breaches is to encourage contractual parties to negotiate upon a release.[80] As he states, under the threat of punitive damages, contractual parties are encouraged to enter *ex post* negotiations, no matter what kind of contingency arises after the conclusion of the contract. However, compensatory damages provide parties with the opportunity to breach as long as they are willing to pay damages. The costs involved in claiming damages through litigation, according to Dodge, are much higher than re-negotiation costs. For these reasons, punitive damages are assumed to lead to a more efficient result than compensatory damages. Thirdly, contractual parties are able to eliminate the rule of punitive damages through a liquidated clause since this rule is only the default rule.[81]

If we further analyse Dodge's arguments concerning wilful breach, we will find 49
at least three problems. First, it is difficult to establish a concrete standard for differentiating wilful breaches from involuntary breaches. For instance, Dodge mentions a situation where a promisor wrongly thinks that the requirements for 'impossibility' are met and decides not to perform. According to him, the promisor's breach is efficient in this situation. In another case, if a promisor decides not to perform only because he thinks the performance is costly (not so expensive as to raise the defence of impossibility), his behaviour should be considered to be wilful and subject to punitive damages.[82] However, in reality, it is often difficult to demonstrate whether or not a promisor thinks the preconditions for an exemption have been met. Some promisors may exaggerate the difficulties that they meet after contract formation in order to make the argument reasonable. Secondly, a default rule should be shaped from the perspective of the contractual parties. However, it is difficult to demonstrate

[79] Ibid, 654–656.

[80] Ibid, 666–687.

[81] Ibid, 679 ('[A]dopting punitive damages for willful breach of contract as the default rule for willful breach of contract would not preclude parties from contracting around that rule').

[82] Ibid, 652.

that people are willing to select punitive damages in all contracts. Dodge argues that the purpose of people entering into a contract is to achieve performance rather than monetary equivalence to performance. However, this statement is not sufficient to justify the introduction of punitive damages. For most risk-averse people, if they know that they are going to be punished as long as they fail to perform the contract, they will not enter into contracts at all. Even if the rules on punitive damages could be ignored, the increased cost of opting out may also deter people from entering into the contract. Moreover, it is sometimes difficult for one party to opt out of a default rule that is disadvantageous to him, especially when the parties have asymmetric access to information or unequal bargaining power. Thirdly and most importantly, the story of wilful breaches is almost extended to all types of breaches except for breaches that are excused by the 'defence rule'.[83] As a result, wasteful performances will be induced and efficient breaches will be deterred. Take the case where performance costs increase after contract formation as an example. As indicated by Dodge, the wilful breach story focuses on people's subjective intention when performing the contract. However, limitation of foresight may lead to people's wrong judgement about the conditions for performance. A direct effect is that people will just increase the cost of performance in order to avoid being punished even when the actual conditions have already amounted to such as 'impossibility' or 'force majeure'.

50 Based on the aforementioned reasons, we suggest the imposition of punitive damages only upon opportunistic breaches which cause inefficient results. However, punitive damages should not be granted merely in relation to the breacher's mental state. In most US cases involving punitive damages, we could find an implied fact that the plaintiffs were vulnerable to the other party's oppressing and malicious acts. For instance, in either the case where an insurer refused to pay for a claim by the insured[84] or the case in which a hotel refused to provide the accommodation according to the reservation,[85] the promisor took advantage of the fact that the other party relied on his performance or had already made payment. A direct effect is that the breacher obtains wealth from the other party without paying reciprocal costs. As is pointed out by Muris, as well as by Thel and Siegelman, such a breach in essence is contrary to the contractual parties' agreement, since it leads to a transfer of wealth without incurring fair payment.[86] One of the most important reasons for

---

83 A typical type of defence rule is the impossibility rule that non-performance of a contract is excused if performance is impossible.

84 *Gruenberg v Aetna Insurance company*, 510 Pacific Reporter, Second Series 1032 (Cal 1973).

85 *Dold v Outrigger Hotel*, 501 Pacific Reporter, Second Series 368 (Haw 1972).

86 *TJ Muris*, Opportunistic Behavior and the Law of Contracts (1981) 65 Minnesota Law Review 521 ('[Opportunism] occurs when a performing party behaves contrary to the other party's

deterring opportunistic breaches is the inefficiency of those breaches. In such cases, the promisor's breaches will not 'increase the size of the economic pie' but are aimed at gain 'simply by capturing a larger share of the pie at the expense of the non-breaching party'.[87] In the end, the promisee becomes the only one who loses but cannot obtain sufficient compensation. An even worse result of opportunistic breach is that the total social welfare will decrease since 'potential opportunists and victims expend resources perpetrating and protecting against opportunism'.[88] Another reason for expanding punitive damages to opportunistic breaches derives from the under-compensation and under-deterrence problem raised by traditional expectation damages. First of all, litigation-based expectation damages are subject to damage limitation rules such as the 'foreseeability rule', the 'reasonably certain rule' as well as the 'material loss rule'.[89] As a result, the amount of compensation that a promisee could obtain is limited to the scope covering the losses that are certain, material, foreseeable and which directly result from the breach. In this sense, expectation damages based on the monetary equivalence of the value of performance can hardly restore the promisee to the status that he would enjoy had the contract been performed.[90] In addition, high costs of litigation as well as judicial errors in assessing damages increase the possibility of under-compensation. Some people may argue that contractual parties could stipulate liquidated damages in order to increase the promisor's cost of breach.[91] However, this hypothesis only works when contractual parties share equal bargaining power and the same opportunity to access information. In most cases where opportunistic breaches may happen, the promisee is vulnerable and enjoys a position that is

---

understanding of their contract, but not necessarily contrary to the agreement's explicit terms, leading to a transfer of wealth from the other party to the performer'); *SS Thel/P Siegelman*, Willfulness versus Expectation: A Promise-Based Defense of Willful Breach Doctrine (2008) 107 Michigan Law Review 1517 ('willful breaches are best understood as those that should be prevented or deterred because the parties have implicitly agreed that the promisor would not breach in those circumstances').

87 *Dodge* (fn 76) 632.

88 *Muris* (fn 86) 524.

89 *Posner* (fn 34) 163–169, 176 f. (According to the foreseeability rule, the promisor is not liable for losses that are not 'foreseeable' at the time when he signs the contracts. The 'reasonably certain rule' provides that the promisee is only entitled to damages for a loss that is reasonably certain. Besides that, US courts do not grant damages for the emotional distress that a promisee suffers from the scope of expectation damages.)

90 *Cooter/Ulen* (fn 33) 309 f. (For instance, in the case of a sales contract, a non-breaching party's expectation loss can be calculated as the market price difference or the value difference. When a buyer breaches, the expectation loss of the seller is normally calculated as the discrepancy between the market price at the time when the breach occurs and the contract price. When a seller breaches, the expectation loss of the buyer is normally calculated as the difference between the contract price and the value that the buyer places on the contracted-for goods.)

91 *U Mattei*, The Comparative Law and Economics of Penalty Clauses in Contract (1995) 43 American Journal of Comparative Law 434–438, 441.

inferior to the promisor's. Moreover, the possibility of making an opportunistic party fully compensate the other party decreases if he commits the breach intentionally by looking for loopholes in the contract or knowing that the other party will not sue.

5) Liquidated Damages

51 Liquidated damages constitute an amount of damages that would have been determined *ex ante* by the parties. In that case it would hence not be the judge but the parties themselves who would, via bargaining, have determined the amount of the compensation that would be due in case of liability.

52 Liquidated damages may only play a role in a case concerning contractual liability. A tort case is by definition a situation where the victim is a third party vis-à-vis the tortfeasor and hence does not stand in a contractual relationship to the tortfeasor. That hence excludes bargaining, which was precisely the reason to make tort liability necessary in the first place.[92] Liquidated damages are, therefore, not discussed in the context of tort in the law and economics literature.

53 The reason that in a contract parties may fix damages themselves *ex ante* is that they may, in some cases, not have confidence in the fact that the court will employ the expectation measure of damages (which is, as indicated, the one that parties would agree to).[93] That may be the reason why parties prefer to stipulate the amount of damages due in the case of breach *ex ante* via a so-called liquidated damages clause. In some cases, courts refuse to award damages that seem excessive (because they constitute a penalty in relation to the value of the performance). Shavell holds that this tendency of the courts is undesirable if the liquidated damages indeed represent what the parties wish. Lower court awards will then reduce the frequency of performance.[94] Generally, economists hold that there are good reasons to enforce liquidated damages clauses, even if they in fact constitute a penalty. Cooter and Ulen hold that there may be three functions of those penalty clauses in contracts:[95] (1) the penalty may be a payment on an insurance contract written in favour of the innocent party by the breaching party;[96] (2) enforcing penalty clauses can convey information

92 *Cooter/Ulen* (fn 2) 325.
93 *Shavell* (fn 5) 352.
94 Ibid, 353.
95 *Cooter/Ulen* (fn 2) 260.
96 This point is made by *CJ Goetz/RE Scott*, Liquidated Damages, Penalties and the Just Compensation Principle: Some Notes on an Enforcement Model and a Theory of Efficient Breach (1977) 77 Columbia Law Review 554.

about the promisor's reliability; and (3) a penalty clause can be restated as a bonus for performance.[97] In addition, Wilkinson-Ryan provides her arguments in favour of the stipulation of damages from a behavioural perspective.[98] The observation is based upon the famous 'Israel day-care centre' case,[99] the 'Boston fire department sick leave' case,[100] as well as two contract experiments conducted by Wilkinson-Ryan.[101] In those cases, people's behaviour became more strategic and self-interested when the punishment of uncooperative behaviour (late arrival, sick leave, or re-rent) was clarified in advance. When a contract does not contain a liquidated damages clause, people view the obligation of performance as a moral obligation even when they know they might pay compensation if they breach. However, a more clear incentive structure provided by liquidated damages clauses may decrease people's moral aversion to breach and makes people become more lenient with uncooperative behaviour (for instance, breach). Given the advantages of liquidated damages clauses, some contract scholars suggest that contract law should deregulate liquidated damages clauses and hold liquidated damages generally enforceable unless there is evidence of fraud, duress or oppression in the process of contract formation.

---

97 *AW Katz*, The Option Element in Contracting (2004) 90 Virginia Law Review 2187.

98 *T Wilkinson-Ryan*, Do Liquidated Damages Encourage Breach? A Psychological Experiment (2010) 108 Michigan Law Review 633–672.

99 In 1998 Gneezy and Rustichini made the famous study of the 'day care centre' in Israel. They researched the relationship between a penalty and the possibility that parents pick up their kids late. It was found that the number of parents arriving late increased significantly after a monetary fine was attached to the behaviour of coming late. As is explained, the introduction of a fine may remove the non-market nature that actors place on being late. Actors are willing to treat a fine as a price for being late and no guilt or shame will be attached to the act of buying a commodity.

100 Wilkinson-Ryan also observed the sick leave case in the Boston Fire Department from 2001 to 2002. It was shown that the total number of sick days increased dramatically after the Boston Fire Department explicitly allowed 15 sick days per year. In Wilkinson-Ryan's illustration, fire-fighters felt more obliged to show up when the sick time had been unlimited in the previous system, while they felt less guilty about missing work when there was an explicit rule about sick leave.

101 *Wilkinson-Ryan* (fn 98) 655–664. Wilkinson-Ryan also conducted two separate experiments under two different contractual contexts. In these two contexts, he asked the participants to act as a promisor (a landlord or an IT firm) and assumed a promisee (a tenant: the Wilsons, or a client: a temp agency). In each context, he presumed a third party who was willing to offer a higher price for the performance of the promisors and examined at what price the participants were willing to breach. A 'willing-to-accept' (WTA) figure is used to represent the price that people would accept to breach. He assumed that someone is more willing to breach if his WTA figure is lower. As was shown, the WTA figure is lower when a penalty (not too high) is attached to the contract; while higher when the condition of penalty or liquidated damages is not satisfied.

54 A different idea proposes that the court should differentiate penalty clauses from liquidated damages clauses and hold the former unenforceable.[102] For those scholars who support this idea, the main reasons are: (1) penalty clauses might induce one party to enter into an unfair contract without carefully reading it;[103] (2) penalty clauses will give promisees an incentive to induce breach;[104] (3) penalties will increase the cost of legal errors;[105] (4) penalty clauses will dissuade people who dislike the risk of high compensation from entering into contracts;[106] (5) penalty clauses might lead to adverse selection;[107] and (6) the goal of penalty clauses is to force a promisor to comply with the contract and hence they will deter efficient breaches.[108]

55 Besides the ideas in favour or against penalty clauses, an alternative perspective is taken by considering the question of whether they are punitive or not. Di Matteo suggests that penalty clauses should be divided into efficient clauses and inefficient clauses, rather than being viewed as efficient or inefficient as a whole.[109] Thus, those damage clauses which are judged as efficient should be enforceable, while inefficient penalty clauses should be deemed non-enforceable. Generally, either penalties or liquidated damages specified in a contract are viewed as the parties' rational response to the uncertainty arising in the ongoing contractual relationship. Therefore, those clauses would be efficient and enforceable. However, some criteria are established in order to exclude penalty clauses which are inefficient. For instance, a penalty clause designed in a purely punitive manner is deemed as inefficient. Besides, a penalty clause included in a contract which is concluded under a premise of unfairness and inefficiency also has the purpose of punishing the weaker party and enriching the other party. In this case, this clause should not be enforceable.

---

102 See eg *E Mackaay*, Economics of Information and Law (1982).

103 See ibid, see also *G De Geest*, Penalty Clauses and Liquidated Damages, in: B Bouckaert/G De Geest (eds), Encyclopedia of Law and Economics (2000) 147.

104 *KW Clarkson/RL Miller/TJ Muris*, Liquidated Damages v. Penalties: Sense or Nonsense? (1978) 54 Wisconsin Law Review 351–390.

105 *De Geest* (fn 103) 148.

106 *P Alghion/P Bolton*, Contracts as Barriers to Entry (1987) 77 American Economic Review 388–401.

107 See eg *RA Posner* (ed), Tort Law: Cases and Economic Analysis (1977) 93. Posner mentions that penalty clauses can be used as a signal for a promisor's reliability. A promisor might be willing to offer a heavy sanction on his non-performance in order to convince the promisee of his creditability and win the opportunity of a trade. This signal function may create an adverse selection problem. If a promisee cannot obtain enough information to assess the risk from transacting with different promisors, one promisor's acceptance of penalty clauses is a signal of a high level of reliability. In this case, a bad entrepreneur might win the chance of contracting if he is willing to accept penalty provisions, while those good traders who prefer real damage computation are excluded.

108 Ibid.

109 *LA Dimatteo*, A Theory of Efficient Penalty: Eliminating the Law of Liquidated Damages (2001) 38 American Business Law Journal 675.

D. DIFFERENCES AS REGARDS 'PURE ECONOMIC LOSSES'

Again, the question as to whether pure economic loss should be compensated is much debated in the economic analysis of tort. The reason is that tort law is supposed to internalise externalities that create social losses. The problem with pure economic loss is that there may be private losses (of, for example, one contractor), which, in some cases, can be offset by private gains for another. As a result, there is no social loss, in the sense of a reduction of total social welfare, but rather a redistribution.[110] The example is provided of the loss suffered by firm A which cannot produce because a power cable was negligently damaged. Although this may lead to private losses for firm A, it could equally lead to increased profits for firm B that steps in and provides a substitutive production. That was traditionally regarded as an important reason not to compensate pure economic loss.[111] However, it is now argued that the substitute by firm B may not be perfect and hence, it cannot be argued either that, in the case of pure economic loss, no social loss would occur whatsoever. For example, for firm B to step in, it would require them to have over-capacity, which in itself would be inefficient.[112] 56

Visscher mentions, moreover, that, in some cases, tort liability for pure economic loss might serve as a surrogate for contractual liability. He provides the example of a public notary who negligently drafts a will as a result of which the intended beneficiary does not become a beneficiary. There is a social loss (since the will of the deceased is not properly executed), but the intended heir cannot sue on the basis of contract (since she does not have a contract with the notary). In this case, allowing the heir to sue the public notary for this pure economic loss on the basis of tort would solve the problem.[113] This is hence an interesting example of a borderline between contract and tort.[114] Allowing compensation for pure economic loss in such a case of flawed professional advice is indeed in line with the economic model of optimal liability. Clients pay an implicit price for the expected liability and thus pay for an implicit warranty of quality.[115] 57

Pure economic loss is not very often mentioned in contract cases, except for the cases involving, for example, product liability or professional malpractice. 58

---

110 *Visscher* (fn 36) 169. For a detailed economic analysis of pure economic loss in the framework of an ECTIL project, see *G Dari-Mattiacci*, The Economics of Pure Economic Loss and the Internalization of Multiple Externalities, in: WH van Boom/H Koziol/CA Witting (eds), Pure Economic Loss (2004) 167–190.

111 *S Shavell*, Economic Analysis of Accident Law (1987) 135.

112 *Visscher* (fn 36) 168.

113 Ibid, 169.

114 And it is close to Case 2 of the questionnaire.

115 *J De Mot*, Pure Economic Loss, in: M Faure (ed), Tort Law and Economics (2009) 210.

In commercial contracts, recoverable losses are normally built into the contract price and hence the court would refuse to award damages for pure economic loss. Hence, this point will be further discussed when referring to professional liability.[116]

E. DIFFERENCES AS REGARDS DEFENCES

1) *In the Tort Case*

59 Several defences are relevant within the tort context. First we already discussed the relative importance of foreseeability in tort cases.[117] Another relevant defence, especially in the context of strict liability[118] is a defence of comparative or contributory negligence which is necessary to provide incentives for optimal care to victims as well as in a bilateral accident situation.[119] The importance of this defence in tort cases has already been analysed in another project for the EGTL and we can therefore refer to this earlier analysis.[120]

60 However, another defence that quite regularly plays a role in tort cases is the so-called 'Act of God' or force majeure defence. This refers to accidents that are caused by an event that cannot be controlled (such as a heart attack) and for which a finding of liability would make no sense since it could not lead to additional incentives for prevention. The important issue is, however, that it should be clear that indeed no preventive measures could have been taken whatsoever by the tortfeasor to avoid a situation of force majeure. Take the case of an epileptic fit while driving: if this were totally unforeseeable for the driver (ie it had never happened before and there is no medical indication that this could happen), a finding of liability would make no sense and the Act of God defence could be invoked. However, if the driver had previously had epileptic fits, driving may constitute an ultra-hazardous activity for him. An exposure to (even strict) liability would be indicated in order to provide incentives for an activity level change, for example to refrain from driving.

---

116 See below sec VI.B.

117 See above sec III.B. But note the remark of Visscher: 'Using legal ideas such as foreseeability or adequacy to limit damages to the losses that the injurer could reasonably foresee, leads to inadequate care incentives for the injurer' (*Visscher* (fn 36) 157).

118 See above sec III.A.

119 See generally *M Artigot i Golobardes/F Gómez Pomar*, Contributory and Comparative Negligence in the Law and Economics Literature, in: M Faure (ed), Tort Law and Economics (2009) 46–79.

120 *M Faure*, Economic Analysis of Contributory Negligence, in: U Magnus/M Martín-Casals (eds), Unification of Tort Law: Contributory Negligence (2004) 233–258.

A similar analysis could also be applied to the Act of God defence in connection to natural disasters. The mere fact that damage was caused as a result of a natural disaster (for example, a nuclear accident triggered by a tsunami) does not make the natural disaster (and hence the resulting damage) totally unforeseeable. The accident at the Fukushima nuclear power plant, for example, shows that, although it was triggered by a tsunami, the resulting nuclear accident could certainly not be considered as an Act of God. Earthquakes and the resulting tsunamis in that region were certainly not unforeseeable in Japan and preventive measures could have been taken, for example concerning the placement of the reserve generators (rather than putting them in the basement as had currently been done, with catastrophic consequences). The government of Japan therefore rightly excluded the Act of God defence and held the Tokyo electrical power company (TEPCO) liable based on the nuclear liability law of Japan for the resulting damage.[121] 61

2) *In the Contract Case*

Also, in contract law, a large number of defences are theoretically available and all certainly have economic relevance as well. Cooter and Ulen even provide a table with no less than 12 defences and excuses applicable in contract law which all have a particular incentive function.[122] In the context of this borderline project, it is most interesting to briefly discuss a few defences which may align most with similar defences in the tort context or which could be relevant from a 'borderline' perspective. 62

Importantly, defendants in contract cases are allowed to defend themselves in the case of unexpected contingencies. A very common doctrine in contract cases is 'force majeure', which is mostly adopted by, for instance, French law or European Union law.[123] Some other legal systems, in contrast, prefer to use the terms 'frustration of contract purpose' or 'impossibility' to deal with the problem to be solved by the rule of 'force majeure'.[124] Although the understandings of 'force majeure', 'impossibility' and 'frustration' defer to some degree, these 63

---

121 For a more detailed analysis of the Fukushima incident, also in relation to the Act of God defence, see *M Faure/L Jing/A Wibisana*, Industrial Accidents, Natural Disasters and 'Act of God' (2015) 43(2) Georgia Journal of International and Comparative Law 383–450.

122 *Cooter/Ulen* (fn 2) 308.

123 See eg Principles of European Contract Law, art 8:108; Code Civil, art 1148.

124 For example, English courts, in practice, very often avoid using the term 'force majeure' although contracting parties in practice frequently use this term in their contracts for a certain category of contingencies. German law, when reacting to unexpected contingencies in contracts, refers to the concept of 'impossibility' and it distinguishes various categories of impossibility: initial, subsequent, temporary or total impossibility. See *E McKendrick*, Force Majeure and Frustration of Contract (2nd edn 2013) 7; see also BGB §§275, 326.

concepts share some common features in most legal systems.[125] The definition of force majeure in contracts is quite similar to that in torts. Force majeure usually denotes the case where non-performance of a contract is caused by an impediment beyond the debtor's control and the debtor could not reasonably be expected to have avoided or overcome the impediment or its consequences.[126] Typical cases of force majeure events are, for example, an earthquake, war, strike or change of laws. As a result of these types of events, the performance of an original contract usually becomes impossible and meaningless. The defendant will then be excused for his non-performance and hence the victim himself will have to bear the risk of non-performance.

64 According to Posner, the effect of the force majeure rule is explained by a theory regarding the contract's insurance function.[127] In an ordinary non-performance case, a promisor failing to perform a contract will be held liable for the non-performance, because an important function inherent to contracts is to provide a form of insurance through shifting the risk of non-performance to a promisor.[128] This creates incentives for the promisor to take proper precautions against risks. However, the costs of preventing force majeure events largely outweigh the benefit of them and hence the party (often the promisor) affected by those events is assumed to be a bad insurer since he is unlikely to be able to prevent the risk with reasonable cost.[129] In such a case, the promisor should be exempted and the risk of non-performance should be shifted to a

---

125 In current contract law literature, there is a certain extent of chaos because of the co-existence of different concepts regarding unexpected contingencies. While most scholars would agree that the contract in some situations should be discharged and there are some preconditions for such a discharge. Force majeure, impossibility and frustration all requires that: (1) the impediment is out of the promisor's risk and control; (2) the impediment must have been unexpected by the promisor when the contract was concluded; and (3) the impediment or its consequence were unavoidable. See *J Elofson*, The Dilemma of Changed Circumstances in Contract Law: An Economic Analysis of the Foreseeability and Superior Risk Bearer Tests (1996) 30 Columbia Journal of Law and Social Problem 2.

126 See eg Principles of European Contract Law, art 8:108; Draft Common Frame of Reference, art III.–3:104 (1).

127 See *RA Posner/AM Rosenfield*, Impossibility and Related Doctrines in Contract Law: An Economic Analysis (1977) 6 Journal of Legal Studies 83–118. Some other law and economics scholars, however, use the foreseeability theory to explain the rules regarding force majeure or discharge of contracts. The foreseeability theory assumes that risk should be allocated to the party who is better informed of the risk in question. For more discussion, see *Elofson* (fn 125) 2.

128 *Posner* (fn 32) 106.

129 According to the test formulated by Posner, the better bearer of a risk is the party that would have incurred lower risk evaluation and transaction costs in insuring against the risk. So this party will estimate the probability and the magnitude of potential losses and calculate the appropriate premium that will be converted into contract price. In the normal non-performance case, a promisor is considered to be the cheaper risk bearer and has to be liable for his non-performance since he has already paid a price for such a risk. *Posner* (fn 32) 107.

better risk bearer who could bear the risk at less cost, such as the promisee or an outsider insurer. For example, the unexpected death of the promisor is always considered as a good reason to discharge a personal-service contract. The risk of non-performance caused by the death of the promisor is unlikely to be prevented by any of the parties unless there is evidence showing that the expectancy of the promisor's life was lower than that of an ordinary person of his age. Reversely, a promisee is able to estimate the cost if the promisor is unable to make the performance and thus is probably the better risk bearer.[130] In this case, the promisee will be asked to bear the disadvantages caused by the promisor's death. Often, in commercial contracts, contract parties will include a force majeure clause in their contract, stipulating under what circumstances non-performance of the contract should be excused as well as what should be done to minimise the losses incurred by both parties. Such a clause has the same effect as a damage limitation clause, which will be discussed in sec IV.B of this chapter.

Some legal systems, furthermore, include a doctrine called 'change of circumstances' in reaction to unexpected contingencies arising after the conclusion of contracts, although there is controversy over the borderline between 'force majeure' and 'change of circumstances'.[131] Instead of excusing the non-performing party directly, the doctrine of 'change of circumstances' leads to the effect that contractual parties have to renegotiate their contract or request the court to modify or terminate the contract.[132] 65

Besides the defence on the basis of unexpected contingencies, it is very common for a party in contract cases to defend himself by claiming the contract to be invalid, illegal, rescinded or there is no contract existing. This would lead to the result that the court refuses to enforce the contract. The common elements that constitute good reasons for contract formation defences include incompetence, fraud, mutual mistake, duress, necessity, etc. For a contract, the presumption that it promotes welfare maximisation is valid only when the parties actually agree on its terms.[133] If the condition of voluntary negotiations is not satisfied, 66

---

[130] Ibid.

[131] Many legal systems disfavour the model consisting of the force majeure rule and the change of circumstances rule separately, such as French law or the United Nations Convention on Contracts for the International Sale of Goods. However, a separate doctrine dealing with change of circumstances is adopted by, for instance, European Union contract law instruments, German law and Chinese law. See eg Principle of European Contract Law, art 6:111; BGB §313.

[132] The creation of a duty to renegotiate as well as the modification or termination of contracts by courts will lead to some adverse effects. For example, imposing an obligation to renegotiate on contract parties may create unnecessary costs; while allowing the court to adapt a contract would interfere with contractual freedom and create more legal errors.

[133] *Posner* (fn 32) 101.

the contract will lead to inefficiency since the enforcement of it takes place at the expense of one party or both parties (mutual mistake). If the promisor is a legally incompetent person (eg child, insane), he could usually not make a genuine estimation of his own interest or fully protect himself from a harmful contract.[134] The law in such a case removes potential risks from the incompetent party and allows him to claim a contract formation defence. A similar example is the case of duress or necessity, where the expression of one party does not truly reflect his willingness and thus the contract is involuntarily formed. For instance, suppose a case where a person is threatening to sell an antique vase to someone at a cheap price. In such a case, inefficiency is created since the antique is passed from the person who values it more to another person who values it less. In order to avoid the loss, the seller should be allowed to claim that the contract is unenforceable. Furthermore, the court might refuse to enforce a contract if the promisee has induced the promisor by lying. Law and economists defend such a rule on the basis of reducing transaction costs. In the case of fraud, a promisee who lies has to invest in producing and disseminating misinformation; while the promisor incurs additional costs to verify information.[135] In order to save those costs, contract law sets fraud as a ground for voiding a contract.

67 A difficult case for a court to decide whether a defence made by the defendant is valid or not, however, is where a party to a contract fails to disclose information. Is one party bound to disclose information? Should the court enforce a contract where a seller withholds information regarding a safety defect in the goods to be sold? Or can a seller defend himself by claiming that he was uninformed of the fact that the market price would increase in a few months? In judicial practice, it is normal that courts might decline the defence based on the non-disclosure of information, such as the famous *Laidlaw v Organ* case.[136] Cooter and Ulen suggest making a distinction between productive information, redistributive information and safety information. In terms of information regarding the safety of a product, contractual parties are supposed to always have a duty to disclose such information since this kind of information helps people to avoid harm. In terms of redistributive information, which does not help to produce economic gains, but only gives the informed party a bargaining advantage,

---

134 *Cooter/Ulen* (fn 33) 343.

135 *Posner* (fn 32) 109 f.

136 In this case, Organ was a merchant from New Orleans and he received private information that the war would end in 1812 before the public knew this. Organ ordered a large quantity of tobacco from Laidlaw at the then market price. However, the market price of this kind of tobacco increased after the public learned the news that the war had ended. Laidlaw sued Organ. In this case, the Supreme Court declaimed Laidlaw's request by holding that Organ was not obliged to disclose all the news within his possession. See *Laidlaw v Organ*, 15 US (2 Wheat) 178 (1817).

the law should require the informed party to disclose it. In contrast, productive information, such as scientific knowledge or an original invention, is used for producing wealth. This kind of information is protected by the law.[137]

IV. LIMITATION OR EXCLUSION OF LIABILITY ARISING FROM TORT AND FROM CONTRACT

A. BY STATUTE OR COURTS

A first question that could be asked is whether tortious liability could be excluded or limited *ex ante* via a statute. The question is not so much whether it could be done; in many cases statutes do limit liability in tort. It is, for example, current practice to limit liability for the nuclear risk as well as for marine oil pollution, often in execution of international conventions that equally provide so-called financial caps on liability.[138] These financial limits on liability are, however, problematic from an economic perspective. 68

In the literature it has been indicated that there may be good reasons to favour a strict liability rule for hazardous activities, the main reason being that only a strict liability rule would lead to a full internalisation of highly risky activities.[139] This strict liability rule is especially put forward in so-called unilateral accident situations; this is where only one party influences the accident risk. Only in the case of strict liability would the potential injurer also have an incentive to adopt an optimal activity level. This full internalisation is obviously only possible if the injurer is effectively exposed to the full costs of the activity he engages in and is therefore in principle held to provide full compensation to a victim. An obvious disadvantage of a system of financial caps is that this will seriously impair the victim's rights to full compensation. But if the cap is indeed set at a much lower amount than the expected damages, this would not only violate the victim's right to compensation, but the above-mentioned full internalisation of the externality would not take place either. From an economic point of view, a limitation of compensation therefore poses a serious problem since there will be no internalisation of the risky activity. 69

Indeed, if one believes that the exposure to liability has a deterrent effect, a limitation of the amount of compensation due to victims poses another problem. There is a direct linear relationship between the magnitude of the accident risk and the amount spent on care by the potential wrongdoer. If the liability 70

---

137 *Cooter/Ulen* (fn 33) 357.

138 See for a discussion in the context of environmental liability, *Faure* (fn 27) 270–274.

139 *Shavell* (fn 17) 8 and 11.

therefore is limited to a certain amount, the potential injurer will consider the accident as one with a magnitude of the limited amount. Hence, he will spend on care to prevent an accident with a magnitude equal to the limited amount from being caused and he will not take the care necessary to reduce the total accident costs. Obviously, the amount of care taken by the potential injurer will be lower and a problem of under-deterrence arises. The amount of optimal care, reflected in the optimal standard, being the care necessary to reduce the total accident costs efficiently, will be higher than the amount the potential injurer will spend to avoid an accident equal to the statutory limited amount.[140] Thus, as a result of the cap, too little care is taken.[141]

71 Moreover, another effect of a financial limit on liability (in addition to providing under-compensation to victims and under-deterrence of operators) is that it would constitute an indirect subsidisation of the industry enjoying a particular limit on liability.[142]

72 An alternative is to limit tortious liability, not *ex ante* generalised in a statute, but ad hoc determined by the court. Visscher rightly mentions that, given the economic point of departure of full compensation, such a restriction of liability is debated.[143] A judicial moderation of the damages can equally jeopardise the loss spreading function of tort law[144] by leaving a part of the victim's losses uncompensated. The only argument in favour of such a judicial moderation would be risk aversion on the side of the injurer in case there would be no possibility to obtain insurance.

B. LIMITATION OF LIABILITY BY CONTRACT

73 The starting point for any economic analysis, including an analysis of contractual limitations, is undoubtedly the Coase theorem.[145] One can argue that the Coase theorem does have relevance in the sense that, via a contractual bargaining setting, parties could in principle *ex ante* agree on the optimal amount of care to

---

140 See *MG Faure*, Economic Models of Compensation for Damage caused by Nuclear Accidents: Some Lessons for the Revision of the Paris and Vienna Conventions (1995) European Journal of Law and Economics 21–43.

141 The reason for the under-deterrence is obviously the same as for the under-deterrence which results from the insolvency of the injurer. Under-deterrence arises because the injurer is not exposed to full liability, either as a result of his insolvency or as a result of a cap.

142 See also *M Radetzki*, Private Arrangements to Cover Large-Scale Liabilities Caused by Nuclear and other Industrial Catastrophes (2000) The Geneva Papers on Risk and Insurance 180–195.

143 *Visscher* (fn 36) 174.

144 These are the so-called secondary accident costs of Calabresi (*G Calabresi*, The Costs of Accident. A Legal and Economic Analysis (1970)).

145 *Coase* (fn 9). For a more detailed discussion, see above sec II.C.

be taken and on the damages, which could be related to the specific preferences of both parties and, for example, to their ability to take out insurance coverage. In this case, the agreement concerning the distribution of risk might also be reflected in the contract price that has to be paid.[146]

A result of this reasoning is that it would, in theory, make no difference where liability is allocated in the supply chain. As long as free negotiations (in a low transaction cost setting) are possible, shifting the liability to the supplier of services or to producers would simply imply that the prices charged for the service or product would increase. In the alternative, it would be the buyer or receiver of the service (assuming that that would be the governing rule) who would bear the liability. This would then also be reflected in lower prices. The allocation of risk between the contracting parties can hence be reflected in an agreement on the price. 74

The Coase theorem of course only applies in situations where the passing on of costs between a seller and a buyer is possible and may hence be important for the question as to whether liability should be allocated to, for example, the buyer or the seller. On the assumption that the conditions of the Coase theorem are met, one could argue that this should, in principle, not make a difference. The allocation of liability does make a difference, however, if a costless passing on of increased liabilities were not possible. 75

The same conclusion could also be reached with respect to the issue discussed in this chapter, being a financial cap on liability, agreed to by contract. Such a so-called financial cap is, from a policy perspective, not too problematic as long as this is (implicitly) agreed upon, for example, between a seller and a buyer within a contractual setting. The same obviously applies when the contract is not for the sale of goods but for the provision of services. In the contractual setting, well-informed parties may agree to cap liability; in that particular case there is as such no specific reason for a legislative intervention to prohibit a cap. 76

From this it follows that a distinction has to be made between the situation where the victim stands in a contractual relationship with the injurer and that where the victim is a third party. 77

As we have just indicated, discussing the Coase theorem, financial caps on liability can be efficient in the contractual setting. In such a case, they could simply signal the division of risk bearing between the contracting parties. Limited liability will, of course, be reflected in the price to be paid for the product or the service. In this particular contractual setting, where informed parties agree to cap liability, this should not cause major worries from a policy perspective. 78

146 See for an application of the Coase theorem to the issue of products liability: *Oi WY*, The economics of product safety (1973) 4 Bell Journal of Economics 3–27.

79 Caps on liability in the contract setting moreover have the advantage that the potential victim (the buyer or receiver of services) could, depending upon his preferences and attitude to risk, purchase individualised insurance coverage. A generalised unlimited liability of a seller could lead to a general increase of prices also for those potential victims who do not want this additional protection. This is a classic argument in the economic analysis of law against strict liability in situations where increased liabilities can be passed on: prices may be increased for all whereas only some (high-risk) individuals may benefit from this increased protection. An efficiency loss and a negative redistribution may be the result.[147] It was already mentioned above that, for the same reason, economic analysis is reluctant to accept generalised compensation for non-pecuniary losses in the case of contracts.[148]

V. NON-CONCURRENCE OF ACTIONS

80 The relationships between contractual liability and tort liability are very complex. Many legal systems (like the French–Belgian model) insist on a priority of the contractual model, thus excluding the possibility to use tort law in the case of a contractual situation. The logic behind this principle is that, as soon as a contract has been concluded, the legal relationships between the parties are regulated through the contract and no longer through the general principles of civil law, including tort liability.[149] As a consequence, it will not be possible to cumulate rights under tort law and contractual torts; in principle contract law will prevail. The economic basis is that an individual drafting a contract is presumed to know better than anyone else (including the legislator) how to maximise his individual wealth. That is the reason why, as we mentioned above, contracts are considered to constitute the law for the parties. Therefore it would, from that perspective, not be logical to allow a creditor to act against a debtor on the basis of tort liability rather than on the basis of contractual liability.

VI. SPECIFIC SITUATIONS OF OVERLAP BETWEEN CONTRACT AND TORT

A. PRE-CONTRACTUAL LIABILITY

81 Many courts will accept tort liability for wrongs committed in the pre-contractual phase. This pre-contractual liability may apply, for example, when one party

147 See *Faure* (fn 50) 143–159.
148 See above sec III.C.3.
149 *Ogus/Faure* (fn 7) 103.

withdraws an offer in bad faith. From an economic perspective, the justification for pre-contractual liability is that both parties may have invested substantial (sunk) costs. Such costs are invested in contractual negotiations with a view to the future benefits resulting from the execution of the contract. There is a danger of an inefficient investment in pre-contractual negotiations if the other party would, for example on the basis of better information, exploit his position and mislead the other party to the contract. The award of tort damages against the party who in the pre-contractual phase acted wrongfully could be considered an instrument to deter that type of wrongful behaviour.[150] Pre-contractual liability is hence, from an economic perspective, an instrument to avoid that one party over-invests in reliance upon the contract which subsequently (as a result of a wrongful act of the other) does not come into being, thus leading to a total welfare loss.[151]

B. PROFESSIONAL LIABILITY

At first sight, the distinction between tort liability and contract liability becomes 82
less clear when it comes to professional liability, particularly regarding a physician's liability for malpractice. A physician might be held liable, on the one hand, for breach of an implied contract term and, on the other hand, for causing injury to another person. In the early law and economic literature, it was suggested that contracting over liability by patients and physicians would be more efficient than relying on tort liability because the parties will make a contract for their own benefit.[152] However, modern law and economists might all agree that the objective of holding a physician liable for malpractice is not only to compensate the patient who is injured by a physician, but also to assure the quality of medical services and to minimise medical errors.[153] According to Shavell, a typical physician should be induced to take optimal care when providing medical services (care); and a relatively unskilled physician should be induced to get more training before engaging in the provision of medical services or reduce his participation.[154] Holding a physician liable for malpractice is considered to be one means to induce optimal care. However, the special structure of a physician–patient relationship, in which only the physician

---

150 For details see *W Wils*, How Should Bear the Costs of Failed Negotiations? A Functional Inquiry into Precontractual Liability (1993) 4 Journal des Economistes et des Etudes Humaines 93.

151 See *Ogus/Faure* (fn 7) 105.

152 *S Boccara*, Medicial Malpractice, in: M Faure (ed), Tort Law and Economics (2009).

153 See *Boccara* (fn 152) 364. See also *S Shavell*, Theoretical issues in medical malpractice, in: S Rotienberg (ed), The Economics of Medical Malpractice (1978) 55.

154 *Shavell* (fn 153) 44.

is usually better informed than the patient and only the physician's activity will impact the risk, determines that both the simple strict liability rule and negligence should be retained.

83 Strict liability for professional malpractice implies that the liability of the professional will only depend on whether or not the injury was caused by the medical treatment. Negligence then does not play a role. This would, however, impose substantial burdens on a physician and create an effect of over-deterrence,[155] as a result of which physicians are likely to practise defensive medicine, such as carrying out additional tests and procedures in order to avoid malpractice suits. Moreover, a strict liability regime also has a danger of inducing a physician's bias in patient selection since a rational physician will generally only accept and treat low risk patients in order to avoid being held liable.[156] However, those problems that arise in strict liability cannot be totally eliminated under a negligence rule. Instead, negligence also has its drawbacks, since it relies on the information regarding the physician's negligent treatment, while such information is usually costly to obtain. Moreover, it should be noted that, where the costs of tort are shifted to the patient, it is often not possible to reflect this in a contractual arrangement, for example leading to a lower price. The reason is that in many countries this will be regulated by the State, excluding contractual arrangements.[157] This also explains why contract liability cannot work well in malpractice cases.

84 Given the weakness of tort liability,[158] malpractice risks in practice are also dealt with via other approaches, such as insurance and regulations. Take insurance, for example. Under strict liability, a physician might purchase liability insurance (third-party insurance) in order to remove the risk of insolvency. The physician will have to pay a premium depending on the probability of the malpractice risk materialising and the loss caused by malpractice. The premium thus induces the physician to take due care and, on the other hand, the compensation paid by the insurer also guarantees that patients can get compensation in the case of malpractice. Under the negligence rule, however, insurance purchased by physicians will not guarantee compensation to patients if it only covers 'designated compensable events' and hence patients will have

155 *Posner* (fn 32) 203.

156 *Shavell* (fn 153) 48. Inducing competence can usually be realised via market mechanisms, such as educational standards and tests for licences.

157 According to the Coase theorem, if transactions are free of charge, both patients and physicians will be fully informed since information becomes less expensive to obtain. As a result, parties can always negotiate about the risks of malpractice via increasing or decreasing the cost for medical service.

158 Besides the problem mentioned in the above text, tort liability also has the problems of being costly and slow.

to purchase first-party insurance.[159] However, insurance has problems that, on the one hand, adverse selection might happen if the premium is calculated incorrectly. Bad physicians will take out such insurance if the premium is too low, while good physicians are deterred if the premium is too high. On the other hand, moral hazard might occur absent an optimal monitoring scheme. Moreover, insurance mechanisms will be applicable only if risk differentiation is possible.

Facing various problems in the malpractice area, lawyers and economists have been working on proposals regarding how to improve the solutions to the malpractice problem, such as reforming tort law or establishing a no-fault liability regime. In contrast to strict liability, which holds a physician liable as long as a causal link is found between his act and the victim's loss, a no-fault liability regime only shifts the burden of proof of no fault to the physician. As for a patient, he will automatically receive compensation without proving the existence of fault. For a physician, he is only bearing the risk of precaution, while not bearing the risk of damages. 85

VII. CONCLUSION

This chapter is devoted to the law and economics approach regarding contracts and tort. We started by looking at the different aims and goals of contract and tort. We also discussed tortious and contractual liability in more detail and established that there are quite a few substantial differences which can be traced back to the diverging aims and characteristics of contract and tort. 86

An important characteristic of contracts is its risk-shifting function. A contract, by its nature, commits the parties to a future course of action and hence it enhances the total social welfare. This leads to a particular policy design of contract law whereby it basically does not regulate contracts but mostly provides various default rules that facilitate risk allocation through voluntary agreements (liquidated damages clauses, force majeure clauses, and liability limitation agreements). The basic idea in contract law is, in contrast to in tort, that well-informed parties will, through voluntary transactions, increase their utility and thereby also social welfare. 87

Of course in this chapter dealing with the borderlines between contract and tort, we largely assumed a professional buyer and a professional seller. The regulation of contractual liability may (at least to some extent) be different in the case of a non-professional buyer, more particularly a consumer. In order to 88

[159] *Boccara* (fn 152) 350 f.

generally address divergences between contract and tort we, however, preferred to address the more general case without specifically focusing on consumer contracts.

89 In recent years, the borderlines between tort law and contract law have become blurred. Traditionally, tort law is supposed to internalise the loss caused by misconduct, while contract law is assumed to facilitate welfare improvement by enforcing a contract that has been voluntarily formed. However, such a distinction seems to have been challenged by the expansion of both tort law and contract law. In an increasing number of cases, overlaps between these two subjects can be found. Tort liability is no longer viewed as an inherently fault-based system, while contract liability is a system of no-fault liability. A large number of examples are found in, for example, environmental cases or product liability cases where tortfeasors who are not at fault are still held liable. Many such examples have been discussed in earlier projects of the EGTL and of the European Centre of Tort and Insurance Law. Moreover, strict liability has also received a basis in the Principles of European Tort Law.

90 Regarding contracts, scholarly efforts have been made to increase the amount of damages (punitive damages) in cases where a contracting party intended to exploit the other party's wealth, such as a contract involving fraud or force. Moreover, tort law seems to have expanded into a contract case if a third party induces a contractual breach or an agreement between two parties creates external effects. This leads to a debate concerning the famous theory of 'tortious inference'. Contract law is also likely to 'invade' the territory to be predominated by tort law.

91 An interesting question is of course to what extent this blurring of boundaries between contracts and tort is to be considered problematic from a normative perspective and whether there would, generally, even be arguments in favour of a stronger integration between contract and tort. The purpose of this chapter was rather to provide a positive (and hence descriptive) analysis of differences between contract and tort rather than to aim at a normative (policy) analysis. Moreover, given the differing starting points of contract and tort from an economic perspective, there are, generally, strong arguments to treat contract law and tort law differently and hence also the ensuing liability rules. Precisely because torts may cause social harm and create market failures connected to externalities, there is a strong argument for society to intervene in the regulation of torts with legal rules. The possibility to deviate from tort rules via contract is therefore most restricted. Since, on the other hand, the basis of the Coase theorem is precisely that well-informed and profit-maximising individuals will in principle bargain in order to make themselves better off via a contract, there is, as long as contracts are freely negotiated between the parties, less to worry about

for the law. As we indicated, as far as contracts are concerned, the major goal of the law from an economic perspective is rather to enforce contracts that have been concluded. Hence, notwithstanding the blurring of boundaries between contract and tort in some domains (like pre-contractual liability or tortious interference in contracts), there generally seem, at least from an economic perspective, to be good reasons to still rely on a different approach concerning tortious or contractual liability, as we have indicated.

THE BORDERLINES OF TORT LAW

Comparative Report

Miquel Martín-Casals

I. Tracing the Borderlines . . . 713
A. Distinction between Tort and Contract . . . 713
B. Existence of a 'Grey Zone'? . . . 716
C. Common or Different Rules Regulating Tort and Contract . . . 719
D. Application of Common Rules in a Different Way . . . 721
II. Main Differences between Tortious and Contractual Liability . . . 722
A. Differences as Regards the Foundations of Liability . . . 722
B. Differences as Regards Causation . . . 726
C. Differences as Regards Remedies . . . 729
1) Degree of Certainty of the Damage . . . 730
2) Compensation for Non-Pecuniary Loss . . . 731
3) Compensation for Loss of Earnings and for Loss of Chance . . . 734
4) Restitutionary Damages . . . 735
5) Aggravated and Exemplary (or Punitive) Damages . . . 738
6) Other Remedies . . . 742
D. Differences as Regards Recoverability of 'Pure Economic Losses' between Contracting and Non-Contracting Parties . . . 745
1) Jurisdictions that Use the Notion of Pure Economic Loss . . . 746
a) Economic Loss between Contracting Parties . . . 747
b) Economic Loss between Non-Contracting Parties . . . 748
i) Relational Economic Loss: The Exclusionary Rule and its Exceptions . . . 749
ii) Negligent Provision of Information and Defective Services . . . 750
2) Economic Loss in Legal Systems that Do Not Acknowledge this Concept . . . 752
E. Differences as Regards Liability for Others . . . 754
1) Liability for Auxiliaries and for Independent Contractors . . . 754
2) Liability for Legal Representatives or Organs of a Company . . . 757
3) Liability of Representatives of Natural Persons . . . 757
4) Liability of the Auxiliary/Organ Itself . . . 758

F. Differences as Regards Multiple Tortfeasors/Breaching Parties...... 759
G. Differences as Regards the Persons Who May be Protected......... 762
H. Differences as Regards Defences 769
I. Differences as Regards Limitation Periods...................... 772
J. Differences as Regards Proof 777
K. Other Differences.. 778
L. Reasons for the Differences?.................................. 779
III. Limitation or Exclusion of Liability Arising from Tort and from Contract 780
A. Statutory Provisions Authorising a Limitation or Exclusion of Liability 780
B. Limitation or Exclusion of Contractual and Tortious Liability by Contract 782
C. Contractual Limitations or Exclusions of Liability as Defences to a Third Party.. 784
IV. Non-Concurrence or Concurrence of Actions...................... 787
A. Overview, Areas of Overlap and the Different Approaches 787
B. Non-Concurrence and Concurrence of Actions for the Protection against Personal Injury or of Property.......................... 790
C. Non-Concurrence and Concurrence in the Case of Interference of Contractual Rights.. 791
V. Specific Situations.. 793
A. Pre-Contractual Liability...................................... 793
1) A Pre-contractual Relationship Governed by 'Good Faith'?..... 793
2) Reliance (Negative) or Expectation (Positive) Interest? 797
3) Specific Situations...................................... 797
a) Duty to Negotiate in Good Faith and Breaking Off Negotiations...................................... 799
b) Duty to Disclose Information 800
c) Duty of Confidentiality................................ 802
B. Liability of Professionals 803
VI. Cases... 806
A. Case 1. The Unattractive Shopping Mall......................... 806
B. Case 2. The Idle Lawyer....................................... 808
C. Case 3. The Defective House.................................. 810
D. Case 4. Apartment in Flames 812
E. Case 5. Injured Skier 813
F. Case 6. Exploding Car.. 815
G. Case 7. Burning Racing Boat 818
H. Case 8. Insidious Report 820
I. Case 9. Circular Letter....................................... 822
J. Case 10. Shortage of Supply 823
K. Case 11. Injured Rock Star 825

L. Case 12. Equipment Destroyed. . . . 826
M. Case 13. Slipping on a Lettuce Leaf 828
N. Case 14. Test Drive 829
O. Case 15. Breaking Off Negotiations 830
P. Case 16. Non-Disclosure of Relevant Facts. . . . 833
VII. Conclusions 835
A. The Issue of Borderlines Over Time and Across Legal Systems. . . . 835
B. The Main Differences between Contract and Tort Law Rules and Their Reasoning 837
1) Fault as a Foundation of Liability and as a Condition for Damages 837
2) Remedies, in Particular Damages 837
3) Liability for Others and in the Case of Multiple Tortfeasors or Breaching Parties 839
4) Defences and Limitation Periods 839
5) Differences as Regards Proof and Other Differences 840
6) Some General Reasons for All these Differences 840
C. The Expansion of Liability in Contract and in Tort 841
D. Grey Zones and Areas of Overlap 842
E. Non-Concurrence and Concurrence of Actions 843
F. Limitation or Exclusion of Liability Arising from Tort or from Contract 844

I. TRACING THE BORDERLINES

A. DISTINCTION BETWEEN TORT AND CONTRACT

Fifteen years ago Professors von Bar and Drobnig published an important study on the interaction of tort with other areas of law which included a very thorough comparative analysis of the interaction between contract and tort in many European jurisdictions.[1] Over all these years, however, many civil codes have been extensively amended or updated in this area, while others, such as the French, are still undergoing what is to be the most major reform for the last 200 years. In common law jurisdictions, the evolution, both through case law and legislation, has also been remarkable. In most jurisdictions, there has also been a growing trend to unify or at least approximate contract and tort law rules in many areas, such as non-pecuniary loss or prescription. 1

1 *C von Bar/U Drobnig*, The Interaction of Contract Law and Tort and Property Law in Europe: A Comparative Study (2004).

2 It is also well known that the distinction between contract[2] and tort[3] varies not only over time but also across legal systems[4] and is still in evolution. Contract and tort appear in the different legal systems with a complex of remedies and rules referring to aspects such as prescription, burden of proof or recoverable damage that may differ depending on whether the legal relationship is qualified as contractual or tortious. When the legal effects are the same, it is immaterial to qualify an action as contractual or tortious, to ask for the borderlines or to discuss whether the remedies in tort and contract overlap or not. Discussing borderlines makes sense only if the claimant can win something with the contractual or tortious classification or, conversely, if this classification may improve the defendant's position. When the approximation of contract and tort rules advances, as has already happened in some legal systems, the interest in the topic of borderline is steadily lost.

3 Additionally, the problem of the borderline between contract and tort is a doctrinal problem and therefore the doctrinal qualifications used in each of the legal systems analysed is very important. To tackle it requires the use of concepts and legal terms that do not have exactly the same meaning in all the legal systems under analysis and to set every question within the doctrinal framework of the corresponding legal system.

4 Classical legal thinking imposed a sharp distinction between contract and tort. It considered that contract is the essential manifestation of the private

---

[2] For a general overview on contract law from a comparative prospective, *H Beale/H Kötz/A Hartkamp/D Tallon* (eds), Cases, Materials and Text on Contract Law (2nd edn 2010); *JM Smits*, Contract Law. A Comparative Introduction (2nd edn 2017); *H Kötz*, European Contract Law (2nd edn 2017); *R Cabrillac*, Droit européen comparé des contrats (2nd edn 2016).

[3] *W van Gerven/P Larouche/J Lever*, Cases, Materials and Text on National, Supranational and International Tort Law (2000) and the corresponding volumes of the 'Principles of European Tort Law' Series of the European Group on Tort Law. Other relevant books for the variety of topics dealt with in this book are: *AS Hartkamp et al* (eds), Towards a European Civil Code (2011) and *J Basedow/K Hopt/R Zimmermann*, The Max Planck Encyclopaedia of European Private Law (2012) (quoted hereinafter as MPI/Author, Word).

[4] *H Koziol*, Basic Question of Tort Law from a Germanic Perspective (2012) 93–107 and *H Koziol* (ed), Basic Questions of Tort Law from a Comparative Perspective (2015) 761–765; *J Cartwright*, Contract Law: An Introduction to the English Law of Contract for the Civil Lawyer (3rd edn 2016) 53–55. Except for England and Wales (abbreviated E&W), this comparative report uses the two-letter codes supplied by the ISO (International Organization for Standardization) at https://www.iso.org/obp/ui/#search (category 'country codes', accessed: 10.4.2019), which bases its list of country abbreviations on the list of names published by the United Nations. The two-letter codes corresponding to the citations of the national reports in this volume are: AT (Austria); CZ (Czech Republic); E&W (England and Wales); FR (France); DE (Germany); GR (Greece); IL (Israel); IT (Italy); NL (the Netherlands); NO (Norway); PL (Poland); ZA (South Africa); ES (Spain); CH (Switzerland); and US (the United States of America). EAL denotes the economic analysis report, and CR denotes this comparative report. The number after the letter coding indicates the paragraph(s) within each report to which reference is being made.

autonomy of the parties, ie the power of self-determination that the legal system confers upon them to organise their legal relationships as they see fit and to make them binding in the pursuance of their own interests.[5] Starting in the 17th century in the continent and reaching its high peak also in the common law world in the 19th century, 'consent' is the normative foundation of contract.[6] Thus, the parties to a contract are bound because they have voluntarily assumed the obligations arising out of their agreement and, in this sense, it is often contended that liability in contract requires the breach of a pre-existing obligation between the parties. Tort law, by contrast, is founded on the breach of a duty imposed by the law and aims at protecting the legal entitlements of private individuals without imposing unbearable restrictions on the freedom of action of others.[7]

It is also generally recognised, however, that this sharp distinction no longer 5
reflects the current situation, since it has been eroded by several factors. In contract, it is no longer true that the duties it establishes are always dependent upon the will of the parties; the increasing interventionism of the State or the need to protect vulnerable parties have given rise to obligations imposed by the law and, in some cases, even to whole new areas of law, such as labour or consumer law. Objectivism in contract law, ie the imposition of objective standards of conduct or externally determined levels of care, has also blurred the boundary between liability based on actual consent and liability imposed by law.[8] This is the case, for instance, with the emergence of a general duty to act in good faith in the negotiation of contracts, in the performance of contractual obligations or, in general, in the exercise of rights.[9] In tort, it is no longer true either that all tortious duties arise independently of the will of the defendant. The emergence and development of tort liability for 'pure economic loss' on the grounds of the existence of a 'special relation', the creation of 'reasonable reliance' or the 'assumption of responsibility' have also brought tort law closer to contract law.[10]

---

5 *R Kreitner*, Fault at the Contract-Tort Interface, in: O Ben-Shahar, Fault in American Contract Law (2010) 108, considers that the distinction between contract and tort was part of a wider project of distinguishing between the public or regulatory realm (ie tort), and the private realm (contract). In contract, the parties had the power to generate obligations independently from the State and intervening in these self-imposed obligations was conceived as a threat to their autonomy.

6 *G Samuel*, Law of Obligations (2010) 16 ff.

7 FR 1 ff, DE 1 ff, GR 1 ff, NL 1 ff, ES 1 ff, ZA 4.

8 See in sense *Kreitner* (fn 5)109.

9 IL 8.

10 *I Gilead*, Non-Consensual Liability of a Contracting Party: Contract, Negligence, Both, or In-Between? (2002) 3 Theoretical Inquires in Law 1–27. In this sense, IL 11 points out that contract liability has a 'tort law foundation' whenever it is based on objective duties imposed by law, whereas tort liability has a 'contractual foundation' when imposing liability on the ground that 'promises should be kept' ('special relations', 'reasonable reliance' and 'assumption of responsibility').

6 This does not mean, however, that contract and tort have merged into a sort of 'contort' common area, where the functions they perform and the applicable rules are the same.

7 Contract is a social economic institution that plays a prominent role in the promotion of individual self-realisation and efficiency.[11] From an economic point of view, contracts aim, through private bargaining, at increasing the expected utility of parties and hence social welfare; accordingly, the main goal of contract law is to enforce the contract that the parties have voluntarily negotiated.[12] Tort law, by contrast, aims to preserve protected interests from the interference of third parties. From an economic point of view, its function is to shift the social costs of an activity from those who suffer its consequences to those who perform it or, in other words, to force them to internalise externalities, when the high transaction costs prevent internalisation through voluntary negotiations.[13]

8 A similar idea as regards the different functions of contract and tort is sometimes expressed with the distinction between the different measure of damages that must apply in one field and in the other. Thus contract law requires compensating for the expectation (or positive) interest, ie placing the aggrieved party in the position where he would have been in if the contract had been correctly performed. Tort law, by contrast, requires compensating for the reliance (or negative) interest, ie placing the victim in the same position he would have been if the tortious act had not taken place.[14]

B. EXISTENCE OF A 'GREY ZONE'?

9 A 'grey zone', as used here, means a zone where it is doubtful whether the situation that gives rise to liability sounds in contract or in tort or, even, where it can be submitted that it is something else beyond this dichotomy (a *tertium genus*). A 'grey zone' is not a zone of overlap. Overlap, as used below in sec IV on non-concurrence and concurrence of actions, means that the same facts can give rise to actions both in contract and in tort, with duplicative cause of actions or at least of applicable rules to the same facts.

10 If we were to follow the view that tort law governs the relationship of absolute legal strangers who become acquainted by an accident, it would be clear that this is not the situation of those who have harmed the other party during

---

11 *Gilead* (fn 10) 20.
12 EAL 20 ff.
13 EAL 6 ff.
14 DE 7, ZA 13 f.

pre-contractual negotiations. This pre-existing relationship, however, is not a contractual relationship, since a contract does not arise until it has been concluded. This gives rise to a double question which is: (a) whether pre-contractual liability is a *sui generis* or specific type of liability on its own and (b) whether either contractual or tort rules apply, or whether it is possible to apply a combination of them. In some cases, the answer to the first question determines the answer to the second, but this is not always the case.

In some legal systems, such as the Austrian, German and the Greek, it is considered that pre-contractual liability is neither contractual nor tortious, but a *sui generis* liability by virtue of law. In Austria, case law holds that this 'third track' or *sui generis* liability based on good faith is governed by contract law rules[15] and also in Germany, where §311 (2) and (3) BGB provide for a specific regulation for these cases, which the Civil Code terms 'obligations similar to legal transactions'.[16] In Greece, however, there is no unanimity on whether the applicable rules are those of contract or of tort. Thus, while some scholars argue that the provisions of contract law apply by analogy, and others contend that the applicable provisions by analogy should be those corresponding to tort law, a third group holds the intermediate opinion that a choice between the two sets of provisions is required depending on each particular case. It is to be noted, however, that art 198 §2 Greek CC explicitly provides that the provision on the prescription of a tortious claim (art 937 Greek CC) applies by analogy to the prescription of the claim deriving from pre-contractual liability, something which is considered in favour of the application of tort law rules.[17] A similar approach is followed in Switzerland, where Swiss courts, to favour victims, apply contractual rules as regards vicarious liability and the burden of the proof of fault. However, they apply tort law rules to prescription which, in fact, are not favourable to them since they entail a shorter prescription period.[18] In the Czech Republic, §1729 CC holds that those who terminate negotiations without just cause act unfairly and establishes that compensation cannot exceed the loss from failing to conclude a contract in similar cases (ie compensation for the reliance or negative interest only).[19] 11

In some jurisdictions, such as Italy and Poland,[20] their respective civil codes remain silent as regards the nature of pre-contractual liability. In the Netherlands,[21] legal writing disagrees on this point, although the opinion 12

15 AT 55.
16 '*Rechtsgeschäftsähnliche Schuldverhältnisse*', DE 3.
17 GR 4.
18 *J Cartwright/M Hesselink*, Precontractual Liability in European Private Law (2008) 459.
19 CZ 12.
20 IT 7, PL 11.
21 NL 91.

that holds that pre-contractual liability is tort liability seems to prevail.[22] For these reasons, pre-contractual liability also constitutes a 'grey zone' in these countries.

13 Some other jurisdictions, finally, tend to be stricter with the contract–tort divide and hold that, since pre-contractual liability does not arise under contract, it must be tort. This is the case in France – at least officially[23] – Spain[24] and South Africa, where legal writing speaks of 'pre-contractual liability *ex delicto*'.[25] In France, the project of the reform of the law of obligations (art 1111 CC) expressly stated that pre-contractual liability was tort liability, but the final wording of the Civil Code does not expressly mention this (cf art 1112 CC). However, although in practice it was sometimes difficult to ascribe liability to either contract or tort,[26] there does not seem to be any reason to think that the new provision has changed what was consolidated case law.[27] In these countries, there does not seem to be a 'grey zone' and the problems posed by pre-contractual liability are solved pursuant to tort law rules.

14 Common law jurisdictions do not recognise the pre-contractual stage as a legally relevant relationship, which, as such, deserves a general protection of the law. The grounds for this approach can be found both in the reluctance of common law to develop broad and general principles and on a different approach to the nature of the negotiation process. An expression of this different approach is the consideration of English judges that a duty to carry on contractual negotiations in good faith is 'inherently repugnant to the adversarial position of the parties when involved in negotiations'.[28] This does not mean, however, that the legal system does not react against the wrongs committed by a party or the unjust enrichment obtained during negotiations, but only that it uses 'piecemeal' solutions. In England, these solutions include, among others, the tort of deceit, in the case of fraudulent misrepresentation, the tort of negligent misrepresentation and the specific provisions of the Misrepresentation Act 1967.[29] In the United States and in other common law jurisdictions, the doctrine of 'promissory estoppel' may also be applicable.[30] In Israel, the recognition of the principle of good faith in pre-contractual negotiations,

---

22 This seems to be the case in IT 7.
23 FR 6 and 83.
24 ES 103.
25 ZA 2 and 60.
26 FR 7.
27 FR 83 and 124.
28 *Walford v Miles* [1992] 2 AC 128, 138 and E&W 15.
29 E&W 16.
30 US 99.

which gives rise to contract remedies, and the existence of liability in tort, usually for negligent misrepresentation,[31] more than to create a 'grey zone', may give rise to an overlap of contract and tort.

Pre-contractual liability refers to a plurality of situations which are dealt with below in sec V.A and in Cases 13–16. 15

Another grey zone in England and Wales is 'bailment', ie a legal relationship whereby a bailor temporarily transfers physical possession of property to a bailee for safekeeping, and the bailee assumes a responsibility to take care of his bailor's goods and not to convert them. Although it is considered contractual when it is onerous, gratuitous bailment does not easily fit either into contract (lack of consideration) or tort (pre-existing relationship) and then it has been disputed whether gratuitous bailment may create a legal obligation independent of that in tort.[32] 16

Finally, it is also submitted that another grey zone, sounding in some countries in contract and in others in tort, is the area of professional liability (on which sec V.B). 17

C. COMMON OR DIFFERENT RULES REGULATING TORT AND CONTRACT

Whether there are rules that are common to contract and tort and to what extent is something that varies among jurisdictions. 18

In a first group of jurisdictions, there are areas which, subject to exceptions, are generally governed by the same rules. This is the case, for instance, in Austria, where contractual and tortious liability are jointly regulated under the same set of provisions in the Austrian Civil Code (§§1293 ff ABGB)[33] and in Germany, where the Second Book (§§241 ff BGB) of its Civil Code, dealing with the Law of Obligations, contains a General Part and a Special Part. Originally, the General Part intended to regulate only those aspects that were common to all kinds of obligations, whereas the Special Part (§§433–853 BGB) provided rules for the single contracts and for non-contractual obligations. Legislative reforms have blurred this clear distinction and there are now a 19

31 IL 2 and 73.

32 E&W 19. As *Cartwright* (fn 4) 54 has pointed out, this is one area in which the common law borrowed concepts from Roman law, but did not place the transplant within the English law of contract but created the separate notion of 'bailment'.

33 AT 1.

number of provisions of the General Part that deal exclusively with contract. There are, however, some parts, such as the general provisions on damages in §§249–254 BGB, which, with some exceptions, are still common to torts and contracts.[34] In Greece, the rules in the Chapter dealing with the performance of obligations (arts 297–300 CC) are also considered to constitute a general part of the law of damages which, with some exceptions, is applicable both to contract and tort.[35] In the Netherlands, the rules on damages are also the same for contract and tort (sec 6.1.10 CC),[36] and in England and Wales and in the United States, contract and tort are also subject to broadly the same (common law) of damages.[37]

20 In Switzerland, in order to avoid a parallel regulation of fault-based contractual and tortious liability, the Code of Obligations legislates on contract law by reference to tort law by establishing that 'the provisions governing liability in tort apply *mutatis mutandis* to the breach of contract' (art 99 para 3 SCO).[38] In Norway, by contrast, although many rules may be similar on some points, they are considered two separate regimes.[39]

21 In some other legal systems such as the French, Italian, Spanish or Polish,[40] although the general provisions on obligations are not specifically restricted to contract law and, accordingly, should be general, they mainly deal with contract. In the French reform of the law of obligations still underway, there have been different views as to the opportunity of drafting rules common to liability in tort and liability in contract. The first reform project, the 2005 Catala Project, set out general rules common to tort and contract, which were followed by tort-specific rules and contract-specific rules. The second project, the 2011 Terré Project, sharply distinguished between tort liability and liability in contract. The *Avant-Projet de Loi de Réforme de la Responsabilité Civile*,[41] which was submitted to consultation in April 2016, and the *Projet de Réforme* 2017[42] deal with civil liability under a common heading and contain common rules on topics such as the definition of damage, causation and damages, and specific

---

34 DE 5.
35 GR 6.
36 NL 9.
37 E&W 21, US 12 ff.
38 CH 4. The Swiss approach was also taken in Poland in the first codification of 1933, but then abandoned in the Civil Code of 1964.
39 NO 3.
40 FR 10, IT 13, ES 11, PL 16.
41 Available at <http://www.textes.justice.gouv.fr/art_pix/avpjl-responsabilite-civile.pdf> (accessed: 1.9.2016).
42 Available at <http://www.justice.gouv.fr/publication/Projet_de_reforme_de_la_responsabilite_civile_13032017.pdf> (accessed: 20.3.2017).

rules for tort and for contract on defences and other topics along the lines of the Catala model.[43]

Finally, in some countries such as South Africa[44] and Israel,[45] the two areas are strictly separated. In Israel, each field is governed by different statutory provisions that are classified as being either tort law or contract law; however, despite contract law following the continental tradition and tort law is based on the common law one, case law and legislature tend to unify some contract and tort rules, as is the case in the proposed Civil Code of 2011 as regards damages.[46] 22

In general terms, it can be said that there is a tendency to unify whenever possible contract and tort rules and not only as regards the regulation of damages, but also in other areas, such as prescription (below sec II.I on limitation periods). However, in some jurisdictions, there are still important differences in many areas. 23

D. APPLICATION OF COMMON RULES IN A DIFFERENT WAY

Generally speaking, if there are common rules, courts do not apply them differently,[47] although the context in which they are to be applied may lead to some differences as, for instance, with regard to what the principle of 'full compensation', ie the need to restore the claimant to the State prior to the occurrence of damage, entails.[48] In some jurisdictions that have general provisions on obligations which, although not specifically restricted to contract law, seem to be mainly tailored to contractual needs, the problem that may arise is whether a provision which theoretically is applicable to all obligations, regardless of their source, also applies to tort. This is the case, for instance, in Spain, with the provision that restricts liability of the 'debtor in good faith' to 'those consequences which are foreseen or which could have been foreseen at the time of contracting the obligation and which are a necessary consequence of his failure to perform', but extends liability of the debtor who intentionally breached his obligation to 'all damages which are known to have arisen from the failure to perform the obligation' (art 1107 Spanish CC).[49] 24

---

[43] FR 15.

[44] ZA 1.

[45] IL 3.

[46] IL 4 and 5.

[47] For instance, GR 7, PL 23 and ZA 3.

[48] DE 7.

[49] ES 13–15.

II. MAIN DIFFERENCES BETWEEN TORTIOUS AND CONTRACTUAL LIABILITY

A. DIFFERENCES AS REGARDS THE FOUNDATIONS OF LIABILITY

25 In contract, the requirement of fault – including here intent and negligence – can be discussed either with regard to the existence of a breach of contract (or 'non-performance') or with regard to the availability of the remedy of damages.

26 As regards non-performance, the question is whether the reasons for failing to perform play any role in this analysis.

27 In continental jurisdictions, fault is not required to claim performance since the right to performance is regarded to be correlative to the debtor's obligation of performance. If the contract is not performed in accordance with its express or implied terms, it is only required that the failure to perform is 'attributable' to the debtor, ie that it is due to causes for which he bears the risk, and his fault can be one of them. This can also be expressed by saying that non-performance must be non-excused, or that there is no force majeure. If there is force majeure, non-performance is excused.[50] In cases of non-performance, the creditor will be able to avail himself of several remedies, such as specific performance, the right to withhold performance, termination, price reduction and damages. The availability of remedies will generally depend on whether non-performance is excused or not, and in some cases, such as damages and termination, the debtor's fault may also be a condition. However, if the failure to perform has been caused by the creditor, either by his fault or by other causes for which he bears the risk, the creditor cannot avail himself of any remedy.[51]

28 By contrast, the starting position in common law jurisdictions is that the reasons for failing to perform do not play any role; contract is regarded as containing a guarantee and when there is a breach of contract, the creditor can exercise the contractual remedies, damages being the most important.[52] Breach of

[50] Art 8:108 (1) PECL summarises the civil law position by saying that: 'A party's non-performance is excused if it proves that it is due to an impediment beyond its control and that it could not reasonably have been expected to take the impediment into account at the time of the conclusion of the contract, or to have avoided or overcome the impediment or its consequences'.

[51] See *O Lando*, Non-Performance (Breach) of Contracts, in: AS Hartkamp et al (eds), Towards a European Civil Code (2011) 681–697; *Smits* (fn 2) 211 ff. See also art II.-3:101 DCFR.

[52] See *Lando* (fn 51) 681–697, *Smits* (fn 2) 211 ff.

contract is understood as non-excused non-performance and can always give rise to the remedy of damages. In the rare case where the failure to perform is excused, in order to escape liability, the debtor may invoke other doctrines, such as frustration, which discharges the debtor from the occurrence of unforeseen events that render impossible or radically different the performance of the contract.

In general terms, the current evolution of the place of fault in the non- 29
performance of contract shows a move away from a moral civil law conception of contract, which requires performance of what has been promised, to a common law conception of contract as an economic device, where the satisfaction of the interest of the creditor is the main aim. This evolution can already be found in some international and uniform principles and legislation.[53] Moreover, the economic analysis of law considers that the distinctions between intent, negligence and strict liability, which may be central to tort law, do not play any role in contract law and that reasons for breach are irrelevant. It is submitted that breach of contract is value neutral and that there is nothing immoral about the conduct of the party who intentionally breaches the contract when he considers that his position, after breach and payment of damages, would be better than if he performed ('efficient breach').[54] However, the theory of 'efficient breach', which denies that breach of contract is wrongful, has attracted few adherents in England and Wales,[55] since it does not take into account important non-economic values (such as reliability and fair dealing) and may also disregard consequences of breach (such as disappointment or inconvenience) which are not measurable in economic terms.

As regards the remedy of damages, although non-performance (or breach), 30
as long as it is non-excused, can take place in continental countries without the need of fault, in many jurisdictions the exercise of the remedy of damages requires fault of the debtor. This is the case, for instance, in Germany, where, when a party breaches his contractual duty, the creditor can exercise all the remedies, except damages. Unless the debtor has given specific guarantees or has undertaken a particular risk, he may resort to the damages remedy only in cases of intentional and negligent conduct (§276 BGB). However, fault of the debtor does not have to be proved by the creditor; it is rebuttably presumed and then it is for the debtor to prove that he has not been at fault if he wishes to escape liability (§280 (1) (2) BGB). Fault is also a condition of liability in Austria,[56] Greece

53 *Cabrillac* (fn 2) 141 f. *Smits* (fn 2) 193 ff.
54 US 28, EAL 24–26.
55 E&W 36. See also *W Liao*, The application of the theory of efficient breach in contract law: a comparative law and economics perspective (2015).
56 AT 4.

(art 330 CC),[57] Italy,[58] Norway,[59] Poland (art 472 CC)[60] and in Switzerland,[61] where the breach gives rise to a presumption of fault, which can be rebutted by the debtor. In Spain, although it is controversial, the prevailing opinion also considers that contract liability is fault based.[62] By contrast in other jurisdictions, such as the Czech Republic (§2913 CC),[63] France,[64] and the Netherlands,[65] liability in contract does not require fault to give rise to the damages remedy. In France, liability in contract is independent from the debtor's fault and, in case of breach, the debtor will have to pay damages 'either on the ground of non-performance or a delay in performance of an obligation, unless he justifies this on the ground that performance was prevented by force majeure' (cf art 1231-1, formerly art 1147 CC), and the new rules in the French Civil Code also provide that the remedy of damages is always available (art 1217 CC).[66] Since breach always gives rise to the remedy of damages and takes place irrespective of the reasons for failing to perform, fault is not required in England and Wales, Israel and in the United States.[67] In South Africa, however, it seems to be controversial whether fault (meaning intention or negligence) is a condition for a claim for damages.[68]

31 In spite of these different starting positions, all legal systems know of cases where liability requires fault and cases where liability is strict, since the debtor's duty depends upon the nature of the obligation incurred. In this sense, under the influence of legal writing, French courts have developed the distinction between *obligations de moyens* and *obligations de résultat*,[69] and this distinction is also known in other jurisdictions.[70] Thus, if the debtor is bound only by a duty of best efforts, he must then make the efforts that would be expected from a person in his circumstances. He will have to live up to the standard of his profession and will be responsible for the fault of his employees and other persons to whom he may have entrusted performance and for the defects of the machines and equipment used in the performance, but he will not have to bring about a

57 GR 6 and fn 11.

58 IT 27.

59 NO 6 and *Lando* (fn 51) 684, who also considers that this is the main rule in the areas not covered in the new Nordic Sale of Goods Act, in spite of the fact that this Act abandoned the fault rule.

60 PL 34.

61 CH 10.

62 ES 17.

63 CZ 21, 31 et passim.

64 FR 20.

65 NL 17.

66 FR 20 and art 1217 French CC: 'Les sanctions qui ne sont pas incompatibles peuvent être cumulées; des dommages et intérêts peuvent toujours s'y ajouter'.

67 E&W 37, IL 17, US 5.

68 ZA 5.

69 FR 20.

70 IL 13, ES 19.

specific result. If he has made his best efforts, he has performed his duty and there is no breach or non-performance. By contrast, if the debtor must bring about a specific result and fails to do so, there will be a case of non-performance. The obligation, however, is not absolute and the debtor will be exempted if he can show that his failure was due to a cause for which he is not responsible, such as force majeure.[71]

In contract, intent and fault may also play an important role when establishing which damage can be attributed to the non-performing party. Thus, the rule of foreseeability,[72] which provides that only damage foreseeable at the time of the conclusion of the contract must be compensated, is displaced in some countries such as France, Italy and Spain, when non-performance was intentional or, in some cases, even grossly negligent, a trend which some uniform texts follow.[73] By contrast, the degree of the debtor's fault, as a general rule, is not taken into account in common law systems for the purpose of assessing damages, and several uniform texts also adopt this position.[74] However, the Austrian position, which generally makes full compensation and recovery of certain losses depend on intent or gross negligence, is an exception in this context.[75] 32

In tort law, intent and fault can also play a role, both as a condition of liability and as regards the extent of damages. Thus, for instance, common law jurisdictions have a tripartite classification of torts according to standards of liability: intention, negligence and strict liability and a whole set of torts can only take place if the tortfeasor acts intentionally. In England and Wales, intentional torts seek to protect a variety of interests, namely persons (eg assault, battery, false imprisonment, the intentional infliction of emotional harm, malicious prosecution); property (eg conversion, trespass to land and chattels, malicious falsehood); economic interests (eg deceit, procuring a breach of contract, intimidation, conspiracy and causing loss by unlawful means) and reputation and privacy (defamation, the misuse of private information).[76] Intention can also be the ground of liability in tort in other jurisdictions.[77] 33

---

71 In France, see however FR 20, contending that currently this distinction is extremely debatable and applies mainly to secondary obligation (*obligations de sécurité*), while 'main' contractual obligations should always be regarded as *obligations de résultat*.

72 See below sec II.B on differences as regards causation.

73 FR 22 and art 1231-3 (formerly art 1150) French CC, covering both now. Also covering intent and gross negligence, art 1107 Spanish CC and art 9:503 PECL: *Foreseeability*, which provides that: 'The non-performing party is liable only for loss which it foresaw or could reasonably have foreseen at the time of conclusion of the contract as a likely result of its non-performance, unless the non-performance was intentional or grossly negligent'. For cases of intent only, IT 26 and art 1225 Italian CC.

74 See *GH Treitel*, Remedies for breach of contract. A comparative account (1988) nos 126, 148 and art 7.4.4 PICC and art 74 CISG.

75 AT 4.

76 ES 33 and 35. See also US 4.

77 As in the case of nuisance in Italy (art 833 CC) and other torts, IT 27.

In most jurisdictions, a wider range of interests is protected in the case of intentional infringements. This is the case, for instance, in Austria and Germany,[78] where pure economic loss is compensated in tort if it is inflicted intentionally and in violation of public morals. Or in Austria in the case of false advice or misinformation where pure economic loss is also compensable under tort when it is given knowingly.[79] Intent and fault play an important role regarding the extent of damages or its amount[80] and may have an impact on other elements to establish or exclude liability.

34 Strict liability also plays an important role in tort law. In continental Europe, expanded systematically during the 19th and 20th centuries through specific Acts that provide for strict liability in different sectors and mainly where high risks brought about by new technological developments are involved.[81] However, its importance varies substantially from country to country,[82] not only between continental and common law jurisdictions, where it is a rare exception, but also among continental jurisdictions, where in countries such as France it plays a central role.[83] In most countries, courts cannot apply strict liability to cases not specifically provided by the law, the analogical application of a strict liability carried out in Austria being rather an exception.[84]

35 As regards wrongfulness, in contract law it can be understood as the breach of an objective duty established by the contractual parties and supplemented by the law. For this reason, in contract it is always necessary for any kind of contractual remedy. In tort, by contrast, wrongfulness is established by the law and is not always necessary to give rise to liability. The actor may incur liability even if his conduct is not wrongful, as is the case in most cases of strict liability, where liability arises out of the mere materialisation of the risks involved in an activity that is dangerous but not necessarily wrongful.[85]

B. DIFFERENCES AS REGARDS CAUSATION

36 Both contract and tort require that the damage suffered by one party has its source in the conduct or activity of the other and this is usually assessed under

---

78 AT 5 and §1295 para 2 ABGB; DE 8 f and §826 BGB. See also E&W 31.

79 AT 5 and §1300 ABGB.

80 See below sec II.C.5 on punitive damages.

81 *M Martín-Casals* (ed), The Development of Liability in Relation to Technological Change (2010) 1–39.

82 *BA Koch/H Koziol* (eds), Unification of Tort Law: Strict Liability (2002) and *F Werro/VV Palmer* (eds), The Boundaries of Strict Liability in European Tort Law (2004).

83 See critically on this point, *JS Borghetti*, La responsabilité du fait des choses, un régime qui a fait son temps, Revue trimestrielle de droit civil (RTD civ) no 1, 2010, 1–40.

84 AT 13, DE 15.

85 AT 9 f, DE 12, CZ 27–30, PL 34.

the *conditio sine qua non* or but-for test rule. In general terms, however, factual causation, or causation in its proper sense, requires less attention in contract than in tort, since in contract the contractual context frames the causal inquiry and the potential causes of damage are limited. For this reason, contractual disputes can be resolved regularly without the need to inquire into causation issues. In tort, by contrast, since in many cases there can be several potential causes of damage, the causal inquiry may become hard to carry out and in the individual case it may be difficult to resolve which of them brought about the harm suffered by the victim.[86]

As problematic in contract as in tort is the question of the scope of liability of the actor, which refers to whether the actor is liable for all damage causally linked to his non-performance or to his tortious conduct. Properly speaking, this is not a causal question, but it refers to the underlying policy reasons which, in a given legal system, are used to limit liability by avoiding the attribution of certain damaging consequences to the actor. The terminology is not uniform. Some legal systems refer to this problem as 'causation in law' or 'proximity';[87] others as 'imputation';[88] and others, such as the French, Italian and Spanish legal systems, displace the question to the definition of recoverable damage by establishing that one of its conditions is that damage must be 'direct'.[89] 37

In contract, a rule that limits liability of the non-performing party is the so-called foreseeability rule, well known both in civil law and common law jurisdictions.[90] The rule, discussed by Pothier, is enshrined in several civil codes,[91] and was also established in the famous English *Hadley v Baxendale* case.[92] In the wording of the French Civil Code, it provides that: '[A] debtor is bound only to damages which were either foreseen or which could have been foreseen at the time of conclusion of the contract, except where non-performance was due to a gross or dishonest fault [*dol* or *faute lourde*]' (art 1231-3, formerly art 1150, French CC).[93] 38

86 See in this sense US 8 f, pointing out that contract law casebooks do not usually devote a section to causation.

87 E&W 8 and 44, IL 21, ZA 7.

88 AT 16.

89 FR 26 and art 1231-4 (formerly art 1151) French CC; IT 37 and art 1223 Italian CC; ES 30 ff and art 1107 Spanish CC, but in tort courts in Spain follow the doctrine of the so-called 'objective imputation', similar to the 'scope of liability' doctrine in art 3:201 PETL.

90 From a comparative perspective, *A Xynopoulou*, Die Voraussehbarkeit als Voraussetzung des Schadensersatzes in der Vertragshaftung (2012).

91 *RJ Pothier*, Traité des Obligations (1761), part 1, chapter 2, article 3, para 160ff and Art 1231-3 (formerly art 1150) French CC; art 1225 Italian CC; art 1107 Spanish CC.

92 (1854) 9 Exch 341, 156 Eng Rep 145.

93 Art 1231-3 French CC: 'Le débiteur n'est tenu que des dommages et intérêts qui ont été prévus ou qui pouvaient être prévus lors de la conclusion du contrat, sauf lorsque l'inexécution est due à une faute lourde ou dolosive'. The new provision follows the same wording than the old art 1150 French CC, but adds gross negligence (*faute lourde*) to intent, FR 24.

In the wording of the *Hadley v Baxendale* case, and leaving out the second part of the rule referring to intention, this foreseeability rule is expressed by saying that the debtor is liable for damage 'either arising naturally, that is, according to the usual course of things, from such a breach of contract itself, or such as may reasonably be supposed to have been in the contemplation of both parties at the time they made the contract, as the probable result of the breach of it'.[94]

39 Foreseeability is also an important rule in tort. However, whether the rule in contract and in tort is basically the same is at least arguable.[95] Those who consider that the foreseeability rule is basically the same underline nevertheless the very important difference in the temporal assessment of reasonable foreseeability. Thus, whereas in contract the relevant time is the time of entering into the contract, not that of the breach, in the case of a tort it refers to whether damage was reasonably foreseeable at the time the tortious conduct took place.[96] Another important difference is that the foreseeability test may be more demanding in tort than in contract and, therefore, include in tort consequences that are further removed. Regardless of the grounds of liability, the required degree of foreseeability may also be lower in the case of personal injury.[97] An obvious difference is, finally, that in contract the parties are able to exclude this rule or to tailor it to their needs, whereas in tort the scope of the risk that the actor is subject to is established by the law.[98]

40 From the point of view of an economic analysis, the foreseeability rule encourages rational behaviour and facilitates risk allocation and information exchange in transactions. It gives incentives to the creditor to indicate to the debtor what the high risks are when concluding a contract. If the debtor wants to run them, that will be reflected in the price or, if not, a limitation clause will be established.[99] Holding the debtor liable for unforeseeable risks could also lead to an increase in the price that he charges to all creditors and it would then give rise to a cross-subsidy flowing from less risky to more risky contracts.[100]

41 German law uses, both in contract and in tort, the theory of adequate causation to exclude from compensation all the losses that were unforeseeable or highly improbable from the point of view of an 'optimal observer' (*optimaler Beobachter*), but since the yardstick of the high improbability of damage is considered rather imprecise, the theory is often supplemented – or even replaced – by the theory

94 *Hadley v Baxendale* (1854) 9 Exch 341, 156 Eng Rep 145.

95 In this sense *S Harder*, Measuring Damages in the Law of Obligations. The Search for Harmonised Principles (2010) 17–69. The opinions are also divided in Spanish law. See also *Beale et al* (fn 2) 1007 f.

96 E&W 45. Foreseeability also plays a role in ZA 7 and US 12.

97 E&W 44, FR 25.

98 In this sense IL 22 f.

99 EAL 28 ff.

100 *Kötz* (fn 2) 259.

of the protective purpose of the rule, which requires examining which damage the violated norm or duty was intended to avoid.[101] In contract, the parties may define the purpose, while in tort it is exclusively the legislature or the judge that establish this protective scope.[102] A similar idea is present in Dutch law, where the breach of duty that the debtor or the victim invokes needs to serve to protect him from the harm for which he tries to obtain compensation,[103] or in the broad rule introduced in the Restatement (Third) of Torts, which provides that a defendant's liability is limited to harm that results from the risks that made the defendant's conduct tortious.[104]

C. DIFFERENCES AS REGARDS REMEDIES

In contract law, damages is only one of the remedies available to the creditor. 42
The creditor can also avail himself of other remedies, such as specific performance, withholding performance, termination of contract or reduction of price. He can also cumulate several remedies as long as they are not incompatible and, under certain conditions, if he has chosen a remedy, he is not precluded from shifting to another one later on. The remedy of damages is compatible with the rest and therefore he can cumulate it to all the others. Accordingly, he can, for instance, claim performance and damages for the loss he suffers for the delay, damages in lieu of performance, ie that replace performance, or another remedy together with compensation for collateral damages or damages for consequential loss.[105] Most of these remedies are out of place in tort, where although theoretically compensation in kind is the preferable remedy,[106] the main remedy in practice is damages. However, in some areas, such as infringements to the rights of personality, several forms of compensation in kind (such as publication of the judgment condemning the infringement in the media) also play an important role. Injunctions can also play a role both in contract and in tort.

In those jurisdictions where the provisions dealing with damages are common 43
to contract and tort, there are no differences,[107] or they are rather minor. This is the case in Austria, where the provisions of the ABGB concerning liability (§§1293 ff) principally apply to both contract and tort law, except for rules on the burden of proof, vicarious liability and compensation for pure

---

101 *Kötz* (fn 2) 260, *Beale et al* (fn 2) 1009 ff.
102 AT 17, DE 17.
103 NL 36 and art 6:98 Dutch CC.
104 US 7.
105 *Smits* (fn 2) 215 ff.
106 Art 10:104 PETL.
107 NL 37.

economic loss. In any case, in contract, the parties may agree in advance on the amount of damages or on the mode of assessment, while this is normally not possible in tort.[108]

1) Degree of Certainty of the Damage

44 All jurisdictions agree that there are no substantial differences between contract and tort as regards the certainty of damage.[109] Swiss law even applies tort law provisions in this respect to contractual damages by establishing that they 'apply *mutatis mutandis* to a breach of contract' (art 99 para 3 SCO).[110]

45 In most continental jurisdictions, the law requires that in both fields the judge is convinced beyond reasonable doubt ('probability bordering on certainty'), or at least with a very high probability, that damage was the consequence of the conduct in question. Preponderant probability does not suffice. However, in Germany, once liability has been established, it is considered that in order to prove the so-called 'liability implementing causation', ie the causal link between the conduct and some consequential losses,[111] the more lenient standard of the clearly preponderant balance of probability is sufficient.[112]

46 In England and Wales and in the United States,[113] proof on a balance of probability is generally sufficient, although contract law may require a higher standard in some cases.[114] When evidence fails to meet the required threshold, the only damages that are permitted are nominal.[115] The same standard applies in Israel as regards past losses; in the case of future losses, the courts are more flexible and may award compensation for future loss, which is discounted by the probability that this loss will occur, even if the probability is less than 50%.[116] Some other jurisdictions also establish special rules to try to solve the uncertainty problem caused by loss of earnings[117] and future losses.[118]

---

108 AT 18, DE 20.

109 For instance, AT 18, GR 12, DE 21, NO 15, NL 38, ZA 9.

110 CH 14.

111 German legal writing, establishing a doctrine unknown in most European countries, distinguishes between two levels of causation. One is the causal link between the conduct of the defendant and the injury suffered by the claimant (*haftungsbegründende Kausalität*). The other is the causal link between the injury suffered by the claimant and the loss claimed by him (*haftungsausfüllende Kausalität*). See *B Winiger/H Koziol/A Koch/R Zimmermann* (eds), Digest of European Tort Law, vol 2: Essential Cases on Damage (2011) 593–611, with examples and comparative notes.

112 DE 21.

113 E&W 49, US 13.

114 US 13.

115 E&W 49, US 13.

116 IL 25.

117 ES 34.

118 E&W 56 ff and 58, ZA 9.

Both in contract and in tort, it is also considered that when the extent of the damage cannot be assessed exactly, it can be estimated.[119] 47

2) *Compensation for Non-Pecuniary Loss*

Compensation for non-pecuniary loss has continued an expanding trend over the last century and, as regards the interaction of contract and tort on this point, contract law has always been trailing in the wake of the development in tort law.[120] In some jurisdictions, such as South Africa and Poland, compensation for non-pecuniary loss is still fully excluded in contract.[121] In some others, there is still an important gap between contract and tort. However, this gap has narrowed over the last few decades and the fundamental difference between jurisdictions, which is still the starting position as regards the recoverability of non-pecuniary loss in general, has also had its impact on the contract–tort divide. 48

Some jurisdictions under survey, such as France and Spain, are very favourable to the recognition of these types of losses. As a matter of principle, they do not discriminate between pecuniary and non-pecuniary losses. They have read the provisions in their Codes as referring to both sorts of loss and placed non-pecuniary loss on an equal footing with pecuniary loss. There are no provisions limiting recovery to those cases expressly provided by the law, and although some legal writing has occasionally contested recoverability of non-pecuniary loss in contract, courts have tended to consider it generally recoverable in this area.[122] 49

Other jurisdictions take the opposite position and, as a matter of principle, require that a specific provision orders compensation and they restrict recoverability of non-pecuniary loss to this limited number of cases specifically designated by the law. Thus, for instance, German law confines compensation for non-pecuniary loss to cases where there is an explicit statutory provision to that effect (§253 para 1 BGB) and only when there is an injury to body, health, freedom of movement or sexual self-determination. Although theoretically there is no difference in contract and in tort, in practice compensation for non-pecuniary loss in contract is the exception.[123] 50

---

119 E&W 49, NL 38 and art 6:97 Dutch CC, PL 113.

120 In the area of contract *VV Palmer*, The Recovery of Non-Pecuniary Loss in European Contract Law (2015). In the area of tort, *U Magnus* (ed), Unification of Tort Law: Damages (2001); *WV Horton Rogers* (ed), Damages for Non-Pecuniary Loss in a Comparative Perspective (2001); and *Winiger/Koziol/Koch/Zimmermann* (fn 111) 11/1–13/29, 493–705 and CR 13/30, 706–718.

121 ZA 10 and PL 50, except where implementation of European Directives so requires.

122 FR 27 and ES 35.

123 DE 22.

51 In a similar vein, Italian law considers that non-pecuniary loss is recoverable only: (a) when non-pecuniary loss is a consequence of a tort which is also a criminal offence; (b) when there is a statutory provision that clearly provides for its recoverability; and (c) when non-pecuniary loss derives from the infringement of a fundamental right related to the person and directly protected by the Constitution.[124] Greece, Poland and the Netherlands adopt a similar position, since compensation requires a specific legal provision, such as the infringement of personality rights (arts 57 and 59 Greek CC; art 448 Polish CC) and, in tort, the infringement of a similar list of absolute rights (physical integrity, personal liberty, sexual liberty, etc). By contrast to Dutch law, Greece and Poland also include compensation for the non-pecuniary loss that relatives suffer in the case of the death of a family member (art 932 Greek CC; art 446 §4 Polish CC; since 2017 also Germany: §844 (3) BGB). In contract, however, the position is even more restrictive, and compensation requires the infringement of a personality right – which in practice is more often the case – or that the breach of contract also amounts to a tort.[125]

52 Some of the restrictive legal systems[126] also take into account whether non-pecuniary loss was caused with intent or gross negligence. Thus in Austria, both in contract and in tort, recoverability requires intent or gross negligence (§§1323, 1324 ABGB), and there are particular provisions that extend, restrict or exclude compensation in specific cases.[127] In the Netherlands, besides the infringement of certain protected interests, intention also plays a role.[128]

53 In English law, it has been pointed out that there is a great difference between tort and contract as regards recoverability of non-pecuniary losses and whereas in tort they are the rule, in contract they are the exception.[129] The main reason is that a large part of the protection given by the law of tort is to interests such as personal safety and personal reputation, which are interests not immediately connected with the monetary considerations that seem to prevail in contract. However, in contract they are also recoverable for the same heads of damage that are available in tort. It has also been recognised that although a contract breaker is not generally liable for any distress, frustration or discomfort that the breach of contract may cause to the innocent party, he will have to compensate for non-pecuniary loss where the purpose of the contract was to provide pleasure, relaxation, peace of mind or freedom from molestation.[130] A similar approach

124 IT 44.
125 GR 13 ff, PL 50, NL 41.
126 AT 20, NL 41 is also a possible condition.
127 AT 20.
128 NL 41 ff.
129 E&W 50 quoting *McGregor* on Damages (19th edn 2014) para 5-001.
130 E&W 54, *Beale et al* (fn 2) 1029 ff and *Kötz* (fn 2) 271 ff.

can be found in the United States, where, starting from a restrictive position, the Restatement (Second) of Contracts provides that recovery for emotional disturbance is excluded 'unless the breach has also caused a bodily harm or the contract or the breach is of such a kind that serious emotional disturbance was a particularly likely result'. Contracts that have been recognised in practice to result in emotional harm include those involving the handling and disposal of human remains and, under certain conditions, hotel and transportation contracts.[131] In the case of travel contracts, this is an idea that has already been present in some of the most restrictive European legal systems (cf §651 f para 2 BGB) and in the European Directive for Package Travel.[132]

In many of the restrictive jurisdictions, legal writing and case law consider that the current approach in their legal systems is too narrow. In Italy, recent legal writing holds that the interpretation of the narrow scope of the provision that limits non-pecuniary loss in the Italian Civil Code (art 2059) is not acceptable and considers that confining compensation to cases of infringement of fundamental constitutional rights would leave out important rights which, although not fundamental, are also important in life and, in the realm of contract law, would also ignore the freedom of contract of the parties who establish obligations affecting non-pecuniary interests.[133] In Germany, it has been considered that the 2002 reform has not gone far enough and some scholars have suggested the introduction of some form of bereavement damages for a very restricted circle of relatives[134] or amending the legislation to introduce the possibility of compensating for non-pecuniary loss in contract when performance aims at protecting immaterial interests of the parties.[135] An Act, which entered into force on 22 July 2017, finally introduced damages for bereavement.[136] 54

131 US 17 f. See also IL 28.

132 Directive (EU) 2015/2302 of the European Parliament and of the Council of 25 November 2015 on package travel and linked travel arrangements, amending Regulation (EC) No 2006/2004 and Directive 2011/83/EU of the European Parliament and of the Council and repealing Council Directive 90/314/EEC, OJ L 326, 11.12.2015, p. 1–33 and PL 50 for the impact of the transposition of the Directive into domestic law in Poland.

133 IT 44 f.

134 *G Wagner*, Angehörigenschmerzensgeld, 2 November 2012, available at SSRN: <http://ssrn.com/abstract=2170334> or <http://dx.doi.org/10.2139/ssrn.2170334>.

135 *G Wagner*, Neue Perspektiven im Schadensersatzrecht, Verhandlungen des 66. Deutschen Juristentages (DJT) (2006) A53.

136 Gesetz zur Einführung eines Anspruchs auf Hinterbliebenengeld, BGBl 2017 I 2421. The Act introduced a new §844 (3) BGB: 'Der Ersatzpflichtige hat dem Hinterbliebenen, der zur Zeit der Verletzung zu dem Getöteten in einem besonderen persönlichen Näheverhältnis stand, für das dem Hinterbliebenen zugefügte seelische Leid eine angemessene Entschädigung in Geld zu leisten. Ein besonderes persönliches Näheverhältnis wird vermutet, wenn der Hinterbliebene der Ehegatte, der Lebenspartner, ein Elternteil oder ein Kind des Getöteten war' (author's own translation: 'The person liable for compensation shall provide the survivor

55 Economic analysis of law, however, does not seem to have reached a clear and unanimous position on this point, since compensation for non-pecuniary loss is still a hotly debated issue both in contract and in tort.[137]

3) Compensation for Loss of Earnings and for Loss of Chance

56 Loss of earnings (*lucrum cessans*) is a recoverable head of damage both in contract and in tort in all jurisdictions and the specific problems that arise in the compensation of loss of earnings (especially uncertainty of its amount) are very similar in contract and in tort. In common law, it is often stressed that in a tort law context, loss of earnings must be consequential upon a physical damage, ie personal injury or property damage, since otherwise this loss of earnings would qualify as a pure economic loss and then it would be recoverable on a very limited basis only.[138]

57 More problematic is the notion of loss of chance, which is not to be confused with future loss of earnings.[139] Although one could formulate both situations in terms of chances, and consider that in both situations positive and negative chances may be involved, in the case of future loss of earnings, uncertainty affects the assessment of damages, its amount, whereas in the case of loss of chance, the enquiry may also affect the very existence of liability, ie whether there is an actionable damage that can give rise to liability. Let us take, for instance, the case of a young student who, as a result of an accident, suffers personal injuries that are so serious that they prevent him from working for the rest of his life. The student suffers no actual loss of earnings, but it is certain that he has suffered a recoverable damage since, sooner or later, he would have carried out some paid activity. Moreover, seen from another angle, he has lost his working capacity, and this already has an economic value. However, the amount of his loss remains very uncertain. The guideline is to ask what would have happened to the future working life of the child according to the usual course of events or by reference to certain circumstances. The assessment can be left to the experience of the judges or to actuarial tables such as the Ogden tables or the Spanish *baremo*,[140] where many 'chances' may be taken into account (such as the chance of obtaining

who at the time of the injury had an especially close personal relationship with the deceased, a reasonable compensation in money for the inflicted mental suffering. An especially close personal relationship is presumed when the survivor is the spouse, the registered partner, a parent or a child of the deceased'). See *C Katzenmeier*, Hinterbliebenengeld. Anspruch auf Entschädigung für seelisches Leid, JZ 18/2017, 869 ff.

137 EAL 38 ff.

138 US 21.

139 *Kötz* (fn 2) 269 ff and *B Winiger/H Koziol/BA Koch/R Zimmermann* (eds), Digest of European Tort Law, vol 1: Essential Cases on Natural Causation (2007) and vol 2: Essential Cases on Damage (2011).

140 E&W 57, ES 37.

promotion after certain years of work, chance of being unemployed, chance of leaving a job temporarily on family grounds, etc).

Loss of chance, by contrast, refers to whether the claimant has a valid cause of action. It is a very controversial issue, which is still evolving, and can be seen as a damage or as a causation problem.[141] According to the damage approach, a chance is a different damage from the final personal injury or property damage that the victim has actually suffered. Thus, in cases of personal injury resulting from medical treatment, for instance, the relevant damage that gives rise to a cause of action is not the injury that the victim has suffered (the final damage), but the chance to be healed, which was prevented by negligent treatment. The final damage could have happened even if the physician had met the required standard of care, but by defining the relevant damage in a different way, this position does away with the problem of establishing causation between the negligent action of the physician and the personal injury suffered. Holding that what the victim has suffered is a loss of chance allows factual causation to be established and then the assessment of the value of the damage suffered (the lost chance) as a fraction of the final damage. This has been the traditional position in France and most of the criticism that can be raised against this position does not make much sense in a system that does not have a list of protected interests and that, in principle, does not object to compensating for pure economic loss. 58

According to a causation approach, by contrast, loss of chance is a problem of uncertain factual causation, which arises when damage can be caused alternatively by negligent conduct or by hazard. In the example mentioned above, there is a single damage only, ie the personal injury that the victim suffers. However, since here the *conditio sine qua non* or but-for test is of no avail, and it cannot be established according to the required standard of proof whether the personal injury was caused by the negligent conduct of the physician or by hazard, the all-or-nothing rule usually required to establish causation is abandoned, and proportional liability applies. The amount of damages is then established according to the probability that the negligent conduct has caused the injury that the victim suffers. 59

4) *Restitutionary Damages*

As a matter of principle, both in contract and in tort, the claimant may claim damages for the harm that the breach of contract or the tortious infringement 60

[141] *MD Green/BA Koch/I Gilead* (eds), Proportional Liability: Analytical and Comparative Perspectives (2012) and *Winiger/Koziol/Koch/Zimmermann* (fn 139) 589 ff and (2011) 1120 ff and the corresponding country reports. See also *C Bolko Ehlgen*, Probabilistische Proportionalhaftung und Haftung für den Verlust von Chancen (2013).

has caused him, but not for the gain that the defendant has made as a result of the breach or infringement. The claimant is entitled to compensation and the principle of full compensation requires compensating for all damage, but prohibits compensating above and beyond the damage suffered. However, if the defendant has made a gain or a profit as a result of his breach or infringement, it can be necessary, on the grounds of prevention, to disgorge the benefits obtained in order to remove an incentive for infringement from his hands. Several questions arise here: Does he have a remedy? Is this remedy still part of damages in contract or in tort? If not, what is the source of this remedy? Is there any difference between contract and tort as regards this disgorging function?

61 There is no uniform terminology in the countries under review to refer the actions that aim at this purpose.[142] The questionnaire calls them 'restitutionary damages', since this is the term that is often used in English practice,[143] but the term 'disgorgement of profits' seems to be becoming the prevailing English term used by European comparatists.[144]

62 In the jurisdictions under survey, a broad rule in this sense, ie a rule which is formulated in general terms and applies both to contract and tort, can be found only in the Netherlands, where art 6:104 CC provides that: '[I]f someone, who is liable towards another person on the basis of tort or a default of complying with an obligation, has gained a profit because of this tort or non-performance, then the court may, upon the request of the injured person, estimate that damage in line with the amount of this profit or a part of it'. Although this rule gives the judge the power to award damages in cases of breach of contract or tort taking into account the profits, it is generally considered that this provision is only a means of assessing the amount of damages, aimed at alleviating the burden of proof that lies on the claimant, and not a specific and independent remedy aimed mainly at prevention. For this reason, it is considered that it is not applicable if no damage has been caused.[145] The possibility of taking into account the gains obtained by the defendant as a measure to assess the amount of damages is also present in other jurisdictions, such as Germany, Poland and Spain, where an infringement of a party's intellectual property rights can give rise to a claim, either for the actual loss suffered, for the reasonable licence fee that should have been paid, or for the profits obtained by the defendant.[146]

---

142 For instance, the French speak about the '*faute lucrative*', Germans about '*Gewinnherausgabe*' or '*Gewinnabschöpfung*', Spaniards about '*absorción de ganancias*' or '*restitución de provechos*', etc.

143 In English sometimes the terms used are also 'gain-based damages' or 'account of profits'. See also as to the latter ZA 13 f.

144 Thus *MPI/T Helms*, Disgorgement of Profits (2012) 485–489 and *E Hondius/A Jansen*, Disgorgement of Profits: Gain-Based Remedies throughout the World (2015).

145 *MPI/Helms* (fn 144) 488, and *Hondius/Jansen* (fn 144) 481.

146 *H Lange/G Schiemann*, Schadensersatz (2nd edn 2003) 356–362, PL 56 and ES 39. See also *Hondius/Jansen* (fn 144) 502 ff et passim, with the additional information that in Germany,

A general remedy for disgorgement of profits in the sense of a specific and independent remedy aimed at prevention does not seem to exist in any jurisdiction. Moreover, when disgorgement comes close to a general remedy, it is not considered a matter of contract or tort, but a matter of an independent source of obligations, such as unjust enrichment or agency without authorisation (*negotiorum gestio*). In some countries, as in Germany, Greece, Italy and Poland, it can have its grounds in a claim for unjust enrichment concurrent with contract and tort.[147] This is also the case in Israel, where the Law of Unjust Enrichment 1979 has been interpreted by the courts as establishing an independent breach of private law, alongside contract and tort. Thus, when a contract is not rescinded or when a tort is committed, restitution of benefits obtained by the breaching party or by the tortfeasor from the breach or the infringement must be claimed under the law of unjust enrichment.[148] In Switzerland, disgorgement can be obtained through the rules of agency without authorisation or *negotiorum gestio*,[149] and a similar solution has been proposed for Germany.[150] 63

Nevertheless, disgorgement of profits appears as a piecemeal remedy in several legal areas. In continental jurisdictions, there are contract rules for cases where the debtor can no longer deliver the thing that was promised, because it has perished, is lost or is in the rightful possession of a third party, and he has already received something in exchange. Then the creditor may subrogate or claim as compensation everything that the debtor has obtained for it, even if the amount of his loss is lower than the sum that the debtor has obtained.[151] This is the case, for instance, when the thing has been destroyed by a fire and the debtor has received compensation from the arsonist or from the insurance company, or where the debtor has sold and delivered the thing to a second buyer when he had already sold it to a first buyer.[152] 64

Disgorgement of profits can also take place in the case of breach of fiduciary or confidence duties, which generally arise in the contract area, as happened in the 2001 English case *Attorney General v Blake*, where the remedy of restitutionary damages was allowed for the first time. Here the defendant was a former 65

due to the deductions permitted in the case of gain-based damages until 2000, 95% of the claimants have opted for claiming the licence fee.

147 DE 24, GR 18, IT 51, PL 56.

148 IL 30.

149 CH 19 and arts 420, 423 SCO. In Germany *Wagner* (fn 135) 110 ff, considers that according to the law in force §687 para 2 BGB (*Geschäftsanmassung*) can fill the existing gap in a similar way.

150 *Wagner* (fn 135) 138 in favour of introducing disgorgement damages in the German law of damages in the case of intentional infringements.

151 See art 1303 French CC; art 1187 Spanish CC; art 475 §2 Polish CC.

152 *Kötz* (fn 2) 270 f and §285 BGB.

member of the Secret Intelligence Service, who had signed an undertaking not to divulge any official information obtained as a result of his employment and who many years later published an autobiography containing substantial parts based on information obtained in the course of his employment. The House of Lords ruled that restitutionary damages could be awarded in exceptional situations where profits are occasioned directly by the breach of contract and compensatory damages would be inadequate.[153]

66 The disgorgement of profits can be relevant in cases such as those related to the infringement of personality rights, intellectual property, competition law and unfair commercial practices.[154] The position of international legal scholars seems to be divided as regards which legal device would be preferable to accomplish the required preventive function. Some of them would prefer an unjust enrichment approach, whereas others would favour a damages approach. In this latter sense, it has been contended that it would be desirable to award disgorgement damages, as a genuine and self-standing remedy independent from the loss that has occurred, when the claimant has not suffered any losses at all, either pecuniary or non-pecuniary (or, if they have occurred, they cannot be proven) or when the unlawful profits exceed these losses.[155] However, it does not seem to make any relevant difference whether the unlawful gains that must be disgorged have been obtained in contract or in tort.

5) *Aggravated and Exemplary (or Punitive) Damages*

67 Aggravated and exemplary (or punitive damages) are not to be confused either with each other or with disgorgement damages.

68 In the case of aggravated damages, we again face a terminological problem. In England and Wales, the term is used to identify a certain type of compensatory damages which seek to provide compensation for non-pecuniary harm that reflects the additional injury (ie separate and independent from pain and suffering) that the claimant suffers in his feelings.[156] A similar approach is adopted in Israel.[157] In the United States, by contrast, the term is rarely used and if it is, it is used as a synonym for punitive damages.[158]

69 In England and Wales, since aggravated damages seek to compensate for additional injury caused to the claimant's feelings or mental distress, as a matter

153 *Attorney General v Blake* [2000] UKHL 45, [2001] 1 AC 268 and E&W 59. See also US 30.
154 *Hondius/Jansen* (fn 144) 483–498.
155 Ibid, 501, favouring the damages approach.
156 E&W 67.
157 IL 33.
158 E&W 67 and *AJ Sebok/V Wilcox*, Aggravated Damages, in: H Koziol/V Wilcox, Punitive Damages: Common Law and Civil Law Perspectives (2009) 257–274, 257–258.

of principle they are available in tort only, although it has been suggested that they could be available in contract as well when the predominant object of the contract is to provide pleasure, relaxation, peace of mind or freedom from molestation.[159] In Israel, they are explicitly allowed in tort, whereas in contract they are allowed implicitly only, since courts, which may allow non-pecuniary loss at their discretion, may also take this aspect into account.[160]

Punitive damages, although preventive, as are disgorgement damages, do not aim at prevention only, but also seek to punish particularly reprehensible conduct. By contrast with disgorgement damages, which are strictly based on the wrongdoer's profits and, for this reason, their amount can never exceed the amount of the profits obtained, punitive damages are not assessed according to the defendant's gains. In fact, they can be awarded even if the wrongdoer has made no profit at all.[161] Basically aimed at the same function, although limited to a few categories of cases,[162] these damages are called 'exemplary damages' in England and Wales.[163] 70

Punitive damages are not awarded in the civil law jurisdictions under survey, where the general position is to reject them and the same position applies to South Africa.[164] By contrast, although they are not as common in England and Wales and in Israel as they are in the United States, punitive damages are allowed in tort in these three countries, but they are not ordinarily permitted in contract. However, by way of exception, punitive damages can be allowed in contract when the breach of contract qualifies at the same time as a tort or in some very specific cases.[165] The policy reasons underpinning this rejection of punitive damages in contract are manifold and include, among others, the idea that the contract is a private arrangement where parties negotiate their rights and duties; the sort of losses suffered in contract, which are mainly pecuniary; the need for certainty that contract law requires or the fact that punitive damages in contract would tend to discourage efficient breach.[166] 71

---

159 E&W 67.

160 IL 33.

161 *MPI/G Wagner*, Punitive Damages (2012) 1403–1406; *H Koziol*, Punitive Damages: Admission into the Seventh Legal Heaven or Eternal Damnation? Comparative Report and Conclusions, in: H Koziol/V Wilcox, Punitive Damages: Common Law and Civil Law Perspectives (2009) 275–308.

162 Following the three categories established in *Rookes v Barnard*: (a) oppressive, arbitrary or unconstitutional action by servants of the government; (b) conduct calculated by the defendant to make a profit for himself which may well exceed the compensation payable to the claimant; and (c) express statutory authorisation. See E&W 65.

163 E&W 65 and *V Wilcox*, Punitive Damages in England, in: H Koziol/V Wilcox, Punitive Damages: Common Law and Civil Law Perspectives (2009) nos 1, 7.

164 AT 25, FR 28, DE 25 f, ZA 15.

165 E&W 64, IL 32, US 32.

166 E&W 64, referring to the reasons given by the English Law Commission.

72 A similar fear of how punishment could negatively affect freedom of contract is also the reluctance that most legal systems, and notably common law systems, show towards penalty clauses, which must be distinguished from liquidated damages clauses. With liquidated damages, the parties agree in the contract that, in the case of breach, the debtor will pay the creditor a specified sum, which is based on the assessment of what the probable damage in the case of breach will be. This clause allows both the parties to avoid the difficulties usually involved in calculating damages and to know beforehand the amount for which they will be liable in the case of breach of contract. Penalty clauses, by contrast, may also fulfil these two functions, but their additional and main purpose is to induce the parties not to breach the contract by establishing for the case of breach an amount of damages that is much higher than any possible pre-estimated amount.[167]

73 In civil law jurisdictions, the two terms are often used interchangeably, since all clauses are valid, although there is sometimes a tendency to refer to them as 'penalty clauses' in order to stress the general power of judges to reduce the amount agreed if they consider it excessive or out of proportion to the damage suffered by the creditor.[168] Thus, in France, art 1231-5 (formerly art 1152) *Code civil* recognises liquidated damages by providing that: 'Where a contract stipulates that the person who fails to perform shall pay a certain sum of money by way of damages, the other party may be awarded neither a higher nor a lower sum'. Since in practice some creditors imposed excessive amounts, a second paragraph was added in 1975, included now in the same new article, which provides that: '[N]evertheless, a court may, even of its own initiative, moderate or increase the penalty so agreed if it is manifestly excessive or derisory'. The second paragraph of the old art 1152 *Code civil* at first created uncertainty about the classification of the clause since, whereas the first paragraph referred to a classical liquidated damages clause, the second relied on a wording that is more connected to the area of contractual penalties.[169] In practice, however, when courts have used this faculty, they have never reduced or increased amounts under or above compensation levels.[170] In Italy, art 1382 *Codice civile*, in case of breach of contract, also recognises the creditor's right to liquidated damages, without any proof either of the existence or of the extension of damages after the breach. In order to avoid abuses, art 1384 *Codice civile* also recognises the judge's power to reduce the original amount of the penalty clause, provided that it may

---

167 *Cartwright* (fn 4) 223–226, *Kötz* (fn 2) 275 ff and *MPI/M Baum*, Penalty Clauses (2012) 1259 ff.

168 *B Pasa*, The European Law of 'Contractual Penalties' (2015) 3 ERPL 355–384, 359.

169 FR 30 and *M Cannarsa*, Contractual Penalties in French Law (2015) 3 ERPL 297–308, 299 referring also to the 'obligations with penalty clauses' formerly regulated in arts 1226–1233 French CC.

170 FR 30.

be considered grossly excessive, or that the obligation has been partly executed by the party in breach, and having regard to the interest of the creditor to the performance.[171] In Germany and Spain, penalty clauses are also allowed and the judge has the power to moderate them in civil contracts (§343 BGB, art 1154 *Código civil*), but not in commercial ones (§348 HGB, art 56 *Código mercantil*). Similar provisions can be found in other jurisdictions under survey.[172]

In common law jurisdictions, the distinction between liquidated damages and penalty clauses is crucial, since whereas the former are valid, the latter are not. 74
Moreover, courts do not have the power to reduce the amounts agreed upon in the contract if they are considered excessive[173] and for this reason they cannot convert an unacceptable penalty clause into an acceptable liquidated damages clause. This position has been favoured by some law and economics scholars, who consider that penalty clauses should remain unenforceable, among other reasons because they give the creditor an incentive to induce the breach and, since their goal is to force the debtor to comply with the contract, they deter efficient breaches.[174] However, recent legal and economics scholars, using insights captured by behavioural law and economics, argue for replacing the common law's penalty rule with one more akin to that found in the civil law. It has thus been submitted that the common law rule providing for unenforceability of all penalty clauses is neither fair nor efficient and is neither rational nor in accord with private autonomy.[175] It is considered that the rule in the common law that forbids penalty clauses should be eliminated and penalty clauses should be presumed to be enforceable and policed like any other term in the contract with a few caveats. The application of the doctrine of unconscionability to police excessive penalties should only require a finding of substantive unconscionability and not evidence of procedural unconscionability. This would be similar to the civil law's not enforcing penalties considered to be manifestly excessive and, as in the civil law, party intent should be honoured by making an adjustment of the amount of the preferred remedy.[176] International soft law texts have long since adhered to the civilian position.[177] However, in England and Wales, the Supreme Court has recently retained the rule against contractual penalty clauses, while redefining some of its underlying principles.[178]

---

171 IT 54 f and *FP Patti*, Penalty Clauses in Italian Law (2015) 3 ERPL 297–308, 309–326.

172 DE 20, NO 27, PL 61, ES 41, NL 45, ZA 15.

173 E&W 66 and US 32. IL 33, pointing out that penalty clauses which significantly exceed the actual loss are not allowed.

174 EAL 53–54.

175 EAL 55 and *LA Dimatteo*, Behavioural Case for Contractual Penalties under the Common Law (2015) 3 ERPL 327–354.

176 EAL 55 and *Dimatteo* (2015) 3 ERPL 353 f.

177 Art 9:509 PECL; art III.-3:710 DCFR; art 7.4.13 PICC.

178 E&W 66 and *Cartwright* (fn 4) 225.

6) *Other Remedies*

75 The array of remedies available in contract is much wider than in tort. Damages, as has already been seen, is a remedy common to both areas, and the differences between contract and tort are rather minor and are more based on historical grounds and on the different position that the debtor and the creditor hold in contract and in tort than on substantive reasons that require them to be different.

76 Different legal systems do not distinguish the various kinds of remedies on the basis of the same criteria. A possible approach to establishing a comparison of the remedies available in contract and in tort, which could be relevant in our borderlines quest, is the place that compulsion can take in order to compel the debtor to perform specifically what he has promised or make good the specific harm that he has caused with his infringement. We refer here to a certain parallelism that can be established between specific performance in contract and restoration in kind in tort. Additionally, compulsion may not only seek, as in this case, to make good the harmful consequences of a breach or of an infringement, but to obviate or overcome the injury, either by preventing the commission of an unlawful act or by removing an ongoing source of harm. Thus, in contract, the creditor may seek injunctive relief, ie try to obtain an injunction to require the defaulting debtor to undo a breach committed in the past or to restrain the debtor of a negative promise from infringing his duty again in the future. In tort, among other functions, injunctions may also be used to put an end to the continuing consequences of an infringement that has already been committed or to prevent the tortfeasor from repeating the infringement in the future. However, the distinction between specific performance or reparation in kind, on the one hand, and injunctive relief, on the other, is not crystal clear in all legal systems.[179]

77 As regards the remedy of specific performance, the different approach from common law and civil law jurisdictions is well known. In English law, priority is given to the claim for damages, and only in exceptional cases can the judge order the debtor to perform what was bargained for if some limitations can be surmounted.[180] The most important limitation to specific performance is the rule that the remedy may only be awarded when the remedy of damages is inadequate, as is the case when the buyer cannot obtain in the marketplace from a third party goods or services that are equivalent to the promised performance.

---

179 See, for instance, US 33 explaining that specific performance is simply a term referring to an injunction enforcing fulfilment of a contractual promise. Or in French law, in the case of the distinction of reparation in kind and injunctive relief in tort law, *van Gerven/Larouche/Lever* (fn 3) 862 et passim.

180 *Kötz* (fn 2) 202–205, *Smits* (fn 2) 200–202.

This is regularly the case in the sale of land, but it can also apply to the sale of goods that are unique, specifically rare or where the claimant has a particular intangible interest in their delivery. A second limitation to specific performance is that, as a rule, it will not be granted to enforce personal services contracts, since otherwise the defendant would be forced into a kind of involuntary servitude. Other reasons behind this limitation are that a court order can hardly restore the relationship of mutual confidence and respect which is necessary in such contracts, or that services performed under coercion tend to be of doubtful quality and it is difficult to determine whether they are performed in accordance with the contract. Finally, other limitations are that specific performance will not be granted when ensuring compliance with the order is likely to require continuous supervision by the court and when specific performance would cause undue hardship to the debtor.[181] By contrast, in civil law systems, specific performance is the routine central remedy and it is assumed that the creditor will seek specific performance regularly.[182] Some limitations, such as impossibility, also play an important role, but the fact that a contract is for services does not prevent the court from granting specific performance, since the concept of specific performance is broader and performance by a third person at the defendant's expense is also considered specific performance.[183] However, this will not be possible if the specific characteristics of the debtor are essential, since then he is the only person who can perform the contract.[184] Nevertheless, provisions that can be found in some civil codes involving others performing in the debtor's place or the debtor destroying something he should not have seem to refer more to restoration in kind than to specific performance.[185]

In tort, only a minority of the legal systems under survey favour restoration in kind as the general principle underpinning compensation in tort law. The majority adopt the view that compensation in tort is primarily owed in money.[186] In favour of this preference it is an obvious fact that, on many occasions, tortfeasors do not have the ability to make good the damage by restoration in kind or it is impossible for anyone to do so. However, there are areas where restoration in kind can better contribute to restoring the victim to the position where he would have been in if the wrong complained of had not been committed. This is notably the case with some infringements to personality rights, such as defamation, where a corrective notice or the publication of the decision establishing the 78

181 E&W 68. In more detail, comparing English and French law, *S Rowan*, Remedies for breach of contract. A comparative analysis of the protection of performance (2012) 25 ff.

182 *Kötz* (fn 2) 198–202, *Smits* (fn 2) 194–200 and, referring to France, *Rowan* (fn 181) 37–47.

183 *Beale et al* (fn 2) 840.

184 Ibid, 868 ff.

185 For instance, arts 1143 and 1144 French CC, or arts 1098 and 1099 Spanish CC.

186 *Magnus* (fn 120) 188 ff.

falsity of the defamatory statements may better contribute to restoring the victim's reputation. For these and similar cases several legal systems provide for restoration in kind[187] and, following them, art 10:104 Principles of European Tort Law (PETL) establishes that victims may claim restoration in kind under the double condition that it is possible and not too burdensome to the other party.[188]

79 Under English law, injunctions can be awarded for both a breach of contract and for a tortious infringement. Injunctions may seek to restrain a defendant from doing a particular thing (*prohibitory injunctions*) or may be directed to the positive performance of a specific duty (*mandatory injunctions*). Either can be perpetual (or final) or interim (or interlocutory). An interim injunction can be issued provisionally, ie before the hearing of an action, in order to prevent the commission or continuance of a harm in the meantime. Both can be awarded '*quia timet*', that is, in order to prevent an act that is threatened or imminent but has not yet commenced. In all cases, an injunction will only be granted where the remedies of specific performance, in contract, or damages, both in contract and in tort, are inappropriate.[189]

80 German law distinguishes between claims for reparation under tort law (*deliktische Schadensersatzansprüche*) and claims to bring an end to or to prevent the occurrence of unlawful interference (*Abwehransprüche*). The latter claims may aim at putting an end to an unlawful interference which has continuing effects (*Beseitigungsanspruch*) or to prevent the imminent commission of an unlawful act (*Unterlassungsanspruch*).[190] In the same vein, Spanish law speaks of an *acción de cesación* in the first case, and of an *acción de abstención* in the second one,[191] but in practice, as in France, it does not seem that there is always a clear distinction between restoration in kind for harm and removal of the source of harm in order to prevent future harm.[192]

81 Injunctions are also considered an alternative or an additional remedy to damages in most reports[193] and they can be important remedies in areas such as infringement of personality rights, unfair competition, intellectual property and other non-material rights, nuisance law, etc.[194] However, there does not seem

---

187 Ibid, 189 with further references. Also ES 44, but considering that publication of the court decision does not have a compensatory nature but merely aims at removing the effects of the damaging event (STS 17.10.2012 (RJ 2012, 9718)).

188 *EPTL Comment/Magnus*, in: European Group on Tort Law, Principles of European Tort Law. Text and Commentary (2005) 159 ff.

189 E&W 69, *van Gerven/Larouche/Lever* (fn 3) 847 ff and *Rowan* (fn 181) 30 ff.

190 *Van Gerven/Larouche/Lever* (fn 3) 856 ff.

191 ES 43 ff. See also Italy, at IT 60–62.

192 ES 44. *Van Gerven/Larouche/Lever* (fn 3) 862 et passim.

193 PL 65–69, ZA 16, CH 22, US 33.

194 See, for instance, ES 43 ff, PL 65 ff.

to be a relevant difference between injunctions issued in the case of breach of contract and those issued in the case of infringement in tort.

D. DIFFERENCES AS REGARDS RECOVERABILITY OF 'PURE ECONOMIC LOSSES' BETWEEN CONTRACTING AND NON-CONTRACTING PARTIES

Economic loss, and more precisely pure economic loss in negligence, has 82
become one of the most debated issues in tort law over the last few decades.[195] Surprisingly enough, the topic is unknown in many legal jurisdictions and, in those that use it, there is no generally agreed definition. Probably the most accurate definition is a negative one, such as that included in the Restatement (Third) of Torts: Liability for Economic Harm, which holds that economic loss is a 'pecuniary damage not arising from injury to the plaintiff's person or from physical harm to the plaintiff's property'.[196]

It has been contended that here the word 'pure' plays a central role. Pure 83
economic loss is a stand-alone pecuniary loss which affects the patrimony of the defendant as such, ie without harming his person or specific items of his property or, as has been graphically described, it 'strikes the victim's wallet and nothing else'.[197] If economic loss is connected to harm to the person or to the property of the claimant, even if it is slight, it becomes a 'consequential economic loss' which gives rise to a completely different situation.[198] Both in countries that use the notion of economic loss and those which do not, if all the other usual conditions for liability are met, consequential economic loss

---

195 *EK Banakas* (ed), Civil Liability for Pure Economic Loss (1996); *WH van Boom/H Koziol/CA Witting* (eds), Pure Economic Loss (2003); *B Feldthusen*, Economic Negligence: The Recovery of Pure Economic Loss (6th edn 2012); *M Bussani/VV Palmer* (ed), Pure Economic Loss in Europe (2003); *VV Palmer/M Bussani* (eds), Pure Economic Loss: New Horizons in Comparative Law (2009); *M Bussani/VV Palmer*, The Frontier between Contractual and Tortious Liability in Europe: Insights from the Case of Compensation for Pure Economic Loss, in: AS Hartkamp et al (eds), Towards a European Civil Code (4th edn 2011) 945–976; *VV Palmer*, A comparative law sketch of pure economic loss, in: M Bussani/AJ Sebok (eds), Comparative Tort Law: Global Perspectives (2015) 300–322. From an economic analysis point of view, *Jef De Mot*, Pure economic loss, in: M Faure (ed), Tort Law and Economics (2009) 201–214.

196 Restatement (Third) of Torts: Liability for Economic Harm, Tentative Draft 1, §2 (2012), which, although recognising that courts often refer to these losses as 'purely' economic, omits this qualification and points out in a Comment that 'economic' loss in this Restatement normally means 'pure economic loss'.

197 In this sense, *Bussani/Palmer*, The Frontier between Contractual and Tortious Liability (fn 195) 947; *Palmer* (fn 195) 302.

198 The Restatement (Third) of Torts, however, after explaining the distinction, uses the term 'economic loss' all through to refer to 'pure economic loss', cf §2. Comment a. Definitional note.

may be recovered without question. A second problematic element as regards recoverability of pure economic loss is that the conduct that gives rise to liability is merely negligent. If pure economic loss is caused by an intentional conduct against *boni mores* or contrary to public policy, legal systems generally agree in recognising recoverability.[199] The problematic notion then is 'pure' or stand-alone economic loss in negligence.

1) *Jurisdictions that Use the Notion of Pure Economic Loss*

84 In the legal systems under survey, countries such as Germany and Austria operate with the notion of pure economic loss, where pure economic loss is not listed among the so-called absolute rights and, therefore, recovery must be sought on the basis of more specific tort provisions or by an expansive application of contract principles.[200] Other legal systems such as England, Israel, the Netherlands, South Africa and the United States also adopt this notion but develop a more pragmatic approach, ie they operate on a case-by-case basis, not driven by a checklist of absolute rights, but by a careful study of the specific socio-economic implications of recovery.[201] In all the above-mentioned common law countries and mixed legal systems like Israel and South Africa, the 'duty of care' concept is also used as a screening device.[202]

85 Legal writing often refers to the 'economic loss rule' when discussing whether a bright-line rule between recoverable and non-recoverable stand-alone economic loss in negligence can be drawn or not.[203] However, no single normative principle can be used to solve all the problems posed by pure economic loss and for this reason it is necessary to organise all the problems that it may give rise to into different groups of cases that analyse different and, sometimes, conflicting rationales.[204]

86 It has been contended that in some legal systems the 'economic loss rule' plays a boundary-line function between contract and tort.[205] For this reason it is important for our borderline endeavour to distinguish whether the parties involved in a claim for pure economic loss in negligence are contracting parties or parties not bound by a previous contractual relationship. Although there

---

199 See, for instance, AT 25 and DE 30 and *Palmer* (fn 195) 314.

200 DE 4, 30 and AT 2, 25.

201 E&W 70 ff, IL 35, NL 47 f, ZA 17–19, 50–52, US 35 ff.

202 In this sense *Bussani/Palmer*, The Frontier between Contractual and Tortious Liability (fn 195) 954 f; *Palmer* (fn 195) 310 f.

203 See in more detail US 37 ff.

204 Which *Bussani/Palmer*, The Frontier between Contractual and Tortious Liability (fn 195) 984 call a 'legal taxonomy'.

205 *V Johnson*, The Boundary-Line Function of the Economic Loss Rule (2009) 66 Wash & Lee L Rev 533.

is no uniform taxonomy of economic loss, this distinction is very important, because the reasons for denying tort liability in one case or another are different. Thus, while recoverability in tort between non-contracting parties may involve, among other factors, concerns about unpredictable and limitless liability, recoverability in tort between contracting parties raises concerns as regards the need to preserve the consensual allocation of risks and interests that the parties have bargained for in the contract.[206] For the rest, the chapter refers occasionally to other classification criteria used by leading scholarship.

a) Economic Loss between Contracting Parties

In a market economy, the protection of economic interests is left to the self-determination of the parties and primarily to contract law. If the parties involved are contracting parties, they have already established their preferences by deciding to enter into a contractual relationship and, through a bargaining process, they have allocated the relevant economic risks involved. In so doing, they may have availed themselves of a wide variety of legal devices, such as warranties, time limitations or exclusion or limitation clauses, to contour the scope of the risk that they are willing to run. If in one aspect or the other the parties have not made any use of the possibilities of the private ordering of their interests offered by the legal system, then the default rules – generally tailored to what the parties regularly agree if they bargain on these aspects – apply. In all legal systems, economic losses resulting from the non-performance or breach of a contract, subject to certain rules such as foreseeability, are considered recoverable without debate, since they refer to the frustration of the expectations of gain that can be rightly founded on the contractual agreement. 87

Needless to say, by entering a contract, the parties do not waive other interests and all legal systems afford them protection against personal injury and property damage arising from the performance or non-performance of the contract. This protection, however, may be carried out differently, ie either by applying tort law rules or by extending contract rules or other sorts of rules. However, economic interests, the infringement of which gives rise to pure economic losses, have been bargained for in the contract and the contractual expectations cannot be overridden by tort law. For this reason, for instance, §3 of the Restatement (Third) of Torts: Liability for Economic Harm (Tentative Draft 1) establishing an exclusionary 'economic loss rule', refers to the preclusion of tort liability arising from contract, which, although it is not absolute ('except as provided elsewhere in this Restatement'), it provides that 'there is no 88

[206] This well-clarified distinction for our purposes is used by *DB Dobbs/PT Hayden/EM Bublick*, Hornbook on Torts (2nd edn 2016) 1061 ff and had been developed in more detail by *Gilead* (fn 10) 14 ff.

liability in tort for economic loss caused by negligence in the performance or negotiation of a contract between the parties'.

89 In the context of contracting parties, a rule that excludes liability in tort between each other like this one serves several purposes. Seen from the bargaining moment, the rule allows the parties to make reliable allocations of financial risk without fear that tort law will be used to undo them later. Seen from the moment when the dispute arises, the rule protects the bargain the parties have made against disruption by a claim in tort. Viewed in the long term, the rule prevents the erosion of contract rules by the use of tort law to work around them and also reduces the confusion that can result when a party brings a claim on the same facts under contract and under tort.[207] The rule has its origin in cases involving product liability, where the demarcation between quality defects, sounding in contract, and safety defects, sounding in tort, has also given rise to serious problems in other legal systems such as Germany,[208] England and Wales,[209] South Africa[210] and the United States,[211] as shown below in Cases 6 and 7.

b) Economic Loss between Non-Contracting Parties

90 When the parties in a claim for pure economic loss are not linked by a contractual relationship, the problem arises in all its crudity in legal systems that start from a tort law system based on the negligent infringement of a more or less closed list of protected interests, which does not include a general protection of economic interests as such – as is the case, for instance, in Germany (cf §823 BGB)[212] – or which, as in the common law jurisdictions, is based on a set of specific torts, where the most general one is the tort of negligence.[213]

91 These legal systems have in common the fact that economic interests enjoy a lower protection in tort and, when necessary, protection is generally afforded through provisions requiring intentional harm which is immoral or against public policy (for instance, §826 BGB[214]) or through piecemeal specific torts (economic torts),[215] which are regularly also based on intention, or through sectoral legislation developed to address particular kinds of economic harm

207 In more detail, §3, Comment b) Restatement (Third) of Torts: Liability for Economic Harm, Tentative Draft 1 (2012).
208 DE 29 f.
209 See E&W 71.
210 ZA 18.
211 US 37 ff.
212 DE 30.
213 E&W 70.
214 DE 8, also AT 25.
215 *Dobbs et al* (fn 206) 1059 ff.

in order to protect business relationships, fair competition and, in general, the good functioning of private law relationships in the market.

Therefore, a general principle of liability for negligently inflicted economic harm does not exist and there is no desire to create it because it could be seriously detrimental to the good functioning of the economy. This does not mean, however, that economic interests whose infringement gives rise to pure economic loss are not protected at all pursuant to the general negligence rules. The constellation of cases where this protection is afforded extends from cases where there is a widespread trend to accept compensation under certain conditions, to cases where the trend is to exclude compensation, with groups of cases in between, which are still in historical evolution and covered today by a dark shadow of doubt. 92

i) Relational Economic Loss: The Exclusionary Rule and its Exceptions

One of the broadest categories is the so-called 'relational economic loss', ie where personal injury or property damage caused by the defendant, D, to a primary victim, X, causes a specific economic loss to a secondary victim, C, who suffers economic loss because of some special relationship that exists between her and X. The case law of most jurisdictions support in these cases a firm exclusionary rule, subject to many exceptions, which would preclude the recovery of pure economic loss in negligence when it is consequent upon personal injury or property damage to a third party.[216] 93

Among the exceptions, the most common and accepted exception to this when the primary victim suffers personal injury is loss of earnings suffered by family members or close persons as a result of the death of a relative on whom they were economically dependent, which is generally considered recoverable. There is, however, a widespread tendency, in this case, to exclude compensation for economic loss suffered by other persons outside a wider or narrower circle of family relatives or close persons, such as employers.[217] If the damage caused has been to the property of the primary victims, the exclusionary rule also tends to apply.[218] 94

Another exception to the exclusionary rule in the case of relational economic loss is the so-called 'transferred loss', ie of a loss ordinarily falling on a primary victim but which is transferred to a secondary victim by the operation of the law or by contracts such as leases, sales or insurance agreements, that separate property rights from rights of use or specifically reallocate risk bearing. 95

216 *Feldthusen* (fn 195) 209 ff.
217 Ibid, 273 ff.
218 Ibid, 235 ff.

Sometimes the claimant is in a position similar to an insurer who needs to recover by subrogation in order to prevent unjust enrichment of the defendant as, for instance, when X retains title but has transferred the risks of property to C and D destroys X's property, so that X, who is the owner, suffers no harm, but C suffers pure economic loss only, because he is not yet the owner.[219] Sometimes the claimant is under an obligation to bear the loss directly as, for instance, when C commits himself by a contract to maintain X's bridge in a good state of repair and D negligently damages the bridge.[220]

96 Transferred loss cases do not increase the liability of tortfeasors, since what is compensated for is the same loss that the primary victim, ie the victim suffering personal injury or property damage, would have suffered. Since the primary victim cannot recover, if it were not recoverable by the secondary victim, the tortfeasor would benefit from the situation and end up scot-free.[221] The difference between this case and the above-mentioned economic loss suffered by relatives is that, in the case of harm suffered by relatives, the secondary victim suffers a harm that is different from any economic harm that the primary victim might have suffered.

97 A subgroup of relational economic losses are those cases where the loss arises through damage to resources not privately owned, as when economic harm results from the destruction or the closure of public infrastructures or from the impairment of natural resources that effects the economic activities of those who thereby suffer economic loss. Here, the most general trend is to award compensation, if any, to the class of victims whose living is more seriously impaired by the event causing economic loss, although in general there is no clear yardstick as to where to delimit the chain of groups of persons adversely affected.[222]

ii) Negligent Provision of Information and Defective Services

98 A second group of cases relates to the negligent provision of information or negligent performance of services that gives rise to economic loss to third parties to the contract who acted on reliance of the information furnished or the services performed.[223]

---

219 Ibid, 261 f.

220 Ibid, 263.

221 *Bussani/Palmer*, Pure Economic Loss in Europe (fn 195) 11 ff et passim, with further examples. Also *van Boom et al* (fn 195) 20–31.

222 *Feldthusen* (fn 195) 267 ff; *Palmer* (fn 195) 304 f; *Van Boom et al* (fn 195) 26 ff.

223 *Bussani/Palmer*, Pure Economic Loss in Europe (fn 195) 13 f; *Van Boom et al* (fn 195) 19 ff. See also Restatement (Third) of Torts, §5 Negligent Misrepresentation and §6 Negligent Performance of Services.

An example regarding negligent provision of information (*negligent misrepresentation*) is the well-known English case of *Hedley Byrne v Heller & Partners Ltd*,[224] where the claimant had relied on the information provided by the defendants regarding the financial position and creditworthiness of a client and who lost £17,000 when the client went bankrupt. The court held that, although there was no contractual relationship between claimant and defendants, if the defendants had not expressly disclaimed their liability – as in fact they did – they would have 'assumed responsibility' towards the claimant by voluntarily entering into a 'special relationship' which created a duty of care. The court considered that it was reasonable for the defendant to have known that the information that they had given would likely have been relied upon for entering into a contract of some sort and this would give rise, the court said, to a 'special relationship', in which the defendant would have to take sufficient care in giving advice to avoid liability in negligence.[225] In this case, negligently inflicted pure economic losses came to be recoverable in tort, albeit only in exceptional circumstances where the fear of indeterminacy is overcome by the close relationship of proximity between the parties involving the defendant's voluntary assumption of responsibility to the claimant either individually or as the member of an identifiable class.[226] 99

A good example regarding the negligent performance of services is also the English case *White v Jones*,[227] where a solicitor was told to draw up a new will, splitting the testator's estate between the two plaintiffs, his daughters. He negligently failed to do this by the time of the testator's death, and the estate passed in accordance with the testator's wishes expressed in a previous will. The daughters sued the solicitor in negligence. It was held that the solicitor had assumed a special relationship towards them, creating a duty of care which he had carried out negligently, and therefore had to indemnify them for their loss. The case has been used as a basis for our Case 2 below and the problems that it gives rise to will be commented upon in more detail there. 100

Since liability should be confined to cases where information or the services are provided in a sufficiently serious spirit to make the claimants reliance reasonable, recoverability of economic loss should be confined to cases where the defendant was acting in the course of his business, profession or employment or in any transaction in which he had a pecuniary interest. Negligence can take place either in obtaining or in communicating information or in the provision 101

224 [1964] AC 465, noted by *K Oliphant/V Wilcox*, England and Wales, in: B Winiger/E Karner/K Oliphant (eds), Digest of European Tort Law, vol 3: Essential Cases on Misconduct (2018) 3e/12, 507 ff.

225 E&W 17 and 71.

226 E&W 71.

227 [1995] 2 AC 207.

of the service. In order to avoid indeterminate or disproportionate liability, claimants must belong to a limited group of persons for whose guidance the defendant intended to supply the information, or who at least knew that their contractual party intended to supply this information, and, in the case of services, they must belong to the group of persons for whose benefit the defendant performed the service. This group would include, among others, cases of pure economic loss caused by legal and financial professionals, such as lawyers, public notaries, insurance brokers, accountants and auditors.[228]

2) *Economic Loss in Legal Systems that Do Not Acknowledge this Concept*

102 'Economic loss' or 'pure economic loss' are not legal notions used either by legal provisions or case law in countries such as France, Italy, Greece, Poland and Spain.[229] A common characteristic of all these legal systems is that tort liability is not based on a closed list of protected interests imposed by the legislature, but on a general clause which does not exclude the protection of pure economic loss as a matter of course. For a legal system to be placed in this group, it is also important that case law and legal writing understand these general clauses as such, ie that, in spite of the silence as regards protected interests and rights, they do not actually read in them a system protecting absolute rights.[230]

103 This does not mean, however, that these legal systems do not have legal devices to control the recoverability of losses infringed purely upon the patrimony of victims, ie without causing them personal injury (or death) or damage to property. It has been contended that one of these devices is the *non cumul* rule, ie the rule that forbids parties contractually bound to each other from bringing claims in tort against each other for any harm connected to the contractual performance which, according to this opinion, would be a 'necessary corollary' of the extension of tort law to economic loss.[231] This would not explain, however, why among all the countries under survey that have a general clause of tortious liability based on negligence, the only one that has adopted this rule is France, while the others opt for one or other form of concurring liabilities.[232]

---

228 *Bussani/Palmer*, Pure Economic Loss in Europe (fn 195) 13 ff; *van Boom et al* (fn 195) 19 ff.

229 FR 33, IT 63 ff, GR 22, PL 70, ES 46.

230 As, for instance, was the case in Italy until the 1970s and is still argued in modern Austrian law.

231 *G Wagner*, Grundstrukturen, in: R Zimmermann (ed), Grundstrukturen des Europäischen Deliktsrechts (2003) 233. In the same sense, *R Zimmermann*, The Law of Obligations: Roman Foundations of the Civilian Tradition (1996) 906, who holds that the admission of an elective concurrence of liability would lead every culpable breach of contract to being actionable in tort too and, as a result, French doctrine has to protect the rules relating to contractual liability by means of the principle of *non cumul*.

232 See below sec IV.

Without denying that the *non cumul* rule can be a useful device to protect contracts from being undermined by tort, it is true that most systems that have a general clause of tort liability can do without it and, as French legal writing has pointed out, the *non cumul* rule is a national French phenomenon that results from the particular doctrine of *responsabilité du fait des choses* to protect contracts against the disruption that this expansion of strict liability could have caused between contracting parties by upsetting the allocation of risk implicitly agreed by them.[233]

Although comparative legal writing ascribes these systems, with the exception of Poland's, to the jurisdictions that adopt what is called 'a liberal approach', ie that in principle they have no objection to allowing compensation for stand-alone economic harm and deal with pure economic losses exclusively on the basis of tort liability,[234] this does not mean that their attitude to compensation for pure economic loss is exactly the same. By contrast, comparative legal writing includes Poland among the countries that adopt a so-called 'conservative' approach, on the grounds that it has developed legal tools such as scope of liability or 'directness of damage' to keep liability for pure economic loss within reasonable limits.[235] 104

In Poland, the prevailing case law and legal scholarship have understood that the provision establishing that, in case of death or personal injury of a primary victim, only secondary victims included in a reduced circle of family relatives are entitled to claim compensation for their own losses (cf art 446 Polish CC) is an exception that proves the existence of the rule that excludes from compensation persons 'indirectly' harmed and operates with the distinction between 'direct' and 'indirect' damage in order to keep economic loss within limits.[236] However, Poland does not seem to stand alone when trying to control the overflow of pure economic losses. Greek legal writing also points out that only directly damaged persons may recover in tort and, although this has been debated, it emphasises that the proof of this rule can be found in the fact that the recoverability of losses of a reduced circle of secondary victims in the case of the death or personal injury of a primary victim or person who suffers a 'direct damage' (arts 928 sent 2 and 929 sent 2 Greek CC) is considered to be an exception.[237] It has been argued, however, that this generalisation is not justified, and that liability cannot be excluded in advance on the directness or indirectness 105

233 *JS Borghetti*, Strict Liability in Tort and the Boundaries of Tort Law, in: H Koziol/U Magnus (eds), Essays in Honour of Jaap Spier (2016) 20, 34.

234 *Palmer* (fn 195) 310.

235 Ibid, 309 f.

236 PL 70 ff and *T Pajor*, Poland, in: VV Palmer/M Bussani (eds), Pure Economic Loss: New Horizons in Comparative Law (2009) 261 f.

237 GR 23.

of the damage, since other factors such as the protective scope of the rule that has been violated and scope of liability will also contribute to determining whether damage suffered by secondary victims is recoverable or not.[238] Spanish law does not use the direct/indirect damage divide, not even as an orientation, and, according to the general clause of liability (art 1902 Spanish CC), every kind of damage is recoverable. However, this does not necessarily mean that every instance of pure economic loss is actually recoverable in practice and courts tend to control the recoverability of these losses with the rules regarding certainty of damage and scope of liability.[239]

E. DIFFERENCES AS REGARDS LIABILITY FOR OTHERS

1) *Liability for Auxiliaries and for Independent Contractors*

106 Whereas all jurisdictions under survey have general rules for liability for auxiliaries in tort, some do not have any general rules dealing with liability for auxiliaries in contract.[240] In fact, the concept of liability for auxiliaries in contract is even regarded as useless in France, where it is considered that in this area the question is not who was in breach of the contract, but only whether the debtor should be liable for that breach. Pursuant to art 1231-1 CC, the debtor is liable for any breach unless he can prove that it was due to force majeure. Obviously, the implication of a third party in the fulfilment of the contract, at the request of the debtor, cannot qualify as force majeure.[241]

107 The rules of most of those jurisdictions with general contractual rules of liability for auxiliaries tend to be more favourable for the claimant than the corresponding rules in tort and this difference often acts as an incentive to fuel borderline disputes. This is the case, for instance, in Austria, where principals

---

238 GR 23.

239 ES 46 and 100 f.

240 This is the case in FR 34, ES 48 and US 40. However, they may have some specific applications of the principle establishing liability of the principal for the acts of his auxiliaries. For instance, in the Spanish Civil Code, the liability of the lessee for damage caused by 'persons in his household' (art 1564 CC); liability of the contractor for work performed by the people he has engaged in the works (art 1596 CC); in the contract of mandate, liability of the agent for the acts of his substitute, when he has not been given authority to appoint him or when he has been given such a power, but without designation of the specific person and the appointee is notoriously incapable or insolvent (art 1721 CC); or, finally, when the innkeeper or restaurateur for damage to the effects of travellers caused by their servants or employees (art 1784 CC).

241 FR 34. The old art 1147 French CC spoke of 'external cause'. For a similar idea, referring to the fact that contract has no notion of vicarious liability, explicitly in US 40 and, implicitly, in E&W 72, IL 39 and in ZA 20, where courts speak about 'delegation of the performance of the obligation'.

are liable for damage caused by all their auxiliaries in contract (§1313a ABGB), but only for damage caused by 'unfit' or 'knowingly dangerous' auxiliaries in tort (cf §1315 ABGB).[242] A similar situation takes place in Germany, where in contract the debtor is responsible for the fault 'of persons he engages for the performance of his obligations as if it were his own' (cf §278 BGB); in tort, however, 'the obligation to compensate does not arise where the principal has exercised due care in the selection of the auxiliary' (cf §831 (1) BGB).[243] The situation is also very similar in Switzerland, where there is – at least, according to the letter of the law – a stark contrast between art 101 SCO, which provides that in contract the debtor who delegates the performance of an obligation is 'liable to the other party for any loss or damage the auxiliary causes in carrying [it] out',[244] and art 55 para 1 SCO, which allows the principal to escape liability in tort by proving that he took 'all due care to avoid a loss or damage of this type'. A similar dichotomy between liability for auxiliaries in contract and in tort can be found in other countries, such as Italy or Poland.[245]

Courts or legal practice, however, have found different mechanisms to work around the exculpatory defence of the principal in tort law in favour of an approximation to the contractual regime that attributes the tort committed by the auxiliary to the principal. One way or another, in most countries under survey, the governing principle is that the principal cannot escape liability and can be held liable regardless of his own fault for damage caused by his auxiliaries when acting within the scope of their employment.[246] The principle has been adopted both by art 6:102 PETL and art VI.-3:201 DCFR, and economic analysis of law seems to confirm its soundness. Thus, it is submitted that a negligence standard does not regulate activity levels efficiently by assuring that principals fully internalise the costs of their torts. Moreover, the negligence standard is poorly suited to inducing principals to adopt other kinds of measures to prevent misconduct (eg reorganising production processes) that do not involve monitoring or do not affect the principal's risk of incurring liability.[247] Accordingly, a vicarious liability regime is considered well suited to the ordinary cases where the costs of an agent's misconduct are appropriately charged to the principal, and misconduct is unlikely to escape detection.[248] 108

---

242 AT 26.

243 DE 31 ff.

244 It is contended that, although based on a very objectivised standard, liability for auxiliaries is still based on fault according to the standard of conduct that would apply to the principal himself if he had personally performed ('hypothetical reproach'), CH 29.

245 IT 65 (art 1228: liability in contract; art 2049: liability in tort), PL 78 ff.

246 For instance, ES 47 ff or in CH 29 and, in general, *S Galand Carval*, Comparative Report, in: J Spier (ed), Unification of Tort Law: Liability for Damage Caused by Others (2003) 300 ff.

247 *RH Kraakman*, Vicarious and corporate civil liability, in: M Faure, Tort Law and Economics (2009) 134–149, 143.

248 However, it is submitted that whenever one of these conditions fails, a better option can be vicarious liability which may be dominated by either a negligence-based liability regime for

109 In any case, even if in a given legal system vicarious liability applies both to contract and tort, some differences remain. These differences, however, rest mainly on those peculiarities of contract not shared by tort, such as the idea that the debtor is the only person responsible for performance, or that in contractual liability it is the contract that establishes the scope of the duties of the parties. Therefore, these differences cannot be easily removed by the legislature or case law. Among others, worth noting are the following.

110 *Liability for independent contractors*: In contract, the debtor is liable for any persons to whom he entrusts performance of the obligation, even if they are independent contractors. In tort, the general rule, subject to some exceptions, is that the principal is not liable for damage caused by independent contractors.[249] Sometimes this difference is also expressed by saying that the relationship of dependence of the auxiliary on the principal, which is essential in order to give rise to liability for auxiliaries in tort, is not required in contract.[250]

111 *Scope of the duties*: In contract, the scope of the duties that have been infringed depends on what the creditor and the debtor have agreed and on the interpretation of the contract; thus, contractual liability of the debtor requires that the auxiliary has breached any of these contractual duties while performing. In tort, however, the principal's liability depends on whether or not the auxiliary acted within the scope of his employment.[251]

112 *Liability of the auxiliary*: The auxiliary is not a party to the contract, he is not a debtor and, accordingly, he cannot be held liable.[252] In tort, however, in spite of a certain tendency to exclude liability of auxiliaries completely or only in some areas, the general rule in most legal systems is still that auxiliaries are held solidarily liable together with their principals.[253]

113 *Exclusion of liability for auxiliaries*: Finally, by contrast to liability duties that arise in tort, at least in some jurisdictions,[254] the principal can exclude liability for auxiliaries regarding duties that arise out of the contract and, sometimes, even if the auxiliary's infringement was intentional.[255]

---

liability for others or a mixed regime that includes elements of both vicarious and negligence-based liability. See *Kraakman* (fn 247) 144. For the factors militating against vicarious liability, such as increase of administrative costs, ibid, 137 ff.

249 AT 26, CZ 58, FR 33, DE 32, IT 65, NO 32, ES 49, ZA 21, CH 31, US 39.

250 FR 35, GR 25, IT 65.

251 See, for instance, NO 35 ff.

252 GR 25.

253 ZA 24, US 42. Cf also *Galand Carval* (fn 246) 304 ff.

254 NO 42, art 101 para 2 SCO, §278 para 2 BGB.

255 See in this sense, for instance, §278 para 2 in relation to §276 para 3 BGB.

2) *Liability for Legal Representatives or Organs of a Company*

Legal representatives or organs of a company are the persons who exercise a managing or controlling function within a certain organisation. They are not auxiliaries and their acts are acts of the legal person itself. The company is identified with their conduct and its liability is not vicarious, but direct. Accordingly, the company is held liable, both in contract and in tort, for the acts or omissions of the organs that represent it, as long as they acted within the scope of the performance of their duties.[256] 114

3) *Liability of Representatives of Natural Persons*

As a preliminary remark, it is important to stress that common law jurisdictions lack the institution of a statutory representative who can represent a minor when making a contract. By contrast, in civil law jurisdictions, parents have the general power to represent their children, which also means that they are able to consent to the contract that a minor entered into.[257] 115

Accordingly, in common law jurisdictions, it is affirmed that a parent does not act in the name of his child and is no more liable to pay a debt contracted by the child with a third party than a mere stranger would be.[258] The question is then whether the contract concluded by the child meets certain requirements for its validity, such as whether the minor is able to understand the nature of the contract or whether it was a 'contract of necessity' (ie a contract for necessary goods and services supplied to the child or a contract of apprenticeship, education or service).[259] 116

In civil law jurisdictions, the legal representative acts as an agent for the minor in all legal transactions, except where the law or usage authorises minors to act for themselves. Contracts concluded by children without the assistance of their representatives are voidable at their request. Liability of parents for their children for contracts they have concluded on their behalf generally follows the general rules regarding legal representation,[260] although in some legal systems liability of parents is milder (cf §1664 (2) BGB, *diligentia quam in suis*). 117

As regards persons with mental disability, in contract, common law jurisdictions broadly apply to these persons the same approach as that taken in the case of liability of minors.[261] In civil law jurisdictions, persons with mental disability 118

256 AT 27, CZ 60, DE 34, GR 26, IL 38, IT 66, NO 40 ff, PL 81, ZA 22, ES 50, CH 33.
257 See *Smits* (fn 2) 92 ff.
258 E&W 76.
259 E&W 76.
260 No special rules in CZ 62.
261 E&W 78.

are also subject to a protection regime, which varies depending on the countries (*curatela*, *curatelle*, *Betreuung*), with the result that the contract entered into by the person suffering mental disability is voidable and can be avoided by the legal representative.[262]

119 As regards liability in tort, common law jurisdictions do not link liability to parenthood, or more precisely, to parental responsibility either. Parents, however, can be held liable if they have been negligent themselves.[263] Moreover, in the United States, some states have enacted statutes making parents vicariously liable for certain acts of their children, such as vandalism, typically with a cap on the total amount of damages for which they can be held liable.[264]

120 In civil law systems, by contrast, liability for children in tort is usually linked to parental responsibility, sometimes requiring further qualifications (such as that the child must live together with his parents[265] or that a parent must exercise 'domestic authority' in order to be liable[266]). The starting point of liability of parents for their children is in many countries a rebuttable presumption of fault.[267] In some of them it is actually rebuttable in practice (eg Germany or Greece).[268] In others, however, this presumption is rarely rebuttable in practice and has developed into a *de facto* vicarious liability regime.[269] France went a step further in the 1990s and now holds parents strictly liable for the acts of their children.[270] The Netherlands combines solutions that are similar to the French (for children under 14), the German (for children aged 14–16) and the English (for children aged 16–18).[271]

4) *Liability of the Auxiliary/Organ Itself*

121 As pointed out, the principle of relativity or privity of contract prevents auxiliaries from being held liable in contract. In tort, however, the general trend – normally subject to labour law rules that restrict or even exclude the auxiliary's liability[272] – is that auxiliaries are solidarily liable with their principals.[273]

---

262 *Smits* (fn 2) 96 ff.
263 E&W 77, US 41 and the same is true for IL 42 and ZA 22.
264 US 41.
265 As in Italy (IT 67), art 2048 Italian CC, and, implicitly, in Switzerland, art 333 para 1 SCO.
266 '*Hausgewalt/autorité domestique*' (art 333 SCO), cf CH 35. Also in the case of France ('*autorité parentale*'), art 1242 (formerly art 1384) French CC.
267 DE 36, GR 27.
268 DE 36, GR 27.
269 CH 35 and *P Widmer*, Unification of Tort Law: Liability for Damage Cause by Others (2003) 267 ff, ES 47.
270 Cf *M Martín-Casals* (ed), Children in Tort Law I. Children as Tortfeasors (2006) 441 f.
271 Ibid, 441 ff.
272 E&W 79 or *H Kötz/G Wagner*, Deliktsrecht (13th edn 2016) no 303 et passim.
273 E&W 79, FR 36.

In their internal relations, however, – and with different sorts of restrictions in favour of the auxiliary – damage may be apportioned according to their respective fault.[274] The bizarre rule of §840 (2) BGB, which holds the auxiliary solely liable in the internal relationship, has traditionally been bypassed by the intelligent legal sensitivity of the German courts and, in practice, auxiliaries are held solidarily liable together with their principals but can, except in the case of intent, claim partial or full redress.[275]

As regards representatives and organs, since the party to the contract is the legal entity they represent or for which they act, it is generally considered that, provided that they do not exceed their function, they are not personally liable.[276] In tort, it is obvious that the fact of being an organ or a representative does not insulate them from the torts they commit which are unrelated to their specific function. However, for the torts they commit acting for the legal entity in their capacity as organs or legal representatives, the general trend is that they are not personally liable.[277] Diverging from this common position, some legal systems, such as the German and the Swiss, hold the organ or representative personally liable in tort. In practice, however, this has very little effect since liability insurance of the legal entity also covers the organ's or representative's liability.[278] 122

F. DIFFERENCES AS REGARDS MULTIPLE TORTFEASORS/ BREACHING PARTIES

It is well known that where there is a plurality of debtors their obligation can be organised in several different ways. In the case of contractual obligations, whether each debtor is bound to full performance (solidary obligation)[279] or only to a part of it (several)[280] depends on what the parties agree in the contract. 123

---

274 E&W 79, IL 43, IT 68.

275 *Kötz/Wagner* (fn 272) no 302.

276 FR 38, GR 31.

277 AT 29, CZ 64, FR 38, GR 31, IL 43, NO 40, PL 83, ZA 24, ES 50.

278 DE 36 and *Kötz/Wagner* (fn 272) no 303, CH 32 and art 55.3 Swiss CC.

279 The term 'solidary obligations' refers to what in English law is commonly known as 'joint and several obligations' and is unanimously followed in harmonisation texts (see, for instance, art 10:101 (1) PECL, art III.-4:102 (1) DCFR, art 9:101 PETL), the term 'joint and several obligations' being in international texts such as art 11.1.1 PICC rather an exception). On solidary obligations, see *MPI/S Meier*, Solidary Obligations (2012) 1573–1577 and *ead*, Schuldnermehrheiten im europäischen Vertragsrecht, Archiv für die civilistische Praxis, vol 211 (2011) 435–490. For solidarity in tort, *WVH Rogers* (ed), Unification of Tort Law: Multiple Tortfeasors (2004) and *C von Bar*, The Common European Law of Torts I (1998) no 50 ff and 315 ff.

280 The terminology used to refer to those obligations where each debtor is bound to perform only part of the obligation, and the creditor may claim from each debtor performance

However, when the parties are silent on this point, all legal systems must provide for a default rule.

124 The traditional default rule, coming from the *ius commune*, which considers these obligations to be several, has been adopted in countries such as France,[281] Greece,[282] Poland,[283] South Africa[284] and Spain.[285] Solidary liability, by contrast, is the default rule adopted in Austria,[286] the Czech Republic,[287] England and Wales,[288] Germany,[289] Israel,[290] Italy,[291] Norway,[292] Switzerland[293] and the Netherlands,[294] and has become common core in international and harmonised texts.[295]

125 Countries that in contract follow solidary liability as a default rule also hold multiple tortfeasors solidarily liable in tort when they have been acting in concert and when they have caused the same indivisible damage.[296] In countries where the default rule in contract is several liability, however, the legislature or case law normally use different legal devices to provide for solidary liability in tort under similar conditions. Thus, for instance, Greece, Poland and South Africa[297] have specific different rules for liability of multiple tortfeasors, which provide for solidary liability when they cause the same and indivisible damage. In Poland, the same rules apply analogically when there is a plurality of debtors on different legal grounds (such as in contract and in tort).[298] In some other countries, such

---

of that part only, varies. Sometimes as 'separate' (art 10:101 (2) PECL), 'divided' (art III.-4:102 (2) DCFR) or 'several' (art 9:101 PETL). This text follows the PETL's terminology. A third category, not recognised in all legal systems and sometimes called 'joint obligation', refers to those cases where the debtors are bound to perform together and the creditor may require performance only from all of them together. In fact, it is the result of the fact that performance is not divisible, and then the category of 'indivisible obligations' covers much of the same area.

281 FR 40 and art 1202 French CC. The new art 1310 French CC remains faithful to this option by providing that: 'La solidarité est légale ou conventionnelle; elle ne se présume pas'.

282 GR 32 and art 480 Greek CC.

283 PL 84 and arts 366–378 Polish CC.

284 ZA 25.

285 ES 51 and art 1137 Spanish CC.

286 AT 30.

287 CZ 67 and §2915 Czech CC (2012).

288 E&W 80.

289 DE 38 and §427 BGB.

290 IL 44.

291 IT 69 and arts 1292–1313 Italian CC.

292 NO 46.

293 CH 39 and arts 50 ad 51 SCO.

294 NL 50 and art 6:102 Dutch CC.

295 Art 10:102 PECL; art III.-4:101 and art III.-4:103 DCFR; art 11.1.1 PICC and art 9:101 PETL; art VI.-6:105 DCFR.

296 See, additionally, *K Oliphant* (ed), Aggregation and Divisibility of Damage (2009) 487 ff.

297 GR 33 ff and 926 Greek CC; PL 85 ff and art 441 Polish CC; ZA 25.

298 PL 90.

as France and Spain, where the rules providing for several liability are general and, accordingly, should also apply to liability of multiple tortfeasors, the courts have felt the need to protect victims and, by making recourse to Roman and pre-codified law, have developed the notion of 'obligations *in solidum*'. Obligations *in solidum* have been defined as a 'watered down version of solidary obligations',[299] which have all their primary effects but not the secondary ones, ie the extension of effects for one debtor to the others in cases such as notice, prescription or *res judicata*. The notion applies regardless of whether liability in tort is fault based or not, fault based in the case of some tortfeasors and strict in the others, or even if the legal grounds for liability of the other debtors are different from tort. The basic condition is, however, that the damage caused is the same and indivisible damage, and this is considered sufficient to hold any of the multiple debtors liable for the whole damage.[300] The difference between these obligations and solidary obligations proper, however, is not very clear, but, at the end of the day, the secondary effects that obligations *in solidum* lack have not been proven very important in practice and the differences with solidary obligations as regards this point have been blurred over the years.[301]

For these reasons, whether a certain obligation is in contract or in tort 126
can make a difference in all the countries where liability in contract is several and liability in tort is solidary, a position which is frankly in retreat following the recent legal developments.[302] It can also make a difference in Switzerland where, although solidarity applies both to contract and tort, art 51 para 2 SCO introduces a hierarchy into the internal relationship between multiple tortfeasors – this being heavily criticised by legal writing – that is normally interpreted in the sense that persons liable in tort and for fault have no right of recourse against their fellow debtors if their liability is exclusively based on contract or results from a strict liability regime.[303]

The differences between contract and tort law rules do not seem rooted in any 127
substantial reasons arising out of the contract–tort divide, but in different legal traditions. Obviously, solidary liability has clear advantages for the victims. It imposes the risk of insolvency of a tortfeasor on the others and, since the claimant can recover his entire damage from any one defendant, it places the burden of bringing a claim against the other tortfeasors for their proportionate share on the defendant rather than the claimant.[304] However, although it is still the

299 In this sense *F Terré/P Simler/Y Lequette*, Droit civil. Les obligations (11th edn 2013) 1311.
300 Ibid, 1306–1308.
301 FR 40 and fn 47 and ES 51 ff. Greek (GR 33 ff) and Polish (PL 89) legal writing also seems to use this notion of obligation *in solidum* to refer to those cases where co-debtors are liable on different legal grounds.
302 However, by contrast to the preceding projects, cf art 1310 new French CC.
303 CH 40 f.
304 See in this sense, US 45.

predominant default rule in contract, the development in the United States over the last few decades shows that there are other ways of organising the plurality of debtors in tort according to hybrid regimes. These regimes combine different elements and provide for solidary liability for specific cases or under certain circumstances only, such as when one of the defendants is insolvent, or exclude it for non-pecuniary loss only, or make it dependent upon a certain threshold of comparative fault that, when overstepped by one defendant, excludes solidary liability for the others.[305]

G. DIFFERENCES AS REGARDS THE PERSONS WHO MAY BE PROTECTED

128 As a general rule, a contract cannot confer rights or impose obligations arising under it on any person except its parties. In England, this rule is known as the doctrine of 'privity of contract'.[306] It was affirmed in 1861 in *Tweeddle v Atkinson*,[307] which held that a promise by a man to pay money to the son of another was not directly enforceable by the son. Among other arguments, this rule was linked to the maxim that consideration must move from the promisee to the promisor, in spite of the fact that it seems clear that one rule can exist without the other.[308] In continental law, the rule is known as the 'principle of relativity of contract'. The principle is laid down expressly in some civil codes,[309] implied in some others,[310] and although it is not mentioned in some others,[311] it seems to be fundamental in all continental legal systems.[312]

129 The principle is considered to be the other side of the coin of the principle of the binding force of contracts, since both principles reflect different aspects of the principle of private autonomy or self-determination. Thus, when two parties enter a contract, they are bound to each other because they give their consent to it. For third parties the contract is a *res inter alios acta*, ie an affair that, in principle is not a matter of their concern. This does not mean, however, that the contract cannot have any effect on third parties or that they can ignore its coming into existence. These effects, in some legal systems, are included in what is known as the 'third party effectiveness' of the contract.[313] What the

305 US 47.
306 E&W 81.
307 (1861)1 B & S 393; 30 LJQB 265, 4 LT 468, 9 WR 781.
308 Cf *M Furstom/GJ Tolhurst*, Privity of Contract (2015) 28 ff.
309 Cf art 1165 French CC; art 1372 Italian CC; art 1257 Spanish CC.
310 Cf §§241, 305 BGB.
311 NL 52.
312 *Kötz* (fn 2) 319 ff; *Smits* (fn 2) 245 ff; *Cabrillac* (fn 2) 123 ff.
313 '*Opposabilité*', in French; '*opponibilità*' in Italian; '*oponiblidad*' in Spanish.

principle of relativity of contract means is that, since third parties have not given their consent to the contract, they cannot be bound by it and, vice versa, that contracting parties cannot be bound to third parties either, since contracts do not regularly involve their assent to it. From this point of view, the principle of relativity of contract follows from the reason why a contract confers rights and imposes obligations on third parties.

The principle of relativity of contract can be easily reconciled with the creation of third party rights if the parties intend to do so, since this doctrine only prevents the recognition of third party rights if they are not based on the will of the parties. Accordingly, its abrogation is not possible without destroying the basis of the law of contract.[314] By contrast, the doctrine of privity in contract had traditionally gone a little bit further in English law, since it was a technical rule which resulted from the requirement of consideration in the formation of the contract. English law finally broke with the rigidity of this doctrine when it passed the Contracts (Rights of Third Parties) Act 1999.[315] According to the Act, 'a person who is not a party to a contract (a "third party") may in his own right enforce a term of the contract'.[316] In spite of not being a full contracting party, he is treated for remedial purposes as if he were, since he may avail himself of 'any remedy that would have been available to him in an action for breach of contract if he had been a party to the contract'.[317] In the United States, the doctrine of privity in the strict traditional common law sense is unknown and §§302 and 304 of the Restatement (Second) of Contracts recognise a duty to an 'intended beneficiary' of a promise and an ability of such a beneficiary to enforce the duty.[318] 130

In the legal systems under survey, there are differences as regards many other aspects, such as whether the third party is considered a party to the contract[319] or not;[320] or whether the creation of a right enforceable by a third party need be explicit or it can be inferred from what the parties have expressed;[321] or, among many other aspects, which defences the promisor may invoke against the third party.[322] In any case, in all of them it is possible for the parties to the contract to establish rights in benefit of parties who, in their turn, may 131

314 *E du Perron*, Contract and Third Parties, in: A Hartkamp et al (eds), Towards a European Civil Code (1998) 331–326, 314.
315 E&W 82.
316 Sec 1(1).
317 Sec 1(5).
318 *EA Farnsworth*, Contracts (4th edn 2004) 651 ff, 655, referring to *Lawrence v Fox* 20 NY 268, 274 (1859) and other influential cases, and *Furstom/Tolhurst* (fn 308) 313 ff.
319 As, for instance, in art 6:254 Dutch CC. Cf *Smits* (fn 2) 248.
320 As in sec 1(1) and (5) Contracts (Rights of Third Parties) Act 1999.
321 *Beale et al* (fn 2) 1189 ff.
322 *Du Perron* (fn 314) 321 ff; *Kötz* (fn 2) 323 ff.

claim performance from the promisor. As regards the different proposals for harmonisation, although they do not coincide with each other in all its aspects, they are also unanimous in acknowledging the validity of contracts in favour of a third party.[323]

132 Nevertheless, the most relevant issue in the context of tracing the borderlines between contract and tort is not whether parties may agree to allow a third party to claim performance, but how the protection of third party interests connected to a contract can be carried out. In order to overcome the shortcomings of tort law, some legal systems have offered this protection by stretching the domain of contract law.

133 There are specific provisions in many legal systems that in particular situations allow a 'direct action' (*action directe*), ie that provide that a third party to the contract may bring a claim against the 'debtor of his debtor' to the extent of anything still owed by both of them. This is the case, for instance, when the landlord who is owed rent by his tenant is allowed to make a direct claim against the subtenant;[324] or when the principal is allowed to bring a claim against the subagent to whom his agent has delegated the contracted task;[325] or, more generally, in the case of the so-called 'direct right of action' that, in cases of traffic accidents, injured parties may bring 'against the insurance undertaking covering the person responsible against civil liability'.[326] However, leaving aside these specific cases provided by the law, most countries under survey do not allow, in general terms, stretching the protective scope of the contract to third parties who have not been mentioned in the contract or, at least, whose protection cannot result from an interpretation of the contractual will of the parties. The two clear exceptions to this trend are the so-called *action directe* in the case of certain 'chains of contracts', awarded by case law in France, and the doctrine of the protective effects of the contract with regard to third parties (*Vertrag mit Schutzwirkung zugunsten Dritter*), developed by German case law in the second half of the 20th century and also followed in Austria and Greece,[327] which apparently has found occasional application in other countries such as Italy[328] and which, in spite of timid attempts in favour of its use, has met with no success in Switzerland.[329]

---

323 *MPI/Du Perron*, Contract in Favour of a Third Party (2012) 387 f.

324 Art 1753 French CC; art 1595 Italian CC; art 1552 Spanish CC; art 599.2 Greek CC.

325 Art 1992 French CC; art 1705 (2) Italian CC; art 1722 Spanish CC; art 716.3 Greek CC.

326 Cf art 18 of the Directive 2009/103/EC of the European Parliament and of the Council of 16 September 2009 relating to insurance against civil liability in respect of the use of motor vehicles, and the enforcement of the obligation to insure against such liability [2009] OJ L263/11.

327 AT 31, GR 41.

328 IT 71 f.

329 CH 42.

134 In France, the starting point was the theory of contract groups ('*groupes de contrats*'), developed in the 1970s and approved in the 1980s by the First Chamber of the Cour de cassation, while it was strongly disapproved by the Third Chamber of that Court. This theory gave a contractual party an action in contract against a contractual party with whom he was not in privity as long as there was, between their contracts, a relationship that was so close that the events occurring in one contract could have effects on the other. After an expansive trend,[330] the *arrêt Besse* (12 July 1991)[331] rejected this theory, since it considered that it violated the principle of relativity of contract (cf art 1165 French CC). Although it did not do away with a general '*action directe*', it confined it to certain chains of contracts. Thus, the current position provides that there is an '*action directe*' in all chains of contracts that have the aim of transferring property, regardless of whether they are homogeneous, ie chains of contracts of sale, or heterogeneous, ie chains including at least one sale together with other commercial contracts.[332] This theory considers that the direct claim is transferred together with the contract, as an accessory to it, a solution that the Cour de cassation has considered to be compatible with the principle of relativity of contract. This direct claim, which is contractual in nature, must therefore respect the terms that the party against whom the claim is addressed has agreed in his contract. In order to honour them, the claimant cannot oblige this party to more than what he owed to his own creditor; conversely, the claimant cannot obtain from this other party along the chain more than what he would have obtained had he brought his claim against his own debtor.[333]

135 A more recent and practically important exception to the principle of relativity of contract results from the 2006 *Myr'ho* decision, where the Cour de cassation ruled that 'a third party to a contract may, on the basis of tortious liability, invoke a breach of contract whenever this breach has caused him harm'. In effect, this rule does away with the principle of relativity of contract in many cases. The liability it creates, however, is in tort and not in contract.[334] The consequences of this decision are not yet fully predictable, but it has been labelled as the outcome of a French taste for very general rules in the field of tort law and a bloating of contract law, especially through the introduction and multiplication of the *obligations de sécurité*. In its turn, the expansion of these obligations is also

330 For the details, *M Fabre-Magnan*, Droit des obligations I (4th edn 2016) 606–612.

331 No 90-13603; D 1991, 549, note *J Ghestin*; JCP 1991, II, 21743, note *G Viney*. For an English version see *van Gerven/Larouche/Lever* (fn 3) Supplement Tort 43/2 ff.

332 More in detail, *Fabre-Magnan* (fn 330) 611 f and *JS Borghetti*, Breach of Contract and Liability to Third Parties in French Law: How to Break the Deadlock?, ZEuP 2010, 279–303.

333 *Fabre-Magnan* (fn 330) 611 et passim.

334 Cass ass Plén, 6 October 2006, *Loubeyre et autres v SATL Myr'Ho et autre*, no 05-13.255, P+B+R+I, Bull, Civ ass Plén no 9; D 2006, 2825, note *G Viney*, JCP 2006, II, 10181, avis *Garazzio* et note *M Billiau*; RTD civ 2007, 123, obs *Jourdain*. FR 44 and *Borghetti* (fn 332) 289 ff.

the result of the *non cumul* rule adopted in the 1930s to try to keep a dividing line between tort and contract in the wake of the adoption and expansion of liability for things (*résponsabilité du fait des choses*).[335] An authorised but still minority opinion has suggested that if the projected French reforms set aside the *non cumul* rule, the contracting parties would thus be able to rely on the ordinary rules of tort law when the execution of the contract provides an occasion for death or personal injury or property damage (ie physical or tangible harm, in economic loss terminology) and then most *obligations de sécurité* would become useless or disappear. This would also enable a reduction of the scope of contract, which would no longer incorporate general duties of care embodied by *obligations de sécurité*, and these would cease to be used as a tool for the protection of the basic interests of the parties to the contract and, instead, would revert to their original function of providing the creditor with a protected interest which, in the absence of a contractual relationship, he would not have.[336] It has been contended that, if these reforms were carried out, it would be far clearer that 'the *Myr'ho* rule is, in fact, an infringement of the principle of relativity and of the legitimate expectations of the contracting parties' and that *Myr'ho* is 'a symptom that something has gone wrong at some point in the way that French law understands the relationship between contract and tort'.[337] Probably for this reason, the *Projet* now under debate devotes an article to providing an express antidote to the *Myr'ho* rule by establishing that where the non-performance of a contractual obligation is the direct cause of damage suffered by a third party, the third party can claim compensation from the debtor solely on the basis of non-contractual liability and only if the conditions required to establish liability in tort are met.[338]

136 With the so-called 'contract with protective effects to third parties' (*Vertrag mit Schutzwirkung zugunsten Dritter*) German law has also developed, from the beginning of the 20th century, a contractual approach to the protection of the interests of third parties.[339] By contrast to contracts for the benefit of third parties,

335 *Borghetti* (fn 332) 302.

336 Ibid, and also in *JS Borghetti*, Strict Liability in Tort and the Boundaries of Tort, in: H Koziol/U Magnus, Essays in Honour of Jaap Spier (2016) 19–54, 33 ff.

337 *Borghetti* (fn 332) 303.

338 Article 1234, al 1: 'Lorsque l'inexécution du contrat cause un dommage à un tiers, celui-ci ne peut demander réparation de ses conséquences au débiteur que sur le fondement de la responsabilité extracontractuelle, à charge pour lui de rapporter la preuve de l'un des faits générateurs visés à la section II du chapitre II'. While this rule appeared absolute in the *Avant-Projet*, the *Projet de Réforme* 2017 creates a major exception to it, by providing that a third party can actually have an option and choose to bring a claim in contract against the party in breach if he proves that he had a legitimate interest in the proper performance of the contract. This exception has been strongly criticised by some French authors, however, and it is not all certain that it will be maintained, should the contemplated reform finally take place.

339 DE 42.

these contracts do not grant third parties a right to claim performance, but only secondary duties of care and protection which, in the case of infringement, entitle them to bring a claim for damages in contract.

During the First World War, the Reichsgericht started including third parties in the protective scope of the contract, on the basis of the interpretation of the contract, by using devices such as the objective meaning and scope of the contract, *boni mores*, supplementary contract interpretation or implied agreement of the parties. The protected interests were regularly personal injury and property damage suffered by family members, workers or tenants and the underpinning idea of this new institution was the protection of vulnerable third parties. In the 1950s, following Karl Larenz, the Bundesgerichtshof coined the current name of this institution and justified it on the grounds of the responsibility of the contractual creditor for the weal and woe (*Wohl und Wehe*) of the third party, and the courts started to loosen ties with the clear fiction of the hypothetical will of the parties without breaking with them. In the middle of the 1960s, starting with a case imposing liability on a notary towards disappointed beneficiaries of a testator,[340] the institution was increasingly used for compensation for pure economic losses. During those years, it also started being applied to the pre-contractual, stage, which was considered by *Canaris* to be a clear 'third track' between contract and tort. In the 1970s, the 'weal and woe' idea lost strength and the institution was increasingly applied to non-vulnerable persons, including legal persons.[341] 137

The 2002 reform included the institution into the German Civil Code (cf §311 III 1 BGB), which now provides that a contractual obligation 'may also come into existence in relation to persons who are not themselves intended to be parties to the contract'. The legal provision does not mention the conditions that must be met, but according to case law: (a) the claimant must be endangered by the defendant's behaviour in the same way as the defendant's contract partner (*Leistungsnähe*); (b) the contract partner must be interested in the extension of the contractual effects and the contract must be able to be interpreted in this way (*Einbeziehungsinteresse*); and (c) the defendant must have been able to know of the claimant's endangerment and interest (*Erkennbarkeit*). However, even if all the previous requirements are met, it is generally contended that a further requirement is necessary, ie (d) that the third party has a need of protection. No such need exists and thus no such protection is required if third parties have a claim – either in contract or in tort – of their own.[342] 138

340 A case similar to the English case *White v Jones*. See below Case 2 (CR 238 ff).

341 *S Vogenauer*, §§328–335, Versprechen der Leistung an einen Dritten, in: M Schmoeckel/ J Rückert/R Zimmermann (eds), Historisch-kritischer Kommentar zum BGB, II/2 (2007) 2031 ff.

342 DE 85 and *H Kötz*, Vertragsrecht (2nd edn 2012) 217 ff and also *Beale et al* (fn 2) 1207 ff and AT 31.

139 A first group of cases to which the institution may apply are those where the third party suffers a harm to interests that are already protected in tort pursuant to §823 para 1 BGB. In these cases, the contractual route is used to circumvent the shortcomings of German tort law, such as the possibility of escaping liability for auxiliaries in tort through the requirement of fault of the principal (§831 BGB), by contrast to vicarious liability in contract (§278 BGB). The important matter here is not whether the interest of the third party is worth protection, but whether a contractual setting exists which, in contract, allows protection of the interest of the third party. The advantage offered by the contract route, however, may come down to the price of having to put up with defences, such as limitation of liability or prescription, that the debtor may have against his contractual party, which in this case he will also be able to invoke against the third party.

140 More important is a second group of cases where the third party does not suffer personal injury or property damage but only pure economic loss. Since this loss is not recoverable under liability for fault as it is not included in the list of the interests protected by §823 para 1 BGB, the main question here is whether it should be recoverable or not. Probably, the bitter criticism raised by some authors against this legal institution should be more focused on these types of cases. The echoes of the floodgates argument seem to reverberate in our ears when these critical voices affirm that this institution has been possible thanks 'to the conversion of contractual obligations into a social institution underpinned with aims of social protection, so that it should generate protective effects to an incalculable number of persons who were unknown to the debtor when the contract was concluded and who had not participated in the contract'.[343] With some exaggeration, the institution is attributed to the 'advancement of socialist ideas in private law' and it is then contended that 'it does not only sacrifice the will of the contractual parties to societal goals, but also demolishes the borders between contractual and tortious liability'.[344]

141 In fact, when pure economic loss is at stake, the constellation of cases solved in practice with this institution come very close to those solved in other legal systems in tort and which constitute exceptions to the recoverability of pure economic losses.[345] Besides Germany, among all the countries under survey, only Austria[346] seems to have adopted this extension of the contract to matters which, in the rest of the countries, are dealt with according to tort law rules. Harmonisation and international texts also ignore 'contracts with protective effects to third parties'.

---

343 *H Hattenhauer*, Grundbegriffe des Bürgerlichen Rechts (2nd edn 2000) 106.

344 Ibid, 106 f.

345 See above on pure economic loss, CR 90 ff.

346 AT 31.

H. DIFFERENCES AS REGARDS DEFENCES

A first caveat as regards 'defences' is that the term may have several meanings. 142
This comparative report follows the meaning adopted in the PETL,[347] which does not embrace, under the terminology of defences, those cases where the claimant fails to establish a basic requirement of liability ('absent element defences'), but only those that apply when all the requirements for liability are established and allow the defendant to escape liability ('affirmative defences') and also to reduce liability.[348] Even more: according to the PETL, all defences which the PETL cover allow not only the exclusion, but also the reduction of liability.[349]

A second caveat as regards defences is that what is considered as a 'defence' 143
is not the same in all jurisdictions under review. Thus, for instance, what some jurisdictions consider defects or vices of consent (such as mistake, misrepresentation, duress and undue influence), others consider to be defences which naturally apply only to contract.[350] This would also be the case, for instance, with some remedies such as the 'right to withhold performance', which the debtor may bring against the creditor's claim when performance is already due and the creditor has not performed (traditionally known as *exceptio non adimpleti contractus*), or when performance is not yet due, but the party who has to perform first has a good reason to believe that the other party is not going to perform.[351] A special type of withholding performance is the so-called 'right of retention', which allows a creditor to retain a good until the owner has met his obligations that relate to it (for instance, a hotel owner keeps luggage or a garage owner keeps a repaired car as long as the guest or the car's owner do not pay the corresponding bill).[352] However, trying to establish a parallelism between

---

347 *European Group on Tort Law*, Principles of European Tort Law. Text and Commentary (2005) 120 f.

348 What Goudkamp does not consider defences properly and would apparently call 'remedy restricting rules'. *J Goudkamp*, A Taxonomy of Tort Law Defences, in: S Degeling/J Edelman/ J Goudkamp (eds), Torts in Commercial Law (2011) 467–469.

349 See art 7:101, 2 PETL for defences based on justifications, and art 7:102, 2 PETL for defences against strict liability. According to art 8:101 PETL, contributory negligence ('contributory conduct or activity') may not only reduce liability, but also exclude it. See also in this sense CH 46.

350 IL 53 and for the United States *RE Barnett*, Contracts (2010) 209 ff, lists under the heading 'Defenses to Contractual Obligations' the most common defences to the enforcement of an otherwise valid contract into three categories: (1) lack of contractual capacity (incompetence, intoxication and infancy); (2) obtaining assent by improper means (misrepresentation, duress, undue influence and unconscionability); and (3) the failure of a basic assumption (mistake of present existing fact, commercial impracticability and frustration of purposes).

351 See, for instance, §§320 and 321 BGB, art 1460 Italian CC, arts 6:262 and 6:262 BW, and art 9:201 PECL. See *Smits* (fn 2) 240.

352 The right of retention is codified in arts 1612 and 2286 French CC (*droit de rétention*), §273 BGB and §369 German Commercial Code (*Zurückbehaltungsrecht*) and art 3:290 Dutch CC (*retentierecht*), as well as in arts 325 and 1095 Greek CC. English law enacts

defences in contract and in tort, these and similar remedies could be grouped under the heading of 'self-help' remedies on the grounds that in these cases the claimant needs no assistance from the court or from any third party to affect them and act as defences that are specific to contract law.[353]

144 Accordingly, some jurisdictions consider that there are a variety of defences found only in contract or in tort because they are particular to the context in which these areas operate,[354] but most of them point out that although contractual agreements may validly vary or exclude defences, there are basically no differences between tort and contract.[355] Although it was debatable whether it referred to the same in both contexts, French law traditionally used the same definition of force majeure in tort and in contract. However, the new art 1231-1 *Code civil* gives a definition of force majeure which only applies to contract law.[356]

145 One of the most important defences is contributory negligence, which in all the countries under survey, except in England and Wales[357] and in South Africa,[358] applies both to contract and tort. In England and Wales, contributory negligence is regulated by the Law Reform (Contributory Negligence) Act 1945 and is not generally available as a defence to a claim for breach of contract. It can only be raised in cases of concurrent liability in contract and in tort, where the defence of contributory negligence is available to the defendant if sued in contract when he could equally have raised it had he been sued in tort. In this sense, it can be said that it is allowed as a defence in the contract so as to avoid the claimant obtaining a better remedy by choosing to sue in tort when the essential nature of the concurrent contract and tort claims is identical.[359] Without this restriction, however, both in contract and in tort, the defendant

---

a right of retention for the unpaid seller (seller's lien) in the Sale of Goods Act 1979, sec 41, but also recognises such a lien in common law, equity and maritime law if further specific requirements are met. See *Smits* (fn 2) 242.

353 *D Campbell* in: D Harris/D Campbell/R Halson, Remedies in Contract and in Tort (3rd edn 2010) 43 ff.

354 US 54.

355 AT 32, CZ 75, DE 44, NL 53, CH 44, PL 98 ff, ES 60 ff.

356 'Il y a force majeure en matière contractuelle lorsqu'un événement échappant au contrôle du débiteur, qui ne pouvait être raisonnablement prévu lors de la conclusion du contrat et dont les effets ne peuvent être évités par des mesures appropriées, empêche l'exécution de son obligation par le débiteur'. Art 1253 al 2 *Avant-Projet* confirms that force majeure should be defined differently in tort law by saying that: 'En matière extracontractuelle, la force majeure est l'événement échappant au contrôle du défendeur ou de la personne dont il doit répondre, et dont ceux-ci ne pouvaient éviter ni la réalisation ni les conséquences par des mesures appropriées'. FR 46.

357 E&W 85.

358 ZA 30 f.

359 E&W 85 and *Cartwright* (fn 4) 296.

may resort to the rules of mitigation. Although these rules have been developed mainly in cases of breach of contract, they also apply in principle to torts.

The distinction between contributory negligence and mitigation (also known as 'avoidable consequences') seems to be between the conduct of the claimant before and after the damage-causing event.[360] In the former case, the conduct of the creditor or victim contributed to the damaging event, whereas in the latter it relates to some consequential loss in the subsequent development. The consequences of the distinction are quite important. Whereas in the case of contributory negligence the 'all-or-nothing' principle has been abandoned and there is an apportionment between claimant and defendant, mitigation may not give rise to apportionment and the claimant who has failed to mitigate may bear the entire loss attributable to his conduct. 146

Most of the legal systems under survey have specific rules that consider mitigation to be a subspecies of contributory negligence and apply the same rules.[361] However, in some of these countries, legal writing still discusses whether the apportionment principle also applies to the duty to mitigate.[362] In this context the only exception establishing a clear rule of no apportionment seems to be Italy, where the Civil Code expressly provides that the additional loss, which the aggrieved party could have avoided by taking reasonable steps, will as a whole stay where it falls and, accordingly, will not give rise to compensation (cf art 1227, 2 *Codice civile*). While most of the international texts on contracts and also the European texts for contract harmonisation favour the English approach, and distinguish contributory negligence and mitigation and reject apportionment in this later case,[363] the PETL follow the continental common approach (cf art 8:101(1) PETL). It has been argued that failing to take measures in order to reduce the loss does not take away the causal connection between the liability-creating event and the additional loss. For this reason, this loss is the result of conduct which is attributable both to the claimant and to the defendant and, therefore, it should also be apportioned between both parties to the degree that each has contributed to the loss. It is also submitted that 147

360 ZA 30 f and *H Rogers* in: U Magnus/M Martín-Casals, Unification of Tort Law: Contributory Negligence (2003) 59.

361 See, for instance, art 44(I) OR; art 6.101 (1) Dutch; §254 (2) (1) BGB; art 300 Greek CC.

362 For a detailed comparative analysis see *A Keirse*, Why the Proposed Optional Common European Sales Law Has Not, But Should Have, Abandoned the Principle of All or Nothing: A Guide to How to Sanction the Duty to Mitigate the Loss (2011) 6 ERPL 951–976. See also *MPI/N Jansen*, Contributory Negligence (Contributory Conduct or Activity) (2012) 401–403 and *H Koziol*, Rechtsfolgen der Verletzung einer Schadensminderungspflicht – Rückkehr der archaischen Kulpakompensation?, ZEuP 6/1998, 593.

363 See arts 77 CISG, 7.4.8(1) PIIC and arts 9:504 and 9:505 (1) PECL; art II.-3:705(1) DCFR. Following the other approach, however, art 8:403 Acquis Principles.

this approach is more balanced and also that it seems to be gaining ground in European scholarship.[364]

I. DIFFERENCES AS REGARDS LIMITATION PERIODS

148 It has been pointed out that one of the policy grounds underpinning prescription is the need to prevent unnecessarily costly and long-drawn-out lawsuits (*ut sit finis litium*) and that for this reason, it would be intolerable if the prescription rules themselves could easily give rise to litigation.[365] Nevertheless, this is what actually happened in many countries before the wave of law reform on prescription swept Europe over the last decades. In fact, in some countries, the main efforts exerted to tracing the boundaries between contract and tort have their origin in very disparate periods of prescription, which have led litigators to try to convince judges that their claims were actually based on one ground (normally contract, since in most cases the prescription period was longer), when they would have already been time-barred if based on the other.[366]

149 One trait that seems common to all countries is that the law of prescription has developed rather by happenstance, depending on which of the conflicting interests was to be considered worthy of protection in a particular type of legal relationship and these differentiated prescription regimes have led to problems of delimitation and to conceptual distortion.[367] This bad

364 *Keirse* (fn 362) 975 ff.

365 *R Zimmermann*, Comparative Foundations of a European Law of Set-Off and Prescription (2002) 80. Also *R Zimmermann/J Kleinschmidt*, Prescription: General Framework and Special Problems Concerning Damages Claims, in: H Koziol/BC Steininger (eds), European Tort Law 2007 (2008) 26–78; *MPI/R Zimmermann*, Prescription (2012) 1306–1310 and *MJ Bonell*, Limitation Periods, in: A Hartkamp et al (eds), Towards a European Civil Code (2011) 715–732.

366 CH 47 f and also ES 66 ff. As regards English law, *NH Andrews*, Reform of Limitation of Actions: The quest for sound policy (1998) 57(3) Cambridge Law Journal 589–610, 605 has pointed out that: '[T]he modern law of obligations has been bedevilled and, arguably, contorted by a conceptual distinction between the accrual of contractual and certain tortious causes of action. It is time for the law of limitation to be changed so that the tail (limitation rules) no longer wags the dog (the substantive principles of liability in contract and tort)'.

367 For instance, as regards the current regulation in England and Wales, the English Law Commission has pointed out that there are cases of 'glaring incoherence' such as that 'the limitation period applicable to actions for personal injury will depend on whether the injury was inflicted deliberately or negligently and, bizarrely, this can sometimes mean that a plaintiff is worse off, as regards limitation, by being the victim of an intentionally-inflicted injury than a negligently-inflicted one' or that 'a claim for latent damage to property which results from a neighbour's use of land will have a limitation period of six years from accrual if pursued in the tort of nuisance, but three years from discoverability or six years from accrual, whichever is the later, if pursued in the tort of negligence'. See Limitation of Actions (Consultation Paper no 151, 1998) 241 and E&W 86 ff.

experience has led legislatures that have amended the rules of prescription to unify not only the prescription periods but also the prescription regimes as a whole.

In some of the jurisdictions under survey, no general legal reform of the regime of prescription has been carried out so far and in these countries one of the most prominent differences between claims in contract and in tort is still the length of the prescription period.[368] However, the reform of the prescription rules carried out in most of the jurisdictions under survey has followed a clear tendency towards: (a) uniformity of general prescription regimes, at least in the area of the law of obligations; (b) much shorter prescription periods, generally between three[369] and five[370] years; (c) the generalisation of the 'discoverability rule', ie the idea that prescription should not start running until the creditor knew or ought reasonably to have known of his claim; (d) as a counterbalance to short (minimum) prescription periods, the use of maximum prescription periods (or long-stop periods), starting at the time the claim accrues and after which no claim can be brought regardless of the creditor's knowledge; and, finally, (e) a more or less extensive freedom of the parties to modify by agreement the regime of prescription established by the law.[371] 150

Leaving aside this last characteristic – which can have no place in the area of tort law, since usually the parties do not have the opportunity to negotiate anything before the accident gives rise to liability in tort – the first question that comes up is whether there is a convincing reason for establishing differentiated prescription regimes for claims in contract and for claims in tort as, for instance, the traditional longer prescription periods for contractual claims, when compared to tortious claims, would seem to indicate. 151

The prevailing legal opinion considers that there do not appear to be any general criteria which would be both sufficiently clear and convincing to provide a basis for a differentiated prescription regime between contract and tort claims and, in general, within the law of obligations.[372] It is submitted that claims 152

368 Greece (GR 44 ff), the general prescription period being 20 years in contract and five in tort, which becomes 20 years from the commission of the act if the injured party continues not to have knowledge of the damage and of the person liable to pay damages; or Italy 10 years in contract and five in tort; or Spain – except Catalonia – 15 (recently amended to five) in contract and one in tort (ES 66 ff); or in Switzerland (CH 47 ff) 10 in contract and one or two in tort.

369 This is the case for instance in AT 33, CZ 76, DE 45 or ZA 33.

370 This is the case, for instance, in NL 55 or in FR 48. However, in France the normal period of five years (art 2224 CC), becomes a 10-year period in case of personal injury (art 2226, 1 CC). In Spain, the only reform carried out so far in general Spanish law has been to reduce the 15-year general period for personal actions to five, ES 66 ff.

371 *Zimmermann*, Comparative Foundations of a European Law (fn 365) 85 ff.

372 Ibid, 81 f, and footnote 89.

in the area of the law of obligations are interconnected and hardly any claim in this field can be dealt with in isolation; this interconnectedness is of particular relevance in the case of prescription and differentiated periods of prescription tend to lead to inconsistencies.[373] Prescription regimes must be clear, certain, predictable and not unnecessarily complex and, for these reasons, require as few exceptions as possible. On these grounds, it is considered that it is distinctly better to have a regime that does not suit all claims equally well than one that makes it difficult for debtors as well as for creditors to assess their position and adjust their behaviour accordingly.[374]

153 This position, however, does not mean that uniformity must be absolute, but only, in our case, that the contract–tort divide is not a sufficient ground for having different regimes and that a single general regime, if its components are properly designed, can apply to both sorts of claims and avoid endless discussion on the contractual or tortious condition of a claim. Thus, for instance, as regards the length of the general prescription period in the context of tort law, economic analysis points out that there are good reasons to believe that relatively short prescription periods are efficient and save the substantial costs of preserving evidence and other expenses.[375] And it can be added that, in the case of contract claims, the freedom of the parties to modify prescription periods by agreement allows them to adjust them to the distribution of risks bargained for in the contract.

154 Since prescription regimes are based on a delicate balance of conflicting interests and on a complex subset of rules that together construct the prescription regime, attention must be paid to all components of the prescription regime in a given legal system. As important as the length of the minimum and the maximum prescription periods and the moment from which they start to run are other components, such as in which circumstances prescription can be suspended or, by contrast, interrupted and start to run afresh, and how this suspension and interruption (or renewal) can take place. All these rules are closely interrelated. Thus, a short limitation period of one year may be too short if it runs from an objective date, such as the date of the damaging event, regardless of whether the victim knew or could have known about the claim. By contrast, it can even be too long if it is subject to the discoverability rule and can be easily interrupted as many times as desired, starting thereby afresh every time the victim brings an out-of-court claim, which can even be filed by a specific certified mail procedure.[376] For this reason, economic analysis also considers

---

[373] Ibid, 85.

[374] Ibid.

[375] *I Gilead*, Economic Analysis of Prescription in Tort Law, in: H Koziol/BC Steininger (eds), European Tort Law 2007 (2008) 112, no 52.

[376] This is the case, for instance, in Spain, ES 66 ff.

that an efficiency analysis of a prescription rule which disregards the other rules that compose the prescription regime is misleading, since questions can only be answered in context, not in isolation.[377]

The practical problems associated with prescription are not related to the contract–tort divide but to the combination of the different components of the prescription regime, such as the discovery rule and long-stop periods, in cases such as latent damage or sexual abuse suffered by children, which even reformed prescription regulations have not solved in a fully satisfactory manner.[378] 155

In the case of latent damage, the problem arises because damage is discoverable only long after the damaging event took place, with the result that even the long-stop period may occasionally have already lapsed before the victim has had the chance to bring the claim. This has been the case with asbestos-related diseases, such as asbestosis and mesothelioma, which have very long latency periods, but it can also be the case with personal injury caused by other substances.[379] 156

A possible solution to these cases is to establish different long-stop periods for personal injury claims. This solution was adopted by the 2002 reform of the German Civil Code, which, by contrast to the regular 10-year long-stop period, provides for a thirty-year period for damages claims for the infringement of life, bodily integrity, health or liberty (§199 (2) BGB).[380] 157

Another possible solution is to do away with the long-stop period in the case of personal injury. This solution was adopted in the Netherlands by an amendment carried out in 2004. Thus in this country, cases of personal injury and death are only governed by the normal five-year period, starting in this case – and by contrast to the general discovery rule – not from actual discovery but from discoverability of the harm, which in this case is equated to knowledge (cf art 3:310 (5) CC).[381] Similar solutions were adopted by the 2008 amendment of the French Civil Code, which now provides that the general long-stop period of twenty years does not apply, among other specific cases, to claims for personal injury (cf art 2232 French CC, in connection with art 2226 French CC);[382] and also in Poland in 2007 where, after a decision of the Constitutional Court,[383] the new amended provision 'suspends' all long-stops of 10 years (or twenty years, 158

377 *Gilead* (fn 375) nos 39 and 40.

378 This is also the case in the United States with the 'statutes of repose', US 65.

379 See *M Martín-Casals*, The Development of Liability in Relation to Technological Change (2010) 33 ff and *Zimmermann/Kleinschmidt* (fn 365) 51 ff.

380 DE 45.

381 NL 56.

382 FR 51.

383 Constitutional Court decision of 1 September 2006 (SK 14/05), reported by *E Bagińska* in: H Koziol/BC Steininger (eds), European Tort Law 2006 (2008) 373, nos 83–90.

in the case of damage resulting from crime or misdemeanour) in personal injury cases.[384] The 2012 new Czech Civil Code does not apply the 10-year general long-stop period to personal injury cases either[385] and this is also the case in Norway.[386]

159 Other solutions are possible,[387] but in any case the problem of damage with a long latency period, asbestos-related diseases being the most conspicuous, must be solved by private law rules if no other sets of rules, regarding social insurance models or special funds, are available.[388] Relaxing prescription rules in one way or another is a valid reason if this is the only way to compensate deserving victims, and the importance of art 6 ECHR and other national constitutional provisions which guarantee all citizens access to justice, as shown in Polish case law, cannot be underestimated.[389]

160 Another problematic area refers to damages claims brought by persons who suffered sexual abuse when they were underage.[390] Although it is true that in this case some legal systems consider that the time limitation of the civil action does not run out as long as the criminal action does not prescribe,[391] and others provide for a specific longer long-stop period,[392] the fact is that occasionally even these long periods will not be long enough to allow the victim to bring a claim. In these cases, leading legal opinion considers that it is preferable to suspend prescription until the minor reaches the age of majority.[393]

---

384 PL 107 ff.

385 CZ 76 ff.

386 NO 51.

387 Such as allowing the long-stop from the time that damage occurs, independently of knowledge, as in the Austria reform draft (see *E Karner*, Geldersatz für ideelle Schäden, Minderung der Ersatzpflicht, Beweislast, Verjährung, in: L Griss/G Kathrein/H Koziol (eds), Entwurf eines neues österreichischen Schadenersatzrechts (2006) 93 or in Catalonia, according to Lamarca's interpretation of art 121-4 of the Catalan Civil Code, in *A Lamarca Marques* in: A Vaquer Aloy/A Lamarca (eds), Comentari a la nova regulació de la prescripció i caducitat en el Dret civil de Catalunya (2005) 281–285. In Italy, case law has established that in cases where damage appears a very long time after the unlawful conduct, the *dies a quo* starts from the time the victim has perceived that his injury was due to a previous specific wrongful act (IT 84). For a more problematic solution, which would allow courts to extend prescription in certain cases, see *Zimmermann/Kleinschmidt* (fn 365) 52.

388 Additionally, one has to bear in mind not only that social security rules, even the German ones, do not furnish full compensation (loss of earnings up to two thirds), but also that not all asbestos-related diseases are occupational diseases and therefore, as in the case of contamination of premises by the use of asbestos as insulating material, are suffered by victims who were not necessarily employees of the tortfeasor.

389 Defending the opposing opinion, *Zimmermann/Kleinschmidt* (fn 365) 56 ff.

390 *Zimmermann/Kleinschmidt* (fn 365) 64 ff.

391 As, for instance, in the Netherlands, art 3:310 (1) Dutch CC, NL 55.

392 For instance, 20 years in Poland (PL 107).

393 *Zimmermann/Kleinschmidt* (fn 365) 76 or, as §208 BGB provides, to his or her 21st birthday.

J. DIFFERENCES AS REGARDS PROOF

In all countries under survey, there are no procedural rules of proof specifically carved out for contract or tort claims. Proof is governed by procedural rules that are common to contract and tort and, as a rule, the claimant bears the burden of proving the elements which give ground to his claim, and the defendant those which oppose it.[394] 161

Accordingly, in contract law, claimants normally have to prove breach or non-performance and the specific facts related to the specific remedy they are seeking. When the remedy sought is damages, in those countries where the applicability of the remedy requires fault,[395] the general rule is that fault is regularly presumed. This is the case, for instance, in Austria, where the burden of proof of fault is reversed at the expense of the defendant, who will have to prove that he was not at fault (§1298 ABGB).[396] The same principle applies to other countries such as Germany, Greece, Italy, Norway, Poland, South Africa, Spain or Switzerland.[397] By contrast, in tort law claims, the claimant will usually have to prove damage, causation, and also fault – provided that fault is required by the corresponding tort law rule. Thus, for instance in Austria, in fault-based tort liability cases, it is for the claimant to prove that the defendant acted with fault (§1296 ABGB) and this is also the case in most countries under survey.[398] However, under specific circumstances, such as when the activity that gives rise to damage is very risky, legislatures or courts may shift the burden of proof of fault in tort.[399] Conversely, in some specific contracts, fault may not be presumed and proof by the claimant is required.[400] 162

There are no differences either as regards the ordinary standard of proof, whether a clear and convincing evidence standard is required, as in most continental jurisdictions,[401] or whether a preponderance of evidence standard or 'balance of probabilities' suffices.[402] 163

---

394 In this sense, AT 34 ff, CZ 82 ff, E&W 22 ff, FR 52 ff, DE 48 ff, GR 48, PL 111 ff, ES 70.

395 See above CR 4.

396 Obviously, as in all countries, this is only true for the requirement of fault as such, whereas it is for the claimant to prove that the defendant acted with gross negligence or intent: AT 2 fn 4.

397 DE 48, GR 48, IT 17–20, NO 54, PL 111, ZA 34, CH 49. The same is true for Spain, although some legal scholars point out that the debtor does not escape liability by proving he was careful, but by proving that breach was caused by a supervening impossibility which was not attributable to him only. Cf ES 71.

398 Such as DE 48, GR 48, IT 21, PL 111, ZA 32, ES 71, CH 49.

399 For instance, IT 34, PL 111 or ES 71.

400 DE 48.

401 AT 35, DE 49, PL 112, CH 50.

402 As in E&W 22, US 71, but also in NO 53.

164 As regards the proof of damage, there are no differences either, although certain heads of loss, such as non-pecuniary loss, future pecuniary loss or loss of chance, which are more common in tort than in contract, may give rise to more problems regarding proof of damage.[403]

K. OTHER DIFFERENCES

165 Most countries under survey point out the different rules governing contractual capacity and tortious capacity.[404] Thus, the requirements for the capacity of persons for the two types of liability are such that, in a given case, a person may be held liable in tort but not in contract. This is the case in some countries where children can be held liable in tort at a certain younger age, usually between seven and 14 years,[405] whereas full contractual capacity is only gained at the age of 18 (or before, if the child has been emancipated[406]). Below this age, children have a reduced contractual capacity depending on their age, the subject matter of the contract (for instance, they have contractual capacity for 'current matters of everyday life'[407]) or the participation of their legal representatives. Occasionally, this different capacity may give rise to problems in the grey zone between contract and tort, as is the case in Austria with pre-contractual liability.[408]

166 A second difference, which refers to the transmissibility of claims has, in fact, more to do with the type of loss that is being claimed than with the contract–tort divide. Especially problematic is the transmissibility of claims for non-pecuniary loss when either the claimant or the defendant die before the court has decided the issue. A typical case refers to victims of accidents who die, normally because of the accident, before being able to bring the claim for personal injury. Although most jurisdictions approve transmissibility with no further conditions[409] and allow their heirs to bring the claim for the non-pecuniary losses suffered by the victim, others do not,[410] or require at least

---

403 See, for instance, E&W 49.

404 AT 36, FR 55 f, DE 50, GR 50, IL 58, IT 89, PL 114, ES 76, ZA 36, NL 58.

405 For instance, seven years, or in some cases 10 in Germany (DE 50), 10 in Greece (GR 70), 12 in Israel (IL 58) or 14 in Austria (AT 36), Poland (PL 114) or the Netherlands (NL 58). In other countries such as the Czech Republic, England and Wales, Italy, Spain or Switzerland, there is no threshold age, and tortious capacity depends on the maturity of the child. In France, since some decisions in 1984, the French Cour de cassation has established that children are always liable for the damage they cause regardless of their age and capacity (FR 56). See in more detail *Martín-Casals* (fn 270) no 5 ff, 425 ff.

406 In this sense, for instance, FR 55 and ES 76.

407 As, for instance, in Poland (PL 115).

408 AT 36.

409 For instance, FR 58.

410 PL 117, with some exceptions created by the courts.

that the claimant had filed the claim before dying[411] or that the victim survived for a reasonable lapse of time before death.[412]

Other differences worth mentioning refer to the jurisdiction of the courts and the applicable rules of conflicts of laws. Thus, as a rule, territorial jurisdiction corresponds to the court of the domicile of the defendant, but in contract the territorial competent court can be the court of the place of delivery or performance of the service and in tort the place where the damaging event took place or where the damage was suffered.[413] As regards the rules of conflicts of laws, in tort claims the most common point of connection is the law corresponding to the place where the damaging event occurred (*lex loci delicti commissi*).[414] By contrast, the contractual claim may be governed by the law to which the parties have expressly submitted to or, subsidarily, by the law corresponding to other connection points, such as the law at the seat of the party that effects the characteristic performance of the contract[415] or the law common to both parties, the place of common residence or the law where the contract was concluded (*lex loci contractus*).[416] 167

L. REASONS FOR THE DIFFERENCES?

The differences can be attributed to the different functions of these two fields, as, for instance, the need to protect the expectation of the parties that have their grounds in the contract they have concluded which, in order to facilitate and protect socially desirable transactions, requires that damages awards include positive or expectation interest. Tort law, however, may confine itself to compensating the negative or reliance interest, since it imposes non-consensual duties that are aimed to protect the public at large from risks of harm that are socially undesirable.[417] 168

The differences are also historical. In continental systems with codes, contract and tort are two separate sources of law[418] and when these codes were drafted, 169

411 As in France before 1976 (FR 58), in GR 51, ZA 39, or as an exception in Poland (PL 119). See in more detail, *WVH Rogers*, Comparative Report, in: WVH Rogers, Damages for Non-Pecuniary Loss in a Comparative Perspective (2001) no 29, 259 f. Moreover in the United States it may affect the scope of the decision making of the juries in the proceedings, see US 75.

412 IT 92.

413 FR 57, IT 90 f, PL 119, ZA 37, ES 76.

414 See for the EU Member States (except Denmark) art 4 Rome II Regulation, although the parties may also choose the applicable tort law under certain restrictions (art 14 Rome II).

415 Again for the EU see arts 3 and 4 Rome I Regulation.

416 ZA 38.

417 DE 52 ff, IL 59, FR 61, IT 47, NO 56, ZA 41, US 79.

418 GR 53, FR 1, IT 93–96, PL 120, ZA 41, ES 78. In France, however, the Government's draft project clearly adopts an approximation approach, FR 62.

tort law was not as important as it is today. In common law, the categories contract and tort are not to be found in the early common law and they began to emerge in England and Wales at the end of the 17th century,[419] developing separately, and tort law became an independent category later on as, for instance, in the United States in the mid- to late 19th century.[420]

170 Finally, some specific differences that we find in particular rules reflect the spirit of the time prevailing when they were drafted. This is the case, for instance, with the differences concerning liability for others in contract and in tort that can be found in the German Civil Code, which still stem from the age of liberalism when the drafters of the Code wanted to secure a far-reaching economic and commercial freedom for employers and enterprises.[421]

III. LIMITATION OR EXCLUSION OF LIABILITY ARISING FROM TORT AND FROM CONTRACT

A. STATUTORY PROVISIONS AUTHORISING A LIMITATION OR EXCLUSION OF LIABILITY

171 Freedom of contract allows the contracting parties to limit or exclude their liability beforehand when they conclude a contract. Some civil codes implicitly authorise limitations of liability in case of breach of contract, by mentioning clauses whereby the parties set in advance damages owed in case of breach[422] (see penalty clauses/liquidated damages above sec II.C.5). However, the validity and effectiveness of such clauses is subject to a certain number of conditions.

172 General limitations to this freedom can be found in a wide variety of statutory provisions preventing the parties from limiting or excluding liability in a certain type of contract, such as contracts concluded with hotel keepers, air carriers, train operators and, in general, travel contracts, or in cases of traffic liability or product liability.[423] Some other statutes provide for caps or limitations in the maximum amount of damages. This is the case in some countries in statutes establishing strict liability, in areas such as traffic liability,[424] transport law, nuclear liability, oil pollution, etc.[425] Sometimes caps can also be found in

---

419 E&W 1.
420 US 78.
421 DE 54.
422 FR 63 and art 1235-1 (formerly art 1152) French CC, and ES 41 and art 1152 Spanish CC.
423 For instance, AT 39 ff and PL 126.
424 DE 55, ZA 43.
425 IT 97 f, ZA 43.

statutes providing liability for fault, if fault is slight only. This is the case, for instance, as regards liability of auditors (€1 million in Germany when not acting with gross negligence or intent).[426] In the Netherlands, caps can also be set by decree, not only in cases of strict liability, but whenever it is necessary to prevent that liability exceeds the damage that can reasonably be covered by insurance (art 6:110 CC).[427] In some jurisdictions, statutory caps are alien to the national legal tradition and to large extent many of them have their origin in international conventions.[428]

Freedom of contract is not paramount either, since in some countries, such as the Netherlands, the Czech Republic, Norway or Poland,[429] there are statutory provisions that give courts the power to limit liability both in contract and in tort under certain conditions, irrespective of what the parties had agreed in the contract. 173

Thus, in the Netherlands (art 6:109 CC), courts may moderate the amount of damages if compensation in full would lead to unacceptable results taking into account the circumstances, among which the provision mentions 'the nature of liability, the legal relationship between the parties and their financial resources'. In these cases, it is also important whether the debtor had covered his liability by insurance 'or was compelled to do so', since then liability cannot be reduced to a lower amount than this insurance coverage.[430] 174

The Czech Civil Code (§2953) also considers that, unless the debtor was a professional in breach of his professional duties or caused damage with intent, courts may reduce damages taking into account the circumstances of the occurrence of the damage and the personal and financial situation of both the wrongdoer and the victim.[431] Something similar also applies under Norwegian law, even if the debtor acts as a professional.[432] 175

In relations as between natural persons, Polish courts may also reduce the awards of damages according to the circumstances of the case, including the economic position of the parties and the degree of the actor's fault if, having regard to the financial circumstances of the injured person or those of the person liable for the damage, the principles of fairness require such limitation (cf art 440 Polish CC). This rule is interpreted strictly and rarely applied by the courts, as it only concerns physical persons (typically uninsured).[433] 176

---

426 DE 56.

427 NL 60 f.

428 FR 65, PL 126.

429 Also in Spain art 1103 CC, but without giving any further guidance to judges.

430 NL 62.

431 CZ 94, IL 61.

432 NO 58–60.

433 PL 123.

177 In Spain, courts are also statutorily allowed to reduce the debtor's liability in the case of contractual liability for fault on a case by case basis (art 1103 Spanish CC). Although the language of the provision conveys the idea that such a reduction may apply 'in every kind of obligations', legal scholarship has suggested that it is only so in the case of damage caused by a contractual breach which, although foreseeable as such, was not foreseeable as regards its amount. However, Spanish courts have made ample use of that judicial power, both in contract and in tort cases. Case law describes such a rule as an exception to the principle of full compensation, which is based on equity and is justified by the lack of proportion between damage caused and the negligent conduct of its author. For many years, the rule was linked to contributory negligence, but now it is clear that the power to mitigate conferred to the courts is not related to this defence (STS 19.2.2014 (RJ 2014, 1129)). By contrast to similar mitigation clauses existing in other jurisdictions, the Spanish provision does not give any yardstick to the courts, which may thus reduce liability according to their discretion and even *ex officio*.[434]

B. LIMITATION OR EXCLUSION OF CONTRACTUAL AND TORTIOUS LIABILITY BY CONTRACT

178 A general rule that is accepted in all jurisdictions is that liability cannot be limited or excluded in the case of damage caused with intent[435] and, in most jurisdictions, this rule also applies to damage caused with gross negligence. This is the case in France where, since art 1231-3 (formerly art 1150) *Code civil* provides that the limitation of damage to foreseeable damage does not apply when breach of contract is intentional, case law considers that liability cannot be limited or excluded in case of intentional breach by the debtor or his auxiliaries, and has traditionally extended this rule to breaches resulting from gross negligence (*faute lourde*).[436] This is also the case in the Czech Republic (§2898 CC),[437] Italy (art 1229 CC), Greece (art 332 CC)[438] and Switzerland (art 100 para 1 SCO),[439] where their respective civil codes specifically provide that any previous limitation or exclusion of the obligation to compensate for damage caused intentionally or by gross negligence is void. In other jurisdictions, such as in Austria, it is also commonly agreed that it is not allowed to limit or

434 ES 24 and 80.
435 AT 43, PL 128, ZA 45.
436 FR 66. See also NO 61.
437 CZ 89.
438 GR 56.
439 CH 53.

exclude damage caused with intent, but the opinions are split in the case of gross negligence.[440] The situation is rather different in Germany, where the German Civil Code also provides that a party can limit or exclude its liability except in the case of intent (§276 (3) BGB). However, this is understood in the sense that liability for gross negligence may be excluded.[441]

In some jurisdictions, the same rule that applies to debtors applies to damage caused by their auxiliaries,[442] whereas in others, such as Germany (cf §278 sent 2 BGB) and Switzerland (art 101 para 2 SCO), debtors may exclude in advance liability for damage caused by their auxiliaries even where liability is for intent.[443] 179

The protected interest is also relevant when it comes to the acceptance of limitation or exclusion clauses. The general rule is that limitations or exclusions of liability for personal injury are not valid.[444] Sometimes the idea of the protected interest is embedded in the idea of public policy or *ordre public*, so that all limitations that infringe the *ordre public* are invalid.[445] For instance, in Spain, it is considered that the *ordre public* prevents from being validly agreed upon clauses that: (a) negatively affect the protection of the physical or moral integrity of the person; (b) impinge upon other fundamental rights; (c) violate human dignity; (d) exclude liability for damage caused with intent or gross negligence; or (e) imply a position of abuse of dominant position.[446] 180

It is also relevant whether the contract was concluded between professionals or whether it is a consumer contract. In consumer contracts, besides the already mentioned exclusion of clauses affecting death or personally injury of the consumer or damage caused with intent or negligence, clauses can be considered unfair or abusive if they exclude or limit in an inadequate manner the legal rights of the consumers in the case of total or partial breach or defective performance by entrepreneurs.[447] Another important factor is whether the clause is included as a standard term or not, ie clauses that have been unilaterally pre-drafted and not individually negotiated. In this latter case, even limitation or exclusion clauses for slight negligence are invalid.[448] 181

---

440 AT 43.

441 DE 58. Liability for gross negligence can also be excluded in South Africa, ZA 45.

442 IT 100 f (art 1229 Italian CC).

443 DE 58 and CH 54. The same positions are held by legal writing in Spain, ES 83.

444 ES 84, IL 61, PL 130, CH 56.

445 Cf art 1229.2 Italian CC and IT 100 f, ES 84–85, NL 64, ZA 46.

446 ES 84.

447 ES 86, IT 103, ZA 47.

448 See art 3 and Annex 1(a) EU Directive on Unfair Terms in Consumer Contracts and IT 102, GR 54, PL 129, ES 85, CH 57, DE 62; however limitations or exclusions of liability for slight negligence are valid in the cases of damage to property.

182 Most jurisdictions accept that parties to a contract may validly limit or exclude their contractual and their tortious liability[449] and consider that whether a clause limits or excludes contract damages only or also affects damages in tort is a matter of interpretation of the corresponding clauses.[450] In other jurisdictions, however, exclusion and limitation clauses may affect liability in contract only, since tort law is considered to belong to *ordre public*. This is the case in French law, where it is not possible to exclude or limit in advance liability in tort, except in the very specific case provided for by art 1245-14 (formerly art 1386-15) *Code civil*, which, in the context of the implementation of the Product Liability Directive, allows exclusion or limitation of liability established between professionals for damage to property not used by the injured party mainly for his own private use or consumption.[451]

C. CONTRACTUAL LIMITATIONS OR EXCLUSIONS OF LIABILITY AS DEFENCES TO A THIRD PARTY

183 The most common situations where the need to protect third parties to the contract arises refer to third parties, whether auxiliaries or independent contractors, who assist a contractual party in the performance of contracts of carriage of goods by air, sea, rail or road, such as crane operators, stevedores, warehousemen, members of the crew, etc.[452] In these and similar cases, the performing party concludes a contract that includes a limitation or exclusion of liability. When the other contractual party suffers harm, since he cannot bring a claim in contract, he tries to bring a claim in tort against the third party in order to circumvent the clause and obtain compensation. Since the principle of privity of contract provides that contracts bind the parties only, the question that then arises is whether these third parties who assist in the performance of the contract can rely on the limitation or exclusion of liability contained in the contract. The problem, however, does not seem to have aroused much interest in some of the jurisdictions under survey, where no case law or clear solutions are reported. As far as international conventions are applicable, in particular in the transport area, they regularly extend their exclusions and limitations to the staff employed by the carrier or other primarily liable persons.[453]

184 A possible solution to the extension of these clauses to third parties is that these third parties become parties to the contract, as could be the case, in most

[449] As a matter of principle, with minor exceptions, CZ 93. Also E&W 107, GR 58, IT 100 f, IL 61, NL 64, PL 121, ES 84, ZA 45.

[450] DE 60, ZA 46.

[451] FR 69.

[452] I use here the terms 'principal' and 'auxiliary' in a very broad sense to refer to those persons.

[453] For instance, art 28 (2) CMR, art 30 Montreal Convention and art 61 Rotterdam Rules.

jurisdictions, by virtue of a contract for the benefit of a third party. Although it is generally the case that in these contracts third parties obtain the right to bring a claim against the contractual party, the benefit conferred to a third party must not necessarily be an enforceable right and may also take the form of an exclusion or limitation of the third party's liability to one of the contracting parties. In this sense, in the Netherlands, art 6:253 CC establishes that a contract can provide a third party not only with the right to performance, but also 'to appeal otherwise against one of them to the observance of their agreement if the agreement contains a stipulation to that effect (third-party clause) and the third party has accepted this stipulation.'[454] In this case, it is no wonder that the effects of the contract extend to third parties, since when all accept this third-party clause, third parties become a party to the contract (art 6:254.1 CC). For this reason, it is possible that other jurisdictions would also accept a similar solution.[455]

The question is, however, whether it is possible that, without the need for third 185
parties becoming party to the contract, the effects of the contract are extended to third parties, firstly in the sense that the contracting parties exclude delictual liability towards third parties; and secondly, in particular, whether third parties can avail themselves of the limitation or exclusion clauses. In many jurisdictions, there is no case law reported,[456] or it is controversial in South Africa as to the first question[457] and legal writing does not seem to have dealt with this problem in detail.[458] However, the Dutch Civil Code contains a provision in this respect establishing that: '[I]f a party to an agreement, in order to ward off his liability for damage caused by one of his subordinates, may raise a defence against his counterparty that directly or indirectly results from their agreement, then his subordinate, if he is held liable for this damage by the counterparty, may also raise that defence as if he himself was a party to that agreement' (art 6:257 CC). Thus, if the third party is held liable in tort, he will be able to avail himself of the limitation or exclusion of liability agreed between the contractual parties 'as if he himself was a party to that agreement'. In Austria and Germany, in the absence of a specific provision, courts reach a similar result, referring sometimes to the doctrine of contracts with protective effects to third parties, which would allow third parties to invoke the benefit of a limitation or exclusion clause in spite of the fact that the clause does not make any express mention of them, provided that, from the terms of the agreement, it can be implied that the contracting parties intended to protect them.[459]

---

454 NL 68 and see also, in this sense, art 5.2.3 PICC and art II.-9:301 DCFR.

455 See, for instance, ES 86, PL 131 f.

456 Thus, for instance, IT 105.

457 ZA 48.

458 NO 63

459 AT 49, DE 65. See also *Kötz* (fn 2) 332.

186 In England and Wales, the traditional common law rules did not allow contracts for the benefit of third parties and, following a strict application of the privity principle, even prevented third parties from obtaining the protection of limitation and exclusion clauses, even if the contract had expressly mentioned them. Contractors sought the protection of their auxiliaries in a variety of clauses included in transportation contracts (the so-called 'Himalaya clauses'),[460] seeking to establish a specific contractual relationship with the third parties as regards the exemption clause (for instance, agency) or holding that the consent to the exemption given by the other contractual party 'nullified the duty of care' that the auxiliary would otherwise have owed at common law.[461] Now sec 1(6) Contracts (Rights of Third Parties) Act 1999 clearly makes the task of the drafters who seek to extend limitation or exclusion to third parties much easier, since it provides that: 'Where a term of a contract excludes or limits liability in relation to any matter references in this Act to the third party enforcing the term shall be construed as references to his availing himself of the exclusion or limitation.' In plain English, this means that if the clause limiting or excluding liability aims at protecting the third party by mentioning or describing him, the third party will be protected by this clause. Thus, a third party may enforce a term in his own right only if he is expressly identified in the contract by name, as a member of a class or as answering a particular description. Enforcement must be consistent with the terms of the contract and the third party is entitled to the same remedies for breach of contract as if he had been a party to the contract.[462]

187 The situation is quite different in France, where the result depends on whether the claim that the contractual party brings against a third party to the contract is in contract or in tort. The first scenario is possible under French law, since it is accepted that a contractual party may bring a claim against a third party under the doctrine of *action directe*, as is the case, for instance, where the buyer of a good brings a claim in contract against the person who sold the good to his own seller. In this case, third parties may avail themselves of these clauses, since contractual parties bringing a claim against third parties must bear any limitation or exclusion of liability contained in that contract. By contrast, when the contractual party brings a claim in tort against a third party and seeks compensation for damage caused by the breach of a contract, the prevailing opinion of legal scholars is that third parties cannot avail themselves of limitations or exclusions contained in the contracts to which they are not a party, a justification that is considered convincing when the breach of contract is also a delictual fault under art 1382 (now art 1240) *Code civil*. The result may be different, however, when, according to the 2006 *Myr'ho* case,

460 After *Alder v Dickson (The Himalaya)* [1955] 1 QB 158.
461 *Furstom/Tolhurst* (fn 308) 140–158, with an analysis of the relevant case law.
462 E&W 109.

third parties acting in tort may invoke a breach of contract whenever this breach has caused them harm, since in these cases third parties should take the contract as it is.[463]

IV. NON-CONCURRENCE OR CONCURRENCE OF ACTIONS

A. OVERVIEW, AREAS OF OVERLAP AND THE DIFFERENT APPROACHES

A breach of contract does not amount to a tortious act against the other party unless this breach would also give rise to liability in tort had the contract not been concluded. Accordingly, for contract to overlap with tort, it is necessary that the breach of contract simultaneously constitutes a tort against the contracting party.[464] 188

Areas of overlap between actions in contract and in tort may appear where breach of contract causes personal injury or property damage as in the case of contracts dealing with medical treatment, carriage of persons or goods, sale of products, rental of premises or labour contracts. In these cases, the party performing the contract is obliged not only to make performance, but also to abstain from harming the other contractual party. In this sense, German law provides that 'an obligation may also, depending on its contents, oblige each party to take account of the rights, legal interests and other interests of the other party' (§241 (2) BGB). In light of the economic loss rule, known in some countries,[465] or of the distinction between 'direct and 'indirect damage', used in some others,[466] the question of potentially overlapping tort and contract claims is largely reduced to cases in which one party to a contract causes physical harm or property damage to the other contracting party. 189

The basic question in these cases is whether contract has absolute precedence over tort and claimants must sue in contract (non-concurrence of actions), or whether they can frame their action in contract, in tort or on both grounds, provided that they do not obtain double recovery (concurrence of actions). By contrast, one can speak of concurrence of actions in a different sense when the same act gives rise to liability in contract and in tort, but with regard to different persons, as when a third party to the contract induces a party to the contract to 190

463 FR 71 and *Borghetti* (fn 332) 279–303.
464 GR 60, IT 106–108, IL 66, PL 123–134, ZA 50, US 91.
465 For instance, US 84 and ZA 50.
466 For instance, GR 63.

breach his contract with the other contractual party, or with regard to different remedies within the same area of law as, for instance, when in the case of non-performance of a contract, the creditor claims at the same time specific performance and compensation for the damage suffered.[467]

191 The practical idea underpinning the question of concurrence of actions is whether or not claimants are entitled to take advantage of the grounds of liability which are most advantageous to them when liability in contract and liability in tort concur and, if they are, whether this concurrence is subject to any limitations or not. In most legal systems, the discussion on this topic is extremely complex, since it involves substantive and procedural issues, and the provided solutions are highly disputed, but while the scholarly discussion may continue to be interesting, its practical interest lessens when the rules applicable to each of these liability regimes is the same, as is the case in the Netherlands.[468]

192 Among the countries under survey, only France sticks generally to non-concurrence of actions (*non cumul*), which means that whenever there is a valid contract between the parties and damage is connected to this contract, the claimant may sue in contract only. The *non cumul* rule established itself in the 1930s, probably as the consequence of the expansion of strict liability regimes such as the so-called *responsabilité du fait des choses* and is justified by the need to prevent contracting parties from circumventing contract rules by resorting to tort.[469] It applies to all types of damage (personal injury, damage to property, pure economic loss, etc) and, therefore, establishes a clear and general precedence of contract over tort.[470] However, there are a few exceptions to this rule, as in road traffic liability or product liability, where the strict tort liability regime that they establish applies regardless of the existence of a contractual relationship between the parties.[471]

193 By contrast, in all the other countries under survey, a general principle of concurrence of actions applies. However, its meaning and scope are all but clear. Some authors consider that there is a plurality of independent actions (*Anspruchskonkurrenz*, following a German terminology that has been echoed in other countries), whereas others consider that there is one legal claim only, but based on two different legal grounds (*Anspruchsnormenkonkurrenz*).[472]

---

467 See *MPI/U Magnus*, Concurrent Claims (2012) 344–348.

468 Cf NL 77, pointing out that once liability is established the rules are the same. However, outside the realm of national law, the distinction may be still worth following, as for instance, as regards the applicable international private law rules.

469 FR 72 ff.

470 FR 72.

471 FR 74.

472 GR 60.

In some countries, the claimant may choose between one or the other, claim on one and, subsidiarily, on the other, or just furnish the court with the facts of the case and let the court then fit them either in tort or in contract rules.[473] In most cases, there are no statutory rules that regulate this situation,[474] but concurrence in one form or another is applied by courts and defended by scholars.

In Germany, the prevailing opinion holds that where there are different grounds for claims referring to an identical protected interest as, for instance, in contract and in tort, concurrence of claims (*Anspruchskonkurrenz*) applies.[475] If there are different requirements for the different claims, the victim can generally choose the most favourable basis. However, exceptions are made whenever the application of tort law would contravene the purpose of the contractual law norm. This is the case, for instance, when the party that rents a car damages the rented vehicle. The owner can claim damages in contract and in tort, since the contractual and tortious protection concerns the same interests (integrity interest). However, contract law provides for a shorter limitation period as regards the compensation claims of the lessor for modifications to or deterioration of the leased property (six months, §548 BGB), in contrast to three years in tort (§195 BGB). The purpose of this shorter limitation period is to clear claims between the parties of the rental contract within a short time after the return of the rented good (car), mainly in order to avoid difficulties of proof clearance. Then courts apply this shorter period only, since the application of the longer limitation period in tort would run counter to the aim of the contractual short period. By contrast, when the interest protected by contract and by tort is different, the limitation period for each claim applies independently.[476] The same disruption of the contractual rules may take place where, to establish liability, contract law requires acting with intent or gross negligence (eg liability of the donor (§521 BGB) or the lender (§599 BGB)), or where liability is established according to the standard of care the depositary (§690 BGB) or the partner (§708 BGB) customarily exercises in his own affairs (*culpa quam in suis*).[477] 194

A similar idea of concurrence of claims (or of legal grounds), coupled with limitations, which basically aim at preventing that the application of tort law 195

473 See with similar solutions PL 137 and ES 94, although this traditional position has been overturned by STS 23.4.2014 (JUR 2014, 181495), which has excluded both an automatic accumulation of actions and an application *ex officio* on the basis of the *iura novit curia* principle. See also IT 106–108.

474 Poland (PL 135 ff) being the exception (see art 433 Polish CC).

475 DE 67.

476 See DE 67, with examples.

477 DE 68 f and G *Bachmann* in: Münchener Kommentar zum BGB, 7.ed. §241 no 43 ff. (hereafter MüKoBGB/author).

rules undermine contract rules, can be found in other jurisdictions. This is the case, for instance, in Poland, where the choice for tort liability rules is excluded when it would circumvent shorter limitation periods or the scope of damages established for certain contracts.[478] Or in England and Wales, where claimants are entitled to avail themselves of the remedies which are most advantageous to them 'subject only to ascertaining whether the tortious duty is so inconsistent with the applicable contract that, in accordance with ordinary principle, the parties must be taken to have agreed that the tortious remedy is to be limited or excluded'.[479] Or in other countries, where concurrence is widely accepted, unless it contradicts contract law rules[480] or where the contractual party could avoid the risk of harm in establishing some contractual terms and failed to do so.[481]

B. NON-CONCURRENCE AND CONCURRENCE OF ACTIONS FOR THE PROTECTION AGAINST PERSONAL INJURY OR OF PROPERTY

196 In France, the exclusion of tort when a contract exists between the parties also applies to personal injury. In some cases, however, the courts disregard the existence of a contract and apply tort law, but they do not do so as a formal exception to the *non cumul* rule. Rather, in such cases the courts displace the boundary of the contract, so that damage, even though it happened on the execution of the contract, will be regarded as having occurred outside the contract. Courts resort to this device where claimants, having entered into a contract with the defendant, are in a situation very similar to those with no contractual relationship with him. This is the case, for instance, of accidents in railway stations, where victims may be passengers with a ticket or visitors without a ticket, or accidents in self-service stores, where the victim may or may not have concluded a contract with the shop at the time when the accident takes place. This allows all claimants to rely on tort rules, which are sometimes more favourable than contractual ones, and avoids them being treated differently in very similar situations.[482] By contrast, in the case of damage to property, the exclusion of tort when a contract between the parties exists applies with no further qualifications.[483]

---

478 PL 139.

479 E&W 118.

480 AT 50 ff, IL 69.

481 ZA 51 ff.

482 FR 75. Moreover, art 1233 para 2 *Avant-Projet* (1233-1 *Projet*) now provides that compensation of bodily injuries should always be governed by liability in tort, even if there is a contract between the parties, FR 76.

483 FR 77.

In all the other countries under survey, concurrence of claims in contract and in tort also takes place in these cases. The most common case of concurrence in cases of personal injury results from medical malpractice or the negligent provision of health care services,[484] although in some countries even medical or health care services provided in the context of private practice are typically treated as a matter of tort law.[485] Other cases are personal injuries suffered in the context of contracts of transport, travel contracts, labour contracts, etc.[486] 197

Concurrence in the case of damage to property is also very common in the other countries in cases such as contracts of lease, deposits, building contracts, provision of professional services, etc.[487] In those countries that acknowledge limitations to prevent circumvention of contract rules through the application of tort law rules, the purpose of statutory provisions must decide whether they will also apply to tortious liability and, in general, remains a matter of interpretation.[488] 198

C. NON-CONCURRENCE AND CONCURRENCE IN THE CASE OF INTERFERENCE OF CONTRACTUAL RIGHTS

Interference with contractual rights by third parties is a matter of tort law, not a matter of contract. Between the contractual party who suffers the breach and the third party there is no contractual relationship and the privity principle prevents the non-breaching party from bringing a contractual claim against the interfering third party.[489] It goes without saying that the creditor concerned will be able to bring a claim in contract against the debtor who is in breach of contract but, in most legal systems, and subject to certain conditions, he will also be able to bring a claim in tort against the interfering third party. These conditions are different from one jurisdiction to another. In most jurisdictions, such as Austria, Germany and Poland, it is necessary that the third party has acted intentionally, with the aim of frustrating the creditor's claim, in collusion with the debtor.[490] In some other jurisdictions, such as in France, acting fraudulently is not necessary and it suffices that the third party knew of the existence of the contract and acted in disregard of it.[491] It has been contended that the first view is more in line with the principle of privity of contract, 199

---

484 AT 55, DE 70, E&W 122, IT 110 f, PL 145, NO 67, ZA 54.
485 EW 122 and ES 108.
486 IT 110 f, PL 145, N.
487 AT 52, EW 123, GR 60, ZA 55, DE 72, PL 146.
488 DE 72.
489 DE 73 ff, E&W 124, PL 147, NL 81, ZA 57.
490 AT 53, DE 73 f, GR 74, PL 147.
491 FR 78.

whereas the second is based on a broad interpretation of the idea of *faute*, considering that a contract is a legal fact which third parties cannot fully ignore in their dealings with one of the contracting parties.[492] In common law jurisdictions, these interferences constitute specific economic torts such as the English torts of inducing breach of contract, or causing loss by unlawful means or intimidation.[493] They seem to adopt a middle position by considering that mere knowledge of the existence of a contract is not sufficient and require that the third party knows that his relationship with the contractual debtor is inconsistent with the contract.[494] Additionally, in most countries these situations are also dealt with under specific unfair competition rules, which, however, do not exclude the general tort law provisions.[495]

200 Loss of business due to personal injury to someone else's employees or clients or to property damage to the entrepreneur in jurisdictions that operate with the notion of pure economic loss regularly falls under the exclusion of this rule and no liability arises. Thus, causing personal injury to someone else's employees allows them to bring a claim in tort, but does not allow their employer to bring a claim for the pure economic loss that he has suffered.[496] Some legal systems also explain this result by saying that pure economic loss is not a protected interest under general tort law provisions, such as §823 (1) BGB in Germany. The result is different, however, if this personal injury takes place in the context of a direct and intentional attack against the enterprise of the employer, where protection could be given, as an infringement of the so-called 'right of an established and operating business' (ie as 'another' protected right).[497]

201 In countries that do not operate with the pure economic loss category, loss of business due to personal injury to one's employees or clients constitutes an 'indirect' damage, which, in principle, should not be compensated in tort. This is the case, for instance, in Greek law, where damage suffered by secondary victims is considered 'indirect damage', which does not fall under the protection of art 914 Greek CC, except in those exceptional cases of liability for wrongful death (cf art 929 Greek CC).[498] Under French law, this damage is also considered a *préjudice par ricochet*, ie damage suffered by someone as a result of someone else's damage, and this damage, whether pecuniary or not, is compensated only when the claimant belongs to a certain circle of relatives of the 'direct' victim. By contrast, courts are reluctant to compensate pecuniary damage suffered by a claimant as a result of damage caused to the direct victim since, although courts

492 *Van Gerven/Larouche/Lever* (fn 3) 247.
493 E&W 124, IL 71, US 100.
494 *Van Gerven/Larouche/Lever* (fn 3) 248.
495 In this sense, for instance, GR 64, IT 118 f and ZA 56.
496 E&W 125, US 101, and the classical position in ZA 58 ff.
497 DE 75 f.
498 GR 66.

do not formulate it this way, they are aware that compensation for these losses would be going too far and could generate massive litigation. This cautious approach, however, has been challenged by a rule developed by courts in 2006 whereby 'a third party to a contract may, on the basis of delictual liability, invoke a breach of contract whenever this breach has caused him harm' (*Myr'ho* decision) (above no 135). The scope of this rule is still unclear in practice. However, since damage suffered by a third party as a result of the violation of a contract is often a consequence of damage suffered by the contractual partner himself, the rule could lead to an extension of compensation for *préjudice par ricochet* suffered by business of professional partners of the contract's creditor.[499]

V. SPECIFIC SITUATIONS

A. PRE-CONTRACTUAL LIABILITY

1) A Pre-Contractual Relationship Governed by 'Good Faith'?

Legislation or case law of most of the jurisdictions under survey establish a general duty to negotiate contracts in good faith, which if breached, may give rise to pre-contractual liability. In common law jurisdictions, however, such a general duty does not exist.[500] 202

In Germany, pre-contractual liability or *culpa in contrahendo* was first established by Rudolf von Jhering for a limited number of cases, especially to protect against damage caused by void or voidable contracts.[501] However, in order to overcome the need to prove fault of the principals to establish liability for the acts of their auxiliaries (§831 BGB)[502] or due to the unavailability of recovery of pure economic loss unless connected to intent (§826 BGB), from the beginning of the last century case law extended liability to other situations, involving personal injury or pure economic loss, and even combined it with the doctrine of contract with protective effects to third parties.[503] As pointed out by 203

---

499 FR 80.

500 *Cabrillac* (fn 2) 42 ff.

501 *R v Jhering*, Culpa in contrahendo oder Schadensersatz bei nichtigen oder nicht zur Perfection gelangten Verträgen, Jherings Jahrbücher für die Dogmatik des bürgerlichen Rechts 4 (1861) 1–112.

502 The German Reichsgericht had to decide a case where a customer was severely injured when a roll of linoleum fell onto her while she was visiting a shop (RG 7 December 1911, RGZ 78, 239). The RG ruled in favour of the customer by applying §278 BGB, a contract law rule which attributes fault of the employee to the contracting party, in order to bypass §831 of BGB, which would have allowed the employer to exonerate himself from liability for the responsible employee if the employer had not been at fault himself.

503 As regards the evolution in case law see *J Dirk Harke* in: Historisch Kritischer Kommentar zum BGB (2007) §311 II, III 1545 ff (quoted hereinafter as HKK-BGB/Author).

von Mehren, the expansion of pre-contractual liability in German law illustrates a phenomenon of covert reform of the branch of tort law by attributing some problems to the branch of contract law in order to bring contractual rules and principles into play.[504]

204 Before the 2002 reform of the German law of obligations, there was a general agreement that cases which involve personal injury – such as the lettuce leaf of our Case 13 below – were tortious in their nature and should have been solved by an amendment that excluded the possibility of exoneration of employer which §831 BGB allows. There was also a widespread opinion that some cases of pure economic loss could have also been solved by a tort law reform by approaching the specific duties of care (*Verkehrspflichten*) created during the negotiation of a contract into statutory duties in the sense of §823 II BGB.[505] However, the 2002 reform of the law of obligations introduced into the German Civil Code all the constellations of cases previously dealt with by case law, which continue to be governed by contract law rules. Thus, §311 (2) and (3) BGB now provide for a specific regulation for these cases which the Civil Code terms as 'obligations similar to legal transactions'. The basic idea behind this regulation is that, when the parties come into contact to negotiate a contract, the law creates between them a special relationship which imposes on both of them the duty to take into account the rights and interests of the other party. §311 (2) BGB lists three different types of cases which can create these duties[506] and §311 (3) BGB extends the scope of the contract to third persons.[507] Thus, the pre-contractual phase of negotiations is regarded as a special relationship which justifies the application of all contract law rules and which often provide a better protection than granted by tort law.[508] The same aim of applying more favourable contractual rules to parties who have not yet entered into a contract has led to a similar application of the doctrine of *culpa in contrahendo* in Austria.[509]

205 Taking each other's interests into account, as established in the BGB, means dealing in good faith (in an objective sense) and this general duty to act in good faith in the course of the negotiations had already been established by Italian case law in the 1920s and included in the 1942 Civil Code, which was the first

504 *AT von Mehren*, The formation of contract, in: International Encyclopedia of Comparative Law VII, ch 9 (1976) 17.

505 HKK-BGB/*Harke* (fn 503) 1551.

506 Namely (1) the commencement of contract negotiations; (2) the initiation of a contract where one party, with regard to a potential contractual relationship, gives the other party the possibility of affecting his rights, legal interests and other interests, or entrusts these to him; and (3) similar business contacts.

507 DE 3.

508 DE 78.

509 AT 55.

one to codify pre-contractual liability (arts 1137 and 1138 CC). Pre-contractual liability is also regulated in other civil codes, such as the Greek (art 197),[510] the Polish (art 72 §2 and art 721 §§1 and 2)[511] and the Czech (§§1728–1730). As a specific relationship which deserves legal protection, it is also known in the Dutch[512] and Norwegian[513] case law. Other countries, such as Spain[514] and Switzerland,[515] to solve some problems arising during the contractual phase, also connect pre-contractual liability, respectively, to the abuse of rights and to the so-called 'liability for confidence' (*Vertrauenshaftung*). In Israel, absence of good faith may also constitute a cause of action under contract law for breach of the pre-contractual duty of 'bona fide' negotiations.[516]

Until the 2016 reform, the French Civil Code did not contain any specific provision on pre-contractual liability, but case law and legal scholarship had recognised a general duty of pre-contractual good faith and inferred several duties from this general obligation of good faith that now have been enshrined in arts 1112, 1112-1 and 1112-2 *Code civil*.[517] 206

Common to all these countries is that they consider that the negotiation of a contract places the parties in a relationship which deserves legal protection. Although negotiations are not yet a contract and the form and the scope of protection cannot be exactly the same, negotiations give rise to duties between the prospective parties the enforcement of which must be made compatible with the basic principle of freedom of contract.[518] 207

A general duty to bargain in good faith is unknown in common law jurisdictions. They do not recognise the pre-contractual stage as a legally relevant relationship which, as such, deserves the general protection of the law. The grounds for this approach can be found both in the reluctance of common law to develop broad and general principles and in a different approach to the nature of the negotiation process. An expression of this different approach is the consideration of English judges that a duty to carry on contractual negotiations in good faith is 'inherently repugnant to the adversarial position of the parties when involved in negotiations'.[519] This does not mean, however, that the legal system does not react against the wrongs committed by a party or the unjust 208

510 GR 3.
511 PL 152 ff.
512 NL 6 and 90 f.
513 NO 2 and 73.
514 ES 103.
515 CH 3.
516 IL 2 and 73.
517 FR 82 f.
518 *Cartwright/Hesselink* (fn 18) 450 ff.
519 *Walford v Miles* [1992] 2 AC 128, 138 and E&W 15.

enrichment obtained during negotiations, but only that it adopts 'piecemeal' solutions. Thus, for instance, when one party has made investments because he trusted in the formation of a contract, English literature has suggested that the principles of unjust enrichment should apply. Yet this institution is not meant to compensate for the loss that occurred on the side of the trusting party, but it aims rather at the reversal of any enrichment obtained by the party breaking off negotiations. However, since in many cases the enrichment may not have taken place, the remedy is not available. A minority opinion suggests solving the problem under tort law as in France, but in English tort law there is no general clause as is the case in the French Civil Code.[520] However, several specific distinct torts may arise, such as the tort of deceit (fraudulent misrepresentation), which is committed where a false representation has been made knowingly or without belief in its truth, or recklessly, without caring whether it was true or false.[521] By contrast, negligent misrepresentation was first recognised in the well-known case of *Hedley Byrne v Heller & Partners Ltd*,[522] where the court ruled that if someone possessing a special skill undertakes to apply that skill for the assistance of another person who reasonably relies upon it or upon his ability to make careful inquiry, a duty of care will arise which, in the absence of a contract between the parties, will give rise to an action in tort for damages for pure economic loss.[523] Additionally, liability for innocent misrepresentation may arise under the Misrepresentation Act 1967.

209 By contrast to some other common law systems, such as the United States,[524] English law does not accept the application of 'promissory estoppel' as a possible remedy to recover expenses incurred in the negotiation while relying on the conclusion of a contract. 'Promissory estoppel' is one of the variations of estoppel which aims at the protection of reliance and is linked to the idea that in some cases it is unconscionable to allow a party to adopt a position which is at odds with the position that he had previously adopted. 'Promissory estoppel' aims at preventing the inconsistent conduct of a party when he has made a clear and unequivocal promise to the other which has affected his position and it is considered that it would be inequitable to allow him to go back on such a promise. While 'promissory estoppel' is well developed in other common law countries and may allow the party relying on the promise not only to recover wasted expenses but also to bypass the requirement of consideration and enforce the promise against the other party,[525] in England it can be used as a defence

---

520 E&W 15.
521 E&W 16.
522 [1964] AC 465.
523 E&W 17. See also ZA 60.
524 US 102.
525 *Cartwright/Hesselink* (fn 18) 463 ff; *M Hogg*, Promises and Contract Law: Comparative Perspectives (2011) 180 ff, 189.

only and it only applies when the promise was one not to enforce an existing right. The situation is, however, different where the promise was to grant the claimant an interest in land or other property. Here the courts have developed the doctrine of 'proprietary estoppel', which is not merely a defence and gives the claimant who has relied to his detriment upon the landowner's promise a cause of action to be brought in the position that he expected.[526]

2) Reliance (Negative) or Expectation (Positive) Interest?

Compensation under the doctrine of pre-contractual liability usually gives rise to reliance or negative interest only, ie a right to be returned to the position in which the claimant would have been if contractual negotiations had not been entered into.[527] The party relying to his detriment on the conclusion of the contract may thus be entitled to recover expenses incurred in reasonable reliance on the conclusion of the contract and which turn out to be wasted. The reliance interest also includes consequential loss, such as lost opportunities to conclude an alternative contract with a third party, if causally connected to failed negotiations and duly proven. As a general rule, expectation or positive interest, ie the right to be returned to the position in which the claimant would have been had a valid contract been concluded, including the profit he would have made with that contract, is not recoverable. However, it can be allowed in exceptional cases as, for instance, in the Netherlands, when one party breaks off negotiations at a very advanced stage (the so-called 'third stage'), which starts when the claimant can reasonably expect that the contract will be concluded. For this reason, breaking off can be considered a wrong that prevents the conclusion of the contract and allowing the claimant to obtain expectation or positive interest is then what he would have obtained if the wrong had not been committed.[528] A similar situation arises in Germany[529] and Norway[530] in cases different to breaking off negotiations and related to public bidding, where it was certain that a contract would have been concluded if the employer who invited the tenders had not violated its pre-contractual duties. 210

3) Specific Situations

Pre-contractual liability refers to a plurality of situations that may arise during negotiations or as a result of them, regardless of whether they end with the conclusion of a valid contract or not. From an economic perspective, 211

526 *Hogg* (fn 525) 188.
527 IT 10, NO 73, PL 156.
528 *Cartwright/Hesselink* (fn 18) 469.
529 *Beale et al* (fn 2) 409.
530 NO 73.

the justification for pre-contractual liability starts from the idea that when the parties begin to rely on the expectation of the successful formation of a contract, they may make substantial investments in the contractual negotiations with a view to the future benefits resulting from the execution of the contract. Thus, for instance, they may spend significant sums travelling, preparing documents or obtaining information, or may even reorganise their business in order to be able to better exploit the opportunities created by the contract once it has been concluded. These investments are usually 'relation specific', ie they are going to be wasted if the negotiations fail and a binding contract is not concluded. Pre-contractual liability is thus an instrument to avoid one party over-investing in reliance upon the contract which subsequently, as a result of an act of the other which is wrongful or, in some systems, contrary to good faith, does not come into being, leading thereby to a total welfare loss.[531] Additionally it also aims at preventing opportunism and at fostering efficient information gathering and exchange, providing thereby an incentive to enter and continue negotiations.[532]

212 When parties come into contact to negotiate a contract, they expose their relative sphere of interests to the action of the other, and the duty to negotiate in good faith means, in particular, that each party may expect that:

(a) the other party is in the position to reach a valid contract, has the intention to do so, cooperates in this common endeavour and does not break off negotiations abruptly or unexpectedly and without any justification (duty to negotiate in good faith);
(b) he receives the information that is necessary to carry out the negotiations and that this information is correct and accurate (duty to disclose information); and
(c) the information that he gives to the other party remains confidential (duty of confidentiality).[533]

213 By contrast to German or Austrian law, most countries under survey would not consider a case where the claimant suffers personal injury on occasion of a contract, such as Case 13 below (lettuce leaf), a pre-contractual liability case, but a plain case of tort liability.[534] The same is true for international texts and texts of European private international law, such as the Rome II Regulation,[535]

---

531 EAL 81 and *EC Melato*, Precontractual liability, in: G De Geest, Contract Law and Economics (2011) 12.

532 *Melato* (fn 531) 20–28.

533 See, for instance, CZ 13, IT 6.

534 See below Case 13 (CR 282).

535 Regulation (EC) No 864/2007 of the European Parliament and of the Council of 11 July 2007 on the law applicable to non-contractual obligations (Rome II) [2007] OJ L199/40.

Recital 30 of which expressly states that art 12, ie '*culpa in contrahendo*', 'covers only non-contractual obligations presenting a direct link with the dealings prior to the conclusion of a contract. This means that if, while a contract is being negotiated, a person suffers personal injury, Article 4 [ie general rule on torts/delicts] or other relevant provisions of this Regulation should apply'.

a) Duty to Negotiate in Good Faith and Breaking off Negotiations

Freedom of contract entails that the parties are free to enter negotiations and to put an end to them when they see fit by freely deciding not to carry them on any longer. Freedom to break off negotiations is, thus, inherent to freedom of contract and for this reason negotiating parties cannot be held liable for failure to reach an agreement. However, negotiations must be carried out in good faith. These two principles are recognised in most continental legal systems and are included in international texts (arts 2.1.15 PICC, 2:301 PECL and II.-3:301 DCFR) and also in some civil codes, such as in the recently amended French Civil Code (art 1112). 214

This means, first, that the parties must enter negotiations with the serious intention to conclude the contract and that it is contrary to good faith to enter negotiations with the sole purpose of preventing the other party from contracting with a competitor or with the aim of obtaining confidential information about the organisation of the other party's business. 215

Additionally, good faith must be present not only at the initiation of the negotiations, but also in the course of their development. Thus, it is against good faith, for instance, to protract negotiations unnecessarily after having decided not to conclude the contract. Conducting parallel negotiations, however, is not generally considered in itself to be contrary to good faith and, in principle, a party is not under the obligation to inform the other about simultaneous negotiations with third parties. However, leading the other party to believe that negotiations are exclusively conducted with him may be contrary to good faith, as may also be continuing negotiations when one has already decided to conclude the contract with a third party. 216

Civil law systems generally acknowledge that under certain circumstances breaking off negotiations can also lead to pre-contractual liability, but the requirements and its effects vary among jurisdictions. One aspect that seems important is whether negotiations are just in their beginnings or have already reached an advanced stage.[536] Dutch law, for instance, distinguishes three stages in the negotiation process. In the first one, both parties are absolutely free to break off negotiations and no claim between them on this ground may arise. 217

536 *Kötz* (fn 2) 32 ff.

In the second stage, the parties are still free, but must pay reliance or negative interest, ie wasted expenses. Finally, in the third stage, the parties are no longer free to break off negotiations and if one party breaks off negotiations, he may be ordered not only to pay damages – and even for the expectation or positive interest – but also to continue negotiations.[537] Although the stage in which negotiations are broken off seems relevant in most jurisdictions, no other jurisdiction reaches in a final stage such an extreme result, which seems to run counter to freedom of contract and it is met with disapproval by most legal writing.[538] This drastic solution, however, can be explained according to the specific meaning of this 'third stage' in Dutch law. It starts when the claimant can reasonably expect that the contract will be concluded and, for this reason, breaking off negotiations can be considered a wrong that prevents the conclusion of the contract. Allowing the claimant to obtain expectation or positive interest is then allowing recovery for what he would have obtained if the wrong had not been committed.[539] However, it is submitted that although the remedies for this third stage are available in theory, they are very difficult to obtain in practice[540] and also that the Dutch leading case on this topic[541] referred to a public procurement case where the claimant would have concluded the contract with all certainty if the defendant municipality had not been negligent.[542]

218 Common law systems, by contrast, consider that as long as the parties have not made a binding promise, committed an established tort, obtained an unjust enrichment or, in some jurisdictions, encouraged the claimant to believe that the contract would be concluded, thereby making applicable the doctrine of 'promissory estoppel', the defendant incurs expenses at his own peril and should be free to withdraw from negotiations, without needing to give any reason, even at a late stage.[543]

b) Duty to Disclose Information

219 The question whether there is a duty to disclose information during negotiations and its extent has been the subject of a passionate debate since Cicero's times.[544]

537 NL 92 and *Cartwright/Hesselink* (fn 18) 468 and *Beale et al* (fn 2) 406.
538 *Beale et al* (fn 2) 407.
539 *Cartwright/Hesselink* (fn 18) 469.
540 Ibid, 470.
541 *Plas v Valburg* HR 18 June 1982, Ned Jur 1983, 723.
542 *Kötz* (fn 2) 36.
543 *Hogg* (fn 525) 468 et passim. See also ZA 60 and 81.
544 As is well known, in De Officiis (III, 12) Cicero presented the case of an honest businessman who imported a large cargo of wheat from Alexandria into Rhodes at a time of dearth and famine. The businessman knew that other ships loaded with wheat had also sailed to Rhodes and were to arrive shortly afterwards. Cicero asked whether the businessman should disclose

It also marks a quite opposite starting position in civil law and common law jurisdictions, although when all the details are analysed, differences diminish.

Among civil law systems, each party is under the duty to disclose information that is relevant for the other party to be able to decide whether to conclude a contract or not. This duty may arise if the other party lacks important information, or is unable to obtain it, and the non-disclosing party is aware of it. Moreover, the information that the parties have the duty to provide must be truthful and accurate. Non-disclosure or misleading information which influences the other's party decision as to whether or not to conclude a contract may not only lead to damages on the grounds of pre-contractual liability but also, if the contract has been actually concluded, to voidability of the contract on the grounds of error or fraud. 220

Thus, for instance, German law on occasion imposes duties to disclose information during the negotiation of a contract (*Aufklärungspflichten*). Italian law considers that the duty to disclose information is a specific duty which derives from the general duty of good faith established in art 1337 CC. French law establishes now in art 1112-1 CC a specific pre-contractual duty of information, which is subject to certain conditions, such as: (a) that the information is available to the non-disclosing party; (b) that the other is legitimately unaware of this information or has legitimately trusted the other party as regards necessary information; and (c) that this information has a direct and necessary link with the content of the contract or the condition of its parties and (d) is crucial for the conclusion of the contract. However, the value of the object of performance is information that the *Code civil* expressly excludes from this duty of disclosure. In the Czech Republic, the parties have to inform each other about the factual and legal circumstances which they actually know or should have known, which are known to only one party and may influence the other party's conduct as regards the conclusion of the contract (cf §1728 para 2 Czech CC).[545] In the Netherlands, liability for failing to inform or incorrectly informing the other party about certain essential facts is partly shaped by the 221

or not the fact of this coming arrival when selling his wheat. An ancient ethicist argued that the seller should declare any defects in his wares, in so far as such a course is prescribed by the common law of the land; but for the rest, since he has goods to sell, he may try to sell them to the best possible advantage, provided he is guilty of no misrepresentation. Another one – with whom Cicero agreed – contented that all facts should be disclosed, that the buyer may not be uninformed of any detail that the seller knows. However, not even the Scholastics later on agreed with him. Thus, for instance, *Luis de Molina* (De iustitia et iure, II Disputation 354-4, 254–257) knew that knowledge was money and by distinguishing between private and public knowledge, held that obtaining profit from private knowledge was acceptable, but to derive it from public knowledge was not.

545 CZ 13.

rules on mistake (art 6:228 CC), but is also an independent duty of care to inform correctly. To what extent such a duty of care exists will depend on the nature of the agreement, the nature of the information, and respective knowledge of the parties about these matters.[546]

222 In common law jurisdictions, no such general duty to disclose information exists. Moreover, it is considered that such a duty would not only encourage feckless commercial practices, but would also be against the basic right to act self-interestedly when entering into contracts.[547] However, if the information given by one party has misled the other, whereas in England, an action for deceit (fraudulent misrepresentation) or for any other piecemeal remedies against misrepresentation might arise,[548] in some other common law jurisdictions 'promissory estoppel' might be additionally available.[549]

c) Duty of Confidentiality

223 Absent an agreement of confidentiality, the information related to the object of performance of the other party, such as know-how, technical details or manufacturing or commercial procedures, which the parties have obtained during negotiations, is not subject to a duty of confidentiality. Good, faith, however, may require the parties not to disclose this information or not to use it for their own benefit and treat it as confidential.

224 This duty is recognised in most jurisdictions under survey. Thus, for instance, in France the new art 1112-2 *Code civil* holds liable those who use or disseminate without authorisation confidential information obtained on occasion of the negotiations of the contract. This is also the case in the Czech Republic, where it is contended that in these cases damages may include disgorgement of the benefits unlawfully obtained from the disclosed information (cf §1730 para 2 Czech CC).[550]

225 Generally speaking, however, if a party enters into negotiations for the sole purpose of confidential information of the other party, the case would also qualify as a general breach of the duty to carry out negotiations in good faith and the breaching party should also compensate for the expenses incurred in negotiating.[551]

546 NL 91.
547 *Hogg* (fn 525) 208 ff.
548 E&W 16 ff. See also ZA 60.
549 See above CR 198.
550 CZ 13.
551 *Beale et al* (fn 2) 426.

B. LIABILITY OF PROFESSIONALS

One of the main reasons to draw as clear a line as possible between contract and tort is to prevent tort rules from interfering with the allocation of risks taken by the contractual parties and to promote their self-determination by leaving to them what they want to regulate and to what extent. These reasons are, however, weak as regards the relationships some professionals establish with persons who require their services. Due to the complexity and the specific characteristics of the services provided and to the imbalance of knowledge between the professional and the other contractual party, those contracting with professionals cannot easily ascertain to what extent professionals comply with their contractual duties. 226

Although in all countries under survey the professions referred to are not exactly the same, the core of the relevant professional activities is related to the provision of health care, legal and financial services. Thus all reports refer to medical doctors and, sometimes also to other health care providers, and to lawyers. Occasionally other legal professions, such as public notaries, are mentioned; providers of financial services, such as accountants, tax advisors and bank employees, are mentioned in some reports, and sometimes also architects and other professions. Probably, the basic distinction would lie between the so-called 'liberal professions' and other professions.[552] 227

The main traits that distinguish liberal professions from the others are that they require formal training, ie the acquisition of the knowledge and the skills specific to the corresponding profession, which usually involve complex activities and decisions which cannot be easily assessed by non-professionals. Regularly, the practice of these professions also requires a licence that empowers and legitimates those who possess it to practise the profession within the relevant community. Additionally, the conduct of these professionals is not governed by contract or tort rules only, but mainly by codes of conduct, codes of ethics or similar internal rules, which are issued by the public or private bodies that are established to organise the profession; these internal rules, usually controlled and enforced by disciplinary bodies, set the standards of conduct that all the members of the relevant profession must follow and from which they cannot deviate in their particular contracts. All these elements create legitimate expectations of the persons who contract with them and show not only that the contractual rules bargained for by the parties are not the main rules setting the standards in the relationship, but also that the general contract or 228

[552] In this sense, *E Hondius*, Professional Liability, in: M Bussani/AJ Sebok (eds), Comparative Tort Law: Global Perspectives (2015) 226–249, 227.

tort law rules would be inadequate if they were not interpreted in the light of this professional setting.

229 As regards the contract–tort divide, most jurisdictions under survey consider that professional liability is primarily a matter of contract law.[553] Thus, for instance, in Greece a 1994 Act dealing with product liability also includes a regulation of liability for service providers moulded on the basis of the unborn European Services Directive. These rules apply to services provided by professionals such as architects and medical doctors but, according to the prevailing opinion, not to lawyers.[554] By contrast, England and Wales,[555] Israel,[556] South Africa[557] and most of the jurisdictions in the United States[558] consider that professional negligence, in general, is primarily a matter of tort law. However, there is a general agreement that both contract and tort law rules may apply, except in France where, due to the *non cumul* rule, liability of professionals is normally in contract to their clients, and in tort to other claimants.[559]

230 Irrespective of the basis of the claim – whether tort or contract – professionals have to abide by a standard of care which is higher than what is required of an ordinary person outside the profession and depends on the specific profession.[560] Professionals are responsible for typical skills of their profession and may not argue that their personal abilities are below average. Normally, the breach of their professional duties gives rise to liability for the ensuing harms.

231 In the case of liability of medical doctors and health care professionals, most jurisdictions have developed specific rules. Thus, art 7:453 of the Dutch Civil Code provides a specific duty of care which, in spite of the wording of the code, is a contractual duty that must be understood according to the specific standards established in the model contract drawn up by the Royal Dutch Society of Medicine and the National Patients Platform.[561] The new Czech Civil Code, effective from 1 January 2014, inspired by Dutch law and under a strong influence of the contract of treatment of the DCFR (art IV. C. 8:101), has also introduced a new contract for health care services (§§2636–2651 NCC) establishing the obligations of the provider towards the patient.[562] A move to contract law has also taken place in Germany, where the Patient

553 DE 79, FR 84, IT 121, NO 74, PL 157, GR 68, NL 96.
554 GR 68.
555 E&W 117.
556 IL 74.
557 ZA 61.
558 US 103 and 104.
559 FR 84.
560 AT 56, NO 74 f, NL 85 f, PL 157 and 158.
561 NL 97 f.
562 *L Tichý*, Czech and European Law of Obligations at a Turning Point, in: R Schulze/F Zoll (eds), The Law of Obligations in Europe: A New Wave of Codifications (2013) 40.

Act 2013 has codified medical liability, so far based on negligence in tort or in contract, in the part of the Civil Code devoted to the 'contract of treatment' (§§630a–630h BGB).[563] In Italy, medical liability was traditionally based on contract, but the wording of 2012 *Legge Balduzzi* caused some confusion.[564] The new Gelli-Bianco Act,[565] overcoming the ambiguities of the Balduzzi reform, has scheduled a double track of liability. Thus, liability is contractual as regards the institution providing health care, public or private, and non-contractual towards health care professionals (art 7). This is an important qualification, since a significant part of case law, in the aftermath of the Balduzzi reform, had continued to qualify health care liability as contractual even in the presence of the explicit reference to the general provision referring to tortious liability (art 2043 *Codice civile*). The new system prompts the patient to go directly to the health care provider, as he will benefit from the much more benevolent rules of evidence (art 1218 ff *Codice civile*) and a more lenient 10-year limitation period (art 2946 *Codice civile*). The legislative choice aims at speeding up recovery for the damage suffered, thereby burdening the subjects economically stronger. Nevertheless, whenever the health care professional and the patient have in fact entered into an actual contract for the provision of health care services, liability will be in contract.[566] In France, there are also special legislative provisions, which apply regardless of the existence of a contract between the doctor and the patient.[567] Finally, some jurisdictions make a distinction depending on whether the health care provider is the public health system (liability in tort of public health care authorities) or a private professional (contract).[568]

Where experts provide opinions, advice, certifications and other services that 232
cause pure economic loss to third parties with whom no contractual relationship exists, courts have also developed stricter liability rules. In Germany, courts in these cases deploy an array of legal devices, which go from *culpa in contrahendo*, contract in favour or with protective effects to third parties to even implied contracts. However, legal rules also try to strike a fair balance between the increased liability of professionals towards third parties and a reasonable extent of their liability by providing that it is subsidiary only (public notaries) or by limiting their amount (statutory auditors).[569] In most jurisdictions, legal and

563 Act of 26 February 2013, BGBl I, 277, DE 79. See also *M Stauch*, The 2013 German Patients' Rights Act - Codifying Medical Malpractice Compensation (2015) Journal of European Tort Law 85–94.

564 Cf Cass civ, 19 February 2013, no 4030, *Ceccioni/Cipriani*, at 35 and IT 121.

565 Law of 8 March 2017, no 24; IT 123.

566 Cf *G Montari Vergallo*, La nuova responsabilità medica doppo la riforma Gelli-Bianco (2017) 68 ff.

567 FR 85.

568 ES 108.

569 DE 82.

financial service providers such as lawyers and accountants may also be liable in tort whenever their standard of care also involves taking care of the interests of third parties.[570]

VI. CASES

A. CASE 1. THE UNATTRACTIVE SHOPPING MALL

D owns a shopping mall and lets a store therein to Z, who is to sell shoes. The contract allows Z to sublet the store and he does so to C, without informing D. In breach of his obligations to Z and other tenants, D fails to keep the shopping mall clean and attractive. Because of this, C's business is on the decline and the number of shoes he sells keeps declining. Can C bring a claim for lost earnings against D (in contract/tort/both)?

233 In this case, C suffers pure economic loss (stand-alone loss of earnings, ie unrelated to personal injury or property damage) when D breaches a contract to which C is not a party. Because of this lack of privity, most jurisdictions rule out that C may bring a claim in contract against D.[571] In most jurisdictions, specific rules governing the relationship between landlords and tenants may occasionally allow claims between C and D in particular circumstances,[572] but they do not allow it in our case. England and Wales seem to be the exception, since the Landlord and Tenant Act 1954 provides statutory protection to C and entitles him to bring a claim against D.[573]

234 Other jurisdictions use several general legal devices to allow C to bring a contractual claim against D for loss of earnings. Thus, Norway, according to the direct claim doctrine accepted by the Supreme Court, allows claims backwards in the chain of contracts and it is the only jurisdiction under survey that grants C a direct claim against D in this case.[574] Germany considers the contract between D and Z as a 'contract with protective effects to third parties' (*Vertrag mit Schutzwirkung zugunsten Dritter*); if the main conditions for the applicability of this doctrine are met,[575] and the third party needs protection because he does not have a claim of his own either in contract or in tort, C is entitled to obtain compensation for the loss of earnings caused by D's omission.[576]

---

570 NL 99, US 104.

571 FR 86, IT 125, GR 74, PL 161, ZA 62, ES 111, CH 72, US 106.

572 ES 111, allowing D to require C to pay the rent when D does not do it. Or GR 74, where C could substitute Z when Z fails to bring his contractual claim.

573 E&W 129.

574 NO 77.

575 See DE 85.

576 DE 85 f.

In Austria, this doctrine would also apply to this case on the grounds that the third party is the beneficiary of the main contractual duty, in spite of the fact that the doctrine of the 'contract with protective effects to third parties, in order to avoid extending the debtor's liability excessively, cannot generally be applied in cases of pure economic loss'.[577] Finally, some other reports hold that C may be also considered a third-party beneficiary who has a contractual claim against D.[578]

As regards a claim in tort, some jurisdictions hold that the claim of C against D is possible,[579] either according to the general clause establishing fault liability,[580] or according to specific general tort law rules.[581] The peculiarity of the French law is that in the *Myr'ho* case,[582] which inspired this hypothetical, the Cour de cassation declared that 'a third party to a contract may, on the basis of tortious liability, invoke a breach of contract whenever this breach has caused him harm'.[583] Most jurisdictions, however, consider that C may not bring a claim against D in negligence or according to the general tort law rules, the main reason being that C suffered pure economic loss[584] and that D violated contractual obligations only and did not act against *boni mores*.[585] 235

However, the opinions are split as regards whether the so-called 'pure economic loss rule' would bar a claim in negligence in this case. The American report considers that the economic loss rule would bar a tort claim by C against D,[586] and so does the South African report, which holds that in this case there are policy considerations (such as lack of foreseeability of damage to C, lack of C's vulnerability, floodgates danger, etc) that do not point to the extension of delictual liability.[587] By contrast, the Israeli report holds that the traditional conditions for holding D liable to C in negligence for C's pure economic loss (special relations between Z and C; reasonable reliance on D's contractual commitments and D's assumption of responsibility toward C) have been met.[588] 236

---

577 AT 1.

578 CZ 100, IL 75, or NL 106, where the fact that Z allowed subletting can be construed as a third party clause.

579 FR 86, IT 125, NO 76; hesitant ES 111, and NL 107.

580 FR 86, ES 111, NL 107.

581 IT 125.

582 Cass ass Plén, 6 October 2006, *Loubeyre et autres v SATL Myr'Ho et autre*, no 05-13.255, P+B+R+I, Bull, civ ass Plén no 9; D 2006, 2825, note *G Viney*; JCP 2006, II, 10181, avis *Garazzio* et note *M Billiau*; RTD civ 2007, 123, obs *Jourdain*.

583 Cf CR 124.

584 AT 58, DE 88, ZA 63, CH 70 and E&W 128 ff and US 106 for a claim based on negligence.

585 AT 58, DE 88, PL 161, or considering simply that such a breach cannot qualify as a tort, GR 73.

586 US 106.

587 ZA 63.

588 IL 76.

237 Additionally, both the English and the American report consider that, under certain conditions, C might be able to bring a claim against D in tort on grounds of (private) nuisance.[589]

B. CASE 2. THE IDLE LAWYER

After having a terrible fight with his two daughters, W had asked his solicitor D to cut his daughters out of his will, which request was duly implemented shortly thereafter. Before W died, however, he reconciled with his daughters. W subsequently asked D to change the will back, so that £9,000 would be bequeathed to each of his daughters, but due to D's unreasonable delay, the will was not prepared for execution before W's death. His heirs were unwilling to share the estate with the two daughters and pointed to the language of the will at the time of death. Can the daughters bring a claim against D in contract/tort/both to recover the amount promised to them by their late father? (Please disregard potential claims against the estate or heirs arising out of the laws of inheritance such as the daughter's legal share).

238 The hypothetical is inspired by the English case *White v Jones*[590] and a German series of cases known, after Kegel's metaphor, as the 'laughing double heirs', because the intended heir who receives compensation from the solicitor could still, in the future, inherit the estate or part of it.[591]

239 Since the daughters (C1 and C2) had not contracted with D, they are not in privity and therefore the starting point is that C1 and C2 cannot bring a claim against D in contract. It is doubtful whether the contract concluded between D and W was a genuine contract for the benefit of a third party. Most reports do not even mention the contract for the benefit of the third party or a third-party clause which, allegedly, would be implicitly contained in the contract between D and W, as a possible solution of the case. Others express their doubts about this solution[592] and finally others reject it expressly.[593] Only the Czech and the Dutch reports consider that C1 and C2 could bring a claim in contract against D on these grounds.[594] However, one should bear in mind that although it is true that C1 and C2 were the intended beneficiaries of the will,

---

589 E&W 130 and US 106.

590 [1995] 2 AC 2007, see E&W 131.

591 DE 89, fn 129. *G Kegel*, Die lachenden Doppelerben: Erbfolge beim Versagen von Urkundspersonen, in: FS für Werner Flume zum 70. Geburtstag (1978) I, 545–558. See also *M Makowsky*, Schadensersatz für entgangene Zuwendungen im Todesfall – von 'lachenden Doppelerben' und 'verzückten Doppelberechtigten', AcP 216 (2016) 497–557.

592 IL 77. US 107 leaves it undecided.

593 FR 87.

594 CZ 101, NL 108.

C1 and C2 were not the intended beneficiaries of the contract that D concluded with W to draft the will. As true third-party beneficiaries of the contract, C1 and C2 should be able to claim performance from D, but this is impossible in this case, since no will can be drafted after the testator's death. One could perhaps say then that, since specific performance is impossible, the only remedy available to C1 and C2 is damages.[595] However, a will cannot be considered a contract for the benefit of third parties because this would be inconsistent with the essence of a will as a legal transaction that the testator can change or revoke whenever he likes.[596]

Considering that such a contract could not be a contract for the benefit of a third party, since only the testator could have claimed performance, the German Federal Supreme Court held back in 1965 that the contract between the deceased and the lawyer to draft a valid will was a contract with protective effects in favour of the intended heir who, therefore, was entitled to the full amount of what he would have inherited if the lawyer had reacted in time.[597] Austria has also followed suit with this doctrine and considers that, although according to Austrian law pure economic losses are usually not recoverable under the doctrine of the contract with protective effects to third parties, there are in this case policy grounds that speak in favour of D's liability, since the danger of an indeterminate liability does not exist here – the parties are well established in advance – and allowing C1 and C2 to bring a claim against D is necessary in this case to enforce the contract between W and D and to prevent thereby D from going scot-free.[598] 240

On similar policy grounds, some other jurisdictions would allow C1 and C2 to bring a claim against D in tort. Although C1 and C2 suffer pure economic loss, the reports corresponding to England and Wales and South Africa, on the one side, and Israel, on the other, do not fully agree as to whether the traditional conditions for holding D liable in negligence are met in this case or not. In favour of the existence of a duty of D towards C1 and C2, the first two consider that here D's assumed responsibility as regards W is extended to C1 and C2,[599] whereas the Israeli report holds that *assumption of responsibility* is at least questionable in this case.[600] In favour of this duty there are also the grounds that D could reasonably foresee that C1 and C2 would suffer a loss as a result of D's negligent omission – but, according to the Israeli report, reasonable reliance 241

595 NL 108.
596 FR 87.
597 DE 89 and BGH NJW 1965, 1955 ff.
598 AT 59.
599 E&W 131, ZA 65.
600 IL 78.

is also questionable here[601] – and the absence of indeterminate liability.[602] Nevertheless, it is admitted that, on the grounds of deterrence, these conditions should be relaxed here if D's liability in negligence is the only way to prevent D from walking free from his contractual obligations.[603]

242 By contrast, most continental law jurisdictions would reject a claim in tort. This is the case in Austria, the Czech Republic, Germany, Greece, Italy, Switzerland and probably France.[604] Others would also likely reject C1's and C2's claim according to general tort rules, but specific professional rules would allow C1 and C2 to bring a claim against D.[605] Finally, the Netherlands stands alone as the only jurisdiction that would consider D's conduct contrary to proper social conduct and hence unlawful, and would allow C1 and C2 to bring a claim in tort against D.[606]

243 In the United States, courts seem divided in this case. Whereas some would allow claims both in contract and tort, some would find grounds for C1's and C2's claim on D's legal malpractice, which is typically addressed as a matter of tort law.[607] And at least a few US jurisdictions would deny C1 and C2 any claim.[608]

C. CASE 3. THE DEFECTIVE HOUSE

Contractor D builds a house for Z. The contract contains an exclusion clause whereby D shall not be liable to Z if the house's negligent construction causes property damage to the latter. Two years after the house has been built, Z sells it to C. Three years later, part of the house falls down due to a defect caused by D's negligence, and C also suffers personal injury. Can he sue D for compensation of his bodily injury and/or the damage caused to the house (in contract/tort/both)?

244 Some legal systems solve most of the problems posed by this case according to specific rules.[609] Thus, for instance, the French,[610] the Italian[611] and the Spanish[612] Civil Codes contain rules providing for the liability of the builder,

601 IL 78.
602 E&W 131, ZA 65.
603 IL 78.
604 AT 59, CZ 101, DE 89, GR 75, IT 126–128, CH 78 and, expressing some doubts, FR 88.
605 PL 162 f, ES 112, and also GR 75 if the claim were not time-barred.
606 NL 109.
607 US 107.
608 For instance, *Baker v Wood, Ris & Hames, Prof'l Corp*, 364 P 3d 872 (Colo 2016).
609 FR 89, IT 129, ES 113, NO 81.
610 FR 89 and art 1792.1 French CC.
611 IT 129 and arts 1655 ff Italian CC.
612 ES 113 and art 1591 Spanish CC.

both in favour of the first buyer and any subsequent buyers, for a period of 10 years. The 10-year period of the warranty starts running when the building was finished and the warranty cannot be excluded by contract. According to these provisions, D would be liable to C as regards both personal injury and property damage and the exclusion clause for property damage would be void. It is disputed whether this is liability in contract or in tort, although the opinion that it is in contract seems to prevail, since the warranty is transferred along with the building when it is sold. However, this is a typical case of professional liability, where the builder's liability is largely independent of the existence of a contract between him and the claimant, and it has been adapted by case law to the participation of new professionals in the building process required by the development of building techniques.[613]

In England and Wales and in some jurisdiction in the United States, there are 245
also similar rules that provide for a warranty of habitability for dwellings that protect the first and subsequent buyers from property damage. Thus, according to the Defective Premises Act 1972 in England and Wales, C could bring a claim against D, not only for property damage but also for personal injury, and any exclusion clause would be void.[614] C would be in a similar situation in some jurisdictions of the United States, but it must be stressed that jurisdictions are split as to whether such warranties extend to subsequent purchasers and to whether exclusion clauses for property damage are void or not. Although all of them would accept a claim in negligence from C against D for personal injury, they also seem split as regards a claim in negligence for damage to the building itself on the grounds of the economic loss rule.[615]

In Austria, the application of the economic loss rule would prevent C from 246
bringing a claim against D for damage to the building itself, both in tort and in contract – on the grounds of doctrine of the contract with protective effects to third parties – since the extension of the effects of the contract refers to duties of protection and care, not to the main contractual duty between D and Z, which was the delivery of a house without any defects.[616] By contrast, both doctrines would allow a claim of C against D for personal injury. In the same vein, the German report would allow a claim for personal injury, but also considers damage to the building as a pure economic loss and, for this reason, holds that for this loss C cannot bring a claim against D pursuant to the general tort law rules (§823 BGB).[617] However, when C has no other grounds for his

613 When it has been considered that such an adaptation could not be carried out any further – as has been the case in Spain – specific statutes have dealt with liability of all professionals involved in the building process which, however, do not include personal injury. ES 113.

614 E&W 133.

615 US 108.

616 AT 60 and 61.

617 DE 92.

claim, the doctrine of the contract with protective effects, as a supplementary 'gap-filler', could be applicable.[618]

247 In some other jurisdictions, apparently, C would also have a claim in tort against D, both for property damage and personal injury[619] or for personal injury only.[620] In the Czech Republic, additionally, C would have a contractual claim on the grounds of a third party clause[621] and in the Netherlands on the grounds that C had acquired certain 'qualitative rights' related to the property, ie rights that were connected in such a way to the house that the owner only had any interest in those rights as long as he retained property. Since these rights, by operation of law, pass to the person who acquires the building, C could bring a claim against D in contract.[622] In this case, the exclusion clause between D and Z would not be of any avail to D in the claim that C files against him.[623] In few jurisdictions, however, the exclusion clause for damage to property could be held valid and thus become an obstacle to recovery for property damage in the claim between C and D.[624]

D. CASE 4. APARTMENT IN FLAMES

C is a tenant living in a rented apartment. Her landlord, D, has negligently failed to monitor the circuit breaker, which causes fire in the apartment while C is inside. She is able to escape the burning apartment, but suffers severe physical injury. Does C have a valid claim against D (in contract/tort/both)?

248 In all jurisdictions but France, D's negligence to maintain or repair the circuit breaker that caused the fire can give rise to concurrent claims in contract and in tort.

249 Common core to all jurisdictions is that D has the duty to maintain the property leased to C in sound condition of use and has to carry out the necessary repairs in order to keep the apartment in a suitable condition of habitability, which refers not only to its utility but also to its safety.[625] In most cases, this is a contractual duty[626] and, accordingly, C can bring a claim

[618] DE 93.

[619] CZ 102, GR 77, IL 80, ZA 66, NL 114 f, PL 165, CH 86.

[620] NO 80.

[621] CZ 103.

[622] NL 112.

[623] NL 113.

[624] IL 80, NO 81.

[625] AT 62, CZ 104, E&W 135, FR 91, DE 96, GR 80, IL 81, IT 134 and 136, NO 83, PL 167, ZA 67, ES 114, CH 93, NL 116, US 109.

[626] In E&W 135 this is a statutory duty, infringement of which would give rise to a tort claim. However, a contractual claim could also exist if there were an implied or express obligation to monitor the circuit breaker.

against D in contract. In France, since there is a contract of lease between C and D, pursuant to the *non cumul* rule, any claim of C against D related to the apartment should be in contract.[627]

250 In the other jurisdictions, however, C can also bring a concurrent claim against D in tort. In these cases, although C may bring a claim on both grounds, he may prefer to sue D in contract or in tort depending on which grounds are more favourable to his interests. Thus, in countries like Austria and Germany, if liability of auxiliaries is involved, he will prefer to sue in contract, due to the restrictive standards existing in tort.[628] Longer prescription periods in contract, in those countries where prescription has not been unified, may also speak in favour of a contractual claim. In other jurisdictions, such as Greece, Italy, Poland and South Africa, where compensation for non-pecuniary loss is fully excluded in contract or subject to severe restrictions,[629] an action in tort can be more favourable to C's interests. When no substantial differences exist, legal practice may consider it more usual either to bring the claim in contract[630] or in tort.[631]

E. CASE 5. INJURED SKIER

C had bought a ski pass which entitled him to use the ski lift in a ski resort during his holidays. For reasons that were not fully clarified, there was a derailment of the ski lift while C was using it, and the cable fell, causing significant personal injury to C. C brings a claim against D1, the owner of the ski resort and issuer of the ski pass, as well as against D2, the insurance company with whom D1 had liability insurance. This policy states that the insurance company 'would cover up to the amount of €900,000, any compensation which the contracting party would have to pay arising from liability in tort pursuant to the general clause of liability for fault by reason of the operation of the resort'. D2, however, refuses to cover the insured accident and to pay any compensation, alleging that this was a case of contractual liability which was not covered under D1's policy.

251 D1 concluded a contract of transport with C, who suffered personal injury during performance of the contract. The first question that arises here is whether D1 is liable in contract, in tort or on both grounds. All jurisdictions but France agree that D1 can be held liable both in contract and in tort. As a matter of principle, French law would not allow a claim in tort on the grounds

627 FR 91.
628 AT 62, DE 51.
629 GR 81, IT 137, PL 167, ZA 67.
630 As in NO 83 and NL 117.
631 As in IL 81, IT 137 and some courts in US 109.

of the *non cumul* rule. According to French law, the operator of the ski lift owes to all those who contract with him an *obligation de sécurité de résultat*, which means that he is liable in contract for any damage caused to the user of the lift, unless it is the result of force majeure.[632] Among all the other jurisdictions that would allow concurring claims in contract and in tort, some of them conclude, however, that it would be quite unusual for C to pursue a claim in contract because, where the harm suffered by the claimant is personal injury, tort law typically prevails.[633] Others, by contrast, consider that a contractual claim would be the most likely course of action and would be better for C, since it would relieve him of the need of having to prove D1's fault when liability in tort is not strict.[634]

252 As regards the claim against D1 in tort, some jurisdictions have rules providing for strict liability[635] or can apply the *res ipsa loquitur* doctrine to this case.[636] Occasionally it is considered that when C has to prove D1's fault, the proof of fault could be so difficult that it might even prevent C from obtaining redress.[637]

253 A direct claim between C and D2 (ie D1's insurer) is not possible in England and Wales, Switzerland and in the United States. In England and Wales, the Third Parties (Rights against Insurers) Act 2010, which came into force on 1 August 2016, allows a third party to pursue a claim directly against a liability insurer only if the insured is or becomes insolvent.[638] No claim of C against D2 seems possible in Switzerland either, unless D2 has contractually subrogated in D1's position.[639] Generally, in the United States, C's direct action against D2 would not be permitted either, since it is considered that the existence of liability insurance would bias a lay jury when deciding whether liability exists.[640] In the other jurisdictions under survey, the success of C's direct claim against D2 would depend on the applicable liability rules in each country and on the interpretation of the insurance clause.[641] However, where concurrence of actions is possible and since insurance is bought to cover damage which

632 FR 92.

633 PL 168, US 110.

634 DE 99, NL 120.

635 In AT 65, NO 83, PL 70, CH 97 this case would be governed by strict liability rules. Also probably in NL 119, in the hypothetical case where they had such facilities in the country, which in fact they do not.

636 ZA 68.

637 DE 100.

638 E&W 136.

639 CH 103 ff.

640 US 111.

641 Thus, for instance, in FR 93 coverage for tort liability would be useless in this case and the insurance contract could be void in those countries where liability is strict.

occurred as a result of the operation of the business, it would be at least odd to suggest that the fact that C bought a ski pass would bring him outside the area covered by the insurance.[642]

F. CASE 6. EXPLODING CAR

C buys a brand new car from D1, produced by D2, which has a two-year full warranty against all defects. Three years later, while on a trip to the mountains, C parks the car, and when he is 300 metres away enjoying sightseeing the car suddenly explodes and is totally destroyed. Experts say that the car's fuel line was defective. C brings a claim against D1 and D2.

The first question that arises is whether C can bring a claim against D1 in contract. According to most jurisdictions, this claim is not possible, since the claim is time-barred. Some jurisdictions have specific national rules for latent defects, which provide for a two-year[643] or shorter prescription period.[644] Other reports refer to the fact that C is a consumer and then the corresponding national rules implementing the Consumer Sales and Guarantees Directive 1999/44/EC would apply. Although C could file a claim against D1 for lack of conformity,[645] the two-year period established by art 5 of said Directive has already elapsed.[646] However, this two-year period aims at protecting consumers and cannot be used to their detriment. For this reason, it cannot prevent C from bringing a claim against D1 according to general contract law rules when they provide for a longer prescription period, as is the case in the Netherlands,[647] or when they provide that time starts running from discovery of the defect and not from delivery of the goods, as is the case in France pursuant to art 1648 *Code civil*.[648] 254

As regards C's claim in contract against D2, most reports answer that this is not possible for the obvious reason that C and D2 are not contractually bound. However, France and Norway, in this case, would allow a direct action of C against D2, provided that C's claim against D1 was not time-barred already.[649] 255

To decide whether C's claim against D2 in tort is possible, most reports refer to their national legislation implementing the Product Liability Directive and 256

---

642 In this sense, NO 84.

643 DE 102, CZ 108, GR 84, IL 83, ZA 70.

644 IT 146–149, one year from discovery of the latent defect; ES 116, six months from discovery.

645 Cf art 3 Directive 1999/44/EC of the European Parliament and of the Council of 25 May 1999 on Certain Aspects of the Sale of Consumer Goods and Associated Guarantees.

646 ES 116, IT 146–149.

647 NL 122.

648 FR 94.

649 FR 95, NO 86.

conclude that this claim would not be possible, since art 9(b) of the Directive provides that damage means 'damage to, or destruction of, any item of property *other than the defective product itself* (emphasis added).[650] However, not surprisingly, some jurisdictions that do not operate with the 'pure economic loss' concept consider that a claim of C against D2 in tort is nevertheless possible according to the general national tort rules.[651] In Spanish case law, for instance, the exclusion of the damage to the product itself seems to be a whim of the European legislator and, although legal scholarship timidly points out that damage to the product itself should remain a matter of contract law, case law resorts to a hodgepodge application of general rules and rules transposing the Directive to allow compensation for damage to the product itself in tort.[652]

257 The reasons why compensation for damage to the product itself in tort should also be excluded according to general tort law rules has been widely discussed in the United States and in Germany. In fact, this hypothetical is inspired by a line of American cases starting with *Seely v White Motor Co*[653] and followed by *Cloud v Kit Manufacturing*,[654] and many others, and also in German cases.

258 American courts consider that when the only harm is the deficiency in the product or its performance, the economic loss rule displaces tort and leaves buyers to the contractual remedies only.[655] However, some courts have made exceptions to this economic loss rule when misperformance occurred in a 'tort-like' accident manner. In *Cloud v Kit Manufacturing* the court admitted how difficult it was to trace a line between contract and tort by saying that: '[W]e recognize that the line between economic loss and direct property damage is not always easy to discern, particularly when the plaintiff is seeking compensation for loss of the product itself. We cannot lay down an all-inclusive rule to distinguish between the two categories'/ Nevertheless, the court added, 'we note that sudden and calamitous damage will almost always result in direct property damage and that deterioration, internal breakage and depreciation will be considered economic loss.'[656] Although courts have occasionally followed other criteria (such as the 'parasitic-damage approach', ie compensating damage for the product itself when personal injury or damage to other property are present,[657]

---

650 AT 10, CZ 108, FR 97, IT 146–149, PL 169, ES 117, CH 111 – if D2 is not the manufacturer of the fuel line; implicitly, also NL 123.

651 GR 87, IT 146–149, PL 169, ES 116. But also E&W 137, NL 122 and ZA 71.

652 ES 117.

653 *Seely v White Motor Co*, 63 Cal 2d, 403 P 2d 145, 45 Cal Rptr 17 (1965).

654 *Cloud v Kit Manufacturing Co*, 563 P 2d 248 (Alaska 1977).

655 US 112.

656 *Cloud v Kit Manufacturing Co*, 563 P 2d 251 (Alaska 1977).

657 For instance *LeSueur Creamery, Inc v Haskon, Inc*, 660 F 2d 342 (8th Cir 1981).

or by distinguishing between consumers and non-consumers[658]), most courts limit the buyer's remedy to contract. This rule has been well entrenched since *East River Steamship Corp v Transamerica Delaval, Inc*,[659] where defective turbines on four chartered ships malfunctioned and forced the charterers not only to pay the cost of repairs, but also to lose profits while the ships were being restored. The charterers were unable to bring a contractual claim against the shipbuilder for breach of warranty and sued the turbine manufacturer for negligence and strict liability, arguing that the defective design of the turbines led to their repair expenses and lost profits. Justice Blackmun declared, however, that 'damage to a product itself is most naturally understood as a warranty claim. Such damage means simply that the product has not met the customer's expectations, or, in other words, that the customer has received "insufficient product value"'[660] and made a strong argument against the conceptual disaggregation of a product into its component parts, pointing out that since all but the very simplest of machines have component parts, a contrary holding would require a finding of 'property damage' in virtually every case where a product damages itself[661] and this would have made warranty law useless.[662] The rule is now being expanded in the Restatement (Third) of Torts as a general preclusion rule of tort liability in all those cases where the claimant and defendant suffer economic loss caused by negligence in the performance or negotiation of a contract that binds them.[663]

The idea that it is possible to establish criteria to distinguish between a contractual interest in the utility of a good (*Äquivalenzinteresse*), preserved by contract law rules, and in interest in safety which would protect against damage to property (*Integritätsinteresse*), preserved by tort law rules, has also been discussed in Germany, where courts have developed the doctrine of the so-called *Weiterfresserschäden* (literally, 'damage which continues to eat up the good'). One of the criteria used has been the 'functional separability' (*funktionelle Abgrenzbarkeit*), ie the distinction between a separate element that serves a functionally separate purpose (such as a floating switch[664] or the back tyres of a car)[665] and can be installed into, and removed from, a greater entity (degreasing machine, car, etc), without great difficulty. If such an element 259

658 For instance *Spring Motors Distributions, Inc v Ford Motor Co*, 98 NJ 555, 489 A 2d 660 (1985).

659 *East River Steamship Corp v Transamerica Delaval, Inc*, 476 US 858, 106 S Ct 2295, 90 L Ed 865 (1986).

660 Ibid, 872.

661 Ibid, 867.

662 Ibid, 867 f.

663 Restatement of the Law (Third) of Torts: Liability for Economic Harm, Tentative Draft 1, §3.

664 *Schwimmerschalter-Urteil*, BGHZ 67, 359 = NJW 1977, 379 = JZ 1977, 343 with notes by *Lieb*.

665 *Hinterreifen-I*, BGH NJW 1978, 2241 and *Hinterreifen-II*, NJW 2004, 1032, with comments by *Gsell* NJW 2004, 1913.

destroys the greater entity, this amounts to property damage and then general tort rules apply. The gist of the whole doctrine is to divide the damaged good into two parts: the defective separate element and the rest of the good that is free from defects. However, in order not to mix up the purpose of tort law and contract law, the damage that the separate element causes to the whole good must not be identical to the originally diminished value of the good on the grounds of its defect (*Stoffgleichheit*).[666] If this were the case, the only remedies available to C would be in contract.[667] According to this doctrine, if the fuel line was a separate element that could be quite easily removed and re-installed in the car, C could bring a claim in tort against D2; since the claim is not time-barred and in this case fault is presumed, the prospects of success for this claim are high.[668] This doctrine, however, has given rise to an endless debate in Germany, where it has been contended that these and other possible criteria cannot properly demarcate the domain of contract law from tort law and, since the doctrine disrupts the risk allocation established by the parties in the contract, it should be abandoned.[669] The impossibility of separating one part of the object and attributing it to the concept of 'other property' is very clear in those cases where the latent defect is discovered before the destruction of the object takes place.[670] The claimant who has no claim in contract because all the possible contractual causes of action have expired has no action in tort either, because the object has suffered no damage yet. The protection of the owner would depend then on whether he has discovered the defect or not, which would then offer him a perverse incentive for not inspecting the object to check whether it has latent defects or not, in order to try to avoid their serious consequences.[671]

G. CASE 7. BURNING RACING BOAT

Y sells a racing boat to D. D adds special electronic equipment to improve navigation on the high seas. After using the boat for two years, D sells it to C with a two-year full warranty against all defects. Three years later, C decides to participate in a race around the world. Once the race has started, and after C has sailed only 400 miles, the equipment added by D, which was defective from the beginning, catches fire, and the fire destroys the boat entirely. C is rescued by X's boat and taken to shore

666 *Gaszug-Urteil*, BGH NJW 1983, 810; *Kompressor-Urteil*, BGH NJW 1985, 2420; *Nockenwellensteuerrad-Urteil* NJW 1992, 1678.

667 DE 105.

668 DE 106.

669 *G Wagner* in: Münchener Kommentar zum BGB, 7 ed. §823, no 252 f.

670 Instructive in this sense is the classical Canadian case *Rivtow Marine Ltd v Washigton Iron Works Ltd* (1973) 40 DLR (3d) 530 (SCC).

671 MüKoBGB/*Wagner* (fn 669) §823, no 253.

where he catches a flight home. C suffers no personal injury but sues D, claiming the value of the destroyed boat and the cost of his repatriation expenses.

The case is inspired by *Saratoga Fishing Co v J M Martinac & Co*,[672] a case decided by the United States Supreme Court, but with the major difference that here the defective product is not the original one (the ship), but the electronic equipment added by the first buyer; by contrast in *Saratoga* the defective product was the ship (the product itself), while the added equipment was considered 'other property'. 260

In *Saratoga*, J M Martinac & Co had built a ship, installed a hydraulic system designed by Marco Seattle Inc, and sold it new to J Madruga. Madruga added extra equipment, used the ship for tuna fishing for several years, and resold it afterwards to Saratoga Fishing Co, which continued to use the ship for fishing. A few years later, due to the fact that the hydraulic system was defective, the ship caught fire and sank. Saratoga Fishing Co brought a claim in tort against Marco Seattle and Martinac. The United States Supreme Court, in a six to three vote, granted compensation in tort for the added equipment, but not for the value of the ship itself. 261

As pointed out in the previous case, 11 years earlier, in *East River Steamship Corp v Transamerica Delaval Inc*,[673] the Court had made a strong argument against the conceptual disaggregation of a product into its component parts. Such disaggregation would have permitted a claimant to argue that his property – the product – was harmed by a component part, and this would have made warranty law useless, since a claimant could have continuously subdivided his product until finding a tort claim against a remote producer beyond the scope of the warranty.[674] In *Saratoga*, however, the Court established that *East River*'s product–component analysis did not apply to the case. Unlike the component of a larger product, the fishing ship had been released into the marketplace before the fisherman added the equipment and the Court held that once a buyer purchases a product from the manufacturer or distributor, any subsequently added equipment ought to be considered 'other property' under the *East River* analysis.[675] The fisherman, in that case, was distinguishable from a manufacturer or a component supplier because he lacked the ability to 'systematically control the manufactured product's quality or … systematically allocate responsibility for [the equipment he added] in similar ways' to those used in the manufacturing process.[676] 262

672 *Saratoga Fishing Co v JM Martinac & Co*, 520 US 875 (1997).
673 *East River Steamship Corp v Transamerica Delaval Inc*, 476 US 858 (1986).
674 Ibid, 867 f.
675 *Saratoga Fishing Co v JM Martinac & Co*, 520 US 875, 884 f (1997).
676 Ibid, 884.

263 Since in our case what is defective is the added equipment, according to *Saratoga*'s doctrine, compensation in tort should be granted for the 'other property' (the ship) and not for the defective added equipment (which is here 'the defective product itself').[677]

264 In our hypothetical, most reports consider that C cannot bring a claim against D in contract since the warranty has already expired. The question that arises then is whether or not the warranty clause intended to cut all contractual claims after its expiration. If this was not the case and the other contractual remedies were not time-barred,[678] C could still bring a contractual claim on other grounds such as breach of contract[679] or consumer law remedies,[680] provided that the conditions required by the application of these remedies (for instance, fault) had been met.

265 The problem arises when C has no contractual claim against D. Can he make recourse to a claim in tort? Some reports mention the corresponding national regulation implementing the Product Liability Directive, but they hold that these rules do not affect C. The reason is not the exclusion of damage to the product itself (art 9(b)), but simply that C is not a producer in the sense of art 3(1) Product Liability Directive.[681]

266 Finally, a claim based on the general national provisions establishing tort liability would require that D was negligent when installing the electronic equipment, and considering that D was negligent, most reports hold that C can bring a claim in tort against D.[682] However, the hypothetical does not say that D was at fault when installing the equipment, but only that the equipment that D added 'was defective from the beginning'. Under this interpretation of the facts, C would not have a claim in tort against D, but possibly, if not expired, could have a claim against the manufacturer of the electronic equipment, from which he could possibly recover for all losses, except for damage to the equipment itself.

H. CASE 8. INSIDIOUS REPORT

D, acting as C's employee, is the contact person for company Z, which manufactures a product exclusively for C. D files a disparaging report on company Z, based

677 US 113.
678 They were in DE 107.
679 E&W 139, FR 98, IT 149, PL 172, ES 118, NL 124.
680 NO 90.
681 In this sense, DE 108.
682 AT 71, DE 109, E&W 139, GR 88, IL 84, IT 146, NO 91, PL 171 (although unlikely), ZA 73, ES 118, CH 124, US 113.

on false and insidious statements, which leads C to terminate its contract with company Z. A few weeks later, D, while still working for company C, sets up his own company and signs a distribution contract for the same product with company Z. C files a claim against its former employee D.

In spite of the fact that D had already been dismissed when C filed his claim 267
('C files a claim against its *former* employee D'[683]), the hypothetical makes clear that D was C's employee both when producing the disparaging report and when starting to compete with him. Accordingly, most reports point out that D has breached several obligations arising from his labour contract with his employer, which include the duty to serve his employer with fidelity and good faith.[684] This duty prevents D from competing with the business activity of his employer and, in this case, it can be immaterial whether a non-compete clause has been negotiated into the employment contract or not,[685] since this illicit competition took place while D was still C's employee, not after termination of employment.[686]

Additionally, in most jurisdictions, C can also bring a claim against D according 268
to general tort law rules and according to the specific rules of unfair competition statutes.[687] Thus, considering that D had intentionally inflicted damage on C, many reports point out that C may claim compensation in tort.[688] In England and Wales, Israel and the United States, C could resort to several specific tortious causes of action, such as malicious[689] or injurious[690] falsehood, defamation,[691] tortious interference with contract,[692] fraud,[693] etc. In some jurisdictions, since D communicated false facts to influence C's commercial contract with Z, it is considered that D's conduct was contrary to public policy or *boni mores*, which allows compensation in tort even for pure economic loss.[694]

Disparagement or denigration,[695] ie D's malicious assertions about C in order to 269
divert his clientele – in particular by discrediting C's products, work or person – and D's illegal competing business activities[696] are recognised as a violation in

683 Some reports consider that what C has done is enough to fire him, AT 72, E&W 141.
684 AT 72, CZ 110, E&W 141, FR 99, DE 110, GR 89, IL 85, PL 174, ZA 74, ES 119, CH 129 f, US 114.
685 E&W 141, IT 150, ES 119.
686 In this sense, DE 110.
687 Thus, DE 110, GR 97, ES 119, CH 126, US 114 f mention both; AT 72, IT 150, NO 92, PL 173 mention unfair competition specific rules only; NL 126 mentions tort only.
688 For instance, see GR 97.
689 E&W 140.
690 IL 85.
691 E&W 140, IL 85.
692 IL 85, US 114.
693 IL 85, US 114.
694 DE 111 and §826 BGB; §2909 Czech CC; ZA 74.
695 For instance, CH 125, ES 119, US 115.
696 For instance, DE 110, ES 119.

the specific statutes on unfair competition. These rules provide not only for damages, but refer to other remedies which would allow C also to request a declaration of unfairness, injunctions regarding the cessation of the unfair conduct and prohibiting its repetition in the future, disgorgement of D's unjust enrichment, etc.[697]

270 For lack of a specific statute, unfair competition is dealt with in France pursuant to art 1240 *Code civil*, ie the general provision on liability for fault. Denigration is a clear instance of fault. However, since here there is a contract between C and D, apparently C can file, against D, a contractual claim only, which regularly requires gross negligence equating to intentional fault to succeed.[698]

I. CASE 9. CIRCULAR LETTER

C is an industrial property agent acting for company D. After many disagreements between agent and company, C leaves D and sets up his own company Z. D then sends a circular to all its customers alleging that C no longer works for the company because he had to be dismissed for misconduct; it claimed further that C's new company Z cannot legally manage industrial property rights; and that C had been reported to the authorities for professional intrusion. Finally, D asks its customers to refrain from dealing with C and to correspond directly with D. C files a claim against D.

271 C may bring a claim in tort against D on several grounds. Most reports point out that the dissemination of facts that are false or that cannot be proven true and which are apt to damage C's commercial reputation and Z's goodwill is one of the many forms of unfair trade practices governed by the rules of unfair competition.[699] Thus, the circulation of the letter and, in particular, the instigation of prospective customers to refrain from dealing with C, can be considered as a tort pursuant to these specific rules. Alternatively, C could sue D according to the general tort law rules,[700] or in some jurisdictions – since the dissemination of false facts regarding commercial conduct in order to harm other market participants is considered a violation of *boni mores* – according to the general tort law rules that allow compensation for pure economic loss in cases of intentional violation of *boni mores*.[701] As regards the dissemination of false facts, in many jurisdictions C could also bring a claim against D according

697 IT 150, ES 119.

698 FR 99.

699 AT 14, CZ 112, DE 114, IT 151, NO 94, ES 120–123, PL 175, CH 133, US 117.

700 Thus FR 100 on art 1204 French, or NL 129, where art 6:106 Dutch CC would allow recovery for non-pecuniary loss.

701 CZ 112, DE 113, CH 132.

to the specific provisions protecting the rights to personality.[702] In common law and mixed jurisdictions, C could use several tortious causes of action such as defamation, malicious falsehood, interference with prospective contractual relations, etc.[703]

Whether there is also a concurrent contractual claim of C against D is at least doubtful in this case. Although some reports hold that a concurrent claim in contract is not possible since the contractual relationship between C and D is already terminated,[704] others consider that, as a secondary effect, the labour contract establishes a contractual obligation to keep confidence after the termination of the contract even if it is not explicitly agreed.[705] If this were the case, or if one way or another there are post-termination obligations between them,[706] a claim in contract would also be possible in all jurisdictions that allow concurrence of claims. 272

The hypothetical is based on the Spanish Supreme Court decision 11.7.2006 (RJ 2006/4977) where the facts were substantially the same. Curiously enough, this is probably the only decision of the Spanish Supreme Court where it referred explicitly to the notion of 'pure economic loss' and it held that in the Spanish system the problem is dealt with by reference to the rules on damage and causation. Accordingly, it held that the claimant had not proved the pecuniary 'indirect damage' that he allegedly suffered in his business and ruled for compensation of non-pecuniary losses only. 273

J. CASE 10. SHORTAGE OF SUPPLY

D, X and Z provide C with the same component parts he needs for his product. When D learns that X is bankrupt and that Z had to reduce its production dramatically for other reasons, D tells C that it will discontinue distribution of component parts if C does not accept a 20% increase in prices, furthermore that payments shall be made in less than 30 days instead of 90 as agreed in the original supply contract. Since C has no alternative supply sources, he accepts the new conditions, but brings an action against D.

D's conduct is *contra bonos mores*, which in this case means lack of fairness in business transactions. In some legal systems, there are specific rules normally requiring the combination of subjective elements, such as levity of character, lack of experience or, as in our case, exploitation of one party's needs, and 274

702 IT 151, GR 93, PL 175, ES 120–123.
703 E&W 143, IL 86, ZA 75, US 116.
704 CH 135, US 116.
705 GR 91 f. Also IL 86.
706 E&W 143.

an objective element, which is gross disparity between performance and counter-performance.[707] Regularly the consequence is that the contract is null and void and then D should return the overpayment made by C according to the rules of restitution or unjust enrichment and could claim damages according to tort law rules. However, since there was a previous contract, full nullity of the second contract could make clear that the only valid contract was the original one and then C could consider that conduct according to this second contract amounts to a breach of the previous one and use the appropriate contractual remedies.[708] Whether the second contract is void in the present case is doubtful, since the price increase is not very high and the changes in the other circumstances in D's favour are not very extreme.[709]

275 Another possible remedy would be to consider that the contract is voidable only because C did not give his consent freely, but under some form of duress (economic duress),[710] undue influence,[711] '*violence économique*'[712] or 'abuse of circumstances'.[713] Attention must be paid to C's acts, to ponder whether they amount to a ratification of the voidable contract or not.[714] If no ratification has taken place, C could ask for restitution and for damages in contract.

276 Although this report does not deal with infringements of competition law, some reports point out that D's conduct might amount to an abuse of a dominant position, which would also give rise to a fine imposed by the market authority and to the corresponding injunctions against D's conduct.[715] The contract would be void and the infringement of rules of unfair competition would allow recovery of damages according to tort law rules.[716] The improper pressure that D has exerted on C could also give rise to a claim according to general tort

---

[707] DE 115, §138 (2) BGB, where, according to case law, the objective element may be sufficient when the disproportion is over 100%; GR 95 (art 179 Greek CC), NO 96 and also PL 177 and IT 152 ff.

[708] For instance, DE 115, IT 152, CH 141 f.

[709] DE 115, PL 177.

[710] E&W 144, referring to a case where a 10% increase might be regarded as economic duress, which finally did not give rise to voidability, because the claimant had confirmed the contract with his acts. See also ZA 76 and US 118.

[711] IL 87.

[712] Art 1143 French CC.

[713] NL 130 and art 3:44 Dutch CC.

[714] E&W 144.

[715] However, abuse of dominant position is more focused on exclusionary abuses than on exploitative ones, which might imply making judgments about a dominant firm's prices and could come close to the role of regulatory supervision. See *K Cseres*, Competition and Contract Law, in: A Hartkamp et al (eds), Towards a European Civil Code (4th edn 2011) 218 f.

[716] FR 101, IT 152 ff, PL 177, ES 124, CH 139; probably also CZ 113, which refers to §8 Czech CC, the general provision on abuse of rights, and GR 96.

rules if it is considered an intentional violation of *boni mores*[717] or amount to specific torts in some jurisdictions[718] but, according to the facts of the case, this would seem a more doubtful solution.[719]

K. CASE 11. INJURED ROCK STAR

X, a famous retired rock star, agrees with C, promoter, to perform a comeback concert. On his way to the concert X suffers an accident caused by D, and the concert must be cancelled. C brings a claim against D for the cancellation costs and for loss of profits.

C and D are not contractually linked, so no contractual claim may arise among them. Here the question is whether C can bring a claim against D when a tort committed by D against X interferes in the contractual relationship existing between X and C. Thus the tort against X prevents X from fulfilling his contractual obligations with C. Or in short: can C file a claim in tort against D as a secondary, indirect or reflex victim for pecuniary loss? The reports from the jurisdictions that acknowledge the notion of pure economic loss point out that C cannot bring a claim in tort against D because C suffers pure economic loss and such a loss cannot be recovered pursuant to the ordinary rules of fault (or strict liability).[720] Some of the jurisdictions that do not acknowledge the notion of pure economic loss hold that this is a case of 'indirect' damage, and recoverability requires that damage is 'direct',[721] or that the general rules on damage, causation or scope of liability[722] would exclude compensation in this case. This is also the case in France where indirect or secondary victims who claim and obtain compensation are nearly always relatives of the direct victim, who suffer financial loss and/or pain and suffering due to the latter's death or injury. As in the other countries, in France, courts also tend to reject claims for financial loss brought by the direct victim's economic partner, but they usually do so on the not very convincing basis that damage is not then a direct consequence of the damaging act.[723] 277

717 Thus considering that this was the case here, CZ 113 and GR 95, and that the facts of the case do not qualify for such a breach, DE 116.

718 As, for instance, the tort of intimidation, in E&W 146.

719 Some other jurisdictions, in general terms, also consider a claim on tort less likely, US 118, IL 87.

720 AT 75, E&W 147, DE 117, IL 88, ZA 77, US 120.

721 GR 97, PL 180, CH 144.

722 NO 96, scope of liability; PL 180, lack of adequate causation; ES 125, lack of causation or damage; NL 132, lack of scope of protection of the infringed norm.

723 FR 102.

278 Probably the only jurisdictions under survey where C could recover the pecuniary losses suffered as a result of X's death are the Czech Republic and Italy. The Czech report considers that, pursuant to §2910 CC, D would be liable in tort because D's liability is not confined to the infringement of absolute rights.[724] In Italy, the Court of Cassation introduced in 1971 a broader interpretation of the notion of *danno ingiusto* (art 2043 CC) and declared, in the legendary case of the Torino football player, the *Meroni* case, that 'who with intent or fault causes the death of another's debtor is obliged to compensate for the damage suffered by the creditor, if the death has resulted in the extinction of credit and in a final and irreparable loss for the same creditor'.[725] Since this decision, subsequently confirmed by others, the expression *danno ingiusto* has been extended not only to the protection of property and personality rights, but also to rights of credit in what has often been called the doctrine of the 'tortious protection of the right of credit' (*tutela aquiliana del diritto di credito*). This protection includes pure economic loss resulting from the breach of a contract due to a tort committed by a third person against the debtor, provided that the creditor, in a very strict test concerning causation, can give evidence of causation and of the damage suffered and that the obligation that the debtor can no longer fulfil was a fundamental personal obligation (*obbligazioni di fare*) for which the creditor cannot obtain a substitute in the market because it was strictly personal or founded on the creditor's personal trust to the debtor or on the debtor's reputation, technical skills or professional abilities.[726]

L. CASE 12. EQUIPMENT DESTROYED

X, a famous retired rock star, agrees with C to perform a comeback concert. C concludes a transport contract with D1 to transport the electronic equipment needed for the concert. On its way to the concert the truck suffers an accident caused by D2, the driver of a colliding bus. The equipment was destroyed and as a result the concert had to be cancelled. C brings a claim against D1 and D2. Does it make a difference if C was the owner of the equipment or not?

279 C's claim against D1, for non-performance of the transport contract, is contractual. The first question that arises is whether non-performance was excused or not. It depends to a large extent on what the parties had agreed in

724 CZ 114 and §2910 Czech CC: 'A wrongdoer who through his fault breaches an obligation set by law and in doing so interferes with an absolute right of the injured party shall compensate the harm he causes by doing so. The duty to provide compensation also applies to a wrongdoer who interferes with another right of the injured party by breaching through his fault a duty established by law for the protection of that right.'

725 Cass Sez Un, 26 January 1971, no 174 (*Meroni*).

726 IT 155.

the contract and on whether a traffic accident can be considered force majeure if D1 is allowed to escape liability or not.[727] Holding that traffic accidents are normal and foreseeable risks in D1's transport business, some reports consider that the risk of non-delivery of the transported object due to a traffic accident could be attributed to D1.[728] If D1 is liable, however, since performance is no longer possible, damages is the only remedy available to C. In this case, if nothing has been agreed between the parties, the rules dealing with the transport contract may also cap the amount of damages[729] and may make recoverability of consequential losses dependant on D1's gross negligence[730] or exclude it altogether.[731] Since the traffic accident was caused by D2 and not by D1, C does not have any concurrent claim in tort against D1.

C's claim against D2, by contrast, if any, can be in tort only. In this claim, it is important whether C was the owner of the equipment or not. If C was not the owner of the equipment, C's claim against D2 is a claim for 'reflex', 'indirect' or '*par ricochet*' damage. The answer of the different jurisdictions would be very similar to the previous case (Case 11), and the Czech Republic and Italy seem to be the only jurisdictions that would allow recovery for pecuniary losses resulting from the cancellation of the concert[732] (subject, however, to a strict proof of damage and causation, including the rules on the scope of liability). Other continental jurisdictions, however, would dismiss C's claim in tort against D2 for lack of damage, causation or on policy considerations referring to the scope of liability.[733] The fact that C was or was not the owner of the equipment does not seem to be crucial in these jurisdictions. 280

For those jurisdictions that operate with the pure economic loss notion, however, whether C was the owner of the equipment or not makes an important difference. If C was not the owner of the equipment, C has suffered pure economic loss only and in this case he cannot bring a claim in tort.[734] However, if C was the owner of the equipment, C may claim against D2 both for the repair or replacement of the equipment and the pecuniary losses resulting from the cancellation of the concert (if duly proven).[735] As the South African report 281

727 Jurisdictions that seem to consider that the traffic accident qualifies as force majeure in this case, CZ 115, IT 156 and, probably, ZA 78 and CH 150. US 121 mentions that the doctrine of impossibility may serve to excuse performance.

728 Considering on these grounds that the traffic accident was not force majeure, FR 103, NL 134.

729 AT 76, FR 103, DE 118.

730 As in AT 76.

731 DE 118, where §433 HGB excludes compensation for consequential losses when the transported goods have been damaged or destroyed.

732 CZ 115, IT 156.

733 FR 103, NO 98, PL 178, ES 126, NL 134.

734 Thus, considering that C was not the owner of the equipment, E&W 148, DE 120, IL 89.

735 Thus, considering that C was the owner of the equipment, AT 76, ZA 78, US 122. The answer in CH 152 is confusing since, although it considers that C was the owner of the equipment, it holds that the cancellation of the concert was pure economic loss.

clearly points out, the difference between this case and Case 11 is that here C has suffered property damage (destruction of the equipment) with consequential financial loss (cancellation of the concert) and not pure economic loss and, for this reason, C may claim damages for his total loss from D2.[736]

M. CASE 13. SLIPPING ON A LETTUCE LEAF

C enters D's premises, a grocery shop. Before buying anything, C slips on a lettuce leaf and breaks her leg. C brings a claim against D (in contract/tort/both?).

282 Suffering an accident by slipping on a lettuce leaf, or on an unidentified vegetable leaf,[737] a cabbage leaf[738] or a banana peel[739] are everyday situations that, if all the required conditions are met, usually give rise to liability in tort. However, when such accidents are related to the conclusion of a contract, in some legal systems pre-contractual liability may be used to avoid the shortcomings of the tort law. This is the case in Germany, where the German Supreme Court decided a case that inspires this hypothetical,[740] and in Austria, where such a case has also become a common classroom hypothetical.[741]

283 Since in this case the parties have not concluded any contract yet, C should base his claim in tort. However, in Germany, this would require proving that D was at fault, which may be extremely difficult in these sorts of situations, or that he was liable for the acts of his employees. In this latter case, in Germany D could also escape liability rather easily by proving that he selected and supervised his employees and organised his enterprise with ordinary care. In order to avoid leaving C empty-handed, courts have considered that in these cases C is in a

---

736 ZA 78.

737 DE 121.

738 ZA 79.

739 NL 136.

740 See the English version of this judgment, BGHZ 66, 51 VIII, Civil Senate (VIII ZR 246/74) *Gemüseblatt*-decision = NJW 1976, 712 = VersR 1976, 589 = JZ 1976, 776, at <https://law.utexas.edu/transnational/foreign-law-translations/german/case.php?id=1487> (accessed: 1.11.2016). The German Supreme Court confirmed *culpa in contrahendo* of a self-service store owner vis-à-vis potential buyers, the latter role being presumed of those entering the store. The court, however, obiter denied such liability if it was clear that the person entering the store had no intention of buying (such as someone merely seeking shelter from the rain). The original precedent was Reichsgericht 7.12.1911 RGZ 78, 239 (English translation RGZ 78, 239 VI, Civil Senate (VI 240/11) *Linoleumrollen*-decision = JW 1912, 191) at <https://law.utexas.edu/transnational/foreign-law-translations/german/case.php?id=807> (accessed 1.11.2016), where the prospective buyer and her child fell on rolls of linoleum floor-cover dropped by a shop assistant. In this case, the court still distinguished between potential clients who had already entered into actual negotiations with the store (as here) and the situation where someone merely enters the store without yet entering into negotiations (in which case the Reichsgericht obiter denied liability).

741 AT 77.

pre-contractual situation where he is already exposed to the risks created by D. This enables them to apply the contractual presumption that damage was caused by D and the more claimant-friendly rules of liability for the auxiliaries in contract where the debtor is responsible for their fault as if it were his own. Since in these situations the debtor is regularly not in the position to rebut the presumption, C would be entitled to damages against D for *culpa in contrahendo*.[742] Austrian courts would also apply the *culpa in contrahendo* doctrine on similar grounds.[743]

Most jurisdictions under survey, however, solve these problems according to tort law rules only[744] and, among those that accept pre-contractual liability based on good faith, some emphasise that this doctrine refers to the standards of reasonability and fairness that are to be observed during the negotiation of a contract. Accordingly, they consider that pre-contractual liability relates to the conclusion or non-conclusion of the contract or to its content, but it does not cover personal injury suffered in the course of negotiations.[745] Liability is then based on the breach of the duty to maintain the shop premises in an adequate condition, which makes them reasonably safe for customers and visitors, either as imposed by specific rules[746] or by the standard of care required by general tort law provisions establishing fault.[747] Some jurisdictions, such as France[748] and Italy,[749] consider, however, that in this case D can be regarded as the keeper or custodian of the lettuce leaf and, accordingly, can be held strictly liable. 284

N. CASE 14. TEST DRIVE

D wants to buy a second-hand car from C, a car dealer. Before buying it D drives the car along the main street in front of C's premises and smashes the front part of the car against a tree. C brings a claim against D.

Most jurisdictions under survey consider that, since the sales contract has not been concluded, liability must be in tort. Also admitting that a claim in tort is possible, the Austrian report mentions that a claim on the grounds of pre-contractual liability or *culpa in contrahendo* of D is possible as well. It points out that, although the sales contract between C and D has not been concluded, the fact that the parties are in the process of concluding it gives rise 285

742 DE 121 f.
743 AT 77 and CR 100 ff. This also seems to be the case in Greece, GR 103.
744 CZ 117, E&W 149, IL 91, IT 157, NO 100, PL 181, ZA 79, ES 127, CH 156, NL 136, US 123.
745 So, for instance, IT 158 f and NL 137.
746 CZ 116, E&W 149.
747 GR 102, IL 91, NO 100, PL 181, ZA 79, ES 127, CH 159, NL 136, US 123.
748 FR 105 and art 1242 al 1 French CC (*responsabilité du fait des choses*).
749 IT 157 and art 2051 Italian CC (*danno cagionato dalle cose in custodia*).

to more extensive duties of protection and care to each other and that, by damaging D's car, C has breached these duties.[750] By contrast, since the damage suffered by D is not related to the negotiation of the contract (information, conclusion, breaking off negotiations, etc) or to its content, some reports do not mention pre-contractual liability[751] or stress that it would not be applicable in this case.[752]

286 Some jurisdictions point out that C may also have a claim in contract, since C may have concluded with D a gratuitous loan of use.[753] By a gratuitous contract of loan of use, C, as the lender of the car allows D, the borrower, to use it at no charge and D is obliged to return the car at the end of the period of time specified for the gratuitous loan, or more probably in our case, after the borrower has used the car in the test as agreed. D will have to return the car in the condition in which he received it and, although he cannot be held liable for the normal deterioration caused by the use of the car in conformity with the contract, he will be liable in contract for property damage caused by the accident.

287 Some reports also take into account that the car crash damaged a tree and contend that the owner of the tree may recover from C for the damage caused to its property in tort.[754] Others consider that in this case the tort claim would be based on the specific road traffic liability provisions, which regularly provide for a strict liability regime for drivers, which is backed by compulsory third-party insurance.[755] These provisions will establish when D as a driver different from the owner C is covered and whether damage to property is covered in all cases or not.[756]

O. CASE 15. BREAKING OFF NEGOTIATIONS

D enters into negotiations to sell an antique to C. C says that he will be on a business trip for a couple of days and that he will continue negotiations on Friday of the same week, to which D agrees. On Thursday D sells the antique to X. C brings a claim against D for the costs incurred.

288 The case may give rise to two related but different issues. The first one is whether parallel negotiations between D and X, which took place when D was already

---

750 AT 79.

751 For instance, NL 137 f.

752 IT 161.

753 DE 123, ES 128, CH 171, NL 139 and probably US 124.

754 ES 128, CH 167, ZA 80.

755 FR 106, GR 104, IT 160, PL 182, CH 166.

756 Thus, as regards to recoverability of property damage, the requirement of fault in ES 128 or certain exclusions in PL 183.

negotiating with C, can give rise to pre-contractual liability or not. The second one, which is the central issue here, is whether breaking off negotiations – which is what D did when he decided not to continue the ongoing negotiation with C by selling to X – can also be a ground for pre-contractual liability in this case.

Conducting parallel negotiations with several potential buyers is by itself not contrary to good faith and the party who carries them out is not under an obligation to inform the other party. However, even when the parties have not agreed exclusivity, these parallel negotiations must be conducted in good faith. Although D did not have the obligation to inform C that he was negotiating with X the sale of the antique, it could be argued that D had implicitly refused parallel negotiations when he accepted C's proposal to continue negotiations on the following Friday.[757] It can also be contended that, on the grounds of this agreement to continue negotiations, C could rely that nothing would change until the following Friday, so that D, before concluding the contract with X, should have told C that he was going to sell the antique to X in order to give C an opportunity to react.[758] 289

Although it can be doubtful whether in this case agreeing to continue negotiations prevents D from carrying out parallel negotiations with other potential buyers, it seems clear that, at least, D had refused to carry any parallel negotiations so far as to prevent the continuation of negotiations as agreed. Here the final result of this parallel negotiation, the sale of the antique to X, prevents any further continuation of the negotiations between C and D and amounts to a breaking off negotiations by D. 290

The freedom to break off negotiations is essential to freedom of contract. However, in exceptional circumstances, a party who has broken off negotiations can be held liable for inducing the other party's reliance that a contract would be concluded or for breaking off negotiations abruptly and without justification. The emphasis on one or several circumstances of the case that are not given in detail in the hypothetical is relevant to decide whether D is liable for breaking off negotiations or not and explain why some reports are for or against D's liability. 291

Probably the most important circumstance is whether C could reasonably expect that the sale of the antique would be concluded. This reliance can arise from objective circumstances, such as the stage in which the negotiations between C and D were when D sold the antique to X. This seems particularly relevant in the Netherlands, since, according to an extensive court practice of pre-contractual liability for breaking off negotiations, at a certain phase of the negotiations, the interests of the other party may have more weight than the 292

[757] IT 163.
[758] ES 129.

principle of freedom of contract.[759] Reliance can also arise from subjective circumstances, such as declarations, actions or omissions of one negotiating party that give the impression to the other party that the contract will be concluded.[760] In our case, it is arguable whether D's agreement with C to continue negotiations the following Friday could give rise to this reliance. Some reports consider that this agreement could not give C the impression that D would conclude the contract,[761] or that it would show that the negotiations between C and D were still ongoing, ie had not reached the point where C could believe that the contract would be concluded and, for this reason, hold that D is not liable.[762] By contrast, most of the other reports consider that in this case D created the expectation that a contract may eventually be concluded[763] or simply that D did not act in good faith,[764] adding sometimes that, by breaking his obligation to continue the negotiations, D had broken his obligation to behave in good faith,[765] and for this reason they hold D liable.

293 In the absence of a valid contract between C and D, the lack of recognition of pre-contractual liability based on good faith would not prevent common law jurisdictions from protecting C according to other grounds such as tort or unjust enrichment – or promissory estoppel in the United States. However, additional facts to those stated in the hypothetical (such as intent to deceive when asking for a two-day delay and reliance by C on D's promise) would be required before these alternative claims could be successfully pursued.[766]

294 Since no contract between C and D has been concluded, if D were to be held liable, his liability would be in tort in most jurisdictions, even in those that specifically include rules on pre-contractual liability in their codes.[767] In some countries, like Austria and Germany, and probably also in Switzerland, although liability is neither in tort nor in contract, contract law rules apply.[768] If C were to be compensated, C could obtain reliance damages,[769] ie damages should aim to return C to the position in which he would have been if no contractual

[759] NL 140.

[760] AT 20, DE 125, PL 184, ZA 81.

[761] DE 126.

[762] AT 23.

[763] ZA 81.

[764] CZ 119, holding that D terminated negotiations without a just cause; GR 105, D did not act in good faith; IL 93, an action for breaching the pre-contractual obligation to act in good faith may succeed; IT 162–164 and probably also PL 184 and ES 129. Undecided NL 141, since the case does not present enough facts to determine that the contractual phase has been reached.

[765] Thus CH 177. Also FR 107, considers that D's is in bad faith, since he did not keep his promise to C.

[766] E&W 124, US 125.

[767] Such as CZ 119, FR 107, IT 12 and 165 (with dissenting opinions in legal writing), PL 184.

[768] See CH 175 and *W Wiegand*, Obligationenrecht (OR) I, Einleitung, arts 97–109, no 10, 594, although with dissenting opinions in legal writing.

[769] FR 107, DE 125, GR 105, IT 10 and 165, PL 184.

negotiations had been entered into. In some jurisdictions, in exceptional cases, expectation damages can also be awarded.[770]

P. CASE 16. NON-DISCLOSURE OF RELEVANT FACTS

C wants to buy a specific machine ('type X') to harvest corn on his land. C does not mention where he intends to use this machine, but D knows through a friend that C owns fields of corn on steep hills in a distant part of the country. Although it works on all terrains, the type X machine has a dramatically reduced performance when used on steep fields. D does not say anything and sells the harvester to C.

The case raises the question of liability for non-disclosure of relevant facts related to circumstances which are neither stated nor implied during negotiations, but which the seller knows on private grounds. If the seller's silence gives rise to any remedy or remedies, a further question is whether the available remedies are in contract, in tort or on other grounds. 295

Since in this case the parties have already concluded a contract, first whether the remedies provided by specific sales law or general contract law exclude pre-contractual liability (either as a 'third-track' or as liability in tort) must be analysed. Some jurisdictions, such as Germany,[771] Greece[772] and Norway,[773] consider that, since a contract has been concluded, pre-contractual liability is excluded as far as the subject matter is covered by sales law, although pre-contractual statements may remain relevant for the contract. Others, such as Italy[774] or Israel,[775] consider that in such cases the buyer can make use of both sets of remedies. In France, art 1112-1 *Code civil* now explicitly provides for the existence of a pre-contractual information duty, violation of which gives rise to liability. Although the nature of this liability is not specified in the *Code*, it is generally accepted that it should be regarded as being in tort, as the violation of the duty took place before the contract was concluded.[776] 296

As regards specific sales rules, it is clear that C did not make an express warranty for the suitability of the machine on steep terrains. It is more doubtful, however, whether there is a breach of an implied warranty. Although the fact is that the machine's performance is dramatically reduced on steep 297

770 NL 143 and CH 179.
771 DE 127.
772 GR 107.
773 NO 104.
774 IT 166.
775 IL 94.
776 FR 108.

fields, this does not make it unsuitable for its general purpose. Accordingly, most jurisdictions stress the fact that the machine was fit for the contractual purpose or for the general purpose of the same kind of machines and that C's one-sided expectations, even when known by D, are not sufficient to establish a warranty, either express or implied. For these reasons, they hold that C cannot avail himself of any remedy under sales law.[777] Other jurisdictions, however, consider that poor performance considerably reduces the utility that C can expect from the machine and that, if it is severe, it may also imply a defective condition of the machine. In this case, the buyer could claim not only damages, but also other contractual remedies such as reparation or replacement of the machine, diminution of price or rescission of the contract.[778]

298 Some jurisdictions consider that in this case C's consent was vitiated when he concluded the contract. D remained intentionally silent on a point which he knew was essential for the other party's consent and about which he had a duty to inform C and fraudulently induced C to contract (*reticence dolosive*,[779] *reticencia dolosa*,[780] *reticenza dolosa*,[781] *misrepresentation* or *fraud*[782]) or, at least, it can be considered that C concluded the contract under a fundamental mistake.[783]

299 Most jurisdictions, however, agree that, alternatively or concurrently to contractual remedies, D's knowledge of the special use to which C intended to put the machine created on D a duty to disclose the poor performance of the machine on steep fields to C. The breach of this duty would then give rise to pre-contractual liability – as either a 'third track' or a tort claim – which would require putting C in the position he would have been in if D had disclosed the relevant facts to him.[784] In this case, since a contract had already been concluded, this might entail not only damages but also rescission.[785] As regards whether D's conduct would give rise to negligent misrepresentation, which would allow C to bring a claim in tort, some jurisdictions consider that D's silence would be sufficient grounds for this claim,[786] whereas others consider that it is doubtful in this case.[787]

---

777 So, for instance, E&W 152, DE 127–130, GR 106–108, PL 185, US 126.

778 NL 146, IT 166, CH 184.

779 FR 108. See also CH 180.

780 ES 130.

781 IT 166 and art 1439 Italian CC.

782 Considering that there was misrepresentation that would allow the buyer to rescind the contract, IL 94. Expressing doubts on the existence of misrepresentation or fraud E&W 152 and US 126.

783 NL 147.

784 AT 81, CZ 120, FR 108, DE 131, IL 94, IT 166, NO 104, NL 148.

785 Thus, for instance, AT 81.

786 IL 94, ZA 82, US 126.

787 E&W 152.

VII. CONCLUSIONS

A. THE ISSUE OF BORDERLINES OVER TIME AND ACROSS LEGAL SYSTEMS

Classical legal thinking imposed a sharp distinction between contract and tort. It considered that contract was the essential manifestation of the power of self-determination of the parties (private autonomy), where the breach of pre-existing obligations created by contract gave rise to different remedies – damages being one of them – that could be claimed for either on its own or in addition to other remedies. In tort law, damages was also an important remedy, probably the most important one, but by contrast to contract, liability arising from tort had its origin in the infringement of interests protected by law rather than by private arrangement. 300

It is also well known that this classical clear-cut distinction has been eroded over time. Probably it never existed to its full extent. Thus, for instance, even the first European civil codes established obligations between contractual parties which were not based on their consent, but on general duties of conduct established by the law, as in the case of good faith in the creation or in the performance of contracts.[788] However, it is also true that these duties and obligations imposed by the law became more important over time. The increasing interventionism of the State or the need to protect vulnerable parties, the imposition of objective standards of conduct or externally determined levels of care (as is the case, for instance, in medical and legal professions) has affected all jurisdictions, to a greater or lesser extent, and has also blurred the boundary between liability based on actual consent and liability imposed by law. 301

The borderlines of tort law and its interactions with contract law also depend, to a large extent, on the basic approach and structure of the system of the law of tort in the corresponding legal jurisdiction. 302

A basic idea is that where the approach to tort law is very stringent, with a more or less closed list of protected interests, an expansion of contract law becomes a way to iron out some of its shortcomings. Sometimes the problems resulting from a rigid tort law system are coupled with the existence of tort law rules which courts sense do not solve the problems properly, and for this reason, they have successfully curbed them over the years. This is the case, for instance, of the so-called 'contract with protective effects to third parties (*Vertrag mit* 303

[788] *R Zimmermann/S Whittaker*, Good Faith in European Contract Law (2000) 675 ff.

Schutzwirkung zugunsten Dritter), which, although it does not grant third parties a right to claim performance, is used as a gap-filler so as to include them in the protective scope of the contract and allow them to bring a claim against a contractual party causing them personal injury and property damage and, in some cases, pure economic loss.[789] In the case of personal injury or property damage, which are interests of third parties already protected by tort law rules, the practical aim of such a doctrine in jurisdictions such as Austria, Germany and Switzerland is to better protect victims in the case of liability of principals for their auxiliaries, since the general contractual rules of liability for auxiliaries tend to be much more favourable to claimants than the corresponding rules in tort.[790] More problematic are those cases where third parties do not suffer personal injury or property damage, but a stand-alone economic loss. Since in these systems pure economic loss is not included in the list of protected interests, it is not recoverable in tort and the constellations of cases this institution tries to solve in practice come very close to those solved in other legal systems by establishing exceptions to the general principle of non-recoverability of pure economic loss in tort.[791]

304 By contrast, legal systems that start from a general clause of liability in tort have the contrary problem. The expansion of tort law rules is used to solve all problems not strictly covered by contract law rules, falling short of flooding contract law with tort. A similar problem arises in common law in the case of the tort of negligence. A strong barrier to ward off this danger is the French general *non cumul* rule, which prevents the application of tort law rules between contractual parties. However, as other legal systems also based on a general clause show, this rule is not essential.[792]

305 The pure economic loss doctrine is an analytical tool that enables problems to be dealt with which are not openly perceived in those jurisdictions that base tort liability on a general clause and which are not familiar with such a doctrine. Since the starting point of these jurisdictions is that all interests, including pure or stand-alone economic ones, deserve legal protection in tort, they try to solve the same concerns about unpredictable and limitless expansion of liability by using other legal instruments such as the concepts of 'damage' and 'causation' or, more precisely, with 'scope of liability' policy rules.[793]

789 CR 132 ff.
790 CR 107 and 136.
791 CR 140 and 238 ff (Case 2. The idle lawyer).
792 CR 103 ff.
793 CR 102 ff.

B. THE MAIN DIFFERENCES BETWEEN CONTRACT AND TORT LAW RULES AND THEIR REASONING

1) *Fault as a Foundation of Liability and as a Condition for Damages*

Fault – including here intent and negligence – plays a different role in contract and in tort. As regards the breach or non-performance of a contract, continental jurisdictions require that it is 'attributable' to the debtor, ie that it is due to causes for which the debtor bears the risk, fault being only one among others. However, in many jurisdictions, the exercise of the remedy of damages requires the fault of the debtor, but the creditor does not have to prove fault because it is rebuttably presumed.[794] By contrast, the starting position in common law jurisdictions is that the reasons for failing to perform do not play any role; contract is regarded as containing a guarantee and when there is a breach of contract, the creditor can exercise all the contractual remedies, including damages, regardless of fault of the debtor.[795] In spite of these different starting positions, all legal systems know of cases where liability requires fault and cases where liability is strict, since the debtor's duty depends upon the nature of the obligation incurred.[796] In contract, fault may also play an important role when establishing which damage can be attributed to the non-performing party (foreseeability rule).[797] 306

In tort, intent and fault can also play a role, both as a condition of liability and as regards the extent of damages or their amount and may also have an impact on other elements which are relevant to establish or to exclude liability. However, the general rule in tort is that fault of the defendant is not presumed and it must be proved by the claimant. Additionally, most jurisdictions protect a wider range of interests in the case of intentional infringement.[798] 307

2) *Remedies, in Particular Damages*

Contract and tort appear in different legal systems with a complex set of rules and remedies which may differ. When the legal effects are the same, it is immaterial to qualify an action as contractual or tortious, to ask for the borderlines or to discuss whether the remedies in tort and contract overlap 308

794 CR 27 and 30.
795 CR 28.
796 CR 31.
797 CR 32.
798 CR 33.

or not. However, the distinction becomes crucial when the effects are different and the claimant can gain something with the contractual or tortious classification or, conversely, when such differences may improve the defendant's position.

309 In contract, the claimant may avail himself of a wider variety of remedies such as specific performance, withholding performance, termination of contract or reduction in price. Damages is only one of the remedies available to the creditor, which he may claim in lieu of performance or, under certain conditions, cumulate to other remedies. Most of these remedies are out of place in tort where, although compensation in kind is theoretically the preferable remedy, the main remedy in practice is damages. However, in some areas, as is the case with some infringements on the rights of personality, compensation in kind may also play an important role. Injunctions may also play a role both in contract and in tort.[799]

310 In those jurisdictions where the provisions dealing with damages are common to contract and tort, there are no differences or the differences are rather minor. It is also submitted that there has been a general trend to unify or at least approximate contract and tort law rules in some areas.

311 This is the case, for instance, of compensation for non-pecuniary loss, which has continued an expanding trend not only in tort but also in contract. In fact, there are very few jurisdictions that still fully exclude compensation of non-pecuniary loss in contract and the gap existing in others between compensation of such losses in tort and in contract has narrowed over the last few decades.[800] Although it may still be true that recoverability of non-pecuniary loss is the rule in tort and the exception in contract, this different approach has more to do with the sorts of interests usually protected in these two areas than with any other fundamental difference.[801]

312 The differences between contract and tort also seem to have little to do either with so-called restitutionary or disgorgement damages, which are often related to a different source of obligations, such as unjust enrichment or *negotiorum gestio*,[802] or with recoverability of loss of chance, regardless of whether it is considered a damages or a causation issue.[803] In those jurisdictions that award punitive damages, the fear that they may negatively affect freedom of contract excludes their application in this area.[804]

---

799 CR 42 f and 75 ff.
800 CR 48 ff.
801 CR 53 ff.
802 CR 60 ff.
803 CR 56 ff.
804 CR 67 ff.

3) *Liability for Others and in the Case of Multiple Tortfeasors or Breaching Parties*

The differences between general contract rules regarding liability for auxiliaries, which tend to be more favourable for the claimant than the corresponding rules in tort, have offered an incentive to fuel borderline disputes.[805] In some of these jurisdictions, such as in Austria, Germany and Switzerland, these differences have also given rise to an expansion of contract law at the expense of tort law that could probably have been avoided with a timely tort law reform.[806] As different proposals for harmonisation suggest and economic analysis of law confirms, establishing vicarious liability in tort would be desirable[807] and would thus harmonise contract and tort law on this point. 313

Another remarkable difference between contract and tort law rules refers to liability in cases of a plurality of debtors or tortfeasors.[808] In many countries, although the default rule in contract is several liability, the rule in tort is solidary liability.[809] This difference does not seem to be rooted in any substantial reasons arising from the contract–tort law divide and, in spite of some resistance,[810] seems to be losing ground.[811] 314

4) *Defences and Limitation Periods*

Most jurisdictions point out that although contractual agreements may validly vary or exclude defences, there are basically no differences between contract and tort on this point.[812] 315

Contributory negligence is probably one of the most important defences, which most jurisdictions under survey apply both to contract and tort,[813] and the same is true when they distinguish between contributory negligence and mitigation of damage.[814] By way of exception, England and Wales and South Africa consider that contributory negligence does not apply to contractual liability and can be raised in contract in cases of concurrent liability only.[815] 316

---

805 CR 106 ff.
806 CR 107.
807 CR 108.
808 CR 123 ff.
809 CR 124.
810 Cf the new art 1310 French CC.
811 CR 124 f.
812 CR 142 ff and 144.
813 CR 145.
814 CR 146 f.
815 CR 145.

317 The reform that has probably had more impact in making the contract–tort distinction less relevant from a practical point of view refers to time limitation or prescription rules. The discussion on the boundaries between contract and tort is still very important in countries such as England and Wales, Spain and Switzerland, which have not carried out such reforms and still have very disparate prescription periods.[816] The reforms carried out in most jurisdictions, such as Germany (2001), France (2008) and the Czech Republic (2012), have followed a clear tendency to unify general prescription periods and regimes, at least in contract and in tort, and this has made the borderline discussion on this point much less relevant, if not obsolete.[817] The prevailing legal opinion considers that there do not appear to be any general criteria which would be both sufficiently clear and convincing to provide a basis for a differentiated general prescription regime between contract and tort law claims.[818] Moreover, it is submitted that the practical problems associated with prescription are not related to the contract–tort distinction, but to the combination of the different components of the prescription regime, which even some reformed prescription regulations have not solved in a fully satisfactory manner.[819]

5) Differences as Regards Proof and Other Differences

318 Procedural rules that govern proof issues are common to contract and tort. However, when the remedy sought in contract is damages, in those jurisdictions where fault is a condition for the applicability of this remedy, fault is regularly presumed. By contrast, when fault is required, the general rule is that it is the claimant who has to furnish proof.[820]

319 Some reports also mention other differences, such as the rules governing contractual and tortious capacity,[821] transmissibility of claims (although this difference has more to do with the type of loss than with the contract–tort divide),[822] the jurisdiction of the courts and the applicable rules of conflict of laws.[823]

6) Some General Reasons for All these Differences

320 As expected, most reports explain the reasons for the differences between contract and tort law rules in their jurisdictions when dealing with

816 CR 148 ff.
817 CR 150.
818 CR 152 ff.
819 CR 155 ff.
820 CR 161 ff.
821 CR 165.
822 CR 166.
823 CR 167.

specific aspects. In spite of this, it was considered that it was necessary to formulate the question again in general terms: what are the reasons for all these differences? Here the reporters have been more laconic – considering, probably, that they had already given all the necessary explanations – and have basically referred to these three reasons: the different functions between contract and tort, historical factors, and the fact that some differences are to be understood in the context of the spirit of the time prevailing when they were drafted.[824]

C. THE EXPANSION OF LIABILITY IN CONTRACT AND IN TORT

Most countries under survey, pursuant to the principle of privity or relativity of contract,[825] do not generally allow an extension of the protective scope of the contract to third parties who have not been mentioned in the contract or, at least, whose protection cannot result from an interpretation of the contractual will of the parties. The two clear exceptions to this trend are the already mentioned doctrine of the protective effects of the contract with regard to third parties (*Vertrag mit Schutzwirkung zugunsten Dritter*) and the so-called *action directe* in the case of certain 'chains of contracts', which gives a contractual party an action in contract against a party to another contract, as long as there is some sort of close relationship between their contracts that shows the events occurring in one contract can have effects on the other. It is then held that the direct claim is transferred together with the contract, as an accessory to it. This direct claim, which is considered to be a claim in contract, must then abide by the terms that the party, against whom the claim is addressed, has agreed to in his contract. Although the doctrine entails a notable expansion of contract law to persons who are not parties to the same contract, it is considered to be compatible with the principle of relativity of contract[826] and many legal systems also apply this doctrine to a limited number of situations.[827] 321

The expansion of tort law, notably through a growing number of exceptions to the so-called bright-line rule that would altogether exclude compensation of pure economic loss in negligence (or according to the general tort law rules, in other legal systems) has also blurred the boundaries of tort law.[828] In these cases, the existence of a close relationship of proximity between the parties, involving the defendant's voluntary assumption of responsibility 322

824 CR 168 ff.
825 CR 128 ff.
826 CR 134.
827 CR 133 and 244 ff (Case 3. The defective house).
828 CR 82 ff.

towards the claimant, either individually or as the member of an identifiable class, has always become a way to solve, within the framework of tort law rules, tort law shortcomings that are similar to those solved by stretching contract law rules in other legal systems.[829]

D. GREY ZONES AND AREAS OF OVERLAP

323 Between contract and tort there is a grey zone, ie a zone where it is doubtful whether the situation that gives rise to liability is contractual or tortious. In most countries there is also an overlap area, ie situations where the same facts can give rise to actions both in contract and in tort, with duplicative cause of actions or, at least, with two sets of rules applicable to the same facts.

324 A typical grey zone in many countries is pre-contractual liability. Here the pre-existing relationship between the parties, properly speaking, is not contractual, since a contract does not arise until it has been concluded. A few jurisdictions consider pre-contractual liability to be *sui generis* or a specific type of liability on its own, although they basically apply contract law rules. Other jurisdictions hold firmly that in these cases liability is in tort and, accordingly, they apply tort law rules. Finally, other jurisdictions hotly dispute whether these situations are contractual or tortious and, in practice, apply contract law rules for some aspects and tort law rules for others.[830]

325 Another grey zone is professional liability,[831] shifting sometimes from tort to contract and vice versa. Although most jurisdictions under survey consider that professional liability is primarily a matter of contract law, others consider it a matter of tort law. Liability of medical doctors and health care professionals is a clear example. In this area the aim of obtaining some specific practical results has led legislatures to move liability back and forth from contract to tort or to split the liability of institutions and professionals that provide health care services between one ground and the other.[832]

326 As regards the overlap issue, all jurisdictions under survey, except France, acknowledge that in some cases breach of contract can constitute a tort against the contracting party simultaneously. Concurrence of actions or rules can give rise to situations which are problematic and can undermine contractual agreements.[833]

---

829 CR 99 ff and 238 ff (Case 2. The idle lawyer).
830 CR 10–14, 202–225 and nos 282–299: Cases 13–16.
831 CR 226 ff.
832 CR 231.
833 CR 188 ff.

E. NON-CONCURRENCE AND CONCURRENCE OF ACTIONS

A breach of contract can simultaneously constitute a tort against the contracting party. This can be the case in contracts dealing with medical treatment, carriage of persons or goods, sale of products, rental of premises and others, in which the breach of contract may give rise to personal injury or property damage. A further question is whether contractual parties who do not suffer personal injury or property damage, but do suffer stand-alone economic loss, may also sue the other contractual party in tort. The basic questions in all these cases are whether contract has absolute precedence over tort and whether contractual parties must always sue in contract (non-concurrence of actions) or whether they can frame their claims in contract, in tort or on both grounds (concurrence of actions), provided that they do not obtain double recovery.[834] 327

All jurisdictions under survey follow the concurrence approach with the exception of France. The French exception derives from the *non cumul* rule, which provides absolute precedence of contract over tort and that, as long as there is a contractual relationship between the parties, claims in tort are excluded. In all the other jurisdictions, although understood in different ways, the basic underlying idea is that when both contract and tort rules are applicable, the claimant may choose the cause of action or the rules that are more favourable to her, but that in no case can the application of tort rules disrupt what has been bargained for by the parties to a contract.[835] 328

When personal injury or property damage are at stake, the possibilities of disruption exist (different limitation periods, different conditions required in contract and in tort), but they are rather limited.[836] Nevertheless, when this happens, the application of tort law rules should also be set aside if they run against what the parties have agreed to in their contract. 329

Much higher are the possibilities of disruption of contract through tort in the case of economic interests. Pure economic losses arising from economic interests that have been bargained for in the contract could easily be overridden by tort law and contractual expectations circumvented by the application of tort rules. The reluctance towards compensating for economic loss in negligence, in some jurisdictions, or the caution shown with 'indirect damage', in others, is to a large extent attributable to this concern. In this context, a rule that excludes liability in tort between contractual parties, with regard to economic interests, may serve several functions, such as allowing the 330

834 CR 188 ff.
835 CR 192–195.
836 CR 196 ff.

parties to make reliable allocation of financial risk without the fear that tort law will be used to undo it later on, protecting the bargain made by the parties and preventing the erosion of contract rules by the use of tort law to work around them. However, it is difficult to establish a bright-line rule in this context as endless disputes in the area of product liability attest.[837]

F. LIMITATION OR EXCLUSION OF LIABILITY ARISING FROM TORT OR FROM CONTRACT

331 As a matter of principle, freedom of contract allows the contracting parties to limit or to exclude their liability beforehand when they enter into a contract. However, statutory provisions may prevent the parties from doing so in some contracts. Statutory provisions may also limit or exclude liability in tort.[838]

332 Courts may also limit liability in contract, and in many cases, also in tort, irrespective of what the parties have agreed in the contract. This is the case in such jurisdictions as the Czech Republic, the Netherlands, Norway, Poland and Spain, where courts may moderate the amount of damages if compensation in full would lead to what they consider to be unacceptable results in the light of the specific circumstances of the case.[839]

333 Validity or invalidity of the limitation or exclusion of liability may depend on several factors, such as the foundation of liability, the type of protected interest or the condition of the parties to the contract. Thus, it is a general rule accepted by all jurisdictions that liability cannot be limited or excluded when damage was caused with intent, and generally, this rule also applies to damage caused with gross negligence (*culpa lata dolo aequiparatur*).[840] Another general rule also provides that the limitation or exclusion of liability for personal injury is not valid either[841] and, finally, many limitations or exclusions, which would generally be valid, are invalid when one of the parties to the contract is a consumer.[842]

334 However, it is disputed whether the parties to a contract may also limit or exclude their liability in tort. While many jurisdictions consider that whether a clause that limits liability in contract also extends to tort is just a matter of

837 Cf CR 254 ff (Case 6. Exploding car) and 260 ff (Case 7. Burning racing boat).
838 CR 171 f.
839 CR 173 ff.
840 CR 178 ff.
841 CR 180.
842 CR 181.

interpretation of the contract, others hold that such a limitation or exclusion may only refer to contract, since tort is a matter of *ordre public*.[843]

Finally, another question that may arise is whether third parties who assist a contractual party in the performance of the contract or are involved with it can rely on the limitation or exclusion of liability established in favour of this party, when the other contracting party brings a claim in tort against them. If the answer is positive, the third party will be able to avail himself of the limitation or exclusion of liability agreed between the contractual parties when he is sued in tort. Although the legal devices used to ensure this protection may vary (contract for the benefit of third parties or with protective effects to third parties) in those jurisdictions that accept this extension, others are hesitant and, indeed, some reject it altogether.[844] 335

843 CR 182.

844 CR 183 ff.